A COMPANION TO THE ANCIENT GREEK LANGUAGE

BLACKWELL COMPANIONS TO THE ANCIENT WORLD

This series provides sophisticated and authoritative overviews of periods of ancient history, genres of classical literature, and the most important themes in ancient culture. Each volume comprises approximately twenty-five and forty concise essays written by individual scholars within their area of specialization. The essays are written in a clear, provocative, and lively manner, designed for an international audience of scholars, students, and general readers.

A COMPANION TO THE ANCIENT GREEK LANGUAGE

Edited by

Egbert J. Bakker

WILEY Blackwell

Library of Congress Cataloging-in-Publication Data

A companion to the ancient Greek language / edited by Egbert J. Bakker.
       p.   cm. – (Blackwell companions to the ancient world)
    Includes bibliographical references and index.
    ISBN 978-1-4051-5326-3 (hardcover :alk. paper) ISBN 978-1-118-78291-0 (pbk. : alk. paper)
1. Greek language–History.   2. Greek philology.   I. Bakker, Egbert J.
    PA227.C58 2010
    480.9–dc22

                                        2009020154

A catalogue record for this book is available from the British Library.

Cover image: Triphylian bronze decree, 2nd half of 4th century BC, Peleponnese. Musée du Louvre,
Paris / photo © RMN Hervé Lewandowski
Cover design by Workhaus

Set in 10/12.5pt Galliard by SPi Publisher Services, Pondicherry, India

1   2014

Contents

List of Figures

List of Tables

Notes on Contributors

Egbert J. Bakker is Professor of Classics at Yale University. Among his interests are the pragmatics of Ancient Greek and the linguistic articulation of Greek narratives. He is the author of *Poetry in Speech: Orality and Homeric Discourse* (1997) and *Pointing at the Past: From Formula to Poetics in Homeric Poetics* (2005). He has (co-)edited *Written Voices, Spoken Signs* (1997), *Grammar as Interpretation* (1997), and *Brill's Companion to Herodotus* (2002).

Victor Bers is Professor of Classics at Yale University. His publications include *Greek Poetic Syntax in the Classical Age* (1984), *Speech in Speech* (1997), *Genos Dikanikon* (2009), and for the University of Texas *Oratory of Classical Greece*, a translation of Demosthenes, Speeches 50–9.

Claude Brixhe is Professor emeritus at the University of Nancy 2, France. Among his interests in the field of Greek linguistics are the study of Greek dialects (ancient and modern), the Greek *Koine*, the non-Greek languages of Asia Minor, and the history of the Greek alphabet. Among his principal publications are *Le dialecte grec de Pamphylie. Documents et grammaire* (1976), *Phonétique et phonologie du grec ancien* I. *Quelques grandes questions* (1996), and *Corpus des inscriptions paléo-phrygiennes*, (1984, with M. Lejeune).

Michael Clarke is Professor of Classics at the National University of Ireland, Galway. His publications include *Flesh and Spirit in the Songs of Homer* (1999) and *Epic Interactions* (co-edited with B.G.F. Currie and R.O.A.M. Lyne, 2006). His work on lexical semantics was supported by a Government of Ireland Research Fellowship awarded under the National Development Plan (2001–2).

Stephen Colvin is Reader in Classics and Comparative Philology at University College London. His main areas of interest are the Greek dialects and the *Koine*, Mycenaean Greek, Greek onomastics, and the sociolinguistic culture of the ancient world. He is the author of *Dialect in Aristophanes* (1999), *A Historical Greek Reader* (2007), and papers on various aspects of Greek language and onomastics, and editor of *The Greco-Roman East: Politics, Culture, Society* (2004).

Eleanor Dickey is Associate Professor of Classics at the University of Exeter, England. She is the author of *Greek Forms of Address* (1996), *Latin Forms of Address* (2002), and *Ancient Greek Scholarship* (2007), as well as of numerous articles on both Latin and Greek. Her research concerns the history and development of the Latin and Greek languages, the way elements of those languages were perceived and explained by their speakers, sociolinguistics, and interaction and influence between Latin and Greek.

Evert van Emde Boas was educated in Amsterdam and Oxford, where he is currently finishing his DPhil in Classical Languages and Literature at Corpus Christi College, and working as a member of the language teaching team of the Faculty of Classics. His research is concerned with the application of modern linguistic methods to Ancient Greek texts, specifically Euripidean tragedy.

Silvia Ferrara is a Junior Research Fellow in Archaeology at St John's College, Oxford. She specializes in the deciphered (Linear B, Cypriot Syllabary) and undeciphered (Linear A, Cypro-Minoan) scripts of the second millennium BCE from Greece and Cyprus. She obtained her PhD from University College London in 2005, and her thesis on the Cypro-Minoan script is in the process of being revised for publication. Her main areas of interest are the development of writing in the eastern Mediterranean in the Late Bronze Age, with a particular focus on the syllabic and alphabetic cuneiform scripts at the Syrian site of Ugarit.

Thorsten Fögen is Assistant Professor of Classics at Humboldt University of Berlin. Among his research interests are the history of linguistic ideas, ancient rhetoric, literary criticism, non-verbal communication and semiotics, ancient technical writers, and women in antiquity, animals in antiquity, and ancient epistolography. He is the author of *"Patrii sermonis egestas": Einstellungen lateinischer Autoren zu ihrer Muttersprache. Ein Beitrag zum Sprachbewußtsein in der römischen Antike* (2000), *"Utraque lingua": A Bibliography on Bi- and Multilingualism in Graeco-Roman Antiquity and in Modern Times* (2003), and *Wissen, Kommunikation und Selbstdarstellung. Zur Struktur und Charakteristik römischer Fachtexte der frühen Kaiserzeit* (2009).

Niels Gaul is Associate Professor of Byzantine Studies and Director of the Center for Hellenic Traditions at Central European University, Budapest. He previously held the Dilts-Lyell Research Fellowship in Greek Palaeography at Oxford University and is the author of *Thomas Magistros und die spätbyzantinische Sophistik* (2009).

Coulter H. George is Assistant Professor of Classics at the University of Virginia. The author of *Expressions of Agency in Ancient Greek* (2005), he has also taught at Rice University and was a Junior Research Fellow at Trinity College, Cambridge. His research interests include the syntax of the Greek verb, particles and prepositions, and contact phenomena between Greek and the other languages of the ancient Mediterranean.

Olav Hackstein is Professor and Chair in Historical and Indo-European Linguistics at the Ludwig-Maximilians-Universität München. His research interests focus on comparative Indo-European linguistics, and particularly on the historical morphology and syntax of the ancient Indo-European languages. Main publications: *Untersuchungen zu den sigmatischen Präsentien des Tocharischen* (1995); *Die Sprachform der homerischen Epen* (2002).

Shane Hawkins is Assistant Professor of Greek and Roman Studies at Carleton University in Ottawa, Ontario. His main interests are Indo-European linguistics and Greek poetry. He has written on Greek inscriptions and early Greek epic, and is currently preparing a linguistic study of Hipponax.

David Holton is Professor of Modern Greek at the University of Cambridge and a Fellow of Selwyn College. His research interests include the history and present-day structure of the Greek language, textual transmission, and Early Modern Greek literature, especially the Cretan Renaissance. He is co-author of two grammars of the modern language and is directing a five-year research project to produce a reference grammar of Medieval Greek.

Luuk Huitink was educated in classics and linguistics at the universities of Amsterdam and Oxford. He is currently completing his DPhil in Classical Languages and Literature at Worcester College, Oxford, working on the expressions of reported discourse in Greek prose, verbal complementation and the intersection of linguistics and narratology. He also teaches Greek and Latin language and literature at the University of Oxford.

Casper de Jonge is Assistant Professor in Ancient Greek Language and Literature at Leiden University. His research focuses on the history of ancient grammar, rhetoric, and literary criticism. His

publications include *Between Grammar and Rhetoric: Dionysius of Halicarnassus on Language, Linguistics and Literature* (2008).

Joshua T. Katz is Professor of Classics and Director of the Program in Linguistics at Princeton University. Broadly interested in the languages, literatures, and cultures of the ancient world, his many publications present new accounts of topics from Indian animals to Irish pronouns and from Homeric formulae to Horatian self-fashioning.

Lawrence Kim is Assistant Professor in Classics at the University of Texas at Austin. His research focuses on Greek literature under the Roman Empire and his publications include articles on the ancient novel, Strabo, and Dio Chrysostom. He is currently completing a book on imperial Greek texts that explore the problem of Homeric poetry's historical reliability.

Peter Mackridge is Professor Emeritus of Modern Greek at the University of Oxford and a visiting professor at King's College London. His books include *The Modern Greek Language* (1985), *Dionysios Solomos* (1989), *Language and National Identity in Greece, 1766–1976* (2009) as well as two co-authored grammars of Modern Greek.

Io Manolessou is a Researcher at the Academy of Athens, Greece, and a collaborator on the "Grammar of Medieval Greek Project" of the University of Cambridge. She has published several articles on the history of the Greek language, which constitutes her main area of interest (together with diachronic syntax, historical dialectology, and the relationship between linguistics and philology).

Gregory Nagy is the author of *The Best of the Achaeans: Concepts of the Hero in Archaic Greek Poetry* (1979; 2nd edn, 1999). Other recent publications include *Plato's Rhapsody and Homer's Music: The Poetics of the Panathenaic Festival in Classical Athens* (2002) and *Homer's Text and Language* (2004). Since 2000, he has been the Director of the Harvard Center for Hellenic Studies in Washington DC, while continuing to teach at Harvard University as the Francis Jones Professor of Classical Greek Literature and Professor of Comparative Literature.

Johannes M. van Ophuijsen is Cornelia J. de Vogel Professor of Philosophy at the University of Utrecht in the Netherlands and is a Fellow of University College, Utrecht. His interests are in ontology and logic in Plato, Aristotle, and the Stoics and the traditions stemming from these. He has contributed to the Ancient Commentators on Aristotle series and to Project Theophrastus and is co-editing with K. Algra and T. Tieleman the fragments of the older Stoics.

James I. Porter is Professor of Classics and Comparative Literature at the University of California, Irvine. His main research interests are in literature, philosophy, and intellectual history. He is author of *Nietzsche and the Philology of the Future* and *The Invention of Dionysus: An Essay on The Birth of Tragedy* (both 2000) and editor of *Constructions of the Classical Body* (1999) and of *Classical Pasts: The Classical Traditions of Greece and Rome* (2006). His book, *The Origins of Aesthetic Inquiry in Ancient Greece: Matter, Sensation, and Experience* is forthcoming from Cambridge.

Philomen Probert is University Lecturer in Classical Philology and Linguistics at the University of Oxford and a Fellow of Wolfson College. She has written *A New Short Guide to the Accentuation of Ancient Greek* (2003) and *Ancient Greek Accentuation: Synchronic Patterns, Frequency Effects, and Prehistory* (2006).

Jeremy Rau is Associate Professor of Linguistics and the Classics at Harvard University. His research focuses primarily on Greek, Latin, and Indo-European linguistics; he is the author of numerous articles and a forthcoming monograph on nominal morphology in Greek and Indo-European.

Bruno Rochette is Professor of Greek and Latin Language and Literature at the University of Liège, Belgium. He is the author of *Le latin dans le monde grec. Recherches sur la diffusion de la langue et des lettres latines dans les provinces hellénophones de l'Empire romain* (1997) and of articles on various aspects of Greco-Latin bilingualism.

Richard Rutherford has been Tutor in Greek and Latin Literature at Christ Church, Oxford, since 1982. He works mainly on Greek literature, especially of the fifth and fourth centuries BCE, but has also published on Latin authors. Among his previous publications are *The Meditations of Marcus Aurelius: A Study* (1989), *Homer: Odyssey 19 and 20* (1992), *The Art of Plato* (1995), and *Classical Literature: A Concise History* (2005).

Francesca Schironi is Associate Professor at Harvard University. Her main interests are Hellenistic scholarship and papyrology. She has published a book collecting the fragments of Aristarchus of Samothrace in the Byzantine Etymologica (2004). She is also the author of *From Alexandria to Babylon: Near Eastern Languages and Hellenistic Erudition in the Oxyrhynchus*

Glossary (2009) and *Tὸ μέγα βιβλίον: Book-ends, End-titles, Coronides in Papyri with Hexametric Poetry* (2010). Her main research focus is currently on Alexandrian scholarship and its interactions with ancient science and cross-borrowing of technical terms.

Andreas U. Schmidhauser is a Postdoctoral Scholar in Classics at UCLA. He received his PhD in Philosophy from the University of Geneva in 2007. The author of various articles on Stoic dialectic and Greek and Latin grammar, he is now preparing a new edition, with translation and commentary, of Apollonius Dyscolus' treatise *On the Pronoun*.

Michael Silk is Professor of Classical and Comparative Literature, and from 1991 to 2006 was Professor of Greek Language and Literature, at King's College London. He has published on a wide range of topics, from Aristotle to Nietzsche, and Homer to Ted Hughes. Forthcoming publications include two books: *Poetic Language in Theory and Practice* (OUP) and *The Classical Tradition: Art, Literature, Thought* (with I. Gildenhard and R. Barrow; Blackwell). His book *Standard Languages and Language Standards: Greek, Past and Present* (co-edited with A. Georgakopoulou) appeared in 2009.

Rupert Thompson is Lecturer in Classical Philology and Linguistics at the University of Cambridge, and a Fellow of Selwyn College. His research interests include the history of the Greek language and its dialects, Mycenaean epigraphy, and Indo-European. He has contributed the section on the Linear B writing system (with T. Meissner) and the *Glossary* (with J. T. Killen) to the third edition of *Documents in Mycenaean Greek*.

Sofía Torallas Tovar holds a PhD in Classical Philology from the Universidad Complutense, Madrid (1995). She was a Postdoctoral Fellow at University College London from 1997 to 2000. Since 2000 she has been a researcher at the Centro de Ciencias Humanas y Sociales (CSIC) in Madrid. She is also the curator of the papyrological collection at the Abbey of Montserrat, Barcelona. Her areas of expertise are Greek and Coptic papyrology, the editing of Coptic literary texts, and the culture and literature of Greco-Roman Egypt.

Olga Tribulato is the Woodhouse Junior Research Fellow in Classics at St John's College, Oxford. She obtained her first degree from the Università degli Studi di Roma "La Sapienza," and her MPhil. and PhD. from the University of Cambridge. During the years 2007–2009 she intermitted her fellowship to take up a temporary lectureship in Philology and Linguistics in the Faculty of Classics, University of Cambridge. Her main interests lie in the field of Ancient Greek language and linguistics (particularly morphology, word formation, and dialectology). She has published articles on Greek compounding and has contributed two chapters on the language of monodic and choral lyric to A. C. Cassio's *Storia delle lingue letterarie greche* (2008).

Arthur Verhoogt is Associate Professor of Papyrology and Greek at the University of Michigan. His publications include editions of papyri and ostraca and studies in the history of Hellenistic and Roman Egypt, including *Regaling Officials in Ptolemaic Egypt* (2005).

Rudolf Wachter is Professor of Greek, Latin, and Indo-European Linguistics at the University of Basel, as well as adjunct Professor of Historical Linguistics at the University of Lausanne. He holds doctorates from Zürich (1987) and Oxford (1991) and is the author of *Altlateinische Inschriften* (1987) and *Non-Attic Greek Vase Inscriptions* (2001). In addition to linguistics, his main interests are epigraphy and the history of the alphabet.

Staffan Wahlgren is Professor of Classical Philology at the Norwegian University of Science and Technology, Trondheim. His main areas of interest are text edition and editorial technique and the history of the Greek language, and he is the author of *Symeonis Magistri et Logothetae Chronicon* (2006) and *Sprachwandel im Griechisch der frühen römischen Kaiserzeit* (1995). Forthcoming is an edition with translation of *Theodorus Metochites' Semeioseis gnomikai* 61–70 and 72–81.

Michael Weiss is Professor of Linguistics at Cornell University. He specializes in Indo-European linguistics, Greek and Latin linguistics, and the interpretation of Sabellic texts. He is the author of *Outline of the Historical and Comparative Grammar of Latin* (2009) and of *Language and Ritual in Sabellic Italy* (2009) and articles on Greek, Latin, Hittite, Umbrian, and South Picene.

Andreas Willi is Diebold Professor of Comparative Philology at the University of Oxford and Privatdozent für Klassische Philologie at the University of Basel. He is the author of *The Languages of Aristophanes: Aspects of Linguistic Variation in Classical Attic Greek* (2003) and *Sikelismos: Sprache, Literatur und Gesellschaft im griechischen Sizilien* (2008) and has edited, among other things, *The Language of Greek Comedy* (2002). His main research interests lie in the fields of ancient sociolinguistics, Greek dialectology, the interaction of language and literature in Ancient Greece, and Greek and Indo-European comparative grammar.

Roger D. Woodard is the Andrew V. V. Raymond Professor of the Classics and Professor of Linguistics at the University of Buffalo (The State University of New York). In addition to the Greek alphabet, particular areas of interest to him include archaic Greek poetry, Greek and Roman myth and religion, and Indo-European culture and language. He is the author of *Greek Writing from Knossos to Homer* (1997) and *Indo-European Sacred Space* (2006) and the editor of *The Cambridge Companion to Greek Mythology* (2007), *The Cambridge Encyclopedia of the World's Ancient Languages* (2004), and *Ovid: Fasti* (with A. J. Boyle; 2000, rev. edn 2004).

Symbols Used

< >	enclose an orthographic symbol or symbols (in most cases one or more letters of the Greek alphabet)
[ ]	enclose a phonetic symbol or symbols representing a particular sound or sequence of sounds
/ /	enclose a symbol or symbols representing a phoneme or sequence of phonemes
[θ]	a voiceless interdental fricative, like the initial sound of English *think*
[χ]	a voiceless velar fricative, like the final sound in the German pronunciation of *Bach*
[ẹ̄]	a relatively high or close long "e" vowel
[ɛ̄]	a relatively low or open long "e" vowel
[ọ̄]	a relatively high or close long "o" vowel
[ɔ̄]	a relatively low or open long "o" vowel
[y]	a high front rounded vowel, like the German vowel written *ü*
C	Consonant
V	Vowel
R	Resonant (liquid)
X > Y	X becomes Y by sound change
X >> Y	X becomes Y by analogical change or a combination of sound change and analogical change

Abbreviations of Ancient Authors and Works

Ael. *VH*   Aelianus, *Varia Historia*

Aesch.   Aeschylus

  Ag.   *Agamemnon*

  Cho.   *Choephori (Libation Bearers)*

  Eum.   *Eumenides*

  Pers.   *Persae (Persians)*

  Sept.   *Septem contra Thebas (Seven against Thebes)*

  Supp.   *Supplices (Suppliants)*

Alc.   Alcaeus

Alcm.   Alcman

Alex. Aphr.   Alexander Aphrodisiensis *in*
  in An. pr.   *Aristotelis Analyticorum Priorum librum I commentarium*

Amm. Marc.   Ammianus Marcellinus

Anac.   Anacreon

Anaximen. Lampsac. *Rh.*   Anaximenes Lampsacus, *Rhetorica*

Andoc., *Myst.*   Andocides, *De mysteriis (On the Mysteries)*

Ant. *Tetr.*   Antiphon, *Tetralogies*

Anth. Pal.   *Anthologia Palatina*

Ap. Dy.   Apollonius Dyscolus

  Adv.   *De adverbiis (On Adverbs)*

Con.	*De coniunctionibus (On Conjunctions)*
Pron.	*De pronomine (On the Pronoun)*
Synt.	*De constructione (On Syntax)*
Apollod. *Bibl*	Apollodorus, *Bibliotheca*
Apul. *Met.*	Apuleius, *Metamorphoses*
Ar.	Aristophanes
Ach.	*Acharnenses (Acharnians)*
Av.	*Aves (Birds)*
Eccl.	*Ecclesiazusae (Women at the Ecclesia)*
Eq.	*Equites (Knights)*
Lys.	*Lysistrata*
Nub.	*Nubes (Clouds)*
Pax	*Pax (Peace)*
Plut.	*Plutus (Wealth)*
Ran.	*Ranae (Frogs)*
Thesm.	*Thesmophoriazusae (Women at the Thesmophoria)*
Vesp.	*Vespae (Wasps)*
[Arc.]	[Arcadius], ἐπιτομὴ τῆς καθολικῆς προσῳδίας
Archil.	Archilochus
Archim.	Archimedes
Meth.	*Method of Mechanical Theorems*
Sph. Cyl.	*De Sphaera et cylindro*
Arist.	Aristotle
[De audib.]	*De audibilibus (On Things Heard)*
[Pr.]	*Problemata*
Cat.	*Categoriae (Categories)*
De an.	*De anima (On the Soul)*
Gen. an.	*De generatione animalium*
Hist. an.	*Historia animalium*
Int.	*De interpretatione*
Metaph.	*Metaphysica (Metaphysics)*

Part. an	*De partibus animalium (On Parts of Animals)*
Poet.	*Poetica (Poetics)*
Pol.	*Politica (Politics)*
Rh.	*Rhetorica (Rhetoric)*
Aristid. *Rhet.*	Aelius Aristides, *Rhetorica*
Aristox. *Harm.*	Aristoxenus, *Elementa harmonica*
Ath.	Athenaeus
Bacchyl.	Bacchylides
Charisius, *Gram.*	Charisius, *Ars Grammatica*
Chrys. *Oppugn.*	Ioannes Chrysostomus, *Aduersus oppugnatores uitae monasticae*
Cic.	Cicero
Acad. post.	*Academica posteriora*
Arch.	*Pro Archia*
Att.	*Epistulae ad Atticum (Letters to Atticus)*
Brut.	*Brutus*
De or.	*De oratore (On the Orator)*
Fam.	*Epistulae ad familiares*
Fin.	*De finibus bonorum et malorum*
Luc.	*Lucullus*
Nat. D.	*De natura deorum (On the Nature of the Gods)*
Orat.	*Orator*
Tusc.	*Tusculanae disputationes*
Verr.	*In Verrem*
Cod. Theod.	*Codex Theodosianus*
Curt.	Q. Curtius Rufus, *Historiae Alexandri Magni*
Dem.	Demosthenes
Demetr. *Eloc.*	Pseudo-Demetrius, *De elocutione (On Style)*
Democr.	Democritus
Deut.	Book of Deuteronomy (OT)
Dexipp. *in Cat.*	Dexippus, *in Aristotelis Categorias Commentarii*

Diod. Sic.	Diodorus Siculus
Diog. Laert.	Diogenes Laertius, *Vitae philosophorum (Lives of the Philosophers)*
Dion. Hal.	Dionysius Halicarnassensis (Dionysius of Halicarnassus)
Amm.	*Epistula ad Ammaeum*
Ant. Rom.	*Antiquitates Romanae*
Comp.	*De compositione verborum*
De imit.	*De imitatione*
Dem.	*De Demosthene (On Demosthenes)*
Isoc.	*De Isocrate (On Isocrates)*
Lys.	*De Lysia (On Lysias)*
Orat. Vett.	*De Veteris Oratoribus (On the Ancient Orators)*
Thuc.	*De Thucydide (On Thucydides)*
Dion. Thrax	Dionysius Thrax
Emp.	Empedocles
Epict.	Epictetus
Diss.	*Dissertationes*
Ench.	*Encheiridion*
Euc. *El.*	Euclides, *Elementa*
Eur.	Euripides
Alc.	*Alcestis*
Bacch.	*Bacchae*
El.	*Electra*
Hec.	*Hecuba*
IA	*Iphigenia Aulidensis (Iphigeneia at Aulis)*
IT	*Iphigenia Taurica (Iphigeneia among the Taurians)*
Med.	*Medea*
Or.	*Orestes*
Phoen.	*Phoenissae (Phoenician Women)*
Troad.	*Troades (Trojan Women)*
Eust., *Il.*	Eustathius, *Ad Iliadem (Commentary on the Iliad)*

Gal.	Galen
De plac. Hippoc. et Plat.	*De placitis Hippocratis et Platonis*
Gell.	Aulus Gellius, *Noctes Atticae (Attic Nights)*
Gen.	Book of Genesis (OT)
Gorg. *Hel.*	Gorgias, *Helen*
Hdt.	Herodotus
Hes.	Hesiod
Op.	*Opera et dies (Works and Days)*
Th.	*Theogony*
[Sc.]	*[Scutum] (Shield)*
Hier., *Ep.*	Hieronymus, *Epistulae*
Hipp.	Hipponax
Hippoc.	Hippocrates
Epid.	*Epidemiae*
Prog.	*Prognosticum*
Hom.	Homer
Il.	*Iliad*
Od.	*Odyssey*
Hor.	Horace
Carm.	*Carmina (Odes)*
Epist.	*Epistulae*
Sat.	*Satirae* or *Sermones (Satires)*
Hsch.	Hesychius
Hymn. Hom.	*Hymni Homerici (Homeric Hymns)*
Hymn. Hom. Ap.	*Hymnus Homericus ad Apollinem (Homeric Hymn to Apollo)*
Hymn. Hom. Ven.	*Hymnus Homericus ad Venerem (Homeric Hymn to Aphrodite)*
Il.	Homer, *Iliad*
Isae.	Isaeus
Isoc.	Isocrates
Juv.	Juvenal

Lev.	Book of Leviticus (OT)
Lib.	Libanius
Decl.	*Declamationes*
Or.	*Orationes*
Long. *Subl.*	[Longinus], *De Sublimitate (On the Sublime)*
Lucian	
Bis acc.	*Bis accusatus (Twice Accused)*
Demon.	*Demonax*
Peregr.	*De morte Peregrini (On the Death of Peregrinus)*
Rh. pr.	*Rhetorum praeceptor*
Lucr.	Lucretius
Lys.	Lysias
Men.	Menander
Dys.	*Dyscolus*
Mon.	*Monostichoi*
Michael Sync. *Synt.*	Michael Syncellus, *De constructione*
Nep. *Att.*	Nepos, *Atticus*
NT	New Testament
Num.	Book of Numbers (OT)
Od.	Homer, *Odyssey*
OT	Old Testament
Paus.	Pausanias
Petron. *Sat.*	Petronius, *Satyricon*
Phld. *De poem.*	Philodemus, *De poematis (On Poems)*
Phot. *Bibl.*	Photius, *Bibliotheca*
Pind.	Pindar
Ol.	*Olympian Odes*
Pyth.	*Pythian Odes*
Pl.	Plato
Alc.	*Alcibiades*
Cra.	*Cratylus*
Gorg.	*Gorgias*

Euthd.	*Euthydemus*
Hp. mai.	*Hippias maior*
Leg.	*Leges (Laws)*
Phd.	*Phaedo*
Phdr.	*Phaedrus*
Phlb.	*Philebus*
Resp.	*Respublica (Republic)*
Soph.	*Sophista (Sophist)*
Symp.	*Symposium*
Tim.	*Timaeus*
Plaut.	Plautus
Aul.	*Aulularia*
Cist.	*Cistellaria*
Poen.	*Poenulus*
Rud.	*Rudens*
Plin. *HN*	Pliny (the Elder), Historia Naturalis
Plin., *Ep.*	Pliny the Younger, *Epistulae*
Plut.	Plutarch
Alex.	*Alexander*
Ant.	*Antonius*
Cic.	*Cicero*
Coniug. praec.	*Coniugalia praecepta (Advice to Bride and Groom)*
Dem.	*Demosthenes*
De Aud.	*De Auditu (On Listening to Lectures)*
De prof. in virt.	*De profectu in virtute (Progress in Virtue)*
De garr.	*De garrulitate (On Talkativeness)*
Mor.	*Moralia*
Quaest. Plat.	*Quaestiones Platonicae*
Them.	*Themistocles*
Thes.	*Theseus*
Poll. *Onom.*	Pollux, *Onomasticon*

Pratin. *Lyr.*	Pratinas, *Lyrica*
Prisc. *Inst.*	Priscian, *Institutiones grammaticae*
Procl.	Proclus
In Pl. Cra.	*In Platonis Cratylum commentarii*
Prot.	Protagoras
ps. Plut. *De mus.*	pseudo-Plutarch *De musica*
Quint. *Inst.*	Quintilian, *Institutio oratoria*
Rev.	Book of Revelation (NT)
Rhet. Her.	*Rhetorica ad Herennium*
RV	*Rigveda*
Sam.	Book of Samuel (OT)
schol. Od.	*scholia in Odysseam*
schol. Techne	*scholia in Dionysii Thracis artem grammaticam*
Semon.	Semonides
Sen.	Seneca
Ben.	*De beneficiis*
Ep.	*Epistulae ad Lucilium (Letters to Lucilius)*
Sen.	Seneca (the Elder)
Controv.	*Controversiae*
Suas.	*Suasoriae*
Sext. Emp. *Math.*	Sextus Empiricus, *Adversus mathematicos (Against the Mathematicians)*
Simpl. *in Cat.*	Simplicius, *in Aristotelis Categorias Commentarii*
Sol.	Solon
Soph.	Sophocles
Aj.	*Ajax*
Ant.	*Antigone*
OC	*Oedipus Coloneus (Oedipus at Colonos)*

OT	*Oedipus Tyrannus (Oedipus the King)*
Trach.	*Trachiniae (Women of Trachis)*
Steph. Byz. *Ethn.*	Stephanus Byzantius, *Ethnica*
Stes.	Stesichorus
Strab.	Strabo
Suda	Greek Lexicon formerly known as *Suidas*
Suet.	Suetonius
Aug.	*Divus Augustus*
Claud.	*Divus Claudius*
Gram.	*De Grammaticis*
Tib.	*Tiberius*
Ter.	Terence
Ad.	*Adelphoe*
An.	*Andria*
Eun.	*Eunuchus*
Heaut.	*Heautontimorumenos*
Phorm.	*Phormio*
Theoc. *Id.*	Theocritus, *Idylls*
Thuc.	Thucydides
Val. Max.	Valerius Maximus
Varro, *Ling.*	Varro, *De lingua Latina (On the Latin Language)*
Verg., *Aen.*	Virgil, *Aeneid*
Vitr.	Vitruvius, *De architectura*
Xen.	Xenophon
Ages.	*Agesilaus*
An.	*Anabasis*
Cyn.	*Cynegeticus*
Cyr.	*Cyropaedia (The Education of Cyrus)*
Hell.	*Hellenica (Greek History)*
Oec.	*Oeconomicus*

Abbreviations
of Modern Sources

A&A	*Antike und Abendland*
Adler	*Suidae Lexicon* edidit Ada Adler, Leipzig 1928–38
AIV	*Atti dell'Istituto Veneto di Scienze, Lettere ed Arti, Classe di scienze morali, lettere ed arti*
AJA	*American Journal of Archaeology*
AJPh	*American Journal of Philology*
Anat. St.	*Anatolian Studies*
Annales ESC	*Annales: histoire, sciences sociales*
ANRW	*Aufstieg und Niedergang der römischen Welt*
Ant. Class.	*L'Antiquité classique*
Arch. Pap.	*Archiv für Papyrusforschung*
AVI	R. Wachter, *Attic Vase Inscriptions*: http://avi.unibas.ch/
BASOR	*Bulletin of the American Schools of Oriental Research*
BCH	*Bulletin de correspondance hellénique*
BÉ	*Bulletin épigraphique*, in *REG*, 1888–
BGU	*Aegyptische Urkunden aus den Königlichen* (later *Staatlichen*) *Museen zu Berlin, Griechische Urkunden*, Berlin
BICS	*Bulletin of the Institute of Classical Studies, London*
BIFAO	*Bulletin de l'Institut français d'archéologie orientale*
BL	*Berichtigungsliste der griechischen Papyrusurkunden aus Ägypten*

BMGS	*Byzantine and Modern Greek Studies*
BSLP	*Bulletin de la Société de linguistique de Paris*
BZ	*Byzantinische Zeitschrift*
C Phil.	*Classical Philology*
CA	*Classical Antiquity*
CAH	*Cambridge Ancient History*
CAVI	H. Immerwahr, ed., *Corpus of Attic Vase Inscriptions*
CCJ	*Cambridge Classical Journal*
CCO	*Collectanea Christiana Orientalia*
CdÉ	*Chronique d'Égypte*
CEG	P. A. Hansen, *Carmina epigraphica Graeca*, 2 vols, Berlin 1983–9
CFHB	*Corpus Fontium Historiae Byzantinae*
CIG	A. Boeckh et al., *Corpus Inscriptionum Graecarum*, 4 vols, Berlin 1828–77
CIL	*Corpus Inscriptionum Latinarum*, Berlin 1862–
CP	*Classical Philology*
CQ	*Classical Quarterly*
CRAI	*Comptes rendus de l'Académie des inscriptions et belles-lettres*
Cron. Erc.	*Cronache Ercolanesi*
CSCO	*Corpus Scriptorum Christianorum Orientalium*
CW	*Classical World*
DAI	Deutsches archäologisches Institut
DGE	E. Schwyzer, *Dialectorum graecarum exempla epigraphica potiora*, Leipzig 1923 (repr. Hildesheim 1960)
DHA	*Dialogues d'histoire ancienne*
DK	H. Diels and W. Kranz, *Die Fragmente der Vorsokratiker*, 6th edn, Berlin 1951–2
Documents	M. Ventris and J. Chadwick, *Documents in Mycenaean Greek*, Cambridge 1956
Documents[2]	M. Ventris and J. Chadwick, *Documents in Mycenaean Greek*, 2nd edn, Cambridge 1973
DOP	*Dumbarton Oaks Papers*

EVO	*Egitto e Vicino Oriente*
FD	*Fouilles de Delphes.* Paris 1902–
FDS	K. Hülser, *Die Fragmente zur Dialektik der Stoiker*, 4 vols, Stuttgart 1987–8
FGrH	F. Jacoby, *Fragmente der Griechischen Historiker*, Berlin 1923–
G&R	*Greece and Rome*
Gram. Rom. Frag.	H. Funaioli, *Grammaticae Romanae fragmenta*, Leipzig 1907
GRBS	*Greek, Roman and Byzantine Studies*
Guide	F. Bérard et al., *Guide de l'épigraphiste. Bibliographie choisie des épigraphies antiques et médiévales.* Paris 1989
Harv. Theol. Rev.	*Harvard Theological Review*
HEL	*Histoire, Épistémologie, Langage*
HSCPh	*Harvard Studies in Classical Philology*
IC	M. Guarducci, *Inscriptiones Creticae*, Rome 1935–50
ICS	*Illinois Classical Studies*
IEG	M. L. West, *Iambi et Elegi Graeci*, 2nd edn, Oxford 1989
IF	*Indogermanische Forschungen*
IG	*Inscriptiones Graecae*, Berlin 1873–
IGSK or *IK*	*Inschriften griechischer Städte aus Kleinasien*, Bonn 1972–
JAOS	*Journal of the American Oriental Society*
JbAChr	*Jahrbuch für antikes Christentum*
JEg. Arch.	*Journal of Egyptian Archaeology*
JGL	*Journal of Greek Linguistics*
JHS	*Journal of Hellenic Studies*
JIES	*Journal of Indo-European Studies*
JMA	*Journal of Mediterranean Archaeology*
JÖB	*Jahrbuch der österreichischen Byzantinistik*
JRS	*Journal of Roman Studies*
JTS	*Journal of Theological Studies*
Joüon–Muraoka	P. Joüon, *A Grammar of Biblical Hebrew*, corrected repr., trans. and rev. T. Muraoka, Rome 1993

Keil, *Gramm. Lat.*	H. Keil, *Grammatici Latini*, 8 vols, Leipzig 1855–1923; repr. Hildesheim 1961–
K-G	R. Kühner, *Ausführliche Grammatik der griechischen Sprache*, 2 vols., rev. B. Gerth, Hanover 1898–1904
Kühn	C. G. Kühn, *Medicorum graecorum opera quae exstant*, Hildesheim 1964–5 (repr. of 1821–33 edn)
Lalies	Lalies, *Actes des sessions de linguistique et de littérature*
LCM	*Liverpool Classical Monthly*
LEC	*Les Études classiques*
LGPN	*A Lexicon of Greek Personal Names*, Oxford 1987–
LSAG	L. H. Jeffery, *The Local Scripts of Archaic Greece*, Oxford 1961; repr. with a *Supplement 1961–87* by A. W. Johnston, 1990
LSJ	Liddell and Scott, *Greek–English Lexicon*, 9th edn, rev. H. Stuart Jones, Oxford 1925–40
MAMA	*Monumenta Asiae Minoris Antiqua*, Manchester 1928–
MEG	*Medioevo Greco*
MH	*Museum Helveticum*
ML	R. Meiggs and D. M. Lewis, *A Selection of Greek Historical Inscriptions to the End of the Fifth Century* BC, rev. edn, Oxford 1988
MSS	*Münchener Studien zur Sprachwissenschaft*
M-W	R. Merkelbach and M. L. West, *Fragmenta Hesiodea*, Oxford 1967
MXG	H. Diels, *Aristotelis qui fertur de Melisso, Xenophane, Gorgia libellus. Philosophische und historische Abhandlungen der königlichen Akademie der Wissenschaften zu Berlin*, Berlin 1900
NAGVI	R. Wachter, *Non-Attic Greek Vase Inscriptions*, Oxford 2001
OCD[2]	N. G. L. Hammond and H. H. Scullard, *The Oxford Classical Dictionary*, 2nd edn. Oxford 1970
OCD[3]	S. Hornblower and A. Spawforth, *The Oxford Classical Dictionary*, 3rd edn revised, Oxford 2003
ODB	A. P. Kazhdan, *Oxford Dictionary of Byzantium*, New York 1991
OGIS	W. Dittenberger, *Orientis graeci inscriptiones selectae*, 2 vols, Leipzig 1903–5 (repr. Hildesheim 1986)
OJA	*Oxford Journal of Archaeology*

OLP	*Orientalia Lovaniensia Periodica*
OSAP	*Oxford Studies in Ancient Philosophy*
P.Amh.	B. P. Grenfell and A. S. Hunt, *The Amherst Papyri, Being an Account of the Greek Papyri in the Collection of the Right Hon. Lord Amherst of Hackney, F.S.A. at Didlington Hall, Norfolk*, London 1900–
P.Batav	E. Boswinkel and P. W. Pestman, *Textes grecs, démotiques et bilingues*, Leiden 1978
PCG	R. Kassel and C. Austin, *Poetae Comici Graeci*, Berlin 1983–
PCPS	*Proceedings of the Cambridge Philological Society*
P.Flor.	*Papiri greco-egizii, Papiri Fiorentini*
PG	J. P. Migne, *Patrologia Graeca*
PGM	K. Preisendanz, *Papyri Graecae Magicae*, 2 vols, Leipzig–Berlin 1928–31
P.Herc.	*Papyri Herculanenses*
Philol.	*Philologus*
P.Lond.	*Greek Papyri in the British Museum*
P.Lugd.Bat.	*Papyrologica Lugduno-Batava*
PMG	D. L. Page, *Poetae Melici Graeci*, Oxford 1962
PMGF	M. Davies, *Poetarum Melicorum Graecorum Fragmenta*, Oxford 1991
P.Mich.	*Michigan Papyri*
P.Mil.	*Papiri Milanesi*
P.Oxy.	B. P. Grenfell, A. S. Hunt et al., *The Oxyrhynchus Papyri*, London 1898–
PP	*La parola del passato*
PPar.	J. A. Letronne, W. Brunet de Presle, and E. Egger, *Notices et textes des papyrus grecs du Musée du Louvre et de la Bibliothèque Impériale*, Paris 1865
P.Strasb	F. Preisigke, *Griechische Papyrus der Kaiserlichen Universitäts- und Landesbibliothek zu Strassburg*, Leipzig
P.Tebt.	*The Tebtunis Papyri*, London 1902–
P.Vat.Aphrod	R. Pintaudi, ed., *I Papiri Vaticani di Aphrodito*, Rome 1980
QUCC	*Quaderni Urbinati di Cultura Classica*

RAAO	*Revue d'assyriologie et d'archéologie orientale*
Radt	S. Radt, *Tragicorum Graecorum Fragmenta*. Vol. 4: *Sophocles*, rev. edn, Berlin 1999
RANL	*Rendiconti dell'Accademia nazionale dei Lincei*
RBPH	*Revue belge de philologie et d'histoire*
REA	*Revue des études anciennes*
REAug	*Revue des études augustiniennes*
REB	*Revue des études byzantines*
REG	*Revue des études grecques*
Rend. Ist. Lomb.	*Rendiconti d. R. Istituto Lombardo di scienze e lettere*
Rev. Ét. Lat.	*Revue des études latines*
Rev. Phil.	*Revue de philologie*
RHM	*Römische historische Mitteilungen*
Rh. Mus.	*Rheinisches Museum für Philologie*
RHS	*Revue d'histoire des sciences*
RO	P. J. Rhodes and R. G. Osborne, *Greek Historical Inscriptions, 404–323 BC*, Oxford 2003
SB	*Sammelbuch griechischer Urkunden aus Ägypten*
SCI	*Studia Classica Israelica*
S-D	E. Schwyzer and A. Debrunner, *Griechische Grammatik*, vol. 2, Munich 1950
SEG	*Supplementum epigraphicum graecum*, Leiden 1923–
SGDI	H. Collitz, F. Bechtel et al., *Sammlung der griechischen Dialektinschriften*, Göttingen 1884–1915
SGLG	*Sammlung griechischer und lateinischer Grammatiker*
SMEA	*Studi micenei ed egeo-anatolici*
SNG	*Sylloge nummorum graecorum*. 2002–
SO	*Symbolae Osloenses*
St.Cl.	*Studii clasice*
SVF	H. von Arnim, *Stoicorum Veterum Fragmenta*, 4 vols, Leipzig 1905–24
Syll³	W. Dittenberger, *Sylloge inscriptionum graecarum*, 3rd edn, 4 vols, Leipzig 1915–24 (repr. Hildesheim 1982)

TAM	*Tituli Asiae Minoris*, Vienna 1901–
TAPA	*Transactions of the American Philological Association*
TAPhS	*Transactions of the American Philosophical Society*
THT	*Tocharische Handschriften Turfansammlung*
TLG	*Thesaurus Linguae Graecae*
TPS	*Transactions of the Philological Society*
UPZ	*Urkunden der Ptolemäerzeit*
Voigt	E. M. Voigt, *Sappho et Alcaeus*, Amsterdam 1971
WJA	*Würzburger Jahrbücher für die Altertumswissenschaft*
WS	*Wiener Studien*
YCS	*Yale Classical Studies*
ZDMG	*Zeitschrift der deutschen morgenländischen Gesellschaft*
ZPE	*Zeitschrift für Papyrologie und Epigraphik*
ZVS	*Zeitschrift für vergleichende Sprachforschung*

Linguistic and Other Abbreviations

abl.	ablative
acc.	accusative
act.	active
Aeol.	Aeolic
Akk.	Akkadian
aor.	aorist
Aram.	Aramaic
Arc.	Arcadian
Arg.	Argolic
art.	article
ath.	athematic
Att.	Attic
Avest.	Avestan
Bithyn.	Bithynia
Boe.	Boeotian
c.	circa
Capp.	Cappadocia
cent.	century
Cilic.	Cilicia

Class.	Classical
Copt.	Coptic
Cret.	Cretan
Cyp.	Cypriot
d.	died
dat.	dative
Delph.	Delphian
Dor.	Doric
du.	dual
E.	East
E. Gk	East Greek
E. Ion.	East Ionic
EMed.Gk	Early Medieval Greek
EMod.Gk	Early Modern Greek
ed(s).	editor(s)
Eg.	Egyptian, Egypt
El.	Elean
ep.	epic
Eub.	Euboean
exx.	examples
fem.	feminine
fl.	*floruit*
fragm.	fragment
fut.	future
fut. pf.	future perfect
Gal.	Galatia
GAves.	Gathic Avestan
gen.	genitive
Germ.	German
Gk	Greek

Heb.	Hebrew
Hier. Luw.	Hieroglyphic Luwian
Hitt.	Hittite
Hom.	Homeric
IE	Indo-European
imp.	imperative
imperf.	imperfect
indic.	indicative
inf.	infinitive
instr.	instrumental
intr.	intransitive
Ion.	Ionic
Iran.	Iranian
Isaur.	Isauria
KN	Knossos tablets (Linear B)
Lac.	Laconian
Lat.	Latin
Lesb.	Lesbian
LMed.Gk	Late Medieval Greek
loc.	locative
Luw.	Luwian
Lyc.	Lycia
Lycaon.	Lycaonia
Lyd.	Lydian/Lydia
masc.	masculine
mid.	middle
Mid. Pers.	Middle Persian
mod.	modern
Mod. Gk	Modern Greek
Mod. Pers.	Modern Persian

Myc.	Mycenaean
Mys.	Mysia
neut.	neuter
nom.	nominative
NW.	Northwest
OL	Old Latin
OP	Old Persian
opt.	optative
Pamph.	Pamphylia
Parth.	Parthian
pass.	passive
PAtt.-Ion.	Proto-Attic-Ionic
pf.	perfect
Phryg.	Phrygian/Phrygia
PIE	Proto-Indo-European
Pisid.	Pisidia
pl.	plural
plupf.	pluperfect
p.n.	personal name
pres.	present
Proto-Gk	Proto-Greek
ps.	person
ptc.	participle
PY	Pylos tablets (Linear B)
r.	reign
Rhod.	Rhodian
SMGk	Standard Modern Greek
s.v.	*sub verbo* (under the headword)
s.vv.	*sub verbis* (under the headwords)
sg.	singular
Skt	Sanskrit

Sogd.	Sogdian
subj.	subjunctive
SW.	Southwest
TB	Tocharian B
TH	Thebes tablets (Linear B)
them.	thematic
Thess.	Thessalian
Toch.	Tocharian
tr.	transitive
Ved.	Vedic
voc.	vocative
W.	West
W. Gk	West Greek
W. Ion.	West Ionic

CHAPTER ONE

Introduction

Egbert J. Bakker

Few of those interested in Greek antiquity, and certainly no one whose interest in ancient Greece is professional and academic, will deny that familiarity with the language, and knowledge about it, is indispensable for any study at any level of critical engagement with Greek antiquity. Those who approach the world of the ancient Greeks without such knowledge will have to rely on a translator's reading skills. For without texts, linguistic evidence, our knowledge of antiquity would not exceed that of other lost civilizations whose ruins and artefacts merely increase the enigma, raising questions that only language can answer.

Yet in spite of such unanimous acknowledgment of the central importance of language, there are widely different attitudes to it within the Classics profession, often coinciding with international fault lines. Whereas in some national traditions the Greek language is seen as an important area of research in its own right – although the angle under which the research is done is not homogeneous – in others the study of Greek as a language is relegated to the pedagogical context of the fresh-men classroom, where instructors are typically graduate students whose own research interests have often nothing to do with the Greek language. In such a context, the Greek language becomes an object of reflection mainly as a pedagogical challenge: learning the language as first step toward, and necessary condition for, access to the ancient world.

The grammars used for reference in this context (in English, e.g., Smyth 1956) are based on nineteenth-century German scholarship that considers deep knowledge of the language as the most powerful – and necessary – hermeneutic tool in the philolo-gist's arsenal. The Greek language is seen as a highly refined (and evolved) means of expressing an author's thought, so that knowing the language's syntax in all its nuances can give the philologist access to this thought and to the world that shaped it. Such a conception of language as indissolubly interconnected with the task of interpretation leads to a natural end point. Critical research into the language comes to a halt when the point has been reached at which the language's refined syntax has been described in such detail that all linguistic obstacles between the critical reader and the author's thought have been removed. Such an end point can be found in the monumental reference grammars of Raphael Kühner and Eduard Schwyzer (K-G and S-D, respectively).

Insofar as the Greek language in itself has traditionally been an object of scholarly, linguistic, interest, the sector studied is not syntax, but morphology and phonology. The perspective is historical-comparative, in that Greek (and Latin) is studied against the background of the reconstruction of Proto-Indo-European, with an eye toward structural similarities between the two ancient languages as well as toward either language's contribution to the reconstruction of the proto-language. Greek was found to be a valuable branch in the Indo-European tree, providing important evidence for what the stem or the root was like. The historical-comparative method has also yielded benefits for the Greek language itself, in the form of deep insight into how linguistic prehistory has shaped the language's morphology and phonology as it can be observed in our texts.

Historical-comparative linguistics is an established subdiscipline of Greek philology and it is practiced in all national traditions. But it is no longer the only way to do critical research on the Greek language. The genetic outlook of historical linguistics, which places Greek in time, the time of the diversification of the Indo-European proto-language, has come to be complemented with a more functional perspective, in which Greek is placed in the geographical space in which it was spoken. The language, we have come to realize, is not only shaped by the regularity of Indo-European sound laws, but also by the interference with the languages, whether genetically related or not, of the peoples encountered by the speakers of Greek. This perspective complements the conception of Ancient Greek as an amalgam of inherited features and involves a variety of language contact phenomena, such as linguistic borrowing, bilingualism on the part of Greek speakers, or the use of Greek by non-Greek speakers.

In another development, the study of the language "itself" has now moved past the pedagogical-hermeneutical positions of the reference grammars. "Greek linguistics" is for some the systematic study of the actual use of the Greek language as we see it deployed in our texts, with reference not only to the understanding of the texts themselves but also to research into the syntax, semantics, even pragmatics, of modern living languages.

The general de-emphasis of "norms" and "default cases" in recent thought in the humanities, furthermore, has stimulated interest in language use other than "standard" or "good" Greek. The "marginal" aspects of the use of the Greek language coming to the fore in this way include spoken language, the "low registers" of the language, the speech of marginal groups such as women, slaves, or foreigners. The margin remains in full focus when we consider the expansion of Greek eastward under Alexander the Great and the profound influence of the resulting "periphery" on what was traditionally the "center." The story of the Greek language is not finished, in more than one way, with the morphology of Homer or the syntax of Demosthenes.

The present volume brings together the traditional perspectives and the newer approaches in what is hoped is a comprehensive overview of the language in its various manifestations (literary texts, papyri, inscriptions) and viewed under a variety of angles: historical, functional, syntactic, pragmatic, and sociolinguistic, to name a few.

Part I deals with the materiality of the Greek language. In order for us to be able to know the language and read its literature, Greek had to be transcoded to written signs in such a way that its sounds and syntax can be recognized; moreover, the objects on which the signs were written physically had to survive the centuries, even the millennia. During its long history the Greek language came to be written down a number of times in a script that was originally designed for another language. The first time was the adaptation, around the middle of the second millennium BCE, of a Cretan syllabary for the purposes of record-keeping in the Mycenaean palatial economy. As *Silvia Ferrara* shows in a survey of the resulting new script (Linear B) and its linguistic and archeological context, much was lost in translation in the way of adequately representing the language's sounds – and due to the nature of the texts not much syntax was committed to writing; but the Linear B texts do provide us with an invaluable window on a stage of the language some 500 years before the earliest surviving archaic inscriptions. *Roger D. Woodard* discusses in detail the second transcoding, the Greek adaptation of the Phoenician alphabet, which in its turn, as recent archeological discoveries have established, was the descendent of an adaptation of Egyptian logograms to stand for the consonants of a West Semitic language. In the adaptation of the resulting consonantal Semitic alphabet, Woodard, argues, Cypriot scribes must have played a key role, and Cyprus must have been the springboard for the expansion of the new invention over the Greek world.

Rudolf Wachter and *Arthur Verhoogt* provide introductions to the study of the main types of documents and their materials that have come down to us from antiquity: inscriptions and papyri. They discuss the types of text that have survived in these documents, which include laws, decrees, transactions, contracts, etc., but also poetry and literature, in the form of funereal or dedicatory epigrams and copies of literary works from Roman Egypt. The great majority of literary texts, however, come to us through Byzantium, heir to the Greek-speaking eastern half of the Roman Empire. *Niels Gaul* discusses – in addition to such material issues as the birth of the codex and of cursive writing – the sometimes violent cultural debates to which the copying of the Classics was subjected through the centuries, reminding us that much of what we take for granted might well not have survived if events had taken a different turn.

Part II presents the Greek language from the perspectives of the traditional linguistic subdisciplines. The type of Greek discussed is mostly the "standard" Classical Attic usage, though diachronic perspectives are also offered. *Philomen Probert* discusses the standard pronunciation of Classical Attic from the point of view of modern phonology, taking into account not only the evidence from inscriptions (the Attic alphabet is discussed), but also from the representation of Greek words in Latin. *Michael Weiss* presents morphology, the "form" of the words of the language and the ways in which they are derived from other words in the language as well as from Proto-Indo-European. *Michael Clarke*, in a new discussion of the meaning of words (lexical semantics), addresses the pedagogically conditioned ways in which classical philology does lexicography. Instead of an organization of lexical entries in terms of "senses" that are – or are not – related by way of metaphorical extensions, he offers a cognitive approach which places not the lexicographer in the center, but the actual speakers of the language, who utter their words with an eye toward their assessment of what their interlocutors take to be the word's basic meaning.

The two final chapters in Part II move from the sound, form, and meaning of words to larger linguistic units. *Evert van Emde Boas* and *Luuk Huitink* present the syntax of Classical Greek, the way in which words combine to form clauses and clauses combine to form larger structures. Among the many topics succinctly presented are the functionally motivated structure of sentences as arguments surrounding a verbal core, the tense, aspect, and mood of the verb, and the order of words in the sentence. In the last chapter, *Egbert J. Bakker* turns to pragmatics, the ways in which language is uttered (and shaped) in conversational discourse contexts. His two case studies are the system of deictics in the language and a cognitively motivated approach to the Greek verb. He shows that the "prototype" of these linguistic features as they are used in interactive conversation in "real life" remains intact also when they are used in formal written texts, arguing that the structure of those texts always remains, to a greater or lesser extent, a matter of interactive communication.

Part III presents the Greek language as subjected to forces deriving from the dimensions of time and space, from its formative period in the second millennium BCE to the end of the Roman Empire and from the traditional Greek heartland to the far-flung regions of the Hellenistic and Roman world. The first two chapters concentrate on the temporal dimension by offering historical-comparative perspectives. *Jeremy Rau* demonstrates the importance of Ancient Greek for the reconstruction of the Indo-European proto-language and, conversely, shows how deeply the inherited features of that language shape Greek as we know it. *Rupert Thompson* then discusses the oldest actually attested Greek. The language of the Linear B tablets, he shows, may be highly archaic in some respects, but it is not to be equated with Proto-Greek: some of its features are shared with only a subset of the dialects we know from the Archaic and Classical ages. Those dialects are the subject of *Stephen Colvin*'s chapter, which shifts the focus from time to space, the space of the Greek language. In his discussion of the geographical variants of Greek, Colvin resists the earlier paradigm of diversity developing out of an original unity in some kind of "autonomous" development. Such a reductive, purely linguistic, model, he argues, obscures such complicating factors as ethnic identity and language contact.

These factors come directly to the fore in the remaining chapters in this section, which deal with the rich set of phenomena, linguistic and social, resulting from the encounter between speakers of Greek with the languages surrounding it, or – and no less important – between the speakers of those languages and Greek. *Shane Hawkins* gives an overview of the evidence we have, directly linguistic or indirectly literary, for the contacts between Greek and its speakers and a variety of languages in the Near East. The picture that emerges is one of a wide variety of contacts over the centuries, from high-level diplomatic exchange in the second millennium to exchanges between Greek and Carian mercenaries in sixth-century Egypt.

With the creation of the Hellenistic world, and continuing under the Roman Empire, Greek comes to be spoken and written by large numbers of non-Greek speakers. *Claude Brixhe* discusses the consequences of this dramatic expansion. He argues that the concept of "*Koine*" commonly used for postdialectal Greek in a world of political and cultural globalization is underspecified and cannot do justice to the complex linguistic reality of the Greco-Roman East. Only the uniform high-register language that artificially preserves Attic grammar can be called "common," whereas the lower, demotic registers display wide variety, even dialects. Brixhe's survey of the epigraphical record in Greco-Roman Asia Minor allows us a glimpse into the real-life laboratory in which the contours of future Modern Greek are taking visible shape. A region where the Greek impact on the local culture, and of the local speakers on the Greek language, was particularly strong and, due to the availability of the papyrological record, particularly visible, was Egypt. *Sofia Torallas Tovar* gives an overview of Greco-Egyptian bilingualism, teasing out the specific Egyptian interferences taking place in addition to the larger patterns in the wider evolution of the *Koine*. Such questions also come to the fore in *Coulter H. George*'s chapter, but here the "interfering" languages are Hebrew and Aramaic and the bilingual context is not everyday interaction, but the translation of the biblical scriptures. George shows that the syntax of the Greek Old and New Testament reflects the patterns of the original text and language, over and above the features that it derives from the evolution of the language itself in the development of *Koine*.

The contact between Greek and Latin, finally, is discussed by *Bruno Rochette*. The interactions between the two languages are intimately connected with Roman identity and the Roman Empire and are apparent in the complex bilingual habits of cultured Romans. Rochette shows that after a period in which the two languages were equivalent (though not without problems or discussion) under the Republic and the early Empire, Greek gradually had to yield, eventually disappearing from the western half of the Empire.

Language is not, as some linguists suppose, a simple algorithm or a value-free "code" for the expression of thoughts. Language is a matter of social empowerment or lack thereof, of speakers' identity or the assignment of identity to them by their listeners, and of social or professional groups either being characterized by it or consciously singling themselves out with it. Part IV offers a selection of the possibilities opened up by such sociolinguistic approaches. *Andreas Willi* discusses register, which he defines as the set of linguistic features reflecting a given "genre" of discourse, a way of speaking conditioned by the framework (social, situational, subject matter, etc.) shared by the speakers in a given situation. Willi's linguistic analysis of register variation in Greek literature also involves a look at parody in literature as well as at the prescriptive discussions of register (*lexis*) in rhetorical theory in terms of "appropriateness" and "decorum." Sometimes a "way of speaking" is not shared or deliberately adopted but attributed to groups of, typically marginal, speakers. Out of the various possibilities here *Thorsten Fögen* selects the speech of women; he discusses the evidence for female speech in Greek and Roman literature, which unsurprisingly reveals more about the male norm with respect to which female speech is "other" than about women's speech itself. The perceived differences between groups of speakers that differ from the male adult norm is "coded" in the form of a language's system of address, which *Eleanor Dickey* presents in the next chapter. Her analysis shows a marked contrast between an egalitarian Classical use of address terms and directives (utterances ordering someone to do something) and increasing social stratification in later ages, complicated by strong influence from the address system in Latin. *Francesca Schironi* finishes the section with a presentation on the language of Greek science (medicine and mathematics). She shows how not only language is conditioned by the special body of knowledge of a given group, but also that the one *Fachsprache* can differ radically from the other. Thus medicine creates its special discourse by lexical means, whereas mathematics employs a specialized formulaic syntax. She also addresses the different communicative needs and goals with which each discipline is faced.

Ancient Greek would not be known to us in the detailed evidence available, if it had not been the language of a literature that has through the millennia been deemed valuable and worthy of transmission. The transmitted literary works thus provide rich evidence for the language, but it would be a mistake to keep language and literature so separate from each other as "form" from "content." As the chapters in Part V show in their different ways, many of the literary genres, even individual works, are a language in their own right. This is a complex phenomenon with many aspects (linguistic, esthetic, social, religious, political) that grew in importance over the centuries as literary works and genres gained an increasingly canonical status. Homeric epic, to begin, is heir to an Indo-European *Dichtersprache*. *Joshua T. Katz* starts the series by considering what this means. The field of comparative-historical poetics he presents is cognate with historical-comparative linguistics as presented earlier by Weiss and Rau, but instead of inherited morphological and phonological patterns it studies inherited phraseology. Katz discusses some well-known Homeric formulae that stand a fair chance of being inherited. In addition to actual phrases he also pays attention to the Homeric evidence for Indo-European stylistic practice as well as to the ever-controversial question of inherited meter. Meter is, of course, one of the most important ways in which poetry as special language reserved for special performance occasions can be set apart from ordinary speech. It is studied by *Gregory Nagy*, who presents his discussion against the background of Plato's critique in *Laws* of contemporary *mousikē* as a state of disintegration of a former integral whole: the contemporary poets have isolated words from rhythm and melody. As Nagy argues, however, meter, taken in the wider sense of "measure," crucially contains rhythm and melody in the form of the double accentuation system of the language, involving both stress and pitch. Meter is thus characterized as a regulation – embedded in the language – of the measures of melody and rhythm, showing both in the rhythmical profile and in the melodic contour of the verse.

Another typifying feature of literature is dialect. *Olga Tribulato* discusses this feature, showing that far from restricting a work's circulation to a limited area, dialect can contribute to a work's, and genre's, panhellenic distribution. Dialects, she states, are consciously adopted literary languages that have often nothing to do with a given poet's native dialect. Moreover, they are conventional stylizations, rather than faithful representations of any local dialect. An important issue Tribulato raises is the question of the transmission of dialect features by Hellenistic and later editors. The question of dialect applies, sometimes controversially, to Homeric poetry with its "multidialectal" character. *Olav Hackstein* addresses the dialectal underpinnings of the epic *Kunstsprache* and offers a comprehensive survey of the diachronic dimension of epic diction, in which archaic features easily combine with recent language in a dynamic interplay of modernization and archaization. He also reviews the extensive evidence for the ways in which Homeric language is conditioned by meter. The chapter ends with a view of the impact of Homeric Greek, as the culture's central poetic language, on contemporary inscriptional poetry and later literary traditions.

Michael Silk continues with a discussion of Greek lyric, in which he includes the language of the choral songs in tragedy and in Aristophanes. The language of Greek song, Silk shows, is throughout indebted to the epic tradition, which sets it apart, along with dialect coloring (never the poet's own native dialect), from ordinary speech, although lyric poets are keen to combine the epic flavor of their compositions with contemporary language. To this dimension of stylistic elevation (which is in part, perhaps, a matter of register) Silk adds the dimension of heightening, the intensification of meaning on an ad hoc basis, e.g., through metaphor. The language of tragedy is further analyzed by *Richard Rutherford*, who sheds more light on both the "elevation" and the metaphorical complexity of tragic language. Rutherford offers a close reading of three sample passages which each exemplify the style of each of the three tragedians.

Prose comes to the fore in the two remaining chapters of Part V. *Victor Bers* discusses the ways in which "prose" (whether as written communication or as enhanced speech) can be turned into an artistic medium. The esthetic concept of *Kunstprosa* sets up poetry as at the same time a source on which to draw and as example to be avoided, and it is not always easy to gauge the artistic impact – or intention – of such phenomena as prose rhythm or poetic coloration in the absence of more comparative material. The Attic texts studied by Bers were destined to become *Kunstprosa* in the second degree in the intellectual and cultural milieu of the Second Sophistic, discussed by *Lawrence Kim* in the final chapter. Kim's discussion of Atticism shows how language came to play a key role in the fashioning of elite Hellenic identity under the Empire, with the attested usage of canonical Attic writers becoming a language in its own right. Tracing the various attitudes toward Classical or Attic language back to Dionysius of Halicarnassus and the Roman *Attici*, Kim warns against simplification and overgeneralization: Atticism is a varied phenomenon, ranging from an uncompromising prohibition on language *not* attested in the Attic models to the loose adoption of an Attic-sounding style. But however one conceived of language and the past among those with access to the highest linguistic registers (from "pure" Atticism to educated *Koine*), the period sees the beginning of a state of diglossia that was to continue till the resolution of the Language Controversy in the modern Greek nation-state.

Part VI offers three essays in reflection on the Greek language within antiquity. There is some overlap between the three chapters, dealing with philosophy, grammar, and rhetoric, respectively, but that overlap is a natural consequence of the fact that the boundaries between these three disciplines were much less clearly drawn in antiquity than they are now. *Casper C. de Jonge* and *Johannes M. van Ophuijsen* provide an overview of the reflection on language in the philosophical tradition from the Presocratics to Plotinus. Their account highlights throughout the wider concerns of Greek philosophers in their dealings with language, such as the Presocratics' questioning of the capacity of nouns and names to grasp the deeper structure of the world, or the Stoics' use of logic, and *logos*, to attain the enlightened philosophical life. While the philosophical tradition is interested in "words," their properties, and classification, mainly insofar as these are indispensable for the correct treatment of *logos* (i.e., the meaningful, declarative sentence), the tradition of *grammatikē*, as it gradually emancipates from philosophy, comes to be interested in the "elements of language" for their own sake. *Andreas U. Schmidhauser*, revisiting some of the philosophical territory and considering it from the viewpoint of the prehistory of linguistics, traces the "birth" of grammar to the Stoics; their hierarchy of constitutive elements of language (writable sound, syllable, word, sentence) as well as their distinction of "parts of speech" will prove very influential. Schmidhauser shows how the great grammarian Apollonius Dyscolus as well as the subsequent grammatical tradition are indebted to it in spite of some important semantic modifications. *James Porter* then offers a further account of what he calls the Greeks' "metadiscursive grasp" of language. Expanding the fundamental idea that language can be broken down various levels into component parts, he speaks of a "componential analysis" of language, of which the *stoicheion* is the atomic building-block – indeed, he traces the concept to fifth-century BCE atomic physics. Porter's discussion of *stoicheion* brings together such diverse topics as esthetics in stylistic theory, "nonsense" inscriptions on early Classical vases, and a new reading of the *Helen* of Gorgias.

Part VII in closing takes the Greek language out of antiquity and brings it to the modern age. *Staffan Wahlgren* in a sequel to Kim's chapter discusses literary language under the Byzantine Empire and writers' attitude toward the classical past. His overview is a useful correction of the common view of Byzantine literature as operating in a one-dimensional space with the classical models at one extreme and contemporary vernacular at the other. Byzantine literature will construe the "high-end" register in different ways in different periods and will sometimes consciously adopt vernacular elements. Emancipation from the ancient language is naturally even stronger in the medieval and early modern vernacular, but the normative bias, sometimes even from within the contemporary Greek-speaking world, is just as strong. *David Holton* and *Io Manolessou* argue that "medieval Greek" is a language in its own right that is not done justice when the ancient language remains the frame of reference. Medieval Greek philology, they argue, can be more fruitfully brought into line with the study of the medieval vernaculars of the Western European languages. Their detailed survey of the changes taking place in the medieval period, many of which originate in the *Koine*, can be profitably read in conjunction with Brixhe's survey of the linguistic changes taking place in Hellenistic and Roman Asia Minor.

Many of those changes are naturally at the basis of the official language of the modern Greek nation-state, but as *Peter Mackridge* shows in the last chapter of the volume, Standard Modern Greek is by no means the direct result of the natural developments in the language (demotic). Conscious choices were made in the wider context of the Language Controversy that sprang into being with Greek independence and that pitted vernacularists (of various "degrees") against purists. The result, as Mackridge shows, is an elaborate compromise in which words from the learned tradition are adopted and subjected to rules of morphology deriving from the popular tradition, if available; if not, ancient morphology is invoked. Modern Standard Greek, of which a detailed overview is offered, thus provides living evidence for the continuous presence of the ancient language.

CHAPTER TWO

Mycenaean Texts: The Linear B Tablets

Silvia Ferrara

Script and language are two uncorrelated, separate entities. In functional terms, a language can be written by means of several writing systems, and, equally, one script can record multiple existing languages. In its long history, the Greek language was recorded by three separate scripts. Following its decipherment in 1952 by Michael Ventris, we can now read the earliest of these, which is commonly called Linear B. This chapter is dedicated to the paleographic origin of Linear B and to its historical significance as the first epigraphic attestation of the Greek language.

Some 400 years before the Phoenician script was adopted for the creation of the Greek alphabet and a few centuries before the Classical Cypriot Syllabary was used to write the Arcado-Cypriot dialect on Cyprus, an early form of Greek, predating the Homeric poems by half a millennium, was recorded by means of a syllabic writing system called Linear B. As opposed to the alphabet, in which the separate sounds of a language are recorded individually, in a syllabary such as Linear B, individual signs consist of two sounds, typically a consonant followed by a vowel (/ka/, /ke/, /ki/, /ko/, /ku/; /ta/, /te/, /ti/, /to/, /tu/; etc.), with a separate set for simple vowels (/a/, /e/, /i/, /o/, /u/). As a result, a syllabary will include a larger number of signs than an alphabet.

The Linear B syllabary was the product of the Mycenaean civilization of the Late Bronze Age in its high phase (1400–1200 BCE) and was instrumental to documenting the administrative transactions of a highly centralized economy focused on palace complexes on Crete (Knossos, Khania) and in mainland Greece (Pylos, Mycenae, Tiryns, and Thebes). But while Linear B is a clear manifestation of the Mycenaean culture responsible for its creation, its origin, from an essentially paleographic perspective, is deeply embedded in the Minoan period, preceding the Mycenaean period by half a millennium. Minoan Crete was the cradle of Aegean writing, and, in the span of five centuries or so, three separate syllabic scripts were fashioned almost uniquely to record the administrative operation of palatial systems.

The Origin: Aegean Syllabaries of the Second Millennium

When, in 1900, Arthur Evans, then keeper at the Ashmolean Museum in Oxford, began excavations at the site of Knossos, he revealed a palace complex centuries earlier in date (Middle Minoan IA) than the Mycenaean palaces unearthed by Schliemann a few decades before on the Greek mainland (Late Helladic I–III).

Evans suspected that this newly discovered civilization of Crete, coined "Minoan" after the legendary king Minos, would yield evidence for literacy. His strong conviction was based on the evolutionarily determined idea that "Man before Writing" could not have reached the level of sophistication displayed in Minoan artistry and craftsmanship in the absence of writing, rather than on the more pragmatic observation that the administration of a complex structure such as a palace would necessitate written records. But he was soon proven right: among the ruins of the palace, more than 4,000 tablets were discovered, which bore hitherto unseen characters, and whose intricate graphic structure was unmistakably recognizable as writing. Most of them consisted of angular signs formed mainly by rectangular and vertical lines. Evans gave this script the imaginative title of "Linear." "Linear" was soon distinguished into two different systems, Linear Script of Class A and Linear Script of Class B, which shared a large common element, but whose distinguishing features were regular and systematically observable. Another deposit of clay documents bore a script vaguely resembling Egyptian hieroglyphs, and was thus termed "hieroglyphic" or "conventionalized pictographic" and dated, in the light of its stratigraphic position, to an earlier phase than the Linear classes (Evans 1909).

Detailing the origin and development of writing on Crete is an enterprise fraught with problems, mainly of a quantitative and chronological nature. We can claim that it is with the appearance of the Cretan "hieroglyphic" script that the history of writing in the Aegean formally begins, but even this assumption is debatable. Four seals that bear the same sequence of five signs, in the so-called Arkhanes script, are attested from the first palatial period (Middle Minoan IA) and thus represent the earliest form of writing on the island, but what they constitute is a repeated "formula" rather than a cohesive graphic system, and even their paleographic relationship with the Cretan hieroglyphic script cannot be persuasively traced (Olivier and Godart 1996).

Quantitative problems are evident even when writing can be formally identified. Cretan hieroglyphic script and Linear A form, together, a corpus of fewer than 2,000 documents, with slightly more than 10,000 individual signs (respectively 350 inscriptions in hieroglyphic adding up to *c.* 3,000 signs, and 1,500 inscriptions in Linear A, with *c.* 8,000 signs). While the paucity of the material impedes our understanding of how writing emerged and advanced on Crete, it equally poignantly reflects onto a problem of a purely linguistic nature: despite several attempts at decipherment, the language, or indeed languages, behind these two scripts remain unidentified. However, even if tracing the history of poorly attested scripts is problematic to the same extent that reading and understanding their language is unfeasible, the functions of these scripts can be evaluated and compared, and the purposes for their creation postulated

Table 2.1 The chronology of the Aegean scripts, with absolute and relative dates

Script	Absolute Chronology BCE	Relative Chronology Crete	Relative Chronology Mainland
Arkhanes	2100–1900	Middle Minoan IA	
	1900–1850	Middle Minoan IB, ***Protopalatial period***	
Cretan hieroglyphic,	1850–1800	Middle Minoan IIA	
Linear A	1800–1700	Middle Minoan IIB	
	1700–1650	Middle Minoan IIIA, ***Neopalatial***	
	1650–1600	Middle Minoan IIIB	Middle Helladic III
Linear A	1600–1480	Late Minoan IA	Late Helladic I
	1480–1425	Late Minoan IB	Late Helladic IIA
Linear B (KN, Chariot Tablets)	1425–1390	Late Minoan II, *Postpalatial*	Late Helladic IIB
Linear A, Linear B	1390–1360	Late Minoan IIIA1 ***Palace of Knossos destroyed***	Late Helladic IIIA1
Linear B	1360–1330	Late Minoan IIIA2	Late Helladic IIIA2
	1330–1250	Late Minoan IIIB1	Late Helladic IIIB1
	1250–1200	Late Minoan IIIB2	Late Helladic IIIB2

with some degree of confidence. This interpretative approach can shed light on the cultural substratum that saw the birth of Linear B.

Cretan hieroglyphic script

Evans infused his analysis of the Aegean scripts with the notion that their graphic structure systematically developed through a unidirectional evolutionary sequence from pictorial to more abstract signs, and that thus the Linear scripts would represent the survivals of a primitive system of picture-writing, stemming directly from the Cretan hieroglyphic. This mechanistic perspective can be challenged on many levels. It can now be safely claimed that the signs of the Cretan hieroglyphic script, although still remaining the less understood of the Aegean syllabaries, do not represent pictograms in the sense of "picture-drawing," and that neither do they genetically stem from the Egyptian hieroglyphs, nor do they have anything "hieratic" or "sacred" about them (Olivier 1989).

The number of distinct signs (96) indicates that the script is syllabic (Olivier and Godart 1996). To the phonographic core, namely the sets of signs representing syllables, it adds a logographic component of about 30 signs, which individually represent a morpheme, or a meaningful unit of language, thus omitting the syllabically spelled-out representation of words in their phonemic structure. Together with these, a series of *klasmatograms* (fractions) and *arithmograms* (numerical notations) are attested. This system already shows a degree of structural complexity that definitely functions as more than an "embryonic instrument for spelling out names and titles" (*Documents*[2]: 30). The inscriptions on archival material, recorded on more than a hundred supports between clay tablets, bars, and medallions, are of a clear administrative nature, as they register the movements of commodities, indicated by the regular usage of logograms, with their respective quantities recorded with a decimal numeric system. This basic layout of information on the clay documents, with the three constituent elements of word-sequence (spelled syllabically), logogram and numeral, will be preserved in the Linear A and B inscriptions produced for comparable accounting purposes and it conclusively indicates that the three scripts had, in their internal structure, a common core.

Half of the total number of Cretan hieroglyphic inscriptions is attested on sphragistic material (seals and seal impressions), probably functioning to register and impress the administrative role of the seal owner. Interestingly, seals are never engraved with Linear A signs. This may be due to more than epigraphic preferences in two different scribal traditions and it may indicate that the basic controlling and recording procedures relating to seals were replaced by the more efficient and far-reaching capabilities of the full phonetic and logographic system which will become the regular practice in Linear B (Palaima 1988a).

Linear A

For decades it was assumed that the Cretan hieroglyphic evolved into a more stylized and more cursive graphic form represented by the Linear A script, in a direct and recognizable line of chronological and paleographic descent. Today this view is problematic. We now know that the two systems were created more or less co-terminously (the earliest attestations of Linear A date to the Middle Minoan IIA period, thus still in the Protopalatial period; Vandenabeele 1985) and in the same cultural context. Moreover, and without intending to dispute a general affiliation, the paucity of the inscriptions in both *corpora* obfuscates their paleographic interrelation: we simply cannot claim, with slightly more than 20 common syllabograms, and about a third of the logograms, that the graphic structural core is wholly shared between the two.

The near totality of the Linear A material is attested from Crete and found in palatial contexts, villas, sanctuaries, and tombs, but also on several Aegean islands and Miletus (Godart and Olivier 1976–85). Its apogee corresponds roughly to the Minoan palace constructions of the Neopalatial period. In stark contrast with the Linear B epigraphic repertoire, Linear A texts are known on a wide range of supports: incised on stone vessels, on precious metal objects (silver and gold pins, a miniature gold axe, a gold ring), painted in cuttlefish ink on the inside of a clay cup and other clay vases, and incised on wall graffiti. The remainder of non-administrative texts is represented by "votive" formulae incised on stone libation tables and other objects dedicated at peak sanctuaries (Brice 1961; Shoep 1994).

More than half of the inscriptions are found in the archival records at the royal villa of Hagia Triada, dating to the Late Minoan IA period, when the script possibly reached its most formalized, and most representative sign repertoire (*Documents*[2]). The Hagia Triada archives bear testimony to the usage of the script in a clearly administrative context. Inventories concerning agricultural and manufactured commodities, personnel and stock transactions were normally entered on page-shaped clay tablets, but also on other independent documents such as nodules and roundels. Roundels were used as receipts for objects leaving the administrative centers, bearing one word on one side and the logogram for the represented commodity on the other. Nodules were holed lumps of clay impressed by a seal and rarely inscribed, used to secure the end of strings and hanging from objects to label them (Hallager 1996). There is evidence that some of the nodules were attached to written documents of either papyrus or parchment and this would open up the possibility that perishable materials were indeed part of the epigraphic supports.

In its graphic structure Linear A presents a composite phonographic and logographic repertoire. The phonograms are 97 (although the exact figure is disputed; Raison and Pope 1977; Godart and Olivier 1976–85) and about 50 logograms (15 of which are regularly attested, the remainder being either *hapax legomena* or very rare). In addition there are as many as 150 "complex" signs formed by the graphic juxtaposition of simple syllabograms (*monograms*), or by superimposing logograms and syllabograms together in one sign (*ligatures*). This complex sematographic repertoire was employed through the space-saving mechanism of recording objects/words both through a more or less reliable "drawing" of their physical characteristics (vessels, animals, etc.) or through acrophonic abbreviations, i.e., the representation of the first syllable of the object/word registered. The result is that the information recorded on Linear A tablets is extremely condensed and shortened, resorting to full phonetic writing only to a minimal degree. Quantities are expressed through a meticulously articulate system of fractions, which dates back to the Cretan hieroglyphs and is likely to be Egyptian in origin (Duhoux 1989; Bennett 1950).

From a paleographic perspective, the affiliation between the two Linear scripts has never been disputed. About 70 phonograms of the Linear A system are common to the Linear B script (see table 2.2, where common signs are marked "**ab**"), thus there would be no theoretical impediment to the idea of "reading" Linear A: determining the phonetic realization of the Linear A syllabograms would be based on the application of the phonetic values of the Linear B signs on their homographic Linear A counterparts. Cross-script recognition and consequent sound transference is, however, a risky procedure since one cannot theoretically exclude the possibility that the phonetic values of the Linear A system were partially modified or reshuffled by the developers of the Linear B system. The general principle prompting us to caution is that paleographical similarity does not go in tandem with phonetic identity, especially when a script is adapted to record different phonological characteristics inherent in a new language.

Even discounting all the possible theoretical *caveats*, and even accepting this method to have proven partially successful in reading Linear A (bearing in mind that "reading" is not "deciphering"), the yielded results of the sound transference have proven inconclusive (Duhoux 1978, 1989). It is today possible to recognize a few Minoan toponyms and anthroponyms and a couple of structural characteristics, such as patterns of sign alternation and affixing and some phonological aspects (for instance, a preponderant use of word-final –u where Linear B uses –o; Duhoux 1989), but these

Table 2.2 The Linear A syllabary, with signs uniquely attested in Linear A (a) and signs shared with the Linear B syllabary (ab)

ab	☓	ab	☓	ab	☓	ab	☓	ab	☓	ab	☓	a	☓	a	☓	a	☓	a	☓	a	☓	a	☓	a	☓	a	☓	a	☓		
ab	☓	ab	☓	ab	☓	ab	☓	ab	☓	ab	☓	a	☓	a	☓	a	☓	a	☓	a	☓	a	☓	a	☓	a	☓	a	☓		
ab	☓	ab	☓	ab	☓	ab	☓	ab	☓	ab	☓	a	☓	a	☓	a	☓	a	☓	a	☓	a	☓	a	☓	a	☓	a	☓		
ab	☓	ab	☓	ab	☓	ab	☓	ab	☓	ab	☓	a	☓	a	☓	a	☓	a	☓	a	☓	a	☓	a	☓	a	☓	a	☓		
ab	☓	ab	☓	ab	☓	ab	☓	ab	☓	ab	☓	a	☓	a	☓	a	☓	a	☓	a	☓	a	☓	a	☓	a	☓	a	☓		
ab	☓	ab	☓	ab	☓	ab	☓	ab	☓	ab	☓	a	☓	a	☓	a	☓	a	☓	a	☓	a	☓	a	☓	a	☓	a	☓		
ab	☓	ab	☓	ab	☓	ab	☓	ab	☓	ab	☓	a	☓	a	☓	a	☓	a	☓	a	☓	a	☓	a	☓	a	☓	a	☓		
ab	☓	ab	☓	ab	☓	ab	☓	ab	☓	ab	☓	a	☓	a	☓	a	☓	a	☓	a	☓	a	☓	a	☓	a	☓	a	☓		
ab	☓	ab	☓	ab	☓	ab	☓	ab	☓	a	☓	a	☓	a	☓	a	☓	a	☓	a	☓	a	☓	a	☓	a	☓	a	☓				
ab	☓	ab	☓	ab	☓	ab	☓	a	☓	a	☓	a	☓	a	☓	a	☓	a	☓	a	☓	a	☓	a	☓	a	☓						
ab	☓	ab	☓	ab	☓	a	☓	a	☓	a	☓	a	☓	a	☓	a	☓	a	☓	a	☓	a	☓	a	☓	a	☓						
ab	☓	ab	☓	ab	☓	a	☓	a	☓	a	☓	a	☓	a	☓	a	☓	a	☓	a	☓	a	☓	a	☓	a	☓						
ab	☓	ab	☓	ab	☓	a	☓	a	☓	a	☓	a	☓	a	☓	a	☓	a	☓	a	☓	a	☓	a	☓	a	☓						
ab	☓	ab	a	☓	ab	☓	a	☓	a	☓	a	☓	a	☓	a	☓	a	☓	a	☓	a	☓	a	☓	a	☓							

scanty data do nothing but underline further how any linguistic solution remains as open as ever. This has not, of course, deterred a number of would-be decipherers from proposing several candidate languages (East Semitic (Gordon 1966; see Hooker 1988, *contra*); Luvian (Brown 1992–3); Lycian (Finkelberg 1990–1)).

What we need for a breakthrough is, simply, more material. When Linear B was deciphered, Ventris had roughly 6,000 tablets and more than 30,000 signs at his disposal: Linear A signs are roughly a fourth. But the obstacle is not just numerical. We need inscriptions of a different kind. Brief dedications and abbreviated inventories or a series of disparate only-once-attested forms cannot offer verification for a recognizable morphological structure and any linguistic interpretation must harmonize with what would be expected in the general historical context of Minoan civilization: to hypothesize, for instance, that the language behind Linear A could have Greek elements (Nagy 1963) vigorously disagrees with the accepted chronological circumstances for the "coming of the Greeks."

The Linear B Script

The graphic repertoire

Although there is considerable overlap in the sign repertoires of the two scripts, a process of selective adaptation is observable in the derivation of the Linear B system from Linear A. The Linear B script constitutes a different writing system, recording a different language. Its working mechanisms are now fairly well understood, primarily because we can read the script and recognize the language, but there are still some problematic aspects.

Syllabograms

Some 30 syllabograms of the donor script were abandoned, and some 20 signs were created *ex novo* (Olivier 1979). Such an adaptation is clearly born out of the necessity

Table 2.3 The Linear B syllabograms

a		*e*		*i*		*o*		*U*		a_2		*ai*		*au*
da		*de*		*di*		*do*		*Du*		*dwe*		*dwo*		
ja		*je*				*jo*								
ka		*ke*		*ki*		*ko*		*ku*						
ma		*me*		*mi*		*mo*		*mu*						
na		*ne*		*ni*		*no*		*nu*		*nwa*				
pa		*pe*		*pi*		*po*		*pu*		pu_2		*pte*		
qa		*qe*		*qi*		*qo*								
ra		*re*		*ri*		*ro*		*ru*		ra_2		ra_3		ro_2
sa		*se*		*si*		*so*		*su*						
ta		*te*		*ti*		*to*		*tu*		ta_2		*twe*		*two*
wa		*we*		*wi*		*wo*								
za		*ze*				*zo*								

Table 2.4 Unidentified syllabograms in the Linear B script

18	19	22	34	47	49	56	63	64	65	79	82	83	86	89

to record more accurately the phonemic structure of the new language, Greek, prompting the creation of new syllables not represented in the Minoan language. Ultimately the number of syllabograms in the two scripts is roughly equivalent, a fact that testifies to a likely similar phonotactical structure, that is a main core of open-syllables (CV) and simple vowel signs (V), with a minority of polysyllabic CCV and complex signs (*pte*, *nwa*, *dwe*, etc. used instead of bisyllabic sequences: *pe-te*, *nu-wa*, *do-wo*). The 73 Linear B syllabograms with known values are displayed in table 2.3. There are more than a dozen further rare graphs whose phonetic values have not been established (table 2.4), as their occurrences are rare, but they are likely to represent complex syllables (Cw/jV or CCV).

Logograms

The adaptors of Linear B streamlined to a great extent the keystone of Linear A accounting practice, namely its complex logographic repertoire of composite ligatured signs. This can be explained by the fact that phonetic abbreviations (which is what ligatured logograms ultimately are) in one language will not make sense in another (Palaima 1988a). Moreover, the tablets in either script deal with different types of commodities: no military equipment, spices, or metals are inventoried in the Linear A records, whereas they abound as logograms in the Linear B ones (tables 2.5–7).

Table 2.5   Frequent Linear B logograms listing people and animals

People and animals											
100	102	104	105		106		107		108		109	
vir	mul	cerv	equ^m	equ^f	ovis^m	ovis^f	cap^m	cap^f	sus^m	sus^f	bos^m	bos^f
man	*woman*	*deer*	*horse*	*foal*	*ram*	*ewe*	*he-goat*	*she-goat*	*boar*	*sow*	*ox*	*cow*

Table 2.6   Frequent Linear B logograms listing commodities

Commodities by dry measure					Commodities by liquid measure			
120	121	122	123	125	130	131	133	135
wheat	*barley*	*olive*	*aroma*	*cyp*	*oil*	*wine*	*arepa (unguent)*	*meri (honey)*

Table 2.7   Frequent Linear B logograms listing commodities

Other commodities											
140	141	145	159	167	200	201	202	204	233	240–242	243
bronze	*gold*	*wool*	*cloth*	*ingot*	*pan*	*tripod ti-ri-po-de*	*jar/goblet di-pa*	*pithos*	*sword*	*chariots*	*wheel*

Some objects represented by the logograms are self-explanatory because they are graphically naturalistic (vessels, horses), others are identifiable only through the phenomenon of double-writing. This is a feature peculiar only to Linear B wherein a full phonetic spelling of an object is followed by the logogram representing it: for instance, *ka-ko* "bronze" (χαλκός) can be followed by the logogram representing bronze, Ḥ. This practice was useful for quick consultation of the contents of the tablet. Logograms can be indicated also by stringing two or three syllabic signs together, for instance the logogram for honey ⅄, spelled in Linear B *me-ri* (normalized in Greek as /*meli*/) is the superposition of the syllables *me* and .

Tables 2.8 and 2.9 Linear B numerals and metrology

Numerical Notations	
I	1
II	2
—	10
○	100
◇	1,000
◈	10,000

Units of measurement										
Dry measure			Liquid measure			Weight				
T	V	Z	S	V	Z	L	M	N	Z	Q
⊤	ꟼ	⌒	⟨	ꟼ	⌒	⚖	⌇	#	⌇	⌇
1/10	1/6	1/4	1/3	1/6	1/4	1	1/30	1/4	1/12	1/6

Numerical system

The decimal system of numerical notations in Linear A was adopted without much alteration (table 2.8), with the minor differences that the sign for 10 in Linear A can be interchangeably represented by a dot or a horizontal line, and the sign for 10,000 is not attested. The most radical change in the logographic repertoire, however, is the fractional system: in Linear A, quantities were calculated in terms of successive numerical fractions of a single whole unit (aliquot system), while the Linear B system re-employed these numerical fraction signs for subsidiary, fixed sub-unit measures for weight, solid, and liquid units (table 2.9). Thus, for instance, a weight for metal would be expressed by successive units of decreasing size bearing a fixed proportionate value: ⚖ 1 ⌇ 22 # 2 ⌇ 6, not much differently from the imperial weight system (ounces, pounds, tons). The highest unit (L) graphically represents a pair of scales (table 2.9), possibly referring to the talent (*c*. 30 kg), divided in turn into 60 minas, so the second unit (graphically redoubled) would represent a double mina (Chadwick 1990). For the absolute values of all the other symbols, see *Documents*[2]: 57–60.

Orthography

Some characteristics observable in the syllabic structure of the script are worth mentioning. Mycenaean (like Classical) Greek presents a variety of complex syllables, with frequent consonantal clusters and word-final consonants. The open-syllable (CV) structure of the Linear B core signary does not record these in plene spelling, and therefore makes the incomplete representation of consonantal clusters primarily responsible for the cumbersome, and often uncertain, interpretation of the texts. This is best witnessed in the deficient rendering of syllable-final liquids (/l/ and /r/), nasals (/n/ and /m/) and sibilant (/s/): for instance, the sequence *pa-te* can be both read as /patēr/ "father" (with final consonant omitted), or /pantes/ "all" (with syllable-final /n/ and word-final /s/ omitted). See also *ka-ko* for /khal-kos/ "bronze" (with syllable-final /l/ and word-final /s/ omitted). Consonantal clusters that include, instead, plosives (velars, dentals, labials) preceding another consonant (cf. /*Kno-sos*/ "Knossos," /*khru-sos*/ "gold," /*tektones*/ "carpenters") are broken into two syllables where the initial one borrows the vowel of the succeeding syllable (*ko-no-so, ku-ru-so, te-ko-to-ne*). This very regular convention is extended to clusters of three consonants (/*Leuktron*/ is, for instance, recorded as *re-u-ko-to-ro*).

Matters are further complicated by the individual function of the voiceless plosive consonant series (/k/, /p/, /t/) to record voiced (/g/, /b/) and aspirated (/kh/, /ph/, /th/) plosive consonants (the only exception being the attested voiced dental /d/).

Several other spelling conventions are deployed (for a full account, *Documents*²) that complicate the linguistic interpretation, leading to the claim that the script clumsily strait-jackets Mycenaean Greek into a system structurally inadequate for recording it. It must be borne in mind, however, that Linear B was not specifically devised to suit the phono-logical characteristics of the Mycenaean language, but was the product of an adaptation from a donor script, whose precise phonological characteristics are unknown.

The Mycenaean Documents

The nature of the evidence

In all likelihood, Linear B was devised solely as a means of keeping records of the eco-nomic activities and concerns of the Mycenaean palaces. Rather simplistically, we could claim that all Aegean scripts are mere palatial instruments or scribal devices fashioned to monitor palatially focused economic systems. However, Linear B cannot be accounted for in the slightly wider uses of writing that were typical of Linear A: no religious inscrip-tions, no dedications on precious objects, no inscribed graffiti, no traces of the script having been employed in areas where we know the Mycenaeans had a strong cultural or trade presence (Cyprus, Rhodes, the Cycladic islands). Linear B seems to be function-ing, uniquely, as an extension of the collective memory of the palace administrators (Chadwick 1990). This use of writing is indeed astonishingly limited: the textual evi-dence we have in Linear B pales in comparison with the versatility and thematic range that we find in the abundance of legal documents or diplomatic correspondence, or of formally literary texts (religious or poetic) in the contemporary archives of the Near East (Ugarit, Nuzi, Alalakh), and even monumental inscriptions (Luvian hieroglyphs).

While we cannot discount the possibility that, for instance, a Mycenaean poetic tradition existed (see chs 24 and 27), or that the Homeric poems may have had their thematic as well as formal origin in the Mycenaean period (Bennet 1997), there is no reason to suppose that poetry, or literature of any sort, had already been committed to writing. This is not because the script was intrinsically unsuited to more complex and articulate purposes than drawing up lists of commodities and personnel, but because literacy was delegated to a small class of palatial administrators and scribes who *chose* to use the script uniquely for a bureaucratic, economic purpose. The reflec-tion of Mycenaean literacy we glimpse is, therefore, if not altogether limited, at least extremely specialized.

This may be the result of a "narrow cultural attitude to writing" (Palaima 1987: 509), or an underestimation of its symbolic power, but the absence of evidence for private and personal use of writing, the total lack of evidence for any literate Mycenaean feeling the urge to mark his possessions or even write his name with the script, is still disconcerting. And to assume that perishable materials were used for such applications of writing does not completely dissolve the perplexity. Regardless of the reasons for such *lacunae*, it should come as no surprise that even the geographical and contextual distribution of the Linear B texts is, as a result, spatially confined: the only sites where inscriptions are attested are the palace archives or, for the inscribed stirrup jars, the palaces' narrow orbits (for the very few exceptions, see Palaima 1987: 502).

That the purpose of writing in Linear B was culturally limited is given further proof by the fact that the records were not intended to be permanent. Linear B was written, mainly, on unbaked clay tablets and the only attestations are those that were accidentally baked in the conflagration that destroyed the palaces in the Late Minoan IIIB period. All we have is a snapshot, "a freeze-frame stopping the action of a motion picture of scribal work" (Palaima 1988b: 172) and of Mycenaean administration at a single, always final moment, a one-year window (some tablets bear the phraseology *za-we-te-jo* "this year's" or *pe-ru-si-nu-wo* "last year's"). Our view is mostly synchronic, blurring the appraisal of changing trends and developments, both in the use of writing and in the economic conditions of the palaces.

The Linear B tablets give us a view of a society right at the end of its existence, as they are chronologically concentrated to the final period of the Mycenaean civilization. Those from the palace of Pylos, on the mainland, are dated to destruction level, thus at the very end of Late Helladic IIIB (in absolute terms 1200 BCE); the archives at Knossos are probably slightly earlier (late Late Minoan IIIA1/early Late Minoan IIIA2, 1375 BCE) and date to the fall of Knossos at the hands of the Mycenaeans. Within the Knossos palace, the Room of the Chariot contains a tablet assemblage that, because of its archeological context, and corroborated by the paleographic analysis of the texts, may be even earlier (dating to Late Minoan II; see Driessen 2000).

Scribal practices

Tablets

The epigraphy of the tablets is remarkably uniform in all palatial assemblages and only a trained eye can distinguish between the script from the Knossos tablets and that in use two centuries later in Pylos (Hooker 1979). This indicates, generally, a fixed established scribal routine in drawing up the documents (*Documents*[2]). Moreover, a remarkable degree of care is lavished by the scribes not only in drawing up the layout of the tablets (with attention to regularly punctuating sections, line by line ruling into columns, formatting of entries in *stoichedon*, and, if necessary, subordinating certain sequences by reducing the size of their characters), but also in spelling out both the phonetic realization of a word and its related logogram (the "double writing" phenomenon mentioned above). This almost redundant emphasis on full clarity is unattested in the abbreviated, stunted information and undisciplined, untidy epigraphic arrangement of Linear A. Ease of consultation, therefore, seems to have been the primary requisite for laying out the information on the documents, and commodity logograms thus played an important role in aiding the identification of the tablet contents at a glance.

Typologically, tablets are of two kinds. The so-called "palm-leaf" shaped tablets are elongated strips of clay, akin to the modern check-book, with the inscription running parallel to the long sides and usually reporting a single transaction (the information entered is usually not longer than two lines). This class is more frequent than the second class, the "page" tablets, rectangular in shape and divided by horizontal cross-lines into columnar layout. On this format the entries are usually multiple and tend to summarize the information recorded on the elongated type. Tablets that treat land tenure records from Pylos, for instance, bear testament to the fact that "palm-leaf" tablets were provisional notations, intended to be re-entered on the more spacious "page" format (scribe "Hand 1" at Pylos, for instance, prepares the summary of two "page" tablet series corresponding to the elongated records written by scribe "Hand 41"). "Page"-shaped tablets thus tend to support longer and more complex lists, usually inventorying personnel and rations, as well as summaries of the entries recorded on the "leaf"-shaped. These larger, more complete documents formed thematic sets that were stored in baskets or boxes and secured by a label (and not, as erroneously assumed, a sealing, cf. *Documents*[2]: 407; Hooker 1980: 180–1).

Other classes of Linear B records

Labels and sealings, while belonging to a very similar typology of records, should not be confused. The contextual contiguity between sealings and tablets led to the assumption that sealings were used to label boxes or baskets containing tablets. That is, conversely, the purpose of *labels*. Tablets of the same subject matter formed *sets* and were systematically filed in the archives and placed inside wicker boxes or baskets (cf. for instance the Pylos Archive complex; Palaima 1988b). Small lumps of clay, the labels, were thus fashioned to identify these tablet-sets with a short inscription and were attached directly to the boxes (some labels bear traces of the basket impressions). Through the painstaking analysis of individual handwriting we can determine that tablets belonging to a set were usually compiled by the same scribe, and it is in this synergic analysis of tablet files and the agents responsible for their compilation, rather than examining single specimens, that we can gain a more holistic picture of how the archives were catalogued.

Mycenaean sealings are clay nodules, pressed about a cord, impressed with a seal and often inscribed (Bennett 1958; Aravantinos 1984). Many specimens bear fingerprints on their unsealed faces. They were generally pressed around cords or affixed to bundles, leather bags, or wineskins, in order to label and identify commodities to safeguard them while they were being transported or deposited in magazines, and thus they functioned as "*documents authentifiés*" (Piteros, Olivier, and Melena 1990: 115). This process took place under the authority of the seal-bearer, who stamped the nodules with a ring bezel or a seal thus providing official documentation that a specific delivery or obligation was fulfilled (some sealings are inscribed with the administrative term word *a-pu-do-si* "due contribution" and also with the much-discussed noun *o-pa* "labor service," "work to be performed"; Melena 1983). In this way they served as contractual and performance records for individual workers or indicated the presence of raw materials or manufactured items in palatial workshops or storerooms as contributions. The concentration uncovered at the palace at Thebes (56) is particularly important as first-stage recording of contributions of domestic animals (indicated by single logograms) sent to the palatial centers for communal sacrifices and feastings (Palaima 2004) and functioned as individual notations, or preliminary records, of livestock, whose entries were to be added to tablets listing miscellaneous provisions, including animals, for the palace banquets.

The last class of inscribed objects are large ceramic vessels, coarse stirrup jars containing oil and bearing on the shoulders between one and three words, usually anthroponyms (in the nominative case), toponyms, and in certain cases with the genitive *wa-na-ka-te-ro* "of the *wanax*," the Mycenaean "king," cf. Hom. ἄναξ. Inscribed stirrup jars (ISJs) are found, in concentration, at Thebes, but they were originally manufactured and inscribed on western Crete. Their several paleographic oddities, often seen as tentative imitations of Linear B signs at the hands of illiterate individuals, can be in fact explained by their manner of inscription, given that they were painted with a brush instead of incised with a stylus (Hallager 1987). The regular word-sequence pattern attested, consisting of personal name of the manufacturer, location, and genitive noun of the possessor indicates that even these short, quirkily written texts were still part of the meticulous Mycenaean administrative *modus operandi*.

Because of the terse and laconic nature of all Linear B documents, and because of their schematic brevity and general lack of syntax, it is impossible to have full access into the mechanisms of the Mycenaean social, economic, and religious structure, as it is equally cumbersome to clarify all problematic aspects of the Mycenaean language. And even if the contents of the tablets are, at first sight, "deplorably dull" (Chadwick 1976b: ix), in their almost obsessive, meticulous listing of personnel, accounts of livestock, inventories of agricultural and manufactured goods, the fact that we can read and value them as historical texts that breathe the authenticity of Greek spoken and written 4,000 years ago, is no little achievement. They do not resound with the heroic echoes of the Golden Age that inspired Homer, but they can guide us, in a way that Homer cannot, into the labyrinths of the Mycenaean age.

Linear B represents the earliest stage of the process of writing the Greek language that we can observe, and marks the starting point in a continuous, and ongoing, line of development since the fourteenth century BCE. However, Mycenaean literacy dies with the collapse of the palaces, leaving no visible trace. Linear B, an instrument so closely associated with the internal workings and the specialized language of the palaces, is no longer needed. And if Greece will plunge into the Dark Ages of literacy, Cyprus will not. There, the Greek language (specifically, its Arcado-Cypriot dialect) will continue to be written syllabically from the ninth century BCE with the Cypriot Syllabary, a script less clumsy and more versatile than the Linear B, which will be consciously and efficiently retained until the third century BCE, in contrast and in competition with the adoption of the alphabet by the rest of the Greek-speaking world.

FURTHER READING

For an accessible account of the decipherment of Linear B, see Chadwick 1967. Most of the literature on Linear B is highly technical and specialized, but Chadwick 1976b offers a comprehensive and engagingly written view on the contents of the tablets. The primary, and not superseded, reference for the texts is *Documents*². A good starting point if one wishes to learn the script and analyze the most important documents is Hooker 1980. The transcriptions of the tablets are organized in accordance with the site of discovery; for Pylos: Bennett and Olivier 1976; for Knossos: Chadwick et al. 1986–98; for Tiryns, Thebes, and Mycenae: Melena and Olivier 1991.

PART ONE

The Sources

CHAPTER THREE

Phoinikēia Grammata: An Alphabet for the Greek Language

Roger D. Woodard

From Egypt to Phoenicia

The moment that counts as the "beginning" of the alphabet has in recent years receded in time, and one wonders if this may be a trend that will continue, at least in small increments, as the desert places of Egypt surrender yet new discoveries – for it is Egypt where the process began. At present, we can with some confidence assign that inaugural event to the early second millennium BCE. The *alphabet* (as the term is used herein – referring to a segmental script having both *consonant* and *vowel* symbols) does not, however, appear full-formed at conception, but passes through a protracted period of gestation.

The earliest evidence of the conceptual act takes the form of recently discovered inscriptions carved on limestone facets at the site of Wadi el-Hôl, located northwest of the ancient Egyptian city of Thebes (Luxor) along the Farshût road (Darnell et al. 2005: 74). While at present a satisfactory semantic sense cannot be assigned to the Wadi el-Hôl inscriptions, the symbols with which they are written are formally consistent with the symbols of the so-called *Proto-Sinaitic* inscriptions found in the vicinity of Serabit el-Khadim in the Sinai, known since Sir William Flinders Petrie's excavations of the area in 1904–05.

The Proto-Sinaitic inscriptions (see Albright 1966) preserve not *Egyptian* language but a form of *West Semitic* spoken by persons involved, in one capacity or another, in the Egyptian turquoise-mining industry of the Serabit el-Khadim region. It was the British Egyptologist Sir Alan Gardiner who first demonstrated that the *language* of these materials is Semitic (Gardiner 1916); in contradistinction, the *symbols* used for recording that language are self-evidently drawn from the repertory of iconographic symbols that comprise the Egyptian *writing system* (which exists in several varieties – the elaborate hieroglyphic, the more utilitarian hieratic, and the later, highly cursive, demotic). Gardiner saw that this relationship of *sound* and *structure* – Semitic *phone* and Egyptian *graph* – is an expression of a so-called "acrophonic" principle or method: in effect, one might say, the aligning (or misaligning) of Egyptian and Semitic linguistic signs (in a Saussurian sense of that term) so as to link the phonetic component of a Semitic sign with the conceptual component of an Egyptian sign. Thus, for example, the Egyptian logogram denoting the Egyptian word meaning "courtyard house" (⌗) was adopted and assigned the Semitic value /b/–that consonantal value being abstracted from the phonetic onset of the West Semitic word meaning "house" (attested by later West Semitic forms such as Hebrew _bet_).

This "acrophonic" method resulted in an inventory of Semitic graphemes (letters) having the value of a single consonant each. The design of this Semitic consonantal system of writing is itself an exploitation of one component of the heterogeneous Egyptian orthographic system. Egyptian graphemes are of two fundamental types: logographic symbols, representing words, and phonetic symbols, representing phonetic components of words (see, _inter alia_, Allen 2000: 13–29; Loprieno 2004: 163–6.). The latter type of Egyptian symbol, the phonetic, represents only consonants – not vowels – and consists of three subtypes: monoconsonantal symbols, each spelling a single consonant; biconsonantal symbols, each spelling two consonants that occur in linear progression (with a vowel potentially intervening in spoken language, but not spelled); and triconsonantal symbols, each spelling three consonants that occur in linear progression (with vowels potentially interspersed in spoken language, but not spelled; on the Egyptian use of a so-called "syllabic orthography" employed chiefly for spelling foreign words, see, _inter alia_, Loprieno 1995: 14, 16, with references).

Probably with (possibly without) Egyptian scribal assistance, some West Semitic speaker(s) found in the monoconsonantal graphemic subtype the inspiration and model for a fully functional script – one that could operate by utilizing only this very simplest element of the already ancient and highly complex Egyptian writing system, jettisoning the remainder as so much orthographic _extranea_. The process is cognitively somewhat akin to, for example, using a graphing calculator with sophisticated algebraic, calcular, and symbolic functions for doing basic addition and subtraction.

And what of the date of these earliest "Proto-Sinaitic" materials? The inscriptions from Wadi el-Hôl likely belong to the period _c._ 1850–1700 BCE (late Middle Kingdom) and can probably be situated more narrowly within the reign of the Pharaoh Amenemhat III (_c._ 1853–1809 BCE; see Darnell et al. 2005: 90). Those from Serabit el-Khadim have in recent decades been dated as late as _c._ 1500 BCE, but in light of the finds at Wadi el-Hôl should probably be assigned to about the earlier second quarter of the second millennium (see the comments of Darnell et al. 2005: 100 n. 130), a date in keeping with that proposed by Gardiner in his 1916 identification of the Serabit el-Khadim materials as West Semitic. The origin of the script, on the basis of paleographic evidence, is probably to be placed somewhat earlier in the Middle Kingdom, perhaps _c._ 1900 BCE (Darnell et al. 2005: 90).

One of the most intriguing aspects of the new finds from Wadi el-Hôl is that of their immediate sociocultural context.

> Through the late second millennium, the Wadi el-Hôl and its associated tracks were a thoroughfare for military units, often supplemented with foreign auxiliaries, who in times of peace ensured safe passage for travelers . . . and in times of war used those same routes for strategic maneuvers. It is into this complex conjunction of activities in a militarized setting that the two early alphabetic inscriptions fit. (Darnell et al. 2005: 75)

Carved in the vicinity of the "Proto-Sinaitic" inscriptions at Wadi el-Hôl are likely contemporaneous Egyptian hieratic inscriptions, a number of which are relevant to an understanding of the Semitic presence at the site. One begins with a reference to the name Bebi, who is called "the general of the Asiatics"; the title must reveal that West Asian mercenaries were under the command of Bebi. Darnell et al. (2005: 88) point out that "Egyptian military units such as Bebi's group also included scribes, and a 'scribe of Asiatics' in fact appears in a Middle Kingdom papyrus." Many of the signs found in the Semitic inscriptions at Wadi el-Hôl, as well as those at Serabit el-Khadim, are modeled on Egyptian lapidary hieratic symbols (with an admixture of hieroglyphic models); this is interpretatively significant in that lapidary hieratic was the predominant script used by Egyptian military scribes. While allowing that the Semitic script "likely emerged initially in a plurality of cultural contexts," Darnell et al. (2005: 90–1) hypothesize that "the Egyptian military, known both to have employed Asiatics (as the Bebi inscription so wonderfully attests) and to have included scribes, would provide one likely context in which Western Asiatic Semitic language speakers could have learned and eventually adapted the Egyptian writing system."

The use of a consonantal orthographic strategy continues to be attested as the evidence of West Semitic writing expands beyond Egypt. Inscriptions produced with the script called *Proto-Canaanite*, a local avatar of Proto-Sinaitic, appear in the archeological record of Syria-Palestine (see Sass 1988) from about the seventeenth to the twelfth centuries BCE. The graphemes of this Proto-Canaanite script continue the pictorial quality of the Proto-Sinaitic characters, the latter being, as we observed, adaptations of iconic Egyptian symbols, both hieroglyphic and, especially, hieratic. The pictorial quality of Proto-Canaanite symbols gives way, however, to characters displaying greater linearity by *c.* 1100 BCE. The Canaanite language recorded by this linear script is recognizably Phoenician by the late eleventh century (but better evidenced beginning in the tenth; see Hackett 2004: 356–66; McCarter 1975: 29–30; Cross 1980: 15–17; Gibson 1982: 1–24). This linear Phoenician script, consonantal in graphemic inventory, was adapted for spelling the Canaanite language of Hebrew, with a national script appearing in Judah and Israel by the tenth century (McCarter 2004: 321), and for spelling the language of the Aramaean city-states, also first attested in the tenth century (Creason 2004: 392–3).

With the flourishing of maritime commercial activities, the quest for raw materials required for producing commercial goods, and affiliated colonial (or para-colonial) expansions among Iron Age Phoenician peoples, the consonantal script with which they recorded their Semitic language was inevitably exported westward across the length of the Mediterranean. Cyprus, Crete, Sardinia, and Spain all provide early evidence of Phoenician writing; that evidence dates to no later than the ninth century BCE in the case of Cyprus, perhaps to the tenth (or earlier) in the case of the more westerly islands (see Negbi 1992 with bibliography). As Phoenicians and Greeks were plying the waters of the Mediterranean, Greek-speaking peoples would have encountered Phoenician writing time and again – and in many different places; compare the Chinese, Japanese, and Korean characters that twenty-first-century speakers of European languages frequently meet at import bazaars and Asian restaurants across Europe and the Americas.

At some Mediterranean locale promoting a mixed Phoenician and Greek context, the Semitic *script* was successfully adapted as a means for giving graphic expression to the Greek *language*. In some respects, the process was fundamentally like the earlier adaptation of Phoenician script for spelling the Hebrew and Aramaic languages: Phoenician consonantal graphemes were employed for spelling phonetically "equivalent" Hebrew and Aramaic sounds in many instances, though in a few cases such equivalence did not exist, with the result that Hebrew and Aramaic adapters adjusted the phonetic values assigned to borrowed Phoenician symbols (see McCarter 2004: 321; Creason 2004: 393, 395–6). Adjustment in phonetic values of Phoenician graphemes likewise characterized the Greek adaptive process; the Greek procedure differed, however, in the radical nature of certain of the adjustments and in the consequent *systemic change* that these adjustments effected.

Within the remainder of this chapter, I would like to explore three questions, and an embedded fourth, with regard to the origin of the Greeks' alphabet – their *Phoinikēia grammata* (Φοινικήια γράμματα "Phoenician letters"). What happened? Where did it happen? Why did it happen and when?

Adapting the Phoenician Alphabet

Though the Greek appropriation of the Phoenician script was indeed "radical" from a systemic perspective, the adaptation of individual graphemes was often minimalistic. The phonemic inventory of the Phoenician *language* consists of 22 consonant phonemes (see Hackett 2004: 369), while that of the Ancient Greek *language* of the eighth century BCE contains only seventeen consonant phonemes (see Woodard 2004a: 616; 2004b: 657–8). The two phonemic systems show, however, extensive overlap, with approximate phonological agreement between thirteen consonants: specifically, these two languages – one Semitic, the other Indo-European – possess in common (allowing for language-specific phonetic details) the voiceless stop phonemes /p/, /t/, /k/; their voiced counterparts /b/, /d/, /g/; the fricatives /s/ and /h/; the nasals /m/ and /n/; the liquids /l/ and /r/; and the glide /w/.

Consider first of all the orthographic treatment of the stop consonant phonemes that are common to the two languages. The Greek adapters of the Semitic script chose to continue the phoneme-to-grapheme mapping of the voiceless and voiced stops that was used within the Phoenician system. Thus, the adaptive equations shown in table 3.1a were produced.

Table 3.1a

Phoenician original		Greek adaptation	
phoneme	*grapheme*	*grapheme*	*phoneme*
/p/	ꀭ *pe*	Π *pi*	/p/
/t/	+ *taw*	Τ *tau*	/t/
/k/	ꓘ *kap*	Κ *kappa*	/k/
/b/	꒙ *bet*	Β *beta*	/b/
/d/	Ꙇ *dalet*	Δ *delta*	/d/
/g/	Ʌ *gimel*	Γ *gamma*	/g/

Table 3.1b

Phoenician original		Greek adaptation	
phoneme	*grapheme*	*grapheme*	*phoneme*
/t'/	⊗ *ṭet*	⊗ *theta*	/tʰ/

The shared set of six stop consonants is, however, augmented by an additional series in each language: Greek has the voiceless aspirated stops /pʰ/, /tʰ/, and /kʰ/ – a full complement to voiceless /p/, /t/, /k/ and voiced /b/, /d/, /g/ (see also ch. 7); Phoenician, on the other hand, has two so-called "emphatic" stop consonants, an emphatic-*t* (conventionally transcribed as <ṭ>) and an emphatic-*k* (transcribed as <q>). The specific phonetic value of these Phoenician consonants is difficult to identify with complete precision, though both are certainly characterized by some additional articulatory event, probably glottalization (involving a forceful expelling of air by a lifting of the glottis): "emphatic-*t*" is thus likely a glottalized (that is, ejective) /t'/ and "emphatic-*k*" a glottalized (ejective) /k'/ (on the phonetics of the Phoenician sounds, see Woodard 1997a: 168–9).

The Greek adaptation of the Phoenician graphemes that spell the emphatic stop phonemes /t'/ and /k'/ is less straightforward than the adaptation of the other six stop phonemes (i.e., /p/, /t/, /k/ and /b/, /d/, /g/). The process looks to be more structurally motivated than (simply) phonetic. The Phoenician grapheme for /t'/ – that is, the phoneme /t/ with an additional phonological component (glottalization) – was adapted for spelling the Greek phoneme /tʰ/ – that is, the phoneme /t/ with an additional phonological component (aspiration); see table 3.1b. The evidence, interestingly enough, suggests that the Phoenician phoneme /t/ was actually characterized by greater *phonetic* aspiration than was "emphatic" /t'/ and, hence, the former Phoenician phoneme (/t/) was closer phonetically to Greek /tʰ/ (see Woodard 1997a: 206–7, 237 n. 8).

One would expect that a consistent application of this structurally motivated adaptive procedure would then result in the Phoenician grapheme for the phoneme /k'/ (/k/ plus an additional component) being taken over and used to spell the Greek phoneme /kʰ/ (/k/ plus an additional component); this did not happen, however, and the failure of this Phoenician symbol to be so adapted is one of several peculiar developments in the Greek conversion of the Phoenician writing system. There is in fact a double oddity here: (1) the Greek adapters made no provision for spelling their phoneme /kʰ/ (the symbol for this sound [i.e., *chi*] was only later appended to the alphabet); and (2) the Phoenician symbol for /k'/ was used by the adapters to spell no Greek *phoneme* at all. In what leaves the impression of being a conspicuously un-ergonomic application (squandering) of Semitic graphic material, the Greek adapters used the symbol for the Phoenician phoneme /k'/ to spell an *allophone* of the Greek unaspirated stop phoneme /k/: that is, a variant of Greek /k/ conditioned by phonetic context – and one with only limited distribution at that – occurring before the *u*- and *o*-vowels; see table 3.1c.

Table 3.1c

Phoenician original			*Greek adaptation*		
phoneme	*grapheme*		*grapheme*		*allophone*
/k'/	Ϙ	*qop*	Ϙ	*qoppa*	"backed" [k]

Table 3.1d

Phoenician original			*Greek adaptation*		
phoneme	*grapheme*		*grapheme*		*phoneme*
/m/	𐤌	*mem*	Μ	*mu*	/m/
/n/	𐤍	*nun*	Ν	*nu*	/n/
/l/	𐤋	*lamed*	⅃	*lambda*	/l/
/r/	𐤓	*reš*	Ρ	*rho*	/r/

Cross-culturally, the dedication of graphemes for this type of allophonic spelling is uncommon, and, in keeping with this tendency, the Greeks began to abandon use of the allophonic symbol *qoppa* in the sixth century BCE, using *kappa* in its stead (i.e., adopting a consistently phonemic spelling of /k/).

The Greek adapters also made no provision for spelling their voiceless aspirated bilabial stop /p^h/. In this instance, Phoenician possessed no corresponding "augmented" bilabial phoneme – in other words, no glottalized stop /p'/ – which could potentially provide a grapheme for Greek /p^h/ in the way that Phoenician /t'/ provided a grapheme for Greek /t^h/. Thus, the adapters designed a Greek alphabet with a grapheme for /t/ (*tau*) and another grapheme for /t^h/ (*theta*), while, in contrast, they determined that a single grapheme (*kappa*) must do double duty for both /k/ and /k^h/ (while a backed allophone of /k/ was given its own dedicated symbol [*qoppa*]) and a single grapheme (*pi*) must do double duty for both /p/ and /p^h/. Only later (as with *chi* for /k^h/) would a distinct symbol for /p^h/ (*phi*) be appended to the alphabet.

As with the voiceless and voiced stops (/p/, /t/, /k/ and /b/, /d/, /g/), many of the graphic symbols for the other consonantal phonemes that Phoenician and Greek shared in common (*mutatis mutandis*) were likewise adapted so as to continue the phoneme-to-grapheme mapping of the Phoenician script. The nasals and liquids fall clearly into this category; see table 3.1d.

The shared glide /w/ departs from this procedure in that the Greek adapters gave the symbol for /w/ a unique (non-Phoenician) shape, though they retained the Phoenician name for the symbol and its position in the alphabetic sequence of letters; see table 3.1e. Greek *wau* (or *digamma*, so called after a shape suggestive of *gamma*) takes its morphology from that of the symbol that precedes it in the alphabetic order, namely Greek *epsilon*, Ε. The non-Phoenician shape of Greek *wau* can be seen in the very earliest examples of Greek writing: one would thus suspect that the form of *wau* is the consequence of intentional morphological deformation on the part of the adapters

Table 3.1e

Phoenician original		Greek adaptation	
phoneme	*grapheme*	*grapheme*	*phoneme*
/w/	Y *waw*	F *wau*	/w/

Table 3.1f

Phoenician original		Greek adaptation	
phoneme	*grapheme*	*grapheme*	*phoneme*
/ħ/	☐ *ḥet*	☐ *ḥeta*	/h/

Table 3.1g

Phoenician original		Greek adaptation	
phoneme	*grapheme*	*grapheme*	*phoneme*
/s/	W *šin*	≤ *sigma*	/s/

(rather than the outcome of some evolutionary process), a matter to which we shall briefly return below.

More complex is the Greek adapters' treatment of the fricative graphemes. The two languages, Greek and Phoenician, share the glottal fricative phoneme /h/ (the so-called *spiritus asper* of Greek – approximately the *h*-sound of English). The Phoenician symbol for the fricative /h/ was not, however, used for spelling Greek /h/; instead, the Greek adapters chose to ignore the (approximate) phonetic equivalence and for spelling their own phoneme /h/ tapped Phoenician *ḥet*, the grapheme that represents a voiceless pharyngeal fricative /ħ/ (essentially the throaty sound that one makes when vigorously exhaling vapor onto a glass surface in order to clean it), traditionally transcribed as <ḥ>; see table 3.1f.

The Phoenician language also has a voiced pharyngeal fricative /ʕ/ (produced in the same way as voiceless /ħ/, except with the vocal cords vibrating), traditionally transcribed as <ʿ>, spelled by the Phoenician grapheme *ʿayin* – a letter assigned a quite different value by the Greeks, as will be seen below.

The Phoenician and Greek languages also share in common a second fricative phoneme, the dental sibilant /s/; see table 3.1g. The value of Phoenician *šin* appears now to have been /s/ generally (see Hackett 2004: 369–70) and certainly so in Cypriot Phoenician (see Woodard 1997a: 184, 188). Here, as elsewhere in this chapter, the names assigned to the Semitic letters are, by convention, those of the comparable Hebrew characters; the probable Phoenician name of this letter was, however, *šan*. Entering Greek as the letter-name *san*, the grapheme continued to be so identified in some local Greek alphabets (see Hdt. 1.139 on the Dorian practice of calling the

Table 3.1h

Phoenician original			Greek adaptation		
phoneme	*grapheme*		*grapheme*		*phonic value*
/dᶻ/	I	*zayin*	I	*zeta*	[z] + [d]
/tˢ/	‡	*samek*	Ξ	*xi*	[k] + [s]
/tˢʾ/	ℾ	*ṣade*	M	*san*	[tˢ]?

letter *san*) and in poetry (see McCarter 1975: 100–01; Woodard 1997a: 185–6, 188.). The now more familiar name of the grapheme Ϛ, *sigma*, is likely derived from the root *sig-*, seen in the Greek verb σίζω (*sizdó*, from **sig-dó*), "I hiss" (Chantraine 1999: 1002), the name denoting the "hissing" fricative that the letter spells (and modern linguists commonly refer to /s/ as one of the "hissing fricatives," distinct from "hushing fricatives," such as the *sh*-sound of /š/. The earlier name *san* would also be attached to a second Greek fricative grapheme (M, discussed immediately below), with which it is now more commonly associated.

Beyond this shared /s/, Phoenician possesses three sounds of which a sibilant is one component, but in the instance of these sounds, the Greek phonemic inventory shows no equivalence. Each of these Phoenician phonemes is likely an affricate (being, in effect, a stop that is released in such a way as to create friction). The value of the Phoenician letter *samek*, it now appears, is generally that of a voiceless dental affricate /tˢ/, that of the letter *zayin* the voiced counterpart /dᶻ/ (see Hackett 2004: 369–70; and the latter was almost certainly so in Cypriot Phoenician; see Woodard 1997a: 172). The third of these sounds, that spelled by the Phoenician letter *ṣade*, was another "emphatic," probably the glottalized /tˢʾ/ (Hackett 2004: 369–70; Woodard 1997a: 169–70; Steiner 1982). This set of three dental affricates thus parallels the pattern of Phoenician dental and velar stops: that is, each set has one voiceless member, one voiced, and one "emphatic."

The Greek adapters had to determine to what use they would put these various graphemes of the Semitic script, most (though perhaps not all) spelling sounds quite distinct from phonemes of Greek. The outcome of that process of adaptation looks like table 3.1h (with graphemes listed in relative alphabetic order).

The values that the Greek adapters assigned to the borrowed Phoenician graphemes *zayin* and *samek* give the *prima facie* appearance of being another puzzling feature of the adaptive process. Perhaps the degree of seeming arbitrariness displayed should come as no surprise: the Greek language, after all, has no comparable phonemes. But it is the design of the seemingly superfluous end products that may surprise. The Greek graphemes *zeta* and *xi* each represents not a unitary consonant phoneme, but *a sequence of two consonant sounds* ([z] + [d] and [k] + [s] respectively). More than that, each of these Greek symbols (*zeta* and *xi*) is fully redundant, in that individual graphemes exist, and are independently required, that could have been used to spell the consonantal sequences equally well: *sigma* + *delta* for [z] + [d] (the /s/ represented by *sigma* is automatically voiced to [z] before a voiced consonant, and the sequential spelling *sigma* + *delta* would in fact come to be used instead of *zeta* in some local Greek alphabets) and *kappa* + *sigma* for [k] + [s]. We shall return to these matters below.

The earliest value of the Greek grapheme commonly called *san* (M) is uncertain. The alphabet-using communities of ancient Greece would early on excise either *sigma* or *san* from the set of letters that constituted each of those epichoric scripts. The surviving symbol, *san* or *sigma*, would then be used to spell the Greek fricative /s/. Both letters can still be seen frozen in certain archaic abecedaria, notably the various examples left by Etruscans (see Pandolfini and Prosdocimi 1990), borrowed from Euboean Greeks who brought with them their alphabet as they colonized sites in the south of the Italian peninsula. Peruzzi (1973: 25), Coldstream (1977: 300), and Heubeck (1979: 123) have proposed that both symbols are used, side-by-side (*sigma* followed by *san*), in a fragmentary graffito from Pithekoussai, dating the inscription, or the form of the alphabet that it preserves, to a moment not far removed from the time of adaptation. Others have read the second letter as *mu* rather than *san* (see, for example, Dubois 1995: 29–30; Johnston 1983: 64).

A variant form of *san*, having the front leg truncated, i.e., И, is used in the Arcadian alphabet and, together with syllabic spelling evidence from the closely related Cypriot dialect, may provide a clue to the phonetic value that the Greek adapters of the Phoenician script assigned to the letter (on Arcado-Cypriot, see ch. 14). The Arcadians employed the *san* variant to spell the sound that arose from the Proto-Greek labiovelar consonant *$/k^w/$ when that consonant occurred before the vowel /i/; in most other dialects, this *$/k^w/$ became dental /t/ in this context. The sound spelled with И in Arcadian likely represents an areally restricted arrested intermediate stage of the geo-graphically widespread change of *$/k^w/$ to /t/ – probably an affricate such as [t^š] (as in English ***church***) or, perhaps more likely, /t^s/ (the latter being close in value to that of the Phoenician source grapheme *ṣade*): thus the indefinite pronoun τις (*tis*) "some-one" is spelled Иις in Arcadian. In the syllabic script of the Cypriot Greeks (who form a dialectal subgroup with speakers of Arcadian), the spelling of the comparable form would be ⌂^{ʮ} (*si-se*, where the vocalic portion of the *se* syllabic grapheme must be read as purely orthographic, lacking any phonetic value): the use of the symbol ⌂ (*si*) to spell what is written in the Arcadian alphabet as the sequence Иι, may indicate that at the time at which such Cypriot spellings are attested a common Proto-Arcado-Cypriot affricate, such as *t^s*, had undergone a further phonological change to become the fricative /s/ in Cypriot (outside of Arcado-Cypriot there was a distinct phonological development to /t/, as noted above). Alternatively, such syllabic spellings may reveal a Cypriot scribal decision to spell an affricate sound of limited occurrence and unique context with *s*-symbols (i.e., a polyphonic strategy, a common phenomenon among the world's writing systems; for a more detailed exposition of these matters, see Woodard 1997a: 177–84).

If earliest Greek *san* had the value [t^s] (whether allophonic [t^s] or phonemicized /t^s/), an interesting parallel would then present itself in the Greek adapters' use of the "emphatic" Phoenician graphemes *qop* (spelling /k'/) and *ṣade* (spelling /t^s'/): both were adapted to spell "comparable" (non-glottalized) Greek sounds, but sounds that had only limited distribution within the language – a distribution that was determined by the quality of the ensuing vowel. Thus *qop* was used to represent a particularly backed variant of velar /k/ that occurred before *u*- and *o*-vowels; while *ṣade* was used to spell a fronted reflex of the labiovelar *k^w that occurred before the *i*-vowel. This

Table 3.1i

Phoenician original		Greek adaptation	
phoneme	*grapheme*	*grapheme*	*phoneme*
/ʔ/	𐤀 'alep	𐤀 alpha	/ă/ and /ā/
/h/	𐤄 he	𐤄 epsilon	/ĕ/, /ē/₁ and /ē/₂

scenario would of course require that the Greek dialect of the adapters be one that was characterized by the synchronic presence of [tˢ], and this would then itself be a potentially valuable clue in the search for the identity of the adapters.

These adapters treated the remaining four consonantal symbols of the Phoenician script with somewhat less impunity. The consonants spelled by these Phoenician symbols do not constitute any particularly natural set of sounds – there are both voiced sounds and voiceless, both obstruent (stops and a fricative) and sonorant (a glide). Traits that these Semitic sounds do *nearly* present in common – though only "nearly" – are (1) an articulatory clustering at the far back of the oral cavity (with one exception), and (2) an absence of comparable consonant phonemes from the Greek language (with one exception).

Two of the Phoenician consonants concerned are glottals (sounds produced by manipulating the glottis, the aperture between the vocal cords): the glottal stop /ʔ/ and the glottal fricative /h/. The former sound does not occur within the phonemic inventory of ancient Greek; the latter, however, does, as we have seen already. The Greek adapters chose, as discussed above, not to use the Phoenician symbol for the glottal fricative /h/ to spell their own /h/; for this they used instead the Phoenician grapheme *ḥet*, the symbol for a voiceless pharyngeal fricative /ħ/. In a simple re-envisioning of Semitic spelling practice that would change from that moment on the mechanical (but not intellectual) potentialities of human writing, the Greek adapters determined to assign to the two Phoenician glottal-consonant symbols the values of *vowels*; see table 3.1i.

Here the symbols /ē/₁ and /ē/₂ stand for two *qualitatively different* (and phonemically distinct) long mid front vowels, one that was inherited from Proto-Indo-European and one that had arisen secondarily within Greek (the sounds that in conventional Attic [i.e., Euclidian-reform] orthography are spelled as η and ει); see also ch. 7 on the Old Attic vs the Ionic alphabet.

The third member of this set of four Phoenician consonants is a voiced fricative produced by constricting the pharynx while forcing air out of the lungs across the vibrating vocal cords, /ʕ/; this is hence a sound made a bit above the articulatory position of the glottal sounds but still at the far back of the oral cavity (for a more detailed phonetic description of the voiced pharyngeal fricative /ʕ/, see Woodard 1997a: 188–9n9). The consonant is represented graphically by the Phoenician letter *'ayin*, and the sound is the voiced counterpart of the fricative /ħ/, which is spelled by the grapheme *ḥet*; see table 3.1j. The Greek adapters again ambiguously assigned to a Phoenician back-consonant symbol the values of three phonemically distinct vowels – all mid back vowels – short /ŏ/ and the qualitatively different long /ɔ/ and /ọ/, one inherited, the other secondary (in conventional Attic orthography spelled as ω and ου; again, see ch.7).

Table 3.1j

Phoenician original		Greek adaptation	
phoneme	grapheme	grapheme	phoneme
/ʕ/	O ʿayin	O omikron	/ŏ/, /ɔ/ and /ǫ/

One sometimes encounters the idea that the Greek adapters were drawn ineluctably to these three consonant-grapheme to vowel-grapheme conversions. Aside from being diametrically opposed as *consonant* versus *vowel*,[1] the three Phoenician consonants spelled by the symbols *'alep*, *he*, and *'ayin* contrast articulatorily with the eight Greek vowel phonemes spelled by *alpha*, *epsilon*, and *omikron*: the Phoenician consonants all cluster at the far back of the oral cavity; on the other hand, two of the Greek vowels are produced in the center of the oral cavity (/ă/ and /ā/), three at the very front (/ĕ/, /ɛ/ and /ę/), and three at the back (/ŏ/, /ɔ/ and /ǫ/). Thus, for some investigators, a motivation for the assigned Greek values devolves upon the initial vowel of the Semitic *name* of the adapted consonant grapheme: for example, in her important survey of local Greek alphabets, Jeffery (1990: 2) writes, "the initial sounds of the words *''ālep*,' *'hē*,' and *''ayin*' would have also to the Greek ear, their nearest equivalents in the vowels ā/ă, ē/ĕ, and ō/ŏ." She continues (p. 22): ". . . for the Greek, listening to the Semitic repetition of the alphabet, those vowels were the approximate Greek equivalents of the initial sounds in the names of the Semitic letters. He did not consciously realize that the sounds which he made were, to a philologist's ear, in a different category from those of the Semite; the Semitic initial sound in *'ālep*, *hē'*, and *'ayin* resembled his own sounds *a*, *e*, and *o* more than they resembled anything else to him, and so he used them as vowels."

Such a scenario obscures the ingenuity of the Greek adaptation: that a clumsy Greek should have stumbled downhill into the creation of humankind's first fully alphabetic writing system (i.e., a segmental script designed to incorporate *both* consonant *and* vowel symbols) seems unlikely. What we have observed so far about the adaptive process reveals that the adapters were proceeding with intentionality and arbitrariness. "The Greek" may have in fact been a "Semite", but regardless of the genotypes of the persons involved, the process of adapting the Phoenician script for Greek usage must have taken place in a setting of Greek-Phoenician interaction and is almost certainly the handiwork of Greek-Phoenician bilingual speakers; such bilingualism would have undoubtedly been common in the eastern Mediterranean of the early first millennium BCE.

The fourth of the Phoenician consonantal symbols to be appropriated for spelling Greek vowels differs from the first three cases in both the articulatory region of the consonant that it symbolizes and in the phonological naturalness of its adaptation for Greek spelling. The Phoenician language is characterized by the presence of a palatal glide /y/; though present in earlier forms of Greek, such a phoneme was absent from the Greek language of the first millennium BCE. The adapters used the Phoenician grapheme for /y/ to devise a symbol for spelling the Greek vowels that are phonetically closely related to that glide; see table 3.1k.

Table 3.1k

Phoenician original		Greek adaptation	
phoneme	*grapheme*	*grapheme*	*phoneme*
/y/	⟨ *yod*	⟨ *iota*	/ĭ/ and /ī/

This orthographic conversion is phonologically natural: cross-linguistically, it is common for the consonant [y] and the vowel [i] to alternate as context-conditioned phonetic variants, as do, in a parallel fashion, [w] and [u].

Beyond these adaptations, certain local Greek alphabets employ yet another consonantal character for vowel spelling. It was noted above that the letter *heta*, from Phoenician *ḥet* (spelling the pharyngeal fricative /ħ/), was adapted for spelling the Greek glottal fricative /h/. Some Greek *dialects* lacked this phoneme, however, such as those of the Ionic Dodekapolis and of Crete; in the *alphabets* that were used to write these dialects, the symbol *heta*, or *eta*, was appropriated for spelling /ē/. There are still other local alphabets that use the symbol to spell *both* the consonant /h/ *and* the vowel /ē/, as in that of the Ionic Cycladic island of Naxos, for example (where the vowel so represented is only that one which had developed secondarily from Common Greek *ā). The Greek use of Phoenician *ḥet* for vowel representation is normally interpreted as a secondary adjustment to the (more or less) recently adapted *Uralphabet*; but it is noteworthy that with the use of *ḥet* for spelling /ē/ the full panoply of Phoenician letters for glottal and pharyngeal consonants has been turned to Greek vowel spelling.

These various graphemic adaptations would have resulted in the engineering of a Greek alphabet of 22 letters, extending from *alpha* through *tau*. A Greek alphabet of precisely this range is attested on three copper plaques, reported to have been unearthed in the Fayum, inscribed with a Greek alphabet in repeating series: these documents likely preserve the most archaic form of the alphabet thus far attested, though perhaps do not themselves constitute the earliest executed examples of Greek alphabetic writing. [2]

While such an alphabet makes provision for spelling most of the Greek vowels using dedicated vocalic characters (though characters typically polyphonous in value, as we have seen), no such provision has been made for spelling the high back vowels /ŭ/ and /ū/. At this stage of the history of the alphabet, *wau* (or *digamma*), the symbol for the glide /w/, would most likely have been used for spelling the phonologically associated vowel /u/ (long and short); such a strategy makes recourse to the same sound relationship that is exploited in the Greek adapters' decision to use the Phoenician symbol for the glide /y/ (i.e., *yod*) as the symbol for spelling the Greek vowel /i/ (i.e., *iota*, the difference between the vowel-value of *iota* and the polyphonous consonant/ vowel-value of *waw* being an artefact of the phonemic structure of the Greek language at the time of the adaptation of the Phoenician script). A similar use of *waw* appears to have characterized the early Phrygian alphabet (see Brixhe 2004a: 283), a script which was itself acquired from the Greeks, by the early eighth century BCE. [3]

Table 3.2 Full list of Phoenician and Greek scripts (cf. table 7 .1)

Phoenician consonantal script			Greek alphabetic script		
/ʔ/	𐤀	'alep	𐌀	alpha	/ă/ and /ā/
/b/	𐤁	bet	B	beta	/b/
/g/	𐤂	gimel	Γ	gamma	/g/
/d/	𐤃	dalet	Δ	delta	/d/
/h/	𐤄	he	Ɛ	epsilon	/ĕ/, /ɛ̄/ and /ę̄/
/w/	Y	waw	F	wau	/w/
/dᶻ/	I	zayin	I	zeta	[z] + [d]
/ħ/	𐤇	ḥet	𐌇	(h)eta	/h/ and /ē/
/tʼ/	⊗	ṭet	⊗	theta	/tʰ/
/y/	𐤉	yod	𐌆	iota	/ĭ/ and /ī/
/k/	𐤊	kap	K	kappa	/k/
/l/	L	lamed	𐌋	lambda	/l/
/m/	𐤌	mem	𐌌	mu	/m/
/n/	𐤍	nun	𐌍	nu	/n/
/tˢ/	𐤎	samek	𐌎	xi	[k] + [s]
/ʕ/	O	'ayin	O	omikron	/ŏ/, /ɔ/ and /ǭ/
/p/	𐤐	pe	Γ	pi	/p/
/tsʼ/	𐤑	ṣade	M	san	[tˢ]?
/kʼ/	𐤒	qop	Φ	qoppa	"backed" [k]
/r/	𐤓	reš	P	rho	/r/
/s/	W	šin	𐌔	sigma	/s/
/t/	+	taw	T	tau	/t/

That strategy would have ceased to be required for Greek spelling with the introduction of the first "supplemental" Greek letter. A distinct vowel symbol having the
value of /ŭ/ and /ū/, *upsilon*, was appended to the end of the Greek adapters'
alphabet. While *upsilon* "supplements" the Phoenician script by extending beyond its
range (i.e., *'alep* to *taw*), the shape of the appended Greek letter is unmistakably
Phoenician. While the Greek adapters had taken over Phoenician *waw* into their
alphabet, retaining its name, its place in the periodic order of letters, and its value
/w/, they chose to alter the morphology of *waw*; as we noted above, the resulting
Greek letter, *wau*, shows no similarity to its Phoenician source (see McCarter 1975:
93–4). In contrast, the first addendum to the Greek adaptation of the Semitic script,
upsilon, preserves the *form* of Phoenician *waw*, but not its name, its position, or its
consonantal value /w/ – being assigned, instead, the value of the vocalic counterpart
of /w/ – that is, /u/. Additional "supplemental" – and non-Phoenician – consonantal symbols were subsequently attached to the expanded *alpha*-through-*upsilon*
Greek abecedarium. A large number of local Greek alphabets show the ensuing
sequence *phi, chi, psi*, with the graphic shapes and phonic values shown in table 3.2a.
Phi and *chi* fill out the graphemic provision for voiceless aspirated stop phonemes:
before the addition of these symbols to the alphabetic repertory, the aspirated stops
/pʰ/ and /kʰ/ would have been ambiguously spelled using the symbols *pi* and *kappa*

Table 3.2a

Grapheme		Phonic value
Φ	*phi*	/pʰ/
Χ	*chi*	/kʰ/
Ψ	*psi*	[p] + [s]

(the graphemes for the unaspirated phonemes /p/ and /k/), a practice attested in the Cretan alphabet (see below), and also paralleled by the syllabic spelling practices of Linear B and the Cypriot Syllabary. With the addition of *phi* and *chi*, the orthographic pattern of distinguishing *voiceless unaspirated*, *voiceless aspirated*, and *voiced* stop phonemes that characterizes the spelling of the dentals (using *tau*, *theta*, and *delta*, respectively), was extended to the bilabial and velar stop phonemes (hence the sets, *pi*, *phi*, *beta* and *kappa*, *chi*, *gamma*). The appending of the symbol *psi*, used to spell a sequence of consonant sounds ([p] + [s]) that could have been, and were, spelled as a sequence of consonantal symbols (such as *pi* + *sigma*) seems idiosyncratic and excessive, but is, again, a decision influenced by an existing pattern: the prior occurrence of a symbol having the sequential value of [k] + [s], i.e., *xi*.

Alphabets characterized by this extended sequence were colored dark blue on the map included in Adolf Kirchhoff's (1877) nineteenth-century classic work *Studien zur Geschichte des griechischen Alphabets*, and are hence at times denoted the "dark-blue" alphabets: included in this set are, *inter alia*, the local alphabets of the Ionic Dodekapolis, some Ionic Aegean islands, Knidos, Corinth, and Argos. Kirchhoff colored as light blue those that differed systemically from the dark-blue alphabets at two points: (1) these light-blue scripts lacked the appended *psi* character (spelling [p] + [s]) of the dark-blues; and (2) they showed excision of the *xi* character (spelling [k] + [s]) from within the body of the Phoenician portion of the alphabet. For spelling the two consonantal sequences [k] + [s] and [p] + [s], the light-blue alphabets opted for a constituent-representation, using, respectively, the letter sequences *chi* + *sigma* and *phi* + *sigma* (i.e., employing the two remaining "supplemental" consonantal symbols); among alphabets of this type are those of Attica and several of the Ionic Aegean islands. Both the dark-blue and the light-blue alphabets thus realize a consistent spelling of the consonantal sequences [k] + [s] and [p] + [s], but they do so by using complementary strategies: one set (dark-blue) achieves this uniformity by the addition of a "supplemental" letter (*psi*), the other (light-blue) by the removal of an adapted Semitic symbol (*xi*).

Kirchhoff colored red those alphabets that utilize – in terms of phonic values – a partially different set of appended consonantal symbols, as shown in table 3.2b. The red-alphabet type shares in common with the blue-alphabet types – both dark and light – the appending of symbols with the values /pʰ/ and /kʰ/. In all three the former (*phi*) has the same graphic shape (Φ); the latter (*chi*) appears as Ψ in the red type, as Χ in the blue types. In contrast, this grapheme Χ is assigned the value [k] + [s] in the red type, and the Phoenician symbol that had been assigned the value [k] + [s] by the adapters has been excised from within the red alphabet, as in the light-blue type. The red alphabets also share with the light-blue alphabets a componential spelling of the consonantal sequence [p] + [s], utilizing the graphemic sequence of *phi* + *sigma*. Notice that while the dark-blue

Table 3.2b

Grapheme		Phonic value
Φ	*phi*	/pʰ/
Χ	*xi*	[k] + [s]
Y	*chi*	/kʰ/

and light-blue alphabets achieve symmetry in the spelling of the consonantal sequences [k] + [s] and [p] + [s] (discussed above), the red alphabets embrace an asymmetric treatment (on the possibility of also identifying a "light-red" alphabetic system, see Woodard 1997a: 215–16). Among red alphabets are the local scripts of Euboea, Boeotia, Arcadia, and Laconia.

A still different alphabetic system is that one which lacks the supplemental consonantal characters of the blue and red alphabets altogether: these alphabets were marked green on Kirchhoff's map. The green-alphabet type is thus systemically close to the alphabet of the copper plaques mentioned above – the initial product of the adapters – though it does show adjustments: (1) the supplemental vowel character *upsilon* has been added; and (2) the [k] + [s] symbol (*xi*) has been excised from within the Phoenician portion of the script (as in the light-blue and red alphabets; on a developmental scenario relating these four systems, see Woodard 1997a: 208–16). The alphabets of Crete, Thera, Melos, and Anaphe are of the green type.

It is important to bear in mind that "red, blue, and green" refer to alphabetic *systems*; distinct (though not necessarily completely unrelated) is the matter of the particular morphology of individual graphemes found in the various local alphabets (see the numerous tables in, *inter alia*, Jeffery 1990, Guarducci 1967, and McCarter 1975). The symbols of the green alphabets have often been assayed as particularly close in form to those of the parent Phoenician script; hence, the green alphabets, especially that of Crete, have been at times denoted as "primitive" (see Jeffery 1990: 8–9, 310).

An additional supplemental letter – another vocalic symbol – was attached to the end of the alphabets used in Ionia, Knidos, Paros, and Melos. This symbol, *omega* (Ω), spelling a long *o*-vowel, appears to have been devised by unrolling *omikron*. It is attested as early the second half of the seventh century BCE (see Guarducci 1967: 101, 265–6; Jeffery 1990: 325.)

Where did it Happen?

What was that locale in which creative and enterprising Greeks adapted the Semitic script for writing their own language? If the social/commercial interacting of some Greek and literate Phoenician individuals were the sole requirement for the "inventing of the alphabet," the totality of potential locales across the Mediterranean could certainly be expressed only as a very large number. Scholars have, however, typically limited the likely points of conversion to only a few: the usual suspects being Al Mina, Rhodes, Crete, and Cyprus. More recently Euboea has garnered some attention.

The proposal that the Iron Age Syrian coastal settlement of Al Mina – located where the Orontes empties into the Mediterranean – was the place of Greek adaptation of Semitic writing followed upon excavations of the site inaugurated by Sir Leonard Woolley in 1936 and 1937 (see Jeffery 1990: 10–12). The discovery of quantities of Greek pottery, much of it Euboean, led to visions of the existence of a Greek *emporion* (ἐμπόριον "trading-station") in the vicinity of Al Mina by 800 BCE (or earlier), a place where Greek merchants lived in close communion with a native West Semitic-speaking population. Recently, however, much doubt has been cast on both the size/significance of the Greek presence at Al Mina (and neighboring areas) and its late ninth/early eighth century dating. Kearsley 1989, for example, argues that the characteristic pendent semi-circle skyphos that suggested the early dating of the Greek presence at Al Mina should be properly assigned to 750 BCE and later (see also Kearsley 1999). Others have contended that the Greeks arrived at Al Mina only in the seventh century (Graham 1986) or later (see, with references, Snodgrass 2004: 4 and Niemeier 2001: 322) and that Al Mina cannot be considered to satisfy the description of a Greek *emporion* (Perreault 1993). The crucial position of Cyprus vis-à-vis Al Mina, and the Levant generally, has tended to be stressed in recent work.[4]

The idea that the culture of Greek Rhodes early intersected with Phoenician orthography is an old one. Writing in the second century BCE, Diodorus Siculus recounts the tale of Cadmus' visit to Rhodes in book 5 of his *Library of History*. Fleeing from Egypt and en route to Argos, the legendary king Danaüs and his daughters passed though Rhodes, where, in the town of Lindos, Danaüs founded a temple for Athena. Soon after, Cadmus the Phoenician arrived on Rhodes, searching for his sister Europa whom Zeus had abducted. There, in Ialysos, he established a sacred precinct (*temenos* [τέμενος]) for Poseidon and left behind some number of Phoenicians as attendants when he continued his search. These Phoenicians, writes Diodorus (5.58.2), "intermingled" (καταμίγνυμι) with local Rhodians and the two groups became co-citizens (συμπολιτευόμενοι); their descendants continued to serve hereditarily as priests of the precinct. Before sailing from Rhodes, Cadmus had also visited the temple of Athena in Lindos and made an offering of a large bronze lebes on which were written *Phoinikika grammata* (Φοινικικὰ γράμματα) "Phoenician letters," and regarding the letters of this inscription, Diodorus adds: . . . ἃ φασι πρῶτον ἐκ Φοινίκης εἰς τὴν Ἑλλάδα κομισθῆναι (. . . which they say were the first carried out of Phoenicia into a Greek place; Diod. Sic. 5.58.3).

Aside from the textual tradition preserved by Diodorus Siculus and the relative easterly geographic positioning of Rhodes, the island offers little to commend itself as "the place." In an important pair of articles on the origin of the Greek alphabet that appeared in the 1930s, Rhys Carpenter first proposed a Rhodian locale.

> The most probable point of entry of the Semitic prototype into the Greek world is Rhodes, whose geographical position exposed it to the oncoming wave of Assyro-Oriental influence brought by the Phoenician westward expansion during the eighth century. Cyprus was exposed to this influence first; but the Cypriote Greeks were immune as far as the alphabet was concerned, because they still preserved their ancient Achaean mode of writing. (Carpenter 1933: 27–8)

In the follow-up article (1938), however, Carpenter relinquished this idea in favor of a Cypriot origin – now realizing, in a rudimentary way, the significance of Cypriot "Achaean" (i.e., Cypriot syllabic) literacy for the Greek adaptation of the Phoenician script.[5]

Crete is no stranger to the claim of "place of invention" of the Greek alphabet. In the tenth century BCE, Crete was a nexus of east–west trade: Cypriot influence is well attested and a Phoenician presence on the island during the tenth century and following is indicated by, *inter alia*, the contents of a pair of tombs at Tekke (see Coldstream 1982: 267–71; Negbi 1992: 607–8) and two temples unearthed at Kommos (see Negbi 1992: 608–9 with bibliography). One of the tombs at Tekke has provided a bronze bowl bearing a Phoenician proprietary inscription. The Phoenician script of this bowl, however, is quite unlike the "primitive" (green) alphabet of the Cretan Greeks (and their island neighbors) and in the balance weakens the case for a Cretan origin of the alphabet (see Johnston 1983: 66n17, 68). The evidence is no more suggestive of a Cretan design of the Greek alphabet than of a Rhodian origin.

In fact, if all that was required for the Greek adaptation of the Phoenician script were a bit of Greek ingenuity situated within the context of a Phoenician social and commercial presence – and this is all that is offered by Rhodes and Crete – the list of potential Mediterranean sites of adaptation could be extended to some length. This is, when extrapolated to its reasonable conclusion, the point that one can read from Boardman's remarks in a recent survey of Mediterranean "colonization": "Whatever the reasons," he writes, "in the eighth century both Greeks and Phoenicians were taking their exploration to the west more seriously. . . . It was in the ports and watering places of the Mediterranean that Greeks, Syrians, and Phoenicians met, and it was on this circuit that a Greek realized and learned the value of an alphabet –" (Boardman 2001: 37). He goes on, "– but not in Cyprus where Greek was already written, for local consumption, in the syllabary devised for it centuries before." Boardman's objection to identifying a Cypriot origin of the alphabet is that same one offered by Carpenter in 1933 (see above).

Carpenter of course subsequently surrendered this objection when he realized, following the work of Nilsson and Hammarström (see Carpenter 1938: 67), that it is the Cypriot Syllabary that provides the crucial motivation for the form that the adapters chose to give to the new alphabetic system. In effect, the orthographic mechanisms of the Cypriot system constitute the missing link between the Phoenician consonantal script and the Greek alphabet.

This author's present view of the evidence adduced by Carpenter is that it should be regarded as supporting in nature (for an earlier summary, see Woodard 1997a: 231–3). There exists other evidence, however, that reveals far more tangibly and convincingly the Cypriot involvement in the adaptation of the Phoenician script for Greek use. Perhaps most persuasive is the Cypriot motivation for the presence of a single symbol with the sequential value of $[k] + [s]$. It seems a remarkably strange choice for inclusion in the new alphabetic writing system – a system also equipped with symbols having the values $/k/$ and $/s/$ individually; and the jittering with this $[k] + [s]$ symbol (i.e., *xi*) evidenced by the early systemic variants of the *Uralphabet* (i.e., blue, red, and green alphabetic systems) must reveal a certain apoplexy regarding its presence. Comparable *syllabic* symbols (i.e., graphemes representing [k] + [s] + vowel) occur in the Cypriot Syllabary: unlike the alphabetic script, where *xi* is *otiose*, the corresponding *ksV*-syllabic symbols are *essential*, being uniquely required by the spelling mechanism of the Cypriot script (an accident of historical Greek phonology intersecting with the Cypriot orthographic strategy of spelling consonant sequences). Among other alphabetic features pointing to a Cypriot origin are the presence of a character having the componential value of [z] + [d] (i.e., *zeta*) and the inclusion of the *san* symbol (with the hypothesized value [tˢ]) alongside the *sigma* symbol (for detailed discussion of Cypriot orthographic mechanisms transferred to the alphabet, see Woodard 1997a, esp. chs 6–8).

Perhaps it would not be injudicious to suggest that something of a consensus seems to be to emerging regarding Cyprus and Cypriots as key to the adaptation of the Phoenician script for Greek use.[6] From (or through) Cyprus the alphabetic script would then have been exported along the heavily traveled trade routes connecting the eastern Mediterranean to the Aegean. Crete was likely an early recipient, as was Euboea, locales directly linked with Cyprus via the sea routes by the tenth century BCE.[7] In the early 1950s, Wade-Gery (1952) espoused the idea that the Greek alphabet was devised expressly for the purpose of producing a graphic record of Homeric epic; this notion was revivified in the 1980s and 1990s by Barry Powell, who located the seminal event in Euboea and identified a sole adapter, the legendary Greek figure Palamedes (see Powell 1991: 231–7). The Wade-Gery/Powell hypothesis, with its premise of lofty literary ideals, does not appear to have attracted a broad following, though Euboea was certainly an important force in the early dissemination of the alphabet. The question of the alphabet's motivation, then, remains.

Why did it Happen?

While the evidence for Cypriot adaptation of the Phoenician script is strong, one must allow the possibility that though the adapters themselves were "scribes," whose literate indoctrination was in the Cypriot syllabic writing system, their adaptive work was (initially or predominantly) carried out on soil other than that of the island of Cyprus. The earliest significant Greek presence in Syria-Palestine appears to have been that of mercenary Greek warriors, dating at least as early as the eighth century BCE. In the eighth and subsequent centuries, Greek mercenaries are evidenced as serving in the armies of various Near Eastern powers, including Assyria, Babylonia, Egypt, Judah, and the Phoenician city-state of Tyre (Niemeier 2001: 16–24; see also Braun 1982a: 14–24; 1982b: 35–7, 44–7, 49–52).

As is well documented in later periods, some of the Greek mercenaries of the early centuries must have been Cypriots. A certain man mentioned in communiqués of the Assyrian king Sargon II who played a leading role in the rebellion of the Levantine city of Ashdod against Assyria (711 BCE) is called Yamani. Assyrian words for "Greek" are *yamnaya* and *yaman* (i.e., *Ionian*; Dalley and Reyes 1998: 95; Braun 1982a: 1, 3); hence, some scholars have interpreted the name Yamani to mean "the Ionian."

This interpretation has been disputed (see Niemeier 2001: 16–17 for bibliography) and this name *Yamani* explained as a homophone of the word for "Greek" (Dalley and Reyes 1998: 95), but the man is also called Yadna, plausibly meaning the "Cypriot" – compare *Yadnana*, the Assyrian name for Cyprus (see Braun 1982a: 17). Boardman (2001: 40n9) writes: "It seems to me very probable that he was a Cypriot Greek, and that other Yamanis of this period in the east may not be unrelated to Greek activity in the area (Saporetti 1990; Rollinger 1997)." Cypriots or other eastern Greek elements appear to have been among those soldiers garrisoned at the Judean fortress of Arad in the late seventh century (see Niemeier 2001: 18 with bibliography). Cypriot mercenaries in Egypt during the fourth century BCE left behind graffiti written with their Cypriot Syllabary (as did other Greek, Carian, and Phoenician mercenaries; see Masson 1983: 356–7 and, generally, 353–88 – see also ch. 15). From the Cypriot town of Amathus comes a Cypro-Phoenician silver bowl of the late eighth or early seventh century BCE engraved with the scene of a military attack on a fortress. Among the attacking force of horsemen and archers in Assyrian dress can be seen four hoplites with Ionic helmets, spears, and round shields having familiar Greek blazons ("These are undoubtedly east Greek hoplites": Niemeier 2001: 21; for detailed description, see Myres 1933). Scaling the opposite side of the citadel are two warriors "protected by their raised shields with spikes of a Cypriote type" (Karageorghis 2002: 176; "a fine example of which [spiked boss] is said to have been found with the bowl," according to Myres 1933: 35); Myres (p. 35 n. 25) had noted that the turbaned headgear of one of the horsemen is otherwise seen on a Cypriot centaur. Within the fortress, figures armed like the hoplites are also depicted, reflecting, as observed by Myres (1933: 36), "their mercenary habit." Niemeier (2001: 21) summarizes: "Whether the scene represented is mythological . . . or a real one . . . , there is no doubt that the Amathus bowl reflects warlike events in the Near East around 700 BCE in which Greek hoplites were involved."

The recent discoveries from Wadi el-Hôl, suggesting that a significant incentive for the creation of the ancestor of the Greek alphabet, the West Semitic consonantal script, was provided by the practical needs of mercenary military activity, lead us to ponder the prospect of the Greek alphabet itself taking shape under similar conditions and for a similar utilitarian end. A sufficient context would be provided by a mixed mercenary contingent consisting of literate Cypriot warriors and illiterate "Ionic" warriors operating in Syria-Palestine (such as that depicted on the Amathus bowl) within the sort of multilingual setting that must have been typical of such military milieus in the Levant and throughout the Near East. The Cypriot syllabic script, with its idiosyncratic (if phonetically natural) spelling strategies, was too unwieldy to be acquired expeditiously by illiterate (non-Cypriot) Greeks, and so – developing this scenario – Cypriots adapted the Phoenician consonantal script, with its small number of symbols, as a readily acquired means for meeting fundamental communication needs among Greek-speaking mercenaries. Such Cypriot adapters (mercenaries) may very well have arrived in Syria-Palestine armed with a knowledge of both Phoenician language and script, acquired in Cyprus – perhaps even arrived with the germ of the idea of a Greek use of Phoenician letters, perhaps having experimented casually with their use, but now finding a practical need for such an adaptation.

When did it Happen?

Prior to Carpenter's 1933 article, scholars had for some decades been situating the origin of the Greek alphabet between the later second millennium and the ninth century BCE (see McCarter 1975: 1–12; Jeffery 1990: 12 n. 4). On the basis of epigraphic comparison of the earliest examples of Greek alphabetic script and its Phoenician parent, Carpenter, however, argued persuasively for a date of *c.* 700 BCE. Since Carpenter, that date has been receding as new discoveries have been made, especially finds in the Euboean colony of Pithekoussai in southern Italy. The later twentieth century saw a consensus movement toward an early eighth-century date (see Johnston's remarks at Jeffery 1990: 426). In the same period certain Near Eastern scholars put forth the case for a Greek acquisition of Semitic script in *c.* 1100 BCE (or earlier), notably Joseph Naveh (see Naveh 1973; 1987; 1991; see also Bernal 1990); most Classicists and many Semitists have not found this view persuasive (see Sass 2005). The recent discovery of a graffito at the Latin site of Osteria dell'Osa in an archeological context of *c.* 830–770 BCE (see, *inter alia*, Bietti Sestieri, De Santis, and La Regina 1990; Ridgway 2004: 42–3), however, seemingly mandates a chronology of hardly later than *c.* 850–800 BCE for the origin of the Greek alphabet. In addition, recent findings at the Phrygian capital of Gordion coupled with new radiocarbon and dendrochronological calibrations have been interpreted as pointing to a date of *c.* 800 BCE for the earliest Phrygian alphabetic writing (see Brixhe 2007b: 278–282). A *terminus ante quem* of the late ninth century for the Greek adaptation of the Phoenician script seems ever more probable (for additional considerations, see the discussions in Woodard 1997a, esp. 218–19, 225–6, 228–9).

If one were to look for the beginnings of the Greek alphabet in a military milieu involving Cypriot and Ionic (including Cycladic and Euboean) mercenaries in a context of Phoenician language and writing within the probable timeframe of the origin of the Greek script, to what moment in Syro-Palestinian history would one turn? Possibly to the Assyrian monarch Shalmaneser III's campaign against Syria-Palestine in 853 BCE where at the Battle of Qarqar he met a massive coalition of forces fronted by Adad-Idrim, king of Damascus, and Irkhuleni, king of Hamath – jointly, the armies of the "twelve kings of Hatti and the sea coast" – an alliance that included the Phoenician cities of Byblos, Irqata, Arvad, Usant, and Siannu (Grayson 1982: 261; Hawkins 1982: 393; Culican 1991: 467; Roux 1992: 297). In 841 BCE Shalmaneser turned against the Phoenician cities of Tyre and Sidon, receiving tribute from both, as well as from the Israelite king Jehu (Culican 1991: 467–8).

Rather than among Greek mercenaries enlisted to oppose Assyrian aggression, perhaps one would expect this new communications system to take shape within the well-organized ranks of the Assyrian army (in which Pythagoras, an Ionian, was reported to have served, though his date does not allow it; see Dalley and Reyes 1998: 97). As noted above, Cypriot Greek mercenaries could have brought with them knowledge of Phoenician language and script. It was in the reign of Shalmaneser III, in 839 BCE, that the Assyrian army marched into Cilicia, making incursions deeper into Anatolia in the following years (Grayson 1982: 263). Could this be the mechanism by which the Greek alphabet so early reached the Phrygians? Shalmaneser was succeeded by his son Shamshi-Adad V, whose throne passed, upon his death in 811 BCE, to his queen Sammuramat.[8] Though the historicity of the account is necessarily uncertain, Diodorus Siculus (2.16.4) writes that in preparing for war the Assyrian queen sent for ναυπηγοί "shipwrights" from "Phoenicia and Syria and Cyprus and other regions by the sea, . . . and commanded them to build river craft that could be disassembled." Military scenarios of "peaceful readiness" from the same era would work as well.

Whether the Greek alphabet took shape on Cyprus itself or under Cypriot guidance in Syria-Palestine (or elsewhere), to be transported west, certainly passing iteratively through Cyprus, it found no foothold on that island. It had no more chance of doing so than the West Semitic consonantal script of Wadi el-Hôl and Serabit el-Khadim had of establishing itself permanently in Pharaonic Egypt. In both locales, Cyprus and Egypt, an established script (both "donor scripts," though in different ways) held sway for reasons of ethnic identity; the illegitimate offspring of the Egyptian and Cypriot scripts would each have to be introduced into regions lacking a scriptic tradition (illiterate locales) in order to become established writing systems and markers of ethnic identity themselves.[9] The Greek alphabet may have reached mainland Greece as eastern mercenaries made their way west – or as mainland Greek warriors returned, like Odysseus, from their war-making in the east. One thinks, for example, of the warrior occupants of eleventh-century tombs in Crete, linked with Homeric Νόστοι "heroic homeward journeys"; see Catling 1994: 136–8; 1995; Karageorghis 2003: 342), but – within a context relevant to the beginnings of the alphabet – especially of the recently unearthed warrior burial of the richly laden Tomb 79 at Lefkandi in Euboea (*c.* 850 BCE) containing, among other items, iron weapons, Cypriote and Phoenician pottery, a Syrian cylinder seal, and a collection of balance weights typical of eastern Mediterranean trade (see, *inter alia*, Popham and Lemos 1995; Kroll 2008). The identity of the ethnicity of the cremated warrior has been a matter of disagreement (see Papadopoulos 1997).

The introduction of the alphabet into Greece was not, however, merely a matter of Greek mercenaries returning home with a knowledge of a military-communications system acquired in the east. Though the alphabet may have perhaps gotten an early start in Euboea in this way, the transmission of the script to Greece was a more complex process: this is suggested by Greek inscriptional practices of word-division and the syllable-division doctrine of Greek grammarians that appear to have a common origin in syllabic Cypriot orthography, itself heir to a Mycenaean tradition.[10] In other words, not only was the alphabet introduced into Iron Age Greece but a learned scribal tradition was as well. One thinks again of Homer and of Odysseus' faithful swineherd Eumaeus, reminding Antinous of "invited strangers from a foreign place" (*Od.* 17.380–6) – itinerant δημιοεργοί, "craftsmen" who, their name suggests, have some affiliation with the community at large ("They could have been paid as they worked, provided only that they were available to the public, to the whole *demos.* That availability would explain the word well enough": Finley 2002: 44). Homer, via Eumaeus, enumerates four types: seers, healers of ills, workers of wood, and bards. Even within this list, certainly not intended to be exhaustive, one could envision the trained scribe.

FURTHER READING

For detailed discussion of the many local forms of the archaic Greek alphabet see Jeffery 1990 and Guarducci 1967. McCarter 1975 provides an invaluable comparison of the early Phoenician letters and their Greek counterparts. On various topics concerning the origin of the alphabet, including Cypriot involvement in the adaptation of the Phoenician script and the continuity between the Bronze Age and Iron Age syllabic scripts of the Greeks and the Greek alphabet, see Woodard 1997a. For a general treatment of the Greek alphabet within a broad historical context of its antecedents and its descendants, see Healey 1990.

NOTES

1 "Whatever definition for vowels and consonants could be considered the most precise, there is not the slightest doubt that this is the cardinal and most obvious bifurcation of speech sounds for linguists, for investigators of speech in its motor, acoustic, and perceptual aspects, for poets, and finally for the intuition of ordinary speakers" (Jakobson and Waugh 1979: 84).
2 See Heubeck 1986; Woodard 1997a: 156–7; Scott et al. 2005; Brixhe 2007a.
3 On the dating of Phrygian texts see Brixhe 2004b: 778–80; Brixhe (2007b: 282) contends that the Phrygian script "reveals a land route for its penetration and suggests a Greek–Phrygian collaboration."
4 Jones 1986; Coldstream 1989: 94; Woodard 1997a: 234–5; and see the remarks of Niemeier 2001: 14 and of Snodgrass 2004: 4.
5 On Carpenter's arguments, see Woodard 1997a: 230–2; for a recent treatment of Rhodes and the Phoenicians, revealing Rhodes's close affiliation with Cyprus in the Iron Age, see Kourou 2003.
6 Recent proponents, with varying degrees of conviction and modes of interpretation, include Heubeck 1979: 85–7; Johnston 1983: 66–7; Robb 1994: 275; Burkert 1992: 27; 2004: 18; and Woodard 1997a.
7 See, *inter alia*, Popham 2004: 14–17, 22; Negbi 1992: 606–7 with bibliography; Coldstream 1982.
8 The legendary Semiramis; for the stele erected by the historical figure in which she touts her accomplishments, see Donbaz 1990.
9 On the Cypriot Syllabary and the alphabet as a problem of ethnic identity, see Woodard 1997a: 217–24; see also Kourou 2003: 253–5; Sherratt 2003.
10 See Morpurgo Davies 1987a, 1987c; Woodard 1997a: 256–60; see also ch. 2 above.

CHAPTER FOUR

Inscriptions

Rudolf Wachter

What is an Inscription?

Inscriptions defy easy definition. We may try to define them and to distinguish the different types by looking at their material and their textual context. Their essential feature is that the material support of the text and its letters date from antiquity. (Of course, there are also inscriptions from later periods, down to modern times, but these do not concern us here.) This also applies to papyri (see ch. 5), of course, but papyri are not considered inscriptions, because papyrus is soft and fragile, whereas inscriptions are typically texts written on solid material. Unlike the literary documents that have come down to us through the mostly medieval manuscript tradition (see ch. 6), a papyrus or an inscription can be the physical text written by its author. This is often the case with, for example, documentary papyri and wooden writing tablets, the latter being counted among the inscriptions. Literary papyri, on the other hand, are in a way just early manuscripts (some Greek literature like Menander is in fact almost exclusively known from papyri). Likewise, epigrams or other metrical inscriptions often share many features with literary texts and are therefore not in every respect a creation by their author. Take, for example, the following dedication on a fired clay stele by a potter at Metapontion:

Νικόμαχος μ᾽ ἐπόε. /
Χαῖρε, ϝάναξ Η(έ)ρακλες· / ὅ τοι κεραμεύς μ᾽ ἀνέθεκε· /
δὸς δ᾽ ἐϝὶν ἀνθρόποις / δόξαν ἔχεν ἀγαθ(έ)ν.

Nikomachos made me.
Enjoy (me), ruler Herakles! That very potter dedicated me to you;
but you grant to him that he may find good acceptance among men!

After the potter's signature (a hemistich, deliberate in view of the imperfect instead of the usual aorist), we have a hymn *en miniature* in which after an invocation with a eulogistic epitheton (ϝάναξ "lord") the donor asks the deity for a favor, in this case professional success, just as the poets of the Homeric Hymns (e.g., *Hymn. Hom.* 10.4f., 15.9) or indeed Solon in his elegy to the Muses (*IEG* 13.3–4):

ὄλβόν μοι πρὸς θεῶν μακάρων δότε, καὶ πρὸς ἀπάντων
ἀνθρώπων αἰεὶ δόξαν ἔχειν ἀγαθήν.

Give me happiness that comes from the gods, and that I from all
humans may find good acceptance!

We note that the pentameter of Nikomachos' dedication bears a striking similarity to Solon's pentameter; this local personal statement is intimately connected with the "international" language of poetry and epigram (see also ch. 26).[1]

Not just in the case of this modest clay stele, but quite generally, inscriptions, even if fragmentary, greatly enhance the scholarly value of an object. The text makes the object literally speak to us. Of course, the Greeks did not write on objects in order to satisfy our scholarly interest, but because they wanted to convey a message to their fellow countrymen and immediate descendants (and, sometimes, to the gods). They were the first people in history to have this possibility for all layers of the population, not just for a privileged elite. This was made possible by the alphabet, one of the easiest and most precise writing systems in history (see ch. 3).

In the following sections we will, among other things, look at editorial conventions, material and application, direction of writing, script style, letter-forms, punctuation, special text arrangements such as *stoichedon*; after this, issues pertaining to language and content will be addressed, such as spelling, dialects, style, sense, and the difficult problem of dating. Finally, we will turn to more technical and bibliographical interests.

Editorial Conventions

Most editions are now made according to the so-called "extended Leiden convention" of 1931 (see Dow 1969). The most important signs are set out in table 4.1.

The latest developments in the editorial conventions as well as in the field of epigraphy as a whole can be followed at the International Congresses of Greek and Latin Epigraphy (the 13th was held in Oxford in 2007, see http://ciegl.classics.ox.ac.uk/; the last published is the 11th, held in Rome in 1997; the 12th was held in Barcelona in 2002, see http://www.ub.es/epigraphiae/).

Material and Application

The majority of inscriptions are on stone. These can be funeral epigrams on stelae or bases (as the Attic funeral inscription for Phrasikleia of *c.* 540 BCE: *CEG* 24), dedicatory epigrams engraved on a statue (as the Naxian Nikandre kore from Delos, *c.* 650

Table 4.1 Signs and conventions in epigraphical text editions (see also table 5.1)

Sign	Meaning	Example
[αβγ]	letters lost	Πλεστιάδας μ' ἀ[νέθεκε] (*CEG* 373)
α(βγ)	letters not written (i.e., an abbreviation)	ἀ(ϝρέτευε) (ML 42*B*)
[[αβγ]]	letters erased or overwritten	ποτ[[ο]]έριον (*CEG* 454, see below)
αβγ	letters damaged but almost certain	Νέστορος : ἐ[. . .]ι̣ : εὔποτ[ον] : ποτ[[ο]]έριον (ibid.)
. . .	letters damaged and not restorable	ὀρκωισ. . .σι (ML 32)
[..]α[.]β[. . .5–7. . .]	lacunae of a determined number of letters	in *CEG* 454, above, more precisely: ἐ[..2–4..]ι̣
[–]	lacuna of an undetermined number of letters	Φυ[– γλ]αυϙόπιδι ϙ[όρει] (CEG 181)
ΑΒΓ	legible but incomprehensible letters	hὸς νῦν ὀρχεστôν πάντôν ἀταλότατα παίζει ΤΟΤΟΔΕΚΛ.ΜΙ̣Ν̣ *vac.* (*CEG* 432)
{αβγ}	superfluous letters deleted by the editor	Στασα{σα}γόραν (*CEG* 859)
<αβγ>	emendation by the editor	ὀρκο{ι}σ<α>ι (ML 32, see above)
vac. (or *v.*, *vacat*)	area left blank	on *CEG* 432, above
|	beginning of a new line	*CAVI* 976 Νέαρχος μ'ἔ|γραφσεν κα̣[ὶ –].

BCE: *CEG* 403) or, again, on stelae, blocks, columns, etc. on top of which there once was a statue or a vessel (e.g., *CEG* 191 by the sixth-cent. BCE Athenian potters Mnesiades and Andokides; see also *LGPN* ii s.vv.).[2] Stone inscriptions can be laws (such as the archaic law code from Dreros concerning the tenure of a κόσμος "local magistrate," ML 2; or the famous civil laws code of Gortyn, *IC* iv.72; see Willetts 1967). Many other official documents, too, were published for the information of politically active citizens in Classical times, in particular at Athens, from where we have financial records, inventories of the treasuries, accounts of building commissions, public dedications, archon-lists, decrees, honorary decrees for cities or individuals, lists of casualties, tribute lists of allies, treaties and alliances, religious calendars, naval lists, and so on (see ML, RO, and *IG* i³, ii). A unique corpus of (semi)private texts is formed by the fourth-century BCE healing reports from Epidaurus (*IG* iv/2.1; Peek 1969; 1972).

The first decades of Greek alphabetic writing have left us mostly graffiti on fired clay (the lightest and cheapest of all durable materials). Early corpora include finds from Eretria (Verdan et al. 2005) and Ischia (Bartoněk and Buchner 1995), but we have now examples of the eighth century BCE from many more places. Particularly famous are the verses on the "Dipylon Jug" from Athens of *c.* 740 BCE (*CEG* 432) and on "Nestor's Cup" (cited in ch. 27) from Ischia found in a boy's tomb of *c.* 715 BCE (*CEG* 454). An important corpus of later clay graffiti are the Athenian ostraka of the fifth century BCE (on which, see Brenne 2002 and Lang 1990).

Relatively few examples of inscribed dedicatory bronze objects have survived. In order to survive, they have to have been buried on purpose or lost; otherwise the precious material would have been reused. The earliest example is probably the statuette of a warrior of *c.* 700–675 BCE, dedicated to Apollo by one Mantiklos in Boeotia (*CEG* 326), with two hexameter lines reflecting the same tradition as the prayer at *Od.* 3.55ff. Later examples are the helmets and other armor from Magna Graecia dedicated to Zeus at Olympia.[3] Some bronze objects were dedicated by victors in the games (*CEG* 362 at Nemea, *CEG* 372 at Olympia).

Quite a few longer texts, mostly of legal content, are on bronze tablets. Important examples are the law of the eastern Locrians concerning their colony at Naupaktos (*IG* ix²/1.718, early fifth cent. BCE, ML 20) and more than 30 shorter treaties and laws deposited in the sanctuary of Zeus at Olympia (see Minon 2007, e.g., her no. 10 (= ML 17), between the Eleans and the citizens of what is now thought to be Εὔα in the eastern Peloponnese).

Not all official texts were published on bronze tablets or stone. Those that were must have been considered important; others were written on wooden boards and have been lost. On the other hand, some texts which were surely not conceived for eternity have survived because of the nearly indestructible material on which they are written, such as the frequent trademarks on vases, which give us interesting information on Greek potters' business, particularly in Athens (see Johnston 1979; 2006). A different case, of a much rarer type, is the private letter on a lead sheet from Berezan on the Black Sea (*LSAG* suppl. 478.60c; *c.* 500 BCE).

Direction, Script Style, and Letter-Forms

The earliest inscriptions are "retrograde," as was (and still is) normal in the Near East, from where the alphabet was borrowed in the first half of the eighth century (see ch. 3). An early example of strict stichic arrangement is Nestor's Cup (one iambic trimeter and two epic hexameters in a separate line each). Some inscriptions keep this direction but go wildly serpentine ("Schlangenschrift"), e.g., a *lex sacra* from Tiryns of the early sixth century BCE (*LSAG* suppl. 443.9a); or they move regularly to and fro in a leftward direction, so that every second line is upside down (so-called "false *boustrophedon*" – βουστροφηδόν meaning "as the ox plows"), e.g., *CEG* 132 from Corinth, *c.* 650 BCE.

But after *c.* 600 BCE Greek script and most scripts derived from it started changing direction (though the Etruscans and those who learnt to write from them never did). For nearly a century, both directions were acceptable, even on one and the same inscription. During that period, (true) *boustrophedon* was often used (mostly on stone, e.g., the Phanodikos bilingual from Sigeion, in East Ionic and Attic dialects and scripts, of *c.* 575–550 BCE; *LSAG* 371.43–4; see fig. 4.1).

This writing style allowed one to read continuously, both without a "return" jump after every line and without having to read upside down as in false boustrophedon. The first line of a boustrophedon inscription may be said to be indicative of which direction the scribe considered normal. On vases, labels to figures, typically starting

Figure 4.1 The Phanodikos inscription[4]

near their heads and leading downwards, could be written either to the left or the right; in the first case they would be from right to left, in the second case from left to right. After 500 BCE, the "retrograde" direction is becoming very rare, and stichic left to right, as we are used to ourselves, is the normal layout (see fig. 4.2).

Figure 4.2 The Telesinos inscription[5]

Letter-forms, synchronically, are different if scratched in clay or stone, painted on clay with a brush, or engraved in marble by a professional stonecutter. People developed individual features in their writing from the very beginning, and not every scribe was (or is) equally skillful. Clearly different styles, however, only developed in the early Hellenistic era, when monumental letters (on stone) and cursive writing (on papyrus) started to grow apart. This was the ultimate origin of capital vs lowercase letters (see further ch. 6). The difference between Ω and ω, for instance, can be traced back to the early third century BCE.

Letter-forms developed also diachronically, according to easy principles (see also ch. 3): at a very early stage, some were turned round in certain local alphabets, whence, e.g., the difference in gammas (Γ, Λ, C) and lambdas (Λ, ʟ, Γ). In particular those lying were turned upright if possible (e.g., *alpha*). Some letters developed strange forms (especially *beta*; see *LSAG passim*). Then they were all simplified as much as possible (i.e., as long as they stayed distinguishable from each other in the particular local alphabet). This was done at first in different ways in the local scripts, but soon the regions started to copy the successful forms from each other: *iota* was straightened almost everywhere (in Corinth it could not be because *gamma* had adopted more or less this form). *Mu* (ᛘ) lost its fifth stroke (except in Euboean). *Heta/eta* (日) lost its upper and lower horizontal. *Theta*'s cross (⊗) was replaced by a dot or short horizontal. *Rho*, which had received an oblique stroke in some local scripts the better to distinguish it from *delta* (R vs D), lost it again when Δ had prevailed over D. *Xi* (Ξ) lost its centered vertical. *Zeta* became zigzag instead of two horizontals and a centred vertical (I). The only exception is *sigma*, whose four-stroke variant (Ϛ) won (in Greece, not in Rome!) over the three-stroke variant after a century-long battle, but that was a Pyrrhic victory as it was soon replaced by the lunate c in cursive writing.

In the Roman Empire, neighboring letters sometimes shared strokes, mostly verticals. Up to four or more letters could be linked in such ligatures, which saved space and time. The practice in stone inscriptions seems to have been taken from cursive writing.

Punctuation and Stoichedon

Most inscriptions of the Archaic and Classical periods do not separate words, but are in *scriptio continua*. In antiquity, the concept of "word" was different from the one we have now. Proclitics (e.g., the article or prepositions) and enclitics (some particles, indefinite pronouns, etc.), which do not have an accent of their own, were considered to belong to the word which formed the center of their accentual unit and on which they "leaned" (κλίνειν); see Morpurgo Davies 1987. Some inscriptions of the fifth century BCE, mostly of very careful execution, punctuate accentual units in exactly this manner, for instance the so-called *Dirae Teiae* of *c.* 470 BCE (ML 30 with add.); others, of roughly the same period, separate units that are sometimes single accentual units, and sometimes groups of two, following the phrase and sentence structure of the texts, for example the Locrian Law and the treaty of the Eleans with Eua, mentioned above. The origin of this practice may lie in dictation (Wachter 1999).

Despite the frequency of *scriptio continua*, punctuation goes far back. The earliest example can be found on Nestor's Cup (see also ch. 27), where in the first line words are separated and in the second and third lines groups of one or two accentual and syntactic units are indicated, coinciding (of course) with the caesura structure of the hexameters. Hence, punctuation seems to be sign of a particularly careful finish of a text. It testifies to a remarkable linguistic awareness and a desire to enhance clarity and legibility. The advantage of structuring a difficult text in this simple way must have been seen already in the early days of the Greek alphabet, and Nestor's Cup gives us a reliable sample of what a written epic text in Homer's time would have looked like.

An invention of late sixth-century Athens, it seems, is *stoichedon*. In this layout, mostly used for official documents, the letters of a text are placed one by one in a grid. The motivation for this would have been to prevent changes to a text (by erasion or insertion). Punctuation is not normally used. *Stoichedon* texts are (and were) not easy to read, but the advantage of being forgery-proof prevailed over the question of legibility. A well-known example is the inscription on the relations between the Athenians and the Phaselites (ML 31, 469–450 BCE; *stoichedon* 22).

Spelling

Spelling partly depends on the type of alphabet. Most local scripts have a *phi* and a *chi*, some even a *psi* and a *xi*; those which do not have those graphemes use combinations of letters (as in Attic, where *phi* + *sigma* is used for /ps/, and *chi* + *sigma* for /ks/).

Dialects which do not need a sign for /h/ use the "*heta*" as "*eta*," i.e., for a long (open) /ē/ (see ch. 7). East Greek even created an equivalent for /ō/, the *omega*, adding it at the end of the alphabet. The others use *epsilon* and *omikron*, e.g., Attic or Euboean (gen. Ἀφροδίτες on Nestor's Cup), Achaean (ἀνθρόποις and ἀνέθεκε of Nikomachos' clay stele), etc.

The sixth letter of the original alphabet was *wau*, or *digamma*. Its phoneme, /w/ (as in *wine*), had already been lost in some dialects when they first adopted the alphabet, in East Ionic for example. In others it was still pronounced in certain positions, e.g., in Aeolic (whence Homer, who did not speak it, knew it) or in Corinth, where κόρη/κούρη is still written κόρϝᾱ in the late fifth century (*LSAG* 132.39).

When around 400 BCE the Greeks gave up their local scripts and replaced them with the (East) Ionic alphabet (officially at Athens in 403/2), those who still needed a sign for /w/ started using β, whose sound was turning into a spirant (which it has been ever since; see chs 16 and 36–37), and for /h/ eventually the rough breathing was created.

Spurious diphthongs, i.e., "long *epsilon*s" and "long *omikron*s" originate either from contraction (e.g., ποιεῖτε < *ποιέετε; δουλοῦμεν < *δουλόομεν; Θουκῡδίδης < Θεο-) or, less frequently, from compensatory lengthening when a following /n/ was lost before /s/ (e.g., βλέπουσα < *-*onsa* < *-*ont-ja*; μιγεῖσα < *-*ensa* < *-*ent-ja* ; see further chs 8, 14, and 26). These sounds were mostly written with single *epsilon* and *omikron* down to the fourth century BCE (this old spelling of spurious ει is seen, e.g., in ἐπόε and ἔχεν on Nikomachos' clay stele, that of ου in gen. καλλιστεφάνō Ἀφροδίτες on Nestor's Cup). However, the diphthong spelling (ει and ου) had already started in the early sixth century BCE at the latest, probably in literary contexts (see *NAGVI*, §§219f.). This was possible because these sounds were similar to the real diphthongs (as in δείκνυμι, πλοῦτος), which had started to become monophthongs, namely closed long /ē/ (almost /ī/) and /ō/ (almost /ū/).

Long consonants are often written with a single sign in pre-Classical times. But double (i.e., "geminate") spelling, which is of great help to the reader, particularly of verse, again is attested as early as Nestor's Cup (καλλιστεφάνō Ἀφροδίτες; late eighth cent. BCE) and Mantiklos' bronze warrior (χαρίϝετταν ἀμοιϝ[άν]; early seventh cent. BCE). Nevertheless, the simple spelling remained acceptable for a long time and should therefore be considered an abbreviation, not a mistake, even in verse: [εἴτ' ἀστό]ς τις ἀνὲρ εἴτε χσένος | ἄλ(λ)οθεν ἐλθὸν, . . . "whether some townsman or a stranger having come from another place" (*CEG* 13; Athens, *c.* 575–550 BCE; not ἄλ<λ>οθεν).

Somewhere in between a mistake and an abbreviation are the frequent cases where a sign for a vowel is omitted because the letter name of the preceding consonant sign contained its sound, e.g., ἀνέθκε, Διονσιος, thus ἀνέθ(η)κε (or ἀνέθ<η>κε), Διον(ύ)-σιος (or Διον<ύ>σιος).[6] Although this principle never acquired official status, it is too frequent to be called an ordinary mistake. We could therefore call it "abbreviated writing" and use round brackets (see table 4.1).[7] The same trick can be observed in Latin inscriptions[8] or modern text messages (*hope 2 c u b4 u dk*).

The velar nasal before occlusive (as in *drink*) is written with *gamma* in the East (e.g., . . . γάρ μιγ καὶ . . . in the letter from Berezan[9]) and with *nu* in mainland Greece and the West (e.g. ἐνγύς *CEG* 16 and 39, Athens; see *NAGVI*, §114 with n. 727). In the Hellenistic and Roman periods both spellings are frequent everywhere (see ch. 16).

There are other unusual spellings which look like, but are not necessarily, mistakes. *CEG* 394 Κλεόμροτος, for instance, rather reflects an archaic pronunciation when the *beta* in -μβρο-, a secondary, merely transitional sound in what is the zero grade **mr̥* of the IE verbal root **mer/mor* "die," was not (yet) felt to be worthwhile noting.

In the Hellenistic and Roman periods, spelling often reflects the changes of the dialects and, as dialects disappeared more and more, of the Greek language in general (e.g. *iotacism*, the ultimate reason of the *etacism/itacism* debate in the Renaissance).

Language and Style

There are many kinds of Greek in Greek inscriptions. First, there are different epichoric, i.e., regional, dialects (see ch. 14). In fact, we know the details of Ancient Greek dialects mostly from inscriptions. Those from Eretria, on the island of Euboea, for instance, show rhotacism of intervocalic /s/ in the Classical period (see ML 82, 411 BCE, with παιρίν instead of παισίν). Plato apparently knew about that, but probably got his example wrong when he says (Pl. *Cra.* 434C) ἡμεῖς μέν φαμεν σκληρότης, Ἐρετριεῖς δὲ σκληρότηρ "We are saying σκληρότης, but the Eretrians σκληρότηρ" (he may have mixed up the Eretrian phenomenon with rhotacism at word end in Olympia).

Second, in a given region, social variants can sometimes be distinguished. In Athens, for instance, someone wrote τὸν Λιμὸν ὀστρακίδ(δ)ō on two (!) ostraka (T 1/79, 1/80; 471 BCE?), which Colvin 2004 plausibly argues to be a local, and probably less prestigious, variant of ὀστρακίζω.[10] Ionian dialect, too, occurs on Athenian ostraka, e.g., T 1/99 (471 BCE?): Μεγακλεῖ Ἱπ(π)οκράτεος (whereas normal Attic pieces have Ηιπ(π)οκράτōς). It must remain uncertain whether the vote was cast by the text's actual writer.

Third, inscriptions can reflect literary language. This is evident in the case of *carmina epigraphica*, dedicatory or funeral, but it can also, for instance, be argued for vases, when labels to mythological figures diverge from local dialect but coincide with well-known literary forms. An instructive example is the name of Odysseus (see also *NAGVI*, §254), which on the archaic Attic vases (sixth and early fifth cent. BCE) is regularly Ὀλυττεύς or Ὀλυτεύς, but from the late sixth century BCE onwards slowly changes to Ὀλυσσεύς or Ὀλυσεύς, and then to the "Homeric" forms Ὀδυσσεύς or Ὀδυσεύς.[11] The co-occurrence on the Boston vase of Ὀδυσσεύς with the perfectly Attic, non-Homeric forms Ἀθηνάα and Κλεοπάτρα suggests that the Attic form of Odysseus' name had gone out of use and been replaced by the literary form even in spoken Attic by the end of the fifth century (for similar observations on non-Attic vases, see *NAGVI*, §§503ff.).

The replacement of -ττ- with -σσ- in Odysseus' name was later continued in normal words by a more general tendency of the Attic dialect to adjust to the majority of dialects and to the *Koine* (see Threatte 1980: 537–41), maybe also to avoid provincialisms (Attic shared -ττ- with Boeotian, a dialect despised by the Athenians: Colvin 2004: 101–2). This case shows that linguistic aspects of education, social class, and region are often not strictly separable.

Sense

One would assume that an inscription must have sense, like any coherent text. That is mostly the case – even abecedaria or writing exercises can be said to have sense (Wachter 2004) – but there is one very frequent group which does not, the so-called *nonsense inscriptions* on (mostly Attic) vases (see also ch. 34), as in fig. 4.3.[12]

Dating

Few inscriptions bear a date, and when they do (e.g., the Halicarnassian law concerning disputed property, ML 32; *c.* 465–450 BCE?), it is often easier to determine the day of the year (despite the diversity of the local calendars, on which, see Trümpy 1997) than the year itself, since we hardly ever know the local eponymous politicians or religious dignitaries and the years of their office – except for Athenian *archontes* (see ML p. 291). Dating Greek inscriptions, even in Roman times, is therefore mostly based on a concurrence of arguments. Sometimes there are historical clues contained in the text. A lucky case is the Battle of Cumae of 474 BCE (see n. 3) referred to on three of the helmets at Olympia dedicated by the Syracusan victors: τὸι Δὶ Τυρ(ρ)άν' ἀπὸ Κύμας "to Zeus, Etruscan (*sc.* spoils) from Kyme." Or arguments can be gained from the style of the monument (statue, vase, etc.), the archeological context (in a sanctuary, cemetery, marketplace, etc.), standardized formulae, the forms of names (e.g., reflecting Roman citizenship or not), dialect, spelling, and letter-forms. The result is sometimes debatable, and there is frequently a danger of circular reasoning, but this does

Figure 4.3 Attic black-figure cup of *c.* 540 BCE, unattributed, with nonsense inscriptions as space fillers[13]

not mean that all dates of the type "first quarter of the fifth century BCE" are hazardous or that we have to take an agnostic view.

Scientific methods (radiocarbon or "C-14," thermoluminescence, amino acid racemization, etc.) play a less important role in Greek and Roman epigraphy than in other historical or prehistorical contexts, as they are hardly ever more precise than the methods mentioned above, and dendrochronology is of no use since there are not enough wooden objects. But they sometimes can contribute welcome independent evidence, for instance in identifying forgeries.

What More to Know?

Epigraphists never know enough. A good knowledge of Greek and its dialects, extensive reading of all sorts of texts, particularly historical ones, and the study of Greek religion should suffice, one might think. But then the next inscription one has to study is perhaps a coin (see *SNG*), or a long literary text like the one by Diogenes of Oinoanda (second century CE, a unique form of self-publication and philosophy for everyone),[14] or it is a Pompeian wall inscription, an ostrakon from Egypt, a fragment of a Corinthian vase, or a Hellenistic amphora stamp.

The first edition of an inscription is hardly ever fully satisfying and needs comments and criticism from the scholarly community. Correcting is more pleasant than being corrected. Both will inevitably happen in an epigraphist's career. Here is an example from my own experience: In my *editio princeps* of a late fifth-century BCE bronze inscription probably from one of the Rhodian colonies of Sicily (Gela or Akragas), I overlooked the (very rare) meaning "to adopt" of the verb τίθεσθαι and thus got the meaning of the inscription, which starts θυγατέρας ἐθήκατο, completely wrong (*ZPE* 142, 2003, 53ff.). Julián Méndez Dosuna duly corrected me (ibid. 151, 2005, 87–90).[15] Yet he did not mention a new inscription from Kaunos, published in 2004 by Andreas Victor Walser (*Epigraphica Anatolica* 37, 101–6), which contains the new word θυγατροθεσία "adoption of a daughter" and would have nicely supported his view (and prevented me from my error). Finally, Laurent Dubois (in *BÉ* 2005.442, 639) gave a synthesis of the entire evidence, and the matter is now settled once and for all. The new inscription also gives support for the attribution of the bronze tablet to a Rhodian context. Sometimes relevant discoveries in epigraphy happen surprisingly quickly one after another.

FURTHER READING

Introductions to epigraphy, the present chapter included, are necessarily to some extent a matter of personal taste. But any of the following introductory books offers the beginner good starting points. Roberts 1887–1905 is somewhat dated; a useful introduction in German is Klaffenbach 1966, and in Italian Guarducci 1987. More recent short introductions in English are Cook 1987 (centered on pieces in the British Museum) and Woodhead 1981. The *Guide de l'épigraphiste* (Bérard et al. 2000) offers ample and useful bibliography.

The most important instruments for the Greek epigraphist are the great editions, especially *IG* (successor to *CIG*), *IGSK*, *MAMA*, *TAM*, *IC*, and *FD*, which are in the care of the national academies, societies, or schools[16] – for the abbreviations, see the list at the end of this chapter. *SEG* and *BÉ* provide yearly updates, and *ZPE* publishes many new finds (duly uniting papyri and inscriptions). Still not fully replaced is the eminent but dated edition of dialect inscriptions, *DGE*. Metrical inscriptions are collected in *CEG* (down to 300 BCE; for later texts, see Peek 1955 and 1957). For vase inscriptions there are *CAVI*, *AVI*, and *NAGVI*. Letter-forms (and countless historical problems) are discussed in *LSAG* and its supplement. Greek proper names and their bearers are found in *LGPN*, which is gradually superseding the old prosopographies and lexica such as Pape and Benseler 1863–70; for Greek names in Rome, see Solin 2003. In all these works there is much more bibliography (see also chs. 3 and 14 in the present volume).

There are excellent selections for historians, primarily the one by Meiggs and Lewis (ML), which is extended till the death of Alexander (adding translations) in Rhodes and Osborne (RO); Moretti 1967–76 covers the Hellenistic period. The Hellenistic and Roman periods are covered by the two large, but old, collections by Wilhelm Dittenberger (*Syll*[3] and *OGIS*), whereas McLean 2002 discusses these periods in his *Introduction* (which is almost a manual). For dialect inscriptions, i.e., all inscriptions other than Attic, in addition to *DGE*, there are *SGDI* (larger but older) and Buck 1955 (smaller but with more explanation), which remain indispensable; more recent finds (earlier than 400 BCE) can be found via *LSAG* and its supplement.

EPIGRAPHICAL ABBREVIATIONS

(For many more, see http://www.arts.leiden.edu/history/seg-abbreviations.jsp)

AVI	*Attic Vase Inscriptions.* Publication and updates of H. Immerwahr, *Corpus of Attic Vase Inscriptions* (*CAVI*), by R. Wachter, on http://avi.unibas.ch/
BÉ	*Bulletin épigraphique*, in *REG*, 1888–
CAVI	see *AVI*
CEG	P. A. Hansen, ed., *Carmina epigraphica graeca*, 2 vols, Berlin, 1983/9.
CIG	A. Boeckh et al., eds, *Corpus Inscriptionum Graecarum*, 4 vols, Berlin 1828–77
CIL	*Corpus Inscriptionum Latinarum*, Berlin 1862–
DGE	E. Schwyzer, *Dialectorum graecarum exempla epigraphica potiora*, Leipzig 1923 (repr. Hildesheim 1960)
FD	*Fouilles de Delphes*, Paris 1902–
IC	M. Guarducci, ed., *Inscriptiones Creticae*, Rome 1935–50
IG	*Inscriptiones Graecae*, Berlin 1873–
IGSK (*IK*)	*Inschriften griechischer Städte aus Kleinasien*, Bonn 1972–
LGPN	*A Lexicon of Greek Personal Names*, Oxford 1987–
LSAG	L. H. Jeffery, *The Local Scripts of Archaic Greece*, Oxford 1961; repr. with a *Supplement 1961–1987* by A. W. Johnston, 1990
MAMA	*Monumenta Asiae Minoris Antiqua*, Manchester 1928–
ML	R. Meiggs and D. M. Lewis. *A Selection of Greek Historical Inscriptions to the End of the Fifth Century* B.C. Rev. edn, Oxford 1988
NAGVI	R. Wachter, *Non-Attic Greek Vase Inscriptions*, Oxford 2001
OGIS	W. Dittenberger, *Orientis graeci inscriptiones selectae*, 2 vols, Leipzig 1903–5 (repr. Hildesheim 1986)
RO	P. J. Rhodes and R. G. Osborne, *Greek Historical Inscriptions, 404–323 BC*, Oxford 2003
SEG	*Supplementum epigraphicum graecum*, Leiden 1923–
SGDI	H. Collitz, F. Bechtel, et al., eds, *Sammlung der griechischen Dialektinschriften*, Göttingen 1884–1915
SNG	*Sylloge nummorum graecorum*, 2002–
Syll³	W. Dittenberger, *Sylloge inscriptionum graecarum*, 3rd edn, 4 vols, Leipzig 1915–24 (repr. Hildesheim 1982)
TAM	*Tituli Asiae Minoris*, Vienna 1901–
ZPE	*Zeitschrift für Papyrologie und Epigraphik*

INTERNET RESOURCES

In recent years, many institutes and projects have started using the internet for publication. The following is a selection, in alphabetical order.

A.I.E.G.L.: Societas internationalis epigraphiae graecae et latinae
  (http://www.aiegl.com/)
Center for Epigraphical and Palaeographical Studies (http://epigraphy.osu.edu/)

Centre for the Study of Ancient Documents at Oxford
  (http://www.csad.ox.ac.uk/ with http://poinikastas.csad.ox.ac.uk/)
Claros (http://www.dge.filol.csic.es/claros/cnc/2cnc.htm)
Cornell Greek Epigraphy Project (http://132.236.125.30/)
EpiDoc (http://epidoc.sourceforge.net/)
Epigraphic Database Roma (http://www.edr-edr.it/)
Guide de l'épigraphiste
  (http://www.antiquite.ens.fr/txt/dsa-publications-guidepigraphiste-fr.htm)
IG (http://www.bbaw.de/bbaw/Forschung/Forschungsprojekte/ig/de/Startseite)
Inscriptiones Graecae Eystettenses
  (http://www.gnomon.ku-eichstaett.de/LAG/IGEyst.html)
Inscriptions of Aphrodisias Project (http://www.insaph.kcl.ac.uk/)
Mysteries at Eleusis. Images of Inscriptions (http://eleusis.library.cornell.edu/)
Searchable Greek Inscriptions (http://epigraphy.packhum.org/)
SEG (http://www.arts.leidenuniv.nl/history/seg.jsp)

INSCRIPTIONS CITED

CAVI:	976, 1999, 2076a, 2403, 2742, 4593, 5055, 5438, 8096 (= fig. 4.3 above).
CEG:	13 (Tettichos), 16 (Archeneos), 24 (Phrasikleia), 39 (Philodemos and Anthemion), 132 (Dweinias, Corinth), 181 (Phy[–]), 191 (Mnesiades and Andokides), 227 (Telesinos, = fig. 4.2 above), 326 (Mantiklos, Boeotia), 362 (Aristis, Nemea), 372 (Akmatidas, Olympia), 373 (Pleistiadas, Laconia), 394 (Kleombrotos, Sybaris), 403 (Nikandre, Naxos/Delos), 432 (Dipylon Jug), 454 (Nestor's Cup, Pithekoussai), 859 (Stasagoras, Rhodos).
CIL:	xiii.3983 (Luxemburg).
LSAG:	132.39 (Corinth), 315.7 (Gortyn), 275.7 (Olympia), 371.43–4 (Phanodikos, = fig. 4.1 above), 443.9a (Tiryns), 454.6a and C, 455.E and F, 458.V, 460.C (Olympia), 478.60c (Berezan).
ML:	2 (Dreros), 17 (Olympia), 20 (Naupaktos), 30 (Teos), 31 (Athens and Phaselis), 32 (Halikarnassos), 42*B* (Argos), 82 (Eretria).

NOTES

1 See Wachter 2002 for the inscription and its relation to the elegy of Solon and especially for the meaning and etymology of δόξα (§3 with n. 22).

2 On epigrams, see Baumbach, Petrovic and Petrovic 2010.

3 *LSAG* 275.7 (a Syracusan), as well as suppl. pp. 454.6a and C (three Messenian), 455.E/F (two Rhegine), 458.V (an Achaean), and 460.C (two more Syracusan dedications) are from the Battle of Cumae of 474 BCE (see below).

4 Drawing by Nicholas Revett of 1764/5, published as an etching by Richard Chandler in 1774 and glued into Boeckh's manuscript of *CIG* in the Berlin Academy (*IG*), where

I took the photo in 2001. All later drawings depend on this etching and are far less accurate, especially with regard to the *rho*s in ll. *a*.2, 3, 7, 9, the *eta* in l. *a*.8, the *delta* in *b*.6, and almost all *mu*s in *b*; the only detail seemingly better in the later drawings is the punctuation in *a*.6, which does not exist in Revett's drawing. But where did the later scholars have it from? The stone itself had suffered much damage in the 50 years before it could be rescued and brought to the British Museum in 1816.

5 *CEG* 227, *c*. 500–480?, from the Athenian Acropolis. The inscription is incised in stichic left to right, irrespective of metrical structure.

6 Ἡ(έ)ρακλες of Nikomachos' clay stele is a very likely case, too, since the inscription uses *epsilon*, not *eta*, for long /ē/ (ἀνέθεκε), and the likely second case, viz. ἀγαθ(έ)ν, suggests that Nikomachos cites Solon, since the form is Ionic.

7 The latest list of examples is found in Wachter 2007, with reference to earlier lists in n. 20.

8 E.g. *b(e)neficiarius* and *coniugi k(a)rissimo* in the monument for C. Iulius Maximinus, *CIL* xiii 3983 (2nd half 3rd cent. CE) in the Musée Archéologique (formerly Musée Gallo-Romain) of Luxemburg, at Arlon.

9 Assimilation of a final /n/ is frequently expressed in writing in the East, rarely in Greece. The same document also contains ἐλθὼμ παρ'/παρὰ, τὴμ μητέρα, and ἐς τὴμ πόλιν. Crasis, too, is written more often in the East. In the spoken language both types of assimilatory sandhi (*sandhi* = phonological change at morpheme or word boundary, a term coined by ancient Sanskrit grammarians) must have been normal in mainland Greece, too, although of course not in the cases where a word started with /h/ (cp. Ion. gen. τ'Ὁρμοκράτεος vs Att. τō Ἡρμοκράτōς in the bilingual from Sigeion).

10 As is observed by Colvin in n. 18 (p. 105), the writer first wrote ὁτ-, then corrected to ὁσ- and continued -τρακίδο (or directly wrote ὁττ . . . and corrected afterwards). We may interpret this mistake as a reflection of a weakly pronounced /s/ before the /t/, i.e. as the exact voiceless pendant to the following spelling of [zd] with a *delta* only. In Spain, /s/ is turning to [h] or Ø before a /t/ in certain regions, e.g. ['aʰta la 'viʰta].

11 Ὀλυτεύς: e.g., *CAVI* 2039 = 2076a, *c*. 570–560 BCE (see also 5128, with Περ(ρ)εύς, from the same vase), Basel, HC 1418; Ὀλυττεύς: e.g., *CAVI* 1999, Basel, BS 477, *c*. 500–475 BCE; Ὀλυσεύς: e.g. *c*. 525–500 BCE, *CAVI* 5438, Naples 81.083, and *c*. 480 BCE, *CAVI* 4593, London E 440; Ὀλυσσεύς: *c*. 440–430 BCE, *CAVI* 2403, Berlin 2588; Ὀδυσεύς: e.g., *CAVI* 5055 = 5773, New York, Market / Malibu, *c*. 480 BCE; Ὀδυσσεύς: e.g., *CAVI* 2742, Boston 1904.18, *c*. 420–400 BCE.

12 Immerwahr (1971: 54) makes the following subdivisions: "mock and near-sense inscriptions, meaningless inscriptions, imitation inscriptions or letters, blots and dots"; now Immerwahr 2006.

13 Würzburg 419, *CAVI* 8096. Photo R.W., June 16, 2004.

14 See the various publications by Martin Ferguson Smith.

15 I should mention here that Fritz Gschnitzer, to whom I sent an offprint of my article, informed me of my error and of the correct interpretation by return of mail.

16 *IG* (and *CIL*): Berlin, Preussische, now Berlin-Brandenburgische Akademie der Wissenschaften; *MAMA*: Manchester University Press, now London, Society for the Promotion of Roman Studies; *IGSK* and *TAM*: Vienna, Österreichische Akademie der Wissenschaften; *FD*: École française d'Athènes, etc.

CHAPTER FIVE

Papyri

Arthur Verhoogt

Greek papyri have much to contribute to the study of the Greek language. They offer a view of Ancient Greek from the "first hand," by showing how residents of Egypt wrote Greek letters and pronounced Greek sounds during a period of more than 1,000 years, from roughly the fourth century BCE to the ninth century CE. They also show the day-to-day use of Greek in Egypt in all spheres of public and private life, illustrating the most technical bureaucratic vocabulary as well as the most intimate private language. In addition, papyri (like inscriptions) keep adding to the known vocabulary of Ancient Greek, requiring a regular updating of the dictionaries.

With few exceptions papyri were found in Egypt, where the circumstances are dry enough to preserve them in large numbers. Egypt, however, was part of the larger world of *Koine* Greek, and the more documents are found outside Egypt, the more it becomes clear that the Greek found in the documents from Egypt, albeit with a local "flavor," was in no way different from the Greek found in other parts of the Mediterranean world (see chs 16 and 17). Although much of current papyrological research focuses on historical and socio-economic matters more than on pure linguistic research, there are still studies of the Greek language found in papyri (e.g. Horsley 1994; Evans 2003, 2009; Vierros 2003).

Papyrus

The writing material papyrus was made from the papyrus sedge (*Cyperus papyrus*) that grew abundantly along the borders of the River Nile in ancient Egypt. It was used as a writing material already in the middle of the third millennium BCE, and its use continued until the gradual introduction of paper from China in the course of the ninth century CE. Papyrus was the product of ancient Egypt, but it was exported and used around the Mediterranean. Only the climate of Egypt, however, was dry enough to preserve papyrus in large quantities.

The papyrus sedge found several uses in ancient Egypt, but most significant for the purpose of the present volume was its use as a writing material. In order to produce a sheet of papyrus, one cut thin strips from the peeled stem, and arranged one layer of these strips vertically, and added another layer horizontally on top of it. Tapping with a flat object then forced the juices of the papyrus to bind the strips and layers together. On one side of the sheet, the fibers of the papyrus run horizontally (often referred to as "recto"), on the other side vertically ("verso").

Twenty papyrus sheets were customarily pasted together to form a roll of about three meters long. The overlap, where two sheets met, is called *kollesis*, and the eventual user of the papyrus would hold the roll in such a manner as to allow him to write "downhill," so that his pen would not bump against the sheet join. The writer would write on the side where the fibers were running horizontally (the "recto"), although sometimes he would turn the papyrus so that the fibers were running perpendicular to the direction of writing (this writing is often called *transversa charta*). The papyrus roll was the basic form, from which all uses were adapted. In the case of smaller documents one would take a small portion of the roll (after, or sometimes before writing on it), or in the case of longer documents (literary works but also tax rolls), one would paste several rolls together. One could also fold several sheets of papyrus together to form a *codex*, similar to, but outside Egypt much less durable than a parchment codex (on which, see ch. 6).

Other writing materials used in the ancient world were *ostraka* (potsherds), wooden tablets, waxed tablets, and lead, all of which bear documents in the Greek language (but also in other languages). "Ostrakon" (ὄστρακον) is the term used for a potsherd with writing. The writing was largely done on the concave side of the sherd. Ostraka were primarily used for more ephemeral texts such as tax receipts, letters, and school exercises. Wooden tablets were used for a variety of documents, from books (like the famous Isocrates from Kellis; see Worp and Rijksbaron 1997) to accounts (an account book from the same site; see Bagnall 1997) and from school exercises to official contracts. Waxed tablets, wooden tablets that were hollowed out on one or both sides and then filled with a thin layer of wax, were used for school exercises, but also for especially Roman legal documents. Lead was used for magical curses.

Greeks wrote on papyrus and ostraka with a *kalamos*, or reed pen, sharpened at the end and cut to form a nib. Ink, *melan*, was made of lampblack, gum, and water. Occasionally we find Greek writing with an Egyptian brush-pen, which allowed varying the thickness of the lines. Since writing with a brush is quite a difficult technique, we can be sure that whenever we find Greek written with a brush, we are dealing with a person coming from an Egyptian background (Clarysse 1993; see also ch. 17 below).

The Greek handwriting on papyri shows distinct traits that allow the texts to be dated to a particular century, and in some periods for which the number of surviving texts is large enough, even to a quarter-century. Whenever a Greek text is not datable internally (by a regnal year or mention of a person known from precisely dated texts), it can only be dated on the basis of the handwriting. Greek handwriting varies according to the use of the text. "School hands" refers to unpracticed and irregular writings of beginning writers in texts that were commonly used in education (Cribiore 1996), whereas such struggling handwritings in functionary texts are known as those of a "slow writer," βραδέως γράφων (Youtie 1973b; Kraus 1999). Fluent and practiced scripts range from beautiful book hands, used to pen the literary works of antiquity, to so-called "personal hands," a term that covers everything from the fairly regular writing found in letters written by somewhat skilled scribes and very regular and sometimes beautiful writings of skilled bureaucrats, to the swiftly scrawled lines of a tax collector, in whose writing it is almost impossible to recognize individual letters.

Most of the papyri were written in the *Koine* dialect that came to be used in the ancient world after Alexander the Great (see ch. 16). The system of Greek education seems to have been reasonably standardized (Cribiore 2001), and, in this light, the consistency of the Greek that a wide range of people was able to produce is not really surprising. It is nonetheless important to realize that papyri reflect the knowledge of Greek of the person who wrote or dictated the text, his or her peculiar pronunciations, word choice, and grammatical constructions, and conform to the use of the text that the writer was planning. Within the greater scheme of *Koine* Greek, therefore, each papyrus text can show local, sometimes even personal, peculiarities, but nonetheless can be easily identified as *Koine* Greek. Many of the phonological (e.g., *iotacism*) and grammatical tendencies that can be seen for Modern Greek can already be discovered in the Greek papyri from Egypt (see ch. 16 for *Koine* Greek, ch. 17 for Egyptian interference in papyrus texts, and ch. 36 for the transition to Modern Greek).

The papyrus texts that most people use in a neat publication with introduction, text, translation, and textual notes, are the end of a long process of transliterating and transcribing traces of ink on papyrus texts (Youtie 1973a; 1974). Greek on papyrus was written continuously, without word divisions, breathings, or accents, which were added only very occasionally in later periods. Also, many texts are more or less severely damaged after 2,000 years in desert sand, mummy casings, or crocodile mummies. Ink may have faded, papyrus has broken off, making the task of deciphering the text even more difficult. The mental process that leads from traces on a papyrus to a readable Greek text involves both reading and interpretation and at the same time leaves room for mistakes. Traces can be misread for letters that in fact they are not, and holes in the papyrus can be filled with a Greek sentence that, in fact, exists only in the papyrologist's mind (sometimes supported, but never proven, by a similar phrase in another text). And although papyrologists will report their doubts and supplements by using various brackets and other signs like dots under letters (see table 5.1), it is easy to read over these and assume too quickly that readings are certain as they stand.

Table 5.1   Signs and conventions in papyrological text editions (see also table 4.1)

Sign	*Meaning*
[ ]	a lacuna in the original, where either the papyrus or the ink is completely lost
( )	the solution of an abbreviation or symbol
{ }	a cancellation by the modern editor of the text
< >	an omission by the ancient scribe
[[ ]]	a deletion by the ancient scribe
\ /	an interlinear addition by the ancient scribe
dots under letters (αβγ)	uncertain letters
. . . .	the approximate number of illegible or lost letters

Papyrology is the field of scholarship where nobody will raise an eyebrow if camels change into ten apples (separating the letter sequence δεκαμηλα into δέκα μῆλα from δὲ κάμηλα), or mice to be caught "pregnant" become mice to be caught in the well-attested village of Toka (separating ἔντοκα into ἐν Τόκα), without changing the actual reading of the traces on the papyrus (see Pestman 1991 for these and other telling examples). Reinterpreting traces on papyri can sometimes lead to even more surprising corrections of a reading on a papyrus. Thus, in a private letter written during the Jewish Revolt of 115–17 CE the author, according to the reading of the first editor, expressed concern that Jews might "roast" (ὀπτήσωσι) the addressee of the letter. This has fed into a large body of scholarship about "atrocities" during this revolt; re-reading of the traces of the papyrus, however, has led to the suggestion, not accepted by all, to read the traces as "conquer" (ἡττήσωσι; cf. Pestman 1991), which is decidedly less atrocious. The surprising thing is, perhaps, that notwithstanding the difficulty of reading papyri there are so few mistakes made by editors, and eventually these mistakes are likely to be caught by further generations of scholars, and collected in the ongoing project of the *Berichtigungsliste der griechischen Papyrusurkunden aus Ägypten* (*BL*). Any scholar using documentary papyrus texts as evidence should consult this project to see whether any correction has been made to the text (s)he is working on.

For many of the writers of Greek texts from Egypt, Greek was not their first language (see also ch. 17). Many Egyptians, but not all, learned Greek, and Greek even functioned as the only written language of Egypt for a brief moment (before Coptic took on this role next to Greek, see Bagnall 1993: 237–8). Soldiers from the Roman army also learned Greek, which was, in the Eastern part of the Roman Empire at least, as important a language as Latin (Adams 2003: 599–608; see also ch. 19). The Greek found in the papyri may show more or less obvious signs of the bilingualism of their authors.

Whence Papyrus?

Papyrus is an organic material, and does therefore not survive archeologically in all climates and circumstances. Most papyri were found in Egypt, especially in the higher- lying portions of the country, at the desert edge, where the groundwater could not reach it. This also explains why almost no papyri survive from the humid Nile delta, including the ancient capital Alexandria. Similar dry and undisturbed conditions were also met in, for example, caves, allowing for the survival of documents from the Judean Desert. In addition, there are also a number of papyrus finds from sites (both inside and outside Egypt) that burned down, where the papyrus has carbonized (inside Egypt: Bubastis and Thmouis; outside Egypt: Herculaneum, Petra, Derveni).

The major source for papyri from Egypt is the region southwest of modern Cairo, known as the Fayum and in antiquity as the Arsinoite nome. Since the late nineteenth century, tens of thousands of texts have been found during (legal and illegal) archeological excavations of the remains of ancient villages, and in cemeteries where the papyrus had been reused in the casings of human and sometimes even crocodile mummies. Many of these papyri found their way to Europe and the United States and now form the backbone of many important collections.

The papyri found in domestic contexts in Fayum villages largely date to the Roman period, before the villages were eventually abandoned or relocated as a result of the desert moving in. Among the more famous of these Fayum towns in terms of papyri found are Bacchias, Karanis, Tebtunis, and Soknopaiou Nesos. Texts from Fayum villages date largely from the first to the (early) fifth century CE, although recent excavations in Tebtunis have also yielded numerous documents from the Ptolemaic period. The audiences of papyrus texts in these contexts are largely village elites, the officials who ran the village for the state, and the property owners. These village elites consisted of a mixture of (sometimes bilingual) Egyptian priests and descendants of the Greek military settlers (*katoikoi*) of the Ptolemaic period. In some villages, like Karanis, there was also a steady influx of Roman veterans who settled there after active service. For many of these village inhabitants Greek was a second language, or rather the language of writing after the various scripts of Egyptian went out of use. What Fayum villages offer for uses of Greek ranges from the finest examples of technical bureaucratic correspondence to the most intimate private letters. The Greek found in especially this latter type of documents may show many features of what we now call "substandard" Greek.

Another famous find spot for papyrus is Oxyrhynchus (el-Behnesa, about 100 miles south of modern Cairo). Here, in the course of a little more than a decade, excavations carried out for the Egypt Exploration Fund in the early twentieth century unearthed more than 500,000 fragments of papyrus in what turned out to be the rubbish heaps of the town. Most texts date from the Roman and early Byzantine period (first through fifth centuries CE) and provide the waste paper of the Greek elite, including many works of Greek literature (Parsons 2007). Oxyrhynchus was a much more "Greek" town than the villages of the Fayum, even in the Roman period, and many of the papyri found there show a Greek that can be recognized even by the non-specialist. Needless to say, however, Oxyrhynchus too knew its abusers of Greek spelling and grammar, and their texts ended up in the same rubbish heaps.

Special mention should be made of papyri coming from the casings of Egyptian mummies. In the third and second centuries BCE discarded papyrus was used in the production of these cases, the technical term for which is *cartonnage*. In the course of the twentieth century, hundreds of these mummy casings have been opened, and the papyri contained in them have been restored. Although in many cases the provenance of the mummy casings themselves is known or can be assumed, the provenance of the documents themselves is difficult to pin down precisely, although most of them come from the Fayum and the region directly to the southeast of it (the Heracleopolite nome). Such mummy casings also preserve the only texts known from Alexandria, from where no papyrus has otherwise survived. Many of these cartonnage papyri are administrative documents, although one mummy casing also yielded the Posidippus papyrus (Bastianini and Gallazzi 2001).

Papyrus Greek

The Greek found on papyri from Egypt (and elsewhere) shows a wide range of different styles. At the one end of the spectrum (just next to people who could not write Greek at all) there is the Greek written by people who were barely literate in that language, but who nonetheless were able to function in society. A famous example in this category is Petaüs, an officially appointed village scribe from Roman Egypt (second cent. CE), who only knew how to write his official signature, because somebody showed him how and he meticulously copied it, letter by letter.[1] At the other end of the spectrum are the highly literate elites of many towns and villages, whose good education shows in the Greek documents they themselves produce. Among them are first-generation Greeks who arrived in Egypt from elsewhere in the Mediterranean world in the late fourth and early third century BCE, but also the Greek-speaking elites of sixth-century CE Egypt, when Egypt was firmly rooted in the Byzantine Empire. An example of the first kind of Greek writer is Zenon, who arrived in Egypt from Kaunos in Asia Minor in the first half of the third century BCE, and part of whose archive (more than 2,000 texts) has survived (e.g. Clarysse and Vandorpe 1995). An example of the latter kind of Egyptian Greek is Dioskoros, a Greek public official in sixth-century Egypt, among whose papers there were numerous copies of Greek literature (Fournet 1999). A large number of documents reveal a knowledge of Greek somewhere between these extremes. All these documents provide a wealth of material for linguistic analysis. It is not often that a language can be followed in this detail in writing for a period of over one millennium.

The number of Greek documents from antiquity will continue to grow as more papyrus texts (and texts on other writing materials) from known collections are edited and published, and at the same time papyrus texts continue to be found during excavations in Egypt (and will be studied and published in due course). Historians can be found in relative abundance to tap into this richness of sources, which is unique for the ancient world, but the attention of linguistic specialists to this wealth of material is relatively minimal (very welcome therefore is Evans and Obbink 2009). Just as the dictionaries of papyrus Greek need to be updated regularly because of re-evaluation of old sources and new discoveries in papyrology, so also the grammars and linguistic studies of papyrus Greek need to be revisited regularly.

FURTHER READING

For an introduction to the field of papyrology, see Turner 1980 (largely for literary papyri), and for documentary papyrology the introduction to Pestman 1994 (with a representative selection of texts). A current list of all abbreviations used for editions of papyrus texts can be found online at http://scriptorium.lib.duke.edu/papyrus/texts/clist.html. The most up-to-date gazetteer of Fayum villages can be found online: http://fayum.arts.kuleuven.ac.be/, and for a general introduction to Oxyrhynchus and its papyri there now is a really splendid book by Peter

Parsons (2007). General introductions to daily life in Greek and Roman Egypt are still Bowman 1996 and Lewis 1999 and 2001. The standard papyrological grammars are Mayser (1906–) for the Ptolemaic period and Gignac (1976–81) for the Roman and Byzantine periods. In recent years there have been many initiatives to make available papyri online, with the Advanced Papyrological Information System still the leader and best: http://www.columbia.edu/cu/lweb/projects/digital/apis/. A good site to start an online adventure into the world of papyrology is the site of the Michigan papyrus collection: www.lib.umich.edu/pap.

NOTE

1   By chance of fate, the sheet of papyrus where we can see him practice this official signature, and leaving out one letter without realizing his mistake, has survived: *P. Petaus* 121; image at http://www.uni-koeln.de/phil-fak/ifa/NRWakademie/papyrologie/PPetaus/bilder/PK328r.jpg.

CHAPTER SIX

The Manuscript Tradition

Niels Gaul

When in 787 CE the second council of Nicaea "placed under anathema those raging against God's church, and issuing a decree, elevated the sacred icons to the glory they had from the beginning" (Duffy and Parker 1979: 127) – after the impious and beastly iconoclastic emperors had defiled them for five decades, as the iconophiles would have it – no manuscript of Ancient Greek or otherwise non-Christian content had been produced for almost two centuries. At least none has yet been dated to this period with certainty, which means there cannot have been many to begin with. Nor were any ancient texts copied in the two decades following this temporary triumph of orthodoxy. At this crucial junction, Byzantine culture might perceivably have gone down an altogether different path, leaving the modern world with few witnesses to the Ancient Greek language indeed. From the Renaissance via Romanticism to nineteenth-century nationalism and beyond, social and political discourses in Italy, England, Germany, and elsewhere would have been construed differently. For better or worse, history might have taken alternative turns ever so often.

Of course the task of this chapter is not to propose counterfactual history; rather, to explain why Byzantine culture emerged from the iconoclastic debates (730–787, 815–843) with an interest in and, in spite of ever-changing circumstances, an unwavering devotion to reading, copying, and annotating Ancient Greek texts for the remaining six centuries of its existence. With huge efforts – economic factors played a major role in this, although usually of little interest to the text-based scholar – the literary and scientific heritage of Classical, Hellenistic, imperial, and late antique (henceforth, ancient) times was preserved within the paradigm of cultural traditionality. It helped build a manuscript tradition of such substance that we can nowadays still study a fair part of the Hellenistic and especially late antique canon of (Classical) Greek texts, that was transmitted to the Byzantine Middle Ages. The wear and tear of taste and time, fires and pillaging – in 1204, less so in 1453, by which date much had reached Italy – reduced it further. Those ancient texts that had reached Byzantium were by and large considered authoritative and preserved in a stable tradition, even if written in dialects other than Attic, which held its sociolectal sway over Byzantine intellectual life. They were, however, prone to the negligence of scribes (whoever copies a text by hand will inevitably commit blunders) as well as the occasional prudery, piety, or prudence of medieval scholars.

Cultural and Material Choices

Rather than assume that the preservation of Ancient Greek writings served a quasi-teleological purpose – a modern world without "the classics" may seem difficult to imagine – it will be helpful to examine the Greek manuscript tradition as a series of conscious and context-related *cultural* and *material choices*.

Its story has been told from different perspectives. Students of the Latin, Greek, and Islamic Middle Ages have tried to explain the roughly parallel Byzantine, Carolingian, and 'Abbāsid revivals of learning as a story of ideological competition in the context of empire-building. Once the struggle for immediate survival following the Muslim expansion had passed, the Byzantines glanced east and west and found the two rival polities well ahead in establishing their cultural ideologies. In order to exploit the glory of the past and to maintain imperial splendor, the Byzantine elite consciously revived ancient learning (henceforth, *paideia*) (Gutas 1998: 175–86). Exclusively in terms of Byzantine history, the ninth-century revival has been interpreted as an answer to the failure of iconoclasm. Once the attempt to restore the victorious empire of Constantine (r. 306–37) – hence the iconoclastic emphasis on the symbol of the cross – had failed, reviving the artificial Attic/ Atticizing sociolect canonized by the Second Sophistic (see ch. 31) along with the literary genres of antiquity, was the best way of pretending nothing in between had ever happened (Speck 1984). Even if this explained the revival of *paideia*, merely evoking categories such as "tradition" (not to be mistaken for traditionality) or "continuity" – the oft-quoted escapist element allegedly prevailing in Byzantine society, locking it in collective longing for a better past – is insufficient to account for its lasting success. In this regard, Byzantium has profited from the recent methodological reversals privileging hitherto marginalized cultures; it can no longer be perceived as a "colony" of the classical world. Highlighting the idea of *choices*, this chapter explores the possibilities of reasons more internal and contemporary to Byzantine society.

Paradoxically, the most convenient starting point – the surviving manuscript evidence – is not necessarily the best; the human mind too readily jumps at what is preserved, and forgets or ignores what was lost. If there existed a comprehensive list of all writings in Greek which perished over the centuries, ancient as well as medieval, it would offer a useful *caveat* against any positivistic approach. It is equally important to consider briefly the different roles that Church and monastic structures played in the production of manuscripts East and West; approaching Byzantium from the perspective of the "Latin" Middle Ages carries danger of distortion. Unlike in the West, *paideia* did not ever move exclusively under the helm of ecclesial and monastic circles. Certainly in Constantinople, lay schoolmasters provided teaching of grammar and, perhaps, rhetoric, even in the bleakest hour. When *paideia* did move into the fold of the patriarchate, in the twelfth century, it was for economic and social reasons, not because the monopoly of *paideia* had come to rest with the Church – a change of patronage rather than of elites. Future clerics and courtiers were trained side by side in the lay schools of the capital studying the same ancient texts; many years of schooling were required to master the artificial sociolect which was, with many concealed ruptures, still perceived as "Attic" and became the only acceptable means of inserting statements into Byzantine public discourse (see ch. 35).

Literate monks copied sacred books and saints' lives. Many were accomplished calligraphers. Catering for the spiritual and liturgical needs of their communities, before long they did not only write different genres but also preferred archaizing hands, which, as *lieux de mémoire*, promised enhanced spiritual benefit (Prato and De Gregorio 2003). However, with regard to the ancient manuscript tradition such scriptoria can be disregarded. Occasionally when monastic structures exerted an extraordinary influence on the course of writing and its materiality, e.g., the spread of minuscule script promoted by the Stoudite monks around their figure-heads, St Theodore (759–826) and his uncle Plato of Sakkoudion (*c.*735–814), it is important to remind oneself that these latter were well-established members of the empire's aristocracy. They had pursued worldly lives before exploiting monastic networks for the pursuit of their anti-imperial agendas, and did not always leave their worldly expertise and connections behind.

Learned monks rarely came from a purely monastic formation. The monk and scholar Ephraim, for example, who copied a number of ancient texts in the mid-tenth century, was a colleague and correspondent of the "anonymous professor" (see below) in charge of one of the lay schools of Constantinople. The polymath, shrewd courtier, and daring philosopher Constantine/Michael Psellos (1018–?1078) donned the monastic robe only when intrigues converged against him. It would be equally misleading to think of the teaching circles established in the Christ Akataleptos and Chora monasteries in the late Byzantine period as "monastic." Manuel/Maximos Planoudes (*c.*1250/5–1305) came dangerously close to the usurper Alexios Philanthropenos and "retired" from a career at court. Nikephoros Gregoras (1291/4–1358/61) inherited his mentor Theodore Metochites' library in the Chora monastery and lived and taught there, without being a monk.

The same *caveat* applies to learned ecclesial figures. While many figures important in the manuscript tradition did pursue ecclesial careers – e.g., Photius (*c.* 810–*c.* 893), Arethas (*c.* 850–?943), and, later, Eustathius (*c.* 1115–95/9) – it would be misleading to assume that "the Church" as an institution was responsible for their formation. Photius, whose noble family tree Mango reconstructed (1977a), was head of the imperial chancery before being promoted to the patriarchate. Arethas, spokesman of the "orthodox," iconodule faction at the court of Leo VI (r. 886–912), must have been from an affluent family in order to afford his choice manuscript collection. Eustathius happened to live in a century when *paideia* as a whole had become associated with the patriarchate – with repercussions for philosophy more than for rhetoric.

Changing Circumstances

Prelude: late antiquity and the birth of the codex

Around the turn from the third to the fourth century, the (parchment) codex superseded the (papyrus) scroll as the predominant book format (Roberts and Skeat 1983). The phenomenon is quite clearly linked to the contemporary rise of Christianity. McCormick (1985) has demonstrated that the codex was the format of the book originally used by traveling professions: physicians, grammarians – and apostles. It must have proved advantageous for performing liturgy. Unlike a scroll, a codex could be opened at any earmarked page and could easily hold the complete text of the four Gospels (Skeat 1994). Economic factors may have been decisive only to the degree that parchment could be used on both sides and produced everywhere while papyrus had to come from the shores of the Nile; it was not much cheaper. This gradual shift from roll to codex did not affect *majuscule* letters as the only acceptable bookscript (Cavallo 1967). It is hardly a coincidence that the earliest surviving complete parchment codices contain the Holy Scriptures: the famous codices Vaticanus and Sinaiticus, commonly dated to the first half of the fourth century (Skeat 1999). Fewer late antique codices containing ancient texts survive; among the most famous examples are the "Vienna Dioscurides" (Vind. med. gr. 1), manufactured in Constantinople in the early sixth century, and the fragments of Cassius Dio surviving in the Vatican Library (Vat. gr. 1288). Fragments of a splendid, illuminated majuscule codex of the *Iliad* are preserved in the Ambrosian Library in Milan (MS F. 205 P. inf.). The practice of illustrating non-Christian texts seems to have died with late antiquity. In the Constantinople of Justinian (r. 527–65), and presumably in other centers of learning across the Mediterranean, book markets existed.

This flourishing world of Greco-Roman late antiquity came to an end in the course of the sixth and seventh centuries, witnessing the culmination of social and political changes that had begun to make themselves felt centuries earlier. Continuous warfare between the two aspiring world empires, the Roman and Sassanid, followed by the Muslim Arab expansion throughout the second half of the seventh century, quickly reduced Justinian's restored empire to two-thirds of its former territory. By 700, the previously multi-centered Greco-Roman Christian *oikoumenē* with its bustling multitude of local, urban, literate elites was left with only one significant cultural center, Constantinople itself. In an attempt to cope with and understand this apparent infliction of God's wrath, the remains of the Roman Empire lapsed into 150 years of theological controversies attempting to adjust "political orthodoxy" to feeble realities. Homiletics, hymnography, hagiography, and patristic florilegia preoccupied the elite's mind (Cameron 1992). Other centers of Ancient Greek learning survived under Muslim rule and outside the reach of the Roman/ Byzantine emperor; until *c.* 700, Greek remained the administrative language of the Umayyad caliphate. They were to play a vital role in the discursive construction of orthodoxy on the one hand (Mango 1991) and of 'Abbāsid, anti-Byzantine "Hellenism" on the other (Gutas 1998).

Paideia *and the imperial "beast" (eighth and ninth centuries)*

For George the Monk the "Triumph of Orthodoxy" in 843, after the end of the second iconoclast period, literally meant that history had fulfilled its purpose. Writing his chronicle around 846, he reported that Emperor Leo III (r. 717–40), when proclaiming the iconoclastic doctrine, had the "imperial university" – which had long ceased to function – in Constantinople burnt, together with the 12 professors and, notably, the library (2.742.1–22, De Boor 1978). Inventions such as these point to the iconophile need to suppress any iconoclastic claim to *paideia*, by inference confirming that such a claim could be made. However, they left their mark on scholarship.

While no manuscript of Ancient Greek content can be dated to the seventh or eighth centuries, training in classicizing grammar and, perhaps, rhetoric was continuously available at least in Constantinople. Early in the ninth century, it seems to have spread again to the provinces (Moffatt 1977). Photius describes a florilegium that seems to have included pagan excerpts not only of Greek, but also of "Persian, Thracian, Egyptian, Babylonian, Chaldaean, and Roman" origin, dating to the later seventh or eighth century (Phot. *Bibl.* 170; Wilson 1994: 154); a certain Theognostos dedicated his rhetorical writings to Leo V (r. 813–20). It is equally evident, however, especially from seventh- and eighth-century writings, that a training in grammar and rhetoric did not need to be put to the service of ancient learning. The much celebrated revival of Byzantine classicizing rhetoric in the two decades following 787 solely suited Patriarch Tarasios' concerted effort to propagate the new theology of icons. The revival of ancient learning does not seem to have been on the agenda of this iconophile elite; nor did it necessarily revert to ancient models (Auzépy 1998a). John Choiroboskos' ninth-century grammatical exercises on the Psalms, privileging them over the Homeric poems while adducing evidence from the latter, are a case in point; they were still being used in the tenth century. The poems of Gregory of Nazianzus were read in school (Simelidis 2009: 75–9). If there had been any such intention and if this route had been pursued further, the traditional curriculum might have become more Christianized over time; Basil of Caesarea's treatise on pagan *paideia*, transmitted through the Middle Ages along with his homilies, did not become an educational treatise before the Renaissance (McLynn 2009).

The most significant innovation pursued by iconophile elite circles was the promotion of *minuscule* letters to the rank of bookscript, hitherto reserved for majuscule (bilinear) letters (Mango 1977b). Greek minuscule (quadrilinear) script had evolved over centuries in the contexts of imperial and provincial chanceries across the eastern Mediterranean – early examples survive on papyri from Egypt under Arab rule (De Gregorio 2000) – as a faster and less space-consuming variant. Codices could contain ever more text and be produced at a quicker pace. Early minuscule writing was known as *syrmaiographein*, literally, "the stringing together of letters" (Cortassa 2003; Luzzatto 2002–3). Stoudite circles may be credited for developing a calligraphic variant of this essentially informal script. It was a script particularly apt for books designed for frequent consultation, e.g., medical manuals kept in monastic hospitals (Fonkič 2000). Truly important texts on the other hand, the Holy Scriptures and any book designed for display in church, continued to be copied in much more prestigious majuscules, often furnished with splendid illuminations, for another three or four centuries (Cavallo 1977).

Why did the classicizing curriculum reassert itself then? It does seem likely that imperial ideology, as inextricably as precariously linked to iconoclasm (Auzépy 1998b), when meeting fierce resistance after 787, needed new, or rather old, ammunition in order to defend its ecumenical position – that powerful imperial "beast" that had been created from the days of Eusebius of Caesarea onwards – and sought it in the "pagan" sciences: astronomy, philosophy, mathematics. Only recently has this iconoclastic contribution been brought back into the picture (Alpers 1988; Magdalino 2006: 55–89).

Theophanes Confessor (see also ch. 35) mentions a certain Pankratios (d. 792), astronomer to the unfortunate Constantine VI (r. 780–96) in the late eighth century. Pankratios' son (?) John (d. ?863/7) became the mastermind of the second iconoclasm. His epithet, *grammatikos*, indicates that he taught grammar, and presumably other disciplines as well. Eventually Emperor Theophilos (r. 829–42) appointed him patriarch (John VII, ?837–42). The famous majuscule manuscripts of the tables accompanying Ptolemy's *Almagest* (Vat. gr. 1291 and Leid. BPG 78), date to his early period of activity around 815, when he was famously charged with collecting books from all Constantinople (Mango 1971: 35). Intriguingly, one of the very few surviving fragments of John's writing champions rhetoric, clearly referencing the rhetorical handbooks of later antiquity:

> It is impossible for any man to be portrayed by any means, unless one has been led to this by words, through which everything that exists is definitely captured. … For if the family or the father from which an individual derives are not depicted – bringing forth his deeds and that he is blessed in his companions and the rest of his manners, which are clearly discernible in the words of which one might judge his praiseworthiness and blameworthiness – then the artwork is a waste of time. Hence it is impossible truthfully to discern the man by such delineations. (Guillard 1966: 173; tr. Barber 2002: 125)

The refusal to accept icons as statements of orthodox discourse must have triggered increasing interest in the ecphrastic, figurative power of language, prompting a two-fold "logocentric" turn: the privileging of the divine Logos inherent in iconoclastic theology resulting in a renewed interest in the ancient *logoi*, rhetoric as well as science and philosophy. The legends surrounding John's nephew and disciple (?), Leo, called *mathēmatikos* (*c.* 790–post 869), whose ingenuity, allegedly, caught the attention of the 'Abbasīd caliph al-Ma'mūn, fit this picture and at the same time indicate a certain cultural rivalry between the two empires. One must not forget that Leo, a formerly avowed iconoclast, was running the "palace school" before *and* after the triumph of orthodoxy in 843, first appointed by Theophilos, later the *kaisar* Bardas (*fl.* 837–66), while Photius was merely maintaining a private circle (Speck 1974: 14–21). The *ex-libris* of a few of Leo's manuscripts have survived and connect him to texts of Plato, Ptolemy, Porphyry, Achilles Tatius, and others (Westerink 1986). His colleague Kometas, teacher of grammar, paid attention to the Homeric epics (*Anth. Pal.* 15.36–38) preceding the earliest surviving minuscule manuscript – the famous Marc. gr. 454 ("Venetus A") – by almost a century. Finally, Leo Choirospaktes, a relative and courtier of emperor Leo VI, who had studied with Leo the *mathēmatikos*, promoted a Neoplatonic, crypto-iconoclastic theology and became the arch-enemy of Arethas, archbishop of Caesarea (Magdalino 2006: 71–79; Vassis 2002: 25–39).

It is this "chain" of iconoclastic scholars who were close to the emperors of the day; they, rather than their iconophile adversaries, had the interest in, and proximity to power would have given them the means of, reviving *paideia*. The "Triumph of Orthodoxy" in March 843, condemning iconoclasm as a "heresy" and anathematizing generations of iconoclast emperors, served a major blow to imperial prestige (Auzépy 1998b). Subsequent emperors must have been toying with the idea of turning back the clock; Photius for one feared the "heresy" might show its head again (Mango 1977a). These ideological and theological struggles at the highest echelon of society may well be the context in which to place the earliest medieval generations of manuscripts carrying Ancient Greek texts, e.g., the so-called "philosophical collection," a group of some 16 manuscripts roughly dating to the middle of the ninth century. The exemplars may well have derived from a late antique school collection; the choice of texts – Plato (Paris. gr. 1807), various Neoplatonic commentaries (Proclus, Damascius, Olympiodorus), Aristotle, Ptolemy (Vat. gr. 1594), next to Pseudo-Dionysius and Theodoret of Cyrrhus (Perria 1991; Palau 2001; Ronconi 2008) – seems to tie well into the iconoclasts' attempts to re-define the *oikoumenē* and the emperor's role in Neoplatonic terms. The careful execution of the manuscripts indicates a patron of high standing; as can be inferred from the codices copied for Arethas a few decades later, a calligraphic manuscript carrying ancient texts came at almost a third of the annual salary of a fairly high-ranking court official, the *prōtospatharios*, who made 72 gold coins a year.

The emphasis here placed on the – lost – iconoclastic contribution allows a slightly different perspective on Photius' *Myriobiblos* (Latinized, *Bibliotheca*) and, about a half-century later, Arethas' famous library. This is not to say that the iconophiles, alarmed by the events of 815, when the empire lapsed into the second iconoclasm under the rule of Leo V, would not have risen quickly to the challenge; but they may have been reacting as much as acting. The *Myriobiblos* makes good sense in the context of the iconoclastic struggle nearing its end, or shortly thereafter; although Photius continued to work on it for decades to come (Markopoulos 2004). Just as iconophile monks had been collecting canons and patristic florilegia in order to defend their cause – e.g., Oxford, Barocci 26 – the *Myriobiblos* provided a safe grounding in *paideia* (omitting all common school texts) as well as an arsenal against heresies. It is generally considered the earliest work of literary criticism surviving from the Byzantine Middle Ages; its religious emphasis (239 Christian and Jewish as opposed to 147 ancient and pagan codices; a word-count reverses this order to 57% and 43% respectively), the attention paid to heretical texts and the neglect of philosophical texts have been noted. Important as Photius' collection of 280 ancient and early Byzantine texts as a source of otherwise lost material is, especially as an indirect witness to the texts in question – 211 did not survive in as complete a version as Photius was able to study, and 110 perished entirely, leaving a mere 89 that still exist – its contemporary purpose may well have been a rather different one (Treadgold 1980; Wilson 1994).

Arethas' library contained some of the most splendid volumes surviving from the late ninth and early tenth centuries. Seven volumes have been identified including the famous manuscript of Plato nowadays in Oxford (E. D. Clarke 39), which contains 24 dialogues (minus the *Republic, Laws,* and *Timaeus*) and cost 21 gold pieces, and the earliest copy of Aelius Aristides' œuvre (Paris. gr. 2951 and Laur. 60.3). Arethas' patristic collection (Paris. gr. 451) cost 26 gold pieces; the parchment required for Aristotle's *Organon* (Urb. gr. 35) six; the copying of Euclid (D'Orville 301) 14.

When young Constantine VII Porphyrogennetos (r. 913/945–59) inherited the throne at age seven, too young to wield power, the link with iconoclastic ideology was effectively broken. Only when he finally assumed sole rule in the mid-940s, did he launch a project of unprecedented scale and complexity to propagate his dynasty's prestige and power (Németh forthcoming). He ordered that 26 Classical and late antique historiographers, ranging from Herodotus, Thucydides, and Xenophon at the far end to Theophylaktos Simokates, John of Antioch, and George the Monk at the near, be excerpted into 53 rubrics, glorifying Roman/Byzantine rulers past and present. Considering that each of these rubrics needed at least one draft before the final de luxe copy could be produced and that several rubrics gathered sufficient material to fill two or more volumes, a minimum parchment supply of 10,000 sheepskins of the finest quality can be calculated. Only two of the original manuscripts survive, MS Tours C 980 and Vat. gr. 73 (palimpsest), a safe indicator that, if ever finished, no second set of the series was produced. The fragmentary œuvres of nine of the 26 historiographers survive almost entirely in the few excerpts that have come down to us (including Dexippus, Eunapios of Sardis, and Peter the Patrician), another six to a substantial degree (Polybius, Diodorus Siculus, Diodorus of Halicarnassus, Appian, Cassius Dio, and Malalas). It remains unclear how many scholars, scribes, calligraphers, and bookbinders were involved in this ideological enterprise of imperial redefinition, or where it was carried out: perhaps in Constantine's newly constructed library overlooking the slopes toward the Marmara Sea. One may speculate that Constantine called on the pupils studying in the palace school which he had refounded, on whom he lavished much attention. The teachers were Constantine the *prōtospatharios* (philosophy), Nikephoros the *patrikios* (geometry), Gregory *asēkrētis* (astronomy), and Alexander one-time metropolitan of Nicaea (rhetoric).

Constantine VII's antiquarianism pertained to other aspects as well, most famously the proper pedigree of imperial ceremonial and imperial administration. In the context of mid-tenth-century court historiography – represented by Joseph Genesios, the so-called *Scriptores post Theophanem,* including Constantine himself narrating the life of his grandfather, Basil I (r. 867–86), and Symeon the *logothetēs* – Plutarch's *Lives* were keenly studied (Jenkins 1954). Revival of iconoclasm was no longer an option. With Constantine Porphyrogennetos' historiographical excerpts, orthodoxy had truly triumphed.

The institutionalization and performance of paideia *(tenth to twelfth century)*

While Constantine's classicizing encyclopedism flourished (a link between the emperor's excerpts and the *Suda* can be safely assumed) a new stratum of society emerged: an urban elite personified in the "middle-class entrepreneur," to use an anachronistic term, striving to improve their, and their sons', social situation. This phenomenon is closely related to the economic revival that had gained in momentum over the course of the tenth century and accelerated further in the eleventh and twelfth (Laiou and Morrisson 2007: 43–165). Acquiring *paideia*, the habitus of the "old elites," became a primary means of social ascent. The correspondence of an "anonymous schoolmaster" (*maïstōr*) – the name was lost in the process of rebinding the volume which is preserved in London, British Library, MS Add. 36,749 – allows insights into a tenth-century Constantinopolitan lay school catering for, and run by a member of, this new class (Markopoulos, ed. 2000). Whereas many of the manuscripts discussed in the previous section had been commissioned by members of the courtly elite and executed by calligraphers, the anonymous schoolmaster and his peers were compelled to copy their own manuscripts.

These tenth-century informal scholarly minuscule hands were rich in space-saving abbreviations; parchment was a costly commodity. Indicatively, the schoolmaster went to quite some effort to distinguish himself from calligraphers such as would have copied the volumes of, e.g., Arethas' collection (*ep.* 53). A manuscript nowadays in Oxford, Barocci 50, is a good example of such a manuscript written by an anonymous scholar-scribe for his own use. The parchment this anonymous could afford was of a much lesser quality than the material of the philosophical collection or Arethas' library; he did not mind accommodating bone-holes in his *mise-en-page*. Barocci 50 is the oldest surviving witness of Musaeus' *Hero and Leander* plus a number of grammatical treatises; its medium, the scholarly miscellany, reflected an innovative trend of Byzantine scholarship (Ronconi 2007: 91–131). Another letter of the anonymous schoolmaster, addressed to the patriarch (*ep.* 88), gives an insight into the practices of collation and, perhaps, textual criticism in the tenth century (Cortassa 2001); about this time the long process of *scholia vetera* entering the margins of ancient texts, excerpted and abbreviated from the much fuller commentaries of late antiquity, must have found its completion. From other letters it can be inferred that the anonymous schoolmaster seems to have been on the patriarch's payroll but could not rely on receiving his annual allowance; he collected fees from his students. Rival schools in Constantinople are mentioned: an atmosphere of competition was born that came to be the characterizing spirit of Byzantine *paideia* in subsequent centuries. Altogether, a bustling market in *paideia* becomes visible, somewhat removed from, but by no means independent of, the imperial palace; the difference to the court-centered, elite scholars negotiating imperial power over the course of the ninth century is immediately evident.

It was now these "new" scholars who championed the study of ancient texts, while the tenth-century aristocratic elite increasingly adopted military values. The earliest copies of the Homeric poems (the famous "Venetus A" with its important corpus of *scholia vetera*), of Aristophanes (Rav. 429), of Aeschylus, Sophocles, and Apollonius Rhodius (Laur. 32.9), of Attic and Hellenistic historiographers and Herodotus (Laur. 70.3), of Thucydides (Laur. 69.2 and Palat. gr. 252), of Xenophon (Erlangen gr. 1, Escor. T-III-14, Vat. gr. 1335), of Polybius (Vat. gr. 124, in the hand of the scribe Ephraim, see above), whose histories were also excerpted into Constantine VII's rubrics, of Isocrates (Urb. gr. 111), and of Demosthenes (Paris. gr. 2934) all hail from this milieu. Almost all of them are written in scholarly, informal hands: these were manuscripts for everyday use in schools and learned circles. The tenth-century *Lexicon Aimōdein* (Dyck 1995), in drawing on Procopius, Arethas, and Theophylaktos Simokates, shows an interest in late antique historiography just at a time when Leo, a deacon of the church of Hagia Sophia, was composing the first "epic" history narrating the reigns of two military "heroes," emperors Nikephoros II Phokas (r. 963–9) and John I Tzimiskes (r. 969–76), taking next to Homer these late antique historiographers as his model. With Leo's *History*, the "Homeric age" of Byzantine rhetoric began; it would reach its apogee about 200 years later in the circle of Eustathius.

The most prominent of these *homines novi* was the polymath Michael Psellos. From one of the new families and gifted enough to seek his fortunes at the imperial court, he seems to have channeled and exacerbated various intellectual trends. He gave lectures on philosophy, theology, and other topics dime a dozen and promoted allegorical readings, thus paving the way for a new understanding of the Homeric epics as well as for the rebirth of the novel in the twelfth century. Somewhat surprisingly, no manuscript once in his possession has been identified. Not least because of Psellos' standing at court, the teaching of philosophy and law seems to have become institutionalized for the first time in Byzantine history when, in 1047, Constantine IX Monomachos (r. 1042–1054) appointed Psellos *hypatos tōn philosophōn*, "consul of the philosophers," and his contemporary John Xiphilinos *nomophylax*, "guardian of the law." The office of *maïstōr tōn rhētorōn*, "master of the rhetors," attached to the patriarchate, seems to have followed suit. The difference from the previous, ninth- and tenth-century palace schools where members of the existing court hierarchy had taught, is striking. Now, new positions were created and integrated into the hierarchy. *Paideia* became an ever stronger social currency; however, when the Komnenos dynasty took over in 1081, the pursuit of philosophy was discouraged in the famous show-trial against Psellos' disciple John Italos in 1082 (Agapitos 1998).

Altogether it is fair to say that the eleventh and the twelfth centuries have received less attention from the paleographical perspective than the previous and following centuries. Growing numbers of students increased competition and ensured that ancient texts were being copied. Competition favored performativity; rhetorical performances celebrating the epic, aristocratic *ēthos* of the age became ever more important. It was the age of the sophists, and of Homer. *Paideia* moved under the auspices of the patriarchate (Browning 1962–3). The social practice of the *theatron* – a place where classicizing rhetoric was performed, social capital gained or lost – resurfaced after a long gap stretching from late antiquity (Mullett 1984; Magdalino 1993: 316–412) and was to become ever more important.

John Tzetzes (*c.* 1110–1180/5), a *grammatikos* and rhetorician attempting to make a living from attracting aristocratic patronage – a way of life unimaginable two centuries earlier – compiled various commentaries on the Homeric poems, some of them in fifteen-syllable verse in order to educate imperial brides from abroad. Tzetzes should be singled out as the one who apparently introduced the concept of the triad to classical scholarship. His commentary on Aristophanes seems to be the first that consciously limited itself to three plays (*Nub., Plut., Ran.*). It provides valuable insights into twelfth-century teaching practice (e.g., *schol. Ar. Ran.* 896b). From elsewhere we learn that a student was supposed to memorize between 30 and 50 verses per day.

Eustathius, deacon, *maïstōr tōn rhē̄ torōn*, finally archbishop of Thessalonike – whose commentaries seem to survive in autograph manuscripts, according to the Renaissance scholar and cardinal Bessarion (e.g., Marc. gr. 460) – played in an entirely different category. As *maïstōr*, he composed his massive commentaries (*Il., Od.*) which surpass the previous Byzantine school commentaries by far. In the atmosphere of courtly, epic chivalry under the Komnenoi, Homer's prestige had increased to such a degree that the epics were transformed from primary school texts into tools for studying rhetoric proper; Eustathius' are perhaps the most sophisticated and multi-layered commentaries surviving from the Byzantine period. (One needs to remember Choiroboskos, who had juxtaposed the Homeric poems with the Psalms as a primary schoolbook.) A certain Ioannikios, who copied at least 17 manuscripts of ancient texts in the later twelfth century (all but one pagan), often in cooperation with an enigmatic anonymous Latin colleague, remains an elusive figure (Wilson 1983a). Most notable among his manuscripts is the archetype of pseudo-Apollodorus' *Bibliotheca* (Paris. gr. 2722). Wilson (1977) rightly observes that these eleventh- and twelfth-century scholars increasingly adopted ornamental fashions and esthetic features of script previously reserved for imperial documents – perhaps as much a sign of scribes of the imperial chancery copying manuscripts on the side as of scholarly self-fashioning, demonstrating familiarity with the scripts employed at court.

This flourishing cultural life came to an end in the wake of the Fourth Crusade. The fires of 1203 and 1204 destroyed more manuscripts than the Turkish conquest in 1453, or any other event for that matter (Madden 1992). One example of a manuscript which survived is the so-called "Archimedes palimpsest," famously auctioned in 1998 and studied with exceptional care over the past decade (Netz 2007): a composite palimpsest codex comprising elements of five original codices of varying date and content, among them one with treatises of the ancient mathematician Archimedes and another with, notably, orations of the Attic orator Hyperides, of whom no manuscript seemed to have survived until this palimpsest surfaced. These original texts were erased, newly arranged, and a *euchologion* (prayerbook) was written on top of the old layers, finished in Jerusalem in 1229. In many regards, the Archimedes palimpsest is typical of the fate that many a codex with ancient texts must have suffered in the turmoil following 1204; it is also indicative of the cultural as well as material choices involved in the process of textual transmission.

From Late Byzantium to Montfaucon and Lachmann

When the usurper of imperial power, Michael VIII Palaiologos (r. 1259–82), in a lucky strike recaptured Constantinople from the Latins in 1261, he invested as much in the revival of *paideia* as in the refortification and rebuilding of the imperial capital, which was a mere shadow of its former self. With a string of well-known teachers active in Constantinople in the second half of the thirteenth century – George/Gregory of Cyprus (*c.* 1240–90) among them (Pérez Martín 1996) – the fruit of this endeavor was to be reaped around 1300, when Michael's son Andronikos II (r. 1282–1328) presided over an "empire" that was rapidly fragmenting from a regional to a merely local power, but flourishing culturally (Constantinides 1982).

In earlier periods, it was either calligraphers or, mostly, individual scholar-scribes who produced manuscripts of ancient content. Additionally, in the later Byzantine period, circles of writing became ever more prominent (Cavallo 2003; Bianconi 2003). Indeed it seems as if these writing circles were at the same time fulfilling the function of teaching circles, with young boys gently guided by a gentleman scholar, the central figure of the circle, and more advanced students. The social practice of common writing seems to have played a key role in this changing concept of transmitting *paideia*. The primary example of such a circle is the school around the famous scholar Manuel Planoudes, whose hand can be traced – often in connection with a number of his disciples – in a substantial number of codices, the famous collected *Moralia* of Plutarch (Ambros. C 126 inf.) and the geographical collection nowadays Marc. gr. XI, 6 among them. Manuel Moschopoulos seems to have been active in this circle but faded from the historical stage around the time of the Planoudes' death (*c.* 1305).

For the first time, *paideia* was at home as much in other cities of the empire as in Constantinople; a retarded development actualizing the potential sown by the twelfth-century learned bishops emerging from the patriarchal school. Following less well-known figures such as John Pothos Pediasimos, Thomas Magistros (*c.* 1280–*c.* 1347/8) in Thessalonike gathered a circle of disciples in his own house, who became instrumental in the compilation of his Atticizing lexicon. Magistros was the first Byzantine scholar who composed commentaries on all four dramatic triads, plus Pindar's *Olympian Odes*. He styled himself as an urban rhetor and ambassador to the imperial court, consciously reviving the example of the deuterosophists. These social interests of the early fourteenth-century rhetors are reflected in two contemporary codices of the minor Attic orators: the Codex Crippsianus (British Library, MS Burney 95) and the less formidable manuscript in Oxford, Auct. T. 2. 8. Magistros left traces in contemporary sources; Triklinios' career on the other hand can be established only by means of autograph codices. The earliest and oldest known codex written by him is Oxford, New College, 258, dating to 1308, the latest Naples, gr. II. F. 31, dating to *c.* 1325/1330. While the former codex carries a de luxe version of Hermogenes' rhetorical treatises, the latter contains Triklinios' state-of-the-art edition of the tragedies of Aeschylus, based on the principle of strophic responsion which he had rediscovered, which poses a challenge to modern textual critics – especially in the "alphabetic plays" of Euripides, of which his autograph recension (Laur. 32.2) is the archetype. In between those two fall the important manuscripts Venice, Marcianus graecus 464, dating to 1316/1319 (Hesiod); Rome, Bibliotheca Angelica, gr. 14, *c.* 1315–1325 (Euripides); and Paris, Supplement grec 463, *c.* 1320/1330 (Aristophanes). Since Triklinios incorporated the scholia and glosses of both Magistros and Moschopoulos, his commentaries conveniently assembled the finest of late Byzantine scholarship. Undoubtedly the most gifted textual scholar of his age and the Byzantine millennium, Triklinios made little impact on his own times; the uncomfortable truth may be that in late Byzantine society editing texts read at secondary-school level carried less social prestige than editing "the classics" nowadays.

Finally, the period between February 2, 1397, when Manuel Chrysoloras arrived at the Studio in Florence for an (unsuccessful) tenure of teaching Greek, and March 1, 1518, when Erasmus published his Latin translation of Theodore Gaza's Greek grammar – which Raphael Hythlodaeus famously recommended to the Utopians – marks a century of transition of Greek studies from the crumbling Byzantine Empire to Italy and beyond (Wilson 1992). Renaissance scholarship, to a certain degree influenced by the methods the Byzantine émigré scholars had brought with them, gave birth to what has become, over the centuries, modern-day classical studies. The systematic collection of Ancient Greek texts commenced; in 1468, Cardinal Bessarion (1403–72) handed over his 746 manuscripts (482 Greek, 264 Latin) to the Serenissima of St Mark. Next to the papal library it constituted the most substantial collection of the day. Venice, attractive to emigrants from the fallen empire, turned into a center of post-Byzantine learning and scholarship. Aldo Manuzio (1449/50–1515) and Markos Mousouros (*c.* 1470–1517) invented the Renaissance pocket book widely disseminating the Greek "classics" (Lowry 1979).

The social prestige associated with Greek led more and more collectors – scholars, merchants, aristocrats, emperors – to acquire Greek manuscripts for their libraries. This lasted well into the sixteenth and seventeenth centuries; nowadays a mere 40 Greek manuscripts are kept in the library of the Serail. Some codices were sent as presents, such as the famous fifth-century Codex Alexandrinus, which reached King Charles I as a gift from the Constantinopolitan patriarch Constantine Loukaris in 1627. But it was not before the Maurist monk Bernard de Montfaucon (1655–1741) published his *Palæographia græca* in 1708 that the ancient manuscript tradition became the subject of more systematic study, ultimately paving the way for the stemmatic method of Karl Lachmann (1793–1851) as a sophisticated tool for reversing the cultural exchanges and transmission outlined in this chapter (Timpanaro 2005). However corrupt the Ancient Greek texts preserved in Byzantine manuscripts may occasionally be, without them our knowledge of the Ancient Greek language would be much reduced.

FURTHER READING

The best account of Byzantine *paideia* is Wilson 1996. Markopoulos 2006 and Browning 1997 offer concise, highly useful introductions. Lemerle 1971 is still valid but in need of revision. Unfortunately, there is no Greek equivalent to Reynolds 1986. Nor is there an up-to-date introduction to Greek paleography and codicology in English; however, Wilson 1972–3 offers a good survey of the evolution of Greek handwriting from late antiquity to the Renaissance. The best way into the subject is a careful perusal of the proceedings of the quinquennial meetings organized by the International Committee for Greek Paleography, e.g., *La paléographie grecque et byzantine* (1977), Cavallo, De Gregorio, and Maniaci 1991, or Prato 2000. Olivier 1989 and the website "Pinakes," hosted by the French *Institut de recherche et d'histoire des textes* (http://pinakes.irht.cnrs.fr) provide a useful survey of library catalogues and manuscript holdings.

CHAPTER SEVEN

Phonology[1]

Philomen Probert

Introduction

The phonology of Ancient Greek varied with time, place, and social factors; indeed, it is inevitable that there was some phonological variation between any two individuals, although we are unable to recover details of variation at this level. This chapter aims to describe the phonology of a relatively consistent and relatively well-attested variety of Greek: educated Classical Attic Greek of the late fifth century BCE. It is necessarily selective and necessarily reflects the prejudices of the author.

Sources of Evidence

Classical Greek is, of course, known to us exclusively from written sources. Nevertheless, it is possible within limits to arrive at a reconstruction of the sounds and the sound system of the language. Sources of evidence include: explicit statements about the language by ancient authors; orthography and especially orthographic variation and mistakes; the treatment of non-Greek words borrowed into Greek or transcribed into Greek script; and the treatment of Greek words borrowed into other languages or transcribed into other scripts. All these sources must be used with caution. Ancient authors operated with concepts and categories that do not always match ours, and they may have had goals very different from ours; in addition, ancient descriptions can be imprecise and difficult to understand, and this has not always helped in their transmission. When we consider the transcription of a word from one language to another, it is necessary to keep in mind that our knowledge of the sound systems of ancient languages other than Greek is likewise limited by our evidence, and that the use of a sound or orthographic symbol from one language to represent a sound from another is significant only in relation to the other choices of sound or symbol available.

Thus, to establish that the sounds represented by <φ>, <ϑ>, and <χ> (see the list of symbols on p. xviii) were aspirated stops in Classical Greek rather than the fricatives found in Modern Greek, one might consider their transcriptions into early Latin as <p>, <t>, and <c>, and then from about 150 BCE as <ph>, <th>, and <ch>. The transcription of Greek <φ> is by far the most significant, since Latin had a sound [f], represented by the symbol <f>, and one would expect this symbol to have been used if Greek <φ> had in fact represented the fricative [f]: the non-use of Latin <f> as a transcription for Greek <φ> is therefore an important piece of evidence. (Latin <f> is in fact used eventually to transcribe Greek <φ> in some words, but there are no clear examples until the first century CE and examples do not become frequent until the second century CE: see Allen 1987a: 23–4.) In this context the use of the digraph <ph> strongly suggests that an aspirated stop is being represented, rather than a fricative (which would have been represented as <f>) or an unaspirated stop (which would have been represented as <p>). By contrast, the early Latin use of <p> cannot be taken as evidence against aspiration of Greek <φ> at this period, since the digraph <ph> was eventually invented specifically to represent Greek <φ>, and its earlier non-use is a natural consequence of its not yet having been invented. (On the development of occlusives into fricatives in *Koine*, see ch. 16.)

Since Latin had no interdental or velar fricative [θ] or [χ], and therefore no symbols to represent these sounds, the use of <th> and <ch> (and earlier <t> and <c>) could, in principle, be attempts to represent such fricatives or to represent aspirated stops. We may, in fact, conclude that Greek <ϑ> and <χ> represented aspirated stops in the Classical period, but only on the basis of other evidence. For example, the phonological behavior of the sounds represented by <ϑ> and <χ> closely parallels that of the sound represented by <φ> (thus all three are replaced by unaspirated stops in reduplication: τίϑημι, καχάζω, πέφυκα), so that if <φ> represents an aspirated stop then <ϑ> and <χ> are likely to represent aspirated stops too.

All three sounds are also normally classified in ancient descriptions as ἄφωνα, "devoid of sound," sounds that cannot be pronounced by themselves, rather than ἡμίφωνα, "half-sounded" consonants like [r] and [l] capable of being pronounced by themselves (so, e.g., Dion. Thrax (?), 11. 5–12. 4 Uhlig).[2]

For an introduction to the sounds of Ancient Greek and the evidence for them, see Sturtevant (1940: 5–105) or Allen (1987a). In what follows, evidence for individual sounds will be mentioned only occasionally.

Old Attic Alphabet and Ionic Alphabet

Throughout most of the fifth century BCE, Attic Greek was written in the local Athenian alphabet (the "Old Attic alphabet"), which consisted of the letters shown in column I of table 7.1. Their approximate sound values are shown in column II. The latter part of the fifth century saw the gradual adoption of a different version of the Greek alphabet, the Ionic alphabet; the Ionic alphabet was officially adopted for public inscriptions in 403/2 BCE (see Threatte 1980: 26–51). The letters of the Ionic alphabet are shown in column III, with their approximate sound values in column IV.

Table 7.1 Letters and sound values of the Old Attic alphabet and the Ionic alphabet (cf. table 3.2)

Old Attic alphabet		Ionic alphabet	
I	II	III	IV
letters	*sound values*	*letters*	*sound values*
A	[a,ā]	A	[a,ā]
B	[b]	B	[b]
Γ	[g,ŋ]	Γ	[g,ŋ]
Δ	[d]	Δ	[d]
E	[e, ẹ̄, ɛ̄]	E	[e]
Z	[zd]	Z	[zd]
H	[h]	H	[ɛ̄]
Θ	[tʰ]	Θ	[tʰ]
I	[i, ī]	I	[i, ī]
K	[k]	K	[k]
Λ	[l]	Λ	[l]
M	[m]	M	[m]
N	[n]	N	[n]
		Ξ	[ks]
O	[o, ọ̄, ɔ̄]	O	[o]
Π	[p]	Π	[p]
P	[r]	P	[r]
Σ	[s, z]	Σ	[s, z]
T	[t]	T	[t]
Υ	[y, ȳ]	Υ	[y, ȳ]
Φ	[pʰ]	Φ	[pʰ]
X	[kʰ]	X	[kʰ]
		Ψ	[ps]
		Ω	[ɔ̄]

The crucial differences between the two forms of the alphabet are the following (for more detail, see Threatte 1980: 19–51):

a) The Ionic alphabet has no sign for [h]. After the adoption of the Ionic alphabet, the sound [h] continued to be part of Attic Greek but simply ceased to be represented in writing. The use of a rough breathing to indicate [h], and of a smooth breathing to indicate lack of [h] before a word-initial vowel, is a post-Classical convention.

b) The Ionic alphabet uses the letter <H> (used for [h] in the Old Attic alphabet) to represent a relatively open long vowel [ɛ̄], and uses the letter <Ω> (not present in the Old Attic alphabet) to represent a relatively open long vowel [ɔ̄]. The short vowels [e] and [o] are written with <E> and <O>, as in the Old Attic alphabet. Attic Greek also had relatively close long vowels [ẹ̄] and [ọ̄], sometimes called "secondary vowels." In the Old Attic alphabet these are normally written with <E> and <O>. In the

Table 7.2 Spelling and pronunciation of original [ei] and [ẹ̄] in Attic, illustrated
with the word λείπειν

	Early fifth *century* BCE	*Mid-fifth* *century* BCE	*Mid-fourth* *century* BCE
Spelling	ΛΕΙΠΕΝ	ΛΕΙΠΕΝ (but some misspellings especially of type ΛΕΙΠΕΙΝ; also ΛΕΠΕΝ, ΛΕΠΕΙΝ)	ΛΕΙΠΕΙΝ
Pronunciation	[leípẹ̄n]	[lẹ́pẹ̄n]	[lẹ́pẹ̄n]

Ionic alphabet these long vowels are (after a period of hesitation) written with the
digraphs <ΕΙ> and <ΟΥ> (see the application of this in chs 14 and 26 on dialects). In
the Old Attic alphabet, these digraphs were originally used for diphthongs [ei] and
[ou]. However, these old diphthongs were monophthongized during the fifth century,
and came to be identical in pronunciation to the existing close long vowels [ẹ̄] and [ọ̄]
(see Threatte 1980: 299–323, 349–52, with further details). As a result, some
instances of the sound pronounced [ẹ̄] were written <ΕΙ> (because in these instances
the sound had originally been [ei]) whereas other instances were written <Ε> (because
in these instances the sound had never been a diphthong). Similarly, some instances
of the sound pronounced [ọ̄] were written <ΟΥ> (because in these instances the
sound had originally been [ou]) whereas other instances were written <Ο> (because
in these instances the sound had never been a diphthong). Some confusion in spelling
naturally resulted, as writers had difficulty knowing when to use which spelling for the
sounds [ẹ̄] and [ọ̄]. Variation in spelling was the norm in the early stages of the use of
the Ionic alphabet, but by the mid-fourth century BCE the writings <ΕΙ> and <ΟΥ>
had become standard for all instances of [ẹ̄] and [ọ̄], whatever their historical origins
(see Threatte 1980: 3, 31, 172–90, 238–59).

c)   The Ionic alphabet uses signs <Ξ> and <Ψ> for [ks] and [ps]. In the Old Attic
alphabet, these combinations are nearly always written as <ΧΣ> and <ΦΣ>, rather
than the <ΚΣ> and <ΠΣ> that one might expect (see further below, under
"Neutralization of phonemic oppositions").

In what follows, Greek words are quoted in the Ionic alphabet, with accents and
breathings included – the form familiar from printed editions of Classical texts – unless
otherwise indicated.

Phonemes and Phonological Contrast

Languages clearly differ in the sets of sounds they employ; for this reason, learners of
a foreign language often find some of its sounds unfamiliar. But beyond this basic difference in the sounds used, languages differ in the status that particular differences
between sounds have in the sound system. For example, English has both unaspirated

[t] and aspirated [tʰ], although most speakers are not consciously aware of this differ-ence. Unaspirated [t] occurs only after [s] whereas aspirated [tʰ] never occurs after [s]: <sty> = [staɪ], <tie> = [tʰaɪ], <steam> = [stīm], <team> = [tʰīm]. (If a hand is held a few inches in front of the mouth when an aspirated stop is pronounced, a small puff of air is felt; when an unaspirated stop is pronounced, no puff of air is felt.) Each of these sounds occurs in English only in environments from which the other is excluded: the two sounds are said to be in *complementary distribution*. Therefore no two English words differ *only* in having [t] in one case and [tʰ] in the other: they must also differ in having [s] in the one case and not in the other. One may say (though rather crudely) that the failure of most English speakers to be conscious of the difference between [t] and [tʰ] is related to the lack of necessity to listen for this difference: one can always listen for the presence or absence of a preceding [s] instead.

Ancient Greek also has both [t] and [tʰ], but unlike English [t] and [tʰ] they can occur in the same environments as each other, and the substitution of one for the other can therefore make the difference between one word and another (e.g., στένει = [sténē] "he groans," σθένει = [stʰénē] "strength (dat.)": one may say that the differ-ence between [t] and [tʰ] is *phonologically distinctive* in Ancient Greek, or that the two sounds *contrast distinctively*.

For a description of English we might say that for the purposes of distinguishing words there is one sound '*t*' that is aspirated in some environments and not in others. For a description of Greek we must say that for the purposes of distinguishing words there are separate sounds '*t*' and '*tʰ*'. A unit such as English '*t*' (with variants [t] and [tʰ]) is called a *phoneme*. The variants [t] and [tʰ] are called *allophones*. A symbol repre-senting a phoneme is written between slashes. Thus, English has a phoneme /t/, with allophones [t] and [tʰ]; Ancient Greek has two separate phonemes /t/ and /tʰ/.

Situations involving sounds in contrast can be more complex than the ones just described. For example, Greek has a velar nasal sound [ŋ] which occurs before [k], [g], or [kʰ] (as in ὄγκος = [óŋkos]; ἄγγελος = [áŋgelos]; ἄγχω = [áŋkʰɔ̄]), probably before [m] (as in ὄγμος = [óŋmos]), and perhaps word-internally before [n] (as in γιγνώσκω, perhaps [giŋnɔ́skɔ̄].[3] Before [k], [g], or [kʰ] there is no phonological con-trast between [ŋ] on the one hand and [n] or [m] on the other: [ŋ] is the only nasal that may appear in this context. Before [m] and perhaps [n], on the other hand, there is no phonological contrast between [g] on the one hand and [ŋ] on the other: word-internally [ŋ] but not [g] may appear (while the <γ> of word-initial <γν> certainly represents [g]: see Schwyzer 1939: 215; <γμ> does not occur word-initially). This situation is not neatly described in terms of phonemes and allophones; [ŋ] appears to behave as an allophone of both [n] and [m] when it occurs before [k], [g] or [kʰ], but as an allophone of [g] when it occurs word-internally before [m] and perhaps [n] (cf. Lupaş 1972: 112). Modern linguistics has tended to move away from treating phonemes as fundamental units of linguistic structure, and thus from trying to answer questions such as whether Ancient Greek [ŋ] should be considered a separate phoneme or whether the same sound can be considered an allophone of different phonemes in different environments. Phonemes and allophones remain convenient concepts for many simple situations involving phonological contrast, and we shall make consider-able use of them in what follows. For more complex situations, which the phoneme concept is ill equipped to model, it is more helpful to describe directly where contrast and non-contrast occur, without reference to the phoneme.

Segmental Phonology I: Consonants

Consonant inventory

The Greek consonant system is usefully described in terms of 15 consonantal phonemes (cf. Lupaş 1972: 105–19):

Phonemes	/p t k b d g pʰ tʰ kʰ m n s r l h/
Spellings (Old Attic alphabet)	Π Τ Κ Β Δ Γ Φ Θ Χ Μ Ν Σ Ρ Λ Η
Spellings (Ionic alphabet)	Π Τ Κ Β Δ Γ Φ Θ Χ Μ Ν Σ Ρ Λ (ʼ)

The stop consonants /p, t, k, b, d, g, pʰ, tʰ, kʰ/ and nasals /m, n/ (also called "oral stops" and "nasal stops" respectively, but we shall use the term "stop" to include /p, t, k, b, d, g, pʰ, tʰ, kʰ/ and not /m, n/), plus the velar nasal [ŋ] that appears in certain contexts (see above, under "Phonemes and phonological contrast"), occur at three places of articulation: labial (the lips are pressed together), dental (the tongue touches the upper teeth), and velar (the tongue touches the soft palate at the back of the mouth). The system of stops and nasals is further structured around oppositions of voicing, aspiration, and nasality (see table 7.3).

Table 7.3   Stops and nasals (The usual orthographic representations in the Ionic alphabet are shown in angle brackets; cf. tables 16.1 and 37.1.)

		Labial	*Dental*	*Velar*
Voiceless	unaspirated	p <π>	t <τ>	k <κ>
	aspirated	pʰ <φ>	tʰ <ϑ>	kʰ <χ>
Voiced	oral	b <β>	d <δ>	g <γ>
	nasal	m <μ>	n <ν>	ŋ <γ>

Consonantal phonemes not included in this table are /h/, the dental fricative /s/, and the two liquids /r/ and /l/.

The aspirate /h/ occurs only prevocalically at the beginning of a word or the second member of a compound or prefixed form (see Lupaş 1972: 30; Threatte 1980: 497–9). In spite of its different distribution, it is treated as the same feature in some respects as the aspiration on an aspirated stop /pʰ/, /tʰ/, or /kʰ/. Thus, when a proclitic word (joined closely in pronunciation to the following word) ending in an underlying voiceless stop (sometimes as a result of the elision of a following short vowel) is followed by a word beginning with /h/, the stop that ends the proclitic is regularly written as (and thus presumably felt to be) an aspirate. Similarly, if a verbal root beginning with /h/ is preceded by a preverb ending in an underlying voiceless stop, the stop is regularly written as an aspirate:

ἀπ(ό) + οὗ	→	<ΑΦ ΟΥ> (Ionic alphabet)
/ap(ó)/ + /hô/	→	/apʰ ô/
κατ(ά) + ἵστημι	→	<ΚΑΘΙΣΤΗΜΙ> (Ionic alphabet)
/kat(á)/ + /hístēmi/	→	/katʰístēmi/

(In Attic inscriptions the root-initial /h/ is not normally represented separately after an aspirated stop resulting from elision or composition, even in the Old Attic alphabet where /h/ could in principle have been represented separately: see Threatte 1980: 497–8.)

Allophonic variation

The evidence for allophonic variation in Ancient Greek is inevitably limited. Since speakers of a language tend not to be conscious of allophonic variation, it tends not to be encoded in alphabetic writing and is rarely discussed explicitly. Some instances of allophonic variation in educated Classical Attic can, however, be identified.

"Aspirated" and "unaspirated" allophones of /r/

The phoneme /r/ has allophones that ancient sources treat as being aspirated and unaspirated:

> τὸ Ρ ἀρχόμενον λέξεως δασύνεται, οἷον· ῥανίς ῥάξ, πλὴν τοῦ Ῥάρος καὶ Ῥάριον.
> τὸ Ρ, ἐὰν δισσὸν γένηται ἐν μέσῃ λέξει, τὸ μὲν πρῶτον ψιλοῦται, τὸ δὲ δεύτερον δασύνεται· οἷον συῤῥάπτω.

> 'ρ has a rough breathing when it begins a word, as in ῥανίς ῥάξ, apart from Ῥάρος and Ῥάριον. When ρ is geminated in the middle of a word, the first one has a smooth breathing, the second a rough breathing, as in συῤῥάπτω.' ([Arc.] 226.24–227.2 Schmidt 1860. From an epitome of a work by Herodian, 2nd century CE)

The distribution of "aspirated" and "unaspirated" /r/ suggested here is also reflected in Latin spellings of Greek words with ρ (e.g. *rhetor, Tyrrheni* but *Socrates*). Its applicability to Classical Attic is supported by inscriptions in the Old Attic alphabet (and some other local alphabets), which occasionally use <H> for [h] before or after ρ at the beginning of the word or after a geminate /rr/ (e.g. ΦΡΕΑΡΗΙΟΣ or ΦΡΕΑΡΡΗΙΟΣ for Φρεάρριος on the Themistocles ostraka of the 480s BCE: see Threatte 1980: 25).

In physiological terms "aspiration" is essentially a period during which air escapes from the vocal tract but the vocal cords do not vibrate. In the case of "aspirated" [r] the aspiration did not necessarily precede or follow the consonant but could be simultaneous with it, i.e., the [r] itself could have been voiceless (see Sturtevant 1940: 62; Threatte 1980: 25; Allen 1987a: 41–2). The statement that in a geminate ρρ the first ρ has a smooth breathing and the second a rough breathing could indicate that the geminate began voiced and ended voiceless (but cf. Allen 1987a: 42). With the obscure exceptions Ῥάρος and Ῥάριον mentioned by Herodian (on which, see Allen

1987a: 42), unaspirated or voiced [r] and aspirated or voiceless [r̥] each occur only in environments from which the other is excluded (they are in complementary distribution) – the classic situation in which two sounds do not contrast distinctively and can be considered allophones of a single phoneme (cf. Lupaş 1972: 112; Sommerstein 1973: 47–8).

Voiced and voiceless allophones of /s/

The phoneme /s/ also appears to have had voiced and voiceless allophones [z] and [s], with [z] appearing before voiced consonants while [s] appeared elsewhere (cf. Lupaş 1972: 26–8, 68–9, 113–14, 116–19, with more details). Evidence comes particularly from confusion between <σ> and <ζ>, which starts to appear on Attic inscriptions from the mid-fourth century BCE. <ζ> for <σ> before a voiced consonant, especially /m/, becomes particularly common (the first Attic example is [E]IPΓAZMENO[N] for εἰργασμένον, *IG* II² 1582, line 79 (probably 342/1 BCE): see Threatte 1980: 547–8). /s/ was probably voiced before any voiced consonant, even before the fourth century BCE, but then in the fourth century the sound written <ζ> (originally [zd]) came to be pronounced [zz] (between vowels) or [z] (in other environments). The letter <ζ> thus acquired the value [zz] or [z], and it became tempting to use the letter for original /s/, when pronounced [z], as well as original /sd/ (see Threatte 1980: 510, 547–9). (Notice that once [zd] has become [zz] or [z], the sounds [s] and [z] are no longer in complementary distribution, so that at that stage there are arguably separate phonemes /s/ and /z/. The new phonological status of [z] at this period, and not only the new availability of a symbol for [z], is likely to have contributed to the tendency to represent [z] differently from [s] even where the traditional spelling was <σ>.)

Neutralization of Phonemic Oppositions

Sounds that contrast distinctively in a language may fail to do so in certain environments. In English, for example, the differences between the nasals [m], [n], and [ŋ] can normally make the difference between one word and another, as in *ram* ~ *ran* ~ *rang* (though the velar nasal [ŋ] is more restricted in its distribution than the others, and various analyses of its status in the sound system are possible). Word-internally before a consonant, however, only the nasal whose place of articulation matches that of the following consonant can appear. Thus, before a labial consonant such as [p] we find the labial nasal [m], as in *impossible*. Before a dental (or, more accurately for English, alveolar) consonant such as [t] we find the alveolar nasal [n] (as in *interminable*). Before a velar consonant such as [k] we find the velar nasal [ŋ] (as in *inconsistent*, with *in-* pronounced [ɪŋ]). No distinctive contrast between the different nasal sounds is possible in English when there is a following consonant, and the only phonologically distinctive characteristic of the nasals in this environment is their nasality. Under these circumstances the phonemic opposition between different nasals is said to be neutralized, and the different nasals that appear are simply realizations of distinctive nasality (sometimes represented with a capital letter between slashes, as /N/). (This account of English nasals does not always apply at the boundary between prefixes of Germanic origin and the following root. Thus, the prefix *un-* is sometimes pronounced with alveolar [n] regardless of the following consonant: *unpack* may be pronounced with [n] or [m].) Neutralization of phonemic oppositions may be identified in the following instances in Greek.

Nasals at the end of a syllable

Before a non-nasal consonant the only nasal that can appear is the nasal whose place of articulation is the same as that of the following consonant, as in English:

πέμπω = /péNpɔ̄/ = [pémpɔ̄], τύμβος = /túNbos/ = [týmbos], ἀμφότερος = /aNpʰóteros/ = [ampʰóteros]

πέντε = /péNte/ = [pénte], σπονδή = /spoNdɛ̄́/ = [spondɛ̄́], ἐνθάδε = /eNtʰáde/ = [entʰáde]

ἀνάγκη = /anáNkē/ = [anáŋkē], ἀγγέλλω = /aNgéllɔ̄/ = [aŋgéllɔ̄], τυγχάνω = /tuNkʰánɔ̄/ = [tyŋkʰánɔ̄]

In archaic inscriptions, nasals before non-nasal consonants are normally written as <N>, regardless of their place of articulation (e.g. ΟΛΥΝΠΙΟΝΙΚΟΣ, *IG* I³ 1213, line 1, *c.* 525(?) BCE; ΕΝΓΥΣ, *IG* I³ 1255, lines 1–2, *c.* 530–520(?) BCE), suggesting that due to the lack of distinctive contrast between nasals in this environment, no necessity to distinguish orthographically between different nasals in this position was felt. After the archaic period, the place of articulation of a nasal before a non-nasal consonant is reflected in spelling more often, but there is considerable spelling variation (see Threatte 1980: 588–638).

There is also no phonological contrast between nasals at the end of a word, since the only nasal that can appear in this environment is [n]: δῶρον, σπλήν. But a nasal at the end of a proclitic word (joined closely in pronunciation to the following word) appears to have been pronounced with the same place of articulation as a following consonant; in Classical inscriptions the place of articulation of a nasal in this position is often reflected in spelling, as in numerous examples of ΕΜ ΠΟΛΕΙ for ἐν πόλει (see again Threatte 1980: 588–638).

Labial and velar stops before /s/

In the Old Attic alphabet, which did not use the signs <Ψ> and <Ξ>, the digraphs <ΦΣ> and <ΧΣ> are nearly always used instead (see Threatte 1980: 20–21, 555). Ancient grammatical texts, on the other hand, treat <ψ> and <ξ> as equivalent to <πσ> and <κσ>:

ἔτι δὲ τῶν συμφώνων διπλᾶ μέν ἐστι τρία· ζ ξ ψ. διπλᾶ δὲ εἴρηται, ὅτι ἓν ἕκαστον αὐτῶν ἐκ δύο συμφώνων σύγκειται, τὸ μὲν ζ ἐκ τοῦ σ καὶ δ, τὸ δὲ ξ ἐκ τοῦ κ καὶ σ, τὸ δὲ ψ ἐκ τοῦ π καὶ σ.

And three of the consonants are double: ζ, ξ, ψ. They are called "double" because each one of them is made up of two consonants. ζ is made up of σ and δ, ξ of κ and σ, ψ of π and σ. (Dion. Thrax(?), 14. 4–6 Uhlig)

Table 7.4 Labial and velar stops before /s/

I (1. sg. pres. indic. act.)	II (1. sg. fut. indic. act.)
/lép-ɔ̄/ = λείπω	/ lép/ + /sɔ̄/ = λείψω
/strépʰ-ɔ̄/ = στρέφω	/strépʰ/ + /sɔ̄/ = στρέψω
/tríb-ɔ̄/ = τρίβω	/tríb/ + /sɔ̄/ = τρίψω
/plék-ɔ̄/ = πλέκω	/plék/ + /sɔ̄/ = πλέξω
/psúkʰ-ɔ̄/ = ψύχω	/psúkʰ/ + /sɔ̄/ = ψύξω
/ág-ɔ̄/ = ἄγω	/ág/ + /sɔ̄/ = ἄξω

It is clear that before /s/ the phonological contrast between voiceless unaspirated stops, voiceless aspirates, and voiced stops is neutralized, so that there are no contrasting sets /ps/ ~ /pʰs/ ~ /bs/ or /ks/ ~ /kʰs/ ~ /gs/. When /ps/, /pʰs/, or /bs/ is expected the sequence written <ΦΣ> (Ionic alphabet <Ψ>) appears, while when /ks/, /kʰs/, or /gs/ is expected the sequence written <ΧΣ> (Ionic alphabet <Ξ>) appears (see table 7.4).

It is likely that these sequences were pronounced voiceless, and without aspiration at least in the normal modern sense (i.e. delay in voicing of a vowel or other voiced sound following the release of a consonant). The writings <φσ> and <χσ> are likely to be due to the perception of voicing delay owing to the voiceless fricative [s] following the stop (see Clackson 2002, also reviewing other explanations).

Sequences of two stops

Two stop consonants in succession always agree in voicing, as in ὀκτώ, ἄχθος, ἕβδομος. (Even prefixed forms such as ἐκβάλλω had at least a variant pronunciation [egbállɔ̄]: see Lupaş 1972: 17–19.) Where two stops come together in the formation of a word or inflected form, the first takes on the voicing of the second (as in τέτριπ-ται, ἐτρίφ-θην as compared to τρίβω; πλέγ-δην as compared to πλέκω; see further below, under "Regular alternations"). Thus the contrast between voiced and voiceless stops is neutralized before another stop, and the voicing of the first stop in the sequence is predictable from that of the second.

The spelling of forms such as those just quoted suggests that successive stops also agree in aspiration (cf. Threatte 1980: 570–1; Allen 1987a: 26–8). However, the spelling convention is different when an aspirated stop is preceded by a stop with the same place of articulation; the normal spellings are e.g., Σαπφώ and Βάκχος rather than Σαφφώ and Βάχχος (see Threatte 1980: 541–6). It is clear that distinctive contrast between an aspirated and an unaspirated stop never arises in Greek before an aspirated stop (see Lupaş 1972: 108–9). It is less clear why a stop followed by an aspirate is written as an aspirate if the two stops have different places of articulation but as an unaspirated stop if the two stops have the same place of articulation. In either case, aspiration in the normal sense (delay in voicing of a vowel or other voiced sound following the release of a consonant) can only have followed the second consonant in

Table 7.5 Assimilation of root-final labial and velar stops to following dental stops and /m/

I *(1. sg. pr. indic.* *act., except where* *otherwise stated)*	II *(3. sg. pf. indic.* *mid./pass.*	III *(1. sg. aor. indic.* *pass.)*	IV *(adv. in –δην* *where attested)*	V *(1. sg. pf. indic.* *mid./pass.)*
λείπω /lép-ō/	λέλειπται /lé-lēp-tai/	ἐλείφθην /e-lép^h-t^hēn/	–	λέλειμμαι /lé-lēm-mai/
κρύφα (adverb) /krúp^h-a/	κέκρυπται /ké-krup-tai/	ἐκρύφθην /e-krúp^h-t^hēn/	κρύβδην /krúb-dēn/	κέκρυμμαι /ké-krum-mai/
τρίβω /tríb-ō/	τέτριπται /té-trip-tai/	ἐτρίφθην /e-tríp^h-t^hēn/	–	τέτριμμαι /té-trim-mai/
πλέκω /plék-ō/	πέπλεκται /pé-plek-tai/	ἐπλέχθην /e-plék^h-t^hēn/	πλέγδην /plég-dēn/	πέπλεγμαι /pé-pleŋ-mai/
ψύχω/psúk^h-ō/	ἔψυκται /é-psuk-tai/	ἐψύχθην /e-psúk^h-t^hēn/	–	ἔψυγμαι /é-psuŋ-mai/
ἐμίγην (aorist passive) /e-míg-ēn/	μέμικται /mé-mik-tai/	ἐμίχθην /e-mík^h-t^hēn/	μίγδην /míg-dēn/	μέμιγμαι /mé-miŋ-mai/

the sequence. In a word such as ἄχθος, the transition from the first stop to the second will have necessitated the release of the first, while in a word such as Σαπφώ, there was no release between the consonant written as <π> and the one written as <φ>, the lips remaining pressed together throughout. The difference in spelling conventions suggests that what was perceived as aspiration involved the *release* of a stop before an aspirated stop. (For various views on the nature of the "aspiration" of the first stop in a cluster <χθ> or <φθ>, see Threatte 1980: 571, with bibliography.)

There are also words such as ῥυθμός, θνητός, φλαῦρος, Ἀφροδίτη, or ἐχθρός, in which an aspirated stop is written before <μ>, <ν>, <λ>, <ρ>, or even a sequence of two aspirated stops before <ρ>. Here the aspiration of the stop or stops may have consisted of voicelessness or delay in voicing of the nasal or liquid (cf. Clackson 2002: 30).

Regular alternations

The oppositions of voicing, aspiration, and nasality play an important role in regular alternations between consonants. For example, a root-final stop may be underlyingly voiceless and unaspirated, voiceless and aspirated, or voiced. Before a vowel, the underlying form of the stop appears (column I in table 7.5). Before a following dental stop, however, an underlying labial or velar stop is realized at its underlying place of articulation but takes its features of voicing and, at least in writing, aspiration (see the previous section) from the following stop (columns II, III, and IV). Before a following /m/, an underlying labial or velar stop is realized at its underlying place of articulation but acquires nasality from the following /m/ (column V).

Table 7.6   Realization of root-final dental stops as /s/ before following dental stops and /m/ (Examples in which an underlying dental stop is followed by /d/ are lacking.)

I *(1. sg. pr. indic. act.)*	II *(3. sg. pf. indic. mid./pass.)*	III *(1. sg. aor. indic./pass.)*	IV *(1. sg. pf. indic. mid./pass.)*
ἀνύτω /anút-ɔ̄/	ἤνυσται /ḗnus-tai/	ἠνύσϑην /ēnús-tʰēn/	ἤνυσμαι /ḗnus-mai/
πείϑω /pét̪ʰ-ɔ̄/	πέπεισται /pé-pḗs-tai/	ἐπείσϑην /e-pḗs-tʰēn/	πέπεισμαι /pé-pḗs-mai/
ψεύδω /pseúd-ɔ̄/	ἔψευσται /é-pseus-tai/	ἐψεύσϑην /e-pseús-tʰēn/	ἔψευσμαι /é-pseus-mai/

The dental fricative /s/ also takes part in phonological alternations. For example, any underlying dental stop is realized as the dental fricative /s/ before a following dental stop (columns II and III of table 7.6). A morphologically restricted alternation also gives rise in many instances to surface /s/ from an underlying dental stop before /m/ (column IV of table 7.6; compare the word πότμος "fate," with no change of /t/ before /m/, and for more details and analysis, see Steriade 1982: 255–9).

Segmental Phonology II: Vowels

Attic at the end of the fifth century BCE had a particularly asymmetric vowel system with five short vowels and seven long vowels (see tables 7.7 and 7.8)

It has been disputed whether the short mid vowels /e/ and /o/ were phonetically equivalent in aperture to the long vowels /ẹ̄/ and /ọ̄/ or to /ɛ̄/ and /ɔ̄/, or whether the aperture of /e/ and /o/ fell between that of /ẹ̄/ and /ọ̄/ on the one hand and that of /ɛ̄/ and /ɔ̄/ on the other. A variant of the latter possibility is that /e/ and /o/ are similar in phonetic height to /ẹ̄/ and /ọ̄/ but nevertheless fall mid-way between /i/ and /a/, owing to /a/ being a higher vowel, *ex hypothesi*, than /ā/ (see Allen 1959: 247–9 and more recently Thompson 2006: 87, 92). Figure 7.1 shows the arrangement envisaged before the fronting of /u/ and /ū/ (inherited as [u] and [ū]) to [y] and [ȳ].

A more rather than less symmetrical short vowel system (however this is seen as relating to the long vowel system) is supported by the observation that the vowel systems of most languages are symmetrical. The force of this observation may be weakened by the fact that both the long and the short vowel systems of late fifth-century Attic are, even so, patently asymmetrical (with two high front vowels and no high back vowel). On the other hand, while the long vowel system is destined for radical change over the centuries to come, the short vowel system remains stable until the much later unrounding of /u/ = [y] (see Threatte 1980: 337); relative symmetry and lack of crowding would contribute to historical stability.

Table 7.7 Short vowels at the end of the fifth century BCE (Orthographic symbols are those of the Old Attic alphabet as well as of the Ionic alphabet.)

	Front	Back
high	/i/ <ι>/u/ <υ> (round)	
mid	/e/ <ε>	/o/ <o> (round)
low		/ɑ/ <α>

Table 7.8 Long vowels at the end of the fifth century BCE (but chronology is disputed) (Orthographic symbols shown are standard in the Ionic alphabet by the mid-fourth century BCE.)

	Front	Back
high	/ī/ <ι>/ū/<υ> (round)	
mid	/ẹ̄/ <ει>	/ọ̄/ <ου> (round)
low	/ɛ̄/ <η>	/ɔ̄/<ω> (round)
		/ā/<α>

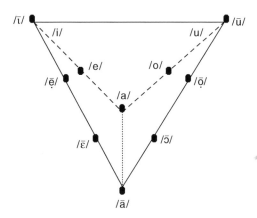

Figure 7.1 Possible arrangement of long and short vowels in early fifth-century Attic, before the fronting of /u/ and /ū/ to [y] and [ȳ]: after Allen 1959: 248 (Cf. Thompson 2006: 87, with a similar arrangement but showing the long and short front axes realistically longer than the respective back axes.)

From a phonological point of view, it is clear that in the late fifth century BCE /e/ and /o/ are treated as the short counterparts of /ẹ̄/ and /ọ̄/ (cf. Allen 1959: 246–7). If vowels are classified as in tables 7.7 and 7.8 (with /ɛ̄/, /ɔ̄/, /ā/ and /ɑ/ forming a natural class as low vowels), the following statements about regular phonological contraction of non-high vowels (which could also be formulated as rules: cf. Sommerstein 1973: 56–9, 102–4) are true:

a) The output vowel is always long;
b) The output vowel is round (/ọ̄/, /ɔ̄/) if and only if at least one of the input vowels is round (/o/, /ọ̄/, /ɔ̄/);

Table 7.9 Present indicative and infinitive active forms of φιλέω, τιμάω, δηλόω (Forms with morphologically conditioned i-diphthongs are underlined; contrast the infinitives of τιμάω and δηλόω.)

Present indicative active

Singular

	Underlying		Surface	Greek
1.	/pʰilé+/ɔ̄/	→	/pʰilɔ̄/	φιλῶ
2.	/pʰilé+/ę̄s/	→	/pʰilḗs/	φιλεῖς
3.	/pʰilé+/ę̄/	→	/pʰilḗ/	φιλεῖ
1.	/timá+/ɔ̄/	→	/timɔ̄/	τιμῶ
2.	/timá+/ę̄s/	→	/timâis/	<u>τιμᾷς</u>
3.	/timá+/ę̄/	→	/timâi/	<u>τιμᾷ</u>
1.	/dēló+/ɔ̄/	→	/dēlɔ̄/	δηλῶ
2.	/dēló+/ę̄s/	→	/dēlois/	<u>δηλοῖς</u>
3.	/dēló+/ę̄/	→	/dēloi/	<u>δηλοῖ</u>

Plural

	Underlying		Surface	Greek
1.	/pʰilé+/omen/	→	/pʰilômen/	φιλοῦμεν
2.	/pʰilé+/ete/	→	/pʰilḗte/	φιλεῖτε
3.	/pʰilé+/ǭsi/	→	/pʰilôsi/	φιλοῦσι
1.	/timá+/omen/	→	/timɔ̄men/	τιμῶμεν
2.	/timá+/ete/	→	/timâte/	τιμᾶτε
3.	/timá+/ǭsi/	→	/timɔ̄si/	τιμῶσι
1.	/dēló+/omen/	→	/delômen/	δηλοῦμεν
2.	/dēló+/ete/	→	/delôte/	δηλοῦτε
3.	/dēló+/ǭsi/	→	/delôsi/	δηλοῦσι

Present infinitive active

Underlying		Surface	Greek
/pʰilé+/ę̄n/	→	/pʰilḗn/	φιλεῖν
/timá+/ę̄n/	→	/timân/	τιμᾶν
/dēló+/ę̄n/	→	/dēlôn/	δηλοῦν

c) The output vowel is low (/ā/, /ɛ̄/, /ɔ̄/) if and only if one of the input vowels is low (/a/, /ā/, /ɛ̄/, /ɔ̄/);

d) The output vowel is back (/ā/, /ọ/, /ɔ̄/) if it is round (/ọ/, /ɔ̄/), or if the first of the input vowels is back (/a/, /o/, /ā/, /ọ/, /ɔ̄/), and not otherwise. (After Sommerstein 1973: 55)

Thus, not only does the sequence /e/ + /e/ contract to /ẹ/, and the sequence /o/ + /o/ to /ọ/, but the other possible sequences of mid short vowels, /e/ + /o/ and /o/ + /e/, both contract to /ọ/. The paradigms of contract verbs (see table 7.9) are related fairly straightforwardly to those of non-contract verbs by the operation of regular contraction (but the outcome of contraction of a non-high vowel with following /ẹ/ is subject to morphological conditioning; under some morphological circumstances, an *i*-diphthong appears).

The accentuation of contract verb forms also supports the status of contraction as part of the synchronic phonology of the language.

Some processes suggest that /e/ can also be treated as the short counterpart of /ɛ̄/, and /o/ as the short counterpart of /ɔ̄/. However, these processes are subject to considerable morphological restriction. Thus, some verbs with stem-initial /e/ have augmented forms beginning with /ɛ̄/ (/egɛ́rɔ̄/ ἐγείρω ~ /ɛ́gēron/ ἤγειρον), while others have augmented forms beginning with /ẹ/ (/ékʰɔ̄/ ἔχω ~ /ệkʰon/ εἶχον). Since an augment for a verbal root beginning with a consonant consists of the prefix /e/, both /ɛ̄/ and /ẹ/, depending on the verb, might seem to behave as the products of /e/ + /e/. However, the augmenting of vowel-initial roots cannot be regarded as simple prefixing of /e/ plus phonologically motivated adjustments: a number of different and partly morphologically or lexically determined operations need to be recognized for different verbs.[4]

A non-high vowel followed by a high vowel normally forms a rising diphthong. The diphthongs that commonly occur are /ai/, /au/, /eu/, /oi/, /āi/, /ɛ̄i/, /ɛ̄u/, and /ɔ̄i/. (Phonetically, /au/, /eu/, and /ɛ̄u/ are realized as [au], [eu] and [ɛu], with the back vowel [u] as second element rather than the front vowel [y] that otherwise realizes /u/: see Allen 1987a: 80). Occasionally, a diphthong /ui/ consisting of both high vowels is also found. The absence of the diphthongs /ei/ and /ou/ is a recent phenomenon at the end of the fifth century BCE. At the beginning of the century, both these diphthongs existed in Attic Greek, but during the course of the century they were monophthongized and merged with existing /ẹ/ and /ọ/ (see above, under "Old Attic alphabet and Ionic alphabet"). The relationship between /ẹ/ and *i*-diphthongs in some morphological contexts (see table 7.9) results from the same process.

The monophthongizations of earlier /ei/ and /ou/ are the first in a series of monophthongizations to come. The first of the "long" *i*-diphthongs to monophthongize was /ɛ̄i/; the evidence from inscriptions is complex but the result of the monophthongization appears to have been /ẹ/. This change possibly began in the late fifth century BCE in some contexts, but it was by no means complete at that date (see Threatte 1980: 208, 353–83, esp. 353–4, 357, 368, 369–70; see also ch. 16 below).

Syllable Structure[5]

Greek has a contrast between heavy and light syllables. Heavy syllables are those containing a long vowel or diphthong, and/or ending with a consonant.

A single consonant between vowels belongs to the same syllable as the following vowel: λείπει = /lḗ.pē/, ἔλιπε = /é.li.pe/. The first consonant of a cluster of two consonants occurring between vowels (including the first part of a geminate consonant, such as /ll/) generally belongs to the same syllable as the preceding vowel, while the second consonant belongs to the same syllable as the following vowel: πίπτω = /píp.tɔ̄/, λείψω = /lḗp.sɔ̄/, ἄλλου = /ál.lɔ̄/. But if a consonant cluster consists of a stop followed by a liquid (/r/ or /l/) or nasal, it is likely that the syllable division regularly fell before the stop in spoken fifth-century Attic: πατρί = /pa.trí/, τέκνου = /té.knɔ̄/, ὕπνῳ = /hú.pnɔ̄i/. When the stop is voiced and is followed by a nasal, however, the syllable division fell between the stop and the nasal: ἔδνοις = /héd.nois/, Κάδμος = /kád.mos/; for the sequences /bl/ and /gl/, syllable division probably fell either before or after the stop. (For the complex evidence especially from meter and from reduplication, see Steriade 1982: 186–208.)

Word-internally, a syllable may thus begin with a single consonant or with a sequence of stop plus liquid or voiceless stop plus nasal after a vowel. It is likely that when a word-internal consonant cluster contains more than two consonants, the syllable division also falls before a single consonant or a stop plus liquid or voiceless stop plus nasal cluster. Otherwise, the syllable division falls before the final consonant of the cluster:

> ἀνθρώπου = /aN.tʰrɔ̄.pɔ̄/
> ὄμβρος = /óN.bros/
> τερπνός = /ter.pnós/
> ἐσθλός = /es.tʰlós/
> θέλκτρον = /tʰélk.tron/
>
> πέμπτος = /péNp.tos/
> ἔμελψα = /é.melp.sa/
> μάρπτω = /márp.tɔ̄/
> ἄρξαι = /árk.sai/

Word-initially, however, and at the beginning of the second member of a compound or prefixed form, some of the syllable onsets found word-internally may be preceded by a further consonant, as follows:

a) A word-initial (or second-member-initial) /s/ may precede a stop or stop+liquid/ nasal sequence or /m/ (e.g., σπένδω, σβέννῡμι, σφάζω, στενός, ζυγόν, σθένος, σκοπός, σχεδόν, σπλάγχνον, σφρᾱγίς, στρατός, στλεγγίς, σκληρός, σμήχω; ἐκ-σκαλεύω, ἐκ-στρέφω)

b) A word-initial (or second-member-initial) non-dental stop may precede a dental stop not followed by a further consonant (e.g. πτερόν, βδελυρός, φθείρω, κτείνω, χθών; ἐκ-φθείρω);

c)   A word-initial (or second-member-initial) /m/ may precede /n/ (e.g. μνῆμα; συμ-μνημονεύω).

Most of these sequences comprise or begin with elements of roughly the same sonority (two stops or two nasals) or even involve a fall in sonority (/s/ followed by stop), while the consonant clusters that may begin a syllable word-internally are of clear rising sonority (stop followed by liquid or nasal). As in many languages, it appears that under some circumstances a consonant extra to the normal limits to syllable onset may appear in word-initial position.

Word-internally a syllable may end with any consonant other than /h/, or with a sequence of nasal or liquid plus stop: cf. again ἀνθρώπου = /aN.tʰrɔ́.pɔ̄/; ὄμβρος = /óN.bros/; τερπνός = /ter.pnós/; ἐσθλός = /es.tʰlós/; θέλκτρον = /tʰélk.tron/; πέμπτος = /péNp.tos/; ἔμελψα = /é.melp.sa/; μάρπτω = /márp.tɔ̄/; ἄρξαι = /árk.sai/. But word-finally, and at the end of the first member of a compound or prefixed form, an extra element may again appear in the form of an /s/ following /p/, /k/, or /Nk/: φλέψ = /pʰléps/, γλαῦξ = /glaúks/, φόρμιγξ = /pʰór.miNks/, ἐξ-μέδιμνος = /heks.mé.dim.nos/.

Word-internal consonant clusters can always be divided into a possible syllable-final cluster followed by a possible syllable-initial cluster. There are, however, constraints on consonant clustering that are not determined wholly by the constraints on syllable structure. Thus, liquid plus nasal clusters are possible (κυβερνήτης /ku.ber.nɛ́.tēs/, τόλμα /tól.ma/) but nasal plus liquid clusters are not, even though a syllable can end with a nasal and a syllable can begin with a liquid. Stop plus stop clusters are either geminates or have a dental as the second stop (except across the boundary between members of a compound or prefixed form: cf. ἐκ-πέμπω).

Greek syllabification rules operate across word boundaries (so that, for example, a single consonant at the end of a word is syllabified with a following word-initial vowel). Nevertheless, word boundaries have a special status. In addition to the behavior of "extrasyllabic" consonants, already mentioned, /h/ occurs only at the beginning of a syllable that also begins a word or the second member of a compound or prefixed form. Furthermore, additional constraints on the occurrence and co-occurrence of consonants apply to word-final position: a full word (not a proclitic) can end only in /n/, /r/, /s/, /ps/, /ks/, or /Nks/ (cf. χθών /kʰtʰɔ́n/, πατήρ /patér/, σθένος /stʰénos/, φλέψ /pʰléps/, γλαῦξ /glaúks/, φόρμιγξ /pʰórmiNks/). Thus, there are no word-final stops (except in proclitics such as ἐκ, οὐκ) although word-internal syllables can be closed by stops (e.g. σκῆπτρον /skɛ̂p.tron/, ἔτνος /ét.nos/, οἰκτρός /oik.trós/). /l/ also is not found at the end of words but can be a syllable-final consonant word-internally (ἄλγος /ál.gos/).

Accentuation

There is very little direct evidence for Greek accentuation until the end of the third century BCE, but indirect evidence (including comparison with other Indo-European languages, especially Vedic Sanskrit, pointing to a considerable amount of shared accentual inheritance) implies a Classical Attic system not far different from the one described by Hellenistic and post-Hellenistic sources (see Probert 2006: 83–96).

There is one main accent per word; the main phonetic characteristic recognized by ancient grammarians is a raised pitch. The accented element is the vocalic mora (a short vowel or half of a long vowel or diphthong), so that an accent on a long vowel or diphthong falls either on the first mora (when it is written as a circumflex, as in σοφῶν) or on the second (when it is written as an acute, as in ἀνθρώπους); over the whole long vowel or diphthong, a falling or rising accent is perceived.

The position of the accent within the word is regulated in part by some phonological restrictions on the position of the accent (primarily the *law of limitation*, which restricts the position of the accent to one of the last three syllables of the word, or one of the last two if the last syllable has a long vowel or is closed by a consonant cluster), in part by the morphological structure of the word (so that, for example, words with certain suffixes are always or usually accented in a particular place), and is in part simply an idiosyncratic characteristic of the word concerned. The complexity of the accentuation system makes it valuable for the theory and typology of accent systems in the world's languages.

There is little direct evidence for intonation or for rhythmic phenomena apart from syllable weight; for a detailed attempt to reconstruct the prosody of the language as far as possible from what can be gleaned indirectly, see Devine and Stephens 1994.

FURTHER READING

On the pronunciation of Greek, see Sturtevant 1940: 5–105; Allen 1987a. For the epigraphic evidence, see Threatte 1980. For traditional (and partly historical) accounts of the regular vowel and consonant alternations, see Goodwin 1894: 13–24; Smyth 1956: 18–33. For a structuralist account of Classical Attic phonology, see Lupaş 1972. For an early generative account with an emphasis on consonant and vowel alternations and on accentuation, see Sommerstein 1973. For a study of Greek syllable structure drawing on and contributing significantly to the theoretical understanding of syllabification, see Steriade 1982. For the basic accentual regularities, see Probert 2003. For a detailed reconstruction of the broader prosodic system, see Devine and Stephens 1994.

NOTES

1   This chapter is based ultimately on teaching materials with input from Anna Morpurgo Davies and from the comparative philology team at Cambridge. I am very grateful to these colleagues and to Eleanor Dickey, who made very helpful suggestions on a draft of this chapter. None of these people is to blame for the decisions I have made on points of fact or on what to include.

2   For further details on ancient classifications of the sounds represented with <φ>, <θ>, and <χ>, see Sturtevant 1940: 76–7; Allen 1987a: 18–19, 23; for further evidence for the

Classical Attic pronunciation of these sounds see Sturtevant 1940: 78–83; Threatte 1980: 469–70; Allen 1987a: 19–22.

3 For word-internal <γ> as [ŋ] before [m] and [n], see Sturtevant 1940: 64–5; Schwyzer 1939: 214–15. For the pronunciation [ŋ] before [m] but not [n], see Ward 1944; Allen 1987a: 35–7. For doubts about <γ> as [ŋ] even before [m], see Lupaş 1972: 20–3.

4 For an attempt to provide phonological rules for augmenting vowel-initial roots, see Sommerstein 1973: 10–12, 18, 51, 61–3, 181; but the use of highly abstract underlying forms is necessitated by the partly morphological and lexical conditioning of the variants; cf. also Sommerstein 1973: 18n 23.

5 This account of syllable structure is heavily based on Steriade 1982. The syllabification of consonant clusters containing more than two consonants, in particular, is disputed and difficult to establish for certain: see also Lupaş 1972: 153–62; Devine and Stephens 1994: 42–3.

PART TWO

The Language

CHAPTER EIGHT

Morphology and Word Formation

Michael Weiss

Morphology

It has long been customary in the Western linguistic tradition to recognize two components in the grammar for the combination of form and meaning. On the one hand, form and meaning combine at the level of the sentence, and this is the domain of syntax. On the other hand, form and meaning combine at the level of the word, and this is the domain of morphology. This traditional view, which has been challenged in recent years, is called the lexicalist hypothesis.

Under the influence of the ancient Indian grammarian Panini, linguists have long realized that many words may be analyzed into smaller, typically meaningful units called morphemes. In older Indo-European languages, it is normally the case that a simplex word conforms to the following structure: Root – Suffix $_{(0...n)}$ – Ending. Roots, suffixes, and endings may be broadly defined in semantico-syntactic terms. Roots give the basic lexical meaning. For example, all derivatives of the root *sed- have to do with "sitting": ἕδος "seat" < *sed-os, ἵζω "I seat" < *si-sd-oh₂. Suffixes provide information about word class (nominal or verbal, *nomina agentis, nomina actionis*) and/or grammatical function (tense, aspect, and mood markers, etc.). Endings provide information that permits a word to be interpreted in a given syntactic context (case, number, person, voice). Suffixes and endings are not required for wordhood. Root nouns, for example, are suffixless, affixing endings directly to the root, and some imperative forms are the bare root with no suffix or ending.

Associations of various strength exist between words with partially overlapping meaning or structure. For example, in English the present tense and past tense of the same verb are strongly associated, and 3 sg. pr. tense of one verb and the 3 sg. pr. of another are also associated but perhaps to a lesser degree. These associations, which are often thought of as rules of inflection and derivation, can lead to the remodeling or creation of forms which are not the simple result of the cumulative workings of *sound change*. These remodelings are said to be the result of *analogy*. For example, the past tense of the verb *strive* in many forms of present-day English is *strove*, not *strived*, which is the historically expected form. It is clear that *strove* has originated on the model of so-called strong verbs with the pattern: present *drive* ~ past *drove*. The creation of *strove* is often represented in the form of a four-part analogy, i.e., *drive*: *drove*: *strive*: x, x = *strove*. Another but not entirely distinct type of analogy is called *paradigm leveling*. In cases of this sort, alternation has been introduced into a formerly unitary paradigm, often as the result of sound change, but one of the two alternates is generalized restoring a non-alternating paradigm. In Greek, for example, the regular outcome of a proto-form **basileu̯-i̯ō* "I rule as king" would have been **basilei̯i̯ō*, but on the basis of extra-present forms which retained the stem form *basileu̯-*, the phonologically expected form of the present stem was replaced in almost all Greek dialects by βασιλεύω. Analogy, broadly defined, is the most powerful mechanism of morphological change and will be frequently mentioned below.

Nominal Morphology

The Attic Greek nominal system expresses the morpho-syntactic categories of case (nom., voc., acc., dat. and gen. with scattered traces of a locative), number (sg., du., and pl.), and gender (masc., fem., and neut.). The case system has been reduced from the earlier PIE eight-case system by the merger of the genitive and ablative singular as the genitive, and the merger of the dative, locative, and instrumental cases as the dative. The survival of distinctive dual forms is a notable archaism of Attic within the realm of the Greek dialects.

The gender system makes a major division between non-neuter and neuter, the latter of which is characterized by identity of the nominative, vocative and accusative in all numbers. The masculine and feminine distinction is not consistently expressed morphologically. Nouns of identical stem types may be either masculine or feminine (ὁ λόγος vs ἡ φηγός, ὁ πατήρ vs ἡ μήτηρ), although stem types do tend to have predominant gender tendencies. Attic Greek is thus a moderately archaic Indo-European language, comparable broadly speaking in terms of nominal morphology to Classical Latin or Gothic.

Case endings

There are two partially overlapping sets of nominal case endings, the so-called thematic and athematic endings. The thematic endings occur in the thematic or *o*-stem declension. The athematic endings occur in all other stem types although the underlying identity of endings has been obscured through sound change, especially in the *ā*-stems.

The athematic endings are:

a) Nom. sg. -ς after a stem ending in a vowel or a stop, e.g., πόλις, φλέψ. After stems ending in continuants there is no surface -ς but the stem vowel is lengthened, e.g., πατήρ, δαίμων. This lengthening results from a pre-PIE rule that eliminates *-s after a sonorant consonant with a compensatory lengthening of the preceding vowel.

b)   Voc. sg. is the bare stem (Σώκρατες, παῖ < *paid) in many cases, but the nominative has been generalized in stems ending in a stop (φύλαξ) and in most oxytone sonorant stems (ποιμήν).

c)   Acc. sg. -ν after a vowel and -α after a consonant. These two allomorphs continue PIE *-m which became syllabic (i.e., *-m̥ > Gk -α) after a consonant.

d)   Dat. sg. -ι, continues the PIE loc. sg. The expected dative ending *-ei (OL VIRTUTEI) is continued in Mycenaean.

e)   Gen. sg. -ος appears on the surface in stems ending in a consonant, for example, in ποδ-ός or ἠδέ(ϝ)ος, but in ι-, substantival υ- and -η(ϝ)-stems the ending is -ως < -ος by quantitative metathesis (πόλεως < *poleu̯os). In σ-stems -ος contracts with the stem vowel to give -ους /-ōs/ (γένους < *genesos) or -ως (γέρως < *gerasos).

f)   Nom. pl. -ες surfaces in consonant stems. In ι-stems, υ-stems and σ-stems the ending -ες combines with the preceding -ε < *-ei̯-, *-eu̯-, and *-es- to give -εις. After stems in -η(ϝ)- the resulting contraction gives -ῆς in Old Att., which is replaced by -εῖς in later Attic.

g)   Acc. pl. -ας after a consonant comes from *-n̥s. By quantitative metathesis -ας became -ᾱς in βασιλέᾱς. In ι-stems, υ-stems and ς-stems the accusative in -εις is identical to the nom. pl.

h)   Dat. pl. -σι is seen in consonant stems like φλεψί, γίγασι < *gigant-si. The dat. pl. may be extended by ν-mobile.

i)   Gen. pl. -ων and under the accent -ῶν. The circumflex intonation reflects the disyllabic Indo-European origin of this morpheme (*-oh_xom; note that the sign "*h_x" [*h_1, *h_2, *h_3] refers to *laryngeals*, a set of reconstructed PIE consonants; see further ch. 12).

j)   Nom. voc. acc. du. The ending -ε < *-h_1e, originally proper only to animate duals, e.g., πόδ-ε has been extended also to neuter athematics, e.g., σώματ-ε. In σ-stems, ι-stems, and υ-stems it contracts with the preceding vowel in hiatus: γένει < *genese, πόλει < *polei̯e, etc.

k)   Gen. dat. du. -οιν and under the accent -οῖν. The exact prehistory of this form is debated.

Neuter forms differ only in nom., voc., and acc., which are always identical. In the singular the neut. nom. acc. is endingless (ἄστυ, γένος). In the plural the ending is -α (ὀνήματ-α), although contraction can obscure this ending, e.g., γένη < *genesa. This ending continues PIE *-h_2. The ending -α, originally belonging to ath. neut. plurals, has been extended to them. neut. plurals, e.g., ζυγά, replacing *-ā from *-eh_2.

Athematic nouns are also characterized in some cases by morphologically governed alternations of vowel quantity and quality (*ablaut*). The different instantiations of the ablauting vowel are called *grades*. For example, in πατήρ, the lengthened grade of the suffix πα-τήρ seen in the nominative alternates with an *e*-grade in the accusative πα-τέρ-α and a zero-grade, i.e., the absence of a vowel, in the gen. sg. πα-τρ-ός. The zero-grade was also present in the dat. pl. πατράσι << *ph_2-tr̥-su, but the development of *$\mathring{r}$* to *ra* has obscured this structure. These ablaut alternations are remnants of more pervasive and systematic patterns of alternation in PIE.

The thematic endings may be derived in most cases by appending the athematic endings to the thematic vowel -*o*-. This is the case in the nom. sg. -*o*-ς, the acc. sg. -*o*-ν, acc. pl. -ους < *-*o-ns*. In the gen. pl. and the gen. dat. du. the thematic vowel is synchronically deleted without trace before the vowel-initial endings -ων and -οιν. In the dat. sg. and nom. acc. du. the relation between the thematic and athematic endings was obscured in pre-Greek times by phonological change. The ending -ω/ results from a contraction of the thematic vowel *-*o*- and the dat. sg. ending *-*ei*. The dual ending -ω is from *-*o-h*$_1$ < *-*o-h*$_1$e by a PIE apocope. In a number of cases the thematic declension shares endings with the pronominal declension. In the gen. sg. -ου /-ō̄/ < *-*osi̯o* (parallel to τοῦ) and the dat. pl. -οισι//-οις this was the PIE state of affairs. In the case of the nom. pl., the replacement of thematic *-*ōs* < *-*o-es* (Ved. *deváḥ* "gods"), by *-*oi* (Gk -οι) of pronominal origin (Gk *o* ~ Ved. *té* < *toi*) happened multiple times in the history of various daughter languages including Greek and Latin. In the dat. pl. the ending -οισι, which is found in Attic documents until about 450 BCE, continues a Proto-Greek remodeling of the loc. pl. *-*oisu* after the loc. sg. *-*i*. The form -οις, which occurs beside -οισι, and which is generalized after 450 BCE, continues the PIE instr. pl. *-*ōis* (Ved. *deváïḥ* "gods").

Neuter thematic nouns, like all neuters, have just one form for nominative, vocative, and accusative. In the singular the ending in -ον (ζυγόν = Lat. *iugum*).

There are two notable subtypes of the thematic declension, the Attic declension and the contracted declension, both resulting from relatively recent sound changes. The core of the Attic declension is made up of nouns and adjectives where the originally long stem vowel and the thematic endings underwent quantitative metathesis, e.g., ληός > λεώς. The contracted declension results from the elimination of the hiatuses created by the loss of stem-final consonants, e.g., *ostei̯on* > ὀστέον > ὀστοῦν, *plói̯os* > πλόος > πλοῦς.

Athematic stem types: the sub-classes

Athematic stems are traditionally divided into a number of sub-classes on the basis of the stem-final consonant. Each sub-class has its own peculiarities.

a) Stop-final stems. Nouns ending in a stop generally do not show any alteration of the pre-stop vowel. Exceptions are ἀλώπηξ, -εκος and πούς, ποδός. Outside of the nom. sg. γυνή, which is archaic, the word has become a stop stem γυναικ-.

b) Σ-stems. In this class the regular loss of intervocalic *s* has lead in Attic to contraction of the suffixal and desinential vowel, e.g., gen. sg. *ĝénh$_1$-es-os* > *génehos* > *géneos* (Ion. γένεος) > γένους. In addition to neuter σ-stems of the γένος type, the class comprises neuters in -ας (κρέας), adjectives and personal names in -ης (εὐμενής), and animate stems in -ως (αἰδώς). These last are normally remade in Attic either as Attic declension forms or as τ-stems.

c) Liquid stems. With the exception of ἅλς, these are all ϱ-stems. Important sub-classes are agent nouns in -τωϱ (δώτωϱ) and -τήϱ (δοτήϱ), relationship nouns in -τηϱ (πατήρ), neuter nouns with a nom.-acc. ending in -ǫ that alternates with an oblique stem in -ατ- < *-n̥-t-, e.g., ὕδωρ, ὕδατος; ἧπαρ, ἥπατος. These continue the PIE *r/n* heteroclites. Cf. Hitt. nom.-acc. *wadar*, gen. *weden-aš* "water."

d) N-stems. Most ν-stems have non-sigmatic nominatives (δαίμων), but a few have added an analogical -*s* (ῥίς < *rhīns, κτείς <*ktens). Some nouns display ablaut of the suffixal vowel (δαίμων, δαίμονος). Others do not (πώγων, πώγωνος). Neuters in -μα, -ματος (σῶμα, σώματος) are also historically *n*-stems since -μα is from *-mn̥. Cf. Lat. *car-men, carminis*.

e) I- and υ-stems. In Attic the unmarked type of ι-stem is the πόλις type with gen. in -εως and a stem in ε in the gen. and dat. pl. (πόλεων, πόλεσι). Outside of Attic this type is virtually unheard of, and instead we find a consistent stem in -*i*- (πόλιος, πόλιες, πόλῑς). The υ-stems are quite parallel showing a stem vowel -ε- in all case forms except the nom., voc., and acc. sg. Υ-stem adjectives have -εος in the gen. sg. (ἡδέος < *suādeu̯os) whereas υ-stem nouns have taken over the form -εως (ἄστεως) from the ι-stems. Beside these ι- and υ-stems there are also some ῡ-stems (ἰχθύς, ἰχθύος) which alternate between ῡ pre-consonantally and υ pre-vocalically. A very productive diphthongal stem type is formed by nouns with nominatives in -εύς. The underlying form of this suffix in most cases is /-ēu̯-/. Before a consonant ēu̯ is shortened to -eu̯- by Osthoff's Law (βασιλεῦσι). Before a vowel the glide was lost and the resulting sequence underwent quantitative metathesis or prevocalic shortening (βασιλέως, βασιλέᾱ, βασιλέων, βασιλέᾱς), and like-vowel contraction (βασιλεῖ, Old Att. βασιλῆς).

The ā/ă-stems and their subtypes

In Attic the first declension has a number of subtypes. First, there are the feminine stems in -η. These continue Proto-Greek * ā-stems (preserved unchanged in non-Attic-Ionic dialects) which have become η-stems by the Attic-Ionic shift of *ā to η [ɛ̄]. By Attic Reversion these have again become ā-stems after ε, ι, and ǫ (subtype ἡμέρᾱ). The endings of this type are derivable from the athematic endings added to the stem in the gen. sg., dat. sg., acc. sg., acc. pl., and the loc./dat. pl. of the Ἀθήνησι(ν) type. The other cases are either anomalous (the nom. sg. -η, which was always endingless, attests to the origin of this declension as a neuter) or analogical (the nom. pl. -αι has been remade after thematic -οι; the gen. pl. -ῶν derives from an *-āsōm of pronominal origin (cf. Ved. *tā́sām* "of these," fem.); the dat. pl. -αις, generalized as the sole dative plural after *c.* 420 BCE, is analogical to -οις. The nom.-acc. du. –ᾱ is modeled on the masc. nom. acc. du. -ω.

A second subdivision of the ā-stems is the μοῖρα, μοίρᾱς type. These nouns have an alternation between short *a* in the nominative (-ă) and accusative (-ăν) and long ā (realized normally as η) in the genitive and dative singular. The plural of this type is identical to the consistent long-vowel type. The suffix of this subtype continues the so-called *devī́* suffix (Ved. *devī́* "goddess"—see also ch. 12). In PIE the ablauting suffix *-ih₂ with a zero-grade in the strong cases (nom. *-ih₂, acc. *- ih₂m) and a full grade in the weak cases (gen. *-i̯eh₂s, dat. *-i̯eh₂ei) made feminines especially to athematic bases. In Greek, the regular phonological development of final *-ih₂ was *-i̯a. The *yod* was mainly eliminated by combinatory sound changes: $*smór\text{-}ih_2 > *mór\underset{.}{r}ia > μοῖρα$; $*mélit\text{-}ih_2 > *méli\underset{.}{t}ia > μέλιττα$.

A third type is constituted by the masculine η-stems. In Attic and many other dialects the nominative of masculine η-stems is characterized by a final -ς: πολίτης. The antiquity of this analogical introduction of -ς from the other declension classes to mark the masculine η-stems is debated. In Attic the genitive singular in -ου has simply been borrowed from the thematic stems and replaces the expected genitive $*\text{-}ās$. Other dialects show the reflex of a form $*\text{-}āo$ (Myc. -*a-o*, Ion. -εω) evidently remodeled in some fashion on the o-stem gen. sg. while it was still disyllabic ($*\text{-}oo, < *\text{-}oho < *\text{-}oh\underset{.}{i}o < *\text{-}os\underset{.}{i}o$).

Adjectives

Most adjectives follow the thematic declension for the masculine and neuter, and the η-stem declension for the feminine ἀγαθός, ἀγαθή, ἀγαθόν. Many compound thematic adjectives and some simplex adjectives do not have a distinct feminine, e.g., ἄδικος, ἄδικον. There are also athematic adjectives of the various nominal subtypes. Some have distinct feminine forms made with the *devī* suffix ($*\text{-}ih_2$) (ἡδύς, ἡδεῖα ἡδύ; μέλᾱς, μέλαινα, μέλαν). Others, predominantly *s*-stems and *n*-stems, have no distinct feminine (ἀληθής, ἀληθές "true," εὐδαίμων, εὔδαιμον "happy"). Gradable adjectives can make synthetic comparative and superlative forms. Primary comparatives and superlatives are made to a limited number of bases directly from the root with the suffixes -ίων or $*\text{-}\underset{.}{i}ōn\text{-}$ and -ιστος respectively (e.g., ἡδύς, ἡδ-ίων, ἡδ-ιστος; ταχύς, θάττων, τάχιστος). This suffixation is also found in the suppletive comparative stems like ἀγαθός, ἀμείνων, ἄριστος. The ν-stem declension of the primary comparative is a post-Mycenaean replacement of an older *s*-stem inflection still surviving in the alternative acc. masc. fem. sg. and nom. acc. neut. pl. βελτίω < $*\text{-}osa$ and nom. pl. masc. fem. βελτίους < $*\text{-}oses$.

The more productive comparative and superlative suffixes are -τερος and -τατος, which are added to the stem of the positive. In origin, the suffix $*\text{-}teros$ had differential or contrastive force mainly with pronominal and adverbial bases: $*k^wo\text{-}teros$ "which of two?," from the interrogative stem $*k^wo\text{-} > πότερος$. When the suffixes -τερος and -τατος are added to thematic bases with a short penultimate the presuffixal vowel appears as -ω, e.g., νέος > νεώτερος vs λεπτός > λεπτότερος. This long-vowel allomorph may be an old instrumental reutilized to fill a prosodic template.

Word Formation

Derivational morphology, also known as word formation, concerns the creation of new words either from roots (primary derivation), or from already derived words (secondary derivation), or the combination of two or more word stems (compounding). In Greek, derivational morphology often involves the addition of affixal material (external derivation), e.g., χάρι-ς → χαρί-εις, but sometimes proceeds by rearrangement of ablaut and/or accent position (internal derivation), e.g., λευκός "bright" → λεῦκος "whitefish." The subject of Greek derivational morphology is extremely complex and can barely be touched upon here. A few notable formants are exemplified below.

a) τόμος type: From a verbal root a *nomen actionis* could be made by adding the thematic vowel to the *o*-grade of the root. In such *nomina actionis* the root bore the accent: τρόχος "a race" ← τρέχω "run". When the τόμος type occurred in the second part of a *bahuvrīhi* (on this concept, see ch. 12), the first member could be interpreted as the object of the verbal noun (type δρυτόμος). This reinterpretation led to the creation of a compound type with an *o*-grade thematic noun in agential sense as second member, e.g., ἀνδροφόνος ← φόνος.

b) τομός type: An *o*-grade deverbal derivative with an accented thematic vowel was a *nomen agentis*, e.g., τροχός "wheel" ← τρέχω.

c) -εο- < *-ejo- made adjectives of material: χρύσεος < χρυσός. Cf. Lat. *argenteus* "of silver."

d) *-ijo- made primary deverbal adjectives, e.g., ἅγιος < ἅζομαι, and secondary genitival adjectives, e.g., σωτήριος ← σωτήρ. This suffix was used in some dialects to form patronymics, e.g., Hom. Τελαμώνιος Αἴας "Ajax son of Telamon," and the neuter was substantivized in diminutive function, e.g., παιδίον ← παῖς.

e) Four related suffixes with corresponding feminine byforms make instrument nouns from verbal bases. These are -τρον//-τρᾱ (λέκτρον ← λέχομαι, Hom. ῥήτρη ← *u̯erh₁- "speak" (ἐρέω)), -θρον /-θρᾱ (βάθρον ← βαίνω, κρεμάθρᾱ — κρεμάννυμι), -τλον (χύτλον ← χέω) and -θλον (γένεθλον ← ἐγένετο). All four variants have matches in other traditions.

Verbal Morphology

The PIE verb system inherited by Greek (see also ch. 12) was characterized by a three-way aspectual distinction into imperfective, perfective, and resultative stems. In the indicative of the imperfective stem a contrast was made between a non-past tense, the present, inflected with the primary endings, and a past tense, the imperfect, built with the secondary endings and the prefixed augment. The perfective did not have non-past forms, since perfective aspect and the descriptive character of the non-past tense are incompatible. The perfective and its past indicative stem are traditionally called the aorist. The non-past of the resultative stem is traditionally called the perfect. The resultative stem developed a past form with the secondary endings and the prefixed augment (at least) in the form of Indo-European ancestral to Greek and Indo-Iranian.

Greek has preserved the Indo-European situation more faithfully than most daughter languages. The chief structural innovation in Greek is the creation of new tense stem, the future, out of a PIE desiderative present formation. The chief semantic innovation, achieved completely only after Homer, was the reinterpretation of the resultative as a true perfect, i.e., a past event with current relevance. This reinterpretation brought the meaning of the perfect fairly close to that of the aorist and ultimately the perfect stem was almost entirely eliminated in post-Classical Greek.

Table 8.1 The Proto-Indo-European tense-aspect system

	Imperfective	*Perfective*	*Resultative*
Non-past	present	————	perfect
Past	imperfect	aorist	pluperfect (?)

Diathesis

The Greek verb also inherited a two-way contrast of diathesis from Proto-Indo-European. The active voice was contrasted with the middle voice at least in the imperfect and perfective stems through different sets of personal endings. The middle voice forms indicated a greater degree of subject affectedness. For some event types this greater degree of affectedness was an inherent feature of the verbal idea. Verbs representing those types are *media tantum*. For other event types, higher affectedness is optionally expressed by the use of middle personal endings. There was no distinct formal expression of passive, but the middle forms of certain event types did permit a passive reading. Overall, Greek preserved this system quite faithfully. The chief innovations were the creation of distinct passive forms for the future and aorist based on the suffix -(ϑ)η-.

Mood

The Greek moods continue the PIE moods in more or less unchanged function. These are the indicative, the subjunctive, and the optative. The imperative, sometimes classified as a mood, stands somewhat apart morphologically since it is expressed through a distinct set of endings and not through a suffixally formed modal stem as the other non-indicative moods are. Modal stems are formed in all three aspects.

The athematic optative is characterized by the suffix -ιη- ~ -ι-. This suffix continues PIE *-$i\acute{e}h_1$- which was added to the usually zero-grade root in the active singular and alternated with the zero-grade allomorph *-ih_1- elsewhere, e.g., *h_1s-$i\acute{e}h_1$-m > εἴην = Old Lat. *siem* ~ *h_1s-ih_1-ent > εἶεν = Old Lat. *sient*. Greek has optionally generalized the full grade of the suffix also to the plural (εἴησαν). The athematic paradigm has spread to ποιέω-type verbs to some extent: ποιοίην beside regular thematic ποιοῖμι. The σ-aorist optative in -ειας, -ειε, -ειαν probably replaced an earlier -ιε still preserved in the Cretan forms δικακσιε "judge," ϝερκσιεν "make." These continue a subtype of optative with zero-grade of the suffix (*-ih_1-) throughout the paradigm. The forms -ειας, -ειε, -ειαν are more common than -αις, -αι- -αιεν in Attic.

When derived from thematic stems the optative has the invariant shape -οι-. This morpheme continues the zero-grade of the optative suffix *-ih_1- appended to the *o*-grade of the thematic vowel: φέροι = Ved. *bháret*. The optative originally required secondary endings. Thus the 1 sg. φέροιμι is an innovation. The expected secondary ending is retained in the famous Arcadian optative ἐξελαυνοια.

The most basic exponent of the subjunctive is at least superficially identical to the thematic vowel. When the subjunctive is formed from an athematic stem the forms were originally identical to a thematic indicative. This pattern is retained in Homer and some dialects in the short vowel subjunctive: Lesb. κωλυσει, Hom. εὔξεαι subjunctives of athematic sigmatic aorist indicatives. Cf. Ved. *ásat*(*i*) subj., Lat. *erit* "will be," both continuing *$*h_1es$-e-ti* subj. of *$*h_1es$-ti* "is" (Ved. *ásti*, Lat. *est*). When the subjunctive vowel was added to a thematic stem the thematic vowel contracted with the subjunctive vowel creating the long vowel subjunctive, e.g., λείπῃ. Cf. Ved. *bhávāt*(*i*) built to the thematic indicative *bhávati* "is." The long vowel subjunctive spreads also to originally athematic stems already in Homer: πέμψωμεν (*Od.* 20.383) etc. Indo-Iranian shows both primary and secondary endings for the subjunctive. Greek may have traces of the same.

In PIE the imperative had distinctive forms in 2 sg. act. and perhaps mid. Elsewhere the forms were either identical to unaugmented forms with secondary endings (2 pl. act. and mid.) or derived from secondary forms by the addition of a particle. In 2 sg. for athematics the ending is either ø (ἴστη "stand!," cf. Lat. *ī* < *$*h_1ei$.*) or -θι (ἴσθι "be!"< *$*est^hi$ < *$*h_1sd^hi$*) < *- *d^hi*), cf. GAves. *z-dī* "be!" Thematic forms have no ending and the *e*-grade of the thematic vowel, e.g., ἄγε "drive" = Lat. *age*. The sigmatic aorist imperative form -σον, e.g., δεῖξον "show!" is an unclear innovation. The aorist imperatives δός, ἕς, θές, σχές may possibly continue old unaugmented secondary forms. The 3 sg. act. ending -τω continues *-*$tōd$. In Indo-Iranian and Latin this ending functions as the marker of the so-called future imperative. This form was originally person, number, and voice indifferent. A trace of -τω in non-third person use may be found in the Hesychian gloss ἐλθετῶ-ς· ἐλθέ (Salamis on Cyprus). In Greek the ending has been reanalyzed and incorporated into the unmarked imperative paradigm. Gk φερέτω < *$*b^heretōt$* ~ OL CAIDITOD. PIE also used *-*$tōt$ in the plural of future imperatives.

This under-differentiation was eliminated in various ways. In Attic a number of different solutions were tried out. The earliest appears to have been combing -τω with 3 pl. ind. -ντ- (cf. Rhod. γραφόντω) and then hyper-pluralizing this with the addition of the secondary 3 pl. morpheme -ν. The end result was Old Att. and Ion. φερόντων. A later solution was the addition of a secondary 3 pl. ending, either -ν or -σαν, directly to the 3 sg. imp. yielding forms like Att. ἔστων and after *c.* 300 BCE ἔστωσαν. For 3 mid. sg. and pl. Greek created a new distinctive form on the analogy 2 pl. act. ind. -τε: 2 pl. mid. indic. -σθε:: 3 sg. act. imp. -τω: X, X = 3 sg. mid. imp. -σθω, e.g., ἐπέσθω "let him follow." This form was originally both singular and plural, a situation preserved in Asia Minor: E. Ion. 3 sg. and pl. θέσθω, Rhod. ἐπιμελεσθω, but in Attic with various differentiations the 3 pl. mid. became -σθων, i.e., σθω + ν (Hom. Class. Att. ἐπέσθων), -ν- . . .σθω(ν), Arg. χρōνσθō < *$*k^hreónst^hō$*, Old Att. ἐπιμελόσθōν and -σθω + σαν in Late Att. and *Koine*.

Personal endings

The primary endings of Greek are used in the present indicative, the future indicative, the perfect middle, and all subjunctives. The secondary endings occur in the imperfect and aorist indicative and in all optatives. The endings of the perfect active remain distinct even in the Classical period, although they are classified as primary endings based on the 3 du. and 3 pl. forms. Greek also continues an inherited distinction between active and middle personal endings. The personal endings of thematic and athematic verbs differ fundamentally in the active singular. In other slots the thematic

Table 8.2   Primary verbal endings in Greek

	Athematic active	*Thematic active*	*Perfect*	*Athematic middle*	*Thematic middle*
1 sg.	-μι	-ω	-α	-μαι	-ομαι
2 sg.	-ς	-εις	-ας	-σαι	-εαι/-η
3 sg.	-σι	-ει	-ε	-ται	-εται
2 du.	-τον	-ε-τον	-τον	-σϑον	-εσϑον
3 du.	-τον	-ε-τον	-τον	-σϑον	-εσϑον
1 pl.	-μεν	-ο-μεν	-μεν	-μεϑα	-ομεϑα
2 pl.	-τε	-ε-τε	-τε	-σϑε	-εσϑε
3 pl.	-νσι	-ουσι	- ᾱσι	-νται	-ονται

Table 8.3   Secondary verbal endings in Greek

	Active	*Middle*
1 sg.	-ν, -α	-μην
2 sg.	-ς -σϑα	-σο
3 sg.	-ø	-το
2 du.	-τον	-σϑον
3 du.	-την	-σϑην
1 pl.	-μεν	-μεϑα
2 pl.	-τε	-σϑε
3 pl.	-ν, -σαν	-ντο

forms are underlyingly the athematic personal endings preceded by the ablauting thematic vowel *e/o.

In PIE the athematic active singular endings were *-*mi*, *-*si*, *-*ti* (see also table 12.5). 1 and 3 sg. continue these forms directly. In 2 sg. the expected reflex of *-*si* is continued in the monosyllabic forms εἶ "you are" < *$h_1ési$ < *$h_1és$-*si* and with recharacterization in φής. Elsewhere the athematic paradigms have introduced -ς (τίϑης, etc.), originally the secondary ending. 3 sg. -σι is regular in Att.-Ion., Myc. and Arc.-Cyp. from *-*ti*; cf. Dor. -τι and, with τ preserved after σ, ἐσ-τί. In 1 pl. some dialects have -μες (Dor., Arc.), which may have been the original primary ending, while -μεν may originally have been a secondary ending. 3 pl. -νσι < *-*nti* (cf. Dor. -ντι) is never seen on the surface in Attic. After the thematic vowel -ο- the *n is lost by the second compensatory lengthening giving -ουσι. In some categories of athematic verbs the 3 pl. ending was *-*enti*, which is continued in Myc. *e-e-si* /ehensi/ < *h_1s-*énti*. In some athematic paradigms, e.g., reduplicated present stem, the 3 pl. ending after a consonant was *-*n̥ti*. By regular phonological development this became *-*ati*. This form was recharacterized as 3 plural by the addition of an *n* and *-*anti* became –ᾱσι. –ᾱσι was generalized to give the 3 pl. forms τιϑέᾱσι, διδόᾱσι, ἱστᾶσι, ἵᾱσι.

The active secondary endings are distinct from the primary endings in the sg., the 3 du. and pl. In PIE these endings differed from the primary endings by the absence of the active primary marker *-i. These were *-m/*-m̥, *-s, *-t, *-teh₂m, *-nt. By sound change these became -ν//-α, -ς, -ø, -την, -ν. Beside 3 pl. -ν, preserved, e.g., in ἔλιπον, the allomorph -σαν extracted from the sigmatic aorist, has been widely extended in Attic, e.g., ἦσαν.

Distinct perfect endings are maintained only in the singular in Greek. The most archaic endings are preserved in the paradigm of "know" 1 sg. οἶδ-α, 2 sg. οἶσ-θα (< *u̯oid- tʰa), 3 sg. οἶδ-ε. Cf. Ved. 1 sg. *véd-a*, 2 sg. *vét-tha*, 3 sg. *véd-a*. These endings continue the PIE *-h₂e endings, which were originally not limited to resultative forms and ultimately are related to the endings of the middle. The 2 sg. -θα has, with the exception of οἶσ-θα, been replaced with -ας, imported from the σ-aorist. In 3 pl. Greek has effaced any trace of the PIE *r*-ending (Lat. *-ēre*, Ved. *-ur*). The first replacement was -ασι (Hom. πεφύκασι) < -ατι (Delph. ἱερητευκατι) < *-n̥ti original to the reduplicated presents. As in the athematic presents this ending was recharacterized by the insertion of *n and when this *n was lost by the second compensatory lengthening the result was -ᾱσι.

The primary middle endings, originally very similar to the perfect endings, have by analogical remodelings become more like the active forms. They have acquired the same primary marker -ι, replacing the earlier distinct middle primary marker *-r (preserved and generalized in Lat. *-tur*, etc.). In most dialects, except Arc., Cyp., and Myc., the *a*-vocalism proper to 1 sg. has been generalized to all of the singular replacing -σοι and -τοι with -σαι and -ται. The 2 and 3 du. form -σθον has been created in Greek on the model -τε : -τον :: -σθε : X, X = -σθον.

The secondary middle endings of 2 and 3 sg. and 3 pl. (-(σ)ο, -το, -ντο) preserve the original *o*-vocalism. The long η of 1 sg. -μην, non-Att.-Ion. -μᾱν, continues *-h₂eh₂e (> *-ā), a reduplicated form of the ending *-h₂e also found in Hittite. The μ- and -ν are the result of approximations to both -μι and -ν in the 1 sg. act.

Stem Formation

Aorist stems may be built in a number of different fashions.

a) Root aorists affix the endings to the uncharacterized root. Full-grade occurs in the singular and originally 1 and 2 pl: ἔβην ἔβημεν = Ved. *ágām ágāma*. Middle root aorists have zero-grade throughout with some exceptions φθάμενος (: ἔφθην). *k*-aorists (of unclear origin) replace the root aorists of δίδωμι, τίθημι, and ἵημι in the singular ἔθηκα, ἔδωκα, ἧκα ~ ἔθεμεν ἔδομεν, εἷμεν. Boeotian preserves an unextended form in ἀνεθη.

b) Thematic aorists are characterized by a zero-grade root and thematic endings. Before the assignment of recessive accent to finite verbal forms the thematic vowel bore the accent. This pattern survives exceptionally in the imperatives ἰδέ, λαβέ, ἐλθέ and regularly in the participle (λιπών) and infinitive (λιπεῖν). Few thematic aorists can be traced to PIE, and many examples replace older athematic root aorists. e.g., ἔκλυον vs κλῦθι, Κλύμενος = Ved. *á-śro-t* "heard." Thematic aorists often pattern with *e*-grade thematic presents: ἔλιπον ~ λείπω, ἔδρακον ~ δέρκομαι, a pattern elaborated in Greek. Another common pattern is co-occurrence with present stems in -N-C-άνω, e.g., ἔλαθον ~ λανθάνω, ἔλαβον ~ λαμβάνω. The thematic aorist is on the decline in Greek. In *Koine* we find forms like ἔπεσα replacing earlier ἔπεσον (see ch. 16).

c) Reduplicated aorist: formula $C_i e C_i C$-*é/ó*-. These forms frequently have factitive sense in Greek though there is no factitive sense in the inherited examples. * $h_1 é$-$g^{wh}eg^{wh}nét$ > ἔπεφνε "killed," aor. of θείνω; *$h_1 é$ -uek^w-*et* > ἔειπε "said" = Ved. *ávocat*.

d) The *s-aorist* or sigmatic aorist was characterized in the form of PIE ancestral to Greek and Indo-Iranian by a marker -*s*- added directly to the lengthened-grade of the root: *($é$)-$deĩk$-*s*-m "showed" > ἔδειξα, GAves. 3 sg. *dāiš*, Lat. *dīxī* "said." In Greek sound change and analogy have eliminated the evidence for the lengthened grade. The sigmatic aorist paradigm was athematic, but has generalized a stem vowel -α- from the reflex of the vocalic nasal in 1 sg. (-α < -m) and 3 pl. (-σαν < *-*sa+n* << *-*snt*). The original athematic status of the sigmatic aorist is also shown by the short vowel subjunctive, found frequently in Homer and the dialects. 3 sg. -ε is probably by analogy to the perfect. The *s* combining with roots ending in a nasal is lost with compensatory lengthening of the preceding vowel in the non-Aeolic dialects: φαίνω ~ ἔφηνα; κρίνω ~ ἔκρῑνα; most liquid final stems follow this pattern (analogically at least in part): στέλλω ~ ἔστειλα; καθαίρω ~ ἐκάθηρα. The sigmatic aorist is very productive. It provides the aorist for most types of denominative verbs and all contract presents: φιλέω ~ ἐφίλησα; τῑμάω ~ ἐτίμησα; δουλόω ~ ἐδούλωσα; βασιλεύω ~ ἐβασίλευσα. The sigmatic aorist, especially when opposed to a root aorist, has transitivizing function: ἔστην "stood" intr., ἔστησα "stood up", tr.

e) The -η- intransitive aorist. The aorist passive in Greek is not essentially a passive but an intransitive: ἐχάρην "I rejoiced," ἐμάνην "I went crazy." This stem form is characterized by the stative suffix -η- < *-eh_1, cf. Lat. *tacēre*, *habēre*. The -θη- aorist, as in τάθη "stretched" ~ τείνω and ἐστάθη ~ ἵστημι is in origin the same as the -η- aorist, but has been extended by a -θ- which arose by analogy: -ἔπλησα (← πίμπλημι), *ἐπλήθη (< πλήθω) :: ἔλυσα, X X = ἐλύθη.

From the present stem were made in PIE the present in all its moods, and the imperfect. The present indicative was characterized by primary endings. The imperfect was characterized by secondary endings and the augment. The augment is found in Greek, Indo-Iranian, Armenian, and Phrygian. The following stem formations are notable:

a) Root presents were formed by affixing the ending directly to the root. The root had accented *e*-grade in the active singular and zero-grade elsewhere, e.g., *$h_1 éi$-*ti* "(s)he goes": > εἶσι,Ved. *éti*, *$h_1 i$-*més* "we go" >> ἴμεν, Ved. *imáh*; *$h_1 és$-*ti* 'is' > ἐστί, Ved. *ásti*.

b) Reduplicated presents. Greek has partially conflated two distinct types of reduplicated presents: i) *i*-reduplicated thematic (originally *-$h_2 e$ presents), e.g., γίγνεται, Lat. *gignit* < *$ĝiĝnh_1 e$-; ii) *e*-reduplicated athematic presents of the type best preserved in Vedic *dádhāti* "makes, puts" < *$d^h é$-$d^h eh_1$-*ti*. In Greek some of the *i*-reduplicated type have been dethematized, e.g., ἵστησι, and the athematic *e*-reduplicated type have been maintained as athematics but have changed to *i*-reduplication, e.g., Gk δίδωσι "gives" vs Ved. *dádāti* < **dé-deh₃-ti*.

c)   Greek inherited from PIE a class of presents which were characterized by an ablauting infix **-né-* in the singular active **-n-* elsewhere inserted into the zero-grade of the root: **ieug-* "yoke" > **iu-né-g-ti, *iu-n-g-énti*. This type of stem often provided presents to root aorists. In Greek the two most productive subtypes of the nasal-infix class are i) those built to roots ending in the second laryngeal (Hom. δάμνημι, δάμναται "overpower" < **dm̥-ne-h₂-ti, *dm̥-nh₂-toi*; aor. ἐδάμασσε). Attic retains only δύναμαι. Otherwise, these presents are replaced with new formations (δαμάζω, κεράννυμι, etc.); ii) those built to roots ending in *-u-*, (Hom. κίνυτο < **(é)-ki-n-u-to*, aor. ἔσσευα < **é-kieu-m̥*). The latter class was widely generalized to become the productive -vῡ- ~ -vυ- suffix, e.g., ζεύγνῡμι "yoke," δείκνῡμι "show," The nasal infix into stop-final roots, which survives in Lat. *rumpō* (pf. *rūpī*) etc., has been eliminated. The productive -N-. . . -ανο/ε- type (πυνθάνομαι ~ ἐπυθόμην) probably arose via a reinterpretation of examples like χανδάνω < **ĝʰn̥d-n-h̥ₓ-e-* which may be analyzed as originally denominative to **-eh₂* stems.

d)   Simple thematic presents are formed by affixing the ablauting thematic vowel **-e-/*-o-* to the root normally, but not exclusively, in the *e*-grade, e.g., ἔχει = Ved. *sáhati* < **seĝʰ-e-*; σείει = Ved. *tvésati* < **tuéis-e-*. This type was highly productive in many Indo-European traditions including Greek, where it is often seen replacing older formations, e.g., λείπω, which replaced a nasal infix present continued in Lat. *linquō*.

e)   **-ie-/-io-* presents. The suffix **-ie-/-io-* made both deverbative and denominal present stems. A variety of sound changes have obscured the suffix. Some deverbative **-ie-/-io-* presents are middle only: **mn̥-ie/o-* > μαίνομαι, Ved. *mányate*. Others are not, e.g., βαίνω < **gʷm̥-ie/o-*, Lat. *veniō*. Some examples of denominative **-ie-/-io-* presents: ὀνομαίνω, from the original *n*-stem ὄνομα. Cf. Hitt. *lamniya-* "to name"; from voiceless dental and velar stems: φυλάττω <**pʰulak-iō*, cf. φύλαξ, ἐρέττω, < **eret-iō*, cf. ἐρετμόν; from voiced velar stems: σαλπίζω < **salping-iō*, cf. σάλπιγξ; from labial final stems: βλάπτω < **blaP-iō*, cf. βλάβη. From -ευς nouns were formed the βασιλεύω type. The regular outcome of **basileuiō* is βασιλείω, which is preserved in Elean, but elsewhere -ευω has been restored on the basis of extra-present forms.

f)   When added to vocalic bases the *yod* of the suffix was lost in the intervocalic position. From thematic bases the suffix added to the *e*-grade produced the φιλέω type, with subsequent contractions in Attic. The τιμάω type derives predominantly from denominals built to *ā*-stems. The δουλόω factitive type is back-formed on the model of the other contract types from denominal adjectives.

g)   **-ske-/*-sko-* presents. Greek inherited a present-stem forming suffix of this shape, but its PIE function is hard to determine. In Latin it forms inchoatives (*crēscō* "increase"). In Tocharian it makes causatives. In Anatolian and in Ionian Greek it makes iteratives/imperfectives (φεύγεσκε "was fleeing" iteratively, Hitt. *peske-* "give" iterative of *pāi-*). The suffix is typically added to the zero-grade of the root, e.g., Hom. βάσκε "go!" < **gʷm̥-ské-*, cf. Ved. *gácchati*. ἔρχεται continues an original **-ske-/*-sko-* presents **h₁r̥-ské-* (Ved. *r̥ccháti*, Hitt. *arškizi*) obscured by sound change.

b) o-grade iterative with suffix *-éịe-/*-éịo-*. Another source for -έω contract verbs are the derived o-grade deverbals with the suffix *-éịe-/*-éịo-*. In Greek these survive only as lexicalized forms in iterative function, e.g., φορέω "wear" < *b^horéịe/o-* "carry around" derived from φέρω "carry." Elsewhere this formation also makes causatives, e.g., Lat. *monet* "warns" < *mon-éịe-ti* "causes to think" < *men-* "think."

With the exception of ((ϝ)οἶδα), which may historically not have been a perfect at all, the perfect stem is always characterized by reduplication. The original ablaut pattern, still preserved in ((ϝ)οἶδα) ~ ϝίδμεν/ἴσμεν and a few other traces in Homer, was o-grade in the indicative singular and zero-grade elsewhere. Most paradigms have leveled the ablaut or introduced the ablaut grade of the corresponding present. There are a number of reduplication peculiarities. "Attic reduplication" is the result of laryngeal lengthening: *h_1l(e)ud^h-* "come" (ἐλυϑ-) → *$h_1$le-$h_1$loud^h-e* > *ἐλήλουϑε* with metrical lengthening Hom. εἰλήλουϑε. When a root began with a consonant cluster, reduplication was replaced with ἐ-: ἔζευγμαι, ἔψευσμαι. This probably originates in perfects like ἔσχημαι < *hesk^{h}ēmai* < *sesk^{h}ēmai*.

The κ formant of the κ-perfects, apparently created on the pattern of the κ-aorist, was originally limited to the singular: ἕστηκα ~ ἕσταμεν; βέβηκα ~ βέβαμεν. In post-Homeric Greek the κ-perfect enjoyed great success, and supplied the perfect for all denominatives, e.g., τετίμηκα.

a) *The aspirated perfect.* In transitive perfects ending in a labial or velar the stem-final consonant was aspirated. The aspiration arose in 2 pl. mid., 3 sg. imp. mid., and infinitive where the *-s-* of the ending was lost with aspiration, e.g., Hom. τετράφϑω < *tetr̥p-st^{h}ō*; τετάχϑαι < *tetak-st^{h}ai*. From there it spread to the 3 pl. mid., e.g., τετράφαται (Hom.) ~ τρέπω, τετάχαται (Thuc.) ~ τάττω, then to the active with transitive sense, τέταχε.

b) The *perfect middle* was perhaps not fully elaborated in PIE, although it exists as a category in Greek and Vedic. In Greek it is characterized by reduplication, zero-grade root and athematic, primary endings: στέλλω ~ ἔσταλμαι τείνω ~ τέταμαι. The Proto-Attic-Ionic 3 pl. ending should have been -αται < *-n̥tai*. This form is well attested in Ionic and other dialects, e.g., τετάφαται (Hdt. 6.103) ~ θάπτω, etc. Attic has replaced this with a periphrasis made up of the perfect middle participle and 3 pl. of the verb "to be," e.g., λελειμμένοι εἰσί(ν).

c) The *pluperfect*, if it existed in PIE, as now seems probable, was made from the (augmented and) reduplicated perfect stem with secondary, athematic (*-mi* type) endings. This type is essentially preserved in Homer in the middle, and in the dual and plural of the active, e.g., Hom. εἵμαρτο < *sesmr̥to*, Att. ἐλέλυτο. But in the active singular, innovative forms have arisen: Homer has 1 sg. ἤδεα, 3 sg. ἤδη and ἤδεε, but in other pluperfects -ει predominates. Classical Attic has introduced the -ε- as a theme vowel throughout the dual and plural, e.g., ἐλελοίπεμεν.

The Greek futures are in origin desideratives, morphologically comparable to the Vedic desiderative formation. Roots ending in an obstruent affix the suffix -σ- and the thematic endings to the e-grade root. Roots ending in a sonorant consonant make so-called contract futures. Many futures to active presents are deponent. This is consistent with their desiderative origin: from the root of ἔλυθε the future is ἐλεύσεται < *$h_1léud^h$-se-; from the root of μένω the future is μενῶ < μενέω. This distribution of future formants in Greek continues a PIE pattern whereby the desiderative morpheme had the shape *-$h_1$se/o- after roots ending in a sonorant consonant and the shape *-se/o- after other roots. The laryngeal-initial form of the suffix led regularly to the contract future type. After long vowels the -σ- of the future is analogically restored, e.g., φιλήσω not †φιλή(*h*)ω, but not after short vowels (with some exceptions) *men-h_1ō > *$menes\bar{o}$ > μενέω > μενῶ. The so-called Doric futures in *-σεο//ε-, e.g., Delph. κλεψεω (in Attic only in the middle, e.g., φευξοῦμαι < φεύγω) are a contamination of *-se- futures and contract futures. The future morpheme was also added to the perfect stem to create the future perfect, which predominantly occurs in the middle (λελείψεται).

Originally the future middle could also be used as passive, e.g., πέρσεται (*Il.* 24.729) "will be destroyed." New distinctively passive futures in -ησε- and -θησε- were built to the aorist passive, e.g., μιγήσεσθαι (the only future passive in Hom.) < ἐμίγην vs μείξεσθαι.

Nominal Forms of the Verb

Participles

The present-aorist participle suffix was built with the suffix *-(o)nt- added to the aspect stem. Cf. Lat. *sōns, sontis* "guilty,", originally the participle of *sum*. In reduplicated and sigmatic aorist participles the suffix appears in the zero-grade -*nt*-. The masc. nom. sg. of these participles is from *-V̥nts, e.g., τιθείς < *tit^hents, λύσᾱς < *$l\bar{u}sants$. This form in thematic paradigms should be †-ους < *-ont-s, but instead we find -ων, identical to the nom. sg. of animate ν-stems.

The perfect participle is formed with the suffix -ότ-, (masc. nom. sg. - ώς) from earlier *-ṷot–. This suffix has become a τ-stem only in post-Mycenaean times since Mycenaean attests s-stem forms like neut. pl. *a-ra-ru-wo-a* "fitted" /arāruoha/ ~ Hom. ἀρηρότα. The archaic character of the s-stem is vouched for by the evidence of the feminine ἰδυῖα < *ṷid-us-ih₂ and the evidence of other traditions, e.g., Ved. *vidúṣaḥ*, Aves. *viduš̄ō* "knowing" gen. sg. < *ṷid-us-ós.

The suffix -μενος of the middle participle is widely thought to continue PIE *V-mh_1nos. Cf. TB -*mane*, Lat. *alu-mnus* "nursling" with *alō* 'nourish'. But if this reconstruction is correct, the middle participle would have had a highly unusual shape for an inflectional morpheme.

Verbal adjectives

The verbal adjective in -τό- has not become a fully integrated participle in Greek as it has in Latin. These forms are usually built to zero-grade of the root *$t\d{n}tós$ > τατός not to a characterized aspect-tense stem. Although typically given a passive reading they were originally diathesis-indifferent e.g., ἄγνωστος "ignorant" and "unknown"; cf. Lat.

pōtus "drunk" (of a person). Verbal adjectives in -τό- originally showed a preference for occurring in the second part of compounds, e.g., Pl. *Soph.* 249d ὅσα ἀκίνητα καὶ κεκινημένα, Myc. *de-de-me-no* = δεδεμένω vs *ka-ko-de-ta* = χαλκόδετα.

The verbal adjective of necessity in -τέος does not occur in Homer. The suffix -τέο- probably continues *-teu̯o-*, a derivative of a verbal noun in *-tu-*; (>> Latin supines like *laudātum*).

Infinitives

The infinitive is usually a fossilized case form of an old verbal noun. In Greek infinitives were integrated into the tense-aspect system. The thematic infinitive -εɩν is from *-e-sen*; cf. Myc. *e-ke-e* /(h)ekʰehen/, ἔχεɩν. This form appears to continue a locative in *-en* made to a neuter *s*-formant appended to a thematic stem; cf. Ved. *neṣáṇ-i* "to lead" < *-s-en-i* from the root *nay-* "lead."

The athematic infinitive *-(e)nai* found in Attic-Ionic, and Arcadian (εἶναι, Arc. ἦναι < *esenai*) looks like a directive case of an *n*-stem. The same suffix is used for the pf. inf. πεποɩθέναι.

Other dialects have infinitives derived from case forms of *men*-stems, e.g., -μεν in Lac. El. ἦμεν, an endless locative to an *men*-stem; cf. Ved. *dā́-mane* "to give" and -μεναι in Lesb. Hom. δόμεναι, ἔμμεναι, perhaps the directive of a *men*-stem or the product of analogy.

FURTHER READING

The best account of Greek morphology is Chantraine 1991, which is the only book-length treatment of the subject. Rix 1992 is also useful. Both are more out-of-date than their dates of publication suggest. For the verb, Duhoux 2000 is an insightful account of morphology and syntax. For nominal derivational morphology, Chantraine 1933 is unsurpassed, and Debrunner 1917, on both the noun and the verb, is still useful. For derivational morphology of Homer, see Risch 1974. For the evidence of Attic inscriptions, see Threatte 1996. Buck and Petersen 1948 is an invaluable tool. Jasanoff 2003 puts the PIE background of the Greek verb in an entirely new light.

CHAPTER NINE

Semantics and Vocabulary

Michael Clarke

I do not really know Ancient Greek, nor do any of the contributors to this *Companion*. To claim knowledge of a language, you must be a member of its speech-community, open to the possibility that the categories of its grammar and vocabulary may mold and be molded by the structures of your thoughts and worldview. This cannot happen if we engage with the language only in a library. Knowledge of language depends on acquaintance; knowledge by description is not enough.

This leads to an uncomfortable paradox. If I learnt enough Arabic or Chinese to order a meal in a restaurant, and if I went to Riyadh or Beijing and did so, I would have a better claim on that language than I have on Homer's mother tongue after many years of daily engagement with his words. Yet, despite this simple fact, for centuries classical scholars have claimed an authoritative understanding of Ancient Greek and the ways that literary artists communicated meaning through its words. Until recently, professors of Classics had typically absorbed the language as children, making the slippage of thought especially easy (cf. Stray 1998: 7–113). Little was written about fundamentals of word-meaning, except piecemeal in textual commentaries; and even among specialists in Indo-European linguistics the reconstruction of lexical semantics was underdeveloped compared to phonology or grammar (see Clackson 2007: 187–215; Benveniste 1969 [1973]). Now things have changed, if only because we typically come fresh to Greek as adults, and we can engage with it as a system of thought and expression which is utterly different from our own, challenging our assumptions about linguistic structure.

Reading the Words of the Greek Language

To read an ancient text is to translate it, mapping its words one by one onto the semantic units of our own mother-tongue vocabulary. The word-to-word match between the two languages can never be perfect. This is familiar from the vocabulary of ethics and cultural institutions. The noun αἰδώς, famously, turns up in translation as "shame" or "pride" or "respect," and it takes 500-odd pages of anthropological and literary study to restore the word's meaning in ancient thought and social practice (Cairns 1993). Such words prompt the classic question of linguistic relativity (Lucy 1992; Gentner and Goldin-Meadow 2003). When the categories of the Greek language fail to match those of our own language, does this imply that there is a corresponding gulf in the ways that speakers of the two languages see the world and categorize experience?

Although this question is prompted most starkly by words for deep cultural or religious concepts, like αἰδώς, it extends in principle to the entire lexicon. Yet the habits we acquire as learners seem designed to hide the depth of our estrangement. Handbooks are full of mismatches and approximations, passed down from the days when perfectionism was a recipe for disaster in the classroom. The learner is taught to match ἀγορά to "marketplace," and on s/he goes until s/he gradually realizes that the ἀγορά was not strictly a place for buying and selling at all – rather, it was the central public space in which adult male citizens carried out the duties and activities of political responsibility. Or s/he is taught to translate the verb τυγχάνω as "I chance to be. . .," even though those English words are virtually meaningless and would never nowadays be spoken; or s/he renders a strange poetic adjective in strange obscure English – for example Homer's famous Ἴλιος ὀφρυόεσσα (*Il.* 22.411) becomes "beetling Troy," glossing over the fact that the adjective seems on the face of it to mean no more and no less than "having eyebrows" (Richardson 1993: 150; cf. Silk 1983). The culprit behind all this is pedagogical strategy: the beginner needs clarity and handy rules to help him or her become fluent, and gradually s/he is supposed to reach a level where his or her mind processes the Greek without a filter of translation. In practice, however, this never really happens: I cannot tell you confidently what the above three words mean, nor have I met anyone who can, but we make a living all the same.

One source of authority remains: the printed dictionary. Consider first what happens when we use a dictionary designed for learners, the *Pocket Oxford Classical Greek Dictionary* (Morwood and Taylor 2002). No difficulty emerges with the rarer and more difficult words. For these, typically, either the referent is precise and limited in definition or the word fits snugly into a particular sociocultural context. We look up ἐρέβινθος or πυράγρα, the dictionary gives "chickpea" and "a pair of fire-tongs"; we look up πρυτανεία or ἴχωρ and the dictionary refers us clearly and helpfully to the contexts in which these words took on their meanings – the term of office of a particular public authority, the immortal substitute for blood that flows in the gods' veins. But what happens when we look up the simple radical words that are central to the functioning of the language? I take as typical examples a verb, a preposition, and a noun:

τίθημι] *put, place, set, lay; inter; ordain, establish, order, fix; reckon, count; estimate, esteem, consider; suppose; make, cause, create, effect, appoint;* [middle] *take up one's quarters, bivouac; lay down one's arms, surrender*

ἀνά] *upwards, above, on high, on the top, thereon;* [preposition with accusative case] *up, upwards; through, throughout, along, about; during; up to, according to, with;* [with dative case] *on, upon* δόξα] *opinion, notion; expectation; false opinion, delusion, fancy; decree, project; judgment; reputation, report, honour; glory, splendour*

These jumbled arrays of handy equivalents do not tell us what the Greek words mean, how they each map out a territory of concepts or experiences. Nor is it clear why the semi-colon and the comma break up each entry: are we to imagine each word as an archipelago, several islands of meaning clustered together in a sea of thought? A learners' dictionary is of course constrained by considerations of compactness and speed of reference, but the same problem will arise wherever the dictionary relies for its entries on a list of English-language alternatives that do not immediately add up to a unified concept. As we will see below, the same problem looms just as large with the most authoritative and scholarly lexicon of them all.

If we are to give an account of a Greek word's meaning, we must move toward the actual shape of the entry in the mental lexicon of a member of the ancient speech-community. This takes us toward a basic problem of psycholinguistics. Common sense as well as neuroscience suggest that the structure of such an entry will be diffuse and unbounded. When the language-user hears a word, this activates the cumulative trace of all previous instances to which he has been exposed, and the mind engages with as much of that trace as is required to understand the word in its context (Pulvermüller 2002: 50–65; Garman 1990: 239–369). It is impossible to squeeze this extended and boundless entity into an account that a reader from another world can grasp. However, idealism can be saved if we focus less on the cognitive basis of comprehension than on the communicative contract that binds speaker and listener together. When the speaker selects a given word and uses it, he does so not because of what it means to himself but because of what he expects it to mean to his listener. So he relies on an internalized approximation of the mental lexicon of his peers. This can be seen as a tool in the apparatus of *metacognition*, of second-guessing the mental realities of others (Carruthers and Chamberlain 2000). If the approximation is to be useful, it must be quick and easy to access its entries and extract meaning from them: in a sense, then, the language-user is making constant reference to something a little like a dictionary. Since people understand each other, the "inner dictionaries" of all competent speakers should be roughly similar, so with only a little simplification we can speak of them collectively as *the public lexicon*. The dictionary's realistic task is to approximate the cognitive realities of the entries in this lexicon.

The key feature of the public lexicon is its practical usefulness, which depends in turn on simplicity and elegance. Each entry must perform a mapping from the diffuse toward the punctual, from the multiplicity of a word's surface uses toward a source or center of meaning which motivates them all and which ensures that each new use will convey meaning in the appropriate way. For us, correspondingly, the lexical reconstruction of an Ancient Greek word becomes the task of uncovering a single center or focus of meaning from which the word's attested uses all proceed. If there are in fact several such centers (or even none at all) this will emerge in the form of a defeat: that is, through our failure to find a unity on examination of the observable usage-patterns (Clarke 1999: 31–6). If on the other hand we begin with a cheerful willingness to split the word into several parts, we will run the risk either of stopping short of the most fundamental level of meaning or (worse) of cutting the word up into fantasy chunks based on the semantic shapes of the foreign language in which we ourselves think and speak. The policy is thus a version of Occam's Razor: "Entities should not be multiplied beyond necessity," not because we can be sure in advance that there is a one-to-one correspondence between word and concept but because we will drag ourselves further toward the Greek realities if we refuse to settle for multiplicity or chaos. Here we enter a territory where there is little help from the academic literature in lexical semantics. A major theme in this literature is the development of tests to establish that a word is polysemous, characterized by several more-or-less distinct meanings; but there is no available methodology for proving the opposite (Cruse 1986: 49-83; Ravin and Leacock 2000; Pustejovsky and Boguraev 1996).

Unity and Disunity in LSJ

We come now to the major resource of the discipline, the *Greek-English Lexicon* of Liddell-Scott-Jones (LSJ). This dictionary has grown continuously from edition to edition since it was first compiled by members of the generation of High Victorian scholars that also gave the world the *Oxford English Dictionary* (Silva 2000: 78–9). LSJ, like the *OED*, is famous for dividing its entries into hierarchies of subtle subsections. Here as a typical example is the outline structure of its account of the familiar verb τυγχάνω:

A. *happen to be at* a place
      2. of events, and things generally, *happen to* one, *befall* one, *come to* one's *lot*
      3. in relative clauses, as *it happened*, i.e. *any*how, at *any* time, place etc
   II. joined with the participle of another verb to express a coincidence

B. *gain one's end* or *purpose, succeed;*
      – participle combined with [a main verb of striking] so that the whole phrase
       means *hit*;
   II. *hit upon, light upon*
      1. *meet, fall in with* persons
      2. light on a thing; attain, obtain a thing.

The two halves of the definition are at loggerheads with each other: the first revolves around the idea of coincidence, of the fortuitous coming-together of events, while the second centers on the deliberate, the well-aimed, that which strikes a target. The arrangement of the entry is thoroughly arbitrary: and there is no better testimony to this than the curious fact that in Liddell and Scott's original editions the two parts were placed in the opposite sequence: "A. to hit, esp. to hit the mark with an arrow . . .; B. to happen, come to pass, fall out, be be by chance . . .". (Liddell and Scott 1847: 1417) – an arrangement that survives to this day in the abridged student version of the work, whose entries have remained frozen for 116 years (Liddell and Scott 1891: 720). There is no telling why the sections were switched; but it is clear that we are left now with a pseudo-definition which has no heart.

Perhaps the most glaring fault of LSJ is the fact that there is no explanation of the intended significance of the subdivisions: are they meant to show how the word separates into parts with distinguishable meanings, or do they merely guide the eye and mind of the reader as he picks his way through a dense paragraph of interchanging Greek and English? The history of the dictionary's younger cousin, the *OED*, throws a remarkable sidelight on the question. The *OED*'s first editor, James Murray, writes as follows in a rebuke to a contributor who was over-fond of dividing his definitions into subsections:

> As Dean Liddell said to me long ago, "Everybody can make distinctions: it is the lexicographer's business to make broad definitions which embrace them; the analytic power is far above the synthetic." (cited by Silva 2000: 86)

The practice of dividing entries into subsections seems to have begun as a way of guiding the reader from the apparent chaos of his first glance toward an ordered analysis of how the word's uses relate to each other: in the words of the original Proposal for the publication of the *OED*, to show ". . . the development of the sense or various senses of each word from its etymology and from each other, so as to bring into clear light *the common thread which binds all together*" (Silva 2000: 79). With hindsight, we can see that this was ambiguous, in that the development of senses over time was not adequately distinguished from the inner organization of the word's semantic structure. This problem is clearly visible in the history of the Greek work: Liddell and Scott modeled themselves at first on the entries in the Greek-German lexicon of Passow, which was based on Homeric Greek alone. Each entry thus began with the Homeric data and further, later uses were fitted in as seemed appropriate, with new subsections added on for uses not found in Homer at all (Jones 1925: i). The mantra was that "each word should be allowed to tell its own story," and it seems to have been implicit in this that the story would be a fluid and continuous one, making the numbered sections no more than an expository tool. But this principle remained unclear, and its basis was obscured as the growth of the book spawned more and more subdivisions within the entries.

The very authority of the book seems to have stifled the possibility of debate on this point. A rare exception is the essay contributed by John Chadwick in the introduction to a series of essays on problem words in LSJ, where he conjures up a striking image:

> [The lexicographer] knows very well that the true relationship between the senses [of a given word] is too complex to be represented by less than a three-dimensional model. The figure of a tree, with a root sending up a trunk which branches in all directions, and each branch sending out boughs and finally twigs, would be hard enough to represent in a linear sequence. But the senses of a complex word can sometimes be shown to have undergone mutual influence, as if the branches have not simply diverged, but at a later stage merged again. (Chadwick 1996: 12)

It is hard to say how the image of the tree relates to a model of psycholinguistic reality, or why any such structure should be characterized by branches that separate out and merge again. In the absence of any positive knowledge as to the appropriate structure to shape an entry in our lexicon, the insistent quest for unities will provide us with the best starting point for a disciplined attempt.

Prototype Semantics

How can we improve on this? Our task is not to jump from a word in Greek to a word in English, from a signifier in one language to a signifier in another. Rather, it is to move from the diverse uses of the Greek signifier back to whatever concept was *represented* by it, explaining in each case the associative logic which allowed the ancient speech-community to link each referent to that concept whenever the word was used. This challenge has been elegantly formulated by Émile Benveniste (1966) for Indo-European semantic reconstruction, but his method leads potentially to vagueness and mystification (Clackson 2007: 194–5). Modern tools for a disciplined approach to the problem can, however, be found in the developing methodologies of the Cognitive Linguistics school, as developed by Charles Fillmore and Dirk Geeraerts (Fillmore 1982; Geeraerts 1998: 12–17 and *passim*; Fillmore and Atkins 1992, 2000; summary overview, Taylor 1995: 39–80; application to Greek materials, Bakker 1988: 14–21).

In the approach developed by this school, the lexical semantics of a given word is separated onto two levels. The underlying concept is termed the *prototype*, and the word's referents exemplify what the speech-community recognized as *instantiations* of the prototype. (Note that "proto-" here refers not to priority in time but to primacy in the structural configuration.) At its simplest, the structure might be plotted as shown in fig. 9.1.

This reduces the data and the challenge to the bare essentials. In fig. 9.1, we have a series of attestations at which the word is applied to a series of points of reference (R1, R2 etc); below, we have the prototypical concept which justified each of those applications and ensured that they conveyed meaning from speakers to listeners. The model refuses to fall back on the traditional labels of subdivision: there is no room for connotation versus denotation, for multiple numbered senses, or for the array of arcane abbreviations – *fig.*, *transf.*, *metaph.* – that traditionally link together the sub-sections of a dictionary definition. Once we accept that the instantiations are likely to have related to the prototype in an ordered rather than chaotic way, it follows that the real challenge is to characterize the prototype – here, to replace "????" with an adequate verbal formula. Since English is our interpretative metalanguage, we will only be able to do that clumsily, because to some unknowable extent the two languages reflect different world-pictures and different systems for the categorization of experience. This leap into a different concept-world is the difficult part, and once that has been made it should be comparatively easy to explain how each instantiation is motivated in the fragments of Greek communication that we find in our texts.

For a given word of the language the task is first to observe the range of instantiations, then to work backwards by trial and error to a hypothetical prototype, arriving finally at the candidate which best explains the motivation of the attested uses and best harmonizes with the overall patterning of lexical semantics in the language (cf. Clarke 2004, 2005). "Occam's Razor" is a key criterion in evaluating any proposed

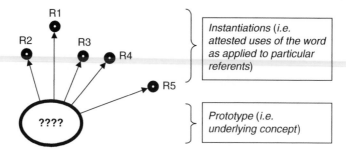

Figure 9.1 Template for semantic structure of a lexical item

reconstruction of a given word. The reconstruction is weakened if arbitrary complexities have to be introduced to justify it, either in characterizing the prototype itself or in motivating the mappings which link it to the instantiations. The converse also applies: if the prototype is excessively abstract the hypothesis will lack explanatory power because it will be unconstrained, or simply because it will be hard to see how a child learning the language could have assimilated the proposed concept on the basis of his exposure to the word in use (cf. Johnson 1999). As an example I will present a classic lexical puzzle, the simple and common verb τρέφω.

The Example of τρέφω

τρέφω is applied from Homer onward to what seem to us several distinct phenomena: often simply the rearing of a child and the nourishment of the body by food, but also such things as the formation of scurf on the body of a long-distance swimmer (*Od.* 23.236–7) or ice on a shield (*Od.* 14.476–7), the curdling of milk into cheese when fig juice is squirted into it (Il. 5.902–3; cf. Od. 9.246–9), and the conception and growth of a child in its mother's womb (Hes. *Th.* 107, 192; Aesch. *Sept.* 753, etc). If we assign primacy to any one of these examples, the others refuse to be explained except through vague metaphorical associations of ideas, and in each case there seems to be at least one instantiation which makes no sense at all. For example, if the basic sense is something like 'nourish, rear a child', how could the word become applicable to salt drying onto the skin? The "Occam factor" would thus be unacceptably high in such a reconstruction. The opposite drawback is represented by Émile Benveniste's explanation of the word: "to facilitate by appropriate means the development of something which is subject to increase" (1966: 293). This is vague and unconstrained, failing to capture why this particular range of phenomena rather than others were felt to be appropriate for this label. Following P. Demont's elegant study (1978; cf. also Moussy 1969), we can characterize the motivating concept in more precise terms as the action of *achieving fulness through thickening or coagulation*. The body literally thickens and fattens as we eat (see esp. *Od.* 13.410), the briny stuff from the sea cakes dry onto the skin, cheese rapidly solidifies when the fig juice is squirted into it; and, remarkably, there is evidence from Aristotle and the Hippocrates that the male's

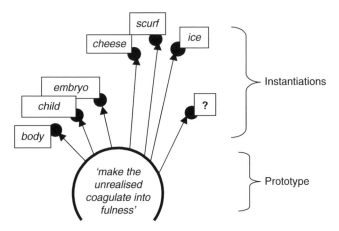

Figure 9.2 Prototype semantics of τρέφω

fertilizing act in conception was understood in a way that invited explicit comparison with the use of juice to curdle cheese (Arist. *Gen. an.* 729a12, 739b20, cited by Demont).

On this basis we might model the lexical structure in the way depicted in fig. 9.2.

Crucial to this model is the fact that the instantiations are ranked in distance from the prototype that underlies them. The nourishing of a child's body with food is a relatively basic or *focal* instance of the phenomenon named by τρέφω, while the coagulation of scurf on a swimmer's body is relatively *peripheral*. What this implies is that an ancient Greek might have had to make a more conscious or more imaginative mental effort to recognize the prototypical concept in the formation of the scurf, while he would have been grasped the nourishing of the child's body as a simple and obvious application. The point is not that the scurf example is metaphorical, or transferred, or figurative: rather, there is a somewhat extended *semantic stretch* in this instance (cf. Lloyd 2003: 9–10), and we can guess that a speaker might find it hard to explain its appropriateness to a child or a foreigner.

The variable ranking of the instantiations is more crucial to the model than is my (clumsy) attempt to render the prototype itself in a verbal formula (cf. Rosch 1975). From the ancient speaker's point of view the prototype is probably apprehended only subconsciously and by inference, but in communicative practice every use of τρέφω was negotiated in terms of its position in the hierarchy of instantiations. By the same token, the model well accommodates the likely patterns by which a language-user would gradually assimilate his internal lexicon from childhood up, continually altering and refining the entries over time. As he is exposed to new uses of the word which apply it to novel referents, he becomes aware of new instantiations (represented here by an arrow leading to a question mark), and his sense of the prototype itself may be progressively modified.

Over a series of generations, this process of continuous modification might gradually change the word's shape in the public lexicon. Many of the species of semantic change listed in the traditional handbooks can be seen as the cumulative effects of

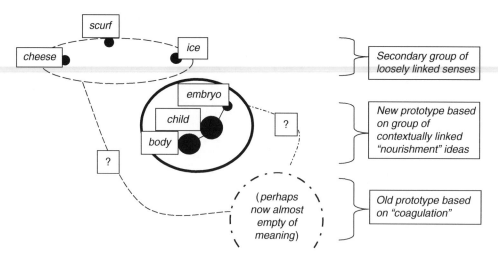

Figure 9.3   Breakdown of the semantic structure of τρέφω

such shifting modifications (Sweetser 1990: 1–22). However, there is the possibility of a more decisive and even destructive kind of change. The prototype model must allow for the likelihood that across the generations a word will become associated more and more closely with a limited cluster of conventional instantiations, which become *salient* among the word's range of uses; and as time and custom proceeds this cluster will be fixed or *entrenched* in the entry in public lexicon. This is clearly seen in the case of τρέφω. In the language of early epic its uses seem to be freely motivated by the prototypical concept, but in Classical and post-Classical Greek it is statistically harder to find instances outside the context of rearing a child, and even within that context there are few signs of any specific reference to physical "thickening" or "making substantial"; so it seems the word's primary reference is to the activity of child-rearing as an undifferentiated whole.

This allows us to plot how the word's semantic logic could gradually change over generations of the speech-community. When a salient usage becomes entrenched, it is possible that the corresponding visual image will achieve the status of a new prototype in its own right, ousting the original prototype from its position of dominance. It may no longer be obvious what made the word appropriate in the more peripheral contexts of its traditional use. The entry in the public lexicon ends up looking very different (fig. 9.3).

A cluster of points of reference has grouped itself around the most salient of all, the rearing of a child; this cluster redefines the prototype, and the remaining senses either fall apart and survive as mere polysemous fossils, or (as in the diagram) they form a shadowy cluster linked loosely to each other and to the main group. If the old prototype survives at all it does so in a vague and shaky way, perhaps carrying meaning only for members of the speech-community with unusual linguistic sensitivities, such as poets.

The second diagram (fig. 9.3) seems to correspond much more closely to the traditional arrangement of academic dictionary entries; but it is valid only as one pole in an opposition between the semantics of the unitary prototype on the one hand and the proliferation of disordered polysemy on the other. In the Classical language the semantic shape of τρέφω has not necessarily reached the stage represented in the second diagram: it represents an extreme *toward* which the word can be seen to be moving over many generations in the history of the language. If we see the life history of a prototype-based category in terms of the unidirectional process of instantiation, entrenchment, and (possible) eventual breakdown, our sense of the public lexicon can begin to accommodate the necessary diachronic element – we are not just defining words but charting their histories as well. In this way, to quote Geeraerts, "Polysemy is, roughly, the reflection of diachronic semantic change" (1998: 6).

Grammaticalization: Syntactic Entrenchment

Our discussion so far shows that the reconstruction of meaning needs to be plotted in three dimensions: the dictionary fails precisely because it lays the word out on a flat plane, when the true logic of word-meaning needs to be understood in terms of time depth as well. We can use a variant version of the τρέφω pattern to cope with τυγχάνω, whose dictionary entry we have already criticized. The story begins with a simple unbounded concept, the action of striking or hitting or colliding – once again, the very simplicity of the prototypical concept makes it hard to express succinctly in English. Among the potentially endless range of contexts in which this word could be applied, one is peculiar to a particular syntactic environment: τυγχάνω contracts a relationship with the participle of another verb and characterizes the action in that verb as a fortuitous or accidental coming-together of events (cf. Jiménez 1999). Here is a typical example, in which a counselor asks his king whether he should speak or be silent:

Ὦ βασιλεῦ, κότερον λέγειν πρὸς σὲ τὰ νοέων **τυγχάνω** ἢ σιγᾶν ἐν τῷ παρέοντι χρή;

O King, is it fitting to tell you what I <u>strike the fulness of</u> knowing, or to keep silence? (Hdt. 1.88.2)

It is easy to see how tempting it is to fall back on the old schoolmasterly gloss "chance to know." Gradually, the participial construction became dominant, while the word continued to be applied to the action of striking a target or encountering a person or phenomenon. A study of typical usage in authors of the fifth century BCE suggests a prototype-based diagram on the lines shown in fig. 9.4.

Does this syntactic entrenchment imply that the word's semantic structure fell apart? Is this the point where the Occam principle becomes impossible to apply, and where we conclude that the word's entrenched role in the participial construction amounts to a separate sub-entry in the public lexicon? Perhaps. However, it is better to see this phenomenon as a first stage in the process of *grammaticalization*, whereby a word takes on a new role through its gradual recruitment as a syntactic prop rather than an independent carrier of referential meaning (Hopper and Traugott 1993: 32–93).

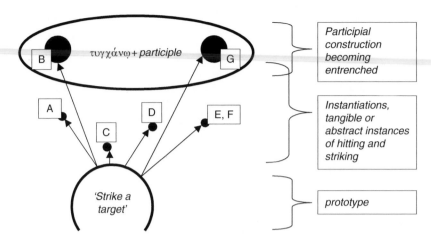

Figure 9.4   Prototype semantics of τυγχάνω

The classic case is the history of English modal auxiliaries like *will, can, may,* which originally had fully active semantic content of their own ("wish," "know how," "have power"). Since the Old English period these words have gradually become entrenched in collocation with other verbs, and have in the process lost their syntactic freedom and undergone further extensions of meaning that depend on their increasingly prevalent role as auxiliaries (Sweetser 1990: 49–75; Traugott and Dasher 2002: 105–51). Vital to the analysis of grammaticalization is the fact that the change is imperceptibly gradual, and that the old meaning can comfortably coexist with the new one for many generations of language-users (Roberts 1993). In this way, again, the apparent multiplicity is underpinned by an emergent and unifying logic. (See also ch. 22 on the development of forms of address.)

Word-Formation and Etymology

Once we start reconstructing meaning in terms of change, we have to wonder how far back in time to push the quest. The movement from prototype to instantiations can also be seen to underlie many simple processes of word-formation. To take a simple example, in Modern English the noun *bit* has three familiar applications: a piece or fragment of something, a piece of metal inserted into a horse's mouth, and the piercing rod on the end of a drill. Historically, all are instantiations based on the simple process labeled by the verb *bite*. The horse grips the bit with his teeth, the "jaws" of the drill grip the rod, and the application of the word to a piece or fragment has been extended from the original image of a piece of food bitten off and taken in the mouth. Historically, then, the prototypical concept has been mapped to a (potentially endless) range of instantiations, of which one became salient and thus entrenched (see fig. 9.5).

Over time the links represented by the arrows became progressively weaker in the sense networks of the language. From the viewpoint of a member of our

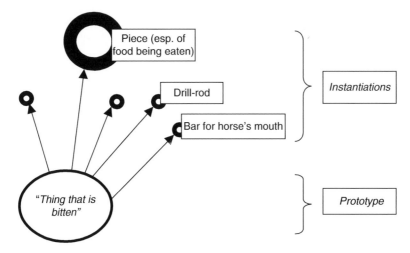

Figure 9.5   Diachronic development of English *bit*

speech-community today, can it even be assumed that the links have disappeared entirely and that the diagram is now no more than a curiosity of linguistic history? Perhaps that will often be a safe guess for a language like Modern English, where words tend not to stand in close relationship to the roots from which they are derived. In Ancient Greek, on the other hand, as also in Old English (Kastovsky 1992: 291–9), the internal structure of the lexicon is strongly *associative*. Much of the basic word-stock falls into families of linked words which share a transparent derivational relationship to each other, whether through formational processes that are active within the language or through patterns of root-based derivation that stretch into prehistory and back to Proto-Indo-European.

To take another of our dictionary examples, the puzzling array of uses of the word δόξα can be restored to order if we look not within the noun itself but to the parent verb δοκέω. The meaning of this verb is relatively easy to represent in English: the prototypical idea is close to our English *seem*, and it refers to the formation of sense-impressions and judgments based on estimation rather than certain knowledge. δόξα, then, names the various possible kinds of instantiations of this prototypical action: the mental act of forming an opinion or judgment, the result of that action, or the manifestation of (good) opinion in the public arena. Thus something like unity can be restored to a noun that the two-dimensional dictionary entry could not cope with.

δοκέω and δόξα are so close formally that we need not doubt the reality of the semantic link in the public lexicon. But how far can we push this kind of associative modeling? λέγω and λόγος are plainly linked: the *e/o* relationship between the vowels characterizes them as derivatives from a single Indo-European root (Szemerényi 1996: 83–5). Greek is full of pairs that chime in the same way, but they are fossils – there is every indication that new words had not been formed on this pattern for many generations before the historical period of the language. Is it sound to consider them together as parts of a single lexical cluster, or is it purely a matter of historical background that they are linked? The answer must lie somewhere between these two extremes, and the likely pattern of influence is complex and contaminated. The evidence (Chantraine 1999: 625) is that the original heart of the meaning of λέγω – the original semantic prototype, in fact – was the action of choosing, arranging, listing, and thus of narrating something in order. The salient instantiation of the original prototype, the act of enumerating the items in a list or the events of a story, eventually dominated the prototype itself, so it comes about that in Classical usage the word can usually be translated satisfactorily as "say" or "tell." The cognate noun λόγος moved in the same direction, cheek by jowl with the parent verb, and is familiar as the term for anything said or narrated or given verbal shape; but a few special instantiations survive which hark back to the old prototype, as for example when λόγος remains the normal name for an account in the book-keeping sense, a reckoning of financial transactions (e.g., Dem. 8.47, Lys. 24.26).

This ambiguous structure gives us pause if we take a step further and consider a further relative, the noun λόγιος. Herodotus, famously, discusses and learns from (or rejects) the information imparted by foreign λόγιοι (e.g. Hdt. 1.1.1, 2.3.1). The word is often rendered as "chroniclers," but this hides a lexical ambiguity (Hornblower 2002: 376–7; Gould 1989: 27). Should the word be heard as a simple derivative of λόγος or does it enjoy a semantic association with the verb? The practical choice is whether we should understand λόγιος as closer to "men with a historical narrative" or "men who have something to say," or "men who have attempted a reckoning." And the question is not an idle academic speculation: on it hangs our interpretation of Herodotus' entire system of investigation.

Questions like the last one can probably never be answered with confidence. But it is vital to pose them: we must resist the temptation either to despair of achieving real understanding, or to fall back on a complacent trust in our ability to impose meaning on the words of an ancient language. This is an exciting time in the study of historical semantics, exciting precisely because we have lost the sense of comfortable ownership which our forebears enjoyed as members of an artificially exalted educational elite. In the twenty-first century we come to a language like Greek as strangers and exiles, not as masters or connoisseurs, and the beginner student and the seasoned scholar stand as equals in the struggle to grasp the elusive meanings of its words.

FURTHER READING

Remarkably little has been published about the general challenge of understanding Ancient Greek words and giving an account of their meanings. A rare exception is Chadwick 1996; this book is remarkable for its willingness to reconsider basic questions of meaning, but it lacks theoretical underpinnings and is best used only as food for thought. On the other hand, many brilliant studies of individual words are scattered through the academic journals, especially *Glotta*, *Revue des Études Grecques*, and *Classical Quarterly*, and in the work of literary commentators. After more than 100 years it is still hard to better many of the subtle semantic insights of Jebb in his monumental commentaries on Sophocles. The available dictionaries are increasingly problematic: the standard LSJ is muddled and treacherous, especially for the commonest words, but becomes much more effective if supplemented by Chantraine's sane and sensitive *Dictionnaire étymologique de la langue grecque* (*DE*; 1999).

Beyond specialist classical scholars, the field of historical semantics has seen some classic advances in recent decades. Grammaticalization theory is all-important: key readings include Hopper and Traugott (1993) and Traugott and Dasher (2000). On the developing discipline of prototype semantics, there is no better introduction than the exuberant speculations of George Lakoff (1987), tempered by the sober and practical essays of Charles Fillmore (1982) and Fillmore and Atkins (1992, 2000). A classic work at the interface between lexicography and semantics is Geeraerts (1998). The insights of Geeraerts and Fillmore substantially motivate the theoretical approach taken in this chapter. An interesting example of the gradual rapprochement between Indo-European linguistics and contemporary cognitive linguistics is provided by Sweetser (1990).

CHAPTER TEN

Syntax

Evert van Emde Boas and Luuk Huitink

Introduction

The study of syntax is concerned with the ways words are combined to form sentences. A well-formed sentence is not a jumble of words randomly thrown together, but a structure built out of words shaped and ordered according to specific rules and principles. By way of introduction to some of the basic features of Greek sentence structure and the terminology we use to describe it, consider the following example:

(1) καὶ διὰ ταύτην τὴν ἐπιθυμίαν ἔδωκε Γοργίᾳ ἀργύριον τῷ Λεοντίνῳ.

And because of this desire he gave money to Gorgias of Leontini. (Xen. *An.* 26.16)

This sentence is built around the predicate ἔδωκε "he gave," which has three "arguments" or obligatory constituents:

a) a subject ("he"), which in this case is expressed only by the third person singular ending of the verb (Greek is a so-called "PRO-drop" language, i.e., the subject can be omitted);
b) a patient-object in the accusative case (ἀργύριον "silver, money");
c) and a recipient-indirect object in the dative case (Γοργίᾳ... τῷ Λεοντίνῳ "Gorgias of Leontini").

The predicate and its arguments form the "core" of the sentence, in that they satisfy the minimal requirements to form a grammatical sentence with the verb δίδωμι "give." Other verbs may have different requirements: for example, τύπτω "hit" has two argument "slots," while χάσκω "yawn" has one.

This sentence core is elaborated by an optional causal adverbial modifier in the form of a preposition-phrase (διὰ ταύτην τὴν ἐπιθυμίαν "because of this desire"). Furthermore, the sentence is embedded in a wider context by the connective particle καί, which establishes a connection between the present and the previous sentence.

On the level of noun phrases, we see that certain principles of agreement are observed: the modifier τῷ Λεοντίνῳ agrees in case, number, and gender and with its head Γοργίᾳ. The same rules show that ταύτην τὴν ἐπιθυμίαν should be taken as a single word group. Note that in the former example, the head and modifier are not adjacent in the sentence: in a heavily inflected language like Greek, the connections between words in a sentence are often made clear by agreement, so that word order is free to serve purposes different from purely syntactic ones (mainly, as we shall see, pragmatic ones).

Naturally, the syntax of Greek differs according to its dialects, has undergone radical changes over time, and may even vary from genre to genre. For example, what is acceptable in a tragic style may not be acceptable in historiographical prose. Below, we shall mainly be concerned with the syntax of Classical Greek prose (fifth and fourth cent. BCE). The chapter is structured as follows. First, we will discuss the system of cases, agreement, and the syntax of noun phrases. Secondly, we will focus on the verb and its use in main clauses. This discussion is followed by an overview of complex sentences. Finally, we deal with word order.

Cases and Agreement

Many syntactic relationships in Greek are expressed by nominal case-endings. Thus, the nominative is the case for subjects of finite verbs and for predicate nouns or adjectives with a copulative verb (2). Of the oblique cases, the accusative is the default case for direct objects (second arguments) (3) and for the subject of infinitives (see below); the genitive to connect one noun to another as attribute (4) and for the genitive absolute construction (see below); the dative is often used for adverbial modifiers (5). The vocative is used in addresses (see ch. 22).

(2) κοινὴ γὰρ ἡ τύχη καὶ τὸ μέλλον ἀόρατον

For chance is universal and the future is invisible. (Isoc. 1.29) *Nominative, as subject (ἡ τύχη, τὸ μέλλον) or predicate adjective (κοινή, ἀόρατον). Copulative verbs, especially εἰμί "be," are frequently omitted, as here.*

(3) τὴν τύχην ὠδυράμην.

I deplored my fortune. (Isoc. 12.9) *Accusative, direct object.*

(4) ὁ δαίμων . . . ἔδωκεν ἡμῖν μεταβολὰς . . . τῆς τύχης.

The god has given us changes of fortune. (Eur. fragm. 554 Kannicht) *Genitive, attribute with μεταβολάς.*

(5) τῇ τύχῃ πέπονθε τὸ συμβαῖνον.

He has suffered the accident by chance. (Dem. 60.19) *Dative, adverbial modifier.*

This basic system is complicated by various factors:

a) a large number of (sometimes semantically related) verbs take second arguments in the genitive or dative: e.g., ἅπτομαι + gen. "touch something/someone," βοηθέω + dat. "help someone";

b) third arguments can be expressed in any of the oblique cases, depending on the predicate: e.g., αἰτιάομαι + acc. + gen. "accuse someone of something," δίδωμι + acc. + dat. "give something to someone" (cf. (1) above); αἰτέω + acc. + acc. "demand something from someone";

c) all oblique cases can be used in specific adverbial expressions: e.g., the accusative of space traversed in ἐξελαύνει παρασάγγας εἴκοσιν "he marches on for twenty parasangs," or the genitive of separation in εἴκουσι τῆς ὁδοῦ "they retreat from the way."

In general, many peculiarities of the Greek case system are due to the fact that its five cases are distilled from the Indo-European eight-case system (see ch. 12), of which, roughly put, the instrumental and (most of the) locative case were absorbed by the dative, the ablative by the genitive, in prose often combined with a preposition. In effect, the Greek cases have to work several syntactic jobs at once.

Mechanisms of agreement (i.e., the correspondence of syntactically connected words in their expression of the inflectional categories case, person, number, and gender) play a much greater role in Greek than in English syntax. The principal rules of agreement are:

a) a finite verb agrees with its subject in person and number: ἡ ναῦς ἀνάγεται (3rd person sg.) "the ship is setting out." Greek often omits an explicit subject, in which case the person and number are expressed only by the verbal ending: τί λέγεις; (2nd person sg.) "what are you saying?";

b) an article, adjective, or pronoun agrees in case, number, and gender with the noun it modifies: ὁ σοφὸς ἀνήρ (nom. sg. masc.) "the wise man," ἐν ταῖσδε ταῖς ὀλίγαις ἡμέραις (dat. pl. fem.) "in these few days";

c) a relative pronoun agrees with its antecedent in number and gender (its case is determined by its function in the relative clause): ἡ ναῦς ἣν ὁρᾷς "the ship which you see" (ἡ ναῦς and ἥν fem. sg., ἥν acc. as object in the relative clause).

Several exceptions to these rules exist. Neuter plural subjects regularly take a verb in the third person singular, and dual subjects may take a verb in the plural. More generally, words sometimes agree in sense rather than precise syntactic form, a construction called κατὰ σύνεσιν or *ad sensum* ("according to sense") (6):

(6) τοιαῦτα ἀκούσασα **ἡ πόλις** (3rd sg.) Ἀγησίλαον **εἵλοντο** (3rd pl.) βασιλέα.

The city, when it had heard such arguments, elected Agesilaus king. (Xen. *Hell.* 3.3.4)

Noun Phrases: The Article, Attributive Modifiers

Greek has a definite article which marks nouns as identifiable, either as a specific entity known from the context (7) or general knowledge (8), or as an entire class (9). There is no indefinite article, though the lack of an article in itself usually expresses much the same as English *a(n)* (7):

(7) ἀλώπηξ καὶ πάρδαλις περὶ κάλλους ἤριζον. τῆς δὲ παρδάλεως . . . τὴν τοῦ σώματος ποικιλίαν προβαλλομένης ἡ ἀλώπηξ ὑποτυχοῦσα ἔφη . . .

A fox and a leopard were engaged in a beauty contest. While the leopard was making his case with the speckled fur on his body, the fox interrupted and said: . . . (Aesop 12.1)

(8) . . . ἐν τῇ ἐσόδῳ, ὅκου νῦν ὁ λίθινος λέων ἕστηκε ἐπὶ Λεωνίδῃ.

. . . at the mouth of the pass, where the (famous) stone lion dedicated to Leonidas now stands. (Hdt. 7.225.2)

(9) πονηρόν, ἄνδρες Ἀθηναῖοι, πονηρὸν ὁ συκοφάντης.

An informant is a vile thing, men of Athens, a vile thing. (Dem. 18.242)

The article of Classical Greek was originally a demonstrative pronominal form (its principal use in Homer); some pronominal uses persist in the Classical period, especially when the article is combined with certain connective particles (ὁ μέν . . . ὁ δέ "the one. . . the other," ὁ δέ (in a topic shift) "and/but he").

Attributive modifiers (usually adjectives, participles, or nouns in the genitive) are positioned either between the article and the head noun (τὸ ἔρημον ἄστυ "the deserted city") or after the head noun and an article ([τὸ] ἄστυ τὸ ἔρημον), with a pragmatic distinction between the possible orderings (S. J. Bakker 2006). When an adjective does not stand in this "attributive" position (i.e., when it is not preceded directly by the article), it expresses not a permanent, identifying attribute of the noun, but the condition that noun is in at the time of the action expressed by the verb ("predicative position," e.g., αἱρέουσι ἔρημον τὸ ἄστυ (Hdt. 8.51.2) "when they took the city it was deserted").

Some pronouns and quantifiers (e.g., ὅδε "this," οὗτος "this/that," ἐκεῖνος "that," ἕκαστος "each," ἀμφότερος "both") always take predicative position when used with a noun, as do so-called "partitive" genitives (τούτων οἱ πλεῖστοι "the majority of them") and genitives of personal pronouns used as a possessive (τὸ βιβλίον σου "your book").

The Verb: Mood, Voice, and Tense-Aspect

The finite forms of the Greek verbal system express, in addition to the categories of person and number, seven forms of tense-aspect (present, imperfect, aorist, perfect, pluperfect, future, future perfect), four moods (indicative, subjunctive, optative, imperative), and three voices (active, middle, passive). There are also two nominal verbal forms: the infinitive and the participle. Each of these verbal permutations may determine the syntactic form of a Greek sentence.

Mood

The verbal category most consequential for the shape of a Greek sentence is probably that of mood. The four moods combine with the two different negatives (οὐ and μή) and the modal particle ἄν to form a complex system of possible expressions, allowing the speaker to express a wide range of attitudes toward the content of his/her utterance. Here, main clauses should be sharply distinguished from subordinate clauses, treated below.

Main clauses can be divided into various sentence-types: declarative (statements), directive (commands), desiderative (wishes), or interrogative (questions), though it should be noted that these types do not always coincide with the communicative intentions of a speaker (as in English, declarative sentences can be used as commands (e.g., "I'm cold," said to someone sitting by an open window), interrogatives as assertions (so-called rhetorical questions), etc.).

The names "optative" (*optare* "wish"), "imperative" (*imperare* "command"), etc., betray a rudimentary understanding of the moods as overlapping with these sentence-types. It is true that the optative can be used in wishes (10) and the imperative in directive sentences (11):

(10)   μὴ πλείω κακὰ **πάθοιεν**. . .

   <u>May they suffer</u> no more. (Soph. *Ant.* 928)

(11)   φέρε δή μοι τόδε **εἰπέ** . . .

   Come on then, <u>tell</u> me this: . . . (Pl. *Cra.* 385b)

But the Greek moods are nowhere near as rigid as their names suggest (this is true for most languages, see Palmer 2001). Their meanings depend on the sentence-type in which they occur (though not all moods can occur in all sentence-types), but also on the presence or absence of ἄν and the choice of the negative. Table 10.1 sets out the relevant parameters.

The labels "counterfactual" and "potential" in table 10.1 merit explanation. When joined with ἄν, a secondary (i.e., past-tense) indicative expresses an action which might occur or might have occurred under certain circumstances, but in actual fact does not or did not (12). An optative with ἄν expresses an action of which the realization is considered possible, but no more than that: the construction often marks a statement as cautious or polite (13); it covers a range of English translations ("may," "might," "can," "could," etc.).

(12)   σίγησε δ᾽ αἰθήρ . . . | θηρῶν δ᾽ **οὐκ ἄν ἤκουσας** βοήν.

   The air fell silent, and <u>you would not have heard</u> a shout of animals [i.e., if you had been there, which you weren't]. (Eur. *Bacch.* 1084–5)

Table 10.1 Parameters of mood in Greek

Mood	Negative	+/– ἄν	"Meanings" and Sentence Types (D = declarative; C = directive; W = desiderative; Q = interrogative)
indicative	οὐ	–	factual statements (D) and questions (Q)
secondary	οὐ	–	(1) unrealizable wishes (W),
(past) indicative			(2) expressions of necessity/appropriateness (D)
	οὐ	+	counterfactual statements (D) and questions (Q)
subjunctive	μή	–	(1) "hortative" (first person commands, C),
			(2) "prohibitive" (second person negative commands, aorist only, C),
			(3) "deliberative" (first person doubtful questions, Q)
optative	μή	–	"cupitive" (wishes, W)
	οὐ	+	"potential" in statements and questions of possibility (D, Q), cautious/polite statements (D)
imperative	μή	–	second and third person commands and prohibitions (second person prohibitions: present only, C)

(13) ὅτι δὲ πολὺ διήνεγκε τῶν ἄλλων ἅπαντες **ἂν ὁμολογήσειαν**.

But everyone <u>might agree</u> that he far surpassed the rest. (Isoc. 11.5)

Voice

The verbal category of voice, too, has immediate consequences for the syntactic make-up of a sentence. Transitive verbs (those that in the active take an object), when put in the passive, have one less slot in their predicate frame ("valency reduction"). That is to say, passive verbs take only a (patient-)subject, no direct object (e.g., ἐώσθην (pass.) "I was pushed," as opposed to ἔωσα αὐτόν (act.) "I pushed him"). The agent is demoted so that it is no longer an argument of the verb: it may be expressed by a preposition-phrase with (usually) ὑπό + gen. (14); for perfect passives the bare "dative of agent" may be used. But explicit mention of the agent is not required (15):

(14) ὁ δὲ χρυσὸς οὗτος . . . **ὑπὸ Δελφῶν καλέεται** Γυγάδας.

And this gold <u>is called</u> 'Gygadas' <u>by the Delphians</u>. (Hdt. 1.14.3)

(15) οἰκοῦσι δ' ἐν μιᾷ τῶν νήσων οὐ μεγάλῃ, **καλεῖται** δὲ Λιπάρα.

They live on one of the islands, of modest size, and <u>it is called</u> Lipara. (Thuc. 3.88.2)

The demotion of the agent, in fact, appears to be a crucial pragmatic consideration for adopting the passive: the focus is on the entity undergoing the action rather than the one performing it (George 2005: 19–42).

The middle voice is found in a densely polysemous network of uses, with the main semantic difference between it and the active seeming to be an indication of "subject-affectedness" (Allan 2003).

Taking the construction of active forms as the norm, the use of the middle often does not, strictly speaking, change the surface structure of a sentence. For instance, the only difference between (16) and the same sentence with the equivalent active form (θηρῶσιν "they hunt") is semantic: the middle θηρῶνται indicates explicitly that the subject, the sophists, themselves benefit from the action (the so-called "indirect-reflexive" middle):

> (16) οἱ (...) σοφισταὶ πλουσίους καὶ νέους **θηρῶνται**.
>
> The sophists hunt the rich and the young. (Xen. *Cyn.* 13.9)

However, just like the passive, the middle of certain types of verb can involve valency reduction, i.e., the deletion of the slot for a direct object. Thus, the middle of certain transitive verbs can be used, without an object, to express habitual physical treatments applied by the subject to himself (the "direct-reflexive" middle, e.g., λούομαι (mid.) "bathe, wash oneself," as compared to λούω + acc. (act., with object) "wash someone, something"). Similarly, some transitive verbs have a "pseudo-reflexive" middle, expressing that the subject changes his own mental or physical situation, rather than that of someone or something else (e.g., κλίνομαι (mid.) "recline," as compared to κλίνω + acc. (act., with object) "cause to lean").

Tense and aspect

The final verbal category requiring discussion is that of "tense-aspect," a label more accurate than merely "tense," since many Greek verb forms express no tense (the location of an action in past, present, or future) at all. Apart from future verb forms, all verbs do express aspect (the way in which an action is "viewed").

The aspectual value of a verb form is determined by the stem on which it is built: present, aorist, or perfect:

a) all forms built on the present stem (pres. and imperf. indic., pres. subj./opt./ imp./inf./ptc.) have "imperfective" aspect, meaning that the action expressed is viewed as incomplete (ongoing or repeated); as a rule, imperfective actions may be interrupted;

b) all forms built on the aorist stem (all moods, inf. and ptc.) have "perfective" aspect, meaning that the action expressed is viewed in its entirety, as an undivided whole;

c) forms built on the perfect stem (pf., plupf. and fut. pf. indic., pf. subj./opt./ imp./inf./ptc.) express the state (or ongoing effects) resulting from an action completed in the past.

Tense is expressed by all future verb forms (which are "aspect-neutral") and the future perfect, otherwise only by indicatives. We may, then, synthesize the following system of indicatives, using κτάομαι "acquire" as our paradigm:

Table 10.2   The indicative paradigm of κτάομαι

			TENSE	
		Past	*Present*	*Future*
A S P E C T	*Present*	imperf. indic. ἐκτώμην ("I was acquiring, I used to acquire")	pres. indic. κτῶμαι ("I am acquiring, I (regularly) acquire")	fut. indic. κτήσομαι ("I will acquire")
	Aorist	aor. indic. ἐκτησάμην ("I acquired, I have acquired")	—	
	Perfect	plupf. indic. ἐκεκτήμην ("I possessed" < "I had acquired")	pf. indic. κέκτημαι ("I possess")	fut. pf. indic. κεκτήσομαι ("I will possess")

Two idiomatic uses of the indicative, exceptions to the tense-values given in table 10.2, should be noted: first the "historic" present, a past tense, which marks crucial events in a narrative (see, e.g., Sicking and Stork 1997, Rijksbaron 2006); second, the "gnomic" aorist, a present tense, which is used to express general tendencies, habits, procedures, etc.

It may be seen from the table that several of the indicatives coincide in their expression of tense, but differ in their expression of aspect. The difference between an imperfect and an aorist indicative, for example, is aspectual: the imperfect is used for ongoing or repeated actions, the aorist to express single actions viewed in their entirety (but see also ch. 11); contrast e.g., imperf. ἐδίδου and aor. ἔδωκε in (17):

(17)   δῶρά οἱ ἀνὰ πᾶν ἔτος **ἐδίδου** . . . καὶ τὴν Βαβυλῶνά οἱ **ἔδωκε**.

He <u>gave</u> him gifts yearly . . . and he <u>gave</u> him Babylon (Hdt. 3.160.2)

This distinction between present-stem forms and aorist-stem forms is crucial to the interpretation of verbs in other moods (which do not express tense) as well. The difference between present and aorist subjunctives, for instance, has nothing to do with tense but everything with aspect. Thus, in (18), the deliberative present subjunctive σιγῶμεν refers to an ongoing action, whereas the aorist subjunctive εἴπωμεν views the "speaking up" as an undivided action in its entirety:

(18)   εἴπωμεν ἢ σιγῶμεν;

<u>Should we speak up</u> or <u>keep silent</u>? (Eur. *Ion* 758)

It is worth mentioning that the description of tense-aspect given thus far is strictly speaking more a semantic than a syntactic one (though the two disciplines are often inextricably linked). In a traditional conception of syntax, which is concerned with the surface structure of sentences as the level of analysis, tense and aspect are not incredibly important (the difference between an imperfect and an aorist indicative is then purely semantic). Even in this narrow view, however, tense has an important syntactic function in that it may determine the usage of moods in subordinate clauses (see on the "oblique" optative below), and aspect, too, may have syntactic repercussions (for a cross-linguistic overview, see Comrie 1976). A complete understanding of the structural functions of tense-aspect (and many other syntactic phenomena), however, is possible only when it is seen to be operating on a level superseding that of individual sentences, lending coherence to larger stretches of discourse (see ch. 11 and compare the discussion of word order below).

Complex Sentences

Predicates may enter into syntactic relationships with other predicates to form complex sentences. One way of combining two predicates is by means of a connective such as καί "and." The result is a "paratactic" construction with two main clauses:

(19) τότε μὲν οὖν ... ἐδειπνηποιήσαντο καὶ ἐκοιμήθησαν.

Then . . . they took dinner and went to sleep. (Xen. *Ages.* 2.15)

However, predicates may also function as arguments or adverbial modifiers with other predicates. In such cases, we speak of "hypotaxis" or subordination:

(20) τότε μὲν οὖν ... δειπνηποιησάμενοι ἐκοιμήθησαν.

Then, . . . having taken dinner, they went to sleep. (Xen. *Hell.* 4.3.20)

In (20), the action "taking dinner" is subordinated to the action "going to sleep" by means of a participle phrase, which has the function of an adverbial modifier. This ordering suggests that the latter action, which is expressed in a main clause, is regarded as the more important one (Buijs 2005). Being conceptually more important, main predicates often pose constraints on the expression of tense, mood, and other features of the subordinate predicate. In (20) for instance, the participle is in the aorist, expressing that the "taking dinner" temporally preceded the "going to sleep": the main predicate functions as the temporal anchor for the subordinate predicate. Furthermore, the participle agrees with the subject of the main predicate.

  Greek displays three major types of subordination: infinitives, participles, and finite clauses headed by a conjunction. In discussing the characteristics of subordination, it is useful to make a distinction between complementary and adverbial subordinate predicates, although the same morphosyntactic categories are used in both. Relative clauses also merit separate treatment.

Verbal complementation

Complement clauses fulfill the role of an (obligatory) argument of the main predicate, usually subject or object. Hence it is to be expected that the main verb plays a crucial

Table 10.3 Complements of semantically determined predicate classes

Predicate class	*Complement*
1. modal (e.g., δεῖ "is necessary")	dynamic inf.
2. ability (e.g., δύναμαι "be able")	dynamic inf.
3. phasal (e.g., ἄρχομαι "begin")	dynamic inf.; pres. ptc.
4. manipulative (e.g., κελεύω "order")	dynamic inf.
5. desiderative (e.g., βούλομαι "want")	dynamic inf.
6. sensory perception (e.g., ὁράω "see")	pres. ptc.
7. fearing (e.g., φοβέομαι "fear")	μή + subj. / opt.
8. effort/contrivance (e.g., φροντίζω "take care that")	ὅπως + indic. fut. / fut. opt.
9. opinion (e.g., νομίζω "believe")	declarative inf.
10. knowledge/emotion (e.g., οἶδα "know," ἥδομαι "be glad")	ptc.; ὅτι "that"/ὡς "that, how" + every mood & tense
11. question (e.g., ἐρωτάω "ask")	indirect question: εἰ "whether"; τίς/ὅστις "who," etc. + mood and tense of direct discourse / opt.
12. declarative utterance (e.g., εἶπον "say")	indirect discourse: ὅτι "that"/ὡς "that, how" + mood and tense of direct discourse / opt.

role in determining the form and meaning of the complement clause. In table 10.3 we list a number of semantically determined predicate classes (partly based on Cristofaro 2003: 99–109) and the complement types they take.

In interpreting the table, it is important to realize that many lexical predicates in Greek are polysemous and belong to more than one predicate class. Some examples:

a) ὁράω "see" and other sensory perception predicates are often combined with ὅτι/ὡς "that" or a participle in a non-present tense, but then they do not express sensory, but "mental" perception and function as knowledge predicates;

b) οἶδα "know" and a number of other verbs from the same class govern a dynamic infinitive in the meaning "know how to," functioning as a predicate of ability; οὐκ οἶδα "I don't know" is semantically equivalent to a question and may select an indirect question;

c) reference grammars universally claim that declarative utterance predicates may govern a declarative infinitive to form indirect discourse. However, this is almost limited to cases in which they denote the expression of an opinion or rumor (always after φημί "claim"; after λέγουσι "they say," passive forms such as λέγεται "it is said," and λέγεις . . .; "do you mean that . . .?") and therefore arguably belong to the predicates of opinion.

The first eight classes listed govern complements which are predicational in nature: the subordinate predicate expresses an action that may or may not occur at some point posterior to or, in the case of phasal and perception predicates, simultaneous with the action expressed by the main predicate. Therefore, the complements have a temporal reference that is predetermined by the semantics of the main predicate. The last four classes govern complements which are propositional in nature, expressing a fact which may or may not be true at any point in time, so that the main predicate does not restrict the temporal reference of the subordinate one.

Some syntactic consequences of this difference (predicational versus propositional complements) may be illustrated by a comparison between the dynamic and declarative infinitive. In the case of the former, having a predetermined temporal reference, the aorist and present infinitive are in aspectual opposition only (the perfect is very rare, and the future infinitive impossible). The negative is μή. In the case of the declarative infinitive, by contrast, the present, aorist, and future infinitive express relative tense, being simultaneous with, anterior to, and posterior to the main predicate, respectively. The particle ἄν may also occur with this infinitive, expressing a potential or counterfactual proposition. The negative is οὐ. In both the dynamic and declarative construction, the subject of the infinitive is not expressed separately if it is co-referential with that of the main predicate: (21) and (23). If there is no such co-referentiality, the subject of the dynamic infinitive is expressed in the case required by the main verb (in the case of δέομαι in (22) the genitive) and the infinitive is added as an extra constituent, while the subject of the declarative infinitive invariably appears in the accusative, which together with the infinitive forms the object of the main predicate (23). Observe that the choice for the dynamic or declarative infinitive influences the meaning of the main verb γιγνώσκω in (21) and (24).

(21)   ἔγνωσαν τούς ... φεύγοντας **καταδέξασθαι**.

They resolved <u>to recall</u> the exiles. (Andoc. 1.107) *Dynamic inf., co-referentiality.*

(22)   ἐδέοντο [αὐτοῦ]$_{OBJECT}$ ... [**ἀπελθεῖν** Ἀθήνηθεν]$_{SUPPLEMENTARY INF.}$

They asked him <u>to leave</u> Athens. (Lys. 13.25) *Dynamic inf., no co-referentiality.*

(23)   ὁ Ἀσσύριος εἰς τὴν χώραν ... **ἐμβαλεῖν** ἀγγέλλεται.

It is reported that the Assyrian <u>will invade</u> the country. (Xen. *Cyr.* 5.3.30) *Declarative inf., co-referentiality.*

(24)   ἔγνωσαν οἱ παραγενόμενοι Σπαρτιητέων ... [Ἀριστόδημον ... ἔργα **ἀποδέξασθαι** μεγάλα]$_{OBJECT}$.

Those of the Spartans who were present judged that Aristodemus <u>had achieved</u> great feats. (Hdt. 9.71.3) *Declarative inf., no co-referentiality.*

In all its usages, the infinitive is opposed to the participle in that it expresses an action which may or may not occur, or a fact which may or may not be true, while the participle always expresses an action which does actually occur simultaneously with the main predicate, or a presupposed fact which has already been established independently (often in the previous context). Thus, ἤρχετο λέγων "he started by saying",

i.e., "at the beginning of his speech he said," but ἤρχετο λέγειν "he started to speak."
The following example bears out the presuppositional characteristics of the participle
(and γιγνώσκω, again, has a different meaning from (21) and (24) above):

(25) καὶ ὃς ἐθαύμασεν . . . κἀγὼ γνοὺς αὐτὸν **θαυμάζοντα** . . . ἔφην . . .

And he was amazed . . . And when I realized <u>that he was amazed</u> . . . I said . . .
(Pl. *Euthd.* 279d)

A final remark on indirect discourse is in order. Unlike for example English, Greek
has no sequence of tenses: instead, in indirect discourse, the mood and tense of the corresponding direct discourse are retained, or, when the main predicate is in a past tense,
the optative may (but does not have to) be used. This "oblique" optative occurs with
question and utterance predicates, but also with predicates of fearing and effort. By
contrast, the tense of the predicate in ὅτι/ὡς-clauses after past tense knowledge predicates such as γιγνώσκω "realize" is usually determined by the standpoint of the narrator,
but they may also be construed as declarative utterance predicates and retain the tense
of the corresponding "direct thought" or use the oblique optative. Thus, for example,
the following three expressions, each of which we would translate "He realized that he
was ill," convey differing perspectives: ἔγνω ὅτι ἐνόσει (imperf.: past for the narrator),
ἔγνω ὅτι νοσεῖ (pres.: standpoint of subject), ἔγνω ὅτι νοσοίη (oblique pres. opt.).

Adverbial clauses

Adverbial relations between predicates can be expressed by the same means as complementary ones, although the adverbial use of the infinitive is much more limited and
that of the participle much more extensive than in the case of complements.

We will start with adverbial finite clauses, of which Greek has many types. Some
conjunctions are semantically specific, while others function as more general "rela-
tors" which do not specify the type of adverbial relation which holds between the
main and subordinate predicate (Buijs 2005: 13–15). Hence, in the following overview, several conjunctions (especially ὡς) are encountered more than once.

a) Purpose clauses: ἵνα/ὡς/ὅπως "in order that", μή "in order that not" + subjunctive. After a past tense, an optative may be used.
b) Causal clauses: ὅτι/διότι + indicative. If the reason given originates with the subject of the main predicate rather than with the narrator, the optative may be used
after a past tense.
c) Consecutive clauses: ὥστε + indicative or infinitive. For the use of the infinitive,
see below.
d) Temporal clauses: ὅτε/ὡς/ἐπεί/ἐπειδή "when, after"; ἐν ᾧ "while"; ἕως "until,"
"as long as"; πρίν "before," "until"; etc. Temporal clauses obey the following
syntactic rules. They have an indicative when they express a single past action
(26). When they express a single future action, we find ἄν plus subjunctive (27).
The same construction is used in the case of a temporal clause expressing an

habitual action in the present (28), while habitual past actions are expressed by the optative (29). In principle, aorist-stem forms signal that the action expressed in the subordinate clause is anterior to that of the main clause ((27) and (28)), while present-stem forms signal simultaneity ((26) and (29)).

(26)   ἐν ᾧ δὲ ὡπλίζοντο ἧκον . . . οἱ . . . σκόποι.

     While <u>they were arming themselves,</u> the scouts came back. (Xen. *An.* 2.2.15)

(27)   τὴν αἰσχροκέρδειαν ἔτι μᾶλλον γνώσεσθε, **ἐπειδάν** πάντων **ἀκούσητε**.

     You will understand their greed still better <u>when you have heard</u> everything. (Isae. 1.8)

(28)   ἐνιαυτὸς δὲ **ὁπόταν** ἥλιος τὸν ἑαυτοῦ **περιέλθῃ** κύκλον.

     And it is a complete year <u>when</u> the sun <u>has been around</u> its orbit. (Pl. *Tim.* 39c)

(29)   ἐθήρευεν ἀπὸ ἵππου, **ὁπότε** γυμνάσαι **βούλοιτο** ἑαυτόν τε καὶ τοὺς ἵππους.

     He used to hunt on horseback <u>whenever he wanted</u> to give himself and his horses exercise. (Xen. *An.* 1.2.7)

e)   Conditional clauses: εἰ "if." The combinations εἰ καί and καὶ εἰ have a concessive value. The moods and tenses are by and large as in temporal clauses. However, when the main clause has a potential optative (with ἄν, see above), the εἰ-clause usually has a potential optative as well, but without ἄν. When the main clause has a counterfactual past-tense indicative (with ἄν), the εἰ-clause usually has a counterfactual past-tense indicative as well, again without ἄν.

Another widely used way to express adverbial relations of any kind is by means of participles. Most commonly, these receive a temporal or causal interpretation. Sometimes, however, a relator is added to the participle to clarify its semantic force: καίπερ (concessive), ἄτε (objective reason), ὡς (subjective reason) (32), ὡς + fut. ptc. (goal), ὥσπερ (comparison).

In principle the participle agrees in gender, number, and case with a constituent of the main clause (in (30) with the subject Κρίτων), but if such a constituent is unavailable, both the participle and its head appear in the genitive absolute (31); impersonal verbs appear in the (neuter) accusative absolute (32). The main predicate functions as a temporal anchor for the participle: an aorist participle expresses anteriority (30), the present simultaneity (31), and the future posteriority (32).

(30)   καὶ ὁ Κρίτων **ἀκούσας** ἔνευσε τῷ παιδί.

     <u>Having heard it</u>/After Crito <u>had heard it</u>, he nodded to the slave. (Pl. *Phd.* 117a)

(31)   **πορευομένων** δ' **αὐτῶν** ἀντιπαρῇσαν αἱ τάξεις τῶν ἱππέων.

     <u>While they proceeded,</u> the squadrons of the enemy's cavalry were passing by on the other side. (Xen. *An.* 4.3.17)

(32) εὐθὺς παρηγγύησε τοῖς Πέρσαις παρασκευάζεσθαι, ὡς αὐτίκα **δεῆσον** διώκειν.

Immediately he ordered the Persians to get ready, because presently it would be necessary to give chase. (Xen. *Cyr.* 3.2.8).

The infinitive, finally, occurs in consecutive clauses after ὥστε and in "before"-clauses after πρίν, in case the action in the subordinate clause does not necessarily occur:

(33) **πρίν** γὰρ δὴ **καταλῦσαι** τὸ στράτευμα πρὸς ἄριστον, βασιλεὺς ἐφάνη.

For before the army could halt for breakfast, the king appeared. (Xen. *An.* 1.10.19)

Relative clauses

Relative clauses (introduced by a relative pronoun, adjective, or adverb, such as ὅς "who/which," ὅσος "as large/many as," ἔνθα "where") are a very flexible form of subordination, with remarkably variegated constructions, depending on the syntactic function they fulfill (syntactically speaking, relative clauses can be attributive or adverbial modifiers, or something "in between"). They may be broadly divided into two categories:

a) "determinative" relative clauses: the information in the relative clause serves to identify the antecedent and cannot be left out (in English punctuation, these are usually not preceded by a comma) (34); the antecedent of determinative relative clauses can be omitted ("autonomous" relative clauses) (35);

b) "digressive"relative clauses: the relative clause gives additional information that is not required to identify the antecedent (normally with a comma in English). These are especially common with proper names (36).

(34) τῷ ἀνδρὶ **ὃν ἂν ἕλησθε** πείσομαι.

I will obey the man you choose. (Xen. *An.* 1.3.15) *The identity of the man whom the speaker will obey cannot be determined without reference to the relative clause.*

(35) ἐγὼ δὲ ... καὶ **ὧν κρατῶ** μενοῦμεν.

But I and (those) whom I command will remain. (Xen. *Cyr.* 5.1.26) *Antecedent omitted; again, the men cannot be identified without the information in the relative clause.*

(36) τρίτον δὲ Ἅλυν, ... **ὃν οὐκ ἂν δύναισθε** ἄνευ πλοίων διαβῆναι.

The third [you will reach] is the Halys, which you will probably not be able to ford without boats. (Xen. *An.* 5.6.9) *The Halys can be identified without the additional information in the relative clause.*

As (34) shows, the usage of moods and tenses in determinative relative clauses is in the main identical to that of temporal and conditional clauses: a single future action in the main clause determines the use of ἄν + subj. in the relative clause (cf. (27) above).

In digressive relative clauses, however, the use of moods and tenses is that of main clauses: thus we find a potential optative with ἄν in (36) (cf. (13) above).

A peculiar feature of Greek relative clauses is "relative attraction," the assimilation of the relative pronoun into the case of its antecedent (regardless of its function in the relative clause). This is a violation of the third rule of agreement we gave above, one which occurs only under specific circumstances: when the pronoun functions as direct object in its relative clause, and when its antecedent is in the genitive or dative:

(37) Μήδων ὅσων ἑώρακα . . . ὁ ἐμὸς πάππος κάλλιστος.

Of all the Medes that I have seen, my grandfather is the most handsome. (Xen. *Cyr.* 1.3.2) *ὅσων is object with ἑώρακα, but assimilated into the gen. of its antecedent Μήδων.*

Word Order

The ordering of words in a sentence is a syntactic issue *par excellence*, and yet Greek word order poses insurmountable problems for traditional methods of syntactic description (leading to its pervasive but inaccurate characterization as "free"). Again, the crux is that individual sentences are not the right level of analysis: the operative patterns become clear only by looking at larger stretches of discourse, and by situating utterances in their communicative context (as mentioned above, this goes for tense-aspect as well; we could further mention particles, pronouns, the article, etc.).

It has long been noted that certain Greek words can only occur in a fixed position of their syntactic unit (sentence, clause, verb phrase, or noun phrase). Prepositive words (the article, relative pronouns, prepositions, conjunctions, negative, and a number of mostly connective particles) only occur in the first position of their syntactic unit. Postpositive or "enclitic" words occur in the second place of their syntactic unit, a feature which Greek shares with many Indo-European languages (Wackernagel's Law). To this class belong most other particles, non-contrastive personal pronouns and the enclitic verbs ἐστί and φησί.

Yet even if we disregard pre- and postpositive words, Greek word order is not free, but conditioned to some extent by pragmatic constraints. The following basic word order for declarative main clauses has been proposed by Dik (1995):

(setting) – (topic) – focus – predicate – rest

Many Greek sentences start with a piece of background information, specifying the circumstances, place, or time in which the following action takes place. Such settings may take the form of a prepositional phrase, a participle, or a subordinate clause. Then follows the topic, the entity about which something is predicated; usually, this entity is already known from the context. If it is the subject, it may be left out, so that not every sentence has a topic. In that case, the sentence starts with the focus, the entity which contributes the most salient and new information to the sentence. Next is the predicate; all constituents which follow the predicate have no specific pragmatic function; often, they contribute more or less predictable information. An example:

(38) ἀκούσας_{SETTING} οὖν ὁ Σωκράτης_{TOPIC} ἡσθῆναί_{FOCUS} τε μοι ἔδοξε_{PREDICATE} τῇ τοῦ Κέβητος πραγματείᾳ_{REST}.

When he heard this, Socrates seemed to me to be pleased by Cebes' earnestness. (Pl. *Phd.* 62e)

In the given context, the fact that Socrates is pleased about Cebes' earnest speech is the most salient information – he could have responded differently – so that ἡσθῆναι appears in focus position. The idea that Cebes' speech is earnest is clear from the context, so that τῇ τοῦ Κέβητος πραγματείᾳ contributes predictable information and takes up the rest position of the sentence.

The basic rule may be subjected to a number of permutations, more than we can go into here. Just two common examples: the predicate may itself be the focus of a sentence (39), and it can even be the topic (40):

(39) Κῦρον_{TOPIC} δὲ μεταπέμπεται_{FOCUS} ἀπὸ τῆς ἀρχῆς_{REST}.

He summoned Cyrus back from his province. (Xen. *An.* 1.1.2) *This sentence marks a topic-shift from Darius to his son Cyrus. The verb is in focus.*

(40) οὗτος ὁ Κροῖσος βαρβάρων πρῶτος . . . τοὺς μὲν κατεστρέψατο Ἑλλήνων . . . τοὺς δὲ φίλους προσεποιήσατο. κατεστρέψατο_{TOPIC} μὲν Ἰωνάς τε καὶ Αἰολέας καὶ Δωριέας τοὺς ἐν τῇ Ἀσίῃ_{FOCUS}, φίλους δὲ προσεποιήσατο_{TOPIC} Λακεδαιμονίους_{FOCUS}.

This Croesus was the first foreigner to have subjugated some of the Greeks and made allies of others. He subjugated the Ionians, Aeolians, and Dorians in Asia, and he made allies of the Spartans. (Hdt. 1.6.2) *In the first sentence, Herodotus names two activities of Croesus, which therefore can subsequently appear in the topic position of their respective clauses when he elaborates on both in the following sentence.*

FURTHER READING

The fullest reference grammars (covering syntax and semantics) of Greek are K-G and S-D, great tomes of late nineteenth- and early twentieth-century German scholarship. In English, the best grammar is Smyth 1956 (based on K-G, but with many valuable independent observations). There are too few studies of the syntax of particular authors or genres in the Classical period: Moorhouse 1982 (on Sophocles) and Bers 1984 (poetic syntax) are worthwhile exceptions.

The syntax of Greek noun phrases is under-studied, but has recently received attention in the work of S. J. Bakker (2006, 2007). On the definite article, see Sansone 1993. There is a mountain of scholarship on the Greek verb: important overviews are Rijksbaron 2002 and Goodwin 1889. For the passive voice, see George 2005; for the middle, Allan 2003. Tense-aspect has been studied primarily in the light of the opposition present-aorist, see, e.g., Jacquinod et al. 2000 (with further references). On the discourse functions of tense-aspect, see Rijksbaron 1988, Bakker 1997c, Allan 2007, and Buijs 2007. A differing view of aspect has been offered by Sicking (1991, 1996).

The reference grammars listed above all have extensive treatments of the infinitive, participle, and subordinate clauses, but good specialized studies are few. Apart from an earlier influential treatment of the infinitive by Kurzová (1968), there is one monograph on verbal complementation in Greek, Cristofaro 1996. Certain types of finite subordinate clauses have also been treated in monographs: e.g., temporal/causal clauses (Rijksbaron 1976), conditional clauses (Wakker 1994) and ὅπως-clauses (Amigues 1977).

A few other detailed studies deserve mention. The negatives are treated in Moorhouse 1959. On particles, the classic text is Denniston 1954; serious modifications and updates are needed, however (some are provided in Rijksbaron 1997). Finally, the study of Greek word order has been given great impetus by Dik (1995, 2007), and by the important work of Slings (e.g., 1992, 1997).

CHAPTER ELEVEN

Pragmatics: Speech and Text

Egbert J. Bakker

After the discussion of sound, of the structure and meaning of words, and the structure of sentences in the preceding chapters, this chapter will present Ancient Greek as
it is actually used in discourse contexts. The branch of linguistics that studies language
in context and in action is often called pragmatics, a slightly infelicitous term insofar
as it suggests the idea of a concrete "thing" or "result" (*pragma*). What is, or should
be, at stake in pragmatics, however, is that language is not a thing done, but a thing
being done, a doing: a *praxis* rather than a *pragma*. In its most principled (some
would say, radical) form, pragmatics sees "linguistic meaning" not as something that
inheres in the words and sentences themselves of the language, but in the strategies
by which speakers convey through language what they mean or intend to achieve.
Words don't mean, speakers do; and a pragmatic account of a language is necessarily
cognitive, in taking account not only the contextual reality within which the speech
action takes place, but also speakers' perception and assessment of that reality.

The step from language as structure, or system, to language as behavior is not an
easy one to make. The language about language that comes naturally to most of us
assumes that language preexists the speech event, as a tool for communication available to speakers. This is most apparent in the use of the verb "use" with as direct
object parts of language, such as "word" or "sentence," or even "language" itself. To
think of a language and its constituents as tools or objects used may be inevitable for
those who have been taught a language for reading and formal instruction, but "language use" is not necessarily the appropriate term for what the language's real speakers do. The words and phrases they utter are shaped in the very context of their
utterance as routinized behavior of many speakers over extended periods of time. In
this perspective, grammar is not what makes speech possible; rather, speech is what
necessitates, and shapes, grammar. The idea of grammar as a work in constant progress is captured in such terms as "grammaticalization" or "grammaticization," denoting functional perspectives on language and a growing body of linguistic literature
(see also ch. 9).

The actual behavior of the speakers of Ancient Greek is forever lost to us, but our corpus of texts allows us to observe the cognitive and discursive praxis of speaking the language in a number of ways. There is first of all the interactive speech as represented in genres that are explicitly concerned with dialogue. Our texts may be the script for an actually occurring speech event, such as a dramatic performance; or they may be a fictional representation of speech, as in the case of dialogues. Those scripted or represented dialogues provide us with a window on actual linguistic behavior, in spite of such potentially distorting factors as metrical constraint, generic convention, or the interference of the written medium. But monologic prose does this too, albeit less directly. Some "prose" is of course stylized speech addressed to an actual audience in an actual context, as in the case of oratory, whether transmitted by itself under the name of its author or as part of a narrative text (as in the case of Pericles' *Funeral Oration*).

But even a thoroughly "readerly" text such as Thucydides' *History*, in order to be coherent and comprehensible, has to resort to communicative strategies, and these come primarily from speech. The dialogue in which Thucydides engages with his reader may not be explicit, but Thucydides will have to make use of at least some of the devices in the speaker's arsenal to situate his speaking voice with respect to its reading listeners and the historical reality it creates.

Central to the study of the discursive strategies behind the coherence of any of our texts is that the idea of "sentence" decreases in importance as object of linguistic analysis. This unit of syntactic and stylistic study is primarily a reality of written composition and stylistic analysis. In the study of Greek as linguistic behavior the units that impose themselves are either smaller or larger than sentences or rhetorical periods: they are either the "intonation units" of speech (Bakker 1997a; 1997b; 2005: 46–55, 66–70) or the "paragraphs" of extended discourses, clusters of continuous speech or text that are shaped by the communicative role they play as a whole (see below on the pragmatic function of temporal subclauses). Units of interest to pragmatics or discourse analysis can also be, regardless of the size of the utterances involved, the "turns" taken by speakers in their dialogic interaction.

This chapter consists of two "test cases," deixis and tense/temporal reference. In each case we will start with interactive speech for the study of the linguistic elements in question and then move on to the role of those same elements in the shaping of "monologic" text.

Deixis in Speech and Text

Deixis is the "pointing" function of language, which involves the strategies by which speakers place themselves in place and in time as well as with respect to each other. Any language has deictic elements (or indexicals), such as personal pronouns ("I," "you," "she/he/it") or demonstrative pronouns ("this," "that"). Any utterance with one or more of these elements, whether in spoken or written form, will need a certain amount of context to be intelligible, either the real-world context in which conversation takes place or the linguistic context created by the written text.

And either context is incomplete without the "subjective" understanding that speakers, hearers, writers, and readers bring to it.

Deictics in speech

Ancient Greek has a fairly complex grammar of three deictic/demonstrative pronouns: ὅδε "this-here," οὗτος "that-there," and ἐκεῖνος "that." It is customary to align these three pronouns, in order of increasing distance from the speaking subject, with the three grammatical persons. Thus ὅδε "this one here" has been seen as the deictic of the first person, whereas οὗτος "this/that one (with you)" is commonly aligned with the second person; (ἐ)κεῖνος is reserved for *Jener-Deixis*, the reference to persons and things that are removed in time and place from the speech situation and its participants, which aligns ἐκεῖνος with the third grammatical person (Havers 1906; K-G 1: 641). Such an objective arrangement, however, useful though it may be for heuristic purposes, does not exhaust the semantic potential of these deictics: in addition to objective distance there is an important cognitive dimension which involves the "subjective" experience of the discourse participants.

Let us begin with the proximal, "first-person" deictic ὅδε, which can be used to point at what is in close, physical proximity to the speaker, e.g.,

(1) ΙΣ   τί γὰρ μόνη μοι **τῆσδ**᾽ ἄτερ βιώσιμον;
     ΚΡ   ἀλλ᾽ **ἥδε** μέντοι μὴ λέγ᾽· οὐ γὰρ ἔστ᾽ ἔτι.

  What life is livable for me alone without <u>her here</u>? Stop talking about "<u>her here</u>"; she does not live anymore. (Soph. *Ant.* 566–7)

Such closeness, incompatible with physical absence, can mean that the thing pointed at is familiar to the speaker (e.g., τῶν ἠθάδων **τῶνδ**᾽ ὧν ὁρᾶθ᾽ ὑμεῖς ἀεί "of these familiar <birds> here that you see all the time," Ar. *Av.* 271). But when the referent of ὅδε is accessible to the speaker *only* (and this happens frequently), it may become a piece of as yet *unknown* information for the hearer and something salient for the speaker to utter. For example, the pronoun is used for what is newly arriving or appearing at the time of the speech; this frequently happens in drama when a new character walks onto the stage, e.g:

(2) ἀλλ᾽ **ὅδε** φύλαξ γὰρ τῶν ἐκεῖθεν ἄγγελος
     ἐσθεῖ **πρὸς ἡμᾶς δεῦρο** πυρρίχην βλέπων.

  But <u>this one here</u>, a guard, a messenger from those out there comes running <u>hither to us here</u> looking like he will perform a war-dance. (Ar. *Av.* 1168–9)

And true to its proximal nature, ὅδε can also be used for "self-pointing," when the speaker's own physical presence is new information to the hearer, e.g:

(3) ΣΥ   τίς ὁ πτερῶν δεῦρ᾽ ἐστὶ τοὺς ἀφικνουμένους;
     ΠΕΙ **ὁδὶ** πάρεστιν

  Who is the one that hands out wings to those arriving here? <u>That's me here</u>. (Ar. *Av.* 1418–19)

The pronoun may even attract the grammatical first person of the verb (e.g., ὅδε τοι πάρειμι "well, here I am," Hdt. 1.115.3). The person indicated with ὅδε, then, is often not simply close to the speaker but also new and salient to the hearer. Objective "givenness," therefore, is matched with subjective "newness."

The second deictic, οὗτος, can be aligned, as mentioned above, with the hearer. The most principled use of οὗτος in speech, in fact, is the direct address of the interlocutor (οὗτος "Hey, you,"; see also ch. 22), e.g., οὗτος, σε καλῶ, σε καλῶ "Hey, you, I'm calling you, I'm calling you," Ar. *Av.* 658: the deixis is the performance of the speech act of address (see ch. 22), which prepares the ground for subsequent interaction between the speaker and the addressee. οὗτος can also be used to indicate the speaker himself, from the perspective of the addressee, e.g.,

(4)   ΑΓ   ποῦ Πεισθέταιρός ἐστιν ἄρχων;
      ΠΕΙ   οὑτοσί

      Where is Peisthetairos our leader? <I'm> <u>that one</u>. (Ar. *Av.* 1123)

The difference between (3) and (4) is instructive. The character who asks the question in the former case does not know the person he is looking for, and so Peisthetairos presents himself with ὅδε, as a new character (for the visitor) at the moment of his appearance. In (4) the entering character, by contrast, knows who he is looking for, and so Peisthetairos presents himself as information that is accessible to the newcomer, deictically referring to himself as οὗτος (cf. Ar. *Nub.* 141).

The deictic can be an answer to a question, as in (4); or it can be the basis for a question, as in (5): a speaker points with οὗτος to something he wants to know more about, knowing or assuming that the hearer can see it too, and is in fact more familiar with it. In such cases the deixis with οὗτος, assuming a joint perception, serves as basis for further interaction, e.g.,

(5)   ΕΥ   ὦ Πόσειδον ἕτερος αὖ τις βαπτὸς ὄρνις **οὑτοσί**.
            τίς ὀνομάζεταί ποθ᾽ **οὗτος**;

      ΕΠ   **οὑτοσὶ** κατωφαγᾶς

      By Poseidon, <u>there</u> is another one, some kind of painted bird. <u>What</u> is <u>that one</u> called? <u>That one there</u> is the Glutton bird. (Ar. *Av.* 287–8)

The deictic, finally, can be the verbal accompaniment of physical gestures, as when Strepsiades demonstrates "giving the finger" to Socrates (πρὸ τοῦ μέν, ἐπ᾽ ἐμοῦ παιδὸς ὄντος, **οὑτοσί** "In the old days when I was a kid, it was <u>this</u>," Ar. *Nub.* 654).

The third demonstrative, ἐκεῖνος, is reserved for what is physically absent for both speaker and hearer, and is as such not often found in a purely deictic ("pointing") function, as in the following extract:

(6)   **οὑτοσὶ** πέρδιξ, **ἐκεινοσί** γε νὴ Δι᾽ ἀτταγᾶς,
      οὑτοσὶ δὲ πηνέλοψ, **ἐκεινοσί** δέ γ᾽ ἀλκυών

      <u>This one here</u> is a partridge, <u>that one there</u> by Zeus a francolin, and <u>this one here</u> is a *penelops*, and <u>that one there</u> a *halcyon*. (Ar. *Av.* 297–8)

The use of the two deictics may imply that the francolin and the *halcyon* are further removed from the speaker than the partridge and the *penelops*, but it is equally possible to assume that the two deictics are differentiated from one another as part of short enumerations ("this one, that one"). Note in any case the affix -ί (always attracting the accent), which in spoken Attic is used only on demonstratives in an explicitly deictic function.

More common is the use of ἐκεῖνος for what is remote, not materially present in the speech situation. Peisthetairos in *Birds* uses the deictic when he refers to the primordial time when birds reigned supreme (ὑπὸ τῆς ῥώμης τῆς τότ᾽ ἐκείνης "through that force he had back then," Ar. *Av.* 489). In the conversation between Gyges and Candaules in the short story at the beginning of Herodotus' *Histories*, the queen, who is not present, is referred to as ἐκείνην (Hdt. 1.8.2). Similarly, the swineherd Eumaios in the *Odyssey* refers to his absent master Odysseus with κεῖνος (e.g., *Od.* 14.70).

Odysseus and the Lydian queen may be away from the speech situations in question, but they are very much on the speakers' minds. The salience of things absent is in fact an important part of the meaning of ἐκεῖνος, the intersection of deixis with the cognitive dimension. What is physically absent may be very present mentally. The person or thing referred to with ἐκεῖνος is frequently someone or something cognitively salient, for example, someone universally known, such as Thales of Miletus (τί δῆτ᾽ ἐκεῖνον τὸν Θαλῆν θαυμάζομεν; "Why do we <still> admire that <famous> Thales?" Ar. *Nub.* 180). Or ἐκεῖνος is used for what is desired, sought, or pursued, e.g:

(7) Στ   οὐ γὰρ ᾤζυρέ
      τούτων ἐπιθυμῶ μανθάνειν οὐδέν
    Σω   τί δαί;
    Στρ ἐκεῖν᾽ ἐκεῖνο, τὸν ἀδικώτατον λόγον.

> No, you loser, of those things I don't wish to learn anything. But what <*do* you want to learn>? That thing, that thing, the most unjust argument. (Ar. *Nub.* 655–7)

When the entity that is mentally present actually comes into the context of utterance, instructive collocations of deictics may occur:

(8) τοῦτ᾽ἐκεῖνο· ποῖ φύγω δύστηνος;

> [The speaker, Euelpides, and his companion Pisthetairos are attacked by the birds] There you have it [lit: 'This/τοῦτο (what both of us are experiencing now) is that/ἐκεῖνο (what I was afraid was going to happen)']; where shall I flee, poor me? (Ar. *Av.* 354)

(9) οὗτος ἐκεῖνος τὸν σὺ ζητέεις.

> This man [who has just been described, a description we now share] is that man whom you are looking for. (Hdt. 1.32.7)

(10) ἥδ᾽ ἔστ᾽ ἐκείνη τοὔργον ἡ ᾽ξειργασμένη.

> This one here is she who carried out the deed. (Soph. *Ant.* 384)

(11)   ὅδ᾽ ἐκεῖνος ἐγώ.

Me here, I <am> that man <whom you are looking for>. (Soph. *OC* 138)

What was in the speaker's and hearer's minds but absent or not yet perceived is identified with something perceived or experienced in the speaker's here and now. Conforming to the difference between ὅδε and οὗτος that we saw earlier, the entity to which ἐκεῖνος refers is pointed at in accordance with its information status. When it is already shared between speaker and addressee, as in (8) and (9), the deictic used is οὗτος; when it is an appearance that is new to the hearer(s), the deictic is ὅδε, as in (10) and (11). Antigone is ἐκείνη, not because she is outside the context of utterance, nor because she buried her brother at another time and in another place than the present place and time, but because she, physically present, is identified with the concept that is on everyone's mind: she is the one. (Note that the "formula" οὗτος ἐκεῖνος "this <is> that" is used by Aristotle (*Poet.* 1448b17) to characterize the mental process of *mimesis*: the correct identification of what a given likeness represents.)

The comparison of ἐκεῖνος with ὅδε/οὗτος yields a number of observations:

a)   physical distance is not the appropriate concept for the characterization of ἐκεῖνος, since the cognitive salience of the concept referred to turns it into something that is experientially very close;

b)   a more adequate description is that ἐκεῖνος, unlike the two other demonstratives, does not point at a person or thing that can physically be perceived in the context of utterance;

c)   unlike ὅδε/οὗτος, the use of ἐκεῖνος is not prompted by perception in the speaker's present: the referent of ἐκεῖνος was already on the minds of both speaker and hearer *before* that moment;

d)   in the case of ὅδε and οὗτος informational disparity occurs: in uttering ὅδε, speakers assume that they have better access to the item in question than their interlocutors (see (2) and (3) above); conversely, in uttering οὗτος they typically assume that their interlocutors have better access to the item pointed at than they do themselves (as in (5) above);

e)   ἐκεῖνος differs from ὅδε/οὗτος in that it does not involve such informational "trade off"; the concept denoted by the deictic is equally accessible to both speaker and hearer;

f)   this means that the utterance of ὅδε is a matter considered by the speaker to be high in "newsworthiness" to the hearer; the utterance of οὗτος, on the other hand, is not so much new or newsworthy to the hearer as a basis from which to launch further exchange (see (5) above); ἐκεῖνος, by contrast, represents referents of low newsworthiness;

g)   note, however, that this does *not* mean that the referent of ἐκεῖνος is unimportant, only that its importance does not derive from a perception in the context and at the moment of utterance.

These various observations can be brought together in table 11.1:

Table 11.1 Perceptual and cognitive modalities of the Greek deictics

Deictic	Perceptual status with respect to speaker	Perceptual status with respect to hearer	Speaker's assessment of hearer's familiarity	Newsworthiness
ὅδε	close/identical	perceptible	lower than speaker's	high
οὗτος	perceptible	close/identical	higher than speaker's	middle
ἐκεῖνος	not perceptible	not perceptible	equal	low

Let us now consider how this use of the deictics in interactive speech is mapped onto the realities of communication in written continuous discourse.

Deictics in text

In continuous written text οὗτος is commonly said to be "anaphoric" and ὅδε "cataphoric," in "carrying" their referent "back up" and "further down," respectively. In other words, an anaphoric pronoun is thought to refer back in the text and a cataphoric pronoun is thought to be referring ahead. This is a very "textual" way of looking, setting deixis within the text (sometimes called "endophora") apart from "exophoric" deixis in actual conversational contexts in the "real world" (on endophora and exophora, see Halliday and Hasan 1976: 33). But what the text's author or represented speaker actually does with the two deictics is not essentially different from what happens in dialogue in the real world. In the implicit (sometimes explicit) communication between the text's narrator/author as speaker and the reader as interlocutor or hearer, οὗτος is the deictic reserved for what is already shared between the two, whereas ὅδε for what can be presented as salient and new to the reader. Thus historiographical narrators typically present the beginning of speeches with a phrase containing a form of τάδε and conclude them with one containing a form of οὗτος, e.g., εἴρετο ὁ Κροῖσος **τάδε** ... **ταῦτα** ἐπειρώτα "Croesus said these/the following things (…) those things he asked" (Hdt. 1.30.2–3); οἱ μὲν Κερκυραῖοι ἔλεξαν **τοιάδε** (…) **ταῦτα** μὲν οἱ Κερκυραῖοι εἶπον "the Cercyaeans spoke words like the following (…) these words the Cercyraeans spoke" (Thuc. 1.31.4–36.4); **τάδε** εἶπεν (…) ἐπεὶ δὲ **ταῦτ'** εἶπεν "he spoke these words … after he had said that" (Xen. *Hell.* 1.6.8–12). Instead of a one-dimensional "up" or "down," the play of pronouns is a matter of dynamic communication. At the moment of its introduction the speech is still "with" the narrator and for the reader it is new information, a situation very similar to the stage entries in drama. At the moment of its conclusion, by contrast, the speech has become "with" the reader as well and can be pointed at as shared information with the appropriate deictic of the second person.

Οὗτος and ὅδε, then, are elements that channel the flow of information between the author (the text's speaker) and the reader (the text's listener), marking the arrival and onset of new information (ὅδε) or the point where information introduced becomes a basis shared between the two parties, from which the discourse can move on. This strategy is not limited to the introduction and conclusion of direct speech; any information can be introduced with ὅδε and concluded with οὗτος; the two deictics punctuate the text, thus setting off specific stretches of discourse, e.g., ἐξηρίθμησαν δὲ **τόνδε τὸν τρόπον** (…) μέχρι οὗ πάντας **τούτῳ τῷ τρόπῳ** ἐξηρίθμησαν "They counted <the army> in the following way (…) until they had in this way counted all persons" (Hdt. 7.60.1–2).

In isolation, ὅδε signals in ongoing narrative the particular salience of a piece of information being introduced, e.g., δηλοῖ δέ μοι καὶ **τόδε** τῶν παλαιῶν ἀσθένειαν οὐχ ἥκιστα· "This/the following point also is not least in making the weakness of the ancients evident to me:. . ." (Thuc. 1.1.3). When this forward-looking use of ὅδε occurs in actual dialogue, the possible interjected question of the interlocutor underscores the status of the proximal deictic as conveying new, salient material not yet shared between the speaker and the addressee:

> (12)   — καὶ μήν που **καὶ τόδε** δεῖ σκοπεῖν, ὅταν κρίνειν μέλλῃς φύσιν φιλόσοφόν τε
>   καὶ μή
>   — τὸ ποῖον;
>
>   — And surely you have to look into this as well, if you are to judge what consti-
>   tutes a philosophical nature and what does not.
>   — What kind of thing? (Pl. *Resp.* 486a1–3)

The interjected question τὸ ποῖον; is of course absent from monologic discourse, but it is never far off; anticipating such questions is in fact what gives the text its structure and its meaning.

Οὗτος does more than "refer back" to what is now known information to the reader or hearer; it recapitulates a stretch of discourse at the moment of its conclusion and so serves as basis on which the subsequent stretch of discourse is built, e.g:

> (13)   **ταῦτα μέν νυν** Πέρσαι τε καὶ Φοίνικες λέγουσι. **ἐγὼ δὲ** περὶ μὲν **τούτων** οὐκ ἔρχομαι
>   ἐρέων …
>
>   This <is what> the Persians and Phoenicians are saying; I for my part am not going
>   to say about these events . . . (Hdt. 1.5.3)

As this extract shows, οὗτος very easily combines with the particles μέν and δέ as markers of "boundaries" in a discourse (see Bakker 1993). In the example just quoted, the deictic ταῦτα stands in "contrast" to the intervention of the narrator himself (ταῦτα μέν … ἐγὼ δὲ), but there is less a contrast strictly speaking than a transition, a meaningful break in the discourse as the narrative moves into a new thematic segment. In other cases οὗτος contributes more to the beginning than to the end of a discourse unit, as in the start of the story of Gyges and Candaules at the beginning of Herodotus' *Histories*:

> (14)   **οὗτος** δὴ ὦν ὁ Κανδαύλης ἠράσθη τῆς ἑωυτοῦ γυναικός, ἐρασθεὶς δὲ ἐνόμιζέ οἱ εἶναι
>   γυναῖκα πολλὸν πασέων καλλίστην. Ὥστε δὲ **ταῦτα** νομίζων, ἦν γάρ οἱ τῶν αἰχμοφόρων
>   Γύγης ὁ Δασκύλου ἀρεσκόμενος μάλιστα, **τούτῳ** τῷ Γύγῃ καὶ τὰ σπουδαιέστερα
>   τῶν πρηγμάτων ὑπερετίθετο ὁ Κανδαύλης καὶ δὴ καὶ τὸ εἶδος τῆς γυναικὸς
>   ὑπερεπαινέων.
>
>   This Candaules, then, was infatuated with his own wife, and in his infatuation he
>   considered that his wife was by far the most beautiful of all. As a consequence,
>   considering these things – and you need to know that there was one of his

> bodyguards, Gyges son of Daskulos, who was especially his favorite – so with <u>this</u> Gyges he used to share his most important business, in particular his excessive praise for the beauty of his wife. (Hdt. 1.8.1)

Candaules, just introduced and hence now known to the listener, is the starting point, marked as οὗτος, from whom the story takes off. The deictic also marks the two other important ingredients of the story, Candaules' ideas about his wife's beauty and the presence of Gyges the bodyguard, thus punctuating the narrative in the leisurely build-up of the story.

Let us now turn to ἐκεῖνος; here, too, the function of the demonstrative in interactive speech that we have briefly reviewed can serve as basis for understanding the way in which the pronoun contributes to the meaning and structure of continuous, monologic discourse. Just as in real life one can point with ἐκεῖνος to something that is farther removed than the item pointed at with οὗτος, so one can use ἐκεῖνος in text to refer back to what is farther removed than the immediately preceding material referred to with οὗτος:

(15) εἰ δὲ εἴη οὕτως ἄκρητον ὥστε καὶ μέλαν φαίνεσθαι, δεινότερόν ἐστι **τοῦτο ἐκείνων**.

And if it [i.e., sputum] should be so unmixed as to appear black, then <u>this</u> is more dangerous than <u>that</u> [i.e., the cases mentioned before]. (Hippoc. *Prog.* 14)

In historiographical narrative we encounter a further, more complicated, way in which the difference between ἐκεῖνος and οὗτος can be exploited in written text. In indirect discourse, when the deictic perspective is that of a third party (i.e., third with respect to the narrator/speaker and the reader/listener), ἐκεῖνος takes the place of οὗτος, a typical strategy in the grammar of narrative to convey that the deixis takes place embedded inside the text, beyond the primary communication between the narrator and the reader:

(16) ὡς δὲ τὰ κατὰ τὸν Τέλλον προετρέψατο ὁ Σόλων τὸν Κροῖσον εἴπας πολλά τε καὶ ὄλβια, ἐπειρώτα τίνα δεύτερον μετ' **ἐκεῖνον** ἴδοι, δοκέων πάγχυ δευτερεῖα γῶν οἴσεσθαι.

When Solon, in saying much about the blessed condition of Tellos, had stimulated Croesus, the latter asked him who he saw as the second [in happiness] after <u>that man</u>, believing that he would at least carry the second prize. (Hdt. 1.31.1)

Our access to Tellos the Athenian is mediated through Solon's account of him and Croesus' listening to it; the reader of Herodotus' text is at one remove from it. The use of ἐκεῖνος instead of οὗτος is the grammatical mechanism effecting such "displaced" communication. In direct speech, we might envisage Croesus asking "Whom do you see as second after <u>this man</u> (τοῦτον)?" The mechanism is even more striking when ἐκεῖνος takes on the second person feature that οὗτος has, as we saw, in real interactive speech:

(17) τοὺς δὲ ὑποκρίνασθαι ὡς οὐδὲ **ἐκεῖνοι** Ἰοῦς τῆς Ἀργείης ἔδοσάν σφι δίκας τῆς ἁρπαγῆς· οὐδὲ ὦν αὐτοὶ δώσειν **ἐκείνοισι**.

> And they [i.e., the Greeks] responded that they [i.e., the Colchians] had not given them [i.e., the Greeks] fair compensation for the abduction of Io of Argos. So they [i.e., the Greeks] would not give them [i.e., the Colchians] any either. (Hdt. 1.2.3)

In hypothetical direct speech we could imagine the Greeks saying: "So we will not give <any compensation> to you either" (whereby "you" comes in the place of ἐκεῖνος).

We see, then, that the availability of a third deictic (in contrast with, e.g., Eng. *this* and *that*) can be exploited for the sake of embedding secondary voices and points of view in narrative: whereas ὅδε and οὗτος are used in the primary (but implicit) communication between the narrator and his listener/reader, ἐκεῖνος is reserved for the secondary communication conducted by the "third parties" contained in the narrative.

But ἐκεῖνος can be used in the communication between the narrator and his audience as well. If it is, the cognitive dimension of the deictic comes into play. As we saw, ἐκεῖνος frequently refers to concepts and ideas that were already in the speaker's and listener's mind before the moment of utterance (see (7) above), whereas ὅδε and οὗτος represent newer, perceptually salient items in the context of utterance. When this difference is transposed to monologic discourse, ἐκεῖνος turns out to be a marker of *continuous topics*, whereas ὅδε and οὗτος tend to occur at moments of discontinuity (as we saw, the transition to explicitly announced new information or the recapitulation of a previous topic as a step to a new one). For example, at the end of the story of Gyges and Candaules, the queen is referred to as ἐκείνη (καί μιν **ἐκείνη** ἐγχειρίδιον δοῦσα κατακρύπτει ὑπὸ τὴν αὐτὴν θύρην "And she gave him a dagger and hid him behind the same door" Hdt. 1.12.2): she has been present throughout the story, whether as concept or as agent, and is a clear case of a continuous topic. To change ἐκείνη into αὕτη would suggest that the queen was somehow being contrasted with another woman or that she had just been introduced into the story, with the demonstrative signaling that the narrative was moving into a new episode from that basis.

The lesser perceptual salience of items referred to with ἐκεῖνος makes it in narrative the appropriate element for reference back to an item from the previous clause without there being any contrast or topic discontinuity involved, as in "the latter" in English, e.g:

(18) ἀρτοφαγέουσι δὲ ἐκ τῶν ὀλυρέων ποιεῦντες ἄρτους, τοὺς **ἐκεῖνοι** κυλλήστις ὀνομάζουσι.

As for their bread consumption, they use starch wheat for their loaves, which they call *kyllestis*. (Hdt. 2.77.4)

(19) οἱ δ᾽ αὐτόν τε ἔβαλλεν καὶ τὰ ὑποζύγια τὰ **ἐκείνου**

And they threw <stones> at him and the pack animals of the latter [i.e., and his pack animals]. (Xen. *An.* 1.3.1)

(20) καὶ διὰ **ταύτην** τὴν ἐπιθυμίαν ἔδωκε Γοργίᾳ ἀργύριον τῷ Λεοντίνῳ. ἐπεὶ δὲ συνεγένετο **ἐκείνῳ**, . . .

And out of that ambition he [i.e., Proxenos] had given money to Gorgias of Leontini <in order to study with him>. When he had been with the latter, . . . (Xen. *An.* 2.6.16)

In (18) and (19) ἐκεῖνος refers back to the subject and object, respectively, of the preceding clause and is little more than a variant of (oblique cases of) αὐτός (cf. K-G i: 649). In (20) the difference between ταύτην and ἐκείνῳ is instructive. The former sets up Proxenos' ambition as *Leitmotiv* for the characterization of this general, whereas ἐκείνῳ is used to refer to "Gorgias" as a topic of only passing importance that will not be mentioned again. We still can call it "continuous" (just as Candaules' wife, who is present as topic throughout the story), since it is easily recoverable from the previous clause.

The considerable contribution of the deictics to the structure of written texts, then, can be traced back to the interplay of perceptual and cognitive factors that lies behind the use of the deictics in interactive discourse. It does not seem appropriate to speak of an anaphoric use as distinct from a deictic use of the demonstrative pronouns. Rather, the function of the pronouns in written texts is an extension of what happens in actual conversation—not unlike the instantiation of prototypes as discussed in ch. 9. This means that the structure of written discourse is not mechanical or impersonal, but a matter of real interaction. In the second case study we will see that the same applies to the use of verbal tense in speech and text.

Tense and Temporal Reference

Tense is commonly seen as the grammaticalized location of events in time. Events are seen as "placed" in time, either before, or after, or simultaneous with the moment of utterance. Such a referential view, however, can become rather abstract and sterile in a conception of language and grammar as something that people actually do. The moment of speech is not just a point on a temporal continuum, but a moment of doing and experiencing things. The act of uttering the verb, i.e., of asserting the event, may have an impact on the event's very temporality and time cannot be isolated as a simple objective space "in which" events are located.

As far as the past is concerned, speakers can of course always state that an event took place at another time (and often another place), but in practice this happens most often when they tell stories, when events are told for their own sake (although many stories told in interactive speech contexts do serve a purpose with respect to the speakers' immediate here and now). More typically, however, the past event that figures in a speaker's utterance is in some way connected with the present speech situation, as in the way Croesus' envoys in Herodotus present themselves to their intended addressees:

(21) ἔπεμψε ἡμέας Κροῖσος ὁ Λυδῶν τε καὶ ἄλλων ἐθνέων βασιλεύς, λέγων **τάδε**.

<The one who> <u>has sent</u> us <is> Croesus, king of the Lydians and of other peoples, saying <u>the following</u>: (Hdt. 1.69.2)

Croesus dispatching his ambassadors of course took place in the past at the beginning of the envoys' long journey from Sardeis to Sparta; but he has not really "sent" his heralds until they arrive at their destination and deliver their king's message. Only the utterance of ἔπεμψε ἡμέας Κροῖσος "Croesus sent us" will complete the mission, as the assertion of a past action that reaches its fulfillment in the present moment.

The use of the *aorist* is crucial in this regard. Had the envoys used an imperfect, as Herodotus does himself in reporting (in his own voice) on this embassy (ὁ Κροῖσος ἔπεμπε ἐς Σπάρτην ἀγγέλους "Croesus sent messengers to Sparta," Hdt. 1.69.1), their audience would presumably have been puzzled, for it would have seemed to them that the envoys were telling them something that happened to them in the past ("<and then> Croesus sent us . . ."). It would also need more context to make sense to the listeners.

We can make a meaningful distinction, then, between referring to an event (or "placing it in time") and asserting it as the action that constitutes the present speech moment. In the latter case, the domain of the aorist, there is something performative – in the sense of Austin's speech act theory (Austin 1975) – about the speech event, in that making the utterance is carrying out, or at least completing, the action denoted by the verb. This phenomenon takes its most extreme form in the so-called "dramatic aorist" or "present aorist" (K-G 1.163–5; Smyth 1956: 432), e.g., ἐπήνεσα "OK" ("I have praised"), συνῆκα "I see" ("I have understood"), ἐδεξάμην "I accept," ἥσθην "Nice!" ("I've had fun"). These are usually considered a peculiar use of the aorist, but are in fact central to the meaning of this "tense" (Bakker 1997c: 23).

The difference between the aorist on the one hand and the present and imperfect on the other stands out clearly when we consider temporal adverbial modifiers such as νῦν "now," οὔπω "not yet," and negation, in particular οὐδείς "nobody" as subject of the verb. Aorists can be modified by νῦν, a combination we do not find for the imperfect:

(22) ΘΕ.   καὶ **νῦν** ὅπερ μαχιμώτατον Θρᾳκῶν ἔθνος
           ἔπεμψεν ὑμῖν.

       And <u>now</u> he <u>has sent</u> you the most warlike tribe of the Thracians. (Ar. *Ach.* 153–4)

Modified with οὔπω "not yet," an aorist is the assertion that something has not happened up to and including the moment of utterance; an imperfect modified with οὔπω, on the other hand, will convey that something that actually occurred in the past was not yet the case at a given point in time in the past (notice also the use of τουτί in (23)):

(23) Ἡράκλεις **τουτί** τί ἦν;
       τουτί μὰ Δι᾿ ἐγὼ πολλὰ δὴ καὶ δείν᾿ ἰδὼν
       οὔπω κόραϰ᾿ **εἶδον** ἐπεφορβιωμένον

       Heracles, what was that?
       <u>That there</u>, by Zeus, I've seen quite a few striking things in my life,
       but <u>never yet have I seen</u> a raven with a mouthband on. (Ar. *Av.* 859–60)

(24) οὐ γὰρ ἔγωγ᾿ **ἐπολιτευόμην** πω τότε

       For <u>I was not yet in politics then.</u> (Dem. 18.18)

In (23) the speaker does not say that something had not yet happened in the past, but that something has not happened until the moment of utterance; in (24), on the other hand, the speaker, Demosthenes, who obviously has a long political career behind him at the time of the utterance of this speech (the *On the Crown*), refers to a time in the past when that career had not yet started. His temporal reference is modified by τότε "then"; this demonstrative temporal modifier contrasts with its indefinite counterpart ποτε "ever," which has a natural affinity with aorists modified by οὔπω, e.g.,

(25) οὐπώποτ' ἐμνήστευσα παῖδα σήν, γύναι

I have never wooed your daughter, woman. (Eur. *IA* 841)

No specific temporal reference takes place here; the past evoked by Achilles' statement includes the present moment of utterance in which the denial takes place.

When the verb has the negative quantifier οὐδείς as subject, the negation is contained in the past when the verb is imperfect:

(26) ἥβων γάρ, κἀδυνάμην κλέπτειν, ἰσχυόν τ' αὐτὸς ἐμαυτοῦ,
κοὐδείς μ' ἐφύλαττ'.

I was young and good at stealing, and was sure of my strength,
And nobody kept a watch on me. (Ar. *Vesp.* 357–8)

But when the verb is aorist, the negation inherent in οὐδείς attracts by a grammatical rule the modifier πώποτε "ever yet," turning the statement again into a denial in the present, e.g:

(27) οὐδ' οἶδ' οὐδείς ἥντιν' ἐρῶσαν πώποτ' ἐποίησα γυναῖκα.

Nor does anyone know any woman whom I have ever represented in my poetry as being in love. (Ar. *Ran.* 1044)

We see, then, that the temporal and deictic orientation of the aorist is quite different from that of the present/imperfect, and also from the way in which "temporal deixis" is usually characterized. Aorists are oriented toward the speaker's present, even if the event they denote is past. The interplay between the two in one and the same discourse is most strikingly displayed in narrative, where the two tenses effect distinct modes of discourse, the evocation of past events vs the assertion of facts from the past in function of the speaker's interests in the present. Oratorical narrative, told by a real speaker, with real interests in the present, to a real audience, provides instructive cases, as in the following passage from *On the Crown*:

(28) Ἑσπέρα μὲν γὰρ ἦν, ἧκε δ' ἀγγέλλων τις ὡς τοὺς πρυτάνεις ὡς Ἐλάτεια κατείληπται. καὶ μετὰ ταῦθ' οἱ μὲν εὐθὺς ἐξαναστάντες μεταξὺ δειπνοῦντες τούς τ' ἐκ τῶν σκηνῶν τῶν κατὰ τὴν ἀγορὰν ἐξεῖργον καὶ τὰ γέρρ' ἐνεπίμπρασαν, οἱ δὲ τοὺς στρατηγοὺς μετεπέμποντο καὶ τὸν σαλπικτὴν ἐκάλουν καὶ θορύβου πλήρης ἦν ἡ πόλις.
τῇ δ' ὑστεραίᾳ, ἅμα τῇ ἡμέρᾳ, οἱ μὲν πρυτάνεις τὴν βουλὴν ἐκάλουν εἰς τὸ βουλευτήριον, ὑμεῖς δ' εἰς τὴν ἐκκλησίαν ἐπορεύεσθε, καὶ πρὶν ἐκείνην χρηματίσαι καὶ προβουλεῦσαι πᾶς ὁ δῆμος ἄνω καθῆτο. καὶ μετὰ ταῦτα ὡς ἦλθεν ἡ βουλὴ καὶ ἀπήγγειλαν οἱ πρυτάνεις τὰ προσηγγελμέν' ἑαυτοῖς καὶ τὸν ἥκοντα παρήγαγον κἀκεῖνος εἶπεν, ἠρώτα μὲν ὁ κῆρυξ 'τίς ἀγορεύειν βούλεται;' παρῄει δ' οὐδείς.

πολλάκις δὲ τοῦ κήρυκος ἐρωτῶντος οὐδὲν μᾶλλον **ἀνίστατ' οὐδείς**, ἁπάντων μὲν τῶν στρατηγῶν παρόντων, ἁπάντων δὲ τῶν ῥητόρων, καλούσης δὲ [τῆς κοινῆς] τῆς πατρίδος [φωνῆς] τὸν ἐροῦνθ' ὑπὲρ σωτηρίας· ἦν γὰρ ὁ κῆρυξ κατὰ τοὺς νόμους φωνὴν ἀφίησι, ταύτην κοινὴν τῆς πατρίδος δίκαιον ἡγεῖσθαι. (...)
ἐφάνην τοίνυν οὗτος ἐν ἐκείνῃ τῇ ἡμέρᾳ ἐγὼ καὶ παρελθὼν εἶπον εἰς ὑμᾶς,

It **was** evening; someone **came** to the office of the *prutaneis* with the news that Elateia had been occupied. Thereafter some of them immediately stood up from their meal and **drove** the <merchants> from their stalls in the marketplace and **burnt** the wicker booths; others **summoned** the generals and **called** the trumpeter, and the city **was** full of noise and commotion.

The next day at the break of dawn the *prutaneis* **convoked** the Council to the council-chamber and you **marched** to the Assembly, and even before the aforementioned (ἐκείνην, i.e., the Council) could consider the matter and pass a motion, the entire *demos* **was already sitting** above (i.e., at the Pnyx). And thereafter, when the Council had arrived and the *prutaneis* had reported the news that had been announced to them, and they had brought forward the man who had come <to bring the tidings>, and when the latter (κἀκεῖνος) had spoken, the herald **asked** "Who wishes to speak?" **No one came forward**. As the herald asked several times still **no one stood up**, with all the generals and all the politicians present. The fatherland was calling for the speaker who would save her (for the voice of the herald under these formal conditions can with justification be called the collective voice of the country).

Well, on that (ἐκείνῃ) day, that one (οὗτος), I, appeared, and having come forward I spoke to you. (Dem. 18.169–73)

Demosthenes' narrative of the arrival in Athens of the news that Philip of Macedon had seized Elateia is meant to bring the audience back to that memorable night and following day; this evocation of the past is articulated as a continuous string of imperfects (in bold face), interrupted only by four aorists in a "backgrounded" temporal subclause (καὶ μετὰ ταῦτα ὡς ἦλθεν κτλ – notice that in the grammatically controlled environment of the temporal clause, the aorist takes on the temporal feature of anteriority and can be translated with a pluperfect in English).

The first independent aorist main verb, ἐφάνην "I appeared" is uttered only when the narrator himself enters on the scene, not as part of the experiential reliving of the past, but as a performance that has a direct bearing on the present of narration and the speaker's interests there. With ἐφάνην τοίνυν the discourse is strictly speaking not narrative anymore and the speaker's actions in the past have become a basis for making claims in the present. (Notice also the use of the deictics in view of the discussion presented earlier: twice the phrase καὶ μετὰ ταῦτα "and thereafter" effects a new step in the narrative; three times we see ἐκεῖνος as a continuous topic, with in the third case, ἐν ἐκείνῃ τῇ ἡμέρᾳ "on that day" the added feature of the distant reality that is present in the mind; and finally, Demosthenes refers to himself pointedly as οὗτος ἐγὼ "that one, me," which lifts him out of the past and points at him as he stands, here and now, before his audience.)

From oratorical narrative, with its live audience, we can now move to the use of the two tenses in written historiography. The communication here is with an absent reader, not with a present listener, but not therefore less real. The present of discourse is here not a real speech situation but a writer's present, in which communication takes place between the historian and his readership, as opposed to the recreation of historical events in the past. An instructive case is the narrative of the battle of Thermopylae in Herodotus (Hdt. 7.207–25). The narrative of the preparations for battle, the Persian spy, Xerxes' reaction to Demaratus' account of the Lacedaemonians, and the first stage of the battle, is largely conducted in a long series of imperfects (for the aorists that do occur occasionally, see below).

The aorist becomes the dominant tense only when Herodotus' account leaves the narrative time-line and digresses on the later death of the traitor Ephialtes:

(29) ὕστερον δὲ δείσας Λακεδαιμονίους **ἔφυγε** ἐς Θεσσαλίην, καί οἱ φυγόντι ὑπὸ τῶν
Πυλαγόρων, τῶν Ἀμφικτυόνων ἐς τὴν Πυλαίην συλλεγομένων, ἀργύριον **ἐπεκηρύχθη**.
χρόνῳ δὲ ὕστερον, **κατῆλθε** γὰρ ἐς Ἀντικύρην, **ἀπέθανε** ὑπὸ Ἀθηνάδεω ἀνδρὸς
Τρηχινίου· ὁ δὲ Ἀθηνάδης <u>οὗτος</u> **ἀπέκτεινε** μὲν Ἐπιάλτην δι' ἄλλην αἰτίην, τὴν ἐγὼ ἐν
τοῖσι ὄπισθε λόγοισι σημανέω, **ἐτιμήθη** μέντοι ὑπὸ Λακεδαιμονίων οὐδὲν ἧσσον.
Ἐπιάλτης μὲν <u>οὕτω</u> ὕστερον <u>τούτων</u> **ἀπέθανε**. ἔστι δὲ ἕτερος λόγος λεγόμενος, ὡς. . .

Later, out of fear for the Lacedaemonians, he **fled** to Thessaly, and when he had fled there a price of silver **was put** on his head by the Pylagoroi when the Amphictyons met at Pylaia. Still later (for he **had come back** to live in Anticyra), **he died** at the hands of Athenades, a man from Trachis. It is true that <u>this</u> Athenades **killed** Ephialtes for an unrelated reason (which I will set out in later accounts), but **he was honored** for it by the Lacedaemonians all the same. <u>This is the way</u> Ephialtes **died** later than <u>the events related here</u>. There is also another account being told, namely that . . . (Hdt. 7.213.2–3)

Whereas the historian is largely absent from his discourse when he seeks to evoke the events from the past for their own sake, he is very much present when he relates events that are explicitly presented as the results of his own research, external to the historical reality recreated. In this extract the narrative is temporarily suspended as the historian focuses on facts that are "timeless," not contained within the temporal frame of the narrative that is under way. (In a similar way Thucydides uses the aorist when he speaks about the end of the Peloponnesian War in the middle of his account of it: Thuc. 5.26.1.) The historian speaks now in his own voice, stating in aorists historical facts that are asserted, and defended against alternative versions.

When the narrative with its "internal" point of view resumes, the imperfects come back. At one point their function is so internal that they do not represent the events themselves but Leonidas' experience and consideration of them:

(30) αὐτῷ δὲ ἀπιέναι οὐ καλῶς ἔχειν· μένοντι δὲ αὐτοῦ κλέος μέγα **ἐλείπετο**, καὶ ἡ
Σπάρτης εὐδαιμονίη οὐκ **ἐξηλείφετο**.

For himself he did not consider moving away an honorable option. Staying <u>would leave</u> him great *kleos* and the prosperity of Sparta <u>would not be wiped out</u>. (Hdt. 7.220.2)

Changing the imperfects here into aorists would be a change from a perspective *ante factum* to one *post factum*; instead of conveying a desire for martyrdom from within the events the passage would become the conferral of fame in the future. The use of the imperfect tense for such represented thought is attested for other languages as well (in English the past progressive serves this function; see Ehrlich 1990: 81–94).

Finally, we may consider the aorists that occur in the narrative outside the digression on Ephialtes. Some of these occur in temporal subclauses, e.g: ὡς δὲ ἐσέπεσον φερόμενοι ἐς τοὺς Ἕλληνας οἱ Μῆδοι "When the Medes threw themselves at the Greeks . . ." (Hdt. 7.210.2); ὡς δὲ εἶδον ἄνδρας ἐνδυομένους ὅπλα "When they saw men arming themselves" (Hdt. 7.218.2). The temporal subclause, when placed before its main clause, is a typical phenomenon in narrative discourse; it states the conditions under which the event denoted by its main clause occurs—in this way the subclause can be said to be "backgrounding," as also in the extract from Demosthenes' *On the Crown*; but it also has a function with respect to the wider flow of the narrative. Preposed temporal clauses, in providing a "frame" for the discourse to come, effect a break with respect to the previous discourse: they signal a new paragraph, or in less textual and more cognitive terms, a new "center of interest" or bundle of interrelated perceptions. Temporal clauses, therefore, in backgrounding an event instead of narrating it in an independent main clause, have a regulatory, or signposting, function: they do not specify "what happened" so much as provide a stage for the events of the story.

Other aorist interruptions of the flow of imperfects occur in recapitulative or explanatory phrases containing οὗτος in the function outlined above (e.g., τότε μὲν οὕτως ἠγωνίσαντο "These ones had delivered battle in this way (Hdt. 7.212.1); οὗτοι δὲ ἐς τὸ ὄρος ἐτάχθησαν "These ones had been positioned toward the mountain" (Hdt.7.212.2)). In these cases the aorist and the deictic are working in concert in phrases that Herodotus explicitly addresses to his readership as interjections to guide and signpost the represented flow of past events.

Speech and Text

Informal interactive speech and formal writing can be and have often been seen as opposite endpoints of a wide continuum. Perspectives on such a continuum include oppositions such as paratactic vs hypotactic, fragmented vs integrated, involved vs detached (see Chafe 1982), or real vs fictional; see also ch. 20 on register. But in spite of such very real differences between speech and text, the idea of a continuum also suggests common ground. If informal interactive speech is where grammar is shaped under communicative pressure and cognitive constraints, then the more formal registers of the language provide venues for adapting the grammatical structures thus created to new but related contexts.

The principle is not entirely different from the relation between the instantiations of prototypes as discussed in ch. 9. The use of the deictics in formal written text, for example, does not involve meanings or senses distinct and separate from that in speech, calling for separate perspectives or terms (such as anaphora/endophora vs deixis/exophora). Rather, text is a domain that, though new, is not so different that the linguistic elements of the "source" domain, speech, cannot be used. A historian such as Thucydides, adopting a detached stance with regard to his distant readership, communicates in ways quite different from the way in which everyday conversation is conducted, or the way in which Aristophanes' characters talk to each other. But communicating he does all the same, and so alongside the many elements that his linguistic register does *not* share with ordinary spoken Greek there are elements that it does share. And some of those elements, including those studied in this chapter, are among the central devices for the structuring of his text.

FURTHER READING

The literature on pragmatics and discourse is overwhelming; there is a proliferation of terms and approaches that is not always justified by the originality of the perspective adopted. And there tends to be an emphasis on models and theories at the expense of careful observation and interpretation of data: actual speech uttered in context. Schiffrin 1994 is an overview of most theories and approaches that are usually subsumed under the general catchword "pragmatics." Chafe 1994 is important for the cognitive aspects of spoken language and Fillmore 1997 is classic on deixis; see also Levinson 1983: 54–96; on tense in narrative, see Fleischman 1990. See (C. S.) Smith 2003 for "modes of discourse" (as, for example, the difference between narrative and historiographical assertion as discussed above).

Deixis in Greek is discussed in Felson 2004 and Bakker 2005. On the demonstrative pronouns, see K.-G. 1: 641–51; Magnien 1922; Ruijgh 2006; and on ἐκεῖνος in particular, Havers 1906 and Bonifazi 2004. The conception of tense in Greek proposed in this chapter is further developed in Bakker 1997c; 2005; 2007. On the discourse function of temporal subclauses in Greek narrative, see Bakker 1991 and Buijs 2005.

CHAPTER TWELVE

Greek and Proto-Indo-European

Jeremy Rau

Greek and the Indo-European Language Family

Greek is a member of the large Indo-European language family, which includes ten or eleven principal branches and hundreds of ancient and modern languages spoken from the British Isles in the far west to western China and India in the east. The genetic ancestor of these languages, which is called Proto-Indo-European (PIE) or simply Indo-European (IE), was spoken some five or six thousand years ago (*c.* 4000–3500 BCE), probably in the steppe zone north and east of the Black Sea. This language, which is not directly attested in written records, has been the subject of intensive linguistic research over the last 200 years; today it is well understood in all aspects of its grammar and has been fully reconstructed through the techniques of comparative historical linguistics. (On Proto-Indo-European and its reconstruction, see also ch. 24.)

The principal branches of the IE language family, in rough order of first attestation, are as follows (excluding Greek):

Anatolian is an extinct language family that was spoken during the second and first millennium BCE in Anatolia, modern-day Turkey. The best-attested and most important representative of this family is Hittite (seventeenth–thirteenth cent. BCE), the language of the Hittite Empire which is preserved in thousands of clay tablets written in cuneiform script. Additional Anatolian languages include Carian (sixth–first cent. BCE), Lycian (seventh–fifth cent. BCE), Lydian (ninth–fourth cent. BCE), and Luwian, a likely candidate for the language of the Trojans (second–early first millennium BCE) – see further ch. 15.

Indo-Iranian, which now includes hundreds of modern languages found mostly in south Asia, has two large and ancient branches: Indo-Aryan (or Indic) and Iranian. The most ancient representative of Indo-Aryan is Vedic Sanskrit, the language of the Vedic literature of ancient India, whose oldest and most important text is the *Rigveda*, conventionally dated to the late second millennium BCE. The oldest attested Iranian language is Avestan, the language of the Zoroastrian *Avesta*, which appears in two dialects, Old and Young Avestan (late second–first millennium BCE). Iranian also comprises Old Persian, the language of the Achaemenid kings of ancient Iran, Median (on these two languages, see also ch. 15), and many other ancient and modern languages of Iran and Central Asia.

Phrygian is an extinct branch spoken during the first millennium BCE in western central Anatolia. It is found in short inscriptions dating from the eighth to the fifth centuries BCE (Old Phrygian) and from the first to second centuries CE (Neo-Phrygian) – see further chs 15 and 16.

Italic includes the majority of the languages of ancient Italy. The family has two main subgroups. The first is Sabellic, consisting of Oscan (fourth–first cent. BCE), Umbrian (seventh–first cent. BCE), and South Picene (seventh–fourth cent. BCE). The second subgroup is Latino-Faliscan, which includes Latin (the ancestor of the modern Romance languages), attested in inscriptions from the seventh century BCE, and its close neighbor and relative Faliscan, which is found in inscriptions dating from the sixth to the third centuries BCE. Venetic, a language attested in inscriptions from northeastern Italy *c.* 600–400 BCE, likely also belongs to this family.

Celtic was spoken in large areas of central and western Europe throughout the first millennium BCE. This branch is normally divided into two subgroups: the extinct Continental Celtic (third cent. BCE–third cent. CE), including Gaulish, Celtiberian, and Lepontic; and Insular Celtic, the languages of the British Isles, including Irish (Old Irish 400 CE +), Welsh (800 CE +), and others. It is likely, though still somewhat controversial, that Celtic and Italic form a distinct sub-branch of IE.

Germanic, which was spoken north and east of Celtic at the beginning of the first millennium CE, is divided into three subgroups. The extinct East Germanic is represented by Gothic, attested in Bible translations from the fourth century CE. North Germanic, which is first attested in Runic inscriptions (third cent. CE +), includes Old Norse (ninth–sixteenth cent.), Modern Icelandic, and the modern Scandinavian languages (Swedish, Norwegian, Danish). Northwest Germanic is represented by Old English (*c.* 700 +), Old High German (*c.* 750 +), Old Saxon (*c.* 850 +), and the modern languages English, Dutch, German, etc.

Armenian is first attested as Classical Armenian in the fifth century CE in a Bible translation and other literature, and continues into the medieval and modern periods. There are several modern dialects, most notably an Eastern (Armenia proper) and Western (Turkish and post-diaspora) variety.

Tocharian is an extinct language family spoken in the Tarim Basin of far western China during the first millennium CE. Two distinct dialects of the language, known as Tocharian A and B, are attested in documents – mostly Buddhist translation literature – dating from the sixth to the eighth centuries.

Balto-Slavic consists of two distinct subfamilies, the Baltic and Slavic languages. The earliest attested Baltic is the extinct Old Prussian (fourteenth–seventeenth cent. CE); the other two Baltic languages, Lithuanian and Latvian, which together constitute the Eastern branch of the family, are attested from the sixteenth century. The Slavic languages fall into three distinct branches: South Slavic (Serbo-Croatian, Bulgarian, Macedonian), which includes the earliest attested Slavic language, Old

Church Slavonic, found in Bible translations from the ninth century; West Slavic (Polish, Czech, etc.); and East Slavic (Russian, Ukrainian, etc.).

Albanian is attested from the fifteenth century CE in and around modern Albania. It appears in two broad dialects, a northern (Geg) and southern (Tosk) variety.

In addition to the well-defined families above, there are a number of poorly attested languages which are clearly members of the IE language family but whose exact position within the family is unclear. These so-called "Restsprachen" include languages like Thracian, spoken north and east of Macedonia in the first millennium BCE, and Messapic, a non-Italic language from ancient Italy found in inscriptions from the sixth to the first centuries BCE.

The Linguistic Periodization of Greek

By looking at linguistic innovations among the IE languages, it is possible to recover facts about the historical development of the IE proto-language and to establish pre-historic subgroups among the individual languages. From research like this it is clear that Anatolian was the first branch to separate off from the IE speech community, followed by Tocharian, a development which left a core group of languages that underwent a series of common innovations. Within this core group, Greek is generally held to be closely related to Indo-Iranian, and further to share a number of characteristic phonological and morphological innovations with Armenian and Phrygian.

The linguistic development of Greek, from late PIE up to the middle of the first millennium BCE, is conveniently arranged in the following four periods:

a) Late PIE/Pre-Proto-Greek. Fourth to third millennium BCE. This period includes the late PIE innovations that are common to Greek and Indo-Iranian, and further the phonological and morphological innovations that seem to characterize Greek, Armenian, and Phrygian. This last set of innovations probably took place in the third millennium once the ancestors (or, possibly, ancestor) of these languages were in the Balkans.

b) Proto-Greek. Late third millennium BCE. This stage of the language includes the changes which distinguish Greek from PIE and all other IE languages and which took place before Greek itself had started to differentiate dialectally. This phase probably coincides with the arrival of Greek speakers in Greece proper, likely dated *c.* 2300/2100 BCE.

c) Second Millennium Greek. This period corresponds to the development and *floruit* of Mycenaean civilization in Greece and Crete, *c.* 1400–1200. It is clear that by the early Mycenaean period Greek has already differentiated into three or four dialects. These dialects probably more or less coincide with what will become the main dialect groups of the first millennium: "Achaean" (Mycenaean, Cyprian, and Arcadian), Attic-Ionic (Attic and West, Central, and East Ionic), Aeolic (Lesbian, Thessalian, and Boeotian), and West Greek, which later differentiates into Northwest (Delphian, Elean, etc.) and West Greek proper (Laconian, Argolic, Cretan, etc.). (See further ch. 14.)

d)   First Millennium Greek. Towards the end of the second and beginning of the first millennium BCE, the Greek dialects undergo a number of Common Greek changes – viz. changes which postdate Proto-Greek but which affect all Greek dialects equally, often with varying results. These changes served to further solidify the dialectal lines that were already present in the second millennium, and include developments like the loss of *-h-* (< PIE *-i̯-* and *-s-*) and the elimination of the labiovelars (see below). The first half of the first millennium is a period of intense dialectal development and diversification, which leads to the large number of dialects that exist by the Classical period. This dialectal diversity is eventually eliminated through the spread of the *Koine* (ch. 16).

Throughout all these periods, Greek remains a remarkably conservative IE language, one rivaled in its preservation of archaic linguistic features only by Anatolian and Indo-Iranian.

Phonology

The PIE stop system distinguished labial, dental, palatovelar, velar, and labiovelar stops, all of which came in voiceless, voiced, and voiced aspirated form:

Table 12.1   Proto-Indo-European consonant stops

Stops	Labial	Dental	Palatovelar	Velar	Labiovelar
Voiceless	*p*	*t*	*k̂*	*k*	*kᵘ*
Voiced	*b*	*d*	*ĝ*	*g*	*gᵘ*
Voiced aspirated	*bʰ*	*dʰ*	*ĝʰ*	*gʰ*	*gᵘʰ*

The consonant system also contained the voiceless fricative *s* (with a voiced allophone *z* before voiced stops), and the nasals *m* and *n*, liquids *r* and *l*, and glides *i̯* and *u̯*. There were also three further consonants, generally referred to as *laryngeals* and represented as h_1, h_2, and h_3 (or alternatively $ə_1$, $ə_2$, and $ə_3$), which have disappeared with various effects from all IE languages but Anatolian. The precise phonetic value of the laryngeals is unclear, although it is likely that h_1 = [h] or [ʔ], h_2 = [ħ] and h_3 = [ʕ]. These consonants are mostly recognized by the effects they had on neighboring vowels and consonants, the most important being the "coloration" effect – viz. backing and lowering or rounding – that h_2 and h_3 exerted on a neighboring *e* – i.e., $h_2 e$, $e h_2 > h_2 a$, $a h_2$ and $h_3 e$, $e h_3 > h_3 o$, $o h_3$.

The PIE vowel system was a typical five-vowel inventory of contrasting long and short vowels *ĭ ĕ ă ŏ ŭ*. It also included four sonorant vowels *r̥, l̥, m̥, n̥*, which with *i* and *u* were automatic allophones of consonantal *r, l, m, n, i̯,* and *u̯* when they appeared between consonants. The PIE word accent was mobile and morphologically conditioned, and was one of pitch as later in Greek, Indo-Iranian, and Balto-Slavic. Together with the vowels *ĕ ă ŏ*, the accent participated in the morphologically conditioned alternations called ablaut (or apophony) that governed all areas of PIE inflectional and derivational morphology. Ablaut involved the movement or non-movement of the accent and the alternation of different vowel colors or lengths, called grades: so $\bar{e}$ alternating with e (so-called $\bar{e}$- or lengthened grade vs e- or full grade); e with zero (e-grade vs zero grade); o with e (o-grade vs e-grade), etc. These alternations can be seen in Greek in the paradigm of nouns like $\bar{e}$-grade nom. ἀνήρ < *$h_2n\acute{e}r$, e-grade acc. ἀνέρα < *$h_2n\acute{e}r\underset{\cdot}{m}$ and zero grade gen. ἀνδρός < *ἀνϱός < *$h_2\underset{\cdot}{n}r\acute{o}s$ or in principal parts like e-grade present λείπω < *$leik^u o/e$-, o-grade perfect λέλοιπα < *$leloik^u$- and zero-grade aorist ἔλιπον < *$(h_1)elik^u o/e$-.

The main Greek phonological developments affecting the PIE sound system are most profitably divided into Proto-Greek and post-Proto-Greek changes. Only a selection of the most important developments is provided below.

Proto-Greek developments

The palatovelar stops (see table 12.1) merge with the velars, so *$\hat{k}$ *$\hat{g}$ *$\hat{g}^h$ > *k *g *g^h > k g k^h–cf., e.g., (ἐ)κατόν < *$\hat{k}\underset{\cdot}{m}t\acute{o}m$, κείϱω < *$ker\underset{\cdot}{i}o/e$- and τίς < *$k^u is$. The three-way velar contrast of PIE was eliminated in all IE languages except Anatolian. Greek, Latin, Celtic, Germanic, and Tocharian preserve the labiovelars and merge the palatovelars with the velars. By contrast, Indo-Iranian, Slavic, Baltic, and Armenian retain the palatovelars, which later mostly become sibilants or palatal affricates, and merge the labiovelars with the velars. These two groups are traditionally known as *centum* and *satəm* languages, respectively, after the Latin and Avestan reflexes of *$\hat{k}\underset{\cdot}{m}t\acute{o}m$ "100" (> Lat. *centum* and Avest. *satəm*).

The voiced aspirated stops are devoiced, so *b^h d^h (g^h, $g^{\prime h}$ >) g^h g^{uh} > p^h t^h k^h k^{uh} – cf. φέρω < *$b^h\acute{e}ro/e$-, θετός < *$d^h h_1 t\acute{o}$-, etc. An important Proto-Greek change following this is the dissimilatory process known as Grassmann's Law, whereby the first of two aspirates in successive syllables – including h < *s – loses its aspiration, e.g., Att.- Ion. τίθησι, Dor. Aeol. τίθητι < *$t^h it^h\bar{e}ti$ << *$d^h\acute{e}d^h eh_1 ti$. This change took place independently in Indo-Iranian. (Note that the symbols "<<" and ">>" in "X <</>> Y" denote "X derives from/becomes Y by means of analogical processes; on analogy, see ch. 8.)

All final stops are eliminated (ἔφεϱε ἔφεϱον < *$(h_1)\acute{e}b^h eret$ $(h_1)\acute{e}b^h eront$) and final m merges with n (ἔφεϱον < *$(h_1)\acute{e}b^h erom$).

The laryngeals are lost and replaced with epenthetic vowels, a process known as the "vocalization" of the laryngeals. A special feature of Greek is the three-way reflex of the laryngeals, according to which the epenthetic vowel that surfaces as the result of the lost laryngeal matches the laryngeal's coloration properties, viz. e-color from h_1, a from h_2 and o from h_3. The actual Greek developments are best arranged by environment:

a) Between obstruents (stops and s) and before or after a consonant at word boundary, the result is a short vowel: θετός < *$d^h h_1 t\acute{o}$-, στατός < *$sth_2 t\acute{o}$-, δοτός < *$dh_3 t\acute{o}$-. The short vowel that surfaces in word-initial position is traditionally termed the "prothetic vowel," e.g., ἀνήρ < *$h_2n\acute{e}r$, ἐϱυθϱός < *$h_1 rud^h r\acute{o}$-, ὀϱέγω < *$h_3 r\acute{e}\hat{g}o/e$-.

b) In pre-consonantal position after vowels, the result is a long vowel, e.g., τίθημι < *$d^h\acute{i}d^h eh_1 mi$, ἵσταμι Att.-Ion. ἵστημι < *$sistah_2 mi$, δίδωμι < *$didoh_3 mi$. Between vowels the laryngeal disappears, and the vowels generally contract, e.g., φοϱᾶς φοϱᾶι < *b^horáh$_2$as b^horáh$_2$ai. This contraction is the source of the Greek circumflex accent.

c)   In the neighborhood of a syllabic sonorant, the result is generally a long or short vowel and a non-syllabic sonorant. In word-initial or word-final position, the outcome is short vowel and non-syllabic sonorant; cf., e.g., word-initial αὐδά Att.-Ion. αὐδή < *$h_2$udáh$_2$ or word-final Att. μέλιττα Ion. μέλισσα < *mélitįa < *mélitih$_2$. In word-internal position – excluding sequences involving *i* and *u* which pattern as under *b)* above – the result is non-syllabic plus long vowel, e.g., γνητός < *ĝn̥h$_1$tó- or κμᾱτός Att.-Ion. κμητός < *k̑m̥h$_2$tó-; or, when the sonorant is under the accent, short vowel plus non-syllabic sonorant plus short vowel, e.g., γένεσις < *ĝn̥h$_1$ti- or κάματος < *k̑m̥h$_2$to.

The sibilant *s* becomes *h* except when neighboring an obstruent or at word end. This *h* is preserved everywhere in the Mycenaean period (see ch. 12), e.g., <pa-we-a$_2$> /p^{h}arweha/ ~ Ion. φάϱεα–, but disappears word internally toward the end of the second millennium. In "psilotic" dialects like East Ionic, it also often disappears word initially, e.g., E. Ion. ἑπτά vs Att. ἑπτά < *septm̥. When *h* is lost between vowels, the result is contraction or hiatus, depending on the vowels involved and the dialect, e.g., Att. γένους vs Ion. γένεος < *ĝénh$_1$esos. For sequences of *h* plus sonorant, see further below.

The glide *-į- is eliminated from all positions in Greek by the end of the second millennium. There are at least two sets of changes involving this consonant that likely took place already in Proto-Greek:

a)   Word-initial *į- becomes an affricate <ζ>, e.g., ζυγόν < *įugóm. Word-initial sequences of laryngeal plus *-į- are simplified to į- and then in the second millennium become *h-* as detailed below, e.g., ἅγιος < *įaĝiįo- < *h$_x$įaĝiįo-.

b)   Clusters of an obstruent plus *-į- undergo various developments depending on the obstruent involved. Sequences of a labial *p*, *b*, *p^h* plus -į- yield <ππ>, e.g., κλέπτω < *klepįo/e-. Sequences of a voiced dental *d* or velar *g*, *g^u* plus -į- give an affricate <ζ> : νίζω < *nig^{u}įo/e-. The voiceless dentals *t*, *t^h* plus -į- have two outcomes depending on whether -į- is part of the denominative verb suffix *-įo/e-, the comparative *-įos-, or the feminine suffix *-ih$_2$-/-įah$_2$- and thus figures at a synchronically transparent morpheme boundary or not. When this boundary is present, the result is -ττ- in Attic and Boeotian and -σσ- in most other dialects, e.g., Att. μέλιττα, Ion. μέλισσα < *melitįa < *mélitih$_2$. Otherwise, the outcome is -σ- in Attic, Ionic, Arcadian, and Myceanean, -σσ- in Lesbian, Thessalian, and most Doric dialects, and -ττ- in Boeotian and Cretan, e.g., Att.-Ion. Arc. (Myc.) τόσος, Lesb. Thess. Dor. τόσσος, Boe. Cret. τόττος < *tótįo-. Sequences of velar *k*, *k^h*, *k^u*, *k^{uh}* plus -į- behave like cases of dental plus -į- at morpheme boundary, e.g., Att. φυλάττω Ion. φυλάσσω < *p^{h}ulakįo/e-.

Long vowels in the sequence long vowel plus sonorant plus consonant are shortened, e.g., dat. pl. -οις < *-ōis (~ Ved. *-ais*) – a sound change named Osthoff's Law. Greek otherwise preserves the PIE vowel inventory more or less intact until the end of the second millennium when some dialects like Attic and Ionic generate new long mid-vowels

/ę̄/ /ǭ/ = Att.-Ion. <ει> <ου> (the so-called "spurious diphthongs"), as a result of contraction and the compensatory lengthenings detailed below – see also ch. 7.

Greek preserves the pitch accent of PIE. It innovates in the creation of the circumflex intonation, which probably arose first as the result of contraction over laryngeal hiatus and was later multiplied by contraction over the hiatus resulting from the loss of intervocalic *-s-, *-i̯- and *-u̯- (see below). Greek also limits the accent to the last three syllables of the word, the so-called "Dreimorengesetz," and generalizes recessive accentuation in the verb.

Post-Proto-Greek developments

The sequence *ti* changes to *si* prehistorically – probably in the first half of the second millennium – in the "Achaean" dialects Mycenaean, Arcadian, and Cyprian and in Attic-Ionic, e.g., "Achaean" Att.-Ion. τίθησι vs Dor. Aeol. τίθητι. The change is also found in Lesbian, where it is probably to be attributed to Ionic influence.

The syllabic sonorants are vocalized in the pre-Myceanean period. In most dialects the results are αρ/ρα, αλ/λα < *r̥, *l̥ and α < *m̥, *n̥, while in "Achaean" and Aeolic the outcome is often ορ/ρο, ολ/λο and o, e.g., Att.-Ion. στρατός vs Aeol. στροτός < *str̥tó- and Att.-Ion. σπέρμα vs Myc. <pe-mo> /spermo/ < *spérmn̥.

Most instances of -i̯- remaining after the changes outlined above become *h* in the course of the late second millennium, a development that can be glimpsed via spelling variants in the surviving Mycenaean corpus (see ch. 13). This *h* falls together with *h* < *s and undergoes the same developments. In word-initial position, it either remains or is lost as above; in intervocalic position it is lost, resulting either in hiatus or contraction depending on the dialect and vowel sequence involved, e.g., Att.-Ion. τρεῖς /trę̄s/ Arc. τρῆς Cret. τρέες < *tréi̯es; in the neighborhood of a sonorant it is lost with compensatory lengthening of the preceding vowel or gemination of the sonorant. The compensatory lengthening result is proper to "Achaean," Attic-Ionic and West Greek, gemination to the Aeolic dialects, e.g., Att.-Ion. φθείρω /pʰtʰę̄rǭ/ Arc. φθήρω Thess. φθέρρω < *pʰtʰéri̯o/e- or Att.-Ion. εἰμί /ę̄mí/ Dor. ἠμί Lesb. ἔμμι < *h₁esmi. This change is known as the first compensatory lengthening. Together with contraction over -h- and -u̯- hiatus and the second and third compensatory lengthenings (see below), it is an important source of Att.-Ion. /ę̄/ /ǭ/ = <ει> <ου> (see ch. 7).

The labiovelars *kʷ gʷ kʷʰ*, which are preserved in all positions in Mycenaean (see ch. 13), e.g., <qe-to-ro-> = /kʷetro-/ < *kʷetr̥ –, merge with the labials or dentals depending on environment and dialect in the late second or early first millennium. In Attic-Ionic the merger is generally with dentals before *e* (and, in the case of the voiceless labiovelar, *i*), e.g., τίσις < *kʷítis, δέλεαρ < *gʷélh₁u̯r̥, θείνω < *gʷʰeni̯o/e-. Elsewhere the labiovelars merge with labials, e.g., ποινή < *kʷoináh₂-, βόλος < *gʷólh₁o-, φόνος < *gʷʰóno-. In Aeolic they merge with labials in nearly all positions, e.g., Lesb. Thess. πέμπε < *pénkʷe.

Long -ā- becomes *-ǣ- in all positions in Proto-Attic-Ionic. This change follows the first compensatory lengthening and precedes the second and third below. In Attic (and partly in West Ionic) *-ǣ- reverts to -ā- after *r*, *i*, and *e* (the so-called "Attic

Reversion"; see also ch. 8), and then later, as everywhere in Central and East Ionic, merges with [ἕ] = <η> – cf., e.g., Att. νέᾱ Ion. νέη < PAtt.-Ion. *néu̯ǣ < *néu̯ā < *néu̯ah₂ vs Att.-Ion. μήτηρ < *mǣtēr < *mátēr < *mátēr.

The nasal in the sequence "vowel plus *n* plus *s*" disappears in the late second or early first millennium from many dialects, resulting either in compensatory lengthening of the preceding vowel, e.g., Att.-Ion. πᾶσα < *pánsa* < *páh₂n̥tih₂*, or in diphthongization, e.g., Lesb. παῖσα. This is known as the second compensatory lengthening.

In the course of the first millennium -u̯-, the so-called "digamma," which is preserved in all positions in Mycenaean, e.g., <ne-wo> /néu̯os/ = Att.-Ion. νέος, is eliminated in many dialects. In Attic and Ionic this loss is prehistoric. In East and Central Ionic, though not in Attic or West Ionic, it is lost from post-consonantal position with compensatory lengthening, e.g., Central East Ion. κᾱλός West Ion. Att. κᾰλός < *kalu̯ó-*. This is known as the third compensatory lengthening.

Nominal Morphology

The PIE noun distinguished three genders – masculine, feminine, and neuter, often referred to more broadly as animate (masculine, feminine) vs inanimate (neuter) – three numbers – singular, dual, and plural – and at least eight cases. In addition to the five familiar from Classical Greek – the nominative, vocative, accusative, genitive, and dative – PIE employed the ablative (motion from), locative (location), and instrumental (instrument, accompaniment). The basic structure of the noun was root plus endings (radical formations or root nouns) or root plus one or more suffixes plus endings (suffixal formations). Stems made with a suffix were further divided between those ending in the thematic vowel *-o-, known as thematic stems, and those formed with any other suffix, including zero, which are referred to as athematics. Thematic formations lacked ablaut and had columnar accent, while athematics belonged to elaborate inflectional classes governed by regular accent and ablaut alternations (see also ch. 8).

Greek preserves the basic outline of the PIE noun, though in somewhat simplified form. This simplification is most conspicuous in the case system, where by the time of the first millennium dialects the eight cases of PIE have been reduced to five by the merger of the ablative with the genitive and the locative and instrumental with the dative. The accent and ablaut alternations that characterized athematic nouns and adjectives have also undergone significant simplification. Most first-millennium dialects further eliminated the dual.

The declensions

The Greek third declension includes the vast majority of PIE athematic formations. The original system of athematic case endings, together with the general outline of their development into second- (Mycenaean) and first-millennium Greek, are schematized in table 12.2.

Table 12.2 Third declension endings in Proto-Indo-European and Greek

	PIE	2nd millennium	1st millennium
sg. m.f. nom.	$*$-s/-ø >	-s/-ø >	-ς/-ø
voc.	$*$-ø	-ø	-ø
acc.	$*$-$m̥$/-m	-a/-n	-α/-ν
n. nom. acc.	-ø	-ø	-ø
gen. abl.	$*$-os	-os	-ος
dat.	$*$-ei	-ei/-i	-ι
loc.	$*$-i	-i (?)	
instr.	$*$-eh_1	-$ē$ (?)	
du. m.f. nom. acc.	$*$-h_1e	-e	-ε
n. nom. acc.	$*$-ih_1 >>	-e	-ε
pl. m.f. nom. voc.	$*$-es	-es	-ες
acc.	$*$-$m̥s$/-ms	-as/-ns	-ας/-(ν)ς
n. nom. acc.	$*$-h_2	-a	-α
gen.	$*$-oh_xom	-$ōn$	-ων
abl.	$*$-$bʰos$		
dat.	$*$-$bʰos$		
loc.	$*$-si	-si	-σι
instr.	$*$-$bʰi(s)$	-$pʰi(s)$	

In the singular, the PIE case system has been more or less preserved up through the late second millennium, when the dative, locative, and instrumental finally fell together. In the plural, the case syncretism was earlier and more extensive. Already in Proto-Greek, distinct ablative and dative case forms were eliminated in favor of the genitive and locative, respectively. As in the singular, the instrumental was absorbed by the new dative-locative plural toward the end of the second millennium. This case, which originally had the shape -hi after vowels and -si after consonants, eventually generalized the post-consonantal variant to all positions. The inherited neut. nom. acc. dual ending $*$-$i̯e$ < $*$-ih_1 survives in the archaic Homeric noun ὄσσε < $*h_3okʷih_1$, but has otherwise been replaced by the animate ending. The remaining dual case forms are difficult to reconstruct, and are omitted from the discussion here and below.

From the PIE perspective, the third declension includes root nouns (abbreviated *R+E*, where "R" stands for "root" and "E" for "ending"), root plus one suffix (*R+S+E*), and root plus many suffix formations (*R+S+S+E*) Each of these stem types was instantiated in PIE by numerous inflectional classes. These classes had characteristic accent and ablaut alternations that affected the root, suffix, and ending in different case forms, with one accent and ablaut shape regularly appearing in the nominative and accusative singular and nominative plural – the strong or direct cases – and another in the remaining cases – the weak or oblique. These classes and their Greek remnants are most clearly seen in root plus one suffix formations, where there were four different accent and ablaut patterns:

a)   Acrostatic. These had fixed accent on the root – with either o/e or ē/e ablaut in the root syllable – and zero-grade suffix and ending: R(ó)-S(z)-E(z)/R(é)-S(z)-E(z) or R(ḗ)-S(z)-E(z)/R(é)-S(z)-E(z). Continuants of this type in Greek include, e.g., *u*-stems γόνυ, γουνός, *i*-stems πόλις, -ιος, and *r/n*-stems ἧπαρ, -ατος or οὖθαρ, -ατος.

b)   Proterokinetic. These had alternation between accented *e*-grade root in strong cases and accented *e*-grade suffix in weak: R(é)-S(z)-E(z)/R(z)-S(é)-E(z). This type includes, e.g., *u*-stem nouns and adjectives πῆχυς, -εος or βαρύς, -έος and *s*-stem nouns γένος, -ους.

c)   Hysterokinetic. These had alternation between accented *e*-grade suffix in strong cases and accented endings in weak: R(z)-S(é)-E(z)/R(z)-S(z)-E(é). This common type includes, e.g., *r*-stems πατήρ, πατρός or δοτήρ, -ῆρος, *n*-stem nouns ὑμήν, -ένος, and *s*-stem compounds εὐγενής, -οῦς.

d)   Amphikinetic. These had alternation between accented *e*-grade root and *o*-grade suffix vocalism in strong cases and accented endings in weak: R(é)-S(o)-E(z) /R(z)-S(z)-E(é). This common type includes, e.g., *r*-stem agent nouns γενέτωρ, -ορος, *n*-stems γνώμων, -ονος, *u*-stems δμώς, -ωός, *i*-stems πειθώ, -οῦς and *s*-stems ἠώς, -οῦς.

Apart from a few archaic stems, the general tendency in Greek has been to simplify these alternations via analogical processes like leveling (see ch. 8). This is most often accomplished by eliminating root ablaut alternations and fixing the accent on either the root or suffix, e.g., *$g^u érh_2 u$-/$g^u r̥h_2 éu$-* >> *$g^u r̥h_2 ú$-/$g^u r̥h_2 éu$-* > Proto-Gk *$g^u arú$-/ $g^u aréu$-* > βαρύς, -έ(ϝ)ος. Stems with hysterokinetic or amphikinetic inflection also tend to level the suffix vocalism of strong cases to weak, e.g., *$dh_3 tér$-/$dh_3 tr$-´* > Proto-Gk *$dotér$-/$dotr$-´* (originally like πατήρ, πατρός) >> δοτήρ, -ῆρος or *$ĝénh_1 tor$-/ $ĝn̥h_1 tr$-´* > Proto-Gk *$génetor$-/$gnētr$-´* >> γενέτωρ, -ορος. Similar developments have taken place in root nouns and more complex suffixal formations.

Athematic nouns in PIE also had the remarkable ability to make derivatives by switching accent and ablaut class, a process termed "internal derivation." Greek preserves traces of this process in the inflectional class shift seen in compound formations like (amphikinetic) ἀπάτωρ, -ορος ~ (hysterokinetic) πατήρ, πατρός or (hysterokinetic) εὐγενής, -οῦς ~ (proterokinetic) γένος, -ους, and further among simplexes like (amphikinetic) γνώμων, -ονος ~ (proterokinetic) γνῶμα, -ατος.

The Greek first declension continues two distinct athematic stem types ending in *-h_2* (see also the discussion of *ā/ă-stems* in ch. 8). The first type, which predominantly made feminine nouns and adjectives to thematic stems, ended in a non-ablauting suffix *-ah_2* and is continued by first-declension stems with consistent long -ā- (Att.-Ion. -η- via the Att.-Ion. sound change Proto-Gk *-ā̆- > -η-): e.g., τομά̄, -ά̄ς (Att.-Ion. τομή, -ῆς). The basic development of the endings in this class are schematized in table 12.3.

Table 12.3 The first declension in Proto-Indo-European and Greek

	PIE	2nd millennium	1st millennium
sg. f.m. nom.	*-ah₂ >	-ā/-ās >	-ā/-ās (: Att. Ion. -η/-ης)
voc.	*-a	-a	
acc.	*-ān	-ān	-ᾰν (: Att. Ion. -ην)
gen. abl.	*-ah₂es	-ās	-ᾱς (: Att. Ion. -ης)
dat.	*-ah₂ei	-āi	-ᾱι (: Att. Ion. -ηι)
loc.	*-ah₂i	-ai (?)	
instr.	*-ah₂eh₁ >/>>	-ā/-āpʰi (?)	
du. m.f. nom. acc.	*-ah₂ih₂ >>	-ō >/>>	-ω/-ᾱ
pl. f.m. nom. voc.	*-ah₂es >>	-ai	-αι
acc.	*-ā(n)s	-ans	-ᾱς/-ανς (: Att. Ion. -ᾱς)
gen.	*-ah₂ohₓom >>	-āhōn	-άων (: Att. -ῶν, Ion.-έων)
abl.	*-ah₂bʰos		
dat.	*-ah₂bʰos		
loc.	*-ah₂si	-āhi >>	-ᾱσι/-ᾱισι, Att. Ion. -ησι/ -ηισι, -αις
instr.	*-ah₂bʰi(s)	-āpʰi(s)	

In the singular, the first-millennium paradigm directly continues its PIE antecedents. The original vocative survives in forms like Homeric νύμφα, the locative in dialectal datives like Boe. ταμίη < -αι. In the plural, inherited forms are preserved in the accusative and further in the W. Gk and early Att. and Ion. datives -ᾱσι and -ησι, which have been remodeled to -αισι/-ηισι or -αις in most dialects after thematic stems. The genitive -άων (: Att. -ῶν, Ion. -έων) and nominative -αι have been borrowed from pronouns. The nominative accusative dual has been variously remodeled after thematic stems. Masculine ā-stems were in the first instance identical to feminines, and later acquired the nominative -ᾱς (: Att.-Ion. -ης) and genitive -āo (> Ion. -εω, >> Att. -ου) by analogy to thematic stems.

The second stem type found in the first declension consists of nouns and adjectives like μοῖρα, -ᾱς, which alternate between -ᾰ- in strong cases and -ᾱ- in weak. This type continues an ablauting suffix of the shape *-i̯a-/-i̯ā- < *-ih₂-/-i̯ah₂-, which is known as the *devī́*-suffix after the Vedic Sanskrit term for "goddess" nom. sg. *devī́*, gen. sg. *devyā́s* (~ Gk δῖα, δῖης << *déi̯uih₂-/diui̯áh₂-).

The Greek second declension is the continuation of the various PIE thematic formations, which made masculine, feminine, and neuter nouns and adjectives exactly as in Greek. Thematic endings were for the most part formed by adding the regular athematic endings to the thematic vowel *-o-. The development of the endings in this class are schematized in table 12.4.

Most of the second declension endings continue their PIE antecedents directly. The inherited locative singular is preserved in οἴκοι as well as in place names like Ἰσθμοῖ, the ablative in adverbs like Delphian Ϝοίκω. In the dual, the original neuter nominative accusative ending *-oi has been replaced with the masculine feminine

Table 12.4 The second declension in Proto-Indo-European and Greek

	PIE	2nd millennium	1st millennium
sg. m.f. nom.	$*-os >$	$-os >$	-ος
voc.	$*-e$	$-e$	-ε
acc.	$*-om$	$-on$	-ον
n. nom. acc.	$*-om$	$-on$	-ον
gen.	$*-os\textrm{i}o$	$-ohio$	-ου, Aeol. –οιο
abl.	$*-oh_2ad$	$-ō$ (?)	
dat.	$*-ō\hat{i}$	$-ō i$	-ωι
loc.	$*-oi$	$-oi$ (?)	(-οι)
instr.	$*-oh_1$	$-ō$ (?)	
du. m.f. nom. acc.	$*-oh_1$	$-ō$	-ω
n. nom. acc.	$*-oih_1 >>$	$-ō$ (?)	-ω
pl. m.f. nom. voc.	$*-ōs >>$	$-oi$	-οι
acc.	$*-oms$	$-ons$	-ος/–ονς (: Att. Ion. –ους)
n. nom. acc.	$*-ah_2 >>$	$-a$	-α
gen.	$*-oh_xom$	$-ōn$	-ων
abl.	$*-o(i)b^bos$		
dat.	$*-o(i)b^bos$		
loc.	$*-oisi$	$-oihi >>$	-οισι/-οις
instr.	$*-ōis$	$-ois$	

ending -ω. In the plural, the nominative $*-ōs$ has been replaced with the pronominal ending -οι, while the neuter has taken over -α from the third declension. In the dative plural, some dialects have generalized the old locative ending -οισι, others the instrumental -οις.

Adjectives

In PIE, adjectives differed from nouns only in showing gender agreement, often realized as an opposition of a single masculine and feminine stem versus a neuter. Gradable adjectives also made synthetic comparative and superlative forms. The suffix of the comparative was an ablauting s-stem $*-\textrm{i}os-/-is-$, which had a further – probably substantival – n-stem variant $*-ison-/-isn-$. The n-stem has been generalized in first-millennium Greek, although the original s-stem survives in forms like the Ion. masc. fem. acc. sg. μέζω $< *még(h_2)ios\textrm{m}$. The inherited superlative is directly continued in forms like μέγιστος $< *még(h_2)ist(h_2)o-$. The productive Greek comparative and superlative suffixes -τερος and -τατος have correspondents in Indo-Iranian (~ Ved. *-tara- -tama-*), and represent a common innovation of these branches.

A peculiar derivational feature of some adjectives inherited from PIE is the so-called "Caland system," named after the nineteenth-century Dutch indologist Willem

Caland who first observed the phenomenon in Indo-Iranian. This designation is used to describe the fact that an important subset of adjectives, typically those denoting gradable qualities, enter into a system of regular suffix substitution when making adjective abstracts, compound first and second members, and stative and factitive verbs. Typical here are ϱο- or υ-stem adjectives (κρατύς/κρατερός "strong"), s-stem adjective abstracts (τὸ κράτος "strength") and compound second members (ἀκρατής "powerless"), i-stem compound first members (Κρατισθένης, p.n.), εω-statives (κρατέω "be strong") and υνω-factitives (κρατύνω "strengthen").

Nominal composition

PIE was rich in compound formations, and Greek has preserved and elaborated this richness, especially in the formation of proper names. Among the many compound formations inherited from PIE, there are two types that have become exceptionally productive in Greek: verbal governing and possessive compounds. Verbal governing compounds serve to nominalize verbal phrases, and consist of a verbal element and a noun or adverb. The internal syntax of the type is flexible, and allows the verbal element to occupy the first, e.g., Στησίχορος (p.n.), or the second member, e.g., Ἱπποδάμος (p.n.). Possessive compounds, which are also known as *bahuvrīhi*s after their name in the Sanskrit grammatical tradition (Skt. *bahuvrīhi* "having much rice"), consist of two nouns and have a basic meaning "having an X (= second member) that is or is characterized by Y (= first member)." This type is made through internal derivation or addition of the suffixes -o- and -ι-, and is frequent among appellatives, e.g., ῥοδοδάκτυλος "rosy-fingered" and proper names, e.g., Ἡρακλῆς.

Pronominal Morphology

PIE distinguished personal, interrogative, indefinite, relative, and demonstrative pronouns. Greek has inherited all these types: personal ἐγώ ἐμέ < *h_1éǵoh$_2$, *$h_1$mé, interrogative (tonic) and indefinite (atonic) τίς τί < *$k^wís$ *$k^wíd$, relative ὅς ἥ ὅ < *$h_x$iós *$h_x$iáh$_2$ *$h_x$ió d$, and demonstrative, e.g., ὁ ἡ τό < *so *sah$_2$ *tod. Greek has also faithfully preserved many of the inflectional peculiarities that originally characterized the pronouns, including stem heteroclisy and a number of peculiar endings. Two important Greek innovations affecting the pronouns include the creation of the deictics οὗτος αὕτη τοῦτο and ἐκεῖνος/κεῖνος out of sequences of demonstrative plus deictic particle and the reinterpretation of the demonstrative ὁ ἡ τό as a definite article, a development still underway in early epic poetry.

Verbal Morphology

As already indicated in ch. 8, the PIE verb distinguished three aspect stems: imperfective (present, imperfect); perfective (aorist); and resultative (perfect, pluperfect). There were two tenses: present (present, perfect) and past (imperfect,

Table 12.5 Athematic verb endings in Proto-Indo-European and Greek

Active	Primary		Secondary	
1 sg.	*-mi >	-μι	*-m̥/-m >	-α/-ν
2 sg.	*-si >>	-ς	*-s	-ς
3 sg.	*-ti	-τι/-σι	*-t	—
1 pl.	*-mes >>	Dor. –μες/–μεν	*-men	-μεν
2 pl.	*-te	-τε	*-te	-τε
3 pl.	*-n̥ti/-nti	-ατι/-ντι/-(ν)σι	*-n̥t/-nt	-αν/–ν

aorist, pluperfect); four moods: indicative, imperative, subjunctive, and optative; and two diatheses: active and middle. It marked three persons (first, second, and third) and three numbers (singular, dual, and plural). As in the noun, the basic inflectional distinction in verbal morphology was between thematic and athematic formations.

Greek preserves intact the basic architecture of the PIE verb. It continues the PIE aspect stems, tenses, moods, and diatheses in their original functions. The main innovations of Greek include the elimination of the dual, the development of a distinct future and an aorist and future passive, and the creation of non-imperfective stems for denominative and derived verbs.

The Endings

(Compare this section with the equivalent section in ch. 8.) The main distinctions in PIE were between primary and secondary endings, active and middle, thematic and athematic. Primary endings were used in the present, the future and perfect middle; secondary endings were proper to the imperfect, aorist, pluperfect active and middle, and optative. The subjunctive could take primary as well as secondary endings. The inflectional endings of thematic stems differed from athematics only in the singular of the primary set.

The PIE athematic endings, together with their development into first-millennium Greek, are set out in table 12.5.

The 2 sg. and non-Doric 1 pl. primary endings have been borrowed from the secondary series. The original zero-grade 3 pl. primary -ατι/-ασι appears in perfect forms like Homeric λελόγχασι; the secondary ending survives in the *s*-aorist where it was remodeled as -αν by addition of the regular 3 pl. ending -ν. The reconstruction of the dual is partly unclear, and is omitted here and below. The Greek thematic endings -ω and -ει continue the pre-forms *-oh₂ and *-ei; the 2 sg. -εις is a special Greek innovation.

The endings -μαι and -μᾱν have been influenced by the 1 sg. act. endings; the original *o*-vocalism of 2 sg. and 3 sg. and pl. primary endings is preserved in Myc., e.g., <e-u-ke-to> /eukʰetoi/, and Arc.-Cyp., e.g., Cypr. κεῖτοι, while other dialects have generalized -αι from 1 sg. -μαι. The -σ- in 2 pl. -σϑε is also a Greek innovation.

Table 12.6 Middle endings in Proto-Indo-European and Greek

Middle	Primary		Secondary	
1 sg.	*-h_2ai >>	-μαι	*-h_2ah_2a (?) >>	-μᾱν (: Att.–Ion. -μην)
2 sg.	*-soi	-σοι/-σαι	*-so	-σο
3 sg.	*-toi	-τοι/-ται	*-to	-το
1 pl.	*-$mezd^bh_2$	-μεσθα	*-med^bh_2	-μεθα
2 pl.	*-d^bue	-σθε	*-d^bue	-σθε
3 pl.	*-$ntoi/-ntoi$	-αται/-ντοι/-νται	*-$nto/-nto$	-ατο/-ντο

The PIE perfect had its own distinct set of endings, which were related to those of the middle. The original form of the singular is well preserved in Greek: -α -θα -ε < *-h_2a *-th_2a *-e. The plural endings have been taken over from the primary active set.

The augment

In Greek, Phrygian, Armenian, and Indo-Iranian, secondary tenses in the indicative also regularly used the augment, ἐ- < *(h_1)e-. Added to laryngeal initial roots, this resulted in the so-called long augment, e.g., ἆγον (Att.-Ion. ἦγον) < *(h_1)$éh_2ag^bom$ or ἤλυθον < *(h_1)$éh_1lud^bom$. The use of the augment was originally non-obligatory in certain circumstances, a situation reflected in early epic poetry.

The tense/aspect stems

The basic morphological structure of the PIE verb was very similar to that of nouns and consisted of a root plus endings or a root plus an infix or suffix plus endings. The main inflectional distinction was between thematic stems, abbreviated *-o/e-, which had columnar accent and ablaut of the thematic vowel, and athematics, which belonged to various inflectional classes that had accent and ablaut alternations between the singular (the strong stem) and dual and plural (the weak). The aspect stems included the imperfective (present, imperfect), perfective (aorist), and resultative (perfect, pluperfect), and were built directly to the underlying verbal root (as in Greek verbs of the type pres. λείπω aor. ἔλιπον pf. λέλοιπα made to the basic root √λιπ-) and not, as often in Greek, to characterized stems.

The present-imperfect or imperfective stem included a large number of different formations. Among athematics, Greek preserves root presents, e.g., φησί φᾱσί < *$b^báh_2ti$ $b^bh_2ánti$; reduplicated presents, e.g., τίθησι τίθεισι << *$d^béd^beh_1ti$ $d^béd^bh_1nti$ (with i-reduplication on the model of the thematic μίμνω-type below); and nasal infix presents (πίτνησι πίτνᾱσι < *$ptnáh_2ti$ $ptnh_2ánti$), which have often been remade as nasal suffix formations in -νῡ-/-νυ- (cf., e.g., ζεύγνῡμι vs Ved. *yunákti yuñjánti* < *$iunékti$ $iungénti$). Thematic formations were slightly more varied, and are continued in Greek by root presents, e.g., φέρω < *$b^béro/e$-; reduplicated presents, e.g., μίμνω < *mímno/e-; iterative-causatives, e.g., φορέομαι < *bʰoréi̯o/e-; and statives, e.g., κρατέω < *kr̥teh₁i̯o/e-.

Two further important thematic types include the suffix *-ske/o-, which has become productive in East Ionic for the creation of iterative imperfects, e.g., φεύγεσκε: φεύγω; and *-i̯o/e-, which made deverbal and denominative formations such as φυλάσσω/ φυλάττω < *pʰulaki̯o/e - (: φύλαξ, -ος). This last suffix was productive in denominative function in the prehistory of Greek. It is at the origin of many of the contract verb types – cf., e.g., φιλέω < *pʰile-i̯o/e- (: φιλός), νῑκάω << *nīkā-i̯o/e- (: νίκη), στεφανόω << *stepʰanō-i̯o/e- (: στέφανος) – and the productive denominative suffixes -ίζω (< *-id-i̯o/e-), -άζω (< *-ad-i̯o/e-), -αίνω (< *-n̥-i̯o/e-) and -ύνω (< *-un-i̯o/e-). The imperfective also contained a number of desiderative formations, one of which has been specialized as the Greek future.

The aorist or perfective stem had three main stem formations: the root aorist (ἔβη ἔβαν (: Att.-Ion. ἔβησαν after the s-aorist) < *(h₁)égʷah₂t *(h₁)égʷh₂ant), the reduplicated thematic aorist (ἔπεφνον < *(h₁)égʷʰegʷʰno/e-), and the s-aorist (ἔδειξα < *(h₁)édēiksm̥), a type that has become extremely productive in Greek. Two further formations elaborated in the history of Greek are the thematic aorist, e.g., ἦλθον (via syncope) < ἤλυθον < *(h₁)éh₁ludʰo/e-, and the k-aorist, e.g., ἔθηκα < *(h₁)édʰeh₁km̥ (~ Lat. fēcī).

The perfect-pluperfect or resultative stem denoted a state resulting from a past action, a usage still well attested in early Greek poetry in forms like τέθνηκα "I am dead." The perfect originally ablauted between o-grade root vocalism in the singular and zero-grade in the plural, e.g., Homeric μέμονα μέμαμεν < *memon-/memn̥-, and in all stems other than the archaic verb οἶδα < *u̯óidh₂a, regularly had reduplication of the root initial consonant (μέμονα < *me-mon-h₂a) or consonant cluster in roots beginning with a laryngeal plus a resonant, e.g., Hom. εἰλήλουθα (by metrical lengthening) < *ἐλήλουθα < *h₁le-h₁loudʰ-h₂a. Greek has innovated by creating the k-perfect, expanding the use of the perfect middle, and generating a distinct set of endings for the pluperfect active.

The moods

The PIE moods, which were formed to all three aspect stems, include the indicative, subjunctive, optative, and imperative. Greek preserves all four categories in their original forms and functions.

The subjunctive was made by adding the thematic vowel *-o/e- directly to the e-grade version of the verbal stem. The subjunctive of athematic stems surfaced as a regular thematic formation, and is continued as such in Greek by the so-called short-vowel subjunctive, e.g., δείξει (: ἔδειξε), still found in early epic, East Ionic, and many other dialects. The subjunctive of thematic stems was made by adding the subjunctive suffix to the thematic vowel; this resulted in a long vowel by contraction, and is found in the familiar long-vowel subjunctive, e.g., φέρῃι (: φέρω), which was generalized in Attic.

The optative was made by suffixing *-i̯eh₁-/-ih₁- to the verbal stem. The optative to most athematic stems ablauted between accented e-grade suffix in the singular and accented endings in the plural, an alternation continued in Greek stems like εἴη εἶεν < *$h_1si\acute{e}h_1t$ *$h_1sih_1\acute{e}nt$. In thematic stems, the zero grade of the optative suffix was added to the *o*-grade thematic vowel, giving the Greek type φέροις φέροι < *$b^h\acute{e}roih_1s$ *$b^h\acute{e}roih_1t$.

The imperative contrasted two formations: a regular imperative and a future imperative which was used for commands relating to the future. The two formations have collapsed in Greek. The regular imperative survives in 2 sg. and pl., the future imperative in 3 sg. and pl.

Nominal forms of the verb

PIE had a full range of nominal forms of the verb, including participles, infinitives, and verbal nouns and adjectives. Active and middle participles were made to all three aspect stems. The active participle had the shape *-*nt*- > -ντ- – often with amphikinetic inflection, cf., e.g., Ion. ἐών, ἐόντος (> Att. ὤν, ὄντος) < *h_1esont-/h_1snt-. The middle participle had the shape *-*mh_1no*- > -μενο-. The suffix of the perfect participle was an amphikinetic ablauting *s*-stem *-*uos-/-*us*-, which though still found in Mycenaean forms like the neut. nom. acc. pl. <a-ra-u-wo-a> /ararwoha/ (~ Att.-Ion. ἀρηρότα) has been remodeled as a *t*-stem in first-millennium Greek. The past passive participle was instantiated by a large number of different suffixes, the most widely attested being the *-*to*- reflected in Greek -τό-.

PIE lacked fixed infinitive formations and regularly employed case forms of verbal nouns – typically the accusative, dative, locative, or directive – in this function. In Greek, several different such formations are preserved, the most conspicuous being the thematic infinitive in -ειν < *-*ehen* < *-*es-en* which has its origins in the locative of an *s*-stem noun. Greek has also inherited many deverbal noun formations, e.g., -τι-/-σι- (γένεσις: γίγνομαι) < *-*ti*- and -μα, -ματος (ποίημα: ποιέω) << *-*men*- for abstract and concrete nouns, -τωρ, -τορος (ῥήτωρ: εἴρω) < *-*tor*-/-*tr*- and -τήρ, -τῆρος (δοτήρ: δίδωμι) < *-*ter*-/-*tr*- for agent nouns, etc.

The Lexicon

As in all other areas of its grammar, Greek is highly conservative in its lexicon and retains a large amount of inherited IE material, both in words preserved directly from the IE parent language and in those made within the history of Greek from inherited material. This conservatism is apparent in all aspects of the language's basic vocabulary, including terms for familial relationships (πατήρ "father," θυγάτηρ "daughter," etc.), body parts (πούς "foot," χείρ "hand," etc.), the physical world (χθών "earth," ἥλιος "sun," etc.), domestic and wild animals (ἵππος "horse," βοῦς "bovine," etc.), agriculture (ἀγρός "field," ἄροτρον "plow," etc.), civilization and technology (οἶκος "house," ναῦς "ship," etc.), and religion (Ζεύς, ἅγιος "sacred," etc.). Greek derivational morphology is also largely of IE origin. As with all living languages, the Greek lexicon includes a certain number of loan words. These are mostly limited to terms for comestibles (σήσαμον, κρόκος), metals (χρυσός, χαλκός), and cultural and technological concepts and implements (χιτών, ἀσάμινθος). A particularly conspicuous category of loans is comprised of Greek place names (Κόρινθος, Παρνασσός), many of which consist of similar morphological elements and likely preserve remnants of the pre-Greek languages of Greece (see further ch. 15).

FURTHER READING

The best introduction to IE linguistics, language, and culture is Fortson 2004. Also useful are Clackson 2007 and the slightly more advanced Meier-Brügger 2003b. The question of the IE homeland is treated in detail by Mallory (1989). Readers who are interested in the theory, method, and results of historical linguistics will profit from the introductory textbook by Hock and Joseph (1996) and the more advanced Hock (1991).

The best IE-oriented historical grammar of Greek is Rix 1992. Sihler 1995, though highly idiosyncratic, is also useful, as is the out-of-date comprehensive treatment by Schwyzer 1939. For the early prehistory of Greek, readers will consult Hajnal 2003a; 2005 and Garrett 2006 and, for the supposed relationship between Greek and Armenian and Phrygian, Clackson 1994 and Neumann 1988. Greek laryngeal treatments are outlined in Beekes 1969 and Peters 1980. Greek dialects in the second millennium BCE are discussed by Cowgill 1966 and Risch 1979. The Mycenaean case system is treated by Hajnal 1995. The function of the augment in epic language is outlined by Bakker 1999; 2005: 114–35.

Greek is served by two etymological dictionaries, Chantraine 1999 and the more IE-oriented Frisk (1960–72), both of which are out of date. Updates to Chantraine's etymological dictionary are regularly published in *Revue de Philologie, de Littérature et d'Histoire anciennes*. A more modern etymological treatment of Greek and IE verbal roots and verbal formations is found in Rix 2001. Pre-Greek elements in Greek are discussed by Morpurgo Davies 1986. An essential resource for bibliography on all aspects of Greek linguistics is provided by Meier-Brügger 1992.

PART THREE

Greek in Time and Space: Historical and Geographical Connections

CHAPTER THIRTEEN

Mycenaean Greek

Rupert Thompson

"Mycenaean" is the name we give to the variety of Greek which was in use in Greece in the Bronze Age in an area encompassing Crete and the mainland as far north as Boeotian Thebes. Our evidence comes from the tablets written in the Linear B script (on which, see ch. 2), primarily from Knossos and Pylos, dating from between 1400 and 1200 BCE. As the earliest written form of Greek, the importance of Mycenaean for the study of the history of the language and its dialects cannot be overstated.

Phonology

Stops

Mycenaean has the same three manners of stop articulation (voiceless, voiced, aspirated) as the later dialects (see ch. 7 for the phonological basics). Although the script does not generally mark it, the feature *voice* is guaranteed by the use of separate signs for /t/ and /d/. Similarly, the optional sign pu_2 = /pʰ/ guarantees *aspiration*. That the aspirated stops are unvoiced is shown by the use of *t*- rather than *d*- series signs for the dental aspirate.

Perhaps the most remarkably conservative feature of Mycenaean phonology is its retention of the PIE labiovelars (see also ch. 12). Adjacent to *$\breve{u}$ or *w these had undergone dissimilation and merged with the velars in Common Greek, and are rendered in Linear B as *ka* etc. In other environments the later dialects (with the exception of Aeolic) turn them into dentals before front vowels (*k^w > τ, *g^{wh} > *k^{wh} > ϑ, *g^w > δ) and bilabials elsewhere (*k^w > π, *g^{wh} > *k^{wh} > φ, *g^w > β), except that *k^{wh} and *g^w give bilabial reflexes also before *$\breve{\imath}$; Aeolic generally has bilabial reflexes across the board. These changes are not shared by Mycenaean, which retains distinct reflexes of the labiovelars in these environments, written using signs which are conventionally transcribed *qa, qe, qi, qo* standing for /kʷ, kʷh, gʷ/. Thus the enclitic particle -*qe*, $k^w e$

"and" is Class. τε; *qa-si-re-u*, *gʷasileus* is the title of a local official corresponding in form though not in meaning to later βασιλεύς "king"; and *-qo-ta*, a common formant in men's names, is either *-kʷʰontās*, later -φόντης, or *-kʷʰoitās*, later -φοίτης. Where one labiovelar is followed by another in a later syllable, the first sometimes undergoes dissimilation to become a bilabial, so we find both *i-po-po-qo-i*, *hippopʰorgʷoihi*, and *i-qo-po-qo-i*, *hik⁽ʷ⁾kʷopʰorgʷoihi* "ostlers" dat. pl. (i.e., later Gk ἱπποφορβοῖς).

Semivowels and fricatives

PIE **w* is preserved in almost all positions: initially, *wa-na-ka*, *wanax* "king," Class. ἄναξ; *we-to*, *wetos* "year," Class. ἔτος; intervocalically, *ka-ke-we*, *kʰalkēwes* "bronzesmiths," Att. χαλκῆς; in word-initial clusters *wi-ri-ni-jo*, *wrīniois* "made of leather" (instr. pl.), cf. Hom. ῥινός "skin, hide"; in internal clusters, *ke-se-nu-wi-ja*, *ksenwia* "related to guests," cf. Ion. ξείνιος, Att. ξένιος. Mycenaean *e-ne-ka*, *heneka* "on account of" thus shows that the lengthening in Hom. εἵνεκα is artificial, and not in compensation for the loss of **w*. The cluster **tw* before a consonant has simplified to *t* in e.g., *qe-to-ro-po-pi*, *kʷetropoppʰi* "four-footed animals" (instr. pl.) < **kʷetwropodpʰi* < **kʷetwr̥podpʰi* (showing that this simplification must postdate the changes to **r̥* described below).

Word-initial **y* shows the same double treatment as in the later dialects. In some roots—those corresponding to Classical forms in ζ—it becomes an affricate, probably [ʣ] or [ʤ], written using *z*-series signs and here rendered *dz*, e.g., *ze-u-ke-si*, *dzeuges(s)i* "pairs" (cf. ζεῦγος). In a second group, those with initial rough breathing in Attic, spellings with signs of the *j*-series alternate with those without (these latter presumably indicating initial *h*). The relative pronominal stem **yo-*, for example, gives an adverb which is spelled both *o-* and *jo-*, *hō*, *yō* 'how', while the temporal adverb from the same stem is always found as *o-te*, *hote* "when," and the indefinite relative is *jo-qi*, *yok⁽ʷ⁾kʷi* < **yod-kʷid*. Either the weakening of **y* to *h* was current at the time the tablets were written, or the spellings with *j-* are historical.

The same phenomenon is observed between vowels. Here, *j*-series signs are usually used to write an epenthetic glide which arises after *i* before another vowel, or to represent the second element of a diphthong in *i*. Intervocalic PIE **y* is normally lost. Occasionally, however, it is represented by *j-*, e.g., the present participle *to-ro-qe-jo-me-no*, *trokʷeyomenos* "touring" from a present in **-eyo-* (cf. τροπέω). The fluctuation between spellings with and without *j-* is common in adjectives of material in **-eyo-*, e.g., *e-re-pa-te-jo* vs *e-re-pa-te-o*, *elepʰante(y)os* "made of ivory." Once again we are either seeing the loss of intervocalic **y* in progress, or the spellings with *j-* are historical. We cannot tell whether **y* weakened to *-h-* or was lost completely, as in the later dialects. Either way, the loss of **y* did not result in contraction of the remaining vowels.

Clusters of a stop and **y* had undergone palatalization before the time of the tablets. The clusters **dy* and **gy* both give a voiced affricate, written *z-*: *to-pe-za*, *torpedza* "table" < **-pedya*; *me-zo*, *medzōs* "bigger" < **megyōs*. Similarly **ky* gives an affricate, presumably voiceless, which is also written *z-* and transcribed here as *ts*: *za-we-te-ro*, *tsāwe(s)teros* "this year's" < **kyāwetesteros*. The same happens when a prevocalic *i* weakens to *y*, as in *su-za*, *sūtsai* "fig trees" < **sūkyai* < **sūkiai* (Dor. and Aeol. συκία).

The sequence **ty* has become *s(s)*, e.g., *to-so*, *tos(s)on* "so much" < **totyo-*. The sign *pte* (see table 2.3) is the only one that represents a cluster of two stops. Its original value was probably *pye*, since there are other signs for syllables with palatalized vowels, but when the cluster **py* became *pt*, it became used for *pte* from any source.

The fricative *s* has weakened to *h* both word-initially and intervocalically. Where followed by *a* the aspiration is optionally noted using the sign a_2 = *ha* (see table 2.3). Thus a_2-*te-ro*, *hateron* "next [*sc.* year]" < **smtero-*. Both spellings are found in the forms of *s*-stem neuters, e.g., *pa-we-a* vs *pa-we-a$_2$*, *pʰarweha* "cloths." The form a_3-*ka-sa-ma*, *aiksmans* "[spear-]points" (Class. αἰχμή) shows that *s* had not yet been lost in the cluster *-ksm-*, despite this being a pan-Hellenic change.

There is some debate about whether Grassmann's Law (i.e., the loss of the first of two aspirations in one and the same word; see also ch. 12) had already operated by the time of the Mycenaean tablets, and thus whether, for example, *e-ke* "(s)he has" should be interpreted as *ekʰei* or *hekʰei*. Traditionally Grassmann's Law has been dated to Common Greek (or earlier), but a post-Mycenaean date has also been argued (Lejeune 1972a: 239; 1972b: 57; Ruijgh 1967: 44–6). In theory, if we saw a word spelled with a_2 or pu_2 before a syllable beginning with another aspirate, we could prove that Grassmann's Law was post-Mycenaean. As it happens, no relevant forms have yet been found. We know that Grassmann's Law operated after the weakening of both **s* and **y* to *h*, and, as already mentioned, the first of these changes has taken place, and the second is at least in progress. Intervocalic *h* < **s* does not, however, trigger dissimilation (hence θεός and not ˟τεός < **tʰehos* < **tʰesos*) and it could be argued that Grassmann's Law thus postdates the complete loss of intervocalic *h*. But we know from spellings such as *pa-we-a$_2$* that intervocalic *h* was still intact in Mycenaean, and this could constitute evidence for a post-Mycenaean Grassmann's Law.

Syllabic nasals and liquids

The regular outcome of the syllabic nasals **m̥* and **n̥* in Greek is α; sporadic examples of apparent o reflexes, such as Arcadian δέκο "ten" < **dekm̥*, are better explained as the result of analogy; they are, as here, largely confined to the numeral system (see Ruijgh 1961: 199). In Mycenaean too the regular outcome is *a*, so, for example, the negative prefix (< **n̥*) always *a-*, e.g., *a-ki-ti-to*, *aktiton* "uncultivated"; *te-ka-ta-si*, *tektasi* "builders" (dat. pl.) < **tektn̥si*. After a labial, however, the usual Mycenaean outcome is spelled *-o-*, though *-a-* is also found. Thus both *a-re-po-zo-o*, *aleipʰodzoos*, and *a-re-pa-zo-o*, *aleipʰadzoos* "unguent boiler," though the noun "unguent" always appears in the oblique cases with *a*-vocalism, e.g., dat. sg. *a-re-pa-te*, *aleipʰatei* < **aleipʰn̥tei*. By contrast **arsmn̥* "wheel" is always written *a-mo*, *harmo*, nom./acc. pl. *a-mo-ta*, *harmota*, dat. pl. *a-mo-si*, *harmosi*. The pair most often cited in this context is *pe-mo*, *spermo* vs *pe-ma*, *sperma* "grain, seed," Class. σπέρμα, < **spermn̥*. There have been attempts to explain away the *o*-vocalism forms, e.g., the suggestion that *pe-mo* is *spermos*, or an abbreviation for *spermoboliā* (*Documents²* 236, 404), or under the analogy of the nom./acc. stem of the *r/n*-stem the declension which could, in some circumstances, have been in *-or* < **r̥* (Ruijgh 1967: 100–1). These have not been generally accepted. Mycenaean is therefore unique among the dialects in showing *o*-vocalism reflexes of syllabic nasals, but it is not difficult to understand how a labial environment could condition such a reflex.

More troubling is the fact that -*o*- and -*a*- forms alternate in a labial environment, since, according to the Neogrammarian Regularity Hypothesis, the same environment should always trigger the same development. It is this unacceptable apparent irregularity that has prompted the attempts mentioned above to relegate the alternation to the realms of morphology or analogy. A radically different approach was adopted by Risch (1966), who saw here evidence of two different dialects of Mycenaean (see below under *The position of the dialect* for further discussion). His theory has found a great deal of favor. Thompson (1996–7) however argues that the distribution of *o* and *a* forms is characteristic of a sound change progressing by lexical diffusion, and that this explains the spelling fluctuation.

The case of the syllabic liquids *$\dot{r}$* and *$\dot{l}$* is rather different. Whereas the majority of dialects have αρ, αλ, ρα, λα (the cause of the fluctuation between *VR* and *RV* is obscure), Arc.-Cyp. and Aeol. show traces of oρ, oλ, ρo, λo as well. The Mycenaean data are hard to interpret. We have -*ar* word-finally in *a-re-pa*, *aleip^{h}ar* "unguent," and medially in *tu-ka-ṭa-ṣi*, *t^{h}ugatarsi* "daughters" (dat. pl.). In a labial environment there is evidence of *or*, *ro*, e.g., *qe-to-ro-po-pi*, *k^{w}etropopp^{h}i* "four-footed animals" (instr. pl.), < **k^{w}etwṛ-* (the *o* cannot be a compositional vowel) and *to-pe-za*, *torpedza* "table," cf. τράπεζα, if < **(k^{w}e)twṛ-pedya* "four-footed." The men's names *a-no-me-de* and *a-no-qo-ta*, if *Anormḗdēs* and *Anork^{wh}ontās*, would show the same development < **anṛ-*, as would *a-no-qa-si-ja* if *anork^{wh}asiās* "manslaughter." Evidence for the same reflex in a non-labial environment has also been claimed, albeit less securely, in *do-ka-ma-i*, if *dorgmahi* "sheaves" (dat. pl.), connected with Homeric δραγμεύοντες; the woman's name *to-ti-ja*, if *Stortiā* and connected with στρατός, Aeol. στρότος "army"; and the man's name *to-si-ta*, if *T^{h}orsitās*, cf. Θερσίτης. If Mycenaean does indeed have *o*-vocalism reflexes of the liquids, this would be a potentially significant link with Arcadian and Cypriot. An alternative suggestion by Heubeck (1972), that both *a* and *o* are attempts to write a still-preserved *$\dot{r}$*, has not found general acceptance.

Simplification of clusters of nasals or liquids and *s

In non-final syllables, clusters involving a nasal or liquid and **s* (i.e., **s{R,N}* and **{R,N}s*) were subject to simplification in the later dialects. In the majority of the dialects the **s* was lost and the preceding vowel lengthened, while in Thessalian and Lesbian the **s* was lost and the nasal or liquid doubled. Allen (1987b: 23) dates this development "very approximately" to 1000 BCE. However, only clusters with inherited **s* are affected. In East Greek, for example, the 3 pl. verbal ending **-onsi* (with secondary **s*, < **-onti*) is affected by a second wave of simplifications, to give Attic -ουσι rather than the *×*-ουνι which would be the result of the earlier change. The first wave of simplifications ought therefore to pre-date the East Greek change of **ti* to *si*; but this is of pre-Mycenaean date.

Further evidence that Mycenaean had undergone the first wave of cluster simplifications comes from the form *a-ke-ra$_2$-te*, which must be the sigmatic aorist participle of the verb ἀγείρω and derive from **ager-s-antes*. The sign *ra$_2$* must originally have had the value *rya*, as shown by the doublet *a-ke-ti-ri-ja* ~ *a-ke-ti-ra₂*, *askētriai* ~ *askētryai* "female decorators," but this cannot be its value in *a-ke-ra₂-te*. It must therefore be able to represent the outcome of both **rya* and **rsa*. Plausible values are *rra* and *rha*, suggesting an Aeolic-like development of these clusters.

The second wave of simplifications, involving word-final clusters and clusters with secondary **s*, was much later and does not affect all of the dialects. The Mycenaean 3 pl. verbal form *e-ko-si* "they have" is thus to be interpreted *hekʰonsi* rather than *hekʰōsi* or similar; and *pa-si* "all" (dat. pl.) is *pansi* (< **pantsi*) rather than *pāsi*.

Morphology

Nominal Morphology

The spelling rules obscure much detail since a large number of potential case forms would be spelled the same way. Of the cases which might exist (nominative, accusative, genitive, dative, instrumental, locative, ablative, vocative), in the *o-stems*, for example, the nom. sg. *-os*, acc. sg. *-on*, dat. sg. *-ōi*, instr. sg. *-ō*, loc. sg. *-oi*, abl. sg. *-ōt*, nom. pl. *-oi*, acc. pl. *-ons*, gen. pl. *-ōn*, and instr. pl. *-ois* would all be written simply *-o*. Beyond the nominative, accusative, genitive, and dative which are universally accepted (we might add the vocative, which happens not to be attested because of the nature of our documents), there is consequently little agreement about how many distinct cases we should recognize.

In the third declension, in the singular, we can see traces of the PIE dat. sg. *-ei* (spelled *-e*) and loc. sg. *-i*, both of which are used with the same dative-locative function. (In fact, at Knossos both endings are found only in the *s*-stems, the C-stems proper showing only *-ei*, while at mainland sites both endings are found in the C-stems. At Thebes the *s*-stems dative always has the *-i* form.) Clearly we are seeing the process by which the locative singular ending replaced the dative singular ending in the third declension in the later dialects. In the first and second declensions both the dat. sg. *-āi*, *-ōi* and the loc. sg. *-ai*, *-oi* would be spelled simply *-a*, *-o*. Should we therefore assume that the formal syncretism of dative and locative had resulted in the replacement of the locative by the dative ending, or do some *-o* forms represent *-oi*, others *-ōi*? In the plural of all three declensions the formal dative-locative syncretism is complete, original locative morphs (*-a-i*, *-o-i*, *-si* = *-āhi*, *-oihi*, *-si*) having replaced the original dative, and in the singular of the third declension, the functional syncretism is complete. Since the *a-* and *o*-stem singular spellings are ambiguous, therefore, most scholars see only the original dative morphs *-āi*, *-ōi*.

Similarly, the spellings *-a*, *-o*, *-e* could hide instr. sg. case forms *-ā*, *-ō*, *-ĕ̆*. In the Classical dialects the instrumental has also syncretized with the dative, in both the singular and the plural. Mycenaean clearly shows traces of an instrumental plural, however: *a*-stem *-a-pi* = *-āpʰi*, *o*-stem *-o* = *-ois*, C-stem *-pi* = *-pʰi*. Should we therefore see a distinct instrumental singular as well, or should we interpret singular nouns which have instrumental function as dative(-locative-instrumental)? As it happens, where such nouns are C-stems, they are always spelled *-e*, never *-i*. Is this significant?

To further complicate the issue, the instrumental plural can also have locatival and even datival function (if *pʰarweha . . . kʰitompʰi* is "cloth *for khitons*"), although the *-a-i, -o-i, -si* endings are never used instrumentally. Evidently Mycenaean is at a stage between that of PIE where instrumental, dative and locative were fully distinct, and that of the later dialects when they were fully formally and functionally syncretized. It is not clear, however, how the available morphs were distributed across the available functions. Morpurgo Davies (1966) has argued convincingly against an ablatival use of the instrumental, but its specter is still sometimes raised.

There is no clear evidence that the *-pi* morph was used in the singular as well as the plural (as it was in Homer). In KN Ld(2) 785 some cloth is described as *kʰrīsta erutʰrāpʰi*, which might mean "dyed (with) red" (i.e., the sg. of the noun "red") or "dyed, [and] with red [attachments]" (i.e., a fem. adj. qualifying an implicit noun or used substantivally, in which case it could easily be plural). The latter is perhaps more likely as on other similar records cloth is described as *erutʰrāpʰi* but without *kʰrīsta*. Similarly in PY Ta 714 two chairs are described as *pʰoinikpʰi* which could mean "[decorated] with purple"; but in one case *pʰoinikpʰi* appears to be qualified by the adj. *ku-ru-so* "gold" and in the other by *ku-wa-no* "made of blue glass paste." They are better interpreted as *kʰrusois-kʷe pʰoinikpʰi* and *kuanois-kʷe pʰoinikpʰi* "and with date-palms rendered in gold" and "and with date-palms rendered in blue glass paste" respectively. A third possible color term has been seen in *ma-ra-pi*, perhaps *malampʰi* "with black," describing an ox on PY Cn 418, but it is in truth opaque.

There are, however, two possible extensions of *-pi* into the *o*-stems (cf. Hom. -οφι). The phrase *e-re-pa-te-jo-pi , o-mo-pi* denotes a decorative part of a chariot and has been interpreted by Chadwick (*Documents*[2] 369) as *elepʰanteiopʰi oimopʰi* "with decorative bands made from ivory" (comparing *Il.* 11.24 δέκα οἶμοι . . . κυάνοιο). Similarly the place name *mo-ro-ko-wo-wo-pi* is probably a composite of a man's name in the gen. sg. and the instr. pl. of *worwos* "boundary" (Attic ὅρος).

The gen. sg. of the *o*-stems is almost always in *-o-jo*, representing *-oγ(y)o < *-osyo* (cf. Skt. *-asya*) and corresponding to Hom. -οιο. Beginning with Luria (1957) some scholars have also seen evidence of an alternative form written *-o*. The data have been discussed in detail by Morpurgo Davies (1960) and more recently by Hajnal (1995: 247–85). A connection with the mysterious Cyp. gen. sg. ending *-o-ne* seems unlikely, as this looks like a purely local development. Nor could it be a lengthened form *-ō* following the loss of intervocalic *y*, as we would expect the resulting *h* to be retained and to block contraction. A relic of the old *o*-stem abl. sg. **-ōt* is a possibility, since the genitive and ablative have syncretized in Greek. The majority of the examples are however problematic. In the Fp series of records of religious offering at Knossos, for example, month names in *-o-jo* alternate with forms in *-o*, some followed by the gen. sg. *me-no, mēnnos* "month" (e.g., *ka-ra-e-ri-jo ~ ka-ra-e-ri-jo-jo*). Where the word *me-no* does not follow we cannot be sure that the *-o* forms are intended to be genitive rather than nominative of rubric. Where *me-no* does follow a genitive of the month name is likely, although often *me-no* has been "squeezed in" in smaller, superscript signs and may be an afterthought. In the majority of cases the short form of the genitive ends in *-jo*, and haplography cannot be ruled out. Risch (1959: 223 n. 234) suggests instead that while *me-no* is singular, the "short" genitives of the month names are in fact plural, denoting the names of festivals. Similarly in PY Fr 1202 *me-tu-wo*, *ne-wo* need not be singular "during the festival of the new wine" rather than plural (Palmer 1963: 248). The example *wi-do-wo-i-jo, i-*65*, perhaps "the son of W." (with *wi-do-wo-i-jo* a "short" gen.) has been joined by the new form *ra-]ke-da-mo-ni-jo-u-jo* from Thebes, perhaps "the son of the Spartan." In both cases haplography is possible, or the scribe might intend "W., the son," "S., the son," in the sense of "Jr." (Killen 2006: 81). For arguments whether forms such as *ra-ke-da-mi-ni-jo-*65* in the Thebes Fq and Gp tablets conceal forms of the word *hyus* "son" (in which case there may be "short" genitives), or whether **65* should be read as the FLOUR ideogram (in which case not), see Palaima (2000–1: 483–4; 2006) and Killen (2006: 103–6).

The gen. sg. of masculine *a*-stems is in *-a-o* = *-āo*, as in the dialects other than Attic (where *-ou* is an import from the *o*-stems; Ionic *-εω* is by quantitative metathesis from earlier *-ηο* < **-āo*; Arc. *-αυ*, Cyp. *-au* is from *-āo* by the regular Arcado-Cypriot raising of final *-o*). It had been generally thought that this ending was formed by analogy with that of the *o*-stems when it was at the stage *-oo* and could be analyzed as a morph *-o* added directly to the stem. The fact that it is present in Mycenaean, where the *o*-stem gen. sg. is in *-oy(y)o* shows this to be false.

The characteristically Greek *-eus* declension is well attested, with nom. sg. *-e-u* = *-eus*, gen. sg. *-e-wo* = *-ēwos*, dat. sg. *-e-we, -e-wi* = *-ēwei, -ēwi*, nom. pl. *-e-we* = *-ēwes*, dat. pl. *-e-u-si* = *-eusi* and instr. pl. *-e-u-pi* = *-eupʰi*.

The dual number is used not just for "natural pairs," but in nouns is attested only in the nom./acc. The feminine *a*-stems have *-o* = *-ō* (e.g., *ktoinō dwo* "two plots of land"). This is also the ending in the *o*-stems. Masculine *a*-stems, however, have *-a-e* = *-āe*; this may underlie the Homeric masc. *a*-stem *-ā* (rather than *-η*). The numeral "two" has the instr. *du-wo-u-pi, dwoupʰi*.

Verbal morphology

The nature of the documents means that the range of verbal forms attested is very limited. We have only third person indicatives, participles, and infinitives. The thematic and athematic conjugations are clearly distinguished.

In the present tense the thematic conjugation has the endings 3 sg. *-ei* (*e-ke, hekʰei* "s/he has"), 3 pl. *-onsi* (*e-ko-si, hekʰonsi* "they have"). The athematic type has 3 sg. *-si* (*pa-si, pʰāsi* "he says"), 3. pl. *-nsi* (*di-do-si, didonsi* "they give"). The verb "to be" is attested in the 3 pl. *e-e-si, ehensi*. The 3 sg. of the athematic type and the 3 pl. of both types show the characteristic E. Gk assibilation of **ti > si*.

The present medio-passive is attested in the 3 sg. of the thematic type as e.g., *e-u-ke-to, eukʰetoi* "s/he claims," and in the athematic as e.g., *di-do-ti, didotoi* sg. or *didontoi* pl. "it is/they are given." The most surprising thing here is the vocalism of the endings *-(n)toi*, vs standard Gk *-(ν)ται*. Arc.-Cyp. too has *-(ν)τοι*. Mycenaean shows that Ruipérez (1952) was right to see *-(ν)τοι* as the original form (see Sihler 1995: 476 for discussion).

The thematic future might be represented in the 3 sg. by *a-ke-re-se*, if this is *agrēsei* "he will take/receive," but this might also be an aorist *agrēse*. In the 3 pl. we have *a-se-so-si, asēsonsi* "they will fatten". The athematic future is represented by 3 sg. *do-se, dōsei* "he will give," and 3 pl. *do-so-si, dōsonsi* "they will give." The medio-passive is not attested in the indicative except perhaps in the verb "to be" in the form *e, so-to, es(s)ontoi* "they will be."

In the aorist: thematic 3 sg. *wi-de*, *wide* "he saw," 3 pl. *o-po-ro*, *opʰlon* "they owed"; athematic 3 sg. *te-ke*, *tʰēke* "he appointed." In the middle only 3 sg. forms are secure, thematic *de-ka-sa-to*, *deksato* "he received", athematic *pa-ro-ke-ne-to*, *parogeneto* "he was present." The lack of augment is somewhat surprising, although *a-pe-do-ke* might be an isolated augmented form *ap-edōke*. Lack of augment cannot be a poetic feature, as was previously thought. There are no secure aorist passive forms; *wo-ke* might be *worgen*, 3 pl. of an -ην type aorist passive (Lejeune 1971: 118). Chadwick (1996–7) proposed to read *o-je-ke-te-to* and *tu-wo-te-to* as *oie(i)kʰtʰēto* "(there) was opened" and *tʰuōtʰēto* "(there) was made fragrant," i.e., as aorist passives of the -ϑη- type with medio-passive rather than active endings, but this suggestion has not been generally accepted. Forms of the aorist middle of τίϑημι, i.e., *tʰeto*, seem more likely.

The perfect medio-passive may be represented by *e-pi-de-da-to*, *epidedastoi* "has been distributed."

The imperfect is not attested, unless *te-ko-to-(n)a-pe* really is *tektōn apēs* "the builder was absent," with *apēs* < **apēst*, the 3 sg. imperfect of the verb "to be," but it seems quite likely that this is a place name rather than a verbal phrase.

The thematic present participle active is in *-ōn*, *-onsa*, *-on* (spelled *-o*, *-o-sa*, *-o*). The fem. form is from **-ontya*, and since it contains secondary *-s-*, the *-n-* is certainly preserved. The present participle of the verb "to be" is *e-o*, *ehōn*. The fem. nom. pl. is attested as *a-pe-a-sa*, *apehasai* < **ap-esn̥tyai*, without the remodeling on the analogy of the masc. which characterizes most of the later dialects; compare Arc. ἔασ(σ)α. The medio-passive participle is in *-omenos* (thematic) e.g., *to-ro-qe-jo-me-no*, *trokʷeyomenos* "touring," *-menos* (athematic) e.g., *ki-ti-me-na*, *ktimenā* "being cultivated."

The only secure future active participle is *de-me-o-te*, *demehontes* "who are to build," showing the **-es-* future in a verb whose stem ends in a nasal. The form *ze-so-me-no* is probably passive in force, *dzes(s)omenōi* "to be boiled" (describing an unguent in the dat.), showing that the future passive and middle were not formally distinguished.

The form *a-ke-ra₂-te*, as already mentioned, is an aorist active participle *agerrantes* or *agerhantes* < **agersantes* "having collected" (cf. ἀγείραντες with compensatory lengthening). The aorist passive is attested as *qe-ja-me-no*, *kʷeyamenos* "having been compensated": as in the future, then, the aorist middle and passive participles are not formally distinguished.

The active perfect participle masc./neut. declines as an *s*-stem, e.g., neut. pl. *te-tu-ko-wo-a₂*, *tetukʰwoha* "finished"; *a-ra-ru-wo-a*, *ararwoha* "fitted." There is no trace of the *-t-* which characterizes the perfect participle in the later dialects; it must be a later development, albeit pan-Hellenic. The fem. form of the same participle is *a-ra-ru-ja*, *araruy(y)a*, with the characteristically Greek ending which appears in the later dialects as -υια. The force is intransitive and stative rather than truly active. Nonetheless, a distinct medio-passive form exists, although its sense is identical: *a-ja-me-na*, *ayai(s)menos* "inlaid."

The thematic present infinitive active is in *-ehen*, e.g., *e-ke-e*, *hekʰehen* "to have." The first *-e-* is, of course, the thematic vowel of the stem. The athematic infinitive has the same ending *-hen*, as shown by *e-re-e*, *ere-hen* "to row" (where the *-e-* immediately before the ending is part of the stem, and derives from **H₁*) and *te-re-ja-e*, *teleyāhen* "to act as a *telestās*."

Syntax

The following true prepositions are attested: *heneka* + gen. "on account of" (as a preposition, not a postposition); *peda* + acc. "to"; *ampʰi* + dat. "around"; *ksun* + dat. "with"; *meta* + dat. "with"; *epi* + dat. has the sense "upon"; its ablaut variant *opi* (cf. Latin *ob*) governs the dat. of men's names with the sense "under the charge of," but also, at Pylos, seemingly governs the instr. pl. in the phrase *opi kʷetropoppʰi horomenos* "watching *over* the four-footed animals." There is no other example of a preposition governing the instrumental, but this may be the result of the dative-locative-instrumental syncretism already described. It may alternatively be a case of tmesis, although this phenomenon is otherwise unattested.

The preposition *paro* + dat. is particularly interesting. In the majority of its instances we cannot tell whether the sense is "*apud*" or "from," but in some cases (e.g., the Pylos personnel records of the An series and the flock records of the Cn series, and the Knossos D– flock/wool and L– cloth records) the locatival sense seems required, in others (notably the Thebes Wu sealings which in all probability record the contribution of commodities for a state banquet) the ablatival sense is needed. This preposition therefore shows the same double value as its Arcadian equivalent παρά + dat. Householder (1959) has observed that formally the nouns following *paro* in its ablatival sense could be instrumentals, but this is unlikely given that the instrumental is part of the dative-locative syncretism rather than the genitive-ablative. Morpurgo Davies (1966) has argued that the ablatival use of the dative in Arcado-Cypriot results from the simplification of case government after prepositions; if the same is true of the dative used after ablatival *paro*, this could be a significant shared isogloss between Arcado-Cypriot and Mycenaean (Thompson 2000).

Even though the prepositional system is well developed, the dative-locative-instrumental is used on its own with locatival function, and the instrumental with instrumental/comitative function: e.g., *e-re-i*, *Helehi* "at Helos"; *pa-ki-ja-pi*, *Spʰagiāmpʰi* "at Sphagianes"; *ararwoha desmois* "fitted with bindings"; *torpedza . . . kuteseyois hekʰmappʰi* "a table with bastard-ebony supports". The postpositional affix *-de* governs the acc.: *te-qa-de*, *Tʰēgʷans-de* "to Thebes."

Preverbs have become fused with their verbs. Unless *opi . . . horomenos* is an example, tmesis is unattested, showing that it is an extremely archaic feature of Homeric syntax.

There are few full sentences with complex syntax, and the majority are found in tablet headings introduced by a particle spelled *o-* or *jo-*. The following is typical:

o-wi-de	*pu₂-ke-qi-ri*	*o-te*	*wa-na-ka*	*te-ke*	*au-ke-wa*	*da-mo-ko-ro*
hō wide	*Pʰugegʷrins*	*hote*	*wanax*	*tʰēke*	*Augēwān*	*dāmokoron*

thus saw (man's name) when king made (man's name) (office)
"Thus Phugegwrins saw when the king appointed Augēwās as dāmokoros."

Here the subordinate temporal clause introduced by the conjunction *hote* has SVO word order, while the main clause has the verb drawn to second position where it is univerbated with the introductory particle. This univerbation is probably motivated by the desire to avoid writing monosyllabic words with a single sign. The particle itself has been variously interpreted: (i) as a survival of a Linear A scribal feature (Hooker 1968: 77); (ii) as part of the demonstrative pronoun **so-* (or the relative **yo-*) used in the same way as the Hittite sentence-connective particles *nu, tu, šu* or Vedic *sá*, the V2 word order following from the verb appearing atonically in Wackernagel's Law position in a main clause, as in Vedic (Watkins 1963a: 13–21); (iii) as the nom. sg. and pl. of the demonstrative and relative pronouns (Gallavotti 1956: 5–10); (iv) as an adverb built to the relative pronominal stem, *hō*, meaning "thus" (*Documents* 91; *Documents²* 563).

Hooker's Linear A survival has the advantage of not being falsifiable, but it does little to explain what is happening. A sentence-connective particle falls foul of the fact that it is invariably used in the first sentence of a document, and so cannot connect to anything preceding. The nom. of a pronoun is awkward when, as in this case, the subject is overtly expressed. Moreover, the frequent word order SOV in the Pylos Ep land-holding records (e.g., *Korinsiā tʰehoyo doelā onāton hekʰei kekesmenās ktoinās* "Korinsia the slave of the god holds a usufruct lease of a plot of land owned by the *dāmos*") shows that the verb is not normally enclitic in main clauses. Ventris and Chadwick's *hō* has found the most favor, but the etymology as a relative does not sit easily with the demonstrative sense "thus" which seems to be required, and the V2 word order is unexplained (see Thompson 2002–3a for a possible solution).

The position of the dialect

Mycenaean shows the assibilation of *ti* > *si* in 3 sg. of athematic verbs and 3 pl. of both athematics and thematics which is characteristic of East Greek. Also characteristic of East Greek is the form *hieros* "holy" (vs ἱαρός) and *hote* "when" (vs ὄκα). Mycenaean is clearly, therefore, an East Greek dialect, along with Attic-Ionic and Arcado-Cypriot (see also ch. 14).

Some features align Mycenaean more closely with Arcado-Cypriot, some of which (e.g., -(*n*)*toi* vs -(ν)ται in the 3 sg. and pl. primary middle endings) are certainly retentions from Common Greek, but others, such as the use of the dative with ablatival sense after *paro*, and the *o*-vocalism reflexes of **Ṛ* , appear to be shared innovations.

In some respects Mycenaean diverges from Arcado-Cypriot: it lacks the raising of word final *o* > *u* (unless *apu* = ἀπύ is an early example, rather than a by-form of ἀπό) or of *e* > *i* before a nasal; but these could easily be post-Mycenaean developments in Arcado-Cypriot. Similarly, Mycenaean has -*āhi*, -*oihi* as the dat. pl. of the *a*- and *o*-stems where Arcado-Cypriot has -αις, -οις; but Mycenaean has an instr. pl. in -*ois* which could underlie the Arcado-Cypriot dative in the *o*-stems and, by analogy, in the *a*-stems. A potentially significant difference is the fact that Mycenaean has extended the ending of the thematic infinitive -*hen* into the athematic conjugation, which Arcadian and Cypriot have not done.

Mycenaean is therefore a dialect related to Arcado-Cypriot – not unexpected, given the geography – but not necessarily to be identified as the direct ancestor of either Arcadian or Cypriot. The precise relationship between the three is difficult to determine. Presumably the Arcadians were the descendants of speakers of a Mycenaean-like dialect who took to the hills when the Dorians invaded the Peloponnese, while the Cypriots were émigré cousins.

The question of dialect differences within Mycenaean itself has been discussed since *Documents* (75–6). Ventris and Chadwick observed that the dialect appears uncannily uniform across both space and time, and attributed such differences as are observable (e.g., the greater use of a_2 on the mainland) to the realm of orthography. They suggest that this was due to the conservative influence of the "scribal schools," the tablets showing not the contemporary state of the language of the twelfth century BCE but that of perhaps the sixteenth or fifteenth.

Modern discussions follow from the observations of Risch (1966). He focuses on three fluctuations in the language of Pylos: (i) *o* vs *a* in the reflexes of syllabic nasals; (ii) *-ei* vs *-i* as the C-stem dat. sg.; (ii) *-i-* vs *-e-* in a group of words e.g., *Artimis* vs *Artemis*. These he explained as the result of a substrate, substandard dialect, the vernacular of the scribes, which he dubbed *mycénien spécial* (with $a < *\underset{\circ}{M}$, dat. in *-i*, and e.g., *Artemis*) showing sporadically through the veneer of the official standard *mycénien normal* (with $o < *\underset{\circ}{M}$, dat. in *-ei*, and e.g., *Artimis*). Nagy (1968) adds a fourth feature: whereas *mycénien normal* shows the standard East Greek assibilation, he attributed the sporadic examples of preserved *-ti-* (e.g., *Milātiai* "women of Miletus") to *mycénien spécial*.

Chadwick (1976a) observes that in this respect *mycénien spécial* resembles West Greek, and proposes that Peloponnesian Doric was the surviving descendant of this substrate. On this account, the Dorians did not invade, but were already present in the Peloponnese as the subjects of East Greek, Mycenaean overlords. They stepped into the vacuum left by the collapse of the palaces. The theory has not found general acceptance: the non-assibilated forms are largely restricted to proper names and ethnics, where conservatism and analogical effects are common, and there are no specifically West Greek features to be seen (Risch 1979). The wider two-dialect hypothesis too has been called into question: other explanations for *o* vs *a* < *$\underset{\circ}{M}$, and for *-ei* vs *-i* in the dat. sg. are possible, and the evidence for the *Artemis* vs *Artimis* fluctuation is restricted to non-Greek words (Thompson 1996–7, 2002–3b).

There are, however, differences to be observed between sites – see Hajnal (1997) for the fullest modern treatment. It seems very likely that the Linear B script hides many differences which may exist, particularly on the phonological level. Most recently Meissner (2007) has argued convincingly that the absence of intervocalic a_2 and the almost completely uniform writing of the non-phonemic glide *-j-* where *h* would have been, indicates psilosis in the Knossian dialect. How this is to be related to the later psilosis of (Doric) Cretan, however, remains unclear.

FURTHER READING

The most comprehensive introduction to Mycenaean in English is still *Documents*[2], although at the time of writing a completely new third edition is in preparation. Bartoněk (2003) is the most recent handbook. Morpurgo Davies (1985) gives an overview of the importance of Mycenaean to the history of Greek.

CHAPTER FOURTEEN

Greek Dialects in the Archaic and Classical Ages

Stephen Colvin

The history of Greek from the introduction of the alphabet until the *Koine* is the history of the dialects. In the Archaic and Classical periods the Greek language is an abstract notion in the sense that there was no standard language, but a collection of dialects that we think were mostly mutually intelligible. One should not overstate the "abstractness" of Greek at this period, however: the notion that a language is a standard with a set of variations (dialects) is a later idea, reflecting the linguistic and socio-linguistic history of languages such as English, French, and Spanish. In these cases centralized political power, printing, and the influence of classical Latin led to the conception of standard and dialect in terms of correctness and deviation: this idea is probably alien to Greek thought about Greek before the *Koine*, though there is some evidence that at the level of the dialects some regional standards had started to emerge by the late fifth century (that is to say, Attic speakers do not seem to have regarded other dialects as less correct or less Greek than Attic, but there may have been "social" varieties of Attic that were regarded as less correct or less prestigious by comparison to an emerging local standard).

In spite of the dialectal diversity, Greek was as real an entity as any language can be because it had been named; it is this metalinguistic event which leads speakers to the view that they have a common language. The Greeks themselves seem to have accepted without worry the idea that they all spoke Greek, though they were typically vague about articulating this (Morpurgo Davies 1987b). There is no reference to the language difference between Greeks and non-Greeks in Homeric epic, let alone to dialectal variation within Greek; there are a few trivial references to the existence of foreign languages, but the epic tradition has no general term for Greek ethnicity or language.[1] However, the spread of Homeric epic is part of the development of pan-hellenic identity that has been connected with the later Geometric period (eighth century BCE); as the first major *Koine* of post-Mycenaean Greece it must have been central to the creation of a centripetal Greek linguistic consciousness, by which the Greeks "rediscovered" and named their common heritage.[2]

Greek willingness to accept the dialects as valid representatives of Greek suggests that they conceived the relationship of dialect to language as one of concrete species (τὸ εἶδος) to an abstract genus (τὸ γένος), "Greek" (the Greek terminology is Aristotelian, though not applied by Aristotle to language). Given the generally low level of anxiety about dialect difference, there is every reason to suppose that in inter-state contact the Greeks would have engaged in dialect accommodation: when the cost is lower than the anticipated reward, speakers of different varieties will converge in interaction (the cost here being the speaker's own sense of identity and integrity). Since the Greeks seem not to have suffered from a high degree of linguistic insecurity, linguistic politics did not play a large role in their culture until the Hellenistic period, when the written standard was fossilized and they began to look back to an earlier period of purity and authenticity.

The term for speaking Greek was rendered with the verb ἑλληνίζω (with the optional specification of a word for language, such as τῇ φωνῇ), or with the adjective "Greek" (ἑλληνικός, ἑλληνίς) applied to a noun for speech, such as γλῶσσα. It is difficult, unfortunately, to be clear from the written sources how the Greeks designated dialectal difference at this period. The various Greek words for "language" were routinely used to refer to the dialects also; the unambiguous use of the term ἡ διάλεκτος "dialect" is hard to pin down before the Hellenistic period. The term derives from the verb διαλέγομαι, in which in the Classical period the pre-verb δια- mostly has the force of "through, across," hence "I converse, talk (with)." There are, however, indications that by the fifth century the verb could perform a different function, one in which the pre-verb had its other possible implication, "in different directions" – hence "I talk separately, in a different way." Herodotus (1.142) uses the verb twice in describing the dialects of Ionia, and a fragment of Aristophanes (706 *PCG*) shows that the derived noun διάλεκτος could also mean "idiom, peculiar way of speaking": the word refers here to a social dialect, belonging to a character who speaks "the normal dialect of the city [διάλεκτον ... μέσην πόλεως], not the fancy high-society accent, nor uneducated, rustic talk." It is probable, therefore, that the word could also be used to denote a characteristic regional idiom, though the context would have to make it clear that the salient differential was region.

Our picture of the Greek dialects is incomplete, in two ways. First, many regions of Greece took up writing late, in the period when the dialects were retreating in the face of the *Koine*, which gradually took over as the written standard. Even before the appearance of the Hellenistic *Koine* (based on Attic-Ionic, see ch. 16), in many culturally backward areas in the northern and western areas of mainland Greece one has the impression that the dialect presented in inscriptions is a local written *Koine* (in fact, a West Greek *koinā*) rather than a close approximation to a regional idiom. Secondly, even in those regions where inscriptions (or literary texts) go back to an early period, it is likely that we are dealing with a standardized or official version of the dialect, which – in the nature of written languages – reflected a conservative variety of the dialect and was largely immune to change (since writing systems quickly become fossilized). There are some exceptions to this, notably in Boeotia, where efforts were made to keep the spelling abreast of rapid phonological changes. Language is so mixed up with politics and collective identity that it is difficult to predict in a given case what the factors influencing the choice of an "official" language variety will be: candidates are likely to include distinctiveness (from neighbors), reference to prestigious literary/

poetic traditions, and the linguistic features of a political elite. With the possible exception of Athens, we can generally only guess at this in the case of the Greek dialects. It is worth remarking that just as the language itself varied across the regions and states of Greece, so too the sociolinguistic culture seems to have varied: some states put up many inscriptions, pay careful attention to matters of spelling, script, etc., and in general seem to have found writing an interesting and valuable thing, while others seem to have been very much less interested.

The modern classification of the Greek dialects is based, with some modifications, on that inherited from the ancient world. The Greeks, like most peoples, associated dialect very closely with ethnicity, and since they distinguished three main ethnic subdivisions amongst themselves, they divided their language into three dialect groupings accordingly: Ionic, Aeolic, and Doric. A well-known Hesiodic fragment sets out the myth-historical background to this division:

Ἕλληνος δ' ἐγένοντο φιλοπτολέμου βασιλῆος
Δῶρός τε Ξοῦθός τε καὶ Αἴολος ἱππιοχάρμης.

From Hellen the warrior king sprang
Doros and Xouthos and Aiolos lover of horses. (Hes. 9 M-W)

The three offspring of Hellen "Greek" are the ancestors of the Dorians, Ionians and Aeolians respectively. The importance of these tribal affiliations can be seen from Thucydides' history of the Peloponnesian War, which is often presented as a conflict between the Ionians (led by Athens) and the Dorians (led by Sparta): Thucydides 7.57 is a *locus classicus* for an analysis of the conflict in ethnic or tribal terms. When Dorians fight on the same side as the Athenians this is worthy of comment, especially when (as at Thuc. 4.3) one side deliberately uses allies who speak the dialect of the enemy for tactical advantage.

Dialect awareness in the early period was based on aural and oral experience: even what we know as literary texts were in most cases encountered orally, since the literary culture until the end of the fourth century and beyond was overwhelmingly oral. In this period we assume that the Greeks made a sharp distinction between "live" dialect that they encountered in various situations (trade, metics, war, panhellenic gatherings) and the language of literature. Thus there would have been no confusing, say, the dialect of Doric-speaking cities with the literary Doric of choral poetry. Familiarity with different dialects will have been a function of proximity, but there will have been "superpower" dialects also (such as Athens and Sparta) which were better known than others. For an Athenian some dialects would have required more effort than others: when Thucydides at 3.94 says of the Aetolians "that their language is the hardest to understand" (ἀγνωστότατοι δὲ γλῶσσαν ... εἰσίν), this is only from the perspective of Attic. Presumably a Messenian would have found Boeotian more of a challenge than the Athenians, for whom it was a neighboring dialect with some significant isoglosses.

However, in the surviving technical literature on the dialects from the Hellenistic and Roman periods, dialect awareness is based mostly on literary dialect: this had the effect, of course, of giving a distorted picture of the ancient dialects at a time when the technical terminology for talking about language and dialect had been expanded (owing to the growth in textual scholarship and exegesis). As a result the ancient scholarly tradition shows almost no awareness of dialects which did not attain literary status, and in general has a number of peculiar ideas about the dialect situation in the Archaic and Classical periods, ones which speakers living in the earlier period cannot possibly have held. These were influential in early modern thinking on the subject (see below; on literary dialects, see ch. 26).

The Dialects

To the three traditional dialect groups inherited from the Greeks, modern scholarship has added a fourth group, Arcado-Cypriot, and an isolate. With these additions, the standard classification of the dialects is as follows (the subgroups listed against each dialect merely reflects the available evidence – or rather, the lack of it in cases where no such groups are recorded):

- Arcado-Cypriot
  Arcadian
  Cypriot

- Attic-Ionic
  Attic
  Ionic: Euboean, Central Ionic, Eastern Ionic

- Aeolic
  Lesbian
  Thessalian
  Boeotian

- West Greek
  Doric: Saronic, Argolic, Laconia/Messenia, Insular, Crete
  Northwest Greek: Phocis, Locris; Achaea, Elis

- Pamphylian (unclassified)

This classification emerged out of nearly two centuries of modern debate on the dialects, grafted onto a history of ancient discussion ranging from random remarks in the classical authors to late grammatical work in the Hellenistic and Roman periods. It is more or less inherited from the Greeks, and is therefore based on non-linguistic (cultural, political) as well as linguistic factors. The grouping indicates as much about the (supposed) evolution of the dialects between the mid-second millennium BCE and the end of the Dark Ages as it does about synchronic relations in the Archaic and Classical periods: for example, the dialects of the Greek colonies are traditionally grouped with the dialect of the mother city in modern handbooks. Thus the dialect of Selinous in Sicily, a colony of Megara, is labeled Megarian in handbooks, though after centuries of interaction in completely different linguistic contexts the two dialects are likely to have diverged in many areas (e.g., in the preservation of ϝ/[w]).

The modern classification

The modern scientific study of the ancient Greek dialects grew out of the publication of the first major epigraphic *corpora* in the early nineteenth century and the advances in historical linguistics which were just taking off at the time. The starting point was Ahrens' *De Graecae linguae dialectis* (1839–43), which remained the fundamental reference during the nineteenth century: it was overtaken by the publication of more inscriptions, and the decipherment of the Cypriot Syllabary in the 1870s. It does not cover Attic-Ionic: the first volume covers the Aeolic and "Pseudaeolic" dialects, and the second volume the Doric dialects. Under Aeolic Ahrens reunited Lesbian, Thessalian, and Boeotian; he rejected Strabo's influential remarks on the classification of the dialects, in particular his classification of Arcadian and the Northwest Greek dialects as Aeolic (Strab. 8.1.2). With the small amount of epigraphic material at his disposal he correctly concluded that the dialect of Elis was closest to Doric, though peculiar in some respects. With a similarly small amount of data for Arcadian he simply noted that the dialect had features in common with Doric and Aeolic. He had very little material on the Northwest Greek dialects, which he treated briefly at the end of the first volume with the "Pseudaeolic" dialects: he could see that they differed very little from Doric, but noticed that the preposition ἐν + acc. (Att. εἰς) is a feature shared between the Northwest dialects and Boeotian. In the second volume he treated Doric as a unitary dialect, and noted variations and exceptions where appropriate. He introduced the distinction between "severe" (*severior*) and "mild" (*mitior*) Doric (still used, though not a significant isogloss), based on the treatment of secondary length-ened *e* and *o* (η, ω or ει, ου).

By the 1880s and early 1890s many more inscriptions had been published, and Cypriot inscriptions were now known. This led to fuller and more accurate accounts of the dialects, notably in two important and unfinished works, those of Meister (1882–9) and Hoffman (1891–8). Strabo's close connection between Arcadian and Aeolic (denied by Ahrens) was revived, and the term *Achaean* was introduced to unite all the non-Doric and non-Ionic dialects in a high-level group (the first volume of Hoffman's work covered Arcadian and Cypriot under the rubric *Der süd-achäische Dialekt*, while *Der nord-achäische Dialekt* covered Lesbian, Thessalian, and Boeotian). Scholars looked for a new classificatory framework for the dialects in the light of the evident connection between Arcadian and Cypriot: the unity was lucidly expounded in Smyth 1887 (followed by Buck 1907), and achieved the status of a dialect subgroup in the handbooks of Thumb 1909 and Meillet 1913. Bechtel's exhaustive three-volume reference work on the dialects (1921–4) was cautious on the status of Arcado-Cypriot (recognizing the connection without formally setting up a new group), and accepted the connection between Aeolic and the dialects of Elis and Arcadia which Ahrens had rejected but the recent handbooks had revived. On the whole, however, Bechtel con-centrated on accurate description rather than historical speculation.

After Bechtel the synchronic relations of the classical dialects were more or less agreed on (e.g., in the second edition of Thumb's handbook: Thumb-Kieckers 1932 and Thumb-Scherer 1959), and scholarly debate was focused on the higher-level (or historical) rela-tions between the dialect groups, a debate which was galvanized by the decipherment of

Linear B in 1952. In 1909 Kretschmer had proposed that the dialectal situation in Greece could be explained by supposing that the Greeks had entered Greece in three separate waves: early in the second millennium BCE the Ionians entered in the first wave, followed a couple of centuries later by the Achaeans (whom he did not distinguish from the Aeolians); finally the Dorians arrived after 1200 BCE. Kretschmer's theory was influential for three decades, but was finally abandoned in favor of more sophisticated attempts to account for the development of the Greek dialects as far as possible on Greek soil. As Cowgill (1966: 78) put it, ". . . the realization that innovations can spread across existing dialect boundaries has led to soberer views of prehistoric migrations."

After the decipherment there was consensus that Achaean (shorthand for Mycenaean and the ancestor of Arcado-Cypriot) was to be connected with Ionic in a high-level grouping distinct from Doric (or West Greek, as the group became known); arguments revolved around the Bronze Age affiliations of Aeolic, the putative ancestor of Lesbian, Thessalian, and Boeotian. In 1955 Risch proposed an explanation which was to dominate thinking on the subject for the next half-century. He saw two dialect groupings in the Bronze Age: on one side, West Greek and Aeolic (which, he argued, differed from West Greek only in developments later than 1200 BCE) formed a group which he called North Greek; on the other, Attic-Ionic and Achaean (Arcado-Cypriot with Mycenaean) formed a group which he called South Greek. Arguments over Aeolic have continued, but for the most part have in common a further diminution of the historical status of Aeolic, emphasizing areal or even social factors over traditional "genetic" ones in the development of the three dialects. García Ramón in an influential study (1975) saw Aeolic as a brief post-Mycenaean development, the result of the overlay of West Greek onto a population speaking an East Greek (Risch's South Greek) dialect; others have rejected the notion of common or proto-Aeolic completely (Brixhe 2006a). Palmer (1980: 67–74) argued against the growing consensus, and made a typically vigorous case for rejecting the premises of Risch's North/South distinction, and for reuniting Arcado-Cypriot and Aeolic in a significant Bronze Age dialectal unity ("Achaean"), distinct from Attic-Ionic and West Greek. In retrospect his arguments merely reinforce the case for not overweighting hypothetical second-millennium dialects and explaining the attested varieties of Greek in terms of mixing and moving. Many explanations of this type proceed on the unspoken and false assumption that languages proceed from unity (homogeneity) to diversity: Greek isoglosses in the second millennium are likely to have been as complex as in the historical period.

In the following brief description of the dialects it will be assumed that there is a high-level connection between Arcado-Cypriot and Attic-Ionic ("East Greek") as against the West Greek dialects. An additional assumption will be that the dialects as we find them in the seventh to fourth centuries BCE were formed *in situ*: developing from a more-or-less eastern or a western variety of Bronze Age Greek, they developed their characteristic traits through normal processes of local innovation, language contact, and the penetration of regional isoglosses. In each "unitary" dialect that we (following the Greeks) identify, there will have been numerous varieties, each perhaps with regional or social implications, and fluctuations in the written record (epigraphic and literary) may reflect this. The distribution of the West Greek dialects lends credence to the Greek view that Doric speakers did not enter the Peloponnese in large numbers until after the collapse of Mycenaean power (*c.* 1200 BCE): before that time they seem to have been concentrated in northern and western regions of Greece.

The decipherment of Linear B shows that a number of characteristic Greek sound changes had not yet happened in Mycenaean, and cannot therefore be ascribed to a stage of "common" (i.e., undifferentiated) Greek (see further ch. 13). This implies that it was not only dialect differentiation that occurred on Greek soil, but also processes of integration or coalescence by which the Greek language (like Greek culture) was formed (see also Garrett 1999).

Dialect differences

The most striking differences between the dialects are in the phonology (but it should be borne in mind that regional phonological differences seem more significant when spelled out than when heard by a native speaker of the language). Regional variations in the lexicon, normal to all languages, may be provoked by phonological change or morphological awkwardness (e.g., ὄϝις "sheep" > ὄις, replaced by πρόβατον in Attic, cf. Ar. *Pax* 929–36); generally they are random developments.

Morphological differences between the dialects are mostly minor: in verbal inflection there are variations in the infinitive endings, the inflection of vowel-stem verbs (thematic in Attic-Ionic and West Greek, athematic elsewhere), and verbal endings (1 pl. -μες in West Greek recalls the Italic ending). There are some small differences in nominal and pronominal inflection: notably variations in the personal pronouns (which were given nominal endings in Att.-Ion.: ἡμέ-ες > ἡμεῖς). Att.-Ion. and Arc.-Cyp. innovated the nom. plur. οἱ of the article τοί.

Phonological differences between the dialects grow out of a number of common developments in Greek which took place before the introduction of alphabetic writing (it is not always possible to tell whether the changes happened before or after the surviving Linear B tablets). As a result of the loss of intervocalic /y/ and /h/ (from *s) in pre-alphabetic Greek, and later by the gradual loss of ϝ/[w], vowels were brought into contact: this led to contraction or synizesis (loss of syllabicity when a vowel is realized as a glide before another vowel) in the various dialects: thus *ϝέτεhα "years" > W. Gk ϝέτεα, Ion. ἔτια, Boe. ϝέτια, Att. ἔτη; *γένεhος > Att. γένους, elsewhere γένεος or γένιος. New long vowels also came about from a process known as compensatory lengthening (see also chs 8 and 12), whereby the vowel was lengthened to "compensate" (preserve syllabic length) for the loss of a consonant from a consonant cluster: thus

> φέροντι "they bear" > E. Gk *φέρονσι > Att.-Ion. φέρουσι, Lesb. φέροισι
> *φθέρyω "I destroy" > φθείρω, φθήρω (but Lesb. φθέρρω)
> τόνς (acc. pl., article) > Att.-Ion. τούς, Lac. τώς
> κόρϝα "girl" > Att. κόρη, Ion. κούρη, Lac. κώρα

The consonant clusters in question are typically a resonant (/l/ /r/ /m/ /n/) plus /s/, /y/, /w/ (note that /s/, /w/, /y/ are all highly unstable in Greek, and disappear at various times and places). The new lengthened *e* and *o* that emerged from contraction and compensatory lengthening merged with inherited IE η/[ɛ̄], ω/[ɔ̄] in "severe" western dialects, but were maintained as long close vowels [ẹ̄], [ọ̄] in Ion.-Att. and were eventually written as ει and ου (the so-called "spurious diphthongs"). On these developments, see also chs 7 and 26).

Consonantal differences obvious in written texts include *a*) loss of ϝ/[w] in the dialects at different times, and *b*) variations in the treatment of palatalized consonants, which resulted from the adjacency of consonant and yod: thus *φυλάκ-yω > Att. Boe. Cret. φυλάττω, elsewhere φυλάσσω; *Dʸeus > Ζεύς, but Boe. and some W. Gk Δεύς. Other differences (loss of the aspirate, the development of stops into fricatives, secondary aspiration, and rhotacism of *s*) are less easy to detect, partly because they were difficult to represent orthographically, and partly because writing systems tend to be conservative.

The West Greek dialects have sometimes been characterized as "conservative," as against "innovative" Attic-Ionic. This is an unhelpful generalization (based on the change of *ti > si* in eastern Greek), and reflects cultural prejudices which can be traced back to the Greeks themselves. Each of the dialect areas was innovative in particular ways: Boeotia (despite the retention of *ti*) had an innovative vowel system, which Attic probably shared to some extent; Laconian turned ϑ/[tʰ] into a fricative [θ], and started to delete intervocalic *s* (νικάσας > νικάhας).

Note: all dialects apart from Attic-Ionic retain inherited ᾱ/[ā] rather than raising it to η/[ɛ̄], an innovation associated with these two dialects only (on "raising," see fig. 7.1). This is not specified in descriptions of dialect features.

Arcado-Cypriot

Neither the Arcadians nor the Cypriots were identified with any of the three tribal divisions in the Greek world. Cyprus was a peripheral part of the Greek world and wrote inscriptions in a local syllabic script that other Greeks would not have been able to read. Herodotus says at 7.90 that the Cypriots of his days were descended from immigrants from Greece, including Athens and Arcadia, and also from the Levant and Africa. Other ancient sources record mythological links between Arcadia and Cyprus: for example, that Paphos was founded by the Arcadian king Agapenor after the Trojan War (e.g., Paus. 8.5; see also Palmer 1980: 66–7). Classical Greek sources on earlier migrations need to be treated with caution, since ethnic identity is fluid and "traditions" are likely to reflect contemporary positions. As Goody and Watt (1963: 33) remark,

> . . . genealogies often serve the same function that Malinowski claimed for myth; they act as "charters" of present social institutions rather than as faithful historical records of times past. They can do this more consistently because they tend to operate within an oral rather than a written tradition and thus tend to be automatically adjusted to existing social relations as they are passed by word of mouth from one member of the society to another.

If any connection was made between the dialects of Arcadia and Cyprus in the ancient world it was not recorded in a form which has survived. The grouping is counterintuitive, given the geographical distance between them: it has traditionally been explained in historical terms by supposing that settlers from the Peloponnese arrived in Cyprus in the late Bronze Age, especially perhaps during the unsettled conditions that prevailed in Greece following the decline of Mycenaean power. The migration has been connected with the Greek tradition that the Dorians entered the Peloponnese after the Trojan War, but this is controversial.[3]

Arcadian and Cypriot share with Mycenaean Greek:

a) The assibilation of [t] to [s] before [i], the feature which is the most obvious diagnostic of the "eastern" dialects. That this change had already occurred in the language of the Linear B tablets (cf. *do-so-si* [dōsonsi] "they will give") shows that it is not the ancestor of all the Greek dialects, in spite of being the earliest attested.

b) Vocalization of syllabic resonants (*$*l$ *$*r$ *$*m$ *$*n$*): *$*l$ *$*r$ are vocalized with *o* (Arc. τέτορτος < *$*k^w etr$-tos*); *$*m$ *$*n$ give both *a* and *o* (in conditions which are hard to define). A similar distribution in the Aeolic dialects.

c) Myc. *po-si* [posi], the likely ancestor of Arc.-Cyp. πός (Att. πρός).

d) ἀπύ "from" (Att., W. Gk ἀπό): this seems to be an inherited variant, not a phonological change.

e) A shared archaism is the 3 sg./pl. middle verbal ending in –(ν)τοι where other dialects have innovated –(ν)ται after 1. sg. -μαι (Arc. γένητοι, Cyp. *keitoi*).

f) Prepositions meaning "out of", "from" (ἀπύ, ἐξ, Myc. *pa-ro* [paro] = παρά) are constructed with the dat.-loc. rather than the gen.

In addition, Arcadian and Cypriot share the following features:

a) A tendency to raise ε > ι before a nasal (thus ἰν < ἐν) and o > υ at word end (Cyp. *genoitu*).

b) Assibilated treatment of labiovelars (see chs 12 and 13) before the front vowels ε, ι: the result of *$*k^w i$* (perhaps an affricate such as [tˢ]) is written ζ/τζ or with a special letter И in Arc. (ὄζις "whoever"), and with an *s* in Cyp. (exclusive to these two dialects).

c) Athematic infin. ending –(ε)ναι, shared with Ion.-Att. (Arc. ἦναι "to be").

d) Athematic (-μι) inflection of vowel-stem verbs.

e) κάς for καί "and" (exclusive to these two dialects).

f) Inherited ἐν (ἰν) with the acc. "into" is retained, as in NW. Gk, Boe., and Thess. (Ion.-Att. and Dor. innovate ἐνς > εἰς/ἐς).

g) ὀν for the prep. ἀνά: also E. Thess. and Lesb.

h) Demonstrative pronoun ὄνι (Arc.), ὄνε (Cyp.), ὄνυ (Arc., Cyp.): ὄνυ also in Cret., ὄνε in E. Thess.

The two dialects also reflect centuries of independent development and local interaction. Arcadian shares εἰ "if" with Ion.-Att. (W. Gk αἰ): the Cyp. equivalent *e* is generally transcribed ἤ, and has parallels in W. Gk (e.g., Cret., cf. Buck 1955: 103). The most striking divergence is in the modal particle: Arc. has ἄν, an isogloss with Att., while Cyp. has κε (with Lesb. and Thess.). No doubt both were possibilities in the Peloponnese in the late Bronze Age (the form is not, unfortunately, attested in Myc.): the Arc. choice of ἄν points to an isogloss with Attic uninterrupted by West Greek at some point when the Achaean speakers were already established on Cyprus with the alternative form. In some cases the Cypriot script is ambiguous: secondary long *e* and *o* merged with inherited η, ω in Arc., as in the neighboring West Greek dialects (Laconia and Elis); there is no reason to assume this for Cyprus.

Pamphylian, a difficult and poorly attested dialect, has traditionally been grouped with Arcado-Cypriot, but shares at least as many features with West Greek (including preservation of -*ti*).

Attic-Ionic

Ionic can divided into three subgroups: western (Euboea), central (the Cyclades), and eastern (Ionia and adjacent islands). Herodotus (1.142) records the existence of four distinct dialects in Ionia, but there is no trace of this in the epigraphic record; this speaks for the early existence of a "chancellery" style in written Ionic. Varieties of Euboean must have been close to Attic, Boeotian, and Locrian.

Attic and Ionic share the following features:

a) The eastern Greek assibilation of [t] to [s] before [i].
b) Raising of [ā] to [ē] (η), universal in E. Ion. and Eub., partial in Att.
c) "Quantitative metathesis" of vowels in hiatus: ηο > εω. A form of synizesis: [ēo] > [ęō]. Thus *βασιλῆος > βασιλέως.
d) Secondary lengthening of *e*, *o* gives ει/[ę̄], ου/[ǭ].
e) Early loss of ϝ/[w].
f) Addition of -*n* (*nu ephelkystikon*) to dat. pl. nouns in -*si* and verbal endings in -*si* and -*e* (3 sg. and pl.).
g) εἰ "if" and the modal particle ἄν in conditional clauses.
h) No apocope of prepositions.

Differences between them are relatively trivial: the change ā > η was inhibited in Attic after ε, ι, ǫ. Ion. has -σσ- from palatalized velars, and compensatory lenthening after loss of ϝ/[w] (*ξένϝος > ξεῖνος, ξένος), and E. Ion. shares loss of aspiration with Lesb. A Eub. peculiarity is the rhotacism of intervocalic -*s*- (παιρίν < παισίν, etc.); it shares -ττ- for -σσ- with Att. and Boe.

Aeolic

We considered above the arguments for supposing that Aeolic was not a unitary dialect in the Bronze Age on a par with the other major groupings, in spite of two isoglosses in unique combination (-τι maintained, and *ṛ > οǫ, ǫο);[4] to some extent the problem reduces to the theoretical question of how many isoglosses constitute a dialect. Such common traits as there are must have spread through the areas north and west of Attica before the last group of settlers left mainland Greece for eastern Aeolis; this eastern dialect (Lesbian) was then in interaction with Ionic. Boeotian shares many features with West Greek (it has been called a "mixed dialect"), but also some with Attica; Thessalian shows a marked West Greek influence in the western region, much less in the eastern region (Pelasgiotis).[5] However, the epigraphic record from Thessaly is poor, and hints at a greater dialectal diversity than the traditional East/West distinction.

Innovations and selections common to the three dialects include:

a) The labial treatment of labiovelars before a front vowel: $*k^w$, $*g^w$, $*g^wh$ > π, β, φ (elsewhere τ, δ, ϑ), though there are exceptions to this.
b) The perfect participle in -ων, -οντος (imported from the present).
c) The third declension (consonant-stem) dat. plur. in -εσσι.
d) ἴα for μία "one" (fem.).
e) A patronymic adjective in *-(e)ios*.

They share with Arc.-Cyp. the vocalization of $*l\,*r\,*m\,*n$ with *o* (data are confused, especially in the case of Thess.): e.g., Lesb. Boe. στρότος "army."

Lesbian and Thessalian show gemination of *m, n, l, r* instead of vowel lengthening to compensate for the dropping of a consonant: ἔμμι < *ἔσμι "I am." They share with Arc.-Cyp. athematic (-μι) inflection of vowel-stem verbs, and ὀν for the prep. ἀνά; and with Cypriot the modal particle κε.

Isoglosses between Thessalian and Boeotian are in general shared with West Greek, and are mostly archaisms (such as the retention of *-ti* where Lesbian joins Ionic in changing to *-si*). A common innovation is the extension of the athematic infinitive ending -μεν to thematic verbs (Thess. πράσσεμεν).

The three dialects are marked by individual peculiarities. Lesbian innovated a predictable recessive accent, and the Thessalian accent seems to have changed into a stress accent (perhaps also recessive). The Boeotian vowel system changed rapidly in the direction of modern Greek from the fifth century. Diphthongs were simplified: [ai] > [ɛ̄], [oi] > [ȳ] > [ī]; and *e*-vowels were raised: ει/[ey] > [ẹ̄] > [ī], η/[ɛ̄] > [ẹ̄].

West Greek

The West Greek dialects have traditionally been known to classicists as "Doric." However, a subgroup of northwestern dialects can be clearly isolated by a number of important isoglosses, and linguists generally use the term Doric to refer to the dialects outside of this subgroup. With the important exceptions of Elis (Olympia) and Delphi, most of the speakers of Northwest Greek lived in culturally and geographically isolated areas: inscriptions are on the whole few and late.

The literary Doric familiar to the postclassical grammarians (see ch. 26) is a non-localized *Koine* with a few minor variations and many extraneous elements. The real Doric dialects covered a vast area, from the colonies in Sicily and southern Italy, across mainland Greece and over the Aegean to Crete, Asia Minor, and North Africa. There are, predictably, a large number of local features, reflecting regional innovations, isoglosses with neighboring dialects, and (probably) local substrate influences. The theory that an early variety of Doric Greek was a "low-class" sociolect in the Bronze Age Peloponnese (Chadwick 1976a) is tempting for a number of reasons, but has now been rejected by most linguists, for whom the arrival of West Greek speakers into the Peloponnese (and across the Aegean) after the end of Mycenaean hegemony is still the most economical way to explain the dialectal data.

West Greek dialects have in common:

a)   The retention of –τι;
b)   The vocalization of syllabic resonants with *a* (*$*ṛ$* > αρ, ρα etc.);
c)   First person plur. verbal ending –μες;
d)   Future suffix -σε- (κλεψέω "I shall steal");
e)   Temporal adverbs ὅκα, πόκα etc. for ὅτε, ποτε;
f)   αἰ "if" and the modal particle κα in conditional clauses;
g)   A range of lexical peculiarities such as λῶ "I want," δήλομαι "id." (from *$*g^welsomai$* – this is merely a variant of Att.-Ion. βούλομαι < *$*g^wolsomai$*).

The inscriptions from the Northwest Greek area show some additional features, including:

a)   A tendency to open ε/[ɛ] to α/[a] before an ρ/[r]: φάρω < φέρω (in Elean the opening is general).
b)   The third-declension (consonant-stem) dat. plur. in -οις (πάντοις).
c)   Inherited ἐν + acc. "(in)to" is retained.

The dialect of Elis has long puzzled scholars. It is marked by a number of unusual features, including rhotacism of final -*s*, a change η/[ɛ̄] > ᾱ/[ā] and (probably) the early development of stops to fricatives: ϑ/[tʰ] > a fricative [θ], etc. We have a large number of Elean inscriptions from an early date, and the Eleans seem to have made a decision to represent the peculiarities of their dialect accurately: if we had similar early epigraphic data from other areas of the West Greek world it is likely that Elean would not appear so anomalous.

The preceding paragraphs have sketched only a small selection of the very many regional variants recorded in Greek before the *Koine*. It has been claimed, presumably on the basis of late grammarians, that the Greeks thought of dialect difference (phonological, morphological) only in terms of different "words." This is scarcely credible of the Classical period, a culture fixated with language, and is in any case implicitly contradicted by the accurate depiction of non-Attic dialect in Aristophanes (*Acharnians* and *Lysistrata*), and by (for example) Theocritus at 15.88, where the poet expects that his audience will understand that the verb πλατειάζω "make broad, flatten" applies to the characteristic lowering of η/[ɛ̄] to ᾱ/[ā] in West Greek.

Most dialects, perhaps all, continued to be spoken for many centuries after the victory of the *Koine* in the written form of the language; there were various nostalgic outbreaks of dialect epigraphy in the Roman period, notably in Lesbos and Sparta, as late as the second and third centuries CE. However, without the underpinning of local institutions and a written standard the dialects must eventually have fallen into the status of local *patois*, continuing to develop perhaps in rural areas, but in urban centers little more than regional accents. This will have been a function of sex, education, and social status, and will have taken time: nevertheless, the "disappearance" of the dialects was none the less real for being social and psychological. Once speakers decided that "Greek" meant the common language, reflecting citizenship in the new Hellenistic world, the old dialects will have gradually lost both their social status and even their names. Some regional features of modern Greek are traceable to ancient dialect features (for example, nasalization in Cypriot, and the Tsakonian dialect of the southern Peloponnese), but in general the neo-Hellenic dialects are thought to derive from regional varieties of the *Koine* (chs 16 and 37).

FURTHER READING

For the ancient Greek conception of dialect, see Morpurgo Davies 1987b; and for the implications of later Greek ideas on dialect for our sources, Cassio 2007. Mickey 1981 discusses the way Greeks used foreign literary dialect in inscriptions, and what this tells us about the way they thought about dialect.

Buck 1955 is an excellent comprehensive introduction to the dialects: invaluable in spite of being out of date in various particulars. Colvin 2007 has a short grammar of the dialects, and a selection of texts with commentary and biblography. Schmitt 1977 is a brief but very useful overview, with a good survey of bibliography on each dialect. Cowgill 1966 is still useful as a lucid and intelligent discussion of the questions raised by the decipherment of Linear B for the dialects, many of which are still pertinent.

Bile et al. 1984 is important reading, giving the manifesto of what has sometimes been called the Nancy school of Greek dialectology: these scholars have sought to shake up traditional thinking about the dialects in the light of modern linguistics (especially structural linguistics and sociolinguistics), in particular by questioning "genetic" relationships between the dialects and associated migrations. Garrett 2006 is also an interesting corrective to "classical" thinking in Ancient Greek linguistics and dialectology, suggesting a model of convergence rather than the traditional differentiation for both Indo-European and Greek.

NOTES

1 On the idea of foreign languages in pre-Classical and Classical Greece, see also ch. 19.
2 For references to language in Homer, see Colvin 1999: 41–50; the question is discussed by Thucydides at 1.3. On Panhellenic consciousness, see Snodgrass 1971; cf. Nagy 1979: 7; 1990a: 52–115.
3 For the late migration of the Dorians (the "return of the Heracleidae"), see, e.g., Pind. *Pyth.* 1.62–5, Hdt. 9.26, and Murray 1993: 9–11. For a sensible critique of simplistic migration theories, see Dickinson 2006: 53–4, 62–3.
4 Pointed out by Ruijgh 1978: 420 in his review of García Ramón 1975.
5 The germ of the Aeolic dialects has traditionally been located in Thessaly: García Ramón 1975: 69 and Drews 1988: 222–3, following the ancient ethnographic tradition (Apollod. *Bibl.* 1.7.3).

CHAPTER FIFTEEN

Greek and the Languages of Asia Minor to the Classical Period

Shane Hawkins

The history of language contact between Greek speakers and languages to the east is a complex story that invokes not only comparative and historical linguistics but the disciplines of archeology, history, religion, and material culture. It is a history impeded by many difficulties and gaps in knowledge, and which has sometimes suffered from fevered speculation, but at the same time the story is both fascinating and one of great importance (not just) to classicists.

This chapter focuses on issues of language contact between Greeks and the languages of Asia Minor down to the Classical period of ancient Greece. Since only a sketch of this story can be given here, an attempt is made to discuss some of the major issues dealt with by scholars in the field and to provide an appreciation of some of the problems that confront them in their work. Not all of the languages under discussion will be familiar to all readers, so the first part of this chapter gives a brief introduction to the languages of Asia Minor. This is followed by a section on the historical and social contexts for language contact, and a final section on 'language artefacts' or phenomena created when speakers of different languages communicate.

The Languages of Asia Minor

Ancient sources provide the names of many different people groups in Asia Minor. Some of these groups can be identified, but the nature or affiliation of their languages remain unknown, while other groups are little more than names to us today (e.g., Keteioi (= Hittites?), Dardans, Zeleians, Pelasgians, Halizones, Mysians, Maeonians (= Lydians?), Solymians, Leleges, Lemnians; see Bryce 2006). Since little can be said for certain about these languages, this chapter focuses on areas where evidence is more readily available: contacts with the Anatolian language family, with Phrygian, and with Old Persian.

The Anatolian languages have the distinction of being some of the oldest attested Indo-European languages (see also ch. 12), while at the same time being among the last recognized as belonging to the family. It is generally agreed that at an early stage a group of Proto-Indo-European (PIE) speakers emigrated to form a separate Proto-Anatolian group, which then further split to form the individual daughter languages of the Anatolian family. By the end of the third millenium central and eastern Anatolia were occupied by three linguistically differentiated groups: Hittite, Palaic, and Luwian speakers. The other five members of the Anatolian family, all first-millenium languages, include Lycian, Carian, Lydian, Pisidian, and Sidetic. The earliest movements of these later languages are largely conjectural.

Hittite was the administrative language of the Hittite empire, which spanned from the seventeenth until the end of the thirteenth century BCE. The language survives mostly on several thousand clay tablets produced by professional scribes and written in a cuneiform syllabary of Mesopotamian origin. Most of the Hittite texts have been discovered in the palace structures of the capital Hattusa (Boğazköy, mod. Boğazkale), where about 25,000 tablets have been found. The subject matter of Hittite texts includes treaties, annals, didactica, law code, and literary texts, but most of them detail cultic material and ritual performance. The writing system is a blend of phonetic syllabic Hittite combined with Sumerian and Akkadian logograms. The work of paleographers and linguists has now made it possible to divide both the script and the language into old, middle, and new categories.

Palaic was the language of north-central Anatolia bordered by the Black Sea to the north and the Halys River to the south. The language was already extinct by the thirteenth century BCE at the latest and survives in about a dozen cuneiform texts of ritual and myth dating to the Old Hittite period (1570–1450 BCE) that were discovered in the Hittite archives at Hattusa. Palaic is conservative and shares certain traits with Hittite.

Luwian (or Luvian) is the only Anatolian language attested in both the second and first millenium. It was spoken mainly in south and southwestern Anatolia and northern Syria, though the influence of Luwian in the northwest and the east, including Hattusa itself, and particularly in the Late Empire (end of thirteenth cent.), may have been considerable. Luwian and Hittite are closely related and Hittite ritual texts are replete with Luwianisms treated either as foreign words or as borrowings with Hittite inflection. There are two closely related dialects of Luwian: cuneiform and hieroglyphic (the latter formerly sometimes called "Hittite hieroglyphs"). Cuneiform inscriptions are primarily devoted to state or private ritual and date as early as the sixteenth but mostly to the fourteenth and thirteenth centuries. Hieroglyphic Luwian is attested as early as the fifteenth century. Most inscriptions are datable to the tenth to seventh centuries, after the fall of the Hittite empire, and are attributable to local rulers of southern Anatolia and northern Syria. These are mostly monumental inscriptions on stone and are dedicatory in nature (though some have lengthy historical sections) and names or titles on seals.

Lycian was spoken along the mountainous coast of southwestern Anatolia between the Gulf of Telmessos and Bay of Attaleia (mod. Gulf of Fethiye and Gulf of Antalya). Lycian survives in inscriptions mostly of the fifth and fourth centuries and was written in an alphabet derived in part from an early Greek model. Inscriptions, numbering around 150, are mostly in stereotypical language inscribed on tombs. There are also graffiti, pottery and object inscriptions, and over 200 inscribed coins. There are only two inscriptions of any size in Lycian. The Letoon trilingual (in Lycian, Greek, and Aramaic) records the founding of a cult of Leto near Xanthos. The Xanthos Stele, a historical account of a local dynasty, is partly written in a more archaic dialect of Lycian called Milyan (sometimes referred to as Lycian B). This text and another also written in Milyan are in verse. There is no direct evidence of the language after Alexander's conquest of Lycia in 334/3.

Lydian was spoken in west-central Asia Minor, and survives in over 100 texts dating as early as the eighth but mostly to the fifth and fourth centuries BCE. Most of these come from the Lydian capital at Sardeis and most are tomb inscriptions on stone in an alphabet related to Greek. At least eight inscriptions are written in a stressed verse containing meter and rhyme.

Carian was the language of the southwestern coast of Asia Minor between Lydia to the north and Lycia to the south. Several Carian graffiti, scrawled by mercenaries in Egypt, date from the seventh to fifth centuries. About twenty short fourth- to third- century inscriptions from Caria itself survive.

The final, meagerly attested, languages are *Pisidian* and *Sidetic*. The former is the language of Pisidia, located north of Lycia and east of Caria (see fig. 16.1). There are about 30 sepulchral inscriptions (containing no more than names and patronymics) of the second or third century CE written in an alphabet related to Greek. Sidetic is the language of Side, located about 15 kilometers east of modern Antalya on the southern coast. There are about ten Sidetic inscriptions, datable to the third century, three of which are Sidetic–Greek bilinguals.

Phrygian is an Indo-European language and shares a few distinguishing features with Greek, Armenian, and Indo-Iranian. It is not well understood, but several elements of the grammar have been worked out. 'Paleo-Phrygian' refers to inscriptions dating from the beginning of the eighth century BCE to about 450 that are written in an alphabet that is perhaps derived from a Greek model. There are over 300 such documents, several of which remain unpublished. Over 100 'Neo-Phrygian' inscriptions, mostly funerary, appear in the first and second centuries CE. They are characterized by phonological changes, such as a reduction in the number of vowels. It appears that the Phrygians were Hellenized rapidly after the conquest of Alexander (see further ch. 16); Neo-Phrygian inscriptions are written in the Greek alphabet and about half of them are Greek–Phrygian bilinguals. It is possible that Phrygian survived to the fifth or even seventh century CE.

Old Persian, one of the languages used in the Achaemenid empire, designates the southwestern dialect of Old Iranian. The language of the inscriptions is an artificial idiom incorporating dialect forms, archaisms, and influences from other languages spoken in the empire. It was written in a cuneiform syllabary perhaps devised in some form already under Cyrus II (*c.* 559–530) and developed by (or under) Darius I (r. 521–486), and which continued to be used at least until Artaxerxes III (end of reign 338). The consensus view that the script was invented solely for the purpose of displaying royal inscriptions as prestigious display pieces has now been undermined by

the appearance of an administrative text from Persepolis recording a modest commodities transaction (Stolper and Tavernier 2007). The language survives primarily in
about 100 royal inscriptions in various media, though a number of proper names and
isolated glosses survive in external sources, including Greek.

Contexts for Contacts

In this section we consider some of the historical and social background that would
suggest points of contact between Greeks and non-Greeks, such as diplomatic relations, the movement of workers, tradesmen, and refugees, and *xenos* and marriage
alliances.

Scholars differ in their determination of the time at which the subgroup of Indo-
Europeans that eventually became known as Greeks migrated to the southern Balkan
Peninsula and settled in what would later become Greece. Whenever exactly the
Greeks arrived, they did not find themselves alone but in the presence of other Bronze
Age populations. Language contact with non-Greek speakers was a linguistic reality
from the moment (pre-)Greeks first arrived.

The most conspicuous *linguistic* signs of substrate influence on Greek are a number
of loan words identifiable by their non-Greek phonology and/or lack of convincing
Greek etymology. Scholars have noted that such words tend to cluster in groups with
certain suffixes or sound sequences. For example, words with a sequence -(υ)μν- (προ-/
τετρα)-θέλυμνα "-foundations," τέραμνα "chamber, house"), words with -ρν- (ἄχαρνος
a small fish, κέρνος type of earthen dish, κόθορνος "high boot"), and words with -μβ-
(διθύραμβος "dithyrambos," θύμβρα "thyme-leaved savory," σίμβλος "beehive").
Words in -ινθος typically designate native flora (ὑάκινθος "hyacinth," (καλα)μίνθη
"mint," τερέβινθος (and variants) "pistachio tree"), novel technologies (πείρινθος
type of wicker basket, πλίνθος "brick," λαβύρινθος "labyrinth" (cf. Myc. *da-pu$_2$-ri-
to-jo*, λάβρυς "ax," Carian Λάβρυανδος), ἀσάμινθος "bath"), and comestibles
(ἄψινθος "absinthe," κήρινθος "inferior-quality honey").

The status of these words and their linguistic affiliation(s) is a much-debated topic.
It is not even certain that all words sharing a suffix or sound pattern can legitimately
be grouped together. As a rule, it is impossible to identify the origins of these words
with any precision, and scholars frequently resort to classifying them with broad labels
such as "Substrate," "Pre-Hellenic," "Aegean," or "Mediterranean." There are, however, two well-known – and also controversial – theories about origins. One posits that
certain words, sometimes dubbed "Pelasgian" (cf. Hdt. 1.57), are non-Greek in origin
but can nevertheless be reconstructed in terms of PIE. For example, Greek τάφος
"funeral rites" is the regular outcome of PIE *d^hmb^hos. However, the same proto-form
appears to be the source of τύμβος "grave mound," which shows a different outcome
of the resonant *m. A similar development with another resonant can be seen in the
word πύργος "tower" for expected †πάρχος from *b^hrg^h- (cf. Germ. *Burg*).

A second theory argues that one of the major constituents of the substrate was from
Asia Minor, and more particularly that it was Luwian. Such a theory partly rests on the
evidence of several toponyms that cannot be explained as Greek but which do look

Anatolian. For example, Greece, Anatolia, and the Aegean are dotted with names in
-σσ- (e.g., Telmessos, Halikarnassos, Knossos) and -νδ- or -νϑ- (e.g., Passanda,
Zakynthos, Korinthos; Finkelberg 2005: 43–6 for maps). These have been related to
Anatolian formations such as the productive Luwian suffix in -*ašša*- that makes possessive adjectives and the Anatolian suffixes -*wanda*- and -*anda*-. A favorite example of
Luwian advocates is the name *Parnassos*, which is meaningless in Greek but explicable
as a derivative of Luwian *parna* "house" + Luwian possessive suffix -*ašša*-. *Parnassa* is
also an Anatolian toponym.

While most of the details regarding contact with substrate languages are lost in the
mists of prehistory or merely suggestive at best, more recently archeology and the
written records of Anatolia have inaugurated a new chapter in the history of early
language contacts in Asia Minor by making clear the extent to which there was early
contact with Anatolia. We can now see that as early as the fourteenth century
Mycenaean contacts and occasionally permanent settlements dotted the coastline of
Asia Minor. By this time Mycenaeans are taking over earlier Minoan sites and establishing bases in places like Miletus, Iasos, and Müsgebi. Certainly the main thrust
behind this movement was trade, the evidence of which sometimes includes surprising
finds such as Hittite ware in late Helladic Miletos, a Hittite cylinder seal in a Mycenaean
building at Thebes, and a fifteenth- to fourteenth-century Mycenaean bowl recovered
as far away as Hattusa.

Shortly after the decipherment of Hittite, the Swiss scholar Emil Forrer announced he
had discovered among the tablets from Hattusa references to a place called *Āḫḫiyā/
Aḫḫiyawā*, which he claimed referred to the land of the Ἀχαιοί "Achaeans" (i.e.,
Mycenaean Greeks). The claim was spectacular and controversial and the "Ahhiyawa
Question" has provoked scholarly debate, occasionally very bitter, ever since. For scholars
interested in the Homeric epics, these texts have yielded a bevy of tantalizing names, such
as *Wiluš(iy)a* (= Ἴλιος/Ϝίλιος "Ilion"), *Tarwiša* (= Τροίη "Troy"), a king of *Wiluša* named
Alakšandu (cf. Ἀλέξανδρος Alexandros/Paris), *Pariya-muwa* (= Priam, Πρίαμος ?), and
Tawagalawa (= Eteocles < *Etewoklēwēs* ?). While disagreement remains over such
equations and many of the details, scholars have made strides in firming up the notori-
ously complex issues of Anatolian geography and a consensus has formed around the
idea that *Ahhiyawā* does refer to Achaea, that it is to be located somewhere on mainland Greece, and that Wilusa is, in fact, to be equated with Ilion/Troy.

The Hittite records show clearly that there existed, already from the sixteenth century, a series of diplomatic contacts and occasional marriage alliances with Mycenaeans.
For example, a late fifteenth-century letter by the Hittite king to a western vassal mentions an Ahhiyawan named Attarssiya, who seems to have attacked the vassal with 100
chariots from his base in western Anatolia. He later reconciled with the vassal and
together they made raids on Alasiya (= Cyprus, or part thereof). The Annals of King
Mursili II (*c.* 1320) record that the king of Arzawa (capital at *Apasa* = Ephesus) and
the land of Millawanda (= Miletus) joined forces with the king of Ahhiyawa against
Mursili. Millawanda was destroyed by Mursili's generals and the Arzawan king appears
to have taken refuge with the king of Ahhiyawa. A treaty was drawn up (*c.* 1296–1272)
between the Hittite king Muwatilli and Alaksandu, ruler of the vassal state of Wilusa.
A letter from the late thirteenth century attests that the people of Wilusa had deposed

their king, Walmu, and that his replacement had not obtained recognition by the Hittite king, who planned to reinstall the deposed Walmu. A letter from the king of the "Seha River Land" to an unidentified Hittite king (*c.* first half of thirteenth cent.) records that Hittite troops attacked Wilusa. The letter also mentions *Lazpa* (= Lesbos), which had been attacked by an Ahhiyawan vassal ruler in Millawanda.

A remarkable letter from a king of Ahhiyawa to the Hittite king (thirteenth century?) appears to form a response to an earlier letter from the Hittite king, quotes an earlier letter, and even refers to an earlier dynastic marriage contracted between the Ahhiyawa and Assuwa of western Anatolia. The extant tablet recording this letter appears to be a Hittite translation of a Mycenaean (oral? written?) communiqué. Another letter from Hattusili III to the king of Ahhiyawa (mid-thirteenth cent.) indicates that Millawanda/Miletus was then under control of Ahhiyawa. The text also appears to mention Wilusa and clearly indicates that a Hittite king and a Great King of Ahhiyawa "were at odds over the matter of Wilusa." Another fragmentary text may say that a Hittite king banished his wife to Ahhiyawa. An oracle text (early thirteenth cent.) indicates that a deity of Ahhiyawa and a deity of Lazpa were going to be brought to an ailing Hittite king.

From the Greek side there is evidence of contact, too. The Linear B documents from Pylos record the presence of female workers, perhaps slaves taken in raids, from the western Aegean. Watkins (1998: 203) has suggested that the Mycenaean name *Aswijos* "man from Aswa = Assuwa," originally applied to refugees from the war conducted by the Hittite king Tudhaliyas against the Assuwan confederacy around 1430.

These texts raise many questions that are difficult to answer at present. What they indicate, however, is that even at this time there were routes of communication between the Ahhiyawan and Hittite kingdoms and the vassal states that lay between them. Already there existed a high level of bilingualism among – at the least – a diplomatic and scribal core, if not the larger population. How exactly the particulars worked, how close the connections, how extensive or widespread the bilingualism, is unknown. It remains to be seen, for example, whether we can assume connections as close as those supposed by the theory of a shared Greek–Luwian oral tradition, which is based on the recognition of the poetic "from steep Wilusa" (*alati . . . Wilusati*) in a Luwian ritual text that is comparable to the Homeric formula "steep Ilion" (e.g., *Il.* 13.773; Watkins 1986). On the other hand, in 1995 a bronze seal with a hieroglyphic Luwian inscription bearing the name of a professional scribe was discovered at Troy. Also, Greeks had a history of experience with foreign-language speakers, and when they moved into Asia Minor they encountered peoples with long traditions of bilingualism from very early times. According to Bryce (2002: 5–6), "no fewer than eight languages are represented in the tablet archives of the Hittite capital and perhaps even more were spoken in its streets on a given day." Similar situations would have existed in western Asia Minor in the following centuries, and trade, diplomacy, and military ventures would have necessitated the creation of bilingual communities and the formation of pidgins (cf. γλῶσσ' ἐμέμικτο "(their) speech was mixed," in reference to the multi-ethnic Trojan army at *Il.* 4.438).

Early Greek epic attests to the idea of close alliances between Greeks and Lycians. Their grandfathers' *xenos* relationship prevents Diomedes and Lycian Glaukos from engaging each other in battle. Glaukos also mentions the early marriage alliance between Proitos, king of Argos, and the king of Lycia. According to Herodotus, the Lycian Sarpedon led a group of Cretan immigrants called *Termilae* to Asia Minor, settling in Lycia. The name *Termilae* is reminiscent of *Trm̃mili*, the Lycian self-designation, and the story "may indicate that part of the Lycian population was Cretan in origin" (Bryce 1995: 1162). Archeological records of close contact in the areas of pottery, alphabet, architecture, and sculpture (e.g., Greek influence in the style of tomb reliefs) begin in the latter half of sixth century. By end of fourth century, however, Lycian culture was in decline and was slowly overwhelmed by Greek expansion east.

The Phrygians migrated from the Balkans and their arrival in Anatolia is usually dated to the end of the Bronze Age, after, but not consequent upon, the fall of the Hittite empire. They settled in central Asia Minor, making Gordion their capital city and forming a confederation of sorts with the Muski and their king Mita (the Midas of legend). The kingdom was destroyed shortly after 700 by Cimmerian invaders, in whose wake were left a number of smaller Phrygian settlements that carried on until the end of the seventh century, when they fell under Lydian subjection. In the *Iliad* the Phrygians appear as allies of Priam, who had fought on an earlier occasion as a Phrygian ally (3.184ff.). Priam's wife, Hekabe, is a Phrygian, and her brother Asios lived in Phrygia (16.717). Evidence from material culture attests to close contact between Greeks of Asia Minor and Phrygians already in the eighth and seventh centuries (Boardman 1999). Ancient sources record the eighth-century marriage of the Phrygian king Midas to Demodike, daughter of a king Agamemnon of Aeolian Kyme (Poll. *Onom.* 9.83). Midas was the first of many eastern kings to dedicate a gift (a throne) at Delphi. Frescoes at Gordion "which are wholly Greek in their style" present "evidence for the work of Greek artists in Phrygia" in the sixth century (Boardman 1999: 93). It seems that Phrygian was the most common ethnic origin of slaves in fifth- and fourth-century Attica, and that "most Athenians had an at least cursory familiarity with Phrygians" (DeVries 2000: 341).

Like the Phrygians, the Carians are also portrayed as the foreign allies of Troy in the *Iliad*. In Homer they alone are described as βαρβαρόφωνος (*Il.* 2.867). Greek contact with Carians must have been close from early on. Herodotus records (1.146–7) that the first Ionian colonists at Miletus brought no women with them, but married the young Carian girls whose parents they had slain when they arrived. Intermarriage must have been common; according to one tradition, Herodotus, who came from Halikarnassos with its mixed Greek–Carian population, was the son of a Carian named Lyxes and was related to the epic poet Panyassis, whose name is also Carian. Thales the Milesian was half-Carian, half-Phoenician. The general Themistocles may have had Carian ancestors.

The Carian economy depended largely on external sources of wealth, a fact that led to extensive emigration and military service under foreign regimes; "the land of Caria was essentially a springboard to action elsewhere" (Ray 1995: 1188). To the Greeks, "Carian" was synonymous with "mercenary," as the denigrating phrase "to run the risk with a Carian" (ἐν τῷ Καρὶ κινδυνεύειν), i.e., to spare citizens by making use of mercenaries, attests. In fact, though, Ionian and Carian mercenaries served together on many occasions from as early as the seventh and sixth centuries in Egypt (see also chs 3 and 17). At Abu Simbel, for example, one finds mixed Greek/Carian graffiti from the sixth century etched by soldiers serving under Pharoah Psammetichos I. One graffito,

Πελεϙός Οὐδάμō "Peleqos son of Eudamos," records a Carian name with Greek patronymic. Bilingualism must have been common in the mixed ethnic cities of Carian Asia Minor and among the soldiers who had served together abroad; Strabo claimed that Carian had "many Greek words mixed up in it" (14.2.28). In 411 Tissaphernes, the Persian satrap, employed Gaulites, a Carian trilingual, as envoy to Sparta (Thuc. 8.85.1f., who however calls him δίγλωττος "bilingual"). More surprising is the story that the Greek oracle at Acraephia in Boeotia answered a Carian representative of the Persian Mardonius in his native Carian (Hdt. 8.135).

The founding of the Lydian empire under Gyges and the Mermnad family came shortly after the fall of Phrygia, around 685. By the end of the sixth century, after waging war against and forging alliances with several major coastal cities, Lydia controlled most of western Anatolia. Although it held a territory smaller than that of its Phrygian predecessors, Lydia maintained hegemony over Anatolian Greece under Croesus. Remains of material culture attest to extensive networks of contact between the two. Greek and Lydian fine wares are sometimes nearly indistinguishable, Lydian dress and music had its vogue in parts of Greece, and Greek tradesmen were known at the Lydian court. Alyattes sent to Delphi a large silver bowl with an iron stand, thought in antiquity to be the work of Glaukos of Chios, and Croesus dedicated two very large bowls of gold and silver at Delphi, which were thought by the Delphians to be the work of Theodorus of Samos (Hdt. 1.25.51). More than one vase painter in Athens signed his name "Lydos."

For lyric poets such as Sappho, Alcaeus, and Anacreon, "Lydian" was already a byword for wealth, luxury, and effeminacy. Some ancients claimed the poet Alcman, who lived in Sparta, was originally from Sardeis, though this was and remains a matter of debate. The Ephesian iambic poet Hipponax lent some local color to his invective by employing some Lydian (and Phrygian) words (Hawkins 2004).

Periander of Corinth sent 300 Corcyrean boys to Alyattes to be made into eunuchs (Hdt. 3.48). Aelian (*VH* 3.26) records a marriage between Alyattes' daughter and an Ephesian ruler, Melas. According to Herodotus (1.29–33, 75ff.), Croesus' court in Sardeis was visited by "all the great Greek teachers of that epoch," including Solon, and Ionians fought on his side, probably as mercenaries, in the campaign against Persia. The inhabitants of Cibyra, located in southern Phrygia near the borders of Lycia and Pamphylia, were said to be descendants of Lydians and Pisidians and to speak Pisidian, Solymian, Lydian, and Greek (Strab. 13.4.17).

Lydian dominance came to an end in 546 when Sardeis, and eventually most of Asia Minor, fell to the Persian King Cyrus. Already by the mid-sixth century a treaty had been arranged between King Cyrus the Great and Miletus (Hdt. 1.141). Initial contacts with Persia appear to have been mostly indirect or through representatives of the empire such as the satrapy at Sardeis. From this time there is growing archeological evidence for trade with Persia in valuables such as Attic pottery, wool, metals, vessels, and statuary. Two of the most important areas of Greek interaction with Persia were skilled labor and manpower. Workers from Ionia with knowledge of stoneworking, building techniques, and sculpture are known to have labored on building projects at Pasargadae, Persepolis, and Susa. The trilingual inscription from the palace of Darius at Susa says that Ionians were among the building's stonecutters. These men, along with Carian and Lydian masons, were possibly forced laborers. Pliny (*HN* 34.68) identifies an Ionian sculptor, Telephanes of Phocaea, who worked for both Darius and Xerxes. Some of the building materials were also imported from Ionia. Caricatures and Greek graffiti survive in a quarry at Persepolis dating from late Archaic period. Notably, the flow of influence was not just one way; it is highly likely that Persepolis exerted a strong influence on the architecture and art of the Athenian acropolis.

Greeks also served in the Persian army, either by compulsion or as mercenaries. The army of general Harpagus included Ionian and Aeolian Greeks (Hdt. 1.171). Ionian and Aeolian soldiers served under Darius in his attack on Eretria in 490 (Hdt. 6.98ff.). In the battle at Salamis and Plataea, Xerxes' army and navy included Greeks and even Demaratus, the exiled Spartan king, served as adviser (Hdt. 6.70). In 401, 10,000 Greeks followed Cyrus as mercenaries in a campaign against Artaxerxes II.

We read of deportations of Greek citizens and their resettlement in Persian-controlled areas, or instances such as the shipment of boys and maidens to the imperial court (Hdt. 6.20, 32). Even Greek nurses have been identified at Persepolis. Villing (2005: 237) suggests that a Greek "may have worked as a scribe in the Persepolis secretariat, since one of the Treasury Tablets dealing with wine transactions is written in Greek." Darius had a Greek physician, Democedes of Croton (Hdt. 3.129–37), whom he found among his other (Greek) slaves.

Much changed with the advent of the war with Persia (499–479), which led to the creation of an Athenian ideology that saw Persians as the barbarian "other," a rhetorical foil comprised of dichotomies like democracy/monarchy, rugged/soft, civilized/barbarian, free/slave. Such antipathy was not, however, universal among Greeks or even Athenians. Sparta, of course, colluded with the Persians against the Athenians and received financial support from Persia. The banished Athenian general Themistocles settled on an estate granted by Artaxerxes I and learned Persian ("as best as he could" – ὅσα ἐδύνατο) in his exile (Thuc. 1.138.1). Alcibiades also is said to have learned the language (Ath. 12.535E). Plato was said to have had a Persian student (Diog. Laert. 3.25). Ctesias (fifth cent.) served as a doctor in the Achaemenid court and as envoy of Artaxerxes. Histiaeus, tyrant of Miletus, was at least able to identify himself in Persian when fleeing in battle (to no avail – he was impaled and his mummified head sent to Darius in Susa; Hdt. 6.29). When Alexander burned Persepolis in 330, he supposedly freed 800 Greeks.

Language Artefacts

Areal features

Pointing to features of language shared by Greek and Anatolian speakers, some scholars have argued for the existence of a *Sprachbund* or linguistic area in western Anatolia. Areal or geographical diffusion is a product of language contact or bilingualism in which linguistic features spread across language boundaries. A frequently mentioned example of morphological diffusion is the inherited *-ske-/*-sko-* suffix that forms the -εσκε/ο- imperfects in Greek. The function of this suffix in PIE is not exactly clear and it shows different uses in different branches of Indo-European; in Latin it mostly forms inchoatives while in Tocharian it makes causatives. It is generally unproductive in Greek, but in both Hittite and East Ionic Greek it indicates ongoing action with iterative/imperfective/durative/habitual sense depending on context and the semantics of the verb. Puhvel (1991: 20) argues that if this is a matter of areal diffusion, it "implies contact if not symbiosis between an eastern form of the Late Mycenaean Greek and thirteenth-century Hittite in or around western Anatolia, and especially of some familiarity with Hittite language and literature on the part of an incipient aoedic tradition." An example of semantic diffusion may be detected in a shared feature of western Anatolian, in which Greek μέϑυ, Cuneiform Luw. *maddu-*, and Hier. Luw. *ma-tu-* all mean "wine," whereas this root is found in words meaning "sweet," 'honey," or "mead" in other cognate languages.

Interpreters

If language difference was ever a hindrance for the Greeks in interstate communication, our sources do not inform us. Occasionally we are told of interpreters, such as the one sent by Xenophon to the Thracian king Seuthes, whose cup-bearer was able to translate Greek into Thracian (Xen. *An.* 7.2.19, 7.3.25). Herodotus notes that when the Scythians went on a trading expedition to the Agrippaei, they took along seven interpreters, each of whom spoke seven different languages (4.24). Darius had a conversation with representatives from an Indian tribe translated for the benefit of Greeks present at his court (3.38). Cyrus used an interpreter to communicate with Croesus (1.86). Cambyses sought Ethiopian interpreters from Elephantine (3.19). The trilingual Carian envoy was mentioned above. Xerxes' heralds were accompanied by an interpreter (Plut. *Them.* 6.2). Xenophon mentions a number of interpreters in the *Anabasis*: the Ten Thousand employed a Persian interpreter (2.5.35; 4.5.10); Tiribazus, a satrap in Armenia, questioned the Greek generals through an interpreter (4.4.4f.); the Persians used an interpreter named Pigres (1.2.17); a peltast who had been a slave at Athens served as interpreter when they encountered his native people, the Macrones (4.8.4ff.); an interpreter was available when they reached the Mossynoeci (5.4.2).

Scripts and alphabets

Herodotus describes (2.106) a relief cut along the Karabel Pass on the road from Smyrna between Ephesus and Sardeis, which he claims was made by the Egyptian king Sesostris and which contained an image of the king and an inscription in Egyptian hieroglyphics reading, "By the strength of my shoulders I possessed this land." In actuality, the relief, which remains *in situ*, depicts Tarkasnawa, a local thirteenth-century vassal of the Hittite king, and the inscription, in Hieroglyphic Luwian, reads "King Tarkasnawa, king of Mira," followed by two fragmentary lines recording the names of the king's father and grandfather.

Thucydides records (4.50) that in 425 the Persians sent documents in "Assyrian letters" to Sparta, and that when the Athenians intercepted the Persian envoy who was carrying them, "The Athenians had the letters translated and they read them." In all likelihood, however, the correspondence was neither in cuneiform nor Assyrian (i.e., Akkadian). Cuneiform was used for permanent and monumental inscriptions, not for letters, and the official language of communication in the Achaemenid empire was not Akkadian but Imperial Aramaic (Schmitt 1992: 26–7).

In general, Greeks recognized the presence of other writing systems, but there is no evidence that there was any general knowledge about how to read them or even about the languages these scripts represented. Translation was a specialist task, but one that was available at least in some major centers of fifth-century Greece. This seems to be implied by the incident recorded by Thucydides, however mangled the facts given there. The passage from Herodotus, on the other hand, indicates that local or popular traditions about such matters could be terrifically incorrect.

It should be remembered, however, that there was a long history of contact with foreign writing systems in Greece and that on at least three occasions Greeks adapted one of these foreign systems for themselves. This is the case with Linear B, which is an adaption of the earlier Linear A used for writing a non-Greek language (see ch. 2). Somewhat later, a large wave of Mycenaean refugees on Cyprus adopted the Cypro-Minoan script, creating the Cypriot Syllabary (attested from the eleventh cent. to the Hellenistic period). Finally, of course, the Greek alphabet was adapted from a West Semitic script (see ch. 3). In turn, we find examples of this alphabet working its own influence, such as in the "Eteocretan" inscriptions (seventh century and later), which use the Greek alphabet to write a non-Greek language and which are sometimes accompanied by Greek. Or, for example, the sixth-century script from Lemnos that is similar to Greek and Phrygian alphabets. The Phrygian, Carian, and Lydian alphabets resemble the Greek alphabet (or epichoric versions thereof) in many aspects and are frequently thought to derive, at least in part, from it. But the exact relationship among them is difficult to work out and it has also been suggested that Phrygian for instance developed its own alphabet from Semitic sources independently (Mellink 1986).

Bilingual inscriptions

Bi- or multilingual inscriptions are *prima facie* evidence of language contact, but their significance is not always easy to assess. Bilingual inscriptions do not necessarily imply extensive bilingual audiences, but they may be a product of various social arrangements: e.g., i) predominately monolingual communities living together who cannot read each others' language; ii) societies that contain one (or more) subgroup of monolinguals; iii) a society of monolinguals with a bilingual elite. Inscriptions may transcend local concerns; one language of a bilingual may be used as an international language of communication or, as in case of the obsolescent Akkadian on Achaemenid inscriptions, to convey prestige.

Scholars are also interested in how the different languages in bilinguals stand in relation to each other, whether they are independent or whether one is primary and the other a translation, to what degree there is equivalence between the languages, whether there is unintentional or deliberate (ideological) interference from one language onto another.

The use of bilingual inscriptions was familiar throughout the Mediterranean and Near East, but only a few short Greek bilinguals survive in Phrygian, Carian, Lydian, and Sidetic. There is a fragmentary sixth-century Carian–Greek bilingual from Athens

and a Carian–Greek bilingual was discovered in Kaunos in 1996 that has had important consequences for the decipherment of Carian. There are about ten Lycian–Greek
bilinguals, the most important of which is the Letoon trilingual and the Xanthos Stele
(mentioned above). Studies of the Lycian–Greek inscriptions have noted instances of
verbal borrowing from Greek into Lycian (*sttala* = στάλα "stele," *triyerẽ* = τριήρης
"trireme") and Lycian interference in the use of Greek prepositions, particles, and
patronymic formulations. It has been argued that parallels in word order, however, are
not to be explained as the result of interference between the languages, but "are generated within the context of the production of the inscription by translators who
consciously seek to preserve cross-language syntactic patterns" (Rutherford 2002:
215–16). They aim at symmetry, since the "order of the main constituents in the
sentence is a higher priority than exact imitation of the syntax" (ibid. 218). According
to Bryce (1995: 1170), the use of Greek represents an "upper-class cultural bias in
Lycian society toward the Greek world."

It is also noteworthy that monolingual Greek inscriptions were occasionally commissioned by non-Greeks. For example, decrees relating to Mausolus were inscribed
in Greek and several Greek authors mention Greek inscriptions on the tomb of Cyrus
and the column set up by Darius on the Bosporus (Hdt. 4.87). The tomb of Darius
contained a Greek inscription (Strab. 15.3.8). A Greek inscription from Magnesia
supposedly preserves a letter from Darius rebuking the satrap Gadatas. This has been
taken to show that Achaemenid administrative correspondence was sometimes conducted in Greek, but the inscription is a late Roman copy and perhaps, it has been
argued, a forgery.

Loan words

Like bilingual inscriptions, loan words are clear indications of language contact and,
also like bilinguals, they involve their own special problems of interpretation. Even if
one can be certain that a given word is a borrowing, there remains the issue of determining what, if anything, that borrowing has to say about the nature or extent of
contact between the two sources. For various reasons, including the fact that the
process of borrowing does not provide the linguist with a set of controls such as inherited or cognate forms do, it is not always possible to determine with confidence
whether a given word is, in fact, a loan. Difficulties are created by the fact that some
loans are attested only in the borrowing language, some are not attested in the language of origin but supported by related words in (an)other related language(s), and
some loan words are not transmitted directly from the original language but indirectly
through a third language.

It is not always possible to be precise about the date of borrowing or the exact source
of Anatolian loans. To illustrate how circuitous a path one might have to trace in hunting a loan down, consider the case of οὐδών, a kind of felt shoe made from goat hair.
The Roman poet Martial refers (14.140) to *udones Cilicii* "Cilician slippers," on the
basis of which some scholars assume an Anatolian source for the word. Or consider
Myc. *di-pa*, δέπας "bowl," which is now widely connected with Hier. Luw. *tipas-* (phonetic /dibas-/) "heaven, sky." The origin of Greek "bowl" seems to have developed

from the Hieroglyphic Luwian sign for "sky," which is a bowl, and the common notion of the sky as a great (inverted) bowl (Melchert 2003: 184; Watkins 2007).

Some of the more commonly accepted Greek–Hittite equations include Myc. *e-re-pa*, ἐλέφα(ν)ς "ivory" and Hittite *laḫaš* "ivory"(?) (although the use of the *Glossenkeil* in one Hittite text may indicate the word is Luwian); Myc. *ku-wa-no* (exact meaning unclear), κύανος "dark-blue enamel," "lapis lazuli," and Hitt. *kuwanna* "copper," ᴺᴬ⁴*kuwanna-* a precious stone; Gk στλεγγίς (with variants) "scraper" and Hitt. *ištalk-* "make smooth, flatten."

Several words attested in late sources can be linked to Anatolian words. Hsch. γυγαί "grandfathers" and Lyc. *xuga*, Hitt. *ḫuḫḫaš* "grandfather"; Hsch. σίλβη kind of cake made from barley, sesame, and poppyseed and Hitt. *šiluḫa* kind of cake; σῶρι, σῶρυ kind of ore and perhaps Hitt. *šuwaru-* "heavy"; τύβαρις "celery pickled in vinegar" and Hier. Luw. *tuwarsa* (see further Neumann 1961).

Lycian loan words include Λήδα (Lyc. *lada* "wife") and the late-attested μίνδις "society of trustees for the care of a tomb" (μενδῖται "members of such a society"). A likely loan word in Lycian from Greek is *sttrat*[= στρατηγός "general."

The lemma ἀρφύτνον, Lydian for "discus" (Hsch.), could reflect the Lydian outcome of a root meaning "turn" seen in Lat. *orbis*, Toch. B *yerpe* "disk, orb." βάκκαρις, an unguent extracted from a plant, is labeled Lydian in ancient sources. Derivatives of καρύκη "rich sauce of blood and spices" appear in the Classical period (e.g., Xen. *Cyr.* 8.3.3), though later sources claim it is particularly Lydian. Hesychius claims the word λαῖλας is Lydian for τύραννος "tyrant" and a connection to Hitt. *laḫḫiyala-* "leader of a military campaign" has been suggested; Myc. *mo-ri-wo-do* and μόλυβδος "lead" come from Lyd. *mariwda-* "dark" (phonetically [marivða-] *vel sim.*). The word πάλμυς "king" (cf. *Il.* 13.792) is taken from *qaλm(λ)uś* "king," which appears about nine times in Lydian inscriptions. Lydian *q*, which is a labiovelar, seems to indicate that the word was borrowed early, sometime before the loss of the labiovelars in Greek. In addition to πάλμυς and βάκκαρις, the iambic poet Hipponax uses the words καύης from Lydian *kaweś* "seer, priest" and σκαπερδεῦσαι, probably to be taken with Lyd. *kabrdokid* "steals" (Hawkins 2004: 267ff.).

Aside from personal names and the designation "Carian" (Κᾶρ), there are no clear examples of Carian loans in Greek. According to Stephanus Byzantius the Carian toponym Ἀλάβανδα is equivalent to ἱππόνικος, being a compound of the Carian words ἄλα "horse" and βάνδα "victory" (cf. Ὑλλούαλα, said to be a compound of Ὑλλος and ἄλα). Likewise, the Carian city Μονόγισσα supposedly contains the native element γίσσα "stone" (< *ĝeis-* "gravel," Germ. *Kies*?) and the Carian city Σουάγγελα (supposed burial place of the eponymous king Karos) is a compound of σοῦα(ν) "tomb" and γέλα "king."

A great number of words have been labeled "Phrygian," but few of these can be supported by any meaningful evidence. The words βέκ(κ)ος or βεκ(κ)ός "bread," called Phrygian in Herodotus (2.2), and ἄκολος "bit, morsel," seem to appear in Phrygian inscriptions as βεκος and ακκαλος. Other words include βέννος "association of believers in a god," γλουρός "gold," and δοῦμος "religious association of women." The σύκχοι/συκχίς (Hsch.) is a type of Phrygian shoe, but the word may be from a third source. There are also some Greek words borrowed by Phrygian speakers: Phryg.

σοροι (dat.), σορου (gen.) from Greek σορός "coffin"; Phryg. κορο, κορου from Greek χῶρος "land, country"; Phryg. θαλαμει from Greek θαλάμη "den."

Most evidence for Old Persian comes from proper names found in literature, inscriptions, and papyri (see "Further Reading"), but there is also a wide range of non-onomastic material: βατιάκη a kind of cup or saucer and OP *bātugara* "drinking cup," Mod. Pers. *bādiya* "vase"; δαρεικός "gold stater," perhaps from OP **darīka-* "golden"; μάγος "Magian," OP *maguš* "Magian"; μαρτιχόρας (and variants) "man-eater," i.e., "tiger," OP **martiya-khvāra-* (cf. Avest. *xʷar-* "eat"), Mod. Pers. *mard-khwār*, ὀρινδης a bread made of ὄρυζα "rice" and Mod. Pers. *brinǰ*, Pashto *wriže* "rice"; παράδεισος "enclosed park" (Avest. *pairi.daēza* "[area] with a wall around it"); ῥόδον "rose" (Myc. *wo-do-we*), Sogd. *wnð* "rose"; (σ)μάραγνα "lash, scourge" and perh. Iran. **māra-gna-* "serpent killer" (cf. Syriac *māralnā*).

Some loans fall into distinct groups:

a)   items of apparel: ἀναξυρίδες "trousers"; γαυνάκης/καυνάκης "thick cloak" (OP **gaunaka-* "hairy," Avest. *gaona-* "hair"); κάνδυς "Median double or upper garment with sleeves" (OP **kantu, *kam-* "cover"); μανιάκης "necklace" (cf. Avest. *-maini-* "collar," Ved. *maṇi* "jewel"); παραγαύδιον/-ης "garment (with purple border)" (cf. Parthian *brywd* "curtain, veil").

b)   measurements: ἀρτάβη a dry measure; μάρις a liquid measure; καπίθη a dry measure (Xen. *An.* 1.5.6, Hsch.; perhaps = καπέτις also a dry measure); παρασάγγης measure of distance (cf. Mid. Pers. *frasang* "league").

c)   military and political terms: (ἀ)κινάκης "short straight sword" (Sogd. *kyn'k*, Hor. *Od.* 1.27.5 *ăcīnăces*); γωρυτός "quiver" (no Iranian evidence); τόξον "bow" from Iran. **taxša* "bow"; ἄγγαρος "(mounted) courier," for carrying royal dispatches (Hdt. 3.126, 8.99; exact origin of term unclear); κάρδακες "mercenaries" (cf. Mid. Pers. *kārdāg* "traveler, migrant"). In some cases we have the Greek designations but the Persian terms are not attested and must be reconstructed: μυριάρχης = **baivarpatiš* "commander of 10,000"; χιλιάρχης = **hazārapatiš* "commander of 1,000"; ἑκατοντάρχης = **θatapatiš* "commander of 100"; δεκάρχης = **daθapatiš* "commander of ten."

The Greek σατράπης "satrap" is not from the OP *xšaθra-pāvan* "protecting the land," but instead mirrors the Median (a northwestern dialect of Iranian spoken by the Medes) form *xšaθra-pā-*. This is not entirely surprising, as Medisms are said to occur "more frequently among royal titles and among terms of the chancellery, military, and judicial affairs" and "not least in the official characterizations of the empire and its countries" (Schmitt in Woodard 2004: 739). Herodotus (1.110) correctly identifies σπάκα "female dog" (**spaka*, cf. Avest. *spaka-*) as Median rather than Persian.

In addition to loan words there are also a number of calques, or loan-translations, such as βασιλεὺς βασιλέων "king of kings" for OP *xšāyaθiya xšāyaθiyānām* and βασιλεὺς ὁ μέγας "the Great King" (e.g., Hdt. 1.188) for *xšāyaθiya vazṛka*. Close advisers to the kings seem to have gone by an Iranian term meaning οἱ πιστοί "the Faithful" (Hdt. 1.108, Xen. *An.* 1.5.15, etc.). οἱ βασιλέως ὀφθαλμοὶ (καὶ τὰ βασιλέως ὦτα) "the eyes (and ears) of the king" (Hdt. 1.114, Xen. *Cyr.* 8.2.10, etc.), has no clear OP equivalent.

There are a few words in Greek that are not loans but glosses: ὀροσάγγαι glossed (Hdt. 8.85) as εὐεργέται βασιλέος "benefactors of the king" = (Iran. *varusanha* "far-famed" has been suggested, cf. Ved. *uruśáṃsa* "far-famed"); ῥαδινάκη a dark, strong-smelling oil (Hdt. 6.119); τυκτά (= τέλειον "perfect, complete" at Hdt 9.110) the name of the royal supper given on the king's birthday (Mod. Pers. *tacht*); πεισάγας is a Persian term for a leper, according to Ctesias (fragm. 14).

Finally, there are a large number of post-Classical loans and glosses (e.g., ἀζάτη "freedom" (Hsch.), Avest. *āzāta* "high born"; δανάκη small coin, Mid. Pers. *dān(ag)*; δεύας "evil gods" (Hsch.), OP *daiva-* "evil god'"), many of which have unclear or complex histories; the interested reader may find these, and more, in Brust 2005.

FURTHER READING

Good introductions to the languages discussed in this chapter can be found in Woodard 2004. On language contact between Greeks and pre-Greeks, see Morpurgo Davies 1986 (somewhat outdated now but methodologically important), Woodard 1997b, and Finkelberg 2005. For material culture, see Boardman 1999. On bilingualism in antiquity, see Adams et al., 2002. A recent account of the Ahhiyawa Problem is Latacz 2004, which must be read with the review by Katz (2005b). Important contributions on the topic include Foxhall and Davies 1984 and Mellink 1986. For Hittite history and society, see Bryce 2002, 2005. An important conference on the Ahhiyawa Question was held at Concordia University in Montreal January 4–5, 2006, and the papers will be published (Teffeteller, ed. forthcoming). On areal features, see Puhvel 1991 and Watkins 2001; on interpreters Mosley 1971. For foreign words in Greek literature (not covered here per se), see Hall 1989 and De Luna 2003. For Old Persian in Herodotus, see Armayor 1978, Schmitt 1967b, Harrison 1998, and Munson 2005; for Old Persian names, Schmitt 1978 and the relevant fascicles of *Iranisches Personennamenbuch* edited by Schmitt et al. Those interested in Greek connections with cultures of the Near East will want to consult Masson 1967, Szemerényi 1974, Burkert 1992, and West 1997a.

An important work on the subject, Collins, Bachvarova, and Rutherford 2008, was published after the completion of this chapter.

CHAPTER SIXTEEN

Linguistic Diversity in Asia Minor during the Empire: *Koine* and Non-Greek Languages

Claude Brixhe

Origins of the Linguistic Situation in the Imperial Period

In order to understand the linguistic situation in Roman Asia Minor, it is necessary to recall the broad outline of the history of this region starting from the end of the Bronze Age.

a)   End of the Bronze Age. Within the loop of the River Halys in central Asia Minor we find the heartland of the Hittite empire; around it are satellites, in particular Mira to the west with its capital Apasa – probably future Ephesos (see Hawkins 1998). Indo-European languages are spoken in this general area, Hittite in the center, Luwian to the south and west. We are in the dark as to the pre-IE languages of the region. Achaeans are present on the Aegean coast, though without real colonization apart from Miletus (see Zurbach 2006).

b)   Beginning of the Iron Age. After the collapse of the Mycenaean and Hittite worlds Greeks of various origins colonize the Aegean coast from the Hellespont to the area south of the Meander river. The various settlements over time constitute three distinct political and dialectal entities: the Aeolis to the north, Ionia on the central Aegean coast, and the Doric region to the south. Achaeans settle in Pamphylia. Furthermore, coming from Macedonia and Thrace, Thracians and Phrygians cross the Hellespont; the former stay on the coast of Mysia and western Bithynia; the latter move up the Sangarios river to Gordion (see fig. 16.1).

c)   Archaic and Classical periods. Greek settlements remain limited to the coast; Miletus colonizes the southern coast of the Hellespont and of the Black Sea, where as a consequence Ionic is spoken, except for Heracleia, which is a Megarian and Boeotian colony. Dorians (of unknown provenance) and Aeolians from Cyme join the Achaeans in Pamphylia. The Rhodians (Doric speakers) colonize the eastern side of Lycia. Of the three hegemonies developing over time in central Asia Minor (the Phrygian, the

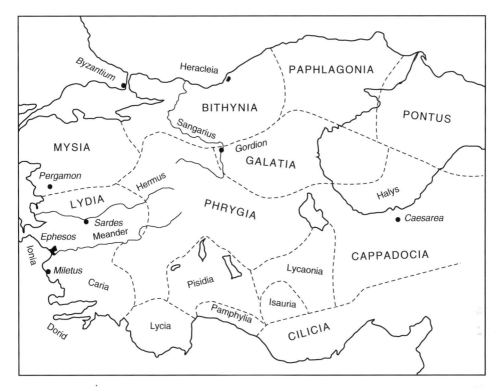

Figure 16.1 Map of Asia Minor in the imperial period

Lydian, and the Persian empires) only the first and the last will have linguistic consequences, respectively in the form of the expansion of Phrygian in the central uplands and of the impact of Achaemenid administration and settlements.

d) Hellenistic period. In 334 BCE, along with the armies of Alexander the Great, Attic Greek, on its way to becoming the common language of the Greek world (Brixhe and Panayotou 1988), penetrates into central Anatolia. Not long after 280 BCE the Galatians add Gaulish to the linguistic landscape by taking possession of western Cappadocia and northeast Phrygia.

e) The arrival of the Romans. With the creation of the province Asia in 133 or 129 BCE, the Romans introduce a new protagonist to the scene, Latin, which they have long tried to impose (Brixhe 1987a: 7–8). Latin, however, has to yield to Greek, the language of the elite and of power in the cities. What the Romans achieve, therefore, is the expansion of Greek in Asia Minor.

Which Greek?

But what is this Greek that was vehiculated in this way? Naturally, we have no access to it but through the written word, inscriptions (see also ch. 4). The Greek of these documents is an Attic that has become "common language" (*Koine*). Its "universal" vocation and form go back to the imperial aspirations and cosmopolitan nature of fifth-century BCE Athens. Certain aspects of the language that Aristophanes gives to his strangers are illustrative in this regard (Brixhe 1988b: 136–7).

Athens was the center of an essentially Ionian empire; as a consequence its language undergoes Ionian influence, a process to which the existence of an already rich Ionian prose tradition was no doubt favorable. Expanding at the expense of the dialects, Attic, in the process of becoming *Koine*, went on to incorporate in addition Dorisms (e.g., ναός for Att. νεώς "temple"; influence from literary language is likely here) or universally non-Attic forms such as φυλάσσω for φυλάττω, which is known only from Attica, Boeotia, and Euboea (on these points, see the articles of López Eire analyzed by Brixhe 1990: 206–7).

But the *Koine* is not merely a heritage. Undergoing a more or less rapid vernacularization process, according to region or social class, it acquires from a very early date a dynamism leading to internal developments. Thus as early as the end of the fifth century BCE we see a flection emerge that foreshadows the modern types κλέφτης/κλέφτη "thief" or παππάς/παππά "priest," with eventually the intrusion of a dental enlargement (-δ-, still present in numerous contemporary plurals, e.g., παππάδες παππάδω[ν], see also further below as well as chs 36 and 37 – for the details, see Brixhe and Panayotou 1988: 250–2 (Macedon) as well as Brixhe 1993b: 68, 78 (Caria and Lycia)).

However, the trajectory thus outlined is a simplification of what is in reality a very complex situation (on which, see also Brixhe and Hodot 1993). This complexity is reflected in the reductive treatments of most modern Hellenists who describe a multifaceted reality as simply "the *Koine*."

To begin with, *Koine* is both a written and a spoken language. The highest written register, the standard language (i.e., Classical Attic as it was fixed at the end of the fifth century BCE and represented linguistically in the language of Demosthenes), and the lowest spoken registers form the poles of a continuum. Just as present-day languages such as French, Spanish, or English, Attic has transcended its original borders to become the language of widely dispersed communities. Such a language, as it comes to cover a wide and heterogeneous territory, is naturally polymorphous. Its unity exists mostly on an abstract level.

Extending from Demosthenes to Julian, that is, seven centuries, the written standard is represented in literary prose, diplomatic documents, and municipal decrees. The latter are from one end to the other of the Greek or Hellenized world written in an identical and homogeneous language, as can be seen in the following two inscriptions:

Ὁ δῆμος ὁ Ταρσέων τῆς μητροπόλεως τῶν κατὰ Κιλικίαν τῆς ἱερᾶς καὶ ἀσύλου Νέστορι Χάρμωνος ἀνδρὶ ἀγαθῷ ἑξηκότι καλῶς καὶ σοφρόνως καὶ εὐνοίας ἕνεκεν τῆς εἰς τὸν δῆμον.

The people of Tarsis, metropolis of the Cilicians, sacred and inviolable, to Nestor son of Charmon, excellent man who has lived beautifully and wisely, and in reason of good intentions to the people. (Tarsis, Cilicia, honorific decree, first cent. CE; Dagron and Feissel 1987: 73)

Ἀγαθῆι τύχηι. Αὐρήλιον Ἀρισταίνετον τὸν δικαιότατον τῆς Φρυγίας ἐπίτροπον ἡ πόλις, τὴν ἐπιμέλειαν τῆς ἀναστάσεως ποιησαμένων τῶν περὶ Αὐρ. Ἀθήναιον Ἀκύλιον πρῶτον ἄρχοντα ἀρχόντων.

With good fortune. The city <has honored with a statue> Aurelius Aristainetos, the most righteous procurator of Phrygia; the archons under Aurelios Athenaios Akulios (= Aquilius) have charged themselves with its erection. (Synnada, Phrygia, base of statue, first half of third cent. CE; Buckler, Calder, and Guthrie 1933: 20)

As we can observe, an Athenian of the *belle époque* would not have been out of his element in reading these texts.

But it is only this superior register of the language that deserves the name *Koine* in a real sense. Since the fourth century BCE, pronunciation has naturally evolved, with consequences for orthography. Still, even adjusted for such change, this written register reflects an elevated spoken register that is superior at least morphologically, syntactically, and lexically, though it occasionally has a regional flavor even with members of the elite. But can we go beyond such formal language and reach the lower strata on the basis of the continuum that is offered by our written documents?

A first observation cannot but lower our expectations. The sector of the population whose language we can reach is necessarily limited to the producers of written documents (scribes, stonecutters), i.e., adult literate males, which excludes children and, with some exceptions, women.

Furthermore, writing distorts "natural" speech in that it presupposes a contact, however minimal, with literature, or at least with the school. The composition of a written statement is a formal act to which the writer devotes his entire linguistic competence. Any written message, however modest or practical, has in the last resort always as model the language of Demosthenes, which continued to be taught. The language teaching in the school tended to reintroduce forms into the written language that had long become defunct in the spoken language. The dative dies at a very early date, as we will see, but it is being reintroduced by schools for centuries. The prepositional phrase εἰς + acc., the expression of direction, is very early substituted for ἐν + dat. as the expression of the locative (see also ch. 36), but the latter expression reappears constantly (Brixhe 1992: 145–50). To complicate matters more, the interaction between the grammatical "norm" and naturally evolving language leads to a host of hypercorrect forms in the texts of semi-literate writers, e.g., dative instead of an expected genitive; ἐν + dat. for εἰς + acc; and while ἔλυσα had created, by analogy, εἶπα besides εἶπον; the reverse phenomenon is the hypercorrect creation of ἔλυσον on the analogy of εἶπον, which was still being taught.

Accordingly, we cannot but have modest ambitions: to reach at least partially the language spoken by part of the population of the first to third centuries CE, in full awareness of the fact that the language was characterized by an infinite number of social and/or geographical variations without there being impermeable boundaries between the numerous registers. In order to reach this goal, we have to scrutinize attentively the orthographical variations with regard to the norm: these variations will be more of interest when they correspond to changes endorsed by the later history of the language.

Greek in Asia Minor in the First Centuries CE: General Tendencies

We will see in this section that generally the *Koine* in Asia Minor has evolved along the same lines as in Greece.

Phonetics and phonology

Vowels[1]

In the first centuries CE the phonological system of vowel articulation is already what it is today, reduced to five isochronous vowels:

$$/i/ \quad /u/$$
$$/e/ \quad /o/$$
$$/a/$$

This corresponds to the following graphemic system:

/*i*/: I, EI, H, HI, Υ, ΥI, OI
/*e*/: E, AI
/*a*/: A, AI
/*o*/: O, Ω, ΩI
/*u*/: OY

This system is the result of a number of earlier mutations: at an early date the phonemes represented by EI and H have become confounded with /ī/, whence /i/ after the elimination of the oppositions of quantity. In contact with the other dialects which did not have /y/, this Attic-Ionic phoneme (written Υ) has become delabialized and so became identical to /i/; /oi/ has evolved toward /y/ and hence OI became over time another graphemic representation of /i/. Just as in Modern Greek, the orthography of /i/ sounds is the most demanding part of the writing system.

Official documents follow Classical orthography in principle, with one exception. According to usage introduced at the beginning of the Hellenistic period, EI has virtually become the norm for ancient /ī/ (hence, e.g., ἐτείμησαν and νείκη for ἐτίμησαν and νίκη). But in other registers we can observe a multitude of exchanges between equivalent graphemes: I for Υ (γινή = γυνή, Pontus); Υ for OI (ἐπανῦξε = ἐπανοῖξαι, Pontus); I for OI (τῖς = τοῖς, E. Phryg.); OI for I (οιατροῦ = ἰατροῦ, Cilic.); E for AI (cf., *supra* ἐπανῦξε); AI for E (καταίστησεν = κατέστησεν, Pisid.); etc. The situation is particularly complex in the case of the succession of two originally different /i/, represented by two different graphemes, as in Class. ἐποίησα (cf. Mod. Gk ποιητής (*piitis*)): ἐπύησεν (*passim*) is manifestly an attempt at representing this pronunciation, but is ἐπόησεν (*passim*) heir to an old Attic form with monophthongized /oi/ or a recent compromise between orthographical norm and actual pronunciation? With substitution of I for H the same question applies to ἐποισε (SW. Phryg.) and the new aorist ἔποιϰε/ἔποιϰα (W. Phryg. – where do we place the accent?); but here we may wonder whether OI does not simply correspond to /*i*/, and hence whether /*ii*/ has not been reduced to /*i*/; cf. περιπυσάμενος (Capp.) and Neo-Pontic *epika* (Drettas 1997: index).

There are three further changes, not apparent from the graphemic system given earlier, which complicate the situation:

a) *The change from /e/ to /i/ before vowel.* This neutralization entails in this phonological context slippage between E or AI (the norm) as well as the graphemes for /*i*/ (I, EI, H, Υ), e.g., ϑιᾶς for ϑεᾶς (Cilic.); ϑυοί for ϑεοί (S. Phryg.); ἐλιοπούλου for ἐλαιοπώλου; and the reverse phenomenon Ἀσϰληπεόδωρος for Ἀσϰληπιόδωρος (Pisid.). In fact, /*i*/ or /*e*/ in hiatus eventually resulted in /*j*/ which (in the absence of an adequate grapheme? or for phonetic reasons?) could be expelled from the writing, e.g., Δογᾶς for Διογᾶς (NW. Phryg.); Δοϰλητιανοῦ for Διοϰλητιανοῦ or ϰυρῶ(ν) for ϰυρίων (Cilic.).

b) *Closed articulation of the mid vowels /e/ and /o/* (on these terms, see ch. 7). This took place at least in entire central Anatolia, in Cilicia, and partly in Lycia (same phenomenon in the Greek of Attica, Macedon, and Egypt), whence the sporadic substitution of I for E, in particular in contact with a nasal (e.g., μηδίνα = μηδένα, Pontus; Μιννέαν = Μεννέαν (E. Phryg.); conversely, E can come to be substituted for a grapheme of /*i*/ (e.g., πύησε = ποιήσει, W. Phryg.; ἐπό = ὑπό SW. Phryg.). By the same token there are exchanges between O/ Ω and ΟΥ, e.g., σωματουϑήϰι = σωματοϑήϰη and, conversely, διαφέροσα = διαφέρουσα (Cilic.).

c) *In final position, reduction of /io/ to /i/.* This happened under all phonetic conditions and with Pamphylia possibly as epicenter; see Brixhe 1994), e.g., Διονύσις and ϰενοτάφιν (Pamph.) for Διονύσιος and ϰενοτάφιον. Note that this phenomenon seems to be prior to the change from /*ēo*/ (EIO) to /*io*/ which remains untouched, whence permanency of the graphemes –ειος and –ειον or variants.

The orthographic system as outlined above shows clearly the elimination of most of the inherited diphthongs. The evolution of the vowel system has resulted in the sporadic appearance of younger diphthongs as well, e.g., ἀείμνηστος > ἀίμνηστος (*[ai]*, Isaur., or βοήϑει > βοίϑι (*[oi]*-, Ionia, W. Phryg.).

Of the ancient diphthongs only /*eu*/ and /*au*/ subsist. They were no doubt pronounced either vocalically (*[au/eu]*) or semiconsonantically (*[aw/ew]*) according to speaker and naturally according to phonetic context. The graphemes ΑΥ and ΕΥ can reflect the norm, as can some variants, e.g., αοὑτοῦ for αὑτοῦ (Cilic.), ϰατεσϰεούασαν for ϰατεσϰεύασαν (Isaur. and Cilic.). The semi-vocal element was no doubt already pronounced as a spirant by some speakers, anticipating Modern Greek pronunciation (e.g., ϰατεσϰέβασεν for ϰατεσϰεύασεν, Mys.). But there was also already a low variant *[a]* and *[e]*, widely distributed and reflected in the graphemes A and E, e.g., ἀτοῦ for αὑτοῦ (*passim*); Ἀξάνοντι for Αὐξάνοντι (Pisid.); πρυτανέσας for πρυτανεύσας (Lyc.). This articulation is not regionally restricted and comes from afar, since we encounter the corresponding written representations already in sixth-century BCE Attic inscriptions.

Words of Latin origin are eventually subjected to this mutation. In virtue of regional and social variation in Latin the sound *[au]* in that language had been integrated in Greek as Ω or ΑΥ. And this ΑΥ was susceptible of being reduced to A *[a]*: Αὐρήλιος >

Ἀρήλιος (E. Phryg.). Sometimes this substitution is explained with Latin itself: Ἀγούστη, Ἀγοῦστα, or Ἀγουστάλιος for Lat. *[aug-]* (E. Phryg.) reflect a low Latin variant, with elimination of *[u]* in *[au]* before following *[u]*.

Consonants[2]

The orthographical norm for *geminated consonants* has obtained to the present day (e.g., γραμμή or κάλλιστος in Mod. Gk). But in linguistic reality they have been reduced to simple consonants for a very long time, e.g., Φιλίπου (Cilic.); κάλιστον (Caria); θάλασα (Pontus). Conversely, we can also encounter στήλλην (*passim*), Ἡλλιόδωρος (Pamph.), or Ἀλλέξανδρος (Capp.). But entirely new geminated consonants are also possible, e.g., at the place of a nasal and a following occlusive or spirant (σύββιον for σύμβιον, Lycaon.).

The weakness of *nasals* at word end as well as word-internally essentially before stops can already be observed in Classical Attic. In early-CE *Koine* in Asia Minor we can observe that word-internally Classic orthography is generally maintained (with sequences such as –ΜΠ-/-ΜΒ-, -ΓΚ-/-ΓΓ-), though from a very early date in the Hellenistic period, N has been generalized regardless of the phonological profile of the following stop. In spite of this, suppression of the nasal is frequent:

- elimination of the letter-sign, e.g., ἐθάδε (Gal.), νύφες (= νύμφαις, Pamph.), σύβιον (σύμβιον, S. Phryg.), ἄδρα (ἄνδρα, Lyc.);
- elimination of the letter-sign with voicing of the following stop, e.g., Ἀδιγόνη for Ἀντίγονη (central Phryg.), but the reverse writing occurs as well, e.g., ἀντρί for ἀνδρί (Pisid.);
- at word end very frequent omission, e.g., πόλη (πόλιν, Gal.), δοῦλο (δοῦλον, W. Phryg.), θήκη (θήκην, Cilic.), see also ch. 37;
- even within a syntagm the nasal can be dropped, e.g., τὸ δοῦλον and τὸ δοῦλο (τὸν δοῦλον, W. Phryg.);
- inverse writing, i.e., addition of an undue nasal happens as well, e.g., παντί τῷ βουλομένων (Lyc.), ἐξέστων (ἐξέστω, Cilic.), or τύχοιτον (Pisid.).

As for *stops* (see also table 7.3), the voiceless stops, as already seen, are voiced after nasal, whether word-internally or within a syntagm (cf. Mod. Gk, τον πατέρα *[tômbatera]*), e.g., κακόν δι (= κακόν τι, SW. Phryg.).

For voiced stops we can observe the generalization of the elimination of /g/ in /gn/ (in itself already old), e.g., γίνομαι, γινώσκω (*passim*). Furthermore, we can observe fricativization in virtually all contexts:

- B can serve to denote the semi-vocalic element of a diphthong (see above) as well as Lat. /v/ (< /w/, e.g., Φλάβιος for *Flavius, passim*) or the ancient /w/ of the Pamphylian dialect, e.g., Διβιδωριανή, Ζώβαλος for Διϝι- or Ζωϝα- (Pisid., Pamph.);
- Δ turns into Θ, sign of a voiceless dental fricative, e.g., Εὐθάμου for Εὐδάμου (Cilic.) or πλαθιμούς for πλαθιμούς (Caria);

Table 16.1 The development of ancient consonant stops in *Koine* Greek (cf. tables 7.3 and 37.1)

		Phonemes			*Graphemes*		
		labial	dental	velar			
Fricatives	*voiced*	/v/	/ð/	/j, γ/	B	Δ	Γ
	voiceless	/f/	/θ/	/ç, x/	Φ	Θ	X
Occlusives		/p/	/t/	/k/	Π	T	K

- Γ can disappear altogether from the writing, e.g., ὀλίος for ὀλίγος (*passim*) or be used to note /i/ in hiatus, i.e., /j/, e.g., γατρός (= ἰατρός, Cilic.). Just as in Mod. Gk, the pronunciation corresponding with Γ varied with the timbre of the following vowel: /j/ before /e, i/, [γ] before /a, o, u/;
- What we see, then, is a series of voiced fricatives: /v/, /ð/ and /j, γ/, with the graphemes B, Δ, and Γ;
- Voiceless aspirated consonants have been fricativized as well;
- Φ is interchangeable with OΥ and Υ in Anatolian names (Οαφα, Ουαουα, Ουανα, southern Asia Minor) and serves to represent Lat. /f/, e.g., Φλάβιος for *Flavius*, *passim*;
- as noted earlier, Δ and Θ are partially interchangeable;
- even if there is no clear clue for X, it is probable that the phoneme represented by this sign has undergone the same development, i.e., /ç/ before /e,i/ and /x/ before /a, o, u/.

This gives us a series of voiceless fricatives, /f/, /θ/, and /ç, x/, parallel to the series of voiced fricatives.

Functionally, then, ancient voiced and aspirated occlusives evolve into two series of fricatives (voiceless and voiced), that are collectively opposed to the series of voiceless occlusives (see table 16.1).

The sounds [b], [d], and [g] certainly existed, but only in allophonic variation (on which, see ch. 7) of voiceless consonants after nasals.

The *liquids* /r/ and /l/ had generally an apico-alveolar pronunciation (i.e., the tip of the tongue touching the alveolar ridge behind the upper teeth), and it is not surprising to see interchanges between the two:

- between vowels, e.g., ἐν μεγάλυσιν for ἐν μεγάροισιν in a funerary epigram of Isauria;
- in particular before fricatives, where the substitution of /r/ for /l/ is frequent, e.g., ἀδερφῷ and ἀδερφοί (= ἀδελφ-, S. Phryg.) or ἀναερϑόντα (= ἀνελϑόντα, Cilic.).

This latter change was destined to a great future and was to be integrated in Mod. Gk (see chs 36 and 37), without, however, touching the totality of the material for any period or the entire geographical space, e.g., Mod. Gk ο αδεϱφός, but Neo-Pontic *o aðelfon*. In this same context, we sometimes see /*n*/, another apico-alveolar, replacing /*l*/ before labiodental fricative /*f*/: ἀδενφόν (Pamph.). These substitutions are evidence for the articulatory weakness of /*l*/ in this position and it does not come as a surprise that it can be eliminated altogether: ἀδεφῷ (Lyc.). Latin words are eventually subject to the same process in the same contexts, e.g., Καϱπουϱνία (*Calpurnia*, Gal.) or Δεματίαν (*Delmatian/Dalmatian*, W. Phryg.).

The composite nature denoted originally by Z (see chs 3, 4, and 7) had long vanished and made place for a voiced counterpart /*z*/ to /*s*/. This phonetic value of the letter can be seen in its use instead of Σ before voiced consonants, e.g., Ἰζμήνου or πϱεζβύτεϱος (Cilic.). Traditional orthography remains the norm, however. From the Hellenistic Age the new pronunciation had given rise to a pleonastic ΣΖ which is still sporadically encountered in our time, e.g., ὀϱκίσζω (Isaur.).

We have seen that Attic, expanding in the process of becoming *Koine*, had substituted the type φυλάσσω with φυλάττω. The Attic revival (see ch. 31), which reached its culmination during the reign of Hadrian, reintroduces the old form sporadically in high-register written language such as municipal decrees.

Morphology and Morphosyntax[3]

Morphology is not an autonomous component of language, but a domain straddling phonology, syntax, even the lexicon. It suffices to project the phonological changes we just reviewed to a few paradigms to see the consequences for morphology as well as for the realization of functions, i.e., syntax: reduction of the number of available forms (in particular in the singular) and confusion of flectional paradigms. The nom. sg. forms πολίτης, εὐγενής, μάντις, and πέλεκυς, morphologically distinct as they may seem to us, all had phonetically the same nominative ending in –*is*; they also had the same accusative and dative ending in –*i*. The singular of κεφαλή was reduced to just two forms (*kefali/kefalis*).

True, the highest register of written language could give the impression of a language that had remained stable since the fourth century BCE, and the Attic models were probably more resistant in the speech of the elites, particularly in regions where Hellenization goes far back (the Aegean rim, Black Sea colonies, Hellenistic foundations). But as appears from the most modest documents (epitaphs, confessions, private dedications) from regions where Greek was competing with another language, many speakers are manifestly baffled by the ancient flectional paradigms (highly complex in themselves) which in addition were now being obscured by numerous clashes between the various endings.

The result is a chaotic situation. For example, for Ἀπελλῆς we find the genitives Ἀπελλοῦ, Ἀπελλοῦς, Ἀπελλέου, and Ἀπελλέους; that of the indigenous name Αττης appears in the forms Αττου, Αττεου, Αττεω, Αττεους, Αττη, and Αττηδος (see Zgusta 1964a *s.vv.*). Nouns of the type πάτϱως, the ending of which was not distinct from that of λόγος anymore, cause the worst difficulties: sometimes the declension is modified (e.g., οἱ πάτρωνες/μήτρωνες, Lyd.), or the word is simply left undeclined: οἱ πάτρως (conforming to the norm), but τὸν μήτρως (see *BÉ* 2007: 452).

Behind this anarchy we can discern the beginnings of the modern flectional paradigms. The evolution seems to have been propelled in particular by proper names. This is not surprising: with their unique referent (which binds them to a restricted communication), anthroponyms have always more freedom with respect to the flectional norm than the rest of the lexicon, and this is even truer for indigenous names integrated in Greek that could not rely on any previous tradition.

It is impossible to go into all the details here; I will limit myself to the general tendencies.

Nominal morphology

Declension of the λόγος-type: acc. sg. and gen. pl. have no doubt lost their word-final nasal (see above) and the dative is probably already defunct. This flection, then, has probably already its modern face.

The elimination of word-final nasal leads by reaction (stigmatization?) to the addition of an unexpected nasal to the acc. sg. in the athematic declension, e.g., μητέραν, πατέραν, γυναῖκαν, μάρτυραν, χεῖραν, and ἐῶναν (for αἰῶνα, Isaur., Pontus, SW. Phryg.). This in its turn leads to a new nominative by analogy (φύλαξ > φύλακας) and the elimination of consonant stems from the language. Furthermore, for the nouns of parenthood a flection-type that is felt as specifically masculine or feminine can now be assigned to either sex, as in Mod. Gk πατέρας vs. μητέρα. This development starts in the first centuries CE: e.g., nom. θυγάτρα in a metrical epigram from Philadelphia (Lyd.) and in particular θυγατέρας (gen. sg., Pontus) and τοῖς ἰδίας θυγατέρης (= ταῖς ἰδίαις θυγατέραις, E. Phryg.).

The identity of nom. and acc. pl. in the types εὐγενής, πόλις, πέλεκυς had favored in certain dialects in pre-*Koine* Greek the extension of nominative to the function of accusative in nouns of consonant stems. This features continues in Asia Minor *Koine*: e.g., acc. ἀνδριάντες or πάντες (Isaur.). This feature is generalized in Mod. Gk, where –ες is the nom. pl. and acc. pl. ending in all flection-types (masc. or fem.) with the exception of that of λόγος.

In its expansion, Attic encounters a flection (essentially Doric) of the type πολίτας/ πολίτα, where gen. sg. is created simply by taking away the final –*s*. But the dialect of Athens had by itself numerous comparable situations, e.g., Διογᾶς/Διογᾶ, νοῦς/νοῦ, χρυσοῦς/χρυσοῦ, or νεώς/νεώ. It is thus not surprising to see from an early date a flection emerge of the type Ἀνδρέας/Ἀνδρέα (Cilic.), which in the natural development of the language spreads to all masculine nouns, e.g., the gen. Ἰωάννη (Cilic.; model: πολίτης), Διοκλῆ (Cilic.; models: εὐγενής, Περικλῆς), Ερμαπι (indigenous name, Caria; model: μάντις), Μακρῦ (W. Phryg.; models: στάχυς or Φωκῦς).

By contrast, the first declension, essentially fem., was always characterized by the inverse reflex: gen. sg. is formed by the *addition* of an –*s* to the nom. form. What we

Table 16.2 Masculine and feminine flection in
Modern Greek

	Nominative	*Genitive*
Masculine	-*s*	-Ø
Feminine	-Ø	-*s*

witness, then, is the gestation period of the situation in Modern Greek, where after
the elimination of consonant stems there are two contrasting flectional types (see
table 16.2, also table 36.2).

Some Mod. Gk masculine nouns: πατέρας/πατέρα, πολίτης/πολίτη, καφές/καφέ,
παππούς/παππού, etc. Examples of feminines: ελπίδα/ελπίδας, θάλασσα/θάλασσας,
νίκη/νίκης, σκέψη/σκέψης, Φρόσω/Φρόσως, ψωμού/ψωμούς; see Triantaphyllidis
1941: 231ff.

In order to resolve the problems posed by word-internal hiatus at the junction of
the root and the ending (whether or not these are caused by a phonetic accident),
the Greek language has used since a very early date a "plug enlargement" –*t*- or –*d*-,
just as, for example, the Mycenaean perfect participles in –*woha* (< **wos-a*) (see ch.
13) have been replaced with those in -(ϝ)ότα in alphabetic Greek. Hence we have
Ἄρτεμις/Ἀρτέμιτος-Ἀρτέμιδος or also Θέτις/Θέτιδος besides Θέτιος (Pindar).
Perhaps initiated by the flection -ᾶς/-ᾶδος of ancient Ionian anthroponymy, the
mechanism has acquired a wider distribution since the end of the Classical period in
nouns ending in -ῶς, -οῦς, etc. (cf. the situation of the Pamphylian dialect). In the
Asia Minor *Koine* this flection fringes the traditional as well as the innovative flection types that we have already reviewed, e.g., Ἑρμῆδι (Pisid., model: πολίτης),
Εὐτύχηδι (εὐγενής, Pisid.), Καλλικλῆδος (Περικλῆς, Pamph.); on the indigenous
name Αττης, see above. Of Οσαεις we find gen. Οσαειτος and Οσαει (Pisid; Pisid.–
Phryg. border); of Πιλλις, gen. Πιλλιτος (Pamph., Pisid., Lyc.) besides Πιλλιος
(elsewhere).

All the phonetic changes had also limited the autonomy of flectional endings in
various feminine paradigms. For example, in the first declension, the singular was
reduced to just two forms: one for nom., acc., and dat. (-α or –η, *[a]* or *[i]*), and
one for gen. (–ας or –ης, *[as]* or *[is]*). The confusion is answered by the same "plug
enlargements" τ/δ and by a recharacterization of the nominative, e.g., Ἀφροδεισιάς
(Lycaon.), dat. Εὐτυχιάδι (E. Phryg.), nom. Ζωτικῆς (W. Phryg.), dat. Ζοῆδι
(E. Phryg.); πενθεράδι (ibid.) in competition with πενθερᾷ This phenomenon
touches naturally on Latin anthroponyms integrated in Greek, such as nom. Ἰουλιάς
(Pamph.), dat. Ἰουλιάδι (Bithyn.), gen. and dat. respectively Φαυστάτος and
Φαυστάτι (Cilic.).

The examples cited show once more that the real *locus* of the development has been
proper names, in particular in the singular. Modern Greek would capitalize on the
-δ- enlargement for the creation of plural paradigms; see the tables in Triantaphyllidis
1941: 239 (masc.) and 247 (fem.).

The disappearance of the dative case

The phonetic changes we briefly reviewed greatly obscured the system of endings and hence the realization of syntactic functions. The circumstances weighed especially heavily on one of the important linguistic characteristics of the age: the decline and eventual elimination of the dative case (see Brixhe 1987a: 95–102; 1992: 145–50; 2002: 263–5).

The first signs of collapse can be observed in private documents from Egypt, ostraka, and papyri (see also ch. 17). These texts go back to the second century BCE; however, it is not until the second and third centuries CE that the decline of the dative acquires real momentum.

The function of the dative is taken over by the accusative, e.g., ἀνάθεμα τοὺς χέζοντας ὧδε "be cursed all those who are defecating here" (Cilic.); βοήθη (= βοήθει) τὸν δοῦλόν σου Ἰωάνην "come to the aid of your slave Ioannis" (Ionia). Three-place verbs (e.g., ἀνίστημι, ἀνατίθημι) with an indirect object (attribution) in the dative in Classical Greek are frequently construed with a double accusative, e.g., τὸν δὲ ἀνδριάντα ἀνέστησεν Ἰα Ἑκαταίου τὸν ἴδιον ἀγώριν "Ia, daughter of Hekataios, has erected <this> statue for her son whose death was untimely" (Pamph.); also single acc. with implicit dir. obj: Εὐτύχης ... τὸν ἀρχηγέτην Ἀπόλλωνα ... ἀνέστησεν "Eutuches has erected for Apollo the Leader <this statue>" (W. Phryg.). The dative is in competition even after δίδωμι, e.g., δώσει τῷ ταμείῳ "he will give to the treasury" (Lyc.), but δώσει ἰς τὸ ἱερώτατον ταμεῖον "he will give to the most holy treasury" (Mys.).

The strongest competition, however, comes from the genitive, e.g., βοήθι Νηκολάωυ μονάχου (= βοήθει Νικολάου) (SW. Phryg.); τὸν δὲ ἀνδριάντα ἀνέστησεν τῆς γλυκυτάτης μητρός "he has set up a statue of/for his sweetest mother" (Pamph.); gen. occurs even after prepositions that govern the dat., e.g., σὺν τῆς μητρὸς Ματρώνης "with his mother Matrone" (Lycaon.).

There is easy fluctuation between case endings expressing the same function in the same syntagm, e.g., ἀνέστησεν ἑαυτῷ καὶ Βαθθιν τὴν γυναῖκα "he has erected for himself and his wife Batthis" (Cilic.); ἀνέσθησα (= ἀνέστησα) τῇ γλυκυτάθῃ (= -τῃ) μου Θεοσεβείης κὲ τῇ ἀδελφῇ μου Κυριακῇ κὲ ἐμαυτοῦ ζῶντος ἀνέστησα "I have set up for my sweetest Theosebeia and my sister Kyriake and for myself <I have set up>' (E. Phryg.); σὺν τῷ γαμρῷ (= γαμβρῷ) μου Πέτρον "with my son-in-law Petros" (ibid.) or σὺν γυνηκὸς Τατει (central Phryg.).

The rest of the story is known: in Modern Greek the prepositional dative has been replaced by the accusative. For the function of attribution (ind. obj.) the northerly dialects have selected the accusative; the southerly dialects the genitive, which is standard modern Demotic which relies on the dialects of the Peloponnese.

But what is the situation in Asia Minor in the second and third centuries, the time that provides most of our documentation? First, even though most of the collapse takes place in the singular of the thematic flection, the plural and the other paradigms are equally affected. Second, the substitutions of the accusative for the dative are on the whole a minority. They seem to be more frequent in the north than in the south, where the genitive tends to be substituted. Still, the two types of exchanges (i.e., accusative for dative and genitive for dative) occur everywhere.

The situation in the spoken language is the more difficult to appreciate when we observe that the dative is still, though with innumerable errors, abundantly present in literary texts till the end of the millennium (see also ch. 35). The pullulation of deviant uses in the period under consideration allows us to suppose that the dative has disappeared, even though its various forms are constantly being reintroduced by the schools and by the standard Attic in use for the highest varieties of the written language. We may wonder whether, in order to replace it, language users did not hesitate between the accusative and the genitive. But there is one region where by virtue of the multiplication of the errors in this sense one has the impression that the genitive has already been elected as replacement. This is the Phrygophone area, i.e., the entire central plateau of Asia Minor. The endings of the obsolete dative seem to be here nothing other than free variants of those of the genitive.

I have shown elsewhere (Brixhe 1992: 139–40) that whereas the semantic affinities between the various functions in question certainly did not impede such an evolution, the process was fueled first and foremost by the phonetic weakening of the endings involved. Multiple homophonies in the case endings occurred as a consequence of (i) the weakening of nasal in final position; (ii) the development of a vocalic genitive singular; and (iii) the closing of /o/ to /u/ in certain regions.

To these observations we may add, first, that Phrygia (where interchange between the dative and the genitive is very frequent) may well have been one of the epicenters of the southern triumph of the genitive, in view of the agreement between Greek and Phrygian on points (i) and (iii); second, whatever the details of the substitution, the anthroponymics, the singular, and the thematic declension have apparently played a major role in the innovation.

In what is no doubt the same development, we can observe from very early onward the substitution of the normal expression of direction (εἰς + acc.) for locative expressions (ἐν + dat.). In the modern language, it is known, verbs for "staying" and for "going" share the same prepositional phrase, an avatar of εἰς + acc. (εἶμαι/ἔρχομαι στην πόλη "I am/go in (into) the city." This neutralization was the more easily tolerated in that with an opposition "staying/going" the semantic opposition between direction and location is already given with the lexical meaning of the verb. Hence it can seem redundant to have two different prepositional phrases for place and for direction (the same neutralization takes place in French and in many other modern languages). Has the Classical expression of the locative prepositional phrase disappeared from the living spoken language? Naturally, it frequently occurs in the written standard. Maintained in the schools, it is found frequently and for a long time to come (see ch. 35), often in hypercorrect fashion as expression of direction, which is proof of its elimination from the spoken language.

Pronouns

Here, too, the discussion will be limited to general tendencies.

a)   The anaphoric τον, του, *etc.* (Brixhe 1987a: 80). The stem αὐτό-, traditionally always accented, was split into an accented form (αὐτός, αὐτόν, αὐτοῦ) for the expression of identity and "ipseity," and an unaccented anaphoric form (αὐτόν, αὐτοῦ) which is frequently reduced in our texts to ἀτόν, ἀτοῦ (see above, "Phonology" under "Vowels").

In order to create between these two an opposition similar to that between ἐμέ and με, the language mutilates the unaccented form to arrive at the modern contrast between αυτός/αυτόν/αυτού . . . (deictic) and τον/του . . . (anaphoric). In the second and third century CE this pair is already present in the language of at least part of the population, as indicated by the sporadic appearance of the truncated unaccented form, e.g., ὁ ἀνήρ της "the husband of-her" (SW. Phryg.) or ἐπὶ τὸ βῆμα του "on the pedestal of-his" (E. Lyd.). When would its generalization have been completed?

b) *The reflexive pronoun* (Brixhe 1987a: 80–2). The singular remained relatively unaffected by the phonetic evolution, but the plural naturally suffered from the confusion between ἡμᾶς αὐτούς and ὑμᾶς αὐτούς.

The written standard remains faithful to the Classical norm, and in spite of the aforementioned confusion we may assume that the same was true of the spoken language of the elite. But the departures from this norm are so numerous, in particular in southern Asia Minor, that to all appearances the spoken language had already found a new equilibrium: to judge from innumerable attestations, ἑαυτο- (ἑατό-) became the sole reflexive pronoun for the three grammatical persons, both in sg. and in pl. Telling examples are ἐποίησα ἑαυτῷ "I have made for myself" (Cilic.) and κατεσκευάσαμεν . . . ἑαυτοῖς "we have prepared . . . for ourselves" (Lyc.).

The language thus economizes on person, which is in any case already expressed by the verb. Eventually the language will reintroduce the reference to grammatical person; hence Mod. Gk του εαυτού μου "of/for me," του εαυτου σου "of/for you," etc.

c) *Expression of possession* (Brixhe 1987a: 82–4). Even though the continuous teaching of the Classical system is attested with numerous examples, it is evident that in the spoken language the modern situation has already been reached: whether or not the possession is reflexive, it is expressed with the genitive of the postposed non-reflexive personal pronoun: μου, σου, αὐτοῦ (ἀτοῦ, τοῦ, etc.), e.g., ἐποίησα ἐμαυτῷ . . . καὶ τῇ γυνεικεί μου "I have made for myself . . . and my wife" (Pontus); ἐκόσμησεν τὴν μητέρα αὐτοῦ "he has paid the funereal honors to his mother" (Lycaon.).

This expression of possession is often in competition with the adjective ἴδιος (τῇ ἰδίᾳ γυναικί, Pontus), which is sometimes combined with the genitive of the personal pronoun, e.g., τοῖς ἰδίοις αὐτοῦ ἀπελευθέροις "for his (own) freedmen" (Pamph.). Would this be the ancestor of the modern idiom ο (ι)δικός μου (σου, του) "the . . . of mine/yours/his"?

d) *The relative pronoun.* ὅς, ἥ, ὅ remain the norm. Note simply the occasional use of the definite article as relative pronoun, e.g., διὰ τὸ ἁμάρτημα τὸ ἐποίησαν "because of the error that they had made" (E. Lyd.). This use is of course ancient and recurrent; it originates in the functional parallelism between the restrictive relative clause and epithetic adjective: ὁ μαθητὴς ὁ σπουδαῖος ~ ὁ μαθητὴς ὃς σπουδαῖός ἐστιν.

Note also the success, in Phrygia in particular, of the use of τίς as indefinite relative pronoun: τίς ἂν τούτῳ ἡρῴῳ κακὴν χέρα προσοίσι (χεῖρα προσοίσει) "whoever will put a hostile hand to this heroon." The usage is ancient, but has always remained infrequent (for its origins, see Brixhe 1987a: 84).

Verbal morphology

In this sector, too, the upheaval caused by phonetic change has at times had decisive syntactic consequences.

a) *Leveling of paradigms.* Conforming to its sense, the verb "be" is given medio-passive endings, e.g., εἶμαι. The athematic –μι verbs are aligned with the thematic conjugation in –ω, which by now is the only one that is productive: τίϑειν (= τιϑέναι, E. Lyd.), δίδι (δίδη, from δίδω = δίδωμι, Cilic.), ἀναστάνι (–στάνει, from ἀναστάνω = ἀνίστημι, Cilic.), etc.

The thematic aorists of the type εἶπον are aligned with the sigmatic aorist (ἔλυσα), e.g., ἀφειλάμενος (= ἀφειλόμενος, Pontus), διενένκαντα (= διενεγκόντα, Caria, Capp.), ἀπέϑανα (= ἀπέϑανον, Pisid.), etc. This feature belongs no doubt to the spoken language, but the school and the written standard are a conduit for this double flection as well and we frequently encounter, even in Greece itself, the reverse phenomenon, the alignment of ἔλυσα with εἶπον, e.g., ἐκολάσετο (SW. Phryg.) or ἔστησον (Lycaon.). Is this a hypercorrection confined to the written language? Can it appear in the spoken language?

b) *Non-declinable participle in gestation.* Fluctuations that can be observed regionally indicate that the language is on its way toward an indeclinable participle with invariant form: in Cilicia, the nom. sg. masc. διαφέρων occasionally modifies ϑήκη or σωματοϑήκη. In Cilicia again as in Isauria and Phrygia the form διαφέροντα, formally acc. masc. sg. or nom.-acc. n. pl., is occasionally epithet to ϑήκη, σωματοϑήκη, or μνῆμα. Literary examples of this feature are attested later as well.

These hesitations are a prelude to the situation in standard Modern Greek: one single form in –οντας, indeclinable, no doubt an ancient nom. masc. sg. modeled on the acc. masc. sg. in –οντα, as πατέρας is to πατέρα(ν).

c) *Weakening of the augment.* The augment of the verb begins to stop being an grammatically obligatory feature of verbs in the past tense, e.g., κόσμησε (W. Phryg.). But since it continued to be taught, we can expect to encounter hypercorrect formations in compound verbs such as ἀπεκατέστησεν (Gal.). In standard Modern Greek, augment has been eliminated when it is unaccented.

d) *Optative* (Brixhe 1987a: 88–9). The optative's functional weaknesses have over the years been exacerbated by the phonetic changes. It certainly still belongs to the standard language, but has gone out of use in the spoken language; in private communication it is used in some fixed formulae only, such as wishes in the 3 sg. and pl., most often in imprecations directed to possible grave robbers, e.g., λίποιτο, περιπέσοιτο, etc. (Phryg.), μὴ γῆ μὴ ϑάλασα καρποὺς δοίη "may neither land nor sea carry fruit" (Pontus); at times competition with the subjunctive also occurs, e.g., εἰ δέ τις ἀνύξι (= ἀνοίξει), τοιαῦτα πάϑη (for πάϑοι) "If anyone opens <this>, may he suffer such things" (*ibid*).

e) *Subjunctive, future, and aspect* (Brixhe 1987a: 89–94; 2001: 106–7). When we remind ourselves that vowels are from now on isochrone, that EI and H indifferently note /i/, and that the oppositions /e ~i/ and /o ~u/ are frequently neutralized with the archiphonemes /I/ and /U/, we can readily understand why in regular verbs the present indicative and subjunctive, future indicative and subjunctive aorist are formally confounded, with a whole series of linguistic and graphemic consequences. In the present, mood is not included anymore in the verbal form, but determined by the syntactic environment (as in Modern Greek, where δένω "I bind" is ind., subj., or fut., according to the presence of the prefixes ∅, νά, or θά, resp. and the negations δέ[ν] or μή[ν].

Hence:

a) use of the written form of the indicative where the subjunctive is expected, e.g., ἵνα μὴ λύει, ἵνα λύονται (E. Lyd.);
b) when confusion between fut. and subj. aor. was excluded, the two forms become free variants of one another, e.g., τίς ἂν προσοίσει (or variants, for –ενέγκῃ, Phryg.), or ἵνα . . . γενήσεται (for γένηται) ἡ στήλλη (E. Lyd.);
c) in the aorist, indicative and subjunctive naturally remain distinct, as they are in Modern Greek (e.g., ἔδεσα vs [νά] δέσω).

In short, from now on verbal forms are not in and of themselves indicative anymore of mood.

Beyond orthography

The language of certain documents, from southwest Phrygia for example, has often been characterized as "barbaric" (Brixhe 1987b: 49–50). Such a judgment is purely philological and does not look beyond mere orthography. A form like πισέτυχει (which in any case has not been understood correctly) is a "barbarism" only for modern correctors of Greek grammatical forms; in light of the above review of phonetic changes, the form is revealed as ἐπεισέτυχε, with aphaeresis (cf. Mod. Gk μέρα < ἡμέρα) or inverse elision (after τὼ χωρί = τὸ χωρίον) and the closing of /e/ to /i/ (Brixhe 1987b: 52, 54, 72). Λημόνησα "I have forgotten" is no more than the first attestation of modern λησμονώ (the replacement of λανθάνομαι), with local reduction of -*sm*- to -*m*- (ibid. 57, 61, 73). And ἐξονπλάριον for ἐξεμπλάριον (Lat. *exemplarium*) is a Phrygian monstrosity only when we ignore ἔξομπλον in Hesychius and ἐξονπλάριν (-ιον) attested in an Egyptian papyrus: our form probably represents a variant of fairly wide distribution (ibid. 56).

The scribes of our documents, in fact, spoke a living Greek, whose differences with the Classical language were in agreement with the general evolution of the language in other hellenophone regions, with some local particularities (on which, see below). They simply did not master a set of orthographical conventions that was fixed five or six centuries before for an altogether different phonetic profile of the language.

If we define a linguistic norm as the total set of rules permitting members of a given language community to understand each other, then the language of our documents, even the most modest ones, conforms to the norm. The written and spoken standard constitutes a kind of "surnorm" which, even if it remains the theoretical target to be reached, remained inaccessible to the modest scribes and engravers who worked at the gates of the necropoles and sanctuaries. The pagan confessions attested from eastern Lydia to southwest Phrygia (Petzl 1994), dating from the first to the third century CE, might well be the transcription of oral statements. In "official" settings, speakers sensing the inadequacy of their language with respect to the "standard," tend to raise the level of their speech, entering in registers they do not master. The result is broken speech in pathological syntax that has nothing to do with the natural development of the language. (We may think in the modern context of humble witnesses to an accident who are handed a microphone for them to give their version of what happened.) In a phrase like ἵνα μηδένι ἐξὸν εἶναι μήτε πωλεῖν μήτε ὑποϑήκην τίϑειν "so that it is not permitted to anybody either to sell (the goods) nor to mortgage them," ἵνα + infinitive cannot be treated as a legitimate linguistic development: this is an occasional formula which is linked to the conditions of its utterance and will have no future (other examples in Brixhe 2001: 113–16).

A Heterogeneous Linguistic Area

This *Koine*, evolving in Asia Minor along the same lines as in other parts of the Greek world, has spread over a vast, linguistically heterogeneous territory where Greek dialects as well as non-Greek languages were spoken. In addition to social variation, normal in any community, there were without fail here and there local variations which lent to the common language a local coloration.

Koine and Greek dialects

a)   *Koine and Asiatic Aeolic.* In the beginning of the Christian era we can observe in the Aeolid, i.e., the area between the Caicos and Hermos rivers, a written revival of the dialect. We do not know when this dialect definitively disappeared from the spoken language. The resurgence in any case seems artificial: as manifestation of identity, it originates in the upper classes and is based, not on a living dialect, but on the epigraphical tradition or on the language of Aeolic lyric (Sappho and Alcaeus), see Hodot 1990: 19–20; 20–3. Aeolic does not seem to have any influence on the *Koine* of the region in the imperial period, at least in the written language.

b)   *The* Koine *of the Pontic region* (Brixhe 1987a: 109). Looking over the Pontic inscriptions of the beginning of the Christian era, one is struck by two features: (i) there is very little exchange between the letter H and the graphemes for /i/, (I, EI. . .); instead, H tends to be substituted for E or AI, e.g., ἐνϑάδη, κατάκιτη, κατάκιντη (= –κειται, -κεινται), πέντη, ἀδήλφια, etc; (ii) whereas elsewhere the final nasal is often eliminated (see above), in the Pontic region it is very frequently explicitly written. In one case (the region of Amasia) it is even strengthened by a supporting final vowel, e.g., ἐστερέσενε (= ἐστέρησεν). This is the more remarkable since the nasal in question is n-mobile. The strengthening in question is also visible in numerous final nasals in the modern language in the third person plural endings in –ουν(ε) and –αν(ε).

We have seen that with the exception of Heracleia all of the coast had been colonized by the Ionians, who took their dialect there. It is this dialect very likely that colors the *Koine* of the region by communicating the two particularities just mentioned, which can be supposed to have touched the Heracleia district (*BÉ* 1996: 436).

c) The Koine of Pamphylia. The originality of the dialect of Pamphylia and its various components is known (see most recently Brixhe 2006b: 31–5). It is very likely that at the very beginning of the Christian era it was still spoken by part of the population. In the written records its influence on the *Koine* is apparent only in personal onomastics, e.g., fluctuations between δ and ρ in Παραμουριανός with respect to Παδαμουριανός /-νή (Termessos, Pisid., territory adjacent to the Pamphylian plain: Brixhe 1976: 83); traces of /w/ become /v/ and now written as β: Διβιδωριανή (Termessos; cf. dialectal ΔιϜίδωρους, ibid: 137), Κορβαλίς, Ζωβαλίμας, Ζωβαλίμα, Ζώβαλος/Ζόβαλος, Ζοβαλίων (< ΖωϜ(ο)-, Termessos, Pamph., Egypt for the Pamphylians: Brixhe and Hodot 1988: 200–1).

Koine and non-Greek languages (except Latin)

Competition for the Greek *Koine* essentially comes, not from the Greek dialects, but from the numerous languages found throughout the region. See also the parallel discussion in Ch. 15.

The Thracians, who occupied the southern coast of the Propontis and of the Black Sea all the way to Heracleia and beyond, have not left any linguistic traces other than onomastic (see below).

The Persian diaspora resulting from erstwhile Achaemenid domination of the region seems to have been assimilated under the diadochs. Its memory nevertheless persisted until the imperial period, with the cult (very much alive in Lydia) of the goddess Anahita, Gr. Αναειτις, who was assimilated with Magna Mater and Artemis. In the late Empire an epitaph from southwest Phrygia still evokes "the gods of the Hellenes and Persians." The descendants certainly kept the memory of their origins (hence the frequent Persian anthroponyms throughout Lydia, Caria, Phrygia, and Kibyratis: see Robert 2007: 348–53; 650–65), but they probably did not speak the language of their ancestors anymore.

Lycian inscriptions more recent than the fourth century BCE have not been found, but survival of the language until the imperial period is not impossible. The persistence of double forms, one being the translation of the other, might be a sign in this regard: at Aperlai and Kyaneai, in Ερπιδαση ἡ καὶ Σαρπηδονίς the second name is the Greek translation of the first, indigenous, one (Schürr 2007: 36–7).

According to ancient sources (see Brixhe 1987a: 11), Mysian, Isaurian, and Lycaonian would have survived until the sixth century CE, an unverifiable assertion in the absence of any documents. Jerome (331–420 CE) informs us that in his time Gallic was still spoken by the Galatians, a suspect testimony according to Lambert 1994: 10. They may have retained for a long time a sense of their ethnic identity (Brixhe 2002: 252), but linguistically they have left us only anthroponyms. Culturally engulfed, first by the Greeks, then by the Romans, the literate members of the population had apparently long abandoned their ancestral language in favor of Greek.

In fact, the only two languages that have left written documents that can be attributed to the imperial period are Pisidian and Phrygian, dominated languages that have found refuge in the cemeteries.

All the inscriptions in Pisidian (a post-Luwian language) have been found at or in close proximity of the Eurymedon: about 40 epitaphs already published and a number of unpublished texts yielded by the territory of Timbriada (southeast of Lake Eğridir) and written in the Greek alphabet of the time (latest review of the corpus in Brixhe and Özsait 2001: 175; the latest general study of the language is Brixhe 1988a).

Neo-Phrygian is attested in about 120 epitaphs ranging from the end of the first century to the middle of the third century CE. A little over half of them are bilingual. These texts, too, are written in the Greek alphabet of the day and all of them, with some exceptions, represent imprecations with respect to looters (Brixhe 2002: 248). They are confined to the central plateau (Brixhe 1993a: 328) and thus cover an area much more restricted than the territory that has yielded Paleo-Phrygian documents (ibid. 325). This is probably a sign of the contraction of the Phrygophone population.

Documented indigenous language in the imperial period, then, is rare. Still, in spite of a relative scarcity of sources it is likely that outside the old Greek territories on the Aegean coast numerous epichoric languages continued to be spoken. In the cities of central Asia Minor bilingualism must have been the norm, as opposed to a frequent non-Greek monolingualism in the countryside.

Such bilingualism surfaces at times, as in the following imprecation which starts with a Greek protasis and ends with a Phrygian apodosis:

ὃς ἂν τούτῳ τῷ μνημείῳ κακῶς προσποιήσει . . . , με δεως κε ζεμελως κε τι τετικμενος ειτου.

Whoever damages this monument . . ., will be marked with infamy with both gods and men.

In a Pisidian epitaph the indigenous names have Pisidian inflection, whereas the other (Greek or Roman) names have Greek inflection, e.g., Μηνι Τίτου "Meni, son of Titos" (Lat. *Titus*) and conversely Νέμεσις Μηνις "Nemesis, daughter of Meni" (Brixhe and Vottéro 2004: 13–17).

But the cohabitation of Greek with the indigenous languages is most manifest in the coloring that the spoken language undergoes. A case in point is the absence of aspirated stops in the indigenous languages, whatever their origin. When speaking Greek, the lower strata of the population assimilated the Greek aspirated occlusive stops (that had become fricatives, see above) to their own voiceless stops. In their writing, T and Θ, Π and Φ, Κ and Χ become interchangeable graphemes for /t/, /p/, and /k/, resp. This feature is widespread in Phrygia (e.g., ἐπολιθεύσατο = ἐπολιτεύσατο or θῆς = τῆς), and also in Isauria (e.g., ἀπελύτροι = ἀπελεύθεροι), in Lycaonia (e.g., κατάχιτε = –κειται), and in Cilicia (e.g., τήκη for θήκη), etc. These spellings naturally also affect names of Latin origin, e.g., Φρείμιλλα for *Primilla* and, conversely, Προντίνου for *Frontini* (E. Phryg.). For general discussion, see Brixhe 1987a: 110–13; 157. The same phenomenon is found in Egypt and in the language of strangers in Aristophanes.

If there is a region where the impact of the indigenous language on the Greek *Koine* was most visible, this must be Phrygia. Phrygian was an Indo-European language, belonging to the same prehistorical cluster as Greek (and Thracian). The local aristocracy certainly spoke and wrote in the same standard language as elsewhere, as shows in the public documents, but in texts from the private sphere we can observe much interference with the local language in addition to the phonetic feature just mentioned. Some remarkable cases include:

- Metathesis of *r* and *l*, particularly frequently in E. Phryg., e.g., Οὐαρελιανόν for *Valerianum*;
- reduction of *st* to *t* word-internally or word-initially in sandhi, e.g., ἀνέτησα or εἰ (= εἰς) τὸν θεόν;
- prothesis, relatively rare in Asia Minor, but particularly abundant in Phrygia and in the adjacent areas, e.g., ἰστήλην, ἰσπουδασάντων (E Phryg.);
- substitution of πος/ποσ- for πρός/προσ-, no doubt because of the existence in Phrygian of a preposition/preverb πος/ποσ- which was functionally identical, e.g., ποστείμου, ποσάξει, πός (SW. Phryg.), ποσαμάρτη (E. Lyd., a zone with a partially Phrygian population);
- adoption of vocabulary of Phrygian origin: τὸ βέννος "association of faithful," ὁ βέκος "bread," and ὁ δοῦμος "religious association."

At times, the variation seems to be stimulated as well by the genetic proximity of the two languages and by convergence phenomena: the closing of middle vowels and the elimination of final nasal in both Greek and Phrygian entails in provincial *Koine* a very high frequency of the confusion of the dative and the genitive and sometimes the accusative (see above).

The distance between the lowest and the highest registers was incontestably very considerable and we have to speak at least of diglossia. But in view of the sheer number of variations we may wonder whether we are not in fact dealing with a separate dialect. This would be one of the first neo-Greek dialects born from the diversification of the *Koine*. The dialect would have been eliminated during the disruptive migrations caused by the Arab incursions of the seventh century CE, and later by the Seljukian invasions of the eleventh and twelfth centuries CE (Brixhe 1987a: 110–16, 158; 2002: 259–63).

Greek and Latin

The last actor to arrive on the linguistic scene is of course Latin. Since the Romans placed the burden of their domination on the local ruling classes (see also ch. 19), the language of power in Asia Minor, for Greek and non-Greek speakers alike, remained Greek. Greek was also the language of a culture manifested in prestigious centers like Ephesos, Nicaea, Nicomedia, or Tarsus.

Latin has yielded written documents only in the cities. Documents deriving from the highest authorities in the Roman Empire arrived from Rome in Latin and were translated into Greek by the provincial chancelleries. Governors and high officials certainly addressed the cities in Latin, and city officials honored the emperors, governors, and their benefactors in Latin till the fourth century CE. In that same period the colonies used Latin for their official documents as symbol of their status and reminder of their privileges. The private documents of the colonists, on the other hand, were frequently in Greek from the second century CE onwards. See Kearsly and Evans 2001 for the decreasing number of bilingual epitaphs and funerary honors. There is general discussion of the question in Levick 1967: 130ff.

Still, in Asia Minor, as in all eastern regions of the empire, Latin was at least partially the language of administration and law, and almost exclusively of the military. Its presence did not fail to leave traces in Greek. Sometimes the Latin feature is structurally unimportant and would not have a future:

a)   Roman realities can be designated through insertion of transliterated Latin syntagms into Greek text, as in an inscription from Attaleia honoring a Roman citizen who was κουαττορουίρουμ οὐιάρουμ κουρανδάρουμ (*quattuorvirum viarum curandarum*, Brixhe and Vottéro 2004: 33; Brixhe 2007c: 906);

b)   Name of tribe frequently in the dative in Greek, modeled on the Latin ablative, e.g., Κυρείνᾳ, Σαβατίνᾳ, etc. (Brixhe and Vottéro 2004: 34; Brixhe 2007c: 906);

c)   Sporadic use of the "dative absolute," in response to Latin ablative absolute (Brixhe 2007c: 906–7).

In view of the institutional differences between the Greek and Roman worlds the area most affected is the lexicon, with at times durable consequences (see also ch. 19); some frequent possibilities:

a)   Periphrasis: οἱ τρεῖς ἄνδρες = *triumviri* (*Res gestae*);

b)   New sense to an old Greek word: ὕπατος "most elevated" (adj.), hence ὁ ὕπατος "the consul";

c)   Calque: δύανδρες, δυανδρία for *duumviri/duumviratus* (Pisid.); ἱκανοποιῶ for *satisfacere* (E. Lyd.); on the model of the couple *consul/proconsul* the couple ὕπατος/ἀνθύπατος is created.

Some of these innovations (e.g., new word [ἱκανοποιῶ] or new sense [ὁ ὕπατος]) subsist in the modern Greek lexicon. Better still, the designation of Roman promagistrates with a compound with the prefix ἀντι- has created a process that is still productive in all sectors of public life, the naming of officials of lower rank, e.g., ἐπίτροπος "commissioner," ἀντεπίτροπος "assistant commissioner," see Brixhe 2007c: 908–9.

Two traits confirm that the influence of Latin on Greek has been more profound than would seem at first sight.

a)   In southern Pisidia, Isauria, eastern Pamphylia and western Rough Cilicia, a derivation in -ιανός/–ιανή (Lat. -*ianus/-iana*) was used as patronymic adjective, e.g., Αὐρήλιος Μανδριανὸς Λογγεῖνος "Aurelios Longinos, son of Mandros," Αὐρηλία Κιλλαραμωτιανὴ Ειη "Aurelia Eie, daughter of Killaramôs" (Pamph.). Note that this adjective occupies precisely the filiation slot in the Roman onomastic formula, see Brixhe 1996: 700; *BÉ* 1994: 599 and 2002: 444, 446.

b) This practice, geographically limited in any case, would not have a future. This is different for the Lat. suffix *–arius/*-άριος, in competition with autochthonous -ᾶς for the names of crafts and professions, e.g., κανναβάριος "hemp worker" (Brixhe 1987a: 107). The suffix has survived till the modern language (Triantaphyllidis 1941: 131).

Note that with respect to the features briefly reviewed here Greek behaves with regard to Latin in the same way as elsewhere; the vocabulary of the lowest strata of the population was never affected.

Onomastics

Asia Minor has always been a zone of encounter and passage. Personal onomastics and toponymy are faithful to this tormented past.

Toponymy

Every new resident people and (since masters like to arrogate the privilege of naming) every new hegemony or dynasty, has left its mark on the toponymy of the region (Calder and Bean 1958; see also ch. 15).

a) *Pre-Hittito-Luwian and Hittito-Luwian toponyms:* Πέργη, Σίλλυον, Ἄσπενδος (Pamph.), Πάταρα, Ἀρύκανδα, Πίναρα (Lyc.), Ἄδανα (Cilic.), etc. Some of these, hellenized, have entered very early in the Greek cultural universe, no doubt toward the end of the second millennium BCE: Μίλητος (*Milawanda/-wata* in the Luwian hieroglyphs), Ἔφεσος (*Apasa*), Ἴλιον (*Wilusa*). The abundance of ethnic adjectives in -ηνός/-ανός probably also goes back to the Hittito-Luwian stratum.

b) *Phrygian toponyms:* Γόρδιον, Κοτιαειον, Μιδαειον (on the Hittito-Luwian and Phrygian toponyms, see Zgusta 1984);

c) *Greek toponyms.* On the coast the following names go back to the very first colonizations: Σμύρνα, Ἡράκλεια, Τραπεζοῦς, etc. Inland we find toponyms deriving from the Macedonian invasion: the various Ἀντιόχεια, Ἀττάλεια, Ἀρσινόη, Λαυδίκεια, and Στρατονίκεια;

d) *Latin toponyms*, e.g., the various Καισάρεια, Σεβαστή (*Augusta*), and Κλαυδιόπολις. These are usually not the names of new foundations but the Latin substitutes for earlier names (e.g., Καισάρεια for Μάζακα or Πομπηιόπολις for Σόλοι).

e) *Hydronymy* is entirely free of Latin influence and offers the same mix of Greek and Anatolian names (tentative classification in Tischler 1977: 153–78). Of the four great rivers of Asia Minor two have Anatolian names (Μαίανδρος and Σαγγάριος) and two Greek (Ἅλυς and Ἶρις). It is not always easy to distinguish between an authentic Greek name and the hellenization of an indigenous hydronym; for example, we now know that Κέστρος (Pisid./Pamph.), previously thought to be Greek (Tischler 1977: 78), is the avatar of Hittito-Luwian *Kastrayas*.

Anthroponymy

It is not surprising that personal names essentially reflect the Greek and Roman hegemonies.

Statistics based on the available text *corpora* show that even in the most remote regions the percentage of Latin anthroponyms often is situated between 25 and 30 percent, for example, in Kibyra, Laodicea-on-Lycus, or Tyana.[4] The Roman naming convention of the *tria nomina* appears very early, the bearers being either native Italians or "naturalized" Greco-indigenous citizens. After the granting of citizenship to all the inhabitants of the empire (212 CE) Αὐρήλιος appears everywhere. The new Roman citizen's usual name (Greek or indigenous) supplies the *cognomen*, e.g., Μᾶρ(κος) Αὐρ(ήλιος) Ἀθηνόδωρος (Pisid.).

As we have seen (see also ch. 19), in exerting their power through the hellenophone elites the Romans effectively achieved the hellenization of Asia Minor. As a consequence, Greek names are almost everywhere an overwhelming majority. In the zones that yield the pagan confessions mentioned earlier (see Petzl 1994), whose Greek has often been considered barbaric, more than 85 percent of the names attested are Greek. The percentage is rarely lower than 60 percent (e.g., 57 percent in Tyana).

Hence the fact that indigenous anthroponymy, even though rich and varied, rarely represents more than ten percent of the onomastic stock of a community. Zgusta (1964a: 539–58) allows us to identify the zones where it resisted most: Caria (with its *ll-ld* fluctuation; e.g., Ὑσσωλλος/Ὑσσωλδος), Lyd., Phryg., Lyc., Pisid., Isaur., and Lycaon.

In the imperial period, Hittito-Luwian Asia Minor of the second millennium BCE is represented by names of two types.

- Names only used among intimates (*Lallnamen* in German), such as Βα(ς), Να(ς), Αβα(ς), Ανα(ς), etc. (typology in Laroche 1966: 241–3). This practice is universal, but was always favored by the Anatolians, sometimes even infiltrating the old Greek territories;
- Names with specifically Anatolian roots. Zgusta (1964b) studies some of these, with maps illustrating their geographical distribution: for example, there are the names produced by *Tarhu(nt)* "the Victorious One" (the Hittite storm and weather god): Ταρκονδας, Τροκονδας, Τερκονδας, etc.; the names containing the element *muwa*- "force, vigor" ([-]μοας, [-]μυας, [-]μουας, [-]μυς, [-]μως in our Greek texts, e.g., Κιδραμουας); and names with *ziti*- "man" (–σητας, –σιτας in the Greek texts., e.g., Μιρασητας), see Houwink ten Cate 1961: 125–8; 166–9; 171–2; Zgusta 1964b: §§ 13, 17, 23. All of these are concentrated in Southern Asia Minor and virtually absent in the West (except for Caria) and the North.

Through the centuries other actors have appeared on the stage and left their traces.

a) The Phrygians, who borrowed the *Lallnamen* from the peoples they subjugated, but have transmitted some specific names, e.g., Ξευνη/Ξευνα or Ιμαν (gen. Ιμενος, dat. Ιμενι);

b) The Persians, with names such as Αρσακης, Αρταπατης, or Μιϑρης (Lyd., Caria, Kibyratid), see Robert 2007: 352–3;

c) The Thracians, in particular on the south shore of the Propontis, around Kyzikos;

d) The Galatians, very modestly represented with names attested in Ancyra till the lands bordering Kyzikos (see *BÉ* 1987: 368 and Brixhe 1993a: 336 and n 51).

We see, then, that personal onomastics perfectly reflects the history of the region, illustrating the consequences of the various interventions.

Conclusions

The linguistic strata that had accumulated since the second millennium BCE, most of which were still active during the imperial period, as substrates or adstrates, have certainly given Asia Minor, its inner regions in particular, an original and variegated linguistic profile. In rural regions non-Greek monolingualism was no doubt the norm from which few individuals were able to escape; those who did, for example, were those whose land yielded an agricultural surplus and who consequently needed to know a little Greek in order to be able to sell their wares in the city, where a situation of bilingualism was constantly being fed by the surrounding countryside.

We have seen the extent of the differences setting apart the various registers of the *Koine*. At the top of the social pyramid there was an elite whose language, at least in official contexts, attained the Attic standard in its morphology and syntax. At the bottom we encounter indigenous populations who naturally had acquired all the low variations of the language – treated in this chapter as its "natural" development – which were to form the basis of modern Demotic. Variations engendered by the local speech were possible, which as we saw could accumulate so as to authorize at times the use of the term "dialect."

But not all the regions have been equally well documented, and we have no access to spoken language but through written texts. This means that we are completely in the dark as to the speech of those who did not have access to writing. We have to be aware, then, that the picture presented in this chapter is necessarily imprecise and incomplete.

FURTHER READING

Numerous collections of inscriptions, by city or by region, are available today. City-based collections are related to the great excavations of which some are old (Pergamum, Magnesia of the Maeander), others constantly being completed (Miletus, Ephesos); region-based collections are published in series in a perpetual state of expansion: *TAM*, and *MAMA*, with essentially regionally oriented bibliographies. The *IK* series, on the other hand, has predominantly city-based bibliographies. The language evidenced by the inscriptions is studied by Brixhe 1987a; see also the numerous remarks in *BÉ* since 1989, in the section "Asie Mineure."

NOTES

1   See Brixhe 1987a: 46–61.
2   See Brixhe 1987a: 31–46.
3   See Brixhe 1987a: 63–102.
4   Note that this percentage applies to onomastic stock in a community, not to the number of individuals.

CHAPTER SEVENTEEN

Greek in Egypt

Sofía Torallas Tovar

The aim of this chapter is to analyze the Greek language spoken and written by the Greek inhabitants of Egypt during the Greco-Roman period, mainly through the source material provided by the papyri. In ch. 5 the difficulties and advantages of working with papyri as a source for the Greek language have been outlined; ch. 16 treats in depth the characteristics of the variety of Greek spoken generally in the Mediterranean in the Hellenistic period, including thus Egypt. Since these two important aspects have already been discussed elsewhere in this volume, I will consider here some aspects pertinent to Egypt only and to the texts provided by Egyptian sources.

Definition of Egyptian Greek

Egyptian Greek is, broadly speaking, the dialectal variety of *Koine* spoken in Egypt in Greco-Roman times, attested not only in literature written in Egypt but also, and mainly, in the documents written on papyrus during this period. This corpus cannot be analyzed as a whole, however, since there are important factors that play a role in the development and diversification of Greek in Egypt. I take as a model the study of the diversification of Vulgar Latin, partly due to bilingualism (Tovar 1964).

Demotic and Coptic are the two "stages" of the Egyptian language as it came in contact with Greek during the Greco-Roman period. The terms define both a stage of the language and a particular writing system. Demotic was used during the period 650 BCE to 400 CE. Coptic script is an adaptation of the Greek alphabet to record the Egyptian language during the Christian era.

The sources

The Egyptian variety of Greek was probably most patent in the spoken language that has obviously not been preserved. The few traces in the written sources are difficult to assess, since – and here comes the intervention of the sociolinguistic problem – it is impossible to know who the writer behind each document is, how deep his linguistic skills are, and what his level of bilingualism is. One cannot study a language but through its speakers, and the speakers of Greco-Roman Egypt were not a uniform group.

The best way to chart the linguistic situation in Greco-Roman Egypt would have been the interviewing of its speakers, as field workers do in modern linguistic research. The closest we can get to that unattainable ideal is through distilling from the written sources the pertinent peculiarities of expression (see Langslow 2002: 23–51). The first problem we are faced with here is the higher register found in many written texts (see also ch. 16; on register, see ch. 20) and in general the requirements of writing as a medium. Simply put, writing conceals most vernacular traits of language (Versteegh 2002: 57–66). This is true not only for literary texts, but also for private and public documents: official documents and even some private texts are often expressed in formulary language. It is also important to note that literacy brings a more conscious and attentive approach to language, since it is conducive to the creation of standard usage and tends to avoid code mixing, which is more typical of popular linguistic registers. Of the sources mentioned, the papyri and ostraka are without doubt the richest and most direct source for our survey. The evolution and characteristics of the sociolinguistic situation can be surveyed through accurate analysis of these documents: a choice of language, orthographic mistakes, popular or vulgar expressions are the only trace of the linguistic behavior of the speakers, members of a society which spoke at least two majority languages and wrote in different graphic systems.

One has also to consider that access to literacy and education in general was limited to a small portion of the population, and written texts are a testimony only for that limited group. The illiterate probably mixed languages more vividly. Another limitation is the fact that we cannot identify the speaker through the preserved testimonies. It is impossible to know whether the author of a text was mainly a speaker of Greek or of Egyptian, whether he was literate or illiterate, or whether he was using an interpreter. Onomastics are of little help in assessing the ethnic or linguistic origin of the writer, since names of different origins often appear in the same family; moreover, many men used double names, an Egyptian one at home and a Greek one in public (Choat 2006: 51–6). In spite of all these limitations, the papyri and ostraka of Greco-Roman Egypt are the only source that can help us understand an extremely complex linguistic situation.

Greeks in Egypt

A historical survey of the contact and presence of Greeks in Egypt has to start very early, in a period for which our written sources provide scant evidence. We know of the presence of Greeks in the land of the Nile before the Classical period. From the seventh century BCE, intense commercial activity in the Mediterranean brought many Greek sailors, traders, pirates, and travelers to the coasts of Egypt. The linguistic situation is that of discontinuous and sporadic contact, which produced minor interference, perceptible only in a few loanwords adopted to name new realities (Torallas

Tovar 2004a; 2004b). As a result of this contact, Naukratis was founded in 650 BCE by Milesian traders. It would be extremely interesting to study the linguistic situation of Naukratis, where Greek merchants from all origins lived in close contact with Egyptians. It is very likely that merchants developed some kind of "pidgin" to understand each other, which unfortunately is not attested in any written source.

But real and permanent contact of the two populations did start early in the seventh century. The first Greek community in Egypt is described by Herodotus (2.153–4; 163; see also Diod. Sic. 1.66.12). During the seventh century the Egyptian armies extensively recruited foreign mercenaries (see also ch. 15). Herodotus reports that the pharaoh Psammetichos I (663–609 BCE) settled the Greek and Carian mercenaries of his army in camps near Pelusium, in the northeastern border of Egypt. These new settlers adopted the local habits, including language and customs. By the mid-sixth century, the pharaoh Amasis transferred these communities to Memphis, where they formed two minority populations: the Hellenomemphites and the Caromemphites (Cook 1937; Thompson 1988). They preserved their identity under the powerful influence of Egyptian culture. The Greeks settled in a district named the Hellenion. They were mostly Ionians, in Demotic the *wynn ms n Kmy*, "Greek born in Egypt" (see Swiderek 1961; Goudriaan 1988: 14–21; Boswinkel and Pestman 1982; Montevecchi 2001). As a result of natural contact, intermarriage (ἐπιγαμία) between the Greeks and the Egyptians occurred (cf. Steph. Byz. *Ethn.* 359).

Shortly before the arrival of Alexander, in the fourth century, there is still some evidence of the preservation of Greek ways of life or even of the Greek language in Memphis. In Abusir, near Memphis, in a necropolis dating back to pharaonic times that was later used in the fourth century BCE (Watzinger 1905), in a typically Greek burial a scroll was found, probably belonging to one of the members of the Hellenomemphite community (Wilcken 1917: 149–203, esp. 192). The scroll contained the text of the *Persae* of Timotheus, the longest fragment preserved by this poet and the oldest Greek papyrus known to date (P. Berl. inv. 9865; the latest edition is Hordern 2002). This papyrus had been copied in the first half of the fourth century and probably not in Egypt. The fact that this papyrus was found here indicates at least some connection between this community and the Hellenic world (Van Minnen 1997: 247–8, 252).

Another document coming from this community is Artemisia's curse, one of the oldest examples of "Egyptian Greek" (*UPZ* 1 = *PGM* II 40). The author of the curse is a woman with a Greek name, though her father's name is clearly Egyptian, Amasis. It is written in the Ionian dialect of the fourth century BCE, and was found in the Serapeum of Memphis. The latest piece of evidence for this community is that of *UPZ* I 116, where a man named Apinchis, son of Inarous – both Egyptian names – is described as an Hellenomemphite.

When Alexander arrived in Egypt, the Hellenomemphites were part of Egyptian society. One would have expected them to have played a key role in the adaptation of Greeks in Egypt in Hellenistic times, but their isolation from Greek culture was too evident: they were no longer Greeks. Conversely, the newly arrived Greeks did not consider themselves simply as "Greeks"; they preserved for some time their local identities, Macedonian, Rhodian, etc. There was even a tendency to preserve the settlers' original dialect in the first century of the Ptolemaic period (Clarysse 1998). Interesting evidence for this is provided by Theocritus, who has Syracusan women in Alexandria claim their right to speak their own dialect:

Συρακοσίαις ἐπιτάσσεις.
ὡς εἰδῇς καὶ τοῦτο, Κορίνθιαι εἰμὲς ἄνωθεν,
ὡς καὶ ὁ Βελλεροφῶν. Πελοποννασιστὶ λαλεῦμες
Δωρίσδειν δ' ἔξεστι, δοκῶ, τοῖς Δωριέεσσι.

These are women of Syracuse you are bullying. Let me assure you, we trace our descent back to Corinth, just like Bellerophon. Peloponnesian is what we are talking. Dorians may, I suppose, be permitted to speak Dorian. (Theoc. *Id.* 15.90–3)

Soon, however, the ethnonyms were dropped from official documents (see Kramer 1991: 69–70) and all immigrants became a single community of Greeks within a cultural, linguistic, and ethnic melting-pot.

Hellenistic Egypt

The conquest of Alexander initiated a much more complicated period, linguistically speaking. The Greeks arrived not as a minority integrated in a fully Egyptian society, but as the dominant section of the population. Even though Demotic Egyptian was not completely dismissed and was kept in some fields of administration, such as financial and juridical documents, the invaders introduced the Greek language as the language of power and culture (Zgusta 1980; Crespo 2007). It is striking that Ptolemaic kings and queens of Egypt never even bothered to learn the Egyptian language, with the exception of Queen Cleopatra VII, whose knowledge of languages was legendary according to Plutarch (*Ant.* 27). Polybius (5.83) informs us that Ptolemy IV used an interpreter when he addressed the Egyptian phalanx of his army. Such small details offer us a glimpse of the social situation that prevailed during the first period after the conquest.

The confrontation between natives and Greeks, due at least partly to the resentment produced by the favorable situation enjoyed by the Greeks, could generate resistance to language mixing. Language is an important sign of ethnic identity, which is difficult to fake. And in this case Egyptian and Greek were two such signs of identity standing face to face. The strong position of Greek limited the written production in the Egyptian language, which already in the first century CE had virtually disappeared from the administration (Bagnall 1993: 237; Lewis 1993; Depauw 2003). From the early Roman period onward, Demotic contracts had to present a Greek subscription in order to be valid, and this brings about an end to Demotic archives. Demotic was progressively restricted to the temples and the religious sphere.

There are some explanations for the demise of the Demotic script. On the one hand it has been claimed that it was an extremely complicated system, accessible to only a reduced part of the population, generally linked to priesthood and administration.

According to this explanation, the hieroglyphic, and also the Demotic script were victims of their own complexity (Quaegebeur 1974: 405). On the other hand, the Roman government imposed the use of Greek in public documents, and this ultimately brought about the downfall of Demotic. The teaching of Demotic writing was linked to the temple, and not to schools as Greek was (Maehler 1983: 192–7). Bagnall (1988) has offered the most convincing explanation for the demise of Demotic, which he relates to the progressive loss of power and influence of the Egyptian religion. The temples, together with their staff, celebrations, belongings, and scripts, suffered increasing decline from the first through the third centuries CE.

The Egyptian language began to be written with alphabetic characters as early as the first century of our era. But this conversion had a long development: it started with the transcription of personal names, or prayers on mummy labels (Quaegebeur 1978: 254). Later on, entire texts were transcribed in this alphabetic system derived from the Greek. These first texts are known as "Old Coptic" (Quaegebeur 1982; Satzinger 1984) and were used mostly for magical purposes. With the addition of seven extra Demotic signs for sounds alien to Greek, a new writing system was introduced and tested. Christianity soon adopted the new alphabet for the translation of the Bible and other Christian writings, as a vehicle of Christianization.

Bilingualism: Society and Language

The interaction of Greeks and Egyptians through the centuries gave birth to a complex and variegated bilingual society. It can be assumed that there were very different levels of bilingualism depending on the speaker, social extract, education, and contact with the second language. The understanding of this complex situation benefits from work on bilingualism in modern linguistics, which suggests patterns observed in modern societies that can sometimes be applied successfully to ancient societies (useful studies are Thomason and Kaufmann 1988 and Thomason 2001). In this way, Fewster (2002) employs the concept of a gradation of bilingual speakers in the modern world presented by Hoffmann (1991), to which I will return later. Vierros (2003; 2007) has resort to studies of language attrition and language contact (De Bot and Weltens 1991; Lambert and Freed 1982) in order to explain the language skills of the scribes of a group of documents.

There is evidence for bilingualism in Egypt as well as for the activity of translators (ἑρμηνεῖς) even before the Ptolemaic period (Peremans 1983b; Rochette 1994). Herodotus (2.154) mentions them in the fifth century BCE and explains that they are the descendants of the children who learnt Greek from the Hellenomemphites. After the conquest of Alexander, hellenization proceeded differently along the Nile in urban and rural areas. The places where mercenaries of the Macedonian army received plots of land were the first territories with mixed populations, since they attracted workers from both origins. In those melting-pots, Greeks were Egyptianized,[1] while Egyptians were hellenized. Intermarriage (Peremans 1981), commercial transactions, and proximity all ensured a certain level of knowledge of the second language.

A higher level of bilingualism developed mostly in cities and among the population of Egyptian origin. In some regions the impact of Greek was less felt. For instance, Theban Pathyris was an Egyptian-speaking environment. *P.Batav.* 4 is a second-century BCE testament where four out of five witnesses are Egyptian and sign in Egyptian because there are not enough Greek-speaking people in the town (τοῖς ἐγχωρίοις γράμμασιν διὰ τὸ μὴ εἶναι ἐπὶ τῶν τόπων τοὺς ἴσους Ἕλληνας "In local script because of the fact that an equal number of Greeks is not present in the area" (see Vandorpe 2002a; Vierros 2003: 720; Youtie 1975). The levels of bilingualism – and literacy – among the population of Greco-Roman Egypt are difficult to assess. Bilingualism should not be understood as a condition of perfect proficiency in two languages in every sphere of the speaker's life – this in fact occurs rarely.

In modern societies the following levels of bilingualism have been described: i) at the basic level stands the monolingual speaker who knows at least a minimum of expressions in the other language; ii) an immigrant (in the case of Egypt it would, conversely, be the case of the natives), who learns the elite language just enough to fit into the social and economic mechanisms; iii) a speaker who has been immersed and trained since childhood in a second language; iv) a speaker who has parents from different linguistic origins, and who has learned both languages during his upbringing; v) lastly, a perfect bilingual, who has no difficulty expressing himself in either language (Fewster 2002: 237 quoting Hoffmann 1991: 16–17).

The monolinguals existed in both ethnic groups in Egypt. The Greeks in the cities did not learn Egyptian, but understood some expressions due to proximity (Peremans 1983a: 262 ; Rochette 1996b). There were also Egyptian monolinguals, especially in the *chora*, and in the south. The subscriptions and Demotic translations of Greek texts bear strong indication that many natives remained un-hellenized. An example is *P.Oxy.* 2.237, a transcript of court proceedings from 133 CE, where the epistrategus Pachonius Felix needs to use an official translator for the interrogation of a witness (see Youtie 1975: 205). The two categories following can be illustrated with the case of the tax collectors in Upper Egypt. Their imperfect knowledge of Greek declension indicates that their use of the language was just enough to report to their superiors (Fewster 2002: 230, 238–9). The Narmouthis texts present a slightly more advanced level of bilingualism. There is at least an attempt at Greek education. In urban areas, all Egyptians working in the central administration needed to write and speak Greek at an advanced level to be able to fulfil their tasks correctly. Some documents illustrate the proficiency of some scribes in writing the Greek language, but not in an absolutely perfect way. For example, many first-century CE documents from the Fayum are translations from Egyptian contracts into Greek that have been made as perfect as possible (κατὰ τὸ δυνατόν). *SB* 1.5231 (CE 11) in particular features some terms that have simply been kept in the original language in Greek characters: λέγει ἐμνεῦθης ὁρπέει [το]π[άε]ις προφήτης . . . νεβοᾶπι ὁι[σ]ῆι ὁι[σ]εγ[έ]του "Amenothes, great one of the temple, first prophet (?) . . . possessor of purity, master of the lake, master of the lake Moeris, says." This can be interpreted as the product of a speaker who knows the second language almost perfectly, but lacking some expressions and terms.

The fourth level is that of bilingual speakers coming closer to perfection. Dionysos in the second century CE, of Egyptian origin, is a competent scribe in both languages and scripts (Boswinkel and Pestman 1982). Many civil servants in high positions in the Greek administration must have had a similar level (Peremans 1983a: 269).

Greek or Demotic as a Second Language

Greek education in schools was not limited to the Greek population in the *metropoleis*. It also extended to the Egyptian population, even in the *chora*. In the Ptolemaic period learning Greek became a necessity if one wanted to find a place in the economy. The bilingual population grew, and eventually mixed into the Greek population (on language and ethnicity, see Bagnall 1993: 203–51). These natives often had a Greek name beside their own Egyptian name, each of them used in the public and private sphere respectively (see Quaegebeur 1978: 244; Clarysse 1985). The Fayum is an example of an area where bilingualism was strongly developed. We have very interesting philological evidence for this, for example in bilingual contracts of sale, first written in Demotic and then translated into Greek. There are also Greek documents featuring subscriptions in Demotic. These examples attest the existence of a bilingual scribal practice and show that at least a portion of the population made the effort to learn to write and speak Greek. The production of these scribes is as heterogeneous as the levels each one of them reached in their mastery of the language. Some of the texts unveil the peculiarities of the Greek spoken by the scribes.

Egyptians learning Greek often reached a high level of proficiency and thus many documents produced by them cannot be distinguished from documents produced by native speakers of Greek, since one cannot identify divergences from the correct language. The signs that would betray an Egyptian scribe are usually orthographic mistakes which show an alternative pronunciation influenced by the mother tongue, or morphological and syntactic mistakes due to a defective knowledge of the language. The use of the brush (Egyptian) instead of the calamus (Greek) is another important fact in identifying an Egyptian scribe (on the brush-pen, see also ch. 5).

As an example of Egyptians learning Greek, there is school material in the ostraka from Medinet Madi, Narmoutis, from the second to third centuries CE, found in a temple (Bresciani and Pintaudi 1987; Pintaudi and Sijpesteijn 1989; Pernigotti 1998). The texts, written by Egyptian scribes (Donadoni 1955), are in Demotic and Greek (see Gallo 1989), often bilingual. These texts also illustrate the phenomenon of code-switching, where the writer alternates between the two languages either by inserting words from the other language in his text, or simply by changing from one to the other. This phenomenon is frequent in spoken language, but very rare in written evidence. In the Narmoutis texts, moreover, there is also "script-switching": the Egyptian texts are written in Demotic, running right to left, but in some cases, when a Greek word is inserted, the direction of the writing changes, since Greek runs left to right. Mummy labels are one more example of the use of Greek by Egyptian priests. It is again the sphere of the funerary, deeply linked to religion (Quaegebeur 1978). These labels often feature bilingual texts. Their minimal content was the name of the deceased, though often one finds other personal details and even a small funerary prayer to Osiris. The question whether they were produced by the same scribe or by two different ones is not entirely clear. Moreover, these texts are evidence for the study of double names and how the transcription system worked (Quaegebeur 1974).

The opposite case of Greeks learning Egyptian is rare but not absent. An example of a Greek learning Egyptian is that of a mid-second century BCE letter, addressed by a woman to her son or husband, to congratulate him on his learning to write in Egyptian characters:

> πυνθανομένη μανθάνειν σε Αἰγύπτια γράμματα συνεχάρην σοι καὶ ἐμαυτῆι, ὅτι νῦν γε παραγενόμενος εἰς τὴν πόλιν διδάξεις παρὰ Φαλουβῆτι ἰατροκλύστηι τὰ παιδάρια καὶ ἕξεις ἐφόδιον εἰς τὸ γῆρας.

> When I heard that you were learning to write Egyptian I rejoiced for your sake and for mine too, because now, when you move back to the city, you will teach the slaves of the medical school of Faloubetis, and you will have an income until you are old. (*UPZ* 1.148; Rémondon 1964)

Despite the uncertainties in the interpretation of this letter, it seems clear that this is the case of someone who probably belonged to a mixed family or was in fact Greek, and was learning Egyptian in connection with the study of medicine. Another area in which Greeks could use Demotic was dream divination, a religious activity.[2] An example of this linguistic speciality is a third-century CE letter, in which Ptolemy writes to Achilles to tell him about his "vision," introducing his description of the dream saying:

> ἔδοξέν μοι καὶ περὶ τοῦ ὁράματος διασαφῆναί σοι, ὅπως ὂν τρόπον οἱ θεοί σε οἴδασιν. Αἰγυπτιστὶ δὲ ὑπέγραψα ὅπως ἀκριβῶς εἰδῆις.

> It seemed convenient to me to tell you about my dream, in order that you understand how the gods know you. I have written it below in Egyptian so that you understand it clearly. (Mitteis and Wilcken 1912: 50)

In spite of the scarcity of the evidence and the uncertainties of the interpretation of the texts, we can conclude that in Ptolemaic Egypt and during the first centuries of Roman rule the Egyptian language in Demotic script was actively used in the spheres of family and religion, especially in the temples, and for activities such as the practice of medicine and oniromancy, as appears from the two examples (Torallas Tovar 2003; 2005). The native population was hellenized at first according to practical need, but soon the interaction between both populations created increasingly strong links, and it is reasonable to suppose that at least a portion of the population was completely bilingual. Clearly, the lower classes intermarried, giving birth to bilingual families. It is however difficult to assess their linguistic situation since the lower classes did not leave as much written evidence.

Some Features of Egyptian Greek

As it has been stated above, written language is always more conservative than spoken language, and the writer, being more conscious of his linguistic medium, tends to avoid the interference of a second language. We can safely assume, therefore, that if a linguistic interference occurs in written language, it was probably more frequent in spoken language. Below I list some possible cases of interference of Egyptian with the Greek text.[3]

Phonology

Some peculiarities of pronunciation can be traced in orthographical mistakes. The Greek papyri are in fact a vast source of information, since they provide documents originating from different social layers and from different levels of alphabetization. There are two competing trends (the reason why the phenomena are not systematic): i) behind orthography lies the pronunciation of the scribe, which may or may not emerge in the documents; ii) orthographic convention plays against phonetic orthography.

The situation in the papyri has been studied systematically by Mayser 1906, Gignac 1976–81, and more recently by Horrocks 1997a. Many of the phenomena can be considered as general for *Koine* Greek (see ch. 16) and can be explained by internal evolution of the Greek language, for which the papyri are a very useful source (reduction of long diphthongs, loss of vowel quantity, iotacism, monophthongization of short diphthongs, fricativization of υ as second element of a diphthong). But other features can be explained as typical of Egyptian Greek, and especially as due to linguistic contact. The papyri feature such a vast variety of cases that, in the words of Gignac (1976–81), there are enough arguments for any theory. One must stick to the most common phenomena, like the confusion of vowels. The Egyptian accent was so strong that vowels in unstressed syllables lost their quality (πάλιν/πόλιν; μετοξύ). Deviating pronunciation and orthography are also due to assimilation and metathesis: ἄνϑραπος for ἄνϑρωπος, σιμιδαίλιος for σεμιδάλιος, εὐσχομονεῖν for εὐσχημονεῖν.

The situation for consonants is clearer than that for vowels. The evidence from Egyptian, Demotic, and Coptic is also more transparent, since vowels have a defective notation, whereas consonants are in general graphically represented. There was a confusion between voiced and voiceless stops: /t/-/d/ and /k/-/g/ as well as a confusion between voiceless and aspirated voiceless consonants. Egyptian did not have a phonological opposition between voiceless and voiced stops, which explains the confusion in Greek as due to linguistic contact. Examples include κείτονες/γείτονες, τημοσίων/δημοσίων, and τραχμάς/δραχμάς (Gignac 1970). The opposition of π and β (which was fricative) was not always so clear: σεπάσμιον for σεβάσμιον or βόλιν for πόλιν.

The process of fricativization of aspirated voiceless stops (see also chs 7 and 16) started as early as the fifth century BCE in Laconia (see ch. 14) and in Asia Minor in the Hellenistic period. In Egypt, however, the voiceless aspirated stop was preserved until the Low *Koine*, perhaps due to the influence of substrate. When the Greek alphabet was adopted by Egyptian, some signs were added to note voiceless fricatives: ϩ hori, for the glottal, and ϥ fai for the labiodental. The Greek signs for the aspirated voiceless, φ, ϑ, and χ, were used only for Greek loanwords in Coptic: ⲯⲩⲭ ⲏ, ⲫⲓⲗⲟ-ⲥⲟⲫⲟⲥ and in some cases when a voiceless stop precedes an aspiration: ⲧ-ϩⲗⲗⲱ, "the old woman" > ⲑⲗⲗⲱ.

The confusion of liquids ρ/λ is common in many languages. However, we find it more profusely in documents from Fayum. The fayumic dialect of Coptic presents lambdacism as very characteristic trait. Here the key for assessing linguistic contact instead of considering a general linguistic trend is the frequency of appearance of this mistake in the Greek of Fayum: καθαλά (καθαρά), καθάπελ (καθάπερ), ἡμέλα (ἡμέρα).

Morphology

Hardly any evidence of contact can be traced in morphology which cannot be interpreted as general *Koine* (Gignac 1981; see also chs 16 and 36): the loss of dual number, reorganization of the pronominal system, analogy changes in some declensions and conjugations, use of hypocoristics in –ιον, etc. The morphology of Greek and that of Egyptian are completely different. Egyptian has no declension, which explains a typical feature of texts written by Egyptians, the uninflected use of personal names (Vierros 2007).

One instance of nominal derivation can be included in this section. This is a case of structural borrowing. Egyptian and Coptic feature a pattern of nominal derivation characterized by juxtaposition of a *regens* and a *rectum* (Loprieno 1995: 56), as in *md.t rmṯ* lit. "the thing of man," "mankind," Copt. ⲙⲛⲧⲣⲱⲙⲉ. In this way, one finds in the Greek *Excerpta* of the Pachomian Rule (ed. Albers 1923), the expression ἐν τῷ τόπῳ τῆς ἑστιάσεως rendering Copt. ⲙⲁⲛⲟⲩⲱⲙ (lit. "place-of-eating," ⲙⲁ "place," ⲟⲩⲱⲙ "to eat"). Similarly ἐν τῷ τόπῳ ἐν ᾧ καθεύδει renders ⲙⲁⲛⲛⲕⲟⲧⲕ (lit. "place-of-sleeping," ⲙⲁ "place," ⲛ̄ⲕⲟⲧⲕ̄ "to sleep").

Syntax

Many of the phenomena general to *Koine* Greek also appear in the papyri: loss of dative, more frequent use of prepositional phrases instead of cases, periphrastic expression of the future with μέλλω, ἔχω, or θέλω, use of subordinate clause with ἵνα instead of infinitive clause, etc. On these phenomena, see also chapters 16, 18, and 36. Other syntactic features of Egyptian Greek are due to linguistic interference:[4]

Loan constructions

Literal translations of Egyptian constructions into Greek often created new syntactic constructions, mainly involving prepositions and adverbs.

a) The numeral "one" in Egyptian (*wꜥ*, Copt. ⲟⲩⲁ) is also the indefinite pronoun. This can lie behind the use of εἷς for τις in *BGU* 4.1044, fourth cent. CE: εἷς λεγόμενος Φαῆσις "someone called Phaesis".

b) The Egyptian polysemy of Copt. ⲉⲓⲥ, meaning both "behold" and "since" (Layton 2004: 390), can also lie behind the use in Greek of ἰδού with a temporal meaning "since," as in: *BGU* 4.948: ἡ μήτηρ σου Κοφαήνα ἀσθενεῖ ἰδοῦ δέκα τρεῖς μῆνες "your mother Kophaena has been ill since three months" (cf. Luke 13.16: ἰδοὺ δέκα καὶ ὀκτὼ ἔτη "since 18 years").[5]

c) The construction known as ὄνος ὑπὸ οἴνου or οἶνον "the donkey under the wine," where the preposition ὑπό is used with the notion of occupation ("donkey loaded with wine"), can be explained by the interference of the use of the Egyptian preposition *ḥr*: *P.Mich.* 9.620 is a third-century CE account of an estate, where rooms are listed with their occupants using this expression: κέλλα ὑπὸ Ὁρσενοῦφιν "cell rented by / occupied by Horsenouphis." Another instance of the same case is *P.Oxy.* 1.76.14–15 (second cent. CE): ἔχων ὑφ᾽ ἑαυτὸν πρὸς οἴκησιν τόπους τρεῖς "he rents three portions of the house." Other examples, not used for persons, include *P.Mich.* 9.620: ἔστιν ταμεῖον . . . ὑπὸ κυριακὸν χόρτον "it is a store-room for the storage of the master's hay", and *P.Flor.* 3.376.1.28 (third cent. CE): αὐλὴ ὑπὸ ταύρους κυριακούς "a yard to keep the master's bulls" (Husson 1982; Erman 1893; Youtie 1950: 103–4).

d)   Similarly, there is the use of the preposition ἐν with an instrumental meaning mostly in the Tebtunis papyri (1.16, 41, 45, 46, 47, 48), as ἐν μαχαίραις or ἐν μαχαίρηι "with the sword(s)." This can be compared to Copt. ϩⲛ ⲧⲁⲥⲏϥⲓ "with my sword." The expression appears frequently in Septuagint Greek (e.g., Num. 31:8, I Sam. 2:33) and NT Greek (Rev. 6.8.5). It can be interpreted as a feature that Egyptian has in common with Semitic (see also ch. 18).

e)   The common use in Egyptian and Coptic of ϫⲉ for introducing direct speech as in ⲡⲉϫⲁϥ ϫⲉ ⲁⲛⲟⲕ ⲡⲉ ⲡⲉⲭ̅ⲥ̅ "He said (that) I am the Christ" can be lying behind the frequent use of ὅτι to introduce direct speech in Egyptian Greek. *P.Oxy.* 6.903, a petition in very vivid language, presents some cases of this phenomenon: καὶ λέγων ... ὅτι δότε πάντα τὰ αὐτῆς, [. . .] λέγων ὅτι διὰ τί ἀπῆλθας εἰς τὸ κυριακόν "and saying ... 'Give me everything she has,' [...] saying 'What for did you come to the Church?'".

f)   The use of the construction εὔχεσθαι ἐπάνω, with ἐπάνω being equivalent to ὑπέρ, can be found in *P.Lond.* 6.1926: ἐὰν εὔξῃ ἐπάνω μου "if you pray for me." This can be compared to Copt. ϣⲗⲏⲗ ⲉϫⲛ–, a preposition meaning literally "upon."

Loan translations

In this case both the construction and the concept are borrowed. The structure is reproduced as accurately as possible with the means available in the target language.

a)   The idiomatic expression in Eg. *3bd n hrw* (lit. "month of days") or Copt. ⲉⲃⲟⲧ ⲛ̄ϩⲟⲟⲩ, can be found in *P.Strasb.* 1.35 (fourth cent. CE) δύο μῆνας ἡμερῶν "two months of days," a literal translation.

b)   Egyptian constructs the numerals with the article in singular (Loprieno 1996: 71–2; Layton 2004: 57). This construction is found in Greek in *P.Oslo* 1.4 (fourth cent. CE) τοῦ δώδεκα στύθχων for τῶν δώδεκα στοιχείων "of the twelve elements."

c)   In a similar way, the transference of gender in nouns can be considered some kind of loan translation. One comes across in the papyri examples such as: *P.Cair. Masp.* 1.67075, πολλὴν σῖτον (dem. Eg. *blbyl3.t*, Copt. ⲃⲗⲃⲓⲗⲉ are fem.) and *P.Oxy.* 6.893, τοῦ ἡμέρας (Eg. *hrw*, Copt. ϩⲟⲟⲩ are masc.).

d)   It is a typical feature of Egyptian to use the repetition of numerals with a distributive meaning (Loprieno 1996: 72; Layton 2004: 53). In Greek this is expressed by the use of the preposition κατά and the numeral. Examples such as κατὰ δύο δύο at *P.Oxy.* 6.886 can be explained by interference.

e) Especially interesting are the relative constructions studied by Vierros (2003). The comparison with the same type of clause in Demotic explains a recurrent divergence in a certain group of documents produced by scribes of Egyptian origin. In Egyptian, relative clauses with a subject different from the antecedent referred to use a coreferential element for this (Loprieno 1996: 203).

The most common way of constructing relative clauses in Demotic is to use a relative converter *nt*, plus a morpheme *iw* and a suffix pronoun which is the subject of the relative clause. An example can show how this suffix pronoun appears in the same place where the relative pronoun in Greek is expected:

n3 mt.w(t) **nt íw** *iw=k ḏ n-im=w*

ART.PL NOUN.PL REL ASP PRS=PRON.2SG VERB PREP=3PL

The words **which you** are saying them (Johnson 2000: 67 E155)

The interference of Egyptian in Greek appears when the construction loses the connection to the antecedent in the relative pronoun, e.g:

προπωλήτρια καὶ βεβαιώτρια τῶν κατὰ τὴν ὠνὴν ταύτην πάντων Θαῖβις ἡ ἀποδομένη, **οὓς** ἐδέξαντο Φῖβις καὶ Ὧρος οἱ πριάμενοι

The negotiator (fem.) and warrantor (fem.) of everything related to this sale, Thaibis, the seller (fem.), whom (masc. pl.) Phibis and Horos, the buyers, accept. (*P.Mil.* I.2)

The relative pronoun οὓς should according to Greek syntactic rules have been ἥν, referring to Thaibis, but the subject of the clause is masculine plural.

f) It is common in Egyptian to use an anaphoric or coreferential pronoun in relative clauses, referring to the antecedent. Its use is pleonastic in Greek, and it can be due to interference of the Egyptian construction, as for example at *P.Oxy.* 1.117: ῥάκη δύο κατασεσημασμένα [τ]ῇ σφραγῖδι μου, ἐξ ὧν δώσεις τοῖς παιδίοις σου ἐν ἐξ **αὐτῶν** "two strips of cloth sealed with my seal, one of which please give to your children" or *P.Mich.* 1.29: κα[ὶ] τὸν δὲ πῶλον αὐτῆς ἀποστελῶ [σοι] **αὐτόν** "and her foal I will send it to you."

Idiomatic expressions can be transferred into the target language in the form of a literal translation. Detecting these cases requires a deep knowledge of both languages. One was noticed by P. Derchain (2001) in Hdt. 2.133: ἔς τε τὰ ἔλεα καὶ τὰ ἄλσεα πλανώμενον, referring to the king Mycerinos. When Mycerinos was told by the oracle that he would live only six years, he decided to feast and enjoy himself unceasingly both day and night, "moving about in the marsh-country and the woods." This mysterious expression is explained when compared to an Egyptian metaphor, *s3b sšw*, literally "to wander in the woods," meaning "to enjoy life."

Lexical borrowings

With almost fifteen centuries of contact it is in fact odd that there is such a limited number of Egyptian loan words in Greek (Torallas Tovar 2004b). Language contact studies generally divide loan words into two kinds (Haugen 1950: 212–13): i) terms natural to the target language, which the speaker does not distinguish from the native terms; and ii) xenisms, which remain as specialized terms to denote foreign objects, practices, or ideas and are generally imported through commercial contact or geographical and travel literature. Fournet (1989) organizes Egyptian loan words in three groups: i) well assimilated loanwords, ii) peregrinisms and iii) loanwords in Egyptian Greek. But these terms may be interpreted differently when appearing in different contexts. The term used to name a special kind of cake – *kakis* – is a good example for two different contexts. Strabo (17.2.5) needs to explain what it means καὶ οἱ κάκεις δὲ ἴδιόν τι ἄρτου γένος "and the kakis are a particular type of bread." But we find a completely different context in *P.Mich.* 5.243, in which the writer uses the term as part of his basic vocabulary, not distinguished from other terms of Greek origin (ἑκάστου παραχρῆμα εἰσφέροντος (δραχμὴν) 1 καὶ κάκεις δύο "bringing each one on the spot one drachma and two loaves of bread"). The two language users have in each case a different conscience and audience, when using the term κάκις.

The adoption of Egyptian terms needed strategies of adaptation into the Greek declension system. One of these resources in the earlier-attested terms was the suffix –ις: βάρις, θίβις, θκυλλάστις "palm," "basket," "rounded bread"). This alternated with another integration suffix -ιον, used for diminutive, which survived until the eighth century CE in coining new terms from a foreign one (Palmer 1945: 79–86; Gignac 1976–81: 2: 25): κολόβιον, ἐμβρίμιον, λακώτιον "sleeveless tunic," "head cushion," "a liquid measure."

Some terms in later texts seem to be the product of code-switching and they preserve the Egyptian non-declined form: κόντσου (*SB* I 1160), a vessel, is Copt. ⲕⲟⲩⲛⲭⲟⲩ. There are however some cases of non-declined forms in earlier periods too, for instance the names of the Egyptian months (Thissen 1993).

Sometimes the writer felt the need to express the same reality in both Greek and Coptic to make sure it would be understood by bilingual or semi-bilingual readers. This was often found in inventories or lists of payments, where things were called by their native names alongside their Greek term (Sijpesteijn 1992: 242). *P.Vat.Aphrod.* 25 (sixth cent. CE) has τοῦ λάκκου ἤτοι τνευπε "the reservoir or *tneupe*"; *P.Lond.* 5.1722, (CE 530) καὶ τὸ ὑποπέσσιον ἤτοι τχηρε "the space under the stairs or *tchrire*."

A semantic borrowing happens when a term in the model language has two meanings, one of them in common with the target language. The polysemy is transferred and the term in the target language acquires an extra meaning. An example is Gk θάλλος "branch," which acquired the new meaning of "present" due to the existence in Egyptian of two etymologically unrelated homophone terms: *mnh* "branch," synonym of θάλλος, and *mnh.t* "present" (Derchain 1955). Gk ὄρος "mountain" acquired the meanings "desert" and "monastery," which can be explained through Copt. ⲧⲟⲟⲩ "mountain," "desert," and "monastery" (Cadell and Rémondon 1967; Kahle 1954: 27–8; other examples in Husson 1986 and 1999).

FURTHER READING

On Latin in Egypt, see Adams (2003: esp. 527–641); Rochette 1998. In general on bilingualism in Egypt, see Adams, Janse, and Swain, eds. 2002 (esp. Fewster); also Peremans 1964 and 1983a, Rochette 1994, 1995, and 1996a, Dieleman 2005, Lüddekens 1980, and Oréal 1999. There is linguistic description of Greek in Egypt in Horrocks 1997a and Ray 2007. On literacy, see Hanson 1991, Harris 1989, Hopkins 1991, Bowman and Woolf 1994 and Wipszycka 1984. On bilingual documents, see Boswinkel and Pestman 1978. On the use of demotic in juridical documents, see Daumas 1972. On the identity conflict, see Goudriaan 1988, McCoskey 2002 and 2004, and Torallas Tovar 2005. On Egyptian scribes and their practice in writing Greek, see Clarysse 1993. On writing materials, see Tait 1986 and Sosin and Manning 2003.

NOTES

1 An interesting example of the Egyptianization of Greeks is the family of Dryton in Upper Egypt; see Vandorpe 2002b.
2 There are dreams told by Greeks in Demotic, like *P. dem. Bologna* 3173, although it is not completely clear who produced this particular text. Apollonius, someone close to Ptolemy, the *katoikos* of the Serapeum at Memphis, mentioned above, could have been the author of these four dream descriptions. See Goudriaan 1988: 44–5.
3 Kapsomenos 1953 represents a trend reticent to recognize the interference of a second language in these phenomena.
4 For many examples I depend on Vergote 1938: 1355–9; cf. Vergote 1984. Others are my own, or else I quote the source. Sometimes I refer to examples in Biblical Greek, mainly Septuagint (see also Torallas Tovar 2007), since there are also traces of linguistic interference which can be compared with the papyri. There are comparative studies by Montevecchi (1957, 1964, 1996, and 1999) and Passoni dell'Acqua (1981). For more on Biblical Greek see ch. 18.
5 But see also the remarks in ch. 18 on ἰδού as due to Hebrew. [Ed.]

CHAPTER EIGHTEEN

Jewish and Christian Greek

Coulter H. George

During the reign of King Ptolemy II Philadelphus (283–246 BCE), the Library of Alexandria became the pre-eminent cultural center of its day. No less a figure than the poet Callimachus catalogued its collection, and, perhaps *c.* 270, his equally famous rival Apollonius of Rhodes became the head librarian. But Alexandria was not just a city of Greek learning. There was also a substantial Jewish population, and Ptolemy's librarian, with his collector's enthusiasm for completing sets, also wanted to have a good copy of Jewish law. He advised his king as follows:

> If it seems a good idea, Your Majesty, we will write to the high priest in Jerusalem, asking him to send men who have led noble lives and are now advanced in years, who have experience in the legal practices of their people, six from each tribe, so that, scrutinizing what is agreed upon in most cases and obtaining accuracy in the translation, we can establish a clear text, worthy both of the state and of your designs. (*Letter of Aristeas* 32)

This, at least, is the story told in the *Letter of Aristeas*, a document generally dated to the second century BCE, which purports to describe the background behind the Greek translation of the Hebrew Bible, called the Septuagint (< Lat. *septuāgintā* "seventy") after the 72 (or, in some versions, 70) scholars who translated it. The letter goes on to describe the elders' remarkable wisdom, as displayed in their sage answers to questions of political philosophy put to them by Ptolemy, but then spends little time on the actual mechanics of the translation. This would be regrettable for those studying the language of the Septuagint were it not for the fact that the letter is a dubious historical source anyway. For instance, it identifies Ptolemy's librarian as Demetrius of Phaleron, who fled to Alexandria after a period as governor of Athens (318–307), but was neither the head librarian nor even on good terms with the king, supposedly because of some maladroit political moves at the time of Ptolemy's accession. Nevertheless, the *Letter of Aristeas* provides a good anecdotal starting point for this chapter, for it brings together the two main linguistic strands that must be teased apart in assessing Jewish and Christian Greek: its temporal location in the Hellenistic Age and its geographical location in the multilingual eastern Mediterranean. Put differently, to what extent does the language of the Septuagint, New Testament, and other Judeo-Christian writings differ from Classical Attic because it represents the natural diachronic evolution of *Koine* Greek? And to what extent does it differ because most of these texts were composed by people who were either translating Semitic-language sources or else themselves speakers of a Semitic language?

The Language of the Septuagint

Many features of the language of the Septuagint that diverge from Classical Attic have traditionally been thought to result from the literal translation of characteristically Hebrew syntactic constructions and lexical expressions into unidiomatic Greek. Three typical examples follow.

   a)   The Septuagint strikes the classically trained reader as unusually *paratactic*: that is, it eschews nested subordinate clauses and participles in favor of a string of syntactically coordinate sentences linked together by καί "and." Compare the Greek account of the creation of light with the Hebrew original:

(1)   καὶ εἶπεν ὁ θεός, Γενηθήτω φῶς. καὶ ἐγένετο φῶς. καὶ εἶδεν ὁ θεὸς τὸ φῶς ὅτι καλόν.

   And God said, "Let there be light." And there was light. And God saw the light, that it was good. (Gen. 1:3–4a)

way-yōmer	*'ĕlōhîm*	*yəhî*	*'ôr*	*wa-yhî*	*'ôr*
and-he.said	God	let.there.be	light	and-there.was	light

way-yarə'	*'ĕlōhîm*	*'et̠-hā-'ôr*		*kî-ṭôb*	
and-he.saw	God	PARTICLE-the-light		that-(it.was.)good.	

The Greek follows the Hebrew word order and syntax very closely. Indeed, there are only two exceptions to an otherwise perfect one-to-one correspondence between the Hebrew and Greek: first, a definite article is added to θεός "God" in Greek; second, the Hebrew particle *'et̠*, which marks definite direct objects, is left untranslated. More important are the similarities. In passing we may note that the structure εἶδεν … τὸ φῶς ὅτι καλόν, with the subject of the subordinate clause raised to be the object of the main clause, parallels the Hebrew precisely. Of more widespread significance is the fact that each Greek καί corresponds to the so-called *waw conversive* of Hebrew. In this construction, *wə* "and" (which in an unvocalized text appears as the single letter *waw*) occurs at the start of a clause, directly followed by a verb form that would otherwise be translated as a future or jussive subjunctive, but is instead "converted" to be the equivalent of a simple past tense. Phonological changes also take place, including the strengthening of the conjunction to *wa* and the doubling of the following consonant. The effect of the construction can be seen in (1) in the contrast between *yǝhî* (γενηθήτω) and *wa-yhî* (καὶ ἐγένετο). (In this case there is an additional complication: when the verb begins *yǝ-*, the schwa is dropped and the initial *y* does not double (Joüon–Muraoka §§18b, 18m).) As the waw conversive is extremely common in the Hebrew Bible, accounting for 29 percent of all finite verb forms (Waltke and O'Connor 1990: §29.1c), scholars have been quick to see the influence of translation language behind the high number of Septuagintal sentences that start with καί + main verb.

   b)   Another feature that distinguishes the language of the Septuagint from Classical Attic is the increased use of the oblique cases of the *personal pronouns*, especially as possessives, direct objects, and resumptive pronouns (for the last category, see Janse 2002: 361–4):

(2)   καὶ ἐγένετο ἐν τῷ εἶναι αὐτοὺς ἐν τῷ πεδίῳ καὶ ἀνέστη Κάϊν ἐπὶ Ἄβελ τὸν ἀδελφὸν αὐτοῦ καὶ ἀπέκτεινεν αὐτόν.

And it happened in their being in the field and Cain rose up against Abel his brother and killed him. (Gen. 4:8)

wa-yhî	*bi-hyôt̲-ām*	*baś-śād̲eh*	*way-yāqom*
and-it.happened	in-being-their	in.the-field	and-he.rose.up

qayin	*'el-heb̲el*	*'ā-îw*	*way-yaharḡ-ēhû*
Cain	to-Abel	brother-his	and-he.killed-him.

In this example, forms of the third-person pronoun αὐτόν occur three times in just twenty words of Greek: once as the subject of an infinitive, once as a possessive pronoun, and once as an object pronoun. All three times there is a corresponding pronominal element in the Hebrew in precisely the same position in the sentence. This is a greater use of this pronominal stem than is generally said to occur in Classical Attic, in which the sense of the possessive αὐτοῦ, for instance, is sufficiently expressed through the definite article on its own, and pronominal objects can be dropped altogether; cf. Thuc. 1.3.3 Δαναοὺς δὲ ἐν τοῖς ἔπεσι καὶ Ἀργείους καὶ Ἀχαιοὺς ἀνακαλεῖ "but [Homer] calls them Danaoi and Argeioi and Akhaioi in his poems," where English requires the pronominal direct object and also favors possessive *his* over the bare article.

   Example (2) also shows once again the prominence of the waw conversive in Hebrew. It occurs with all three main verbs, and it is translated into Greek with καί + main verb each time. Particularly typical of the syntax of the Hebrew Bible is the expression of a subordinate temporal clause with the sequence *wa-yhî* + preposition + infinitive construct (of the subordinate verb) (*bi-hyôt̲-ām*) + waw conversive (of the main verb) (*way-yāqom*) (Waltke and O'Connor 1990: §§33.2.4, 36.2.2). This leads to the Greek structure καὶ ἐγένετο + preposition + articular infinitive + καί + main verb, where one would otherwise expect a participial construction or a subordinate clause introduced by, e.g., ὡς or ἐπεί "when."

c) A third feature of Septuagintal language that can be attributed to Semitic influence is its non-Classical use of *prepositions*. This is most obvious at the lexical level: certain verbs take prepositions in constructions that are not found in Attic authors, but which do have analogues in the Hebrew original. The verb φοβέομαι "fear," for instance, usually construed with an accusative object in Attic, can take ἀπό + genitive in the Septuagint. This reflects the Hebrew construction of the verb *yārē'* "fear, be afraid" (seen in the form *ṯîr'ûn* in example (3)) with the preposition *min* "from," which often assumes the combining form *mē-*:

(3) μὴ πτήξητε μηδὲ φοβηθῆτε ἀπ᾽ αὐτῶν

Do not tremble and do not be afraid of them. (Deut. 1:29)

lō'-ṭaʿarṣûn	*wə-lō'-ṯîr'ûn*	*mē-hem*
not-tremble.2pl	and-not-be.afraid.2pl	from-them.

Such non-standard prepositional use can also be found more systematically in the marking of agents of passive verbs. Classical Greek typically has ὑπό + genitive, but Hebrew often uses *min* (as well as compound prepositions formed from *min*). As it happens, the closest Greek counterpart of *min* is ἀπό, a preposition found only rarely as an agent marker in Classical Greek. Even so, nearly invariably, when the Hebrew Bible uses *min* or its compounds in this function, the Septuagint has ἀπό. When, however, the Hebrew does not predispose the Greek to one preposition or another, ὑπό remains the agent marker of choice (George 2005: 232–40). Contrast in this respect (4) and (5):

(4) καὶ γυναῖκα ἐκβεβλημένην ἀπὸ ἀνδρὸς αὐτῆς

and a woman divorced by her husband (Lev. 21:7)

wə-'iššāh	*gərûšāh*	*mē-'îš-āh*
and-woman	divorced	from-husband-her

(5) κατὰ τὰ εἰρημένα ὑπὸ Φαραώ

according to what was said by Pharaoh (Gen. 45:21)

ʿal-pî	*p̄arʿōh*
according.to-(the.)mouth.of	Pharaoh.

Such a pattern strongly suggests that ὑπό remained the default agent marker for the translators of the Septuagint and that ἀπό was only used because of interference from the constructions in the Hebrew original.

Now, all three of these features – parataxis with καί, increased pronoun use, and non-standard prepositional constructions – have also been claimed as representing merely the simple historical evolution of Greek. In the examples just presented, however, the regularity of correspondence between the Greek and the Hebrew points rather to interference from the source language as the cause of the non-Classical constructions. Still, it remains the case that some potential Semitisms do reflect straightforward diachronic developments in *Koine*. But since Greek is developing at this period in a direction that is on the whole bringing it closer to Hebrew, considerable effort is often necessary to work out whether diachronic development or interference from Hebrew is more important in accounting for the presence of such features in the Septuagint.

One such development was the gradual loss of the optative (Evans 2001: 175–97; see also ch. 16). Starting soon after the Classical period, Greek first lost the optative as a marker of secondary sequence in subordinate clauses; next, the potential optative disappeared; finally, the optative of wish was lost, although it survives even today in a couple of fossilized phrases (e.g., ο μη γένοιτο "God forbid!"). The Septuagint appears to represent a relatively advanced stage in this progression, insofar as the optative of wish is by far the most common use, accounting for approximately four-fifths of the total number of optatives. As Evans shows, however, caution is required in interpreting this statistic. Because the Hebrew verbal system does not employ non-indicative moods in as wide a range of uses as Greek, the only Hebrew construction that naturally lent itself to translation with a Greek optative was the jussive. Moreover, the potential optative, though relatively infrequent, still shows enough flexibility in its Septuagintal use to be considered a living part of the literary language. That the optative of wish is much more common than the potential optative is thus likelier to result from Semitic interference than from the gradual decline of the optative in *Koine*. It must also be noted, however, that the Pentateuch, at least, has no examples of the optative in subordinate clauses apart from in a curious set of comparative clauses introduced by (ὡς) εἰ. In this case, it is reasonable to posit that the early decline of this use of the optative explains its rarity in Septuagintal Greek.

Along these same lines, we may consider the dative case, which, in this period, was beginning to lose ground to various prepositional usages (Horrocks 1997a: 57–9; see also ch. 16). While the Septuagint often does maintain the old preposition-less dative, there are also many instances where a prepositional construction, such as ἐν + dative or ἐπί + accusative is used instead. Here too, however, one must be wary of underestimating the extent to which the choice of dative or preposition in the Greek was motivated by the Hebrew original. In the passage that Horrocks uses to illustrate this phenomenon (2 Kings 18:17–21), the following constructions potentially show prepositions used where one might earlier have expected the dative on its own: with εἶπον "said" and βοάω "shout," πρός + acc. (v. 18, v. 19 (2×)); with πέποιθα "trust in," ἐπί + acc. (v. 21 (3×)); with στηρίζομαι "lean on," ἐπί + accusative (v. 21); with ἀθετέω "deny, refuse assent," ἐν + dat. (v. 20); and a comitative dat. ἐν δυνάμει βαρείᾳ "with a strong force" (v. 17). In every one of these constructions, the Greek preposition matches the one used in the Hebrew: the three examples of πρός correspond to 'el "to," the four examples of ἐπί all translate 'al "upon," and both examples of ἐν render bə "in." Furthermore, the translator did find use for the dative on its own in three places. Twice, in verse 21, it translates *lə* "to, for" (once with πέποιθα, once in the phrase οὕτως. . . πᾶσιν "thus he is to all"); the final dative, τίνι πεποιθώς "trusting in whom" is particularly striking because it is the sole example in this passage where the dative or prepositional construction fails to match the Hebrew, for the dative translates *'al* (elsewhere here rendered by ἐπί) rather than *lə*. In other words, the one time that the translator has departed from the Hebrew construction, it is in the direction of *favoring* the dative. This particular example may be the exception that proves the rule, as it is certainly true that the general decline of the dative should have encouraged its replacement or reinforcement by prepositions in the Septuagint. Still, the unusually close correspondence between the particular replacement for the dative employed by the translator and the construction found in the original text means that we cannot fully evaluate the use of prepositions in the Septuagint without reference to the Hebrew.

In the end, perhaps we should not be surprised that the Septuagint does not offer particularly explicit evidence of diachronic development in Greek: if most of it was indeed translated in the third century BCE – and the features Evans examines in the Pentateuch are "consistent with the consensus view of a date of *c*. 280–250 BCE" (2001: 263) – there simply had not been that much time since the Classical period for changes to take place in the language. But there will be more evidence for such diachronic development once we allow another three hundred years to pass and turn to the New Testament.

A Semitic Interlude

Before moving on to the Greek of the New Testament, however, a few words about the Semitic languages are in order. As far as the Septuagint is concerned, it is Hebrew that is the chief source of potential Semitisms. But the question becomes more complicated when we turn to the New Testament, for another Semitic language comes into play: Aramaic. Aramaic and Hebrew are closely related to each other. First, they are both placed in the Northwest Semitic branch of the Semitic language family tree on the basis of shared linguistic innovations, such as the change of Proto-Semitic **w-* to *y-* (Heb. *yeleḏ*, Aram. *yald-ā* "child," but Akk. *walādum* "give birth to"). Second, there are historical reasons for considering the two languages in conjunction with each other. While Hebrew had been the primary spoken language of Israel and Judah up to the time of the Babylonian Captivity, after the sixth century BCE it was gradually confined to use as a learned religious language, and Aramaic, the *lingua franca* and chancellery language of the Persian Empire, replaced it as the spoken vernacular. Indeed, a couple of the books of the Old Testament that were written last include lengthy passages in Aramaic, notably Ezra 4:8–6:18 and 7:2–26 (fifth–fourth century BCE) and Daniel 2:4b–7:28 (mid-second century BCE). Hebrew continued to co-exist with Aramaic, as is shown for example by the presence of both languages in the Dead Sea scrolls, but the exact sociolinguistic relationship between the two languages in the first century CE – the main period of interest for those examining the language of the New Testament – remains uncertain. Still, it is generally accepted that Aramaic (not Hebrew or Greek) was the language in which Jesus is most likely to have taught.

But even though Hebrew and Aramaic are closely related languages, there are still differences between them, and these provide a foothold that occasionally enables us to determine whether a particular Semitism in the New Testament is more probably a Hebraism or an Aramaism. First, the treatment of the Proto-Semitic interdental fricatives shows that Aramaic, though very similar to Hebrew, still belongs to a separate branch: Proto-Semitic *ḏ, for instance, becomes z in Hebrew, but d in Aramaic (Heb. zāhāb : Aram. dəhab, both "gold"). More important, however, for teasing apart Hebraisms and Aramaisms in the New Testament are a number of morphological and syntactic differences. The waw conversive, so typical of Hebrew, is not a feature of Aramaic, which is generally much happier to allow asyndeton: see table 18.1 for the contrasting figures for the Hebrew and Aramaic sections of the book of Daniel. Aramaic also uses the participle, which serves as a historical present, to a greater extent than Hebrew. Finally, the Aramaic treatment of the definite article is different. Whereas Hebrew has a prefixed article (*haz-zāhāb* "the gold"), Aramaic has a suffixed article (*dahb-ā* "id."). Furthermore, the Aramaic article gradually underwent semantic bleaching, and, by the time of Late Aramaic dialects like Syriac, the form of the noun with the article had become the unmarked form of the noun (the so-called emphatic), thus creating the need for other strategies – notably proleptic pronouns, discussed below – to mark definiteness.

One final topic that deserves mention is the nature of the sources that can be used as evidence for the Aramaic of the first two centuries CE. There is, as it happens, a rather unfortunate gap in the attestation of Aramaic. A relatively abundant amount of Aramaic survives from its use as a *lingua franca* in the Persian Empire, and the texts written in Late Aramaic (*c.* 200–700 CE), including both the Aramaic of the Jewish targums (translations) of the Old Testament and Syriac, the dialect associated with Christian writers in and around Edessa, are even more extensive. But until the discovery of the Dead Sea scrolls from Qumran, there was little that could be dated to the intervening period of Middle Aramaic. Accordingly, much of the scholarship on Aramaisms in the New Testament has revolved around the extent to which it is permissible to use the Aramaic of better-attested periods to assess the validity of a putative Aramaic construction thought to underlie a curiosity in the Greek of the New Testament. Paradoxically, as our knowledge of the Aramaic of the appropriate period has grown, this question has somewhat receded in importance: the dissemination of an increasing number of Middle Aramaic texts has shown that many constructions previously known only from other periods of Aramaic are in fact attested in New Testament times as well (Casey 1998: 35–6).

The Language of the New Testament

As Aramaic is the language in which Jesus is most likely to have taught, it would be surprising if it had not left some imprint on the Greek of the New Testament. Nevertheless, some features characteristic of New Testament Greek once attributed to the influence of the Semitic languages have been shown to represent nothing other than the natural evolution of *Koine* Greek. In the following section, we will examine some of these features, first looking at the evidence that suggests that they are due to contact with Semitic languages, then turning to the papyri used to support the alternative position.

We may begin with one clear sign of Semitic influence on the language of the New Testament, namely the occasional quotation of untranslated Aramaic words:

(6)   καὶ ἔλεγεν· Ἀββα ὁ πατήρ

And he said: Abba, Father. (Mark 14:36)

Aram. *abbā* "father"

(7)   καὶ κρατήσας τῆς χειρὸς τοῦ παιδίου λέγει αὐτῇ· Ταλιθα κουμ, ὅ ἐστιν
μεθερμηνευόμενον· Τὸ κοράσιον, σοὶ λέγω, ἔγειρε.

And he took hold of the child's hand and said to her: "Talitha qum," which, translated, is: "Child, I say to you, get up." (Mark 5:41)

Aram. *ṭəlīṯā* [emphatic state] "girl," *qûm* "arise"

The exact reason for such switches into Aramaic is uncertain, but it is likely that several motivations must have been in play. Turner proposed that Jesus was quoted in Aramaic whenever he was speaking to people who did not know Greek, but Casey (1998: 64) rightly criticizes this explanation as incompatible with extract (6): it seems safe to assume that God the Father could get by well enough in whatever language he chose. What does stand out about these passages, however, is that they occur more in Mark than in Matthew or Luke, suggesting, in line with the standard view that Mark pre-dates the other two synoptic gospels, that Aramaic quotations were gradually edited out of the text.

More valuable, however, for assessing the various influences on New Testament language are those features that, in addition to being more pervasive, are integrated into the text at a more structural level. We will consider three in turn: parataxis and asyndeton, pronouns, and subordinating conjunctions.

a)   Paralleling our look at Septuagintal language, we turn first to questions of coordination: both *parataxis* and, comparatively more prominent in the New Testament, *asyndeton*. Certainly, the καὶ ἐγένετο construction that is so typical of the Septuagint is also found in the New Testament, although it is not evenly distributed: seven times in Matthew, seven times in Mark, 28 times in Luke, and six times in Acts, but never in John. When it occurs in the New Testament, it generally looks very similar to the Septuagintal construction. With example (2) above, compare the following:

(8)   καὶ ἐγένετο ἐν τῷ εἶναι αὐτὸν ἐν μιᾷ τῶν πόλεων καὶ ἰδοὺ ἀνὴρ πλήρης λέπρας

And it happened in his being in one of the cities and, behold, a man full of leprosy. (Luke 5:12)

Table 18.1 Contrastive figures for asyndeton in Hebrew and Aramaic sections of Daniel and in the New Testament

Text	Sentences starting with connective particle	Sentences starting with asyndeton
Daniel 1:1–2:4a (Hebrew as original language)	22	1 (the opening verse)
Matthew 3	13	0
Mark 1	36	2
Luke 8	58	2
Daniel 2:5–49 (Aramaic as original language)	22	22
John 1	28	34

Once again, rather than a subordinate temporal clause, we find καὶ ἐγένετο followed by the preposition ἐν governing an articular infinitive. Also Septuagintal is the use of καὶ ἰδού introducing a nominal main clause: this construction stems from the frequent use of *hinnēh* "behold" at the start of such clauses in Biblical Hebrew (Waltke and O'Connor 1990: §40.2.1; but see also the remarks on ἰδού in ch. 17).

But, as has already been noted, such parataxis with καί is more typical of Hebrew than it is of Aramaic. The Hebrew sections of Daniel nearly invariably have a connective particle while those in Aramaic use asyndeton and connective particles in roughly equal measure. As foreshadowed by the frequency counts for καὶ ἐγένετο given above, the synoptic gospels line up with Hebrew practice in almost always using a connective particle, while John mirrors the relatively high frequency of asyndeton found in Aramaic (Burney 1922: 49–52; see also table 18.1).

While the figures given here throw all three synoptics into sharp contrast with John, on the whole Mark appears to have had more asyndeton than the other two, which again might reflect the position that that gospel is closer to an Aramaic original than Matthew and Luke are (Black 1967: 55–61) – though Maloney, it should be noted, argues that Mark's asyndeton is not an Aramaism, but rather straightforward Hellenistic Greek (1981: 77–81). Finally, Luke's particular fondness for καὶ ἐγένετο may be connected to the generally Septuagintalizing style of passages like the hymns in the birth narrative (ibid. 151–6).

b) A second feature of the language of the New Testament to show possible Semitic influence is once again, as in the Septuagint, an increased use of third-person *pronouns*. This may take several forms. First, we have already seen that the postposed Aramaic article gradually lost its force as an article; new strategies were thus necessary for marking definiteness, among them the use of a proleptic third-person pronoun, originally a demonstrative, but later weakened to an article. The sort of construction seen in Biblical Aramaic in the first extract below would then be the ultimate source of the anomalous use of αὐτῇ in the second (Black 1967: 96–100, 108–12):

(10)　*bēh-zimnā* (Daniel 3:7, 8, etc.)

　　　in.it-the.time → at that time.

(11)　ἐν αὐτῇ δὲ τῇ οἰκίᾳ μένετε ἐσθίοντες καὶ πίνοντες τὰ παρ' αὐτῶν.

　　　But stay in that house [not: in the house itself], eating and drinking what is given by them. (Luke 10:7)

Second, Aramaic also appears to have used a proleptic pronoun with the discourse-cohesive function of marking the topic of a clause. Thus, an Aramaic clause like the first item in the following pair could have led to the peculiar Greek of the second (but cf. Maloney 1981: 113–16):

(12)　*hû*　　　*ṣalmā*　　　*rēš-ēh*　　　　　*dî-dhab*　　　*ṭob*

　　　it　　　the.statue　　head-its　　　　　of-gold　　　good

　　　The statue, its head was made of pure gold (Daniel 2:32)

(13)　αὐτὸς δὲ ὁ Ἰωάννης εἶχεν τὸ ἔνδυμα αὐτοῦ ἀπὸ τριχῶν καμήλου

　　　And this (aforementioned) John had his garment made from camel hair. (Matthew 3:4)

Finally, Aramaic uses the preposition *lə* "to, for," together with a suffixed pronoun, in an indirect reflexive construction roughly equivalent to the Greek middle. This is particularly common with verbs of motion, such that a construction like that of the first item below could have given rise to that of the second (Black 1967: 101–4):

(14)　*'zlt*　　*ly* (*Aḥiqar* 22 (Cowley 1923: 212, 228))

　　　I.went　for.me → I betook myself, I went away

(15)　ἀπῆλθεν πρὸς ἑαυτὸν θαυμάζων τὸ γεγονός

　　　He went off to himself (?), marveling at what had happened. (Luke 24:12)

The last three Greek passages thus exemplify three of the environments in which the writers of the New Testament used pronouns where a strict Atticist would have avoided them; however, as we shall see below, such pronominal use is by no means certain to be a Semitism.

　　c)　A third class of New Testament syntactic oddities often ascribed to Aramaic influence lies in the confusion of various *subordinating conjunctions*. This state of affairs would result from the multifunctionality of the Aramaic particle *də* (< earlier *dî*), a word polyvalent enough to make Greek ὡς look quite straightforward by comparison. For *də* not only overlaps with ὡς as a causal and temporal conjunction and as a marker of indirect statement, but also shares with ἵνα and ὥστε the function of introducing purpose and result clauses, with ὅς that of the relative pronoun, and, last but not least, stands in as a marker of possession, virtually equivalent to the genitive case. This last function can be connected to the same shift in nominal morphology that led to increased pronominal use in Aramaic. At an earlier date, Aramaic, like Hebrew, could mark the possessive relationship by putting the head noun in the so-called construct state, leaving the dependent noun unmarked. But the increased use of the suffixed article across the board gradually obscured this distinction, apart from in a few lexicalized phrases, thus creating the need for an alternative genitive marker. At any rate, the fact that this particle had these manifold uses means both that there was opportunity for mistranslation (or at least a skewed translation) when *də* in an existing Aramaic text was turned into Greek and that a native Aramaic speaker composing in Greek might not have always hit upon the correct Greek usage in constructions belonging to this general sphere.

In particular, there appears to have been a movement, especially in the Gospel of John, toward increased use of ἵνα as a catch-all conjunction (Burney 1922: 69–76; Black 1967: 76–8). Now the rise of ἵνα is certainly not restricted to *Koine* that is subject to Aramaic influence: one need only point to the replacement of the Classical Greek infinitive by the Modern Greek construction with να (see chs 36 and 37) to show the general trend. But the overwhelming prevalence of ἵνα in John requires special explanation (127 times, as opposed to 33 times in Matthew, 60 in Mark, and 40 in Luke, according to Burney's count). Interference from Aramaic might well be responsible. Consider the following passage, where Black argues that confusion of ὅς and ἵνα by an Aramaic speaker who did not understand the difference between the functions of *də* as a marker of relative and purpose clauses could have led to the use of ἵνα where one expects the relative:

(16)   κἀγὼ ἐρωτήσω τὸν πατέρα καὶ ἄλλον παράκλητον δώσει ὑμῖν, ἵνα μεθ᾽ ὑμῶν εἰς τὸν αἰῶνα ᾖ.

And I will ask my father and he will give another intercessor to you so that he might be with you for ever. (John 14:16)

. . . *ut maneat uobiscum in aeternum* (Vulgate)

. . . *qui uobiscum sit in aeternum* (Vetus Latina, Codex Monacensis, *q*; for the Old Latin of John, see now http://www.iohannes.com)

In this passage, one manuscript of the Vetus Latina even offers textual support for the position that the Greek ought to have a relative pronoun instead of ἵνα. We may reasonably surmise that the anomalous use of ἵνα in similar passages was at least sometimes due to interference from Aramaic, even in the absence of any textual smoking guns.

Still, one can go too far in this direction and start to see Semitisms as the explanation for every last curiosity in New Testament syntax. For the New Testament is very different from the Septuagint: it is not a wholesale translation of a Semitic-language text (although it is likely that Aramaic sources lie behind parts of it), and it was written about three hundred years later. There is thus much more prima facie reason to attribute divergences from Attic to diachronic development rather than to Semitic interference. This certainly seems true at the morphological level: the near complete loss of the optative (only the optative of wish is found, except in the more literary Luke and Acts), the substitution of first for second aorist forms (e.g., ἔπεσαν for ἔπεσον in Matthew 17:6 and elsewhere), and the increase of -ω verbs at the expense of -μι verbs (e.g., ἱστάνω and στήκω for ἵσταμαι and ἕστηκα) are all features that reflect the regular development of *Koine*, as was shown in chapter 16. But the same may also be true of potential Semitisms as well. The scholar most associated with this position is Adolf Deissmann, whose chief breakthrough was to note that features, especially at the lexical level, that had previously been thought peculiar to Biblical Greek in fact had parallels in Hellenistic papyri not connected with the Judeo-Christian tradition. His *Bibelstudien* (1895), for instance, contains numerous examples from papyri illustrating the non-biblical use of supposedly Christian words, arranged alphabetically from ἀγάπη "(Christian?) love" to ὁ υἱὸς τοῦ θεοῦ "the son of God" (1895: 80–170). Albert Thumb did similar work on syntax (1901). Consider, for example, the frequent use of αὐτόν as a third-person pronoun discussed above. This is in fact paralleled in the papyri (see ch. 17):

(17)   κατατρέχω αὐτὴν λέγων οὐ μὴ ἀφῶ αὐτὴν φυγῖν. καταλαμβάνω αὐτὴν καὶ ἐμβάλλω
        αὐτήν

        I run after her saying I will *not* let her run away. I catch her and hit her. (*P.Par.*
        50.17; example from Maloney 1981: 112)

Moreover, the fact that this use of αὐτόν, after aphaeresis of the initial syllable, developed into the Modern Greek enclitic third-person pronoun τον further suggests that its appearance in Christian texts is due to the internal development of Greek rather than external interference from Semitic (Horrocks 1997a: 208). The situation is similar with paratactic καί. If such parataxis is common in many different sorts of low-register texts in many different linguistic traditions (Trenkner 1960), then why shouldn't we attribute its presence in the New Testament not to Semitic influence but to the simple fact that this collection of texts is the product of writers of little education who couldn't be expected to compose elaborate Atticizing periods replete with hypotaxis?

There remain two objections, however, to considering all linguistic features found both in the papyri and in the New Testament to be simple *Koine*. First, there is the nature of the papyri themselves. They do not represent *Koine tout court*, but merely the *Koine* of Egypt, and so they too may have been subject to linguistic interference, though in this case from Egyptian rather than Semitic (see ch. 17). As Vergote points out, however, Egyptian behaves rather like the Semitic languages in many of the syntactic features under consideration (1938: 1353–60): for example, it is more prone to use third-person pronouns than Attic is. Thus, a papyrus like that given in the above example should perhaps not be used as evidence for the frequent use of third-person pronouns in "garden-variety" *Koine* (Maloney 1981: 112–13). This can be taken too far, of course: as already mentioned, the later Greek development gives us good reason to think that this high level of pronoun use would have been common to most, if not all, forms of *Koine*. But the fact remains that we must be wary of assuming that the papyri are free from non-Greek influence – warier, at any rate, than Deissmann was when, as Burney pointed out (1922: 5), he cited as an example of paratactic καί in non-Semitic *Koine* a papyrus letter that contains the word μαγδωλοφύλαξ "tower guard" (< Heb. *miḡdāl* "tower").

A second problem with too strong an adherence to the Deissmannite position concerns the distribution of the features in question. Some of them may well occur in plain *Koine*, but are they as frequent in such documents as they are in the New Testament? And, when they do occur, is the general shape of the construction the same in terms of word order, tense usage, and so forth? In other words, it is not enough simply to find individual examples of paratactic καί in low-register papyri: one also has to show both that it is as common a construction there as in the New Testament and that the overall feel is the same. Trenkner, for instance, in asserting that "style καί" was too widespread a phenomenon to be associated too closely with Semitic influence, adduces such examples as the following (1960: 17; cf. example (28) in ch. 11):

(18) ἔξω δ' αὐτῆς οὖσ' ὑπὸ τοῦ κακοῦ καὶ τοῦ πράγματος ἡ γυνή, ἀναπηδήσασα προσπίπτει πρὸς τὰ γόνατα τῷ Ἰατροκλεῖ, **καὶ** τὴν τράπεζαν ἀνατρέπει. **καὶ** εἰ μὴ 'κεῖνος ἀφείλετο, ἀπώλετ' ἂν παροινουμένη ... **καὶ** περὶ ταύτης τῆς ἀνθρώπου καὶ ἐν Ἀρκαδίᾳ λόγος ἦν ἐν τοῖς μυρίοις.

And, as she was driven insane by this awful treatment, she leapt up and fell at the knees of Iatrocles, and she overturned the table. And if he hadn't taken her away, she would have perished in a drunken frenzy ... and even in Arcadia there was talk of this woman among the Ten Thousand. (Dem. 19.198)

But this repeated use of καί is clearly something very different from what we saw in the examples from the Septuagint and New Testament: in those examples, there is less subordination, and καί is followed directly by the verb (or ἰδού), both traits that align those passages more closely with Hebrew models.

In the end, the truth, as so often, is likely to lie somewhere in the middle. Indeed, the general consensus seems to be that the pendulum, having swung in the Deissmannite direction in the early twentieth century, has returned to more neutral ground now (Voelz 1984: 952; Janse 2007: 647). The language of the Septuagint and the New Testament does not represent a special dialect of Jewish-Christian Greek altogether cut off from the regular development of *Koine*, nor is it completely free from Semitic influence. Instead, as one would expect of writings produced in Hellenistic Alexandria and Roman Palestine, it reflects both the broader evolution of the Greek language as a whole and the more specific influence of the Semitic milieu in which it arose.

FURTHER READING

As space has permitted discussion of only a small number of illustrative problems – and texts other than the Septuagint and New Testament have been passed over altogether – readers are advised not to neglect the many other recent accounts of Jewish and Christian Greek. Summaries with different emphases from the present chapter include: De Lange 2007, covering Jewish Greek and including reference to texts other than the Septuagint as well as discussion of distinctively Jewish uses of individual words like προσευχή; Drettas 2007 on the translation of the Septuagint; and Janse 2007, which discusses New Testament Greek, including convenient lists of lexical items particularly characteristic of Christian Greek. A more thorough account, focusing on New Testament Greek and the many responses to Deissmann's work over the course of the twentieth century, may be found in Voelz 1984. Though older, Vergote 1938 still offers a good picture of the earliest scholarly reaction to Deissmann; he also examines the potential for interference from Egyptian on Jewish and Christian Greek. Despite its somewhat parochial title, Maloney 1981 also provides a very convenient overview of many of the issues discussed here.

For the Septuagint in particular, Fernández Marcos 2001 is a useful introduction with rich bibliography; it also covers the other Greek translations of the Hebrew Bible. For the many variations in the legend of the 72 (or 70) translators, see Wasserstein and Wasserstein 2006. Evans 2001 shows how much can be accomplished by close linguistic study of verbal syntax in the Pentateuch, while Janse 2002 looks at the Septuagintal use of resumptive pronouns in relative clauses, causative verbs, and the position of clitic pronouns (contrasting the conscious influence of Hebrew in the Septuagint with the unconscious influence of Turkish in Cappadocian Greek).

For Semitic influence on New Testament syntax, Beyer 1968 is a central study. Wilcox 1984 looks at New Testament Semitisms more generally. Fitzmyer 1979 is a helpful collection of essays on topics such as the languages of Palestine in the first century CE and the chronological phases of Aramaic. Chancey 2005 argues that Greek was spoken less in first-century Galilee than previously thought (making Aramaic influence on the New Testament all the more likely), although it should be emphasized that there is very little evidence we can use to determine the relative sociolinguistic positions of the two languages. Important works seeking to reconstruct the Aramaic sayings thought to underlie some of the Greek of the New Testament include the classic Black 1967 and, more recently, Casey 1998 and 2002.

CHAPTER NINETEEN

Greek and Latin Bilingualism

Bruno Rochette

Introduction

Greco-Roman bilingualism is without doubt one of the clearest manifestations of the close cultural ties between Greece and Rome. The scope of this phenomenon, extending to numerous aspects of the ancient world, including diplomacy, literature, law, medicine, religion, administration, the military, commerce, and philosophy, reveals it as one of the principal foundations on which Greco-Roman cultural unity is based. This importance fully justifies the interest it has evoked in the linguistic, literary, and cultural sectors of classical scholarship. Whereas Greco-Roman bilingualism was until the 1930s chiefly used to illustrate the symbiosis of two languages and two cultures in the Greco-Roman world (e.g., Boyancé 1956; Marrou 1965: 374–88), since the 1980s new perspectives have been opened up that have benefited from work in general linguistics, in particular the pioneering study of Weinreich (1953). The most recent developments in the study of Greco-Roman bilingualism are concerned with notions such as language contact (Dubuisson 1992b), linguistic interference (Biville 2001–3), *diglossia* (Adams 2003: 754–5), code-switching (Wenskus 1998), mixed language (Leiwo 1995), and language choice (Adams 2003: 35–6). Moreover, research in these areas has turned from quantitative to being qualitative in nature, in differentiating situations of bilingualism according to type of context. And advances in sociolinguistics have brought questions to the fore such as "Who speaks what language to whom and when?" In this respect the study of Kaimio (1979) and the work of Dubuisson (1992a) are typical of the shift in focus from the words spoken to their speakers in their actual contexts (see also Valette-Cagnac 2003: 149–51), with constant attention being paid to such parameters as the concrete speech situation, the speakers' linguistic competence, their motivations, their sociocultural level, and their attitude toward foreign elements (see also the overview in Dickey 2003a).

Bilingualism in Classical Greece

The evidence on bilingualism in the world of Archaic and Classical Greece is scant. Before the fifth century BCE there is little to go by. The Homeric poems make only sporadic and largely inconclusive mention of linguistic diversity (e.g., *Il.* 2.867; 4.438; *Od.* 19.175; see Werner 1989). It is not until the fifth century that authors show awareness of the existence of linguistic diversity and of an opposition between foreign languages and Greek as one of the key elements of Greek identity (e.g., Hdt. 8.144; on non-Greek languages in Herodotus, see Munson 2005). At *Politicus* 262d Plato takes issue with a classification that divides humanity into two parts, τὸ Ἑλληνικόν, the Greeks, on the one hand, and on the other all the other peoples that are referred to with a single name, "barbarians," even though they do not all speak the same language (ἀσύμφωνοι). The languages of the barbarians lack a recognized status and are compared to the chirping of birds (Soph. *Trach.* 1060). Only Greek is considered to be a real language (Strab. 14.2.28). In the comedies of Aristophanes, the Persian Pseudartabas and the barbarian Triballus utter unintelligible sounds that are opposed to Greek. Such a lack of linguistic curiosity is not necessarily sheer ignorance, for Ar. *Ach.* 100 is authentic Persian. In such a context it is normal for polyglots to be looked upon as exceptions (Werner 1983). The adjective πολύγλωσσος in the sense of "speaking various languages" is rare (Rotolo 1972: 409 n. 52; Dubuisson 1983: 214–15). We know of some δίγλωσσοι, persons who know Greek and a barbarian language, either a Greek who can speak a foreign language, like Themistocles, who had learned Persian in a year, or a barbarian who knows Greek (Dubuisson 1983: 206–13; Rochette 2001). The Greek world remains monoglot at least until the Hellenistic period. Great Greek travelers such as Herodotus and Hecataeus do not feel the need to learn the languages of the peoples they visit, since they are convinced that Greek is universally understood and that they will always find people who are capable of translating the texts in which they are interested. We know from Herodotus (2.154) that Pharaoh Psammetichos I had entrusted Ionian colonists with Egyptian infants, in order to produce bilingual speakers who would become interpreters.

The Encounter of the Greek World with Rome

Flexible linguistic policies

The conquests of Alexander the Great had the effect of imposing Greek as the *Weltsprache* of the entire Macedonian Empire, thus supplanting Aramaic, the *lingua franca* of the Persian Empire (Zgusta 1980: 137). After the completion of his campaigns Alexander intended, according to Plutarch (*Alex.* 47.6), to unify his empire by establishing Greek as the sole administrative language of his provinces. After the king's death, Greek became in fact the language used in the various kingdoms resulting from the division of the vast empire.

In the west, meanwhile, the rise of Roman power did not come at the expense of philhellenism: *Graecia capta ferum uictorem cepit et artes | intulit agresti Latio* "Greece, conquered, has conquered its wild victor and has imported the arts into rural Latium" (Hor. *Epist.* 2.1.156–7). The process of hellenization of Rome begins with the Punic Wars (Gruen 1992: 223–71). Greek becomes the language of choice of the educated class in Rome. The reading of Greek literary works spread among the elite due to the arrival in Rome of libraries taken as booty (such as that of Perseus, king of Macedon, brought to Rome by Emilius Paulus in 167 BCE). The Romans were accordingly aware of the prestige of Greek as an international language: *Graeca leguntur in omnibus fere gentibus, Latina suis finibus, exiguis sane, continentur* "Greek texts are read by virtually all peoples, Latin texts are contained within their own restricted boundaries" (Cic. *Arch.* 23). Military exchanges between Italy and the Greek world as well as trade were also favorable to the diffusion of the two languages. From the second century BCE onward, *negotiatores* criss-cross the eastern Mediterranean and leave numerous epigraphical documents as traces of their passage. The epigraphical record at Delos shows that this island had become a meeting-place for merchants from Latium or Campania, who sometimes have been buried there (Adams 2002: 103–27; 2003: 642–86).

But increasing levels of bilingualism did not prevent the Romans from being aware of the prestige of their own language. Cato, even though he was capable of expressing himself in Greek, used Latin even when he was addressing native Greek audiences, such as the Athenians in 191 BCE.[1] In fact, it was customary for Roman magistrates to respond only in Latin to foreign ambassadors, whether in the Senate or abroad (Val. Max. 2.2.2: *magna cum perseuerantia custodiebant, ne Graecis umquam nisi Latine responsa darent . . . non in urbe tantum nostra, sed etiam in Graecia et Asia* "They took care with the greatest perseverance never to respond to the Greeks in any language but Latin, . . . not merely in our own city, but also in Greece and in Asia"). In spite of being bilingual the Roman magistrates attached much importance to the use of Latin for diplomatic discourse in order to underscore the *maiestas* of the Roman people (Gruen 1992: 236 n. 61). In the Senate the use of Latin was mandatory for the same reasons (ibid. 238 n. 69). Interpreters would translate resolutions in Latin, whether in Rome (so C. Acilius during the embassy of the three philosophers of 155 BCE) or in the Greek world.[2] Augustus, whose knowledge of Greek was insufficient to speak the language fluently (*expedite*, Suet. *Aug.* 89; cf. Dubuisson 2002) and Tiberius, a perfectly bilingual speaker, make efforts in the same sense to promote pure Latinity as unifying cement for the Empire (Suet. *Tib.* 71). According to Kaimio (1979: 96), Valerius Maximus' statement cited above could be explained as a wish to support the policy of Tiberius in favor of Latin.

Still, it was not Roman policy to impose by force the use of Latin on Greek-speaking provinces (Rochette 1997). Bilingualism functioned in a flexible and practical way, Roman policy being well adapted to the circumstances (Dubuisson 1982). Proof of this is provided by the formal request addressed by the citizens of Cumae to the Roman Senate in 180 BCE: *Cumanis eo anno petentibus permissum est, ut publice Latine loquerentur et praeconibus Latine uendendi ius esset* "That year it was granted to the Cumaeans, at their request, to use Latin for their civic discourse and for the merchants to use it in their transactions" (Livy 40.42.13). Cumae wished to obtain authorization to replace Oscan with Latin in their public discourse, in particular in their auctions. This example shows that the inhabitants of regions subjected to Roman power were not obliged to use Latin, even though they frequently wished to do so. The Romans did not have a rigid linguistic policy (Dubuisson 1982).

Promotion of Latin

In the Republican period the primacy of Greek gave rise to an anti-hellenic movement led by Cato the Elder, who was the first to write a Roman history in Latin, the *Origines*. Varro, pupil of the very conservative L. Aelius Stilo, can be placed within this same movement. Author of *De Lingua Latina*, he contributed to the autonomy of Latin toward which the Romans had been striving since the conquests of the second century and the definitive victory over Greece. He was not ignorant of the debt of Latin to Greek (*Ling.* 9.31) and is the author of an entire treatise on the Aeolian origins of Latin (Collart 1954: 205–28). But he maintains that certain words in Latin do not derive from any other language (*Ling.* 5.3). At the level of literary registers, Cicero took great pains to show that the Latin language is equally well, if not better, suited for the articulation of philosophical concepts, parting company with Lucretius on the subject of the *egestas patrii sermonis* "poverty of the language of the fathers" (e.g., Lucr. 1.139, 832; 3.260; see Fögen 2000: 77–141). In opposition to this formula, he tried to promote the language of Latium by using it for his philosophical treatises, thus endowing Rome with a corpus of literary works in its national language (Cic. *Fin.* 1.10). In creating numerous neologisms according to various mechanisms (Nicolas 2005), he made a monumental contribution to the enrichment of the Latin language.

The ambiguous status of Greek

In spite of its favorable position in the Roman Republic, the Greek language has always had an ambiguous status in Rome, being at the same time a foreign language and an integral part of Roman society (Dubuisson 1981a: 27–8 n. 6). Greek is both internal and external to Roman society. The ambiguous relation of Augustus with Greek as described by Suetonius (*Aug.* 89) is enlightening in this respect. According to the biographer, Augustus was greatly drawn toward Greek studies (*Graecae disciplinae*) and he excelled in them, having as rhetoric teacher Apollodorus of Pergamon. Nevertheless, he never learned to speak Greek fluently and he refrained from writing in that language (*aut loqueretur expedite aut componere aliquid auderet*). He wrote his text in Latin and had it translated (*Latine formabat uertendumque alii dabat*).

Bilingualism was strongly favored in education and is most apparent at the level of the individual.[3] Many educated Romans boasted excellent knowledge of Greek to the point of speaking it as a second maternal language. Cicero (Cic. *De or.* 2.1.2) says of Crassus that he spoke Greek as if he did not know any other language. According to Cornelius Nepos (Nep. *Att.* 4.1), Atticus spoke Greek so well that one could have believed he was a native Athenian. Still, Greek was not universally used and known in

Rome (Quint. *Inst.* 12.10.57). Even Cicero could make mistakes (Holford-Strevens 1993: 209). Romans who knew Greek did not all understand the language in the same way: an educated aristocrat knew a homogeneous and codified Greek, whereas members of inferior classes would speak the Hellenistic *Koine*. Cicero himself did not have a uniform attitude toward Greek.

Did Romans use Greek in daily conversation with each other? There are few sources that allow us to form a precise idea on this subject (Kaimio 1979: 193). What is certain is that Greek was widely used for the composition of works on archeological, historical, and philosophical subjects (Henriksson 1956). Cicero had projected a Greek *hypomnêma* on his consulate (*Att.* 1.19.10; 2.1.2; Lendle 1967). His remarks in the letter to Atticus of 60 BCE (*Att.* 1.19.10) show that there existed a "Roman" variety of Greek, a Greek that allowed Romans to stay Roman. Cicero asks his friend, who speaks Greek like a native Athenian, to be indulgent if he finds un-Greek turns of phrase or a less elegant style (*quod homini Attico minus Graecum eruditumque uideatur*). According to Cicero, Lucullus deliberately committed solecisms and barbarisms in order to sound Roman.

Bilingualism is thus closely linked with identity. The only bilingualism acceptable in Rome is the one that makes it possible to identify the speaker. This is why Romans who speak or write Greek never use the Greek of the Greeks, since they are eager to be different. The problem of identity is illustrated by an anecdote, reported by Cicero (*Fin.* 1.8–9), of Albucius being greeted in Greek in Athens by the praetor Scaevola, an apparently absurd gesture (Valette-Cagnac 2003: 170–9).

Latin is Greek

Greek and Latin are so closely linked in the linguistic consciousness of the Romans that they came to assume a total assimilation of Latin to Greek: Latin is a form of Greek. This is the thesis that has come to be formulated at Rome from the time of Sulla to the reign of Claudius: Latin is presented as a Greek dialect, Aeolic (Werner 1996). The grammarian Philoxenos of Alexandria, who is perhaps to be dated prior to Varro, wrote a dialectical treatise to this effect (Funaioli, *Gram. Rom. Frag.* I, p. XVI, 206–8; Collart 1954: 206–18). The cultural context underlying this theory is well understood. Annalists and early Roman historians who had prepared the framework within which the theory could develop (Gabba 1963) include Fabius Pictor, Hyperochos of Cumae, even Cato, who states that Evander upon his arrival in Latium made Greek and the Greek alphabet known to the barbarians of this region (*Origines* 1.19). Since Cato can hardly be credited with sympathy for the Greeks, such a statement is surely an echo of a *communis opinio* of the time (Gruen 1992: 235). Dionysius of Halicarnassus, who serves the cause of Augustus, takes up the theory in the first book of his *Roman Antiquities* (Dion. Hal. *Ant. Rom.* 1.90.1), insisting on its three dimensions, cultural, religious, and linguistic, with the object of proving the ethnic unity of Greeks and Romans. In his view the Romans speak a language that is neither completely barbarian nor completely Greek. Speculations of grammarians on the origins of the Latin language would lead linguists of the generation of Charisius (fourth cent. CE) and Priscian (*c.* 500 CE) to emphasize, on the basis of parallels, the similarities between the two languages (Schöpsdau 1992). Macrobius (fourth cent. CE) would link the two languages so tightly as to confirm that the study of the one leads necessarily to the mastery of the other (Keil. *Gramm. Lat.* V.631).

Greek in Rome

Latin borrowing from the Greek

Rome is a bilingual city. The Greek epitaphs of the city, engraved by and for persons of foreign origin, slaves, freedmen, or immigrants from the East, but equally for Roman natives, reflect a cosmopolitan society and provide evidence for widespread bilingualism in the capital of the Empire (Kajanto 1963: 43–4). Greek was the first language of numerous slaves and immigrants. Kaimio (1979: 315) even speaks of a Greek pidgin. Greek has infiltrated in the linguistic habits of Rome's lower classes before it exerted influence on the higher echelons of society. The language of every-day speech in fact has undergone foreign influence from a very early date. Latin has borrowed not only Greek words, but also words from other Italic languages even when typically Latin words were available for the concepts in question. *Popina* "tavern" and *rufus* "red" are Latin borrowings from Oscan-Umbrian and Faliscan, whereas the Latin equivalents are *coquina* (<*quoquina) and *ruber* (Meillet 1977: 100–1). These words have been completely "naturalized" and become generalized along with their host language.

From the Greek, Latin has borrowed two categories of words (Biville 1990–5: 1: 31).

a) *Written and learned borrowings* drawing directly on Greek texts. These words keep their original form fairly conservatively and are thus "ageless" (Biville 1992: 232–3). *Aer* (ἀήρ, ἀέρος), for example, is a Greek word completely naturalized in Latin. The "welcoming" of a Greek word in Latin is expressed by Seneca (Sen. *Ep.* 120.4) with the evocative image of civil rights, *civitas*, a term adopted by the grammarians (*civitate donaverint*).

b) *Oral or "vulgar" borrowings* subject to various types of deformation in their progressive integration within the Latin language. These phonetic phenomena, studied by Biville (1990–5), depend on the period in which the borrowing takes place and loan words continue to be modified along with the host language. Greek βαπτίζω becomes *baptidio* in Christian authors, since the Greek sound [z], at first assimilated to Latin s(s), comes to be written as *di* by the third century CE (pronounced [dz], Biville 1990–5: 2: 417–18). When entering into the language a Greek word undergoes deformations that render it suitable for the phonetic structures into which it is inserted and which make it lose its foreign character, e.g., suppression of a phoneme: λέων > *leo*; inversion: ψυχή > *spyche*; addition: μνᾶ > *mina*. Such adaptations can be formulated as rules of phono-graphemic correspondence between the systems of Greek and Latin (Biville 1990–5; 1991: 51–2). Once it has adapted to the rules of the host language the borrowing is part of the language and undergoes the same phonetic developments as purely Latin words (Biville 1986: 852–4), e.g., πλατεία enters as *platea* (Plautus) and subsequently becomes **platya* from which derive It. *piazza* and Fr. *place*. Far from being closed, this system is productive. It generates a Greco-Roman language system of neologisms created by hybridization (e.g., *Romulidae, Anti-Catones*) as well as a purely Greek presence within the Latin language, a "Greek Latin" composed of neologisms of entirely Greek provenance, but created by Latin speakers for whom Greek is not the primary language (Biville 1993).

The degree of receptivity of Latin to external influences can be best measured in the imperial period, particularly in subliterary texts (Adams 2003). Yet in spite of all the linguistic and cultural influences Latin has not lost its identity nor its force (Verg. *Aen.* 12.834–9).

Code-Switching

Besides borrowing, a further language-contact phenomenon manifests itself from a very early date in Latin literature: code-switching, the switch from one language to another within one and the same discourse. As early as the *comoedia palliata* the transition from Latin to Greek is very frequent (Jocelyn 1999). In Plautus this process appears in various passages, particularly in the responses of slaves or other characters of the lower social strata (Jocelyn 1999: 184–9). For Plautus, who addresses an audience that is largely bilingual, the use of Greek is clearly a sign of the condition of slave (Shipp 1953). But in everyday life code-switching was a living reality too and is frequently attested for the second and first centuries BCE (Jocelyn 1999: 177–84).

The best-known case in literature is that of Cicero, who was, as we saw, fluent in Greek both in speech and in writing. In 70 BCE he addressed the senate of Syracuse in Greek (*Verr.* 2.4.147) and he communicated with various Greek correspondents (Plut. *Cic.* 24.8–9). Whereas his public speeches present a pure Latinity, as symbol of Rome's prestige, his letters abound with Greek words and expressions – up to 850. The switch from Latin to Greek in Cicero as well as in the writings of other members of the Roman elite has often been interpreted as a form of intimacy, or even of a "language of intimacy" (Pabón 1939), the maternal language of the Roman so to speak. According to some scholars, the language switch could be provoked by emotive and psychological contexts. Dubuisson attaches great importance to this aspect and extends it to the general use of Greek among the Roman upper class. Caesar's καὶ σὺ τέκνον would be due, according to him, to the fact that at the moment of his death he "refinds his mother tongue or at least his first language."[4] Pabón (1939: 129) sees proof that Greek was used as the language of the emotions in a passage in Juvenal's sixth Satire (184–99), where Greek is presented as women's language of sexuality. But that passage also points up a distinction between two linguistic spaces: the private sphere, where Greek is permitted, and the public sphere, where it was frowned upon. The use of either language is thus closely linked to the speech context. In private, the use of Greek signals culture and an element of recognition for an educated class. In public, in particular in the Senate, one abstains from speaking Greek, since Latin is the language of formal civic discourse. Similarly, to speak Greek in the countryside produces unusual effects, since Greek is associated with urban life (Plin. *Ep.* 7.25.2–5). The Greek language is endowed with qualities that make it the preferred language in certain contexts: smoothness (Quint. *Inst.* 12.10.27–8), charm, grace, and cheerfulness (Plin. *Ep.* 4.3; cf. Valette-Cagnac 2003: 164–6).

The switches from Latin to Greek in Cicero's letters cannot all be explained by the intimate character of the use of Greek in Rome. First, the Greek words we find in his letters are not all of the same status. Cicero uses many Greek medical terms in the absence of a fully developed medical vocabulary in Latin at the time. Code-switches also depend on the correspondent and the date of the letter in question. When he writes to politicians and dignitaries of the State, Cicero uses Latin without any code-switches, just as in letters to his wife and daughter, which are in general free of Greek (Wenskus 2001: 218–19). He reserves Greek for certain intimate friends, such as Atticus, who presents himself as more Greek than the Greeks themselves (Valette-Cagnac 2003). The use of Greek, language of "connivance," serves to create rapport with the addressee of the letter.

Chronology plays a role as well (Venini 1952). At certain points in his career Cicero makes a more extensive use of Greek than at others. During his exile (April 58 to September 57) he refuses any use of Greek words, but within a month of his return he resumes the habits of the past. In the letters of the year 56 we find 63 Greek words, but we can observe a total absence of Greek in the letters of the years 48 and 47, another period of political crisis. But in the years 45–44, when he is composing his philosophical treatises, Greek appears again. However, in February of 45 during the days following the death of his daughter Tullia which greatly affected him, Cicero avoids Greek. We can conclude from this that there is a psychological dimension in Cicero's code-switches. In periods of tension and anxiety he tends to avoid Greek, whereas when he is more relaxed, he uses it again. The use of Greek, then, is for him a conscious choice.

The Balance of the Two Languages in the Empire

Utraque lingua

Under the Empire the two languages coexist on a basis of complete equality, as is shown by the expression *utraque lingua* "in either language" (Dubuisson 1981a) or the formula used by the Emperor Claudius, *uterque sermo noster* "either of our two ways of speaking" (Suet. *Claud.* 42.1). Whereas the adjective *bilinguis* never means "bilingual" (Poccetti 1986), *utraque lingua* underlines the close connection between the two languages, since it sets Greek and Latin together apart from all other languages, thus signaling the unity, parity, and complementarity of Greek and Latin. By contrast, *bilinguis* has a negative connotation (Verg. *Aen.* 1.661) and designates a language that is mixed and corrupted, like that of the Brancchides, who had gradually abandoned their native language to adopt a foreign language (Curt. 7.5.29; Hor. *Sat.* 1.10.30).

In the western part of the Empire Latin gradually won out over Greek, which remained the principal language of the *Pars orientis*. A passage in Plutarch (*Quaest. Plat.* 10.3 = *Mor.* 1010D) seems to signal the decline of Greek, even though his expression ("Latin. . . which nowadays is spoken by everyone") is probably a rhetorical exaggeration. Plutarch himself knows Latin (see below), but admits that he does not know it sufficiently well to appreciate the stylistic finesses in Cicero's speeches (Plut. *Dem.* 2.2).

Some authors write both in Greek and in Latin, depending on the occasion: the Christian apologist Tertullian, the Platonist Apuleius of Madaura, both Africans, and also the Emperor Marcus Aurelius, who wrote his *Reflections* in Greek, but in his younger days preferred Latin in his correspondence with his teacher, the purist Fronto. Greek is the learned language, adapted to such domains as history, philosophy, or science. The mathematician L. Tarutius of Firmum, a friend of Cicero and Varro, wrote a book on the stars in Greek. The Emperor Claudius wrote in Greek books on the history of Etruria and Carthage (Suet. *Claud.* 42.5). A number of philosophers (mostly Stoics), all full-blooded Italians, wrote their treatises in Greek so naturally that philosophers writing Latin, like Seneca, are the exception (Gauly 2004: 38–51).

But after the reign of Marcus Aurelius, which marks the culmination of the collaboration between the two cultures (Swain 2004), Greek gradually loses its favored position in the *Pars occidentalis*. At the personal level, this change is already visible in the correspondence of Pliny the Younger. Whereas Cicero's Greek presents all the characteristics of a real *Umgangssprache*, Pliny's is more artificial and tied to the literary tradition. After having been bilingual for various centuries, the West became exclusively Latin (Hier. *Ep.* 50.2). Toward the end of the fourth century CE it became difficult to find Greek teachers in the cities of the West (*Cod. Theod.* 13.3.11).

Bilateral unilingualism

In the domain of official communication the Roman conquest of the Greek world had not changed anything in the status of either language. Latin did not replace Greek, but rather was added as an instrument of social and economical advancement. Greek remained the language for official documents addressed to the cities of the Greek world. With some rare exceptions, such as the *Res Gestae diui Augusti*, all the *senatus consulta* and *epistulae* of the Republican period (Sherk 1969) as well as imperial constitutions (epistles, edicts, rescripts, instructions) from Augustus till the reign of Diocletian (Oliver 1989) are in Greek. But after 284 CE till the beginning of the fifth century Latin gradually takes over.

In the Greek provinces the use of Latin in the administration is limited to four principal domains: exchanges between the central government, i.e., the emperor and the Roman magistrates in function in the provinces (the correspondence of Pliny the Younger with Trajan is a good example); communication between the Roman magistrates and the Roman colonies; the administration of the Roman colonies; and, to a certain extent, administration relative to the *ciues Romani*. Roman administration thus uses Latin in the East for external communication, whereas Greek serves the purposes of internal communication, even though Latin can also be used for political communication between cities in the East (Eck 2000). Before the Roman conquest Greek was of course already the language for international communication in the Mediterranean basin. It was also the administrative language for the Hellenistic monarchies and the language of culture enjoying considerable prestige in Roman society. The Roman administration needed Greek equivalents to the notions necessary to Roman government and so the scribes of chancelleries had to translate the documents into the other language (Mourgues 1995). The result was what Kaimio calls a bilateral unilingualism, since the Roman Empire is divided in two *partes*, one latinophone, the other hellenophone (Adamik 2006: 24–8). But alongside the two official languages, the local languages continue to have their place in the government of the provinces, often through the intermediary of interpreters (Eck 2004).

Latin in the Greek World

A new linguistic policy?

As indicated in the previous section, the situation gradually changes, starting from the second half of the third century CE and in particular in the fourth century. Diocletian and his successors are often thought to have pursued an aggressive linguistic policy that aimed at generalizing the use of Latin throughout the Empire. Marrou (1965: 378) sees support for this in a passage in Libanius (314–93). In his autobiography (Lib. *Or.* 1.234) the rhetor from Antioch expresses concerns about the future of Greek rhetoric and holds Roman law and the Latin language responsible for the demise of his school (Cribiore 2007: 206–12). However, Libanius also specifies that the decline as he sees it is not caused by any decree or law (γράμματα μὲν οὖν καὶ νόμος τοῦτο οὐκ ἔπραττεν). Rather, it seems that the decline of Greek was due to the public prestige and influence that came with the knowledge of Latin. Arguments *e silentio* are always delicate, but if a systematic language policy had existed, it would have been very likely that Libanius, great defender of Greek language and culture, would have mentioned it and fought it energetically.

However this may be, the increasing importance of Latin in the Greek world, in particular from the fourth century CE, is no stranger to the creation of new imperial residences, that is, new administrative centers, in the Greek orient. With Nicomedia, where Diocletian took up residence, and in particular, somewhat later, Constantinople, the "New Rome" at the heart of the Greek-speaking world founded by Constantine in 324 CE, the faraway capital comes closer to its Greek subjects, who from now on have reasons to learn the language of Rome. The central administration uses Latin, the "language of the rulers" which is linked to the person of the emperor.

When the Tetrarchy came to an end with Constantine the Great, the administrative system that the Tetrarchs had established survived the organization in prefectures. Besides quantitative and territorial factors, there was also the qualitative factor in the increase in prestige of Latin among the hellenophones. A career in the bureaucracy of the Empire or in the Roman army was attractive, and knowledge of Roman law, and hence of Latin, was indispensable for such a career. This is the reason why the Greeks began to attend in great numbers the law school at Beirut, which was considered as early as the first century CE an island of Latinity in a Hellenophone world (Suet. *Gram.* 24). Libanius, who forbade himself the knowledge of Latin, complains of this phenomenon, which emptied the schools of traditional Greek παιδεία (Lib. *Or.* 1.214). But knowing Latin permitted one to rise faster on the social ladder (Chrys. *Oppugn.* 3.12 = *PG* 47.368), as is shown by the career of Strategius Musonianus, *praefectus praetorio orientis* in 354 under Constantine II (Amm. Marc. 15.13.1; Drijvers 1996). For efficient Latin language acquisition special textbooks appear, such as the *Hermeneumata Pseudodositheana* (Debut 1984). This method is based on scenes of daily life composed in order to teach hellenophones Latin. In the fourth century CE, authors who are native Greek speakers, such as Claudianus of Alexandria or Ammianus Marcellinus of Antioch, use Latin for the composition of their works (Geiger 1999).

Latin influence on Greek

The importance of linguistic policy in favor of Latin, if it existed at all, has probably been exaggerated (Adams 2003: 635–6), but the prevalence of Latin in the eastern provinces toward the end of the Empire is a historical reality. The influence of Latin on Greek has long been presented as relatively unimportant and less significant than the reverse phenomenon. Such a perspective may be justified if one takes only literary language into consideration. The majority of Greek authors during the Empire are impervious to the influence of Latin, especially when they attempt to reproduce the purity of Classical Greek. This is especially clear in the case of the authors of the Second Sophistic (see ch. 31), such as Lucian, who nevertheless must have known Latin. But the Greek historians, some of them working at Rome (Dubuisson 1979), all undergo influence of Latin, partly due to the subject matter of their writing, as was also the case with their Hellenistic predecessor Polybius (Dubuisson 1985). Examples include Diodorus Siculus, Dionysius of Halicarnassus, Strabo, Plutarch, Arrian, Appian (Famerie 1998), Cassius Dio (Freyburger-Galland 1997), and Flavius Josephus (Ward 2007). As Dubuisson (1979: 99) notes, all these writers understood and spoke Latin and were capable of reading Latin literature.

In order to present Roman realities to his audience, the Greek historian had three methods at his disposal: (i) transcription pure and simple (*per transcriptionem*), by which *consul* is rendered as κωνσούλ; (ii) the calque (*per translationem*), the creation of a word composed of Greek elements which correspond to the original, *consul* becoming σύμβουλος; (iii) equivalence (*per comparationem*), by which *consul* becomes ὕπατος (Dubuisson 1992b: 102). The same three-fold strategy can be applied to *quaestor* (Famerie 1999: 218–25): *transcriptio* (κ(ο)υαίστωρ) is rare, but *translatio* (ταμίας) is frequent in many Greek cities; *comparatio* (ζητητής) does not appear until very late.

Plutarch's rapport with Latin is instructive in this regard (Dubuisson 1979: 95–7; De Rosalia 1991: 450–1; Setaioli 2007). This author deals with Latin in two ways, first at a practical and later at a formal and theoretical level. He was certainly able to communicate with his interlocutors in Rome and Italy when he was living there.

The duties resulting from his official appointments under Trajan and Hadrian must have made extensive knowledge of Latin a necessity for him. Later, no doubt during his retirement at Chaeronea when he composed the majority of his works, he must have spent much time and energy on the study of Latin texts, which he cites frequently and which he understands well in general. Geiger (2002) shows that at *Cato Minor* 11, in the narrative of the death of Cato's half-brother, Caepio, and Cato's reaction, Plutarch renders *verbatim* a Latin expression used by Munatius Rufus in his polemic against Caesar.

But it is the papyrological documents of the imperial period that give us the best idea of the receptivity of Greek to the influence of Latin (Daris 1991; Cervenka-Ehrenstrasser 1996-2000; see also ch. 37 in this volume). The borrowings are (i) in the sphere of public life, in particular government administration and the military; (ii) in social life (industry, commerce, agriculture); and (iii) private life (home and furniture, food, and clothing). Examples are αὐγουσταλιανός *augustalianus* "functionary of the *officium* of the Augustal in Alexandria"; βορδωνάριος *burdonarius* "mule driver"; δέκρητον *decretum* "decrete"; κεντηνάριος *centenarius* "centurio"; κορτίνη *cortina* "tapestry."

Dickey (2003b) has analyzed the chronological distribution of Latin borrowings in Greek papyri. The statistics that she has established show clearly that the fourth century CE represents the period in which Latin borrowings are most numerous: 3,365, which is 102 Latinisms for 100 documents as against 1,380 for the second century and 1,329 for the third. The influence of Latin also shows in expressions that are directly translated from conventional Latin formulae. Thus the epistolary concluding formula ἐρρῶσθαί σε εὔχ(ομαι), φιλτ(ατε) is nothing other than the translation of *ualere te opto* (Dickey 2004a: 506). By the same token, the vocative title κύριε frequently found in the Greek papyri of the imperial period seems to be a translation of Latin *domine* (Dickey 2001; see also ch. 22).

As we saw, not only the translation, but also the transliteration of Latin administrative terms is possible. The latter allows of a direct import of Latin terms in Greek. The use of calques, which was prevalent for centuries, can still be seen as a sign of resistance to Latinization through the opposition to direct borrowing, which would signal acceptation. First-century BCE borrowings are still concerned with objects, titles, or customs that were unfamiliar to Greeks (e.g., κεντυρίων *centurio*, λεγιών *legio*), but fourth-century CE borrowings enter the language even when a Greek word existed for the reality in question (e.g., βέστη *uestis*, ὅσπες *hospes*, φαμιλία *familia*; cf. Dickey 2003b: 257).

The epigraphical record, too, is witness to this influence of Latin. The Roman government units stationed all over the Greek world, as well as the numerous commercial exchanges, brought a never-ending stream of latinophones to the Greek world. The epigraphy of the Near East shows evidence of Latin influence on Semitic languages through Greek. The term *legio*, λεγεών in the New Testament, is found in the inscriptions of Palmyra as LGYWN (Millar 1995: 405). In Asia Minor, where the influence of Latin clearly manifests itself in the borrowings evident in Greek inscriptions (Kearsley and Evans 2001: 157–62), bilingual funereal inscriptions, whether translations or Greco-Latin assemblages, show that the persons commemorated desire in the choice of language to show their belonging to the one or the other community (Levick 1995: 399).

FURTHER READING

On multilingualism in the Greco-Roman world, see Rotolo 1972 and Werner 1983 and 1992. Kaimio 1979 offers a broad synthesis and rich bibliography on the attitude of the Romans to the Greek language. His perspective is sociolinguistic theoretically, but in practice his approach is historical and literary, as he discusses historical and social contacts between Greeks and Romans, the use of Greek in official documents, the use of Greek in private life, and Greek as language of high culture. On these issues, Dubuisson 1981b and 1992b, Weis 1992, Rochette 1996c, Valette-Cagnac 2003, and Dupont and Valette-Gagnac 2005 should also be consulted. On the subject of linguistic politics, Petersmann 1998 offers a well-documented synthesis. For the linguistic aspects, in particular Latin borrowing from Greek, see Biville 1990–5. Biville 2001–3 discusses the various aspects of linguistic contact: interference, transfer, and fusion. Code-switching in Cicero has attracted much attention and has led to various lines of interpretation, e.g., Wenskus 1993 and 1998, Dunkel 2000, Adams 2003: 297–416, Swain 2002, and Dubuisson 2005. For contacts between Latin and other languages, see Adams 2003, who opens wide perspectives and surveys a wide range of materials. He insists in particular on the need to consider the phenomenon of bilingualism comprehensively and takes into account not only literary texts, but also subliterary sources that are closer to the actual experience of the language user. The study offers a wealth of bibliographical material. On the process of latinization of the Greek world, see Rochette 1997. The collective volume edited by Adams, Janse, and Swain (2002) is of great interest for methodological purposes; it approaches the phenomenon of bilingualism from various perspectives and goes far beyond Greco-Roman bilingualism proper. For the Byzantine period, see Zilliacus 1935.

NOTES

1 On Cato, see Gruen 1992: 52–83; on his knowledge of Greek, Weis 1992: 139; on Athens, Gruen 1992: 237.

2 On embassy, see Gell. 6.14.9, with Kaimio 1979: 104–5, and Greek world, Livy 45.29.3, with Kaimio 1979: 100. See also Moatti 1997: 82–3.

3 E.g., Quint. *Inst.* 1.1.12–14, a text that highlights the respective status of Greek and Latin. See also Dubuisson 1992a: 195–9.

4 Dubuisson 1980: 887–90, with the objections of Wenskus 1993: 214–15 taken up by Adams 2003: 310.

PART FOUR

Greek in Context

CHAPTER TWENTY

Register Variation

Andreas Willi

Dialects, Sociolects, Registers

The term "register" is not always used consistently. Its core value is captured best when we compare "registers" with other varieties of language. Whereas "dialects" and "sociolects" are varieties defined by groups of speakers, other varieties are constituted by a shared topic ("technical languages") or by a shared situational framework: it is the latter which should be referred to as "registers."

The theoretical basis for the modern study of registers was laid when Malinowski (1923) and Firth (1935) first paid close attention to the interaction between linguistic usages and their cultural settings (Malinowski's "context of situation"). To take a simple example, one and the same sentence may be offensive when uttered in conversation with one person, but perfectly acceptable when said to another: already Protagoras allegedly objected to Homer's use of the imperative ἄειδε "sing" in the first line of the *Iliad* because he felt an imperative to be inappropriate in a prayer to the Muse (Arist. *Poet.* 1456b15–18 = DK 80A29). Since ancient prayers routinely used imperatives, we may not agree with Protagoras – nor did Aristotle – but the general point remains true: a prayer is a different "genre" from, say, an everyday conversation between equals, and therefore it follows different linguistic rules. Not to observe these rules may render a text awkward, inefficient, improper, or simply ridiculous, as the poets of Ancient Comedy knew when they made their characters speak in a paratragic or paraepic manner: in real life, no cook would have been so pretentious as to speak Ὁμηρικῶς all the time, as does the cook in Strato's *Phoinikides* when he asks his exasperated employer how many μέροπες (i.e., ἄνθρωποι "people") are invited to dinner and whether the plan is to sacrifice μῆλα (i.e., πρόβατα "sheep") (Strato fragm. 1; cf. also Arist. *Poet.* 1458b31–4: Ἀριφράδης τοὺς τραγῳδοὺς ἐκωμῴδει ὅτι ἃ οὐδεὶς ἂν εἴπειεν ἐν τῇ διαλέκτῳ τούτοις χρῶνται, οἷον τὸ δωμάτων ἄπο ἀλλὰ μὴ ἀπὸ δωμάτων κτλ. "Ariphrades made fun of the tragic poets because they use expressions which no one would ever utter in ordinary conversation, like δωμάτων ἄπο instead of ἀπὸ δωμάτων 'from the houses' etc.").

Register, Style, Genre

Traditionally, the varieties highlighted in the preceding examples would have been referred to as Homeric/epic and tragic *style* respectively. Even in some specialist literature the term "style" is preferred to "register" on the grounds that the latter "has been applied to varieties of language in an almost indiscriminate manner, as if it could be usefully applied to situationally distinctive pieces of language of any kind" (Crystal and Davy 1969: 61). While this criticism is justified to a degree, to use "style" instead only makes things worse. One may speak of the "style" of an author or even of an epoch (e.g., the "style" of Thucydides/of Hellenistic literature), but given the wide range of linguistic usages adopted by Thucydides in different parts of his work or by different Hellenistic authors, any overall description of these would end up being banal; and one might even argue that the peculiar "style" of a poet like Aristophanes arises precisely from the *mixture* of "registers" belonging to different communicative situations. Hence, the danger of imprecision is at least reduced when we use the term "register," and as long as we define at what level of generality we are conducting our investigations, "register" is actually quite a useful concept. After all, the same is true for its counterpart "genre": the fact that we may refer to, say, love-letters as a "genre" at a low level of generality, whereas at a higher level personal letters on all kinds of topics might constitute a "genre," does not reduce the usefulness of the concept of "genre." Rather than set registers and genres against each other, by associating the former with regularly recurring *communication situations* and the latter with regularly recurring *message types* (Ferguson 1994: 20–1), we should therefore understand register as the form (or *signifiant*) plane of an utterance or text, which corresponds to genre as the content (or *signifié*) plane: genres are "text categorizations made on the basis of external criteria relating to author/speaker purpose" or "text categories readily distinguished by mature speakers of a language" (Biber 1988: 68; 1995: 9), whereas registers are constituted by the linguistic features identifying these text categories. For instance, all those features (of intonation, syntax, lexicon, etc.) which were typically used in a funeral speech constitute the "register" of the "genre" ἐπιτάφιος λόγος.

Register Markers and Co-Occurrence Patterns

Many genres are of course not characterized by specific linguistic features: unless we pay attention to the *content* of an ἐπιτάφιος λόγος, there may be little to tell us *formally* that we are dealing with one. Formal linguistic features that are exclusive to one genre – so-called "register markers" – are indeed rare. In English, we may perhaps think of the itemizing "Whereas . . ." in legal texts, and it is feasible that the obscure sequence *o-da-a₂* in Mycenaean lists fulfilled a similar function (cf. Palmer 1963: 57, "paragraphing-itemizing"); it might not have survived into alphabetical Greek because it was tied to a specific administrative genre which was discontinued during the "Dark Ages." Similarly, text-initial ἀλλ᾿ ὅταν/ὁπόταν/ὁπότε (often followed by καὶ τότε δή or the like) seems to have been a characteristic feature of oracular verse responses in Classical times, as suggested by instances like the famous oracle given to Croesus and cited by Herodotus:

> ἀλλ᾿ ὅταν ἡμίονος βασιλεὺς Μήδοισι γένηται,
> καὶ τότε, Λυδὲ ποδαβρέ, πολυψήφιδα παρ᾿ Ἕρμον
> φεύγειν μηδὲ μένειν, μηδ᾿ αἰδεῖσθαι κακὸς εἶναι.

> But when a mule becomes king to the Medes, then, o tender-footed Lydian, flee to the many-pebbled Hermos, do not stay, nor be ashamed of being a coward. (Hdt. 1.55.2; cf. Hdt. 3.57.4, 6.77.2, 8.77, Plut. *Mor.* 399c, and Paus. 9.17.5; Fontenrose 1978: 166–70)

In this case, the linguistic peculiarity must have arisen from a transitional connector in chresmologic collections, but because oracles are normally cited in isolation, it has lost its original function and become a register marker. That it was consciously perceived as such is shown by the fact that parodistic oracles regularly adopt it, as in Aristophanes:

> ἀλλ᾿ ὁπόταν μάρψῃ βυρσαίετος ἀγκυλοχήλης
> γαμφηλῇσι δράκοντα κοάλεμον αἱματοπώτην,
> δὴ τότε Παφλαγόνων μὲν ἀπόλλυται ἡ σκοροδάλμη,
> κοιλιοπώλῃσιν δὲ θεὸς μέγα κῦδος ὀπάζει,
> αἴ κεν μὴ πωλεῖν ἀλλᾶντας μᾶλλον ἕλωνται

> But when the leather-eagle with crooked claws snatches with his jaws the blood-sucking booby snake, then the garlic-sauce of the Paphlagonians perishes and the god grants great fame to the tripe-sellers, unless they rather choose to sell sausages. (Ar. *Eq.* 197–201: cf. further Ar. *Av.* 967–8, Lucian *Peregr.* 29–30)

However, we must not think that such a beginning was a *necessary* ingredient of verse oracles, whether taken from chresmological collections or actually formulated by the Delphic Pythia and similar institutions (*if* their responses were versified). For instance, a common alternative marker is the imperative φράζευ/φράζεο/φράζου, which is also found both in serious and in mock oracles (e.g., Hdt. 8.20; Paus. 3.8.9; Ar. *Eq.* 1030–4, *Pax* 1099–1100). Yet again, not every utterance in which the imperative φράζευ occurs is also an oracle: neither *Od.* 13.376, where Athena urges Odysseus to think about how to deal with the suitors, nor the *skolion* at *PMG* 903 is. So we must not concentrate exclusively on register markers. Instead, the linguistic description of a given register should rather focus on the co-occurrence of entire sets of features, none of which may be exclusive to the register under consideration, even though the specific mixture and alternation patterns are (cf. Ervin-Tripp 1972; Biber 1994: 35–6).

The "correct" description of the register of verse oracles does not, then, stipulate an introductory ἀλλ᾿ ὅταν/ὁπόταν/ὁπότε and/or an imperative φράζευ/φράζεο/

φράζου; it just observes that there is a significant likelihood for either of these features to occur, *in conjunction* with further features such as a hexametrical rhythm, an Ionic-epic base dialect (Μήδοισι, γαμφηλῇσι), epic vocabulary and phraseology (κῦδος ὀπάζει, αἴ κεν), the ample use of metaphors (often from the animal world: ἡμίονος, βυρσαίετος, δράκοντα), a high incidence of compound epithets (cf. ποδαβρέ, πολυψήφιδα, ἀγκυλοχήλης, αἱματοπώτην), an injunction formulated in the jussive infinitive (φεύγειν, μηδὲ μένειν, μηδ᾽ αἰδεῖσθαι), a condescending or even aggressive but occasionally also a honorific form of address (Λυδὲ ποδαβρέ; elsewhere, e.g., ὦ μέλεοι "wretches," ὄλβιε "blessed": Fontenrose 1978: 173–4), and so on.

Register Allusions and Parodies

If registers are mainly characterized by co-occurrence patterns, rather than register markers, one difficulty arises: in order to make meaningful comparisons between registers, we need large text samples. It would be impossible to substantiate the above claims about typical verse oracles on the basis of only three or four recorded responses. Moreover, the literary scholar in particular will want to know when a given passage, whose surroundings belong to one register, contains a sufficiently distinctive mix of features to have evoked another register in the minds of the primary audience. When Empedocles addressed his listeners with the words ὦ πόποι, ὦ δειλὸν θνητῶν γένος, ὦ δυσάνολβον "Woe, o wretched race of mortals, fatefully doomed" or told them δειλοί, πάνδειλοι, κυάμων ἄπο χεῖρας ἔχεσθαι "Wretches, more than wretches, keep your hands from beans" (DK 31B124.1, 31B141), these utterances are likely to have been consciously designed so as to sound "oracular," for elsewhere the poet does proclaim to be consulted as a μάντις (DK 31B112.10; cf. Willi 2008: 235–8); but how could we ever *prove* this in the absence of ancient testimonia?

Because of such difficulties of demarcation, one particular source of evidence for register variation in Ancient Greek is of prime importance: parodies. Unlike other forms of allusion, parodies are the more effective the more recognizable they are. In the parody of a genre, the genre's register features and co-occurrence patterns are therefore faithfully highlighted (though possibly exaggerated), whereas the *contents* of the message are often incongruous (cf. Willi 2003: 5–6). In a fragment of Aristophanes' contemporary Cratinus, we find for example a parodic attack on Pericles which formally imitates early epic genealogies, without actually being hexametrical (Cratinus fragm. 258): Στάσις δὲ καὶ πρεσβυγενὴς | Χρόνος ἀλλήλοισι μιγέντε | μέγιστον τίκτετον τύραννον | ὃν δὴ κεφαληγερέταν | θεοὶ καλέουσι "Discord and Time born of old having intercourse with one another bring forth the greatest tyrant, whom the gods call head-collector"; apart from the non-Attic forms (ἀλλήλοισι, καλέουσι) and the epic or pseudo-epic epithets (πρεσβυγενής, κεφαληγερέταν ~ Hom. νεφεληγερέτα "cloud-collector"), the semantics of μιγέντε and the historic present τίκτετον are most characteristic since the former is largely restricted to epic, and the latter is at least likely to have been a stock ingredient of early genealogies, just like its counterpart γίγνεται (cf. Lilja 1968: 101–19; Dover 1997: 67–8).

Similarly, we could infer from the parody at Ar. *Av.* 1040–1, where the Decree-Seller visits Cloudcuckooland and proposes the law χρῆσθαι Νεφελοκοκκυγιᾶς τοῖσδε τοῖς μέτροισι καὶ σταθμοῖσι καὶ ψηφίσμασι καθάπερ Ὀλοφύξιοι "That the Cloudcuckoolanders may use these measures and weights and decrees just as the Lamentians," that the "officialese" style of Classical Athenian laws and decrees typically used jussive accusative-with-infinitive constructions (cf. Thesleff 1967: 77; Bers 1984: 167) and possibly also the conjunction καθάπερ, which is otherwise rare in pre-fourth-century Attic prose. In this case, of course, we would have known these things anyway from actual fifth-century laws (see, e.g., Andoc. *Myst.* 96–8 with phrases like ὀμόσαι δ᾽ Ἀθηναίους ἅπαντας "that all the Athenians may swear" and καθάπερ Ἁρμόδιόν τε καὶ Ἀριστογείτονα "just as Harmodios and Aristogeiton"), but we are not always so fortunate. Without comedy, for example, we would not know for certain that official proclamations by the Athenian κῆρυξ were standardly introduced by the words ἀκούετε λεῴ "listen, people," followed by jussive infinitives (cf. Ar. *Ach.* 172, 1000–21, *Pax* 551–3, *Av.* 448–50), for the supporting evidence in other genres is limited and, apart from Lucian *Bis acc.* 12.4, mentions only the formula as such, without indicating the following construction (cf. Susario fragm. 1; Plut. *Thes.* 13.4; Eust. *Il.* p. 4.60.17).

Register Boundaries

So far we have operated with a somewhat intuitive notion of what counts as a distinct "genre" (with its associated register) in ancient Greece. Although this may be unavoidable, the resulting picture is not always quite satisfactory. Let us consider oracular responses once again. At first these might seem to constitute a coherent as well as clearly demarcated group of texts. The latter is no doubt true, but the former much less so. The oracular passages cited above (and many others that could be added) do show considerable formal similarities, but our faith in the adequacy of a register description based on them is shattered when we look at the Delphic oracle quoted by Demosthenes:

συμφέρει Ἀθηναίοις [. . .] θύοντας καλλιερεῖν Διὶ ὑπάτῳ, Ἀθηνᾷ ὑπάτῃ, Ἡρακλεῖ, Ἀπόλλωνι σωτῆρι, καὶ ἀποπέμπειν Ἀμφιόνεσσι· περὶ τύχας ἀγαθᾶς Ἀπόλλωνι ἀγυιεῖ, Λατοῖ, Ἀρτέμιδι, καὶ τὰς ἀγυιὰς κνισῆν, καὶ κρατῆρας ἱστάμεν καὶ χορούς, καὶ στεφαναφορεῖν καττὰ πάτρια κτλ.

It is profitable for the Athenians [. . .] to sacrifice with good omens to Zeus the Highest, Athena the Highest, Herakles, Apollo the Saviour, and to send to the Amphiones; about good luck to Apollo of the Streets, Leto, Artemis, and to make the streets steam with sacrifice, and to set up mixing-bowls and choruses, and to wear wreaths in the traditional way. (Dem. 43.66)

The non-Attic forms in this piece (τύχας ἀγαθᾶς, κνισῆν, ἱστάμεν, καττὰ πάτρια) suggest that at least the second part has undergone no editorial adjustment (e.g., by a transfer of an original verse text into prose); and yet, the response does not show any of the "typical" register features previously discussed. Would an Athenian audience therefore have thought of two entirely separate oracular registers: "verse oracles" vs "prose oracles"? Or should we admit only one oracular register, but one with considerable internal diversity (cf. the "mixed" oracle at Dem. 21.52)? As long as we want to say anything meaningful about the most characteristic linguistic components of a given register, the former view is preferable, but the problem persists: both the Demosthenic and the Herodotean oracles would have been covered by the same generic name μαντεία (μαντηίη).

At the same time, we cannot simply postulate invariant cross-cultural genres associated with certain situational contexts. No doubt there are some parallelisms between communicative situations in a modern European culture and in the ancient world – e.g., writing a personal letter, delivering a defense speech, praying to a divinity, etc. – but the divergences are likely to be greater than the similarities, and this not only when one culture lacks a given genre and its register altogether (e.g., ancient oracles, modern police reports). Thus, while communal religious acts certainly played a major part in the lives of many people in ancient Greece, and while they still do so for some people in modern Britain, there is nothing to suggest the existence of one coherent "religious/liturgical register" in Greek (Willi 2003: 8–50): as far as we can tell, there was much less of a linguistic overlap between the language of Greek hymns and official prayers than between the language of traditional church anthems and liturgical prayers in the English tradition (on which, see Crystal and Davy 1969: 147–72: distinct vocabulary, morphological archaism, reversals of word order, etc.). To judge again from some parodic evidence (which is the main evidence we have: cf. esp. Ar. *Av.* 864–88, *Thesm.* 295–311, 331–51; Kleinknecht 1937; Horn 1970), the most noticeable feature of official communal prayers in Classical Greece was the enumeration of long lists of divinities, which is unknown in hymns, whereas some of the main features of Greek hymns (e.g., the use of elaborate epithets, a high incidence of relative clauses, the avoidance of definite articles, etc.; see Adami 1901) played no visible role in official prayers: several of these hymnic features are rather shared with other forms of choral poetry. The absence of a unified religious/liturgical register thus illustrates the need not to overlook culture-specific genre and register boundaries.

Synchrony and Diachrony

Moreover, allowance must be made for diachronic changes in the history of registers. This is obvious where standard expressions are replaced or altered. A conspicuous ingredient of the register of decrees in Classical Athens is the introductory formula ἔδοξε τῇ βουλῇ /τῷ δήμῳ "the council/people decided" + accusative with infinitive. In Classical Elis, the structure is quite different, since a typical decree there begins with ἁ Ϝϱάτϱα τοῖς Ϝαλείοις "the decree of (lit.: to) the Eleans" (with an adnominal dative). However, at some point, presumably under Athenian influence, Elean decrees adopt the ἔδοξε-type formulation (Rhodes and Lewis 1997: 550–1).

In other cases, the changes are less obtrusive. Dover (1997: 62–3) observes that casual oaths such as νὴ Δία "by Zeus" and μὰ τοὺς θεούς "by the gods," which serve as a means of intensification in comedy and in prose dialogues (Plato, Xenophon) but not in tragedy, are rare also in early oratory (Antiphon, Lysias, Andocides, Isocrates); only in the speeches of Isaeus and Demosthenes do these oaths suddenly occur with some frequency, thus indicating "a change towards informality, no doubt very carefully calculated, in the middle of the fourth century" (cf. also the increased frequency of the deictic affix -ί attached to pronouns and adverbs such as οὑτοσί, ὁδί, οὑτωσί, etc.). Of course, we do not know what happened when these speeches were actually delivered – Andocides and Isocrates might have inserted the occasional νὴ Δία on the spot – but the emerging overall pattern agrees with observations made cross-linguistically about the diachronic evolution of written registers, for even in the case of Greek oratory we are dealing with the *written* representation of (an) oral genre(s). "When written registers are first introduced in a language, they are already quite different in their linguistic characteristics from pre-existing spoken registers," and "over the early periods of evolution [they] develop linguistically to become more sharply distinguished from typical spoken registers," but "in later periods, written registers begin to show a fundamental split between specialized, expository prose, and other more popular kinds of writing," the latter showing "a reversal of the trend towards more literate characteristics and a marked transition back towards more oral linguistic characteristics" (Biber 1995: 311). In view of this third period, it makes sense if features such as oaths and deictic -ί, which were banned from early oratory as well as, say, historical prose, were allowed "back" into written Greek by later orators like Demosthenes and Isaeus, but not by the contemporary historiographers.

Given the possibility of such diachronic changes, a complete description of the register system of Ancient Greek would have to consist of two parts: the first would provide a synchronic picture of the entire register landscape at several points in time, taking into account all the problems regarding the establishment of register boundaries mentioned above, and the second would then trace the changes between these synchronic pictures (noting in particular the loss or emergence of registers as well as their mutual interaction). Obviously, to do all of this would be a Herculean task, and it is therefore understandable if no one has ever tried. More surprisingly, however, even the major registers of Ancient Greek have never been comprehensively described and compared: there is no such thing as a "Handbook of Greek Registers," to match the handbooks of Greek dialects. This is all the more remarkable since the study of (at least some) registers was already pursued by the Greeks themselves.

The Beginnings of Register Studies

When a comedian parodies a register, this presupposes an aprioristic notion of its linguistic norms. The same is true when Plato's Socrates remarks about himself that he is talking "almost in dithyrambs" (Pl. *Phdr.* 238d): clearly, Plato's readers knew what this meant just as well as the audience of Aristophanes' *Birds* was able to appreciate a dithyrambic parody (Ar. *Av.* 1372–1409). On a different level, Thucydides must have a precise idea of the usual register of historiography when he announces that his work will be a challenge to his addressees: for τὸ μὴ μυθῶδες, "the lack of leisurely story-telling," which they are about to face, no doubt refers to the linguistic as well as the content plane of his exposition (Thuc. 1.22.4).

Next to such impressionistic statements, there is one domain in which the reflection about registers was more systematic: the teaching of rhetoric. Here, apart from the principal dichotomy between the macro-registers of poetry and prose (see, e.g., Isoc. 9.9–10, according to whom ξένα and καινὰ ὀνόματα "strange and newly coined words" are the prerogative of the former; cf. Arist. *Rh.* 1404b26–33), several more specific registers were distinguished: thus, Aristotle (*Rh.* 1406b1–5) saw in the frequent use of compound words the defining feature of dithyrambic poetry, as opposed to epic and iambic poetry with their preferences for γλῶτται "strange words" and metaphors respectively, and Dionysius of Halicarnassus (*Dem.* 2; cf. *Thuc.* 5) observes that natural philosophers, local historians, and genealogists regularly wrote in the "plain style," which is structurally similar to ordinary spoken language.

However, these issues are discussed in more detail only with regard to register differentiation within oratory (though oratory in the widest sense: Demetr. *Eloc.* 223–35 devotes an entire section to the register of letter-writing): δεῖ δὲ μὴ λεληθέναι ὅτι ἄλλη ἑκάστῳ γένει ἁρμόττει λέξις. οὐ γὰρ ἡ αὐτὴ γραφικὴ καὶ ἀγωνιστική, οὐδὲ δημηγορικὴ καὶ δικανική "one must not forget that a distinct register is appropriate for each genre; for the register of writing is not identical with that of debating, and the register of assembly speeches is not the same as that of lawcourt speeches" (Arist. *Rh.* 1413b3–5). Epideictic, deliberative, and forensic speeches must be kept apart, because the addressee groups are different (Arist. *Rh.* 1358a36–b8; cf. Dover 1968: 59 with further passages), and, within these, different stylistic rules obtain for different sections (προοίμιον "introduction," διήγησις "narrative," πίστεις "proofs," ἐπίλογος "conclusion" in Aristotle's taxonomy): for instance, asyndeta such as εἴρηκα, ἀκηκόατε, ἔχετε, κρίνατε "I have spoken, you have heard, keep it, judge it" (which are to be shunned in written style: Arist. *Rh.* 1413b19–20) are appropriate at the end of ἐπίλογοι (Arist. *Rh.* 1420a6–8). More generally, features such as the artificial avoidance of hiatus, periodic sentence structures, and frequent figures like antitheses may be suitable for ceremonial (epideictic) speeches (Dion. Hal. *Isoc.* 2), but not for public or private forensic speeches, which must both (though to different degrees: Dion. Hal. *Dem.* 56) follow the artless conventions of ordinary speech (Dion. Hal. *Lys.* 3).

The foundations for these theoretical statements were laid long before Aristotle, by the sophists if not earlier. Both Gorgias and Protagoras are said to have paid attention to the concept of καιρός in their teaching, i.e., to how a speech can be adapted to the particular circumstances and communication situation in which the speaker finds himself (Gorg. DK 82B13, Prot. DK 80A1.52; cf. the modern concept of "audience design": Bell 1984). But before them, Pythagoras had already become famous for his gift of making his speeches suitable for different types of audience, and we may therefore perhaps regard this elusive early thinker and teacher as the true founder of register-variation theory (Nicomachus *FGrH* 1063F1; cf. Willi 2008: 173, 284–6).

Taxonomies and Statistical Comparisons

One crucial difference between ancient and modern approaches to register variation lies in the strong prescriptivist element which is found in the major sources mentioned above: for example, Aristotle censures Gorgias for not following the "rules" of oratory as he uses too many compound words (Arist. *Rh.* 1405b35–1406a1) and Dionysius of Halicarnassus finds fault with Thucydides because his liking for nominalized adjectives, among other things, is supposed to be inappropriate in the writing of history (Dion. Hal. *Thuc.* 31: e.g., τὸ συγγενές and τὸ ἑταιρικόν for συγγένεια "kinship" and ἑταιρία "party"). In contrast, modern register studies aim to be exclusively descriptive (unlike style guides). In order to achieve this, it is essential to compare like with like.

One way to ensure the comparability of the material is to set up as precise a register taxonomy as possible. The most detailed proposal to date is that of Biber (1994: 39–44), who draws on earlier classifications by Crystal and Davy (1969), Hymes (1974), and Halliday (1978). Biber's analytical framework includes the following main components:

a) Communicative characteristics of participants (i.e., number of addressors and addressees, presence/absence of an audience);
b) Relations between addressor and addressee (i.e., relative status and power, extent of shared knowledge, personal relationships);
c) Setting (i.e., characteristics of the place of communication, extent to which place and time are shared by participants);
d) Channel (i.e., written vs spoken communication, medium of transmission);
e) Relation of participants to text (i.e., planned vs on-line production, personal evaluation by the addressor and addressee);
f) Purposes, intents, and goals (i.e., entertainment value, amount of transferred information);
g) Topic/subject (i.e., popular vs specialized level of discussion, specific subject area).

When classified according to this taxonomy, probably no two texts will share exactly the same configuration, but the model is able to establish the level of generality at which a comparison is made: one might for instance ignore differences of topic or channel as long as all the other criteria are identical. Such decisions are particularly necessary in dealing with ancient texts since the textual basis would otherwise be excessively reduced. Thus, the symposiastic songs (*skolia*) collected by Athenaeus (15.694c–696a, our main source for *skolia*, providing 26 out of just over 30 items in *PMG* 884–917) must all have arisen in communicative situations in which categories *a)*–*f)* were fairly homogeneous (the symposium), but they widely diverge with regard to category *g)* (topic/subject). Even disregarding this, however, their register is by no means uniform: one might note a general tendency towards the co-occurrence of first-person verbs and other references to the addressor with directive utterances (χρή, ἄριστον [ἐστι], imperatives) and evaluative vocabulary (ἄριστος, ἀγαθός, καλός, φίλος, δειλός, etc.), but it is unclear whether similar patterns could not also be detected in other genres.

Let us therefore consider an alternative approach to register variation, which, at least initially, abstracts from all aprioristic notions about genre boundaries. Instead, we might simply take a number of texts of equal length and analyze their constituent linguistic elements (phonological, morphological, lexical, pragmatic, etc.). The distribution of these elements will make the texts fall into groups: for example, the addressor–addressee relationship in texts with frequent second-person pronouns is obviously different from the one in texts without such pronouns. Moreover, we might look for co-occurrence patterns again (for example, some of the texts with frequent second-person pronouns might also use more present-tense than past-tense verbs). Only after establishing such patterns would we then ask whether the corresponding texts also belong to the same genre on non-linguistic grounds. We would thus obtain a methodologically unobjectionable register description, but there is one drawback: each of the surveyed texts would have to be of a certain minimum length (a few hundred words at least) to make comparisons statistically meaningful. A single *skolion*, oracular response, or public decree might not be long enough to be assessed. This second method of ensuring comparability can therefore never entirely replace the more intuitive one described before. Still, it would make it easier to establish how "typical" (or deviant) a particular passage is within the framework of the genre to which it supposedly belongs.

A Sample Study of Non-Poetic Registers in Classical Greek

Unfortunately, in the absence of a tagged electronic corpus the work required to produce comprehensive results in such a manner would be enormous. For our present purpose, however, a small sample study may illustrate the methodology, its potentials, and pitfalls.

While the 23 linguistic variables figuring in table 20.1 were somewhat randomly selected, to reflect syntactic, morphosyntactic, and pragmatic divergences alike, the same is admittedly not true of the six roughly contemporary text samples, each consisting of the first 1,000 printed words of the given text in a standard edition. Had it been possible to compare dozens of samples, randomness would have been mandatory, but given the time needed to count the occurrences of even such a limited set of variables across six passages, a little streamlining seemed advisable. Thus, the beginnings of Lysias' defense of Euphiletos (Hude) and of Andocides' speech *On the Mysteries* (MacDowell) could be expected to "represent" the macro-genre "forensic oratory"; the beginnings of Herodotus Book Two (Hude) and Thucydides Book Six (Hude) (each including some paragraphs of a more geographical type) that of historiography; and the beginnings of Plato's *Gorgias* (Dodds) and Aristophanes' *Clouds* (Hall-Geldart) that of casual conversation (or at least an approximation thereof). Table 20.1 shows that certain distribution patterns do in fact coincide with these generic classifications.

Table 20.1 The distribution of 23 variables in six 1,000-word samples of Classical Attic Greek

Linguistic feature	Lys. I	Andoc.	Hdt. II	Thuc. VI	Pl. Gorg.	Ar. Nub.
Nouns (incl. proper names, but excl. nominalized adjectives and participles)	131	147	241	290	149	205
Attributive adjectives (excl. pronominal adjectives ἄλλος, οὐδείς, τοιοῦτος, τοσοῦτος, πᾶς as well as ordinal numbers)	11	11	18	11	3	18
Demonstrative pronouns I (οὗτος, αὕτη, τοῦτο)	22	16	18	1	15	25
Demonstrative pronouns II (ὅδε, ἥδε, τόδε)	–	4	–	–	3	1
Pronouns with demonstrative -ί	–	1	–	–	–	8
First-person verbs	41	25	9	1	30	54
Second-person verbs (excl. imperatives)	9	16	2	–	25	24
Past-tense indicatives (aor., imperf., plupf.; excl. counterfactual ind.)	74	36	37	55	13	35
Perfect indicatives	5	6	3	1	6	7
Future indicatives	2	9	5	–	8	18
Subjunctives (excl. subj. as negative aor. imp.)	10	8	1	1	7	11
Potential optatives	7	6	2	1	4	6
Finite passives	4	8	3	18	1	2
Imperatives (incl. subj. as negative aor. imp.)	3	4	–	1	15	28
Infinitives	38	52	36	12	45	15
Participles	65	56	62	69	26	44
Relative clauses, specific (ὅς, etc.) and general (ὅστις, etc.) (excl. adverbial relative clauses, e.g. οὗ "where")	10	15	12	6	17	9
Conditional clauses	3	5	–	1	11	8
Direct questions	–	5	–	–	34	28
Average sentence length (number of words, accepting the punctuation of the editions used)	19.6	20.4	21.3	23.3	8.2	7.5
Vocative phrases	11	9	–	–	29	17
Oaths	–	–	–	–	2	5
Particles (ἀλλά, ἄν, ἄρα, ἀτάρ, αὖ, γάρ, γε, γοῦν, δέ, δή, δήπου, δῆτα, ἦ, καίτοι, μέν, μέντοι, μήν, οὖν/ὦν, περ, τοι, τοίνυν; also embedded in combinations like ἐάν, νυνδή, ἔγωγε, οὐδέ, but excl. lexicalized items like ὅδε, οὐδέν)	89	91	80	70	148	104

a)   The frequency of *nouns and proper names* is much higher in Hdt. Book Two and Thuc. Book Six than elsewhere; only Ar. *Nub.* comes close, but the condensation there might be due to the restrictions imposed by the meter and admissible overall length of a comedy.

b)   Unsurprisingly, *first-person verbs* are far more common in the forensic speeches and in "conversation," but the table also shows considerable internal variation in the historiographical data (cf. the deictic pronouns); this distribution is similar to that of second-person verbs (but note that the second-person verbs in the Lysias sample are mostly found in embedded speech).

c)   *Past-tense indicatives* are rarer in "conversation" than in the other registers, but the figures are not uneven enough to ensure that different samples would not have produced different distribution patterns. Conversely, future forms as well as modal forms are more frequently found in the "oral" registers of oratory and "conversation."

d)   The two "oral" registers differ in their use of *imperatives*: while virtually absent from historiography, imperatives seem to be most easily accommodated in "conversation," and the same holds for questions, oaths, and vocative phrases. Whether the slightly higher figures for perfect forms in the "oral" registers are meaningful, must be left open.

e)   The *average sentence length* also differentiates between forensic oratory and "conversation," but here the former is close to historiography. Interestingly, the difference is not correlated with a smaller number of relative or conditional clauses in "conversation"; it rather goes hand in hand with a more restrictive use of participial phrases (whereas the number of infinitives appears to be unrelated to sentence complexity).

f)   No clear pattern emerges for *passives* and *demonstrative pronouns* (except that the use of deictic -ί is rare outside the comic sample), but this is mainly the fault of the wide divergence of the Herodotean and the Thucydidean passage; already Dion. Hal. *Amm.* 2.8 comments on Thucydides' weakness for the passive. Similarly, there is some inconsistency in the "conversational" representation of attributive adjectives (where, as under *a)* above, Plato may be nearer the truth than Aristophanes).

g)   Finally, *particles* are rarest in historiography, more usual in forensic oratory, but distinctly most common in "conversation." The figures for Plato and Aristophanes are in broad agreement with those counted by Duhoux (1997), but I am no longer sure that, with Duhoux, ordinary colloquial Attic must have been less particle-friendly than Plato's rendering of it (cf. Willi 2003: 261); again, we must not forget the technical restrictions a poet like Aristophanes was facing.

Register Dimensions

By way of conclusion, we may ask how the results of such individual register analyses can be integrated into a larger framework providing overall parameters for register classification. A very basic way of proceeding would be to adopt a unidimensional scale of increasing "formality" (cf. Biber 1994: 34, and 37–9 on further simple frameworks: e.g., Chafe's (1982) "involved vs detached" and "integrated vs fragmented"). Toward one end of the scale we might locate an Aristophanic conversation, toward the other a Thucydidean exposition. Accordingly, linguistic features could be classified as more or less formal (e.g. "informal" deictic -ί vs "formal" passives). However, such a categorization would soon encounter problems, because the institutional "formality" of a communicative situation need not be reflected by a "formal" register. The writing, recitation, and deposition of a curse-tablet (*defixio*) was certainly an act of high formality for the addressor/sender, but the language of curse-tablets is far from "formal": where there is more than just a list of names, the vocabulary (including "technical terms" like καταδέω or καταγράφω "to write/bind down") is simple, and instances of muddled syntax or doubtful orthography are common; the mere presence of certain *formulaic* phrases (e.g. καταδέω τὸν X "I bind down X," ὁ X καὶ ἡ τοῦ X γλῶσσα ἀπεστραμμένη "X and the tongue of X [are to be] paralyzed") does not change this, since formulaicity is not the same as formality. Meanwhile, there is also nothing distinctly informal about these curse texts, unless we choose to qualify as "informal" everything that does not conform with certain grammatical standards.

Hence, a more sophisticated framework is needed. In a cross-linguistic study of English, Korean, Tuvaluan, and Somali, Biber (1995) has argued that the register dimensions that are necessary to describe the co-occurrence patterns of register features in these languages reflect a small number of over-arching categories: orality vs literacy, interactivity, production circumstances (on-line vs planned), informational focus, personal stance, argumentation/persuasion, and narration. Extrapolating a universal from this, we might try to define each register of Ancient Greek accordingly; the number of nouns and names in the historiographical samples above would for instance indicate a strong informational focus, whereas the limited number of first- and second-person verbs and the absence of direct questions or vocative phrases would point to a low interactivity score, and the number of participial constructions as well as the sentence-length parameter to a high degree of planning.

Alternatively, we might adopt a classification which starts from a more general reflection on the uses of language in communication. Jakobson (1960) distinguishes six basic functions: emotive (focused on the addressor and his/her attitude to what (s)he is saying, e.g. through evaluative terms), referential (focused on the referent), conative (focused on the addressee, e.g. through second-person forms), poetic (focused on the message for its own sake, e.g. through poetic figures), phatic (focused on the (dis)continuation of the communication, e.g. through requests for attention), and metalingual (focused on the code, e.g., through glossing of difficult words); see fig. 34.1. Jakobson himself stresses that "the diversity [sc. between different types of verbal messages] lies not in a monopoly of some one of these several functions but in a different hierarchical order of functions" (1960: 353). So, a Thucydidean exposition would score low for all the functions but the referential, whereas a forensic speech would score higher with regard to the emotive and conative functions (and also, less prominently, for the phatic one: cf. the vocative phrases in the above samples). Even a strongly metalingual register is imaginable when we think of an ancient commentary like the Derveni papyrus in which the verbal choices of another text (here, an Orphic cosmogony) are explained with sentences including terms such as ὀνομάζειν, σημαίνειν, καλεῖν, etc. (e.g., col. XVIII.6–7 Ὀρφεὺς γὰρ τὴν φρόνησ[ι]ν Μοῖραν ἐκάλεσεν "Orpheus called the thinking Moira"; col. XVIII.2–3 τοῦτ᾽ οὖν τὸ πνεῦμα Ὀρφεὺς ὠνόμασεν Μοῖραν "this breath, then, Orpheus named Moira"). Once again, the predominance of one or the other communicative function is associated with specific co-occurrence patterns.

Of course, the picture of the register landscape of Ancient Greek we obtain by adopting Biber's dimensions, Jakobson's functions, or any other classification, will not be revolutionary. We are perfectly able to state that a Platonic dialogue is more "argumentative" or "conative" than an epic catalogue without analyzing its linguistic set-up. But that is not the point: we can also enjoy a cake without knowing the ingredients that went into it. A true connoisseur, however, will want to know. In other words, we cannot truly understand and appreciate Greek literary culture without understanding how the texts that constitute it work.

FURTHER READING

There is no comprehensive study of the registers of Ancient Greek. Even studies on individual registers (however broadly defined) are rare: apart from those cited in the main text, note for instance Ausfeld 1903 and Pulleyn 1997 on prayers, Nehrbass 1935 on the healing reports of Epidauros, Koskenniemi 1956 and Kim 1985 on letters, Lazzarini 1977 on votive inscriptions, van der Eijk 1997 on medical texts, and Walser 2001 on the Greek of texts belonging into the context of the Jewish synagogue. Mostly, relevant observations therefore have to be collected from works dealing with either specific variables (e.g. Meyer 1923 on compounds, Trenkner 1960 on paratactic structuring, Denniston 1954 on particles, Dickey 1996 on forms of address) or very large topics such as colloquial language (e.g. Stevens 1976, López Eire 1996) or the style of Greek prose (e.g. Denniston 1952, Rydbeck 1967, Lilja 1968, Dover 1997) and poetry (e.g. Bers 1984); to these one may add the many stylistic studies on individual authors (e.g. Breitenbach 1934 on Euripides, Dover 1968 on Lysias, Hummel 1993 on Pindar), highlighting for example Thesleff 1967 on registers in Plato or Allan 2007 on narrative modes in Thucydides.

Recent sociolinguistic findings are brought to bear on Ancient Greek register variation in Willi 2003; because of its cross-linguistic implications, the work by Biber (1995) is of particular interest here. The papers in Biber and Finegan 1994 can be read as a diverse introduction to modern register studies more generally.

CHAPTER TWENTY-ONE

Female Speech

Thorsten Fögen

Introduction

Since the 1980s there has been a remarkable concern in classical studies with the role of women in ancient Greece and Rome, as can be seen, for example, from the recent research report by Scheer (2000) and from the internet website "Diotima" (http://www.stoa.org/diotima). The majority of investigations concentrate on aspects of gender and sexuality, the legal status of women (e.g., marriage laws, the regulation of inheritance), and general patterns of behavior in various spheres of society. However, no wide-ranging attempt has been made so far to systematically collect and discuss the literary evidence on gender-specific communication in Greco-Roman antiquity. The few contributions touching upon this topic are rather eclectic in their approach: they either do not pay much attention to metalinguistic documents, or they concentrate on a single genre or author, such as analyses of women's language in Greek comedy or tragedy. Moreover, some classicists tend to ignore modern linguistic studies on female speech, a fact that is occasionally responsible for a lack of rigorous methodology as well as of a critical distance from the ancient texts.

This chapter attempts to provide an overview of how the Greeks and Romans portrayed the forms of speech that were used by women. It is not the aim here to reconstruct *actual* linguistic patterns of communication that were used by this group of speakers; the evidence for such an endeavor would be too sparse. Rather, the main focus will be on *metalinguistic* reflections presented by a wide range of Greek and Roman literary writers. How do these authors describe the forms of speech deployed by women? What kind of value do such reports have, especially those that have nothing in common with linguistic analysis proper? Although very few, if any, of the statements to be examined demonstrate a neutral and objective approach to their topic, they serve as important documents for the reconstruction of the Greeks' and Romans' awareness of marginalized social groups. They thus have a sociological rather than linguistic value.

Methodological Problems

Before we move on to the actual examination of the literary evidence, it is crucial to say a few words on the methodological difficulties and limits of the analysis of ancient texts on women (see, e.g., Blundell 1995: 10–11).

a) The extant Greco-Roman literary evidence on women does not only consist of texts from a number of different genres, each of which may take a special perspective; it also spans a period of approximately 1,300 years from the Homeric poems (*c.* 800 BCE) to pagan and Christian texts from late antiquity (*c.* 500 CE). Furthermore, some genres are rather problematic sources for the precise reconstruction of social conditions affecting the lives of women. Especially texts that are based upon myths from the remote past (such as epic and tragedy) or located in a fantastic world (such as some comedies) may not portray their female protagonists in a way that could be directly related to the real situation of women in Greece and Rome (see Fantham et al. 1994: 69–70, 121–2). Satire and invective provide even less reliable information, as it is part of their generic conventions to distort reality.

b) The vast majority of sources was not written by women themselves, but by elite Greek and Roman males. This includes texts that purport to have been composed by women such as the courtesan letters by the two epistolographers Alciphron (second/third cent. CE) and Aristaenetus (*c.* fifth century CE). Other voices, especially non-elite ones, are seldom heard, although one may gain some insights from non-literary evidence such as graffiti and private letters preserved on papyrus (see Bagnall and Cribiore 2006), provided these texts were actually written by women themselves and not by scribes; however, many private letters were penned or at least dictated by upper-class females, though their literacy was by no means standard for women of lower social ranks. The scope of analysis is further constrained by the fact that our evidence is limited to written material, not spoken language from which conclusions about female communication might be derived. It is therefore questionable whether the available data reflect women's speech accurately.

c) There is also the problem of the general marginalization of women in ancient societies. In Classical Athens, but also in later periods, education and participation in politics was a male privilege. Although some women were literate and a few even produced literary texts, this tended to be the exception. Forms of visual evidence such as vase paintings which depict women holding book-rolls or girls being taught in a domestic environment mirror upper-class activities and cannot be interpreted as representative of the entire Greek and Roman societies (see Blundell 1995: 132–4). Political and intellectual independence was not a goal ancient women were supposed to strive for; rather, they were expected to define themselves through their fathers or husbands. But although they are rarely represented as public figures or speakers, they participated in public life through certain forms of ritual speech such as lamentations (see Alexiou 1974; Holst-Warhaft 1992: esp. 98–170; McClure 1999: 40–7) and scurrilous joking (αἰσχρολογία), as it occurred in the context of religious festivals such as the Thesmophoria, the Stenia, and the Haloa, all celebrated to honor the goddess Demeter (see McClure 1999: 47–52).

d) While women in antiquity have been the object of numerous scholarly investigations, the fact is often ignored that they do not constitute a homogeneous entity. As Griffith (2001: 136) rightly says, "the term 'woman' is too clumsy an umbrella for too many separate categories (daughter, sister, virgin, bride, wife, mother, princess, captive, etc.), whose several duties and expectations cannot be expected to cohere tidily." In the case of many female figures in ancient literature and history, it depends on one's perspective with which social group they may be associated. For a character such as the seer Cassandra in Aeschylus' *Agamemnon*, it is crucial to note that she is not only a woman but also a captive, and being a Trojan, she is viewed by the Greeks as a foreigner. Medea is a comparable case: as the daughter of the Colchian king Aietes she is a woman with an aristocratic background, through her grandfather Helios (the sun god) she is connected with the divine sphere, and as the niece of the sorceress Circe she is familiar with the powers of magic; at the same time, she embodies the "barbarian," even for her husband Jason, who expects her to be grateful to him for having brought her to the "civilized" world (Eur. *Med.* 534–44). Therefore, when women such as Cassandra or Medea speak, the question arises of how we are to view their speech habits: as typical of "barbarians" (or, to use a modern linguistic term, of "foreigner talk") or as characteristic for female speakers? Quite often, such a distinction would not even make sense, since it would impose artificial boundaries. It thus turns out to be difficult to extrapolate characteristic traits of female speech habits.

For reasons of space and in order to avoid any major inconsistencies, this overview limits itself to an investigation of the literary sources, mainly from early Greece to the early Roman Empire. Christian authors have not been taken into account, although some of them may not radically deviate from pagan writers in their approach to the topics in question (see Fögen 2004: 230–5). Although the subsequent outline cannot hide its very selective character and makes no claim to be exhaustive, it nevertheless tries to describe typical elements of Greco-Roman thought.

Research on Female Speech in Modern Linguistics

Before the ancient evidence is considered, it will be helpful to give a brief introduction to some of the findings of modern linguistics on female speech (for details, see Fögen 2004: 200–15). Some connections between speech and gender were already observed in the nineteenth century, most notably by Wilhelm von Humboldt (1767–1835) and Jacob Grimm (1785–1863), and in the early twentieth century, especially by the Danish linguist Otto Jespersen (1860–1943) in the chapter "The woman" of his book *Language: Its Nature, Development and Origin* (1922), and by the American sociologist Paul Hanly Furfey (1896–1992). In a succinct article from 1944, Furfey starts from the assumption that diverging forms of language usage of men and women are less prominent in the languages of Europe than in those of primitive peoples. He then adduces instances of phonetic, grammatical, and lexical idiosyncrasies which are restricted to the usage of female speakers. One of his examples, taken from the language of the Chiquito of Bolivia, may serve as an illustration of phenomena situated on the grammatical level:

> In the men's language two genders are distinguished. Nouns designating gods, daemons, and men are masculine, while those designating women, the lower animals regardless of sex, and all other concepts are feminine. There is an elaborate system of gender inflections involving, not only nouns, but all the words of the language except a few invariable particles. This results in a sharp distinction between constructions containing masculine nouns and those containing feminine nouns. . . . In the women's language these gender distinctions do not exist. Men, therefore, use masculine constructions when speaking of masculine nouns and feminine constructions when speaking of feminine nouns, while women use the feminine constructions in all cases regardless of gender. . . . The language of the Chiquito probably represents the most radical distinction between men's and women's speech which is known to exist anywhere. . . . (Furfey 1944: 219)

Furfey points out that, from the sociologist's perspective, linguistic evidence on gender-specific modes of communication has intriguing implications for a better understanding of gender roles within a given society. According to Furfey, the assertion of masculine superiority can be recognized from the system of the language used in a hierarchically structured community. Since he notes that comparable sex differences also occur in the languages of Europe, one may argue that he anticipates *in nuce* key points of much later research regarding women's language.

Research on female speech was not very intensive in modern linguistics until the 1980s. Important impulses came from the works by Robin Lakoff (1973) and Mary Ritchie Key (1975) as well as from Barrie Thorne's and Nancy Henley's reader *Language and Sex: Difference and Dominance* (1975). In her famous article "Language and woman's place," Lakoff started from the assumption that "[t]he marginality and powerlessness of women is reflected in both the ways women are expected to speak, and the ways in which women are spoken of" (1973: 45). In the first part of her paper, she tries to identify several traits that in her opinion characterize female speech (1973: 49–57): women tend to use a wider and more precise range of color terms which are absent from the active vocabulary of most men (e.g., *ecru, aquamarine, lavender*); they have the inclination to employ supposedly meaningless particles such as *goodness* or *oh dear*; another significant feature of female speech is the use of evaluative adjectives for the purpose of approbation or admiration (e.g., *adorable, charming, divine, lovely*); a further characteristic is constituted by tag questions such as *isn't it* to avoid straightforward assertions and a conflict with the addressee; also conspicuous is rising instead of falling intonation in declarative sentences, often interpreted as a sign of women's lack of self-confidence and of a clear opinion.

Lakoff has been criticized for her method of basing her conclusions on data which, as she admits herself, were "gathered mainly by introspection" (1973: 46) and analyzed rather intuitively. Her claim that many of her findings may be universally true has also provoked objections. Most importantly perhaps, it must be questioned whether lists of context-independent features that are supposedly characteristic of female speech are really useful, since "the same linguistic features can, when used by different persons in different contexts and cultures, often mean very different things" (Romaine 1999: 5; similarly Cameron 2007: 45–51, 118–19, 163–4; see also ch. 20). Despite its obvious deficits, however, Lakoff's investigation has stimulated discussion in scholarly circles as well as in the public sphere. Two years after its publication, the article was turned into a short book with an extended list of characteristic features of women's speech (Lakoff 1975),[1] and it has since been re-edited as a revised and expanded version with a commentary (Lakoff 2004).

With regard to methodology we note that some studies seem to be inclined to grasp "women's language" as a uniform concept. However, modern sociolinguistics, following ancient rhetoric (consciously or unconsciously), has convincingly demonstrated that sex or gender alone is not the only parameter that determines the communicative behavior of a speaker. Thus the simple fact that a speaker is female cannot be used to draw far-reaching conclusions. In addition, criteria such as the cultural and social background (including religion), regional origin, level of education, and age of a speaker, as well as the communicative context of an utterance ("Who speaks to whom and when?"), must be taken into account (see, e.g., Nabrings 1981: 118). It is open to question whether the category of gender can be sufficiently isolated from these other factors. Therefore, "the study of men's versus women's speech is much more complicated than it at first appears" (Romaine 1999: 131).

During the last three decades, the investigation of "women's language" from a wide range of different angles has attained a vital role within linguistics, as can be seen from the sheer abundance of publications.[2] Perhaps in no other branch of linguistics has the scholarly output been so high; this is also due to the fact that gender and communication are analyzed in many disciplines neighboring linguistics, such as communication studies, sociology, psychology, anthropology, education studies, and gender studies. However, the vast majority of these enquiries lack a historical dimension and completely ignore the fact that some ancient authors already raised the problem of gender-specific languages (now called, for example, *genderlects* or *sexolects*[3]) and thus made at least a first step toward a diaphasic sketch of the linguistic levels and varieties of both Greek and Latin, however far such sketches may be from a scholarly analysis.[4]

Ancient Evidence on Female Speech

The ancient sources on women's language are admittedly not very ample or elaborate. Moreover, they are scattered: there is no single treatise that deals entirely with female speech. In the following paragraphs, some relevant metalinguistic passages have been collected and combined with a closer reading in order to obtain a more differentiated impression of the ancients' views on gender-specific language and style. Ancient authors point out gender-based differences not only in pragmatic respects, but also on the phonological, morphological, and lexico-semantic levels.

In the following outline the analysis of the sources will be structured according to their content and contextual criteria, although cases of overlap cannot be entirely avoided. This emphasis on the contexts of the documents may help prevent a grossly anachronistic approach, without restricting the corpus to a too narrowly focused period of time. The following topics will be treated in six sections: (i) physiological differences between men and women, especially with regard to voice; (ii) the linguistic influence of mothers and nurses; (iii) passages from rhetorical treatises on "unmanly" appearance; (iv) the phenomenon of language change and the question of the openness of women toward change; (v) the stereotype of the loquacity of women; (vi) some other aspects of communicative strategies that are described as typical of women, such as forms of address, diminutives, and oath formulae.

It should be noted that this contribution is not concerned with literary texts written by women[5] and the minute analysis as to their linguistic peculiarities. Such an investigation must be reserved for the future and may serve as a valuable supplement and touchstone to the documentation of metalinguistic sources on gender-specific communication.

Physiological differences between men and women

The bodily constitutions of men and women are the topic of ancient medical and biological treatises (see Lloyd 1983: 86–111), among which the works of Aristotle belong to the most extensive sources. In his *De generatione animalium*, he classifies women as infertile males and as constitutionally retarded, which is why they cannot produce semen (Arist. *Gen. an.* I 20 727b33–729a33, V 3 784a4–11). According to him, most relevant for speech differences is the fact that female voices tend to be higher and less robust than male ones, and this not only among humans but among all species that have a voice, except in the bovine (*Gen. an.* V 7 786b7–788b2, *Hist. an.* IV 11 538b13–15). Aristotle views a deep voice as the mark of a nobler nature (*Gen. an.* V 7 786b34–787a2). Similarly, Epictetus observes that nature has provided the female voice with a softer sound (*Diss.* 1.16: ἁπαλώτερον). As will be demonstrated below, this has wide-ranging implications for the speech training of the rhetorician who is expected to train his voice to be sonorous and masculine in order to avoid any vocal signs of effeminacy.

The linguistic influence of mothers and nurses

Some literary sources accentuate the great influence of the language of women on children. For the purposes of assuring a most effective education of very young children, Quintilian, professor of rhetoric in first-century Rome, recommends employing only those nurses who are not only morally impeccable, but who also have a flawless diction. It is to be expected that by permanent contact with the nurse the children will imitate her ways of speaking. As all kinds of impressions are likely to be engraved in children's minds to a significant extent, one ought to take care, he says, that children do not adopt bad language from a supposed model; later in their life, they might have severe problems in getting rid of certain defective accents or incorrect grammar (Quint. *Inst.* 1.1.4–5). Similar remarks can be found in Cicero's dialogue *Brutus* (§ 210). Both Cicero and Quintilian demonstrate how influential the contact with an ideal female speaker of Latin can be for children with the example of Cornelia, the mother of the Gracchi Gaius and Tiberius: she is said to have contributed much by her own high linguistic standards and her erudition to the rhetorical talent of her sons, and her sophisticated style could still be recognized from her letters (Cic. *Brut.* 211; Quint. *Inst.* 1.1.6). But in some cases, it was the father himself who not only attended to the more advanced education of his sons, but who also taught them to read and write, like the Elder Cato. He thought the elementary instruction of his son to be so crucial that he did not want to leave it to a slave, and he even tutored him in the principles of Roman law and physical education, as Plutarch reports (*Cato maior* 20.5–6).

It is interesting to note that in Latin, in contrast to many other languages of Europe, there is no term that corresponds exactly to "mother tongue." There are, however, the terms *sermo patrius* or *lingua patria*, referring to the "tongue of the father(s)," or expressions consisting of a word for "language" and a possessive pronoun such as *sermo noster* or *lingua nostra*. The coining of *materna lingua* with the meaning of "mother tongue" does not occur until the twelfth century CE and even then it still coexists for quite a while with the more common *lingua patria* or similar expressions (Fögen 2000: 51–6, with full references). Greek terms such as φωνὴ πατρῴα or πάτριος are loan translations of the Latin *patrius sermo* and are not attested in literary documents before the third century CE (Fögen 2000: 58–60).

Rhetorical treatises on "unmanly" appearance

In addition to the practical training in the forum as part of the *tirocinium fori*, normative rhetorical treatises and handbooks were used to prepare the future orator for his professional career. They contained important advice on the successful appearance of the rhetorician in public. To achieve this goal, not only stylistic aspects were to be taken into account, but also the impression which the orator made on his audience by his nonverbal behavior, i.e., the use of gestures, posture, facial expression, and voice (see Fögen 2001: 207–9; cf. Richlin 1997).

Quintilian starts his own outline with the earliest level of rhetorical education. Already in his very young years, the future orator ought to concentrate on a proper diction in his grammatical and stylistic training: poetic texts should not be read without a certain gracefulness, but at the same time their recitation must sound manly and dignified (Quint. *Inst.* 1.8.2). But this postulate is not only applied to the reading aloud of literature; it is a maxim for all speaking in public: a feeble and thin voice is associated with female speech and thus to be avoided by the future orator (Quint. *Inst.* 1.11.1, 11.3.32). This goal is achieved by a rigorous speech training during the rhetorical instruction. At the same time, the teacher of rhetoric guides his pupil toward a skillful use of nonverbal elements to enhance the effectiveness of his presentation (Quint. *Inst.* 1.11.3–19).

Why does Quintilian so emphatically point to the danger of effeminacy in an orator? In the twelfth chapter of the fifth book of his *Institutio oratoria*, he complains about the degeneracy of rhetoric in his own time. According to him, declamations have become oriented increasingly toward superficial beauty, the goal of which is to enhance the pleasure of the audience. In earlier times, good speeches were characterized by brevity and vigorous style; they were comparable to a male body, by nature strong, powerful, and robust. However, this old ideal has now been abandoned in favor of a "castrated" style, as it were, which has lost all the natural qualities of manly speech. In particular, verbosity, contrived expressions, and long-windedness are denigrated in this context (Quint. *Inst.* 5.12.17–21). The same analogy between style and

the human body is taken up by Quintilian in the preface to the eighth book. As he
bases his definition of good style upon the principles of naturalness and unaffected-
ness, he transposes the concept of established Roman virtues to the linguistic level
(Quint. *Inst.* 8 pr. 19–28, esp. 20–1; similarly *Inst.* 8.3.6–11, 10.1.43, and
12.10.40–7). This does not mean that he pleads for a fully archaic style or for the
complete renunciation of rhetorical devices; rather, archaisms and embellishing
elements should both be deployed moderately and with great care, not just for
cheap showmanship, but as a means of making one's case effectively (Quint. *Inst.* 8
pr. 32–3).

   Quintilian's contention that a man's appearance as well as his style ought to differ
significantly from that of a woman also appears in earlier rhetorical treatises as a postulate of a pronounced normative character. As in many other cases, he follows certain
tenets developed by the rhetorical tradition, in particular Cicero (e.g., *De or.* 3.41,
3.199; see also *Rhet. Her.* 3.22). The key to understanding the rejection of female
elements in a male speech lies in the contention of Roman authors that a man's style
indicates his morals, and that his morals will affect his style (*talis oratio qualis vita*) – a
motto which is of Greek origin (e.g., Diog. Laert. 1.58 on Solon and Cic. *Tusc.* 5.47
on Socrates). This principle is discussed at greater length in epistle 114 of Seneca the
Younger with reference to Maecenas as an example of effeminate style and, earlier on,
in some passages of Seneca the Elder's *Controversiae* and *Suasoriae* where in particular
the "soft" style of the orator Arellius Fuscus is censured (*Controv.* 1 pr. 7–9, 2 pr. 1,
and *Suas.* 2.23; see Richlin 1997: 94–8).

   This all demonstrates that in the later Roman Republic and early Empire there
existed fixed concepts as to how men were expected to communicate in public discourse. In many areas of Greek and Roman society, especially in rhetoric, the ideal of
masculinity prevails in every respect: the model-rhetorician is set apart from effeminate speech as well as from bodily behavior allegedly typical of women. Groups such
as women, children, slaves, and barbarians that are perceived as linguistically as well as
physically different, in particular as far as their body movements, gestures, facial
expressions, and voices are concerned, are often associated with political irrelevance,
a lack of sufficient education and knowledge, and a high degree of emotionality as
well as a lack of restraint and sometimes also with immorality. These perceptions of
the ancients frequently result in marginalization of the groups that diverge from the
"male norm."

Language change: the openness of women toward change

In a passage of Plato's *Cratylus* it is maintained that women's pronunciation differs in
certain respects from men's (Pl. *Cra.* 418b7–419b4). Socrates remarks that words
change their phonological shape over the course of time, some so much so that their
original meaning is no longer discernible. According to him, the semantic value of a
word becomes particularly evident if it has retained its original shape or if it can be
traced back to it. With this background, Socrates describes two phenomena of sound
change which are obviously related to Attic Greek: first, the change from /i/ to /ei/
or /ē/, supported by the example ἱμέρα > εἱμέρα and later ἡμέρα, and, second, the

change from /d/ to /z/, illustrated by the example δυογόν > ζυγόν. The motivation for this change is explained by euphony: the sounds that are in use now are perceived by the speaker to be more sublime (μεγαλοπρεπέστερα). It is added that women in particular tend to stick to the archaic pronunciation, as they do in the case of phonological change (Pl. *Cra.* 418b7–c3).

On the basis of the findings provided by historical Greek grammar we may dispute that the phenomena of language change outlined by Plato really took place in the way he described. However, it seems plausible that Plato sketched a phonological feature occurring in the first half of the fourth century BCE that was indeed restricted to female speech, namely the pronunciation of Attic /e/ as /i/ and of /zd/ as /d/. However, this development cannot be interpreted as a feature of archaizing tendencies, but, on the contrary, as a phonological innovation which has its origins in nonstandard Greek.[6] The prestige forms of Standard Attic seem to have been retained by men rather than women; they were learned by men at school and used in assemblies as well as in the public sphere more generally. Nonetheless, the excerpt from the *Cratylus* sheds an interesting light upon the way in which linguistic peculiarities of female speakers were perceived. Therefore, it may serve as an intriguing document of language awareness in ancient Greece. It seems to be very unlikely that the passage is to be interpreted as an ironic exaggeration or even as conscious distortion, as in many other instances in Platonic dialogues.

Further evidence of the supposedly archaizing speech of women comes from a passage from the third book of Cicero's treatise *De oratore*, in which Crassus discusses the significance of earlier Latin for contemporary rhetoric (*De or.* 3.39–46). It cannot be denied, he says, that most early Roman orators had a plain, unambiguous, and correct style, since in this epoch of simplicity one did not yet strive for embellishment. Certainly, a blind imitation of this unadorned and straightforward style is not recommended by Crassus, as the usage of Latin has changed in many respects. He therefore advocates the moderate use of uncommon words and forms that belong to the past, and then only for the sake of special stylization of certain passages. Moreover, antiquated style should not be confused with coarse and boorish diction, as so often happens. That an uncultivated and peasant-like way of speaking must not be equated with the refined and urbane style of old Roman aristocracy is illustrated by the example of Laelia, Crassus' own mother-in-law (b. around 160 BCE), who was married to the augur Quintus Mucius Scaevola. For aristocratic women of that time, Crassus continues, it was typical not to adopt common phenomena of language change into their own idiolect because they lived a secluded life in private and thus did not have the opportunity to perceive new tendencies of language usage. By hearing Laelia's diction with its natural plainness, one felt reminded of the language of old Roman dramatists such as Plautus (d. 184 BCE) and Naevius (d. after 201 BCE). According to Crassus, it would be possible to conclude that Laelia's ancestors also used a similarly simple, but nonetheless cultivated style, which had nothing to do with the crude diction of peasants (Cic. *De or.* 3.45; see *Brut.* 211). It is obvious that Crassus herewith gives an example of early forms of the linguistic variety characteristic of the city of Rome, which was typically described as not having any external admixtures and as being characterized by a specific euphony. Frequently termed *sermo urbanus* and thus defined as a mainly diatopic (i.e., local/regional) variety, it is clearly distinguished from other varieties of Latin (cf. Fögen 2000: 119–41).

The loquacity of women

The claim that speechmaking (μῦθος) is male and not female business is first made in Homer's *Odyssey* when Telemachus tells his mother Penelope to go back into the house and take care of her female duties, namely weaving (*Od.* 1.356–9). Given Penelope's intelligence and courage with which she administers the court of Ithaca during her husband's absence, this may be seen as a rather rude outburst of an adolescent. At the same time, it needs to be borne in mind that Telemachus wants to demonstrate that he has become mature enough to take charge. His words could be interpreted as an indispensable part of his transition from boy to man which enables him to deal with the suitors at Odysseus' court.

The notion that women are well advised to remain silent is a stereotype of which one can find several instances in earlier Greek literature. For Greek drama, there is a passage in Sophocles' *Ajax*: it is Ajax himself who gives this sort of recommendation to his beloved Tecmessa, the daughter of the Phrygian king Teleutas, when she attempts to prevent him from leaving the house and from killing the Greek army commanders Agamemnon and Menelaus (Soph. *Aj.* 292–3). In her report to the chorus, Tecmessa speaks of Ajax's reaction as of an "old song" (ἀεὶ δ' ὑμνούμενα) and thus provides us with a hint that the exigency for women to be quiet had attained proverbial status in fifth-century Athenian conceptions of the ideal communicative behavior of women.[7] At the same time, Ajax' response illustrates his brusque behavior toward his beloved. Indeed, Tecmessa follows Ajax' advice and keeps silent (Soph. *Aj.* 294); he leaves the house and, blinded with madness by the goddess Athena, murders the cattle instead of the army commanders (*Aj.* 294–326). In the further course of the tragedy, Ajax refuses to answer Tecmessa's questions and turns her away, asking her not to besiege him any further, as she has already spoken far too much and for too long (*Aj.* 585–92). The servant, who brings along Ajax' son Eurysaces, is encouraged by Ajax not to cry about the fatal incidents, as laments are the domain of women (*Aj.* 578–80).

For Greek men, female silence or at least verbal restraint was a sign of self-control and moderation (σωφροσύνη), as can be seen from a passage in Semonides' iambic catalogue of women in which the only praiseworthy character is the "bee-woman" who abstains from female talk about sex (Semon. IEG 7.90–1: ἀφροδισίους λόγους). Women's gossip, especially when it has a sexual content, is perceived here and elsewhere to have the potential of subverting social hierarchies (see McClure 1999: 56–62). Moderation in words frequently entailed the subordination of the wife to her husband. This social expectation of female passivity is expressed by Plutarch in a passage of his work *Advice to the Bride and Groom*, where he recommends that "a wife should speak only to her husband or through her husband, and should not feel aggrieved if, like a flute-player, she makes a nobler sound (φθέγγεται σεμνότερον) through another's tongue" (*Coniug. praec.* 32 142d; cf. Xen. *Oec.*). A much earlier example is Andromache's self-description in Euripides' *Troades* as a woman who has achieved a flawless reputation through her devout behavior toward her husband: she exhibited σωφροσύνη by guarding the house, shunning conversations with other females, and practicing silence (Eur. *Troad*. 643–58).

In comedy and related genres the image of the loquacious woman is exploited as a topos, employed to evoke laughter and ridicule, and often developed into the grotesque. Comedy allows for intentional exaggerations, like those in Plautus' *Aulularia*, in which the matron Eunomia says that women are rightly held to be garrulous, as something like a silent woman has never existed (*Aul*. 123–6; cf. *Rud*. 1114, *Cist*. 120–9, and *Poen*. 32–5; see also Ter. *Heaut*. 621, 879–81, 1006–11). But Aristophanes already plays with this stereotype (e.g., *Eccl*. 120, *Thesm*. 393; cf. Willi 2003: 168–9), which is taken up after him by various other authors such as Alexis (96 PCG), Menander (581.13 PCG), Lucian (*Rh. pr.* 23) and Libanius (*Decl*. 26.34).

Particularly impressive is the fifteenth idyll of Theocritus, which portrays the conversation of the Syracusan women Gorgo and Praxinoa in a parodistic manner. With their vicious tongues they make nasty comments about their husbands, before they move on to speak about the Adonis festival. When they go together to the palace of Queen Arsinoë in order to attend the festival in person, they encounter a man who is surprised at their torrent of words and also at their Doric accent. Praxinoa tells him to mind his own business (Theoc. *Id*. 15.87–95).

Almost four centuries later, Juvenal takes up the stereotype in his so-called Satire on Women and supplements it with references to women's inclination to spread rumors and fabricate horror stories in an unrestrained fashion (Juv. 6.408–12). This proclivity for exaggeration is mirrored in Juvenal's verses by hyperbolic formulations (Juv. 6.410–11: *magno . . . diluvio, cuncta arva*) as well as emphatic plural substantives (ibid.: *populos, urbes, terras*). The fact that crude and grossly made-up stories were usually called "old women's tales" (γραῶν μῦθοι or *aniles fabellae*) or "old wives' prattle" (γραολογία, a term employed by Sextus Empiricus (*Math*. 1.141) to criticize the supposedly idle talk of his opponents) indicates that older women in particular were thought to be quite inventive in their narrations. Quintilian relates such stories to the fables of Aesop (Quint. *Inst*. 1.9.2) and thus to the world of fantasy (cf. Quint. *Inst*. 1.8.19; Cic. *Nat. D*. 1.94; Apul. *Met*. 6.25.1; Sen. *Ben*. 1.4.6). But literary evidence on women's talkativeness is also found outside the tradition of comedy and parody. The rhetorician Seneca the Elder, for instance, mentions *muliebris garrulitas* to denote the opposite of his description of a woman who is not only perfectly capable of keeping a secret even in a most precarious situation, but who is also a paragon of female modesty (*Controv*. 2.5.12).

The stereotype of female loquacity is ubiquitous in ancient literature, in particular in comedy and satire. It recurs in these and other literary genres, but also in proverbs and sayings of all centuries thereafter. In addition to their garrulity, female speakers are often described as noisy and gossiping. They are said to be unreliable in what they utter, to reveal secrets, and to have a tendency to lie, and sometimes their language would mirror their irrationality (see Kramarae 1982: esp. 87–90; Bußmann 1995: 135–6; Bierbach 1995). In general, these proverbs show that it is women who deviate from social norms with their communicative behavior, and it is evident that the perspective in these sayings is almost always a male one. The "norm" is thus equated with male speech, as is the case in many other respects. The simplistic statement that "women talk too much" has therefore been rightly contested by modern linguists (e.g., Tannen 1990: 74–95, 96–122; Holmes 1998; see also Yaguello 1978: 61–6).

Interestingly, various sources prove that the ancients' distaste for loquacity did not only apply to women but also to men. Theognis has a few verses on how unbearable the company of a talkative man is for others (Theognis 295–8). Theophrastus devotes three sketches in his *Characters* to types of men who suffer from garrulity (ἀδολεσχία), talkativeness (λαλιά), and the spreading of false rumors (λογοποιία). Later on, Plutarch composes a separate essay on the problem of "garrulity," an annoying antisocial behavior which, as he says, is difficult for philosophy to cure, since the typical babbler will not be prepared to listen to anyone, not even to words of reason (*De garr.* 1 502b). Plutarch, who approaches the topic from an ethical perspective, warns that a talkative person often creates the impression of being untrustworthy and prone to lies (e.g., *De garr.* 3 503c–d). Uncontrolled talking may even harm friends, aid enemies, and ultimately lead to self-destruction (*De garr.* 7–15 504f–10c). In the second part of this work (*De garr.* 16–23 510c–15a), he offers various methods for treating this disease (νόσος): especially by developing a disciplined habit of reticence and by exercising self-control.

Forms of address, diminutives, oath formulae

Finally, some minor topics will be discussed that are associated in ancient texts with female speech. Certain forms of address are classified by the *Suda* lexicon as being used only by women, although earlier on they were also employed by men (s.vv. ὦ μέλε (vol. III p. 609 Adler) and ὦ τάν (vol. III p. 628–9 Adler); cf. Bain 1984: 33–5, with special reference to Menander; Sommerstein 1995: 73–8; and Willi 2003: 186–8, 192–3, with special reference to Aristophanes).

The fourth-century grammarian Donatus writes in his commentary to Terence's comedy *Eunuchus* that the vocative of the possessive pronoun *meus* fits very nicely with the flatteries of women (Donatus in Ter. *Eun.* 656.1; similarly, Donatus in Ter. *Phorm.* 1005, *Ad.* 289, *Andr.* 685). It is generally typical of women, he adds, that they flatter and lament (Donatus in Ter. *Ad.* 291.4). A further characteristic trait of female speech that is recorded by some sources is the frequent usage of diminutives termed in Greek ὑποκορισμοί or ὑποκοριστικά (Gilleland 1980: 181; Sommerstein 1995: 76–7). One may interpret statements like these as an indication of the belief that the general tendency of women to be more affective or emotional than men could be perceived on the linguistic level. Some of the sources pointing in that direction could also be related to the frequently expressed attitude of ancient authors that women use language for trickery and cheating. Hesiod's Pandora is the classic example in this respect (Hes. *Op.* 54–104, esp. 77–9; cf. Hes. *Op.* 372–4 and *Th.* 570–612), and Aristotle in his *Historia animalium* (IX 1 608a21–b18) states that, while the nature of men is most consummate and complete, women are, among other things, more compassionate than men, more easily moved to tears, more mendacious (ψευδέστερον), and more deceptive (εὐαπατητότερον) (*Hist. an.* IX 1 608b8–15). But already in Homer there are various female figures who use their speech, with its soft-ness or its sweet sound, to beguile men (see Bergren 1983: esp. 69–75; Cantarella 1996: esp. 3–13; McClure 1999: 62–8), like the Sirens (*Od.* 12.39–54, esp. 12.39–40), the sorceress Circe (*Od.* 10 *passim*), and the nymph Calypso (esp. *Od.* 1.55–7). All of these female characters have in common that they symbolize sexual attractiveness, that they are *femmes fatales*; by their conscious instrumentalization of their erotic appeal and charm they try to interfere with Odysseus' plan to return to his faithful wife Penelope who, as Odysseus himself admits, cannot compete with the immortals' looks (*Od.* 5.215–18). Thus they present a serious danger to the male protagonist that he must overcome in order to pursue his goal.

Other gender-specific differences are observed for the use of vows and oath formu-lae (see Sommerstein 1995: 64–8; Adams 1984: 47–55; Moreau 1995: 54–6). In Aristophanes' *Ecclesiazusae* (produced probably in 392 or 391 BCE), one of the women is rehearsing a speech which she wants to deliver at the assembly in male guise and which should therefore sound like the speech of a man (ἀνδριστί). However, when she swears μὰ τὼ θεώ "by the Two Goddesses," i.e., by Demeter and Persephone, she is harshly criticized by the female protagonist Praxagora, as this formula was only used by female speakers and would most definitely betray her sex (Ar. *Eccl.* 148–60, cf. 189–92; see Bain 1984: 39–42). The exclamation *mehercle* is, according to Gellius, reserved for men, whereas *mecastor* is an expression exclusively employed by women. Gellius even gives a reason for this: women never swear by Hercules because they do not participate in his festivals (Gell. 11.6.1–3). However, the oath formula *edepol* "by Pollux" was uttered by both men and women. Gellius closes with the statement that he disbelieves the hypothesis brought forward by Varro that in early Rome *edepol* was only used by women during the celebration of the Eleusinian mysteries and only later taken up by men, who were not informed about the original context of the formula (Gell. 11.6.4–6). Part of the evidence provided by Gellius is supported by a note of the grammarian Charisius, who adds the exclamation *eiuno* "by Juno" to the list of formulae that are reserved for women and *mediusfidius* "I call heaven to witness," "so help me God") to the formulae used by male speakers (Charisius, *Gram.* 1.198.17–23 Keil). In Petronius, however, the female character Quartilla uses *mediusfidius* (Petron. *Sat.* 17.4: *misereor mediusfidius vestri* "By the god of truth, I pity you"); one may argue that the author consciously puts a "male" expression in the mouth of a woman who is on the whole portrayed rather negatively as lacking proper female conduct and being vulgar.

Conclusions

This survey has had to be restricted to the discussion of a few exemplary passages. Further topics could have been taken into account, such as linguistic taboo, the lan-guage of love, and the way in which women communicate with small children (see Boscherini 1995: 57–60). Then there is some evidence on women's knowledge of foreign languages. To give just one example, Plutarch (Plut. *Ant.* 27.2) reports the

Egyptian queen Cleopatra's talent to turn to whatever language she pleased, so that in her interviews with barbarians she very seldom needed an interpreter, but made her replies to most of them herself and without any assistance, whether they were Ethiopians, Troglodytes, Hebrews, Arabians, Syrians, Medes, or Parthians.

Nevertheless, it is possible to draw at least some conclusions from the material considered here. One can group the documents examined in this contribution along the following lines. These are:

a)   texts that contain remarks on the language of women in general;
b)   sources that are related to the language of specific groups of women and thus take into account social (diastratic), age-related, education-related, and regional (diatopic) differences;
c)   documents that are concerned with individual women and thus relate to a specific idiolect typical of one particular female speaker;
d)   passages from normative rhetorical treatises that characterize the speech of certain men as "unmanly" and thus proceed from a more or less clear idea of what prototypical female speech is like, at least with regard to pitch and voice quality.

Women's language was almost always understood in antiquity as a deviation from the male norm. If, on the other hand, women did not behave as they were expected to and acted more like male speakers, this was perceived as a transgression of boundaries and a threat to male domains and spheres of power. Greek drama provides instructive examples of "dangerous" female characters, such as Clytemnestra, Antigone, and Medea, whose bold behavior and words disrupt the masculine order (Griffith 2001: 124–5, 127–35).

In particular the documents reporting on women's loquacity reveal that the majority of the texts concerned with female speech are loaded with stereotypes, though in certain literary genres like comedy and satire admittedly on purpose and for the sake of parodic exaggeration. But on the whole, the use of clichés is so pronounced and importunate even in non-humoristic texts that it is impossible to claim that ancient texts provide a reasonably neutral description of the characteristics of women's language. Nonetheless, many of the documents, in particular those embedded in a rhetorical context, reflect relatively precise societal expectations regarding the communicative behavior of both men and women. Those who did not adopt the system of strategies of communicating that was held to be ideal committed an offense and had to reckon with sanctions. On the other hand, as has been pointed out, prescriptive rules "are of limited value in determining how females really spoke" (Adams 1984: 44).

Most intriguing and perhaps also most reliable are documents like those on certain forms of address or oath formulae, the use of which is described as being restricted to women. Further, remarks on pronunciation (the phonological level) and the personal style (the lexical and pragmatic level) of individual women, as they occur in Plato's *Cratylus* and in Cicero's description of Laelia, should not be totally discarded, although it must be underscored that sketches like these can be criticized for incorrect explanations of phonological phenomena or for the lack of a more detailed description of the idiolect of a particular female speaker.

Most ancient sources offer far-from-nuanced and often misogynistic analyses of elements of gender-specific communication; instead they contain a large number of prejudices and stereotypes toward female speech that, along with many other texts, have unwittingly set the agenda for modern criticism and in particular feminist linguistics. But however one-sided and biased ancient approaches may have been, it cannot be denied that some of the texts, notably rhetorical treatises, are noteworthy for their attempts to provide the first steps toward a sociolinguistic outline of Greek and Latin. It was recognized in ancient rhetoric that there are a number of parameters that determine the communicative behavior of a speaker, namely social background, regional origin, level of education, age, and also gender (see, for example, Fögen 2000: esp. 117–41). This perception provided the basis for elaborate research in modern sociolinguistics that has been undertaken mainly from the 1970s onwards, and it would not be completely mistaken to maintain that it laid at least some of the groundwork for contemporary studies on gender-specific communication.

The informative value of ancient sources regarding gender-specific forms of language may be rather limited from the viewpoint of modern linguistics, in particular because of the biased and stereotypical character of the majority of the ancient texts in question. But their importance can certainly not be denied from a historical perspective, since "[t]hrough an historical approach we can learn how our present attitudes toward women's and men's speech were shaped" (Kramarae 1982: 87).

FURTHER READING

Among contributions from modern linguistics, Romaine 1999 is particularly valuable. Those who read German may refer to Samel 2000.

Gender-specific communication in Greco-Roman antiquity is dealt with more extensively in Lardinois and McClure 2001 and in the article by Fögen (2004), which also contains a broad documentation of scholarship on female speech and related topics. For an analysis of speech and gender in Greek drama, McClure 1999 is to be recommended.

NOTES

1   For a convenient summary and critical discussion of Lakoff's revised catalogue of features in her 1975 book see, for example, Fasold 1990: 102–7, 116 and Romaine 1999: 154–7.

2   Among the more extensive surveys, see in particular the books by Yaguello (1978), Talbot (1998), Romaine (1999), Samel (2000), and Eckert and McConnell-Ginet (2003), but also the useful volumes edited by Hellinger and Bußmann (2001–3) and Holmes and Meyerhoff (2003). See the extensive bibliography in Fögen 2004.

3   To give just a few examples: Glück 1979 employs the corresponding Germanized term "Sexlekte." Nabrings (1981: 113–22) speaks predominantly of "gender-specific varieties" ("geschlechtsspezifische Varietäten"), Tannen (1990: 42, 279) of "genderlect." Jespersen (1922: 241) uses the phrase "sex dialects."

4   Among the commonly used introductory surveys on gender and language Romaine 1999
    is a notable exception; see also Bußmann 1995 and Kramarae 1982: esp. 87–90.
5   Collections of literature written by women are, for example, Rayor 1991, Churchill, Brown,
    and Jeffrey 2002, and Plant 2004; see also Snyder 1990.
6   For details, see Boscherini 1995: 55–6 and in particular Sommerstein 1995: 81–3.
    Sommerstein's interpretation of the passage has now been questioned by Willi (2003: 161–2,
    171, 194–5), who assumes "(1) that women prominently furthered linguistic innovation in
    Attic because they regarded the innovatory variety as prestigious, and (2) that this variety
    had prestige connotations also for those (male) social groups who aimed at cultural refine-
    ment (ἀστειότης) although that meant to be on the 'female' side of the established gender-
    model" (Willi 2003: 162).
7   See also Democr. 68 B 274 DK and Eur. *El.* 945–6. Sophocles' line is quoted by Aristotle,
    Pol. 1 13 1260a30, and slightly modified by Menander (*Mon.* 139).

CHAPTER TWENTY-TWO

Forms of Address and Markers of Status

Eleanor Dickey

The use of language communicates many things besides information. The two utterances, "Boy! Open that door!" and "Excuse me, sir, do you suppose you could open the door for me?" both convey the basic information that the speaker wants the addressee to open the door, but the first one also conveys the speaker's sense of superiority to the addressee, while the second also conveys the speaker's respect for the addressee. Forms of address, that is words or parts of words that refer to the addressee, are a common place for languages to encode references to status and respect, though there are also many other ways in which such references can be signaled linguistically.

In many modern languages, such as French, German, and Italian, social differences are indicated by the use of two different sets of second-person pronouns and accompanying verb forms. With this "*tu / vous*" distinction, one pronoun indicates familiarity and/or lack of respect, while the other indicates distance and/or respect. Ancient Greek, like English, does not have such a distinction in pronoun and verb usage: there is only one second-person singular pronoun for all addressees.

In both Greek and English, linguistic encoding of status is most obvious in "free" (not grammatically bound) forms of address, that is, vocatives. Thus the difference between "boy" and "sir" in the two utterances quoted above is striking (but it is not the only difference, as even if both these words were removed the second sentence would be more respectful than the first). For this reason far more scholarly attention has been devoted to vocatives than to other linguistic status markers in Ancient Greek, and the term "address system" is generally used to refer to the body of vocatives in normal usage and the way in which those vocatives are employed.

The Greek address system is not a unified, monolithic whole. Not only did it evolve over time, but at any one point in time different systems were in use in different types of Greek – not, of course, that we can always recover enough information to reconstruct the whole range. As with many features of the Greek language, a radical split in usage is particularly visible in the later period, between classicizing and non-classicizing systems. Some address systems, such as the one in daily use in Classical Sparta, are no longer recoverable from the information we have, but that information does allow us to recover a number of address systems with varying degrees of completeness.

Forms of Address in the Classical Period

The address systems about which we have the most information are those used in Classical literature. Classical texts containing vocatives fall into two groups: in one type of text a fairly small group of vocatives is used in a consistent and predictable fashion, and in the other type of text a much larger group of vocatives, many of them unique, is used in a varied and largely unpredictable fashion. Texts of the first type are prose and Menander, and texts of the second type are Homer, tragedy, and Aristophanes. Later prose by Atticizing authors such as Lucian tends to use an address system resembling that of the first group of classical texts and can to all intents and purposes be treated as an extension of it, except in a few particular areas (for which see next section).

Sociolinguists investigating modern languages have undertaken extensive study of the address systems of a wide variety of languages, and in every case they have found predictable patterns of usage in the address system of ordinary conversation. Indeed such predictability is essential for the proper functioning of a language's primary address system and allows it to operate and develop naturally. Address systems develop as follows: a word that is not normally used as a form of address is imported into the address system because it has a lexical meaning that some speakers find useful, and other speakers then pick it up and start using it. As it becomes more common, the word develops a particular social meaning, and that meaning gradually eclipses the lexical meaning in the minds of speakers and addressees. The social meaning often evolves over time as the word continues to be used, sometimes to the point where it seems to be in direct conflict with the lexical meaning, which may continue unchanged in the word's use in non-vocative contexts. Thus in Icelandic the word for "anus" has become a term of endearment when used as an address but is still very far from an endearment in other uses. This development requires consistent use of the same vocatives by numerous speakers over an extended period of time; without such use vocatives cannot develop a social meaning distinct from their lexical meanings (Braun 1988: 260–5; see also the discussion of "grammaticalization" in ch. 9).

The address system of prose and Menander contains numerous terms with social meanings distinct from their lexical meanings (see below), as well as the consistent usage and relatively small core group of terms that would be necessary for such meanings to develop. The address system of Homer, tragedy, and Aristophanes, though it contains many elements of the prose system, also tends to employ many other terms in their lexical meanings. This suggests that prose and Menander provide a fairly accurate reflection of the address system of ordinary conversation (at least of conversation among educated Athenian citizens), and that other poetic genres have a tendency to replace those simple and predictable vocatives with unique, creative, and elaborate alternatives. In attempting to recover conversational address usage, therefore, it is important to pick one's literary sources carefully (Dickey 1995).

The Classical address system, as used in ordinary conversation and preserved in prose and Menander, was divided into two parts. There was a basic, unmarked set of addresses that functioned as the standard terms for certain individuals, and then there was a second set, including but not limited to categories such as insults and endearments, that were used to convey particular feelings. Because the basic addresses were not the same for all addressees, some terms belonged to both groups and could function as standard, unmarked terms in one context and as more emotional terms in another. The same basic division is common in address systems in other languages. For example in English a schoolteacher might be standardly addressed as "Mrs Smith" by her pupils and as "Jane" by her friends, and either address would convey something particular if produced by the other set of speakers, while "idiot" would always convey something particular regardless of the speaker.

Standard addresses

The basic, unmarked address in Classical Greek was always the addressee's name unless the addressee was a woman, a child, a slave, a foreigner, or a close relative of the speaker. As Greeks in the Classical period had only one name it was not possible to make distinctions by using a first, middle, or last name, as in the Roman address system or that of modern English speakers. Thus as long as speakers were dealing with adult male citizens unrelated to themselves, which is most often the case in extant literature, the address system was very simple: the addressee's single name would be used unless some particular feeling needed to be conveyed. When Greeks addressed Romans, of course, the simplicity of the address system was interfered with by the addressees' having several names. Romans themselves made complex distinctions among those different names (see Dickey 2002), and at first the Greeks did not understand those distinctions, simply using the Latin *praenomen* like a Greek single name. Eventually, they learned to employ the Latin name system as the Romans did.

People other than adult male citizens, that is women, children, slaves, and foreigners, could be addressed by name like adult men, but they could also be addressed by the characteristic that distinguished them from adult male citizens. Thus women tended to be called γύναι "woman," boys tended to be called παῖ "boy" or τέκνον "child," young men νεανία, νεανίσκε, or μειράκιον "young man," slaves παῖ "boy," and foreigners ξένε "foreigner." Our surviving evidence does not indicate how girls unrelated to the speaker were addressed, and it is possible that such addresses were in practice rarely needed because of the seclusion in which young females lived.

The extent to which such generic designations were used instead of names depended on the category into which the addressee fell. In surviving literature young men and foreigners are normally addressed by name and comparatively rarely by terms indicating their youth or national origin; for boys names are less common but still the preferred option. For slaves the most common option is παῖ, but names are also possible (especially from other slaves), while women are normally called γύναι and rarely addressed by name (in Classical literature; see below for a shift in the later period) unless they are prostitutes or the speaker is also female. This latter name avoidance is connected to a general tendency in Classical Attic to avoid using the names of respectable women in public at all (see Schaps 1977: 323–8, Sommerstein 1980: 406–7). Since the status of women in Sparta was notably different from that in Athens, it is not unlikely that the Spartan address system differed from the Athenian on this point, though we have no direct evidence of such difference owing to the scarcity of surviving literature from Sparta.

The address choices described so far of course depended on the addressee's name being known; if it was unknown, the name was obviously not a viable address option. In real life this problem would only have arisen when the name was unknown to the speaker, but in literature it can also occur when an author wants to depict interaction with a character whose name would have been known to the speaker but is not known to the author. In such circumstances it was not easy to get around the issue by avoiding the use of any vocative, as the absence of direct address at the start of an interaction was rude. For women, children, slaves, and foreigners there was a simple solution available in the generic addresses that were often used instead of names, and therefore unknown or unnamed characters in these categories were almost always addressed with γύναι, παῖ, etc. But in the case of adult male citizens the generic term that might seem most obvious to us, ἄνερ "man," was not used. The state of being an adult male seems not to have been a distinguishing characteristic in the way that being young or female was; the vocative ἄνερ meant "husband" and was restricted almost entirely to women addressing their husbands, although in cases other than the vocative ἀνήρ meant "man" much more frequently than it meant "husband." Instead, speakers employed an interesting group of very broad generic terms, chiefly οὗτος "this one" (see ch. 11) and ἄνθρωπε "human being." Since these addresses are not used to unknown women, ἄνθρωπε was exclusively masculine in the vocative, though in other cases ἄνθρωπος was gender-neutral.

The other major category of exceptions to the rule of unmarked address by name comprised the speaker's close relatives, who were often addressed by terms indicating kinship. People addressing their parents normally used πάτερ "father" or μῆτερ "mother" as appropriate, and names were never used, regardless of the age of the speaker. Older relatives other than parents seem to have received kinship terms (e.g., θεῖε "uncle," πάππε "grandfather") from children and names from adult speakers, though the evidence on this point is not extensive. Parents addressing their sons and daughters normally used kinship terms (υἱέ "son," θύγατερ "daughter," παῖ or τέκνον "child") until the children were clearly adults. In extant literature names are never used by parents to offspring who are still children, rarely to youths, but often to adults – although the use of kinship terms by parents is not uncommon even to adult offspring, particularly from parents of the same sex as the child they are addressing. Spouses can be addressed either by name or with the kinship terms γύναι "wife" and ἄνερ "husband"; in the case of wives γύναι is more common than names, but in the case of husbands names are preferred to ἄνερ.

Expressive addresses

Any departure from the system just described communicated a particular attitude or emotion. The most obvious example of such departure is insults, terms with a specifically offensive lexical meaning. These are difficult to study effectively with our surviving evidence because they are not common in the texts that provide the most reliable evidence for the address system. (Aristophanes makes frequent use of insults, but his are too clever and elaborate to be typical of ordinary interaction.) Nevertheless it is clear that addresses like κάκιστε "worst" or καταγέλαστε "ridiculous" were always rude. Another obvious example of expressive address is terms of pity, such as ταλαίπωρε "miserable" or ἄθλιε "pitiful." These terms were often used to convey sympathy for the addressee, but they could also be employed as insults.

Another set of terms used for marked departure from the normal system comprises those indicating affection or admiration, as φίλε "dear, friend," ἀγαθέ "good," ἑταῖρε "comrade," or βέλτιστε "best." Such vocatives were sometimes used simply to express the affection or admiration that their lexical meanings suggest, but often they were used as a form of exaggerated politeness by a speaker who wanted to indicate his own intellectual superiority to the addressee. This usage is particularly characteristic of Socrates as depicted in both Plato and Xenophon, and of other Platonic characters who take on the dominant role in dialogues that do not involve Socrates, but it is also found in the Attic orators. The agreement between Plato and Xenophon on this point suggests that frequent, somewhat ironic usage of such terms was a characteristic of the speech of the historical Socrates.

Titles could be used to convey particular respect, but such usage was less common than we might expect from parallels in other languages. The only context in which titles can have been at all common in Greek society is addresses from slaves to their masters and mistresses. In literary representations of such addresses δέσποτα "master" and δέσποινα "mistress" frequently occur, but they are by no means the rule, and in Menander address by name is more common. Free men and women who were not a slave's own master or mistress did not receive titles or any other type of respectful address from slaves, merely names or γύναι as appropriate. Such a distinction between masters and others in address by slaves is interesting, given that in address to slaves there is no such distinction: παῖ "boy" is used by masters and others alike.

Speakers other than slaves normally did not use titles at all. All our evidence on Classical Greek society suggests that titles of office were rarely or never used by one citizen to another, even if the addressee was an archon, a general, or a king. Such egalitarian behavior is not unexpected in democratic Athens, but it is more surprising that, if we can believe our sources, it appears to have been equally the rule all over Greece, including Sparta and cities with tyrannies. Of course it would be possible to argue that our chief sources for this information, Herodotus and later historians and biographers, did not know or did not care how Spartan kings were addressed. Nevertheless their evidence on this point is worthy of serious consideration, because of the distinction they draw between Classical Greek kings and tyrants, who almost never receive titles except from servants, and Persian and other oriental rulers, who are often called βασιλεῦ "king" even by speakers of high status in their own right. It is unlikely that Herodotus or his successors knew a great deal about actual Persian practice in addressing the monarch, but the picture they produce, with a sharp contrast between Greek and Persian practice, shows both that they were paying attention to the issue of address and that they saw the use of titles by free men as fundamentally non-Greek. It is unlikely that they would have drawn such distinctions had Athenian practice in this respect been idiosyncratic in comparison to the rest of Greece.

Subtler departures from the standard address system involve terms that belong to the standard system but would not normally be used for the particular addressee in question, at least not by that particular speaker. The most obvious example of such usage in Greek is the use of a kinship term to an unrelated addressee (e.g., πάτερ "father" to an older man or τέκνον "my child" to a younger one); this was considered a friendly gesture, as Menander explicitly states (*Dys.* 492–5). Address by name could have meaning in a context where another term would be expected; for example addressing one's wife by name rather than with γύναι "wife" appears to have been a sign of emotional strain, and a man addressing an unrelated woman by name could be implying that she was not entirely respectable. Terms for youths (νεανία, νεανίσκε, and μειράκιον) were sometimes applied to adults, and when so used were offensive; interestingly there is no evidence that παῖ could be used insultingly in the same way.

Even more interesting are the implications of using the generic terms for strangers (οὗτος "this one," ἄνθρωπε "human being") to an addressee known to the speaker: such usage was generally impolite. In this respect Classical Greek was strikingly different from languages such as English, where strangers tend to be addressed with terms (such as "sir") that are polite rather than impolite when used to acquaintances. One result of this unusual characteristic of Greek is that when an author was prevented from using a name by his own ignorance rather than by that of the speaking character, he would take care to point this fact out with a phrase such as οὗτος, ἔφη προσειπὼν τὸ ὄνομα . . . "'This guy,' he said, addressing him by name . . ." (Lucian *Demon.* 14).

Another aspect in which Greek differs from many other languages is the lack of connection in the address system between advanced age and respect. Most of the time, old men and women are addressed with the same terms that younger adults would receive. A few vocatives are reserved specifically for older addressees: γραῦ "old woman," γέρον "old man," πρέσβυ "old man," etc. Such terms seem on the whole to be more impolite than polite, though there is some variation among them and in general the feminine variants are ruder than the masculine ones. They are relatively rare except in comedy, perhaps because comedy is our only major source of impolite addresses. The tendency for terms indicating advanced age to be inherently respectful, as illustrated in other languages by the derivation of titles like *sir* and *señor* from Latin *senior* "older," is not found in Classical Greek.

All of this, of course, applies only to addresses directed at individuals. When groups of people were addressed the situation was very different: names were not practical as terms of address, and therefore generic terms were essential. Some generic terms were part of the address system both as singulars and as plurals, but with very different meanings, since in the singular they were expressive addresses contrasting with a more expected alternative and in the plural they acted as neutral addresses since they were the only practical option. For example plural ethnics such as Πέρσαι "Persians" or Λακεδαιμόνιοι "Spartans" tend to be used in polite or neutral contexts, whereas singular ethnics such as Πέρσα "Persian" or Λάκων "Spartan" tend to be forms of address used by superiors to inferiors. And while the singular ethnic carries an implication that the speaker is of a different nationality, the plural has no such implication.

Forms of Address in Postclassical Greek

For several centuries after Menander there is a gap, during which few vocatives are preserved. Examination of the literary record might lead one to believe that this gap has to do with accidents of preservation: the surviving literature, for example Polybius' history, happens to contain less dialogue and therefore fewer forms of address than Classical works in similar genres, for example the histories of Herodotus and Thucydides. But starting in the middle of the third century BCE our understanding of the Greek language is augmented by the appearance of large number of papyrus documents from Egypt, including letters and petitions, two genres in which one might well expect to find vocatives. It is notable that until the beginning of the Roman period these documents very rarely contain vocatives of any type, with the exception of βασιλεῦ in highly formulaic petitions to the king of Egypt.

This use of βασιλεῦ is interesting, given the evidence mentioned earlier that Greek kings did not receive this title in address and the fact that the Ptolemaic rulers of Egypt were largely Greek in language and culture. One might even want to consider it evidence that the portrayal of address to Greek kings we find in Herodotus and later literary authors is inaccurate, and that they in fact received titles all along. But such a conclusion would be unwise, for literary texts make a distinction between address to Classical (and Archaic) Greek rulers and address to Hellenistic and Macedonian rulers, so that members of the latter group frequently receive the title βασιλεῦ. This distinction can be seen not only between authors (e.g., Herodotus vs Diodorus Siculus), but also within a single author in the case of Plutarch. If we did not have the papyri, we might think that Plutarch had no idea how Hellenistic monarchs were addressed, but as it is we know that he depicted such address accurately, which makes it more likely that Herodotus depicted address to Classical Greek monarchs equally accurately.

In the later first century BCE and first century CE vocatives start to appear again in our written record, both in literary texts and in papyrus documents (chiefly but not exclusively letters); in the second and later centuries they become common in both types of source. The address system of the papyrus documents, however, is sharply divergent from that visible in literature. The papyri reveal an address system completely different from that of the Classical period, while the literary texts have a whole range of systems according to how heavily Atticizing they are: those with the least literary pretensions, such as the New Testament or the works of Epictetus, show significant similarities to the addresses of the papyri, while those with the most Atticizing tone use an address system nearly identical to the Classical one; other works fall on a scale between these two extremes.

The address system of the papyri at this period, and for the next several centuries, is heavily influenced by Latin, the new language of power in the Greek world (see also ch. 19). It is striking that the address system of the early Roman period shows so much more Latin influence than do many other aspects of the Greek language at the same time. This peculiarity, combined with the lack of evidence for most types of vocative in the Hellenistic period, suggests that direct address in the vocative case had genuinely become rare or even died out after the end of the Classical period, so that the Latinate address system was introduced as a new element to the language rather than ousting a previously existing system.

The main features of the Roman-period address system, which persisted until around the fourth century CE, were a set of titles indicating conventionalized affection and respect. The most common of these titles was κύριε "lord" (= Lat. *domine*; cf. ch. 19), followed by ἀδελφέ "brother" (= Lat. *frater*) and φίλτατε "dearest" (= Lat. *carissime*). One might suppose that κύριε showed respect and ἀδελφέ and φίλτατε affection, but such is not the case; all three were highly conventionalized and could be applied both to inferiors and to addressees with whom the writer had no personal relationship. The similarity between the usage of κύριε and of ἀδελφέ is underscored by the fact that they were often combined to form the address κύριε ἀδελφέ (= Lat. *domine frater*).

In this address system personal names were used infrequently, and the main distinction encoded in the Classical system, that between adult male citizens and others, was no longer marked in the address system at all. Close relatives were still normally addressed with kinship terms, but these terms (not only ἀδελφέ "brother," but also πάτερ "father," μῆτερ "mother," υἱέ "son," θύγατερ "daughter," and ἀδελφή "sister") were also freely used to addressees unrelated to the writer, making the address distinction between kin and non-kin much less sharp than it had been in the Classical period.

The practice of calling women γύναι had completely disappeared by the Roman period. In papyrus letters women are very rarely addressed by name, but this restriction has nothing to do with gender since it applies to men as well; address by name was simply no longer usual. In referring to (as opposed to addressing) women the writers of Roman-period letters use names as freely as they do when referring to men. It is possible that this change was related to a change in the Roman system of nomenclature, around the beginning of the Empire, by which Roman women for the first time acquired individual names.

An interesting echo of this change in the status of women makes its way into the Greek literary texts. Lucian, writing in a highly Atticizing language showing few traces of the changes the lower registers of the language had undergone since the fourth century BCE, of course makes heavy use of address by name and never employs the newer vocatives like κύριε or non-literal ἀδελφέ. But he is almost completely oblivious to the Classical distinctions of gender in the address system: Lucian's female characters are addressed freely by name just like his male characters, and γύναι is very rare.

This element of Lucian's address system tells us that the literary language was not immune to influence from contemporary culture. Yet it is not clear how extensive the contact between users of the two systems was. The subliterary address system found in the papyri must have been used orally as well as in writing; this would be clear from the low level of education displayed by many writers who use it, even if we did not have explicit testimony about oral usage (e.g., αἱ γυναῖκες εὐθὺς ἀπὸ τεσσαρεσκαίδεκα ἐτῶν ὑπὸ τῶν ἀνδρῶν κυρίαι καλοῦνται "women are called 'ladies' by men from the time they are 14 years old," Epict. *Ench.* 40). But such evidence does not in itself suggest that the Atticizing address system existed only in writing during the Roman period. Certainly educated men like Lucian made an effort to speak as well as to write strictly Classical Greek; so much is clear from Lucian's essay entitled *On a slip of the tongue in greeting*. Though we have no direct evidence for the oral use of an Atticizing address system in the Roman period, it is likely that it existed at least to some extent among the most educated speakers.

From the fourth century onwards the address system changed again, with the introduction of more elaborate polite formulae that developed further in the Byzantine period (see Zilliacus 1949; Dinneen 1929). These formulae were often abstractions, formed on the same principle as English "your majesty": ἡ σὴ ἐνδοξότης "your glory," τὸ σὸν ὕψος "your elevation," etc. They therefore necessitated addressing the recipient in the third person.

A separate issue concerning the Greek address system is the circumstances in which the particle ὦ was used with vocatives. In Classical prose most vocatives are preceded by ὦ (in Plato the particle is used 98 percent of the time), but usage in poetry is less regular (ten percent in Homer, 80 percent in Aristophanes, with the tragedians in between). For a long time it was believed that omission of ὦ was meaningful, though there was little agreement as to what that meaning was (see, e.g., Brioso Sánchez 1971; Lepre 1979), but it is now thought that its use or omission had less to do with meaning than with other considerations such as avoidance of hiatus (Dickey 1996: 199–206). In the postclassical period the use of ὦ declined sharply, and it is almost never found with vocatives in papyrus documents. Given the other Latin influence on the postclassical Greek address system it is tempting to connect this shift with Latin usage, for *o* is not normally used with vocatives in Latin prose. Such a connection would be illusory, however, since the Greek shift occurs too early for Latin influence to be plausible. The few vocatives that occur in Hellenistic papyri are already uniformly without ὦ, and even in Menander only 12 percent of vocatives are accompanied by ὦ.

Other Markers of Status

Status could also be indicated by means other than vocatives. The headings of letters, petitions, etc., in which the addressee's name and/or titles appeared in the dative, offered a natural opportunity for such indication. The terms used in headings are not identical to those used as vocatives, and one can never assume that a given term has the same implications in both uses; for example in papyrus letters to the writer's son it was customary to use the dative υἱῷ "son" in the heading but the vocative τέκνον "child" in the body of the letter (see Stanton 1988: 464; Dickey 2004b). This is particularly true in cases where the heading had to provide unambiguous identification of the addressee and therefore offered a great deal of information.

There are nevertheless some similarities between vocatives and headings: in the Classical period they tend to be simple and are unlikely to involve titles, whereas in the Roman period they regularly employ titles such as κύριος and ἀδελφός, and in the late Roman and Byzantine period they become extremely elaborate (e.g., Αὐρηλίῳ

Διοσκόρῳ τ[ῷ κα]ὶ ['Ελλαδίῳ γυ(μνασιάρχῳ)] βουλ(ευτῇ) ἐνάρχῳ πρυτάνει τῆς λαμ-
(πρᾶς) καὶ λαμ(προτάτης) 'Οξυρυγχιτῶν πόλεως Αὐρήλιος Τιμόθεος Σαραπιάδου{ς}
ἀπὸ τῆς αὐτῆς πόλεως "To Aurelios Dioskoros also called Helladios, gymnasiarch, senator, prytanis in office of the glorious and most glorious city of the Oxyrhynchites,
(from) Aurelios Timotheos son of Sarapiades, from the same city," *P.Oxy.* 65. 4491.
4–8). In contrast to vocatives, however, headings do not disappear during the
Hellenistic period, and (presumably for practical reasons) personal names remain very
common in headings at all periods. Therefore there was a gradual divergence between
the terms used in headings and in vocatives: in the Classical period they were very
similar, but after that they began to diverge, and by the Roman period the differences
between them were marked.

Status is also communicated in letters by the writers' references to themselves. Since
ancient letter headings tended to include a reference to the writer as well as to the
addressee (e.g., Πλάτων Διονυσίῳ εὖ πράττειν "Plato to Dionysius, greetings," the
heading of several of Plato's letters), such self-references are found at all periods and
can be seen to evolve over time. In the Classical period simple, unadorned names are
the rule, for writer even more than for addressee. This tendency generally continues
in the Hellenistic and early Roman periods, but in private letters from later centuries
one can also find terms of relationship, such as τῇ κυρίᾳ μου ἀδ[ελ]φῇ Μανατίνη
Πρώβ[ο]ς ἀδελφὸς χαίρειν "to my lady sister Manatine Probos her brother sends greetings" (*P.Oxy.* 14.1683.1–3). Official letters from the later Roman period frequently
contain as many (or more) of the writer's titles as of the addressee's titles, for example
Αὐρήλιος Βίων ὁ καὶ 'Αμμώνιος γυμνασίαρχος βουλευτὴς ἔναρχος πρύτανις τῆς
'Οξυρυγχιτῶν πόλεως Αὐρηλίῳ Δίῳ τῷ καὶ Περτίνακι στρατηγῷ τοῦ αὐτοῦ νομοῦ τῷ
φιλτάτῳ χαίρειν "Aurelius Bion also called Ammonios, gymnasiarch, senator, and
prytanis in office of Oxyrhynchus, to his dearest Aurelius Dios also called Pertinax,
strategos of the same nome, greetings" (*P.Oxy.* 14.1662.1–7).

In the late antique and Byzantine periods there is an interesting tendency for writers to use conventionalized abasement of themselves as a way of showing respect for
the addressee, on the same principle as the use of formulae such as "your obedient
servant" in older English letters. Thus we find writers referring to themselves with
terms like ὁ δοῦλός σου "your slave" or with abstractions such as ἡ ἐμὴ ταπείνωσις "my
lowliness" (Zilliacus 1949: 5).

It is striking that linguistic self-abasement of this type is almost entirely absent from
most Greek before the fourth century CE. An exception is some of the interaction with
the Persian king as described by Herodotus (for example a nobleman using the servile
vocative δέσποτα "master" to address the king at 3.35.4). Such interaction, however,
was intended as a depiction of Persian practice (whether real or imagined) intended to
seem strikingly alien to Greek-speaking readers.

Status can also be indicated by the use of a plural for a single person. As noted
above, Ancient Greek did not use the second person plural as a polite form of address
in the way that, e.g., French does. But the use of the first person plural either as a
plural of majesty (like the English "royal we" in contexts such as "we are not amused")
or as a plural of modesty (the opposite usage of the same construction) is attested in
Greek from a relatively early period. In Classical literature it is a sporadic, poetic

phenomenon, but it becomes more regularized in the Hellenistic period, when it appears in royal letters, and later (see Zilliacus 1953).

A very different type of status marker is found in the phrasing of requests and commands (imperatives, optatives, and other ways of indicating that one would like the addressee to do something, collectively known to linguists as directives). In Classical Attic directives were not regularly used as markers of status: the normal way of making a request was to use the imperative, regardless of the relative status of speaker and addressee, and such imperatives were not normally accompanied by softening modifiers like our "please" or "if you wouldn't mind." This is not to say that other ways of making requests did not exist, but that they were not very common, and the unsoftened imperative did not have the rude implications that it does in modern English, where "please" is so common that its absence is immediately remarkable.

In postclassical Greek, on the other hand, and particularly in the subliterary language, the unmodified imperative was much more likely to be used to subordinates than to superiors, as is the case in English. It therefore became a marker of the addressee's lower status, and other directive strategies became markers of higher status. Requests too polite to use the unmodified imperative did not normally employ the imperative with some sort of softener (like English "please do this"), but rather avoided the imperative altogether by using a different construction (like English "could you do this?," though in Greek the alternative construction was rarely a question). Thus for example we find παρακαλῶ οὖ[ν], ἀδελφέ, γράψαι μοι "so I ask you, brother, to write to me" (*P.Oxy.* 14.1666.19) and καλῶς οὖν ποιήσεις ἐλ[θοῦσα] τῷ Μεσορῇ πρὸς [ἡμᾶ]ς "you will do well if you come to us in Mesore" (*P.Oxy.* 14.1676.29–32).

Nearly all these different types of status marker show a parallel development toward more frequent and more elaborate indications of status as the language evolved from the Classical to the Late Antique period. These changes clearly reflect changes in social structure from democratic Athens to the intense stratification of the early Byzantine world.

FURTHER READING

The main works on Greek address usage are Wendel 1929 (for poetry) and Dickey 1996 (for prose). Studies of particular words abound; among the most useful are the discussions of *kyrie/ despota* by Hagedorn and Worp 1980 and Dickey 2001, of *daimonie* by Brunius-Nilsson 1955, and of words for "god" by Wackernagel 1912. Studies of usage in particular situations include Dineen 1929 on Christian letters and Exler 1923 on papyrus letters. Bain 1984 discusses women's language, Zilliacus 1949 the abstractions used as titles in late antiquity, Zilliacus 1953 the use of plural for singular, and Dickey 2004*a* the influence of Latin on Greek address usage in the Roman period.

CHAPTER TWENTY-THREE

Technical Languages: Science and Medicine

Francesca Schironi

Definitions and Problems

A technical language can be defined as a subcategory of common language containing all the linguistic elements employed by a restricted group of speakers to name, define, and discuss the contents of a particular discipline. Since the ideas and the objects of any technical discipline need to be defined unambiguously, terminology is the landmark of any technical language. Technical terminology tends to be (cf. Willi 2003: 69):

a) Standardized, economic and concise, i.e., monosemy is preferred over polysemy;
b) Expressly neutral, i.e., the lexeme does not entail any judgment: e.g., gonorrhea vs the slang term "the clap";
c) Seldom used—though possibly understood—by the non-specialists. For this reason, technical terms often have lay synonyms in common language; this is particularly evident in medicine where technical and lay terminology coexist (e.g., *tinea pedis* vs "athlete's foot") and often physicians use the latter in order to be understood by their patients.

Studies of Greek technical languages need to take into account two basic features of Greek science. First, when speaking of "technical languages" we assume that there is a well-defined group of disciplines that uses them, but in ancient Greece this is far from being true. The term τέχνη was widely used by Greek writers to indicate a discipline founded on knowledge (ἐπιστήμη) and rationality (λόγος), but it was not clear which disciplines could be defined as τέχναι. We can reasonably speak of Greek science during the Hellenistic period, when mathematics (Euclid, Eratosthenes, Archimedes, Apollonius of Perge), astronomy (Aristarchus of Samos, Hipparchus), mechanics (Ctesibius, Philo of Byzantium), and medicine (Erophilus, Erasistratus) were highly developed and used what we can indeed call "technical languages." However, in earlier periods the status of τέχναι is difficult to define. Medicine (with the Hippocratic school) and mathematics (with Hippocrates of Chios and Eudoxus) were flourishing, but their terminology was not yet fixed. For other fields things are even worse. For example, the Presocratics did have an interest in the physical aspect of the world, but it is difficult to consider them "scientists," because in the sixth and fifth centuries BCE philosophy takes the place of science. In addition, in antiquity the distinction between a technical text and a literary text is not as clear as in our societies. Didactic poetry consisted of "technical" topics not directed to specialists and primarily intended to "entertain" rather than to "inform;" in such works language follows poetic and metrical rules rather than clarity and monosemy.

Secondly, in many cases the Greeks were the first to discover even basic phenomena of the physical and biological world, or develop new disciplines. Even when they might have been influenced by other cultures (i.e., Egyptian or Middle Eastern lore), they did not adopt their technical vocabulary. As a consequence, the Greeks had no words readily available to describe their discoveries. Modern science can build on the experience of previous generations of scientists and on their vocabulary even when dealing with breakthrough new results. In addition, technical terms in modern scientific languages often derive from Greek or Latin roots and hence are "extraneous" to the common language. The Greeks could not draw on the work of predecessors, nor could they rely on other languages, because they were the first to give a name to something previously unknown. All Greek technical terms are thus Greek-based. As a consequence, on the one hand Greek technical language was more accessible to non-specialists than modern technical languages, but on the other hand it was a completely new (sub)language to develop from scratch.

In this overview of Greek technical language, the main goal is to outline the different strategies that the ancient Greeks adopted when they had to convey "scientific" content. The focus will be on two fields, medicine and mathematics, since these are the disciplines for which we have by far the most evidence: the Hippocratic Corpus, Hellenistic physicians and Galen for medicine, and the works of Euclid, Apollonius of Perge and Archimedes for mathematics. Medicine and mathematics are central also because many of the other technical languages in ancient Greece borrowed from mathematical or medical *Fachsprache*, due to their strong similarities to either or both these τέχναι. For example, harmonics, optics and astronomy, which were considered part of the μαθηματικὴ ἐπιστήμη, used mathematical language, while botany and zoology adopted medical linguistic expressions. Mechanics shares linguistic features of both disciplines.

Interestingly, medicine and mathematics employed quite different linguistic strategies to express their results. A comparison between them will thus highlight some important features of technical languages and the motivations behind certain linguistic choices.

Technical Terminology

Naming new objects, phenomena and concepts discovered in a scientific discipline is the main task of its technical vocabulary. There are three strategies to create a technical terminology: (i) use of existing terms; (ii) coinage of new terms through suffixation or compounding; (iii) borrowing of existing terms from other semantic fields (metaphors). The medical language of anatomy and pathology is the best area in which to analyze these three strategies and to show how a new technical terminology was developed in ancient Greece.

Use of existing terms

This procedure consists of giving a more specific meaning to an existing word. This already happened in Presocratic philosophers, who endowed common Greek terms such as φύσις "nature" or ἀρχή "beginning" with new meanings to express their ideas about reality. Using common words with a technical meaning is attested also in medicine. Hippocratic and later physicians use Homeric words such as καρδίη, φρένες, φλέβες. Among diseases, σπασμός "convulsion" and φῦμα "what grows," hence "tumor," are words used by both Herodotus and Hippocrates. This practice, however, carries the risk of polysemy, since a term can have both a general and a technical meaning, which can be difficult to distinguish.

Coinage of new terms

To avoid ambiguity, neologisms are the most common solution for building up a technical vocabulary. The Greek language is especially versatile at creating new words. Its derivational morphology and its compounding capability are extraordinary resources to "name" something previously unknown. Medical neologisms created by the Hippocratic and Hellenistic schools are the best examples, also because many of these terms are still used by modern medicine. There are two strategies to create new terms: suffixation and compounding.

Suffixation

In Greek, new words, especially nouns, are created through particular suffixes conveying a particular meaning, such as the ending –της for *nomina agentis,* -μα for *nomina rei actae,* -σις for *nomina actionis* (see also ch. 8). The latter two suffixes are used also in medicine to distinguish the process from the result: ἕλκωσις "ulceration" and ἕλκωμα "ulcer"; οἴδησις "swelling" and οἴδημα "tumor." Greek medicine has the additional peculiarity of using specific suffixes, which, though also used in common Greek, eventually became particularly associated with medical terminology:

a) Suffix –ίη/-ία for many abstract nouns of diseases or symptoms: e.g., αἱμορραγία "hemorrhage"; λειεντερία "passage of undigested food into stools" → lientery; ὀφθαλμία "disease in the eyes" → ophthalmia; περιπνευμονία/περιπλευμονία "disease of the lungs" → pneumonia;

b) Suffix -ῖτις to indicate an inflammation in a particular part of the body (originally these are adjectival forms modifying νόσος, but eventually they came to be used substantively): e.g., ἀρθρῖτις "inflammation of the joints" → arthritis; ἡπατῖτις "inflammation of the liver" → hepatitis; φρενῖτις "inflammation of the brain" → phrenitis;

c) Suffix -αινα for diseases characterized by weeping/pus-filled sores: e.g., γάγγραινα "gangrene"; φαγέδαινα "cancerous sore"; φλύκταινα "blister made by a burn";

d) Suffix –ότης for feminine nouns, sometimes used to express a quality or durable attribute: e.g., ἐρυθρότης "redness"; ἐφθότης "languor"; καμπυλότης "crookedness"; χλωρότης "greenness";

e) Suffix –σμός for masculine nouns indicating a medical condition: e.g., μετεωρισμός "swelling"; κνησμός "itching"; λεπτυσμός "thinning";

f) Suffix -δών for feminine deverbal nouns: e.g., σηπεδών "putrefaction"; πρηδών "swelling"; σπαδών "cramp."

The following adjectives are particularly common in Greek medical language:

g) Adjectives in –ώδης (or -ιώδης) indicating any kind of similarity or quality: e.g., ἀλφώδης "leprous"; ἰκτερώδης/ἰκτεριώδης "jaundiced"; κνησμώδης "affected with itching"; σαρκώδης "fleshy"; ὑδεριώδης "suffering from dropsy";

h) Adjectives in –ειδής to indicate similarity (εἶδος): θρομβοειδής "full of clots or lumps"; πυοειδής "like purulent matter"; σποδοειδής "ashy";

i) Adjectives in -ικός often meaning "suffering from. . .": e.g., κεφαλαλγικός "suffering from headache," "of the headache"; σπληνικός "of the spleen" → splenetic; τετανικός "suffering from tetanus"; ὑστερικός "suffering in the womb" → hysterical.

Verbs are typically denominal: they are mostly derived from the names of the diseases and convey the idea of suffering from them. Hence the typical suffixes of denominal verbs are very much used:

j) Verbs in –ιάω: ἰκτεριάω "have jaundice"; ποδαγριάω "have gout"; ὑδεριάω "suffer from dropsy"; ψωριάω "have itch";

k) Verbs in -αίνω: e.g., προσγλισχραίνω "make more viscid"; πυρεταίνω "to be feverish"; παραχλιαίνω "warm slightly"; ὑδεραίνω "suffer from dropsy";

l) Verbs in –έω: e.g., αἱμορραγέω "have a hemorrhage"; κεφαλαλγέω "suffer from headache"; λευκοφλεγματέω "have dropsy."

In this process, derivational morphology comes also into play, so that from the one basic form, often a noun, verbs, and adjectives are also created. The result is a family of words, as for example, from νεφρός "kidney" we have: νεφροειδής and νεφρώδης "like a kidney," νεφριτικός and νεφριαῖος "of the kidneys," and the noun νεφρῖτις "inflammation of the kidneys."

Compounding

Compounds have the advantage of condensing in one word a complex concept, even an entire phrase. The Greek language allows extensive use of compounds in any field, starting from common and poetical language. Among medical compounds, Greek physicians used the typical prefixes privative ἀ-, δυσ- and εὐ- to compound nouns, adjectives and verbs:

a)   Privative ἀ-: e.g., ἄκοπρος "with little excrement in the bowels"; ἄσαρκος "without flesh"; ἀσφυκτέω "to be without pulsation";

b)   δυσ-: e.g., δυσέμβλητος "hard to set," of dislocations; δυσεντερία (→ dysentery); δυσεπίσχετος "hard to check," of bleeding; δυσθενέω "to be weak";

c)   εὐ-: e.g., εὐέμετος or εὐήμετος "vomiting readily"; εὐεξανάλωτος "easy of digestion"; εὔσαρκος "fleshy," "in good condition"; εὔχροια "goodness of complexion."

In some cases the opposition between the prefixes δυσ- and εὐ- is used to create an antinomy with a technical meaning: εὐελκής "favorable for healing of sores" opposed to δυσελκής "unfavorable for healing of sores"; εὔπνοια "easiness of breathing" opposed to δύσπνοια "difficulty of breathing."

Some prefixes are used in medicine to give a more specific meaning to verbs, nouns, or adjectives. The prefix ὑπο- has a local meaning of "below," as in ὑπογλωσσίς "swelling under the tongue" and "the under side of the tongue," but it is also often used as a diminutive: ὑπαλγέω "have a slight pain," ὑπόγλισχρος "somewhat slippery," ὑπόλευκος "whitish," ὑπομέλας "blackish." The prefix περι- intensifies: περίψυχρος "very cold," περιωδυνάω and περιωδυνέω "suffer great pain."

Borrowing of existing terms from other semantic fields (metaphors)

A particularly interesting aspect of technical terminology is the use of metaphors. Metaphors can be linked with a typical scientific approach: analogy, by which new discoveries can be explained after something known that shares some features with them. Thus language can "visualize" a new phenomenon by naming it after a more common object that has some kind of resemblance. In this way, the name already contains some sort of explanation. The examples of metaphorical language in medicine and zoology are numerous, especially for anatomy and pathology. (See also the discussion of word meaning in ch. 9.)

Metaphors from common language

In metaphors, the link between the new object and the common object is usually a similarity in their aspect or, more rarely, in their function.

The first group includes some names for bones: for example, κερκίς "weaver's shuttle" is the name for the tibia or for the radius; περόνη "pin of a buckle" indicates a small bone in the leg (Lat. *fibula*); κοτύλη "cup" indicates the socket of a joint. Among body organs, τὸ ἔντερον τυφλόν or simply τὸ τυφλόν is the part of intestine without outlet (the "blind" gut); δακτύλιος "ring" becomes the anus. The name ἶρις "rainbow" indicates the colored part of the eye. The pupil is called (not only among physicians) κόρη "girl" (cf. Lat. *pupilla*), a metaphor which might have a more popular origin: people believed they saw a little image of a girl in the pupil (cf. Pl. *Alc.* I 133a).

Among the metaphors derived from similarity in function we can mention πυλωρός "gate-keeper" (→ pylorus), which is the lower orifice of the stomach that serves as a "watcher" for what gets out from the stomach; moreover, πύλαι "gates" is the name of various orifices in the body such as in the liver. Similar is the case of πόρος, literally "ford" or "strait" in the sea; in medical terminology, it indicates a passage through the skin (→ pore) or many other ducts of the body (womb, ovaries, esophagus, arteries and veins). Many internal membranes (of the heart, of the eyes and of the testicles) are called χιτών "tunic," because they defend the organ by wrapping it up. The ζύγωμα "bolt" indicates the arcus zygomaticus, because it connects the cranial with the facial bones.

Herophilus employs various metaphors to name the new organs and bones he discovered through human dissection. He calls a pointed bone in the skull "pharoid process" (fragm. 92, ed. Von Staden 1989) in analogy with the Pharos of Alexandria, whose pointed shape was similar to the bone; he also (fragm. 88) calls the retina "spider's-web-like tunic" (χιτὼν ἀραχνοειδής) and describes (fragm. 89) it as similar to a net (ἀμφίβληστρον), from which the name χιτὼν ἀμφιβληστροειδής "net-like tunic" was derived (and the modern term "retina" is the Latin translation of this metaphor). The term "calamus scriptorius," designating a cavity in the fourth ventricle of the brain similar to the groove of a "reed pen" (κάλαμος), is also due to Herophilus (fragm. 79).

In pathology, χάλαζα "hail" indicates a small cyst on the eyelids or a pimple in the flesh of swine; ἄνθραξ "burning carbon" is a disease of the skin; φλεγμονή "heat" indicates an inflamed tumor. Also, verbs are used metaphorically to describe an anatomical process: "to digest" is συμπέσσειν, which means "to cook" (cf. the derivative noun: πέψις "cooking" and "digestion").

Metaphors from other technical languages

Metaphors can also be taken from other technical terminologies. The main semantic fields from which Greek physicians drew names were human and animal anatomy, plants' names and their parts, and architecture.

Human anatomy is particularly interesting: some internal parts of the human body are called with the same name given to external (hence known) ones similar to them. Κεφαλή "head" is probably the term most often "reused" to name other parts of the human body. It indicates the biggest part of an organ: so we have a κεφαλή of the humerus, of the femur, or of the heart. The femur has also an αὐχήν "neck," as does the uterus. Equally common is στόμα "mouth" for various orifices, such as in the uterus (where it indicates the same as the κεφαλή). The ball of the hand is the στῆθος χειρός "breast of the hand." The second (or sometimes the first) vertebra of the neck or its apophysis is called ὀδούς "tooth" because of its protruding shape. And the heart has "ears" (οὔατα or ὦτα).

The animal world also offers examples of metaphors. Muscle comes from μῦς "mouse" probably because of the rounded shape of a contracted muscle, similar to the body of a mouse. The cuckoo names the coccyx (κόκκυξ), as it resembles the beak of a cuckoo. The term χέλυς "tortoise" is used for the chest because of the similarity of shape with the tortoise's shell (and the chest also emits "sound" like the lyre, also called χέλυς, as Hermes made the first lyre from a tortoise's shell).

Pathology too uses names of animals. The καρκίνος "crab" indicates cancer because of the aspect of the ulcers and their resistance to cure. A πολύπους "octopus" designates an anomalous excrescence on the skin similar to the shapeless body of the octopus. Βάτραχος "frog" is the name of swelling under the tongue in analogy with the frog's uneven body. Other diseases are named using the same stem of the animal's name: ἀλωπεκία, the disease "of the fox" (a disease in which hair falls off) is so called, because ancient physicians believed that it also affected foxes; or ἐλεφαντίασις (→ elephantiasis), because the swollen limbs resembled elephant legs. The κυνικὸς σπασμός, the "canine spasm," designates a facial paralysis with a tic, which makes the human face similar to that of a barking dog.

Plants and parts of plants too provide metaphors to physicians. In anatomy there is ῥίζα, the "root" of a tooth, of the eye, of the tongue; ἄκανθα "thorn" to designate the spinal column and also the apophysis of vertebras (→ spinous process). In pathology the names of plants are many, especially to describe skin disease. Ἄνθος "flower" together with the neologism ἐξάνθημα are used to indicate an "efflorescence" on the skin, an eruption, a pustule. Λειχήν "lichen" is a lesion on the skin, which resembles the vegetal organism; φακός "lentil" is the mole on the skin. Τέρμινθος is the terebinth tree and a disease of the olive; in human pathology, it indicates a swelling like the fruit of the terebinth tree. The name of the fig, σῦκον, indicates a fig-like excrescence, especially in the eye; in the eye too we can find a grain of "barley," κριθή. Σταφυλή is the "grape" of the vine and in pathology it means an inflammation of the uvula, swollen at the end and thus similar to a grape.

Metaphors for parts of the body and for diseases are taken from other fields too; for example, γίγγλυμος, technically a "hinge" in architecture, is the "articulation." Γομφίος "molar tooth," is derived from γόμφος "bolt," because the molars are "fastened with bolts" in the mouth. Another name for the molar is μύλη "mill," as it grinds food. Ἧλος "stud," for the "callus," because of its shape and hardness, also comes from architecture.

Metaphors working on similarities between the new thing and a known one are thus one of the most powerful means to name new objects, concepts, and phenomena in disciplines where description of a new reality is paramount. Metaphors taken from daily life and human activities are the clearest and easiest to understand by laypeople, but medical language takes metaphors also from other technical vocabularies, such as those of zoology or botany. The phenomenon is not one-directional. There are cases of botany using terms of human medicine: ψωριάω means "to have the itch" (in the human body), but Theophrastus uses it also for a disease of trees in the sense of "to be scabby." In the same way, a leaf of a plant can be defined σαρκώδης "fleshy," as a human body would be. Mathematics takes from Greek anatomy words like πλευρά "rib," used to indicate the "side" of a triangle or another figure.

A particularly interesting cross-borrowing between two technical languages happens between mechanics and anatomy. Since the human body can be seen as a "machine," Erasistratus describes the heart as a pump with valves similar to the water pump invented by Ctesibius in the same period (fragm. 201, ed. Garofalo 1998). He also explains respiration in mechanical terms (fragm. 108). Physicians borrow from mechanics' names for their tools: πλινθίον, originally both "brick" and "frame" used in molding bricks, in medicine indicates the "bandage," which "molds" the limb, as well as a machine invented by Nileus to reduce dislocations. Conversely, machines can be described as human bodies.

Engines, especially the torsion-engine, can have legs (σκέλη), heels (πτέρναι), arms (ἀγκῶνες), eyebrows (ὀφρῦς, the woodwork enclosing the bore of a torsion-engine). Mechanics, like anatomy, borrows words from other disciplines: χελώνη "tortoise," to name a machinery used to transport heavy weights, comes from zoology. The torsion-engine has a χελώνιον "tortoise-shell" (the knob against which the butt-ends of the arms of a torsion-engine rest) and πτέρυγες "wings" (the front-frame).

Connotative metaphors: the battle against the diseases

Another metaphorical usage in Greek medicine concerns the way physicians see their τέχνη. Descriptions of symptoms and diseases often adopt expressions belonging to the language of war, aggression, and force. For example, a colic is a malignant "twist" (στρόφος). Diseases are an "attack" (ἐπίθεσις, ἔφοδος) on the patient; they are painful "like a bite" (δακνώδεις) and "take possession of him" (ἐπιλαμβάνειν), while the patient "toils" (κάμνειν) and is "tormented" (ἐπιτείνεσθαι). This metaphorical language describes how the ancient physicians used to see their profession: as a battle against the disease.

Limits and recognition of medical language

A technical language requires a certain degree of self-awareness by its speakers, since they are often its "creators" and almost its only users. In terms of self-awareness, medical terminology was the most advanced in antiquity.

The appearance of lexica of medical terms already in the Hellenistic period demonstrates that medical language was already perceived as a *Fachsprache*, not normally used (and understood) by laypeople. The development of medical lexicography in third-century BCE Alexandria parallels the development of literary lexicography (on Homer or lyric poets) and indicates that the language of Hippocrates needed interpretation like that of Homer.

However, Greek medical language was not "perfect." Polysemy often caused confusion, especially in the earlier period and for smaller organs like muscles, nerves, and the vascular system. The same term could be used for different organs: φάρυγξ meant "pharynx," "esophagus" but also "trachea" and "larynx." The δίδυμοι "two-fold" were both the ovaries and the testicles; θαλάμη "lurking place" indicated the ventricle of the heart, the nostrils, the optic thalamus, the recesses in the cranial bones and the eye socket. In other cases, the same term indicated both the anatomical part and a disease affecting it: σταφυλή meant the uvula as well as its inflammation. The opposite problem was also present: one organ was called with different names. The retina was ἀμφιβληστροειδής "net-like," as we have seen, or ἀραχνοειδής "spider's-web-like," or ὑαλοειδής "glass-like"; the bronchi were called βρόγχια, σήραγγες, and ἀορταί.

This fluid situation in medical terminology is symptomatic of the status of the discipline that, from the very beginnings, had to invent its language but was divided in many different schools with different principles and terminology. Studying its technical language is thus a way to study the history of Greek medicine.

Syntax

The creation of a technical lexicon is an important feature of technical languages, but not the only one. There are many cases where technical texts manipulate syntactic tools in order to better convey their scientific content. For example, contrary to common language, technical languages tend to use nominal constructions (e.g., "energy flux") rather than verbal constructions (e.g., "energy flows"). As a consequence, a technical language tends to be richer in deverbal abstract nouns than common language. Specifically, scientific writings use language in a denotative rather than a connotative way, since their scope is to "communicate" a content rather than "comment" upon it. Thus, a scientific text needs to be clear and concise; in Greek terms, its characteristics are σαφήνεια "clarity" and συντομία "brevity," two fundamental principles of ancient rhetoric. The best example is Greek mathematics, because it uses syntactical devices rather than lexicon, the opposite strategy of medicine, which is instead based on a highly developed terminology and common syntactical features.

Greek Mathematics

The most striking feature of Greek mathematical texts is the homogeneity and repetitiveness of their language. There are only few neologisms and the vocabulary is standard and rather limited. However, the text is far from easy to understand. The reason lies in the syntactic constructions used by Greek mathematicians to express relationships between, and properties of, geometrical objects.

Naming geometrical objects

The Greek geometrical lexicon is not as rich and diversified as the medical one. Still, it has interesting features, especially when compared with medical terminology. First, mathematical words are not normally created *ex novo*, but rather they are taken from everyday language: σημεῖον "sign," hence "point"; γωνία "corner," hence "angle"; κύκλος "ring," "circular object," hence "circle"; στερεός "firm," "solid," hence geometrical "solid" figure; σφαῖρα "ball," hence "sphere"; or verbs like δείκνυμι "demonstrate"; δίδωμι "give," as in ἡ δοθεῖσα γραμμή/γωνία "the given line/angle"; τέμνω "cut," hence "divide" a line. All these are common Greek words used with a more specific meaning. Other words seem more "geometrically oriented," such as γραμμή "line," τετράγωνος "square," and κύλινδρος "cylinder," but they are still used in common Greek. Some words are used by mathematicians with a technical meaning derived from but not identical to the original one: μέρος changes meaning from singular to plural, as the μέρος of a number is one of its divisors, whereas its μέρη are all the numbers less than the given one that are not divisors of it (cf. Euc. *El.* 7, def. 3–4).

Metaphors, unlike in medicine, are rare. For example, κέντρον, the "center" of a circle, at first sight might seem metaphorical. Literally, κέντρον is the "horse-goad," a spike used to spur on the animals. From this, κέντρον then indicated many pointed objects: the point of a spear, the sting of bees and wasps, and the pin or rivet in mechanics, and also the point of a pair of compasses. Since compasses draw circles and the point is the "center" of the circle, κέντρον was then used by mathematicians in the latter sense. This use, however, is not metaphorical but metonymic.

In terms of lexicon, mathematics is easier than medicine. However, this does not mean that mathematical texts are simple, but that they use a different strategy to convey their content. Words like σημεῖον, γραμμή, γωνία, κύκλος, and τετράγωνος are the "technical" terms to name a point, line, angle, circle, and square in the definitions. However, in the demonstrations, which are the real core of the mathematical deductive reasoning, the way of expressing these geometrical objects is different. In fact, particular points are here identified by a letter, as in τὸ Α σημεῖον or, in the most abbreviated form, τὸ Α. Just to give some examples, we can mention:

ἡ ΑΒ (γραμμή)→ the (line joining the points) A (and) B.
ἡ ὑπὸ τῶν ΑΒ, ΒΓ (γωνία) → the (angle contained) by (the straight lines) AB (and) BC.
ἡ πρὸς τῷ Β (γωνία) → the (angle originating) at (the point) B
ὁ ΑΒΓ (κύκλος) → the (circle passing through the points) A B C
τὸ ΑΒΓ (τρίγωνον) → the (triangle whose vertexes are the points) A B C
τὸ ΑΒΓΔΕ (πολύγωνον) → the (polygon whose vertexes are the points) A B C D E
τὸ ἀπὸ τῆς ΑΒ (τετράγωνον) → the (square described) on (the segment) AB
τὸ ὑπὸ τῶν ΑΒ, ΒΓ (ὀρθογώνιον) → the (rectangle contained) by (the straight lines) AB (and) BC

These syntagms are familiar to us because they are also used in modern geometry based on Euclid's systematization. However, they reveal many interesting details about Greek mathematical reasoning and its expression. The complete phrase behind the cryptic τὸ ὑπὸ τῶν ΑΒ, ΒΓ is to be understood as τὸ ὑπὸ τῶν ΑΒ, ΒΓ εὐθειῶν περιεχόμενον ὀρθογώνιον "the rectangle contained by the straight lines AB, BC." None of the elements expressing these geometrical objects are "technical terms." There are definite articles, letters (Α, Β, Γ), and prepositions (ἀπό, πρός, ὑπό), and they all have a specific function. The article "points to" real geometrical objects, a very important function, since Greek mathematics deals with geometrical objects drawn in diagrams accompanying the texts, rather than with the abstract idea of a geometric figure. Letters indicate the most important points of a line, plane, or solid figure, so they "identify" these objects. Finally, prepositions "place" each object in the space and help defining their relative position, thus avoiding ambiguity.

This vocabulary is extremely flexible and fit for what Greek mathematics is: the study of geometrical objects and their relations. It is not, as Netz (1999: 134) claims, uneconomical. An angle can be called ἡ ὑπὸ τῶν ΑΒ, ΒΓ and ἡ πρὸς τῷ Β, because the two expressions are just two different ways to look at the same geometrical object, according to whether we decide to focus on the lines enclosing it or on the vertex. The use of articles, letters, and prepositions comes almost naturally from the use of diagrams in the text. Thus, when a Greek mathematician is writing ἡ ὑπὸ τῶν ΑΒ, ΒΓ, he is doing nothing more than "describing" what he sees on the diagram. Hence, in this perspective, there is no need of "lexical economy," as long as the name is clear, unambiguous, and meaningful.

This language is immediately recognizable as belonging to mathematics. The technical element has been reached not through suffixation, compounding, or neologisms, but rather through the interplay of simple words (articles, prepositions, and letters) in peculiar syntactic constructions (especially the attributive positions and the substantivation of any part of speech through the article) that privilege the visual side of the discipline.

The reason for this linguistic choice is that, unlike modern mathematics, Greek mathematics did not have any symbols. Language using mathematical symbols is more concise, but Greek mathematics could only use Greek common language. To express what we would write as: $\angle\, A = \angle\, D$ (i.e., the angle in A is equal to the angle in D) Euclid had to write a much longer sentence: ἔστι δὲ καὶ ἡ πρὸς τῷ Α ἴση τῇ πρὸς τῷ Δ (Euc. *El.* 6, prop. 7, 36). Moreover, the written text was not easy to read: in antiquity, Greek words were written in *scriptio continua* and without marks for accents and breathing, making the text even more complex to divide into elements.

Thus the problem for Greek mathematicians was not to "create" new terms to name new geometrical objects, because all geometrical objects can be described using their basic components: points, lines, angles, and circles. It was to reduce common language to the "bare bones" to be as clear and concise as possible. Streamlining the syntax and fully exploiting the possibilities of Greek language was their solution. The problem in reading a Greek mathematical text is that reduced forms, though syntactically intelligible, are very difficult from the mathematical point of view, unless the reader is trained in mathematics and in its language. As happens now with modern mathematical symbolism, one needs to know exactly the mathematical concept behind each reduced form in order to understand phrases like τὸ ὑπὸ τῶν ΑΒ, ΒΓ.

Discussing geometrical objects

Because Greek mathematics is deductive, conjunctions play an important role. With conjunctions and connective particles the strategy is the same: reduction to the minimum in favor of conciseness and clarity. For example, the same conjunctions always introduce the same kind of clause: καί for coordinate clauses, δέ or ἀλλά for coassumptions, ἤτοι for disjunctive clauses (see Acerbi 2008). The conclusion of an inference is usually introduced by ἄρα or sometimes by ὥστε. A postpositive explicative assertion is marked by γάρ or διά. Anteposed explications are introduced by ἐπεί (or ἐπεὶ γάρ, καὶ ἐπεί, ἐπεὶ οὖν).

Syntax is shaped by content. In the case of mathematics, most theorems are inferential; hence the most common syntactic construction is the conditional clause of the type "If A, then B" (Acerbi forthcoming). The typical form is always ἐάν with aorist or present subjunctive in the protasis, and present or future indicative in the apodosis, to express the idea that whenever something happens, something else will follow, i.e., a general truth (e.g., Euc. *El.* 1, Prop. 6 Ἐὰν τριγώνου αἱ δύο γωνίαι ἴσαι ἀλλήλαις ὦσιν, καὶ αἱ ὑπὸ τὰς ἴσας γωνίας ὑποτείνουσαι πλευραὶ ἴσαι ἀλλήλαις ἔσονται "If two angles of a triangle are equal to one another, also the sides subtended by the equal angles will be equal to one another"). Instead, the conditional clause with εἰ and present indicative in the protasis and present or future indicative or imperative in the apodosis is a simple condition: if something happens, something else will follow but without implying that what is stated in the protasis may possibly apply. The latter form is therefore often used for *reductio ad absurdum* proofs: εἰ γὰρ δυνατόν ἐστι, . . . ἔστω . . . 'For if it is possible, let (some property) be true . . .'.

Geometrical constructions in Euclid are characterized by particular tenses and moods in the verbs. Normally, we find the perfect imperative in the middle passive such as ἐπεζεύχθω "let [a straight line] be joined . . .," κύκλος γεγράφθω "let a circle be drawn." The impersonal form and the passive voice help the reader to focus on the geometrical object rather than on who must draw the geometric figure. The perfect is a resultative form, which helps to visualize the result of the construction. The same use of the imperative (but not necessarily in the perfect tense) is found also in mechanics when the construction of a machine is described, for example in the mechanical works by Hero of Alexandria.

Essential and concise language was a necessary choice in mathematics. Since the basic principles were few, and the rest was deductive and inferential, the required lexicon was small and easy to learn. Therefore, unlike medical language, Greek mathematical language in the Hellenistic and early Roman period was standardized.

Technical Language and Formulae

Mathematical language tends to be repetitive. It uses set phrases, easy to recognize after reading a few texts. This has led scholars to apply the concept of "formula," known from Homeric studies, to Greek mathematical language. Formulae are used to name geometrical objects (e.g., τὸ Α, ἡ ΑΒ); in the enunciation of a problem (e.g., περὶ τὸ[ν] δοθέν[τα] + name of a figure (e.g., κύκλον) + name of a figure (e.g., τετράγωνον) περιγράψαι "Let (a square) be drawn around a given (circle)"); to open proofs (e.g., ἔστω γὰρ . . . followed by the name of the geometrical object discussed in the proof). The imperatives of the constructions are also formulaic, e.g., ἤχθω "let be drawn," ἐπεζεύχθω "let be joined."

Other very common formulae are found in demonstrations, such as . . . ἄρα . . . ὅπερ ἔδει δεῖξαι ". . . therefore . . . QED" at the end of the demonstration, which can also be considered a sort of "ring composition" within the demonstration. Another example is found in the *reductio ad absurdum*: Εἰ γὰρ δυνατόν, . . . ἔστω. . . ὅπερ ἐστὶν ἀδύνατον. Οὐκ ἄρα . . . "For if possible, let [some property] be true. [Then, consequence of the assumed property,] which is impossible. Therefore, negation [of the property]."

There are formulae typical of the theory of proportions: the relationship of proportionality is introduced by: ὡς . . . οὕτως . . . "as . . . so . . .," while the different possible modifications of the terms of a proportion are expressed by the adverbs ἐναλλάξ "alternatively" and ἀνάπαλιν "inversely," and by forms of a so-called *dativus iudicantis*, e.g., συνθέντι "in composition" (literally "for one who puts things together)," διέλοντι "separately," and ἀναστρέψαντι "by conversion."

Another formula, used mainly in *Elements* Book Five (dedicated to the theory of proportion), is used when applying the definition of proportional magnitudes: καὶ εἰ ἴσον, ἴσον, καὶ εἰ ἔλαττον, ἔλαττον "if it is equal, equal, and if less, less" (with the variant καὶ εἰ ἴσον ἐστίν, ἴσον, καὶ εἰ ἐλλείπει, ἐλλείπει).

The application of the concept of Homeric formulae to Greek mathematical language explains the same sense of "repetitiveness" found in Greek mathematical texts and epic poetry. However, Homer composed poetry and mathematicians wrote prose. Also, Greek mathematicians were literate and wrote their texts, while literacy and writing are considered the antithesis of orality and hence of formulae. According to Aujac 1984, the origin of Greek mathematical formulae might be didactic: Greek mathematical education was oral and hence worked like Homeric poetry. More simply, in mathematics, the repetitiveness of set phrases helped logical necessity, a function that now is fulfilled by mathematical symbolism. Indeed, formulae can be found also in other Greek technical texts, where it serves the purpose of articulating logical reasoning. In medicine, we find recurrent linguistic patterns, especially introductory and concluding formulae, such as νῦν δὲ ἐρέω "and now I shall say"; μέλλω ἐρεῖν "I will say"; ταῦτα δέ μοι ἐς τοῦτο εἴρηται "this has been said by me up to this point."

Style and Rhetoric

Greek "scientific style" has been described as "a continuous, systematic, and discursive, though non-rhetorical and non-emotional prose" (Thesleff 1966: 89). However, scientific discourse in ancient Greece sometimes uses language in a connotative way when it needs to convey some emotion to convince the audience/reader about its contents.

One of the most striking uses of rhetoric aimed at persuading can be found in the Hippocratic Corpus, especially *The Art of Medicine* and *On Breaths* (Jouanna 1984). These texts are characterized by long introductions and conclusions, antitheses, anaphoras, and sound effects typical of Gorgianic style (see also ch. 30). Rhetorical elements are also found in other works, not primarily composed for laypeople, such as *The Sacred Disease*, *Air, Waters and Places*, *Fractures*, *Prognostics*, just to quote the most famous examples. The reason why medicine, unlike other technical disciplines, uses rhetoric can be explained by looking at the historical context. Medicine, especially in the fifth and fourth centuries BCE, had to establish itself against other common healing practices performed by magicians, priests, and other types of healers. The first physicians not only did "medical research," but also had to fight against these practices to prove that "real" medicine was better and more effective than magic. This meant convincing a general audience who would go to magicians rather than to physicians. Thus, according to a common practice of Greek society, rhetoric was necessary to "persuade" both colleagues and prospective clients.

Mathematics, by contrast, makes a much more sparing use of rhetorical devices, because it did not need to fight against any similar but unscientific discipline, as medicine had to do against magic. As a consequence, mathematical language does not so much "persuade" as "demonstrate," and it achieves this not so much by rhetorical means as by using logical connective particles, which are part of dialectic, as developed by Aristotle and then by the Stoics.

Technical language sometimes admits personal elements in scientific texts. Both the Hippocratic Corpus and Euclid use verbs of "saying" in the first person singular (φημί or λέγω and, in medicine only, ἐρέω) when stating something or clarifying a key passage. This use of the *Ich-Stil* (Regenbogen 1961: 171) is a feature of the Ionic tradition of the ἱστορίη, and Greek "scientists" use it to underline their own results or to explain important concepts. In medicine, this sense of individual scientific achievement and of the ἱστορίη through first-person statements is particularly evident. In mathematics, instead, the first person is much less used, with the exception of prefatory letters that mathematicians like Archimedes or Apollonius of Perge address to a colleague. In these prefaces, first and second persons are much used, as the incipit of Archimedes' letter to Eratosthenes (the dedicatee of the *Method*) shows:

Ἀρχιμήδης Ἐρατοσθένει εὖ πράττειν. Ἀπέστειλά σοι πρότερον τῶν εὑρημένων
θεωρημάτων ἀναγράψας αὐτῶν τὰς προτάσεις φάμενος εὑρίσκειν ταύτας τὰς ἀποδείξεις,
ἃς οὐκ εἶπον ἐπὶ τοῦ παρόντος ·

Archimedes greets Eratosthenes. Before, I sent you some theorems I found, limiting
myself to their propositions and asking you to find out these demonstrations which
I did not indicate at that time. (*Method* 426.3)

Apart from these letters, which are not, strictly speaking, "mathematical writings" but belong to the genre of the "preface," mathematical texts tend to be characterized by highly impersonal style and passive forms. However, there are some interesting cases of *Ich-Stil* in Archimedes, who is more personal than Euclid. Archimedes intrudes in his own persona in the discussion by frequently using verbs in the first person singular: for example in the *De sphaera et cylindro* he uses καλῶ many times in the axioms (eg., Archim. *Sph. Cyl.* 6.25 ῥόμβον δὲ **καλῶ** στερεόν, ἐπειδὰν … "I call it a solid rhombus when . . ..") or λαμβάνω in the sense of "I take it/assume (that . . .)" to introduce postulates (which he calls λαμβανόμενα "things taken"). By contrast, Euclid's first-person forms λέγω "I say" and ὁμοίως δὴ δείξομεν "similarly we will prove" sound more like formulae than real "personal statements."

Non-Normative Syntax

Technical prose is sometimes characterized by what, at first sight, can be defined as an elliptic and anacoluthic syntax. This is certainly evident in the Hippocratic writings, in particular the *Epidemics*, for example:

Ἐρασινόν, ὃς ᾤκει παρὰ Βοώτου χαράδρην, πῦρ ἔλαβε μετὰ δεῖπνον· **νύκτα ταραχώδης.**
Ἡμέρην τὴν πρώτην δι' ἡσυχίης, νύκτα ἐπιπόνως.
Δευτέρῃ πάντα παρωξύνθη· ἐς νύκτα παρέκρουσεν.
Τρίτῃ ἐπιπόνως · παρέκρουσε πολλά.
Τετάρτῃ δυσφορώτατα · ἐς δὲ τὴν νύκτα οὐδὲν ἐκοιμήθη · ἐνύπνια καὶ λογισμοί· ἔπειτα χείρω,
μεγάλα καὶ ἐπίκαιρα, **φόβος, δυσφορίη.**
Πέμπτῃ πρωῒ κατήρτητο, καὶ κατενόει πάντα · πουλὺ δὲ πρὸ μέσου ἡμέρης ἐξεμάνη · κατέχειν
οὐκ ἠδύνατο · **ἄκρεα ψυχρά, ὑποπέλια · οὖρα ὑπέστη** · ἀπέθανε περὶ ἡλίου δυσμάς.

A fever seized Erasinus, who lived near the Canal of Bootes, after supper. [He was] agitated during the night.
During the first day [he was] quiet, during the night [he was] in pain;
On the second day, everything exacerbated, at night he became delirious.
On the third day, [he was] in pain; he was in great delirium.
On the fourth day, [he was] in a most uncomfortable state; he did not sleep at night; dreams and talking; then (every symptom became) worse, strong and serious; [he had] fear, discomfort
On the fifth day, in the morning he recovered and was in full possession of his senses; but long before midday he fell in great delirium; he could not restrain himself; [his] extremities [were] cold, livid; urines stopped. He died around sunset. (Hippoc. *Epid.* 1, Case 8)

The syntax, rich in non-consequential constructions, is typical of notes, rather than of elaborated prose text. Many predicates are suppressed in nominal clauses with a simple nominative (φόβος, δυσφορίη) or with an adjective referring to the sick person (νύκτα ταραχώδης) or with a prepositional phrase or an adverb (ἡμέρην τὴν πρώτην δι' ἡσυχίης, νύκτα ἐπιπόνως). There are harsh changes of subjects (δευτέρῃ πάντα παρωξύνθη · ἐς νύκτα παρέκρουσεν). Sometimes, nominal phrases are followed by a clause with predicate, creating an odd *variatio* (ἄκρεα ψυχρὰ, ὑποπέλια · οὖρα ὑπέστη).

Sometimes the syntax is not only brachylogic as here, but even grammatically incorrect, as when necessary articles are missing as in *Epid.* 1.3.1–3: ... πυρετοὶ ... **μακρὰ δὲ νοσέουσιν, οὐδὲ περὶ τὰ ἄλλα δυσφόρως διάγουσιν** ἐγένοντο "... fevers ... attacked persons who had been sick for a long period, but who were otherwise not in an uncomfortable state," where a definite article τοῖσι before μακρὰ δὲ νοσέουσιν, οὐδὲ περὶ τὰ ἄλλα δυσφόρως διάγουσιν is necessary in order to substantivize the participle. Another typical trait is the *nominativus pendens*, a nominative that is not followed by any predicate and seems thus disconnected from the rest of the clause, but which can serve as a topic marking, as in *Epid.* 3.14.4–6: Τὸ μελαγχολικόν τε καὶ ὕφαιμον · οἱ καῦσοι καὶ τὰ φρενιτικὰ, καὶ τὰ δυσεντεριώδεα τούτων ἥπτετο "And the melancholic and the sanguine (complexions); bilious remittent fevers, the symptoms of phrenitis and those of dysentery attacked them." This loose syntax is typical of notes, whose purpose is to keep track of important events without any interest in style and elegance. The result is a "brachylogic" prose, that must be considered not a mistake but a personal choice of the scientific writer. This "minimalist" style suits didactic texts and reference works well, since it contains only the relevant data and highlights the most important logical steps through the process of topicalization, as the *nominativus pendens* or other absolute word-usages.

In this survey, brief and limited for obvious reasons, I have tried to show how Greek technical writers were able to exploit the lexical, morphological, and syntactic possibilities of their language in order to express new scientific ideas and reasoning. They adopted various strategies. Technical terminology was created by reusing old generic terms, by creating new ones with suffixes and compounding, as well as by adopting "visual" metaphors. Syntax too was used to communicate scientific content (especially by using argumentative particles to articulate proofs) as well as to "persuade" a larger audience of the soundness of the "scientific" approach to a discipline. Beyond doubt, medicine and mathematics are the best examples of technical languages in ancient Greece. However, behind them and their linguistic achievements there is Aristotle. Not only did he use the technical languages of both medicine (in his biological works) and mathematics, he also made a crucial contribution to scientific language and its syntax and style by setting out the principles of both dialectic and rhetoric, which, as we have seen, are at the core of ancient scientific discourse.

FURTHER READING

On technical languages in general, see Fluck 1985 and Hoffmann 1985. On modern terminology for diseases, see Goltz 1969. Snell 1953: 227–45 and Barnes 1987: 18–22 discuss the language of the Presocratics. On Ancient Greek scientific style in general, see Thesleff 1966, Eijk 1997, and Willi 2003: 51–95. Langslow 2000 and Fögen 2003 are more focused on Latin, but still very useful.

On Greek medical terminology, see Lanza 1983, Lloyd 1983: 149–67, and López Férez 2000. Metaphorical language in Greek medicine is discussed in Vegetti 1983 and Skoda 1988. On Greek medical style and rhetoric, see Langholf 1977, Lloyd 1979: 86–98, Wenskus 1982, Hellweg 1985, Jouanna 1984, Nutton 1992: 16–27, Von Staden 1997, and Eijk 1997. Von Staden 1996 and 1998 deal with the interactions of medicine and mechanics.

A general approach to Greek mathematical language is Acerbi 2007: 213–18, 259–313, 532–4. On the other hand, Netz 1999: 89–126 must be approached with caution due to several inaccuracies in terms both of collection of data and linguistic analysis. A good reference work is the dictionary by Mugler 1958. Aujac 1984 covers formulae in Greek mathematics. For Aristotle's influence on mathematical language, see Einarson 1936. On language and logic in Greek mathematical language, see Acerbi forthcoming. Various and specific aspects of Greek mathematical language are covered by Federspiel 1992, 1995, 2003, 2005, and 2006, by Vitrac 2008, and by Acerbi 2008.

PART FIVE

Greek as Literature

CHAPTER TWENTY-FOUR

Inherited Poetics

Joshua T. Katz

Western literature begins with the *Iliad*. This statement is uncontroversial as long as we define the first two words conventionally, with "Western" describing the area that stretches west from the shores of Asia Minor and "literature" not including such things as administrative records. And yet what about the very next words, the verbal phrase "begins with"? The fact is that Homer's foundational text, which has had an incalculable influence on written works and other cultural artefacts the world over in the nearly three millennia since it was composed, did not spring fully formed from the void but itself has a prehistory that scholars have over the past two hundred or so years been endeavoring to uncover. The purpose of this chapter is to give a sense of what we know, or suspect, about the tradition that hides, so to speak, behind the imposing poetic practice that most readers of Greek – whether the general public or professional classicists – take for granted.

In order to get at this shadowy tradition, we need first of all to understand my title: what does "inherited poetics" mean? The adjective, "inherited," is easy enough to define but takes some work to explain in the context of language. By contrast, "poetics," like "literature," is nearly impossible to define, and yet most of the time we know its effects when we see them.

Let us begin with "inherited." The basic idea of inheritance is, of course, that something or someone takes over one or more features from a prior (or at least contemporaneous) thing or person. Virgil's *Aeneid*, Ingres' painting of Thetis supplicating Zeus, and Christopher Logue's new *War Music* (an English-language "account" of the *Iliad*) all owe a large debt to Homer, and we can readily say that this debt is in each case an inheritance, for these post-Homeric figures "receive or take over from a predecessor" (*American Heritage Dictionary*, 4th edn (2000), s.v. *inherit* 2) motifs, diction, or both from the great poem of Achilles' wrath. Obviously Homer and Virgil did not know each other and obviously, too, Virgil did not "receive [his material] from [his] ancestor by legal succession or will" or "by bequest or as a legacy" (ibid., definition no. 1), but it is perfectly normal for artists to borrow deliberately from or somehow be influenced by one another. Indeed, a principal occupation, not to say preoccupation, of classicists today (especially Latinists) is uncovering what are regularly referred to as allusions and intertexts (see above all Hinds 1998).

But there is another meaning of "inherit" to consider as well, one that has to do with nature rather than culture: "To receive (a characteristic) from one's parents by genetic transmission." This definition (no. 3 in the *American Heritage Dictionary* s.v. *inherit*) is headed by the label "*Biology*," but in fact it applies in only lightly modified form to linguistics as well. Although languages do not (typically) have two parents, they (not unlike cellular organisms) do develop, multiply, and die – and this natural, unintellectual transmission and reception of linguistic characteristics via everyday parent-to-child communication generation after generation is what lies behind the following two (necessarily simplified) observations. On the one hand, you, your parents before you, and your children after you share many sounds, intonational patterns, and idioms; and on the other hand, the language of your great-great-great-. . .-great-grandmother (Old English, say, or Classical Greek) is evidently very different from and yet at its core also the same as your modern (English or Greek) tongue. Both facts are consequences of oral tradition (see for an interdisciplinary overview the 82 short notes in a special issue of the journal *Oral Tradition* (vol. 18), which include many on Ancient Greek and Katz 2003 on linguistics).

The development of languages, which takes place orally and aurally, is thus quite a bit like the party game that Americans call "Telephone" and the British "Chinese whispers," but with a significant difference: to a remarkable degree, linguistic change – in particular, phonological change – is regular. (The idea that sound change admits of no exceptions at all, the so-called "Neogrammarian Hypothesis," has been the subject of sustained criticism for well over a century. This is obviously not the place to consider whether there really are no exceptions or whether regularity is just an essentially correct guiding principle, though for a forceful defense of Neogrammarianism, see Hale 2003 and 2007: 124–45.) It is not possible to predict with confidence how some sound now (call it t) will develop over the next ten, hundred, or thousand years, but it is possible to chart developments *ex post facto*, to demonstrate (for example) that every (or nearly every) instance of the sound d in the speech of your great-great-great-. . .-great-grandmother has turned into what you pronounce as t and, furthermore, to demonstrate that among your many cousins, all of whom share with you the same Ur-grandmother as ancestor, some still say d while others have turned it into z.

Compare, for instance, these six sets of three words: *two, tame, foot* (English) ~ *twā* (fem.), *tam, fōt* (Old English) ~ *zwei, zahm, Fusz*[1] (Germ.) ~ δύο, δαμ-, ποδ- (Gk) ~ *duo, dom-, ped-* (Lat.) ~ *dvā̆, dam-, pád-* (Skt). There is no obvious semantic or pragmatic reason for each triplet to behave in the same way, and yet the patterns are perfectly clear: t in English (both Modern and Old) corresponds to z in German and to d in Greek, Latin, and Sanskrit. This cross-linguistic systematicity is what gives the study of linguistic history its essential scientific rigor and allows scholars to produce a family tree, not unlike the way genealogists do: the only way to explain the regularities is to say that English, German, Greek, Latin, and Sanskrit are all (more or less closely) related to one another – and what this means is that they all inherited material from one and the same source, a long-dead language that today goes by the name of Proto-Indo-European (on which, see also ch. 12). In this language, spoken five or six thousand years ago, probably in the steppe north of the Black and Caspian Seas, the sound *d (the asterisk indicates that it is not attested as such but must be inferred) is in effect the lowest common denominator, that is to say, the reconstruction that most easily accounts for all the evidence that we actually do possess. This straightforward application of the Comparative Method, a simple procedure that remains, after nearly two centuries, the most consistently validated theory of language ever put forward (see now Campbell and Poser 2008), yields the result that the word for "two" is PIE *$dwoH$ (probably specifically *$dwoh_3$) and the roots of "tame" and "foot" are *$demh_2$- and *ped-, respectively.[2] (Occasional phrases in this paragraph and throughout the present essay are taken more or less directly from Katz 2005a, which may be consulted for further discussion of much of the material treated here; see also Katz 2007b for general remarks on the relationship between linguistics and classics.)

There is, needless to say, a lot more to language than just sounds: sounds combine to form morphemes, which in turn combine to form words, which in turn combine to form phrases, clauses, sentences, and larger narrative structures (in which there usually rest, sometimes only below the surface, all kinds of socially important information about dialect, class, genre, and the like). It is hardly surprising that the bigger and more unusual the units of analysis, the more difficult they are to assess synchronically in any given language; and since reconstruction involves in the first place the careful cross-linguistic assessment of synchronic data, it is obvious that engaging in responsible, reliable diachronic analysis is a very tricky business. In principle, though, the Comparative Method *can* take on larger units, and in practice it does do so, with scholars sometimes obtaining truly illuminating and exciting results, most prominently in the area of poetics.

Formula

In Indo-European studies, poetic language (often referred to with the German phrase *indogermanische Dichtersprache*) is one of the most vibrant areas of study, and Greek naturally plays a leading role. Of particular importance has been the recognition of pre-Greek – typically Proto-Greco-Indo-Iranian, but in some cases plausibly Proto-Indo-European – antecedents of Homeric formulae (e.g., ἱερὸν μένος, which literally means something like "holy vigor"), the archaic but flexible backbone of epic that has been the subject of such a variety of high-profile scholarly inquiry since the pioneering work of Milman Parry in the 1920s and 1930s (collected in Parry 1971). Leading references on inherited poetic figures and motifs since Rüdiger Schmitt's *catalogue raisonné* (1967a) include Durante 1976, Watkins 1995, Matasović 1996, Pinault and Petit 2006, and West 2007; note also the papers collected in Schmitt 1968 and Watkins 1994 (esp. vol. 2: *Culture and Poetics*).

The Homeric formula ἱερὸν μένος, just mentioned parenthetically, is of evident synchronic interest. It is found a number of times in the *Odyssey* (e.g., 7.167), always after the penthemimeral caesura and before a personal name in the genitive that closes the verse with an adonic; the name is in almost every instance Ἀλκινόοιο "of Alkinoos" (there is one example of Ἀντινόοιο "of Antinoos" (*Od.* 18.34), and Ἠελίοιο "of Helios" appears once in a Homeric hymn (*Hymn. Hom. Ap.* 371)). Aside from two (obviously allusive) examples in Quintus of Smyrna's *Posthomerica*, which lack the following personal name, and aside from Homeric quotations (in, e.g., the works of scholiasts and grammarians), the formula is unattested outside Homer. But as for Homer, it is difficult to see that the formula could have any function aside from a space-filler since "the holy vigor of Alkinoos" – whatever that would even mean – is nothing but a periphrasis for "Alkinoos," the name itself (as already the fifth-cent. CE lexicographer Hesychius states).

Now, the combination of semantic obscurity with evident archaism is precisely what the historical linguist looks for since one of the main mantras of comparative philology is this: if you encounter a synchronic oddity, look for a diachronic explanation. And at least the beginnings of such an explanation are at hand, as was recognized already in 1853 by the German comparative mythologist and philologist Adalbert Kuhn (see Kuhn 1853a: 274): ἱερός "holy" and μένος "vigor, strength, fighting spirit" find their (nearly) exact cognates in the Sanskrit words *iṣirá-* "vigorous" and *mánas-* "mind, intellect," respectively – and in the oldest text from India, the *Rigveda*, we find the collocation *iṣiréṇa . . . mánasā* "with vigorous mind (instr. sg.)" in a hymn to the intoxicating god Soma (*RV* 8.48.7). It is true that *iṣiréṇa . . . mánasā* is found but once and appears, furthermore, with the genitive singular pronoun *te* "of you" between the two words (which, if it were Greek, would mean according to some scholars, whose views on this subject are in my opinion intellectually stifling, that the pairing could not possibly count as a "formula"), but this is not to say that it holds no interest for the Hellenist. While there remain details that we do not know, it is surely the case that something like *$h_1is(h_2)ro-$* (see García Ramón 1992) + *$menos-$* existed before the Greek and Indic languages went their separate ways (perhaps much earlier: Matasović 1996: 42 suggests a parallel in Old English, but the link is tenuous at best) and that what we find in Greek is the semantically bleached vestige of this tradition. The adjective ἱερός has shifted meaning from "vigorous" to "holy" (but this makes little sense in connection with Alkinoos) while the noun μένος has gone from meaning "mind" (this English word likewise goes back to the root of mental activity *par excellence*, PIE *$men-$*, on which there is an enormous body of secondary literature; see most recently Bakker 2008) to conveying basically the same sense that the adjective once did, namely "vigor, strength" – except that in this old collocation, μένος does not synchronically mean much of anything. And it will not have escaped the notice of the reader who knows Greek that Alkinoos is a "speaking name": ἱερὸν μένος Ἀλκινόοιο from a diachronic point of view effectively means "the strong mind of Strong (ἀλκι-) Mind (νόος)."

There are, of course, dozens of tales to tell about Homeric formulae and the tradition from which they are inherited, stories that highlight their diachronic as well as synchronic interest. Let me briefly mention three. First of all, some formulae seem straightforward, even banal. For example, is it really so interesting that ὠκέες ἵπποι "swift horses (nom. pl.)" (e.g., *Il.* 5.257; cf. also acc. pl. ὠκέας ἵππους (e.g., *Il.* 3.263)) finds correspondents (with the noun preceding the adjective: "horses . . . swift") in Vedic *áśvās . . . āśávaḥ* (*RV* 10.119.3; nom. pl.) and Young Avestan *aspā̊ŋhō . . . āsauuō* (*Yašt* 17.12; nom. pl.) – given, after all, that speed is a proverbial equine feature (Matasović 1996: 40, 73–4 adduces parallels in early Celtic, Germanic, and Slavic literatures, but also in Tamil, which is not Indo-European)?

Other formulae, however, have for one reason or other proved to be anything but straightforward, with the famous, not to say infamous, example of κλέος ἄφθιτον leading the pack. The study of Indo-European poetics began (it is conventionally said) with a passing comment by Kuhn (1853b: 467) about the essential equivalence of the unique Homeric phrase κλέος ἄφθιτον "imperishable fame" (*Il.* 9.413) with the like-meaning Vedic *ákṣiti śrávaḥ* (*RV* 1.40.4, 8.103.5, and 9.66.7) and (even closer, though Kuhn did not explicitly note it) *śrávas . . . ákṣitam* (*RV* 1.9.7). The controversy over this correspondence – in particular, whether it is appropriate (as I believe it is) to speak of **ḱlewos n̥dʰgʷʰitom*, whose two parts are individually the evident precursors of the words for "fame" and "imperishable" in both Homer and the *Rigveda*, as a "formula" – is fiery and shows no signs of abating.

And finally, in at least one case, detailed morpho-phonological analysis has actually taken away, in my view conclusively, what has generally been considered a formula. It has been claimed since the 1870s (see the extensive treatment in Schmitt 1967a: 10–11, 142–8) that the verse-final vocative phrase δῶτορ ἐάων "o giver of good things," used of the god Hermes in *Od.* 8.335, as well as in *Hymn. Hom.* 18.12 and 29.8 (cf. likewise verse-final nom. pl. δωτῆρες ἐάων in *Od.* 8.325) has nearly exact equivalents in Vedic (e.g., nom. sg. *dātā́ vásūnām* (*RV* 8.51.5; said of the leading deity Indra)) and Young Avestan (e.g., nom. sg. *dāta vaŋhuuąm* (*Videvdad* 22.1, 8, and 14; said of the highest god Ahura Mazdā, whose name, by the way, reflects the PIE root **men-*)). The Proto-Indo-European reconstruction would be something like **deh₃tor- h₁weswoHom*, but while this preform yields *dāta vaŋhuuąm* directly, Nussbaum (1998: 130–45), building on doubts that some other scholars have had over the years as well, seems finally to have demonstrated that ἐάων[3] reflects **h₁es-u-* (cf. Gk εὖ and Vedic *sú*, both adverbs meaning "well"), a derivative of the root **h₁es-* "be" (cf. English *is*, Gk ἐστί, etc.), rather than **h₁wes-u-* (seen also in, e.g., Old Irish *fíu* "worthy"); for discussion, see now Wodtko in Wodtko, Irslinger, and Schneider 2008: 241–2 n. 13, 253, 255 n. 8, with references. Though phonologically, morphologically, and semantically nearly identical, the Greek and Indo-Iranian phrases thus do not share an ancestor. Still, we can well imagine that their two Ur-grandmothers were friends: the Proto-Indo-Europeans do seem to have spoken of their gods as givers of good things, but either they did so with more than one phrase or the single one they used is unrecoverable on the basis of the attested evidence.

Let us go back to ὠκέες ἵπποι and κλέος ἄφθιτον. In fact, the former *is* interesting. In the first place, it presents a salutary reminder that much of language, even poetic language, is actually pretty ordinary. From another and entirely different point of view, however, there is something quite remarkable behind the ordinariness, for although ὠκέες and ἵπποι appear to be in no way alike (they have no letters or sounds in common), the Indo-Iranian evidence strongly suggests that "swift horses" is actually a *figura etymologica*, **h₁ṓḱ-ewes h₁eḱ-wōs* ("swift swifties"), with two different derivatives of a Proto-Indo-European root that is sometimes set up as **h₁eḱ-* "swift" (for references, some skeptical, see now Wodtko in Wodtko, Irslinger, and Schneider 2008: 200–1, 230-3, esp. 231 n. 1). And as for "imperishable fame," its importance in "standard" Homeric studies presumably comes in no small part from the fact that Achilles speaks of κλέος ἄφθιτον in his great speech to the embassy, in which he muses on the choice between returning home and winning undying glory through death on the battlefield. Instead of summarizing the extensive literature, I send readers to the latest two articles on the subject: Volk 2002, which presents a clear and original line of argument in favor of taking Homer's phrase as a reflection of the inherited poetic tradition, and Finkelberg 2007, which resumes and amplifies earlier arguments that there is no good reason to believe it to be inherited at all.

Poetics

By talking about Homeric formulae, I have evidently been sliding from an explanation of inheritance into the realm of poetics. Whatever exactly is meant by "poetics" (see Brogan in Preminger and Brogan 1993: 929–37), it clearly has to do with formal concerns. In the second chapter of his 1995 book, Calvert Watkins treats the history and study of Indo-European poetics as having three parts (Watkins 1995: 12–27): formulaics (at which we have already looked), metrics, and stylistics, the last a necessarily vague term for the study of "all the other linguistic devices, figures, and other recurrent phonological, morphological, and syntactic variables which may be in play in verbal art in cognate languages" (1995: 12). Let us consider the matter with reference to one of the similes that precede the Catalogue of Ships in book 2 of the *Iliad* (459–68):

> τῶν δ', ὥς τ' ὀρνίθων πετεηνῶν ἔθνεα πολλά,
> χηνῶν ἢ γεράνων ἢ κύκνων δουλιχοδείρων,   460
> Ἀσίῳ ἐν λειμῶνι, Καϋστρίου ἀμφὶ ῥέεθρα,
> ἔνθα καὶ ἔνθα ποτῶνται ἀγαλλόμενα πτερύγεσσι,
> κλαγγηδὸν προκαθιζόντων, σμαραγεῖ δέ τε λειμών,
> ὣς τῶν ἔθνεα πολλὰ νεῶν ἄπο καὶ κλισιάων
> ἐς πεδίον προχέοντο Σκαμάνδριον· αὐτὰρ ὑπὸ χθὼν   465
> σμερδαλέον κονάβιζε ποδῶν αὐτῶν τε καὶ ἵππων.
> ἔσταν δ' ἐν λειμῶνι Σκαμανδρίῳ ἀνθεμόεντι
> μυρίοι, ὅσσα τε φύλλα καὶ ἄνθεα γίγνεται ὥρῃ.

And as the many tribes of winged birds, wild geese or cranes or long-necked swans on the Asian meadow by the streams of Caÿstrius, fly here and there, glorying in their strength of wing, and with loud cries settle ever onwards, and the meadow resounds, so their [*sc.* the Greeks'] many tribes poured out of the ships and huts into the plain of Scamander, and the earth resounded terribly beneath the tread of men and horses. And they stood in the flowery meadow of Scamander, countless, as are the leaves and flowers in their season. (Murray–Wyatt 1999: 95)

From the point of view of the Indo-Europeanist, the second verse, χηνῶν ἢ γεράνων ἢ κύκνων δουλιχοδείρων "of geese or cranes or long-necked swans" (460) is perhaps especially remarkable, for every syllable goes back to something in the proto-language (compare Watkins 1998: 204). The genitive plural ending -ων is exactly cognate with Lat. gen. pl. -*um* (cf., e.g., *ānserum* "of geese") and such other genitive plural endings throughout the family as Skt -*ām* and Avest. -*ąm* (cf. *vásūnām* and *vaŋhuuąm*

(~ ἐάων)), Old Hitt. -*an*, and Lithuanian -*ų*; they all go back to (quasi-)PIE *-*ōm*, from a still earlier *-*oHom*. The precise morphology of the repeated conjunction ἤ "or" is not entirely clear, but it is a contraction of ἠέ (well attested in Homer as such), whose first element is generally believed to be the (independently well-known and in the first place asseverative) particle ἦ (which probably reflects a deictic element or interjection of the form PIE *eh₁ (*vel sim.*) and is cognate with a Vedic particle *ā́*; compare Dunkel 1997: 18–23, 25–6) and whose second element, -(ϝ)έ, is certainly cognate with Latin -*ue* "or" (PIE *-*we*).

As for the compound adjective "long-necked," both parts are of inherited stock: δολιχός "long" – here with a metrically lengthened first syllable (see, e.g., Chantraine 1973: 99) – goes back to something like PIE *dolh₁igʰo- (certain morpho-phonological matters remain disputed) and is cognate (more or less exactly) with the like-meaning Skt *dīrghá*-, Hitt. *daluki*-, etc., while δειρή "neck" (cf. Arc. δερϝα) goes back to something like *gʷer[*H*ʔ]*weh₂* and is evidently related (but the details are difficult) to such words as Skt *grīvā́*- "neck" and Russian *griva* "mane." Whether the combination itself goes back to the proto-language is uncertain.

Finally, all three birds have good Indo-European names: χήν "goose" is cognate with (the first syllable of) Lat. *ānser*, as well as with English *goose* (Old English *gōs*), Skt *haṁsá*-, etc. (PIE *ǵʰans-); the precise Proto-Indo-European preform of γέρανος "crane" is not securely reconstructible, but the Greek word is cognate at the level of the (almost certainly onomatopoetic) root (PIE *ger(*h₂*)- "cry hoarsely") with such other designations of the bird as English *crane* (Old English *cran*), Welsh *garan*, and (a bit more distantly) Lat. *grūs*; and κύκνος "swan" seems to mean literally "whitey" and be the nominalization of PIE *kuk-no- "shining, white," an adjective that makes its way into Sanskrit in a slightly different guise, *śukrá*- (PIE *kuk-ro-; cf. the Sanskrit verb *śoc*- "shines"). All three birds are indigenous to all the likely candidates for the Eurasian homeland of the Proto-Indo-Europeans (compare Mallory 1991, J. A. C. Greppin in Mallory and Adams 1997: 66–8, 140–1, 236, 558, and also Mallory and Adams 2006: 143–5).

The formulaic nature of the passage is not in dispute. A glance at Pavese and Boschetti 2003: 60–1 shows that at least parts of seven of the ten verses are found elsewhere in the Homeric corpus, from the disjunct phrase Σκαμάνδριον· αὐτάρ "Skamandrian [meadow]. But . . ." (465), which reappears in the same metrical position in *Il.* 6.402; to the iconic collocation ἔνθα καὶ ἔνθα "hither and thither" (462), which is found over 30 times in the *Iliad* and the *Odyssey*; to the whole verse on which I was just concentrating, χηνῶν ἢ γεράνων ἢ κύκνων δουλιχοδείρων, and also ὡς τῶν ἔθνεα πολλὰ νεῶν ἄπο καὶ κλισιάων "so [poured] the many tribes from the ships and huts" (464), both of which are found in full elsewhere as part of similes, in *Il.* 15.692 and 2.91, respectively. (Two components of the latter are formulae in themselves: verse-final νεῶν ἄπο καὶ κλισιάων and also ἔθνεα πολλά, a significant phrase, discussed further below, that appears in the first verse of the quoted passage as well and yet again in the verse that immediately follows, *Il.* 2.469 (see n. 4 below).) Some passages are more formulaic than *Il.* 2.459–68, some less so, but this simile suffices to demonstrate something that essentially every Homeric gobbet could, namely the existence of "building blocks" that are the hallmark of oral composition.

Meter

Since formulae are generally considered to be repositories of linguistic archaism (passed down by oral transmission, as already explained), the next question to ask concerns meter. Diachronically perfect lines are highly unusual, but what does "perfect" mean? Is there, for example, any reason to think that *Il.* 2.460 directly reflects something like *$\hat{g}^h$ansoHom eh_1-we $gerh_2noHom$ eh_1-we kuknoHom dolh$_1$i$\hat{g}^h$o-g^{w}erwo-Hom* in the proto-language? The simple answer is that there is not, and this in itself makes clear that the relationship between inheritance and poetics is not always straightforward.

For one thing, the cumbersome asterisked verse I have just posited is neither a dactylic hexameter (scanned according to usual principles) nor an instance of any other conventionally recognized metrical form. But – and this is the more important point – since the hexameter has no immediately recognizable analogues in other Indo-European traditions and is generally believed to be a Greek innovation, we have no cause to try to reconstruct whole hexametric lines anyway. The origin of the hexameter remains high on the list of problems that all Hellenists should wish to see resolved, for it is obviously difficult to say anything authoritative about the deep background of Homeric formulae unless one has a plausible theory of the relationship between these linguistic units and the prosodic template that guides (or is guided by) them. And furthermore (though I have no room to talk about this here), if early Greek poetry is filled with such inherited motifs as "imperishable fame," then what does the lack of a reconstructible hexameter say about the antecedents of the very genre of epic (compare Katz 2005a), which classicists typically view as fundamental?

A number of views of the origin of Greek heroic poetry's defining meter may be found in the relatively recent scholarly literature (see Magnelli 1996); not surprisingly, the details are highly technical, and it is not easy to provide a summary. What is nearly certain, though, is that the hexameter arose out of one or more shorter "lyric" lines, and this is interesting to the historical/comparative linguist since the (synchronically very complicated) metrical underpinnings of archaic Greek lyric poetry – a genre that exists as such alongside the epic hexameter – correspond to well-known forms in Indic (e.g., the meters of the *Rigveda*), Iranian, and very likely other traditions and thus probably go back to Proto-Indo-European times. The work of Antoine Meillet (see especially Meillet 1923) was fundamental for establishing the genetic relationship between Greek and Indic meters, but this great linguist could do nothing with the hexameter, which he thought had to be of foreign origin (see 1923: 57–63). My own preferred view of the hexameter is that of Nagy (1974), who, building on work by Meillet, Roman Jakobson, and Watkins, sees its "Aeolic" archetype in a sixteen-syllable internally expanded pherecratean, which is itself a catalectic version of another lyric base, the octosyllabic glyconic. Nagy's arguments (which he has often repeated and lightly revised: see Nagy 1998, with references) are not without significant problems, as distinguished and basically sympathetic reviewers have pointed out (West 1974 and Haslam 1976), but the linchpin of his case is very attractive: the appearance of κλέος ἄφθιτον at the end of an expanded glyconic in Sappho (44.4 Lobel–Page/ Voigt) – with which one might indeed cautiously compare the consistent appearance in the *Rigveda* of *ákṣiti śrávaḥ* at the end of an octosyllabic *pāda* – is probably not to be attributed to Homeric borrowing but is rather an important piece of evidence for the lyric background of this significant "formula" and for its metrical deployment prior to the creation of the hexameter.

Whatever the precise origin of the hexameter may be – significant alternatives to Nagy's scheme include the coalescence of a hemiepes and a paroemiac (compare West 1973a: 185) or otherwise of a glyconic and a pherecratean (see first Berg 1978 and, for more recent discussion and literature, Haug and Welo 2001 and Hajnal 2003b: 61–100, esp. 70–9, and 2003c; see also ch. 27 below) – the interplay between formula and meter needs to be recognized, and one of the more significant aspects of Nagy's work is his insistence on the importance of trying to give a formal diachronic account of this relationship. Just how important it is, and how difficult, can be seen from the controversy over the Iliadic verses

> ψυχὴ δ' ἐκ ῥεθέων πταμένη Ἀϊδόσδε βεβήκει,
> ὃν πότμον γοόωσα, λιποῦσ' ἀνδροτῆτα καὶ ἥβην

> and his soul flying from his limbs went to Hades,
> bewailing its fate, leaving manliness and youth,

said first of Patroklos (*Il.* 16.856–7) and then of Hektor (*Il.* 22.362–3). If you try to scan λιποῦσ' ἀνδροτῆτα καὶ ἥβην, you will immediately encounter a really quite dramatic difficulty: the first syllable of ἀνδροτῆτα "manliness (acc. sg.)" can hardly not scan long since the alpha is followed by no fewer than three consonants, and yet it has to scan short according to the regular rules of the dactylic hexameter; if it scanned long, the first three syllables of the word would form what is in this meter an impossible sequence, a cretic ($-\cup-$). The standard response to the problem (see, e.g., Watkins 1995: 499, with some references in n. 1) is to say that whatever the synchronic scansion of ἀνδροτῆτα may be, the verse was composed at a time when -ρο- was still a syllabic *ṛ* (and there was not yet an epenthetic *d*): *"*anṛtāt-*" ($\cup\cup-$), from PIE **h₂nṛ-*"man" (cf., e.g., Skt *nár-* "man"). An alternative view (see Tichy 1981) holds that when the verse was composed, the proto-hexameter did in fact allow a cretic: specifically, ἀνδροτῆτα καὶ ἥβην really does scan the way it looks ($-\cup-\cup\cup--$), that is, as a trochee-opening pherecratean (Tichy explicitly – and, it must be said, very elegantly – builds on Berg 1978). I favor the former, but the whole matter will have to be revisited in the light of a brilliant forthcoming paper by Timothy Barnes (see also ch. 27 below). An awkward but rarely acknowledged truth is that most reconstructions of archaic poetic language yield preforms whose metrical properties sit uneasily with the prosodic schemes we are used to: for example, καί goes back to disyllabic *kati and the pluperfect ending -ει (3 sg. act.), as in βεβήκει "went" at the end of the previous verse, is probably a contraction of -εε (see Katz 2006a, with 13–15 n. 30). Working out in detail the implications of this would be a worthwhile project.

Stylistics

Having considered formulaics and metrics, we come finally to the omnium-gatherum of stylistics and return to χηνῶν ἢ γεράνων ἢ κύκνων δουλιχοδείρων. One striking feature of this verse is that each of the avian names begins with one of the three velar stops in the language: k^h, g, and k. (I have already mentioned that the root of the word for "crane" is thought to be onomatopoetic; the gutturalism of all three birds is perhaps meant to evoke their cries.) Furthermore, the two parts of the adjective "long-necked" (on the use of compounds in Indo-European poetry, see now West 2007: 79–81) both begin with a delta, and the only other oral stop in the word is another velar; indeed, with the exception of the two *d*'s (one of which reflects a labiovelar, as we have seen), all oral stops in the line are velars, and this makes a striking contrast with the immediately preceding verse, which begins the simile, for it contains no velar stops at all, only dentals and labials. Alliteration is a feature of stylized language the world over, of course, but it played a larger role in early Greek poetry than most scholars readily admit (see Silk 1974: 173–93, 224–8) and was arguably a significant tool in the kit of the Proto-Indo-European bard (see, e.g., Watkins 1995: 23 and *passim*; West 2007: 58–9 is a bit more cautious). What phonetic repetition does is call attention to the words in question, and there are other interesting examples of this effect in *Il.* 2.459–68 as well. One case belongs in a class of its own: the consonants *p* and *t* found at the start of πετεηνῶν "winged (gen. pl.)" in 459 and ποτῶνται "fly about (3 pl. pres.)" and πτερύγεσσι "wings (dat. pl.)," both in 462. There is a good historical reason for this: all three words are derivatives – each with a different form of ablaut: *e*-grade πετ-, *o*-grade ποτ-, and zero-grade πτ- (see Watkins 1995: 21–2 on anaphora and polyptoton as stylistic devices) – of the PIE root *peth₂- "fly." But there is more to say (compare Bader 1997–8: 111–13 and *passim*). Not only is πετεηνῶν picked up morphologically by ποτῶνται and πτερύγεσσι, but the words on either side of πετεηνῶν, ὀρνίθων "of birds" and ἔθνεα πολλά "many tribes," are picked up phonetically by ἔνθα καὶ ἔνθα . . . ἀγαλλόμενα "hither and thither . . . exulting" (462) and then again, to form a ring, by φύλλα καὶ ἄνθεα "leaves and flowers" at the end of the simile (468; cf. also 467 ἀνθ-): ὀρνίθ- + ἔθνεα ~ ἔνθα καὶ ἔνθα ~ ἄνθεα and πολλά ~ -αλλόμ- ~ φύλλα. The repetition of the sounds in the phrase "the many tribes of winged birds" is a sort of proleptic reinforcement of the point of the Catalogue of Ships, namely to list the many tribes of men – who will be going into battle and, like the φύλλων γενεή "generations of leaves" (*Il.* 6.146) to which men are likened in what is the most discussed of all early Greek similes, will very likely die (compare Latacz 2003b: 136).[4]

There are also poetic features at play that point to inherited material of greater complexity than simple sounds and morphemes. The most obvious one concerns the entirety of verse 460. "Geese or cranes or long-necked swans" is a paradigmatic example of what is often known as Behaghel's Law, a stylistic figure named after the Germanist Otto Behaghel that was evidently part of the repertoire of the artful Proto-Indo-European: NOUN$_x$, NOUN$_y$, and/or [EPITHET + NOUN]$_z$ (in general, the number of syllables also increases from *x* to *y* to *z*). This figure (it is not a "law" at all) forms a subset of the *Gesetz der wachsenden Glieder* ("law of increasing members"), one of four general principles of discourse that Behaghel formulated in the first half of the twentieth century; West (2004 and 2007: 117–19), who notes that it is found with special frequency in the Catalogue of Ships (West 2004: 34–5), has now dubbed it the "Augmented Triad." The nouns are frequently proper names (as in *Il.* 1.145 ἢ Αἴας ἢ Ἰδομενεὺς ἢ δῖος Ὀδυσσεύς "whether Ajax or Idomeneus or godly Odysseus" (all three are vowel-initial; the list continues with further augmentation in the next verse) and – for an early example outside epic – Alcm. *Partheneion* 75–6 Φίλυλλα / Δαμαρ[έ]τα τ' ἐρατά τε Ϝιανθεμίς "Philylla and Damareta and lovely Wianthemis" (Watkins 1995: 31 notes the phonetic effect in the middle of 76)) and in one other instance in Homer are names of birds: σκῶπές τ' ἴρηκές τε τανύγλωσσοί τε κορῶναι "owls and hawks and long-tongued crows" (*Od.* 5.66). Examples abound in Indo-European poetry from India to Ireland, as documented by West (see also now Galjanić 2008: 138–43), who does not ignore the tricky matter of trying to square the idea that "Behaghel triads" are a poetic inheritance with a plausible picture of Proto-Indo-European meter, which for him involves, quite reasonably, hepta- and especially octo-syllabic sequences (West 2004: 44–5, 47–8, referring back to West 1973b). Also desirable are investigations into the status of these triads as a purely Indo-European phenomenon (is it really?) and also into their relationship with the wider *Gesetz*, whose rhetorical effects are said to be visible in languages all over the world and occur by no means just in poetry. One example among many from Ciceronian Latin of what classicists generally call a "rising tricolon" or a "tricolon crescendo" is *si acerbe, si crudeliter, si sine causa sum a tuis oppugnatus* "if I have been attacked bitterly, cruelly, without reason by your family" (*Fam.* 5.2.10); Morgan (1983), suggesting that triads of various kinds may be one of the "bas[e]s of a grammar of folk-poetry" (55), gives examples of triads of various kinds in Sumerian, Egyptian, and Biblical Hebrew, as well as in Indo-European languages, ancient, medieval, and modern.

Finally, it can hardly be forgotten that the entire passage *Il.* 2.459–68 – like the immediately preceding verses 455–8 and the immediately following verses 469–73 and again 474–83 – is a simile. West (2007: 95) writes that "[s]imiles are perhaps a universal feature of poetry and colourful discourse," adding, however, that "[t]he long simile that is such a familiar ornament of the Homeric poems, where the picture is developed by successive clauses and a whole situation is sketched, is very rare elsewhere." So this most prominent stylistic feature of early Greek epic poetry presumably does not have Proto-Indo-European roots. Instead, it is probably a borrowing from the Near East, an example of a poetic "areal feature," as suggested by Puhvel (1991: 21–9 (= 2002: 169–77 + 308 n. 17)) and West (1997a: 217–19, 242–52). The simile on which I have been concentrating describes, after all, birds and warriors along the Skamander, near Troy in what is now the Turkish province of Çanakkale, where Hittite and other Anatolian languages were spoken in the second millennium BCE. And indeed, an increasingly important line of research in Greek poetics involves sorting out Proto-Indo-European inheritance from relatively low-level borrowing from Indo-European and non-Indo-European Anatolia. To take just one example, Oettinger (1989–90) has argued that γαῖα μέλαινα "black earth" (e.g., *Il.* 2.699) is more likely to be a (culturally interesting) Hurrian-inspired borrowing from Hittite than a formula of Proto-Indo-European date.

There are many aspects of the inherited poetic tradition on which I have not touched: for example, the fact that Skamander (Σκάμανδϱος) is actually only the name of the river for men, while the gods, who in a number of Indo-European traditions have a different vocabulary, call it Ξάνϑος "Tawny" (see *Il.* 20.74), with a rearrangement of sounds (on the cultural significance of this pairing in the shared Greco-Anatolian context, see Watkins 1998: 206–9, esp. 209). And it would certainly have been appropriate for me not to have concentrated almost exclusively on Homer and instead to have said more about other poetic genres (West 2007: 63–74 gives a brief overview; see also Katz 2006b on riddles): I note the synchronic description and diachronic background of Sappho's syntax and style in Tzamali 1996 and the same for Pindar in Watkins 2002 (and other publications). Fascination with what came before our earliest poetry does not take away from Homer's genius (or Sappho's or Pindar's) or imply that archaic Greek bards were hacks who did little but unthinkingly assemble bits of the inherited tradition. On the contrary: much of the power of great verbal art, from all times and all places, derives from the ability of poets to work innovative magic with traditional material. I have recently tried to demonstrate this point in some detail with respect to the unexpectedly rich interaction in Homer between formulaic instances of the inherited particle (-)ταϱ and examples of what I call "unetymological ταϱ" (Katz 2007a). In the present chapter, however, there is only so much space, but I hope nonetheless to have offered a fair and engaging account of what "inherited poetics" means and why it is both important and interesting to study the inheritance, the poetics, and the combination of the two.

FURTHER READING

Inheritance is a linguistic matter, poetics a stylistic one. Campbell 2004 is a very good textbook of historical/comparative linguistics; Fortson 2004 is the best introduction to the older Indo-European languages and what they tell us about Proto-Indo-European inheritance. For poetics, see Preminger and Brogan 1993 in general and Schmitt 1967a and Watkins 1995 on Indo-European in particular, each with plenty of discussion of Greek. Recent works worthy of attention are Pinault and Petit 2006 and West 2007.

NOTES

1   The conventional spelling is *Fuß*, where the final letter is an "Eszett," i.e., a ligature of *s* and *z* (zed). The word is *fuoz* at an earlier stage of German known as Old High German (in which today's forms *zwei* and *zahm* are respectively *zwā* (fem.) and *zam*).

2   Along with h_1, the symbols h_2 and h_3 make up the so-called "laryngeals" (cover term: *H*), a series of sounds, quite possibly all post-velar fricatives, that were posited for Proto-Indo-European in 1879 by a very young Ferdinand de Saussure (1857–1913) – on the basis of structural considerations rather than any direct evidence. Saussure's audacity was vindicated shortly after his death with the decipherment of Hittite (1915), which has at least one consonant that goes back directly to the laryngeals, conventionally transcribed as *ḫ(ḫ)* and

thought to have been pronounced something like [x] (as in Germ. or Scottish *Lo_ch_*). In Greek, laryngeals are responsible for such things as the "prothetic vowel" in a number of words whose familiar cognates begin simply with a consonant: e.g., ὀδοντ- "tooth" vs English *tooth* (Old English *tōþ*), Germ. *Zahn*, Lat. *dent-*, and Skt *dánt-* (all go back to PIE *h_1d-(e/o)nt-*, literally "eat-ing"). On laryngeals, see also ch. 12.

3 The word is sometimes printed with aspiration and sometimes not; the former is correct.

4 The collocation ἔϑνεα πολλά, found only in similes in *Iliad* 2, is used exclusively of winged animals and humans with which they are compared: bees in 91, birds in 459 and 464, and flies in 469. On the likely Proto-Indo-European antiquity of the arthropodan metaphor that lies behind μυιάων ἀδινάων ἔϑνεα πολλά "many tribes of swarming flies" at the start of the immediately following simile, see Watkins 1979 (= 1994 (vol. 2): 622–5).

CHAPTER TWENTY-FIVE

Language and Meter

Gregory Nagy

The term *meter*, as used in the study of literature, is ordinarily associated with rhythm in poetry. As such, this word is more specialized in its applications than the Ancient Greek word *metron* from which it is derived, which means simply "measure." In this chapter, the term *meter* is analyzed in this more basic sense of "measure." As we will see from the Ancient Greek evidence, meter was a "measure" in the sense that it gave "measure" to language, so as to create a special language that was differentiated from whatever was understood to be everyday language. Such special language was understood to be a form of art – a verbal art as distinct from visual arts like painting and sculpting. The most comprehensive term for such verbal art was *mousikē*.

Like the derivative term *meter*, which is more specialized than the ancient term *metron*, the derivative term *music* is more specialized than the ancient term *mousikē*, which referred not only to music in the sense of playing a musical instrument. Instead, *mousikē* referred to all forms of verbal art, not only to the art of playing musical instruments. In terms of *mousikē*, as we will see, the playing of musical instruments was in fact an aspect of verbal art.

The word *mousikē* derives from a combination of the feminine noun *tekhnē*, which means "art" or "craft" with the feminine adjective *mousikē*, which means "belonging to the Muses." The expression *hē mousikē*, with or without the word *tekhnē* explicitly added to it, means the "art" or "craft" of the Muses.

Who, then, are the Muses, who preside over this *tekhnē*? The noun *Mousa*, from which the adjective *mousikē* derives, derives in turn from the root **men-*, which conveys the basic idea of "have in mind" (Nagy 1974: 249–50, West 2007: 34). In the plural, the noun *Mousai* refers to the Muses, goddesses who inspire the special state of mind required to create the special language that they control. And the creation of that special language is *hē mousikē*.

The mythical dimensions of visualizing the acquisition and the creation of this special language can be seen most clearly in the *Theogony*, a composition attributed to a prehistoric figure named Hesiod. In this composition, the definitive form of which dates back to the sixth century BCE, the figure of Hesiod describes the moment when he acquired the special language of the Muses: it happened when these goddesses appeared to him in an epiphany and gave him a special voice that enabled him to practice his verbal art (Hes. *Th.* 21–34). The poet is literally "inspired" by the voice that the Muses literally "breathed" into him (Hes. *Th.* 31).

In this chapter, the focus is not on the myths that tell about the creation of the ancient poetic language but rather on the realities of such a special language. These realities are expressed in the surviving evidence about the "art of the Muses," which is *mousikē*. And this concept of *mousikē* is essential for understanding the ancient Greek concept of what we call meter.

The most informative sources for understanding the realities of *mousikē* are two major exponents of philosophical thinking in the fourth century BCE, Plato and Aristotle. I will mine these sources not for their philosophical agenda but for the linguistic information they provide about the usage of key words like *mousikē*.

The Evidence of Plato's *Laws*

Especially relevant is a passage in Plato's *Laws* (2.668e–670b). In this passage, we see an anonymous Athenian speaker engaged in an ongoing conversation with a Cretan and a Spartan about the problem of making a distinction between the Muses as divine practitioners of *mousikē* and the human practitioners of *mousikē*, whom the speaker calls *poiētai*. Essential for understanding this distinction is the meaning of this word *poiētai*. The ancient term *poiētēs* (sg.) / *poiētai* (pl.), unlike the modern term *poet* that derives from it, refers not only to composers who compose in the medium of *poetry* as we know it. Like the Muses, who are the ideal practitioners of *mousikē*, the *poiētai* compose not only in the medium of *poetry* but also in the media of *song* and *dance* and *instrumental music*.

In a moment, we will look at the relevant wording used by the Athenian speaker in Plato's *Laws*, which will show clearly that the Muses are in fact being imagined as the perfect model for the *poiētai* to follow as practitioners of these multiple media of *mousikē*. Before we do so, however, I must highlight a basic fact about this wording. The fact is, the Ancient Greek words *mousikē* and *poiētai* are used by Plato's Athenian speaker in a traditional rather than an innovative way. It is not a philosophical innovation for Plato to think of *mousikē* as the art of composing in the various media of poetry and song and dance and instrumental music. In the historical era of Plato, such a way of thinking about the art practiced by *poiētai* was perfectly traditional. What is innovative and untraditional about Plato's way of thinking is merely his negative attitude toward this art as it existed in the real world of his era – which he holds up as a foil for the ideal and therefore perfect world of the Muses.

According to the Athenian speaker in Plato's *Laws*, the Muses themselves are divine *poiētai*, to be contrasted with the human *poiētai* (2.669d: ποιηταὶ . . . ἀνθρώπινοι). By contrast with the ideal that is represented by the divine Muses, whose compositions must be perfect, the compositions of the all-too-human *poiētai* are imperfect and therefore inferior. And this inferiority, according to the Athenian speaker, is the actual cause of an all-important distinction between the Muses and the *poiētai* as practitioners of *mousikē*, of the "art" or "craft" of the Muses (669c: διὰ τὸ τοὺς ποιητὰς φαυλοτέρους εἶναι ποιητὰς αὐτῶν τῶν Μουσῶν "because of the fact that the *poiētai* are inferior, as *poiētai*, to the Muses themselves").

What, then, is this distinction? As we are about to see, it is the fact that the human *poiētai*, unlike the divine Muses who practice their art in their ideal world of *mousikē*, are unable to produce compositions that integrate perfectly the media of poetry and song and dance and instrumental music.

The Athenian speaker in this passage from Plato's *Laws* gives an example of the imperfect *mousikē* of the *poiētai*. These craftsmen, he says, make the mistake of *mixing things up* when they are composing song and dance. What happens in the imperfect world of *mousikē* as practiced by these *poiētai* would never happen in the perfect world of *mousikē* as practiced by the divine Muses themselves. These goddesses would never make the mistake of confusing what goes with what in the process of composing song and dance:

οὐ γὰρ ἂν ἐκεῖναί γε ἐξαμάρτοιέν ποτε τοσοῦτον ὥστε ῥήματα ἀνδρῶν ποιήσασαι τὸ χρῶμα γυναικῶν καὶ μέλος ἀποδοῦναι, καὶ μέλος ἐλευθέρων αὖ καὶ σχήματα συνθεῖσαι ῥυθμοὺς δούλων καὶ ἀνελευθέρων προσαρμόττειν, οὐδ᾽ αὖ ῥυθμοὺς καὶ σχῆμα ἐλευθέριον ὑποθεῖσαι μέλος ἢ λόγον ἐναντίον ἀποδοῦναι τοῖς ῥυθμοῖς.

You see, they [= the Muses] would never make such big mistakes as the following: if they composed words having to do with men, they would not produce the coloratura and melody [*melos*] of women; or, if they composed the melody [*melos*] and the dance poses [*skhēmata*] of free men, they would not add to them the rhythms [*rhuthmoi*] of slaves and captives; nor would they, if they composed the rhythms [*rhuthmoi*] and dance pose [*skhēma*] of a free man, produce a melody [*melos*] or wording that was the opposite of those rhythms [*rhuthmoi*]. (Pl. *Leg.* 2.669c)

Clearly, the Athenian speaker is referring to the actual artistic practices of *poiētai* contemporary with Plato and Aristotle. These *poiētai*, as we see from the examples cited here by the speaker – and as we can see also from the testimony of other sources surviving from that era and from even earlier eras – indulged themselves in the artistic bravura of mixing the existing forms of composition in the media of song and dance.

But Plato's speaker does not think of such mixed forms positively as evidence for the artistic bravura of these *poiētai*. Rather, he thinks of them negatively as evidence for the imperfection of the art of *mousikē* as actually practiced by *poiētai* who composed in the media of song and dance.

Counting himself among the exceptional few who are perceptive enough to notice all such confusions, the Athenian speaker now goes on to give another example of outrages committed against the art of *mousikē* by the *poiētai*:

ταῦτά γε γὰρ ὁρῶσι πάντα κυκώμενα, καὶ ἔτι διασπῶσιν οἱ ποιηταὶ ῥυθμὸν μὲν καὶ σχήματα μέλους χωρὶς λόγους ψιλοὺς εἰς μέτρα τιθέντες, μέλος δ᾽ αὖ καὶ ῥυθμὸν ἄνευ ῥημάτων ψιλῇ κιθαρίσει τε καὶ αὐλήσει προσχρώμενοι, ἐν οἷς δὴ παγχάλεπον ἄνευ λόγου γιγνόμενον ῥυθμόν τε καὶ ἁρμονίαν γιγνώσκειν ὅτι τε βούλεται καὶ ὅτῳ ἔοικε τῶν ἀξιολόγων μιμημάτων

So they [= the perceptive ones] see all these confusions [created by the *poiētai*]. But the *poiētai* go even further [when they compose in the special medium of poetry]: they separate the rhythm [*rhuthmos*] as well as the dance poses [*skhēmata*] and, without any melody [*melos*] either, they put into measures [*metra*] the words thus made bare, or, alternatively, [they separate] the melody [*melos*] as well as the rhythm [*rhuthmos*], and, without the words, they use the instrumental music of the cithara [*kithara*] or the reed [*aulos*], thus making it extremely difficult to recognize what is intended by way of the rhythm [*rhuthmos*] and the tune [*harmonia*] without wording, and what is being imagined in the world of representations that would need to be expressed with words. (Pl. *Leg.* 2.669d–e).

In terms of this formulation, the *poiētai* create the special media that we know as *poetry* and *music* by dismembering the components of the general medium of *mousikē*. In order to create the special medium of poetry, the *poiētai* separate – and exclude – the components that we know as instrumental music and dance, while they include only the component that we know as the words of poetry. Alternatively, in order to create the special medium of music, the *poiētai* separate – and include – only the components that we know as instrumental music and dance, while they exclude the component that we know as the words of poetry.

The word that the Athenian speaker uses here in referring to the "measures" of the words of poetry, stripped bare of instrumental music and dance, is *metra* (μέτρα). In general, the word *metron* means "measure." In particular, as we are about to see, a *metron* is a way of measuring two irreducible elements that cannot be taken out of the words of the special language that is *mousikē*. These two irreducible elements are *rhythm* and *melody*.

Rhythm and Melody

What we mean by these two words *rhythm* and *melody* is different from the meanings of the Ancient Greek words from which they are respectively derived, ῥυθμός and μέλος, as we can see from the usage of the Athenian speaker in Plato's *Laws*.

Let us begin with the word *rhuthmos*. In the passage I have quoted from Plato's *Laws* containing the formulation of the Athenian speaker, this word *rhuthmos* can be translated not only as "rhythm" but also, more generally, as "dance movement." That is because the noun *rhuthmos* derives from the verb *rhein*, in the sense of "flow" (Chantraine 1999: s.v.). The basic idea inherent in *rhuthmos* is that whatever bodily movement there is in dance has a "flow" to it. But the question remains, how does "flow" become "rhythm"? The answer has to do with the fact that the flow of movement in dance is counterbalanced by a holding up of the flow, as expressed by way of the noun *skhēma*. This noun, which I have translated up to now as "dance pose," derives from the verb *ekhein* in the sense of "hold" or "hold up." As we can see from the combination of the words *rhuthmos* and *skhēma* in the passage I have quoted from Plato's *Laws* as also in other passages, dance is pictured as a counterbalancing of movement and non-movement.

But how does this picture square with the fact that dance is basically a motor activity? How can dance be seen as a counterbalancing of movement and non-movement, of motor- and non-motor activity, of *rhuthmos* and *skhēma*? The answer is this: the actual counterbalancing of motion and non-motion can be seen overall as motion in its own right. That is why the "rhythm" of dance can be seen overall as *rhuthmos*. I will now restate this in terms of Prague School linguistics: in the opposition of *rhuthmos* and *skhēma*, *rhuthmos* is the *unmarked and inclusive* member of the opposition, while *skhēma* is the *marked and exclusive* member. (For a relevant commentary on the inclusiveness and exclusiveness of unmarked and marked members of oppositions, see Nagy 1990a: 5–8.)

Besides the unmarked rhythm of dance, there is also a marked kind of rhythm: as we will see later, this marked kind of rhythm is the *meter* that frames the verses of poetry. Those aspects of rhythm that are needed only for song and dance can be taken out of the words that are the building blocks of poetry. But there are other aspects, as represented by what we call *meter*, that cannot be taken out of the words. These aspects are irreducible and inherent in the words of *mousikē*. And these irreducible aspects of rhythm, as we will also see later, correspond to a phenomenon that can best be described as *stress accentuation* in the Ancient Greek language.

Earlier, I said that a *metron* "measure" is a way of measuring two irreducible elements that cannot be taken out of the words of the special language that is *mousikē*. So far, we have examined the first of these two irreducible elements, *rhythm*, derived from the Greek word ῥυθμός. We turn now to the second of these two irreducible elements, *melody*, derived from the Greek word μέλος.

In the passage I quoted above from Plato's *Laws* (2.669d–e), *melos* actually refers only to an unmarked kind of melody, which is the melody that is sung and danced in song. But there is also a marked kind of melody: as we will see later, this marked kind of melody is the *melodic contour* that frames the verses of poetry. Those aspects of melody that are needed only for song and dance can be taken out of the words that are the building blocks of poetry. But there are other aspects, as represented by what I call the melodic contour, that cannot be taken out of the words. These aspects are irreducible and inherent in the words of *mousikē*. And these irreducible aspects of melody, as we will also see later, correspond to a phenomenon that can best be described as *melodic accentuation* in the Ancient Greek language.

So far, on the basis of the passage I quoted from Plato's *Laws*, we have seen that the ancient *poiētēs* can practice the art of *mousikē* by composing either in the medium of poetry or in the medium of music. But there is more to it. The ancient *poiētēs* can practice the art of *mousikē* by composing also in a medium that is more basic than either poetry or music. He can compose also in the medium of *song*, and he can combine the danceable rhythm and the danceable melody of his words with the danceable music played on musical instruments like the *kithara* "cithara" and the *aulos* "reed." This third and more basic medium is highlighted in another passage from Plato, where we see Plato's Socrates eliciting a simple answer to a simple question:

— τίς ἡ τέχνη, ἧς τὸ κιθαρίζειν καὶ τὸ ᾄδειν καὶ τὸ ἐμβαίνειν ὀρθῶς;
— μουσικήν μοι δοκεῖς λέγειν

[Socrates asks the question:] What is the *tekhnē* that has the elements of playing the *kithara* and singing [*āidein*] and executing the right dance steps?
[Alcibiades gives the answer:] You must be talking about *mousikē*. (Pl. *Symp.* 205c–d)

The term for referring to the composer of such *mousikē*, as we have seen from Plato's *Laws*, is *poiētēs*. Unlike the derivative term *poet*, which refers to the composer of only one medium, which is poetry, the ancient term *poiētēs* refers to the composer of multiple media – not only poetry but also song and dance and instrumental music.

But the problem is – and the Athenian speaker says so in the wording I already quoted from Plato's *Laws* – the *poiētai* in the real world fail to integrate these multiple media of *mousikē*. Only the Muses in the ideal world of *mousikē* do not fail. By contrast with these goddesses, who are of course perfect, the imperfect *poiētai* do fail. One reason for their failure, as we have seen, is that *they mix things up*. Another reason, as we have also seen, is that *they leave things out*, as when they compose poetry by leaving out dance and instrumental music from song, or when they compose unsung instrumental music by leaving out of song the actual words of song.

The very idea that *poiētai* supposedly leave things out in the composition of *mousikē* is a key to understanding the media used by the *poiētai*. When the *poiētai* are using the medium of unsung instrumental music, they are not composing either poetry or song, since both poetry and song require words. Conversely, when the *poiētai* are using the medium of poetry, they are not composing instrumental music, since this kind of music has various kinds of rhythms and melodies that poetry does not have. More than that, the *poiētai* are not even composing song, since song too has various kinds of rhythms and melodies that poetry does not have.

I return to an essential point that is being made by the anonymous Athenian speaker in Plato's *Laws* (2.668e–670b). The point is, only the divine Muses in the ideal world can succeed in integrating the media of poetry and song and dance and instrumental music in practicing their own divine *tekhnē*, the "art" or "craft" that is *mousikē*. By contrast, the all-too-human *poiētai* in the real world fail to integrate these media. Their *tekhnē* of *mousikē* has disintegrated.

The Differentiation of *Mousikē*

This point about the art or craft that is *mousikē*, as spoken by the Athenian Plato in the words of his anonymous Athenian speaker, is a remarkably insightful appreciation of the actual state of the art in Athens in the era of Plato and Aristotle. At that time, *mousikē* as the *tekhnē* of the *poiētai* was not an integral whole, even if the meaning of the word *mousikē* as the *tekhnē* of the Muses idealizes the idea of an integral whole.

But the integral whole that is *mousikē* had not really disintegrated. To say that *mousikē* had disintegrated is to take literally the metaphorical world of Plato. Rather, *mousikē* had become differentiated. To say this much is simply to describe the state of the art at the time of Plato. The form of art known as the *tekhnē* of the Muses had become differentiated into multiple forms of art, multiple *tekhnai*, as it evolved over time. In terms of the evolution of *mousikē*, the difference between the idealized *tekhnē* of the Muses and the actual *tekhnē* of the *poiētai* is a matter of differentiation, not disintegration.

There are indications of these multiple *tekhnai*, as practiced by *poiētai*, in the examples used by Plato's Athenian in his efforts to show the disintegration of *mousikē*. I will focus on analyzing examples of *poetry without music*, *song with music*, and *music without words*. These examples have to do with not one but five distinct *tekhnai*, as we know from historical evidence. This evidence can be summarized in terms of two historical facts: (i) There were *mousikoi agōnes* "competitions in *mousikē*" held at a festival in Athens known as the Panathenaia, which was one of the two major festivals of the Athenians in the era of Plato and Aristotle; (ii) These competitions had to do with the actual performance of *mousikē*.

Up to now, we have been considering the art of *mousikē* only in terms of *composition*. From here on, however, we must consider the same art also in terms of *performance*. In the real world of the art of *mousikē*, as practiced at the Panathenaia in the fourth century BCE, the performance of the four media of poetry and song and dance and instrumental accompaniment was differentiated from the composition of these four media.

In the era of Plato and Aristotle, there were basically five *tekhnai* or "arts" of performance in play at the *mousikoi agōnes* held in Athens during the seasonally recurring Panathenaia. The first of these five *tekhnai* was the *tekhnē* of performing poetry. This *tekhnē* was known as *rhapsōidikē*, the "art" or "craft" of *rhapsōidoi* "rhapsodes" (Pl. *Ion* 538b, 538c, 538d, 539e, 540a, 540d, 541a). At the Panathenaia, this *tekhnē* was practiced by performers called *rhapsōidoi*, who competed with each other in performing poetry – without musical accompaniment (Nagy 2002: 36, 41–2).

The second and the third of these five *tekhnai* were the *tekhnai* of singing to the musical accompaniment of the *kithara* and the *aulos*. These two different forms of *tekhnē* were known as *kitharōidia* and *aulōidia* (Pl. *Leg.* 3.700d). At the Panathenaia, these two different *tekhnai* were practiced separately by performers called respectively *kitharōidoi* "*kithara*-singers, citharodes" and *aulōidoi* "*aulos*-singers, aulodes," who competed separately with each other in singing songs accompanied by the *kithara* and by the *aulos* respectively. In the case of the citharodes, the accompaniment was performed by the singers themselves. In the case of the aulodes, on the other hand, the singers and the accompanists were different competitors.

The fourth and the fifth of these five *tekhnai* were the *tekhnai* of performing music without words. These two different forms of *tekhnē* were known as *kitharistikē* and *aulētikē* (Pl. *Gorg.* 501e) or, more simply, *kitharisis* and *aulēsis* (Pl. *Ion* 533b). At the Panathenaia, these two different *tekhnai* were practiced separately by performers called respectively *kitharistai* "*kithara*-players, citharists" and *aulētai* "*aulos*-players, auletes," who competed separately with each other in performing instrumental music – without words – on the *kithara* and on the *aulos*.

It is essential to keep in mind that these five different *tekhnai* – that is, *rhapsōidikē*, *kitharōidia*, *aulōidia*, *kitharistikē*, *aulētikē* – were involved in five separate *mousikoi agōnes* at the festival of the Panathenaia in Athens. Corresponding to these five different *tekhnai* were five separate competitions at the Panathenaia – of *rhapsōidoi*, of *kithāróidoi*, of *aulōidoi*, of *kitharistai*, and of *aulētai*. We learn about these separate categories of competition from an Athenian inscription dated at around 380 BCE (*IG* II² 2311), which records the winners of Panathenaic prizes (Nagy 2002: 38–9, 42 n. 16, 51). And we learn about these separate categories of competition also from Plato's *Laws* (6.764d–e), where we read about rhapsodes, cithardes, and auletes – and where the wording makes it clear that the point of reference is the Panathenaia (Nagy 2002: 38, 40, 42).

These five separate *tekhnai* as practiced in five separate *mousikoi agōnes* at the Panathenaia were all subcategories of one overall *tekhnē* – which was *mousikē*. Direct confirmation comes from the Aristotelian *Constitution of the Athenians* (60.1), where the author refers to "the overall *agōn* 'competition' in *mousikē*" at the Panathenaia (τὸν ἀγῶνα τῆς μουσικῆς).

Although the word *mousikē* was applicable as an overall term for the five separate and differentiated *tekhnai* as practiced at the Panathenaia, it was generally not applied to other *tekhnai* that were practiced at the festival of the City Dionysia, which was the other of the two major seasonally recurring festivals of the Athenians at the time of Plato and Aristotle. At this second major festival, there were four separate and differentiated *tekhnai*, which were *tragedy* and *comedy* and *dithyramb* and *satyr drama*.

Even though all four of these *tekhnai* having to do with the competitions at the City Dionysia accommodated all four of the media of *mousikē* as described by the Athenian speaker in Plato's *Laws* – poetry and song and dance and music – we find a striking absence of any overall reference to these competitions in terms of *mousikē*. There is a simple explanation for this absence. It has to do with the dramatic frame for all the performances at the City Dionysia. The composers of the poetry and song and dance and music to be performed at this festival were composing for performers who represented characters *inside* the composition and who, as non-composers, had no claim to any direct inspiration by the Muses. Only the *poiētēs*, as the maker of the given composition, could have claimed to be inspired. So the concept of *mousikē* as the "art" or "craft" of the Muses could in principle apply only to the *composition* of the poetry and song and dance and music at the City Dionysia, not to the actual *performance* of these media.

By contrast, the performers at the Panathenaia represented the composers themselves, and they could thus claim, like the composers, to be inspired by the Muses. So the ancient concept of *mousikē* as the "art" or "craft" of the Muses could apply to performers as well as composers at the Panathenaia. That is one reason why the performers at the Panathenaia, unlike the performers of drama at the City Dionysia, did not wear masks.

Mousikē and *Poiētikē*

We have seen, then, that the differentiation between composer and performer is linked with a pattern of differentiation in the actual use of the word *mousikē* as practiced by the *poiētai*. By the time of Plato and Aristotle, the word *mousikē* was being used not only in referring to the craft of composition as practiced by the *poiētai* but also in

referring to the craft of performance as practiced by craftsmen who directly represented the *poiētai*. These craftsmen were the rhapsodes, citharodes, aulodes, citharists,
and auletes who competed at the Panathenaia.

The use of the word *poiētai* itself is a sign of this differentiation. Whereas *mousikē*
as a *tekhnē* is practiced by the Muses themselves in the ideal world, there are no corresponding ideal practitioners in the real world of Athens in the era of Plato and
Aristotle. In this real world, there are merely *poiētai*, who compose but do not necessarily perform what they compose. Unlike the divine Muses, who practice their integral art of *mousikē* by simultaneously composing and performing in their ideal world,
the *poiētai* are primarily composers, not performers. And so the *tekhnē* of these *poiētai*
is not so much *mousikē* as it is simply *poiētikē*.

This word *poiētikē*, derived from the word *poiētai* and meaning literally "the art of
the *poiētai*," is essential for understanding the differentiation between the art of the
Muses as practiced by *poiētai* in the real world and the art of the Muses as practiced
by the Muses in the ideal world. This differentiation is made explicit in the *Ion* of
Plato, where *poiētikē* is used in the specialized sense of referring to the *tekhnē* of composing only, not performing. In this Platonic dialogue, such a specialization of the
word *poiētikē* becomes overt when Socrates traps the Panathenaic rhapsode Ion into
agreeing with the argument that rhapsodes, since they are performers and not composers, have no mastery of the art that is *poiētikē*.

Here is how Plato develops this argument. First, Plato's Socrates induces the rhapsode Ion to agree that *poiētikē* is a *tekhnē* and that this *tekhnē* is a *holon*, an "integral
whole," just like other *tekhnai* (*Ion* 532c). Then he induces Ion to agree that the
tekhnē of painters, *graphikē*, is likewise a *holon*; and the same goes for the *tekhnē* of
sculptors (532e–3b). Comparable is the pairing of *mousikē* and *graphikē* in Aristotle's
Politics (8.1337b24–5). It follows, then, that the multiple *tekhnai* practiced by performers such as auletes, citharists, citharodes, and rhapsodes are disintegrated aspects
of a single *tekhnē*, to which Socrates had referred earlier as that integral whole, *poiētikē*
(*Ion* 533b–c).

In terms of Plato's argument, the word *poiētikē* has replaced the word *mousikē* in
conveying the integrated totality of the *tekhnē* of the *poiētai*. And these *poiētai* are
primarily composers, not performers. Accordingly, *poiētikē* is primarily the *tekhnē* of
composing, not the *tekhnē* of performing.

The same pattern of replacement is evident in the work of Aristotle on *poiētikē*,
known to us as the *Poetics*, which is in Greek terms a discourse about *poiētikē tekhnē*.
In the opening of the *Poetics*, we see a listing of the various forms of composition as
practiced by *poiētai* (1447a13–15): these forms are epic, tragedy, comedy, dithyramb, and the various forms of composition for the *aulos* and the *kithara*. All these
forms, as listed by Aristotle in the opening of the *Poetics*, correspond to the forms
of composition that were actually performed at the two major festivals of the
Athenians.

At the Panathenaia, there were five separate forms of composition, corresponding
to five separate *tekhnai*: (i) epic accompanied by no instrument; (ii) song accompanied by the *aulos*; (iii) song accompanied by the *kithara*; (iv) instrumental music
played on the *aulos*; (v) instrumental music played on the *kithara*. I have listed these

five forms here in the order indicated by Aristotle's own listing. At the City Dionysia, there were four separate forms of composition, corresponding to four separate *tekhnai*: (i) tragedy, (ii) comedy, (iii) dithyramb, and (iv) satyr drama (Nagy 1996: 81–2; 1999: 27; Rotstein 2004).

Meter in Poetry and Song

Now that we have seen the state of the art of *mousikē* in the historical context of Athens in the lifetimes of Plato and Aristotle, the time has come to assess how the realities of this historical context, as captured by the alternative term *poiētikē*, relate to the idealization of *mousikē* as the "art" or "craft" of the Muses.

From a synchronic point of view, the realities of *poiētikē* in the Athens of Plato and Aristotle during the fourth century BCE indicate the existence of multiple differentiated systems of verbal art; from a diachronic point of view, on the other hand, the idealization of *mousikē* as pictured by the Athenian speaker in Plato's *Laws* indicates the pre-existence of a single and undifferentiated system. (For a relevant commentary on the terms *synchronic* and *diachronic*, see Nagy 1990a: 4–5.)

Although the Athenian speaker is using a mythological instead of a scientific model in explaining the idea of *mousikē* as a single undifferentiated system of verbal art, picturing this system as an integrated and perfect whole that disintegrates into imperfect parts in the real world of the *poiētai*, this mythological explanation is nevertheless most intuitive. That is because it approximates an explanatory model that is truly scientific, not mythological.

Such a scientific explanatory model is supported by the empirical and comparative perspectives of not one but two sciences: linguistics and musicology. In terms of these two sciences, as we will now see, the multiple differentiated systems of Ancient Greek poetry and song and dance and even instrumental accompaniment can all be explained on the basis of one single undifferentiated system, which is the Ancient Greek *language*.

Applying such an explanatory model, I start by reassessing the formulation of the Athenian speaker:

> So they [= the perceptive ones] see all these confusions [on the part of the *poiētai*]. But the *poiētai* go even further: they separate the rhythm [*rhuthmos*] as well as the dance poses [*skhēmata*] and, without any melody [*melos*] either, they put into measures [*metra*] the words thus made bare, or [they separate] the melody [*melos*] as well as the rhythm [*rhuthmos*], and, without the words, they use the instrumental music of the *kithara* or the *aulos*, thus making it extremely difficult to recognize what is intended by way of the rhythm [*rhuthmos*] and the tune [*harmonia*] without wording, and what is being imagined in the world of representations that would need to be expressed with words. (Pl. *Leg.* 2.669d–e)

In attempting to describe here the differentiation of (i) poetry and (ii) music in terms of (i) words without song and (ii) song without words, the Athenian speaker is forced to use terms that are imprecise in expressing that differentiation.

A case in point is the term *metra*, which the Athenian speaker applies to the "measures" or "measuring units" of elements that are built into the words of poetry. As I have argued, these measurable elements are *rhythm* and *melody*. The problem is, the term *metra* is imprecise for such an application. As we will see, *metra* in the sense of "measures" or "measuring units" can apply to the elements of rhythm and melody not only in poetry but also in song. And we already know that song is distinct from poetry. Although song is like poetry in having rhythm and melody, it is unlike poetry in having patterns of rhythm and melody that are more varied than the reduced patterns of rhythm and melody that we find in poetry. Also, song is unlike poetry in having dance and instrumental music as optional features, whereas poetry has no such options.

A related case in point is the pair of terms that the Athenian speaker applies to the elements of rhythm and melody: *rhuthmos* and *melos*. I have already argued that these terms are likewise imprecise. First, let us review the case of *rhuthmos*. This term can apply not only to rhythm as sung in song (or as recited in poetry) but also to rhythm as produced by instrumental music, with or without song. Further, as we have already seen, this term can apply not only to rhythm but also to the motion or motor activity of dance. In the case of *melos*, this term can apply not only to melody as sung in song but also to melody as produced by instrumental music, with or without song.

These cases of imprecision in the references made by the Athenian speaker to the uses of rhythm and melody in the four media of poetry and song and dance and instrumental music provide valuable evidence for reconstructing an earlier phase in the evolution of Ancient Greek verbal art when these four media were as yet undifferentiated from each other.

Such an earlier phase is evident in the usage of the Athenian speaker when he speaks about *rhuthmos* in poetry. This linking of *rhuthmos* and poetry points to an earlier phase when poetry was as yet undifferentiated from song. To be contrasted is the later phase – as reflected in what the Athenian speaker says about the state of the art that is *mousikē*. In this later phase, song and poetry were already differentiated from each other. In this later phase, the differentiated medium of song could still be coordinated with the medium of dance, but such coordination had already broken down in the differentiated medium of poetry.

Meter, Stress, and Melody

Here we must reckon with a salient fact about the state of the art that was poetry in Athens in the fourth century BCE. At that time, the basic metrical feature of poetry was rhythm as embedded in the words of poetry. This fact is the single most noticeable and most obvious reality we find in the surviving texts of Ancient Greek poetry. The study of ancient Greek meter as we know it is basically a study of rhythm. This kind of rhythm in poetry was differentiated from rhythm as sung and danced in song and as played on a musical instrument.

What is a less noticeable and less obvious reality about Greek poetry at that time is the fact that melody, like rhythm, was also embedded in the words of poetry. This kind of melody in poetry was differentiated from melody as sung and danced in song and as played on a musical instrument.

These twin facts about rhythm and meter as embedded in the words of Greek poetry are exemplified in the use of the word *metron* "measure" by Herodotus, who flourished in the fifth century BCE. There are two cases to consider.

The first case is straightforward, involving a reference to the measuring of rhythm in terms of *metron*. Herodotus (1.12) uses the expression ἐν ἰάμβῳ τριμέτρῳ "in an iambic poem that has three measures" with reference to verses of Archilochus, dated to the seventh century BCE. Herodotus is referring here to a form of invective poetry (*iambos*) composed of verses containing three *metra* or "measures." The meter of these verses is known to us as the *iambic trimeter*. In terms of the embedded rhythms of this meter, as produced by the alternation of long and short syllables, the iambic trimeter can be described as three consecutive units shaped ‿–◡– (– = long syllable; ◡ = short syllable; ‿ = short or long syllable). As we see from the internal evidence of all attested verses composed in iambic trimeter, this meter is in fact a "trimeter" in terms of its rhythmical structure of three consecutive units measured as ‿–◡–.

The second case is less straightforward and more complicated, involving a reference to the measuring of both rhythm and melody in terms of *metron*. Herodotus (1.47) uses the expression ἐν ἑξαμέτρῳ τόνῳ "in a tune [*tonos*] that has six measures [*metra*]" with reference to verses uttered by the Delphic Oracle, which are actually quoted in this context. Herodotus is referring here to a form of epic or oracular poetry composed of verses containing six *metra* or "measures." The meter of these verses is known to us as the *dactylic hexameter*. In terms of the embedded rhythms of this meter, as produced by the alternation of long and short syllables, the dactylic hexameter can be described as six consecutive units shaped –◡◡ or ––, with the sixth unit truncated from –◡◡ to –‿ (again, – = long syllable; ◡ = short syllable; ‿ = short or long syllable). As we see from the internal evidence of all attested poetry composed in dactylic hexameter, this meter is in fact a "hexameter" in terms of its rhythmical structure of six consecutive units measured as –◡◡ or as –– or, at the end of the line, as –‿. (In Aristophanes' *Frogs* (650–1), there is talk of two kinds of *rhuthmoi* "rhythms," and one of these is described as κατὰ δάκτυλον "dactyl by dactyl," which is evidently a reference to the dactylic hexameter.) But now we run into a complication. Although the six *metra* or "measures" of the dactylic hexameter, as we see from the internal evidence of the alternating long and short syllables in this meter, are basically six units of rhythm, these same six units, as Herodotus describes them, are being measured in terms of melody rather than rhythm, that is, in terms of the "tuning" or *tonos* of a string instrument, which is the *kithara* by default. Evidently, Herodotus is thinking of this meter in terms of the "measures" of singing it to the musical accompaniment of a *kithara*.

So it appears that in this case Herodotus is thinking of poetry primarily in terms of melody and only secondarily in terms of rhythm as a working component of the *metron* that is the "measure" of the dactylic hexameter. We can see other cases of this way of thinking. For example, in terms of what the Athenian speaker says in Plato's *Laws*, we have already seen that poetry contains *melos* "melody" as well as *rhuthmos* "rhythm." Or, to say it in Greek terms, the *metron* that measures the basic measurable units of poetry is measuring *melos* as well as *rhuthmos*.

A rare and most precious example of the use of the term *melos* with reference to melody as embedded in poetry composed in dactylic hexameter is a passage in Plato's *Ion* (536b–c) where we see a mention of the melody inherent in the dactylic hexameters of epic poetry attributed to Homer. In this passage, Socrates finds fault with the rhapsode Ion for being a specialist in the poetry of Homer as *poiētēs* or "poet" – to the exclusion of all other *poiētai*. Socrates playfully describes how this Panathenaic rhapsode is inattentive and dozes off whenever he has to hear the poetry of *poiētai* other than Homer, but he wakes up whenever he hears a performer sing a *melos* or "melody" that is typical of the verses of Homer himself.

καὶ ἐπειδὰν μέν τις ἄλλου του ποιητοῦ ᾄδῃ, καθεύδεις τε καὶ ἀπορεῖς ὅτι λέγῃς, ἐπειδὰν δὲ τούτου τοῦ ποιητοῦ φθέγξηταί τις μέλος, εὐθὺς ἐγρήγορας καὶ ὀρχεῖταί σου ἡ ψυχὴ καὶ εὐπορεῖς ὅτι λέγῃς ·

And when someone sings something from some other *poiētēs*, you tend to fall asleep and have absolutely no control of what you say [about such poetry], but when someone sings a melody [*melos*] that belongs to this poet [= Homer], then you immediately wake up and your soul [*psukhē*] starts dancing, and now you have good control of what you say. (Pl. *Ion* 536b–c)

Plato's Socrates goes on to compare the behavior of the Corybantes, who are figured as mystical Phrygian dancers: those dancers, he says, are attentive to one single melody that inspires them to dance and to sing the words that go with the dance. One single *melos* or "melody" can activate for those dancers the *skhēmata* "dance poses" and the *rhēmata* "words" that go with that one single melody.

ὥσπερ οἱ κορυβαντιῶντες ἐκείνου μόνου αἰσθάνονται τοῦ μέλους ὀξέως ὃ ἂν ᾖ τοῦ θεοῦ ἐξ ὅτου ἂν κατέχωνται, καὶ εἰς ἐκεῖνο τὸ μέλος καὶ σχημάτων καὶ ῥημάτων εὐποροῦσι, τῶν δὲ ἄλλων οὐ φροντίζουσιν.

. . . just as the Corybantic dancers are keenly attentive only to that one melody [*melos*] that comes from whichever divinity possesses them, and they have good control of the dance poses [*skhēmata*] and of the words [*rhēmata*] that are meant for that one melody [*melos*] – but they do not care about other dance poses and other words. (Pl. *Ion* 536c)

Although there is an element of metaphorical play here in what Plato's Socrates says about the rhapsodic soul that dances to the distinctive *melos* of Homeric verses, the actual presence of melody in Homeric verses is not a metaphor but a reality. The meter known as the dactylic hexameter, which was the one single rhythmical frame for the composition of epic verses attributed to Homer, was simultaneously a melodic frame for these verses. To state it more technically, each hexameter had its own distinctive *melodic contour*.

There is documentary confirmation in papyrus texts of the Homeric *Iliad* and *Odyssey*: in some of these texts, most of which can be dated to the second and the third centuries CE, we can see markings of accents that correspond to the melodic contour of the hexameter (Nagy 2000). The markings are placed over vowels of selected syllables within the wording framed by each hexameter. These markings correspond to *pitch accents* that are built into those same syllables – accents that exist within the individual words of the overall wording. Also, these markings correspond to *melodic peaks* that are built into the *intonation* of the overall wording. (The importance of the overall wording is indicated by the fact that Ancient Greek was normally written in *scriptio continua*: that is, the overall wording was written out without any indication of word breaks, without leaving spaces between words.)

In using the term *intonation* here, I am referring to the patterns of *melodic accentuation* in Ancient Greek, which are not only word-bound but also phrase-bound. The term *melodic accentuation* derives from the research of W. S. Allen (1987a: 116–31), who shows that the Ancient Greek accents that we know as *acute* (´) and *grave* (`) and *circumflex* (^) are reflexes of a system of melodic accentuation that operates on the level of phrase-units as well as word-units. He describes these patterns of Ancient Greek accentuation not only in terms of *intonation* or *contonation* but also in terms of *melodic accent* (Allen 1987a: 131). The term *melodic*, as used by Allen, is most fitting for describing the phonetics of Ancient Greek accentuation. It points to an understanding of melody as a metrical feature that derives from the Ancient Greek language itself (Nagy 1990a: 34–5, 39–41; for more on accent and melody, see Probert 2006: 47–8, also 45–7 on evidence from the papyri).

When we examine the evidence of Homeric texts as transcribed in papyri dated mostly to the second and third centuries CE, we find that there are generally no more than two or at the most three *melodic peaks* indicated for each hexameter, and the selective marking of these peaks in the *scriptio continua* of these poetic texts is a way of recording the traditional patterns of intonation embedded in the poetry itself (Nagy 2000). These patterns of intonation are embedded in the traditional phrases contained by the metrical framework of Homeric verses, and these patterns, which are traditional in their own right, combine to form the melodic contour of these verses (Nagy 2000: 17).

Accentuation

In what follows, I show an example of the marking of melodic contour in the Homeric text of the so-called Bankes Papyrus (= Papyrus 14 in the Oxford edition of the *Iliad* (Monro and Allen 1920), which is a fragment from a papyrus manuscript of the *Iliad* produced in the second century CE. The Homeric verse I have chosen as an example from the Bankes Papyrus corresponds to line 796 of *Iliad* 24. I first give the wording of the verse as written in the *scriptio continua* of the papyrus (i), and I then give the same wording as it is written in the Byzantine spelling system (ii):

(i) ΠΟΡΦΥΡΕΟΙϹΠΕΠΛΟΙϹΙΚΑΛΎ†ΑΝΤΕϹΜΑΛΑΚΟΙϹΙΝ
(ii) πορφυρέοις πέπλοισι καλύψαντες μαλακοῖσιν
covering his body with purple robes (Hom. *Il.* 24.796)

It would be insufficient to say that the pitch accents we see built into the words καλύψαντες and μαλακοῖσιν in this verse actually determined the melodic contour of the overall wording contained within the frame of the hexameter. Rather, the melodic contour was determined by the intonation of the overall wording, within the overall syntax of the Homeric verse. And it was this melodic contour that ultimately preserved the older phrase-by-phrase pattern of pitch accentuation (Nagy 2009, with reference to Laum 1928).

Such markings of pitch accentuation can also be found in texts containing other forms of poetry and song, as in the case of papyri featuring the songs of the poet Bacchylides, who flourished in the fifth century BCE (Nagy 2000).

In the case of song, it must be added that its melodic patterns are more stylized than the melodic patterns of poetry – and far more stylized than the melodic patterns of everyday speech. That is because melodic stylization in song is measured in terms of melodic intervals – corresponding to melodic intervals produced by the accompanying musical instruments. The testimony of the ancients highlights the distinctions between the melodic intervals of song, which is *diastēmatikē* "marked off by intervals," and the melodic contours of everyday speech, which is *sunekhēs* "continuous" (Aristox. *Harm.* 1.8–9 ed. Da Rios 1954; also Dion. Hal. *Comp.* 11.13–18 ed. Aujac and Lebel 1981; see Probert 2003: 4–7).

By now we have seen that the irreducible element of melody as embedded in ancient Greek poetry, as also of course in ancient Greek song, corresponds to the phenomenon that Allen describes as *melodic accentuation* in the Ancient Greek language.

This formulation about melody can be matched with a formulation about rhythm – or, to be more specific, about rhythm in song and about meter in poetry. That is, the irreducible element of rhythm/meter as embedded in ancient Greek song/poetry corresponds to a system of *stress accentuation* in the Ancient Greek language.

Although the system of stress accentuation was not indicated in traditional ways of writing Greek, the existence of such a system has been argued persuasively by W. S. Allen (1966, 1973; a similar but in many ways different argument is offered in the work of Devine and Stephens 1984, 1994; Allen 1987a: 139 comments on their work). In following Allen's argument, I distance myself from the position taken by Meillet (1923: 11), who argued that ancient Greek rhythm/meter was determined exclusively by *quantitative* or *durational* differences between syllables (for a critique of this position, see especially Allen 1973: 98).

The basic rules of stress accentuation in Ancient Greek can be summarized as follows (Nagy 1972: 26–7):

a) Words were primarily stressed on their last heavy syllable. (On the concepts of "heavy" and "light" syllables, see Probert 2003: 2.) Words containing only one syllable could have either stress or no stress on that syllable.

b) A secondary stress fell on preceding heavy syllables if separated from the primary stress by at least one mora of quantity. (On the concept of a "mora" of quantity, see Probert 2003: 16.)

For illustration, I show two sample verses, one composed in dactylic hexameter and the other in iambic trimeter. The highlighting of vowels indicates the placement of stress on the syllable occupied by those vowels:

ἄνδρα μοι ἔννεπε Μοῦσα, πολύτροπον, ὅς μάλα πολλά (Hom. *Od.* 1.1)
ὦ κοινὸν αὐτάδελφον Ἰσμήνης κάρα (Soph. *Ant.* 1)

(The line-final syllable ᴗ counts as latent ᴗ or – when the preceding verse-rhythm is . . . –ᴗ. . . or . .ᴗ–. . . respectively; Allen 1987a: 134 explains this "law of indifference.")

As we see from these illustrations, the patterns of stress accentuation were independent of the patterns of pitch accentuation in Ancient Greek. (In later phases of the ancient language, however, the old patterns of pitch accentuation were replaced by corresponding new patterns of stress accentuation, which persist into Modern Greek, while the old patterns of independent stress accentuation were lost; see Horrocks 1997a: 67.)

The model built by Allen for describing the Ancient Greek system of stress accentuation "gives an immediate and simple explanation of a number of the 'laws', 'canons', 'bridges', etc., regarding the positions at which heavy word-finals may or may not occur; all reduce simply to the avoidance of word-division where this would produce conflict between stress and ictus – more particularly in the coda section of a metrical structure" (Allen 1966: 146; on *ictus*, see Allen 1973: 276–9). Especially productive is the application of this model to "Porson's Law" in iambic trimeter (Allen 1966: 129–35).

Allen's use of the term "metrical structure" highlights a differentiation in terminology. The concept of *rhythm* as a general term may be contrasted with *meter* as a specific term referring primarily to *a stylization of rhythm in poetry*. Applying a combination of synchronic and diachronic perspectives, I have built a model for explaining such a stylization.

> At first, the reasoning goes, traditional phraseology simply contains built-in rhythms. Later, the factor of tradition leads to the preference of phrases with some rhythms over phrases with other rhythms. Still later, the preferred rhythms have their own dynamics and become regulators of any incoming non-traditional phraseology. By becoming a viable structure in its own right, meter may evolve independently of traditional phraseology. Recent metrical developments may even obliterate aspects of the selfsame traditional phraseology that had engendered them, if these aspects no longer match the meter. (Nagy 1974: 145; see also Allen 1973: 13–14, 258; further analysis in Nagy 1990a: 39–42)

This model also helps explain the relationship of *meter* and *formula* in the making of Homeric verse (on the concept of *formula* see Nagy 1990b: 29). An alternative model is the formulation of Hermann Fränkel (1960) concerning what he sees as four "cola" contained by the dactylic hexameter of Homeric verse. (On the concept of the "colon," see West 1982: 5–6.) Such a model cannot account for the full range of formulaic variation in the making of Homeric verse (Nagy 1990b: 29–35; 1998; see also Clark 1994, 1997).

In terms of this argumentation, then, rhythm in ancient Greek poetry and song was a function of stress accentuation, just as melody was a function of melodic accentuation.

Conclusion

In closing, I stress that the patterns of rhythm and melody in song may diverge as well as converge with the patterns of stress and intonation in speech, and that such divergence is actually an aspect of the overall metrics of song, despite the ultimate derivation of song from speech. More than that, there is an actual esthetic at work in such divergence. A striking example is the relatively greater degree of divergence between stress and rhythm in the opening as opposed to the closing of the iambic trimeter (Allen 1966: 125; Nagy 1972: 27–8). Another example is the interplay of partial convergences with partial divergences between rhythm and stress or between melody and intonation in the dynamics of responsion, that is, in the matching of strophe and antistrophe, stanza and counter-stanza. Studies of this phenomenon of responsion show that the convergences are more pronounced in the rhythm than in the melody.

A pioneering example of studies in melodic responsion is the work of Wahlström (1970). For a critique, which is overly negative in my opinion, I cite Devine and Stephens (1994: 169). For another critique, I cite Probert (2006: 48 n. 88): "apparent accentual responsion in poetry (significantly greater than that found in prose) can result from the fact that sequences of words with similar distributions of word boundaries and heavy syllables are more likely to have similarly-placed accents than sequences of words with no such constraints on the location of word boundaries or heavy syllables."

I also stress that the elements of dance and instrumental music are both relevant to the linguistic basis of rhythm and melody in the overall metrics of song (Nagy 1990a: 33–42).

a)   In the case of *dance*, which is basically a stylization of *movement* as produced by any part of the human body, I quote a formulation by Allen (1973: 100): "Implicitly or explicitly underlying [the] identification of stress as the basis of rhythm is the conception of rhythm as movement, and of stress, in the production of audible linguistic phenomena, as the motor activity par excellence." (See also Nagy 1990a: 38.)

b)   In the case of *instrumental music*, which is basically a stylization of *rhythm* and *melody* as produced by the human voice, I refer to a generalized formulation by the musicologist Bruno Nettl (1965: 41), who points out that the limitations of the human voice (not to mention the limitations of the human ear), as contrasted with the relatively greater freedom of sound-range in musical instruments, may lead to differences in the patterns of evolution for vocal and instrumental music. Instrumental music may not only diverge from the human voice: such patterns of divergence may become part of an esthetic of interplay between the human voice and its instrumental accompaniment. (See also Nagy 1990a: 34.)

From a diachronic point of view, dance and instrumental music may be seen as differentiated elements that derive from song – elements that can become further differentiated as either contrasting with song or parting with song altogether. (Examples of such a parting are forms of dance or instrumental music that exist independently of song.)

From a synchronic point of view, on the other hand, any such contrast may be seen as the basic state of affairs. That is, song and dance and instrumental music may be seen as separate elements that happen to come together in the art of *mousikē*.

Either way, separate or unified, song and dance and instrumental music are regulated by the measures of their rhythm and their melody. And such measures are based on language. That is the essence of meter.

FURTHER READING

The basic facts about ancient Greek rhythm and melody as linguistic phenomena can be found in the introductory books of Allen 1987a and Probert 2003. There are specialized accounts in Allen 1973 and Nagy 1990a: 33–42. Another specialized account is the book of Devine and Stephens 1994, which offers alternative views. A standard work on Greek meter is West 1982. The work of Blanc 2008 is a model of sound methodology in studying the interactions of meter and poetic language. For alternative views on stress and pitch accent, see David 2006.

CHAPTER TWENTY-SIX

Literary Dialects

Olga Tribulato

For much of its history Ancient Greek was fragmented into a multiplicity of regional dialects, each sharing a number of common features (isoglosses) with one or more other dialects which allow their classification into a number of dialect groups. Three of these groups take their names from the ancient theory of the Greek ἔθνη "races": Ionic, Aeolic, and Doric (see also ch. 14). Two other groups, Arcado-Cypriot and Northwest Greek, take their names from the regions in which they were spoken (overview in García Ramón 2004). Each of these groups is further divided into sub-varieties, such as Ionic and Attic within Ionic, Thessalian and Boeotian within Aeolic, Laconian and Cretan within Doric, etc.

The same linguistic fragmentation also surfaces in most of Greek literature, the bulk of which is written in various literary "dialects." These, however, never entirely correspond to the local dialects; hence the use of general labels such as "Doric" and "Aeolic" instead of more specific ones like "Laconian" or "Thessalian," a practice which we have inherited from the ancient Greeks themselves (Morpurgo Davies 1987b: 17–19). The literary dialects are almost never pure, admit frequent interference from other dialects, and may also display elements that were never part of any spoken variety. Rather than "dialects," it would be more correct to describe them as "literary languages."

On a general level, each literary genre is associated with a specific dialectal group. For instance, epic poetry is largely Ionic, choral lyric Doric, and monodic lyric Ionic (with the notable exception of Sappho and Alcaeus, who write in East Aeolic), while tragedy and oratory employ Attic. This association was originally made on the basis of the reputed land of origin of a given literary genre or of its founder: Homer was thought to be a native of Ionia; the first music and poetic schools connected with choral poetry were all located in the Doric-speaking Peloponnese; tragedy and oratory flourished in Athens, etc.

As a rule, ancient Greek authors do not write in their native dialect, but in the dialect appropriate for the genre they practice: Pindar was native of Cynoscephalae in

Boeotia, but his odes are all written in the Doric-based language of choral poetry. A familiar modern example may be the long-standing use of Italian as the international language of melodrama. Even after *Koine* became the common language of the Greeks, eventually permeating literary communication as well, many literary (predominantly poetic) works remained free of any *Koine* influence. While the citizens of third-century BCE Alexandria spoke *Koine*, Apollonius Rhodius wrote his epic poem *Argonautica* in the blend of Ionic and Aeolic characteristic of Homer.

The Greek association between genre and dialect – one of the most steadfast rules in the whole of Greek literature – admits very few exceptions. Pindar does not use his native Boeotian dialect because it did not have a connection with choral poetry, nor any literary prestige. Seen in this perspective, the use of Boeotian on the part of Pindar's fellow countrywoman Corinna is remarkable. Regrettably, however, we do not know enough about this local poet. While we read her poetry in a Hellenistic edition showing Boeotian phonological traits that cannot be more ancient than the third century BCE, there is no consensus as to whether she lived in the fifth or third century BCE, and whether she composed choral or monodic odes. Unless new papyri surface, we must accept that we do not know enough about Corinna to draw firm conclusions as to why she used Boeotian; one possible explanation is that the local destination of her poetry justified the adoption of her native dialect.

At a deeper level, dialects and genres do not match in a perfectly tight one-to-one correspondence. Epic poetry is not exclusively Ionic, as it also has a solid Aeolic layer, while the Doric of choral lyric leaves much room to Aeolic and epic-Ionic elements. To describe these linguistic blends, scholars often use the German term *Kunstsprache* "art language." Cross-linguistically, characteristics of *Kunstsprachen* are their relative artificiality and distance from natural languages. A *Kunstsprache* may also develop out of a real spoken variety which rises to the dignity of a supra-regional literary language. For instance, in early modern Italy the Tuscan dialect was at some point selected as *the* language of poetry and in the 1800s came to constitute the basis of the national Italian language because of the influence of the great medieval poets Dante, Petrarch, and Boccaccio. Not all Greek literary languages can be termed *Kunstsprachen*, though, as they may be relatively close to the local dialects; the term better applies to the dialectal blend of Homer or of choral lyric, in which the degree of artificiality and linguistic artistry is at its highest point.

If the composite nature of the Greek literary languages makes it difficult to give texts a fast and ready dialectal label, the vicissitudes of the textual transmission further complicate the analysis of their dialectal *facies*. This particularly concerns Archaic and Classical poetry, which was sung and recited before being "read," and which in the Hellenistic period underwent editorial work aimed at preserving it from the risks of linguistic degeneration. Yet the Alexandrian philologists, inspired by current grammatical theories and/or contemporary dialects, may also have consciously altered this dialectal *facies*.

A much debated question is that of Laconian traits such as the writing <σ> for <ϑ> (e.g., σιῶν = ϑεῶν) in Alcman's language, which underlies the fricativization of the aspirated dental [tʰ]. This writing never features in archaic Laconian inscriptions, and only appears from the fourth century BCE onwards. We do not know whether this might be due to the conservatism of official documents: in this case, the underlying phonetic change [tʰ] > [θ] would be much older. In particular, it has been suggested that the instances of <σ> for <ϑ> may have made their way into the text because of the way in which the sound was pronounced in oral recitals after the age of Alcman (Hinge 2006). On the other hand, E. Risch (1954/1981) proposed that this and other features – which, crucially, are purely phonetic and not morphological – were introduced by the Alexandrian editors who marveled at Alcman's lack of those traits which in the Hellenistic period singled out Laconian from other Doric dialects. Both hypotheses draw our attention to the complex history of archaic lyric compositions before they became the "texts" which we read nowadays.

Ionic

Ionic is a dialect bearing a close resemblance to Attic, most prominently in that both dialects change /ā/ (<ᾱ>) to /ē/ (<η>). It is further subdivided into West Ionic (Euboea and colonies) and East Ionic (Asia Minor and most of the Cyclades). Of the two varieties only the latter acquired any literary prestige: East Ionic is the dialect of Homer, epic, and "didactic" poetry down to Nonnus (fifth cent. CE); it is also employed in iambic and elegiac poetry, as well as in historical and scientific prose (e.g., Hecataeus, Heraclitus, Herodotus, Hippocrates, down to Arrian). Owing to Homer's influence Ionic elements are found in all of Greek poetry.

Epic Ionic

As the epic songs that later came to constitute the Homeric poems had a long oral life before being fixed in written form, the Homeric *Kunstsprache* is the most composite of all the Greek literary languages, being formed of ancient elements – which may even go back to a pre-Mycenaean period – and more recent traits. In a nutshell (more in ch. 27), dialectal features generally belong to either Ionic or Aeolic, with very few later additions from Attic. In the long process of stratification preceding the final fixation of the poems, a fundamental role seems to have been played by Ionic bards: it is now largely accepted that this was the last phase in chronological terms, to be dated in the tenth and ninth centuries BCE.

The most striking Ionic elements (see also ch. 14 under "Attic-Ionic") in Homer are as follows: the passage of inherited /ā/ to /ē/ also before ι, ε, and ρ (e.g., χώρη); quantitative metathesis in the gen. pl. of ā-stems (βουλέων vs Att. βουλῶν) and in the gen. sg. of masculine nouns in -ā- (e.g., Ἀτρείδεω vs the more archaic Ἀτρείδᾱο); lack of contractions, e.g., in the personal pronouns ἡμέων/ὑμέων and ἡμέας/ὑμέας (vs Att. ἡμῶν/ὑμῶν and ἡμᾶς/ὑμᾶς); "compensatory lengthening" in ξεῖνος, μοῦνος, κᾱλός (vs Att. ξένος, μόνος, καλός); -σσ- from *$k^{(h)}j$-, *$t^{(h)}j$-, and *tw- e.g., φυλάσσω (vs Att. φυλάττω); "psilosis" (lack of initial aspiration) e.g., οὖρος "border" (vs Att. ὅρος).

Since the epic language is a *Kunstsprache*, the dialectal elements are mixed together and often played against each other to achieve the highest level of metrical flexibility.

To give one example, the dative of the first person plural pronoun may take the shape of two metrically convenient alternatives: Ionic ἡμῖν (– –) and Aeolic ἄμμι (– ᴜ).

The Homeric *Kunstsprache* also characterizes the languages of later epic works (Homeric Hymns, the Epic "Cycle," Apollonius Rhodius, Quintus of Smyrna, down to Nonnus), as well as of "didactic" and philosophic poetry (Hesiod, Epimenides, Parmenides, Empedocles, Aratus, Nicander, etc.).

Elegy, epigram, and iambic poetry

A heavily epic Ionic is the dialect chosen by the elegiac poet Tyrtaeus to incite the Spartans to war – in so doing, the Doric poet placed himself in the trail of a tradition which clearly connects elegy with Ionic. Not only Ionic citizens such as Mimnermus, Callinus, and Xenophanes, but also Theognis of Megara and Solon of Athens chose to use Ionic. Elegiac Ionic is relatively free from colloquial influences, but features a vast number of epic forms: disyllabic scansion of vocalic groups such as -εο-, -εω-, -εᾰ-, -εη- (as in Homer, but unlike iambic poetry, where they are contracted); gen. sg. -οιο; lack of augment in some verbal forms; dat. pl. in -εσσι; modal particle κε, etc. Elements of Ionic vernacular are more frequent in authors from Ionia (e.g., κοτε and κως in Callinus vs the standard ep.-Ion. ποτε and πως), whereas non-Ionic poets may accept elements from their dialect of origin: the dual χειροῖν in Sol. 13.50 is an Attic feature, while -αις and -οις dative plurals are more frequent in non-Ionic poets (Ionic has -ῃσι and -οισι).

The hegemony of Ionic yields to a dialectal kaleidoscope in archaic epigraphic epigrams from all over Greece. Here "national" allegiances and personal considerations make the use of the local dialect a more pressing necessity: Ionic <η> and quantitative metathesis are not found outside Attica and Ionia, while local features such as -ττ- for -σσ- in Boeotia or the written representation of /w/ through *digamma* (in areas where the sound was still pronounced) are common elements. And yet, the local constituents of archaic epigrams are not as frequent as one might expect. There seems to have been a ban on having too many vernacular forms, as if the composers of these epigrams selected only a few elements to complement the standard Ionic-based diction. The general impression is that of an imperfect *lingua franca* which served as a model of intra-dialectal communication, a sort of historically unsuccessful compromise between the literary languages and the local dialects (Mickey 1981; Passa 2008).

The use of Ionic in iambic poetry is rather different. Stemming from the geographical provenance of the first authors (Archilochus of Paros, Semonides of Amorgos, Hipponax of Ephesus), this language includes numerous elements of the spoken dialect. Morphological features include -οισι and -ῃσι datives, the "Ionic" declension of i-stems (e.g., πόλιος vs πόλεως), and the thematic inflection of μι-verbs; from the phonological point of view there is a tendency toward vowel loss through crasis (e.g., κὠπόλλων, τοὐτέρωϑεν), aphaeresis (e.g., δὴ'πίκουρος), and contraction. At the same time, iambic authors avoid those Ionic traits that are common in epic or elegiac poetry but are far from the vernacular, such as uncontracted vowels (contraction or synizesis being the norm in spoken Ionic). Hipponax's lexicon also abounds with low and colloquial terms (e.g., βαμβαλύζω "chatter the teeth," σαμβάλισκα "little sandals," or the Lydian word πάλμυς "king" – see also ch. 15) and hyperbolic neologisms such as συκοτραγίδης "fig-nibbler" and ποντοχάρυβδις "sea-gulf" (epithet of a glutton).

The iambic genre enjoyed huge popularity in the Hellenistic period. In the literary experimentation typical of the Alexandrians, Callimachus and Herodas (both third century BCE) adopted the iambic meter and Ionic dialect to compose poetry that also treats topics far from the original intentions of the ἰαμβικὴ ἰδέα "iambic form/idea." Thus Callimachus' sixth iambus contains the description of the statue of Zeus at Olympia, while the eighth iambus is an epinician (victory ode). Herodas composed dramatic mimes ("mimiambi") using the choliamb, Hipponax's meter; the dialect presents the most striking Ionic features (cf. κοτε and κόσος for ποτε and πόσος, or the crasis in κὤμμασιν; see further Schmidt 1968), but also admits Doric and Aeolic elements (e.g., the Doric anaphoric pronoun νιν and the ep.-Aeol. gen. μαχάων).

Prose

Since its beginning, Greek prose (on which, see also ch. 30) was associated with Ionia, which by the sixth century BCE embodied the heart of Greek culture and trading. The first prose authors we know of are the philosophers Heraclitus of Ephesus and Anaxagoras of Clazomenae, and the historians Hecataeus of Miletus and Herodotus of Halicarnassus. Only the work of the latter survives in an extended form: the writing of the very first prose authors, not unlike that of most Ionic thinkers (Democritus, Protagoras, Pherecydes, etc.), has come down to us in fragments, through indirect attestations which have altered the original dialectal aspect by adding an Attic patina.

The following are the most important Ionic features in the language of Herodotus: forms such as κως, κοτε (for πως, ποτε); the elimination of hiatuses through contraction; genitives of -εύς stems ending in –έος (e.g., βασιλέος for βασιλέως); the reflexive pronoun ἑωυτός; the thematic conjugation of some athematic verbs (τιθεῖ instead of τίθησι, ἀπολλύω instead of ἀπόλλυμι); and 3 pl. verbs ending in -αται, -ατο (e.g., βουλοίατο). In antiquity Herodotus was also known as ὁμηρικώτατος "the most Homeric" (Long. *Subl.* 12). This claim principally rests on his frequent use of Homeric words, as well as on morphological formations such as the iterative imperfects in -σκον (e.g., κατελίπεσκε "he used to abandon"). Herodotus' text clearly underwent rewriting at some stage of its transmission. There is no sign of the East Ionic lack of aspiration (psilosis), and hiatuses in place of contractions seem to have been reintroduced in verbal endings such as -εε, -έεσθαι, and -έειν (Thumb and Scherer 1959: §304).

After its Ionic beginnings the language of prose splits into three branches: Ionic, Attic, and Doric. Ionic is used to write history (for example, Antiochus of Syracuse, a Doric city in Sicily, wrote in Ionic) and characterizes the language of the *Corpus Hippocraticum* (Hippocrates himself was a native of Doric Cos). Later pseudo-Hippocratic treatises often contain mistakes or non-Ionic elements, indicative of an ignorance of the dialect. Conversely, in the Hellenistic and imperial periods antiquarian interest in the dialect fostered the production of several Ionic texts, with authors like Arrian and Lucian adopting an artificial and often hypercorrect Ionic to write minor historical or scientific works.

Aeolic

Aeolic (on which see also ch. 14) is a dialectal group comprising Thessalian, Boeotian, and East Aeolic (often also reductively named "Lesbian"). Of these only East Aeolic ever enjoyed a literary status (for Corinna's Boeotian, see above) and is mainly used in epic and lyric poetry. Features which *may* belong to the two continental dialects appear in both epic and choral poetry, but elude any clear-cut definition.

Epic Aeolic

The Homeric language contains a number of prominent Aeolic features: geminated forms such as ὔμμι, ἄμμε, ὄππως, ἐρεβεννός; -εσσι datives extended from neuter stems in -ος to other nouns of the athematic declension (e.g., ἄνδρεσσι vs ἀνδράσι); -μεν and -μεναι infinitives (e.g., φευγέμεν vs φεύγειν, ἔμμεναι vs εἶναι); perfect participles in -οντ- (e.g., κεκλήγοντες); ποτί "toward" vs πρός; the preposition ζα- vs δια-; apocopation in prepositions such as κάτ, πάρ; modal particle κε (vs ἄν); as well as a number of lexical elements.

More difficult is the question of the origin and date of these Aeolic elements (see also ch. 27). According to the traditional theory of "phases" (which goes back to A. Fick), Aeolic features entered the Homeric poems at a very early stage (overview in Janko 1992: 15–16). This idea was later superseded by the view that the Homeric language descends from the same "East Greek" of which Mycenaean was a member. According to this perspective, there never was an Aeolic phase: the Aeolic elements entered the Homeric diction only through diffusion from neighboring, yet independent, poetic traditions. The Ionic bards chose to borrow forms from such independent traditions whenever they afforded alternative metrical shapes (Horrocks 1997b: 214–17). The "diffusion" theory, however, still leaves a number of questions unanswered: for instance, the question of why the Homeric poems contain "unnecessary" Aeolic features in place of metrically identical Ionic ones. An example is the close of *Il.* 14.481 κατακτενέεσθε καὶ ὔμμες, which contains the Aeolic ὔμμες even though the Ionic equivalent ὑμεῖς would fit the end of the line equally well.

Lyric Aeolic: Sappho and Alcaeus; choral poetry

The case for the existence of a parallel Aeolic epic tradition rests heavily on a fragment of Sappho (44 Voigt) in which the seventh-century BCE Lesbian poet narrates the wedding of Hektor and Andromache in a language that, while clearly Aeolic, also shows unequivocal epic reminiscences. The mixture of the Lesbian vernacular with Homeric suggestions famously induced E. Lobel to name this and other Sapphic compositions "abnormal poems." This definition implies that the "normal" language of the Lesbian poets is a real vernacular void of artificial elements and literary allusions (a view that goes back to L. Ahrens).

Such an assumption, however, entirely misses the point of the nature of the Greek literary dialects. While it is true that the dialect of Sappho and Alcaeus is less of an artificial blend than the Homeric or choral *Kunstsprachen*, a countercheck on the Aeolic inscriptions from Lesbos and Asia Minor also shows that it contains features that have little to do with the genuine form of the dialect. Already in the 1890s W. Schulze demonstrated that epic suggestions surface in the Lesbian lyrics more frequently than one would readily admit: for instance, χρυσοστέφαν᾽ Ἀφρόδιτα at the beginning of Sappho's "Hymn to Aphrodite" may be the Aeolic translation of *Hymn. Hom. Ven.* 1 χρυσοστέφανον καλὴν Ἀφροδίτην; and κῦμα κυλίνδεται in Alc. 208.2 Voigt is reminiscent of *Il.* 11.307. Our perception of the Lesbian poets' relation with epic is dim because of the loss of all the epic works which are not "Homer" (the so-called "Epic Cycle"), as well as of more work by Sappho and Alcaeus. The latter was clearly active in the hymnal and mythological genres: when the extant fragments allow one to make comparisons between Alcaeus' poetry and that of Homer or Hesiod, what emerge are either Homeric formulae adapted to Aeolic or unquestionably epic forms.

This brings us back to the question of whether a form of Aeolic epic ever existed. While the possibility that it did cannot be ruled out *a priori*, the evidence to substantiate such a claim is only indirect and somewhat controversial. On the other hand, it is possible that Aeolic poets active in the *lyric* genre employed much of the mythological and heroic material which was also at the center of epic poetry. Clear evidence suggests that a number of Lesbian poets from a generation earlier than Alcaeus and Sappho played a fundamental role in the definition of the style and motifs of Greek archaic poetry. Hellanicus attributes the authorship of the *Parva Ilias* to a Lesches of Mytilene; Arion is credited with the invention of the dithyramb; Periclitus of Lesbos won the prestigious citharodic competition at the Spartan Carnea festival. According to the pseudo-plutarchean *De Musica* this competition had been set up and won for the first time in 676 BCE by Terpander of Lesbos.

We know nothing about the linguistic character of the compositions of these early poets: for us, the Aeolic of lyric poetry coincides with the language of Sappho and Alcaeus. In addition to the features mentioned above with regard to epic, the most prominent elements are the preservation of inherited /ā/ (e.g., Ἀφροδίτᾱ); labial realization of inherited labiovelars (e.g., πέμπε for πέντα "five"); *o*-outcome of syllabic resonants (e.g., στρότος for στρατός); -οι-, -ει-, and -αι- outcome of -νσ- (the so-called "diphthongization"), e.g., in the pres. ptc. φέροισα vs φέρουσα (< φέρονσα) and acc. pl. of the ā-declension in -αις instead of -ᾱς; dat. pl. -αισι and -οισι; athematic conjugation of contracted verbs (e.g., φίλημμι vs φιλέω); more features in Hamm 1957.

Perhaps because of the enormous prestige of Sappho and Alcaeus, the tradition of poetry in the Lesbian dialect later seems to have died out. Two notable exceptions are Theocritus' *Idylls* 28–31, in which the Alexandrian poet pays homage to the Lesbian lyrics, and the conventional verses heavily reminiscent of Sappho that the noblewoman Julia Balbilla had inscribed on the colossal statue of Memnon in Luxor, Egypt, when she visited it with Hadrian in 130 CE.

More long-lived is the Aeolic component of choral poetry, where the Doric *Kunstsprache* leaves room for elements borrowed from epic (both Ionic and Aeolic) as well as from the lyric tradition. The most striking features are the so-called

"diphthongized" forms which, however, are only limited to feminine present participles and personal names (φέροισα, Ἀστυμέλοισα, Μοῖσα, etc.) against the wider
employment in the Lesbian poets (note that the textual tradition also attributes aorist
masculine and feminine participles in -αις/-αισα to Pindar). Similar forms have been
interpreted in the past as borrowings either from an alleged pre-Doric substrate in the
Peloponnese (E. Schwyzer, C. Buck, and others; Thera and Cyrene, both Spartan
colonies, have -οισα instead of the Doric -ωσα) or from the dialect of Argos. For
E. Risch (1954), on the other hand, these forms were never part of the original language of choral poetry, but were introduced by the Alexandrian editors who were
familiar with the Doric dialect of Cyrene. Neither hypothesis explains why the only
diphthongized forms in choral poetry are feminine names and participles. This distribution suggests that choral poetry borrowed diphthongized feminine forms directly
from lyric poetry in East Aeolic, a theory that goes back to L. Ahrens. They were only
borrowed in the feminine as prestige forms, perhaps from a kind of poetry in which
feminine personal names abounded ("catalogue poetry," Cassio 2005). Given the
influence that poets from Lesbos had on the poetic and musical climate of the
Peloponnese, this seems the most balanced view.

Doric

Doric dialects were spoken in a vast area of the Peloponnese (including Argos, Sparta,
and Messenia), on Crete, Rhodes, Cos, Thera, in several western colonies (Syracuse,
Gela, Tarentum, etc.), and in Cyrene (see again ch. 14, under West Greek). All these
local varieties share features such as the preservation of /ā/, retention of -τι in verbal
endings and numerals; first ps. pl. ending in -μες; athematic infinitives in -μεν; πρᾶτος
for πρῶτος and ἱαρός for ἱερός. L. Ahrens further divided Doric dialects into a *Doris
severior* characterized by the open quality of secondary vowels [ē] = <η>, [ɔ̄] = <ω>
(as in most of the Peloponnese and in the Spartan colonies) and a *Doris mitior*, in
which the secondary vowels have a close quality ([ẹ̄], [ọ̄] = ει, ου, as in Corinthian and
Cretan).

Choral lyric

The first texts to employ Doric appear to be Alcman's choral odes (*c.* 650–600 BCE);
yet the origins of the genre must be more ancient and should probably be sought in
the activity of poets and citharods of a generation earlier such as Xenodamus of
Kythera, Sacadas of Argos, and Eumelus of Corinth, all active in the Peloponnese
(cf. ps. Plut. *De mus.* 1134B.8–9). Although we do not know in what language these
poets composed, their connection with the Doric world has long been seen as the
principal cause for the Doric character of choral poetry.

Choral authors share the following linguistic elements: preservation of /ā/ (ā);
contraction of -ᾱο- and -ᾱω- into -ᾱ- (e.g., gen. pl. τιμᾶν vs Att.-Ion. τιμῶν); contraction of -αε- into -η-; frequent preservation of /w/ at the beginning of a word; 2 sg.

pronoun τύ; pl. art. τοί/ταί; the conjunctions αἱ and πόκα; 3 sg. pres. in -τι and 3 pl. in -ντι; and athematic pres. inf. in -μεν. More sporadic, but probably equally Doric elements are short present infinitives such as γαμέν in Stes. *PMGF* 148 and short pl. acc. such as παγάς in Stes. *PMGF* 184. For the sake of completeness it should be mentioned that most of these Doric traits may also be interpreted as belonging to a continental Aeolic dialect. The advocates of such interpretation are inclined to believe that choral poetry originated in Aeolic-speaking areas of continental Greece (Pavese 1972).

Alcman's language – as we read it today – is the one most strongly characterized as Doric: it shows features such as the gen. of o-stems in -ω and the *severior* form Μῶσα "Muse," whereas all the other choral poets have -ου and Μοῦσα. The version of Alcman's text that has come down to us also contains traits which may be the result of a later editorial intervention (see above). The language of all the other poets, on the other hand, is Doric only to an extent, and it harbors frequent Ionic and Aeolic elements. Such linguistic differences probably stem from the different purpose of their poetry: Alcman's poetry was composed for Spartan religious festivities, whereas that of Stesichorus, Simonides, Ibycus, Pindar, and Bacchylides traveled across Greece and was performed at various panhellenic festivals. If the panhellenic destination probably contributed to the avoidance of any markedly local traits, the provenance and later *floruit* of some authors may also have triggered a more frequent use of non-Doric features. For instance, it is undisputed that Ionic elements are more prominent in Ibycus and Simonides, both of whom came from Ionic-speaking areas (Rhegium and Ceos respectively) and composed much of their poetry for Ionic clients.

The transmission of these texts remains a problematic issue. Much of what we perceive as "Doric" or "Ionic" is due to the quality of /ē/ and /ō/. At first sight, a text which contains the grapheme <ου> representing [ọ] looks Ionic to us. Yet the question we must ask is whether this was the vocalism that the poet originally intended. The archaic alphabets in which the first copies of the choral lyrics are likely to have been written do not have separate graphemes for long and short /e/ and /o/. In speculative terms it cannot be ruled out that an original Doric *severior* [ọ] written with an <O> was later transliterated as <ΟΥ> rather than <Ω> (which represents [ɔ̄] in the post-Euclidean alphabet; see ch. 7). Theories concerning the origin of a poet may have triggered the interpretation of <O> as <ΟΥ>: for instance, ancient editors may have believed that an Ionic vocalism was more appropriate to the language of Ibycus than to that of Pindar. Another, no less likely, possibility is that the <ου> and <ει> digraphs in some authors are not at all Ionic, but Doric *mitiores*: such interpretation would fit Stesichorus, who came from a *mitior* area. Whether such vowels are authentic or the outcome of editorial intervention is impossible to tell, but this issue provides a good glimpse of the difficulties involved in the dialectal analysis of archaic poetic texts.

With the decline of choral poetry in the fifth century BCE poetic Doric underwent a period of decline that lasted until in the early third century BCE. Theocritus (a Syracusan) revived the language and used it in his bucolic *Idylls*, while Callimachus with his customary penchant for experimentation, used Doric for two of his *Hymns* (5–6), a genre traditionally associated with Ionic.

The Doric of attic tragedy

It is often stated that lyric parts of tragedy "are in Doric." This is not an accurate description of the language of Attic choruses, as their most prominent Doric trait is the preservation of /ā/ (ᾱ), representing the arrival point of the prestigious choral tradition. Attic tragedy pays homage to it, but within a linguistic framework that, albeit highly poetic, is far from the original language of choral odes: there are no other Doric vocalisms in tragedy, nor -οισα participles, nor verbal endings in -τι/-ντι.

Doric comedy

A comic genre flourished in Sicily in the early fifth century BCE. Its representatives are the Syracusan playwrights Epicharmus, Phormis, and Deinolochus, and the writer of mimes Sophron. Of these, Epicharmus is the author we know best; yet only short fragments (*c.* 240) of his work survive, and their cultural and sociolinguistic context is hard to reconstruct. As far as we can tell, Epicharmus's comedy dealt with mythological matter in a burlesque tone, parodying "serious" literature and philosophy. Among the general Doric features of Epicharmus' dialect it is worth mentioning the following: the preservation of /ā/; contractions of αε into η and of αο into ω; 3 sg./pl. endings in resp. -τι and -ντι (e.g., λέγοντι, ἐντί for λέγουσι, εἰσί); "Doric" futures (λεξοῦμαι vs λέξομαι); the numeral πρᾶτος (vs πρῶτος); the nasalization of laterals before dentals (e.g., φίντατος < φίλτατος); and the preservation of /w/ (e.g., in fragm. 34.2 *PCG* τὺ δὲ ἑκὼν), though this is not constant (cf. fragm. 18.1 *PCG* ἔσθοντ᾽ ἴδοις).

The most ticklish question concerns the quality of secondary vowels. Syracusan is a dialect of the *Doris mitior*, which means that its /ē/ and /ō/ have a closed quality, i.e., what in the Classical alphabet would be written with the digraphs <EI> and <OY>. In Epicharmus' papyri the treatment oscillates between η and ει, and ω and ου; this may in turn suggest that the original text was ambiguous in this respect. This is possible if the original Epicharmean text used archaic graphic conventions (i.e., <E> for both [ē] and [ẹ] and <O> for both [ɔ̄] and [ọ̄]), so that the text we read must be the result of a Hellenistic interpretation (Cassio 2002: 58–61). It is again thanks to Alexandrian editorial practice that we possess important information on Doric accentuation and vowel quantity in those cases in which these differed from the standard Attic or *Koine* ones. In *P. Oxy.* 2427 (second cent. BCE; = fragm. 113 *PCG*), for instance, the accusative plural ἀμυγδάλας (l. 279) has a short macron on the last alpha. The syllable is metrically long as it occurs before a pause, but the editor obviously wanted to draw the readers' attention to the fact that in Doric it was pronounced short.

Doric prose

Historical, philosophical, and rhetorical prose in Doric flourished at various stages of Greek literary history, in a chronological span extending roughly from the fifth century BCE to the second century CE (and perhaps beyond). The extant sources are often scanty, but the bulk of scientific works by Archimedes of Syracuse (mid-third cent. BCE) provides a glimpse of the importance of Doric as one of the languages of Greek prose.

The information we possess suggests a strong link between production in Doric and the western Greeks of Sicily and Magna Graecia. Apart from Archimedes, we know that one Akron of Akragas, a contemporary of Empedocles, compiled a medical treatise in Doric (*Suda* α.1026), while Plato states that the famous Syracusan cook Mithaecus wrote works on cookery (*Gorg.* 518.b; Cassio 1989: 143–4). In Magna Graecia Doric prose was the means of expression of the Pythagorean school, whose main representatives are Philolaus (fifth to fourth centuries BCE) and Archytas of Tarentum (fourth century BCE). Whereas in Sicily Doric prose seems to have died out with Archimedes, in Magna Graecia the later production of several pseudo-Pythagorean texts suggests an enduring link down to the second century CE.

A fundamental difference between the two western productions lies in the quality of secondary long vowels, which – in accordance with the Syracusan dialect – are closed (ει, ου) in Archimedes, but open (η, ω) in Philolaus and Archytas (Thumb and Kieckers 1932: §§106, 165). As is often the case, we cannot be sure of whether the dialectal coloring of such texts is authentic or due to later editing (not an unlikely event in the case of Pythagorean literature). One wonders what induced so many authors to choose Doric in a period when Ionic and, increasingly, Attic had become the dialects of prose. Cultural pride must have played a leading role: for Sicilians, Epicharmus stood as a model of successful authorship in a local dialect; the association between Pythagoras and Tarentum must have done the trick for the other side of the strait. A comparable mixture of local pride and political interests may have prompted the use of a moderately Argive variety of Doric by Hagias and Dercylus, authors of *Argoliká* "Facts of Argolis" around the fourth century BCE.

Attic

With the emergence of Athens in the fifth century BCE as a cultural and artistic center the Attic dialect, which is the great absentee in the age of archaic literature, makes its entree on the Greek literary scene. It is a grand entree: for Attic was soon associated with tragedy and oratory, the two new genres that most influenced Greek cultural life in the fifth and fourth centuries. Attic enjoyed a long-standing prestige over the other dialects, to the point of playing a leading role in the development of *Koine* and of Medieval and Modern Greek. Among the most prominent Attic characteristics are the passage of /ā/ to /ē/ (in common with Ionic), except before ε, ι, and ϱ (in contrast to Ionic: the so-called Attic reversal); -ττ- from *$k^{(h)}j$-, *$t^{(h)}j$-, and *tw-; and dative plurals in -αις and -οις.

Tragedy and comedy

The essence of Athenian tragedy and comedy is Attic, with different degrees of closeness to the spoken or vernacular variety depending on genre (comedy is more colloquial), author (of the tragedians, Aeschylus is the less informal), and moment in the play. It is frequently the case that this Attic core includes more distinctly Ionic features, or epic and lyric expressions, particularly when tragic dramatic moments require a more heightened language. Comedy may likewise consciously elevate the tone in connection with particular meters and situations: this especially shows in Aristophanes' parodies of tragic or epic style. For instance, at Ar. *Av.* 976 (a hexameter) one finds the Ionic vocalism in κοῦρε "o boy" instead of Attic κόρε, while datives in -εσσι feature only in hexameters.

New Comedy, whose main representative is Menander (*c.* 244/3–290/1 BCE), testifies to a different kind of Attic: less parochial than the Attic of Old Comedy, it is the "Great Attic" in use in a vast part of the Hellenic world. At the same time, Menander's language is devoid of Ionic or epic elements taken from the literary language.

Prose and oratory

Attic prose begins with Gorgias (*c.* 485–380 BCE), a Sicilian rhetorician active at Athens, and Thucydides (*c.* 460–400 BCE) – see also ch. 30. In both cases "the leap toward writing Attic prose was not made without concessions" (Adrados 2005: 152): if Attic features such as ξύν for σύν mark the distance from Ionic, more local traits like -ρρ- for -ρσ- and -ττ- for -σσ- are avoided at this early stage. Only a generation later, though, the orator Isocrates (436–338 BCE), the historian Xenophon (born *c.* 430 BCE), and the philosopher Plato (*c.* 429–347) use a dialect which is both purer and more confident, in that it allows, for example, local elements such as -ττ-.

The contemporary spoken variety of Attic, however, had gradually become something altogether different. The blend of Attic and Ionic (*Grossattisch* "Great Attic" in the popular definition of A. Thumb) that was the official language in the early fourth century BCE period gradually gave way to *Koine* towards the end of that century. Many authors of the Hellenistic and imperial periods used *Koine* rather than Attic proper: Polybius, Plutarch, the Stoic and Epicurean philosophers, to name only a few, all wrote in an elevated form of *Koine*.

During the early imperial period, a cultural renaissance marked by a degree of nationalism triggered nostalgia for the mythical past of fifth-century Athens. In this new atmosphere, the purist literary and linguistic phenomenon known by the name of Atticism was born (see ch. 31). Rebelling against the technical and undignified aspects of *Koine*, the Atticists predicated the return to the style and language of the best Attic writers. The orator Aelius Aristides (*c.* 117–81) and the biographer Philostratus (*c.* 170–244) are two of the most representative authors of this movement – which also engendered an Atticist lexicography – aimed at teaching second-century CE Greeks how to speak like their Classical ancestors. In spite of its anachronism, such classicizing literary style was employed up until the modern period, determining – *de facto* – a condition of diglossia between the spoken variety of Greek descending from *Koine*, known as *dimotikí* "popular language," and the archaic written language which significantly was named *katharévousa* "pure language." More on this in ch. 37.

FURTHER READING

Good comprehensive overviews of the Greek literary dialects are Cassio 2008, Adrados 2005, Forssman 2004, Meier-Brügger 1992: 80–6, Hiersche 1970, and Hoffmann et al. 1969. For the wider linguistic context, see Colvin 2007, García Ramón 2004, Morpurgo Davies 2003, Mickey 1981, Palmer 1980, and Meillet 1975. For the dialect of Homer, see Janko 1992 and Horrocks 1997b; on literary Ionic, see Passa 2008 and Schmidt 1968; on literary Doric, see Hinge 2006, Cassio 1989 and 2002, and Risch 1954; on literary Aeolic, see Cassio 2005 and Hamm 1957.

CHAPTER TWENTY-SEVEN

The Greek of Epic

Olav Hackstein

The present chapter is intended to give an overview of the central features characteristic of the language of Homer and to present the major problems and controversies
surrounding Homeric language. Another focus shall be on the way in which "hexametric Greek" exerted a formative influence on the language of subsequent Greek
literature.

Controversies: Old and New Homeric Questions

The specification of Homeric Ionic

There is not a single line in the Homeric epics without Ionic (see also ch. 26 under
"Epic Ionic" and ch. 14 under "Ionic-Attic"). Ionic forms are all-pervasive. Their
specification has been the matter of some debate. Certain features point in the direction of Central or West Ionic (West 1988: 166; Forssman 1991: 271; Peters 1995;
Strunk 1997: 150; Nussbaum 1998: 62ff.). Among these West Ionic features are:

a) The *failure of compensatory lengthening* to occur, e.g., in ξένιον (*Od.* 14.389)
in contrast to E. Ion. ξείνιον (*Od.* 9.356) from **ksenϝo-* or in μονωθείς (*Il.* 11.470)
in contrast to E. Ion. μουνωθέντα (*Od.* 15.386) from **monϝo-*.

b) The *labial onset of the interrogative-indefinite pronoun*, e.g., ποῖος, πόσος, ποῦ,
πῶς "what kind, how much, where, how," is characteristic of West Ionic and at the
same time all-pervasive in Homer in contrast to sixth-century E. Ion. κοῖος, κόσος,
κοῦ, κῶς, as found in Herodotus. "The true explanation seems to be that it was in the
central Ionic area that epic particularly flourished during the period when the labiovelar was assimilating itself to other phonemes, so that the π-forms became established
as the epic norm" (West 1973a: 189).

c)   The *loss of word-initial aspiration* (psilosis) occurs in Homer only infrequently (Wackernagel 1916: 41f.). In general, *spiritus asper* is preserved in epic Ionic in accordance with West Ionic (for attestations, see Wackernagel 1916: 44), but in contrast to sixth-century East Ionic, as illustrated by Hom. ἀφίκετο (*Il.* 13.645) vis-à-vis E. Ion. ἀπίκετο (Hdt. 5.11.1). A scenario according to which the non-psilotic character of epic Greek simply reflects an archaism, i.e., the aspiration of the (West) Ionic idiom imported by (West) Ionic colonists to Asia Minor, cannot be ruled out (Jacobsohn 1908: 352; West 1988: 163; Rix 2005: 388). It is further supported by archaic epic Ionic epithets like ἑκήβολος "hitting from afar," the aspiration of which is independently proven to be authentic by its inscriptional Naxian attestation as ℎεκηβόλοι ἰοχεαίρηι (seventh cent. BCE; *CEG* I 403).

Closer inspection might reveal more instances of West Ionic forms in Homer. It can be argued, for instance, that θέᾱ "goddess" as found in the opening line of the *Iliad* is not an Aeolicism, as customarily assumed, but a West Ionic form with its characteristic reversion of η to ᾱ after ε. The recurrence of θέᾱ on a piece of West Ionian seventh-century pottery found on Ischia might be adduced in favor of its West Ionic origin (Bartoněk and Buchner 1995: 194; Peters 1995).

Aeolicisms

Aeolic words and morphemes (for lists, see Thumb and Scherer 1959: 209–12; West 1988: 162–5; Forssman 1991: 270–4; Janko 1992: 15f.; also ch. 26 under "Epic Aeolic") are a fixed component of epic Greek. Many of these Aeolicisms serve merely as useful metrical alternatives (Meier-Brügger 1986) or as ornamental stylistic devices (Heubeck 1981: 76). Apart from metrical necessity, however, there are Aeolic function words, e.g., πότι, πρότι (Ion. πρός "toward"); ἄμμες (Ion. ἡμεῖς "we"); ὔμμες (Ion. ὑμεῖς "you" pl.; see West 1988: 162ff.); and the particles κε(ν) (see Witte 1972: 187), αἰ, and μάν (see Wachter 2000: 64 n. 4), which are deeply embedded in epic language. These have been diachronically explained according to the theory initiated by A. Fick as remnants of an earlier Aeolic phase of epic diction.

The theory of an Aeolic phase antedating the Ionic phase is still a matter of some debate. On occasion an Ionic variant is definitely older than its Aeolic pendant. For instance, it is not Aeol. κύνεσσιν "dogs" dat. pl. (◡◠◡, *Il.* 1.4, altogether four attestations) but Ionic κυσί ((⊥)◡◡, *Il.* 11.325, altogether ten attestations) that is shared with Myc. *ku-si* (*kunsi*) TH Fq 130, as attested on the "new" Theban fragments. (See Hackstein 2002: 186 n. 33 on the reconstruction.)

Furthermore, alongside the Ionic tradition there may also have existed a parallel Aeolic epic tradition. Accordingly, some scholars have suggested a concurrence and confluence of Aeolic and Ionic epic traditions with some mutual diffusion of dialect features (cf. Drerup 1903 apud Witte 1972: 178; Horrocks 1997b: 214–17).

There are also manifold examples of interdialectal translation of epic verses and formulae shortly after the eighth century. Intertextuality must have been a long-established tradition in Greek poetry, and crucially, it would have been an ideal catalyst for the interdiffusion of Aeolic and Ionic epic forms.

Homer and Mycenaean

The existence of heroic poetry of some sort in the second millennium BCE is uncontested, despite the fact that the "smoking gun," i.e., an actual piece of Mycenaean poetry, is missing. But there is indirect evidence. Thus, Mycenaean "singers of tales" occur on frescoes from Pylos, and these are now complemented by the mention of two lyre players on the recently discovered Mycenaean tablets from Thebes, Myc. *ru-ra-ta-e* /lurātāhe/, TH Av 106,6 (Meier-Brügger 2003a: 233; cf. West 1988: 165).

Likewise uncontested is the existence of an oral tradition bridging the Dark Ages after the fall of Troy until the socio-political rebirth of Greek culture in the eighth century BCE, involving the Greek expansion, the (re)establishment of literacy (Latacz 1998: 156ff.), and the "sudden resurgence of interest in the heroic past" (appearance of heroic scenes in art; West 1973a: 182).

Despite its potential for preserving archaisms, the linguistic nature of poetry, like that of non-poetic linguistic varieties, will always remain dynamic, even if conservative as compared to natural spoken language (Hackstein 2002: 17f.). Even archaisms are not exempt from linguistic renewal in the long run. Given this, the prospects of finding vestiges of Mycenaean, whether frozen or in slightly renewed guise, are meager.

Generally, the probative value of different kinds of archaisms in determining the age of epic diction can differ markedly. Less probative are archaisms in the domain of names or technical terms because of their tendency to become frozen entities, partially exempt from the operation of sound laws also outside of poetry. More probative are archaisms in the domain of function words, and especially an accumulation of archaic function words; for these by their very nature are less accessible to intentional, purely poetic, and artistic archaizing. The domain of additive conjunctions is an ideal testing ground; these are crucial for epic diction because of the "adding" and paratactic nature of oral poetry.

As it turns out, the Mycenaean and the Homeric systems diverge significantly. Whereas Mycenaean distinguishes progressive δέ from inclusive k^we, Homer uses a formally renewed and functionally redistributed system. Like Mycenaean, epic Greek uses progressive δέ; but unlike Myc. *de*, Hom. δέ, in contrastive use, is preceded by non-Myc. μέν. Instead of Myc. inclusive k^we, epic Greek uses inclusive καί (Hajnal 2003b: 98f; 2003c: 228.). Hom. Gk καί (Arcad., Cypr. κας) "and" represents the post-Mycenaean development of the original adverb *$kati$* "(together) with" into a coordinating conjunction. Crucially, Greek καί has the properties of being both post-Mycenaean and a ubiquitous function word in the *Iliad* and *Odyssey* (with altogether over 5,400 occurrences; Meier-Brügger 2003a: 236), found in all compositional and linguistic layers of the poems. As such it marks both epics as creations of post-Mycenaean date (Hajnal 2003c: 228f.; Meier-Brügger 2003a: 240). The frequent occurrence of adverbial (originally non-clitic) καί "also, even" as a longum in the thesis of the third foot (collection: La Roche 1895: 173f.) makes it likely that the word should be reconstructed as having originally had a disyllabic shape, since the third foot clearly prefers to be dactylic if it contains the penthemimeral caesura and is followed by word-division. It may thus phonologically betray a remarkable archaism dating from before the eighth century BCE while functionally postdating the Mycenaean period.

Generally, one should heed the caveat that dating a text, a formula, a word by linguistic archaisms may be slippery ground, except in case of an accumulation of archaisms.

Conservatism and Modernization

The Homeric epics are both the culmination of a very long oral tradition and at the same time the foundation of a literary language constituting the "Greek of epic" and setting the linguistic standards for all post-Homeric epics. Two opposing factors, the conservative potential of the tradition and the innovative potential of the creative composition, have led to the linguistic shape of Homeric Greek with its constant combining and intertwining of linguistic archaism and innovation.[1]

Verse-end formulae show a potential for being both remarkably conservative on the one hand and linguistically innovative on the other. A prominent example is the inherited vocative syntagm Ζεῦ πάτερ "father Zeus" (e.g., *Il.* 1.503), besides which the nom. Ζεὺς πατήρ (as in Archil. fragm. 122,2) yields a non-hexametric word shape. In the hexameter the nominative was usable only with an interposed monosyllable, e.g., Ζεύς με πατήρ, Ζεὺς δὲ πατήρ (Strunk 1982: 429–31).

Both an inherited formula and its modernization are shown by Διὶ πατρί (ᴗᴗ⌣ᴗ, *Il.* 13.818), which while continuing an Indo-European formula shows the dative ending in its modernized form, i.e., short -ι (the old locative ending). By contrast to Διί (ᴗᴗ), certain old formulae preserve traces of the archaic dative διϝεί by metrically retaining the iambic structure of Διί (ᴗ–), e.g., διί- φιλε (*Il.* 1.74; cf. West 1998: xxviii), . . . Διὶ μῆτιν ἀτάλαντος "equal to Zeus in counsel" (verse-final, 2 x *Il.*, 4 x *Od.*; cf. Watkins 1987: 288; West 1982: 38 n. 21, 1997b: 230; Meier-Brügger 2003a: 239).

The modernization of the text as an ever-present and ongoing phenomenon is demonstrated by epigraphic adaptations of epic line-end formulae such as *Il.* 7.200 . . . Διὶ Κρονίωνι ἄνακτι, which in sixth-century Doric appears as . . . Δὶ ϙρονίōνι ϝάνακτι (*CEG* 362.1, Cleonae, Nemea, *c.* 560 BCE). In its Doric adaption, epic Διί has been replaced by its younger contracted form Δί, although the meter still presupposes disyllabic Διί.

The verse-end formula δῶτορ ἐάων "giver of good things" (*Od.* 8.335; *Hymn. Hom.* 18.12, 29.8; Callim. *Hymn* 2.91) is an old inherited formula. It is demonstrably inherited from Proto-Indo-European, forming an indirect equation with Ved. dātā́ vásūnām (*RV* 8.51,5).[2] But δῶτορ ἐάων was not exempt from innovation. The inherited verse-end formula δῶτορ ἐάων was not usable in the plural, where it would have yielded the metrically impossible tribrach δῶτορες ἐάων. Artificial reshaping generates the hexametric verse-end plural version δωτῆρες ἐάων (*Od.* 8.325; Hes. *Th.* 46, 111, 633, 664), by maintaining the root δω- "give" and replacing -τορ- with the suffix -τηρ- of the oxytone agent noun type; see Nussbaum 1998: 132 n. 120.[3]

The verse-end formula at *Il.* 1.290, . . . θεοὶ αἰὲν ἐόντες, contains two remarkable archaisms: the present participle in its older shape without apheretized initial, a feature still alive in Mycenaean but moribund in East Ionic; and more remarkable still, the form αἰέν, an archaic *en*-locative, variant of the otherwise customary adverb αἰεί.

All-pervasive archaisms

There are two all-pervasive archaisms in the *Iliad* and *Odyssey* which serve to set Homeric language *in toto* apart linguistically from later Attic and Ionic Greek. These are the still incomplete use of the demonstrative pronoun as the definite article and the omission of the augment.

Homeric Greek preserves a linguistic stage prior to the development of the demonstrative pronoun into a definite article. Hence, in Homeric Greek, semantically definite noun phrases often lack the article where it would be mandatory in later Greek (Chantraine 1953: 158ff.). Examples of this are the first words of the *Iliad* and the *Odyssey*, i.e., μῆνιν "wrath" and ἄνδρα "man" respectively, introducing the basic topic of both epics, which is assumed to be known to the audience and consequently is definite. The definiteness of both topics and noun phrases would require them in later Greek to be preceded by the definite article, i.e., τὴν μῆνιν and τὸν ἄνδρα, as witnessed by later commentators who quite naturally gloss the opening line of the *Iliad* as τὸ μὲν γὰρ ἔργον Μουσῶν δι᾽ ἀκριβείας διελθεῖν τὴν μῆνιν, ἣ ἐμήνισεν Ἀχιλλεὺς ἐν Τροίᾳ "It is the task of the Muses to treat in detail the wrath which Achilles cherished at Troy" (Aristid. *Rhet.* 1.14.1). Likewise ἄνδρα, where contextually definite and specific, must be preceded by the definite article in Attic, as exemplified by λέγε οὖν ... τὸν ἄνδρα (Pl. *Soph.* 240a6).

Homeric Greek, likewise, preserves a linguistic stage in which the augment in preterite tense forms was still optional. In contrast to later Greek, the augment can be omitted in the imperfect, aorist, and pluperfect. Recent research has shown that the augmentation of preterite forms is not merely an artistic option but rather an archaic and rule-governed phenomenon. The augment serves as a foregrounding device attaching salience to the proposition (Bakker 1999: 56; 2005: 127; Mumm 2004). Functionally, the primarily affirmative (and only secondarily temporal) value of the augment accords with its long-presumed etymological identification with the PIE affirmative hic-et-nunc particle *e (Strunk 1994), which after undergoing monosyllabic lengthening survived into Homeric Greek as ἦ, the affirmative particle of direct speech.

Archaisms in morphemes

The epic long-vowel subjunctive φέρηισι represents an archaism, being replaced by φέρῃ in post-Homeric Greek. The equation of φέρηισι with Skt *bhárāti* was borne out by the discovery of πίηισι in the Nestor's Cup inscription (West 1998: xxxi).

The epic use of the morpheme -φι, which had fallen out of general use by post-Mycenaean Greek, is remarkably archaic. So is the singular use of -φι in epic ἶφι, which is shared by Mycenaean (see Risch 1980: 267 n. 33 and Hajnal 1995: 139ff., 147); cf. also δεξιτερῆφι "with his right hand" (*Il.* 24.284).

The poets avail themselves of the morpheme -φι for various poetic purposes. Thus, -φι clearly is exploited for metrical reasons (avoidance of cretic sequences; Witte 1972: 76) or on stylistic grounds, e.g., for archaizing purposes or out of a desire for a diction removed from everyday contemporary speech (Hackstein 2002: 15).

Lexical archaism: particles

We find archaic function words inherited from PIE, e.g., PIE *nu, occurring in inherited locutions in Homer, e.g., μή νύ τοι (*Il.* 1.28; cf. Skt *mā́ nu*, Toch. A *mā nu ākāl knäṣtär ñi* (68a5 +), *mā nu täṣ THT* 639, 6b4, Toch. B *mā no* "but not"); or relative ὅς νυν … (*CEG* I 432), on which, see Watkins 1976b: 438 n. 8.

Linguistic change yields unmetrical forms

Since language change and the accompanying linguistic modernization affected the traditional epic language over the entire course of its existence, there are also many instances of pre-Homeric modernizations. Such pre-Homeric modernizations often led to metrical or prosodic anomalies (West 1982: 39; 1997b: 226f.).

   a)   *Quantitative metathesis.* Linguistic modernization of ἧος ὅ ταῦθ' ($\stackrel{\_}{}$ ‿‿ $\stackrel{\_}{}$) to the transmitted ἕως ὃ ταῦθ' ($\stackrel{\_}{}$ ‿ $\stackrel{\_}{}$, *Il.* 1.193) has caused the line incipit to become unmetrical (West 1997b: 230).

   b)   The *genitive ending* -ου represents a pre-Homeric contraction of earlier disyllabic –οο, as can be seen from the meter in a few cases (Witte 1913: 2219; West 1997b: 230; 1998: xxxiiif.). The restitution of -οο seems plausible for old formulae like *Il.* 9.440 *ὁμοιΐοο πτολέμοιο (printed by West; see Wachter 2000: 79 n. 40). The hypothesis that *ὁμοιΐοο πτολέμοιο was the authentic form is rendered even more likely by the observation that the onset πτ- in πτολέμοιο (rather than the variant π-) is chosen only where metrically necessary (Jacobsohn 1909: 268).

   Moreover, Leumann's explanation of ὀκρυόεις alongside κρυόεις (1950: 49 following Payne Knight) as resulting from reanalysis and misdivision of a syntagm like *Il.* 9.64 *ἐπιδημίοο κρυόεντος (= West) as *ἐπιδημίο ὀκρυόεντος, modernized to ἐπιδημίου ὀκρυοέντος (‿‿ $\stackrel{\_}{}$ ‿‿ $\stackrel{\_}{}$ ‿‿ $\stackrel{\_}{}$ ‿), lends additional credence to the supposition of an underlying *-οο.[4]

   Especially doubtful are cases in which an attempted linguistic reconstruction of the "original" text emends transmitted forms out of the text which are elsewhere presupposed by other poetic variants (cf. Hackstein 2007). The reconstruction *Il.* 2.325 *ὅο κλέος $\stackrel{\_}{}$‿‿ (printed by West) replaces the transmitted ὅου, an old artificial form (Forssman 1991: 280), which is otherwise presupposed by the artificial form ἕεις (Führer and Schmidt 2001: 18 n. 89).

   c)   In some cases where the *contracted biceps of the fifth foot* infringes the avoidance of word-end after a spondaic fifth foot (Meister's bridge), the meter can be emended by resolving the contraction, e.g., ἠῶ (-οα) δῖαν *Il.* 11.723; Πατρόκλεις (*-κλεες) ἱππεῦ *Il.* 16.20; δήμου (*-οο) φῆμις *Od.* 14.239; ἣν (*ἕεν) ἄλσος *Od.* 17.208; or by proclisis: μὴ δῶ Hes. *Op.* 354 (see Meister 1921: 7f.; Hoenigswald 2004: 179–81).

   To be distinguished from these early modernizations are later post-Homeric modernizations which certainly do have to be emended (Hackstein 2002: 19f., 88f. exx. 15–16).

   There are borderline cases in which it is difficult to distinguish Homeric from post-Homeric modernizations. Within the Homeric transmission the inherited invocational formula κλῦθι μοι (see West 2007: 316f.) shows vacillation between older μοι (= Av. *mōi*) and younger μεο. The younger form μεο is likely already an authentic component of eighth-century Ionic (Wachter 2000: 96 n. 38). Nevertheless, West is justified in printing κλῦθι μοι because of the unanimous presence of κλῦθι μοι in the parallel transmission of archaic lyric poetry (cf. Meier-Brügger 1986: 352f.; Hackstein 2002: 81–2).

Heterogeneity

From its earliest attestations on, epic Greek appears as a patchwork of linguistic retention and innovation. This can be demonstrated by the following examples, showing older and more recent variants of the same morpheme or word within the same line or within successive lines; for more examples, see Hopkinson 1982.

a) Digamma. In the following line, *digamma* blocks hiatus in ἄρα (*ϝ)εἶπε ($\smile\smile\overset{3}{-}\smile$) but fails to make position in πρὸς (*ϝh)ὅν ($\smile\overset{4}{-}$):

ὀχθήσας δ' ἄρ**α εἶπε πρὸς ὃν** μεγαλήτορα θυμόν (*Il.* 11.403)

b) Quantitative metathesis. The occurrence and non-occurrence of quantitative metathesis in the same line occurs in Μενέλαος with maintenance of the archaic *-lā(u̯)o-*, as opposed to the (by three steps) further developed *ēu̯os > *-eōs > -εος in Ἀτρέος (on which, see Meister 1921: 149f. and Nussbaum 1998: 62f.):

τόφρα δέ τοι Μενέλ**αος** ἀρήϊος Ἀτρ**έος** υἱός (*Il.* 17.79)

c) Contraction. Depending on the meter the poet may avail himself of the contracted or the uncontracted variant of the same word or morpheme. *Il.* 10.249 nicely contrasts the uncontracted 2 sg. pres. imp. ending in αἴνεε with contracted νείκει (as is mandatory in verse-end position):

Τυδεΐδη, μήτ' ἄρ με μάλ' αἴν**εε** μήτέ τι νείκ**ει** (*Il.* 10.249)

d) Muta cum liquida. In *Il.* 24.324, the compound τετράκυκλον shows a double treatment of word-internal plosive plus liquid. While -κῡκ.λον exemplifies the heterosyllabic treatment and long scansion, as is customary word-internally, the first compound member deviates in scanning and syllabifying τĕ.τρά-:[5]

πρόσθε μὲν ἡμίονοι εἷλκον τĕτράκῡκ.λον ($\smile\smile\overset{5}{-}\smile$) ἀπήνην (*Il.* 24.324)

e) Syllabification of y. According to word-sandhi, /i/ before vowel may optionally be syllabified as a non-syllabic /j/. This option mostly occurs in cases of metrical necessity, e.g. Αἰγυπτίη > Αἰγυπτjη (West 1982: 14), or in allegro speech, e.g. πόλιος ($\smile\smile\overset{4}{-}$, *Il.* 21.608), πόλjος ($\smile\overset{4}{-}$, *Il.* 21.567) (Hackstein 2002: 30f.).

f) Dialectal variants. In *Od.* 7.203 we find the 1 pl. pronoun co-occurring in its Ionic (ἡμεῖς) and its Aeolic form (ἄμμι):

δαίνυνταί τε παρ' **ἄμμι** καθήμενοι ἔνθά περ **ἡμεῖς** (*Od.* 7.203)

In *Il.* 9.440 we find the genitive ending of the first declension co-occurring as -oo and -οιο:

νήπιον, οὔ πω εἰδόθ' ὁμοιίοο πτολέμοιο (*Il.* 9.440 West)

And in *Il.* 23.280 as -ου and -οιο:

τοίου γὰρ σθένος ἐσθλὸν ἀπώλεσαν ἡνιόχοιο (*Il.* 23.280)

g) Morphological variants. Od. 18.267 shows the side-by-side occurrence of two variants of the same morphological type, once with zero-grade suffix -τρ- (πα-τρ-ός "father" gen.) and once with full-grade suffix -τερ- (μη-τέρ-ος "mother" gen.), the latter complying with the highly favored dactylic word-end before the bucolic dieresis:

μεμνῆσθαι πατρὸς καὶ μητέρος ἐν μεγάροισιν (*Od.* 18.267)

Language and Meter

The influence of meter on epic Greek is enormous. The basic property of the meter was concisely described by Witte both as conservative and innovative ("konservierend und fördernd", Witte 1913: 2214; Hackstein 2002: 278). On the one hand meter constrains the shape of words; on the other it is innovative in inviting multifarious reshaping of words. Despite metrical constraints, and despite the formulaicness of the inherited epic diction, the placement and employment of words does show a degree of freedom of poetic diction; the poet may exchange words or artificially reshape them so as to make them fit the needs of the hexameter.

Some mechanisms

To ensure and heighten metrical flexibility, the poet can avail himself of a pool of variants. These are of three kinds (Parry's three elements): archaic, foreign, and artificial elements, yielding diachronic variants, dialectal variants, and artificial variants.

This formulaic flexibility is also part and parcel of the nature of oral composition, as recent research has confirmed; see Visser 1997, conveniently summarized in Latacz 2000 and Hajnal 2003b: 93–6; see also Bakker 2005: 1–37. Beyond prefabricated phrases, the nature of oral composition provides room for free, not metrically dictated formulation. Formulae can be viewed as stylized speech-units of ordinary discourse (Bakker 1997a and 1997b).

a) Older and younger forms. The genitive of Ὀδυσσεύς occurs in altogether four forms ranging from the phonologically archaic Ὀδυσ(σ)ῆος to the phonologically recent form Ὀδυσεῦς, as set out in table 27.1.

b) Dialectal variants. Ionic and non-Ionic forms are shown in table 27.2.

c) Artificial and authentic forms. Non-hexametric word structure requires the reshaping of a word to fit the hexameter (alteration of vowel length, expansion,

Table 27.1 Forms of the genitive of Ὀδυσσεύς

Ὀδυσῆος	. . . Ὀδυσῆος| (Il. 1.138)
	πῶς ἂν ἔπειτ' **Ὀδυσῆος** ἐγὼ θείοιο λαθοίμην (*Od.* 1.65)
Ὀδυσσῆος	μῦθον ἐπαινήσαντες **Ὀδυσσῆος** θείοιο (*Il.* 2.335)
	νόστον **Ὀδυσσῆος** ταλασίφρονος, ὥς κε νέηται (*Od.* 1.87)
Ὀδυσσέος	τοῦ μὲν ἅμαρθ', ὁ δὲ Λεῦκον, **Ὀδυσσέος** ἐσθλὸν ἑταῖρον (*Il.* 4.491)
Ὀδυσεῦς	ἀμφοτέρας, **Ὀδυσεῦς** δὲ λαβὼν κύσε χεῖρ' ἐπὶ καρπῷ (*Od.* 24.398)

Table 27.2 Ionic and non-Ionic forms

Ionic	*non-Ionic*
Ion. ἠελίου ($\overset{1}{-}$ ⏑⏑ $\overset{2}{-}$, *Il.* 8.538)	ἠελίοιο ($\overset{5}{-}$ ⏑⏑ $\overset{6}{-}$ ⏑, *Il.* 1.605)
Ion. θυρέων (⏑ $\overset{4}{-}$, *Od.* 21.191)	. . . θυράων| (⏑ $\overset{6}{-}$ –, *Il.* 9.473)
Ion. κυσί (($\overset{1}{-}$) ⏑⏑, *Il.* 11.325)	. . . κύνεσσι (⏑ $\overset{6}{-}$ ⏑, *Il.* 1.4)
Ion. νηυσί (*Il.* 1.26 etc., 175x)	νήεσσι (*Il.* 2.175 etc., 38x), νέεσσι (*Il.* 3.46 etc., 10x)
Ion. ἀγορεύειν (always at verse-end; *Il.* 1.571)	ἀγορευέμεν (⏑⏑ $\overset{4}{-}$ ⏑⏑, *Il.* 2.10, 9.369, 12.213)
Ion. εἶναι ($\overset{6}{-}$ –, *Il.* 1.92)	ἔμεν (⏑ $\overset{2}{-}$, *Il.* 4.299), ἔμεναι (⏑⏑ $\overset{4}{-}$, *Il.* 3.40)
Ion. ἡμεῖς ($\overset{1}{-}$ –, *Il.* 2.126), ὑμεῖς ($\overset{1}{-}$ –, *Il.* 2.75)	ἄμμες ($\overset{3}{-}$ ⏑, *Il.* 21.432), ὔμμες ($\overset{3}{-}$ ⏑, *Il.* 1.274)
Ion. τέσσερας (*Il.* 5.271)	πίσυρας (⏑⏑ $\overset{4}{-}$, *Il.* 15.680)
Ion. ἅμαρτε (⏑ $\overset{3}{-}$ ⏑, *Il.* 8.311)	ἤμβροτες ($\overset{1}{-}$ ⏑⏑, *Il.* 5.287)

truncation): i) metrical lengthening, e.g., ἀθάνατος becomes ἀ̄θάνατος; ἄνερα becomes ᾱ̆νερα (Wachter 2000: 82f.); ii) expansion of word length, e.g., στένων becomes στενάχων, στεναχίζων (Forssman 1991: 263); iii) reduction of word length by truncation of a syllable, e.g., προ[τι]θέουσιν becomes προθέουσιν (*Il.* 1.291), δεδουπ[η]ότος becomes δεδουπότος (*Il.* 23.679), and προ[πε]φυλάχθε becomes προφυλάχθε (*Hymn. Hom. Ap.* 538) (Hackstein 2002: 195).

Interaction of meter and artificial alteration

The meter may constrain and influence the employment of words in either of two ways: i) if intractable in the hexameter, words are either avoided or reshaped, so as to comply with the meter (Chantraine 1973: 94–102); ii) non-hexametric word shape apart, another factor prompting reshaping is the inner metrics of the hexameter itself, requiring the word shape to change as the word occurs in different positions within the verse.

a) Non-hexametric words can be brought to comply with the meter as demonstrated in tables 27.3–7.

b) Structural constraints and tendencies of the hexameter (inner metrics). The position within the line of an otherwise hexametric word may require it to be reshaped so as to comply with the inner metrics of the hexameter, including bridges and caesuras.

Table 27.3   Adaptation of cretic word shape –⏑–

	(*) Proto-form	(*) Scansion 1	Adapted form	Scansion 2
Il. 19.88	ἀγρίην	⏓⏑–	ἄγριον	⏓⏑⏑
Il. 6.469	ἱπποχαίτην	⏓⏑⏓–	ἱππιοχαίτην	⏓⏑⏑⏓–

Table 27.4   Adaptation of tribrachic word shape ⏑⏑⏑

	(*) Proto-form	(*) Scansion 1	Adapted form	Scansion 2
Il. 5.477	μαχόμεϑ(α) ∇–	⏑⏑⏑	μαχόμεσϑ(α)	⏑⏑³
Il. 1.423	Αἰϑίοπας	–⏑⏑⏑	Αἰϑιοπῆας	⏓⏑⏑⏓⏑
Il. 11.270	μογοτόκαι	⏑⏑⏑–	μογοστόκοι	⏑⁴⏑⏑
Il. 2.338	πολέμια	⏑⏑⏑⏑	πολεμήϊα	⏑⏑⏓⏑⏑
Od. 1.143	οἰνοχοέων	–⏑⏑⏑–	οἰνοχοεύων	⏓⏑⏑⏓–

Table 27.5   Adaptation of iambic word shape ⏑–⏑–

	(*) Proto-form	(*) Scansion 1	Adapted form	Scansion 2
Il. 10.364	διωκέτην	⏑–⏑–	διώκετον	⏑⁴⏑⏑
Il. 18.583	λαφυσσέτην	⏑–⏑–	λαφύσσετον	⏑⁴⏑⏑

Table 27.6   Adaptation of trochaic word shape –⏑–⏒

	(*) Proto-form	(*) Scansion 1	Adapted form	Scansion 2
Il. 5.785	χαλκοφώνῳ	–⏑–⏒	χαλκεοφώνῳ	⏓⏑⏑⏓
Od. 6.185	εὐμενέσσι	–⏑–⏑	εὐμενέτῃσι	²⏑⏑³⏑
Il. 2.723	μοχϑέοντα	–⏑–⏑	μοχϑίζοντα	²–³⏑

Table 27.7   Adaptation of antispastic word shape ⏑––⏑

	(*) Proto-form	(*) Scansion 1	Adapted form	Scansion 2
Il. 12.379	Σαρπηδόνος	(⏑)––⏑⏑	Σαρπήδοντος	⏘–²⏑
Od. 2.190	ἀνιηρότερον	⏑––⏑⏑⏑	ἀνιηρέστερον	⏑⁴–⁵⏑⏑

Verse-end position requires a longer word to end in – ⏓. However, if placed verse-internally before ⏘ or the bucolic dieresis (⏓), the same word is subject to the preference rule favoring a dactylic word-end.

As was already seen in the nineteenth century, the avoidance of word-end after spondaic fourth and fifth foot (bucolic bridge: ⁴–⁵, and Meister's bridge: ⁵–⁶, respectively) is tied up with the preference for dactylic word-end before the bucolic dieresis and before the sixth foot (for the fourth foot, see Bekker 1863: 144–7; Witte 1915: 484f.; Meister 1921: 9, 12–22; Witte 1972: 88-90; and for the fifth foot, Bekker 1863: 147f.; Meister 1921: 7f.). These two preference rules creating dactylic word-ends constitute a powerful mechanism behind the frequent dactylization of word-ends in the fourth and fifth foot. In these two positions there is a tendency for trochaic and spondaic word-ends to be reshaped as dactyls, i.e., $\overset{4}{-}/\overset{4}{-}\cup \rightarrow \overset{4}{-}\cup\cup$ and $\overset{5}{-}/\overset{5}{-}\cup \rightarrow \overset{5}{-}\cup\cup$. These mechanisms take effect if a given word is displaced from verse-end to the fifth or fourth foot. For instance, the self-same goatherd who appears at verse-end as nom. Μελανθεύς (*Od.* 17.212, etc.), voc. Μελανθεῦ (*Od.* 21.176), is forced to change his name to nom. Μελάνθιος (*Od.* 17.247, etc.), acc. -ον (*Od.* 21.175) and voc. Μελάνθιε (*Od.* 22.195) before the bucolic dieresis.

Another impressive example is the system of intransitive perfect participles of the shape $\cup\cup --$ (δεδαηκώς), which, when occurring in the fourth and fifth foot, systematically change their ending to middle voice (δεδαημένος) to attain the metrical value $\cup\cup - \cup\cup$; see Hackstein 1997/8: 42–6, 51–3, e.g., |… τετιηότι θυμῷ| (*Il.* 11.555) → |… τετιημένος ἦτορ| (*Il.* 11.556).

Likewise, the spondaic acc. pl. ὀφρῦς "eyebrows" has to be expanded to dactylic ὀφρύας when placed before the bucolic dieresis:

ἀμφοτέρας δ' **ὀφρῦς** σύνελεν λίθος, οὐδέ οἱ ἔσχεν (*Il.* 16.740)
πάντα δέ οἱ βλέφαρ' ἀμφὶ καὶ **ὀφρύας** εὗσεν ἀϋτμὴ (*Od.* 9.389)

The genitive forms of kinship terms normally show the zero-grade suffix -τρ- but expand it to -τερ- before the bucolic dieresis:

μεμνῆσθαι πατρὸς καὶ **μητέρος** ἐν μεγάροισι (*Od.* 18.267)

Before the bucolic dieresis, the pronoun σφίν is changed to σφίσι(ν) (*Il.* 1.368). The preference for dactylic word-end before the bucolic dieresis has generated many artificial nominal compounds of the shape $(\cup)\cup\overset{4}{-}\cup\cup,\overset{4}{-}\cup\cup$; for a collection, see Witte 1972: 50f., 89. Exclusively found in the fourth foot are ἀνόστιμος (*Od.* 4.182, replacing ἄνοστος); περιμήκετον (*Il.* 14.287, *Od.* 6.103, replacing περίμηκες; Witte 1913: 2228ff.; 1915: 484f.); μελανόχροος (*Od.* 19.246, replacing μελανοχροής/μελανοχροίης; Witte 1913: 2230). Verb forms, too, prefer dactylic word-end before the bucolic dieresis. The infinitive ending -εμεν is preferred over -ειν, and the uncontracted endings -εε, -εο (ἔπλεε, αἴδεο) over the contracted ones (Witte 1972: 88).

Depending on its prosodic structure, the displacement of a word before the bucolic dieresis or to line-end position can require it to be augmented by one syllable. This can be done by turning an active form into a middle form as exemplified in tables 27.8–9.

The extension of words at verse-end is amply attested and can be achieved by turning a first-declension genitive singular into a genitive plural (see table 27.9).

Table 27.10 shows how, in other cases, entirely new, artificial, forms can be created.

Table 27.8 Change of active into middle form

Line-end position –ει	Before the bucolic dieresis -εται
. . . ἱϰάνει| (e.g., *Il.* 1.254)	ἱϰάνεται . . . (e.g., *Il.* 10.118)

Table 27.9 Extension of word by change of singular to plural

Verse-internal –η	Line-end position -άων
ἱπποσύνη (*Il.* 16.809)	ἱπποσυνάων (*Il.* 16. 776)
	τεϰτοσυνάων (*Od.* 5.250)

Table 27.10 Creation of artificial forms

Verse-internal -ον	Line-end position -ῆα
βάλ' **ἡνίοχον** θεϱάποντα| (*Il.* 5.580)	**ἡνιοχῆα**| . . . βάλε (*Il.* 8.312)
Ἀντιφάταο (*Od.* 10.106)	Ἀντιφατῆα (*Od.* 10.114, hapax)

Owing to its trochaic word shape, the abstract noun ποτή "drink" can only be used verse-internally, e.g., dative ποτῇ (*Od.* 5.337). In verse-final position the word must be reshaped. At verse-end, the genitive ποτῆς is artificially expanded to ποτῆτος: ἐδητύος ἠδὲ ποτῆτος "of food and drink" (*Il.* 11.780). ποτῆτος represents an infringement of the early Greek word-formational rule requiring abstract nouns in -της, -τητος to be formed only from adjectives and agent nouns designating persons (Meister 1921: 30f.; Fraenkel 1952: 145). The underlying ποτή, however, is an abstract noun.

In sum, the placement of a word at verse-end has a twofold linguistic effect. It favors the preservation of archaisms, such as the highly archaic acc. Ζῆν, or the instr. pl. δεξιτεϱῆφι and many other linguistic retentions. At the same time, the verse-end shows a potential for generating innovative and artificial forms on metrical grounds. For more examples, see Meister 1921: 30f, 172ff., 241ff.

Analogy

Analogy is another prime factor underlying the reshaping of words. If a word occurs within a formula, then normally it will maintain its syllabic structure (even contravening normal morphological rules) when the formula, and the word within it, is inflected. This concept of "inflection with metrical equivalence" is a guiding principle of formulaic inflection (see Witte 1913: 2214; 1972: 139; Latacz 2000: 49f.).

For example, the epithet εὐϱύοπα "wide-eyed," an accusative in origin and as such justified only in juxtaposition with an accusative (specifically, the highly archaic accusative Ζῆν), comes to modify the vocative Ζεῦ under the same metrical conditions:

... εὐρύοπα Ζῆν| Zeus of the broad brows (*Il.* 8.206).
... εὐρύοπα Ζεῦ| (*Il.* 16.241).

The verse-end formula μερόπων ἀνθρώπων| (7x *Il.*) acquires a nom. pl. μέροπες ἄνθρωποι| (*Il.* 18.288) by analogy (cf. West 1982: 39), even at the expense of a metrical violation scanning μέροπες as ∪∪⁻.

Verse-end position requires active verb forms to shift to middle inflection in the 3 pl. preterite, e.g., ... εἰσορόωντι| (*Il.* 23.464) becomes ... εἰσορόωντο| (*Il.* 23.448); ... μητιόωντι| (*Il.* 18.312) becomes ... μητιόωντο| (*Il.* 12.17); ... ὑλάουσι| (*Od.* 16.9) becomes ... ὑλάοντο| (*Od.* 16.162).

The Prehistory of the Greek Hexameter: Linguistic or Metrical Archaism?

(On some of the issues addressed here, see also ch. 24.) Many scholars from the late nineteenth century onwards (Witte 1913, 1972; West 1973a: 188; Watkins 1963b: 199f.) have pointed out that the hexameter may have arisen from the conjunction of two shorter verses, an octosyllabic plus a heptasyllabic verse – henceforth the conjunction theory. (For a survey of the research, see Sicking 1993: 70f.; Hackstein 2002: 8f.; Hajnal 2003b: 70–9.) Two basic variants were proposed (see Hajnal 2003b: 74f. for a recent summary):

Type A: glyconean + pherecratean: |××–∪∪–∪⁴| + | ××–∪∪––|.
Type B: choriambic dimeter + pherecratean: | ××××–∪∪⁴| + | ××–∪∪––|.

(Note that "×" stands for a syllable that can be either short or long.) An assessment of the conjunction theory must take into account that, first, the presumed origin of the hexameter as the conjunction of two shorter verses is not just an abstract postulation since it finds a concrete precedent in the Indian Śloka, which is certain to have arisen out of the conjunction of two shorter verse types attested in Vedic; second, the proposed origin of the hexameter has explanatory power. It is capable of accounting for certain anomalies found in the hexameter, and it explains some constraints of the inner metrics (metrical syntax) of the hexameter.

Starting with metrical anomalies, the conjunction theory opens the door to an entirely different metrical assessment of a phrase like ἀνδροτῆτα καὶ ἥβην "manhood and youth" (on which, see also ch. 24) and its metrically irregular trochee ἀνδρο- in the biceps of the fourth foot, since there is a different way to apply Meillet's principle (anomalies as possible archaisms) to the line in question. Instead of explaining a synchronic metrical irregularity as a linguistic archaism, it is also possible to explain the metrical irregularity as a metrical archaism. (On the special role of the fourth foot of the hexameter, see Tichy 1981 and Hajnal 2003b: 77ff., neither of whom mentions Witte's detailed observations, reprinted in Witte 1972: 83ff., 88ff.)

Indeed, the metrical irregularities found in the epic hexameter often occur at the caesura at the join of the two cola of the proto-hexameter, i.e., in the fourth foot.

Metrical irregularities of the hexameter such as a trochaic biceps in the fourth foot then resolve to metrical regularity if seen as the Aeolic base (××) at the beginning of the second colon. Thus some of the metrical anomalies indeed stand a chance of being metrical archaisms; see Tichy 1981; Hackstein 2002: 10ff.; Hajnal 2003b: 70ff., 76f., 84; Rix 2005: 387. For instance, anomalous verse elements of the shape ⊥ ⌣/⌣– or (⁴) – ⌣⁵ (στίχοι ἀκέφαλοι "headless verses" and λαγαροί "sunken [verses]") can be explained as a continuation of the Aeolic base.

Turning to the inner metrics, it has gone unnoticed so far that the posited antecedent of the Homeric hexameter explains not only irregularities but also regular limitations and preference rules of the meter, in particular the preference for dactylic word-end over a spondaic word-end before the bucolic dieresis and before the sixth foot (on which, see also above).

The presumed onset of the second half of the protohexameter was ×× ⌣⁵ ⌣⌣⁶–, and directly upon the change from syllable-counting meter to quantitative meter the Aeolic base ×× at first remained disyllabic, i.e., pyrrhic (⌣⌣), so that at verse-end the structure ⌣⌣⁵⌣⌣⁶– came closest to the shape of the proto-hexameter, preserving the disyllabicity of the Aeolic base and the choriambic element ⌣⁵ ⌣⌣⁶. Put differently, placing ⌣⌣–⌣⌣ in the fifth foot was ideal. This is the underlying motivation for Meister's bridge, i.e., the preference for dactylic word-end before the sixth princeps.[6]

Relatable to this same phenomenon, the shift of ××⁵ to ⌣⌣⁵, are the preference for dactylic word-end before the fifth princeps (bucolic dieresis), and, Witte's pyrrhic prefix (⌣⌣ +⁵). Witte (1972: 65ff., 68–70) observed the tendency of verse-end word types of the adonean shape (⁵ ⌣⌣⁶–) to be (artificially) prefixed by a pyrrhic biceps – i.e., ⁵ ⌣⌣⁶– is extended to ⌣⌣ +⁵⌣⌣⁶–. The pyrrhic prefixation rule (or tendency) is necessary to fill the empty slot of the pherecratean, e.g., τεθνηῶτος (⁵–⁶ ⌣, *Il.* 9.633) → κατατεθνηῶτος (⌣⌣⁵–⁶⌣, *Il.* 7.89), *ἅρματα ἄξω (⁵ ⌣⌣⁶–) → κατά θ' ἅρματα ἄξω (⌣⌣⁵⌣⌣⁶–, *Il.* 8.403).

Finally, the posited seam between the two halves of the protohexameter, i.e., after ⁴ |⁷, accounts for the absence of a caesura after the fourth trochee, i.e., after ⁴|⁷ ⌣, because a metrical or syntactic pause after a monosyllabic first element of a verse is unlikely.

In sum, some of the preference rules concerning the inner metrics of the hexameter can readily be understood as continuations of the protohexameter.

The Poetic Exploitation of Diachronic Variants

The poets exploit linguistic variation to ensure formulaic flexibility. This holds true not only for synchronic but also for diachronic variation. Thus, it is not rare for phonemic change to be indirectly exploited by the poets. Owing to its long prehistory, epic Greek often preserves the same morphemes and words at different developmental stages. The poets, though unaware of the diachronic changes per se, were quite aware of their reflexes in attested formulae of the language and interpreted diachronic variants as free variants, which then led to their use as metrical alternatives. This can be exemplified by three cases: the loss and metrical reflection of the phoneme *digamma*; the assimilation of certain word-initial clusters to simple consonants; and the sandhi-conditioned syllabification of *muta cum liquida* clusters.

Digamma

Though lost in Ionic before the beginning of the textual transmission of alphabetic Greek in the eighth century, *digamma* never ceased to be reflected metrically (Ludwich 1885: 29ff., 270–87; Chantraine 1973: 116–57; Wachter 2000: 72f.). The historic reality of *digamma* is impressively demonstrated by Doric and Aeolic adaptations of certain Homeric formulae, notably Διὶ Κρονίωνι ἄνακτι (*Il.* 7.200), translated into sixth-century Doric as Δὶ ϙρονίōνι ϝάνακτι (*CEG* 362.1), and Ποσειδάωνι ἄνακτι (*Il.* 15.57), translated into seventh-century Corinthian as Ποτε͂δᾶϝο͂νι ϝανακτι (*CEG* 357; Corinthian *pinakes* 3 (Wachter 2001): 125, 327).

Once it was lost phonetically, *digamma* was replaced by a lexically defined list of exceptions: the onsets of certain vowel-initial words acquired the potential for (i) making position, (ii) leaving preceding final vowels unelided, and (iii) leaving preceding final diphthongs or long vowels uncorrepted, e.g:

(i) τὸν δ' ὁ γέρων Πρίαμος **πρῶτος (*ϝ)ἴδεν** ὀφθαλμοῖσιν (–⁴ ϝ‿, *Il.* 22.25)
(i) ... χαριζομένη **πόσεϊ (*sϝ)** ᾧ (‿‿⁶ sϝ–, *Il.* 5.71)
(ii) ἔνθά κεν **οὐκέτι (*ϝ)ἔργον** ἀνὴρ ὀνόσαιτο μετελθών (²‿‿ ϝ³‿, *Il.* 4.539)
(iii) ἄρνε δύω **καὶ (*ϝ)οἶνον** εὔφρονα, καρπὸν ἀρούρης (– ϝ³‿, *Il.* 3.246)

(Note that the portions of the text above in bold face correspond to the metrical analysis in brackets.) In the aftermath of the phonemic loss of *digamma*, the rules for its metrical observance came to be relaxed through two processes, namely analogy and contextual ambiguity. In the course of analogical formulaic inflection, the position-making of *digamma* and the non-elision before digammatic onset were sometimes suspended, e.g., allowing μελιηδέα (*ϝ)οἶνον (*Il.* 10. 579) to form the genitive μελιηδέος (Ø)οἴνου (*Il.* 18.545); see Hoekstra 1965: 48.

The faithfulness of *digamma* reflexes and the aversion to analogical spread can be demonstrated by minimal pairs such as the reflexive and possessive pronoun (ϝ)ος and the relative ὅς or demonstrative ὅ(ς). Crucially, their phonetic coalescence within Ionic has not led to their metrical merger. Compare the position-making reflexive ᾧ in Πηλεὺς **μὲν ᾧ** [²–] παιδὶ γέρων ἐπέτελλ' Ἀχιλῆϊ (*Il.* 11.783) to relative ᾧ not making position in χάλκεον, ᾧ πέρι (¹‿‿² ‿‿, *Il.* 23.561). Or compare the hiatus-breaking reflexive ὅν in οὐδὲ Σκάμανδρος ἔληγε **τὸ ὃν μένος** [‿⁴‿‿], ἀλλ' ἔτι μᾶλλον (*Il.* 21.305) to relative ὅν not making position in οὐ γὰρ ἔα πόνος **ἄλλος, ὃν** (³ ‿) Ἀργυρότοξος ἔγειρεν (*Il.* 5.517). The two pronouns may be found metrically contrasting even within the same line, as in Πάτροκλον, |³ **ὃν** (² ‿) **ἑταῖρον·ὃ** (³‿‿) δ' ἐν πυρὶ βάλλε θυηλάς (*Il.* 9.220).

Assimilation

Another case of phonemic change reflected in the metrics is that of initial /s/ plus resonant clusters, i.e., *sn*, *sl*, and (less often) *sm*. Such onsets ran through an intermediate stage as geminates *nn*, *ll*, *mm*, until they ultimately were simplified to *n*, *l*, *m* (La Roche 1869: 46–65; Chantraine 1973: 175–7; Eben 2004).

a) Occasionally the meter reflects the double position-making of such onsets. In these cases, the resonant onset is always preceded by a princeps plus caesura:

αἶψα δ' ἐπὶ νευρῇ κατεκόσμει πικρὸν ὀϊστόν (‿²sn‿³, *Il.* 4.118)
καὶ ἔπεα νιφάδεσσιν ἐοικότα χειμερίῃσιν (‿‿²sn‿‿³‿, *Il.* 3.222)
Ἠνοπίδην, ὃν ἄρα νύμφη τέκε νηῒς ἀμύμων (‿³sn‿⁴, *Il.* 14.444)
θυγατέρες δ' ἀνὰ δώματ' ἰδὲ νυοὶ ὠδύροντο (‿⁴sn‿‿, *Il.* 24.166)

b) As in the case of *digamma*, the position-making in these cases can be suspended:

... ποτε νύμφη | (‿‿sn‿⁶‿, *Il.* 6.21; PIE root **sneubʰ-*)
... εἵνεκα νύμφης | (≟ ‿‿ sn‿⁶‿, *Il.* 9.560)
ἑλκομένας τε νυοὺς ... (‿¹‿‿²‿ sn ‿³, *Il.* 22.65; PIE **snusos*)

c) In contrast with the treatment of *digamma*, the position-making ability of initial *n-, m-, l-* is extended beyond its original etymological bounds, i.e., to words with initial non-geminate *m-/n-/l-*:

| ... τέκετο **νεφεληγερέτα** Ζεύς| (‿³‿‿, *Il.* 20.215; νεφ- < PIE **nebʰ-*)
|ἔλπομαι ἐκτελέεσθαι, **ἵνα μὴ** ῥέξομεν ὧδε | (‿⁴-, *Il.* 7.353; μή < PIE **mḗ*)
|τῷ δ' ἄρ' ὑπὸ **μήτηρ** μοῦνον τέκεν Ἰλιονῆα| (‿²-³, *Il.* 14.492; μήτηρ < PIE **méh₂tēr*)
|χρυσέῳ ἐν δέπαϊ, **ὄφρα λείψαντε** κιοίτην | (-⁴-, *Il.* 24.285 = *Od.* 15.149; λειπ- < PIE **leib*)

Muta cum liquida

A final case of the artificial exploitation of linguistic variants is the treatment of *muta cum liquida* (La Roche 1869: 1–45; Wathelet 1966; Chantraine 1973: 108–11). By contrast with *digamma* and resonant clusters, we are dealing here not with developmental variants but with synchronic sandhi-variants.

a) Word-internally between vowels, *muta cum liquida* is heterosyllabic with long scansion of the preceding syllable, e.g.,

|πολλάκι γάρ σεο **πατ.ρὸς** ἐνὶ μεγάροισιν ἄκουσα| (*Il.* 1.396).

(Note that the dot indicates syllable boundary.)

b) Word-initially, *muta cum liquida* normally is tautosyllabic with the short scansion of the preceding syllable, as seen in:

|καί μιν φωνήσας ἔπεα πτερόεντα **.προσηύδα**| (*Il.* 1.201)

This is especially so when a caesura intervenes, e.g. the feminine caesura:

|νηῒ πολυκ.λήϊδι **.πλέων** ἐπὶ οἴνοπα πόντον| (*Il.* 7.88)
|ἀντίον ἀΐσσουσι **.θρασειάων** ἀπὸ χειρῶν| (*Il.* 11.553)
ὣς οἱ μὲν ποιαῦτα **.πρὸς** ἀλλήλους ἀγόρευον| (*Od.* 4.620)

c) When preceded by a clitic, however, or when part of a word-group, post-vocalic word-initial *muta cum liquida* may either show the word-internal treatment as per rule *a)*, or else rule *b)* applies: cf. heterosyllabic treatment after clitic με in μή με π.ρίν (⌣–⌣, *Il.* 19.306), but otherwise tautosyllabic treatment in τέρπετο, .πρίν (⌣⌣⌣, *Il.* 19.313); heterosyllabic treatment after clitic προ in ἀλλὰ π.ρὸ Τρώων (⌣–⌣–⌣, *Il.* 24.215), but otherwise tautosyllabic treatment in κυρτὰ φαληριόωντα, |ᵗʳ πρὸ μέν τ' ἄλλ', αὐτὰρ ἔπ' ἄλλα (⌣⌣⌣, *Il.* 13.799).

d) Rules *a–c* may be suspended due to metrical necessity: Ἀφροδίτη (⌣⌣ _ _, *Il.* 2.820); Ἀμφι.τρύωνος (_ ⌣⌣_ ⌣, *Il.* 5.392); φαρέτρης (⌣⌣⌣, *Il.*8.323).

e) The two possibilities of syllabifying *muta cum liquida* clusters are sandhi variants in origin, but were consciously exploited by the poets for metrical purposes. For instance, to accommodate longer words in the hexameter, the poet can avail himself of either option for the same word depending on metrical needs. Compare μή μοι, Πάτ.ροκ.λε, σκυδμαινέμεν, αἴ κε πύθηαι (*Il.* 24.592) with Πάτ.ρο.κλέ μοι δειλῇ πλεῖστον κεχαρισμένε θυμῷ (*Il.* 19.287) and τὸν μὲν ἐγὼ δάκ.ρυσα ἰδὼν ἐλέησά τε θυμῷ (*Od.* 11.55) with φῇ δὲ δα.κρυπλώειν βεβαρηότα με φρένας οἴνῳ (*Od.* 19.122).

Epithets, Formulae, and Language Change

During the long prehistory of the oral tradition of verse-making, there never was a linguistic standstill. Despite the absence of attested Mycenaean poetry and despite the Dark Ages it can occasionally be proven that poetic words were liable to semantic change before the eighth century. A case in point involves the epithets ξουθός "golden yellow, rapidly moving to and fro" (*Hymn. Hom.* 33.13), αἰόλος "quick-moving, nimble" (epithet of horses), κορυθαίολος "moving the helmet quickly, with glancing helmet." These occur as poetic epithets in both Homer and Hesiod. Crucially, their Mycenaean counterparts *aiwolos* and *ksouthos* differ in being non-poetic words and designating cattle, a prosaic usage which is no longer found in Homer. Their semantic divergence and non-poetic status in turn marks ξουθός and αἰόλος as components of a post-Mycenaean poetic language (Risch 1992: 91).

A formula may contain archaisms that have fallen out of use. The obsolete and archaic character of words is frequently revealed:

a) by formulaic inflection violating the historically expected inflection, e.g., acc. εὐρύοπα Ζῆν >> voc. (*acc.!) εὐρύοπα Ζεῦ, see above;

b) by reanalysis, e.g., ἀγγελίην ἐλθόντα "coming [to give] message (= ἀγγελίη)" (*Il.* 11.140) is reanalyzed as "coming as messenger (= ἀγγελίης)," (Forssman 1974);

c) by the post-Homeric employment of Homeric epithets, e.g. Homeric ἀτρύγετος (m. = f.) "undryable" (Vine 1998: 62–4), a compound adjective in contrast to Stesichoros' (seventh cent.) innovative treatment of ἀτρύγετος as a simplex adjective with new feminine form ἀτρυγέτα as in δι' αἰθέρος ἀτρυγέτᾱς (32.I.4P);

d)   by the fact that early glossators (from the sixth cent. BCE; Latacz 2003a: 14f.)
       deemed poetic words and phrases worth being glossed;
e)   by an epithet coming to be traditional and habitual to such a degree that it has
       undergone semantic bleaching. The context-independent use of such epithets
       may (but need not) be indicative of such a situation, for examples see Latacz
       2000: 39–42 on the so-called ἀδύνατα-verses.

An instructive summary is presented by Edwards 1997: 272–7 ("Do formulaic
epithets have any meaning?") and Latacz 2000: 39–59. The cumulation of (quasi)
synonymous formulae attests to the semantic bleaching of formulae, which over the
course of time underwent routinization, generalization, and automization, a natural
process observable already in the *Iliad* and *Odyssey*. The contamination or cumulation of speech-act formulae have been regarded as the model case (Witte 1972:
9–14) to show that formulae can lose their function. For example, the simple speech
introduction εἶπε|ᵗʳ placed before the trochaic caesura (*Il.* 17.237, 20.375) and |ᵗʳ ἔπος
τ᾽ ἔφατ᾽ ἔκ τ᾽ὀνόμαζε "made a speech and named (him)" (*Od.* 2.302, 3.374, 4.311) are
combined to yield the pleonastic combination εὐχόμενος δ᾽ ἄρα εἶπεν|ᵗʳ ἔπος τ᾽ ἔφατ᾽ ἔκ
τ᾽ ὀνόμαζε (*Od.* 8.330). Cratinus (fragm. 355 *PCG* IV: 294) is reported to have made
fun of Homer διά τὸ πλεονάσαι ἐν τῷ "τὸν δ᾽ ἀπαμειβόμενος" "because of his pleonastic
use of 'τὸν δ᾽ ἀπαμειβόμενος'" (Witte 1972: 11 n. 2).[7]

Formulae and poetic freedom

Like meter, formulae, despite their limiting influence, do not dictate the diction of
epic. The poet is free to coin new expressions and formulae. The poet's unrestricted
creativity and flexibility becomes especially manifest in the case of word-games. Word-
games show the poet at work, deliberately playing with words for poetic purposes.
Especially noteworthy are mimetic word-games. (Consider also the mimetic use of
the meter; West 1997b: 232f.) In *Od.* 4.451–3 the confusion of Proteus, who is
unable to distinguish his seals from Odysseus' comrades hiding among the seals, is
mirrored by the alliterating and partially homonymic succession of λέκτο-λέγε-λέκτο,
presenting a confusingly similar phonic structure (parechesis) overlaid on two altogether different verbs; on parechesis, see the recent summaries by Latacz 2000: 51
and Hackstein 2007: 103–13, to which add Bekker 1863: 185–95. At *Il.* 1.291, the
rage of Achilles is mirrored by the omission of the reduplicating syllable in προ-
[τι]θέουσιν (Hackstein 2002: 114f.; 2007: 111).

The Impact of Hexametric Greek

Inscriptional epic Greek and para-Homeric elements

The earliest attested vestiges of epic Greek (taken as a purely linguistic label) are
inscriptional. The earliest attestations are the dipylon vase inscription (*CEG* I 432)
and the Nestor's Cup inscription (*CEG* I 454; see also ch. 4), which can be transcribed as follows:

Νέστορός ἐμι εὔποτον ποτήριον·
ὃς δ᾽ ἂν τόδε πίησι ποτηρίο᾽ αὐτίκα κῆνον
ἵμερος αἱρήσει καλλιστεφάνō Ἀφροδίτης.

I am the cup of Nestor, good to drink from:
Whoever drinks from this cup, right away
Longing for Aphrodite of the beautiful crown will seize him.

(For a commentary, see Watkins 1976a.) The inscription contains three verses, two epic-style hexameters, and at the beginning an iambic trimeter with choriambic onset (this is a metrical mixture typical of parodistic poetry; cf. West 1982: 40 n. 27). Although this and the dipylon vase inscription slightly postdate the *Iliad* and the *Odyssey*, their value is heightened by the fact that they are the earliest attested documents of epic diction, greatly antedating the earliest transmitted documents of the Homeric epics.

Both inscriptions are neither exclusively dependent on nor solely repetitive of Homeric diction. Instead of copying, they are innovative in coining epithets and phrases not found in the *Iliad* and *Odyssey*. Such non-Homeric words and phrases, however, can be shown to be generated by the same generative mechanisms that lie behind the diction of the large-scale epics *Iliad* and *Odyssey*. For instance, the compound καλλιστέφανος "with beautiful crown" found in the third line of the cup inscription, has no direct counterpart in Homer. Yet it can be generated by a technique attested in Homer that requires compound initial ἐü- after the trochaic caesura to change to καλλι- after the penthemimeres (Risch 1987: 7–9). Just as ἐüπλόκαμος "with beautiful locks" ($|^{tr} \cup {}^{4} \cup \cup {}^{5}$, *Il.* 11.624) alternates with καλλιπλοκάμῳ ($|^{5-} {}^{4} \cup \cup {}^{5}$, *Il.* 18.592), so ἐüστεφάνου ($|^{tr} \cup {}^{4} \cup \cup {}^{5}$, *Od.* 8.288) would automatically change to καλλιστεφάνου, if placed after the penthemimeres, hence καλλιστεφάνō ($|^{5-} {}^{4} \cup \cup {}^{5}$, *CEG* I 423,3). While unattested in Homer, the non-Homeric compound καλλιστέφανος of the cup inscription is nevertheless generated by epic techniques implicit in Homer. The suppletive formulaic-metrical system, interchanging ἐü- and καλλι- in compounds, was already available in the eight century BCE both to Homer and to contemporaneous composers of inscriptions. Hence the generative mechanism is very likely not a Homeric invention but an older part of the traditional oral language predating Homer. It is para-Homeric.

In the same vein, the second line of the Nestor's Cup inscription ὃς δ᾽ ἂν τόδε πίησι "whoever drinks from this <cup>", as in ὃς δ᾽ ἂν με κλέφσει "whoever steals me" (W. Ion., Cumae, seventh cent. BCE; *DGE* 786 = *IG* xiv 865) and Homeric ὅς δέ κε can be brought together as involving both a pre-Homeric formula and pre-Homeric technique. The interchange of inscriptional ἄν and Homeric κε(ν) is governed by metrical and stylistic factors. In Homer, κε(ν) is predominantly placed in the thesis of a dactylic foot, while ἄν is placed in the thesis of a spondaic foot (Witte 1972: 187). The selection of an aeolicism is the mark of an elevated solemn style (Hackstein 2002: 43; Peters 1998: 587 n. 38).

Beyond the formula, other indications are also provided by morphological and orthographical peculiarities. Thus the Nestor's Cup inscription preserves the archaic long-vowel subjunctive ending and the old ablative ending in their older guise without *iota adscriptum*, as -ησι and -ω: πίησι, τῶδε. The endings and their spelling without *iota adscriptum* represent an archaism; the later literary epic tradition introduced the analogical spelling -ηισι and -ωι with unetymological iota in the course of the transmission after the eighth century.

Homeric echoes and independent traditions

By contrast to the earliest inscriptional Greek, which is not strictly dependent on Homer and may reflect para-Homeric traditions, the later Greek of epic becomes increasingly dependent on Homer. The literature subsequent to Homer is influenced by Homeric diction in many ways. (On the formative influence of Homeric Greek, see in general Hunter 2006.) Especially instructive in this respect are complex and all-pervasive Homeric systems of artistic variation. Such systems can be shown to have been faithfully replicated by later epic poets.

An example is the Homeric system of resonant lengthening, recently studied by Eben (2004: 101–29) and see also above. Post-Homeric poets preserve this Homeric system, and there is "no wholesale generalization of a disembodied license to any and all words beginning with a resonant" (Eben 2004: 101).

Another example is the complex interchange of active and middle endings in a metrically and lexically defined class of perfect stems; see Hackstein (1997/8: 38–46, 51–3). It is more common for Hellenistic and later epic writers to reproduce quasimechanically Homeric systems than to consciously revive and innovatively extend them beyond their original Homeric lexical domains (Hackstein 1997/8: 40). The Homeric system which stipulates that intransitive active perfect participles of the metrical shape ⏑⏑––, if placed in the fourth or fifth foot, be replaced by ⏑⏑–⏑⏑, is repeated for the same lexical items by later poets (see tables 27.11 and 12).

Table 27.11   The Homeric system of perfect endings

(1)	βεβαρηώς *	[⏑⏑⁴–]	→	βεβαρημένος	(⏑⏑⁴⏑⏑)
(2)	δεδαηκώς *	(⏑⏑⁴–)	→	δεδαημένος	(⏑⏑⁴⏑⏑)
(3)	τετιηώς *	(⏑⏑⁵–)	→	τετιημένος	(⏑⏑⁵⏑⏑)
(4)	κεχαρηώς *	(⏑⏑⁴–)	→	κεχαρημένος	(⏑⏑⁴⏑⏑)
(5)	κεκορηώς *	(⏑⏑⁴–)	→	κεκορημένος	(⏑⏑⁴⏑⏑)

Table 27.12   The post-Homeric system of perfect endings

	Ap. Rhodius	Theocritus	Nicander	Oppian	Nonnus
(1')	βεβαρημένος		βεβαρημένος		βεβαρημένος
(2')	δεδαημένος			δεδαημένος	δεδαημένος
(3')	τετιημένος			τετιημένος	
(4')	κεχαρημένος	κεχαρημένος	κεχαρημένος	κεχαρημένος	
(5')		κεκορημένος			

Translation and intertextuality

The practice of translating hexametric epic poetry from one Greek dialect into another is widely attested. Instructive examples are the Boeotian translations of Homeric formulae. Thus the Boeotian rendering of two Homeric verse-end formulae, ἀργυρότοξος Ἀπόλλων "silver-bowed Apollo" (e.g., *Il.* 2.766) and δίδου χαρίεσσαν ἀμοιβήν "give recompense full of charm" (*Od.* 3.58) is contained in the oldest datable inscription from Boeotia:

Μάντικλός μ' ἀνέθεκε ϝεκαβόλοι ἀργυροτόξξοι
τᾶς {δ}ε|κάτας· τὺ δέ, Φοῖβε, δίδοι, χαρίϝετταν ἀμοιϝ[άν]

Mantiklos donated me from his tithe to Apollo shooting/hitting from afar with the silver bow. You, Phoebos, give me a pleasant recompense.(700–675 BCE; *CEG* 326)

(For commentary, see Wachter 2001: 119-123 and West 1981: 120.) Similarly, the verse-end formula ἑκηβόλῳ Ἀπόλλωνι (e.g., *Il.* 1.438) recurs in Boeotian as καλϝὸν ἄγαλμα ϝάνακτι ϝ[εκαβόλοι Ἀ|πόλονι:] (*c.* 550–525 BCE; *CEG* I 334,1). This state of affairs very likely had a prehistory reaching back several centuries and may plausibly have served as a catalyst for the diffusion of dialect features; cf. Horrocks 1997b: 214–17.

To be distinguished from synchronic, interdialectal translations like these, there is also intertextuality of the diachronic kind. Particularly instructive are Corinthian inscriptions which, although postdating Homer's eighth-century Ionic by one or two centuries, still represent epic formulae in their pre-eighth-century linguistic guise.

To take an example, Corinthian vase inscriptions preserve *digamma* in the sixth century where epic Ionic had already lost it two centuries before: cf. cases like Corinthian sixth-century ϝιφι-κλεδας (Getty Handbook 2002: 55) in contrast to eighth-century Homeric Ἰφι-άνασσα (*Il.* 9.145) or the formula [αὐτῷ] δέ ϝοι [ὅλπα] (*c.* 580–575 BCE; *CEG* I 452,2) in contrast to Homeric [τὼ] δέ οἱ [ὄσσε] (e.g., *Il.* 13.616), ἠδέ οἱ αὐτῷ (*Il.* 15.226). The sixth-century knowledge of epic ϝιφι- and δέ ϝοι can be straightforwardly explained by an oral para-Homeric transmission line extending from sixth-century Corinthian back to the Dark Ages when digammatic onsets were still present.

Homeric echoes in Greek prose

Homeric echoes in Greek are not confined to poetic literature. They are also frequently found in Herodotus, who was perceived as ὁμηρικώτατος "most Homeric" already in antiquity (Long. *Subl.* 13.3), e.g., κοῖον ἐφθέξαο ἔπος "what word did you utter?" (Hdt. 5.106), οἷον ἐφθέγξαο ἔπος (Hdt. 7.103). In many cases Herodotus even goes so far as to maintain the hexametric structure of such Homeric phrases, which serve the stylistic purpose of solemnification. A collection of examples is provided by Mansour 2007. See also Mansour 2007: 158f. on Homeric speech-act formulae and Witte 1972: 9ff., to which add Leumann 1950: 303–8. For the diffusion of poetic words outside poetic literature, see Leumann 1950: 262–320.

FURTHER READING

For the most recent survey of research on Homeric Greek, see Meier-Brügger 2003a. Wachter 2000 is a 48-page descriptive account of the phonology, morphology, and syntax of Homeric Greek. For the linguistic and metrical prehistory of epic Greek poetry, see West 1973a and 1988. On the relationship between Homeric and Mycenaean Greek, see Hajnal 1998. West 1997b gives a concise and accessible description of Homer's meter, and for the metrical placement of words in the hexameter, see West 1997b: 224–6 and Clark 2004: 120–3. A concise and accessible survey of research on the issue of formularity of epic diction is provided by Latacz 2000: 39–59. Bakker 2005: 1–37 covers the complexity of factors determining the semantics of epithets and ornamental adjectives. On Homer and the Near East, see Morris 1997. On the transmission of myths and themes, and on linguistic issues involving language contact, see Watkins 1998 and Hajnal 2003b.

NOTES

1 For examples, see Hackstein 2002: 17f., and for partial or complete lexical renewal in fixed expressions, Meid 1978 and Hackstein 2006: 95f.

2 Despite the etymological difference between Gk ἐάων from PIE *h_1esu- "good" and Ved. *vasu*- "good" from PIE *h_1wesu-, the two words very likely were either synchronically suppletive lexemes in PIE or replaced each other diachronically, thus providing another case of lexical substitution and renewal in inherited formulae. See also ch. 24.

3 It is possible that later documents may attest archaisms that are absent from earlier documents (Hackstein 2002: 81–7); linguistic gaps due to accidents of attestation do occur. To name another example, Gk πέρυσι "last year" – an archaism of PIE date – is accidentally unattested in the Homeric epics, in contrast to its attestation in Myc. *pe-ru-si-no-wo* and choral lyric. The poetic word ἔαρ "blood," an archaic heteroclitic noun inherited from PIE and akin to Hitt. *eshar*, Skt *ásr̥j*- (PIE *$hₑeshₐ-r̥$), is unattested before the Hellenistic period, but preserved as prose term for blood and lexical archaism in Cyprian (ἔαρ αἷμα. Κύπριοι Hsch. sub ε-31).

4 Nevertheless, it is likely that the eighth-century version of the text already had the contracted forms, so that this metrically based reconstruction runs a certain risk of editorial archaization of the text; see Führer and Schmidt 2001: 18 and Hackstein 2002: 19, 21, 91. Meier-Brügger 2003a: 240 marks the -oo forms with an asterisk, for they are nowhere so transmitted.

5 This deviation is explainable from metrical necessity. The expected scansion τέτ.ρά- is actually attested in *Od.* 9.242 ἐσθλαὶ τέτ.ράκυ.κλοι (² ᷉³) ἀπ' οὔδεος ὀχλίσσειαν.

6 The glyconean stipulates that the fifth foot be dactylic; cf. Hajnal 2003b: 74 n. 117. According to the statistics of O'Neill (1942) a long monosyllabic never occurs in the thesis of the fifth foot.

7   It must be noted, though, that the doubling of speech-act verbs is not necessarily just redundant and artificial by virtue of its pleonastic nature, rather it can be an authentic component of oral grammar. This holds true for the speech-act construction with double speech-act verb, as exemplified by τὴν δὲ Πάρις μύθοισιν ἀμειβόμενος προσέειπε (*Il.* 3.437). The second speech-act verb is functional in marking the transition from narrative to direct speech. This construction was first documented by Kieckers (1912 and 1913) for all Indo-European languages and a number of non-Indo-European languages.

CHAPTER TWENTY-EIGHT

The Language of Greek Lyric Poetry

Michael Silk

"Greek lyric poetry" is the long-established name for the words of Greek song: words, minus music. Despite many endeavors (e.g., West 1992, Mathiesen 1999), the effect of Greek music, and its significance for the words of Greek song in particular, is lost to us – except that we do possess the rhythms of Greek song in the shape of what is customarily called Greek lyric meter (see ch. 25). As far as the poetry is concerned, in any event, the loss is less serious than might be supposed, because ancient testimony, from the Classical period (Pratin. *Lyr.* 708, 6–7 *PMG* and Pl. *Resp.* 398 c–d; cf. West 1992: 39), makes it clear that the music (unlike the music most of us are used to) was strictly subsidiary to the words themselves.

The scope of Greek song extends beyond what is usually discussed under the heading of Greek lyric poetry, insofar as it is usual to exclude from "Greek lyric" the many songs in Attic drama (but see, e.g., Hutchinson 2001). There are good reasons, though, for considering dramatic and non-dramatic song on a par. In this chapter, accordingly, "Greek lyric poetry" and (the words of) "Greek song" are effectively synonymous; and the two designations will be used indifferently here.

Song implies performance; and Greek song subsumes two types of performance, monodic (solo) and choral (group), and various performative contexts. Songs may involve public devotion (like paeans to the god Apollo) or private ritual (like wedding songs). They may be public and celebratory (like epinician "victory odes") or more intimate (like love songs, satirical songs, drinking songs); functional in an immediate sense (like work songs, traces of which are preserved among the surviving bits and pieces of ancient "folk song") or elements of a larger artistic entity – like the lyrics of Attic drama, which, collectively, constitute roughly half (and, along with Pindar's epinicians, much the best-preserved part) of Greek lyric poetry as a whole. Songs of various kinds were composed throughout antiquity; this discussion will confine itself to the Archaic and earlier Classical periods, from the seventh to the fifth centuries BCE.

Alongside song proper, the Greeks of this period also composed a variety of semi-musical types of verse, from the (solo) elegiac and iambic poetry of Archilochus in the late seventh century to the (usually choral) "recitative" poetry of Attic drama in the fifth. These types (or at least their non-dramatic versions) are sometimes subsumed under the heading of "lyric poetry" (as by, e.g., Fowler 1987), but will not be so subsumed here.

Our concern, therefore, is with the Greek of Archaic and Classical sung poetry, beyond, or within, drama, which will be discussed here primarily with reference to internal dynamics, rather than external context (including performance). Within this poetic corpus (preserved very imperfectly and unevenly), the most important names are:

a) Alcman, Sappho, Alcaeus, Stesichorus (seventh to sixth cent. BCE); Ibycus, Anacreon (sixth); Simonides, Bacchylides, Pindar (sixth to mid-fifth) – these nine were later treated as a canon of "nine lyric poets" by the Alexandrian scholars;
b) Archilochus (seventh cent.) – Archilochus' whole *oeuvre* is generally classified under "iambic poetry," but his "epodes" are songs; so too are the "epodes" of the sixth-century "iambic" poet, Hipponax, of which scanty traces survive;
c) Corinna (uncertain date);
d) the great dramatic poets of fifth-century Athens: the tragedians Aeschylus, Sophocles, Euripides, and the comic poet Aristophanes. (The innovative work of the dithyrambic poet Timotheus (fifth to fourth cent.) does not concern as: its significance, arguably, is largely musical, with the words tending towards the status of "a libretto rather than a poem" (Mountford and Winnington-Ingram 1970: 711; cf. Mathiesen 1999: 65–8).)

The linguistic character of Greek lyric, as thus defined, is, in the first instance, a product of dialect and (a not entirely separate matter) traditional poetic idiom. As far as dialect is concerned, there is a broad, though inexact, correlation of usage with the choral/monodic distinction (see also ch. 26). Most choral poetry (beyond or within drama) contains Doric features to a greater or lesser degree, and shows little relation to the poet's own presumed vernacular – unless that happens to be one of the Doric dialects itself. For instance, the poems of Bacchylides (from Ionic-speaking Ceos) and Pindar (from Aeolic-speaking Thebes) are dialectally almost indistinguishable, with (positively) just such Doric features and (negatively) minimal acknowledgment of their own, very different, native dialects; see, e.g., the summaries in Gildersleeve 1890: lxxvi–lxxxvii (Pindar) and Maehler 2004: 10–13 (Bacchylides). Monodic lyric rarely has any Doric element; instead, it does generally involve a pattern of usage related to that presumed vernacular (again, to a greater or lesser degree). More specifically, most solo song involves versions of Aeolic dialects (as with the broadly Lesbian Aeolic of Sappho and Alcaeus) or of Attic-Ionic dialects (as with Anacreon, Simonides, and Attic comedy). The reality of this broad correlation – choral lyric, more or less Doric; monody, largely non-Doric – is confirmed by correspondences on the level of formal organization. Monody generally comes in short repeated stanzas (a – a – a etc.), choral lyric more commonly (especially by the fifth century) in larger and more complex forms, often in a triadic pattern (A – A – B, A – A – B etc.), as generally in epinician poetry and tragedy.

In practice, however, the dialectal situation is more complicated, above all because conventionalization is the norm. It has been plausibly argued (Ruijgh 1980) that in early lyric, in particular, "the" dialect never fully corresponds to any purely local speech-form – even if some sung poetry comes fairly close to it, notably the work of Alcman, of Sappho and Alcaeus, and (in fifth-century drama) of Aristophanes (much of which approximates to the known or presumed usage of Laconian Doric, Lesbian Aeolic, and Attic, respectively). As far as Doric usage is concerned, furthermore, a particular qualification is in order. It is a crude, if convenient, misstatement to describe the poetry of any lyric (even the poetry of Alcman's lyric) as "Doric" *tout court*, if only because of the variable, but widespread, presence there of traditional poetic idiom.

The Legacy of Epic

"Traditional poetic idiom," in the first instance, is the traditional idiom of epic poetry. From our earliest examples of lyric poetry, the language of lyric is seen to be under the influence of that remarkable composite of dialectal variants and features new, old, and eccentric: the epic *Kunstsprache* (see ch. 27). Virtually no choral lyric, in particular, is without an epic, or epic-related, element; and in choral lyric, above all, the "Doric" presence characteristically impinges as a stronger or weaker coloration (often largely a matter of superficial phonology) on an idiom shaped, more or less, in epic-related terms. At one extreme, then, the dialect is effectively an epic-based composite with (so to speak) a generalized Doric accent. This extreme is represented by much of the extant poetry of Stesichorus, e.g., fragm. 222b (on which, see also Bremer et al. 1987: 128–72):

> οὔτε γὰρ αἰὲν ὁμῶς
> θεοὶ θέσαν ἀθάνατοι κατ᾽ αἶαν ἱρὰν
> νεῖκος ἔμπεδον βροτοῖσιν
> οὐδέ γα μὰν φιλότατ᾽ . . .

> Not for all time, in like measure,
> Did the immortal gods on holy earth ordain
> Strife unchanging for mankind,
> No, nor friendship either . . . (Stes. fragm. 222b, 204–7 *PMGF*)

The only distinctively Doric features of this sequence are the *alpha*s (long and short) in ἱράν (= ep. ἱρήν), γα (= γε) and φιλότατ᾽ (= φιλότητ᾽). There is one Doricized modernism: the combination γα μάν (first attested here and at Hes. [*Sc.*] 139; see Denniston 1954: 347–50). Everything else is either indistinctive (universal Greek), like γάρ, or epic-relatable. Specific epic indicators here include: the archaizing omission of the definite article (as with θεοί) and of the temporal augment (in θέσαν); the Ionic dative plural in βροτοῖσι(ν); the generic epithet ἱράν (though, as epithet of αἶαν, not itself either a stock or literally Homeric epithet; see Bremer et al. 1987: 139); phraseological groups (like θεοὶ θέσαν: as, e.g., *Il.* 9.637); and, not least, epic word-forms (αἰέν and the contracted ἱρ-) and lexemes (αἶα and ἔμπεδος). This last feature, the epic lexeme, belongs to a larger, and important, category of "verse words," as they are often characterized in scholarly exegesis. Such words pervade Greek poetry, especially lyric, and most especially choral lyric, in the epic-poetic tradition. Lyric usage of this kind serves to maintain that tradition, but also to determine that the tradition itself impinges, not as the mechanical re-use of epicisms necessarily, but as a developing continuum, which may, in its development, subsume "verse words" not in fact attested in epic as such. (And one need not assume that it is only *our* limited knowledge of ancient epic texts that produces this impression.)

Of the epic-poetic features cited, verse words and archaizing omissions (notably omission of the article) are especially common in lyric usage. Additional indicators, not present or not obvious in the Stesichorus passage cited, are: a tendency (again archaizing) to favor uncompounded ("simplex") verbs (as θέσαν there); a parallel tendency to favor (and sometimes to stretch) grammatical relationships involving oblique cases of nouns instead of prepositional phrases; a free use of heavy-compound adjectives; and a freer word order than is characteristic of more "ordinary" Greek in any period – here represented by the modest separating of noun θεοί and adjective ἀθάνατοι by the verb between them.

For obvious reasons, specifically epic phraseology is most likely to occur in a passage with some rhythmic affinity to the epic, which tends to mean a passage with a dactylic (or dactylic-relatable) character. This is indeed the case with our Stesichorus passage (dactylo-epitrite, including dactylic sequences like the hemiepes, – ᴜ ᴜ – ᴜ ᴜ –, in 204; on the rhythmical/metrical varieties of Greek lyric, see West 1982, Dale 1968, and Parker 1997). In later lyric, in particular, such usage is often turned into opportunities for specific epic evocation or ironic allusion (see, e.g., Silk 2007: 178–9 on Pind. *Ol.* 12, and Dunbar 1995: 433 on Ar. *Av.* 688–9).

In the choral lyric of Stesichorus' contemporary, Alcman, Doric coloring is both strong and as specific as it ever gets (approximating, as noted above, to the features of Laconian; see also ch. 26). Even here, though, the epic presence is apparent. Take fragm. 1. 90-91 *PMGF*:

> ἐξ Ἁγησιχόρας δὲ νεάνιδες
> ἰρήνας ἐρατᾶς ἐπέβαν.

> Through Hagesichora, maidens
> Have found a way to lovely peace.

Here the phonology is Doric: Ἁγ- (Att.-Ion. Ἡγ-), ἰρήνας ἐρατᾶς (Att.-Ion. εἰρήνης ἐρατῆς), νεάνιδες (Att. νεά-, ep./Ion. νεή-/νή-). But the idiom is epic; witness the suppression of articles, epic diction (νεῆνις and ἐρατός are Homeric "verse words"), generic epithet (ἐρατᾶς), and stereotyped epic-poetic idiom with ἐπιβαίνω (see LSJ s.vv.).

In reconstructing the profile of such usages, it is important to acknowledge that we have no option but to generalize from the evidence that we have, however limited and patchy it may be (especially for some periods and some genres). It is also essential to grasp precisely what the suggested reconstructions mean. For instance, "epic" means something more than: "this is attested in epic." "Epic" in such a case means: "on all available evidence (which may be hard to assemble, and may or may not be assembled in convenient secondary sources like LSJ), this may be regarded as *distinctively* epic, because its *distribution* in earlier and Classical Greek is largely or entirely restricted to verse (and, specifically, epic plus later poetry), with the usage *not* found – this is crucial – in more 'ordinary,' more 'standard' Greek." That latter category of (more) "ordinary" Greek is typically represented by plain prose, and perhaps comic dialogue (on the principle of distributional "literary lexicography," see Silk 1974: 33–51, 82–4). Conversely, the poeticism ἐπιβαίνω in the given sense is also attested – as often happens – in postclassical, less-than-plain prose: first in the ps.-Platonic *Epinomis* 981e.

At the opposite extreme from Stesichorus, Aristophanic choral usage typically eschews both Doric coloration and any epic allegiance. In Aristophanes, even choral lyric often impinges on more or less ordinary Attic:

> οἷον τὸ πραγμάτων ἐρᾶν φλαύρων· ὁ γὰρ
> γέρων ὅδ᾽ ἐρασθεὶς
> ἀποστερῆσαι βούλεται
> τὰ χρήμαϑ᾽ ἁδανείσατο.

> Wrong dealings: what a disaster, flirting with this.
> He's been flirting, our old man:
> He wants to hold onto
> The money he borrowed. (Ar. *Nub.* 1303–6)

Here, only a slight inversion of word order (with the adjective φλαύρων separated from its noun, πραγμάτων) faintly evokes the idioms of poetic usage that look back, ultimately, to Homer, while "alien" dialectal coloration, Doric or other, is entirely absent. Even in Aristophanes, though, special circumstances can make a difference:

> ἀέναοι Νεφέλαι,
> ἀρϑῶμεν φανεραὶ δροσερὰν φύσιν εὐάγητον
> πατρὸς ἀπ᾽ Ὠκεανοῦ βαρυαχέος . . .

> Clouds everlasting,
> Raise we to view our glittering form dew-laden,
> Far from our father, deep-voiced Ocean . . . (Ar. *Nub.* 275–8)

For these first words of his chorus of cloud goddesses, Aristophanes specifically evokes the tradition of Doricized epic-poetic language (the rhythms of this sequence, not irrelevantly, are dactylic). On the epic side, note in particular the suppression of articles and the generic epithets (even if, as often, these particular epithets are not Homeric as such). On the Doric side, the long *alpha* of βαρυαχέος is a tell-tale if minimal sign (see further Silk 1980: 106–7 and 2000: 169–72).

In Attic tragedy, by contrast, choral songs invariably have minimal Doric features, alongside the familiar epic cast, even in lyric "conversation":

> σὲ δ᾽ αὐτόγνωτος ὤλεσ᾽ ὀργά.

> Thy self-willed temper hath destroyed thee. (Soph. *Ant.* 875)

So sing the chorus to Antigone, with, on the one hand, conventional "Doric *alpha*" (ὀργά: Att.-Ion. -ή) and, on the other, suppression of the article (with ὀργά), along with epic-archaic simplex verb ὄλλυμι (~ standard fifth-century ἀπ-όλλυμι).

The fifth-century choral lyric of Bacchylides and Pindar assumes epicizing as a norm (cf. Gildersleeve 1890: lxxvii: "The basis [of Pindar's dialect] is the language of the epic, itself composite"), along with a more extensive Doric coloration (and also occasional non-epic aeolicisms – perhaps the residue of Aeolic poetic tradition from an earlier age; see Verdier 1972; Bowie 1981: 49–67). This is the opening of Bacchylides' fifth epinician ode, in honor of Hiero, tyrant of Syracuse.

> εὔμοιρε Συρακοσίων
> ἱπποδινήτων στραταγέ,
> γνώσῃ μὲν ἰοστεφάνων
> Μοισᾶν γλυκύδωρον ἄγαλμα, τῶν γε νῦν
> αἴ τις ἐπιχθονίων,
> ὀρθῶς.

> Blessed commander
> Of horse-riding Syracusans,
> The violet-crownèd
> Muses' sweet-given honor thou,
> If any mortal now alive, wilt judge
> Correctly. (Bacchyl. 5. 1–6)

Doric color is unmistakable (στραταγέ . . . αἴ τις: Att.-Ion. στρατηγέ . . . εἴ τις), as is a touch of Aeolic hue in the Μοι- of Μοισᾶν (Att.-Ion.-ep. Μου-, Dor. Μω-). Epic-poetic allegiance, however, is more fundamental: heavy compounds ἱπποδινήτων (cf. Homeric compounds like ἱππόδαμος), γλυκύδωρον (cf. Homeric ἀγλαόδωρος), ἰοστεφάνων (which alone of these forms has an attested epic pedigree: *Hymn. Hom.* 6.18); omission of articles (with τῶν νῦν a special case – see below); epic-poetic vocabulary, ἐπιχθονίων and ἄγαλμα "honor" (the latter word is used in Classical prose, but of physical objects: LSJ s.v. 2–5). At the same time, the poet addresses this "commander" by the more modern στραταγέ (not epic, and not distinctvely poetic) and then, after ἄγαλμα, adjusts the idiom to a contemporary range (despite ἐπιχθονίων), with τῶν γε νῦν (οἱ νῦν is fifth-century usage), αἴ τις (not much earlier; see Maehler 2004: 111) and ὀρθῶς (again fifth-century). None of these modernisms is abrasively modern (they are not colloquial, for instance), but collectively they serve to inform the celebration of a man of the poet's own time with more contemporary resonance.

Bacchylides' "modern" aspect is representative. Whatever their allegiance to epic-poetic tradition, the lyric poets do not usually let the ghosts of ancient usage dominate their poetry entirely. It is not just that the ghosts probably have another – and less venerable – dialect mask on. It is also that the epic element is usually mediated or accompanied by what are and feel to be specifically post-Homeric usages. This is especially obvious with the Bacchylides passage, but also true of the others cited. In the *Antigone* example cited earlier, the noun ὀργά hardly recalls epic idiom: it occurs once in the Hesiodic corpus (at Hes. *Op.* 304), but is standard usage in fifth-century prose and verse. In the Alcman passage, again, the opening phrase ἐξ Ἀγησιχόρας feels much closer to Classical usage (ἐξ ἐμέο τάδε ποιεύμενα ὑπὸ Μήδων "these things were done by the Medes *thanks to* me," Hdt. 8.80.1) than to anything in the epic age. And even our heavily epicized bit of Stesichorus (p. 426 above) has its γα μάν. The epicizing practiced by the lyric poets, then, is not some mindlessly backward-looking traditionalism. It is a way of preserving a productive continuum between the authoritative traditions of the past and the living usage of their own day. It is only in later ages, after the Hellenistic era, that looking back becomes an obsessive ideological norm, in lyric verse as elsewhere (cf. Silk 2009).

In solo song, meanwhile, the traditional element (along with "alien" dialectal coloration) is in any case less prominent, and the modern vernacular presence generally stronger. Exceptions are not hard to find. Antigone's sung reply to the chorus (like their accusation to her) is in conventionally Doricized Greek, with Homeric echoes. Her cry ἀ ταλαίφρων ἄγομαι "wretched me, I am led away" (Soph. *Ant.* 877: cf. Homeric ταλάφρων, in the – ironically? – different sense of "stout-hearted"), embodies both. Or consider the beginning of Sappho's prayer to Aphrodite, accented according to Sappho's vernacular (with Lesbian-Aeolic recessive accentuation and "Aeolic shortening" in the final vowel of the goddess's name), but composed mostly of verse words and heavy-compound generic epithets:

> ποικιλόθρον᾽ ἀθανάτ᾽ Ἀφρόδιτα,
> παῖ Δίος δολόπλοκε, λίσσομαί σε
>
> Immortal Aphrodite, thou of the well-wrought throne,
> Scheming daughter of Zeus, I pray thee . . . (Sappho fragm. 1.1–2 Voigt)

After these opening words, though, the traditional-poetic cast weakens, and the poem soon has Sappho finding something closer to her "own voice," τὰς ἔμας αὔδας (1. 6) – in which phrase, symptomatically, a lexeme of pure epic-poetic pedigree (αὐδή: note the distribution in LSJ s.v.) is attached to an everyday usage with article.

In Sappho's poetry overall, in any case, the balance between epic-traditional and vernacular-modern is strongly in favor of the latter. Take:

> τᾶς κε βολλοίμαν ἔρατόν τε βᾶμα
> κἀμάρυχμα λάμπρον ἴδην προσώπω
> ἢ τὰ Λύδων ἄρματα κἀν ὄπλοισι
> πεσδομάχεντας.
>
> I'd rather see her lovely walk
> Or a bright dazzle in her face
> Than the chariots of Lydia
> And men marching to arms. (Sappho fragm. 16.17–20 Voigt)

Dialectal features of Lesbian Aeolic are abundant: a mechanical translation into Classical Attic would produce a host of differences (from ἧς ἂν βουλοίμην to πεζομαχοῦντας). Echoes of the epic tradition (like the lack of an article with προσώπω, in particular, and the all-but-generic use of the favorite verse adjective ἐρατός) are faint by comparison.

In Aristophanes' solo songs, as in most of his choral sequences, contemporary Attic is again the norm, while in Anacreon's love poetry the staple is generally contemporary Ionic, though with more significant accommodation to poetic tradition. Such accommodations, however, are not allowed to override a broad vernacular effect, although they may be quite extensive in fact; and indeed the accommodation itself may have its own significance:

> σφαίρῃ δηὖτέ με πορφυρῇ
> βάλλων χρυσοκόμης Ἔρως
> νήνι ποικιλοσαμβάλῳ
> συμπαίζειν προκαλεῖται.

> Once again, with his purple ball
> Love starts touching me, golden-haired,
> Calling me out to come and play
> With a girl in fancy sandals. (Anac. fragm. 358.1–4 *PMG*)

Alongside the passage's Ionic features (most obviously σφαίρῃ . . . πορφυρῇ, Att. –α . . . –α; νήνι, Att. νεάνιδι), a cluster of items – separation of noun and adjective in the first line, verse words (δηὖτε, νήνι), classic heavy-compound generic-epithet verse word χρυσοκόμης, without article – all strongly evoke the traditional-poetic continuum. However, the co-presence of contemporary and traditional-poetic here is one that Anacreon can be seen to be exploiting constructively in the contrast between two heavy-compound adjectives, χρυσοκόμης (traditional) and ποικιλοσαμβάλῳ (in substance, quirky and modern): love is age-old, but this girl and her assets are brand-new.

There has been extensive debate about the vernacular authenticity of Greek lyric, especially in respect of Sappho and her fellow-Lesbian poet, Alcaeus. It has been argued, for instance (e.g., by Bowie 1981), that, quite apart from epic-traditional elements, their Lesbian Aeolic admits both contemporary Ionic features and Aeolic archaisms. Any such archaisms would surely impinge as "epic-traditional," even if historically "traditional" rather than "epic" – but in any case, the qualification is less significant than it may sound. All literary embodiments of particular versions of languages, in all cultures at all times, are liable to involve some degree of "artificial" conventionalization. Even "spoken prose" in modern fiction or films is "far more different from conversation than is normally realized" (Abercrombie quoted by Colvin 1999: 33). For modern readers, as for ancient audiences, an overall vernacular impression is surely what counts for most, and the overall vernacular impression of a Sappho, an Aristophanes, or (even?) an Anacreon is hardly in doubt.

High and Low

This account of the language of Greek lyric – broadly conventional in its terms of reference – can be profitably (and less conventionally) restated. Modern scholarly emphasis on dialect and the monodic/choral distinction tends to obscure what is arguably a more decisive issue: the distinction between high and low levels of linguistic usage (see also ch. 20 on "register"). The high/low issue is one of lasting importance in the history of Greek poetry. It is not indeed that there is one single high range of language, or one single low level: there are many versions and gradations of each. Nevertheless, the broad distinction is unmistakable. It corresponds – roughly – to the distinction between traditional myth and contemporary life: between (on the one hand) the typical and universal within the realm of the divine and heroic and (on the other) the topical and immediate within the human environment of ordinary man; it corresponds – very roughly – to what Aristotle, in the fourth century, perceived as a determinative opposition between "serious" epic and tragedy and less-than-"serious" comedy (Arist. *Poet.* 2–5: *c.* 340 BCE). Here, we shall speak of "the" high style, in particular, as both convenient and intelligible shorthand.

Within the varieties of Greek lyric, the high/low distinction serves, certainly, to differentiate Attic tragedy and comedy (in particular Aristophanic Old Comedy – see Silk 1980, esp. 117–29). Tragic usage, in both choral song and monody, assumes a certain stylistic range, below which it never falls. It is not just the *Antigone* chorus, in its address to the heroine, or the heroine in her response to the chorus, that sing high: it is all the singing choruses and soloists in Sophocles, in Aeschylus, in Euripides (notwithstanding a notorious satirical slur by Aristophanes, esp. at Ar. *Ran.* 1342–3b; see Silk 1993: 487–90), and, as far as we know, in all tragedy of the Classical age. For a poet like Sophocles, the imperative (one infers) is that new lyric practice should acknowledge the traditions of high lyric from the past, in terms both of recognizable features from (ultimately) the epic tradition and of appropriate dialectal coloration from (in this case) "Doric." The epic is plainly an ultimate point of reference because of the authority of Homeric poetry (in the broad sense, not just the two great epics as we know them). The rationale of the Doric gesture may seem less obvious: why should singing in Attic tragedy with a bit of a Doric accent make the song any "higher"? The answer is surely that this kind of gesture itself amounts to an acknowledgment of tradition: in this case, the tradition that the main line of sung poetry is a Dorian line, represented for us by poets like Alcman. However slight and conventionalized the Doric gesture in any given sequence (maybe just the use of "Doric" long *alpha*s where Attic would have an *eta*), and however slight and conventionalized the actual epic presence (maybe recreated largely by a few "verse words" not even attested in Homeric epic, but now used *à la* Homer without articles), there will be a sense of continuity with these traditions.

In all such cases, continuity is assured as much by negative omission as by positive usage, and the stronger the sense of high style, the more obvious this will be. It is obvious, too, that omission is operative on two levels. Take the start of Sophocles' choral ode in *Oedipus Tyrannus* on the news from Delphi, a close translation of which (with notable "omitted" items italicized) is clumsy but illuminating:

> ὦ Διὸς ἁδυεπὲς φάτι, τίς ποτε τᾶς πολυχρύσου
> Πυθῶνος ἀγλαὰς ἔβας
> Θήβας;

O Zeus' sweet-worded tidings, what-are-you-that *from* gold-rich
Pytho *to* glorious Thebes
Came? (Soph. *OT* 151–3)

Here, omission is unmistakable on the level of idiom. We have: compound adjectives instead of wordier locutions; exploitation of oblique noun case-forms instead of prepositional phrases (gen. Πυθῶνος "from Pytho," acc. Θήβας "to Thebes"); suppression of articles (except for one, τᾶς, with Πυθῶνος). But omission operates equally on the level of lexical choice. In the high style, certain ranges of contemporary language are excluded altogether (obscenities and slang catchphrases being the most obvious), while other ranges of putatively contemporary usage are exploited selectively and, probably, unobtrusively, so that neither the new composite nor, even, the particular modernisms in question impinge as aggressively "modern." A simple example is the phrase τίς ποτε here. The locution, on available evidence, is fifth-century, prose and verse, and perhaps distinctively Attic (see the evidence in LSJ s.v. ποτε III.3) – but its elements, τίς and ποτε, are standard Greek (in whatever dialect form) in all periods.

To a large extent, then, high/low corresponds roughly to old/new, and what the high style features and accommodates above all is archaisms, especially the authoritative archaisms (lexemes, idioms, whatever) from the earlier poetic tradition – *but* (as we have seen from various examples) the accommodation is such that contemporary ("new") usage (like the innocent-seeming τίς ποτε here) is not excluded. In the low style, conversely, archaism is exceptional, whereas almost any contemporary register or resource, from matter-of-fact allusion to contemporaries to colloquial obscenity, is available. Take the lyric duet (very unlike the one in *Antigone*) in Aristophanes' *Lysistrata*, where old woman and old man threaten each other in down-to-earth terms (on this passage, see Silk 2000: 164; on σάκανδρος, Henderson 1991: 133):

— τὴν γνάθον βούλει θένω;
— μηδαμῶς· ἔδεισά γε.
— ἀλλὰ κρούσω τῷ σκέλει;
— τὸν σάκανδρον ἐκφανεῖς.

O. W. Want me to smash your face in?
O. M. Now you're making me cringe.
O. W. Rather I put the boot in?
O. M. Go on, show us your minge! (Ar. *Lys.* 821–4)

However, in Aristophanic song – unlike Aristophanic speech or recitative – such out-and-out obscenity is rare (and this *Lysistrata* passage is read as recitative by some, as implicitly by Parker 1997: 378; as song by, e.g., Zimmermann 1987: 65). Perhaps significantly, our earliest examples of low lyric, Archilochus' epodes, also show little sign of outright obscenity, but, alongside less abrasive colloquialism, foreground euphemistic sexual metaphor. Thus in Archil. 196a.31 and 21 *IEG* we find, respectively, ἐς κόρακας "to hell with her" and πύλαι "gates," euphemistic for "cunt."

More representative of low lyric in general is Aristophanes' satirical treatment of the politician Cleon in *Knights*:

ἥδιστον φάος ἡμέρας
ἔσται τοῖς τε παροῦσι καὶ
τοῖσιν εἰσαφικνουμένοις,
ἢν Κλέων ἀπόληται.

Sun will shine as never when
On immigrant and citizen
The day Cleon drops dead. (Ar. *Eq.* 973–6)

The instance provides a convenient reminder that "low" does not necessarily mean monodic (this is the start of a choral song); that "low" may be symptomatized by linguistic ordinariness of various kinds (as here partly by the matter-of-fact allusion to a named contemporary); likewise that "low" and "high" are relative terms: on a scale from 0 (lowest) to 10 (highest), this might get a 4 (where the *Lysistrata* duet might get a 1). But also that degrees of low or high are not necessarily constant within a single poem: this lyric is predominantly low, but starts high (with epic-poetic φάος for Attic φῶς; see Silk 2000: 187–8), then dips. That particular contour tends in fact to characterize much Aristophanic lyric (Silk 1980: 133–4, 142–3; 2000: 189–90), and the existence of this tendency neatly confirms the reality and significance of the high/low distinction itself. The comic poet Aristophanes, a master of hybrids, both enriches the linguistic range of low lyric and gestures towards high-lyric tradition, before settling back into a lower level, which is his norm (Silk 1980; 2000: 160–206). In this, Aristophanes' lyric premise is surely paradigmatic (and it is no accident that something like the Aristophanic contour is recognizable in a not-very-high piece of Sappho; see p. 430 above). In Classical Athens, as in Archaic Greece, as surely in any culture overall, high is not normal but special. In linguistic terms, the high is the marked form, the low the unmarked – except that there *is* no one form of high or of low.

Elevation and Heightening

These last points take us onto another significant restatement. The high/low distinction does not imply an opposition so much as a spectrum, the middle-to-lower section of which corresponds to a relatively unstylized version of (in the poet Wordsworth's classic words of 1802) "the language really spoken by men" (preface to *Lyrical Ballads*: Brett and Jones 1965: 244; cf. Silk 1983: 303), whereas the middle-to-upper section comprises (as one moves "upwards") increasingly stylized forms of poetic *elevation*. In these terms, the elevational tendencies of Greek lyric are exceptional. That is, all "serious" Greek poetry, from Homer onwards, is more or less elevated; the most elevated examples of all are to be found in lyric (especially choral lyric), but even low lyric (as our Aristophanic evidence suggests) is broadly less low than low poetry elsewhere (for instance, in Aristophanic dialogue; cf. Silk 1980: 120–36; 2000: 160–2).

To a post-Wordsworthian sensibility, the stratified relationship between high and low, and the logic of the high style itself, are alien. We expect our poetry, including sung poetry, to relate directly to vernacular, idiomatic, spoken norms. In effect, we find the Greek-lyric low more or less "natural," but the high artificial, and the relationship of the two enigmatic. Greek practice, and also Greek theory, tells a different story.

Two millennia before Wordsworth, Aristotle offers the Western world its first theoretical formulation – *and* privileging – of elevation. In a famous discussion in *Poetics* 22, Aristotle suggests that poetic language *should* be elevated ("not low," μὴ ταπεινή: *Poet.* 1458a18), and lists what he takes to be the types of usage that produce the requisite effect: γλῶττα "borrowed word," μεταφορά "metaphor," ἐπέκτασις "lengthened form" and in general "everything that diverges from standard use" (1458a22–3) – with these various types summed up as "alien expressions" (τοῖς ξενικοῖς, 1458a21–2). Here, "borrowed words" means "names which others [= other Greek-speaking communities] use" (1457b3–4), by which Aristotle refers – if awkwardly – to dialectal coloration like (though he hardly has this at the forefront of his mind) the use of Doric coloration in Attic and other sung verse. In Greek usage, his word γλῶττα is generally used to refer to obsolete words (as already by Aristophanes, fragm. 233 *PCG*) – that is, archaisms, like the wealth of epic archaisms employed in the high lyric tradition – but Aristotle does not seem to be thinking of such usages as archaistic but as, again, "names which others use." His "lengthened forms" is evidently shorthand (as an afterthought, he adds "shortened" and "modified" forms, ἀποκοπαί and ἐξαλλαγαί, 1458b2) for what a modern analyst would see as non-Attic morphological features (Aristotle's starting point is Attic usage) – like, again, those originally associated with the epic tradition. His "metaphor," which he calls "much the most important" of the features cited (1459a5–6), does not belong here; we shall return to this point shortly. Meanwhile, his catch-all, "everything that diverges from standard use," also turns out to subsume additional features, notably the kind of heavy compound (his word is διπλᾶ "double forms," 1459a8–9) that, once again, we may associate with the epic-poetic tradition.

To his great credit, then, Aristotle, surveying the Greek poetic traditions known to him, offers a pioneering characterization of elevation, as a key feature of "serious" poetry (his term is σπουδαῖος), and correctly distinguishes elevation from the "standard" (contemporary) linguistic norm. He further points to dialectal coloration and (obliquely) to archaism as characteristic features. Unhelpfully, though, he prescribes elevation as the only proper linguistic mode for poetry: poetic language *should* be "not-low." In our terms, then, he dismisses the possible propriety of low-lyric usage, as in Aristophanes and Archilochus, and ultimately of the less than consistently elevated usage of Sappho and Anacreon. Unhelpfully again, Aristotle's pioneering formulation conjoins "borrowed words" (and the rest) with "metaphor." As such, it confuses two distinct kinds of non-ordinariness. "Borrowed words," as Aristotle calls them, are indeed a determinant of poetic elevation. Metaphor (under which heading he subsumes what later ages will identify as separate tropes: metaphor, metonymy, and the like) is rather a representative element of poetic *heightening*. Elevation is in general a matter of conventional stylization and formal dignity, heightening of *ad hoc* intensification and enhanced meaning.

This distinction, between elevation and heightening, may be taken as fundamental for any productive understanding of poetry, although within literary theory the distinction is only made fully explicit in the twentieth century. Heightened language is what Ezra Pound (1954: 23) called "language charged with meaning to the utmost possible degree." Such extra "meaning" is created by what T. S. Eliot (1920: 128) called "words perpetually juxtaposed in new and sudden combinations," that is, by unexpected mobilization of the connotations of words or of their sound or rhythmic properties in the cause of the sensuous enactment of meaning or the suggestion of new meaning, and by defamiliarizing subjects, as Russian Formalist theorists argued that poetic language should: through poetic eyes, the world is shown to be, is experienced as, different (on "defamiliarization" (Russian *ostranenie*), first formulated by Shklovsky in 1917, see Lemon and Reis 1965: 12; also Silk forthcoming, and briefly Silk 2007: 179–80). And one especially powerful mechanism for such uses of language is metaphor, especially new, disconcerting metaphor. It is at once apparent why Aristotle's association of metaphor with (what may well be) a reassuring restatement of tradition is unhelpful.

As our earlier Anacreon example indicated, and as the Pindar and Aeschylus examples to be considered shortly will confirm, there can be a relation between elevation and heightening in practice, but there is no correlation between the two tendencies as such. Elevated poetry may or may not be significantly heightened; heightened poetry may or may not be significantly elevated. The entrance song of Aristophanes' cloud chorus we saw earlier is strikingly elevated and minimally heightened. Contrast the end of his phallic song in *Acharnians*, proclaiming free love in place of costly war. The addressee is Phales, god of the phallus:

> ἐὰν μεθ᾽ ἡμῶν ξυμπίῃς, ἐκ κραιπάλης
> ἕωθεν εἰρήνης ῥοφήσει τρύβλιον·
> ἡ δ᾽ ἀσπὶς ἐν τῷ φεψάλῳ κρεμήσεται.

> Drink with us now and, come the morning,
> You'll slurp a cup of peace to stop your headache;
> We'll hang our shield up in the chimney. (Ar. *Ach.* 277–9)

Here, only a certain freedom of word order in the second clause (whereby the noun τρύβλιον "cup" is separated from its dependent genitive εἰρήνης by the verb ῥοφήσει) marks the writing off significantly from what one might take to be ordinary Attic usage. But if this passage is not noticeably elevated, it is significantly heightened. One notes the simple but powerful metaphor (ῥοφήσει: not just "drinking" but "slurping" peace) and a sharply immediate metonymy (ἀσπὶς . . . φεψάλῳ: the symbol of the ordinary citizen's participation in a war is "hung up," out of use) (see further Silk 1980: 131–3; 2000: 122–3, 181–7).

Within the range of surviving Greek song, one can hardly point to poets whose language is never heightened, but there are some whose lyric usage is often less heightened than elevated: Alcman, Stesichorus, Bacchylides, and (perhaps surprisingly) Euripides. There are at least two whose characteristic language is more heightened than elevated: Archilochus and Aristophanes. And there are two whose language is both consistently elevated and also intensely heightened: Aeschylus and Pindar. In their usage, heightening is taken to its ultimate, as a means of exploring realms of reality as far beyond ordinary experience as the language goes beyond ordinary language.

In Aeschylus' *Agamemnon*, intense sound-patterning and imagery are used to make something special, and deeply disturbing, of the cautionary tale of Paris, woman-thief and violator of hospitality:

> κακοῦ δὲ χαλκοῦ τρόπον
> τρίβῳ τε καὶ προσβολαῖς
> μελαμπαγὴς πέλει
> δικαιωθείς, ἐπεὶ
> διώκει παῖς ποτανὸν ὄρνιν,
> πόλει πρόστριμμα θεὶς ἄφερτον.

> [The guilty man,]
> Like base bronze
> Rubbed, beaten,
> Turns black
> Brought to justice: child,
> Chasing bird on wing,
> Brings on community damage intolerable. (Aesch. *Ag.* 390–5)

The passage features an overwhelming assonantal progression that involves everything from initial alliteration to (almost) auditory anagram. From κα-κοῦ . . . χαλ-κοῦ and τρ-όπον τρ-ίβῳ we move through one cluster of "p"s (προσ- -παγὴς πέλει) to another (παῖς ποτανόν etc.), via the aurally distinct sequence δικαιωθείς . . . διώκει. The "p"s in the two clusters are all immaculately stem-initial; they tend, therefore, to enforce the semantic relationships that the "p" words carry (on alliteration as semantic enforcement, see Silk 1974: 173–87; 2003: 193–4). Aurally isolated between the clusters, thus foregrounded, the δικαιωθείς . . . διώκει sequence impinges as an enacted equation: δικαιωθείς is the anticipated and inevitable corollary of διώκει παῖς; "crime and punishment" works by deep necessity. The startlingly new, and swiftly successive, images, meanwhile, target the essentials of the situation as much by additional connotative suggestion as by felt analogy: μελαμ- "black," connotes darkness and death; παῖς "child," both the powerlessness and the seeming innocence of the guilty, caught in a cosmic trap.

The passage is of course elevated, though not overpoweringly. There is light Doric coloring (the long *alpha*s in –παγής, ποτανόν), while epic-derived, or epic-related, usage includes: the lexeme πέλει, the heavy compound μελαμπαγής (Homeric μελανόχροος, εὐπηγής, etc.), and the suppression of article with (above all) πόλει (itself exemplifying expansive high-style non-prepositional case usage), along with post-Homeric verse vocabulary (ποτανόν, ἄφερτον). Against this, the passage accommodates some ordinary modern Attic (τρόπον "after the way of," "like"; LSJ s.v. τρόπος II.2) and, at one point, perhaps, even prosaic modern Attic (πρόστριμμα "damage": cf. the distribution in LSJ s.v. προστρίβω III). In these terms, the idiom may be seen as a paradigm of lyric usage: in touch with both authoritative poetic tradition and contemporary living Greek, and thus able to draw on the strengths of both.

A classic Pindaric passage shows how poetic-traditional habits, in the usage of a great poet, can be converted into a mechanism of intense heightening (on the passage as a whole, see Silk 2001: 30–3):

ἐν δ᾽ ὀλίγῳ βροτῶν
τὸ τερπνὸν αὔξεται· οὕτω δὲ καὶ πίτνει χαμαί,
ἀποτρόπῳ γνώμᾳ σεσεισμένον.
ἐπάμεροι· τί δέ τις; τί δ᾽ οὔ τις; σκιᾶς ὄναρ
ἄνθρωπος. ἀλλ᾽ ὅταν αἴγλα διόσδοτος ἔλθῃ,
λαμπρὸν φέγγος ἔπεστιν ἀνδρῶν καὶ μείλιχος αἰών.

Enjoyment
In quick time grows, but so too falls to ground,
By recoiled judgment shaken.
Creatures ephemeral! One is what? One is not? Shadow's dream,
Mankind. But when god-given radiance comes,
Fame's light is left to us and gracious time. (Pind. *Pyth.* 8.92–7)

With such a passage, translation is peculiarly inadequate, because the poet is stretching to the utmost the distinctive possibilities of the Greek language – possibilities partly unrelated to elevation, partly arising from peculiarities of elevated language, partly created by a bold contrast between more elevated language and less. Like the Aeschylus excerpt, this passage is marked by successive images (the metaphorical complex of plant growth at the start, the elusive complex of shadows and light at the end). Very unlike the Aeschylus, though, Pindar here makes significant use of open-ended, even ambiguous expression. In part, this is a matter of inexplicitness. How is the "judgment" ἀποτρόπῳ? – is it, in one or other sense, "turned away" from us? is it "abhorrent" to us (makes *us* recoil)? And whose is the γνώμα anyway? – our own? a human judge's? the gods'? And what is the αἴγλα referring to? – success? recognition? a pagan equivalent to the Christian "state of grace"? Then again, we have multiple senses of words within the two images, where αὔξεται is both "grows" (with the vehicle of the metaphor) and "increases" (with the tenor), and λαμπρόν, likewise, both "bright" and "notable" (Silk 1974: 90, 119). In addition, the staccato questions carry alternative meanings, to some extent matters of alternative emphasis: "*what* is one?"/"what is *any*one?" and "*what* is no one?"/"what is one *not*?" ἐπάμεροι, too, is open to alternative interpretations: "lasting for a single day" or "changing every day." And what is the syntax of that word? Is it (despite the δέ following) a momentary vocative in the second person? – or (with the copula, "to be," suppressed) a statement in the third person (picking up βροτῶν)? or even (very unusually, with suppression of the copula) a statement in the first person? (the ambiguities are mostly played down by commentators, e.g., Pfeijffer 1999: 593–8).

These striking uncertainties might well be said to enact the existential elusiveness of Pindar's big questions in a suitably poised way. Even more striking, though, is the contrast of tone and phraseology between these questions and the words surrounding them. It is characteristic of the high style, as we have seen, to squeeze out "little" words: articles, particles, prepositions, and the like. In linguistic terms, elevation tends to eliminate semantically "empty" ("function") words (in Greek, as in modern English, often very short items, as befits their frequency of usage) and to promote the use of "full" ("content") alternatives. And what Pindar does here is articulate his big questions in a sudden flurry of little (literally little) "empty" words, yet frame them between two versions of the opposite: words that impress us as more weighty, in content as in form. We start with the majestic . . . πίτνει χαμαί, | ἀποτρόπῳ γνώμᾳ σεσεισμένον. | ἐπάμεροι – then switch to an extraordinary run of six monosyllables (or seven, with one elided), and then (as if these stylistic manoeuvres were not sufficiently arresting in their own right) switch back to three more "full" words, but in a self-contained, three-noun sentence (σκιᾶς ὄναρ | ἄνθρωπος, with copula again suppressed), to which there is no known parallel in Classical Greek, until a five-noun imitation of this very passage by Plato (Pl. *Resp.* 617d; cf. Silk 2001: 33–6). The big questions come out in empty words; the answer is unimaginably full.

Overall, Pindar's passage contains its requisite share of elevated features, from the Doric phonology of ἐπάμεροι (Attic-Ionic ἐφήμεροι) to the verse vocabulary of βροτῶν and μείλιχος. But though the staccato-question sequence is not exactly low (in the sense that Aristophanic lyric may be low), it is perceptibly less elevated – and the dynamic contrast requires that it be so. For this poetic exploration of such large realities, one might say, only such huge dynamics will do.

The way that Pindar here mobilizes and extends the resources of the Greek language cannot be paralleled outside lyric poetry itself (though the usage of the prose-poet Heraclitus points the same way) – and, within lyric poetry, only by Aeschylus, along with Pindar himself elsewhere (see further Silk forthcoming). The lyric poetry of Pindar and Aeschylus embodies the most intensely heightened language, not just in all Greek lyric, but in all Greek literature; and though exceptional, even within the lyric corpus, amply confirms the special distinction of the language of Greek lyric as a whole.

FURTHER READING

The secondary literature is overwhelmingly concerned with high-style lyric. Surveys of dialect and related features (mostly on individual poets) include Risch 1954, Forssman 1966, Nöthiger 1971, Bowie 1981, Brillante 1987, and Poltera 1997. Studies focused on linguistic/stylistic features of elevated usage include Dornseiff 1921, Meyer 1933, and Breitenbach 1934; see also Harvey 1957 and Fowler 1987: 3–53 (both on epicizing, the latter angled towards elegiac/iambic poetry). Helpful perspectives, from a variety of literary and literary-theoretical standpoints, are: Renehan 1969, Steiner 1986, and Race 1990 (Pindar and Bacchylides); Petersmann 1983 (tragedy); van der Weiden 1991: 11–14, 21–6 (dithyrambic style); Gentili 1989, Segal 1998, and Danielewicz 1990 and 2001 (various).

There is, however, little systematic discussion of linguistic heightening in Greek lyric, elevated or not. The following contain much of relevance, but are not confined to lyric: Stanford

1939 and 1942, Bers 1974 and 1984, and Silk 1974, 1983, and 2000: 98–206. The present writer has assessed heightened lyric usage (along with the high/low distinction) more specifically in Silk 1980 (Aristophanes; see also Silk 2000: 160–206); Silk 1999 (choral lyric in Attic tragedy, comedy, satyr-play); Silk 2001 and 2007 (Pindar). Anyone wishing to confront the issues here should consult more wide-ranging discussions of poetic language, such as Nowottny 1962, Tambling 1988, and Silk forthcoming.

CHAPTER TWENTY-NINE

The Greek of Athenian Tragedy[1]

Richard Rutherford

When we are dealing with a highly developed literary genre such as tragedy, the study of language cannot be restricted to formal features: one must also bear in mind the generic conventions, the context and purposes of the form, and its evolution in time. This chapter will therefore be concerned not only with linguistic aspects but with stylistic practice in a wider sense.

The texts to be considered are not homogeneous: several distinctions need to be made at once. First, there is the chronological span. Discounting early fragments (some of them of doubtful authenticity), our 32 surviving tragedies cover the period from 472 BC (Aeschylus' *Persae*) to 401 (Sophocles' *Oedipus at Colonus*, posthumously produced); if, as is likely, the *Rhesus* is not genuinely Euripidean, it may date from the early fourth century. Second, we are dealing with the works of three very different poets (five, if the *Prometheus Bound* and *Rhesus* are spurious), and they themselves evidently developed, both as dramatists and stylists, in their long careers: we are told that Sophocles observed such a development in his own style (Plut. *de prof. in virt.* 79b: Pelling 2007). Third, the language of drama varies in its different parts, for tragedy is a hybrid genre, embracing a wide range of meters and employing differing styles in sung and spoken parts; distinctions can also be drawn between the various spoken portions, especially between *rhesis* (extended speech by one actor) and *stichomythia* (fast-moving exchanges between actors involving one line in turn from each, a form which encourages compression and ellipse). In all parts of the play, however, the tragedians employ an elevated poetic style, remote from both formal prose and everyday speech: the presence of occasional vivid colloquialisms (Collard 2005), especially in Euripides, modifies but does not dispel the characteristic tragic "dignity" (σεμνότης).

Some guidance is available from the traditions of ancient criticism, though little from the earlier period. It is clear that the tragedians were keenly conscious of their own art, including the linguistic resources of the genre. This is not only probable *a priori* (Pindar and Aristophanes include extensive reflections on their own work), but suggested by the evidence that Sophocles himself wrote a work on the chorus (T2.7 Radt); there are also self-conscious allusions to formal features within the texts (e.g., Aesch. *Eum.* 585–6, on the stichomythia about to commence; Eur. *Med.* 546, on the *agon* in progress). Contemporaries, notably Protagoras and Prodicus, scrutinized poetic texts and analyzed their weaknesses in terms of *orthoepeia* "correct use of words" (see also ch. 32). Gorgias clearly had views on tragedy (fragm. B11 and 23–4 DK), and Aristophanes in *Frogs* uses critical ideas (redundancy, ambiguity, metrical laxness, and so forth) and terminology in the extended comparisons and contest between Aeschylus and Euripides (see Pfeiffer 1968: 16–56; Dover 1993: 24–37 minimizes the technical aspect). In the next century Aristotle, while pursuing many important independent ideas of his own, also gives us some impression of the state of critical opinion, notably in his relative neglect of Aeschylus (Halliwell 1986). Many insights can also be gained from the ancient scholia, especially those on Euripides, and from a variety of later sources: the short essay by Dio Chrysostom which compares the three tragedians' very different versions of the Philoctetes story is a particularly valuable case (*Oration* 52).

In this chapter I shall first give a general account of the tragic poetic style which is valid for all three major tragedians, and then try to describe some of the ways in which each differs from the others.

Tragic Style

We have already noted that tragic diction is elevated (see also ch. 28): the Aristophanic Aeschylus remarks that lofty diction, like rich garments, suits a genre which presents the actions of heroes and gods (Ar. *Ran.* 1058–61). Although the dialect used is basically Attic, some very recognizable Attic forms are strictly avoided: thus πράσσω and τάσσω, never πράττω or τάττω. Epic forms are commonly admitted, and epic tmesis, the separation of prefix from verbal root, is frequent. Many prepositions which would normally precede their noun may follow it in tragedy; and in general, hyperbaton and mannered word order are common, especially in sung lyric. The poets use many words which would not have been used in prose: e.g., δάμαρ "wife," γόνος "son," ὅμαιμος "brother," στέρνον "breast." Numerous elements of vocabulary and morphology come from epic, no doubt often mediated through lyric (πτόλις, πίτνω, ἔκτα, σέθεν, σφε, νιν).

An important feature is the so-called Doric *alpha*, where Attic η is replaced by a long α, recalling Doric choral lyric (see also chs 26 and 28): this mainly happens in the sung portions, but is not consistent even there (it is commonest in the genitive singular and plural of nouns and adjectives). The inconsistency of practice suggests a generic mannerism (Björck 1950). The definite article, obligatory in prose, is very frequently omitted: when the article does appear, it often has a demonstrative ("this") force. Among the devices which are shared with other verse genres are the poetic plural (Bers 1984: 22–61; Moorhouse 1982: 4–10) and the elaborate periphrasis, sometimes based on epic formations (e.g., Aesch. *Cho.* 893 Αἰγίσθου βία "the might of Aegisthus"). Clytemnestra's florid reference to the tapestries laid out for the returning Agamemnon illustrates several of these points:

> τρέφουσα πολλῆς πορφύρας ἰσάργυρον
> κηκῖδα παγκαίνιστον, εἱμάτων βαφάς,
>
> (the sea) nurtures dye of ample purple, equal in worth to silver
> all-renewable, bathings of cloths. (Aesch. *Ag.* 959–60)

These periphrastic phrases are part of the elevated diction of the genre; unless viewed in this light, they can seem absurd. Aristophanes mocked "the foot of Time," and Housman "mud's sister."

The vocabulary of tragedy is also rich in rare or unique words, above all compound adjectives. Some of these no doubt existed in earlier poetry, but it is overwhelmingly likely that many of them are coined for the occasion by the dramatists; this is especially likely with those which are absolute hapax legomena, words which are not taken up in later literature. Some of these compounds are intensifying, such as σεμνότιμος "revered and honored," some ornamental and strongly visual, e.g., λασιαύχην "shaggy-necked," μελισσοτρόφος "bee-nurturing"; others express more complex ideas, sometimes dark or paradoxical, e.g., ἀνδρόβουλος "with a man's mind," τεκνόποινος "child-aveng-ing," μειξόμβροτος "of mixed mortal form" (of Io, part woman, part cow). Numerous words are formed by the addition of prefixes such as εὐ-, δυσ-, ἀ-, παν-, κακο-, αὐτο-, πολυ-, ὁμο-, χρυσο-, and χαλκο-. A notable feature is that the sense of compounds may be flexible according to context, as the poet draws on the associations of the word rather than on a strictly defined meaning. Active and passive senses may be present in different places. A good example is ἀκόρεστος, used by all three dramatists. Normally it means "insatiable," but at Aesch. *Ag.* 1331, applied to prosperity, it must mean "impossible to get enough of": the basic idea of abundance and excess is preserved, but viewed from a different angle.

Another very popular area of tragic coinage is that of "abstract" nouns ending in -μα. These are not infrequent in earlier Greek, but the tragedians are especially fond of them: at this date they evidently convey a note of dignity or grandeur (Clay 1958: 12–15 finds 441 examples, more than for any other category of noun). They may be used as substitutes for even very common words: thus δοῦλος "slave" is sometimes replaced by δούλευμα, μηχανή "device" by μηχάνημα, often in the plural. But usually the term is more exotic and may have no very obvious simple equivalent (σκίρτημα "leap," λάκτισμα "kick," παροψώνημα "dainty," παραγκάλισμα "darling," etc.). Often they permit a periphrastic expression, sometimes grandiose, even affected, as when Agamemnon says to Clytemnestra, "Do not address me gawping with submissive crying-out from the ground" (i.e., groveling acclamation): μηδὲ ... χαμαιπετὲς βόαμα προσχάνῃς ἐμοί (*Ag.* 919–20) (for further discussion, see Long 1968: 35–48).

At this point it will be convenient to revert to the distinction drawn above between spoken and sung parts of the text. (Strictly there is also recitative, chanted passages, usually choral utterances, but this third category is less important.) In general, the spoken parts of the drama, dialogue between actors and sometimes involving the chorus-leader, become steadily more important as the century goes on, and the choral songs diminish in length and seem more tangential to the main line of the plot. Alongside this, we can observe an increasing naturalization of the dialogue. In Aeschylus the spoken verses are almost as rich and polysyllabically elaborate as the lyrics, but in his successors the greater simplicity of spoken verse is evident: though still distant from prose, it is much less markedly "poetic" or linguistically peculiar than the sung portions. Aristotle remarked that the iambic trimeter was chosen for the dialogue sections because of its closeness to the rhythms of ordinary speech (*Poet.* 4.49a24ff.). Moreover, the handling of the trimeter is more varied: lines may be divided between speakers ("antilabe," found nowhere in authentic Aeschylus), and long syllables are more freely resolved, loosening up the meter. In these parts of the drama the style is more argumentative and dialectical or rhetorical. Characters often present a case, defending their own actions and character: in Euripides in particular, scenes commonly involve sustained debate in terms which recall the lawcourts (Collard 1975b, Hall 1995). There are also narrative passages, of which a special category is constituted by the messenger speeches: these often include reminiscences of epic narration. Lucidity, vigor, and pungency of expression are prominent. Even in less markedly rhetorical passages, balance and antitheses are common, and telling juxtapositions can sharpen the expression. ὦ τέκνα, Κάδμου τοῦ **πάλαι νέα** τροφή "My children, *young* offspring of *ancient* Cadmus," is how Oedipus opens his address to the Thebans (Soph. *OT* 1); πρὸς **διπλῆς** μοῖρας **μίαν** | καθ᾿ ἡμέραν ὤλοντο "They perished on a *single* day by a *double* fate," says Creon of the two sons of Oedipus (Soph. *Ant.* 170); and more elaborately, Antigone describes the same occasion: ἐξ ὅτου | **δυοῖν** ἀδελφοῖν ἐστερήθημεν **δύο**, | **μιᾶι** θανόντοιν ἡμέραι **διπλῆι** χερί "from the hour when *we two* were deprived of *two* brothers, who died on *one* day by a *double* hand" (ibid. 12–14). More powerful is the grim prophecy of Oedipus (predicting future disaster for invading forces): ἵν᾿ οὑμὸς εὕδων καὶ κεκρυμμένος νέκυς | **ψυχρός** ποτ᾿ αὐτῶν **θερμὸν** αἷμα πίεται "sleeping and hidden, my body, *cold* though it be, in time to come drinks their *hot* blood" (Soph. *OC* 621–2).

In the lyrics, by contrast, there is greater freedom of syntax and word order; imagery is denser and more complex, and there is as much focus on creation of mood and heightened emotional tension as on exposition or narrative. Choruses in their song do not generally present an argument, though they may reflect on or circle round a moral or religious issue. Certain types of song can be identified (partly by analogy with lyric genres, though these are often subverted: the paean, the wedding song, and so forth). Some songs evoke ritual: hymnic openings and invocations are frequent, but the phenomenon goes deeper (Kranz 1933: 127–37). The prayers for Argos in Aeschylus' *Suppliants* (625–709) and for Athens in his *Eumenides* (916–1020) presumably owe something to actual cultic songs (Furley and Bremer 2001: 1: 273–96); the repeated cries of the Bacchants (ἐς ὄρος "to the mountain") also probably echo authentic ritual shouts (Eur. *Bacch.* 116, 164; see Seaford 1996: 162).

Lyric passages, however, are not confined to the choral odes. Already in Aeschylus actors also erupt into song, particularly at moments of intense emotion (e.g., Cassandra breaking silence at Aesch. *Ag.* 1072). Sometimes an actor sings alone (monody), sometimes together with another singer, whether a second actor or the chorus; very commonly, one sings and another speaks in response, a structure traditionally called "epirrhematic." Whatever the terminology, this combination makes possible significant shifts of emotional tempo, sometimes colored by contrast of age or sex or state of mind (the singer may be mad – or female!). A particularly effective case is the scene near the end of the *Eumenides* where the Furies, outraged and insulted by the acquittal of Orestes, sing a series of stanzas dominated by the dochmiac meter (which regularly indicates violent emotion), expressing their fury and determination on revenge, while Athena answers them with placatory spoken verses, employing all her gifts of persuasion to calm their anger, and eventually succeeding (Aesch. *Eum.* 778–915: that the Furies *repeat* their stanzas expresses their intransigence): when her words finally make an impression, this is shown by the chorus' finally reverting to spoken trimeters (at 892). Who sings and who does not in tragedy is a fertile topic for enquiry (Hall 1999).

Although all tragedy makes use of repetitions and related figures, these are particularly frequent in lyric. (Rhetoricians judged repetition a particularly important resource for heightening emotion, e.g., Long. *Subl.* 20, Quint. *Inst.* 9.3.28–47.) Simple iteration is common enough ("sing sorrow, sorrow, yet let good prevail" at Aesch. *Ag.* 121, 139, 159); it was especially cultivated by Euripides, as the well-known parody of his lyrics by Aristophanes makes plain (cf. Breitenbach 1934: 214–21). More complex are the various devices whereby different forms of the same word, or of cognate words, are combined, often with a rhyming effect or some other kind of assonance (so-called *Klangfiguren*: see esp. Fehling 1969, e.g., 139ff.). Examples occur in all three dramatists: Aesch. *Pers* 1041 δόσιν κακὰν κακῶν κακοῖς "an ill gift of ills in answer to ills"; Soph. *OT* 284 ἄνακτ᾿ ἄνακτι "a lord to a lord"; Eur. *Med.* 513 ["I shall be exiled"] σὺν τέκνοις μόνη μόνοις "alone with my children alone"; *Supp.* 614 δίκα δίκαν δ᾿ ἐκάλεσε καὶ φόνος φόνον "justice has called forth justice and slaughter slaughter." More elaborate structures may be composed of several repeated elements:

> αἰαῖ αἰαῖ, τρομερὰν φρίκαι
> τρομερὰν φρέν᾿ ἔχω· διὰ σάρκα δ᾿ ἐμὰν
> ἔλεος ἔλεος ἔμολε μα-
>   τέρος δειλαίας.
> δίδυμα τέκεα πότερος ἄρα
> πότερον αἱμάξει—
> ἰώ μοι πόνων, ἰὼ Ζεῦ, ἰὼ Γᾶ—
> ὁμογενῆ δέραν, ὁμογενῆ ψυχὰν
> δι᾿ ἀσπίδων, δι᾿ αἱμάτων;

Alas, alas, my heart trembles, it trembles with shuddering dread; and surging through my frame comes pity, pity for an unhappy mother. Those two sons, which of the two will cause which one's blood to flow – ah! my sufferings! ah Zeus, ah earth! – from the kindred neck, the kindred soul, amid shield-wielding, amid blood-shedding? (Eur. *Pho.* 1284–92)

More eloquent are combinations in which the one term negates or casts a blight on the other: Soph. *Aj.* 665 ἄδωρα δῶρα "gifts that are no (true) gifts"; Soph. *El.* 1153 "a mother that is no mother"; Eur. *Hec.* 612 "a bride that is no bride, a virgin unvirginal" (of Polyxena, about to be sacrificed). Negative expressions, especially combined in asyndeton, are something of a tragic mannerism (though Homer already has a fine example at *Il.* 9.63): the "alpha-privative" prefix is frequently used in such passages: e.g., Aesch. *Ag.* 412, with Fraenkel's note; Eur. *IT* 219 δυσχόρτους οἴκους ναίω ἄγαμος ἄτεκνος ἄπολις ἄφιλος "I dwell in a barren home, with no husband, no child, no city, no friends"). The verbal expression can expand into dark and vivid imagery: "lyreless hymns" (Eur. *Alc.* 447); "the bride of Hades" (Eur. *IA* 461; cf. Soph. *Ant.* 806–16); "a paean for a dead man" (Aesch. *Cho.* 151); "revelers unsuited to Bacchus" (Eur. *Or.* 319). Oxymoron and other expressions embodying contradiction form a suitable vehicle for the tragic vision of a world out of joint, where normal rituals or conventions are distorted (Kranz 1933: 135–6; Collard 1975a: 2: 127, 352). A more extensive example is the comparison in the *Agamemnon* of the Furies infesting the house of Atreus first with a chorus that is discordant, and then more specifically with a κῶμος, a party of drunken revelers – but the Furies are "drunk" on blood, and the pregnant adjective describing their band as "hard to send away" (δυσπέμπτος) unites the inconvenience of dispersing a bunch of rowdies with the impossibility of exorcising an accursed presence which threatens the household for generations (Aesch. *Ag.* 1186–93).

A figure of speech particularly common in tragedy is etymologizing, especially of names. Some of these were no doubt embedded in the myths (Polynices, "Much strife," opposes his nobler brother Eteocles, "True glory"), but it remains true that tragedy draws out the implications and dwells on the *nom parlant* in significant contexts, often for irony. Either the true aptness of the name is not yet seen (Pentheus, "Sorrow," has "a name well-suited for calamity," says Dionysus ominously at Eur. *Bacch.* 508), or its truth is bitterly recognized in retrospect (Ajax recognizes the lament αἰαῖ in his own name (Soph. *Aj.* 430)). There are also places where a less obvious connection is made: Helen as "the taker," from the Greek root for "take/take away" (ἑλ-) as at Aesch. *Ag.* 687–9, and also in other plays; Apollo as "destroyer" (ἀπόλλυμι) as at Aesch. *Ag.*1080–2). Zeus can be linked both with "life" (ζῆν) and with causation (διά); cf. Aesch. *Supp.* 584 and *Ag.* 1485). Oedipus' name means "swell-foot" (οἰδέω + πούς), a sense alluding to his childhood mutilation, and this point is made in Sophocles' *Oedipus Tyrannus* itself (1036); but connections with knowledge (οἶδα) are also made explicit for ironic effect (Soph. *OT* 397). The poets were not concerned with philological accuracy: far more important is the sense of the numinous, of a force of destiny at work in the world, so that names are tokens of a fate already foreordained (Kranz 1933: 287–9; Silk 1996).

Still on the subject of emotional intensification, it should be emphasized that lamentation, and the vocabulary of exclamation or inarticulate outburst, is far more abundant in tragedy than in any previous genre (cf. Hutchinson 2001: 429–31; Schauer 2002). In Homer the aggrieved god or hero may occasionally exclaim ὢ πόποι, but this seems to amount to little more than "oh bother"; there is no parallel for the exclamatory cries, often extrametrical, which are uttered by tragic characters in moments of stress: ὀτοτοτοτοῖ πόποι δᾶ (Cassandra), ἰὴ ἰὴ ἰὼ ἰώ (Xerxes), παππαπαππαπαῖ and ἀτταταῖ (Philoctetes). The dramatic impact of these cries, no doubt accompanied by violent movement (in Philoctetes' case a positive paroxysm), can hardly be overstated;

but here it is their linguistic novelty that needs to be noted. Tragedy used every device to call forth the audience's emotional responses. Lamentation and even self-mutilation in honor of the dead were represented on stage to a degree which would have been reprehensible in life (Foley 2001: 19–56).

Given the artificial nature of the tragic language (*Kunstsprache*), it is natural to ask how much scope is available for characterization (itself a controversial topic), and how far linguistic variation plays a part in this (see also ch. 20 on register). Although the genre does not admit such a range of styles as Shakespearian drama (which makes use of prose and dialect amongst other devices), there is some modification in many cases (Katsouris 1975). Differentiation is partly by typology and role in the drama (the chorus rarely indulges in extended rheseis, while the messenger speech has its conventions, including the tendency to end with gnomic wisdom), partly by gender, status, and power-relations. Characters of lower status seem to be permitted rather more down-to-earth speeches and mention more trivial matters: examples include the guard in the *Antigone*, and above all Orestes' nurse in the *Choephori*, who reminisces about her charge's childhood (εἰ λιμὸς ἢ δίψη τις ἢ λιψουρία "if (he felt) hunger or thirst or a need to urinate," Aesch. *Cho.* 756). Her counterpart, the nurse in Euripides' *Hippolytus*, warns her mistress of Aphrodite's power with a chatty colloquialism: "and if she finds someone who's too high and mighty, she takes him and you wouldn't believe (πῶς δοκεῖς) how badly she treats him" (446). Yet the same character a moment later is allowed to utter a few sublime lines about the omnipotence of Aphrodite ("she moves in the ether, she dwells in the waves of the sea . . ."), before the stylistic level shifts downwards again.

Characterization is most effectively conveyed through contrast: in the prologue to *Antigone* Ismene and Antigone speak to one another in different ways (Griffith 2001, an outstanding essay) and use value terms which reflect their differing priorities. Antigone uses short sentences, blunt and direct questions, insistent repetition, future indicatives; Ismene prefers more involved periods, potential and conditional constructions, generalizations which move away from the crucial choice with which her sister is confronting her. Imagery can also make a contribution: tyrannical figures such as Clytemnestra and Creon favor cruel metaphors of taming, yoking, and goading (Aesch. *Ag.* 1066–7, Soph. *Ant.* 477–8; see Goheen 1951: 26–35). Racial characterization might also be expected to play a part, in a genre and in a period that make so much of the opposition of Greek and barbarian; but apart from the special case of the *Persians*, a historical drama set at the Persian court and with no Greek characters, this seems less fully exploited than one might expect. (Kranz 1933: ch. 3 discusses "non-Hellenic elements," including foreign vocabulary, of which βαλλήν, a term for "king," is the most certain (Aesch. *Pers.* 657).) The most likely other case is the Egyptians who attempt to carry off the Danaids toward the end of Aeschylus' *Suppliants*, but the text of the passage is hopelessly corrupt. (See further Hall 1989: 76–9.)

An example of colloquialism in Euripides was given above. Valuable work has been done on identifying colloquialisms in tragedy; not surprisingly, they seem to be most frequent in Euripides (Stevens 1976, West 1990, Collard 2005). Even in his work, however, they make only occasional appearances; it is not the case that a particular character, even a slave, speaks consistently in a lower style (as the guard does in Seamus

Heaney's translation of *Antigone*). Rather, a vivid phrase from a different register in everyday language may be introduced for a particular effect, often in excited or unusual circumstances: delighted excitement is one such context, e.g., the watchman shouting ἰοῦ ἰοῦ at Aesch. *Ag.* 25. Abusive exchanges also call forth colloquialisms, e.g., ἔρρε, ἄπερρε "get out, be off with you," and οὐκ ἐς φθόρον "go to hell" (Aesch. *Sept.* 252, cf. *Ag.*1267), or the exclamation "isn't this an absolute outrage" (ἆρ᾽ οὐχ ὕβρις τάδε. . ., Soph. *OC* 883, with parallels in comedy). Perhaps the most telling sequence is the scene in the *Alcestis* in which Heracles is drunk and indulging himself: his lecture on hedonism to the indignant servant contains an unusual incidence of colloquialisms (773ff.; see Stevens 1976: 66–8); when he learns the truth about Alcestis' death, however, he swiftly sobers up and his diction becomes markedly more elevated, as he prepares to undertake the heroic task that awaits him (883ff.).

In the remainder of this essay I offer a few further comments on each of the individual tragedians, focused in each case on a single short extract. I have tried to choose a passage which shows the characteristic techniques of the author; also, the form is different in the three examples, in an effort to illustrate the different modes available in the genre. For Aeschylus, in whose work lyric is most important, a passage from a choral ode seems appropriate; from Sophocles comes an extract from an extended rhesis by the main character; and the Euripidean example is a passage of stichomythia. Of course, this procedure truncates long and complex passages and oversimplifies the picture; it must be understood that each of these poets is capable of excelling in all these styles and others besides.

Aeschylus

Aeschylus' achievement is summed up admiringly but with a sting in the tail by Aristophanes' chorus: "O thou who first among Greeks built walls of awesome words (ῥήματα σεμνά) and brought form to tragic blathering" (Ar. *Ran.* 1004–5). By the time of *Frogs* Aeschylus had been dead for over 50 years and his work could be represented as archaic, his lyrics ponderous and even unintelligible. The account along these lines in the *Frogs* itself is of course comic distortion. That Aeschylus'style is often dense and difficult cannot be denied (though textual damage will sometimes be the reason for the obscurity), but his linguistic and imaginative power is second to none. More than the later dramatists, he thinks with metaphor and imagery; they are not employed as supplements but are part of an organic conception, fundamental to the meaning (see also ch. 28 on "heightening").

> ὁ χρυσαμοιβὸς δ᾽ Ἄρης σωμάτων
> καὶ ταλαντοῦχος ἐν μάχῃ δορὸς
> πυρωθὲν ἐξ Ἰλίου
> φίλοισι πέμπει βαρὺ
> ψῆγμα δυσδάκρυτον, ἀντ-
>   ήνορος σποδοῦ γεμί-
> ζων λέβητας εὐθέτους.

στένουσι δ εὖ λέγοντες ἄνδρα τὸν μὲν ὡς μάχης ἴδρις,
τὸν δ᾿ ἐν φοναῖς καλῶς πεσόντ᾿
ἀλλοτρίας διαὶ γυναικός·
τάδε σῖγά τις βαΰζει·
φθονερὸν δ᾿ ὑπ᾿ ἄλγος ἕρπει
προδίκοις Ἀτρείδαις.
οἱ δ᾿ αὐτοῦ περὶ τεῖχος
θήκας Ἰλιάδος γᾶς
εὔμορφοι κατέχουσιν· ἐχ-
θρὰ δ᾿ ἔχοντας ἔκρυψεν.

Ares, the goldchanger whose trade is in corpses, who handles the scales in the conflict of the spear, sends back from Ilium dust that has felt the fire, heavy for the kindred and fit for hard tears, loading the vessels, so easily stowed, with ashes that were once a man. And they groan for them, praising one who was expert in combat, another who fell nobly in the slaughter, thanks to another man's wife. This is how a man mutters in secret, and pain creeps upon them, resentful towards the sons of Atreus, chief advocates in the case. And there are others, around the wall, who fair of form occupy graves in the soil of Ilium, and the land of the enemy covers its occupiers. (Aesch. *Ag.* 437–55)

The chorus of the *Agamemnon*, having heard the news of Troy's fall, brood on the import of this event. Wars are normally thought to involve winners and losers, but here the winners' losses are central to their concerns – so many good men died at Troy, all for a questionable cause. The war-god Ares is naturally seen as responsible for the losses of war (that he, not the Greeks, is made the subject of the sentence is expressive: cf. Macleod 1983: 136 nn. 14–15), but here a remarkable metaphor is used, comparing the god to a merchant, a gold-changer. The precise concept is ambiguous: either Ares is returning ashes in return for bodies (of living men who set out to Troy), or weighing lives and bodies in his scales; perhaps the poet had not fully distinguished these ideas. The picture of the god weighing with scales can hardly fail to recall the *Iliad*, where Zeus is twice shown using the scales of death, to determine which warrior is to die. The vocabulary is choice: the compounds χρυσαμοιβός, ταλαντοῦχος, and δυσδάκρυτος all seem likely to be Aeschylean coinages. The dust that is sent back to the kinsmen is far lighter than the original bodies (just as the urns are "easily stowed"), but it is "heavy" in that it brings pain and grief. The dead men win praise: their kindred remember them for their skill in battle, they died "nobly"; "fair of form," they now occupy Trojan soil; but the repeated syllable εὐ- contrasts with the prefix of δυσδάκρυτον, just as "noble" death in battle is tarnished, or at least qualified, by the motive for the war – to recover a faithless woman. By ascribing these words, partly praise, but also a hint of blame, to other citizens, the chorus are able cautiously to distance themselves from disloyal complaint. Even those who are quoted seem to be speaking guardedly: the words are muttered in secret (449), and the resentment "creeps" or "crawls" into the minds of the bereaved (ὑπ᾿. . .ἕρπει). The reference to the Atreids as "chief advocates" (προδίκοις) in a single word recalls another view of the war and a different strand of metaphor (the conflict as a legal prosecution); this was introduced in the parodos (41) and will be important again, but it sits uncomfortably here with the personal losses of those caught up in the wake of the supposed lawsuit. The concluding lines of the stanza shift perspective again (with a marked change of meter): we are given a glimpse of those who have not come home, even as ashes, those who remain in tombs of foreign, Trojan soil; they have "occupied" the land only in the sense that they will never leave it; and the territory they have conquered, and which still represents *enemy* soil (ἐχϑρά), now covers them: this hollow "victory" is brought out by the change from the dead Greeks as subjects of κατέχουσιν to their inert role in the accusative case of the participle of the root verb (ἔχοντας) in the next line. All of this brings out by implication, though less than explicitly, some of the reasons for the chorus's dissatisfaction with the expedition and its misgivings regarding the return of the king. It also suggests a political aspect to the situation in Argos: in a drama performed under a democracy, it is not surprising that the old saga of ambition and adultery is no longer confined to the royal household.

Sophocles

The style of Sophocles is more supple and less majestic than that of his predecessor, though his work is full of echoes and imitations of Aeschylean themes and *topoi* (not least the *Electra*, which treats the same mythic material as the *Choephori*). Dialogue is more important and more flexibly handled (including three-cornered exchanges). The choral songs are more compact and often enigmatic. But the qualities of elusiveness and complexity of language and thought which characterize such odes as *Ant.* 583–625 and *OT* 863–910 are also evident in many spoken passages, including the following extract from Oedipus' proclamation to the Thebans.

> νῦν δ᾿ ἐπεὶ κυρῶ τ᾿ ἐγὼ
> ἔχων μὲν ἀρχὰς ἃς ἐκεῖνος εἶχε πρίν,
> ἔχων δὲ λέκτρα καὶ γυναῖχ᾿ ὁμόσπορον,   260
> κοινῶν τε παίδων κοίν᾿ ἄν, εἰ κείνῳ γένος
> μὴ ᾿δυστύχησεν, ἦν ἂν ἐκπεφυκότα - -
> νῦν δ᾿ ἐς τὸ κείνου κρᾶτ᾿ ἐνήλαθ᾿ ἡ τύχη·
> ἀνϑ᾿ ὧν ἐγὼ τάδ᾿, ὥσπερεὶ τοὐμοῦ πατρός,
> ὑπερμαχοῦμαι, κἀπὶ πάντ᾿ ἀφίξομαι,   265
> ζητῶν τὸν αὐτόχειρα τοῦ φόνου λαβεῖν,
> τῷ Λαβδακείῳ παιδὶ Πολυδώρου τε καὶ
> τοῦ πρόσϑε Κάδμου τοῦ πάλαι τ᾿ Ἀγήνορος.

But as things are, since I am now in possession of the authority which that man held before, and in possession of his marital bed and the wife that we have shared, and since if his stock had not been unfortunate, common birth of common children would have been born to us – but as things are, mischance has landed upon his head; and so for these reasons I shall fight this battle as if for my own father, and go to every length, in my quest to seize the perpetrator of the murder, for the sake of the son of Labdacus, sprung from Polydorus and Cadmus before him and from Agenor in time long past. (Soph. *OT* 258–68)

The phrase "as if for my own father" has been noted since antiquity (Easterling 2006) as a paradigm case of Sophoclean irony, where the character speaks more truly than he knows. But other less obvious points about this passage deserve comment. For one thing, it seems to be conceived as a single, unusually long sentence (10.5 lines: on sentence length see Griffith 1977: 214–17), building to an impressive climax with the ringing names of the royal genealogy (Oedipus' own ancestors, if he only knew it). But the sentence does not advance straightforwardly. The first startling feature is the use of ὁμόσπορον to describe Jocasta. The word should mean "of the same seed," but here, bizarrely, it must mean "in whom both he and I have placed our seed"; this is an extreme case of the redefining of compound adjectives mentioned above. The strained expression already suggests the question whether that seed bore fruit; and this point is developed in the following lines, which raise grammatical and logical difficulties. Oedipus must mean "if he had had children, they would have been akin to/ on a par with mine," but the vagueness of the "if"-clause allows for ambiguity: does Oedipus in fact know that Laius had children or not? The point appears to be new to him later in the play.

The use of the adjective κοινῶν, and the repetition of the term in κοίνα, allows further ambiguity as to what kind of bond there would have been. Oedipus thinks of half-brothers and sisters, but the truth is far different. The sentence runs into anacoluthon at this point; in 263 Oedipus restarts, adding the point that "mischance" has "landed upon" the head of Laius – a disturbingly violent image with parallels later in the play (esp. lines 1300, 1311). Several of these points – the abnormal usage, the contorted syntax, the breaking-off and making a new start – suggest language under strain; it is possible that Sophocles is using the shape of the sentence to suggest the unnatural horrors lurking beneath the surface. Language is equally stretched in some later references to the incest, above all at 1214–15 τὸν ἄγαμον γάμον πάλαι τεκνοῦντα καὶ τεκνούμενον, a contested passage rendered by Jebb as "the monstrous marriage wherein begetter and begotten are one" (differently Lloyd-Jones and Wilson 1990: 107–8). This is not to suggest that Sophocles was deliberately writing incoherently, but rather that the horrors of the myth call forth particularly bold and unconventional language.

Euripides

Euripides, Sophocles' younger contemporary, has always been regarded as the most "modern" of the dramatists, whether this is taken to refer to the political or the philosophical influences on his plays. It is easy to exaggerate this, but we can certainly trace connections with the developments in prose writing (notably the rhetoric of Gorgias) and the theories of sophists such as Protagoras and Prodicus (e.g., the sketch by Allan 2005). Greater lucidity and crispness in dialogue (e.g., *Hec.* 1272–83) are balanced by an extravagance of emotion and self-conscious lyricism in the sung sections (e.g., *IT* 1089–1152, *Helen* 1451–511). But it is Euripides the dramatist of moral issues pungently articulated who dominates the critical tradition, and this final extract, in which Menelaus encounters the despairing Orestes in the aftermath of his matricide, gives some idea why.

Με. ὦ θεοί, τί λεύσσω; τίνα δέδορκα νερτέρων;   385
Ορ. εὖ γ᾽ εἶπας· οὐ γὰρ ζῶ κακοῖς, φάος δ᾽ ὁρῶ.
Με. ὡς ἠγρίωσαι πλόκαμον αὐχμηρόν, τάλας.
Ορ. οὐχ ἡ πρόσοψίς μ᾽ ἀλλὰ τἄργ᾽ αἰκίζεται.
Με. δεινὸν δὲ λεύσσεις ὀμμάτων ξηραῖς κόραις.
Ορ. τὸ σῶμα φροῦδον, τὸ δ᾽ ὄνομ᾽ οὐ λέλοιπέ με.   390
Με. ὦ παρὰ λόγον μοι σὴ φανεῖσ᾽ ἀμορφία.
Ορ. ὅδ᾽ εἰμί, μητρὸς τῆς ταλαιπώρου φονεύς.
Με. ἤκουσα· φείδου δ᾽, ὀλιγάκις λέγων κακά.
Ορ. φειδόμεθ᾽· ὁ δαίμων δ᾽ ἐς ἐμὲ πλούσιος κακῶν.
Με. τί χρῆμα πάσχεις; τίς σ᾽ ἀπόλλυσιν νόσος;   395
Ορ. ἡ σύνεσις, ὅτι σύνοιδα δείν᾽ εἰργασμένος.
Με. πῶς φῄς; σοφόν τοι τὸ σαφές, οὐ τὸ μὴ σαφές.

M. Gods above, what do I see? What being from the world below am I looking at?
O. Well put. For in my misfortune I live no more, yet I still look upon the light.
M. You poor devil, how wild you look with your squalid locks.
O. It is not my appearance but my actions that disfigure me.
M. How dreadfully you glare at me, with those parched eyes.
O. My body is no more, but my name has not abandoned me.
M. Your appearance is hideous, beyond my expectations.
O. Here I stand, the murderer of my wretched mother.
M. Yes, I've heard. But spare me that; say as little as possible of that disaster.
O. I am sparing with my words; but my fortune lavishes disaster on me.
M. Whatever's the matter with you? What disease is making you waste away?
O. Conscience, for I am conscious of the dreadful crimes I have committed.
M. How do you mean? Intelligence consists in intelligibility, not its opposite. (Eur. *Or.* 385–97)

Stichomythia is part of the repertoire of all tragedy, but Euripides is particularly fond of it, and has the most extended examples (Collard 1980). This extract shows some of its advantages: rapid exchange of information and reactions, but also an opportunity to put a point across repeatedly, in almost epigrammatic form. The format also permits a kind of dialectic or competition in which speakers pick up ideas or cap one another's points, often adapting the expressions just used. (Thus νερτέρων in the first line is picked up by οὐ . . . ζῶ in the next, and Menelaus' φείδου answered by Orestes' φειδόμεθα, but the idea is countered by developing the metaphor of poverty with the opposite notion in πλούσιος). The love of antithesis is tangible in each of Orestes' first three responses, and indeed reaches a degree of self-indulgence in the third (where the opposition body-name, significant in the playwright's *Helen*, has little or no import here; Orestes presumably means only that he cannot escape his identity). Still more mannered is the half-punning opposition of σοφόν and σαφές (cf. Ar. *Ran.* 1434). The formal constraints encourage brief clauses; the circumstances make a question-and-answer sequence inevitable, but the poet varies this with exclamations and changes of direction. The tone is subtly modulated: in 394 talk of a divine power hints at the supernatural background, but Menelaus' reply brings the conversation down to earth (τί χρῆμα appears colloquial; see Stevens 1976: 20–1, 33) and also treats the youth's affliction in more physical terms ("what disease . . ."; the ambiguity is a recurring one in this play). Finally, Orestes' famous claim that it is σύνεσις that torments him marks the passage as quintessentially Euripidean. The noun does not occur in Aeschylus and Sophocles, but is frequent in Euripides (x8, plus 13 of adjective or adverb), as in his contemporary Thucydides; Aristophanes makes his Euripides pray to Ξύνεσις, there meaning "Intelligence," as one of his patron gods (Ar. *Ran.* 893). In this passage the sense comes close to "conscience" (as the explanatory phrase makes clear), and the intellectual expression of moral and emotional reactions owes an evident debt to the debates of philosophic teachers. Tragedy had always been deeply concerned with values and morality, but in Aeschylus the most important personified abstractions were formidable figures such as Ate, Hubris, Stasis, or the ambiguous Peitho; in Sophocles some of these recur, while special significance seems to attach to the embodiment of Time, Chronos, under whose auspices all change and revelation takes place. It is in Euripides that such entities acquire a more conceptual edge.

Aristotle's definition of tragedy has been quoted innumerable times, but usually with the emphasis on such controversial key terms as *mimesis* and *katharsis*. Less attention has been paid to the clause that briefly refers to the verbal medium, ἡδυσμένωι λόγωι χωρὶς ἑκάστωι τῶν εἰδῶν ἐν τοῖς μορίοις "in language which is pleasurably embellished in various forms in its different parts" (*Poet.* 6.49a25–7). This chapter has, I hope, gone some way to put flesh on these tantalizing words. Much remains to be done.

FURTHER READING

Computer programs, especially those designed to work with the *TLG*, now make it possible to search for and collate some features of the tragic corpus more swiftly; but far more valuable are the man-made lexica which provide the raw data on the diction of the tragedians (Italie 1964, Ellendt and Genthe 1872, and Allen and Italie 1954, supplemented by Collard 1971). Clay 1958 is hard to obtain, awkward to use, and not free of error, but does supply useful wordlists arranged by formal categories, and makes it possible to see the common ground in the tragedians' usage.

Useful essays on the language of tragedy include Palmer 1980: 130–41; Goldhill 1997 (mainly on rhetoric); Mastronarde 2002: 81–96; and Valakas 2007. On Sophocles, Campbell 1871, i.1–98 and Bruhn 1899 retain value as compilations of linguistic detail, now supplemented for syntax by Moorhouse 1982; for Euripides there is Breitenbach 1934 (on lyric diction). Griffith 1977 and Ritchie 1964 were mainly concerned to assemble evidence relevant to the authenticity of the *Prometheus Bound* and the *Rhesus*, respectively, but their material is more widely applicable: see, e.g., Griffith, ch. 8 on vocabulary, with appendices F–J, esp. on compounds.

Important studies of a more discursive nature include Stanford 1942, Long 1968, Silk 1996, Easterling 1973, 1999, Budelmann 2000, and de Jong and Rijksbaron 2006. Less useful, but not useless, are Earp's two books (1944, 1948). Kranz 1933 remains a classic on the generic forms, with the emphasis on the lyric portions. On imagery, besides Lebeck 1971 and Barlow 1971, there is an excellent survey-article by Porter 1986. On the interplay between tragedy and rhetoric, especially in the *agon*, see Lloyd 1992, Hall 1995, and Halliwell 1997. For the comparison with comedy, see Willi 2003 and Willi, ed. 2002 (esp. the editor's bibliographical essay). For comparison with prose usage Denniston 1952 remains essential, supplemented by Dover 1997.

I discuss these and other aspects of Greek tragic language, style, and rhetoric in a forthcoming book, to be published by Cambridge University Press.[2]

NOTES

1 Citations are normally from the current Oxford Classical Text editions. Translations are my own.
2 I am indebted to Dr. P. Finglass, Professor C. Collard, and Professor C. B. R. Pelling for valuable comments on a draft of this chapter.

CHAPTER THIRTY

Kunstprosa: Philosophy, History, Oratory

Victor Bers

The title of this chapter requires an explanation. Why reach for a German word when "prose" looks clear enough? To a large degree, the title is an homage to a single influential book, Eduard Norden's *Die antike Kunstprosa* (1971), which first appeared in 1898. Norden insisted that the sensibility of the ancient Greeks and Romans differed from that of moderns in its preoccupation with the formal qualities of texts. For him, "artistic prose," *Kunstprosa*, denoted a style of composition first established in the late sixth century BCE by some of the early philosophers, including Gorgias, Democritus, Heraclitus, and Thrasymachus. This style is characterized by the use of figures of speech, "poetic coloration," and rhythm (though later Norden (1923: 368 n. 1) revised his views on the extent of poetic influence on prose). Thanks to the conservatism and prestige of literary traditions, *Kunstprosa* lived on not only in Greek and Latin, but also in the vernacular languages of writers of the Middle Ages and Renaissance. Since contemporary scholarship can see artistry in much non-verse Greek that does not meet his specific criteria, Norden's focus has come to be seen as rather too narrow. Still, beyond those texts he identified as *Kunstprosa* there is very little surviving Greek prose that clearly reflects esthetic, not just utilitarian, purposes. There must have been striking, indeed beautiful, non-metrical speech that has gone unrecorded, but we can only guess what that was like.

Greek terminology meant to denote the phenomenon we call "prose" is directly or indirectly negative, e.g., "not in meter," or is even mildly derogatory. The verb *poiein* "make, create" and the noun *poíēsis* "creation" could, in principle, accommodate prose, but these words were almost never applied to any but metrical texts. Of course prose is also "made," but the preferred fifth- and fourth-century BCE terms indicated a less creative action: *suggraphein*, roughly "to assemble, or put together, by writing," and the corresponding nouns. *Logos* does make a famous appearance in the sense of non-metrical language at Gorgias' *Praise of Helen* (DK 11.9), where he insists with an emphasis suggesting he anticipates stiff opposition that poetry (*poiêsis*) is (merely) *logos* with meter. There are other attestations of *logos* in the sense of "prose" in fifth- and fourth-century texts, as well as a related adverb, *katalogadēn* (as at Pl. *Leg.* 811e). Sometimes *logos* is qualified by *psilos,* an adjective meaning "bare of what one would rather have," including armor or hair atop the head. The adjective *pezos* "pedestrian, moving on feet" could still be used in the fifth century BCE for "verse unaccompanied by music" (LSJ s.v. II 2). By the first century, however, *pezos logos* became a slightly demeaning word for language that "treads on the ground," as Shakespeare says of the ordinary woman who is his mistress.[1] Still, the polysemous character of the word (the entry in LSJ occupies nearly six columns) appears to have worked against *logos* becoming a common usage for "prose" : see Dover 1997: 182–6 and Silk 1974: 210–23 for useful surveys of the problems in much ancient discussion of "poetic," "metaphoric," etc. In time, certain prose texts acquired enormous prestige, but the earliest practitioners exhibited signs of diffidence. Even Plato, the greatest of all Greek prose stylists, seems to work in poetry's shadow, borrowing some of its methods and devising compensatory strategies (see below). (For an entirely different approach, stressing prose as the form making the loudest claims for "authority," see Goldhill 2002.)

J. D. Denniston opens his *Greek Prose Style* with an encouraging remark (1952: 1): "The student of Greek prose expression can certainly not complain of lack of materials." He goes on to speak of an abundance of texts by great authors and by "second-raters" useful for establishing general trends. This is, regrettably, too optimistic. Bad luck has deprived us of a full set of texts that share enough characteristics that would allow many close comparisons, for instance, actual speeches delivered before the fifth-century BCE Athenian assembly contemporary with speeches in Attic tragedy. We often have to make do with, say, comparing the latter to historiographical speeches written in a different dialect, reporting events in another city and time, or to actual speeches delivered a century after the play was performed.

This survey, by necessity highly abbreviated, will touch on a number of principal genres and authors, often recurring to several matters of form: dialect, vocabulary (especially in its relation to poetry and "natural language"), figures of speech, and acoustic qualities, including rhythm. Some minute stylistic details are introduced, not because they are in themselves of great moment, but to indicate the intricacy of workmanship to be expected in literature of this quality.

A Pervasive and Persistent Menu of Choices

Once he had settled on prose rather than verse as his medium, any Greek author aspiring to win the esteem of a wide audience, whether of a small leisured class or massive crowds in a panhellenic milieu, needed to make a number of choices. Except for some pioneers, however, the choice of dialect was probably not entirely his to make.

Classical Greek is a language of numerous, mutually intelligible dialects, and a pervasive conservatism associates specific dialects with specific forms of literary expression (see ch. 26). Within prose, a spectacular example is the language of the medical texts of the Hippocratic Corpus, where Ionic held sway in the earliest texts – though Hippocrates' own dialect was presumably Doric – and persisted for many centuries, whatever the "mother dialect" of the physician and the geographical area of his practice

(Bers 1984: 10 n. 32). In time, most of the prestigious and influential classical prose texts came to be written in Attic, a sub-category of the Ionic dialect, but surviving texts clearly show that for prose writers working in Athens in the fifth century BCE, whether natives or immigrants, the choice of dialect was no simple matter. Rhetorical works attributed to Antiphon the Orator, the earliest of the known Athenian speechwriters (he was executed not later than the spring of 410 BCE), are of special interest for their inconsistency of dialect. Especially clear is the variation in the aorist tense of a single important word (*apologeisthai* "to speak in defense") between a speech of Antiphon's written for delivery in an actual court and several model speeches, evidently written by the same man, primarily to train students in forensic argumentation. In the former we find the contemporary Attic form, in the aorist middle voice (as at 5.13.6 ἀπολογησαμένῳ); in the latter, the Ionic form, in the aorist passive (as at ἀπελογήθην; Ant. *Tetr.* 1.7). It is generally assumed that by the end of the fifth century BCE, the language of the Athenian courts and deliberative bodies, as well as the epideictic speeches ("display oratory") delivered at state funerals, very rarely deviated from Attic as it is known from inscriptions and comic drama.

The same is *not* true of Plato and Xenophon, two of the prose authors, both Athenian born and bred, most commonly and intensively studied, especially in elementary and secondary schools, by boys of the European elite (see below). Vagaries of transmission, however, sometimes make it impossible to be certain about the dialect characteristics of various periods, genres, and authors.

The most obvious signal that a prose text is exploiting a feature associated with poetry is the appearance of a sequence of long and short syllables, e.g., an iamb (short–long), identical to those sequences that poetry employs in repeated units (*metra*, e.g., *trimeter*) – see also ch. 25. Any sort of language is bound to contain some of these sequences. The difficulty lies in determining whether a rhythm is sufficiently pronounced that it will arouse in the hearer a brief recollection, preconscious or conscious, of a meter built on repeated sequences of the rhythm. Dover (1997: 160–71) has shown, in some detail, the difficulties in establishing whether a particular rhythm is intentional or accidental, and in my opinion the intentional use of poetic rhythms is highly unlikely in the absence of strong contextual clues.[2] Aristotle (Arist. *Rh.* 1409a2–3) credits Thrasymachus of Chalcedon (active in the second half of the fifth century BCE) with promotion of the paeanic rhythm (Dover 1997: 173 suspects Aristotle slipped here, meaning some other man), but long before these aspects of composition were the subject of explicit discussion or became a marked feature in surviving texts, there were loud pre-echoes in the Greek language.

The opening of what might be the earliest surviving prose text, attributed to Pherecydes of Syros (DK 7B1), has a spondee (long–long) and at least four dactyls (long–short–short). Here, the formal similarity to hexameter poetry is not likely to be an accident. Doubt can be countered, if not decisively neutralized, by considering what the fragment says: Ζὰς μὲν καὶ Χρόνος ἦσαν ἀεὶ | καὶ Χθονίη · Χθονίηι δέ "Zeus and Time always existed, and also Earth; but Earth . . .") These words challenge Hesiod's *Theogony* in the only two rhythms permissible in his metrical form, dactyls and spondees (Dover 1997:160). Nevertheless, Pherecydes breaks the rhythmic sequence before it can form a full hexameter line, as if anticipating Aristotle's admonition, written more than a century later, that prose should have rhythm, but not meter, lest it turn into a poem (Arist. *Rh.* 1408b30–1). And another section of the same piece (DK 7B63) is written in a notably simple, indeed naive, style, an indication that one must not assume that style is uniform within a single work, even within a short compass.

More generally, the Greek prose writer needed to consider how to make a composition intelligible and persuasive, adjusting his text to his audience and the mode in which they would take in his work. A philosopher not interested in swaying a listening audience would be quick to exploit the post-Homeric use of the definite article for its advantages in advancing abstract thought, for instance in the naming of an action or state with a neuter article, inflected as necessary, together with the infinitive, e.g., τῷ γράφειν for "by means of writing." He needed to assess his own vocal abilities and sang-froid. Any author writing for the Assembly or the law courts would need to consider how to hold the attention of a large, often boisterous, and easily bored crowd. Judging by contemporary political rhetoric in the United States, one might assume that short sentences, all grammatically independent, would be the obvious expedient, but Classical Athens had different tastes and skills. In distinguishing two speaking styles, the paratactic or "beads along a string" style (λέξις εἰρομένη), or the hypotactic or "turned around or back" style (λέξις κατεστραμμένη), Aristotle recommends the latter as more satisfactory because it is easier for an audience member to comprehend and remember. Hearing the periods gives him a sense of the magnitude of the larger unit (normally what we call a sentence) and, we may add, of a predictable structure, cues that are missing from the paratactic style (Arist. *Rh.* 1409a27–1409b8; note that Aristotle compares both these prose styles to poetic forms, cf. Bakker 1997a: 127–9). A speaker can more easily hold an audience if it is following the contours of the exposition. It must be said, nevertheless, that the skilled use of the paratactic style, notably in parts of Herodotus, could achieve the same effect (a notable example is the "Thief's Tale" at 2.121, which is built almost entirely on participles and infinitives).

A speaker needed to decide whether to memorize a text, a process that Aristophanes (Ar. *Eq.* 347–50) seems to describe, or to trust himself to speak *ex tempore*, as Alcidamas, a fourth-century rhetorician, advised. He would also do well to minimize his audience's suspicion of precisely that which he was cultivating, i.e., craftiness in speechmaking. He might want to give the impression of spontaneity, even if that too was a maneuver planned in advance (Andersen 2001: 3–16; Hesk 2000: ch. 4; Schloemann 2002: 133–46.). If he was writing for another man (Bers 2009: chs 4–7), deluxe service would include assessing his client's abilities to contend with a large crowd packed into a very large space.

At first glance, some choices seem to have entered the menu rather late. The treatment of hiatus, the "collision" of word-final and word-initial vowels as the Greeks normally perceived it, for instance, looks like a preference that arose late in the fifth century BCE and became an obsession in some authors of the fourth century BCE. Verse texts cannot be scanned if the extremely common word ἀλλά "but" retains its last letter before vowels. At an even more basic level, οὐ "not" becomes οὐκ or οὐχ before a vowel; and short stretches of some early prose texts are plausibly interpreted as incorporating rhythms familiar from poetry.

First Texts: Anaxagoras and Others

Some early epigraphical texts might display elements of conscious artistry, for instance Draco's homicide laws (Aly 1929: 8–29). Aside from the esthetic evaluation of that text, there is the problematic relation of what we read on the stone, a re-scription ordered in the last decade of the fifth century BCE, to the original text. Most accounts, though, hold that Greek prose had its beginnings in the writings of the Ionian philosophers.

Philosophy, it should be noted, was not quick to settle on prose as its preferred medium. In the sixth century BCE Xenophanes of Colophon, an Ionian city less than 50 miles north of Miletos, employed elegiac couplets. Remarkably, Parmenides of Elea in southern Italy, who lived well into the fifth century BCE, and the Sicilian Empedocles, born in the fifth century, both chose to write in dactylic hexameters. Aristotle (*Poet.* 1447b13–20) insists that Empedocles' subject matter makes him more a scientist (*physiologos*) than a poet, but that was an eccentric opinion: nearly everyone else was certain that Empedocles' meter placed him in the same category as Homer, "the poet."

The earliest philosophers known to have written prose are Anaximander (born in the last decade of the seventh century BCE) and Anaximenes, said to have been his student. Both lived in Miletos on the coast of Asia Minor. At most, one fragment each of any size of Anaximander's and Anaximenes' own words has survived. Our source for the first, writing nearly a millennium later, remarks that Anaximander's expression is "rather poetic," probably because as applied to matter coming into existence and perishing, words for justice and retribution seem metaphorical (Simplicius quoted at DK 12B1; Anaximenes DK 13B2 is not so characterized). Some scraps assigned to Pherecydes of Syros have already been mentioned for the apparent coexistence of poetic and naive elements. Perhaps a false naivety might be adopted as a strategy to compete with poetry by evoking the atmosphere and delivery style of storytelling ("Once upon a time . . .") or a feeling of the portentous engendered by concentrated simplicity (Denniston 1952: 4 speaks of "statuesque grandeur").

From Anaxagoras of Clazomenae we have fragments substantial enough to display a full repertory of devices in Ionic prose of the fifth century BCE. Particularly famous, though not of unchallenged authenticity, is DK 12. In presenting his argument that mind alone stands apart from the great flux in which all matter is forever commingled, Anaxagoras makes extensive use of word patterning: positive statements reinforced by negatives (X, not not-X), repeated sounds, and repeated words, most strikingly when a word that ends one clause starts the next one (the figure known as *anastrophe*, e.g., . . . πλὴν νοῦ, νοῦ δὲ . . .). As none of these devices is necessary to present the basic proposition or posit elusive nuances of meaning, they must be considered deviations from straightforward language meant to make the text both clearer and more persuasive. (Admittedly, even routine legal documents sometimes employ synonyms or lists fuller than logically necessary, but the *Kunstprosa* phenomena under discussion here are more complex and variegated.) Though we know virtually nothing for certain about how these Ionic texts circulated and were read, their aural qualities are undeniable, and that characteristic must count as strong evidence for reading aloud, whether by an individual with the text in his hands, a group listening to a single reader, or even a group listening to the philosopher himself.

Heraclitus

An anecdote related by Diogenes Laertius (*Lives of the Philosophers* 9.6) has it that Heraclitus of Ephesos, a philosopher whose literary acme was about 500 BCE, buried his work in the foundation of the temple of Artemis to keep it from the view of riffraff. If true, and it is very likely not, this action would put considerable distance between most, perhaps all, human audiences and his speaking voice. The disdain for his audience suggested by the anecdote is certainly in harmony with Heraclitus' riddling presentation, but his prose style has a strong esthetic appeal and is hard to categorize, as befits a writer known as "the obscure" (ὁ σκοτεινός). His vocabulary includes a number of words that he *might* have chosen for their poetic ring, but not a single one can with complete confidence be assigned to this category (Lilja 1968: 26–8). A tantalizing example comes at fragm. DK B29: αἱρεῦνται γὰρ ἓν ἀντὶ ἁπάντων οἱ ἄριστοι, κλέος ἀέναον θνητῶν · οἱ δὲ πολλοὶ κεκόρηνται ὅκωσπερ κτήνεα "In exchange for absolutely everything, the best choose ever-flowing fame, but most men are sated like cattle." In Homer the noun *kleos* "fame, that which is heard" modified by an approximately synonymous adjective plays a prominent part in the matter of Achilles' choice (*Il.* 9.413), and Simonides (fragm. 26.1.9) chooses the same noun-adjective combination that we meet in Heraclitus.

At the very least, Heraclitus seems to be dipping into the edges of epic and lyric poetry to add flavor to his prose. Rhythms suggestive of hexameter poetry are likewise possible, e.g., ἀντὶ ἁπάντων in the fragment just quoted, a dactyl and a spondee, as in the ending of many hexameter lines; but textual problems and the "unpoetic" content of many candidates preclude any certainty on the point (Lilja 1968: 29–30). Even more likely are instances of alliteration and repetition devised to ring in the reader's ear, with an acoustic effect often intrinsically bound to Heraclitus' argument, as in the repeated "p"- sounds at DK B52: αἰὼν παῖς ἐστι παίζων, πεσσεύων · παιδὸς ἡ βασιληίη "Life is a boy playing at draughts; kingship is the boy's." That fragment also illustrates Heraclitus' use of concrete language to advance, though not too clearly, an abstract proposition. The same can be said of his most famous image, the river that is never the same, as at DK B12, which according to Cleanthes, who supplies the quotation, refers to the soul: ποταμοῖσι τοῖσιν αὐτοῖσιν ἐμβαίνουσιν ἕτερα καὶ ἕτερα ὕδατα ἐπιρρεῖ· "As they step into the same rivers, others and still other waters flow upon them" (trans. C. Kahn).

Compression itself can suggest the complex responses associated with poetry, and Heraclitus' style is nothing if not compact. His remark on the Delphic Oracle (DK B93), whose pronouncements in the Archaic and Classical periods come down to us in hexameter, both asserts the indirection associated with the metaphors and metonymies frequent in poetry and seems to describe his own form of expression: ὁ ἄναξ, οὗ τὸ μαντεῖόν ἐστι τὸ ἐν Δελφοῖς, οὔτε λέγει οὔτε κρύπτει ἀλλὰ σημαίνει "The lord of the oracle in Delphi does not say and does not hide; instead, he signals." Plutarch, himself a priest at the oracle some five centuries later, reports that the Pythia's language was poetic (*Mor.* 405d), and this might have been Heraclitus' perception as well. But if the transmission of his writings favored apothegms over continuous prose, the stylistic impression made by the fragments may be a grossly misleading accident.

Gorgias

Gorgias of Leontini in Sicily is reported to have come to Athens in 427 BCE as a member of an embassy seeking an alliance of his town with Athens. A first-century BCE source, whom we must suspect of inflating the importance of a fellow Sicilian, says that Gorgias stunned the Athenians with a speech style marked by parallel sense units of exactly or nearly exactly equal syllable counts, antitheses, and clauses ending in the same syllable (Diod. Sic. 12.53). Much of Gorgias' technique was anticipated by early composition, particularly in tragic poetry (Finley 1939), and elements of his style are often found in epideictic oratory and in Isocrates (see below), but it is not clear whether in imitation of Gorgias, rather than as deliberate concentration of inherent properties of the Greek language, especially its recurring desinences (case endings and the like). Gorgias is unique in maximizing the use of these natural features, often emphasizing them by very short clause lengths, and playing on etymology or accidental similarities among words. The last sentence of a funeral oration, said to have been composed in honor of valorous Athenians, plays on repeated forms of nouns, verbs, and adjectives for life and living, death and dying:

> τοιγαροῦν αὐτῶν ἀποθανόντων ὁ πόθος οὐ συναπέθανεν, ἀλλ᾽ ἀθάνατος οὐκ ἐν ἀθανάτοις σώμασι ζῆ οὐ ζώντων

> Therefore, longing for them who have died did not die with them, but in bodies not deathless lives deathless for those not living. (Gorg. fragm. DK B6)

It takes some effort to imagine the survivors of fallen soldiers deriving consolation from what to most of us sounds downright silly.

Herodotus

> Ἡροδότου Θουρίου [or Ἀλικαρνησσέος] ἱστορίης ἀπόδεξις ἥδε

> This is the presentation of the inquiry of Herodotus of Thurii [or Halicarnassus].

Many contemporary scholars understand the word ἀπόδεξις in Herodotus' proem to signal public reading, or at least a performance in an oral tradition, but this is a controversial matter. (For discussion of this notion and some variants, see Bakker 2002: 8–13; Bakker 2006: 95 remarks on "Herodotus' prose style" as having a

> "performative quality" which means, most importantly that . . . the *Histories* itself, whether in actual oral delivery or in the fictional orality of the act of reading, performs

and enacts the speaking historian's research. The text is the very accomplishment of the researches and investigations that led to its existence; the *logos* itself "seeks out" its subjects, leading us to the goals it indicates.

For the currently *less* fashionable view of ἀπόδεξις, see Drexler 1972: 4, 11–14.)

In any case, there can be no doubt that the text is molded by the contours of skilled public storytelling. It is, then, not surprising that discourse analysis has been especially successful when applied to Herodotus (see, e.g., Slings 2002: 53 on "downslip," 60 on "chunking"), bringing greater precision to earlier studies that had observed some of the narrative techniques that make him easy to follow down long narrative paths with only the signals used in paratactic construction (see above on the paratactic style). Denniston 1952: 95, for instance remarks on a sort of "pivot-by-redundant-participle" (my term, not his) whereby "a participle picks up a preceding word." Significantly, this device is virtually restricted to Herodotus and Plato, with only a few examples from oratory, which frequently uses μὲν οὖν . . . δὲ . . . to signal a summing up of what has been said followed by a transition to another subject. Similarly, the particle combination μέν νυν to introduce a stretch of narrative appears hundreds of times in Herodotus, but never in Thucydides, Aristophanic comedy, the Attic orators, or Plato (Bakker 2006: 95).

His use of poeticisms at the level of vocabulary is far from clear, since many of the candidates are very likely words that were routine in Ionic and not likely to evoke the recollection of epic or any other sort of poetry. As we are denied a good range of comparative texts, sound method requires that a word or phrase not be declared poetic unless there is a close or perfect match in an earlier or contemporary verse text and, most important, a context appropriate for stylistic elevation. The mutilation and death of Zopyus (3.153–60) provides such a context for the phrase οἱ ἐδόκεε μόρσιμον εἶναι ἤδη τῇ Βαβυλῶνι ἁλίσκεσθαι "it seemed to him that it was now Babylon's fate to be captured," making it probable that Herodotus expected his audience to hear a Homeric echo, μόρσιμον . . . δαμῆναι "fated to be overcome" or even more specifically, to recall that these words were addressed to Achilles, as it happens by his divine horse (*Il.* 19.417; see Dover 1997: 90–5).

Thucydides

There are good reasons to think that Herodotus, even with pen in hand, composed with the cadences and other aspects of oral performance in his head. Thucydides stands at nearly the opposite pole. Although many scholars, following in the long train of Francis Cornford's *Thucydides Mythistoricus* (1907), have seen affinities to poetry in Thucydides' history of the Peloponnesian War, the verbal surface very rarely reproduces features of oral performance. His language is in some passages so involuted as to make almost plausible Collingwood's vigorous condemnation of Thucydides' style: "The style of Herodotus is easy, spontaneous, convincing. That of Thucydides is harsh, artificial, repellent. In reading Thucydides I ask myself, What is the matter with the man, that he writes like that? I answer: he has a bad conscience. He is trying to justify himself for writing history at all by turning it into something that is not history" (1946: 29). In a phrase that looks like a jeer aimed at Herodotus, Thucydides dismisses "pleasure in hearing" (1.22.4), and he seems to carry through by writing in a style oblivious to hiatus and very rarely falling into a rhythm reminiscent of poetry.

As in the testing of proposed instances of poetic lexicon in Herodotus, one should in evaluating Thucydidean candidates for alleged poetic flavor demand that the linguistic surface be appropriately reinforced by the explicit content. A few passages do qualify, for instance at 3.59.2, where Thucydides represents the desperate Plataean speakers as using a poetic word for the dead (κεκμηκότες) (Dover 1997: 109, *pace* Bers 1984: 11, which is excessively skeptical).

With Antiphon (see below), Thucydides shares a penchant for abstract expression far beyond any other historian. This can be seen in both authors' heavy use of nouns of certain morphological categories, like -*sis*, and of abstract nouns used as a grammatical subject displacing the far more usual construction with a human subject and a verb (Denniston 1952: ch. 2, esp. 28–32, and more generally Allison 1997). But whereas Antiphon softens the abstractions, Thucydides appears to make them both more conspicuous and more difficult to comprehend by frequent use of another stylistic turn, *metabolê*, a variation of form in parallel sense units (Ros 1938). At 2.39.1 in the Funeral Oration, for instance, he has Pericles contrast the Spartans' "laborious practice" (ἐπιπόνῳ ἀσκήσει – not only a noun with the -*sis* suffix, but an abstraction itself modified by an adjective) with the Athenians' way of "living without restraint" (ἀνειμένως διαιτώμενοι), a more normal expression using an adverb and a participle. Thucydides' motives for writing "like that" remain controversial. A number of writers take up Thucydides' narrative at the point it breaks off in the middle of his narrative of the year 411 BCE; strikingly, we know of no text that offers a version competing with the portion covered by Thucydides, nor of any of the several "continuators" who perpetuated his unusual style.

Plato

In his *Poetics* (1447b), Aristotle says that there is no specific term for "Socratic dialogues," by which he almost certainly means those by his teacher Plato; and if we can trust a late report, Aristotle characterized Plato's writings as "between poetry and prose" (*pezos logos* fragm. 73 Rose 1886). If it were only for the range of styles he expertly reproduced, Plato must be regarded as the greatest master of Classical Greek prose. Among the styles he adopted, sometimes for parodic purposes, are those of sophisticated conversation, inscribed laws, forensic and epideictic oratory, and mythic narrative (Thesleff 1967: 62–80). Late anecdotes report that he had tried out every possible permutation of word order before settling on the opening sentence of the *Republic*, and some of his texts are replete with explicit comments on style, which together with the variations in his style over time make his acute sensitivity to this aspect of writing indubitable.

Beginners are seldom aware how far Plato stood from his contemporaries in the use of archaisms and from his Athenian neighbors in his use of Ionic forms. Just as

Xenophon's popularity in Greek instruction during the nineteenth century CE and part of the twentieth misled teachers and students (see below) for much of the twentieth century and even now, Platonic writing is mistaken for a paradigm of Attic usage. Even advanced students are sometimes unaware that the frequent quotatives ἦν δ' ἐγώ, ἦ δ' ὅς "I said, he said" are not found in any fourth-century texts other than Plato, or that his use of particles puts Plato into what Denniston (1954: lxxi) calls a "semi-Ionic group." A likely motive for the occasional fifth-century usage is a desire to produce *via* style something of the flavor of Attic Greek as it was spoken by Socrates and his contemporaries before Plato was around to hear them. That would render *ben trovato* the remark in the pseudonymous *Second Letter* that descriptions of his teacher are of a Socrates grown "handsome and young" (314c). There are also archaisms of a more panhellenic cast, as at *Republic* 614b7 near the start of the Myth of Er, where the linking of clauses by immediate repetition of a verb ("he came back to life, having come back to life") recalls Herodotus (see Halliwell 1988 *ad loc.*).

Plato is often mischievous, as in a passage of the *Republic* (393c11–394b1) where he has a *faux naïf* Socrates demonstrate the difference between *mimesis* (imitation) and *diēgēgis* (narrative) by presenting a paraphrase of *Iliad* 1.12–42 (this passage is the *locus classicus* illustrating the absence of the article in Homer and its near ubiquity in Classical Attic prose). Socrates apologizes for not being *poiētikos* (poetic), but sneaks into his prose a Homeric form for a small word (*his* ἃ [δάκρυα] tears (394a6)) and perhaps a dialect form of the word for "temple" (ναῶν (394a4), a form common in tragedy, for the expected Attic νεῶν). In the *Phaedrus* Plato has Socrates describe himself as a man highly susceptible to incursions of the poetic, as at 238d3: "I am nearly speaking in dithyrambs" and at 257a5, where he says he was compelled to make his palinode in "somewhat poetic language." In the *locus amoenus* passage (230b2–c5) Socrates describes the shaded grove where he and Phaedrus will talk about rhetoric and love, using language exceptionally dense in stylistic refinements: archaism (a sentence-connective τε), numerous aural and rhythmic effects that play on chains of repeated vowels and consonants and reproduce stretches of iambic and dactylic rhythms, and abstract expression using the neuter article in a manner suggestive of scientific analysis ("the element of the grass" for "grass"). The unmistakable parody of Gorgianic style in the *Symposium* that starts at 194e3 concludes with a paragraph in which Plato has Agathon, tragic poet and host of his celebration party, move from one identifiable poetic rhythm to another (197d1–e5: see Dover 1997:169–71; see also his important remarks (164–5) on the variations in pronunciation and articulation that complicate assessment of prose rhythm).

At times Plato turns to a style deeply affective in its simplicity, for example in the description of Socrates' last minutes of life at the close of the *Phaedo*. As he grew older, Plato joined other prose writers, notably Isocrates, in avoiding hiatus, but unlike Isocrates he was no aficionado of the long balanced clauses that intimidate students whose own languages do not enjoy the inflectional characteristics, but in fact ease the comprehension, of a hypotactic style. Plato also became increasingly fond of complex word order (a phenomenon not yet fully understood): he also dropped much of the polite formulae and conversational bits that lightened his earlier style (on "interlacing" word order, see Denniston 1952: 54–5, Thesleff 1967: 79–80, and more generally on Plato's later style, Rutherford 1995: 278–9).

Oratory

Oratory was the genre of Greek prose that most influenced the writing styles of later Greeks, Romans, and indeed the vernacular prose of the educated classes of Europe as long as Classics dominated the elite schools. For purposes of stylistic analysis, oratory offers the advantage of preservation in a large corpus of texts of essentially uniform dialect that fall, more or less cleanly, into sub-categories explicitly identified – and sometimes revealingly parodied – by contemporaries or near contemporaries: forensic (or "dicanic"), political (or "symbouleutic"), and display (or "epideictic"). The tripartite division in precisely this form goes back to Aristotle, *Rh.* 1358b7–8. There is abundant evidence for how orators prepared and the conditions in which they delivered their speeches. Moreover, courtroom oratory was unique in being a verbal performance forced on numerous men with no public literary aspirations whatsoever; the prestige forms of court speech show signs of reacting to the inadequate performances of those men too poor to pay for skilled assistance (Bers 2009, esp. ch. 7). In consequence, rhetorical style can be studied with greater precision than any other surviving Greek literature.

True, the earliest specimens of prose oratory preserved on their own, rather than incorporated in and modified for the historiographical or poetic forms that report them, are later than the founding of the democracy that gave persuasive speech great power. The oldest surviving speeches cannot have been delivered much earlier than about 430 BCE. Still, once Cleisthenes brought the mass of common, rather poor citizens into politics at the end of the sixth century BCE, if not before, artful public speaking became a more powerful tool for acquiring and wielding power. There is, regrettably, very little evidence on the use of writing in the preparation for the oral presentation and preservation of public speech.

For us, preserved oratory begins with Antiphon. As noted earlier, his corpus allows dialect comparisons between speeches actually delivered (those numbered 1, 5, and 6) and the *Tetralogies,* each one with short speeches for both prosecution and defense, evidently written to demonstrate Antiphon's skills and teach argumentation from a set of stipulated facts. As compared to preserved oratory contemporary or only a little later, Antiphon's style appears stiff, overly abstract, and at least in a few passages in *Against the Stepmother*, imitative of tragic poetry. But if his style seems bent on impressing jurors by its slightly formal, or even alien, phraseology, there are also devices that seem meant to ensure it was comprehensible. For instance, in the narrative portion of the *Murder of Herodes* the speaker tells of a guileless transfer from one boat to another, using a *-sis* noun *nomen actionis* as the grammatical subject (22.5: ἡ μετέκβασις ἐγένετο εἰς τὸ ἕτερον πλοῖον οὐδενὶ μηχανήματι οὐδ᾽ ἀπάτῃ "The transfer from one boat to the other occurred with no machination or deceit"). After witnesses attest to the veracity of his account, the speaker recapitulates this part of his story using conventional syntax, namely the corresponding verb with a first-person plural subject (23.1: ἐπειδὴ δὲ μετεξέβημεν εἰς τὸ ἕτερον πλοῖον, ἐπίνομεν "After we went over to the other boat, we drank").

With surprising rapidity, Attic oratory took on a far more natural and entirely indigenous cast in the hands of Lysias and, possibly, a number of other writers whose words found a place under his name. (This qualification is not pedantic, since Dover 1968 has shown the problems in assigning authorship, or sole authorship, of a speech to Lysias, with the sole exception of the twelfth speech, *Against Eratosthenes*, where the legal issue was his own brother's murder.) Not only were the rapidly emerging generic qualities of oratory easy, by virtue of their intrinsic qualities, to imitate, but there are grounds for suspecting that Lysias' assistance as a *de facto* professional could range from total authorship of every word of a speech, at least in its written form, to a few words of general advice to a litigant writing his own speech. Among the generic qualities Dover demonstrates are subtle differences between the signaling of temporal sequence in the narratives of forensic oratory and those found in the narratives of Old Comedy. This is an extremely important observation, for it establishes a *differentia* that distinguishes artistic prose taken from the least mannered corpus of Attic speech, moreover in the sub-category of oratory regarded as the least deviant from everyday speech.

Differences between forensic and political speeches are not easily detected, and we are hampered by a delay in the preservation of the latter: the certain examples come from the middle of the fourth century BCE. Display speeches, on the other hand, were composed in an unmistakable, easily parodied style. It is convenient to take examples of this category from the corpus of works attributed to Lysias, although their authenticity cannot be taken for granted. One is a *Funeral Oration*, a genre best known from the speech by Pericles that Thucydides reports in his second book (2.35–46).[3] The first phrase of Lysias 2.20 (a tiny sample, chosen at random) is typical in having ornamental sound qualities virtually impossible to suggest in translation: καὶ γάρ τοι καὶ φύντες καλῶς καὶ γνόντες ὅμοια "And further, both nobly sprung and likewise minded . . .". Though the sentence begins with a three-particle combination found also in forensic speech (but virtually never outside Attic oratory), an accomplished speaker performing in an Athenian courtroom would be careful to avoid the pair of rhyming, isosyllabic participles in parallel positions. To the extent our sources can show, epideictic is also thick with vocabulary rarely or never found in colloquial speech or professional courtroom oratory, and only occasionally attested in poetry. Surviving epideictic shows little hiatus, but this characteristic is more fully developed in Isocrates.

Isocrates wrote in the most obviously elaborate style and, not coincidentally, his oratory is the most self-conscious about its resources and methods. In the *Evagoras* he complains that prose writers must confine themselves to words in common use and must deny themselves the unfair advantages metrical language bestows on even inferior poets (8–11). He was querulous and conceited, but also candid about the personal inadequacies that made him unfit for tumultuous public debate (*Letter to Philip* 81) and forced him to turn to the publication of speeches with, at best, a notional relation to public performance. Nevertheless, technical mastery and his cultural and political program (shallow and opportunistic as it seems to many) made him the most celebrated teacher of rhetoric in the fourth century BCE. It is easy to mock Isocrates for his obsessive avoidance of hiatus and the unremitting stream of long balanced clauses, a paradigm of the subordinating style favored by Aristotle (see above). His *Kunstprosa* is among the monuments of classical literature, but among modern Hellenists only a small band of enthusiasts read him with much pleasure.

In the nearly unanimous opinion of ancients and moderns, Demosthenes was the greatest of all the classical orators. His speeches are dramatic and stylistically varied, qualities that make him utterly different from Isocrates. His corpus is clearly contaminated, or "supplemented," by speeches composed by others, notably Apollodorus (see Trevett 1992), but among those accepted as genuine there are interesting variations between the two sub-categories of oratory, forensic and political, that resemble each other much more than either resembles epideictic. For instance, Demosthenes employs a way of saying "both . . . and" (corresponsive τε . . . τε) in forensic, but not political speeches. This fine point is a matter of personal style not dictated by genre, for the public speeches deemed spurious do not exclude the usage (Denniston 1954: 503). The best known of Demosthenes' personal, and possibly unconscious, preferences is an avoidance of a sequence of three short syllables known as "Blass's law" (see McCabe 1981). None of this stylistic skill ultimately protected Athens from being swallowed up by Macedon, but the subsequent establishment of Alexander's kingdom made Hellenists of much of the known world, and an audience for Greek prose up to the present.

FURTHER READING

An introduction with texts and commentary, starting with Ionic prose and continuing to writers of the late Roman Empire is Russell 1991. Still useful for its discussion of prose within the general development of Greek is Meillet 1975. Important works bearing on various aspects of Greek prose (syntax, lexicon, figures of speech, etc.) include Dik 1995, Denniston 1952 and 1954, Dover 1968 and 1997, and Volkmann 1885. Most recent commented editions have good remarks on style, including Dover 1980, Rusten 1989, Whitehead 2000, and Yunis 2001.

NOTES

1 Sonnet 130, and cf. Callimachus fragm. 112.9 αὐτὰρ ἐγὼ Μουσέων πεζὸν [ἔ]πειμι νομόν, but his meaning is controversial.
2 Hence I am skeptical of Norden 1909: 64–5 and Bakker 1997a: 144 on the rhythm of Gorgias' manifesto. The phrase ἐγὼ δὲ βούλομαι "and I want" is certainly not meant to be heard as a bit of iambic verse at Dem. 21.3. I do acknowledge that Gorgias is talking about meter, but I understand his rhetorical drift to be couched in very narrow terms, as if he is saying "*metron*, and I mean *metron* so narrowly that it precludes rhythm."
3 That Pericles gave the official oration for the war dead no one doubts, but the degree to which Thucydides' account is faithful to the original is controversial in the extreme.

CHAPTER THIRTY-ONE

The Literary Heritage as Language: Atticism and the Second Sophistic

Lawrence Kim

In his *Lives of the Sophists* (early third cent. CE), Philostratus describes the curious figure of Agathion, a primitive "survival" from the hinterlands of Attica who was nearly eight feet tall, wrestled wild animals, subsisted only on milk and the occasional barley-cake, and dressed in a patchwork garment fashioned from wolfskins. Agathion's isolation has kept him free of civilization's corrupting influences, and he disdains tragic performances and athletic competitions in good "noble savage" fashion (*Lives* 552–4). But it has also preserved, and this is what gives the portrait its particular Second Sophistic touch, Agathion's language (γλῶττα). As he explains in an interview with the famous second-century orator Herodes Atticus, he has been taught by "the interior" (μεσογεία) of Attica, which is (unlike the city of Athens) "untainted by barbarians" (ἄμικτος βαρβάροις); its "accent is healthy" (ἡ φωνὴ ὑγιαίνει), and its "language sounds the purest strain of Attic" (γλῶττα . . . τὴν ἄκραν Ἀτθίδα ἀποψάλλει)" (*Lives* 553). Perhaps no anecdote more vividly illustrates the quasi-mythical status enjoyed by the Attic dialect in the imperial era. Agathion is more than just a "native speaker" of Attic; he embodies the qualities of the dialect itself as it was imagined by his sophistic contemporaries – archaic, ethnically pure, morally and physically "simple," and uncorrupted by the passage of time.

Atticism – the emulation of the style and language of Classical Athens – reached its height in the second century CE, and became a defining emblem of an Imperial Greek elite that privileged *paideia*, or culture and education, above all else. The factors that played a role in Atticism's ascendance – an insistence on language purity (ἑλληνισμός: Vassilaki 2007), a widespread archaizing nostalgia for the past, the prestige of oratory – had always been important features of Greek culture. But in the Second Sophistic, their impact is more profound. Rhetorical prowess is now associated with wealth and status, and as a result proper language and education become increasingly important in defining one's place within the social hierarchy. The policing of language purity produces an atmosphere of intense anxiety – one in which the satirist Lucian of Samosata (*c.* 120–85 CE) feels compelled to write an entire treatise

(*On a Slip of the Tongue in Greeting*) apologizing for his incorrect use of the saluta-tion ὑγίαινε "good health," and in which unthinkingly referring to a breadbox as πανάριον instead of ἀρτοφόριον could make one the object of ridicule (Sext. Emp. *Math* 1. 234). The idealization of the past so prevalent in the period led to a general revival of archaic literary dialects, such as Doric and Ionic, but it was Attic that became the dominant model of "correct" Greek, due to the cultural, political, and literary centrality of Classical Athens in the imperial imagination. Orators and lit-térateurs thus "Atticize" (ἀττικίζειν), that is, they imitate not only the style of Classical authors like Plato, Xenophon, Isocrates, and Demosthenes, but also their dialect, employing Attic orthography, morphology, vocabulary, and syntax and simultaneously "purifying" their own language of postclassical forms, words, and constructions.

Our knowledge of Atticism comes from two different types of sources: (i) explicit discussions, dictates, or complaints about Atticizing language, and (ii) texts written in Atticizing Greek. Taken separately, the two sets of evidence present a somewhat dif-ferent picture: the first, an oppressive polemical milieu populated by an elite obsessed with recreating the minutiae of the Attic dialect and catching the mistakes of their peers; the second, of a body of literary texts in which Atticizing language is skillfully employed in a fairly relaxed and creative way in a manner faithful to rather than slav-ishly dependent upon Classical models. The two are not necessarily incompatible, since there is no reason for the discourse on Atticism to match up precisely with its practice. But the vivid anecdotes of (i) have tended to overshadow the less spectacular and harder to analyze evidence of (ii). Moreover, the best recent treatments of Atticism (Swain 1996 and Schmitz 1997) have spotlighted (i) in order to demonstrate Atticism's role in consolidating elite identity. These are valuable and necessary correctives to the often confused and less comprehensive studies that preceded them (based on analyses of individual authors' usage of "Attic" words and forms), but they naturally privilege the repressive and normative thrust of Atticist discourse over its less coherent textual practice. My goal here, in the brief space available, is to present an overview of Atticism that attempts to reconcile, or at least juxtapose, Atticist theory with its practice. I also spend some time examining the question of Atticism's origins because much of the confusion concerning the nature of second-century Atticism derives from the super-ficial understanding of this evidence. But first, a few words about the place of Atticizing language under the Empire.

Atticism and Diglossia

Without an Agathion at hand as a guide, composition in an idiom and dialect which was no longer current required the extensive study only the elite, who had sufficient resources and leisure, could afford. As a result, their language became even more distant from the everyday speech of the majority of the population. A sociolinguistic situation of this sort, in which two moderately distinct varieties of the same language are used for different societal functions – a "high" register reserved for formal con-texts and a "low" for colloquial ones – is traditionally called *diglossia* (Ferguson 1959).

The paradigmatic modern examples include Classical and vernacular Arabic, High and Swiss German, and modern Greek *katharevousa* and *dimotiki* (see also ch. 37), but the case of Imperial Greek adheres closely to the pattern (Niehoff-Panagiotidis 1994: 106–26). The high dialect (elite Atticizing *Koine*) is considered more prestigious and esthetically superior than the low (popular colloquial *Koine*); it is linked to the culture's literary heritage, acquired through schooling rather than "naturally," associated with written discourse, and hence remarkably stable over a long period of time. High grammar (considered more "complex") and orthography and vocabulary (more "pure") are described and standardized in linguistic scholarship, while that of the low is ignored. Both share a great deal of vocabulary, but high and low terms often exist for the same referent, with each reserved for a corresponding "proper" context; incorrect application of a given word constitutes a serious breach of etiquette (cf. the Sextus passage alluded to above).

The gap between the two registers is customarily illustrated by comparing the strictures of the surviving second-century Attic lexica and the language of Atticizing authors (e.g., Aelius Aristides and Lucian) to texts believed to reflect the spoken popular *Koine*, like the Gospels (Luke excepted) and other early Christian literature, or Egyptian papyri (on the characteristics of this *Koine*, see Blass and Debrunner 1961 and Adrados 2005: 192–6, as well as chs 16 and 17 above). Atticizing authors were careful to maintain the phonological and morphological peculiarities of the Attic dialect that had largely been lost in the popular language: e.g., preferring ττ over σσ (e.g., γλῶττα vs γλῶσσα) and ρρ over ρσ (e.g., θαρρεῖν vs θαρσεῖν), and employing the "Attic" second declension (νεώς instead of ναός), the contracted forms of certain first and second declension nouns, athematic verb endings, and γίγνομαι and γιγνώσκω for γίνομαι and γινώσκω. The Atticists also sought to deploy the dual number, the dative case, the middle voice, the perfect tense, the future infinitive, and the optative mood, among others, in their full range of Classical functions, which were used in more restrictive contexts, if at all, in low texts.[1] The most striking contrast between Atticist and colloquial language, however, is in vocabulary; Atticizing writers avoid using words not attested in Classical texts, substituting the Attic equivalent. To take a popular example (Browning 1983: 47; Zgusta 1980: 126; Horrocks 1997a: 94), the late second-century lexicographer Phrynichus (*Selection* 10) recommends the Attic χάριν εἰδέναι "to give thanks" instead of εὐχαριστεῖν, a postclassical word that appears frequently in the New Testament.

Presented in this way, the artificiality of Atticizing Greek and its distance from popular spoken language seems great indeed. But while the development of second-century Atticism undoubtedly exacerbated the divide between the language of the elite and the masses, a state of diglossia had probably already existed right from the beginning of the spread of the *Koine* in the late fourth century BCE (Versteegh 1987, Niehoff-Panagiotidis 1994: 124–5), and possibly even earlier in Classical Athens itself (López Eire 1991; Adrados 2005). The Hellenistic literary *Koine* (*Normalprosa* (Palm 1955) or "artistically 'developed'" *Koine* (Horrocks 1997a: 48)) always remained much closer syntactically and morphologically to Classical Attic than to the spoken vernacular. The Greek of the historian Polybius (*c.* 150 BCE), for example, is written in a much higher register than the "low" *Koine* of the papyri or "vulgar" texts such as the *Life of Aesop*. The gap between written literary Greek and spoken colloquial was not ushered in by Atticism.

It is thus slightly misleading to compare Atticizing texts with those of the "low" register without taking into account Atticism's relationship with the Hellenistic literary *Koine*. The implication drawn from the χάριν εἰδέναι – εὐχαριστεῖν example cited above is that Atticists advocated replacing the standard *Koine* term with one "revived" from Attic. But even if the spoken colloquial used εὐχαριστεῖν exclusively, *both* terms were standard in the written literary *Koine* (e.g., Dion. Hal. *Orat. Vett.*1.4), and for all we know in the educated spoken language as well. Rather than introducing an obsolete term, Phrynichus is reacting against what he feels is the overly accommodating stance of literary *Koine*, identifying and approving of the "pure" Attic χάριν εἰδέναι while proscribing εὐχαριστεῖν as postclassical and vulgar. Comparison of the prescriptions of the Attic lexica with the vocabulary of first-century CE authors, such as the novelist Chariton of Aphrodisias (Ruiz-Montero 1991), point to similar conclusions: pre-Atticizing literary prose often already employs both the lexica's prescribed and proscribed variants, and the same goes for phonology and morphology. Atticism can be seen as essentially a reduction and "purification" of the literary *Koine* to its perceived Attic roots (Schmid 1887–97: iv: 642). Perhaps only with certain morpho-syntactic features, such as the optative or the future, can we speak of an Atticizing "revival," and even here we are not dealing with an artificial resuscitation of "dead" forms, but with an increase in usage of forms and constructions that had declined, but never disappeared from the literary language.

Atticism then, arose from the desire to cultivate a more rarefied style of Greek than that of the existing literary language, one closer to that of the ancients, purged of "vulgar" postclassical accretions, and hence more appropriate for certain kinds of literary discourse, such as oratory and belles-lettres, although the old literary *Koine* remained appropriate for other genres, such as philosophical or grammatical writing. But the gulf separating both of these, at least in the mind of the elite, from the "low" language was vast. For instance, the philosopher-doctor Galen of Pergamum (*c.* 130–200 CE) eschews Atticism, claiming that he will follow the "usage of the Greeks" (συνήθεια) instead, but he is quick to add that this is *not* the language of merchants and traders but one cultivated "in the books of the ancients" (*Distinctions between Pulses* 587.5–8). And while Galen is no Atticist, he is appalled by the Greek of the pharmacologist Dioscurides (first cent. CE) whom Rydbeck (1967: 200–3) has identified as a good example of an "in-between" register typical of Hellenistic technical treatises (*Zwischenschichtsprosa*). So while we can speak of a basic diglossic framework in which the educated language of the elite is separated from that of the non- or less educated masses, within the high category one should imagine a hierarchy of stylistic registers corresponding to particular social contexts and functions – high Attic rhetorical style, various levels of educated speech, less Atticizing literary language, the language of technical literature and popular philosophy, etc.[2] In the second century CE, prose authors such as Galen, Marcus Aurelius, Pausanias, Ptolemy, or Sextus Empiricus are arrayed along a spectrum below the high Atticism of the orators but still far above the popular vernacular. And as we shall see, the range of styles among Atticists is also quite varied, depending on the genre and the predilections of individual authors.

Dionysius of Halicarnassus and the Origins of Atticism

How then did this Atticizing phenomenon arise and become the normative standard for the highest levels of literary prose? An investigation into Atticism's origins requires identifying and correlating the earliest examples of the two categories of evidence mentioned above: (i) explicit remarks advocating the imitation of Attic, or asserting its purity or superiority to *Koine*, and (ii) prose that shows signs of Atticizing. As we shall see, neither of these tasks is without its difficulties. One reason is the multivalence of the term "Attic," which can refer to the geographical area or the dialect, the written or the spoken language, prose or poetry, and in looser fashion invokes temporal (Classical Athens), stylistic ("pure," plain, and direct), or ideological ("archaizing" in general) associations. For instance, the polemical debates of Hellenistic scholars over the authenticity of certain "Attic" words (particularly in Old Comedy) has been taken as evidence for Attic purism in the third and second centuries BCE.[3] But this interest in the Attic dialect is primarily descriptive, and refers to Attic poetry, not prose. Although later Atticist lexicographers would use the results of this research for *pre*scriptive purposes, there is no indication that Hellenistic scholars had any interest in laying down rules for writing prose or speaking in the Attic dialect.

The problems caused by the semantic vagaries of Atticism are perhaps best on display in discussions of its putative founder: the rhetorician, critic, and historian Dionysius of Halicarnassus, active in Rome during the reign of Augustus (27 BCE–14 CE). In the preface to his *On Ancient Orators* (1) Dionysius praises the recent revival of the "ancient, sober Rhetoric" – the "ancient and autochthonous Attic Muse" – that has overcome the "intolerably shameless and histrionic, ill-bred . . . vulgar and disgusting" ("Asian") style of oratory that had been ascendant since the late fourth century BCE. As a proselytizer of this archaizing trend, Dionysius advocates emulating the "best" orators, all active at Athens in the fourth century – Lysias, Isocrates, Isaeus, Demosthenes, Hyperides, and Aeschines – and devotes the rest of his work to a careful study of their style.

Dionysius nowhere refers to his campaign as Atticism, but its similarities with an earlier Roman Atticist movement of the mid-first century BCE make the attribution a reasonable one, since both were modeled on fourth-century Attic orators and polemically set against an "Asian" rhetoric (cf. Cic. *Brut.* 13.51; 82.284–91; *Orat.* 7.23–9.32; 70.234–71.236). The precise relationship between Dionysius and the Roman Atticists (*Attici*) has been the subject of much controversy (a good account in Wisse 1995; cf. Hidber 1996), but for now I only want to point out that both treat Attic rhetorical *style*, not grammar, orthography, or vocabulary (although Roman Atticism may have been caught up in Latin grammatical disputes; see Dihle 1977). Roman Atticists took writers like Lysias and Thucydides as their models, but they could hardly advocate imitation of their Attic Greek dialect. Dionysius, under no such restrictions, nevertheless refrains from recommending Attic words or forms; Attic and Atticism (ἀττικισμός) always refer to an author's style (e.g., Dion. Hal. *Lys.* 1; *De imit.* 31.5.1). "Asianism" is likewise marked as a stylistic, not linguistic, failing. Hegesias of Magnesia (third cent. BCE), the archetypal Asian orator despised by Dionysius, is criticized for his word arrangement and prose rhythm rather than vocabulary or morphology (*Comp.* 4; 18). From a very early stage scholars thus distinguished Dionysius' stylistic, early first-century CE Atticism from the grammatical and lexical variety of the second century CE (Schmid 1887–97. i: 10; Wilamowitz-Möllendorff 1900: 41 speaks of rhetorical vs linguistic).

But closer examination of Dionysius' account reveals some complications. His Athenian models are all active *before* the beginning of Asianism's rise to prominence – the death of Alexander the Great (323 BCE). The oratory of the entire period from this moment until Dionysius' own time (what we call the Hellenistic era) is thus implicitly tarred with the Asian brush. The broadening of the opposition of Attic and Asian style into one between Classical (pre-Alexander) and Hellenistic is reflected elsewhere in Dionysius' work: e.g., when he criticizes the unreadable style of nine Hellenistic historians (including Polybius) or champions Classical, but non-Attic, authors like Homer, the Archaic lyric poets, and Herodotus as models for imitation (*Comp.* 4; *De imit.*). Some scholars (e.g., Gelzer 1979, Lasserre 1979) have thought it more accurate to characterize Dionysius' program as "classicist" or "classicizing" (although he does not use the terms), in order to convey both its stylistic ("classical" as expressing a certain formal and moral propriety) and temporal concerns ("Classical" as opposed to Hellenistic). On this model, the term Atticism is reserved for the second-century variety; Dionysius, newly baptized as a classicist, seeks a return to the stylistic purity and power of the "ancient" authors in reaction to both a degenerate, flowery Asian oratory *and* a poorly composed, inartistic Hellenistic prose style. In terms of his theoretical stance, then, Dionysius is the first to articulate certain ideological positions which would be fundamental to later Atticism, but these are both broader in focus and directed toward slightly different goals.

Dionysius also plays a significant role in the history of Atticizing practice, as well as theory. After all, he wrote a twenty-book *History of Ancient Rome*, and one might expect that the prose of a critic who advocated the careful study and imitation of Athenian orators and historians would be recognizably more "Attic" than that of the Hellenistic authors he disdains. At first glance, however, Dionysius' prose seems quite similar to that of the historians Polybius and Diodorus Siculus (mid-first cent. BCE), the only previous literary *Koine* writers whose works survive in comparable length. For example, Polybius retains, albeit to a lesser degree, the distinctive Attic dialectal forms and grammatical constructions that had disappeared in the "low" vernacular (de Foucault 1972), but alternates between these and non-Attic *Koine* forms and usages; his verbose, "bureaucratic" style (Horrocks 1997a: 48–9; on Polybius' preference for extended articular infinitive clauses, see Hewlett 1890) and his greatly expanded vocabulary most conspicuously mark his drifting away from Attic. For all his insistence on imitation of Classical authors, Dionysius' style is as characteristically "Hellenistic" – discursive and circumlocuitous – as Polybius' and Diodorus' (Usher 1982: 827–8), and like them he is far from an Attic grammatical purist; he is inconsistent with Attic orthography – using both *Koine* οὐθείς and Attic οὐδείς, both γίνομαι and γίγνομαι – and uses as many postclassical words as Polybius.

That said, closer examination reveals isolated glimmers of "Atticizing": stylistically, in the increased use of the historical present, the optative, or hyperbaton (cf. Usher

1960: 360; Lasserre 1979: 144–5), lexically, in the avoidance of typically postclassical words like the conjunctions διό and διόπερ, and morphologically, in the replacement of *Koine* forms (ἱστάνω, ἀπεκρίθην) with their Attic equivalents (ἵστημι, ἀπεκρινάμην). These relatively limited, unsystematic attempts to capture the flavor of Attic are paralleled in other writers active at roughly the same time (20 BCE–50 CE): the historian Nicolaus of Damascus, the historian and geographer Strabo of Amasia, and the Hellenized Jewish scholar Philo of Alexandria (Wahlgren 1995). The distribution of individual "Atticisms" among these authors displays no particular pattern, suggesting that they were operating without a consistent set of guidelines as to what constituted "Attic."

What are we to make of this? There is clearly no comprehensive attempt to replicate Attic language. But even if these authors could be said to be merely haphazardly adorning an underlying literary *Koine* with Atticizing ornaments, their practice does still constitute a change, however minor, from that of Polybius and Diodorus. Another observation is that the neat distinction between a Dionysian stylistic classicism and a later grammatical Atticism falls apart in practice; these early imperial Atticizing features range from style to syntax, morphology, and vocabulary. But does this Atticizing language derive from Dionysius' classicizing imperatives? Or, as is more likely, was Dionysius giving programmatic expression to a state of affairs that already existed *de facto*, in which the imitation of the ancients was encouraging the adoption of Atticizing features of style *and* language? A significant difficulty in answering these questions is the paucity of Hellenistic literary prose before Dionysius to use as comparanda; Polybius and Diodorus might not be truly representative of the range of Greek literary style. The *Love Stories* of Parthenius of Nicaea, a contemporary of Diodorus, belongs to a different genre, but displays Atticizing features akin to those found in Dionysius' work (Lightfoot 1996: 283–97) as do papyrus fragments of early Hellenistic historical speeches (or are they declamations?) (Lasserre 1979: 157–62). One wonders, given the close connection between Classical Attic and literary *Koine*, whether the evidence of a wider body of artistic Hellenistic prose might force us to push back the beginnings of "Atticist" practice even further.

From Dionysius to the Second Sophistic

By the second century this relatively unsystematic emulation of Classical models had developed into a full-fledged purist movement which sought to imitate Attic style and required adherence to Attic grammar, morphology, and vocabulary. Older views attributing this shift to the archaizing efforts of an influential individual (e.g., Herodes Atticus (Schmid) or the Augustan grammarian Apollodorus (Wilamowitz)) have fallen out of favor, replaced by a more credible, yet vaguely conceived model of gradual development over the first century CE (e.g., Swain 1996).

A glance at the divergent styles of the two major literary authors of the late first century, the popular philosopher and orator Dio of Prusa (*c.* 40–110 CE) and Plutarch of Chaeronea (*c.* 50–120 CE), demonstrates the difficulties of mapping individuals onto this model. Plutarch's prolixity and immense postclassical vocabulary are characteristic of literary *Koine* (even if he writes more elegantly than Dionysius and his contemporaries),[4] while Dio is arguably the first Atticist writer, closer to Classical Attic in morphology, vocabulary, use of particles, syntax, and style than any other postclassical author before him (although he is far from strict: Schmid 1887–97: i: 70–191). Both authors evince the archaizing nostalgia characteristic of the Second Sophistic, but only Dio's reverence for the past extends to the stylistic and linguistic emulation of Classical authors. Philostratus tells us that he used to carry Plato's *Phaedo* and Demosthenes' *On the False Embassy* with him at all times (*Lives* 488), and Dio himself has high praise for Xenophon as a stylistic model, advocating the careful study, rewriting, and memorization of his prose (*Oration* 18.14–19). One factor for this discrepancy in style is surely genre; as someone with a deep interest in scientific and philosophical issues, Plutarch was immersed in Hellenistic texts, and generally seems distant from the world of public oratory and moral diatribe in which Dio thrived (more on genre below).

This suggests that, just as in Dionysius' day, the continuing push toward Atticism came from rhetorical circles. Debates over Atticizing oratorical style were still alive and well in the late first century: compare Quintilian's long rehash of the old Roman Atticist–Asianist debate (Quint. *Inst.* 12.10.16–26) and Plutarch's mocking of speakers who insist upon a "severe Attic style" (τὴν λέξιν Ἀττικὴν . . . καὶ ἰσχνήν) as akin to men who refuse overcoats in winter, content "in a delicate, thin jacket of Lysian language" (Plut. *De Aud.* 42d).

The first unambiguous reference to grammatico-lexical Atticism also occurs in a rhetorical context. Around 100 CE, Pliny the Younger refers to the "Greek, or rather Attic language" (*sermo Graecus, immo Atticus*) of the sophist Isaeus, and bestows special praise on his "well-chosen and polished words" (*verba – sed qualia! – quaesita et exculta*: Plin. *Ep.* 2.3). Pliny had seen Isaeus, whom he calls a teacher of rhetoric (*scholasticus*), performing declamations – fictitious speeches, often on historical themes, in which an orator could display his skills in argument, impersonation, and improvisation. Declamation had been a part of rhetorical education since the early Hellenistic period, but under the Empire it developed into a literary form in its own right, performed by teachers to their students, but also to larger elite audiences (Heath 2004: 299–308). The classicizing tendencies of the curriculum ensured that historical declamations (the more difficult variety) centered on Classical Athens, and imitation of the Attic dialect would have been one way to make a speech sound historically appropriate. Isaeus' declamations served, at least notionally, as models for his students, who were thus presumably being taught to write and speak in Attic. This accords with the evidence of an epigram by the Neronian poet Lucillius, in which he criticizes a rhetorician for teaching his students stereotypically Attic terms (although Lucillius does not specify their origin) like πολλοῦ δεῖ, ἄττα, μῶν, τετταράκοντα, ταυτί (*Anth. Pal.* 11.142). Two other phrases included in the list (δικασταὶ ἄνδρες "gentlemen of the jury" and λέγε δὴ τὸν νόμον ἐνθάδε μοι "now read out the law for me") are from Attic courtroom speeches, suggesting that the teacher has encouraged his students to copy the most obvious "Attic" words and phrases from their reading in order to make their compositions sound more authentic.

Similar Attic word-lists are criticized in second-century epigrams (Cerealis *Anth. Pal.* 11.144; Ammianus *Anth. Pal.* 11.157) and Lucian's *Lexiphanes* and *Teacher of Rhetoric* (16), and the two surviving declamations of the famous sophist Polemo of

Laodicea (early second cent. CE) seem to have been composed along these lines, with conspicuous words bestowing an Attic veneer on otherwise typical postclassical prose (Schmid 1887–97: i: 48–67). By the latter half of the second century CE, we hear of bolder strategies for dazzling audiences, such as digging up recondite archaic words (*Lexiphanes* 24; *Teacher* 17; Ps.-Dionysius, *Mistakes in Declamation* 365) or inventing outlandish neologisms out of Attic roots (Ath. 3.97d–98f; see Schmitz 1997: 117–23 on other methods). This evidence points to the continuing centrality of rhetorical training and performance to the practice and development of Atticism.

Attic Lexica and Linguistic Purism

Two significant changes, however, occur in the second century. First, the issue of language use moves from the fringes of elite debate to its center, and second, the "positive" adoption of Attic dialectal features is supplemented by a "negative" proscription of anything that appears non-Attic or postclassical. Questioning the legitimacy and purity of certain words becomes a formidable weapon that provokes equally powerful rejoinders: Lucian devotes an entire treatise, *The False Critic* (*Pseudologista*), to defending his use of the word ἀποφράς in an allegedly unattested construction, and the sophist Philagrus egotistically (or desperately) cites his *own* authority when a suspicious word is publicly questioned by Herodes Atticus' students (Philostratus *Lives* 578). Ulpian of Tyre, one of the guests in Athenaeus' *Sophists at Dinner* (early third cent. CE), continuously interrupts the other speakers to ask them whether or not a given word has been used by the ancients (κεῖται ἢ οὐ κεῖται "is it attested, or not attested?"), earning him the nickname Keitoukeitos. And the title character of the (Ps.-?) Lucianic *Solecist* is criticized not because he makes mistakes, but because he cannot detect them in his interlocutor's speech (on the competitive atmosphere, see Anderson 1993: 86–94 and Schmitz 1997: 110–27).

It is hard to see how this kind of debate could have been conducted without the support of grammatical and lexical scholarship; utilizing an Attic phrase found in one's reading is one thing, being certain that a given word or syntactical construction does *not* appear in any Classical author quite another. The growing influence of grammar on rhetoric in the second century CE is embodied in the group of Attic lexica that survive from the period. Dictionaries or glossaries of Attic terms had existed for a long time, necessitated by the increasing distance between the literature read in school and everyday vocabulary. But until the second century these seem to have been descriptive and designed for reading Attic texts (e.g., those by Irenaeus and Pausanias in the first cent. CE). Traces of prescriptive intent, however, can be detected in the fragments of Aelius Dionysius' early second-century CE lexicon (Erbse 1950), and by the latter half of the century the majority of surviving lexica are oriented toward writing Attic Greek. These include Phrynichus' *Sophistic Preparation* and *Selection of Attic Words*, Pollux of Naucratis' *Onomasticon*, Moeris' *Atticist*, and two anonymous lexica: that of the so-called Anti-Atticist, and the Ps.-Herodianic *Philetaerus*, a later work based on a second-century original (possibly by Aristides' teacher, the grammarian Alexander of Cotiaeum: Alpers 1998).[5]

The extant examples are not identical in organization, content, or tone. Some arrange their entries alphabetically, others at random, and Pollux does so according to topic; the consistency with which they cite Attic authors varies, as does their choice of sources (see below). But all are aimed at the same goal: to define Attic usage. This covers more than vocabulary; many entries deal with phonology, morphology, and occasionally syntax, as these examples from Moeris' *Atticist* show:

δεδιττόμενος Ἀττικοί· ἐκφοβῶν Ἕλληνες (Moeris δ 7: vocabulary)
βελτίους Ἀττικοί· βελτίονες Ἕλληνες (β 8: morphology)
ἤρεσέ με Ἀττικοί· ἤρεσέ μοι κοινόν (η 6: syntax)

δεδιττόμενος [scaring], Att.; ἐκφοβῶν [scaring], Gk
βελτίους [better; nom. pl.], Att.; βελτίονες, Gk
ἤρεσέ με [it pleases me], Att.; ἤρεσέ μοι [it pleases to me], common usage

Moeris establishes a simple polarity between "Attic" on the one hand and *Koine* on the other (referred to as "Greek" or "common"; his criteria for distinguishing them are unclear) that often masks a more complicated reality. For instance, both βελτίους and βελτίονες ("better"; nom. masc./fem. pl.) appear in Classical Attic and literary *Koine*, although the former is found more often in Attic, the latter in *Koine*. But Moeris is concerned not so much with descriptive accuracy as prescriptive utility; the contracted βελτίους is undoubtedly the alternative that *seems* more Attic, and this is what matters. The normative intent underlying Moeris' categories is explicit in Phrynichus' labeling of words as "approved" and "unapproved" (δόκιμον/ἀδόκιμον) and his simple injunctions to the reader: "do not say X, but Y" or "avoid X."

Phrynichus' judgments extend beyond the linguistic realm. For him "approved" terms are those used by "ancient," "Attic," and "educated" writers (παλαιοί, Ἀττικοί, πεπαιδευμένοι), while "unapproved" words are denigrated as "foreign" and "barbaric" (ἀλλόκοτον; βάρβαρον) and uttered by "the uncultured" (οἱ ἀμαθεῖς), the "masses" (οἱ πολλοί), and "the vulgar" (οἱ ἀγοραῖοι). It is clear that there is more at stake here than just mastering Attic; the skill with which one did so was closely tied to the outward determination of social status and Hellenic identity. It should not be a surprise, then, to learn that the lexicographers were not dispassionate scholars, systematically describing Classical Attic grammar and vocabulary, but active participants in the same sophistic disputations in which Lucian, Athenaeus' Ulpian, and Philagrus were engaged. Pollux, for instance, held the Imperial Chair of Rhetoric at Athens (Philostratus *Lives* 592–3) and was a practicing orator, while Phrynichus relishes pointing out the "errors" of famous second-century sophists like Polemo (*Selection* 236), Lollianus of Ephesus (140), and Favorinus of Arelate (215, 218, etc.).

Outside the lexica, the contentious battles over language purity are most apparent in the work of Galen and Lucian. Galen is a particularly fascinating case (Swain 1996: 56–62). As a doctor, he belonged to a group whose "impure" Greek was criticized by Atticists like Phrynichus; in response he ridicules their use of obsolete Attic terms for plants, foods, and animals whenever he gets the chance (collected in Herbst 1911). As mentioned above, however, Galen's own standards of language purity may have been different from the Atticists, but they were no less stringent. In fact Galen took the fight to the Atticists' own turf, composing his own lexicographical works (now lost), such as *On False Attic Usage* and his enormous 48-book Attic dictionary in order to elucidate the differences between Attic and modern usage (*The Order of My Own Books* 60–1K).

If Galen attacks Atticism from the outside (although the pull of the Attic norm affects his style as well), Lucian satirizes it from the perspective of a practitioner. His *Lexiphanes* (on which, see Weissenberger 1996), *Teacher of Rhetoric*, *A False Critic*, *The Ignorant Book Collector*, *How to Write History*, and (if it is his) the *Solecist* present a colorful rogues' gallery of language abusers that collectively conveys the absurdities of a culture obsessed with linguistic purity.[6] Both Lucian and Galen have been interpreted as targeting "hyper-Atticists" (a term apparently coined by Lucian: e.g., *False Critic* 29) who go "too far" in their insistence on purity; Lexiphanes and the Teacher of Rhetoric, for instance, are derided for unearthing recondite words and inventing Attic neologisms (the same faults that Ulpian and his associate Pompeianus are accused of in Athenaeus). But Lucian is equally harsh on *pseudo*-Atticists, who are ignorant of the meanings of the Attic words they use, employ faulty forms, resort to word-sprinkling, and fail to properly study ancient authors.

In their desire to police the boundaries of what constituted "correct" language, and to judge when it crossed the line into vulgarity or preciosity, Galen and Lucian, despite their significantly different linguistic ideals, are engaged in the same game as the lexicographers. While Phrynichus is uncompromising in his strictness, rejecting the testimony of authors like Xenophon, Aristotle, and Menander, and even judging approved authors as sometimes mistaken (e.g., *Selection* 330 on Lysias, probably an attack on Anti-Atticist 82, 21; more examples at Schmitz 1997: 123), Lucian's and Galen's strategy is to stake out a "sensible" middle ground from which they can criticize the linguistic usage of those who try too hard to be "pure" *and* those who don't try hard enough (Whitmarsh 2005: 45–7). This ground, however, was constantly shifting, since "proper" Greek, as an abstracted linguistic ideal, was essentially a mirage. Even Classical Attic was not stylistically, grammatically, or lexically unitary, and debates over what genres, periods, and authors should be included could never be objectively resolved. Because it was both closely tied to the determination of social status *and* constantly open to renegotiation, correct language use became an ideal focal point for elite polemic. It is perhaps no accident that Lucian and Galen, who both had reason to be sensitive about their own status vis-à-vis language – as a doctor and a non-native Greek speaker respectively – are our best sources for the excesses and anxieties of second-century language purism.

Styles of Atticism

Viewing Atticism solely through the lens of this normative discourse, however, risks distorting the extent of its control over literary production (Bompaire 1958: 116). Although there is no denying that the Attic standard exercised a powerful influence on all educated (and even semi-educated) writing, the traditional image of Atticizing language as a straitjacket that stifled originality and resulted in an imitative and artificial literature removed from real life is far from accurate. As Albert Wifstrand pointed out long ago, "one ought not to base one's appraisal of the literature of an age on the *theory* of its authors and critics" (2005 [1942]: 146). The theory itself was probably more varied than the bulk of our evidence suggests: for instance, Phrynichus' narrow canon of approved authors was not universally accepted among lexicographers – Pollux is more inclusive, and the Anti-Atticist is so called because he cites a broad range of sources comprising non-Attic authors like Hipponax, Herodotus, or the poets of New Comedy (Schmid 1887–97: i: 204–10). Moreover, if we turn to the evidence of surviving Atticist texts, a similarly varied picture of Atticism emerges. Rather than only a strict adherence to the prescriptions of the lexica, or slavish imitation of Athenian writers, second-century authors employ a wide variety of individual Atticist styles with correspondingly different attitudes toward "purity," suggesting that the successful emulation of Attic was a more complicated business than most of the lexica would care to admit.

At one end of the spectrum is the historian Arrian (90–150 CE), who wrote works in Ionic, Attic, and *Koine*. While he was far from a purist, Arrian's Atticism is marked by stylistic choices reminiscent of the reductive precepts of Moeris and Phrynichus (Tonnet 1988: 299–351). For instance in indefinite temporal clauses, Arrian uses ἐπείδαν "whenever" with the subjunctive but never ὅταν – a decision that is completely arbitrary from the perspective of Classical Attic, which has both alternatives. In other cases, similar choices seem motivated by Arrian's desire to avoid association with *Koine*: e.g., his preference for χρῆ over δεῖ, which are both Attic, can be explained by the fact that in *Koine* δεῖ had taken over the semantic field of both terms, and hence sounded more like *Koine* than the rarer χρῆ. Such attempts to fashion a coherent, unambiguous Atticism in which certain words are used in only one prescribed fashion give Arrian's style an idiosyncratic Atticizing patina, but seem more concerned with sidestepping accusations of vulgarism than with actually recreating Classical Attic.

A considerably different approach is taken by the orator Aelius Aristides (117–80 CE), recognized by ancients and moderns as one of the "purest" Atticists due to the unparalleled rigor with which he excludes postclassical words and forms from his writing (Schmid 1887–97: ii: 309–13). But Pernot (1981: 117–46) has shown that Aristides' practice, at least in his *Sicilian Orations*, diverges from that advised by the lexica in two significant ways. First of all he models his vocabulary and morphology primarily on two authors – Thucydides, from whom the historical situation (the Sicilian Expedition) is taken, and Demosthenes – rather than an unwieldy "ideal" Attic compiled from an entire set of approved Classical texts. Secondly, the "Attic" purity of the *Sicilian Orations* also arises from Aristides' imitation of Atticizing *style* (e.g., periodic structure, characteristic constructions, figures of speech, etc.), a matter absent from the discussions in the lexica, Galen, and Athenaeus. Moreover, he bases this style on that of a particular model – Demosthenes – rather than a generalized group of stylistic phenomena considered "Attic." The result is a remarkable display of rhetorical and linguistic virtuosity that emulates the spirit as well as the letter of his chosen models, and demonstrates that successfully composing Attic at this level required considerably more knowledge and expertise than the lexica could provide.

The extreme purism of the *Sicilian Orations* (which, as historical declamations, naturally demanded a close approximation of Classical Attic) is not, however, entirely representative of Aristides' Atticism, which varies in its strictness throughout his corpus. The "high" Isocratean Attic of his urban panegyrics, for example, contrasts with the far less "purist" style he employs in his prose hymns or the autobiographical *Sacred Tales* (Boulanger 1923: 399–400). In his groundbreaking work on Atticism, Schmid (inspired by ps.-Aristides' *Art of Rhetoric*, on which see Schmid 1917; Rutherford 1998: 64–79) accounted for this variety by distinguishing two Atticizing registers: a "political discourse" (λόγος πολιτικός) appropriate to declamation and public oratory and a "simple discourse" (λόγος ἀφελής) employed in less formal writing, such as letters, philosophical dialogues, biographical or fictional narratives, moral and satirical essays, etc. (Schmid 1887–97: ii: 8–12; iv: 733). Moreover, practitioners of each brand of writing embraced a separate set of Attic authors as their paradigms of diction and style: Isocrates, Demosthenes, and Thucydides for the "political," Xenophon, Plato, and Herodotus for the "simple." In line with their models, "political" authors adhered to a fairly rigorous standard of grammatical purity and cultivated an elevated periodic style, while "simple" ones sought a more casually constructed style that attempted to capture the "charm" and "simplicity" of their models' prose and permitted a reasonable amount of Ionicisms, poeticisms, and postclassical words and forms.

Schmid's division may be overly schematic – the stylistic landscape of imperial rhetoric is bewildering in its complexity (Pernot 1993 is an excellent introduction; cf. Rutherford 1998) – but is useful nonetheless. In fact, it is the looser, less purist "simple" style that dominates the extant Atticizing texts of the Second Sophistic; no examples of the "political" style have survived other than those of Aristides. The four major Atticist authors of the period – Dio, Lucian, Philostratus, and the Italian sophist Aelian (*c.* 170–235 CE) – take Xenophon and Plato as their primary models, adopt a liberal approach toward Atticizing lexical and morphological standards, make heavy use of poetic words, and avoid (for the most part) the elevated tones and complicated periods characteristic of declamatory and epideictic oratory. Of course, within these parameters, each author's methods are quite distinctive. Dio is the least purist of the four in terms of diction, but stylistically the closest to Xenophon and Plato. Lucian draws heavily from Old Comedy vocabulary, and is technically the most "Attic," but still frequently diverges from Classical syntax, and nearly a quarter of his vocabulary is not attested in Attic prose. Philostratus and Aelian employ even more postclassical vocabulary, share a penchant for brachylogy and odd word order, and generally seem more mannered and self-conscious in their striving for Attic "simplicity" (Anderson 1986: 14–17). But all four embrace a fairly relaxed Atticism that seems quite alien to the purist worldview evoked by Phrynichus and Moeris and criticized by Lucian and Galen. To be fair, some of their divergences from Attic usage may stem from ignorance, but most "errors" are either intentional attempts to avoid an overly purist style, or simply the result of an attitude that did not look with horror upon "unapproved" words, forms, or constructions.

For writers of the "simple" style (and arguably even for some "political" writers) the goal was never to produce perfect imitations of Attic prose that could pass for fourth-century BCE documents, but rather to maintain a vital connection to their literary and cultural heritage by inhabiting the same linguistic milieu as the illustrious writers of the Hellenic past. To this end, they fashioned a contemporary style based on a comfortable familiarity with a wide range of Classical models, shaped according to the kind of work being produced, but marked by their own individualized predilections and innovations. The apparent split between the liberality of Atticist practitioners and their more purist theoretical counterparts is perhaps not surprising; those who prescribe rules and engage in polemic tend to reduce the messiness of actual performance to an easily comprehensible choice between right and wrong. But as we have seen, there are lexica like that of the Anti-Atticist that almost seem designed for writers of the "simple" style (as Schmid himself suggests), and conversely the picture of a lenient Atticizing practice offered here might change significantly if we had a larger body of more purist "political" speeches.

The texts we possess, however, reveal enough variety to allow us to conclude that Second Sophistic Atticism was a far from monolithic phenomenon, either in theory or in practice. Atticism has often functioned as a convenient all-inclusive label to characterize Imperial Greek, concealing the incredibly complex linguistic and stylistic variation in the second century CE; aside from that discussed in this chapter, there are several literary authors such as Pausanias and Maximus of Tyre who Atticize in a lower register, and others like the novelists Longus or Achilles Tatius who Atticize in their diction but adopt a poetic, rhythmic *style* that is reminiscent of Dionysius' "Asianism." The ideology of Atticism was powerful, but it did not affect everyone in the same way, and much more work needs to be done on the ways in which individual authors used Atticizing language as a means of connecting to the past, appropriating and transforming their Classical models.

FURTHER READING

The most important recent studies of Atticism's role in maintaining social boundaries and fashioning elite Hellenic identity are Swain 1996: 17–64 and Schmitz 1997: 67–96, 110–127. For Atticist practice, Schmid's five-volume *Der Atticismus* (1887–97), covering Dio Chrysostom, Aristides, Lucian, Aelian, and Philostratus, is still indispensable (cf. Anderson 1993: 86–100). Schmid's analyses have been critiqued and supplemented: by Tonnet 1988: 299–351 on Arrian; by Boulanger 1923: 395–412 and Pernot 1981: 117–46 on Aristides; by Deferrari 1916 and Bompaire 1994 on Lucian; and by de Lannoy 2003 on Philostratus. General accounts in handbooks of Greek literature or language are not always accurate and should be used with caution (e.g., Reardon 1971: 64–96; Zgusta 1980; Browning 1983: 44–50; Dihle 1994: 49–59, 67–70, 250–5; Adrados 2005: 198–202; Kazazis 2007); notable exceptions are Horrocks 1997a: 71–101 and Whitmarsh 2005: 41–56. On Hellenistic and early imperial prose, see the useful introduction in Wifstrand 2005 and, more specifically, Palm 1955 (on Diodorus), Anlauf 1960 (on optative use), Rydbeck 1967 (on scientific prose), Lasserre 1979 (on Dionysius), and Wahlgren 1995 (on Atticizing). Latte 1915 is still informative on the lexicographers; for a more recent appraisal, see Alpers 1997. On the sociolinguistic background, see the rather abstract, but still insightful comments in Frösén 1974.

Fasold 1984: 34–60 is a good introduction to the concept of diglossia, and Niehoff-Panagiotidis 1994 applies it to Imperial Greek. Finally, for more on "Asianism," which I have only touched upon, see Wilamowitz-Möllendorff 1900, Sirago 1989, and Pernot 1993: i: 371–80.

NOTES

1 See further: Schmid 1887–97. iv: 579–734; Horrocks 1997a: 83–4; Browning 1983: 24–43; and, more comprehensively, Blass and Debrunner 1961. See also chs 16, 17, 18, and 36 in this volume.
2 Frösén 1974: 168–79; Schmitz 1997: 79–80; Swain 1996: 29. For similar expansion of diglossia more generally, see Fasold 1984.
3 Aristophanes of Byzantium: fragm. 1-36 (Slater 1986); Crates of Mallos: fragm. 106–21 (Broggiato 2001); Eratosthenes of Cyrene: schol. Ar. *Ran.* 1263. See Tosi 1998.
4 On Plutarch's Atticism and style, we have only the rather limited study of Weissenberger 1895.
5 Available editions are: of Phrynichus, de Borries 1911 (*Preparation*) and Fischer 1974 (*Selection*); of Pollux, Bethe 1900–37; of *Philetaerus*, Dain 1954; of Moeris, Hansen 1998; of Anti-Atticist, Bekker 1814, 75–116. Other second-century lexica like Harpocration's *Lexicon of the Ten Orators* were meant for readers, not composers.
6 See Swain 1996: 45–9 and Hall 1981: 252–309, who also summarizes debates over the possible real-life targets Pollux, Pompeianus, Philagrus, and the sophist Hadrian of Tyre, among others.

CHAPTER THIRTY-TWO

Greek Philosophers on Language

Casper C. de Jonge and Johannes M. van Ophuijsen

Introductory

Philosophy is an irredeemably verbal and linguistic discipline. Its founders and early practitioners in Greece were aware of some of the ways in which their projects tied up with structures of speech, and they had a sense of there being something special about Greek and the community of its speakers. Yet they developed neither a full-fledged philosophy of language in general nor an explicit account of what was distinctive about their native tongue. Their interests were on the whole in external reality and the ways human thought could attain to it. Language served as a reflection of other domains, and served as a tool rather than an object of enquiry valued independently; the deep structure of what would later be called logical grammar counted as more revealing than linguistic phenomena observable at the surface, and comparison with other languages remained strictly *ad hoc*.

Significantly, there is no single word in Ancient Greek with more or less the same reference as our term "language." What we do find are nouns for speech "sounds and voice" (φωνή), for "tongue and tongues" (γλῶσσα), and for what is typically alleged to be the most distinctively human capacity: the capacity for articulate speech as the stating of accounts, which is the natural expression and indeed the inseparable companion of discursive reason (λόγος), the obverse of one and the same coin. Later on we find, from the same root and more particularly from the cognate verb for counting, listing, telling, and stating (λέγειν), the verbal noun (λέξις), which might properly refer to any such act but is most often used either of expression and style or of single words; and from the compound verb for talking (διαλέγεσθαι), a noun (διάλεκτος) for the practice and ways of speaking and so, just like its modern derivative, for dialects.

"Accounting" (λέγειν) and "account" (λόγος)

The concept of λόγος as the oldest and, for philosophical purposes, most central of the concepts involved, has in modern times been generalized so as to provide an inclusive characterization of the emergence of recognizably rational thinking at an early stage of the Greek cultural tradition. It has indeed proved difficult to narrow the concept down to anything at all unambiguous and unitary, as witness the fact that interpretations of the term as it occurs in the extant prose fragments of Heraclitus (*c.* 500 BCE) range between a *rational proportionality* foreshadowing the Stoic notion of cosmic harmony named by the same Greek word, and a minimalist reading limiting the connotation to "the account," in the sense of the true explanation of things furnished exclusively by Heraclitus.

While it is plausible that many later readers have projected Stoic refinements onto Heraclitus' formula, the view here taken is that λόγος as early as Heraclitus does indeed conceptualize the conviction that the universe of our experience displays an *order* which we may hope and attempt to express in terms of proportions and, more generally, relations between components into which it could be analyzed, and which, even though "nature likes to conceal itself" (φύσις κρύπτεσθαι φιλεῖ, DK 22 B123), our thought and speech are in principle fit to trace and recover. As far as language is concerned, this sets the stage for the position voiced by Socrates in Plato's *Phaedo*, that words are only a second best when we are trying to deal with realities (Pl. *Phd.* 99e4–6), but they are at least less misleading than the conflicting phenomena of sense perception.

In Heraclitus, the most conspicuous structural pattern enabling rare individuals of exceptional insight to reduce the phenomenal manifold to a unitary veridical perspective is that of *coinciding opposites*. The senses present a never-ending alternation of contraries. The common tongue is fit only to capture each of these partial, fragmentary aspects in separation from the complement that lends it integrity in the deep structure of things. The reason, rationale, and ratio that is λόγος, at once represents to us and *is* the essence that encompasses them, as well as the focus into which they converge. Any perception short of the noetic grasp (νοῦς) of this foundational principle is not so much wrong as hopelessly inadequate and partial, missing the entire point; but rarely if ever do the words of ordinary language, undisciplined by Heraclitus' hieratic management of them, bear witness to underlying unity (cf. Sluiter 1997: 169; Schmitter 2000: 352). Even where, exceptionally, one word (βιός "bow") succeeds in conveying notions as contradictory and as inseparable as those of "life" (βίος) and death, we need a Heraclitus to point out just what it is that we have all along been implying (DK 22B48: τῷ οὖν τόξῳ ὄνομα βιός, ἔργον δὲ θάνατος "the name of the bow is life, but its work is death"). The tacit understanding between the two organizing principles, reason-*cum*-speech (λόγος) and intelligence-*cum*-intellect (νοῦς), one spreading out and articulating, the other contracting and unifying, is Heraclitus' legacy to mainstream ancient Greek metaphysics, and is presupposed by medieval and modern systems betraying its influence.

Its first transformation, in Parmenides (*c.* 480 BCE), enlists "stating" (λέγειν) together with "affirming" (φάσθαι) and "expressing" (φράζειν) in the cause of highlighting "being" and "what is" as the only real bearers of truth, in opposition to naming (ὀνομάζειν) as a use of words fatally compromised by its association with false opinions (δόξαι) that divide being into whatever *it* is not, and therefore *is* not. The names involved are said to be "set down" and "instituted" (DK 28B8.39; DK 28B19.3), with a verb κατέθεντο "they [sc. humans] set down" that is related to θέσει "by institution," a term that is attested much later. They are credited with a limited and qualified validity as far as they go, i.e., for the everyday commerce of mortals.

The Investigation of Names:
Presocratic Philosophers on Language and Reality

Throughout antiquity, philosophers share the interest of poets in *etymology* (a term coined by the Stoics). As early as Homer and, especially, Hesiod, we find many interpretations of proper names, some of them more plausible than others by the standards of modern linguistics. It is the least plausible ones that reveal best what is the object of the exercise: to lend authority to an interpretative claim about the real nature of the person or object denoted by the name. An intriguing complication is provided by a class of doublets: persons who are given different names by different sets of people, or one name by humans, another by gods, e.g., the river Xanthos *a.k.a.* Skamandros (Pl. *Cra.* 391e4–6 on *Il.* 20.74). The fact may be traceable to an identification between putative persons of different origin, but the solution bears witness to an implicit awareness of *perspective* as a factor in establishing natures and identities. The recognition that there is an interpreting *subject* involved in name-giving opens the door to criticism of incorrect names, such as we find in the claim by Xenophanes (*c.* 570–475 BCE) that the rainbow is wrongly called Iris (DK 21B32), and to the notion of *degrees* of correctness, developed in Plato's *Cratylus* (e.g. Pl. *Cra.* 392d8–9: cf. Sedley 2003: 78–80).

In the fragments of the Presocratic philosophers, we find clear signs of discomfort with the inadequacy of customary human names, which they suppose are in many cases not, or only partially, capable of grasping the world as it is. Thus, for Heraclitus, the name of Zeus, which is traditionally associated with "living" (ζῆν), captures only one of two opposites that are really one (DK 22B32). Parmenides (DK 28B8.38–41; DK 28B19) also thinks that the names human beings apply are mistaken, since they reflect opinion (δόξα) rather than truth (ἀλήθεια) and being or "what is" (ἐόν). Empedocles (*c.* 490–430 BCE) objects to what human beings call "coming into being" (γενέσθαι), while conceding that he, too, uses this expression "as custom will have it" (νόμῳ; DK 31B9). For Empedocles, "coming into being" (γενέσθαι) is a name that does not describe any real process in nature because, on his view, the world consists of four elements that continually mix with each other. Democritus (*c.* 460–370 BCE), finally, is said to have listed four types of connections between names and things, each of which demonstrates that language fails to be a successful representation of reality (Sluiter 1997: 172–3): the phenomena of homonymy or "polysemy" (πολύσημον);

multiplicity of names or synonymy (ἰσόρροπον, literally an "equal balance" or "match"); change of names (μετώνυμον); and deficiency of certain names or forms of names (νώνυμον). Each and all of these four show that there is no one-to-one relationship between names and things (DK 68B26 – but it is uncertain how much of this text from Proclus (Procl. *In Pl. Cra.* 6.20ff. Pasquali) may be attributed to Democritus.

There is, then, an increasingly articulated uneasiness among the Presocratic philosophers about the appropriateness of customary names: different as the views of the various thinkers mentioned above may be, they seem to agree that the common tongue of humans is in many cases not an adequate instrument to speak about the world.

The Sophists on Language

This feeling of unease triggers a more systematic investigation of its object among the sophists, who seem to have promoted the awkward relationship between language and reality to a topic in its own right. It is natural that language was a primary interest of the sophists, since they professed a competence to turn their students into successful public speakers, able to deploy arguments effectively so as to influence the opinions of their audience.

The connection between names and things, or language and reality, was sometimes discussed in terms of "nature" (*physis*) and "convention" (*nomos*). It should be observed that this debate was in fact concerned with two different problems, which have often been confused, both in antiquity and in modern times (see Fehling 1965: 218–29 and Gera 2003: 169–70). On the one hand, there is the problem of *how* names are *related* to things: is this relationship a natural or a conventional one? Or, in more Platonic terms: does correctness of names arise "by nature" (φύσει) or "by custom" (νόμῳ)? This is the question tackled by Plato in *Cratylus* (see below); it reflects the interests of contemporary thinkers, many of whom appear to have argued for a conventionalist position. On the other hand, there was much speculation about the *origin* of language: did it have a natural origin (φύσει, again), or was it instituted (θέσει "by institution, imposition") by one or more "namegivers"? Most sophists seem to have argued for imposition and institution (θέσις) as the most plausible origin of names: this view is presupposed, for instance, in Plato's *Cratylus*, where "namegivers" (νομοθέται) are portrayed in several different ways: they are either human or divine, operating either as individuals or in groups (Gera 2003: 168–9). Even a barbarian namegiver is mentioned (Pl. *Cra.* 390a4–5: τὸν νομοθέτην τόν τε ἐνθάδε καὶ τὸν ἐν τοῖς βαρβάροις "the namegiver, whether he be here or among the barbarians"). The author of the Derveni papyrus, who is clearly interested in the process of namegiving, presents Orpheus as the man who assigned names to all things (esp. col. 22.1–3; Betegh 2004: 46).

Three sophists in particular are noteworthy for their linguistic interests: Prodicus, Gorgias, and Protagoras. Whereas Democritus had emphasized that the relationship between language and reality was in many respects asymmetrical by pointing to synonymy and related phenomena (as we have seen in the preceding section), Prodicus (*c.* 465–415 BCE) argued that genuine synonymy is nowhere found: he made a practice of demonstrating that apparently synonymous words in fact bore slightly different meanings (DK 84A19). Since Democritus is usually regarded as a supporter of the conventionalist thesis, Prodicus might be understood as arguing for the naturalist thesis, and thus against relativism (Heinimann 1945: 156ff.; Sluiter 1997: 176). At the same time, however, Prodicus' subtle distinctions between similar words – his characteristic procedure (Plato's *Protagoras* 337a1–c4 gives a wonderful parody) was appropriately called διαίρεσις, literally "taking apart," "dividing" – may be understood as part of a primarily rhetorical training in speaking effectively.

Gorgias (*c.* 487–376 BCE), the champion of artfully contrived and conspicuous rhetoric, was on the whole more interested in the acoustic effects and the enchanting power of words than in the relation between names and things (see also ch. 30). Yet according to one substantial fragment, Gorgias "claimed that nothing exists; that if it exists, it cannot be known; and that if it both exists and can be known, it cannot be communicated to others" ([Arist.] *De Melisso, Xenophane Gorgia* 979a12–13; cf. DK 82B3). The consequence of this argument is that the role of language is reduced to that of a magic wand that can be used at will to impress and manipulate an audience (cf. Sluiter 1997: 177).

The pioneering "sophist" Protagoras (*c.* 490–420 BCE) is often credited with being a kind of proto-grammarian, but we should not ignore the philosophical context in which he made his linguistic observations. From Plato's *Phaedrus* (267c3–5 = DK 80A26), we know that Protagoras used a term for "speaking correctly" or "correctness of diction" (ὀρθοέπεια). The context of this passage throws little light on what Protagoras meant by it, but testimonies from Aristotle's *Rhetoric, Poetics,* and *Sophistici Enlenchi* (DK 80A27–9) and Diogenes Laertius (DK 80A1, 254,13–17) inform us about Protagoras' linguistic interests. Protagoras (i) introduced distinctions of gender and (ii) classified different types of "speech" (λόγος) such as wish, question, answer, and command (πυθμένες λόγων "basic forms of speech" or, as we would now say, "speech acts"). These two observations can be connected with Protagoras' criticism of Homer's usage in the first line of the *Iliad* (μῆνιν ἄειδε θεά . . .) (Fehling 1965). According to Protagoras, the poet makes two mistakes: (i) he treats "wrath" (μῆνις) as feminine instead of masculine, as its inner nature would dictate; (ii) with "sing" (ἄειδε), he issues a command (ἐπιτάττει), whereas praying (εὔχεσθαι) would have been more appropriate to the divine addressee.

Do these testimonies support the view that "correctness of diction" (ὀρθοέπεια) is equivalent to "correctness of names" (ὀρθότης ὀνομάτων), as Plato's *Cratylus* might suggest (391c3–4)? Some scholars think that Protagoras criticized the incorrectness of language in general and that he advocated a reform of language, demanding an exact correspondence between words and things, or between the structures of grammar and those of reality (see, e.g., Di Cesare 1996: 100–4; Schmitter 2000). We should, however, bear in mind that Protagoras' term for "correct diction" (ὀρθοέπεια) is closely connected with the Greek for "uttering, saying, speaking a word" (εἰπεῖν) and for the "word spoken, uttered utterance" (ἔπος) (Fehling 1965: 215–16). Hence it refers primarily to (our acts of) "speaking correctly," to our *use* of language rather than to the correctness of language as such, or to that of isolated names, which is the topic of Plato's *Cratylus*. If so, then Protagoras did not criticize the incorrectness of names so much as the incorrect way in which poets, especially, express themselves: his linguistic observations, then, are to be understood in the context of his criticism of Homer, which in its turn may be interpreted as a demonstration of his notorious *relativism*: by showing that, in the very first words of his *Iliad*, the most famous and authoritative poet of the Greeks has made two mistakes, Protagoras demonstrates that the Greeks are wrong to suppose they can rely on Homer as a model for linguistic usage or, for that matter, as a source of knowledge in general.

Plato and Aristotle on Language, Thought, and Reality

The relations between the domains or dimensions of reality, thought, and speech are among the most central subjects of philosophical and meta-philosophical enquiry. Reflection on these relations comes of age in the seminal opening chapters of Aristotle's *De interpretatione* (on the expression of thought in assertions that form contradictory pairs: see Whitaker 1996). The claim there made is that the mental grasp of objects is as natural and intersubjectively universal as the nature of the objects themselves, but that the names we impose upon the objects in order to communicate this mental content are of human contrivance, arbitrary and variable.

This seems at first sight at odds with what may arguably be propounded as the upshot of Plato's *Cratylus*, in which Socrates does not give up hope of a natural basis for the words we use to refer to things, even if this basis may not reveal itself on their phonological surface. Yet it can be argued that the outcome hinted at is precisely that this natural basis is not as such to be found in natural language as we know it, but at most in a logical grammar to be distilled from it by rigorous and radical revision. If so, then Aristotle's position in *De interpretatione* is not fundamentally different from the perspective approximated to by Socrates and his partners in the dialectic of *Cratylus* – to which Aristotle supplies fairly unmistakable references (Arist. *Int.* 16a26 κατὰ συνθήκην "by convention," repeated at 17a1; see below). Still, the tenor is much more upbeat: Plato was warning against the pitfalls of speech unsupported by a firm grasp of what is enduringly real, whereas Aristotle is sanguine about the chances of overcoming the imperfections of human language and collectively achieving an empirically adequate understanding of the world.

Here Aristotle is able to capitalize on one step forward taken by Plato in a different dialogue, usually supposed to be later than *Cratylus*. In his *Sophist*, Plato has embarked on a distinction between two complementary classes of expressions, that of a "name" (ὄνομα) or referring word, hence our "noun," and that of a word saying something *of* the referent, a predicating word (ῥῆμα), often one denoting a disposition or act of this, hence leading to our "verb" (see de Rijk 1986: 218–25). This major leap toward abolishing a naive picture of words as representing the world by labeling things individually in the way of quasi-proper names, is an accomplishment that Aristotle can thus afford to take for granted, specifically as a move in logical analysis, cleared of any implications for Plato's ontology of Forms and Kinds.

Plato's *Cratylus*: The Correctness of Names

Admittedly, almost any general claim about the upshot of a Platonic dialogue is disputable. More precisely, what we find in *Cratylus* is a discussion of a question concerning the "correctness of names" (ὀϱθότης ὀνομάτων). Such a correctness might be taken to be guaranteed if names pertain to their referents "by nature" (φύσει); but what if they have been imposed "by custom and habit" (νόμῳ καὶ ἔθει; Pl. *Cra.* 384d6–7) resting on some form of "contract and agreement" (συνθήκη καὶ ὁμολογία; ibid. 384d1)? Do we have as many varieties of correctness as we find different conventions?

In the dialogue named after him, Cratylus defends the view that there is a single natural correctness of names, which is the same for both Greeks and barbarians (ibid. 383a4 ff.). His opponent, Hermogenes, argues that there is no other correctness of names besides "contract and agreement" (384c10 ff.). Socrates, who is invited to participate in the debate between the two, first refutes Hermogenes, by demonstrating that nature does play a distinct part in the process of naming. Later on, however, he forces Cratylus to admit that convention is equally involved, so that, for someone who aims to understand reality, it is not enough to investigate the names of things.

Although *Cratylus* does not systematically deal with the relationship between Greek and other languages, there is a clear awareness in this dialogue of the variety of tongues. The difference between names barbarian and Greek plays a considerable role in the debate between the two opponents. In Hermogenes' view, the existence of different languages supports his thesis that the correctness of names is based on convention (Pl. *Cra.* 385d9 ff.). Socrates, however, points out that a natural correctness does not entail that people use names of identical phonetic sound all over the world: barbarian and Greek names do not have to be composed of the same letters and syllables, as long as they express the same "being" or "essence" (οὐσία); similarly, weaving experts in Greece and elsewhere make use of shuttles that, even if they look very different, share the same "being," and all of which perform the duty of a shuttle. "A name," then, "is a tool for teaching and the dividing up of reality" (διδασκαλικόν τί ἐστι ὄργανον καὶ διακριτικὸν τῆς οὐσίας; ibid. 388b13–c1). This is the definition that Aristotle will react against when arguing for the conventional character of language (Arist. *Int.* 17a1; cf. 16a26–8): "Every statement," he claims, "is meaningful, not as an instrument but, as we observed, by convention" (ἔστι δὲ λόγος ἅπας μὲν σημαντικός, οὐχ ὡς ὄργανον δέ, ἀλλ᾽ ὥσπερ εἴρηται κατὰ συνθήκην).

In the long middle part of the dialogue, Socrates proposes an overwhelming number of etymologies of Greek names, drawing partly on the poetic tradition and partly on the repertoire of contemporary thinkers; parallels are found in the Derveni papyrus, which may reflect fifth-century views. In many cases it turns out that Socrates' analysis of names reveals the Heraclitean worldview of the original "namegivers" (νομοθέται), who appear to have thought that all things move in a continuous flux. The etymologies are more creative than plausible, but there are moments when even Socrates is forsaken by his divine inspiration: at these moments, it is the supposedly foreign origin of certain names that excuses Socrates from further enquiring into them (Pl. *Cra.* 409d–10a on πῦρ "fire," ὕδωρ "water," and κύων "dog"). Socrates' claim that κακόν "bad" is originally a barbarian word as well (Pl. *Cra.* 416a) may be regarded as part of the playful mode that characterizes his etymological investigations.

Despite its importance in the history of linguistics, Plato's *Cratylus* was certainly not intended as an attempt at etymology in a modern sense, or more generally at a systematic study of language as such. In the etymological section of the dialogue, Socrates and Hermogenes investigate whether the analysis of names can reveal the truth, or any truths, about the world; it turns out, however, that the highest goal one may possibly achieve is to reconstruct the views of one or more namegivers. Yet how can we tell whether these namegivers were right? In the final part of the dialogue, Socrates concludes that it is much better to learn from truth itself (ἐκ τῆς ἀληθείας) than from its likeness, i.e., names (439a–b). In this sense, *Cratylus* can be read as at once a demonstration and a review of a method that is ill conceived, but that was none the less popular among Socrates' contemporaries. For Socrates, and certainly for Plato, it is not the investigation of names but, if anything, the dialectical scrutiny of their application that may finally lead us to truth.

Aristotle on the Production of Speech

Of Aristotle's further pronouncements about language, besides his contribution to the disputes between nature and both institution and convention (see above), and his development of Plato's distinction between the roles of "name" (ὄνομα) and "predicate" (ῥῆμα) in what in this context may be glossed as a "statement" (λόγος; see below), a number concern the production of speech (esp. *De an.* II.8; *Hist. an.* I.1 and IV.9: on these texts, see also Ax 1978 and 1992, Weidemann 1996, and Arens 2000: 371–2). Not every noise (ψόφος) is a vocal sound (φωνή): the latter qualification is limited to noises produced by specifically vocal organs, and conveying a particular meaning or sense. The production of vocal sounds meeting these two criteria is not confined to humans; many other animals know how to express pleasure and pain, to communicate a sense of danger. What is distinctive of human speech is precisely that the form of its chunks, of its soundbites so to speak, rests on a convention to the extent that it is understood within one particular linguistic *community*; their sense could have been conveyed by different sounds, and is in fact conveyed by different sounds in other communities. A word is a "symbol" (σύμβολον) in the full, original sense of a *token* which receivers may supplement from their own resources in such a way that communication and an understanding arise, and are seen to arise; not merely is the word a sign with a sense; human speakers also have to use words in order to be able to "signpost," i.e., to signify and convey their meaning.

It is no accident that the coupling of sound and sense in speech leads naturally to the subsequent fixation of speech in writing: this increases dramatically the range of experience capable of being conveyed and communicated, and on the receiver's part, the resources for successful interpretation that consist in relevant pragmatic information. From the perspective of the subject, writing increases the power of a human community collectively to process input, preserve remembrance, and develop the body of shared insights that single out rational animals from the others, and among the rational ones a few tribes in particular. The natural basis for these developments is ultimately the human capacity to distill from the modifications of our sense organs, with the help of an intellectual "intuition" (νοῦς), the "account" (λόγος) of a "universal" (καθόλου, literally what may be said "of [some thing as a] whole'), and to that extent assimilate ourselves mentally to the enduring and unitary, immanent forms of things: to frame, or rather to become, a replica (ὁμοίωμα; Arist. *Int.* 16a7) of such forms in our souls.

The combination of articulate sounds – articulated, first of all, into "voiced" and "voiceless" elements – to make up meaningful chunks and the recording of structures of chunks thus formed serve purposes of generalization, both "extensive," ranging over indefinite numbers of thinking and speaking subjects as well as of objects envisaged and investigated, and "intensive," dissecting the noetic structures underlying phenomena down to laying bare the finite set of their very first principles. But the primary use of these options is in the constitution of the distinctive life-forms of the human "political" animal par excellence: the core community of a family, and the larger-scale civic society with its customs and laws. Both of these associations necessarily involve communicating (in addition to pain and pleasure) notions of what is useful and harmful, good and bad, right and wrong. In expressing these, humans do not so much avail themselves of speech as something given, but rather in the process create language as we know it.

The Stoics on Form and Meaning

Stoic observations on language were offered as part of what the Stoics called "logic" (λογική), which included rhetoric as well as dialectic (see also fig. 33.1), but we should not ignore the close connections between logic thus understood and the other principal divisions of Stoic philosophy: physics and ethics. The goal of human life – to lead an enlightened and thereby "happy" life – was supposed to be attained only by "the wise man," who has freed himself from emotional distractions – who has achieved a benign "apathy" (ἀπάθεια) – by making correct judgments about everything that happens to him; these judgments are expressed in propositions, one of the main objects of study in Stoic logic (cf. Sluiter 1997: 200). The *ratio* (λόγος) that guides the wise person, who lives "according to nature," is the same λόγος that pervades the entire cosmos – but it is also the same λόγος, in the sense of meaningful, articulate speech sound, that is analyzed in Stoic grammar, which distinguishes five "parts of speech" or μέρη λόγου (see below).

In their discussion of language, the Stoics are the first to draw explicitly the fundamental distinction between *form* on the one hand and *meaning* on the other (Sluiter 1997: 201; Sluiter 2000: 377–8). They hold that when we speak, three different items are combined: the signifier (σημαῖνον), the referent in the extra-linguistic world (τυγχάνον), and "that which is signified" (σημαινόμενον), or what we may call the "meaning." The linguistic expression "Cato walks" is corporeal, as is the walking person Cato that we name and describe, but the meaning "that Cato walks" is incorporeal, since it cannot act (ποιεῖν) or be acted upon (πάσχειν; *SVF* II.387; *FDS* 892). The distinction between corporeal form and incorporeal meaning is at the root of the distribution of Stoic pronouncements on language over two different departments, a "section on (formal) sound" (τόπος περὶ φωνῆς) and one "on things signified" (τόπος περὶ τῶν σημαινομένων).

The section on sound comprises various observations on formal aspects of language. Here "(speech) sound" (φωνή) taken in its most general sense is defined as "battered air" (ἀὴρ πεπληγμένος); it may be inarticulate or articulate. Articulated sound, which may be written down, is called λέξις, literally, "speaking." Such λέξις may or may not be meaningful, but "discourse" (once again, λόγος) always is: this is "meaningful sound that is sent forth from the mind" (Diog. Laert. 7.55). The "elements" (στοιχεῖα) of λέξις are the letters of the alphabet (but see also ch. 34), whereas the "elements" of λόγος are the "parts of speech" (see below).

The central topic in the section on things signified or on meanings was what has come to be called a "sayable" (λεκτόν), with a more specific term than that for "what is signified" (σημαινόμενον); see Frede 1994b; Sluiter 2000: 377–8). This "sayable" does not properly exist, since it is incorporeal, yet it still is "something" (τι), coming under the most general heading in Stoic ontology, which covers both existing, i.e., corporeal items and non-existing ones: void, place, time, as well as the "sayable." More specifically, the sayable is "what subsists in accordance with a rational impression" (τὸ κατὰ φαντασίαν λογικὴν ὑφιστάμενον; *FDS* 696 = Diog. Laert. 7.63; *FDS* 699). A "rational impression" (φαντασία λογική) is a presentation that is formed in our (material) soul, and which, unlike irrational presentations, can be expressed in discourse (λόγος). In other words, the λεκτόν may be regarded as the semantic content of the verbal expression that corresponds to a rational (and material) impression; since "meaning" is incorporeal, however, the sayable cannot be said to "exist" (εἶναι), which is why its definition features the term "subsist" (ὑφίστασθαι). Sayables are either complete or incomplete. Complete ones include the "proposition" (ἀξίωμα), which is the bearer of truth and falsity, but also the content implied in other "speech acts," such as questions, commands, and oaths. Only one example is mentioned in our sources of an incomplete "sayable:" the predicate (κατηγόρημα), i.e., the incomplete meaning of predicating something, which needs at least a nominative case in order to yield a complete proposition.

Stoic linguistic theory had a great impact on the development of grammatical theory (see also ch. 33). The Stoics' achievements in the field of *etymology* – the term ἐτυμολογικά is first attested in the title of a work by Chrysippus (*c.* 280–207 BCE; see *SVF* II.16; *FDS* 195K) – were particularly influential, and their analysis of the combination of different propositions stood at the basis of syntactic analysis in the linguistic as well as the logical sense. Grammarians such as Apollonius Dyscolus (2nd cent. CE) adopted the Stoic distinction between form and meaning and borrowed numerous Stoic philosophical terms – e.g. οὐσία "substance," συμβεβηκός "accident," σύνταξις "syntax" – often reinterpreting them so as to serve their own more practical purposes (see Blank 1982; Sluiter 1990).

"Parts of Speech"

Perhaps the most influential linguistic doctrine to survive from antiquity is that of the μέρη λόγου "parts of speech" (see Matthaios 1999 and 2002; De Jonge 2008: 96–104). Ancient grammarians traditionally distinguished eight word classes: noun (ὄνομα), verb (ῥῆμα), participle (μετοχή), article (ἄρθρον), pronoun (ἀντωνυμία), preposition (πρόθεσις), adverb (ἐπίρρημα), and conjunction (σύνδεσμος). These are part and parcel of the grammatical system that we find in Apollonius Dyscolus and in the *Grammar* (Τέχνη γραμματική) attributed to Dionysius Thrax but now most often dated to the fourth century CE (see also ch. 33). The division into these parts of speech is central to ancient grammatical treatises, but its origins may be traced back to the much earlier philosophical interest in λόγος and its parts. Although the word class system can thus be considered as the result of a long development beginning with Plato, we should be aware that the philosophers' conception of "parts" of λόγος differed in important ways from the grammarians' notion of parts of speech: Plato, Aristotle, and the Stoics were not in fact interested in the characteristics and behavior of different types of *words* so much as in the analysis of the minimal unit of speech called λόγος as the potential truth-bearer; what they referred to as ὄνομα, ῥῆμα, etc. were essentially or primarily constituents of the declarative, assertoric sentence.

In *De interpretatione*, as was noted above, Aristotle first distinguishes two ingredients in such a "statement-making stretch of speech" (λόγος ἀποφαντικός): ὄνομα "name" and ῥῆμα "predicating expression" (Arist. *Int.* 16a19–17a7). Although he also in this treatise employs the term σύνδεσμος "conjunction," he does not consider this a part of his *logos*: it merely refers to the "joining" of primitive assertions each of which does constitute such a *logos*. Aristotle's distinction between "name" and "predicating expression," then, is the outcome of a logical analysis of the statement-making sentence (e.g., "Socrates walks"), the bearer of truth or falsity, which Aristotle needs for his enquiry into contradictory pairs.

In his *Rhetoric* too, Aristotle considers "name" and "predicating expression" the sole components of a λόγος (Arist. *Rh.* 1404b26–7). However, a very different approach to language is found in *Poetics*, where Aristotle discusses the μέρη λέξεως "parts of expression"; Arist. *Poet.* 20): στοιχεῖον "element," hence "letter," συλλαβή "syllable," σύνδεσμος "conjunction," the familiar ὄνομα and ῥῆμα as what in this context may fittingly be glossed "noun" and "verb," ἄρθρον "joint," πτῶσις "case," and λόγος "utterance, stretch of speech" (see also chs 33 and 34). This list contains all and only items that may be considered as "components of diction," whether these are words, less than words (as, obviously, both "element" and "syllable"), or combinations of words. It is to be noted, then, that Aristotle has no word for "word." From the stylistic viewpoint of *Poetics*, the "utterance, stretch of speech" (λόγος) is that "part of expression" (μέρος λέξεως) which is defined as "a compound, significant utterance, some of whose parts have independent significance" (λόγος δὲ φωνὴ συνθετὴ σημαντικὴ ἧς ἔνια μέρη καθ᾽ αὑτὰ σημαίνει τι; Arist. *Poet.* 20.1457a23–4, tr. Halliwell). In short, Aristotle's "parts of expression" and his "parts of speech" represent two very different approaches to language, *neither* of which corresponds to the later grammatical perspective, from which language is viewed as a collection of different types of words with their own "accidentia."

The fact that the Stoics developed a different logic and ontology from Aristotle is mirrored in their list of "parts of speech" (μέρη λόγου; *FDS* 536–49). They identified five of these: ὄνομα "proper noun," προσηγορία "appellative," ῥῆμα "verb," ἄρθρον an "article" that encompasses the pronoun as well as our definite article, and the "conjunction" (σύνδεσμος); at a later stage the "adverb" (μεσότης) was added, presumably under the influence of Alexandrian philology. Chrysippus' distinction between ὄνομα "proper noun" and προσηγορία "appellative" rested upon the ontological difference between individual quality and common quality (Diog. Laert. 7.58); see also ch. 33. Like Aristotle, the Stoics distinguished between λόγος and λέξις, but they did so in a different way (see above). For the Stoics, λέξις is articulated sound, which may be either meaningless or meaningful. By contrast, λόγος is a *semantic* unity which is always meaningful, whether it refers to (in non-Stoic terms) a word, a series of words, or an entire text (Diog. Laert. 7.56–57). In later times, grammarians would reinterpret the difference between λέξις and λόγος as one between "word" and "sentence," a distinction that was not germane to either Stoic or Aristotelian thought.

Alexandrian philologists and, later, technical grammarians, used in part the same terms as the Stoics, but they did so in different ways and for different purposes. The eminent critic Aristarchus (*c.* 216–144 BCE) already, as has been been shown by Matthaios (1999), distinguished the eight word classes that were to remain traditional (though he called the adverb μεσότης, not ἐπίρρημα). The use of μέρη λόγου to refer to "word classes" in this sense is first attested in fragments of writings by two grammarians of the first century BCE, Tyrannio and Asclepiades of Myrlea (see Blank 2000: 407–11).

Late Antiquity

The Platonist mainstream of philosophy during the Roman Empire objects to the Aristotelian and Stoic focus on the categories and propositional contents of ordinary, natural language, and parts company with the study of grammar as an empirical phenomenon. Plotinus (*c.* 205–70 CE) devotes to Aristotle's *Categories* three treatises (VI.1–3), in which he argues that these apply only to the realm accessible to sense perception. To his dedicated student Porphyry (*c.* 234–305 CE) we owe the hugely influential *Introduction* (εἰσαγωγή, or in the Latin travesty of this title, *Isagoge*) which posed in classic form to Boethius (*c.* 480–524 CE) and to the medieval tradition feeding on him what has become known as the problem of universals: the question of the ontological status of the referent of terms of multiple application, especially adjectives and common, sortal nouns as opposed to proper names—what is now more usually discussed under the heading of "abstract objects." From this metaphysical vantage-point, words (φωναί, pl.) and speech (φωνή, sg.) appear as mere trappings, the tokens and tools of soul in the process of its self-redemption and reconstitution as pure intellect; the linear nature of speech at best serves to reflect and record the steps of discursive reason, stepping-stones in retrospect once they have been surmounted, but liable until then to distort and distract from the required focus on the constancy of true being and the unity beyond it. The ontological bias shines through in Plotinus' etymological association of ὄν "being" (as a participle, in the sense of "what is") with ἕν "one" and, even more fancifully, in his wholesale adoption of Plato's association (cf. Pl. *Cra.* 401c1–d7) of οὐσία "Being" (as a gerund or noun) with ἑστία "hearth."

In Plotinus' wake, Platonists continue to debate such traditional issues as the natural or conventional basis of language and the correctness of names. If they succeed in throwing new light on these issues, this is partly thanks to the need to face realities that are not Greek in origin; not, as with some of the grammarians, the demand for codification of the language on behalf of non-native speakers, but confrontation with phenomena of syncretism, the assimilation and identification of foreign deities with putative Greek counterparts, raising afresh the hoary question by what name the divine is most properly called.

Within the confines of a Greek-speaking civilization, these various stimuli to escape from Hellenocentric parochialism were never coordinated to inform the bird's-eye view of one language in contrast and comparison with others that would long afterwards enable students from different linguistic communities to penetrate the Greek language from new directions and with deepened insight. For a long time this made it easy to dismiss the Greek philosophers', and to an only slightly lesser extent the Greek grammarians', concerns with their native speech or adopted cultural *lingua franca* as partial, indeed patchy, misguided, and obsolete. Now, when the positivist faith in a story of steady scholarly progress has been shaken and no one paradigm of descriptive linguistics occupies central stage to the point of discrediting others, we are in a position more favorable to valuing the Greek contributions for what they are worth: as a rich and varied palette of applications, with sometimes striking effect, of critical acumen to the analysis of a language richly repaying the effort by the subtleties thus revealed.

FURTHER READING

General introductions to the ancient history of linguistics can be found in Pinborg 1975 and Robins 1997. For beginning students, Law 2003 is an accessible introduction to the field. The international handbook edited by Auroux, Koerner, Niederehe, and Versteegh (2000) includes useful contributions on the Presocratic philosophers, sophists, and Plato (Schmitter 2000), on Aristotle (Arens 2000), and on Stoic philosophy (Sluiter 2000). The handbook on philosophy of language by Dascal et al. (1992) contains important articles as well (Ax 1992 on Aristotle and Hülser 1992 on the Stoics). Classen 1976 and Di Cesare 1996 deal with Presocratic views on language. For Protagoras, see especially Fehling 1965: 212–17. The literature on Plato's *Cratylus* is vast. Baxter 1992 and Sedley 2003 offer sensible readings of this difficult dialogue, with helpful bibliographies. For Aristotle, Weidemann 1996 is an important addition to the essays by Ax 1992 and Arens 2000 already mentioned. Hellenistic philosophy of language is the topic of the rich volume edited by Frede and Inwood (2005), which explores many themes that figure in the survey written by Barnes and Schenkeveld (1999) in the *Cambridge History of Hellenistic Philosophy*. The Stoic fragments on dialectic have been collected and translated (in German) by Hülser (1987–8). Blank (1982) and Sluiter (1990) demonstrate the importance of (Stoic) philosophy to the grammatical works of Apollonius Dyscolus. The collection of papers edited by Swiggers and Wouters (2002) focuses on the close connections between philosophy of language and grammatical theory, with an important contribution by Matthaios (2002) on the history of the theory of the parts of speech. For the development of semantic theory in Greek linguistics, see Sluiter 1997. Herbermann 1996 offers a useful discussion of ancient etymology. Ancient Greek views on the origin of language are discussed in Gera 2003.

PART SIX

The Study of Greek

CHAPTER THIRTY-THREE

The Birth of Grammar in Greece

Andreas U. Schmidhauser

Grammar as one understands it today gives an account of the system of rules governing the construction of syllables, words, and sentences in a certain language. The science thus called was independently – and very differently – developed at about the same time in ancient India and Greece: Sanskrit grammar is the work of Pānini (*fl. c.* 400 BCE); Greek grammar is the creation of Chrysippus of Soli (*fl.* 240 BCE). Both Pānini and Chrysippus not only inaugurate a new field but also represent the culmination of centuries of linguistic thought: what distinguishes them from their predecessors is that they, for the first time, integrated the results obtained into one theory.

The term "grammar" itself is of Greek origin: literally ἡ γραμματική (or in full: ἡ γραμματικὴ τέχνη) is the skill, expertise, or knowledge belonging to a person considered γραμματικός; and the adjectival γραμματικός is derived from the noun γράμμα "letter," which in turn derives from the verb γράφειν "write, draw." Over time the meaning of γραμματικός and thus also of γραμματική changed. One can distinguish four stages:

a) In the fourth century BCE, when γραμματικός first appears, it is used to describe someone who knows the "letters": a person versed in grammar, that is, knows how to read and write, can set apart vowels, consonants, and semiconsonants, and such (e.g., Pl. *Cra.* 431e; *Phlb.* 18d; *Soph.* 253a).

b) From the third century BCE, γραμματική comes to be used for what one now would call philology and criticism (e.g., Dion. Thrax ap. Sext. Emp. *Math.* 1.57; cf. Di Benedetto 2007: 2: 522). Thus the oeuvre of Aristarchus of Samothrace (*fl.* 160 BCE) – ὁ γραμματικώτατος "the most grammatical" to some (Ath. 15.12.2) – consists in editions of and commentaries on Homer, Hesiod, Archilochus, Alcman, Pindar, Herodotus, and others, as well as in a number of critical treatises on Homeric questions (see, e.g., Pfeiffer 1968: 210).

c) From the early first century BCE, the content of the grammarians' discipline is enlarged; in particular, it includes a new so-called technical (τεχνικόν) part or tool, which corresponds to what one would now term grammar (e.g., Asclepiades ap. Sext. Emp. *Math.* 1.91; 1.252; cf. Blank 1998: 146). A "technical grammarian" such as Apollonius Dyscolus (*fl.* 140 CE) no longer edits texts nor comments on them – instead, he composes treatises on the elements, the parts of speech, etc. (*Suda* α 3422; cf. Ap. Dy. *Con.* 213.10).

d)   From the end of antiquity, the τεχνικόν progressively comes to be seen as the γραμματική *par excellence* (e.g., Michael Sync. *Synt.* 46 (*c.* 813)). Thus Priscian (*fl.* 520), the author of, *inter alia*, a voluminous and immensely influential Latin grammar, can now refer to Apollonius as *summus artis auctor grammaticae* "the greatest authority on grammatical science" (Prisc. *Inst.* 8.439.22). It is this use of γραμματική which has given rise to the modern notion of grammar.

(Two precisions to the above quadripartition: first, the use of the term evolved of course gradually; and secondly, the creation of a new use did not, in this case, entail that the older uses passed away entirely.)

Now some might argue the semantic shift just outlined makes it impossible to write a historiography of Greek grammar from Plato to, say, Planoudes (*fl.* 1300) insofar as there does not exist a single discipline called γραμματική, the history of which one could study. Yet to renounce the project entirely would be rash. For there still remains the possibility of focusing on one relatively stable acception of the term γραμματική, and studying the history of *that* discipline. Furthermore, one must not forget that past nomenclatures are immaterial to the question whether the enquiry is the same as, or similar to, the one practiced later. Hence if one intends to study the history of grammar qua science of language, one should not want to restrict oneself to studying the history of the τεχνικόν and of γραμματική in its last use. For it is well known, and I shall show below, that the subject as such was first recognized by the Stoics (see also ch. 32).

Because the Stoics' enquiry was done under the umbrella of philosophy, it is often declared – generally without further argument – that theirs was not yet an "autonomous science" (e.g., Di Benedetto 2007: 2: 497). Some scholars have even gone so far as to argue that philosophy "blocked" the emancipation of grammar (e.g., Ildefonse 1997: 15). Both claims are anachronistic and false, for they presuppose that philosophy and science are radically different in nature – which, at least in antiquity, they were not: any historiography of biology, for example, starts with Aristotle, who invented the discipline (see, e.g., Lennox 2001: xx). As for the alleged lack of autonomy, depending on how one understands the notion, this need not necessarily be a point of criticism: after all, for half a century now most linguists who reflect on such questions consider their discipline a branch of cognitive science (e.g., Chomsky 1968: 1).

Grammar – and from now on, I shall use that term to speak of linguistic science – was one of the pillars of education in antiquity and the Middle Ages. Thus one encounters examples of grammatical analysis in ancient texts of all genres – from rhetoric and philosophy, to medicine and theology. Its influence went far beyond the Greek world. Latin, in the late second century BCE, became the first language to which the Greek system was adapted; and for the next 600 years Latin grammarians continued to be inspired by their Greek homologues (the reverse does not hold). In the sixth and seventh centuries, the *Techne* (a brief school grammar) and other works were translated into languages as diverse as Syriac, Armenian, and Georgian. In each case, the resulting grammars were the first for that language. And so it spread. The Greek heritage, then, was vast.

One is so used to speaking of nouns and pronouns, of the first person and the past tense, of case and gender, that it may sometimes prove difficult not to forget that these are all technical notions we inherited from antiquity. They may – or may not – have been appropriate for describing Ancient Greek. Yet to decide whether they are suited to other languages, or to language in general, one first has to know what they meant, and why they were introduced. The study of the origins of the study of language is thus indispensable to the study of language itself.

The Beginnings

Some situate the genesis of grammar in the Dark Ages, regarding the creation of the Greek alphabet, in the late ninth century BCE, as "the first achievement of linguistic scholarship in Greece" (Robins 1997: 16). This is confused on two counts. First, on such an inclusive conception of linguistic scholarship, one surely ought to start at least 700 years earlier, for the creation of a syllabary – Linear B (see ch. 2) – requires linguistic proficiency, too – indeed, *every* script presupposes some linguistic analysis. Second, the changes in respect to the Phoenician consonantal alphabet are but few: the graphemes for the glottal and pharyngeal obstruents (resp. /ʔ/ and /ʕ/) – which do not occur in Greek – were set to represent the vowels /a/ and /o/ (see ch. 3); and with the grapheme for /ħ/ already assigned to Greek /h/, the grapheme for /h/ was set to represent the vowel /e/. Otherwise the Greek alphabet closely resembles its model; even the order of the letters and their names are the same (see Burkert 2005: 294).

In the fifth and fourth centuries BCE, a variety of linguistic phenomena were for the first time identified and labeled and, sometimes, explained. The sophists, in particular, appear to have shown an intense interest in language. (Their writings on the subject have been lost entirely, so that one is dependent on later authors for information.) Protagoras (*fl.* 450 BCE), the most celebrated of that heterogeneous group, "divided up the kinds of names (τὰ γένη τῶν ὀνομάτων): male (ἄρρενα), female (θήλεα), and inanimate (σκεύη)" (Arist. *Rh.* 1407b6); "distinguished the parts of time (μέρη χρόνου)" (Diog. Laert. 9.52); and "divided speech (λόγος) into four kinds: prayer, question, answer, order" (ibid. 9.53). There can be little doubt that one has here the ancestors of the grammatical categories of gender, tense, and sentence (see also ch. 32).

Plato (*fl.* 380 BCE) is the most important figure in the prehistory of grammar. On every linguistic level – element, syllable, word, sentence – the distinctions he draws, the terms he introduces, the arguments he advances (and also those he thinks he refutes) have left their imprint on the Stoic and thus the Apollonian system. An illustration – one influential passage – must here suffice: When, in the *Sophist*, he analyses λόγος, he distinguishes between names (ὀνόματα) and verbs (ῥήματα), characterizing them in semantic terms: a verb is "an indication applied to actions" (ἐπὶ ταῖς πράξεσιν), whereas a name is "a vocal sign applied to those performing them" (262a). To say something, then, one cannot just utter a list of names or of verbs: the smallest sentence (λόγος) is a combination (συμπλοκή) of a name and a verb (262b–d). This brilliant – and now seemingly trivial – insight permits Plato to provide a precise account of truth and falsehood: to be true, a sentence must say of "what is that it is" (τὰ ὄντα ὡς ἔστιν)": Θεαίτητος νεῖ "Theaetetus swims," for instance, is false insofar as what is said or predicated of Theaetetus is not something that he is – for Theaetetus is not swimming now, but talking to the Stranger (263a–d; cf. Frede 1992: 412).

Aristotle (*fl.* 340 BCE) touches on matters of language in many of his writings. The closest he comes to presenting his ideas in a systematic fashion is in chapter 20 of the *Poetics*. He there first lists, and then discusses the several parts of speech (τὰ μέρη τῆς λέξεως; see also ch. 34): "element (στοιχεῖον), syllable (συλλαβή), connective (σύνδεσμος), name (ὄνομα), verb (ῥῆμα), article (ἄρθρον), case (πτῶσις), and saying (λόγος)" (1456b20). Elements, syllables, names and verbs, and sayings (or sentences) are known from Plato (e.g., *Cra.* 424e). Cases, for Aristotle, are modifications of a name or a verb: nominal cases include both inflectional and derivational modifications, as one would now call them – that is, not only forms such as φίλου "of a friend" (gen. sg.) or φίλοι "friends" (nom. pl.) but also words like φιλικός "friendly" (adj.) and φιλικῶς "friendly" (adv.); verbal cases are, for example, βάδιζε "Walk!" and βεβάδικα "I have walked" (e.g., *Poet.* 1457a18; *Cat.* 1a13; *Int.* 16a32, 16b16; cf. Vahlen 1914: 120). Aristotle's class of connectives comprises words such as δέ "and, but" (e.g., *Poet.* 1457a4; *Rh.* 1407a20); his class of articles contains, it appears, words like ὅδε "this one" (the text is corrupt – but see Anaximen. Lampsac. *Rh.* 25.4; Dexipp. *in Cat.* 32.30). Articles and connectives differ from names and verbs in that they lack signification. They are like glue, explain the commentators: they cannot signify anything on their own – their role is to "co-signify along with the other parts of saying" (Dexipp. *in Cat.* 32.24; see Barnes 2007: 231). (For an account of Plato's and Aristotle's ideas on language, within the context of their philosophy, see ch. 32.)

Chrysippus

Chrysippus, a native of Soli in Cilicia, became the third head of the Stoa, after Zeno and Cleanthes, in 230 BCE. His position within the school was *sans pareil* – hence the quip "Were there no Chrysippus, there would be no Stoa" (Diog. Laert. 7.183). With an oeuvre of over 700 books, he was also one of the most prolific authors antiquity had seen. What remains are a few hundred fragments: a handful of papyri, notably of his *Logical Investigations* (*P.Herc.* 307; cf. *FDS* 698); a few dozen quotations; and many reports from mostly much later sources which in general are hostile or incompetent or both. There are, in addition, a few thousand anonymous fragments – pieces attributed to the Stoics in general. Scholars ascribe many of them to Chrysippus, too. Though in theory this seems the right thing to do, in practice the selection is often exceptionally difficult. Chrysippus' system has not yet been reconstructed satisfactorily; to this day no consensus has been reached on even the basic issues (see, e.g., Frede 1994a and Gaskin 1997 on cases).

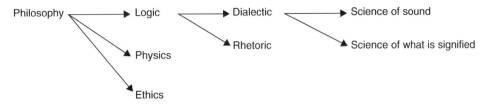

Figure 33.1 The division of philosophy according to Chrysippus

Philosophy, according to Chrysippus, divides into three species: logic (λογική) studies λόγος, that is, both language and reason; physics investigates the world; and ethics examines how one can live in accordance with the world (Diog. Laert. 7.39). Logic divides into the two sciences of dialectic and rhetoric (7.41). Dialectic, in turn, subdivides into a part concerned with "sound" (φωνή), and a part dedicated to the items signified (σημαινόμενα) (7.43; see fig. 33.1).

The study of dialectic is indispensable to one's success in life – even the Wise Man, that elusive creature, is a dialectician (7.83): for otherwise he "would not be infallible in argument" (7.47).

At the heart of Chrysippus' reflection on language stands the theory of what he called "the elements of language" (τὰ τοῦ λόγου στοιχεῖα) – name, verb, etc. That theory is a self-contained part of his science of sound. Sound (φωνή), he claims, is either writable (ἐγγράμματος) or unwritable (ἀγράμματος): writable sound is speech (λέξις), for this is the only sound that can be written down with letters (γράμματα); unwritable sound, on the other hand, is mere noise (ἦχος) such as the crash of thunder. Speech that is significant (σημαντικός) is what one calls language (λόγος) (Diog. Laert. 7.55–57; cf. Ax 1986: 138).

Speech is sound which can be divided into smaller items which themselves can be divided into smaller items which…. The smallest parts of this division, the elements of speech" (τὰ τῆς λέξεως στοιχεῖα), are the letters (Diog. Laert. 7.56). When letters are constructed with one another, they form syllables (συλλαβαί); syllables, in turn, can be constructed with one another to form words (λέξεις); and words constructed with one another form sentences (λόγοι). Language thus exhibits three degrees of complexity.

A letter, then, is a part of a syllable – but not any part. A letter is a part of a syllable that does not have any parts itself. For example, the sounds represented by ε and τ are said to be letters; I shall refer to them as /e/ and /t/. Hence the sound corresponding to τε – henceforth /te/ – could not count as a letter because there are two parts to it, viz. /t/ and /e/. Note, however, that /te/ could qualify as a part of a syllable, for instance if one analyzed the word στέγη. It is because the sound /e/ does not have any parts itself that one considers it a letter. "Wait a moment," someone might object, "surely one can split it up further. Suppose your utterance lasts one second. Mine will last just half a second. Hence the sound /e/ does have parts and is not a letter." Well, this is true as far as the argument goes. It does not apply to the present case, though: for the point is that /e/ does not have any part that would count as a part of a syllable.

The short and the long /e/ do not count as two different parts of a syllable. Suppose we both pronounce /te/ in our way, once with a long and once with a short /e/. Surely both would agree that they produced twice the same syllable. By contrast, were I to produce the sound /te/ and you the sound /de/, there would seem to be a difference. In point of fact, the two Greek words which correspond to the two syllables in question – τε and δέ – do not mean the same: the one means "and", the other "but." Hence the two component syllables could not be the same. Hence the two component sounds /t/ and /d/ constitute two different letters. Accordingly, one could define the letter as follows (cf. *schol. Techne* 316.24; Gal. *De Plac. Hippoc. et Plat.* 8.2.5): For any sound *x*, *x* is a 'letter' (γράμμα) if, and only if, *x* is the smallest part of any syllable in which *x* may occur.

How many letters are there? That is an empirical question. The traditional answer is 24 (Diog. Laert. 7.56; cf. Sext. Emp. *Math.* 1.100.3; see Blank 1998: 154). These letters can be ordered by various relations. Following again the tradition, Chrysippus divided them into two subsets: the seven "vowels" (φωνήεντα), and the seventeen "consonants" (σύμφωνα). The criterion for inclusion is whether a letter may be uttered alone – or rather, whether when uttered alone it may constitute a syllable (cf. *schol. Techne* 500.23). The condition is straightforward: letters were defined as the smallest parts of a syllable; if one desires to differentiate them further, it seems reasonable to investigate the contribution each letter makes to the constitution of a syllable. (On such a "componential analysis," see also ch. 34.)

One may look at the syllable from two different viewpoints. On the one hand, a syllable appears to be a construction of letters. But not any construction. To give an example, νυν – that is, the sound corresponding to it – counts as a syllable, whereas νχυδφ does not. To know which letters, in a syllable, may be combined with which demands a fair amount of work. Vowels, as we just saw, are peculiar in that they can constitute a syllable on their own. Such a syllable would thus have only one part, namely itself: ἠώς "dawn," for instance, has two syllables, the first of which consists in the element η.

On the other hand, the syllable seems to be the result of a partition of the next greater unit, viz. the word (cf. Gal. *De Plac. Hippoc. et Plat.* 8.2.5). Yet a syllable is not any part of a word. Take the word Σωκράτης "Socrates." Someone might want to distinguish here the two parts σωκρα and της. The first part, however, is not really a part of the word Σωκράτης but rather two parts in one. The objection is the same as in the case of the letters; and the answer, too. One may thus define the syllable as follows: *x* is a 'syllable' (συλλαβή) if, and only if, *x* is the smallest part of a word. Notice that a word can have only one part, that is, consist of a single syllable: such an example would be the sound corresponding to νῦν "now."

Words, too, can be described under two aspects. On the one hand, as just illustrated, words are a construction of syllables (cf. Diog. Laert. 7.192). On the other hand, they are themselves parts of yet another entity – the sentence. Thus: *x* is a 'word' (λέξις) if, and only if, *x* is the smallest part of a sentence. Why "smallest"? Is, say, γυνὴ ἐρᾷ "a woman loves" not a part of the sentence γυνὴ ἐρᾷ κυνός "A woman loves a dog"? Well, of course, it is; yet as in the case of the parts of a word or of a syllable, there is no use in taking into account alternative partitions – Chrysippus appears to believe that syntactic relations of any kind apply only to the ultimate constituents.

Words – all words – signify. That is why Chrysippus insisted on calling the different subsets not the parts of speech but "the elements of language" (τὰ τοῦ λόγου στοιχεῖα); for words are peculiar in that their significates constitute the semantic atoms, as it were, out of which the significates of sentences and other complex structures will be built (cf. *schol. Techne* 514.36).

Chrysippus recognized five elements of language: "articles" (ἄρθρα) such as the definite οὗτος "this one" or the indefinite τις "someone"; "names" (ὀνόματα) such as Δίων "Dio"; "appellatives" (προσηγορίαι) such as κύων "dog"; "verbs" (ῥήματα) such as περιπατεῖν "walk"; and "connectives" (σύνδεσμοι) such as καί "and" (Diog. Laert. 7.57).

Connectives signify what is called a "connective" (σύνδεσμος), too (e.g., Diog. Laert. 7.71; cf. Ap. Dy. *Con.* 214.4, 248.1). Verbs signify a "predicate" (κατηγόρημα) (e.g., Diog. Laert. 7.58, 7.70). Appellatives, names, and articles signify a "case" (πτῶσις) (e.g., Diog. Laert. 7.70; Sext. Emp. *Math.* 11.29) – or alternatively: appellatives signify a "common quality" (κοινὴ ποιότης); names, a "peculiar quality" (ἰδία ποιότης); and articles, it appears, a "substance" (οὐσία) (Diog. Laert. 7.58). (A substance, for the Stoics, is a bit of matter; a peculiar quality is what makes a certain bit of unqualified matter the unique thing it is; and a common quality is constitutive of the thing it qualifies, but, in a sense, not peculiar to it insofar as there may be, and generally are, other things which have the same quality.)

A sentence is a construction of words. Occupying the last place in the hierarchy of writable sound, it cannot be characterized as being a part of something else, which is why it is defined semantically: *x* is a 'sentence' (λόγος) if, and only if, *x* signifies a complete 'sayable' (λεκτόν).

Consider, for example, the sentence Δίων τρέχει "Dio runs." The name Δίων signifies the case Dio; the verb τρέχει signifies the predicate run. When the two words are constructed together, they signify the "statable" (ἀξίωμα) or state of affairs that Dio runs (Diog. Laert. 7.65; cf. Frede 1994b). States of affairs constitute one kind of "sayable" (λεκτόν). Another such kind are questions: for example, the sentence ἆρα Θέων τρέχει; signifies the question whether Theo runs. One also finds commands, oaths, etc. (Diog. Laert. 7.76; cf. Barnes 1999: 200). Any sound signifying a complete sayable therefore counts as a sentence. If a single word does so, it counts as a sentence, too. Examples of a one-word sentence include verbs in the imperative like λέγε "Speak!", and nouns in the vocative such as Πάτροκλε "Patroklos!".

Chrysippus refers to the words and sentences one utters as τὰ σημαίνοντα "the signifiers" (Diog. Laert. 7.62). The items signified by the signifiers are called τὰ σημαινόμενα "the significates" or τὰ πράγματα "the things" (ibid.): for example, in the sentence Δίων τρέχει, these are the state of affairs that Dio runs and its constituents, viz. the case Dio and the predicate run.

Truth and falsehood do not belong to sentences, but to states of affairs: a state of affairs is true if it obtains or "is the case" (ὑπάρχει), and false otherwise (e.g., Sext. Emp. *Math.* 8.85). To know whether a certain state of affairs obtains, one has to look at the world. When assessing Δίων τρέχει, for example, one will have to determine whether the predicate run is truly said of the case Dio – one will try to ascertain whether Dio is now running.

A negative sentence such as οὐ Δίων περιπατεῖ is simple according to Chrysippus: indeed, it signifies a "negative" (ἀποφατικόν) state of affairs, viz. the simple state of affairs which obtains if it is not the case that Dio walks (Diog. Laert. 7.69; cf. Frede 1974: 70). Chrysippus also recognizes non-simple states of affairs: a complex sentence such as Δίων τρέχει καὶ Θέων περιπατεῖ, for example, signifies the complex state of affairs that Dio runs and Theo walks (ibid.).

Logically speaking, the article οὗτος, the name Δίων, and the appellative ἄνθρωπος signify the same, viz. a case. From a physical viewpoint, however, their semantics is not the same: whereas οὗτος, for example, signifies the mere matter of which Dio consists, Δίων signifies his peculiar quality. Since according to Stoic doctrine Dio's substance and his peculiar and common quality are bodies, cases should be considered corporeal, too; they are thus not sayables.

Verbs signify a predicate, which is an incomplete sayable and thus incorporeal. Take the verb in Δίων τρέχει. Plainly it could not signify a body. For suppose τρέχει signified Dio's running (a disposition Chrysippus considers a body); then whenever one said Δίων τρέχει, one would speak truthfully. There is, of course, a link between the verb, the incorporeal predicate, and the corporeal disposition of running: the predicate run, which is signified by the verb τρέχει, is true of something if, and only if, that thing has the disposition of running.

Connectives appear to function like verbs in that the connective they are said to signify must be incorporeal and thus an incomplete sayable. For were the connective a body, the resulting complex state of affairs would always obtain whatever the circumstances – which is absurd.

Chrysippus' theory of writable sound constitutes a generative grammar – from the set of the 24 letters (and with the help of three sets of rules), one can "generate" (γεννᾶν), first, syllables, then words, and then sentences (Gal. *De Plac. Hippoc. et Plat.* 8.3.13; cf. *schol. Techne* 514.36). On the level of sound alone, there thus exist three syntaxes. His lost writings – three works in eight books – and the number of fragments preserved suggest that Chrysippus focused especially on the syntax of the elements of language (cf. Diog. Laert. 7.192). Let me give a brief specimen of how the reconstruction of that part proceeds:

None of the syntactic rules is directly preserved. To some extent, however, one can derive them from passages where they are presupposed. Consider, for example, the definitions of the elements of language and of their significates – our sources happen to confuse the two (e.g., Plut. *Quaest. Plat.* 1009c; *schol. Techne* 356.10). On the linguistic level, the few definitions that we have are all purely semantic: the verb, for instance, is defined as signifying a predicate (e.g., Diog. Laert. 7.58; *schol. Techne* 161.7). Yet in Chrysippus' eyes the elements of language must have certain syntactic properties themselves, for otherwise he would not have written at least two books on their "construction" (σύνταξις) (Dion. Hal. *Comp.* 4.20; cf. Alex. Aphr. *in An. pr.* 404.7). On the ontological level, the definitions are more informative: the predicate, for instance, is defined as follows:

> ἔστι δὲ τὸ κατηγόρημα . . . λεκτὸν ἐλλιπὲς συντακτὸν ὀρθῇ πτώσει πρὸς ἀξιώματος γένεσιν.

The predicate is . . . an incomplete sayable which, if constructed with a straight case (i.e., a nominative), generates a state of affairs. (Diog. Laert. 7.64)

From this one can derive the following rule: *case + predicate → state of affairs*. (The two symbols "+" and "→" are used only for the sake of brevity: the rule should be read "If a case is constructed with a predicate, a state of affairs is generated".) The corresponding rules on the linguistic level immediately follow: *name + verb → sentence; appellative + verb → sentence; article + verb → sentence*. According to another definition, the predicate is "constructible" (συντακτόν) with one *or several* cases (Diog. Laert. 7.64). Which suggests that for predicates such as the significate of ὁρᾶν "see," the rule is as follows: *case + predicate² + case → state of affairs.*

To this one ontological rule correspond nine linguistic rules: one can see why Chrysippus chose to base the latter on the former (Egli 1987; Frede 1993).

From Diogenes to Trypho

Chrysippus' pupils were mostly concerned with preserving the doctrine of the Master. Zeno of Tarsus, who on Chrysippus' death (*c.* 205 BCE) became the fourth scholarch of the Porch, did not write much, but he left a great number of disciples (Diog. Laert. 7.35; cf. *SVF* 3: 209). Diogenes of Seleucia, called the Babylonian, the fifth scholarch, had been a student first of Chrysippus and then of Zeno, and he became one of the dominant intellectual figures of the second century BCE (cf. *SVF* 3: 210–43). His handbook *On Sound* (περὶ φωνῆς) appears to be the main source lying behind Diogenes Laertius 7.55–9, which is one of our principal sources for that part of the Stoic doctrine (Diog. Laert. 7.55, 7.57; cf. Mansfeld 1986: 367). During his long career, Diogenes formed scores of students – among them not only philosophers such as his successors Antipater and Panaetius, but also grammarians like Apollodorus of Athens and Dionysius Thrax. The Babylonian seems to have played a cardinal role in the transmission of the Stoic science to the Alexandrian γραμματικοί (cf. Frede 1987: 358).

Antipater of Tarsus, the sixth scholarch (from *c.* 140 BCE), was one of the "leading dialecticians" of his time (Cic. *Luc.* 143; cf. *SVF* 3: 244–58). To students of the history of linguistics, he is known especially for having introduced, in his *On Speech and What is Said* (περὶ λέξεως καὶ λεγομένων), the so-called "middle" (μεσότης) (Diog. Laert. 7.57). As in the case of "connective," the term "middle" is used to speak both of an ontological class (e.g., Simpl. *in Cat.* 388.24) and of the corresponding linguistic class – instances of the latter include ἀνδρείως "bravely" and καλῶς "well" (ibid. 37.12). It is with Antipater that the most innovative period in the history of Stoic dialectic ends.

The contribution to linguistic theory made by the early Alexandrian grammarians – from Zenodotus of Ephesus (*fl.* 280 BCE) to Aristophanes of Byzantium (*fl.* 200 BCE) – is modest. The position occupied by Aristarchus of Samothrace (*fl.* 160 BCE) is more difficult to determine: in recent years, it has been argued that the system of the eight parts of speech as one knows it from Apollonius Dyscolus' writings was to a great extent already in place in his time, and had presumably been partly created by him (Ax 1982; Matthaios 1999).

Aristarchus himself did not write any books on what was later called technical grammar; but some of his many pupils did – for instance, Dionysius Thrax (*fl. c.* 120 BCE). The little one knows of Dionysius' system (and setting aside the grammatical *aide-mémoire* known as *Techne*, which apart from its opening postdates Apollonius) suggests he defended a Stoic theory: names and appellatives, in Dionysius' eyes, constitute two different word classes; verbs he defined as signifying a predicate; and words such as ἐγώ he did not (unlike Apollonius) call pronouns but deictic articles – Chrysippus had referred to them as definite articles, but regarded all definite articles as deictic (cf. Di Benedetto 2007: 2:522; Schmidhauser forthcoming).

The first century BCE witnessed an explosion of interest in grammar and a corresponding number of specialized publications, ranging from orthography and pneumatology (the theory of aspiration), to pathology, the theory of the various parts of speech, and dialectology. The most important figure of that age was Trypho of Alexandria (*fl. c.* 50 BCE). As far as one can tell from the scattered remains of his writings, the general theory he defends is, if not the same, certainly very similar to the Apollonian one – half of the preserved fragments in fact stem from Apollonius.

Apollonius Dyscolus

Apollonius is the greatest and most influential of the Greek grammarians; he is also the first of whom we possess original writings – and not just a thin essay but hundreds of pages. His theory of language in many respects resembles that of Chrysippus, as the famous second paragraph of his *Syntax* may illustrate:

> ἤδη γὰρ καὶ ἡ πρώτη ῥηθεῖσα ἀμερὴς ὕλη τῶν στοιχείων τοῦτο πολὺ πρότερον κατεπηγγείλατο, οὐχ ὡς ἔτυχεν ἐπιπλοκὰς ποιησαμένη τῶν στοιχείων, ἀλλ᾽ ἐν τῇ κατὰ τὸ δέον συντάξει, ἐξ ἧς σχεδὸν καὶ τὴν ὀνομασίαν εἴληχεν. ἤ τε ἐπαναβεβηκυῖα συλλαβὴ ταὐτὸν ἀνεδέξατο, εἴγε αἱ ἐκ τούτων συντάξεις ἀναπληρούμεναι κατὰ τὸ δέον ἀποτελοῦσι τὴν λέξιν. καὶ σαφὲς ὅτι ἀκόλουθόν ἐστι τὸ καὶ τὰς λέξεις, μέρος οὔσας τοῦ κατὰ σύνταξιν αὐτοτελοῦς λόγου, τὸ κατάλληλον τῆς συντάξεως ἀναδέξασθαι· τὸ γὰρ ἐξ ἑκάστης λέξεως παρυφιστάμενον νοητὸν τρόπον τινὰ στοιχεῖόν ἐστι τοῦ λόγου, καὶ ὡς τὰ στοιχεῖα τὰς συλλαβὰς ἀποτελεῖ κατὰ τὰς ἐπιπλοκάς, οὕτω καὶ ἡ σύνταξις τῶν νοητῶν τρόπον τινὰ συλλαβὰς ἀποτελέσει διὰ τῆς ἐπιπλοκῆς τῶν λέξεων. καὶ ἔτι ὃν τρόπον ἐκ τῶν συλλαβῶν ἡ λέξις, οὕτως ἐκ τῆς καταλληλότητος τῶν νοητῶν ὁ αὐτοτελὴς λόγος.

> Much earlier already, the elements – mentioned first qua indivisible matter – announce this, for the combinations of the elements are not made at random but according to the rules of the construction – from which they in effect have also received their name. The syllable, at the next level, obeys the same principle, since to produce the word, the constructions of the syllables must be realized according to the rules. And clearly it is logical that also the words, which are the parts of a well-formed complete sentence, obey the congruence of the construction: for the thinkable underlying each word constitutes an element, as it were, of the sentence – and just as the elements produce the syllables according to their combinations, so also the construction of the thinkables will produce syllables,

as it were, through the combination of the words; and again, just as the word comes into being from the syllables, so does the complete sentence come into being from the congruence of the thinkables. (Ap. Dy. *Synt.* 1.2.3–3.2; cf. Prisc. *Inst.* 18.108.5–109.3)

Like Chrysippus, Apollonius starts with the elements of writable sound, and derives from them, first, syllables, then, words, and then, sentences (cf. *schol. Techne* 4.2); like Chrysippus he regards a construction of words as a sentence if and only if it signifies a certain underlying entity; etc. (see Frede 1987: 354).

Yet the similarities – striking though they may be – should not lead one to overlook the differences between the two theories. Most importantly, Apollonius introduces an additional level of analysis. A sentence, in his eyes, is a construction of words that signifies a complete thought – a mental item, that is (cf. *schol. Techne* 214.4, 354.7; Prisc. *Inst.* 2.53.28). For Chrysippus, on the other hand, the significate of the sentence was a state of affairs – which is an element of the ontology, alongside predicates, cases, qualities, etc. Again, for Apollonius a word is a part of a sentence that signifies a thinkable – something that is, so to speak, an indivisible element of a complete thought. In fact, he presupposes that to each word-class there corresponds a thinkable-class, and he generally calls the two by the same name: an ἀντωνυμία, say, can be a pronoun (e.g., *Pron.* 23.6) or the thinkable signified by a pronoun (e.g., *Pron.* 8.4). Sometimes he also uses circumlocutions such as ἡ τῶν ῥημάτων ἐκφορά "the form of verbs" to speak of the word (e.g., *Pron.* 23.19); or he specifies what one finds on the noetic level by means of expressions such as τὸ γὰρ νοούμενόν ἐστι … "for what is thought is … " (e.g., *Pron.* 43.17).

Sometimes we might wish to be more precise. Let us therefore stipulate the following:

> If α is an expression of Greek that signifies a thinkable, then <α> is the thinkable signified by α; likewise, if αβ is an expression of Greek that signifies two thinkables, then <αβ> are the two thinkables signified by αβ; etc.

And:

> If *x* is a word-class, then <*x*> is the corresponding thinkable-class.

These are not modern sophistries. In his commentary on the *Techne*, for example, Heliodorus (ninth cent. CE) once reports a distinction between pronouns and <pronouns>: the latter, he says, are called ἀντωνυμίαι, the former, ἀντώνυμα (*schol. Techne* 77.21). The use of such twin terminologies did not become generalized, however – presumably the risk of confusion was deemed small.

In principle, a word is a writable sound that signifies exactly one thinkable. In reality, however, the one-to-one correspondence between words and thinkables often fails to hold. Indeed, sometimes a word includes more than one thinkable: an inflected verb like γράφω "I write," for instance, signifies two thinkables, viz. <ἐγώ> (or rather its enclitic but unrealized sibling) and <γράφω> (e.g., *Synt.* 2.165.2). Sometimes, on the other hand, a single thinkable is expressed by two words: thus, for instance, when Homer (as read by Apollonius) splits certain words and writes κατὰ … ἤσθιον "(they) ate down" instead of κατήσθιον "(they) devoured" (e.g., *Od.* 1.8ff., with *schol. Od.* ad loc.; cf. Ap. Dy. *Synt.* 1.6.11). It is inexact, then, to describe the relation between the two structures as isomorphism (*pace* Sluiter 1997: 207; cf. 1990: 140).

Apollonius wrote a treatise called *On the Doric, Ionic, Aeolic, and Attic Dialects* (*Suda* α 3422). The title alone illustrates that he regarded Attic as one dialect among others – it certainly was not the standard against which he measured Greekness (cf. e.g., *Pron.* 50.4). As for the Greek used in Apollonius' time – what we call "Common Greek" or *Koine* – it, too, is considered a dialect (e.g., *Con.* 223.24). For to Apollonius, all varieties of Greek seem to stand on the same level – the linguistic level. Each dialect represents a different realization of what is to be found on the noetic level. This does not entail, as is frequently claimed, that "he still has a synchronic view of the Greek language" (Schironi 2002: 155). On the contrary, Apollonius was well aware that some linguistic forms were older than others – as can be seen, for example, in his brilliant demonstration that Homer did not yet know the reflexive pronoun ἐμαυτός (*Pron.* 44.11).

In fine, let us take a brief look at three parts of speech: pronouns, verbs, and nouns.

A *pronoun* is defined as a word which is used in place of a noun and which indicates a definite person (*Pron.* 9.11). The first criterion seems to be syntactic: a pronoun is the sort of word which, when joined to a verb, yields a sentence – that is, a <pronoun>, constructed with a <verb>, produces a thought: *pronoun* + *verb* → *sentence* (linguistic); <*pronoun*> + <*verb*> → <*sentence*> (noetic). The second criterion is semantic: by means of a pronoun, one defines or identifies a certain item. Elsewhere, Apollonius further explains that the sort of thing one identifies is a "substance" (οὐσία) (e.g., *Pron.* 26.14; *Synt.* 101.12). Ordinarily it is thought that Apollonius intends to speak of "Aristotelian substances" – things like me or my bike (e.g., Lallot 1997: 2.64; cf. Arist. *Cat.* 2a11). It appears more likely, however, that he uses οὐσία in the Stoic fashion, that is, in the sense of "(bit of) matter" (cf. *Synt.* 2.155.6).

The *verb*'s syntax has been outlined above: when constructed with a noun, or a pronoun, a verb such as γράφειν "write" yields a sentence. Most verbs signify an "action" (πρᾶγμα): γράφειν, for instance, signifies the action of writing (e.g., *Pron.* 114.28; *Synt.* 3.323.9; see p. 501 above). Actions in all likelihood are incorporeal items, akin to Stoic predicates. For were they corporeal, one could not entertain erroneous thoughts. Apollonius recognizes various kinds of action. Running, flying, etc. constitute one group: these belong to one person or thing only; seeing, killing, etc. form another group: they involve two or more things (e.g., *Synt.* 3.395.13).

A *noun* is defined as a word that "assigns" (ἀπονέμει) a "quality" (ποιότητα) (*schol. Techne* 524.9; *Synt.* 2.142.1). The noun ἀνήρ "man," for example, assigns the quality of being a man to some bit of matter. Thus when I combine the noun with a verb and say, for example, ἀνὴρ τρέχει "a man runs," what I say is that an underlying substance qualified as man is engaged in the action of running. A quality is either "peculiar" (ἰδία) or "common" (κοινή) (see above). A common quality is one had by many (*Pron.* 26.10). Manhood is an example of such a quality; and ἀνήρ "man" would thus be an example of a noun that signifies a common quality – Apollonius refers to it as an "appellative noun" (προσηγορικὸν ὄνομα). A peculiar quality, on the other hand, is one had by one person only (e.g., *Pron.* 105.18). An example would be the quality of being Andreas, for no one save me is qualified in this way: hence Ἀνδρέας "Andreas" is a noun that signifies a peculiar quality – Apollonius calls it a "proper noun" (κύριον ὄνομα). Sentences with a proper noun such as Ἀνδρέας τρέχει "Andreas runs" are analyzed in the very same way as sentences with an appellative noun like ἀνὴρ τρέχει "a man runs": the action of running belongs to a certain substance qualified as being a man or as being Andreas.

Among the verbs that do not signify an action, one finds the so-called verbs of being such as εἶναι "be" or ὑπάρχειν "be." (The standard translation of ὑπαρκτικὰ ῥήματα as "verbs of existence" – e.g., LSJ s.v. ὑπαρκτικός – is obviously mistaken.) Two examples of what Apollonius has in mind: Τρύφων γραμματικός ἐστι "Trypho is a grammarian"; φιλόσοφος σοφὸς ὑπάρχει "A philosopher is wise." Verbs of being are peculiar in both syntax and semantics. They are constructed with two nominatives. They signify the ὕπαρξις "being" or οὐσία "being" of something (e.g., *Synt.* 2.207.8). That is to say, these verbs are used to "predicate a quality" (κατηγορεῖν ποιότητος) (e.g., *Synt.* 1.91.2). Given that an ἐστί "is," on its own, cannot signify a quality, Apollonius might have intended to say that a verb of being serves to predicate the quality signified by the second noun, of the person signified by the first noun. What a sentence such as Τρύφων γραμματικός ἐστι thus means is – the quality of grammarian is predicated of the substance with the peculiar quality of Trypho.

FURTHER READING

The best surveys of the history of Greek grammar are Pinborg 1975 and Blank 2000.

The remains of Stoic dialectic have been collected and translated into German by Hülser (1987–8); a selection of the fragments, with English translation and commentary, may be found in Long and Sedley 1987. For a general account of Stoicism, see the contributions in Algra et al. 1999 and Inwood 2003; for Stoic grammar in particular, see especially chs 16 and 17 in Frede 1987.

A full bibliography on Apollonius Dyscolus – including editions and translations to download – can be found in Schmidhauser 2000. For a general introduction to Apollonius, see Blank 1993; much can be learned from Lallot's notes to his French translations of the *Syntax* (1997) and the *Techne* (1998).

CHAPTER THIRTY-FOUR

Language as a System in Ancient Rhetoric and Grammar

James I. Porter

Language as Metalanguage

In book 3 of *De Anima*, Aristotle draws a nice distinction between perceiving and perceiving that we perceive ("perceiving that we see and hear"). Not content with the distinction, he soon collapses it with the argument that simply to perceive is to perceive in second-order sense: it is to be aware of the fact that one is perceiving while one is perceiving. In modern terms, it is to be self-conscious of one's activity. More drastically, it is to be self-conscious, pure and simple (Kosman 1975). The point is of interest, because moments of attained self-reflexive awareness in antiquity are normally regarded, rightly or wrongly, as watershed moments in the history of the evolution of the mind. The question naturally arises, what corresponding moment of attained awareness might exist in the realm of language? The answer, I wish to suggest, lies in the insight that language operates as a system and as a totality. Grasping this thought leads to the distinction between speaking and knowing that we are speaking: it leads, in other words, to a meta-discursive grasp of language. This theoretical grasp first became available in Greek antiquity towards the end of the fifth century, and it continued to organize the study of Greek to the end of the rhetorical and grammatical tradition. To be provocative, we might say that rhetoric as a science became possible only once this theoretical insight into the systematic totality of language was had. But before going on to explore this claim, let us consider what might be meant by a meta-grasp of language.

In a much-cited and foundational essay in formalist and structuralist linguistics, Roman Jakobson (1960) designated six speech functions of the paradigmatic speech act, which were meant to hold true of "any act of verbal communication," and which he illustrated with a diagram (see fig. 34.1; Jakobson 1960: 353; for a rudimentary equivalent, see Arist. *Rh.* 1.2.3.1356a1–4).

The ingenuity of this scheme is that it shows how six different kinds of speech acts are generated merely by shifting the weight of the speech function from one area to another. Thus, if the focus is placed on the context, the speech act is predominantly referential; if

Figure 34.1 Jakobson's communication model

it is placed on the addressee, it becomes conative (attempting to produce an effect in the recipient); if the emphasis falls on the addresser, the speech act is emotive (expressive); if on the contact, it is phatic ("uh huh, uh huh," "do you hear me?" "well, now"); if on the message itself, which is to say on "the palpability of signs" (the medium rather than the message), the act is poetic; and if on the code, which is to say the means of expression itself, the act becomes concerned with the very code that is being used. In this last case, the speech act becomes metalinguistic. In Jakobson's words,

> metalanguage is not only a necessary scientific tool utilized by logicians and linguists; it plays also an important role in our everyday language. Like Molière's Jourdain who used prose without knowing it, we practice metalanguage without realizing the metalingual character of our operations. Whenever the addresser and/or the addressee need to check up whether they use the same code, speech is focused on the CODE: it performs a METALINGUAL (i.e., glossing) function. "I don't follow you – what do you mean?" asks the addressee, or in Shakespearean diction, "What is't thou say'st?" And the addresser in anticipation of such recapturing questions inquires: "Do you know what I mean?" . . . Any process of language learning, in particular child acquisition of the mother tongue, makes wide use of such metalingual operations. (Jakobson 1960: 355)

In its most obvious use, the metalingual function serves a pedagogical need: it is how users of a language get clear about the meanings of their own language. But as Jakobson hints (but fails to develop in his essay), at a deeper level the metalingual function serves another purpose, one akin to the second-order perception described by Aristotle in the *De anima*: through it, language users become conscious of the fact that they are language users. Like Molière's Monsieur Jordain, it is how they discover that they are using prose. In ancient Greece, rhetoric performed this job. It was the way in which the metalingual function learned to express itself for the first time, and it was through rhetoric, especially in its more theoretical dimensions, that language users became self-conscious language users, far more so than they did through any exposure to poetry. It was, after all, Gorgias who taught the Greeks that they had, in effect, been speaking prose all their lives, when he explained to them that poetry was prose (*logos*) with meter added to itself (Gorg. *Hel.* 9; see also ch. 30). Such an insight became available only in the wake of a concept of language as a system, or if one prefers, with the concept of *logos* as such. Esthetic functions in the medium of prose, conveyed in the first instance by rhetoricians, reinforced this fundamental lesson about language.

Stoicheia: The Componential Analysis of Language

The idea that language comprises a system and is made up of primary constituents seems to have originated in the latter half of the fifth century. The basic model was simple, though its variants, its implications, and its applications were both many and complex. The starting points were the letters of the alphabet, known as *grammata* when written, *phônai* when spoken, and *stoicheia* or *dunameis* in either capacity. The components were said to "combine" into larger aggregates, for instance into "syllables," then into words and sentences, as in chapter 20 of Aristotle's *Poetics*, which summarizes earlier grammatical and linguistic knowledge (see also ch. 32 above).

> Verbal expression as a whole (τῆς δὲ λέξεως ἁπάσης) has the following parts: element, syllable, linking word, articulatory word, noun, verb, termination, statement (στοιχεῖον συλλαβὴ σύνδεσμος ὄνομα ῥῆμα ἄρθρον πτῶσις λόγος). An element is an indivisible sound (φωνὴ ἀδιαίρετος), not any sound, but that capable of producing intelligible utterance (ἀλλ᾽ ἐξ ἧς πέφυκε συνθετὴ γίγνεσθαι φωνή [lit., "from which composite, viz., articulated, sound can arise"]) . . . (Arist. *Poet.* 20.1456b20–3; trans. Hubbard 1989)

Implicitly, elements belong to a complete whole, namely to the whole that constitutes language itself. That they do lies behind the very idea of the *stoicheion*-model, which in fact derives not from linguistic analysis but from Presocratic physics, though it would take some time before the thought of language as a totality was fully articulated (or else simply attested) in ancient linguistics. We might compare Plato in the *Timaeus*, where he speaks about "the ABC of everything," which is to say, of the universe (στοιχεῖα τοῦ παντός), and contrasts them with those that comprise the "syllables" of words (48b8–c2; trans. A. E. Taylor 1928: 306). Whether or not Plato calqued the physical sense of *stoicheion* onto the pre-existing grammatical term (Crowley 2005: 381), he did not invent the model of elements combining into a whole: that was derived from the *phusikoi*, and it is the model, not the terminology, that is our primary concern. That elements belong to a complete whole is further implied by the very definition of element as "smallest part" which is itself "indivisible," as in Aristotle's inherited usage above (cf. also *Metaph.* Δ 3.1014a26-34). For at the other end of the scale lies not simply a syllable or a word, but the entire realm of combinations of articulated voice (συνθετὴ φωνή), which, while in principle infinite in its expressions, in another way is finite: when elements are combined, the threshold of recognizable utterance is attained. Language is the sum of all such possible utterances. Whence the phrase τῆς λέξεως στοιχεῖα "elements of expression," found first in Xenocrates, Plato's pupil (fragm. *120 Isnardi Parente 1982 = Sext. Emp. *Math.* 10.253), and then in the Stoic Diogenes of Babylonia (Diog. Laert. 7.56), though, oddly, no satisfying single equivalent for the abstract concept of language ever quite emerges in antiquity. (*Logos* sometimes carries this meaning, but not consistently or unequivocally – see also ch. 32.) The best representative of the notion that elements comprise language as a totality appears in a fragment from Crates of Mallos in the second century BCE to be discussed below. Obviously, the thought is crucial: once it is achieved, the idea of language as such has been achieved. And with it comes the notion, or practice, of metalanguage, in the sense defined above.

The physical origins of the componential model of language more or less guaranteed the idea that language is the totality to which the elements belong and which they jointly comprise. The elements were originally the material constituents of the universe, as in Empedocles (Arist. *Metaph.* A 4.985a32) and the atomists (ibid. 985b4–19), and later Plato (*Timaeus*, see above). Leucippus and Democritus seem to have drawn an analogy between the combinations of atoms and those between letters of the alphabet (ibid.). Other clues suggest that they played a crucial role in linking the two models, or rather in propagating the one model across the two domains. It matters little if the term *stoicheion* in the sense of *letter* does not appear before the fourth century with one exception, known through a reference by Aristotle to the sophist Euthydemus of Chios (*Rh.* 2.24.3.1401a28–30), because it is the model, not the terminology, that counts: "There is also the argument that one who knows the letters (τὸν τὰ στοιχεῖα ἐπιστάμενον) knows the whole word (τὸ ἔπος οἶδεν), since word is the same thing [as the letters that compose it] (τὸ γὰρ ἔπος τὸ αὐτό ἐστιν)."

Euthydemus' point has further bite if *epos* refers not to *word*, but to *epic* (Burkert 1959: 179): what if the whole – say, the *Iliad* – is nothing beyond the sum of its constituent parts (here, the letters that make it up, or for an atomist, the atoms that comprise its sounds)? From the start the componential model has a reductionist and materialist tinge that it never sheds, likewise an inheritance from physics (cf. Cic. *Nat. D.* 2.93). Language cannot be reduced to an irrational residue. Aristotle will express this worry in a *reductio* when he insists that the syllable "ba" is something else (*heteron ti*) besides "b" plus "a" – otherwise it would be a mere "heap," a σωρός (*Metaph.* Z 17.1041b11–33). Presumably, this something-more has to do with the formal nature of the syllable *qua* linguistic entity. And Plato will marshal similar arguments in the *Philebus* when he notes that what unifies language is not the mere succession of the alphabetic letters, but the grammatical knowledge that collects them in their totality and indeed allows us to recognize any given letter *as a letter* at all (Pl. *Phlb.* 18 c–d).

At any rate, the reference to Euthydemus is one of the many indices from the fourth century that point back to knowledge in the fifth about the componential system of language. Both Plato and Aristotle presuppose its existence among rhythmicians and metricians (Pl. *Cra.* 424b–c; Arist. *Part. an.* 2.16.660a2–8; cf. Arist. *Poet.* 20 1456b33–4), and the allusion to Euthydemus suggests that the term *stoicheion* may in fact have evolved in sophistic circles (Burkert 1959). But the model of parts in synthesis had a life of its own, and a flow of concepts between physics and the arts of language, music, painting, and the plastic arts seems inevitable (the key terms being synonyms for synthesis: *harmonia, mixis, sugkeimena, sustasis, par'allêla thesis,* and *sullabê,* but also *summetria,* as in Polyclitus' Canon: ἐν τῇ τῶν μορίων συμμετρίᾳ (Gal. *De plac. Hippoc. et Plat.* 5.448 Kühn); and, e.g., *constitutio,* as in the theory of the architectural *embatêr,* or building module (Vitr. 4.3.3). A picture of rapid and increasingly fervid intellectual activity during the second half of the predisciplinary fifth-century world begins to emerge. Nevertheless, in order to reconstruct these developments, we will need to turn to our best attested sources in the next century.

Let's begin by quoting a passage from Plato's *Cratylus*, which throws a telling light on the contemporary scene. Socrates is asking how best to approach language systematically:

> Since an imitation of a thing's being or essence (τῆς οὐσίας) is made out of syllables (συλλαβαῖς) and letters (γράμμασιν), wouldn't it be most correct for us to divide off the letters or elements (τὰ στοιχεῖα) first, just as those who set to work on [speech(?)] rhythms first divide off the forces or powers (τὰς δυνάμεις) of the letters or elements (τῶν στοιχείων), then those of syllables, and only then investigate rhythms themselves? (Pl. *Cra.* 424b–c; trans. Reeve, adapted)

What we have here is a merger of Platonic and pre-Platonic terms and concepts: Socrates is plainly overlaying a search for essences onto existing grammatical, rhetorical, and/or musicological criteria and methods. Of interest, and I think a fair reflection of earlier method, is the isolation of terms in a progression. *Stoicheia* is the neutral, scientific, and colorless equivalent of *grammata*. The label converts the 24 letters of the Greek alphabet into the potentially more numerous (cf. *Schol. Techne* (Hilgard 1901: 32–3); Sext. Emp. *Math.* 1.99–111, a parody), but in any case smallest components of a systematic whole, into units that themselves can be divided no further. Strictly speaking, linguistic *stoicheia qua* purely systematic entities are themselves soundless: they are arrived at by mentally subtracting the *dunameis* (breathings, pitches, accents, and so on) that give voice to letters (*grammata*). By the same token, a linguistic *stoicheion* can resound and be linguistically recognizable (and "readable") only in the context of a system and (in the predominantly oral culture of antiquity) in the environment of sounds. Consider the schema set out in table 34.1:

Table 34.1   The hierarchy of constitutive elements in a compositional conception of language

stoicheia	non-phenomenal, functional, indivisible elements
grammata/phônê	letters of the alphabet/voice
dunameis	phenomenal (audible, sonorous) features of *stoicheia*
sullabê	syllable
onomata, rhêmata, etc.	nouns, verbs, etc.
sunthesis	compositional unit (word, colon, sentence, etc.)
logos	speech act/sentence/discourse/language
sustêma	totality of the language system

The atomistic analysis provided a suitable model, not just analogue, for this line of grammatical analysis, which involves a "phenomenalization" (and not merely a phonation, or ἐκφώνησις) of the constituent elements of speech. It was, indeed, the source of this original fissuring into system and sonority. But the label *stoicheion* (or its equivalents) can be applied to any element of any systematic whole, be it in language, music, architecture, painting, astronomy, mechanics, or, more abstractly, a theoretical system of rules, as in harmonics or in mathematics, where *stoicheia* are simply "elementary" or "first" "principles." A *stoicheion* is thus a kind of methodological "atom" (it is literally partless: ἀδιαίρετος "indivisible," φωνῆς μέρος τὸ ἐλάχιστον "the smallest part of sound," ἄτομος "indivisible," ἀμερής "without parts," *atomos* in Latin) and the building-block upon which are built, successively, the various analytical parts that conspire to make up the entity under examination (universally called a *suntheton*) – in the present case, the rhythms of a linguistic utterance (whether spoken or sung). Similarly, when Dionysius of Halicarnassus speaks of "the elements (στοιχείων) out of which (ἐξ ὧν) an argument" is constructed, he is reverting to the language of methodological atomism (Dion. Hal. *Lys.* 15). In the very next breath he talks about the "differences" (διαφοράς) that exist between the parts, "down to the smallest cut" (ἄχρι τῆς εἰς ἐλάχιστον τομῆς; "the last detail," Usher 1982). Beyond that point, the constitutive elements exist no longer, for they are the partless "atoms" of the argument. The idea that (imperceptible) elements combine to make perceptible (phenomenal) differences derives from the atomists themselves (Arist. *Metaph.* A 4.985b12–16). The transformation from physics to language is never forgotten, though the atomistic origins of this model would never be quite fully explicit again (but see *Schol. Techne* 506.25 (Hilgard 1901): ἄτομα).

The sophist Hippias of Elis (late fifth century) is the next thinker we find deploying a similar incremental analysis, again in Plato. As Pfeiffer says (1968: 53), "Hippias seems to have been the first 'literary' man, not a musician, to treat language together with music, distinguishing 'the value (δυνάμεως) of letters and syllables and rhythms and scales (ἁρμονιῶν)'" in a sequence that runs from the smallest discernible units to ever larger combinations, and that finally culminates in harmonics, which is to say the largest-scale arrangement of sounds in a sentence (Pl. *Hp. mai.* 285d = DK 86A11). The sequence clearly anticipates the lessons of a schoolmaster in the classroom: the progression mimics the way one learns one's ABC's. Pfeiffer's wording ("language together with music," "traditional Greek unity of word and 'music'") can be made more precise: Hippias was not only combining linguistic and musical analysis; he was also attempting to discover a *single* model for capturing *the music of language* whenever it is sung, set to rhythm, accentuated with pitches, and so on.

The key term *dunamis* (value) – among Latin grammarians, *potestas* – designates the audible, esthetic, and prosodic value or quality of *stoicheia* once they are "realized" in a given context. We might compare the grammatical scholia to Dionysius Thrax: "*Dunamis* is the <sound> that results from and completes the *stoicheia*" (197.29 (Hilgard 1901)). It "completes" them inasmuch as it gives them their material realization (phonation). Dionysius of Halicarnassus in the first century BCE is a crucial link in the same tradition: "It is from this number of letters (γραμμάτων), with the properties (δυνάμεις) described, that are formed what we call *syllables*" (*Comp.* 22). The language of Hippias, but also of his later heirs, is identical to that of the *Cratylus* passage quoted above.

The most sophisticated expression of this model appears with Crates of Mallos, the early to mid-second century BCE Homerist, critic, and grammarian. His theory of the *stoicheion* is preserved in the scholia to the grammar attributed to Dionysius Thrax in a short paragraph that is astonishingly modern-sounding.

ὁρίζεται δὲ τὸ στοιχεῖον ὁ μὲν Κράτης οὕτω· 'φωνῆς μέρος τὸ ἐλάχιστον <τῆς κατὰ σύνταξιν>· 'μέρος ἐλάχιστον' δ' εἶπεν ὡς πρὸς τὸ ὅλον σύστημα τῆς ἐγγραμμάτου φωνῆς>. ὁ δὲ Ἀριστοτέλης οὕτως· 'ἁπλῆ καὶ ἀδιαίρετος φωνή' ⟦ ⟧· ἄλλοι οὕτως, κτλ. (*< > transposed by Mette 1952, following Hilgard 1901, from ⟦ ⟧)

Crates defines the *stoicheion* thus: "[It is] the smallest part <of ordered voice>." He called it the "smallest part" inasmuch as it stands in relation to the entire system of voice capable of being articulated into letter-sounds. Aristotle [defines it] thus: "simple and indivisible voice." Others define it in the same way. (fragm. 52a Mette 1952 = fragm. 95 Broggiato 2001 = *Schol. Techne* 316.24–7 (Hilgard 1901))

A further definition is given in the Grammar (τέχνη γραμματική) attributed to the great second-century BCE grammarian Dionysius Thrax but now most often dated in the third or fourth cent. CE:

γράμματά ἐστιν εἰκοσιτέσσαρα ἀπὸ τοῦ ᾱ μέχρι τοῦ ῶ .[. . .] τὰ δὲ αὐτὰ καὶ 'στοιχεῖα' καλεῖται διὰ τὸ ἔχειν 'στοῖχόν' τινα καὶ τάξιν.

Grammata are the twenty-four letters of the alphabet from *alpha* to *omêga* . . . . The same entities are called *stoicheia* due to their occupying some "place" [or "row"] (*stoichos*) and position. (*Ars Gramm.* §6; Περὶ στοιχείου, Uhlig 1883: 9.25–32)

Synthesizing, we can say that whereas *grammata* stand for the 24 letters of the alphabet, *stoicheia* are clearly the same items viewed now from a different perspective and according to different criteria: they are the same signs regarded, not for their property of following one another in an established sequence, but simply for their property of occupying a position in that sequence at all. To be a *stoicheion* is not to possess any particular value but just to be a place-holder for particular values and to occupy a place in a system. Crates' innovation, if it was one, was to bring out what was implicit in the componential model all along: the systematic character of the *stoicheion*. Hence, he defined it as "stand[ing] in relation to the entire system (πρὸς τὸ ὅλον σύστημα) of [linguistic] voice." That is, *stoicheia* are abstract, differential units, purely relational entities that are defined by two aspects: (i) according to their differences from one another rather than according to any positive features they carry intrinsically (for this reason, *stoicheia* have no sound: they are, by definition, intrinsically featureless); and (ii) according to their standing within the system or totality of language. The *stoicheion*, in other words, is very much the relative of the modern-day phoneme (see Zirin 1980; Belardi 1985: 91–7; Ax 1986:136), however much the latter notion may be contested among linguists (Lüdtke 1969).

Stoicheia and Stylistics

Phonemes do not *have* a sound, because they represent the *potential for* sound. The idea of a theoretical entity such as the phoneme would have made intuitive sense to any late fifth-century Greek interested in discovering the foundations of language, precisely at a time when the conditions of orality and literacy were undergoing a dramatic revolution. The rise of linguistic reflection at this time, and in particular the theory of the *stoicheion* as the foundational element in the new sciences of language, can only have been a reflex of this larger change.

But that is not all. With the introduction of writing to ever more numerous spheres of private and public life, the eye became highly sensitized as never before to the physical appearance of texts: texts had a materiality that one could actually touch and see. But what about the same texts when they were sung or read aloud? Or speeches? Or texts in the mind's eye? What kind of materiality did these have? The concept of the *stoicheion* was a partial answer to questions like these. It at least provided a uniform basis, in theory, to the various manifestations of *logos*. And if the term *stoicheion* (or the concept behind it) did in fact arise out of the context of *phusiologia,* or natural philosophy, then it also carried the suggestion of being a material or at least quasi-material entity. This uncertain origin will have sufficed in itself to provoke doubts and some consternation should anyone have chosen to press the issue of the status of the *stoicheion* as an entity: was it a concept, a thing, a bit of matter, or an abstract element of language conceived as a system of relations? Was it audible or not, visible or not? Different answers led to different views about the materialism of language, with inevitable implications for esthetics.

Analysis by way of *stoicheia* has further implications for the perception of the objects in question. Componential analysis creates a *double articulation*: to every abstract, methodological entity there corresponds an embodied material equivalent, be this a proportional body length, a building unit (such as the architectural *embatḗr*), a slice of time (in rhythmical theory, a *chronos prôtos,* or primary duration), or a part of the color spectrum. In the realm of language or music, to discover the materiality of the entities in question one normally has to seek out *stoicheia* in the dimension of *sound,* for it is as sound that the productions in language and music strike the sensorium (following the principle enunciated above concerning the subjective impact of esthetic impressions). As a rule, one has to look for *stoicheia* at their point of articulation on the body or within the material that gives rise to their expression and appearance: they exist to be embedded there. In spoken language, this means looking to the sources of sound, be this "according to the shape of the mouth," "the place of contact <of the lips and teeth>" (Arist. *Poet.* 20.1456b31–3) or in the gaps and spacings and clashings or blendings amongst the letter sounds. Though Aristotle attests to the antiquity of the tradition, one might compare Dionysius of Halicarnassus, who adds a subtle factor, the element of time: "The process of the mouth's altering from one shape (σχηματισμόν) to another, that is neither akin to it nor like it, entails a lapse of time (χρόνος), during which the smoothness and euphony of the arrangement is interrupted (διίσταται)" (Dion. Hal. *Comp.* 22; trans. Usher).

Attention to *stoicheia* brings the focus on esthetic minutiae, but also on the constructed nature of large esthetic effects. The dimensional disparity creates interesting perceptual dilemmas: to zero in on a small quantity takes greater amounts of time; the longer the perceptual duration, the more palpable the object's sensuous qualities will be. One way in which we can conceive of roughening in Dionysius' terms is to notice how in the grand style (what Dionysius calls the austere style) the elements of language and the mechanisms of style are gradually pulled apart and exposed to view. In contrast to the blurring effect of the smooth style, where "lights and shadows melt into one another," here all the materials stand exposed, in part thanks to the slow-motion effects of the thickening and stuttering of rhythms and sounds. Individual letter sounds protrude; combinations break down; the illusory mechanisms that once produced *phantasiai* grind to a halt. In Shklovsky's terms (1965), complementary to his language about thickening, the "technique" of the artistry is laid bare. But so too is the basic structure of language itself. For what stand exposed now are the individual *stoicheia,* their *suntheseis,* and the euphonic effects they no longer produce – though they of course continue to produce further esthetic effects, albeit of an opposite but still positive nature. Indeed, just given their contrastive nature, being so tiny and discreet, so jarringly material and disaggregated, and their tendency to pull structures apart whenever one focuses upon them, *stoicheia* can be *sublime*. Euphonic criticism as a rule tended to emphasize the power (*dunamis*) of individual letters and their resulting combinations (*suntheseis*). Such criticism works in two directions at once: it knows that euphony in its pure form exists in only three open vowels – *alpha, êta,* and *omêga* ("because they are sounded for a long time, and do not arrest the strong flow of the breath") – and that in practice these rarely or never occur except in combination with other letters that, by contrast, are *not* euphonic (Dion. Hal. *Comp.* 22, trans. Usher). The job of *sunthesis* is to create an appearance in the ear – that of an aural illusion (ibid., 23).

It is here that critics come to an appreciation of the *technê* of literary composition, but also to disagreements about the sources of literary effects: are they to be found in the *stoicheia,* in the *sunthesis,* or in the sound that supervenes on the surface of the *sunthesis?* Here, one might be obliged to speak of a *triple articulation* that bears upon (i) the linguistic material, (ii) the resulting sound, and (iii) the abstract entities (phonemes) lying behind both. This unresolved ambiguity is the source of endless disputes among the euphonists reported by Philodemus, who seem unable to agree whether the criterion of good poetry is to be sought for in the *sunthesis* (the combination of letters/elements) or in the euphony that supervenes on the *sunthesis* and finally reaches the ear. That is, they cannot agree on how to articulate, in theory, the division of labor between the *stoicheia* of language and the effects they collectively produce (Phld. *De poem.* 5; col. 24.27–33 Mangoni 1993).

Similar quandaries that arise in writing can in theory be traced back to the same dilemmas. After all, a *stoicheion* names, abstractly, what its graphic realizations do. Here, the *stoicheion* would in modern terminology be labeled a *grapheme.* The marked fascination of sixth- and early fifth-century vase painting with writing for writing's sake, sometimes taking the form of "pseudo-inscriptions" or pure nonsense inscriptions (strings of letters that seemingly exist to represent the fact and materiality of writing but which combine into no known lexical items – see fig. 4.3), could well serve to capture the (new) strangeness of writing itself, rather than serving a purely calligraphic function, as is sometimes thought. These stochastic sequences of letters could, that is, be an attempt to capture something of the surdity of written language, its opaque otherness (its brute materiality) – the more so if the norm in painted vase inscriptions was to read them out to one's peers in social settings, for instance at symposia. What better way to express the otherness of writing in visual terms than by reducing words to decorative strokes or meaningless sequences of letters? If "inscriptions inherently emphasize the nature of the surface *as* surface" (Hurwit 1990: 192), nonsensical and calligraphic inscriptions inherently emphasize the materiality of inscription and of language generally. They present visual strings of *stoicheia,* at once luring and congesting the eye, parallel to the "thickening" of sound-perception witnessed above in the case of euphonistic criticism, where questions of meaning dissolved before the sheer attentiveness to sound as a perceptual phenomenon. Tongue-twisters (so-called *chalinoi*), a recommended pedagogical staple in the ancient rhetorical schools, served a similar end: they brought language back down to the level of pure (a)grammaticism, and its nearly pure *stoicheia*-like nature. An example from an Egyptian papyrus of the first century CE is κναξζβιχθυπτηςφλεγμοδρωψ, a pangram consisting of all 24 letters of the alphabet, albeit in unsayable and unreadable form.

Gorgias and the *Stoicheion*: Structure, Sign, and Play

I want to conclude with a brief speculation about Gorgias' theory of *logos*. Gorgias, in pressing to the point of aporia the problem of the identity of *logos*, was probing the exact same issues as have been explored so far in this essay. My analysis will bear on the question of Gorgias' presumed materialism and will throw further light on the materiality of the *stoicheion* in its stylistic arenas.

Gorgias has been widely viewed as a linguistic materialist, indeed as a mechanically reductive materialist. The strongest arguments in favor of this thesis draw their greatest hope from a single phrase in *Helen* §8, namely that *logos* carries out its effects either "by means of" or "in" "the smallest and most invisible body" (σμικροτάτῳ σώματι καὶ ἀφανεστάτῳ). All manner of philosophical and scientific precursors to Gorgias have been proposed as models for this claim, from Empedocles and Anaxagoras to Democritus and the Hippocratics. None of these candidates is particularly convincing, and the very breadth of the options on offer attests to the true nature of the problem: the ambiguity of his own language. Any kind of "body" could be meant, so what kind did he mean? Even the precise sense of the dative construction is unclear from Gorgias' statement, and much hangs on that too. (Is it locative or instrumental?) And how is the unapparent body of matter related to appearances and sensations, which are the foundation of his esthetics of seduction (Porter 1993)? What if the gap between invisible body and visible consequences is meant to provoke reflection on the very dilemmas of Gorgias' own explanatory model, and on the echoes it evokes from contemporary discourses?

The best proposal to date for making sense of the problematic phrase in *Helen* §8 is that the body in question is not atoms or some other esoteric Presocratic matter, but the linguistic material from which speeches are made (Buchheim 1989: 164). This is surely more plausible than the suggestion that Gorgias has in mind the human tongue (Immisch 1927: 23)! But the tongue at least has the advantage of being unapparent – some of the time. In what way is linguistic material this too? A direct connection with sound might look promising, were it not for the same objection: sound, the matter from which speeches are made, is anything but "unapparent" because it appears to the senses (cf. Arist. [*De audib.*] 803b37; Arist. [*Pr.*] 901a20). I believe we can press the proposal of linguistic material a step further by reverting to the componential model of material parts discussed in this essay. One could try to line up "the smallest and least visible body" directly with "the smallest and least divisible" parts of language (its "atoms"), to wit, its *stoicheia* – not only in the sense of the letters of the alphabet, but above all in the sense of their theoretical counterpart, the *stoicheion*. The *stoicheion* would be truly "smallest and most invisible," though it would only metaphorically speaking be a "body." Or rather, it would be a body in a potential sense, as I will try to explain.

To invoke a modern textual theorist, G. Thomas Tanselle (1989), the "text" – for Gorgias, the expression of the *logos* – is in effect really another way of stating what the material contingency of the work (the *logos*) is in its momentary embodiments. But by the same token, each and every material contingency *alters the experience of the work*, the way the conditions of lighting alter the colors of a painting or the way the variable tuning of an instrument can alter a melody – nor is there any way to measure colors or melodies against some invariable original: *they can only be measured against other alterations*, the same picture or score seen or heard under different conditions. The net effect of this esthetic encounter is that of a *divided* materialism: a highly specified materiality for the text, and, in direct proportion to that, an equally uncertain materiality and identity for the work. Once again, the parallel with Gorgias ought to be evident: there is *logos* in its manifestations, each radically contingent and experienceable, and then there is the puzzle of *logos* apart from these (a point stressed in *On Not Being* and carried over, I believe, with a vengeance in the *Helen* too; see Porter 1993). *Stoicheia* would be one of the *loci* of this division: they are the elements in which the division replicates itself, being as we saw the site of a double articulation of system and physical embodiment, while the structures they build in their mutual (and mute) relations are another such *locus*, and the resulting realizations, visual or aural, form a third.

We can, I believe, demystify both our image of Gorgias and his phrase about *logos* in *Helen* §8 by bringing them both in line with contemporary fifth-century linguistic analysis. Gorgias need be stating no more than a simple and obvious fact about language: that its workings are extraordinarily remarkable, even "divine," and the more so since they are founded on primary elements that can be understood to be either letters of the alphabet and so "invisible" when they are spoken aloud, or the same letters (or, more abstractly, the *stoicheia* that represent them) that combine into syllables, rhythms, words, and sentences and are used in speech and poetry but that have no phenomenal correlate in themselves. *Logos* names this transparent or non-apparent aspect of language, language in its invisibility to the eye or ear, as it goes about its everyday business, clothed in materiality. But above all, *logos* names that which the materiality of language must clothe, the abstract skeleton or structure on which language is founded, in the same way that "meter" represents a sensuous feature that *logos* can have but need not have. Once it has this or any other feature, *logos* will resound.

Gorgias did not invent figures of sound like antithesis, isocolon, homoeoteleuton, and parisosis, but he experimented in them and pushed them to such an extreme that they later became known simply as "Gorgianic figures." To modern ears these jingles may sound frigid, even if they did not to every ancient ear, though they were controversial (see Norden 1971: 1:51–52; also ch. 30). As techniques for achieving euphony, these figures of sound were also acknowledged by euphonist literary critics in antiquity who could legitimately be called materialists in language insofar as they privileged sound over other aspects of language (such as sense). Gorgias' speeches are filled with such ringing turns of phrase. But that is because those speeches are self-trumpeting embodied *logoi*, not "non-apparent" *logoi*. If Gorgias in the *Helen* is toying with a kind of reductionism, this time that reduction can be argued to exhibit a coherent rationale, because it appears to be conducted in the name of linguistic science. At the very least, the reduction of speech – not to a body, but to a *logos* conceived as an abstraction minus its materializations – can be seen to mimic one of the enigmas that contemporary Greek linguistics (or its logic) had produced, that of the uncertain status of language organized around its component *stoicheia*.

Yet at the same time, and by the same token, if Gorgias appears to be drawn to the sensuous surface of language or of images, he seems no less drawn to the hidden element, to a kind of *je ne sais quoi*, that might or might not lie behind these. Rhetoric, after all, is as much an art of silence as it is an art of speaking (DK 82B6). And as another little quoted fragment from Gorgias suggests (it is among his least well-attested fragments, though it has every right to be deemed genuine), Gorgias found a special beauty in what is "hidden" in art, in that which painters, and presumably poets and speechwriters like himself, struggle to capture "with their tried and true colors" but which resists depiction and expression, "the outstanding beauty of something that is hidden … [and] splendid in its concealment … That which no hand touches and no eye sees – how can the tongue say it or the ear of the hearer perceive it?" (DK 82B28; trans. after Buchheim 1989: 99). And so in the end, the best artists, Gorgias felt, must bow to the inevitable beauty of what, in the most interesting of cases, they may themselves have produced – for it is just as likely that the enigma they are trying to express is one they create while trying to express it – and then seal it with the greatest rhetorical act there is: "their silence." If the sensible world contains a parallel enigma, and this hidden element is the world's "art," then we can only admit that Gorgias, who has to have been one of antiquity's most ardent and self-conscious metalinguists, was also one the great lovers of the world's beauty, and that his paradoxical writing *On Not Being* and his other accounts of sensation, especially in the *Helen*, are the ultimate testament to this love.

FURTHER READING

On the early nexus of grammar, rhetoric, and music, see the groundbreaking discussion in Kroll 1907. The concept of the *stoicheion* has been much studied: see Diels 1899, Koller 1955, Gallop 1963, Wismann 1979, Ferrari 1981, and Steiner 1994. On Sextus Empiricus and the grammatical tradition, see esp. Blank 1998. On the Latin tradition, see Vogt-Spira 1991. On the larger cultural revolution of literacy in the fifth century and its implications, see most recently Thomas 1989 and 1992 and Yunis 2003. None of these studies links the revolution in literacy to the nascent sciences of language (a topic that would deserve a study of its own). On vase inscriptions, calligraphic and other, see Lissarrague 1987, Hurwit 1990, Snodgrass 2000, and Boardman 2003. A famous instance of an ancient puzzle that plays on the ambiguities of *graphai* and *stoicheia* is Callias' *Letter Tragedy* (post *c.* 421 BCE), as transmitted in *On Riddles* by Clearchus of Soli, a pupil of Aristotle's, and reported by Athenaeus (see most recently [J. A.] Smith 2003). On the euphonistic critical tradition, see Porter 1989, and 1995 and Janko 2000. For more on the componential method and its relation to the various arts and sciences of Greece and Rome, see Porter 2010.

CHAPTER THIRTY-FIVE

Byzantine Literature and the Classical Past

Staffan Wahlgren

The language of Byzantine literature has been very little studied. The main reason for this, and especially for the lack of studies of the higher registers of the language, seems to be that Byzantine Greek has been simply considered identical with Ancient Greek as far as the intentions of its users are concerned. In addition, the deliberate use of language spoken and written many centuries earlier does not incite much linguistic interest, since linguists are more interested in "natural" language. The consequence has been that Byzantine authors in their relation to each other have not attracted much attention, and there has been little interest in defining or describing Byzantine linguistic usage on its own terms, as a language with its own rules and dynamics. Instead, Byzantine authors have been described, if at all, in terms of how well they live up to the rules of the grammar of Ancient Greek. This has been done, moreover, without critical attention to the question whether the authors really were trying to achieve correctness in this sense (for the issues raised here, see Wahlgren 2002 and Hinterberger 2007a).

All this indicates that Byzantine Greek has been considered as what we may call a set of registers, with the spoken language at one end and actual Ancient Greek at the other (for the concept of register, see Trosborg 1997 as well as ch. 20 above). This view is fallacious: even a high-level Byzantine language form can be at best no more than a reflection of how the ancient language was perceived in the Byzantine language community. Another important factor is the interference between different registers. For these reasons, it would probably be more appropriate to think of Byzantine Greek as a register continuum, or scale, ranging in each period from the spoken language (which is subject to constant change; see chs 16 and 36) to a "high-end" register which may be defined in different ways in different periods.

These claims are not made in denial of the importance of tradition, of which Greek literature is rarely independent. Byzantine literature usually employs language that is reminiscent of the past and which almost always bears greater resemblance to the Greek of antiquity than does the spoken language. Yet even in the most extreme cases of high-register language it is an open question to what extent direct contact with the Greek of antiquity has motivated the linguistic choices made. Ancient texts were certainly read in Byzantium, and there is a certain amount of deliberate imitation – the concept of *mimesis* is very important – but there may also be other reasons for the similarity. Contemporary or earlier Byzantine writers can be the immediate source of a particular usage and an object of emulation.

It can be said, then, that progress in the understanding of Byzantine literary Greek can be made only on the basis of more work of a descriptive character and of internal comparison within the corpus of Byzantine texts. To provide impulses for this kind of work will be the main object of the present chapter.

Despite a lack of relevant studies, various categorizations of Byzantine texts have been proposed. Around 1980 Herbert Hunger and Ihor Ševčenko initiated a discussion of levels of style in Byzantine literature. Several, mostly short, studies of the usage of a wide range of authors were published (some in *JÖB* 32.3 (1982)). Ševčenko (1981 and 1982) also attempted a synthesis defining three levels of style: high, middle, and low:

> a work in high style is one that uses periodic structure; its vocabulary is recondite, puristic and contains *hapax legomena* made up on a classicistic template; its verbal forms, especially its pluperfects, are for the most part Attic; its Scriptural quotations are rare or indirect and its classical ones, plentiful.
>
> In a work of middle style, periods are rarely attempted and fill-words and clichés, more abundant; it requires the use of a patristic lexicon; and its Scriptural quotations are more frequent than its classical ones.
>
> A work in low style uses largely paratactic structures; its vocabulary contains a fair number of words unattested in standard dictionaries or coming from languages other than Greek; its verbal forms are not Attic; its Scriptural quotations, more frequently than not, come from the New Testament and Psalter. (Ševčenko 1981: 291)

One of Ševčenko's aims is to establish a solid linguistic basis for the evaluation of texts. In earlier research there had been a tendency to consider linguistic form and literary genre as an inseparable whole (often combined with sociolinguistic speculations on writer and reader), even though language and literary genre do not always follow suit. Even Beck's (1971) classic history of Byzantine *Volksliteratur* incorporates literary texts in a learned language and is not a history of a specific linguistic form: it deals, not with literature in the supposed language of the people, but with literature supposed to be somehow "of the people." Also, the use made of terms such as "vernacular" and "vulgar" has often been confusing.

Unfortunately, Ševčenko's attempt at categorization remains a sketch. As it stands it is admittedly impressionistic. The linguistic criteria used are few and rather predictable. Byzantine Greek is not considered as a system in its own right, and, just as older research did, the description tends to strengthen the conception of main text types or genres as entities that are stable across the centuries without being influenced by each other.

Hinterberger 2007a and 2007b are investigations of the pluperfect and the syntax of conditional sentences, respectively. They interestingly demonstrate that, to a great extent, it is possible to talk of a distinct Byzantine usage which transcends genres and which, when deviating from Ancient Greek, is not necessarily to be considered an example of incompetence or unfortunate accident. A case in point is the omission of the temporal augment for the pluperfect. Although modern scholars have often described this as a deviation from the Classical norm (and even condemned it as a sign of ignorance), it can be shown to be the normal usage in Byzantine literary Greek, even among writers of the greatest ability: what is normal is classified as exception, with reference to an implicit rule (see Hinterberger 2007a, esp. 111 n. 12).

Like Wahlgren 2002, Hinterberger's studies argue for the need to look at the linguistic usage in Byzantium in greater independence of antiquity, and to embrace a truly descriptive attitude with regard to Byzantine Greek. They also signal the danger of oversimplifying divisions of Byzantine Greek into levels of style. This problem, for which there can be no remedy at present, should be kept in mind in the following brief overview of Byzantine literature.

Epochs

The Byzantine Greek Empire existed with Constantinople as its capital during the years 330–1204 and 1261–1453. Yet Byzantine culture existed before as well as after these dates, and 1453 does not mean an immediate end to Byzantine culture. Byzantine tradition also existed in exile during the days of the Latin Empire (1204–61). But instead of arguing for an extension of the limits set by the years 330 and 1453, it is also possible to see Byzantine culture as a more restricted phenomenon. It may be claimed that antiquity continues into at least the seventh century CE and that Byzantium proper comes to an end when it opens up to other cultures, in particular to the West, as a consequence of the Crusades (from *c.* 1100). Exact dates, therefore, are useful only for practical purposes. This also applies to my subdivisions below into shorter periods. Our survey will start with the roots in antiquity prior to 330 CE, and it will take authors active after 1453 into consideration, as well as those active in the period 1204–61.

From Antiquity until the End of the Early Byzantine Era (*c.* 650 CE)

The foundations for the linguistic and literary situation prevailing in early Byzantium were laid down in antiquity.

Atticism

The most prestigious literary language has some of its roots in Classical Athens, but also in old and admired literature in general (Homer, Herodotus), and not least in the

Atticism of the Roman Empire (on which, see ch. 31). Postclassical authors such as Libanius may be used as models and considered paragons of style, and the language allows of constructions that are atypical of, or even unknown to, writers of the Classical period (for this, see Fabricius 1962 and 1967, and Jenkins 1963; the greatest collection of facts on atticistic Greek is Schmid 1887–97). An example of such a construction is the so-called separative genitive which becomes very frequent and, although it is apparently used with classicistic intentions, it is, in the way it is used, unclassical (constructions such as ἀπάγειν τινά τινός "to lead someone away from someone," i.e., those involving verbs of movement, are totally unknown in Classical Greek). For this phenomenon the term "conceptual classicism" has been coined (Browning 1978: 107).

Of the greatest importance for the future is the process by which the Church adopts pagan learning and thus provides the option of using atticistic language. This starts early: atticizing language was used for the purpose of evangelization, i.e., outreach communication, already by such writers as Clement of Alexandria (early third cent. CE). From the fourth century the Fathers of the Church write in an atticizing Greek (this is discussed by Fabricius (1967) who provides a list of characteristic features), so that Christians and the dwindling pagan community come to share a literary and linguistic framework in many genres.

In this way, ecclesiastical historiography, starting with Eusebius of Caesarea (c. 263–c. 340), becomes atticistic and comparable with secular historiography. Secular historiography may sometimes, at least early in the period, still be the work of pagans (Zosimus), but the tradition is soon to be carried on by Christians. From the sixth and seventh centuries we have a continuous narrative, in the works of Procopius, Agathias, Menander Protector, and Theophylaktos Simokates and, although some earlier historians are now lost (fragments excepted; for these, see Blockley 1981–3), the tradition from antiquity was unbroken. Procopius is a particularly classical author and adheres closely to the linguistic usage of the ancient historians. His followers represent a gentle decline, although all of them are still steeped in the rhetorical tradition.

Written Koine *and the spoken language*

A great amount of prose, however, is not, atticistic, or only infrequently so. Such prose is often summarized as "literary *Koine*" (*Schriftkoine*), an uncomfortably vague term covering heterogeneous literary material.

In antiquity there are modes of expression particular to Christians, derived from their Holy Book (see ch. 18). There are in addition different kinds of technical language (see ch. 23). And finally the official administration represents a linguistic tradition in its own right, for *Koine* is the language of officialdom and the administrative language form of the state. There is probably a certain amount of interference between these subtraditions. (On the various manifestations of *Koine*, spoken and written, see ch. 16.) Aspects of the problem of diversification and variation within the *Koine* of antiquity are discussed by Rydbeck 1967 (New Testament Greek as *Fachprosa*) and Walser 2001 (Biblical Greek as a literary variety). Although *Koine* is part of the heritage from antiquity, the Byzantine era must to a certain extent have meant the breakdown of the differences between the various subtraditions. To name just one example,

Christians now assumed control of the state, and the Church turned into another bureaucracy, adopting a conventional *Koine*.

Examples of Byzantine *Koine* include the legal writings of Emperor Justinian, the writings of the brothers Anthemios and Alexander of Tralles (the architect of Hagia Sophia and a physician, respectively) and of John Lydos (a state official), and the military handbook of Emperor Maurice. Similar to this is a new type of historiography that emerges in the sixth century CE. First stands John Malalas (sixth cent.), followed by the *Chronicon Paschale* (*c.* 630; for the roots in antiquity of such chronography, see Wallraff 2007).

Narrative texts of a hagiographical or edifying kind are also extant (see Browning 1981). These are further removed from more formal literature and likely to be closer to the spoken language. To this category belong the main text of *The Spiritual Meadow* by John Moschos (540/550–619/634) and *The Life of St John the Almsgiver* by Leontios of Neapolis (mid-seventh cent.) as well as the text of Kosmas Indikopleustes' *Christian Topography*. These texts contain features of the spoken language known to us from papyri (cf. Browning 1978: 112 and Browning 1983: 19–52, 53–68; *ODB* notes: "Leontios' professed intention . . . [was] to provide an account in a Greek style plain enough for uneducated readers to understand"). Some of these features (see also chs. 16, 17, 18, and 36) are:

a) elimination of the dative case, with as consequence some restructuring of the use of the other cases and of prepositional constructions;
b) restructuring of μι-verbs into thematic forms: (e.g., δίδω replaces earlier δίδωμι);
c) contract verb stems are liable to restructuring: -άω and -έω are confused, and -όω is replaced by -ώνω;
d) convergence of the aorist and perfect;
e) signs of the eventual elimination of the participle;
f) periphrastic constructions are used for progressive tenses (ἦν διδάσκων);
g) gradual disappearance of the optative and the synthetic future.

The proems of authors such as John Moschos and Leontios of Neapolis, are more formal. This may serve as a memento that authors employing elements of the spoken tongue are not necessarily doing so out of inability to write differently.

In any case, the span from formal written *Koine* (reflecting the stylized speech of an educated elite) to the least learned forms ever found in writing, does not seem to have been great. Most texts could probably be understood with only limited schooling. Greek was still one language, understandable to all its users, in quite another sense than in the late Middle Ages.

Poetry

The classical tradition remains for a long time essentially unbroken in poetry as well. Epic language and the hexameter are handled competently by Nonnus (fifth cent.) and in a similar way, although with a less classical subject, by Paul Silentiarios (sixth cent.). Epigrams in classical form are written by Agathias and Paul Silentiarios.

A more conscious break with the tradition of ancient poetry comes with the emergence of new genres, possibly influenced by Syriac tradition. This occurs in the sixth century, and the great innovator is Romanos the Melode, the creator of the *kontakion*.

Romanos writes a kind of *Koine* which we may suppose to be not too far removed from the spoken language with occasional "vulgar" forms (he uses the accusative form μητέραν, on which, see also ch. 16). At the same time he uses some striking classicisms: the dual ἀμφοῖν and the specifically Athenian -ττ- for -σσ-. His vocabulary is often poetic and archaic. One must bear in mind the exigencies of meter, and of lost melodies, in order to understand the variations in his language.

A comparable case is George of Pisidia. The language of Romanos and George is said to demonstrate a "breakdown of the boundaries between . . . prose and poetry" (Browning 1978: 114).

The Dark Age (*c.* 650–*c.* 800)

It has been claimed that a kind of cultural catastrophe takes place during this period. The challenges posed by a competing religion (Islam), and by the loss of Egypt and Syria-Palestine are mentioned among the triggering factors; the breakdown of ancient learning has been considered their ultimate effect (for this epoch, see Lemerle 1971: 74–108 and Browning 1978: 114–15; a good linguistic study with a comparative approach (as far as this is possible) is Rosenqvist 1981).

In recent scholarship there has been a tendency to modify this picture. Little is preserved, and probably not much was produced, but it may be an exaggeration to talk of a breakdown. Although important genres of ancient literature seem to be discontinued, ancient literature was still being read by some, and the few texts preserved to us reveal, even when not couched in high-register language, an awareness of ancient modes of expression.

There is a fair amount of literary activity pertaining to the Church. Examples of texts are those of Maximos the Confessor (580–662), of John of Damascus (*c.* 675–749), the *Vita Theodori Syceotae*, the *Canons of the Council in Trullo 692*, the *Ecloga*, and the *Miracula S. Demetrii*. These texts are written in a mostly non-classicizing language – in different shades of *Koine*, though not quite devoid of ancient rhetorical stylistic devices.

In the tradition of Romanos and George of Pisidia stand Andrew of Crete (*c.* 660–740) and Kosmas the Hymnographer (*c.* 675–*c.* 752).

Around or shortly after 800 we find the chroniclers George the Synkellos (see below), Theophanes the Confessor, and Patriarch Nikephoros I (these authors are investigated by Psaltes 1913).

Theophanes (and George to a lesser degree) belongs to the dark age from a linguistic point of view. He uses the dative and the optative sparingly. The accusative is on the way to becoming the only case after a preposition. ἐν with dative is fairly common, and probably employed in order to strengthen the dative, considered semantically void. Absolute participles in other cases than the genitive hint at the artificiality of the syntax of the participle (which is dying in the spoken tongue) as well as at uncertainty in case syntax. ἐχεῖ and ἐχεῖσε (originally "there" and "thither") are indiscriminately used for place and direction, and the same applies to εἰς "into" and ἐν "in." Some of these phenomena might reflect the spoken tongue of the day.

Some writers active at the end of the era seem to strive for a return to a more classical language, e.g., Theodore of Stoudios (759–826) and Ignatios the Deacon (*c.* 770/780–after 845; see Browning 1978: 116 and Lemerle 1971: 109–47). To the same category belongs the aforementioned Nikephoros, whose language is more classicizing than that of the other chroniclers. Unfortunately, the language of these authors has not been the object of much study.

The Macedonian Renaissance (*c.* 800 to 1000)

There are many signs of a new attitude toward ancient learning around the year 800. Some authors who demonstrate this have already been mentioned. This awakening takes on the appearance of a conscious effort, and institutions of higher education receive support from the highest quarters. Photios the patriarch (*c.* 810–after 893) is active as a promoter of ancient learning; he is also a writer of high-register language in many genres (letters, homilies, theology, etc.). His most important contribution, and the most significant exponent of the new attitude, is his *Bibliotheca*, in which older writers are judged from a stylistic point of view. In this he rejects a *Koine* which resembles the spoken language and the official language of his day (Browning 1978: 117).

During the rest of the ninth and tenth centuries there are several other writers of high-register language, often active in different genres (letter-writing, speeches, theology, etc.), such as Arethas of Caesarea and Patriarch Nicholas I Mystikos.

Parallel to this, a great amount of literature, often of a technical kind, is produced in a lower register. Such a language form is employed by Emperor Constantine VII Porphyrogennetos (905–59). He declares that the reason for his making use of the language of daily intercourse (χαθωμιλουμένη) is the need to be readily understood.

Of similar kind are many texts in the chronographical genre, such as parts of the chronicles of George the Monk (ninth cent.) and of Symeon the Logothete (tenth cent.), and in particular the early parts of these chronicles, which are, in fact, taken over from texts written by Theophanes the Confessor and others, in the 800s or earlier (yet it should be noted that the greatest deviations of Theophanes from high-register language seldom occur in George and never in Symeon).

Increasingly, a returning interest in antiquity can be seen in chronography too. The section in Symeon's chronicle which deals with the tenth century is in a higher style than earlier parts of the same work. The continuators of Theophanes (see Jenkins 1954) and, somewhat later, Leo Diakonos, are further exponents of a new awareness of ancient models. Genesios is an interesting case of classical ambition not matched by corresponding ability.

A parallel to the development in the chronographical genre can be observed in hagiography. The saints' lives associated with the name of Symeon Metaphrastes (sometimes equated with Symeon the Logothete) are written not only with attention paid to rhetorical means (Høgel 2002). Even the language is at a higher level than that of earlier hagiography, at least of that from before *c.* 900 (cf. Hinterberger 2007a: 121).

How close to the spoken language some of these examples lie, is hard to say. Discussing the date of the *Vita of Andreas Salos*, written by a certain Nikephoros, Rydén (1982: 175–83), who bases his argument mostly on vocabulary but also on some grammatical features, concludes that this is not a genuine product of the sixth century but a kind of pastiche from the tenth. The low style of earlier days does not exist genuinely any longer and, according to Rydén, this text is an "island[s] in a sea of tenth century language."

In poetry the tradition from Romanos and Andrew of Crete is carried on by Joseph the Hymnographer (816–86) and others. Also, Byzantine adaptations of the iambic trimeter are common (twelve-syllable and fifteen-syllable verses). Further, some authors demonstrate an ability to handle ancient meters and the corresponding linguistic form, e.g., Constantine Kephalas and John Geometres (epigrams).

From the Macedonians to the Angeloi (Eleventh to Twelfth Centuries)

High-register literature in this period is rich and varied. There are some writers of history of the highest rank, especially Michael Psellos (1018–after 1081?), Anna Komnene (1083–*c.* 1153/54), and Niketas Choniates (*c.* 1156–1217). Other historians, generally less ambitious, are Michael Attaleiates, Nikephoros Bryennios (married to Anna Komnene), John Skylitzes, John Zonaras, and Michael Glykas.

There is also high-register prose literature of every other imaginable kind, such as orations and letters, by writers such as Michael Psellos, John Italos, Eustathios of Thessalonike, and Michael and Niketas Choniates.

The twelfth century seems to be a time of increased study of ancient literature. An indication of this is the existence of four romances in learned language. Three of these (Manasses, Prodromos, Eugeneianos) are in verse (mostly iambic twelve-syllable), one in prose (Makrembolites).

Even more indicative of an interest in antiquity is *Timarion* (early twelfth cent.?), which is a pastiche of Lucian, and, probably also from the twelfth century (though sometimes ascribed to Gregory of Nazianzus or dated in the fifth–sixth cent.), *Christos Paschon*, a cento compiled from lines from ancient tragedy, especially Euripides.

There are also translations from languages other than Greek into high-register language: *Syntipas*, and Symeon Seth's *Stephanites and Ichnelates*.

Some research has been done on eleventh and twelfth century high-register language, in particular by Böhlig (1956), Browning (1978: 119–23), and Buckler (1929: 481–522; on Anna Komnene). Böhlig points out that the rhetorical policy of the time is very liberal as to the kind of ancient literature that may be accepted as model (the range is from Homer to the Fathers of the Church). She also notes that rhetorical language is negatively determined: stylistically desirable is whatever deviates from contemporary spoken language. Thus, as in earlier classicizing literature, there is no direct imitation of classical models and the actual classical usage is not decisive.

Even fairly technical discourse is characterized by high registers and there is a tendency toward the elimination of middle registers. Although certain authors active in more than one genre, such as Psellos or Eustathios, can master a range of registers – this is more apparent in vocabulary than in syntax – the tendency of the age, as in the dark age of 650–800, is convergence rather than divergence of expression. An interesting question, difficult to answer, is to what extent the language of the administration is affected by the tendencies in the literary language.

An author with little concern for the learned tradition is Kekaumenos (between 1020 and 1024–after 1070s), the author of the *Strategikon*. His work can be compared to that of Constantine VII Porphyrogennetos: both authors write for a very restricted circle and do not seem to belong to an acknowledged literary genre.

Poetry and a new form of language

In the eleventh and twelfth centuries much the same tendencies as in the previous epoch can be observed. Some poets, e.g. Symeon the Theologian, continue a more or less Byzantine tradition, with simple language and Byzantine meters. Several authors use ancient and Byzantine meters alternately and make a creative use of the classical past, especially in the epigrammatic genre. To these belong Christopher of Mytilene and John Mauropous (both eleventh cent.) and, in the twelfth century, Theodore Prodromos and John Tzetzes.

However, in the twelfth century at the latest poetry in a kind of vernacular language emerges. Michael Glykas uses this in his *Verses from the Prison*, and another example is the work of Ptochoprodromos (perhaps the Theodore Prodromos who has already been mentioned). These texts, as well as the didactic poem known as *Spaneas*, give the impression that the contemporary expression is used to achieve comic effect, and we can assume that we are witnesses to communication within a small group of learned writers and readers.

It may well be that the epic of *Digenis Akritis*, which was probably written down in the twelfth century, belongs here: one version of it, the Escorial version, uses language similar to that of Glykas and his like; another version, that of Grottaferrata, uses language of a somewhat higher register.

A proper evaluation of this kind of language involves many problems and does not so much belong in the present chapter as in the study of Medieval Greek vernacular (see ch. 36). However, it remains unclear how close it really is to actual everyday speech, in particular whether the forms that we know from learned varieties of the language testify to a wide span of variation in the spoken language or should be considered as concessions to the conventions of literature.

Late Byzantium (Thirteenth to Fifteenth Centuries)

In 1204 the Greek empire based in Constantinople was destroyed as a consequence of the Fourth Crusade. Yet, despite the political turmoil of the day a break is not obvious in literary culture, which continued in the empires in exile. This was especially so in Nicaea, where we have several examples of authors writing in high-register language of the same kind as in the previous epoch, e.g., Nikephoros Blemmydes (philosophy, autobiography) and Demetrios Chomatenos (theology, letters). The case of Emperor Theodore II Laskaris (a learned writer in many genres) proves that the cultivation of tradition was taken seriously.

Some writers active in this period are known from before 1204, e.g., Michael and Niketas Choniates. Also some men of learning, such as George Akropolites and George Pachymeres, returned to Constantinople after the re-establishment of the Greek empire there in 1261.

In Palaiologan Byzantium (1261–1453) the highest registers are strained towards the extreme in accordance with general rules derived from the ancient language system. This has been compared to the development of Classical Sanskrit, where texts are written which respect Panini's standard grammar to the letter but display a language very different from that of Panini (see also p. 530 above on "conceptual classicism"). This kind of Byzantine Greek has seldom appealed to readers of later generations – Browning (1978: 125) speaks of a "mandarin-like classicism" – and sometimes did not do so even to contemporaries: Theodore Metochites was already the target of criticism during his lifetime.

There also exists outright imitation of classical models, not least among historians, e.g., John VI Kantakouzenos and Michael Kritoboulos (both imitate Thucydides) and Laonikos Chalkokondyles (Herodotus and Thucydides). Different is Doukas, who writes in a lower style with occasional extreme archaisms (such as the dual of the declination), and, probably, George Sphrantzes (there is some doubt about the authenticity of the texts transmitted under his name).

There are many other kinds of narrative in high-register language, such as Church history (Nikephoros Kallistos Xanthopoulos), hagiography (Gregory II of Cyprus), and autobiography (Joseph Rhakendytes). There are likewise orations and letters. It may be supposed that the particularly high register in these genres can be sustained because their informational purpose is negligible.

There are further many kinds of scientific discourse (also in high registers), such as philology (Maximos Planoudes and Demetrios Triklinios) and philosophy and theology (George Gemistos Plethon and Gennadios Scholarios).

Some poetry from this period has come down to us, for example Theodore Metochites' hexameter verses which well illustrate to what extremes the learned language of the time may go. The poems are extremely difficult and recherché, and while general principles of word formation (to mention one aspect of the language) tend to be respected, the result arrived at is very far indeed removed from Homer.

Sample investigation

I will now present some results of a comparative study of the use of the dative case and particles in the *Semeioseis gnomikai* of Theodore Metochites (1270–1332), in the letters of Matthew of Ephesus (also known as Manuel Gabalas; 1271/72–before 1359/60), in Isocrates (*Speeches*), and in Plutarch (*Lives*).

There is a much greater frequency of the dative per text unit in the two Byzantine texts than in Isocrates and Plutarch. The dative is used with a greater variety of prepositions than in the texts from antiquity and in lower-level Byzantine texts: not only, or even chiefly, with the preposition ἐν, a construction which may have been avoided as too common.

Particles (such as μέν, δέ, γάρ, etc.) are more frequent in Isocrates than in the other texts, but the length of the cola probably affects frequency in such a way that mere numbers are not very telling (the smallest number of particles occurs in Metochites). In Isocrates all particles seem to have a connective force. This is not so in Plutarch, Metochites, and Matthew. As demonstrated by Blomqvist 1969, the Hellenistic era is a period of great changes with regard to the use of particles. Many of these changes are fairly subtle and do not affect the surface structure. Thus Byzantine texts on the highest level are no more classical than the postclassical texts of antiquity.

To sum up: the fourteenth-century authors always agree closely with each other, and they agree with Plutarch more than with Isocrates – with imperial Greek more than with Classical Attic.

Metaphrastic literature

In the Palaiologan era, as in the previous period, middle registers are rare. Possibly as a substitute for this (see below), Palaiologan literature comes up with the *metaphrasis*, a text form in which high-level texts are paraphrased and somewhat simplified. Examples of this are versions of the *Histories* of Anna Komnene (Hunger 1981) and Niketas Choniates (van Dieten 1979), and of the *Basilikos Andrias* of Nikephoros Blemmydes (Hunger and Ševčenko 1986); the chronicle of Manasses is also translated into language of a lower register.

We may wonder for whom the metaphrases were meant. Browning (1978: 125) thinks of a common readership for low-register (see next paragraph) and metaphrastic literature, a readership "not educated in the classicising language." Ševčenko (1982: 228–9), on the other hand, points out that it is people with the highest education who seem to be reading these texts. He also argues (1982: 226–7) for a system of equivalences common to the new versions of different texts, i.e., an agreement as to what word or phrase should be used to represent a particular word or phrase of the classicizing language. This, if confirmed by systematic study, would be particularly interesting as proof of generally acknowledged rules in Byzantine Greek.

A breakthrough for the spoken language?

In the fourteenth century a vast literature comes into being in a language comparable to that of the literature mentioned above under the heading "Poetry and a new form of language." Of this kind are romances, epics, and various other kinds of texts, in verse and in prose, original products as well as translations and adaptations. Some texts, such as the *Physiologos*, show traces of an original version's postclassical *Koine*, and there are traces of ancient literary strategies and an awareness of ancient rhetoric. Some of this literature belongs to Frankish and other milieus outside the boundaries of the Byzantine state and may in some cases stand in no contact with the learned Greek tradition. This should probably be seen as the final breakthrough of a language recognizable as Modern Greek.

Latin

In Palaiologan Byzantium there is also a growing awareness of the existence of traditions other than that which uses Greek as its language. A competence in Latin is acquired among literates, and the Latin classics are spread. Translations from Latin (Cicero, Ovid, Boethius, etc.) are made by Maximos Planoudes (*c.* 1255–*c.* 1305), Manuel Holobolos (*c.* 1245–*c.* 1310), and the brothers Demetrios and Prochoros Kydones (fourteenth century).

FURTHER READING

General histories of the Greek language such as Palmer 1980, Horrocks 1997a, Nesselrath 1997, and Adrados 2005 contain very little information on the high-register language of Byzantium. A valuable overview of the language of Byzantine literature is Browning 1978. See also *ODB* s.v. language. For questions of method and the research deficit, see Wahlgren 2002 and Hinterberger 2007a and 2007b.

Problematic but not superseded as an attempt at a grammar of all kinds of postclassical Greek is Jannaris 1897. The only investigation of a genre of Byzantine Greek is Psaltes 1913 on the chronicles; this study deals only with phonetics and morphology. Apart from this, descriptions of the language of a great many individual Byzantine authors exist, although, as has been said, these tend to focus on deviations from Classical grammar (this is almost always the case with *Indices graecitatis* which accompany editions, e.g. in the *CFHB* series). Investigations of individual authors can be retrieved through literary histories (see below), *ODB*, and Apostolopoulos 1994.

On the particular problems of Byzantine lexicography, see Trapp 1988 and Hörandner and Trapp 1991; see also the *Lexikon zur byzantinischen Gräzität*, a tool to be used alongside with *LSJ*, Lampe, and older dictionaries.

For a history of Medieval Greek with focus on the forerunner of demotic Modern Greek, see Browning 1983; see also Debrunner and Scherer 1969.

For the history of Byzantine literature and general information on Byzantine authors, see Beck 1971, Hunger 1978, Kazhdan 1984, 1999, and 2006, and *ODB*. For cultural perspectives, see Lemerle 1971, Wilson 1983b, and Treadgold 1984.

Anyone interested in general linguistic interpretations of the development of Greek diglossia and related phenomena may consult Frösén 1974 and Niehoff-Panagiotidis 1994.

PART SEVEN

Beyond Antiquity

CHAPTER THIRTY-SIX

Medieval and Early Modern Greek

David Holton and Io Manolessou

Introduction

Preliminaries

When Henry George Liddell died, Thomas Hardy wrote a light-hearted poem as a tribute to the lexicographers Liddell and Scott. He imagines Liddell musing on the enormity of the task and wondering:

> What could have led me to have blundered
> So far away from sound theology
> To dialects and etymology;
> Words, accents not to be breathed by men
> Of any country ever again!

Not true, of course. In fact, the subsequent history of the Greek language already extends over a longer period than that covered by *A Greek–English Lexicon*. The aim of the present chapter is to plot the development of the language from late antiquity to the early modern era. Two clarifications are immediately called for: first, we are concerned here with the evolving, non-learned language – the language of everyday communication – insofar as it is accessible via the surviving written texts, as opposed to the learned, archaizing language of scholars and littérateurs, which is the subject of ch. 35. The second clarification relates to the geographical spread of the language in this period, which coincides with neither that of Classical and *Koine* Greek nor that of the modern period. Greek-speaking areas grow and contract, partly following the fortunes of the Byzantine Empire. Thus, around 560 CE Greek must have been spoken (as a first or second language) throughout the southern Balkans, most of Asia Minor, and parts of southern Italy, Egypt, Palestine, and Syria (see map in Horrocks 1997a: 147). Areas that later came under Western or Turkish rule continued to be

Greek-speaking in our period, whereas the southeastern regions (Egypt, Palestine, Syria) ceased to be Greek-speaking when they were conquered by the Arabs. On the other hand, in the early modern period there are sizeable Greek-speaking diaspora communities in European cities such as Venice, Vienna, and Budapest. During this long period, the main metropolitan center and constant point of reference for the Greek-speaking Orthodox world is the city of Constantinople.

Chronological issues

In this and the following section we intend to discuss what we mean by "Medieval and Early Modern" Greek, first in chronological and then in linguistic terms.

The delimitation between the end of the *Koine* and the beginning of the medieval period has variously been set at around 300, 500, 600, or even 700 CE. The earliest limit is due to mainly historical considerations: 330 is the conventional start of the "Byzantine" period, corresponding to the foundation of Constantinople; many histories proper, and histories of literature or art, start there. The later datings also involve historical landmarks, such as the closing of Plato's Academy in Athens by Justinian (529, supposedly marking the end of "true" classical literature), the publication of the Justinianic laws known as the *Novellae* (535–, marking the "hellenization" of the Eastern Roman Empire through the replacement of Latin by Greek as the language of law and administration), and the conquest of Egypt by the Arabs (fall of Alexandria in 641, marking the end of available papyrological evidence for spoken Greek in the area, and any other area for that matter). Others draw the dividing line based more on literary criteria, such as the appearance of the first "Byzantine" texts, i.e., Christian chronicles and lives of saints (e.g., the *Historia Lausiaca*, fourth cent.), or the appearance of poetic works in which the classical metres have been influenced by the "new" stress-based accentual system of the language (Nonnus, fifth cent.).

Coming now to the end of the story, here again opinions are divided, and alternative chronological boundaries are proposed on the basis of historical, literary, and linguistic criteria. A very obvious, and frequently employed, *terminus* is 1453, the conquest of Constantinople by the Ottomans, which conventionally corresponds to the end of Byzantine history and literature. However, by 1453 most areas of the Greek-speaking world had been under Western or Ottoman rule for up to two and a half centuries. In 1453 Byzantine rule was limited to a very small area around Constantinople itself, Trebizond and part of the Peloponnese. Thus this date is merely symbolic and does not relate to linguistic realities. Alternative proposals include 1509, the date of publication of the first printed book in vernacular Greek (the *Apokopos* of Bergadis); 1669, the completion of the conquest of Crete by the Ottomans (putting an end to the flourishing Cretan Renaissance literature); or even 1821, the start of the war of independence that led to the establishment of the modern Greek state.

The medieval era thus covers, according to preference, between ten and fifteen centuries, making it arguably the longest period in the history of Greek. Its internal periodization is yet a third matter of controversy: some scholars believe it displays a fundamental linguistic unity rendering subdivision unnecessary, while for others it is possible to distinguish both linguistic and cultural/ideological differentiation between sub-periods. Important internal landmarks are the twelfth century, during which vernacular literature starts to reappear after a considerable period of "silence," and the fifteenth century, when the disintegration of the Byzantine Empire through the Turkish conquest leaves more room for the development of local vernacular varieties, and prose (as opposed to verse) vernacular texts appear in significant quantity. In the course of the eighteenth century, we see the beginning of the ideological and political developments that will bring about the birth of the modern Greek nation-state and the emergence of a national language (see ch. 37).

The periodization adopted here does not ignore external (historical, literary, etc.) criteria, but gives more weight to internal (linguistic) ones on the basis of clusters of significant linguistic changes, which will be discussed below and presented in a summary table at the end of the chapter.

On the basis of the above discussion, the division employed is the following (with all dates approximate):

1. Early Medieval Greek (EMed.Gk)   500–1100
2. Late Medieval Greek (LMed.Gk)   1100–1500
3. Early Modern Greek (EMod.Gk)   1500–1700

Terminological issues

As stated above, this chapter is concerned with the evolution of Greek in everyday use. Naturally we have no access to the spoken language as such: we are entirely dependent on written texts. These texts are composed in a wide spectrum of linguistic levels, or *registers* (see ch. 20) according to their function, genre, intended readership, and the education of the writer. We can make a rough and ready division between *learned* (high) and *non-learned* (low) registers. The former make extensive use of linguistic features from older forms of Greek (see ch. 35), require a considerable degree of education on the part of the writer and reader, and are employed for literary, scholarly, or formal purposes. In non-learned registers, while some archaizing elements *may* occur (especially in morphology and lexis), mainly under the influence of ecclesiastical language, they tend to be sporadic rather than systematic. From a linguistic point of view, the main difference between the low and high registers is that only the former may be acquired as a native tongue through the mechanism of first-language acquisition, while the second is only accessible through instruction (Toufexis 2008).

The range of "low-register" texts is great – from dialect to a semi-formal mixed language – but it is through such texts that we can trace developments in the *vernacular*, if not the actual spoken language, the closest we can get to it via its written representation (on issues of terminology, see also Hinterberger 2006). Our use of the terms "vernacular," "Medieval," and "Early Modern" thus implies comparability with other European vernaculars of these historical periods.

Scholars, editors, and publishers from the sixteenth century onward have used various terms to refer to these non-learned registers: "vulgar Greek/grec vulgaire/ Vulgärgriechisch," *lingua barbaro-graeca*, and *Romaic* (which, before Independence, was the usual term in Greek: ῥωμαίϰα from the fact that in Byzantine times its speakers were Ῥωμαῖοι, subjects of the Roman Empire).

Lastly, we should elucidate our use of *Byzantine* and *postclassical* in relation to language. "Byzantine Greek" can refer to any form of Greek used in a text written during the Byzantine era (330–1453) and within the empire's borders (or at least its sphere of influence), although some scholars would use the term only for the more learned, non-vernacular registers. However, the language of a vernacular text written in Crete or Cyprus in the fourteenth century is clearly not Byzantine Greek. "Postclassical" is an extremely broad term, indicating that a particular feature or development is located some time after the end of the Classical period, with possibly negative implications.

Linguistic Sources

Early Medieval Greek

As discussed elsewhere (chs 31 and 35), the later history of Greek can only be described in diglossic terms (even though the applicability of the term "diglossia" as understood by modern sociolinguistics is questionable for earlier periods of Greek): ever since the Atticist movement and until modern times, there is an ever-increasing rift between texts written in imitation of past linguistic forms, enjoying high prestige as well as educational and state support (ranging from the purest Classical Attic to a "simplified" administrative *Koine*), and texts written in the everyday spoken language of the period (ranging again from brief illiterate scrawls to literary prose and poetic works). For the first part of the early medieval period, evidence for spoken Greek comes principally from one area, Egypt, in the form of non-literary papyri (phonology and morphology discussed in Gignac 1976–81, syntactic description lacking). After the Arab conquest of the seventh century, however, this source rapidly disappears; furthermore, unfavorable historical conditions (Slav invasions, defensive and civil wars) led to a lowering of the educational and cultural level, and a corresponding radical diminution of literary production, to the point that one frequently speaks of a second "dark age" in the history of Greek (the first being the period twelfth to eighth cent. BCE).

As a result, the available sources for tracing the history of the language are hard to come by: the non-literary sources are almost exclusively inscriptions, which are fairly short and formulaic in character, published disparately in hundreds of archeological publications, and for which there exists no comprehensive linguistic description. Literary texts approaching the vernacular, in varying degrees, come in the following types (see Browning 1983: 55–6; Horrocks 1997a: 161–5): (i) chronicles, such as the *Chronographia* of Ioannes Malalas (sixth cent.), the anonymous *Chronicon Paschale* (seventh cent.); (ii) hagiographical texts, such as the works of Bishop Leontios of Neapolis, the *Life* of Patriarch Euthymius, *The Spiritual Meadow* of John Moschos; (iii) short poems (known as *acclamations*) and satirical songs in praise or derision of the emperor, transmitted by Byzantine historians (see Maas 1912); (iv) works by learned authors, but in a consciously simplified register, with conservative phonology and morphology but considerably innovative syntax and vocabulary, such as the works of Emperor Constantine Porphyrogennetos, *De Caerimoniis* and *De Administrando Imperio* (tenth cent.), or the *Strategikon* of Kekaumenos (eleventh cent.).

The form of language appearing in these texts is of course not uniform – it varies according to period and genre. None of them can claim to be direct representations of everyday language, and the linguistic changes that will be discussed below are attested sporadically in them, and sometimes only indirectly, through hypercorrection. Furthermore, it is difficult to distinguish genuine changes datable to the period of the work's composition from changes datable several centuries later, when the manuscripts were copied.

Late Medieval Greek 1100–1500

The twelfth century is a landmark for the study of the later history of Greek, as it is mainly from this century onward that textual sources close to the spoken language appear again in comparative abundance. However, this statement needs qualification. The vernacular sources are for the most part literary (documentary sources such as letters, legal documents, etc. written in the vernacular are still quite scarce) and in verse (prose works such as historical and fictional narratives only appear at the very end of the period). Furthermore, even the most vernacular of texts contain some admixture of learned archaizing elements, since literacy involves some training in Ancient Greek. Additionally, the process of copying vernacular literature differed greatly from that of Classical literature, as there was no model standard language which the copyist needed to emulate and as the texts themselves were not treated as "fixed" entities to be meticulously preserved. This resulted in many different "versions" of the (usually anonymous) vernacular literary works, frequently quite divergent from one another.

Linguistic research in the language of medieval vernacular texts therefore requires careful distinction between what constitutes authentic usage of the period under examination and what can be attributed to either the influence of earlier literary language or the linguistic habits of a copyist one or more centuries removed from the original (see Manolessou 2008).

The most important of the available vernacular texts from this period (see Beck 1971) fall in the following categories: satirical "begging" poems known as the *Ptochoprodromika*, moralizing and didactic poems (the anonymous *Spaneas* and two poems by Michael Glykas), a few examples of heroic poetry such as the *Song of Armouris* and the "epic" *Digenis Akritis* (eleventh–twelfth cent.), verse romances, some of them original Greek creations (*Kallimachos and Chrysorrhoe, Livistros and Rodamne*) and some adaptations of Western romances (*Imberios and Margarona, Theseid, Achilleid, War of Troy*). Of particular importance is the verse *Chronicle of the Morea*, describing the Frankish conquest and rule of the Peloponnese, because of its length and relative independence from learned language.

Cyprus is a case apart, since from this area only there appear, at the end of this period (fifteenth cent.), two extensive prose chronicles, by Leontios Machairas and Georgios Boustronios. Cypriot literature is the first truly dialectal literature.

Early Modern Greek 1500–1700

A major help in the investigation of EMod.Gk is the appearance, from around 1550, of grammatical descriptions of the contemporary language (about fifteen in number; see Legrand 1874: 175–98). Although the phonological sections are somewhat sketchy, nominal and verbal morphology is treated in detail. Geographical variation in this period is more easily studied than in the previous one, due to the abundance of non-literary sources. However, their provenance is mainly from Venetian-occupied areas (Crete, Cyclades, Heptanese), while for the areas under Ottoman rule (Thessaly, Macedonia, Thrace) evidence is hard to come by.

Literary texts become more abundant in this period, again particularly from areas under Western European rule, although verse texts continue to outnumber prose; romance and other narrative works, popular texts of a religious or moralizing texts (some translated from Italian, such as the *Fior di Virtù*), and intralingual translations from Ancient Greek (*Iliad, Batrachomyomachia*) are the main text types we encounter. With the advent of printing, many of these texts enjoy wide circulation, from the early sixteenth century onward. From a linguistic point of view, there may well have been a tendency for editors and printers to prioritize texts that were not markedly dialectal, and perhaps even to eliminate dialectal features.

Two main areas of literary production can be identified in the early modern period: (i) Crete, where Renaissance influences are fruitfully assimilated, and comedy, tragedy, pastoral, and other genres are successfully cultivated by writers of the stature of Georgios Chortatsis and Vitsentzos Kornaros (Holton 1991) until the completion of the Ottoman conquest in 1669; (ii) the Heptanese (especially Corfu and Zakynthos), which enjoyed close relations with Venice.

Language Change in the Medieval Period

Phonology

Most of the changes that radically transformed Ancient Greek into its medieval and modern successor(s) had already taken place during the *Koine* period (see ch. 16), especially in the phonological domain. The only major phonological changes in EMed. Gk are: (i) the merger of /y/ and /i/ (dated around the ninth–tenth cent.), which resulted in the modern five-vowel system /a e o i u/; (ii) the appearance of the affricate phonemes /ts/ and /dz/ around the sixth century. A number of conditioned sound changes make their (sporadic) first appearance in this period, but never achieve full regularity, i.e., never encompass the totality of the vocabulary, in any period of Greek, due to the strong conservative influence of learned language (see Newton 1972 and Moysiadis 2005). Some of these are shown in table 36.1.

These changes achieve a certain degree of regularity in LMed.Gk: they appear in all the texts included in the sources discussed above, and with a quite high rate of frequency. Therefore, although it is rare to find a text in which the innovative form appears to the exclusion of the older, "unchanged" variant, in most cases it can

Table 36.1 Phonetic changes first appearing in Late Koine–Early Medieval Greek

	Change	Example
vowels	Deletion of unstressed initial vowels	ἡμέρα > μέρα, ὀφρύδιον > φρύδιν [iméra] > [méra], [ofrýðion] > [frýðin]
	/o/ > /u/ unstressed, adjacent to labial/velar	κοκκίον > κουκκίν, πωλῶ > πουλῶ [kocíon] > [kucín], [poló] > [puló]
	/i/ > /e/ unstressed, adjacent to liquid/nasal	κηρίον > κερίν, ὑπηρεσία > ὑπερεσία [ciríon] > [cerín], [ypiresía] > [yperesía]
consonants	Manner dissimilation of stops	πτωχός > φτωχός, ἕκτος > ἔχτος [ptoxós] > [ftoxós], [éktos] > [éxtos]
	Manner dissimilation of fricatives	φθονερός > φτονερός, ἐχθές > χτές [fθonerós] > [ftonerós], [exθés] > [xtés]
	Deletion of final /n/	τὸν λόγον > τὸ λόγο [ton lóγon] > [to lóγo]
	/l/ > /r/ before consonant	ἀδελφός > ἀδερφός, τολμῶ > τορμῶ [aðelfós] > [aðerfós], [tolmó] > [tormó]

be assumed that in spoken language the change has been established, and the unchanged forms are a result of learned influence (see Manolessou and Toufexis, 2009).

In EMod.Gk, the most important phenomenon in the phonological domain are some changes which constitute major isoglosses within Greek, and serve to distinguish between the various dialects (see Trudgill 2003 and Newton 1972 for Modern Greek dialectal phonology). Unfortunately, there is insufficient information concerning their emergence, which must date at least to the previous period; however, evidence for them becomes sufficient only in this era.

The foremost dialectal phonological phenomenon is the so-called "northern vocalism," which affects unstressed mid and high vowels, raising the first and deleting the second (on vowel phonology, see also tables 7.7–8 and fig. 7.1). Thus (i) /e/ > /i/ and /o/ > /u/ and (ii) /i/ and /u/ > ∅. The phenomenon affects northern Greek-speaking areas and forms the basic isogloss dividing Modern Greek in two groups, northern and southern. Some scholars claim that it can be traced as far back as the end of the *Koine* period (e.g., Panayotou 1992a, on the basis of inscriptions from Macedonia). The examples are few for the LMed.Gk period but become numerous in EMod.Gk. (Note that the abbreviations of medieval Greek texts cited below refer to the list at the end of this chapter.)

ὄριξιν (< ὄρεξιν) (*Chr.Tocc.* 2684)

ἀρσινικόν (< ἀρσενικόν) (document from Athos, thirteenth cent.)

δίδου (< δίδω) καὶ ἐγὼ (document from Skyros, sixteenth cent.)

A second dialectal feature is the strong palatalization of velar consonants, which affects southern dialects (Crete, Cyprus, Dodecanese, parts of the Peloponnese). The earliest (LMed.Gk) examples come from Cyprus, and other areas display the phenomenon only in EMod.Gk times:

ψυχικόν > ψυσικόν [psiçikón] > [psiʃikón] (Mach. 224.9)

κόκκινο > κότζινο [kókino] > [kótsino] (document from Peloponnese; 1688)

Morphology and Syntax

In the morphological and syntactic domain, it is difficult to follow evolutions, as they are often obscured by the consciously archaizing form of the texts. The nominal and verbal system, however, must have been radically restructured, and at least the following changes are evident.

Loss of grammatical categories

a) The *dative case* is replaced by the genitive or accusative (Humbert 1930, Lendari and Manolessou 2003; see also ch. 16) in the function of indirect object and various personal uses (ethical, personal gain, etc.). The change starts from clitic forms of personal pronouns already in Egyptian papyri, spreads later to full lexical phrases, and must have been completed around the tenth century, although dative forms still appear even in late medieval vernacular texts. In EMed.Gk texts, the accusative seems to be the preferred variant, but in LMed.Gk both alternatives are equally frequent. The choice between the two constitutes a major dialectal isogloss in Modern Greek, with accusative preferred in the northern and Asia Minor dialects, and genitive in southern and island dialects, as well as in Standard Modern Greek; however, the fixing of the choice between the two alternatives cannot be narrowed down, as some texts have fixed choice as early as the ninth century while others as late as the nineteenth century present variation:

εἴρηκά **σου** ὅτι δὸς ἐμοί κέρμα . . . καὶ εἶπες **με** ὅτι . . .
I told *you* that "give me coin . . ." and you told *me* that . . . (*P.Oxy.* 1683; fourth cent. CE)

δηλοῖ **αὐτὸν** ὁ γέρων · δεῦρο ἕως ὧδε
The old man declares *to him*: come here (Mosch. 2877A)

ὁ οὖν Δαυίδ, ὁ μέγας, τὴν ἑαυτοῦ χώραν οὐκ ἐδίδου **τὸν βασιλέα**
And David, the great, was not giving his land *to the king* (*DAI* 46.118)

ἐνταῦτα **τὸν ἐλάλησεν** κ' εἶπεν **του** τὰ μαντᾶτα
There *he spoke to him* and *told him* the news (*Chron.Mor.* H 2249)

As a direct object and a prepositional complement, the dative is everywhere replaced by the accusative, which gradually becomes the only possible case for this syntactic usage. The first instances of the change date from *Koine* times, and in EMed.Gk they increase greatly. In LMed.Gk vernacular texts the dative is no longer a possible verbal and prepositional complement except as an archaism:

πῶς νῦν ὑμῶν πιστεύσομεν **τοὺς ὅρκους**;

How can we now believe *in your oaths?* (Theoph. 209.3)

καὶ οἱ φάρες ἂν **σὲ** ἀκολουθοῦν, ἐσὲν κανεὶς οὐ φθάνει.

Even if the steeds pursue *you*, no one will overtake you. (*DigE* 281)

καὶ πρὸς τὸ ἡλιοανάτελμα πλησιάζουσιν **τὸ κάστρον**

and towards sunrise they approach *the castle.* (*Achil.N* 477)

Exceptionally, especially in southern and island areas, there appear from LMed.Gk onwards, as a dialectal feature, verbs governing the genitive instead of the (otherwise universal) accusative:

βόηθα **τοῦ δουλευτῆ** σου

Help *your servant.* (*Thys.Avr.* 117)

ἤμνογε καὶ τοῦ φίλου του, ὀγιὰ νὰ **τοῦ πιστεύῃ**

He swore to his friend, so that he would *believe him.* (*Erotokr.* 1.403)

εἰς τὴν στράταν ἐπάντησε 'νοῦ **καραβίου** σαρακήνικου

On the way [the galley] met *a* Saracen *ship.* (Mach. 194.18)

Another alternative to the dative in most functions (verbal complement, personal, instrumental, adverbial, etc.) is replacement with prepositional phrases governing the accusative (see also ch. 16):

ἐγύμνωσεν δὲ τὰ ἱμάτια αὐτοῦ καὶ εἶπεν **πρὸς αὐτὸν**

he took off his clothes and said *to him* . . . (*V.Sym.Sal.* 90.19)

αὐτὸν τὸν βλέπεις ἔδωκεν **εἰς τὴν μονὴν** εἰκόναν

He that you see gave *to the monastery* an icon. (*Ptoch.* 4.90)

εὐχὴν καὶ παρακάλεσιν ἀπέστειλεν **εἰς ὅλους**

He sent a wish and a request *to all.* (*Chron.Mor.* H 487)

b) The *active participle* is lost, replaced by an uninflected gerund functioning as a manner/temporal adverbial (Mirambel 1961, Manolessou 2005). The change, caused perhaps more by the double (verbal and nominal) nature of the participle than by its difficult (third declension) inflectional paradigm, started from singular neuter participles around the fourth century CE and was completed around the fifteenth, with the addition of an adverbial marker –[s] to the uninflected –[onta] form.

παιδαρίου τελευτήσαντος, **ζῶντα** ἀπέδωκεν τῇ μητρί

When a child died, he gave it back to its mother *living*. (*Chron.Pasch.* 186.1)

θεοῦ σπορὰν **μέλλοντα** καλεῖσθαι τὸ τικτόμενον

Because the child *was going to be* called a god's seed. (*V. Alex. L* 1.10.32)

ἦλθες σὺ ὁ καθηγούμενος μονῆς [. . .] **κομίζοντα** γραφὴν

You, the abbot of the monastery [. . .], came *bringing* a letter. (Cusa 432.3; 1183)

ὁ πρίγκιπας [γὰρ] **ἐβλέποντας** τὴν τόση ἀλαζονείαν

ἀπὸ χολῆς του καὶ θυμοῦ ὤμοσε εἰς τὸ σπαθί του

The prince, *seeing* their great arrogance,

in anger and resentment swore upon his sword. (*Chron.Mor.* H 2917–18)

During the LMed.Gk period, an aspectual distinction between present (imperfective) and aorist (perfective) gerund was still possible, a difference which persisted in EMod.Gk but has disappeared from Modern Greek:

ἀκούσοντά το οἱ ἄρχοντες [. . .] μεγάλως τὸ ἀνεχάρησαν

Upon hearing it, the lords were greatly pleased. (*Chron.Mor.* H 351)

καὶ **περάσοντας** πέντε χρόνους ἐσυφωνήσαμεν

Five years *having passed*, we agreed. (document from Peloponnese; 1683)

c)   The *infinitive* is reduced in use, replaced by finite complement clauses, in a long process that lasts until the end of the medieval period. The causes of the evolution are multiple, but probably include the achievement of greater semantic transparency (since the infinitive could not express person distinctions) and of simplified subject case assignment mechanisms. The process might have been strengthened by a phonetic factor, the homonymy of some infinitive forms with the third singular active indicative/subjunctive, which resulted from the falling together of /ei/, /ē/, and /ɛ̄/ as /i/ and the debility of final /n/, dated already to *Koine* times (Joseph 1990: 23–4):

γράφειν ≠ γράφει ≠ γράφῃ   >   γράφει(ν) = γράφει = γράφῃ

graphēn ≠ graphei ≠ graphēi   >   γrafi(n) = γrafi = γrafi γράψειν ≠ γράψει ≠ γράψῃ   >   γράψει(ν) = γράψει = γράψῃ

grapsēn ≠ grapsei ≠ grapsēi   >   γrapsi(n) = γrapsi = γrapsi

γραφθῆναι ≠ γραφθῇ   >   γραφθεῖ(ν) = γραφθῇ

graphthēnai ≠ graphthēi   >   γrafθi(n) = γrafθi

The above schema also presents two morphological evolutions of LMed.Gk, which have enhanced the phonetic similarity between infinitive and finite third person forms: –σειν /si(n)/ replaces –σαι /se/ as the active aorist ending, and –ειν /i(n)/ replaces –ηναι /ine/ as the passive aorist ending, both in analogy to the active present.

The first to be lost was the infinitive dependent on verbs of saying, thinking, etc. It is replaced by clauses introduced by ὅτι, ὡς, and in LMed.Gk also πῶς and ὅπου, in a process which began in the *Koine* period:

λέγουσιν ὅτι Πλούτων ἥρπασε τὴν κόρην

They say that Pluto ravished the girl. (Mal. 63.2)

φανερὸν ἦν ὅτι αὐτὸς ἦν ἡ νίκη

It was obvious that he was (the cause of the) victory. (*V.Alex. L* 13.22)

The infinitive dependent on verbs denoting ordering, wanting, and in general future-referring actions involving will is ultimately replaced by complement clauses introduced by ἵνα > νά /hína/ > /na/:

καὶ **εἶπεν** αὐτῇ ὁ βασιλεὺς Ζήνων **ἵνα** αἰτήσῃ τὸν πατρίκιον Ἰλλοῦν

and King Zeno *told* her *to* ask the patrician Illous. (Mal. 387.3)

This change begins in *Koine* times, but the infinitive in such uses is maintained throughout the medieval period, albeit in alternation with finite clauses. The faster rate of loss of the first type of infinitive clause is probably due to the fact that the subject of the infinitive clause is usually non-co-referential with that of the matrix clause, thus requiring a different and more complex case assignment mechanism (nominative for finite verbs, accusative for infinitives), while in the second case the subject of the matrix and the infinitive clause are most frequently identical. Thus, it is structures where the accusative and infinitive (AcI) syntax predominates which are lost first, whereas control structures are retained longer (Horrocks 1997a: 45–6; Kavčič 2005: 190).

Obligatory control verbs ("want," "can/be able," "begin/end") are precisely the ones which retain infinitival structures in LMed.Gk; research (Joseph 2000, Mackridge 1996) shows that in this period the infinitive can be still be claimed as a "living," "authentic" category, regularly appearing even in the lowest registers, and being retained up to modern times in peripheral Modern Greek dialects (Pontic and Southern Italian).

οὐκ ἠμποροῦν τὴν **εὕρειν**

they can't *find* her (*DigE* 124)

ἀλλὰ καβαλλικεύοντα ἄρχασαν **συντυχαίνει**

but, having mounted their horses, they began *to converse* (*Chron.Mor.* H 5261)

οὐκ ἐπόρεσα **σταθῆναι** [utʃ epóresa staðíne]

I wasn't able *to stay* (Modern Pontic; Mackridge 1996: 197)

τί ἤρτετε **κάμει** ὦδε; [ti írtete kámi óðe]

what did you come here *to do*? (Modern Calabrian Greek; Karanastasis 1997: 143)

A characteristically LMed.Gk use is the development of a new type of infinitival construction, the so-called circumstantial infinitive. Its origins lie in the articular infinitive governed by prepositions which was a widespread *Koine* phenomenon:

διὰ **τὸ** ἀνθρωποφάγον αὐτὸν **εἶναι**

because he [Bucephalus] *is* a man-eating beast (*V. Alex. L* 1.17)

μετὰ **τὸ διελθεῖν** ἐκεῖνον, εἴσελθε ὡς εἰς πάντων ἡμῶν

after *he passes,* enter like one of us (*V. Euth.* 12.79.1)

In LMed.Gk and EMod.Gk, the infinitive appears without a preposition, with a subject co-referential to that of the matrix verb, and having a temporal/causal meaning. The construction is very widespread in texts of the period, but has disappeared from Modern Greek and its dialects:

τὸ ἀκούσει το ὁ μισὶρ Ντζεφρὲς σπουδαίως ἐκεῖσε ἀπῆλθε

Upon hearing it, messire Geoffroi hurriedly went there (*Chron.Mor.* H 2491)

τὸ ἰδεῖ τὴν κόρην ὁ ἀμιρᾶς μετὰ τοῦ νεωτέρου . . . πονεῖ, στενάζει, θλίβεται

When the emir *sees* the girl with the young man, he aches, he sighs, he's sad (*Flor.* 1710)

Creation of periphrastic forms

a) The *future* is replaced by the indicative and various periphrastic constructions (Markopoulos 2009). The causes of the change are multiple, including the inability of the future to express aspectual distinctions and the formal identification of the ancient future indicative with the aorist subjunctive after the loss of phonological vowel quantity. The change starts from the *Koine* period, when the first alternatives to the ancient future appear. In EMed.Gk the usual variants are: present indicative, aorist subjunctive, ἔχω + infinitive (the dominant periphrasis around the eighth–tenth cent.), and, less frequently, μέλλω + infinitive (often used interchangeably).

ὄμοσόν μοι, ὅτι οὐδενὶ **λέγεις** ἃ **μέλλω** σοι **λέγειν**

Swear to me that *you will tell* no one what *I am about to tell you.* (Mosch. 2900.22)

καὶ ἐὰν λαλήσῃς τὸν στρατόν, ἵνα δέξωνταί με, καὶ τὰς ῥόγας αὐτῶν **ἐπαυξῆσαι ἔχω** καὶ εἰρήνην **ποιῶ** μετὰ τοῦ βασιλέως Ῥωμαίων

If you tell the army to accept me, *I shall increase* their pay and *I shall make* peace with the king of the Romans. (Theoph. 326.1)

In LMed.Gk, by far the most frequent future periphrasis is formed by the verb θέλω [θélo] "want" + present/aorist infinitive:

θέλω γενεῖν καλὰ καὶ **θέλομεν φαγεῖν** καὶ **πιεῖν** ὁμοῦ

I shall get well, and *we shall eat* and *drink* together. (Sphrantz. 16.26)

ὡς πότε **θέλω κυνηγᾶν** λαγούδια καὶ περδίκια;

Until when *shall I be hunting* hares and partridges? (*DigE* 744)

This construction, following a well-studied but still controversial path (Joseph and Pappas 2002, Markopoulos 2007) ends up, in EMod.Gk, as a periphrasis involving an uninflected and reduced form of the verb, θὲ or θά, plus a finite replacement of the infinitive with (νὰ +) subjunctive present or aorist. The θά + subjunctive form, which constitutes the single Modern Greek future expression, is first attested in the late sixteenth century, but the older forms persist and co-occur with newer ones:

τὰ θαλάσσια ἐγνωρίζουσιν ὅταν **θέλη νὰ ἀλλάξῃ** ὁ καιρός

the fish know when the weather *is going to change* (Landos 131.8)

γιατὶ **θέλω θανατωθῶ** τὴν ὥρα ποὺ **θὲ φάγω**/ τὸ ξύλον τὸ τῆς γνώσεως

because *I shall die* the moment *I shall eat* the tree of knowledge (Vestarchis 33)

ἔνας μας **θὲ νὰ σκοτωθῆ** κι ὁ ῥήγας του **θὰ χάσῃ**

One of us *will die* and his king *will lose* (*Erotokr.* 4.1778)

b) The *perfect and pluperfect* are lost, and in their place several periphrases arise, with the new auxiliary verbs "to be" and "to have" plus various forms of the infinitive or participle (see Aerts 1965, Moser 1988). The loss is motivated by the identification in meaning of the ancient perfect and aorist (already completed during the *Koine* period), evident from the fact that in EMed.Gk texts the (ancient) perfect forms are used interchangeably with the aorist:

[ὁ βασιλεὺς] τὰ ἐξ ἔθους γινόμενα ἄριστα εἰς τὰ ιθ´ ἀκούβιτα **ἔπαυσε** καὶ τὴν τούτων ἔξοδον τοῖς πτωχοῖς **δέδωκεν.**

[The emperor] stopped the traditional dinners at (the hall of) the nineteen couches, and gave their cost to the poor. (Theoph. 232.5)

The change starts in *Koine* times and takes many centuries to reach completion. In the EMed.Gk period, the variant perfect/pluperfect periphrastic constructions in the lowest registers are εἰμί + active aorist participle, εἰμί + passive aorist participle, and εἰμί + passive perfect participle. Many of them, however, can arguably be viewed as a combination of copula + adjectival participle rather than as true periphrases:

κτίσας τὸ βουλευτήριον· **πεσόντα** γὰρ ἦν

building the assembly hall, because *it had fallen into disrepair* (Mal. 211.18)

καὶ λαβὼν αὐτὸν ἀπήνεγκεν ὅπου **ἦσαν θάψαντες** αὐτὸν

And taking him he led him where *they had buried* him (Mosch. 107.82)

τὸ δὲ αὐτὸ δημόσιον **ἦν κεκτισμένον** παρὰ τὸ ὄρος

and this public bath *was built* by the mountain (Mal. 263.14)

In LMed.Gk a peculiar change occurs: what was previously the dominant future-referring periphrasis, the auxiliary ἔχω "have" + infinitive, becomes a past-referring perfect/pluperfect expression. The change starts from the contexts in which the past form of ἔχω + infinitive was used as a future-in-the-past, i.e., expressing unrealized possibility in the past, in conditional and counterfactual clauses (see Moser 1988, Horrocks 1995):

εἶχον δὲ καὶ τὰς ἡμῶν ναῦς **καῦσαι** οἱ βάρβαροι, εἰ μὴ νὺξ ἐπῆλθε

the barbarians *would have been able to burn/would have burnt* our boats, if night had not fallen (Mal. 128.5)

The formation "had" + infinitive was initially used only in the apodosis of conditional clauses, but later in the protasis also:

ἂν τό 'χεν **μάθει** πρότερον, ἂν τό 'χεν **ἐγροικήσει**, τὴν βασιλείαν τῶν Ρωμαίων **κληρονομήσειν εἶχεν**

If *he had learned it* earlier, if *he had heard it*, he *would have inherited* the kingdom of the Romans. (*Velisar.χ*.371–2)

In this position, expressing a presupposition for the realization of the apodosis, it could easily be re-analyzed as expressing an action/event anterior to the apodosis:

ἐκεῖνοι ἂν σὲ **εἶχαν εὑρεῖ**, Συρίαν οὐκ ἐθεώρεις

If *they had found you*, you would not have seen Syria (*DigE* 141)

From this interpretation, anteriority in the unreal past, there derives the use of the periphrasis as a true pluperfect, expressing an action/event anterior to another action/event in the "real" past. This "true" pluperfect use appears around the thirteenth century, and is quite frequent in LMed.Gk texts and present in most Modern Greek dialects.

καὶ οὐκ ἀπῆλθεν μετ' αὐτοὺς καθὼς τοὺς **εἶχε ὁμόσει**

and he did not leave with them, as *he had sworn* to them (*Chron.Mor.* P 81)

However, the corresponding perfect use, employing the present form of the auxiliary "have" appears much later, is extremely rare in the texts, and most Modern Greek dialects lack this formation, despite the fact that it is the only means of expressing the perfect in Standard Modern Greek:

ἐκεῖνοι ὁποὺ δικαίως **ἔχουν ἀποκτήσει** μεγάλην φήμην

Those who *have* rightfully *acquired* great fame. (*Don Quixote* 164.13–14)

Instead, both LMed.Gk texts and dialects present alternative formations, the most frequent being those employing the verbs "to be" and "to have" with the perfect participle passive:

ἐκεῖνος ὁποὺ **ἔχει** τὸ πρᾶγμαν **χαμένον** ἐντέχεται νὰ τὸ λάβῃ ὅλον

He who *has lost* the thing must take it all. (*Assiz.* B 426.22)

ἔχει κλειδωμένα | τὴν πόρτα ἡ κεράτσα μου

My lady *has locked* the door. (*Katz.* 2.105)

στὸ Νίκλι γὰρ τοῦ εἴπασιν ὅτι **ἔνι διαβασμένος**

They told him that he *is gone* to Nikli. (*Chron.Mor.* H 2298')

c) The *imperative mood* must have lost the third person already during *Koine* times, but the second person remains unchanged (apart from analogical re-formations of the endings). It is complemented by a periphrastic formation made up of the subjunctive (present or aorist) introduced by the uninflected particle ἂς [as], a grammaticalized form of the imperative ἄφες of the verb ἀφίημι "let" (Nikiforidou 1996):

καὶ εἴτι θέλεις **ὅρισε**, αὐθέντη, καὶ **ἂς μὲ ποιήσουν**.

And whatever you want, lord, *command*, and *let them do to me.* (*Achil.N* 920)

εὐθὺς "**ἂς βράσῃ** τὸ θερμόν" λέγει πρὸς τὸ παιδίν του

Straightway he says to his son, "*Let* the water *boil.*" (*Ptoch.*2.116)

The grammaticalization process begins in the *Koine* period, when the verb appears still in unreduced form, accompanying non-co-referential hortative subjunctives:

ἢ πῶς δύνασαι λέγειν τῷ ἀδελφῷ σου· ἀδελφέ, **ἄφες ἐκβάλω** τὸ κάρφος τὸ ἐν τῷ ὀφθαλμῷ σου . . . ;

Either how canst thou say to thy brother, Brother, *let me pull out* the mote that is in thine eye . . .? (Luke 6:42)

Early attestations of reduced [as] are from Egyptian papyri dated to the sixth to seventh centuries, and several examples can be found in texts from that period onwards:

καὶ **ἃς λάβ[ω]σι[ν]** οἱ ὀνηλάται μίαν ἀρτ(άβην) κριθῆς ὑπὲρ ἑκάστου γαϊδαρίου

And *let* the donkey-drivers *receive* one artaba of barley for each donkey. (*P.Amh.* 2.153; sixth–seventh cent.)

ὅμως ἄνω τὰ ἱμάτιά σου · **ἃς ἴδω**, τί ἔχεις

But up with your clothes, *let me see* what's wrong with you. (*Miracula* 66.13)

Leveling of nominal paradigms

The nominal paradigms undergo radical analogical leveling, originally due to phonological changes of the *Koine* period, namely the deletion of final /n/, the loss of quantity distinctions, and the monophthongization of diphthongs. These resulted in the homophony of previously distinct case-endings (see also table 16.2).

First declension singular accusative /ān/	
First declension singular dative /āi/	all just /a/
Third declension singular accusative /a/	
First declension plural accusative /ās/	both /as/
Third declension plural accusative /as/	
First declension plural nominative /ai/	> /e/
First declension plural dative /ais/	> /es/
Third declension plural nominative /es/	> /es/

Thus the ancient first declension (masc./fem. a-stems) and a large part of the ancient third declension (masc./fem. consonant stems) gradually merged into a single paradigm, in which the /a/ vocalism of the first declension prevails in the singular, and the /e/ vocalism of the third declension in the plural.

The schema shown in table 36.2 (details in Seiler 1958 and Ruge 1969) shows that: (i) the inflection of the nouns belonging to the first and third declensions becomes identical, except for the accentuation of the genitive plural (paroxytone for the "old third " nouns, oxytone for the "old first"), causing considerable variation in the accentuation of this case form in later Greek; and (ii) morphologically, the ancient five cases are reduced to two, although functionally they remain apart. Of course this is an oversimplifying schema, which omits some residual third declension paradigms not amenable to this

Table 36.2 Evolution of nominal inflection

	First declension		Third declension	
	Singular	*Plural*	*Singular*	*Plural*
Feminine				
Nom.	/hēmérā/	/hēmérai/	≠ /elpís/	/elpídes/
Gen.	/hēmérās/	/hēmerɔ́n/	/elpídos/	/elpídɔn/
Dat.	/hēmérāi/	/hēmérais/	/elpídi/	/elpísi/
Acc.	/hēmérān/	/hēmérās/	/elpída/	/elpídas/
	⇓⇓⇓⇓⇓⇓⇓⇓⇓⇓		= ⇓⇓⇓⇓⇓⇓⇓⇓⇓⇓	
Nom./Acc./Dat.	/iméra/	/iméres/	/elpíða/	/elpíðes/
Gen.	/iméras/	/imerón/	/elpíðas/	/elpíðon/
Masculine				
Nom.	/tamíās/	/tamíai/	≠ /kanɔ́n/	/kanónes/
Gen.	/tamíū/	/tamiɔ́n/	/kanónos/	/kanónon/
Dat.	/tamíāi/	/tamíais/	/kanóni/	/kanósi/
Acc.	/tamíān/	/tamíās/	/kanóna/	/kanónas/
	⇓⇓⇓⇓⇓⇓⇓⇓⇓⇓		⇓⇓⇓⇓⇓⇓⇓⇓⇓⇓	
Nom.	/tamías/	NAD	/kanónas/	NAD
Gen./Acc./Dat.	/tamía/	/tamíes/	/kanóna/	/kanónes/
		G /tamión/		G /kanónon/

evolution. These are the neuter paradigms (s-stems, t-stems, etc.) and the masc./fem. -i- and -u-stems, which retain (some of) their original inflectional forms.

The evolutions described above are only sporadically evident in texts of the early medieval period, in inscriptions, papyri, chronicles, and lexica (data in Hatzidakis 1892: 77–80; Dieterich 1898: 156–67; Jannaris 1897: 106–9, 120–3), although some of them make their first appearance in *Koine* times.

Frequently cited EMed.Gk attestations of the changes described above include those shown in table 36.3.

The ancient second declension (masc./fem./neut. o-stems) shows less change, as the masculine o-stems are the most conservative nominal inflectional paradigm, retaining the ancient inflection intact (apart from the loss of the dative and the final -n). However, the feminine and neuter paradigms undergo important modifications. A new and well-populated subset of neuter nouns evolves, through a change first appearing in *Koine* times: the deletion of /o/ following /i/ in inflectional endings (i.e., -ιος, -ιον > -ις, -ι(ν)). Scholars disagree whether this is a phonetic or morphological evolution. Due to the extreme frequency of -*ion* as a diminutive (often in order to replace "difficult" third declension inflectional patterns which involved stem allomorphy, e.g., ὀφρύς > ὀφρύδιον, παῖς > παιδίον), the –ιον > -ιν suffix lost all semantic force as a diminutive and was seen as simply the inflectional ending. Thus the neuter

Table 36.3 Early evidence for changes in nominal inflection

Phenomenon	Example
First decl. pl. –ες for –αι	οἱ δὲ ῥινοτομηθέντες **Πέρσες** (Mal. 331.7)
Third decl. nom. sg. –α	σεισμοῦ λαβροτάτου γενομένου ἐν Κύπρῳ, **Σαλαμίνα** πόλις κατέπεσε (Theoph. 29.25)
Third decl. gen. sg. –ας for –ος	φορῆσαι τὸ **τῆς Δημήτρας** σχῆμα (Mal.173.22); ἐκ τῆς **προίκας** (Pieria, Kitros; third cent.; Panayotou 1992b: 20)

o-stem class now contains two subtypes of nouns, those ending in -o(ν) and those ending in –ι(ν), but inflection otherwise remains unchanged.

The restructuring of feminine o-stems is more substantial: the feminine second declension inflection, being identical to the masculine o-stems, was felt to be "untypically" feminine, having as it does {presence of -s} in nom. sg. and {absence of -s} in gen. sg., in contrast to the reformed first and third declension paradigm, which had the reverse. As a result, feminine o-stems (a not so numerous class anyway) were reformed in the following ways:

a) they became masculine (ἡ ἄμμος > ὁ ἄμμος). This tendency had already begun in the Classical period (cf. the examples from Aristophanes and Aristotle in Hatzidakis 1892: 24) and became stronger in *Koine* times. Gignac (1976–81: 2: 39–40) mentions forms like τὸν γύψον (second cent.), τοῦ βώλου, τοὺς πλίνθους (third cent.).

b) they acquired first declension endings (ἡ παρθένος > ἡ παρθένα). Again, this is a change first appearing in late *Koine*, e.g., καμίνη, ἀντιδίκαις (Gignac 1976–81: 2: 39-40), ἵνα πολλὰς παρθένας διαφθείρῃ (*De fallacia* 7.7; fourth cent.).

c) they were replaced by diminutives. Thus ἀμπέλιον (< ἄμπελος) appears already in Hippocrates, νησίον (< νῆσος) in Strabo and ῥαβδίον (< ῥάβδος) in Theophrastus (LSJ s.vv.) and these become more frequent in later periods, to the point that in Modern Greek they have replaced the original feminine form (except in very formal or scientific registers).

d) they adopted an inflectional pattern similar to that of first declension feminines (ἡ ἄμμος τῆς ἄμμου > ἡ ἄμμο τῆς ἄμμος, ἡ μέθοδο sg., but οἱ μέθοδες pl.). This change is never attested in EMed.Gk texts, first appearing around the fourteenth century, e.g., τῆς Κόρινθος (*Chron. Mor.* H 1476), but becomes frequent only in EMod.Gk, e.g., ἡ Ρόδο ἐθλίβηκε, τῆς Χίος ἐκακοφάνη (*Symfor.* 189).

Turning to verbal morphology, in the inflectional domain there develops a tendency for analogical unification of past tense endings (Babiniotis 1972). The -a- vowel characteristic of the aorist and perfect spread to the imperfect (with the exception of the second singular where the -e- vowel of the imperfect prevailed in the aorist and perfect), while the –ασι ending of the perfect spread to the imperfect and aorist. The change encompassed the "strong aorist" inflectional paradigm, which disappeared, replaced by its weak aorist counterpart. The result is a merged past personal ending system (see table 36.4), which in LMed.Gk also spreads to the passive voice.

Table 36.4 Merger of past active endings

	Imperfect		*Aorist*		*Perfect*
1 sg.	e-graph-on	≠	e-graps-a	=	ge-graph-a
2 sg.	e-graph-es	≠	e-graps-as	=	ge-graph-as
3 sg.	e-graph-e	=	e-graps-e	=	ge-graph-e
1 pl.	e-graph-omen	≠	e-graps-amen	=	ge-graph-amen
2 pl.	e-graph-ete	≠	e-graps-ate	=	ge-graph-ate
3 pl.	e-graph-on	≠	e-graps-an	≠	ge-graph-asi
	⇓ ⇓ ⇓ ⇓ ⇓ ⇓ ⇓ ⇓		⇓ ⇓ ⇓ ⇓ ⇓ ⇓ ⇓ ⇓		⇓ ⇓ ⇓ ⇓ ⇓ ⇓ ⇓ ⇓
1 sg.	e-γraf-a	=	e-γraps-a		
2 sg.	e-γraf-es	=	e-γraps-es		
3 sg.	e-γraf-e	=	e-γraps-e		
1 pl.	e-γraf-ame(n)	=	e-γraps-ame(n)		
2 pl.	e-γraf-ete/-ate	=	e-γraps-ate		
3 pl.	e-γraf-an/ -asi	=	e-γraps-an/ -asi		

The change probably originated from the 3 sg., which was identical in the three paradigms, and is also the most frequent, and therefore basic, form in many languages, and was strengthened by the semantic merger of aorist and perfect which produced a large majority of forms with the characteristic -a- vowel. The identity of 1 sg. and 3 pl. in the imperfect might also have been an original motivation for change in both persons. The change begins in *Koine* times, where several cases of fluctuation between allomorphs of the personal endings are attested (Mandilaras 1972: 127–8, 148–56; Gignac 1976–1981: 2: 331–50).

The best-studied syntactic change in the medieval period involves word order, and in particular the placement of weak personal pronouns (clitics) with respect to the verb (Horrocks 1990, Mackridge 2000, Pappas 2004). In Ancient Greek, personal pronouns are enclitic, and governed by Wackernagel's law, according to which they appear in second position in the clause. Already in this period there emerges a tendency for them to appear immediately after the verb, in order to ensure semantic transparency, which becomes even stronger in the *Koine* period (Janse 2000). Thus in EMed.Gk, most clitic pronouns are immediately postverbal (see, e.g., statistics for Moschos in Kissilier 2003), although pre-verbal position adjacent to a focused element is possible:

Ἐὰν καύσῃ με τὸ πῦρ, ἐκ τῶν καιομένων μου ὀστέων λάβετε

If the fire burns *me*, take from my burning bones. (Mal.18.16) γύμνωσον σεαυτόν, ὅπως ἴδω **σε**, ἀδελφέ

Take off your clothes so I can see *you*, brother. (*Miracula* 3.12)

ἐὰν τελευτήσῃς, ἐν μέσῳ τῆς πόλεώς **σε** θάψομεν καὶ οὐκ ἐξάξομέν **σε** ἔξω τῶν τειχῶν.

If you die, in the middle of the city we'll bury *you*, and we won't take *you* outside the walls. (*DAI* 53. 378).

In LMed.Gk however, a more complex system of object clitic pronoun placement evolves, which depends on the type of constituents preceding the verb (if any): (i) a clitic is postverbal if the verb is first in the clause or preceded by a co-ordinating conjunction or the subordinating conjunction ὅτι, e.g:

καὶ πίνει **τα** καὶ ἐρεύγεται, κιρνοῦν **τον** ἄλλον ἕνα

And he drinks *them* and belches, they treat him to *another* drink. (*Ptoch.* 3.122)

διατὶ μὲ τὸ ὥρισε ὁ ἰατρὸς κ' εἶπεν ὅτι ὠφελεῖ **με**

because the doctor prescribed it for me and said it does *me* good (*Chron. Mor.* H 8209–13)

and (ii) it is pre-verbal when the verb is preceded by a subordinating conjunction or a fronted constituent, e.g.,

μὲ δύναμης **τὰ** ἄρπαζαν κ' ἐρρίχτασίν **τα** κάτω,

κι ἂν ἦτον τόσα ἀπότολμος νὰ **τοὺς** ἀντιμιλήσῃ,

εὐτὺς χάμω **τὸν** ἔρριπταν, πολλὰ **τὸν** τιμωροῦσαν.

With force they seized *them* and cast them down,

and if anyone was so bold as to speak against *them*,

they would throw *him* to the ground and punish *him* severely. (*Chron.Mor.* P 15–17)

After the medieval period this pattern changes, and object clitics become increasingly pre-verbal, to the point that in Modern Greek the pre-verbal position is the only available option with finite verbs, and the postverbal one with gerunds and imperatives. Cretan Renaissance literature still largely adheres to these rules, but prose texts begin to show the modern pattern:

ὅμως, **σὲ** παρακαλῶ, ἀνασηκώσου

But please, get up. (*Don Quixote* 524.39)

καὶ ἐζεμάτισε ξίδι καὶ **τοῦ** ἔρριξε 'ς τὰ μάτια καὶ **τὸν** ἐτύφλωσε·

and he boiled vinegar and poured it in *his* eyes, and blinded *him* (*Chron.Tourk.Soult.* 25.14–15)

However, some Modern Greek dialects (such as Cretan and Cypriot) preserve the older pattern, while others (Pontic) have developed in the opposite way, generalizing the postverbal position.

Lexicon

The vocabulary is the domain in which the greatest amount of change is evident. Change in EMed.Gk consists mainly of borrowing from Latin: initially military, legal, and administrative terminology (e.g., κάστρον < *castrum* "castle," ἀππλικεύω < *applicare* "camp," μανδᾶτον < *mandatum* "message"), but also everyday words, such as ὁσπίτιον < *hospitium* "house," φοῦρνος < *furnus* "oven" (Kahane and Kahane 1982). Latin influence decreases when Greek becomes the official language.

Loans from Slavic languages also began to enter Greek in this period, but very few of them (mostly military and administrative terms) are attested in early sources, e.g., ζάκανον "law" (*DAI* 38.52), τζελνίκος "general" (Kekaum. 172.30) (see Schreiner 1986), and possibly though controversially, the diminutive suffixes –ίτσα, -ίτσι. In LMed.Gk and EMod.Gk, Slavic loan words are slightly more frequent (there are 28 recorded in Kriaras 1976–), and also include everyday terms (βάλτα "swamp" (*DigE* 1138), καράνος "penitent" (*Ptoch.* 1.257), καρβέλι "loaf" (*Spanos* 5.392). Slavic influence is more easily detected through toponyms and ethnic and personal names (Miklosich 1870).

The third source of foreign influence in the EMed.Gk period is Persian and Arabic (sometimes difficult to distinguish, because loan words from the first enter Greek via the second), giving terms such as ἀγγούριον "cucumber" < *'agur*, ἀμιρᾶς "emir" < *amir*, χάνδαξ "trench" < *khandaq*. Kriaras (1967–) gives 80 words of Arabic origin for the LMed.Gk period.

In LMed.Gk, the influence of Latin and Arabic naturally decreases, and the main source of loan words and constructions are the Romance languages, coming into contact with Greek through the Frankish conquest of Greece (Kahane and Kahane 1982). Areas under French occupation, such as the Peloponnese and Cyprus, present many loan words from Old French, especially terms of feudal administration, e.g., φίε < *fief*, σεργέντης < *serjent*, μπαρούνης < *baron*, κλέρης < *clerc* (all from the *Chron.Mor.*), ἀπλαζίριν < *plaisir*, κουβερνούρης < *gouvernour*, τζάμπρα < *chambre* (all from Mach.), which however slowly drop out of the language in the EMod.Gk period, as contact with French decreases. Areas under Venetian occupation (Crete, Cyclades, Heptanese) are the centers of Italian influence. The supremacy of the medieval Italian cities in sea trade was also a major source of Italian influence on Greek (Hesseling 1903). Italian influence proved more lasting than French, due to the much longer and stronger period of contact (the Heptanese remained under Venetian rule until the Napoleonic wars), and is still apparent in Modern Greek dialects.

Towards the end of the LMed.Gk period, Turkish becomes the main source of influence on vocabulary, since most Greek-speaking areas fall under Turkish rule: Kriaras (1967–) reports 273 words of Turkish origin in medieval vernacular texts, including administrative and military terms (πασάς "pasha," βεζίρης "vizier," ἀσκέρι "army") but also everyday words (ἄτι "horse," καζάνι "pot," κονάκι "house," κουβάς "bucket")) (see Moravcsik 1943).

Table 36.5   Major linguistic changes by period

Period	Phonology	Morphology–Syntax	Lexicon
Early Medieval	Change of /y/ > /i/ Appearance of /ts/, /dz/	Loss of dative Loss of declarative infinitive -οντα active gerunds ἔχω + inf. = future εἰμί + pass. part. = perfect	Latin borrowings
Late Medieval	Deletion of unstressed initial vowels Manner dissimilation of stops and fricatives	-οντας active gerunds Inf. only in control structures θέλω + inf. = future ἔχω + pass. part. = perfect Merger of first and third declension masc./fem.	Italian and French borrowings
Early Modern	Dialectal phonology: Northern vowel raising Palatalizations	Loss of aorist gerund Total loss of infinitive θὲ νά, θὰ + subj. = future ἔχω + inf. = perfect Change in clitic word order	Italian and Turkish borrowings

In table 36.5, the changes discussed above are classified by period.

Conclusions

The author of one of the few contemporary grammars of Medieval (or rather, Early Modern) Greek, Mitrofanis Kritopoulos (Dyovouniotis 1924), explained in 1627 that in writing his linguistic description he was motivated by the hope that αἰσχυνθήσονται οἱ νῦν Ἕλληνες ὁρῶντες ἐν τῇ βίβλῳ, καθάπερ ἐν κατόπτρῳ, τὴν σφῶν ἀμορφίαν καὶ εἰς ἀνάμνησιν τῆς πάλαι ὡραιότητος ἐπανήξουσιν "the present-day Greeks will be so ashamed to see their own ugliness reflected in this book, as if in a mirror, that they will return to the recollection of their erstwhile beauty." The aspiration of the present chapter, although its subject is similar to that of Kritopoulos' book, is quite the reverse: we hope that readers will realize that knowledge of and research into Medieval Greek need not be inextricably linked to Ancient Greek; we regard Medieval Greek as an autonomous language, and a fascinating subject in its own right. Phonologically speaking, the all-pervasive changes which took place in the *Koine* period have ensured that the Medieval (and Modern) Greek system is entirely different in sound and structure from that of Ancient Greek; grammatically, Medieval Greek displays constant variation and change over a period of more than a millennium, very far from any notion of a rigid, codified "Classical" language. It can perhaps be more fruitfully compared to the medieval phase of other modern European languages (coexistence of a vernacular and an alternative – high – linguistic code, complex textual tradition of literary works, chaotic spelling, issues of orality/literacy, thematic similarities, insufficient modern linguistic research).

Then why, one might ask, is this chapter included in a book dedicated to Ancient Greek? First, it is a natural inclination to want to know what happens next, how the story ends – although in this case it is still going on. Secondly, a purely linguistic motive: Greek offers a rare opportunity, among the world's languages, to study language change over more than 3,000 years of continuous recorded tradition (well, with a small gap for the Dark Ages, 1200–800 BCE); strangely, this opportunity has often been ignored. Finally, the fact that ancient, medieval, and modern forms of the language share the same name should remind us that the disciplines of Classical, Byzantine, and Modern Greek Studies are not separate, watertight categories of scholarship, but can frequently inspire mutually beneficial collaboration.

FURTHER READING

There is no comprehensive grammatical description for any sub-period of Medieval Greek. However, there are five scholarly works which constitute indispensable contributions, though now considerably out of date: Hatzidakis 1892 and 1905–7, Jannaris 1897, Dieterich 1898, and Psaltes 1913. Recent accounts of the history of later Greek are Browning 1983 and Tonnet 2003; the most linguistically informed description is Horrocks 1997a. The University of Cambridge hosts a major research project which will shortly produce a grammar of LMed.Gk and EMod.Gk (details at www.mml.cam.ac.uk/greek/grammarofmedievalgreek; see also Holton, forthcoming). Many examples in this chapter come from the electronic corpus and database of the project. The vocabulary of LMed.Gk and EMod.Gk is well served by the dictionaries of Kriaras (1967–), (available online in a concise version, at http://www.greek-language.gr/greekLang/medieval_greek/kriaras/index.html) and Trapp et al. (1994–); both, however, have yet to reach completion. EMed.Gk is only partially covered by Lampe 1969, Sophocles 1887, and Konstantinidis and Moschos 1907–95 (the Greek translation of the eighth edition of Liddell and Scott, with additional material on *Koine* and EMed.Gk). Loan words in Medieval Greek, their sources and phonetic adaptation, are discussed in Triantaphyllidis 1909. Bibliographic surveys of linguistic research on the period are Kapsomenos 1985, Apostolopoulos 1994, Janse 1996–7, and Jeffreys and Doulavera 1998.

MEDIEVAL AND EARLY MODERN GREEK SOURCES

Achil.N   Smith, O. L. 1991. *The Byzantine Achilleid. The Naples Version* (Wiener Byzantinische Studien 21). Vienna.

Assiz.   Σάθας, Κ. Ν., 1877. Ἀσσίζαι τοῦ Βασιλείου τῶν Ἱεροσολύμων καὶ τῆς Κύπρου, in Μεσαιωνικὴ Βιβλιοθήκη ἢ συλλογὴ ἀνεκδότων μνημείων τῆς ἑλληνικῆς ἱστορίας, vol. 6. Venice and Paris.

Chr.Tocc.   Schirò, G. 1975. *Cronaca dei Tocco di Cefalonia; prolegomeni, testo critico e traduzione* (*CFHB* 10). Rome.

Chr.Pasch.   *Chronicon Paschale. Patrologia Graeca*, vol. 92.

Chron.Mor.   Schmitt, J. 1904. *The Chronicle of Morea*, Τὸ Χρονικὸν τοῦ Μορέως. London.

Chron.Tourk.Soult.   Zoras, G. Th. 1958. Χρονικὸν περὶ τῶν Τούρκων σουλτάνων *(κατὰ τὸν Βαρβερινὸν ἑλληνικὸν κώδικα 111).* Athens.

Cusa   Cusa, S. 1868–82. *Diplomi greci ed arabi di Sicilia, pubblicati nel testo originale, tradotti ed illustrati.* Palermo.

DAI   Constantine Porphyrogenitus, *De administrando imperio.* Greek text ed. Gy. Moravcsik, English trans. R. J. H. Jenkins, 1967. Washington DC.

De Caer.   Reiske, J. J. 1829. *Constantini Porphyrogeniti imperatoris de cerimoniis aulae Byzantinae libri duo*, vol. 1 (Corpus scriptorum historiae Byzantinae). Bonn.

De fallacia   Casey, R. P. 1935. "An early homily on the devil ascribed to Athanasius of Alexandria." [St Athanasius, *De fallacia diaboli*] *Journal of Theological Studies* 36: 4–10.

DigE   Jeffreys, E. M. 1998. *Digenis Akritis. The Grottaferrata and Escorial Versions* (Cambridge Medieval Classics 7). Cambridge.

Don Quixote   Δον Κισότης της Μαντσίας. In Kechagioglou, G. 2001. *Πεζογραφική Ανθολογία. Αφηγηματικός γραπτός νεοελληνικός λόγος. Βιβλίο πρώτο: Από το τέλος του Βυζαντίου ως τη Γαλλική Επανάσταση.* Thessaloniki.

Erotokr.   Alexiou, S. 1980. *Βιτσέντζος Κορνάρος, Ἐρωτόκριτος.* Athens.

Flor.   *Florios kai Platzia-Flora.* In Kriaras, E. 1959. *Βυζαντινὰ ἱπποτικὰ μυθιστορήματα*, 141–214. Athens.

Fort.   Vincent, A., 1980. *Μάρκου Ἀντώνιου Φόσκολου Φορτουνάτος .* (Ἑταιρία Κρητικῶν Ἱστορικῶν Μελετῶν, Κρητικὸν Θέατρον 2). Herakleion.

Katz.   Politis, L. 1964. *Γεωργίου Χορτάτση Κατζοῦρμπος* (Ἑταιρία Κρητικῶν Ἱστορικῶν Μελετῶν, Κρητικὸν Θέατρον 1). Herakleion.

Kekaum.   Ioannes Cecaumenus, *Strategicon.* In Wassiliewsky B. and V. Jernstedt. 1896. *Cecaumeni Stategicon et incerti scriptoris De officiis regiis libellus.* St Petersburg.

Landos   Kostoula, D. D. 1991. *Αγάπιος Λάνδος. Γεωπονικόν.* Επιμέλεια κειμένου–Εισαγωγή –Σχόλια – Γλωσσάριο. Volos.

Liv. V   Lendari, T. 2006. *Ἀφήγησις Λιβίστρου καὶ Ροδάμνης (Livistros and Rodamne). The Vatican Version. Editio princeps* (Βυζαντινὴ καὶ Νεοελληνικὴ Βιβλιοθήκη 9). Athens.

Mach.   Dawkins, R. M. 1932. *Recital concerning the sweet land of Cyprus entitled "Chronicle". By Leontios Makhairas.* Oxford.

Mal.   Dindorf, L. 1831. *Ioannis Malalae chronographia* (Corpus scriptorum historiae Byzantinae). Bonn.

Miracula   *Miracula Sancti Artemii.* In Papadopoulos-Kerameus, A. 1909. *Varia graeca sacra* (Subsidia Byzantina lucis ope iterata 6). St Petersburg.

Mosch.   Ioannes Moschos. *Pratum Spirituale. Patrologia Graeca*, vol. 87.3.

Ptoch.   Eideneier, H. 1991. *Ptochoprodromos. Einführung, kritische Ausgabe, deutsche Übersetzung, Glossar* (Neograeca Medii Aevi 5). Cologne.

Sphrantz.   Maisano, R. 1990. *Giorgio Sfranze, Cronaca* (*CFHB* 29). Rome.

Spanos	Eideneier, H. 1977. *SPANOS. Eine byzantinische Satire in der Form einer Parodie.* Berlin and New York.
Symfor.	Bouboulidis, Ph. K. 1955. Ἡ συμφορὰ τῆς Κρήτης τοῦ Μανόλη Σκλάβου. Κρητικὸ στιχούργημα τοῦ ΙΣΤ΄ αἰῶνος. Athens.
Thys.Avr.	Bakker, W., and A. F. van Gemert. 1996. *Η Θυσία του Αβραάμ. Κριτική ἔκδοση.* Herakleion.
Theoph.	de Boor, C. 1883–5. *Theophanis Chronographia.* Leipzig.
V. Alex. L	van Thiel, H. 1983. *Vita Alexandri Magni. Recensionem Graecam codicis L edidit Helmut van Thiel.* Darmstadt.
V. Euth.	Karlin-Hayter, P. 1970. *Vita Euthymii patriarchae Constantinopolitani* (Bibliothèque de Byzantion 3). Brussels.
V. Sym.Sal.	Festugière, J. A., ed. and trans. 1974. *Vie de Syméon le Fou et Vie de Jean de Chypre* (Bibliothèque archéologique et historique 95). Paris.
Velisar. χ	Bakker W., and A. F. van Gemert 1988. Ἱστορία τοῦ Βελισαρίου. (Βυζαντινὴ καὶ Νεοελληνικὴ Βιβλιοθήκη 6). Athens.
Vestarchis	Μιχαήλ Βεστάρχης, Ὁ Πρόλογος τῆς Ὑπεραγίας Θεοτόκου. In M. Manoussakas and W. Puchner. 2000. Ἀνέκδοτα στιχουργήματα τοῦ θρησκευτικοῦ θεάτρου τοῦ ΙΖ΄ αἰώνα. Ἔργα τῶν ὀρθόδοξων Χίων κληρικῶν Μιχ. Βεστάρχη, Γρηγ. Κονταράτου, Γαβρ. Προσοψᾶ. Ἔκδοση κριτικὴ μὲ εἰσαγωγή, σχόλια καὶ εὑρετήρια. Athens.

CHAPTER THIRTY-SEVEN

Modern Greek

Peter Mackridge

Synchronic Variation in Greek since the Eighteenth Century

Regional spoken varieties

Up to the present day, Greek has continued to be spoken not only in Greece and Cyprus, but in parts of Turkey and Italy. During the compulsory exchange of minorities between Greece and Turkey under the Treaty of Lausanne (1923), religion rather than language was the factor deciding whether one was to be deported or not. For this reason, linguistic minorities remained in both countries.

In Turkey there are still descendants of Greek-speaking Muslims who were expelled from Greece, most of these originating from the island of Crete. In addition, there are communities of Greek-speakers in Pontus in northeast Turkey, who stayed behind when their Greek-speaking Christian neighbors were expelled. At the other geographical extreme, there are Greek-speaking Catholics in the regions of Calabria and Terra d'Otranto in southern Italy. While they have been deeply influenced by Turkish and Italian respectively, the Pontic and Italic dialects of Greek today can provide valuable information about the history of the Greek language in medieval and modern times. The fact that the infinitive can be used after certain types of verb in some of these dialects, for instance, indicates that the infinitive was still a living category in medieval spoken Greek (see ch. 36).

The modern Greek dialects of the Aegean and Balkan regions can be divided along a north–south axis and along an east–west one. The dialects of southern Greece were spoken in the Peloponnese and the Ionian Islands, while those of northern Greece were spoken on the mainland north of the Gulf of Corinth and on some northern islands in the Aegean. Dialects of the Cretan-Cycladic group were spoken in islands of the central and southern Aegean, while those of the southeastern group were spoken in the islands of the southeast Aegean and in Cyprus. Cyprus is the only region where a Greek regional dialect is still spoken today in everyday life by the majority of the population, including highly educated people.

The phonology and morphology of the dialects of the southern mainland have developed less far from the Hellenistic *Koine* (see ch. 16) than the rest. The phonology of the northern dialects is characterized by changes in the pronunciation of unstressed vowels: high vowels are deleted, while low vowels are raised (on high and low vowels, see also ch. 7). Thus το πουλί /topulí/ "the bird" becomes [tuplí]. Conversely, the Cretan-Cycladic and southeastern dialects are characterized by changes in consonants. In Cyprus, for instance, /k/ before a front vowel becomes [č], while voiced fricatives between vowels are deleted: thus καί /ke/ "and" becomes [če], while the underlying form *κοπελλούδιον "lad" /kopellúðion/ becomes [kopellúin]. The last example also shows that Cypriot preserves the ancient final /n/ and (unlike all the Greek dialects outside the southeastern group) pronounces double (long) consonants.

While the Greek speech of the coastal regions of western Asia Minor tended to be similar to that of the neighboring islands, the two other chief dialects of Asia Minor, namely Cappadocian and Pontic, presented some similarities with the southeastern dialects, but some of their characteristics distinguished them markedly from the rest of the Greek dialects. The dialects of Cappadocia and the southeastern group differ from mainland dialects in the position of the weak object pronoun in relation to the verb: in independent, positive declarative clauses containing verbs in the present and the past, the object pronoun follows the verb, while in other contexts it precedes: thus, in Cyprus, [mílisatu] "I spoke to him" but [ennatumilíso] "I'll speak to him." In Pontic the weak object pronoun follows the verb in all contexts. In mainland and southern Italian dialects the weak pronoun always precedes a verb in the indicative or subjunctive: thus the standard equivalent of the first of these examples is [tumílisa].

The only Modern Greek dialect that is not descended from the Hellenistic *Koine* is Tsakonian, spoken in a small area of the southeastern Peloponnese. Tsakonian presents some features of ancient Doric and is in general markedly distinct from the other dialects of Modern Greek.

Competing written varieties

Every successive stage of the Greek language has coexisted with earlier stages, since most Greek writers in the recent and distant past have believed that they would render their texts more refined and intellectually more elevated if they used some features of Ancient Greek vocabulary and grammar in their own discourse.

In the nineteenth century a continuum of varieties of written Greek was used at any one time, extending from ancient Attic to versions of the modern colloquial language. In 1800 texts could broadly be distinguished into three categories, according to whether they were written in Ancient Greek, the modern vernacular, or a hybrid variety consisting of features from the ancient and the modern language. Some writers used the whole gamut of varieties, varying their language according to their topic, their intended audience, and generally the effect they wished their writing to have on the reader.

Ancient Greek was written particularly by schoolteachers, who tended to teach exclusively the ancient language, whether in its classical or its ecclesiastical manifestations. Such writers believed that the best way to raise the educational level of their compatriots was to place them in contact with the great works of classical literature. In addition, it was considered that all Greek Orthodox Christians should ideally be able to understand the New Testament and the liturgical texts in the original.

By 1900 the use of Ancient Greek had completely died out except as a scholarly exercise, while there were two competing written varieties, known by then as demotic and *katharevousa* (καθαρεύουσα, literally "[language] aspiring to be pure"). By this time most poetry and much prose fiction was being written in demotic, which was based on the common features of the spoken dialects. *Katharevousa* was a mixture of ancient and modern features. It used much of the vocabulary and morphological system of Ancient Greek, though it employed certain forms that were intermediate between Classical Greek and the modern spoken language, such as εἴμεθα "we are" (Class. Gk ἐσμέν, common Mod. Gk εἴμαστε) and ἦτον "he/she/it was" (Class. Greek ἦν, common Mod. Gk ἦταν). In syntax *katharevousa* tended to be closer to Modern than to Ancient Greek, employing the particle νὰ + finite verb rather than the infinitive and the negative particle δὲν rather than the ancient οὐ, but it used most of the ancient participles where the spoken language used subordinate clauses.

The language controversy

The language controversy has been one of the most contentious issues in the history of modern Greece. Especially from the 1880s until its resolution in 1976, it split intellectuals into two opposing camps, each supporting one of the rival varieties of written Greek. In 1901 and 1903 it gave rise to riots in Athens against the translation of the Bible and Greek Classical texts into Modern Greek, during which a number of demonstrators were killed by security forces.

A plurality of varieties of Greek was available to writers in the late eighteenth century. Until then, there was no language controversy, and authors felt free to use whichever variety suited them. From the 1760s onwards, however, as Enlightenment ideas began to penetrate into Greek high culture and Greek educators and others sought to transfer the new ideas into their own language, they began to disagree openly as to which was the most appropriate variety of Greek for use in educational and scholarly publications. The language controversy began as a dispute between advocates of the continuing use of Ancient Greek for scholarly writing, and those who argued that Modern Greek should be used in both teaching and writing. Very soon, however, disagreement began to manifest itself between vernacularists, who supported the written use of the spoken language, and compromisers, who advocated a hybrid version of Modern Greek containing a large number of ancient lexical and grammatical features.

The controversy came to a head between 1808 and 1821, when Greek intellectuals came to realize that political autonomy from the Ottoman Empire might be feasible. Under these circumstances, there was a prospect that the choice of language variety would no longer be confined to education and scholarship, but would predetermine the official language of the independent Greek state. Most of those who participated in the controversy were driven, at least partly, by their differing conceptions of the relationship between the modern Greeks and their ancient forebears. Archaists argued that, in order to become more like the ancients, the moderns should write in the ancient language; indeed, some of them even proposed that the Greeks should gradually abandon their current spoken language and learn to speak Ancient Greek. By contrast, the vernacularists urged that education should be available to all and that the most effective way for pupils to study was through the medium of their mother tongue; besides, they argued, the best way for the modern Greeks to show themselves worthy of their ancient forebears was to imitate them by writing in the spoken language of the time. The compromisers used similar arguments to the vernacularists, except that they asserted that the spoken tongue was vulgar and corrupt, and that the modern written language should be a lexically and grammatically elevated version of the spoken. During the last dozen years before the outbreak of the revolution in 1821, Greek intellectuals expended considerable effort on publishing often vituperative attacks on each other's linguistic theory and practice.

The controversy died down in 1821 and continued to lie comparatively dormant for more than 60 years, during which a hybrid language was used for most written purposes, with the exception of some poetry and a very small amount of literary prose; almost all of the literary prose in demotic in this period was produced by writers from the Ionian Islands. In 1888 the linguist Psycharis (1854–1929), living in Paris, published the manifesto of the demoticist movement, Τὸ ταξίδι μου (*My Journey*). The demoticists advocated the use of demotic for all written purposes, arguing that the language and culture of the traditional rural population represented the genuine continuation of ancient Greek civilization. By 1900 most literary writers were writing their work in demotic, while the written use of demotic gradually spread into other areas of public life. A delayed reaction to the riots of 1901 and 1903 was the decision to include, for the first time, a clause in the 1911 Constitution of the Greek state specifying the official language. Even though the formulation was not explicit, it is clear that it referred to *katharevousa*. The clause went on to state that any intervention aimed at corrupting the official language was forbidden.

Nevertheless, the teaching of demotic was introduced into primary schools in 1917 and, despite the increase and decrease of this teaching over the following half-century according to the views of the political party that happened to be in power, demotic retained its foothold in education. As the twentieth century proceeded, however, the language controversy became increasingly more politicized. After the Russian Revolution it became common for reactionary politicians and intellectuals to allege that demoticism was connected with Communism. This drove non-Communist demoticists to publicly dissociate the two movements. During this period each of the two sides in the controversy claimed to be defending the language variety that would guarantee the unity of the Greek nation in the face of external and internal threats to its existence.

The military junta that ruled Greece from 1967 to 1974 promoted *katharevousa* so vigorously, and used the language so clumsily, that when it fell, the use of *katharevousa* was discontinued almost overnight. The current constitution, passed in 1975, makes no mention of an official language. In 1976 a law was passed specifying that "Modern Greek" (defined as demotic) was to be the language of education at all levels, and in the following year demotic was officially recognized as the language of government and the civil service. Since that time the old language controversy has ceased to exist. However, the education law of 1976 removed the obligatory teaching of Ancient Greek from the *gymnasio* (the compulsory first three years of secondary school). Soon many Greeks began to believe that the standard of Greek used by younger people and in the media was deteriorating, and that this was because Ancient Greek was no longer a compulsory subject. Since then, the compulsory study of Ancient Greek has gradually been re-introduced into the *gymnasio*. This measure has usually been justified on the grounds that it will enable Greeks to use their own language more correctly and more effectively.

Written versions of the vernacular

The few writers around 1800 who used a variety of Greek close to colloquial speech aimed at removing education from the hands of the Church and at following the example of western European nations in using the vernacular to disseminate knowledge. The first of the vernacularists was Dimitrios Katartzis (*c.* 1730–1807), a Constantinopolitan living in Bucharest, where he wrote a grammar of "Romaic" (Modern Greek) and a number of essays in a remarkably faithful transcription of the phonology and morphology of the spoken language. His vocabulary consisted of a mixture of vernacular and ancient items, but the inflected words among the latter were made to conform to the grammatical rules of the modern language. This was a radical departure from tradition, since earlier – and later – adherents of the vernacular tended to use a certain proportion of ancient morphological features in their writing. However, since his writings were not published during his lifetime, they had little influence outside his circle of followers.

In 1805 Athanasios Christopoulos (1772–1847), also living in Bucharest, published a *Grammar of Aeolodoric, or the Spoken Language of the Present-Day Hellenes*. In this hurriedly written book, Christopoulos attempted to prove that the colloquial spoken language was not derived from Attic but from a combination of the ancient Aeolic and Doric dialects. The evidence he adduced in support of his argument consisted of superficial resemblances between ancient and modern phonological and morphological features rather than any systematic relation. His purpose was to show that the spoken language was as ancient as Attic, and therefore that it should be no less prestigious. Christopoulos' Aeolodoric theory of the origins of spoken Modern Greek was highly influential in Greece, and it was frequently reiterated until it was finally demolished in 1881 by the linguist G. N. Hatzidakis (1848–1941), who demonstrated that spoken Greek was derived from the Hellenistic *Koine*.

In the 1810s two writers living in Ioannina in northern Greece, Athanasios Psalidas (1767–1829) and Giannis Vilaras (1771–1823), developed a phonetic version of Greek script, in which they wrote a variety of Greek very close to colloquial speech in an attempt to make literacy more readily attainable. Vilaras published a little book in Corfu in 1814, which contained samples of this language and script in both prose and verse, including translations of passages from Thucydides and Plato. The title of the book, Η ϱομεηϰη γλοσα (*The Romaic Language*), provides a sample of Psalidas' and Vilaras' phonetic transcription; in the normal orthography of the time it would have been written Ἡ ῥωμαïϰη γλῶσσα.

Once the Greek Revolution broke out in 1821, the neoclassical ethos of the new nation made the use of "vulgar" language decidedly unfashionable. Nevertheless, some writers, especially in the Ionian Islands, persisted in writing in the vernacular. One of these was Dionysios Solomos (1798–1857), whose *Hymn to Liberty*, written in 1823, eventually became the Greek National Anthem in 1865.

In the 1880s Psycharis began his campaign to persuade the Greeks to abandon *katharevousa* and use demotic for all written purposes. However, the variety of the vernacular that he chose to write in was not acceptable to many other Greek writers, who considered it to be the product of linguistic science rather than a version of the Greek that was actually spoken. Younger linguists and writers after 1900, notably Manolis Triantaphyllidis (1883–1959), took a more pragmatic view, developing a written version of demotic that accepted many of the learned phonological and morphological features that had become incorporated into the speech of educated Greeks.

Hybrid varieties

Most Greek writers until the early twentieth century used hybrid varieties, in which the proportion of ancient and modern features varied according to the intentions and the educational level of the author. The most renowned author who promoted such a variety was Adamantios Korais (1748–1833), a self-taught classical philologist from Smyrna who lived in Paris from 1788 onwards. From 1804 until his death he made regular public pronouncements about Greek language and education. Like other enlightened Greek educationalists before him, he argued that Greek children should be taught Ancient Greek, but that they should learn it through their mother tongue rather than using the ancient language as the medium of instruction. Nevertheless, he believed that the spoken language had been barbarized as a result of the Greeks' lack of proper education since the end of antiquity and that consequently it needed to be "corrected" according to the rules of Ancient Greek morphology. In practice this meant the rules of Hellenistic *Koine* rather than Classical Attic.

Korais claimed to ignore the written tradition of hybrid Modern Greek and to start from first principles by correcting the spoken language. However, the variety that he used in his writing is remarkably similar to those used by other authors of his time, although he introduced some trademark forms which belong neither to Modern nor to Ancient Greek and which provoked exaggerated expressions of righteous indignation from those who opposed his methods. Yet, while still a hybrid, the variety he proposed tended to be more consistent than those of his predecessors and contemporaries, and he preferred to use modern syntax where others followed ancient usage; for example, for the indirect object he used either εἰς + acc. or the accusative of the object pronoun instead of the dative case, and he construed ἀπό "from" with the accusative (as in the spoken language) rather than the genitive. Whereas some authors wrote "it seems to me" as μοὶ φαίνεται (using the dative), Korais wrote μὲ φαίνεται (with the accusative), while the form that has prevailed in Standard Modern Greek is μοῦ φαίνεται (using the genitive), which both Korais and the archaists considered to be an error.

Despite Korais' judicious combination of ancient and modern features, he encouraged his readers to introduce progressively more archaisms into their writing. For instance, he believed that the lack of the infinitive was "the most frightful vulgarity of our language," and for this reason he formed the future of γράφω "I write" as θέλω γράψειν "I will write" and θέλει γραφθῆν "it will be written" (where the second word in each case is derived from the ancient infinitive forms γράψειν and γραφθῆναι), instead of the forms normally written in his day, namely θέλω γράψη and θέλει γραφθῆ (using the ancient subjunctive). He believed that readers would become so accustomed to seeing infinitive forms used in this way that they would eventually be encouraged to use them in the contexts in which they were used in Ancient Greek.

Korais' encouragement to others to introduce more ancient features gradually into the modern language licensed later generations of Greek writers to attempt to bring their written language progressively closer to Ancient Greek. Some authors proclaimed that Ancient and Modern Greek were the same language, and that they were proud of the fact that they had been able to write whole books without a single occurrence of the particles νά, θά, and δέν – the three items that no extended text in Modern Greek can do without. Nevertheless, such extreme archaists tended to stop short of using the ancient negative particle οὐ, which meant that they were obliged to avoid writing negative indicative sentences. This archaizing process reached a peak in the late nineteenth century, when even moderate purists – let alone demoticists – came to believe that it had gone too far.

Nevertheless, *katharevousa*, as the hybrid written language became known from the 1850s onward, continued to be the medium of official written communication until 1976, when it was replaced by demotic as the official language of the Greek state.

The Origins of Standard Modern Greek

Since 1976 the official language of the republics of Greece and Cyprus has been Νεοελληνική (Δημοτική) "Modern Greek (Demotic)," which is sometimes called Κοινὴ Νεοελληνική "Common Modern Greek" but which I prefer to call Standard Modern Greek (SMGk).

In contrast to the purists of the nineteenth century, who argued that the spoken language consisted exclusively of regional dialects, the demoticists consistently argued that there was a single common spoken language. They claimed that this common demotic had been developed by the Greek people through their folk songs. According to this theory, first articulated by Fauriel (1824), as a song was transmitted from one area to another, it shed the original regional features of its language and gradually came to be formulated in a supra-regional variety. This theory has been reiterated by those who argue that the anonymous Greek folk, like another Homer, have developed a poetic language that can and should form the basis of the standard written language of the Greek nation. This view was expressed by Triantaphyllidis in the prologue to his standard grammar of demotic (1941).

In fact, little is known about precisely how, when, and where common demotic developed, and out of what components. According to Pantelidis (2007), who has undertaken a critical scrutiny of these questions, major factors in the development of common demotic included the avoidance of features that were felt to be regional and the restoration of many modern forms to their ancient etymological origin. As for the origin of the language spoken in Athens and other cities today, the consensus has been that it resulted from the influx of people into the capital of the new state. These were chiefly from the Peloponnese, which was the largest area of Greece that was liberated in the 1821 revolution. They were joined by a number of influential Greeks from Constantinople and the Ionian Islands, whose dialects, especially on the level of phonology, were similar to those of the Peloponnese. However, Pantelidis (2001) has challenged this received idea, arguing that many morphological features of Athenian Greek are not to be found in the Peloponnesian dialects. This issue has yet to be resolved. Suffice it to say that Constantinople, which still had more Greek inhabitants than Athens as late as 1900, must have been a melting-pot for the regional speech of people who settled there from all over the Greek-speaking world.

To the extent that SMGk is based on common demotic, then, it is a mixture of features from various regions. But it is also a mixture of features from the popular and the learned traditions.

Interplay of popular and learned features

The result of the coexistence of different varieties of Greek in everyday life is that there has been a certain convergence between what are conveniently called the popular and the learned traditions. The popular tradition can be defined as the demotic language used by the rural populations in colloquial speech and in their folk songs, while the learned tradition covers the hybrid varieties known as *katharevousa*. The standardization of demotic as a written language usable in all forms of writing is due in large part to the efforts of Triantaphyllidis. This standardizing process took place between the first decade of the twentieth century and 1941, when Triantaphyllidis' *Modern Greek Grammar (of Demotic)* was published by a state-run organization. No government agency ever published a grammar of *katharevousa*, even though it was the official language.

Katharevousa contained a set of consonant clusters that were absent from the spoken dialects. These included [kt] and [xθ], which had become [xt] in all the dialects; [pt] and [fθ] had become [ft], while the dialectal equivalents of [mv] and [nð] were [mb] and [nd]. Psycharis argued correctly that these *katharevousa* clusters were the result of using the written forms of Ancient Greek words but pronouncing each letter as it is pronounced in Modern Greek. Thus ἄνδρα "man" (acc. sg.), thus spelled in Ancient Greek, was pronounced [ánðra] in *katharevousa*, whereas the equivalent form in the spoken dialects was pronounced [ándra], just as it was in Ancient Greek. Since he believed that the sound system is the basis of every language, Psycharis asserted that demotic was essentially closer to Ancient Greek than *katharevousa* was; *katharevousa*, he argued, was based only on the visual appearance of Ancient Greek rather than on its sound and for this reason contained sequences of sounds such as [nð] that had never been uttered naturally by Greek vocal organs. He then set about altering learned words that were normally used in educated speech to make them conform to the sound system of the spoken dialects. Thus he rejected the form διεύθυνσις [ðiéfθinsis] "direction, address" on the grounds that it contained the learned clusters [fθ] and [ns]; he proposed that the word should be written διέφτυση [ðjéftisi]. These artificial demoticizations of learned phonology did not become widely accepted. Psycharis' obsessive refusal to make any concession to lexical and grammatical features that had entered the spoken language from the learned tradition resulted in a variety that many Greeks felt to be almost as distant from their own speech as *katharevousa* was.

The chief innovation made by Triantaphyllidis and his associates in relation to the proposals made by Psycharis was that they recognized that the learned tradition had exerted a substantial influence on the phonology and morphology of the Greek that was spoken in their time.

SMGk includes words that conform to the phonology of the spoken dialects and words that conform to the phonology of *katharevousa*. Thus there are pairs of words such as δέντρο "tree" (with [nd]) and δενδροστοιχία (with [nð]) "avenue of trees," of which the first has come down through the popular tradition and the second is a creation of the modern learned tradition. The fact that SMGk embraces the phonological systems of both the spoken dialects and the learned written tradition means that its phonology is richer than that of either of the two traditions. Thus, for instance, SMGk includes forms such as the popular άχτι [áxti] "grudge, rancor" (from Turkish *ahd* "oath, promise") and the learned άχθος [áxθos] "burden" and ακτή [aktí] "coast," the first of which would have been rejected by *katharevousa* because of the sequence [xt] (let alone its foreign origin), while the second and third would have been rejected by Psycharis' version of demotic on phonological grounds.

As a matter of principle, Triantaphyllidis attempted as far as possible to make every inflected word in the modern language conform to the morphological rules of demotic. All *katharevousa* nouns inflected according to the ancient third declension were adapted, in demotic, to conform to the first declension. Thus, for instance, all learned feminine nouns in /sis/, such as διεύθυνσις (gen. sg. διευθύνσεως), were recast in the form διεύθυνση (gen. sg. διεύθυνσης), by analogy with ancient first declension nouns such as φήμη (gen. sg. φήμης) "fame."

In some cases Triantaphyllidis promoted new forms that shared characteristics of both the learned and the popular traditions. For example, the plural of μαθητής "pupil" was μαθηταί in the nominative and μαθητάς in the accusative in the learned tradition, but μαθητάδες for both cases in the popular colloquial language. Rejecting both of these forms, Triantaphyllidis promoted the intermediate form μαθητές for both cases, by analogy with nouns stressed on the penultimate syllable such as κλέφτης "thief." For ancient and learned third declension feminine abstract nouns in /tis/ such as ολότης (gen. sg. ολότητος) "entirety," the spoken dialects had equivalent forms ολότη and ολότητα; of these, Triantaphyllidis preferred ολότητα (gen. sg. ολότητας), which was formed by analogy with first declension nouns such as θάλασσα (gen. sg. θάλασσας) "sea."

Most speakers had become so habituated to the separation between the popular and the learned traditions that it did not come naturally to them to transfer the morphology and phonology of the former to words originating from the latter; they had to be encouraged to do so by demoticist grammarians. In fact, such compromise forms as μαθητές and ὁλότητας did not come to be used universally in speech until after 1974. Indeed, some demoticized verb forms such as καταναλώνω (ancient and *katharevousa* καταναλίσκω) "consume" and διαβρώνω (created from the aorist form διέβρωσα of ancient and *katharevousa* διαβιβρώσκω) "erode" have become generally accepted even more recently.

In addition, however, Triantaphyllidis promoted certain morphological forms that originated in the learned tradition. Learned feminine nouns in /sis/ are a case in point again. Psycharis and other demoticists of a similar persuasion made them decline like demotic nouns in the nominative and accusative plural (διεύθυνσες or διέφτυσες according to whether their demoticism was moderate or extreme) but were unable to propose a genitive plural form. By contrast, Triantaphyllidis promoted the ancient and learned plural forms of these words (nom./acc. διευθύνσεις, gen. διευθύνσεων), which were in any case the forms that were normally used in speech. Thus the morphological paradigm of such words in SMGk is a hybrid, the singular conforming to the popular pattern and the plural to the learned one. Similarly, whereas Psycharis attempted to demoticize the ancient and learned συγγραφεύς "author" as συγραφιάς, Triantaphyllidis and his colleagues promoted συγγραφέας in the singular (the final /as/ conforming to demotic forms such as πατέρας "father"), but the ancient and learned form συγγραφεῖς in the plural.

Certain classes of words from the learned tradition have been accepted into SMGk together with their ancient inflectional paradigms (except the dative). This is the case with words following the patterns of ἔθνος (gen. sg. ἔθνους) "nation", πρᾶγμα (gen. sg. πράγματος) "thing," and ἀκριβής (gen. sg. ἀκριβοῦς, neut. nom./acc. sg. ἀκριβές) "precise." Some of these classes of word were hardly or not at all used in traditional colloquial speech, while others had problematic paradigms. For instance, the genitive singular of πρᾶγμα (pronounced [práma]) was not commonly used in the dialects, where it was variously formed as πραμάτου or πραματιού. Psycharis attempted to impose one of these, but it was not accepted by educated people.

In sum, in SMGk learned words have been made to conform to the morphology of the popular tradition as long as the relevant paradigms are available; otherwise they are inflected according to ancient morphology. In phonology, however, learned words have not been adapted so as to conform to the phonology of any spoken dialect. The result is that, whereas Psycharis was prepared to reject a large proportion of words of learned origin on phonological and/or morphological grounds, SMGk has been able to import any word from Ancient Greek or *katharevousa* without altering its stem. Thus SMGk potentially includes within it the whole of the Greek vocabulary, irrespective of whether it is of popular or learned origin.

In syntax, too, SMGk has made some compromises between the popular and the learned traditions. In the popular tradition, "until" (in time) and "as far as" (in space) were expressed by ὥς or ἴσαμε + acc., while the equivalent in *katharevousa* was μέχρι + gen. SMGk normally uses μέχρι + acc., which used to be condemned by demoticists as a "bastard construction." In such cases, as with phonology and morphology, SMGk has achieved a synthesis and reconciliation between the two traditions that had previously been viewed as antithetical rather than as simply coexisting.

The origins of the vocabulary and idiom

The vast majority of words in Modern Greek are either identical to words in the ancient language or derivatives of Ancient Greek morphemes. Examples of words whose written form, at least, has not changed since ancient times are γῆ "earth," ἥλιος "sun," οὐρανός "sky, heaven," θάλασσα "sea," βλέπω "I see," ἀκούω "I hear."

Over the centuries Greek has borrowed many words from other languages (chiefly Latin, Italian, and Turkish; see also ch. 36). Many of these are still in common use today, e.g., πόρτα (Latin *porta*) "door," σπίτι (Latin *hospitium*) "house," βέρα (Venetian *vera*) "engagement or wedding ring," πιάτσα (Italian *piazza*) "market, taxi-rank," τζάκι (Turkish *ocak*) "fireplace," τζάμι (Turkish *cam*) "window-pane." Many other loan words have now been replaced by native equivalents.

In the nineteenth and twentieth centuries a large number of French words were borrowed, such as ἀσανσέρ (French *ascenseur*) "elevator" and μοβ (French *mauve*) "mauve." A new characteristic of most of these nouns and adjectives borrowed from French was that – unlike almost every other noun and adjective in Greek – they were indeclinable. The words that have entered Greek in large numbers from English in recent decades are also mostly indeclinable. Many educated Greeks see the presence of these indeclinable words as a threat to the Greek morphological system, and hence to the survival of the language itself.

Widespread bilingualism and multilingualism in the southern Balkan region during the early modern period resulted in the use of a large number of common metaphorical expressions and idioms in all the local languages (Greek, Turkish, Aromanian, Albanian, and Slavonic). In such cases idiomatic usages appear to have been translated literally from one language to another. However, it is practically impossible to identify which is the language in which each of these usages first developed.

Since the late eighteenth century, a large number of idioms has been literally translated from western European languages, notably Italian, French, German, and, in more recent times, English. Unlike the Balkan idioms mentioned above, these more recent semantic borrowings have been introduced through the written language and have therefore tended to be dressed in archaic Greek garb. An interesting example is ἐντάξει "OK," nowadays written as one word, which originated in the early nineteenth century as a literal translation of the German phrase *in Ordnung* into pseudo-Ancient Greek, using the preposition ἐν "in" and the dative case of the noun τάξις "order"; neither ἐν nor the dative case was normally used in any of the spoken dialects. In addition, the meaning of a large number of words of Ancient Greek origin has been adjusted to the semantics of western European languages.

The task of enriching the modern Greek language, which has been undertaken since the late eighteenth century, has focused particularly on neologisms and discourse markers.

Since the late eighteenth century a wealth of new Greek words have been invented to cover aspects of modern culture and science and are still in use today, e.g., πολιτισμός "civilization," πανεπιστήμιο "university," ισολογισμός "balance sheet," λογοκρισία "censorship," γραφείο "office," στρατοδικείο "court martial," αμερόληπτος "unbiased," νηπιαγωγείο "infant school," ἀντιπολίτευση "opposition party," νομοσχέδιο "draft law," ψυχραιμία "*sang-froid*," and the considerably more recent ὑπολογιστής "computer," διαδίκτυο "internet," ἱστοσελίδα "web page," and ἱστολόγιο "[we]blog." The success with which Greeks have created neologisms out of Ancient Greek morphemes is indicated by the fact that, on his website "Akropolis World News" (http://www.akwn.net), in which he summarizes the latest world news in Ancient Greek, the classicist Juan Coderch uses many neologisms that he has found in Modern Greek dictionaries. Greeks have been fortunate in that many scientific terms invented in modern times by western scholars have been based on Greek roots and could therefore be imported into Greek ready-made. Where necessary, these have been linguistically corrected in the process, e.g., λευχαιμία "leukaemia," ὀξυγόνο "oxygen."

In addition, many ancient words have been revived to denote modern institutions, e.g., Ἄρειος Πάγος "supreme court," βουλή "parliament," γυμνάσιο "high school," δήμαρχος "mayor," δραχμή "drachma (currency)," μουσεῖο "museum," νομός "prefecture (administrative region)," οἰκογένεια "family," περίπολος "patrol," πρύτανις "vice-chancellor," στάδιο "stadium," συνέδριο "conference," and φροντιστήριο "private tutorial school."

The other area in which Modern Greek has been greatly enriched by the learned tradition is discourse markers, and in particular logical connectives. These include ἐπειδή "since," διότι "because," ἀφοῦ "since (cause and time)," ὅμως "however," ἄρα "therefore," ἐφόσον "provided that," ἀπεναντίας "on the contrary," ἐξίσου "equally," and ἐπίσης "also."

In addition, the period since the eighteenth century has seen a massive extension of the uses of the genitive case. In most of the spoken dialects, the use of the genitive had been confined to expressions of possession, e.g., τοῦ Γιάννη ἡ ἀδερφή "John's sister." This meant that nouns that did not denote animate referents were hardly used in the genitive. Many of the new uses of the genitive that entered SMGk through the learned tradition were based on uses of French *de* and Italian *di*. These included the so-called subjective and objective genitive, e.g., ἡ ἀπόρριψη τῆς αἴτησής μου "the rejection of my application." In addition, the genitive is used to express a wide range of other abstract relationships, such as ξενοδοχεῖο πολυτελείας "de luxe hotel" and σύστημα ποιοτικοῦ ἐλέγχου "quality control system" (the use of the adjective ποιοτικός here is based on the attributive use of the English noun *quality*).

Finally, many ancient phrases are used in SMGk, taken from either classical or ecclesiastical texts. These are often equivalent to Latin phrases used in English. Examples include ἐκ τῶν ὧν οὐκ ἄνευ "sine qua non" and ἐκ τῶν ὑστέρων "a posteriori, after the event," from Classical Greek, and ἀποδιοπομπαῖος τράγος "scapegoat" from the Bible.

Description of Standard Modern Greek

What follows is no more than a sketchy outline. Greek is written according to the monotonic system throughout this section, except in the subsection on "Orthography."

Table 37.1　The consonant system of Modern Greek

	Bilabial	Labio-dental	Dental	Alveolar	Velar
Plosive	p	t			k
Fricative		f v	θ ð	s z	x γ
Nasal	m		n		
Lateral			l		
Flapped				r	

Phonology

The sound system of SMGk consists of the following distinct segments:

five vowels: /i/ /e/ /a/ /o/ /u/
fifteen consonants: /p/ /t/ /k/ /f/ /θ/ /x/ /v/ /ð/ /γ/ /s/ /z/ /l/ /r/ /m/ /n/

The relative position of articulation of the vowels may be represented as:

/i/　　　/u/

/e/　/o/

/a/

(See also the vowel triangle in ch. 16, p. 232, and table 7.7, p. 97)

The chief features of the distinct consonant segments are as set out in table 37.1 (see also the section on consonants in ch. 7)

There is no space here for a detailed coverage of allophones. Suffice it to say that velars become palatal before the front vowels /e/ and /i/, while /n/ becomes velar [ŋ] before the velar /k/. Plosives are voiced after nasals: thus /mp/ becomes [mb], /nt/ becomes [nd] and /nk/ becomes [ŋg].

Demotic did not allow certain sequences of consonants that are found in *katharevousa*. In particular, demotic operated manner dissimilation on sequences of two consonants of the same manner. For instance, the aorist of παύω "I stop" was έπαυσα [épafsa] in *katharevousa* but έπαψα [épapsa] in demotic. Features of *katharevousa* phonology are currently used side by side with demotic Features in SMGk, so that, for instance, the aorist of δουλεύω "I work," which is of popular origin, is δούλεψα [ðúlepsa], while the aorist of δημοσιεύω "I publish," which is of learned origin, is δημοσίευσα [ðimosíefsa].

Orthography

There is no one-to-one relationship between sounds and letters in SMGk. However, even though there are alternative ways of writing the same sound, native speakers normally have no difficulty in pronouncing an unknown word when they see it written. The sounds listed in the "Phonology" subsection are represented graphically as follows:

i	η, ι, υ, ει, οι, υι
e	ε, αι
a	α
o	ο, ω
u	ου
p	π
t	τ
k	κ
f	φ
θ	ϑ
x	χ
v	β
ð	δ
γ	γ
s	σ
z	σ, ζ
l	λ
r	ϱ
m	μ
n	ν

In addition, αυ represents [av] or [af] and ευ represents [ev] or [ef], according to whether it is followed by a voiced or voiceless sound. Μπ, ντ, γκ may represent [b], [d] and [g] respectively, while γγ normally represents [ŋg].

Until the 1830s Greek orthography did not normally distinguish between the sounds [ts] and [dz], both being represented by τζ. The influential dictionary by S. Vyzantios (1835) explicitly distinguished between these sounds, representing [ts] by τσ and [dz] by τζ, and this distinction was soon universally adopted.

Until the twentieth century, the orthography of Modern Greek words attempted to display their supposed etymology or at least to make them look as much like Ancient Greek forms as possible. Today Greek orthography is still broadly historical, but certain simplifications have taken place. However, there is still disagreement about the spelling of a considerable number of individual words.

One of the twentieth-century innovations was the abandonment of the old (pseudo-)etymological principle in favor of an analogical principle in inflectional morphemes. Before 1900 the nominative plural of ἡ κόρη "the daughter" was normally written ἡ κόραις or ἡ κόραις. The –αις ending was used because it was believed (without any evidence) that this form originated in the Ancient Greek dative plural, which was thus spelled. Even those who did not subscribe to this belief wrote κόραις because this was a form found in Ancient Greek. Those who used the first of the alternative spellings of the plural article ἡ implied that it was the singular form transferred to the plural. Those who wrote ᾑ followed the same reasoning, but added the iota subscript as a reminder of the ι of the ancient feminine plural article αἱ. Since 1900 it has become universally accepted that the medieval and modern feminine plural article developed by analogy with the masculine plural form οἱ. It has also been accepted that the /es/ ending of first declension feminine plural nouns resulted from the merging of the first and third declensions, in which the third declension plural -ες ending had been transferred to the first declension (see ch. 36). Thus the plural of ἡ κόρη is now spelled οἱ κόρες.

Similarly, until 1900 feminine abstract nouns in /si/ in demotic were normally spelled with -ι (nom. sg. κυβέρνησι, gen. sg. κυβέρνησις "government") in order to show their etymology (the nominative form in Ancient Greek and *katharevousa* being κυβέρνησις). Since 1900, however, it has gradually become usual to write the /i/ as η (nom. κυβέρνηση, gen. κυβέρνησης) on the grounds that these nouns decline according to the pattern of first declension nouns. These spellings have now become almost universally accepted. In addition, an orthographic distinction is no longer made between the ancient indicative and subjunctive endings of verbs, which in any case are pronounced alike; thus "He wants to leave," which used to be written Θέλει νὰ φύγῃ, came to be written Θέλει νὰ φύγει.

Most of the orthographic reforms that took place in the twentieth century have focused on the use of diacritics. Until 1982 the polytonic system was almost universally employed. This used the diacritics that were introduced in Classical, Hellenistic, and Byzantine times, namely the two breathings, the three accents, and the iota subscript. In Modern Greek none of these diacritics serves a synchronic purpose except the accent, which indicates the stressed syllable; yet only one kind of accent is needed for this function. Because the diacritics served little synchronic purpose, schoolchildren used to spend an inordinate amount of time attempting (and usually failing) to master the system. For this reason, since the early twentieth century, there had been calls for the polytonic system to be replaced by the monotonic, in which the acute accent is written on the stressed vowel in words of more than one syllable.

In the meantime, some simplifications were made to the polytonic system. One of the difficulties of the polytonic system for modern Greeks is that it is geared to a language which distinguished between long and short vowels, yet vowel length is not a distinctive feature of Modern Greek. One of the simplifications made to the polytonic system was a rule that in words stressed on the penultimate syllable where the last vowel of the word was not obviously short (i.e., it was not either ε or o), the accent could be acute rather than circumflex; thus, γλῶσσα "language" could be spelled γλώσσα, while the plural continued to be γλῶσσες.

In 1982 a presidential decree ruled that the monotonic system would be taught and used in all schools. This continues to be the case today, despite the protests of many intellectuals who see words as incomplete when they are not wearing the traditional diacritics. Most publications are printed in the monotonic system, but a considerable number of books and journals still use the polytonic.

According to the monotonic system, the sentence Ὁ Παῦλος ἔφαγε μῆλα καὶ ἀχλάδια "Paul ate apples and pears" becomes Ο Παύλος έφαγε μήλα και αχλάδια.

Inflectional morphology

The Modern Greek system of inflectional morphology is remarkably similar to that of the ancient language. Modern Greek retains all three genders and most of the characteristics of the ancient systems of noun and verb inflection. The dative is the only case that was lost from all the spoken dialects, and in SMGk it is only used in set phrases. There is no dual and no optative, while the ancient indicative and subjunctive have merged. The future and the perfect are represented by analytical constructions.

An important characteristic of SMGk morphology is the coexistence of learned and popular stems, which are sometimes inflected in slightly different ways. In particular, certain verbs formed with ancient prepositional prefixes behave differently from the base verb or from other such verbs. For example, δίνω "I give" originates from the popular tradition, whereas μεταδίδω "transmit," with a slightly different stem, is a learned derivative of the same ancient verb, δίδωμι. Similar phenomena are φέρνω "I bring" but μεταφέρω "I transport," and καταλαβαίνω "I understand" (from the popular tradition) but καταλαμβάνω "I capture" (from the learned).

Nouns, adjectives, pronouns, and numerals

The inflection system of nouns can be conveniently divided into first and second declensions, though there are some patterns that do not conform to these general rules. Few exceptions will be covered here.

First declension. The ancient third declension disappeared from the spoken dialects of Modern Greek, and those third declension nouns that remained in the language are inflected according to first declension patterns. Thus:

Masculines

nom. sg.	πατέρας "father"
voc./acc./gen. sg.	πατέρα
nom./voc./acc. pl.	πατέρες
gen. pl.	πατέρων

Feminines

nom./voc./acc. sg.	μητέρα "mother"
gen. sg.	μητέρας
nom./voc./acc. pl.	μητέρες
gen. pl.	μητέρων

Nouns that belonged to the ancient first declension shift the stress to the final syllable in the gen. pl.: κλέφτης "thief," gen. pl. κλεφτών; θάλασσα "sea," gen. pl. θαλασσών. This shift of stress is a borrowing from the learned tradition, since the genitive plural was not commonly used in the spoken dialects, and, even where it was used, the stress tended not to shift in the gen. pl.; thus one finds forms such as κλέφτων in older vernacular texts.

Some first declension nouns insert an additional syllable in the plural. Thus the masculines παπάς "priest" and καφές "coffee" form the pl. παπάδες, παπάδων, καφέδες καφέδων, while the feminines μαμά "mummy" and γιαγιά "grandmother" have plural forms μαμάδες μαμάδων, γιαγιάδες γιαγιάδων.

Second declension. This is broadly similar to ancient patterns:

Masculines

nom. sg.	άνθρωπος "person, human being"
voc. sg.	άνθρωπε
acc. sg.	άνθρωπο
gen. sg.	ανθρώπου
nom./voc. pl.	άνθρωποι
acc. pl.	ανθρώπους
gen. pl.	ανθρώπων

Neuters

nom./acc. sg.	δωμάτιο "room"
gen. sg.	δωματίου
nom./acc. pl.	δωμάτια
gen. pl.	δωματίων

In words stressed on the antepenultimate syllable, oblique cases normally follow the ancient pattern with regard to the position of the accent. This applies to basic words inherited through the popular tradition from Ancient Greek, such as θάνατος "death" and πόλεμος "war." However, some popular medieval and modern formations do not change the position of the stress, e.g., χωματόδρομος "dirt road," which preserves the stress on the antepenultimate throughout the paradigm. The singular of second declension masculines is the only part of the morphological system in which the vocative has a distinct form.

Most adjectives follow the second declension paradigms in the masculine and neuter, but always retaining the position of the stress in oblique cases, e.g., όμορφος "beautiful," gen. sg. όμορφου. Feminines are normally formed with –η and follow first declension patterns, e.g., όμορφη, gen. sg. όμορφης. But if the stem-final vowel is /i/ or is stressed, the feminine endings have –α: ωραίος "lovely," fem. ωραία.

The chief morphological departure from Ancient Greek is the paradigm of neuter nouns in –ι, originally diminutives:

nom./voc./acc. sg.	χέρι "hand, arm"
gen. sg.	χεριού
nom./voc./acc. pl.	χέρια
gen. pl.	χεριών
nom./voc./acc. sg.	παιδί "child"
gen. sg.	παιδιού
nom./voc./acc. pl.	παιδιά
gen. pl.	παιδιών

Personal pronouns are divided into strong (emphatic) and weak. The strong forms are set out in table 37.2.

Table 37.2   Strong forms of personal pronouns in Modern Greek

	Singular	*Plural*
1st nom.	εγώ "I"	εμείς "we"
1st acc./gen.	εμένα	εμάς
2nd nom.	εσύ "you"	εσείς
2nd acc./gen.	εσένα	εσάς

For the third person, αυτός (masc.) αυτή (fem.) αυτό (neut.) "he/she/it" (also "this") is used. The weak forms are set out in table 37.3.

Table 37.3   Weak forms of personal pronouns in Modern Greek

	Singular	*Plural*
1st acc.	με	μας
1st gen.	μου	μας
2nd acc.	σε	σας
2nd gen.	σου	σας
3rd acc.	τον/τη[ν]/το	τους/τις/τα
3rd gen.	του/της/του	τους (all genders)

The third-person pronouns distinguish between masculine, feminine, and neuter. There is no nominative form of the weak pronoun, except in the third person; it is used in very circumscribed contexts.

The numerals ένας "one" (also used as the indefinite article), τρεις "three," and τέσσερις "four" are inflected. The paradigm of ένας is set out in table 37.4.

Table 37.4   The paradigm of ένας (The –ί- in μία is accented (and stressed in speech) when used emphatically.)

	Masculine	*Feminine*	*Neuter*
nom.	ένας	μια/μία	ένα
acc.	ένα(ν)	μια(ν)/μία(ν)	ένα
gen.	ενός	μιας	ενός

Verbs

Apart from person, number, and voice, the chief forms of the Modern Greek verb are distinguished by tense and aspect. As regards tense, verb forms are either past or non-past. In terms of aspect, they are either perfective or imperfective. Perfective forms convey a single action or series of actions, whereas imperfective forms convey an action that is perceived as being performed continuously or repeatedly. Tense and aspect combine to give the basic forms for the active voice (see table 37.5).

Table 37.5   Tense and aspect in Modern Greek in the active voice

		Aspect	
		imperfective	perfective
Tense	non-past	γράφω	γράψω
	past	έγραφα	έγραψα

The forms γράφω "I write, I am writing" and γράψω "I write" are traditionally called the present and the aorist subjunctive respectively, while έγραφα "I used to write, I was writing" and έγραψα "I wrote" are known as the imperfect and the aorist indicative.

The present active inflects according to table 37.6.

Table 37.6   Inflection of the present active

	Singular	*Plural*
1st	γράφω	γράφουμε
2nd	γράφεις	γράφετε
3rd	γράφει	γράφουν(ε)

The third person plural displays an alternation, typical of SMGk, between a more formal (without -ε) and a more colloquial (with -ε) form. The aorist subjunctive active inflects in the same way.

As for the past tenses, the syllabic augment is used only in stressed position. Thus the aorist indicative active of γράφω is as shown in table 37.7. The imperfect active inflects in the same way.

Table 37.7   Aorist indicative active of γράφω

	Singular	*Plural*
1st	έγραψα	γράψαμε
2nd	έγραψες	γράψατε
3rd	έγραψε	έγραψαν/γράψανε

The future is formed by a non-past verb form preceded by the particle θα (for the development, see ch. 36). This means that perfective aspect is distinguished from imperfective in the expression of future as well as past time:

Θα σου γράψω αύριο "I will write to you tomorrow,"

Θα σου γράφω συχνά "I will write to you often."

The perfect tenses are formed by the infinitive (identical to the 3rd sg. of the aor. subj.) preceded by the relevant tense of έχω "I have": thus έχω γράψει "I have written", είχα γράψει "I had written."

The imperative active forms are sg. γράφε, pl. γράφετε (imperfective) and sg. γράψε, pl. γράψτε (perfective). There is also an indeclinable gerund γράφοντας "writing" (i.e., "while writing" or "by writing").

The passive equivalents are set out in table 37.8, and the inflection of the present passive and the imperfect passive in tables 37.9 and 37.10.

Table 37.8   Tense and aspect in the passive voice

	Imperfective	*Perfective*
non-past	γράφομαι	γραφτώ
past	γραφόμουν(α)	γράφτηκα

Table 37.9   Inflection of the present passive

	Singular	*Plural*
1st	γράφομαι	γραφόμαστε
2nd	γράφεσαι	γράφεστε/γραφόσαστε
3rd	γράφεται	γράφονται

Table 37.10   Inflection of the imperfect passive

	Singular	*Plural*
1st	γραφόμουν(α)	γραφόμασταν
2nd	γραφόσουν(α)	γραφόσαστε/γραφόσασταν
3rd	γραφόταν(ε)	γράφονταν/γραφόντουσαν

The aorist passive γράφτηκα inflects like the active past tenses, while the aorist subjunctive passive γραφτώ inflects like the present active of θεωρώ (see below).

The perfective passive imperative is γράψου, but its imperfective counterpart has more or less dropped out of the language. The past participle passive is γραμμένος "written." A present participle passive (γραφόμενος "being written") has come into SMGk from the learned tradition, but the other ancient participles are not so commonly used.

The modern manifestations of the ancient verbs in /ao:/ such as αγαπώ "I love" are conjugated in the present as shown in table 37.11.

Table 37.11   Modern forms of αγαπώ

	Singular	*Plural*
1st	αγαπώ/αγαπάω	αγαπούμε/αγαπάμε
2nd	αγαπάς	αγαπάτε
3rd	αγαπά/αγαπάει	αγαπούν/αγαπάνε

The imperfect active is αγαπούσα or αγάπαγα, while the passive forms are αγαπιέμαι (pres.), αγαπιόμουν(α) (imperf.), αγαπήθηκα (aor. indic.) and αγαπηθώ (aor. subj.).

The modern conjugation of verbs in /eo:/ such as θεωρώ "I consider" is close to the ancient paradigm (see table 37.12).

Table 37.12   Modern forms of θεωρώ

	Singular	*Plural*
1st	θεωρώ	θεωρούμε
2nd	θεωρείς	θεωρείτε
3rd	θεωρεί	θεωρούν

The imperfect active is θεωρούσα, with present passive θεωρούμαι, but with imperfective passive normally only in the third person: sg. θεωρείτο, pl. θεωρούντο. The aorist indicative passive is θεωρήθηκα.

Ancient verbs in /oo:/ have become /ono/ in Modern Greek, e.g., δηλώνω "I state."

The verb "to be" conjugates irregularly, but shares many similarities with passive paradigms (see tables 37.13 and 37.14).

Table 37.13   Present forms of the verb "to be"

	Singular	*Plural*
1st	είμαι	είμαστε
2nd	είσαι	είστε/είσαστε
3rd	είναι	είναι

Table 37.14 Imperfect forms of the verb "to be"

	Singular	*Plural*
1st	ήμουν(α)	ήμαστε/ήμασταν
2nd	ήσουν(α)	ήσαστε/ήσασταν
3rd	ήταν(ε)	ήταν(ε)

There is also a set of modern contracted verbs, such as λέω "I say" (see table 37.15).

Table 37.15 Forms of modern contracted verbs

	Singular	*Plural*
1st	λέω	λέμε
2nd	λες	λέτε
3rd	λέει	λένε

The verbs ακούω "I hear," καίω "I burn," κλαίω "I weep," πάω "I go," τρώω "I eat," and φταίω "I am to blame" conjugate in a similar way in the present active, but always preserving the same stem vowel. A –γ- is added in the imperfect active and in the imperfective tenses of the passive: έλεγα, λέγομαι.

A number of commonly used verbs that have been passed down through the popular tradition form their aorist stem in a highly irregular manner (see table 37.16).

Table 37.16 Irregular aorist forms of common verbs

Present	*Aorist indicative*
δίνω "I give"	έδωσα
έρχομαι "I come"	ήρθα
λέω "I say"	είπα
ντρέπομαι "I am ashamed"	ντράπηκα
παίρνω "I take"	πήρα
τρώω "I eat"	έφαγα
φαίνομαι "I appear"	φάνηκα

Among the legacies of the learned tradition are modern versions of some of the ancient verbs in –μι. These have only partially been adapted to the regular Modern Greek morphological system. The most commonly used of these morphologically problematic verbs are the modern versions of the ancient verbs τίθημι "I place" and ἵστημι "I stand (tr.), set up." The present active form of the first of these verbs in Modern Greek, θέτω, behaves normally throughout the active (aorist έθεσα), but in the present passive it reverts to its ancient form τίθεμαι, which is normally only used in the 3rd ps. sg. τίθεται and pl. τίθενται, the corresponding imperfect forms being ετίθετο and ετίθεντο. The aorist passive is τέθηκα.

There are various Modern Greek manifestations of ἵστημι. One of the three that came into SMGk through the popular tradition is στήνω "I set up," which conjugates quite regularly (aor. έστησα). A second, στέκω "I stand up," is normally used in its passive form στέκομαι, aor. στάθηκα. The third is –σταίνω, which is normally only found in ανασταίνω "I resurrect." However, SMGk has inherited from the learned tradition a number of versions of ἵστημι formed with prepositional prefixes. In the present active most of them end in –ιστώ, e.g., εγκαθιστώ "I install," aor. act. εγκατέστησα, pres. pass. εγκαθίσταμαι (imperf. almost exclusively in the 3rd ps.: sg. εγκαθίστατο, pl. εγκαθίσταντο), aor. pass. εγκαταστάθηκα, and past ptc. pass. εγκατεστημένος. There is also a verb in –ιστάνω, namely παριστάνω "I represent."

Syntax

As in Ancient Greek, the nominative is used to indicate the subject, the accusative for the direct object, and the genitive for the possessor. The genitive of personal pronouns (and sometimes nouns) is also used for the indirect object. More frequently, however, a noun phrase functioning as the indirect object is introduced by the preposition σ[ε] "to": Του το έδωσα "I gave it to him"; Το έδωσα στον Αντώνη "I gave it to Anthony." Weak pronoun objects immediately precede the verb except in the case of the imperative and the gerund, where they immediately follow the verb.

The Modern Greek infinitive is only used to form the perfect tenses. Some of the functions of the infinitive in other languages are performed in SMGk with a finite verb preceded by the particle να: Θέλω να έρθω "I want to come"; Θέλω να έρθεις "I want you to come." Να is also used in independent clauses to express wishes, commands, and the like: Να έρθεις αύριο "You should come tomorrow."

The particle ας is used to express permission, indifference, or mild command: Ας έρθει αύριο αν θέλει "Let him/her come tomorrow if s/he wants."

The negation of a verb is achieved through the use of the particle δεν or μη before the verb. Δεν is used in negative statements, while μη is used in negative commands and after να and ας: Δεν θα μιλήσω "I won't speak"; Μη μιλάς! "Don't speak!"; Μπορεί να μη μίλησαν "It's possible they didn't speak"; Ας μη μιλήσουν, αφού δεν θέλουν "Let them not speak, since they don't want to."

Unless it is neuter, a noun phrase normally indicates whether it is the subject or the direct object of a verb. For this reason, word order in Modern Greek is flexible, and the subject, verb, direct object, and indirect object (unless it is a weak pronoun) may appear in whatever order the speaker chooses. In fact, word order, together with the presence or absence of a weak pronoun, normally plays a part in conveying semantic emphasis, e.g., Είδα τη Μαρία "I saw Maria" (neutral); Την είδα τη Μαρία/Τη Μαρία την είδα "I did see Maria" (emphasizing the verb); Τη Μαρία είδα "It was Maria I saw" (emphasizing the direct object).

Register variation

Now that the learned and popular traditions have merged, it is possible to use different vocabulary items for different registers while still employing the same grammar. Words from the popular tradition tend to be used in informal speech, while words from the learned tradition are often preferred in formal writing. In the following pairs of examples, the first word of each pair is of popular origin, while the second is of learned origin: παπάς or ιερέας "priest"; φαγητό or τρόφιμα "food"; πάω or μεταβαίνω "I go."

Sometimes two synonyms are distinguished by context rather than register: φεγγάρι is the everyday word for "moon" (i.e., the moon as normally seen from Earth) but σελήνη is the astronomical term (the moon as visited by astronauts); συκώτι "liver" is the everyday and culinary term, but ήπαρ is the medical term.

In other instances the difference between two synonyms of popular and learned origin (which may both be of native Greek origin) is similar to the stylistic difference in English between words of Germanic and Romance origin: e.g. μπαίνω "I go in" vs εισέρχομαι "I enter"; αφήνω "I let" vs επιτρέπω "I permit"; ψάχνω "I look for" vs αναζητώ "I search for"; γίνεται "it happens" vs συμβαίνει "it occurs."

In some cases a word of popular origin is used in a literal sense, while its learned equivalent is used for metaphorical purposes: e.g., σπίτι "house, home," but (εκδοτικός) οίκος "(publishing) house"; σπρώχνω "I push," but ωθώ "I impel" as in Τον έσπρωξα "I pushed him," but Τι σας ώθησε σ' αυτή την εκλογή; "What impelled you to [make] this choice?"

FURTHER READING

For the history of Greek, see Horrocks 1997a. For a systematic account of the phonology of the Modern Greek dialects, see Newton 1972, and for more on the dialects in general, Kontosopoulos 1994. Mackridge 2009 has a full historical account of the language controversy. For the relationship between language and ideology in modern Greece, see the contributions by Christidis 2007, Skopetea 2007, and Liakos 2007 in Christidis, ed. 2007. For intra-lingual convergence in SMGk, see Holton 2002. For grammars of SMGk see Holton, Mackridge, and Philippaki-Warburton 1997 and 2004. Mackridge 1985 is a more informal description of SMGk. Comprehensive monolingual dictionaries of SMGk are Babiniotis (1998) and *Lexiko* (1998).

Bibliography

For abbreviated titles of journals, see Abbreviations of Modern Sources at the front of the book.

Acerbi, F. 2007. *Euclide. Tutte le opere. Introduzione, traduzione, note e apparati di Fabio Acerbi*. Milan.

Acerbi, F. 2008. "Disjunction and Conjunction in Euclid's *Elements*." *HEL* 30: 21–47.

Acerbi, F. Forthcoming. *La logica della matematica greca*.

Adami, F. 1901. "De poetis scaenicis Graecis hymnorum sacrorum imitatoribus." *Jahrbücher für classische Philologie, Supplement-Band* 26: 213–62.

Adamik, B. 2006. "Offizielles Kommunikationssystem und Romanisierung." In C. Arias Abellán, ed., *Latin vulgaire-latin tardif VII. Actes du VIIème Colloque international sur le latin vulgaire et tardif* (Séville, 2–6 septembre 2003). Seville: 17–29.

Adams, J. N. 1984. "Female Speech in Latin Comedy." *Antichthon* 18: 43–77.

Adams, J. N. 2002. "Bilingualism at Delos." In Adams, Janse, and Swain, eds., 2002: 103–27.

Adams, J. N. 2003. *Bilingualism and the Latin Language*. Cambridge.

Adams, J. N., M. Janse, and S. Swain, eds. 2002. *Bilingualism in Ancient Society: Language Contact and the Written Word*. Oxford.

Adrados, F. R. 2005. *A History of the Greek Language: From its Origins to the Present*. Leiden.

Aerts, W. J. 1965. *Periphrastica: An Investigation into the Use of εἶναι and ἔχειν as Auxiliaries or Pseudo-Auxiliaries in Greek from Homer up to the Present Day*. Amsterdam.

Agapitos, P. A. 1998. "Teachers, Pupils and Imperial Power in Eleventh-Century Byzantium." In Y. Lee Too and N. Livingstone, eds., *Pedagogy and Power: Rhetorics of Classical Learning*. Cambridge: 170–91.

Ahrens, H. L. 1839–43. *De Graecae linguae dialectis*, 2 vols. Göttingen.

Albers, P. B. 1923. *S. Pachomii Abbatis Tabennensis Regulae Monasticae* (Florilegium Patristicum 16). Bonn.

Albright, W. F. 1966. *The Proto-Sinaitic Inscriptions and their Decipherment*. Cambridge, MA.

Alexiou, M. 1974. *The Ritual Lament in Greek Tradition*. Cambridge.

Algra, K., et al., eds. 1999. *The Cambridge History of Hellenistic Philosophy*. Cambridge.

Allan, R. J. 2003. *The Middle Voice in Ancient Greek: A Study in Polysemy*. Amsterdam.

Allan, R. J. 2007. "Sense and Sentence Complexity: Sentence Structure, Sentence Connection and Tense-Aspect as Indicators of Narrative Modes in Thucydides' *Histories*." In Allan and Buijs, eds., 2007: 93–121.

Allan, R. J., and M. Buijs, eds. 2007. *The Language of Literature: Linguistic Approaches to Classical Texts*. Leiden.

Allan, W. 2005. "Tragedy and the Early Greek Philosophical Tradition." In J. Gregory, ed., *The Blackwell Companion to Greek Tragedy*. Oxford: 71–82.

Allen, J. P. 2000. *Middle Egyptian*. Cambridge.

Allen, J. T., and G. Italie. 1954. *A Concordance to Euripides*. Berkeley, CA.

Allen, W. S. 1959. "Some Remarks on the Structure of Greek Vowel Systems." *Word* 15: 240–51.

Allen, W. S. 1966. "Prosody and Prosodies in Greek." *TPS*: 107–48.

Allen, W. S. 1973. *Accent and Rhythm. Prosodic Features of Latin and Greek: A Study in Theory and Reconstruction*. Cambridge.

Allen, W. S. 1987a. *Vox Graeca: The Pronunciation of Classical Greek*, 3rd edn. Cambridge.

Allen, W. S. 1987b. "The Development of the Attic Vowel System: Conspiracy or Catastrophe?" In J. T. Killen, J. L. Melena, and J.-P. Olivier, eds., *Studies in Mycenaean and Classical Greek Presented to John Chadwick*. Salamanca: 21–32.

Allison, J. W. 1997. *Word and Concept in Thucydides*. Atlanta, GA.

Alpers, K. 1988. "Klassische Philologie in Byzanz." *CP* 83: 342–60.

Alpers, K. 1997. "Griechische Lexikographie in Antike und Mittelalter." In H.-A. Koch, ed., *Welt der Information. Wissen und Wissenvermittlung in Geschichte und Gegenwart*. Stuttgart: 14–38.

Alpers, K. 1998. "Lexicographica Minora." In Chr.-F. Collatz et al., eds., *Dissertatiunculae Criticae. Festschrift für Günther Christian Hansen*. Würzburg: 93–108.

Aly, W. 1929. *Formprobleme der frühen griechischen Prosa*. Leipzig.

Amigues, S. 1977. *Les subordonnées finales par ὅπως en attique classique*. Paris.

Andersen, Ø. 2001. "How Good Should an Orator Be?" In C. W. Wooten, ed., *The Orator in Action and Theory in Greece and Rome*. Leiden: 3–16.

Anderson, G. 1986. *Philostratus: Biography and Belles Lettres in the Third Century* A.D. London.

Anderson, G. 1993. *The Second Sophistic*. London.

Anlauf, G. 1960. *Standard Late Greek oder Attizismus? Eine Studie zum Optativgebrauch im nachklassischen Griechisch*. Cologne.

Apostolopoulos, Ph.D. 1994. *Inventaire méthodique de linguistique byzantine (grec médiéval). Essai d'une bibliographie raisonnée des travaux sur la langue byzantine (1880–1975)*. Thessaloniki.

Aravantinos, V. L. 1984. "The Use of Sealings in the Administration of Mycenaean Palaces." In T. G. Palaima and C. W. Shelmerdine, eds., *Pylos Comes Alive: Industry and Administration in a Mycenaean Palace*. New York: 41–8.

Arens, H. 2000. "Sprache und Denken bei Aristoteles." In Auroux et al., eds., 2000: 367–75.

Armayor, O. K. 1978. "Herodotus' Persian Vocabulary." *Ancient World* 1: 147–56.

Aujac, G. 1984. "Le langage formulaire dans la géométrie grecque." *RHS* 37: 97–109.

Aujac, G., and M. Lebel., ed. and trans. 1981. *Denys d'Halicarnasse, Opuscules rhétoriques. Tome III: La composition stylistique*. Paris.

Auroux, S., E. F. K. Koerner, H.-J. Niederehe, and K. Versteegh, eds. 2000. *History of the Language Sciences*, vol. 1. Berlin and New York.

Ausfeld, C. 1903. "De Graecorum precationibus quaestiones." *Jahrbücher für classische Philologie, Supplement-Band* 28: 503–47.

Austin, J. L. 1975. *How to do Things with Words*, 2nd edn. Cambridge, MA.

Auzépy, M.-F. 1998a. "Manifestations de la propagande en faveur de l'orthodoxie." In L. Brubaker, ed., *Dead or Alive? The Byzantine World in the Ninth Century*. Aldershot: 85–99.

Auzépy, M.-F. 1998b. "Le Christ, l'empereur et l'image (VIIᵉ–IXᵉ siècle)." In *ΕΥΨΥΧΙΑ. Mélanges offertes à Hélène Ahrweiler*. Paris: 35–47.

Ax, W. 1978. "Ψόφος, φωνή und διάλεκτος als Grundbegriffe aristotelischer Sprachreflexion." *Glotta* 56: 245–71.

Ax, W. 1982. "Aristarch und die Grammatik." *Glotta* 60: 96–109.

Ax, W. 1986. *Laut, Stimme und Sprache. Studien zu drei Grundbegriffen der antiken Sprachtheorie*. Göttingen.

Ax, W. 1992. "Aristoteles." In Dascal et al., eds.,1992: 244–59.

Babiniotis, G. 1972. *Τὸ ῥῆμα τῆς ἑλληνικῆς. Δομικαὶ ἐξελίξεις καὶ συστηματοποίησις τοῦ ῥήματος τῆς ἑλληνικῆς (ἀρχαίας καὶ νέας)*. Athens.

Babiniotis, G. 1998. *Λεξικό της νέας ελληνικής γλώσσας*. Athens.

Bader, F. 1997–8. "Aspects de l'hermétisme d'Homère. Phonologie poétique (allitérations, inventaires phonologiques et prosodiques) et liages en composition discontinue." *AIV* 156: 103–77.

Bagnall, R. S. 1988. "Combat ou vide: christianisme et paganisme dans l'Égypte romaine tardive." *Ktèma* 13: 285–96.

Bagnall, R. S. 1993. *Egypt in Late Antiquity*. Princeton.

Bagnall, R. S. 1997. *The Kellis Agricultural Account Book (P. Kell. IV Gr. 96)* (Dakhleh Oasis Project: Monograph No. 7). Oxford.

Bagnall, R. S., and R. Cribiore. 2006. *Women's Letters from Ancient Egypt, 300 BC–AD 800*. Ann Arbor, MI.

Bain, D. 1984. "Female Speech in Menander." *Antichthon* 18: 24–42.

Bakker, E. J. 1988. *Linguistics and Formulas in Homer: Scalarity and the Description of the Particle* Per. Amsterdam.

Bakker, E. J. 1991. "Foregrounding and Indirect Discourse: Temporal Subclauses in a Herodotean Short Story." *Journal of Pragmatics* 16: 225–47.

Bakker, E. J. 1993. "Topics, Boundaries, and the Structure of Discourse: An Investigation of the Ancient Greek Particle *Dé*." *Studies in Language* 17: 275–311.

Bakker, E. J. 1997a. *Poetry in Speech: Orality and Homeric Discourse*. Ithaca, NY and London.

Bakker, E. J. 1997b. "The Study of Homeric Discourse." In Morris and Powell, eds., 1997: 284–304.

Bakker, E. J. 1997c. "Verbal Aspect and Mimetic Description in Thucydides." In Bakker, ed., 1997: 7–54.

Bakker, E. J. 1999. "Pointing to the Past: Verbal Augment and Temporal Deixis in Homer." In J. N. Kazazis and A. Rengakos, eds., *Euphrosyne: Studies in Ancient Epic and its Legacy in Honor of Dimitris N. Maronitis*. Stuttgart: 50–65.

Bakker, E. J. 2002. "The Making of History: Herodotus' *Historiês Apodexis*." In Bakker, de Jong, and van Wees, eds., 2002: 3–32.

Bakker, E. J. 2005. *Pointing at the Past: From Formula to Performance in Homeric Poetics*. Washington, DC and Cambridge, MA.

Bakker, E. J. 2006. "The Syntax of *Historiê*: How Herodotus Writes." In Dewald and Marincola, eds., 2006: 92–102.

Bakker, E. J. 2007. "Time, Tense, and Thucydides." *CW* 100.2: 113–22.

Bakker, E. J. 2008. "Epic Remembering." In E. A. Mackay, ed., *Orality, Literacy, Memory in the Ancient Greek and Roman World*. Leiden: 65–77.

Bakker, E. J., ed. 1997. *Grammar as Interpretation: Greek Literature in its Linguistic Contexts*. Leiden.

Bakker, E. J., I. J. F. de Jong, and H. van Wees, eds., 2002. *Brill's Companion to Herodotus.* Leiden.

Bakker, S. J. 2006. "The Position of the Adjective in Definite Noun Phrases." In E. Crespo et al., eds., *Word Classes and Related Topics in Ancient Greek.* Louvain-la-Neuve: 91–104.

Bakker, S. J. 2007. "Adjective Ordering in Herodotus: A Pragmatic Explanation." In Allan and Buijs, eds., 2007: 188–210.

Barber, C. 2002. *Figure and Likeness.* Princeton.

Barlow, S. 1971. *The Imagery of Euripides.* London.

Barnes, J. 1987. *Early Greek Philosophy.* Harmondsworth.

Barnes, J. 1999. "Logic and Language." In Algra et al., eds., 1999: 65–83, 193–213.

Barnes, J. 2007. *Truth, etc.: Six Lectures on Ancient Logic.* Oxford.

Barnes, J., and D. M. Schenkeveld. 1999. "Language." In Algra et al., eds., 1999: 177–225.

Barnes, T. Forthcoming. "Homeric ἀνδροτῆτα καὶ ἥβην." *JHS.*

Bartoněk, A. 2003. *Handbuch des mykenischen Griechisch.* Heidelberg.

Bartoněk, A., and G. Buchner. 1995. "Die ältesten griechischen Inschriften von Pithekoussai (2. Hälfte des VIII. bis VI. Jh.)." *Die Sprache* 37: 129–231.

Bastianini, G., and C. Gallazzi. 2001. *Posidippo di Pella. Epigrammi (P. Mil. Vogl. VIII 309).* Milan.

Baumbach, M., A. Petrovic, and I. Petrovic. 2010. *Archaic and Classical Greek Epigram: Contextualisation and Literarisation.* Cambridge.

Baxter, T. M. S. 1992. *The Cratylus: Plato's Critique of Naming.* Leiden.

Beard, M., et al., eds. 1991. *Literacy in the Roman World* (Journal of Roman Archaeology Suppl. 3). Ann Arbor, MI.

Bechtel, F. 1921–4. *Die griechischen Dialekte,* 3 vols. Berlin.

Beck, H.-G. 1971. *Geschichte der byzantinischen Volksliteratur* (Handbuch der Altertumswissenschaft, XII, 2, 3). Munich.

Beekes, R. S. P. 1968. *The Development of the Proto-Indo-European Laryngeals in Greek.* The Hague.

Bekker, I. 1863. *Homerische Blätter.* Bonn.

Bekker, I., ed. 1814. *Anecdota Graeca,* vol. 1. Berlin.

Belardi, W. 1985. *Filosofia grammatica e retorica nel pensiero antico.* Rome.

Bell, A. 1984. "Language Style as Audience Design." *Language in Society* 13: 145–204.

Bennet, J. 1997. "Homer and the Bronze Age." In Morris and Powell, eds., 1997: 511–33.

Bennett, E. L., Jr. 1950. "Fractional Quantities in Minoan Bookkeeping." *AJA* 54: 204–22.

Bennett, E. L., Jr., ed. 1958. *The Mycenae Tablets II. TAPhS* n.s. 48.1. Philadelphia.

Bennett, E. L., Jr., and J.-P. Olivier. 1976. *The Pylos Tablets Transcribed.* Rome.

Benveniste, E. 1966. "Problèmes sémantiques de la reconstruction." In *Problèmes de linguistique générale,* vol. 1. Paris: 289–307.

Benveniste, E. 1969. *Vocabulaire des institutions indo-européennes.* Paris. Trans. 1973. *Indo-European Language and Society.* London.

Bérard, F., et al. 2000. *Guide de l'épigraphiste. Bibliographie choisie des épigraphies antiques et médiévales,* 3rd edn. Paris.

Berg, N. 1978. "Parergon metricum. Der Ursprung des griechischen Hexameters." *MSS* 37: 11–36.

Bergren, A. L. T. 1983. "Language and the Female in Early Greek Thought." *Arethusa* 16: 69–95.

Bernal, M. 1990. *Cadmean Letters.* Winona Lake, IN.

Bers, V. 1974. *Enallage and Greek Style.* Leiden.

Bers, V. 1984. *Greek Poetic Syntax in the Classical Age*. New Haven.

Bers, V. 2009. *Genos Dikanikon: Amateur and Professional Speech in the Courtrooms of Classical Athens*. Washington, DC and Cambridge, MA.

Betegh, G. 2004. *The Derveni Papyrus: Cosmology, Theology, and Interpretation*. Cambridge.

Bethe, E., ed. 1900–37. *Lexicographi Graeci. 9, Pollucis Onomasticon*, 3 vols. Leipzig.

Beyer, K. 1968. *Semitische Syntax im Neuen Testament. Band I. Satzlehre Teil 1*, 2nd edn. Göttingen.

Bianconi, D. 2003. "Eracle e Iolao. Aspetti della collaborazione tra copisti nell'età dei Paleologi." *BZ* 96: 521–58.

Biber, D. 1988. *Variation across Speech and Writing*. Cambridge.

Biber, D. 1994. "An Analytical Framework for Register Studies." In Biber and Finegan, eds., 1994: 31–56.

Biber, D. 1995. *Dimensions of Register Variation: A Cross-Linguistic Comparison*. Cambridge.

Biber, D., and E. Finegan, eds. 1994. *Sociolinguistic Perspectives on Register*. New York and Oxford.

Bierbach, C. 1995. "Normes et représentations de comportement langagier: la parole féminine dans les proverbes." In G. Marcato, ed., *Donna & Linguaggio. Convegno Internazionale di Studi: Sappada/Plodn (Belluno) 1995*. Padua: 267–84.

Bietti Sestieri, A. M., A. De Santis, and A. La Regina. 1990. "Elementi di tipo cultuale e doni personali nella necropoli laziale di Osteria dell'Osa." *Scienze dell'Antichità* 3–4: 65–88.

Bile, M., C. Brixhe, and R. Hodot. 1984. "Les dialectes grecs, ces inconnus." *BSLP* 79: 155–203.

Biville, F. 1986. "Du modèle à l'imitation ou les avatars des mots grecs en latin." *Latomus* 45: 848–54.

Biville, F. 1990–5. *Les emprunts du latin au grec: approche phonétique*, 2 vols. Paris and Louvain.

Biville, F. 1991. "L'emprunt lexical, un révélateur des structures vivantes des deux langues en contact." *Rev. Phil.* 65: 45–58.

Biville, F. 1992. "Les interférences entre les lexiques grec et latin, et le Dictionnaire étymologique de P. Chantraine." In F. Létoublon, ed., *La langue et les textes en grec ancien. Actes du colloque Pierre Chantraine (Grenoble – 5–8 septembre 1989)*. Amsterdam: 227–40.

Biville, F. 1993. "Grec des Romains ou latin des Grecs? Ambiguïté de quelques processus néologiques dans la koiné." In C. Brixhe, ed., *La koiné grecque antique I: Une langue introuvable?* Nancy: 129–40.

Biville, F. 2001–3. "Les contacts linguistiques." *St.Cl.* 37–8: 195–200.

Björck, G. 1950. *Das Alpha impurum und die tragische Kunstsprache*. Uppsala.

Black, M. 1967. *An Aramaic Approach to the Gospels and Acts*. Oxford. (3rd edn., with intr. by C. A. Evans. Peabody, MA: 1998.)

Blanc, A. 2008. *Les contraintes métriques dans la poésie homérique. L'emploi des thèmes nominaux sigmatiques dans l'hexamètre dactylique*. Louvain and Paris.

Blanc, A., and E. Dupraz, eds. 2007. *Procédés synchroniques de la langue poétique en grec et en latin*. Brussels.

Blank, D. L. 1982. *Ancient Philosophy and Grammar: The Syntax of Apollonius Dyscolus* (American Classical Studies 10). Chico, CA.

Blank, D. L. 1993. "Apollonius Dyscolus." *ANRW* 34.1: 708–30.

Blank, D. L. 1998. *Sextus Empiricus: Against the Grammarians (Adversus Mathematicos I)*. Oxford.

Blank, D. L. 2000. "The Organization of Grammar in Ancient Greece." In Auroux et al., eds., 2000: 400–17.

Blass, F., and A. Debrunner. 1961. *A Greek Grammar of the New Testament and Other Early Christian Literature*. Trans. R. Funk. Chicago.

Blockley, R. C. 1981–3. *The Fragmentary Classicising Historians of the Later Roman Empire*. Liverpool.

Blomqvist, J. 1969. *Particles in Hellenistic Prose*. Lund.

Blundell, S. 1995. *Women in Ancient Greece*. London.

Boardman, J. 1999. *The Greeks Overseas: Their Early Colonies and Trade*, 4th edn. London.

Boardman, J. 2001. "Aspects of 'Colonization.'" *BASOR* 322: 33–42.

Boardman, J. 2003. "'Reading' Greek Vases." *OJA* 22.1: 109–14.

Böhlig, G. 1956. *Untersuchungen zum rhetorischen Sprachgebrauch der Byzantiner mit besonderer Berücksichtigung der Schriften des Michael Psellos*. Berlin.

Bompaire, J. 1958. *Lucien écrivain. Imitation et création*. Paris.

Bompaire, J. 1994. "L'atticisme de Lucien." In L. Pernot, ed., *Lucien de Samosate*. Paris: 65–75.

Bonifazi, A. 2004. "ΚΕΙΝΟΣ in Pindar: Between Grammar and Poetic Intention." *CP* 99: 283–99.

Boscherini, S. 1995. "Come parlavano le donne a Roma." In *Studi Linguistici per i 50 anni del Circolo Linguistico Fiorentino*. Florence: 55–60.

Boswinkel, E., and P. W. Pestman, eds. 1978. *Textes grecs, démotiques et bilingues*. Leiden.

Boswinkel, E., and P. W. Pestman, eds. 1982. *Les archives privées de Dionysios, fils de Kephalas (P.Lugd.Bat. 22)*. (Textes grecs et démotiques). Leiden.

Boulanger, A. 1923. *Aelius Aristide et la sophistique dans la province d'Asie au IIe siècle de notre ère*. Paris.

Bowie, A. M. 1981. *The Poetic Dialect of Sappho and Alcaeus*. New York.

Bowman, A. K. 1996. *Egypt after the Pharaohs, 332 BC–AD 642, from Alexander to the Arab Conquest*. London.

Bowman, A. K., and G. Woolf, eds. 1994. *Literacy and Power in the Ancient World*. Cambridge.

Boyancé, P. 1956. "La connaissance du grec à Rome." *Rev. Ét. Lat.* 34: 111–31.

Braun, F. 1988. *Terms of Address: Problems of Patterns and Usage in Various Languages and Cultures*. Berlin.

Braun, T. F. R. G. 1982a. "The Greeks in the Near East." In J. Boardman et al., eds., *CAH* 3.3, 2nd edn. Cambridge: 1–31.

Braun, T. F. R. G. 1982b. "The Greeks in Egypt." In J. Boardman et al., eds., *CAH* 3.3, 2nd edn. Cambridge: 32–56.

Breitenbach, W. 1934. *Untersuchungen zur Sprache der euripideischen Lyrik*. Stuttgart.

Bremer, J.-M., A. M. van Erp Taalman-Kip, and S. R. Slings. 1987. *Some Recently Found Greek Poems*. Leiden.

Brenne, S. 2002. "Teil II: Die Ostraka (487–ca. 416 v. Chr.) als Testimonien (T 1)." In P. Siewert, ed., *Ostrakismos-Testimonien*. Vol. 1: *Die Zeugnisse antiker Autoren, der Inschriften und Ostraka über das athenische Scherbengericht aus vorhellenistischer Zeit (487–322 v. Chr.)*" (Historia Einzelschriften, 155). Stuttgart: 36–166.

Bresciani E., and R. Pintaudi. 1987. "Textes démotico-grecs et gréco-démotiques des ostraca de Medinet Madi: un problème de bilinguisme." In S. P. Vleeming, ed., *Aspects of Demotic Lexicography*. Louvain: 123–6.

Bresciani, E., et al., eds. 1978. "Una rilettura dei Pap.dem. Bologna 3173 e 3171." *EVO* 1: 95–104.

Brett, R. L., and A. R. Jones. 1965. *Wordsworth and Coleridge, Lyrical Ballads*, rev. edn. London.

Brice, W. C. 1961. *Inscriptions in the Minoan Linear Script of Class A*. Oxford.

Brillante, C. 1987. "Sulla lingua della lirica corale." *QUCC* 56: 20–37.

Brioso Sánchez, M. 1971. "El vocativo y la interjeccion ὦ." *Habis* 2: 35–48.

Brixhe, C. 1976. *Le dialecte grec de Pamphylie*. Paris.

Brixhe, C. 1987a. *Essai sur le grec anatolien au début de notre ère*. Nancy.

Brixhe, C. 1987b. "La langue comme critère d'acculturation." In. R. Lebrun, ed., *Acta anatolica E. Laroche oblata* (= *Hethitica* VIII), 45–80. Louvain-la-Neuve.

Brixhe, C. 1988a. "La langue des inscriptions épichoriques de Pisidie." In Y. L. Arbeitman, ed., *A Linguistic Happening in Memory of Ben Schwartz*. Louvain-la-Neuve: 131–55.

Brixhe, C. 1988b. "La langue de l'étranger chez Aristophane." In R. Lonis, ed., *L'étranger dans le monde grec*. Nancy: 113–38.

Brixhe, C. 1990. "Bulletin de dialectologie grecque." *REG* 103: 201–30.

Brixhe, C. 1992. "Du 'datif' mycénien aux protagonistes de la situation linguistique." In J.-P. Olivier, ed., *Mykenaïka* (= *BCH* Suppl. XXV). Paris: 129–57.

Brixhe, C. 1993a. "Du paléo- au néo-phrygien." *CRAI* 137: 323–44.

Brixhe, C. 1993b. "Le grec en Carie et en Lycie au IVe siècle: des situations contrastées." In C. Brixhe, ed., *La koiné grecque antique* I. Nancy: 59–82.

Brixhe, C. 1994. "Le changement <IO> → <I> en pamphylien, en laconien et dans la koiné d'Egypte." *Verbum* 16: 219–41.

Brixhe, C. 1996. Review of J. Nollé, *Side im Altertum*. *Gnomon* 68: 697–701.

Brixhe, C. 2001. "Individu, langue et communauté sociale. À propos des confessions païennes du Moyen Hermos." In C. Consani and L. Mucciante, eds., *Norma e variazione nel diasistema greco*. Alexandria: 101–18.

Brixhe, C. 2002. "Interactions between Greek and Phrygian under the Roman Empire." In Adams, Janse, and Swain, eds., 2002: 246–66.

Brixhe, C. 2004a. "Nouvelle chronologie anatolienne et date d'élaboration des alphabets grec et phrygien." *CRAI* 148: 271–89.

Brixhe, C. 2004b. "Phrygian." In Woodard, ed., 2004: 777–88.

Brixhe, C. 2006a. "Situation, spécificités et contraintes de la dialectologie grecque. À propos de quelques questions soulevées par la Grèce centrale." In C. Brixhe and G. Vottéro, eds., *Peuplements et genèses dialectales dans la Grèce antique*. Nancy: 39–69.

Brixhe, C. 2006b. "De la filiation à l'héritage." In C. Brixhe and G. Vottéro, eds., *Peuplements et genèses dialectales dans la Grèce antique*. Nancy: 7–37.

Brixhe, C. 2007a. "Les alphabets du Fayoum." *Kadmos* 46: 1–24.

Brixhe, C. 2007b. "History of the Alphabet: Some Guidelines for Avoiding Oversimplification." In Christidis, ed., 2007: 277–87.

Brixhe, C. 2007c. "The Greek of the Roman Texts." In Christidis, ed., 2007: 903–10.

Brixhe, C., and R. Hodot. 1988. *L'Asie Mineure du Nord au Sud*. Nancy.

Brixhe, C., and R. Hodot. 1993. "À chacun sa koiné." In C. Brixhe, ed., *La koiné grecque antique* I: *Une langue introuvable?* Nancy: 7–21.

Brixhe, C., and M. Özsait. 2001. "Nouvelles inscriptions pisidiennes et grecques de Timbriada." *Kadmos* 50: 155–76.

Brixhe, C., and A. Panayotou. 1988. "L'atticisation de la Macédoine: l'une des sources de la koiné." *Verbum* 11: 245–60.

Brixhe, C., and G. Vottéro. 2004. "L'alternance codique ou quand le choix du code fait sens." In R. Hodot, ed., *La koiné grecque antique V: Alternances codiques et changements de codes*. Nancy: 7–43.

Broggiato, M. 2001. *Cratete di Mallo: I frammenti. Edizione, introduzione e note*. La Spezia.

Brown, E. L. 1992-3. "The Linear A Signary: Tokens of Luvian Dialect in Bronze Age Crete." *Minos* 27–8: 25–54.

Browning, R. 1962–3. "The Patriarchal School at Constantinople in the Twelfth Century." *Byzantion* 32: 166–202; 33: 11–40.

Browning, R. 1978. "The Language of Byzantine Literature". In S. Vryonis, ed., *The Past in Medieval and Modern Greek Culture*. Malibu: 103–33. Repr. Browning 1989.

Browning, R. 1981. "The Low Level Saint's Life in the Early Byzantine World." In S. Hackel, ed., *The Byzantine Saint*. London: 117–27. Repr. Browning 1989.

Browning, R. 1983. *Medieval and Modern Greek*, 2nd edn. Cambridge.

Browning, R. 1989. *History, Language and Literacy in the Byzantine World*. Northampton.

Browning, R. 1997. "Teachers." In G. Cavallo, ed., *The Byzantines*. Chicago: 95–106.

Bruhn, E. 1899. *Anhang*. F. W. Schneidewin and A. Nauck, *Sophocles*, vol. 8. Berlin.

Brunius-Nilsson, E. 1955. Δαιμόνιε: *An Inquiry into a Mode of Apostrophe in Old Greek Literature*. Uppsala.

Brust, M. 2005. *Die indischen und iranischen Lehnwörter im Griechischen*. Innsbruck.

Bryce, T. 1995. "The Lycian Kingdom in Southwest Anatolia." In Sasson, ed., 1995: 1161–72.

Bryce, T. 2002. *Life and Society in the Hittite World*. Oxford.

Bryce, T. 2005. *The Kingdom of the Hittites*. Oxford.

Bryce, T. 2006. *The Trojans and their Neighbours*. London and New York.

Bryer, A., and J. Herrin, eds. 1977. *Iconoclasm*. Birmingham.

Buchheim, T., ed. 1989. *Gorgias von Leontini. Reden, Fragmente und Testimonien*. Hamburg.

Buck, C. D. 1907. "The Interrelations of the Greek Dialects." *CP* 2: 241–76.

Buck, C. D. 1955. *The Greek Dialects*, 2nd edn. Chicago.

Buck, C. D., and W. Petersen. 1948. *A Reverse Index of Greek Nouns and Adjectives, Arranged by Terminations with Brief Historical Introductions*. Chicago.

Buckler, G. 1929. *Anna Comnena: A Study*. London.

Buckler, W. H., W. M. Calder, and W. K. C. Guthrie. 1933. *Monuments and Documents from Eastern Asia and Western Galatia* (= *MAMA* IV). Manchester.

Budelmann, F. 2000. *The Language of Sophocles*. Cambridge.

Buijs, M. 2005. *Clause Combining in Ancient Greek Narrative Discourse: The Distribution of Subclauses and Participial Clauses in Xenophon's* Hellenica *and* Anabasis. Leiden.

Buijs, M. 2007. "Aspectual Differences and Narrative Technique: Xenophon's *Hellenica* and *Agesilaus*." In Allan and Buijs, eds., 2007: 122–53.

Burkert, W. 1959. "ΣTOIXEION: Eine semasiologische Studie." *Philol.* 103: 167–97.

Burkert, W. 1992. *The Orientalizing Revolution*. Cambridge, MA.

Burkert, W. 2004. *Babylon, Memphis, Persepolis: Eastern Contexts of Greek Culture*. Cambridge, MA.

Burkert, W. 2005. "Near Eastern Connections." In J. M. Foley, ed., *A Companion to Ancient Epic*. Oxford: 291–301.

Burney, C. F. 1922. *The Aramaic Origin of the Fourth Gospel*. Oxford.

Bußmann, H. 1995. "*Das Genus, die* Grammatik und – *der* Mensch: Geschlechterdifferenz in der Sprachwissenschaft." In H. Bußmann and R. Hof, eds., *Genus. Zur Geschlechterdifferenz in den Kulturwissenschaften*. Stuttgart: 114–60.

Cadell, H., and R. Rémondon. 1967. "Sens et emplois de τὸ ὄρος dans les documents papyrologiques." *REG* 80: 343–9.

Cairns, D. 1993. Aidos: *the Psychology and Ethics of Honour and Shame in Ancient Greek Literature*. Oxford.

Calder, W. M., and G. E. Bean. 1958. *A Classical Map of Asia Minor*. London and Ankara.

Cameron, A. 1992. "Byzantium and the Past in the Seventh Century: The Search for Redefinition." In J. Fontaine and J. N. Hillgarth, eds., *The Seventh Century: Change and Continuity*. London: 250–76.

Cameron, D. 2007. *The Myth of Mars and Venus*. Oxford.

Campbell, L. 1871. *Sophocles, the Plays and Fragments*. Cambridge.

Campbell, L. 2004. *Historical Linguistics: An Introduction*, 2nd edn. Cambridge, MA.

Campbell, L., and W. J. Poser. 2008. *Language Classification: History and Method*. Cambridge.

Cantarella, E. 1996. "La comunicazione femminile in Grecia e a Roma." In M. Bettini, ed., *I signori della memoria e dell'oblio. Figure della comunicazione nella cultura antica*. Florence: 3–21.

Carpenter, R. 1933. "The Antiquity of the Greek Alphabet." *AJA* 37: 8–29.

Carpenter, R. 1938. "The Greek Alphabet Again." *AJA* 42: 58–69.

Carruthers, P., and A. Chamberlain, eds. 2000. *Evolution and the Human Mind: Modularity, Language, and Metacognition*. Cambridge.

Casey, M. 1998. *Aramaic Sources of Mark's Gospel*. Cambridge.

Casey, M. 2002. *An Aramaic Approach to Q: Sources for the Gospels of Matthew and Luke*. Cambridge.

Cassio, A. C. 1989. "Lo sviluppo della prosa dorica e le tradizioni occidentali della retorica greca." *AION* (filol.) 11: 137–57.

Cassio, A. C. 2002. "The Language of Doric Comedy." In A. Willi, ed., 2002: 51–83.

Cassio, A. C. 2005. "I dialetti eolici e la lingua della lirica corale." In F. Bertolini and F. Gasti, eds., *Dialetti e lingue letterarie nella Grecia antica. Atti della IV Giornata ghisleriana di filologia classica (Pavia, 1–2 aprile 2004)*. Pavia: 13–44.

Cassio, A. C. 2007. "Alcman's Text, Spoken Laconian, and Greek Study of Greek Dialects." In I. Hajnal and M. Meier-Brügger, eds., *Die altgriechischen Dialekte. Wesen und Werden*. Innsbruck.

Cassio, A. C., ed. 2008. *Storia delle lingue letterarie greche*. Florence.

Catling, H. W. 1994. "Cyprus in the 11th Century BC: An End or a Beginning?" In V. Karageorghis, ed., *Cyprus in the 11th Century: Proceedings of the International Symposium*. Nicosia: 133–40.

Catling, H. W. 1995. "Heroes Returned? Subminoan Burials from Crete." In J. B. Carter and S. P. Morris, eds., *The Ages of Homer: A Tribute to Emily Townsend Vermeule*. Austin, TX: 123–36.

Cavallo, G. 1967. *Ricerche sulla maiuscolo biblica*. Florence.

Cavallo, G. 1977. "Funzione e strutture della maiuscola greca tra i secoli VIII–XI." In *La paléographie grecque et byzantine*. Paris: 95–137.

Cavallo, G. 2003. "Sodalizi eruditi e pratiche di scrittura a Bisanzio." In J. Hamesse, ed., *Bilan et perspectives des études médiévales*. Louvain-la-Neuve: 65–80.

Cavallo, G., G. de Gregorio, and M. Maniaci, eds. 1991. *Scritture, libri e testi nelle aree provinciali di Bisanzio*. Spoleto.

Cervenka-Ehrenstrasser, I.-M. (unter Mitarbeit von J. Diethart). 1996–2000. *Lexikon der lateinischen Lehnwörter in den griechischsprachigen Texten Ägyptens*. 2 fasc. (Alpha; Beta–Delta). Vienna.

Chadwick, J. 1967. *The Decipherment of Linear B*, 2nd edn. Cambridge.

Chadwick, J. 1973. "The Linear B Tablets as Historical Documents." *CAH* 2: 609–26, 3rd edn. Cambridge.

Chadwick, J. 1976a. "Who Were the Dorians?" *PP* 31: 103–17.

Chadwick, J. 1976b. *The Mycenaean World*. Cambridge.

Chadwick, J. 1990. "Linear B and Related Scripts." In J. T. Hooker, ed., *Reading the Past: Ancient Writing from Cuneiform to the Alphabet*. London: 137–95.

Chadwick, J. 1996. *Lexicographica Graeca*. Oxford.

Chadwick, J. 1996–7. "Three Temporal Clauses." *Minos* 31–32: 293–301.

Chadwick, J., et al. 1986–98. *Corpus of Mycenaean Inscriptions from Knossos*. Cambridge.

Chafe, W. L. 1982. "Integration and Involvement in Speaking, Writing, and Oral Literature." In D. Tannen, ed., *Spoken and Written Language: Exploring Orality and Literacy*. Norwood, NJ: 35–53.

Chafe, W. L. 1994. *Discourse, Consciousness, and Time: The Flow and Displacement of Conscious Experience in Speaking and Writing*. Chicago.

Chancey, M. A. 2005. *Greco-Roman Culture and the Galilee of Jesus*. Cambridge.

Chantraine, P. 1933. *La formation des noms en grec ancien*. Paris.

Chantraine, P. 1953. *Grammaire homérique. Tome II: Syntaxe*, 2nd edn. Paris.

Chantraine, P. 1973. *Grammaire homérique. Tome I: Phonétique et morphologie*, 5th edn. Paris.

Chantraine, P. 1991. *Morphologie historique du grec*, 3rd edn. Paris.

Chantraine, P. 1999. *Dictionnaire étymologique de la langue grecque*. With suppl. Paris.

Choat, M. 2006. *Belief and Cult in Fourth-Century Papyri*. Turnhout.

Chomsky, N. 1968. *Language and Mind*. Cambridge.

Christidis, A.-F. 2007. "General Introduction: Histories of the Greek Language." In Christidis, ed., 2007: 1–22.

Christidis, A.-F. ed. 2007. *A History of Ancient Greek: From the Beginnings to Late Antiquity*, 2 vols. Cambridge.

Churchill, L. J., P. R. Brown, and J. E. Jeffrey, eds. 2002. *Women Writing Latin: From Roman Antiquity to Early Modern Europe*. Vol. 1: *Women Writing Latin in Roman Antiquity, Late Antiquity, and the Early Christian Era*. New York and London.

Clackson, J. 1994. *The Linguistic Relationship between Armenian and Greek*. Oxford.

Clackson, J. 2002. "The Writing of χσ and φσ for ξ and ψ." *Glotta* 78: 22–35.

Clackson, J. 2007. *Indo-European Linguistics*. Cambridge.

Clark, M. 1994. "Enjambment and Binding in Homeric Hexameter." *Phoenix* 48: 95–114.

Clark, M. 1997. *Out of Line: Homeric Composition beyond the Hexameter*. Lanham, MD.

Clark, M. 2004. "Homeric Metre." In R. L. Fowler, ed., *The Cambridge Companion to Homer*. Cambridge: 119–23. Repr. 2006.

Clarke, M. 1999. *Flesh and Spirit in the Songs of Homer: A Study of Words and Myths*. Oxford.

Clarke, M. 2004. "The Semantics of Colour in the Early Greek Word-Hoard." In K. Stears and L. Cleland, eds., *Colour in the Ancient Mediterranean World*. Oxford: 131–9.

Clarke, M. 2005. "Etymology in the Semantic Reconstruction of Early Greek Words." *Hermathena* 179: 13–38.

Clarysse, W. 1985. "Greeks and Egyptians in the Ptolemaic Army and Administration." *Aegyptus* 65: 57–66.

Clarysse, W. 1993. "Egyptian Scribes Writing Greek." *CdÉ* 68: 186–201.

Clarysse, W. 1998. "Ethnic Diversity and Dialect among the Greeks of Hellenistic Egypt." In A. M. Verhoogt and S. P. Vleeming, eds., *The Two Faces of Graeco-Roman Egypt: Greek and Demotic and Greek-Demotic Texts and Studies presented to P. W. Pestman*. Leiden: 1–13.

Clarysse, W., and K. Vandorpe. 1995. *Zénon, un homme d'affaires grec à l'ombre des Pyramides*. Louvain.

Classen, C. J. 1976. "The Study of Language amongst Socrates' Contemporaries." In C. J. Classen, ed., *Sophistik*. Darmstadt: 215–47.

Clay, D. M. 1958. *A Formal Analysis of the Vocabularies of Aeschylus, Sophocles and Euripides*, Part II. Athens.

Coldstream, J. N. 1977. *Geometric Greece*. London.

Coldstream, J. N. 1982. "Greeks and Phoenicians in the Aegean." In H. G. Niemeyer, ed., *Phönizier im Westen*. Mainz: 261–75.

Coldstream, J. N. 1989. "Early Greek Visitors to Cyprus and the Eastern Mediterranean." In V. Tatton-Brown, ed., *Cyprus and the Eastern Mediterranean in the Iron Age.* London: 90–6.

Collard, C. 1971. *A Supplement to the Allen and Italie Concordance to Euripides.* Groningen.

Collard, C. 1975a. *Euripides, Supplices: Edition, Introduction, and Commentary,* 2 vols. Groningen.

Collard, C. 1975b. "Formal Debates in Euripidean Drama." *G&R* 22: 58–71. In J. Mossman, ed., *Oxford Readings in Classical Studies: Euripides.* Oxford, 2003: 64–80.

Collard, C. 1980. "On Stichomythia." *LCM* 5: 77–85.

Collard, C. 2005. "Colloquial Language in Tragedy: A Supplement to the Work of P. T. Stevens." *CQ* 55: 350–86.

Collart, J. 1954. *Varron grammairien latin.* Paris.

Collingwood, R. G. 1946. *The Idea of History.* Oxford.

Collins, B. J., M. R. Bachvarova, and I. C. Rutherford, eds. 2008. *Anatolian Interfaces: Hittites, Greeks and their Neighbours.* Oxford.

Colvin, S. C. 1999. *Dialect in Aristophanes: The Politics of Language in Ancient Greek Literature.* Oxford.

Colvin, S. C. 2004. "Social Dialect in Attica." In J. H. W. Penney, ed., *Indo-European Perspectives: Studies in Honour of Anna Morpurgo Davies.* Oxford: 95–108.

Colvin, S. C. 2007. *A Historical Greek Reader: Mycenaean to the Koine.* Oxford.

Comrie, B. 1976. *Aspect: An Introduction to the Study of Verbal Aspect and Related Problems.* Cambridge.

Constantinides, C. N. 1982. *Higher Education in Byzantium in the Thirteenth and Early Fourteenth Centuries, 1204–ca.1310.* Nicosia.

Cook, B. F. 1987. *Greek Inscriptions.* London.

Cook, R. M. 1937. "Amasis and the Greeks in Egypt." *JHS* 57: 227–37.

Cornford, F. M. 1907. *Thucydides Mythistoricus.* London.

Cortassa, G. 2001. "Un filologo di Bisanzio e il suo committente: la lettera 88 dell' 'Anonimo di Londra'." *MEG* 1: 97–138.

Cortassa, G. 2003. "Συρμαιογραφεῖν e l'antica minuscola libraria greca." *MEG* 3: 73–94.

Cowgill, W. C. 1966. "Ancient Greek Dialectology in the Light of Mycenaean." In H. Birnbaum and J. Puhvel, eds., *Ancient Indo-European Dialects.* Berkeley, CA: 77–95.

Cowley, A. 1923. *Aramaic Papyri of the Fifth Century B.C.* Oxford.

Creason, S. 2004. "Aramaic." In Woodard, ed., 2004: 391–426.

Crespo, E. 2007. "The Linguistic Policy of the Ptolemaic Kingdom." In M. B. Hatzopoulos, ed., *Actes du Ve Congres international de dialectologie grecque.* Athens: 35–49.

Cribiore, R. 1996. *Writing, Teachers, and Students in Graeco-Roman Egypt* (American Studies in Papyrology 36). Atlanta, GA.

Cribiore, R. 2001. *Gymnastics of the Mind: Greek Education in Hellenistic and Roman Egypt.* Princeton and Oxford.

Cribiore, R. 2007. *The School of Libanius in Late Antique Antioch.* Princeton.

Cristofaro, S. 1996. *Aspetti sintattici e semantici delle frasi completive in greco antico.* Florence.

Cristofaro, S. 2003. *Subordination.* Oxford.

Cross, F. M. 1980. "Newly Found Inscriptions in Old Canaanite and Early Phoenician Scripts." *BASOR* 238: 1–20.

Crowley, T. J. 2005. "On the Use of *Stoicheion* in the Sense of 'Element'." *OSAP* 29: 367–94.

Cruse, D. 1986. *Lexical Semantics.* Cambridge.

Crystal, D., and D. Davy. 1969. *Investigating English Style.* London.

Culican, W. 1991. "Phoenicia and Phoenician Colonization." In J. Boardman et al., eds., *CAH* 3.2, 2nd edn. Cambridge: 461–546.

Da Rios, R., ed. 1954. *Aristoxeni Elementa Harmonica*. Rome.

Dagron, G., and D. Feissel. 1987. *Inscriptions de Cilicie*. Paris.

Dain, A., ed. 1954. *Le Philetaeros attribué a Hérodien*. Paris.

Dale, A. M. 1968. *The Lyric Metres of Greek Drama*, 2nd edn. Cambridge.

Dalley, S., and A. T. Reyes. 1998. "Mesopotamian Contact and Influence in the Greek World: 1. To the Persian Conquest." In S. Dalley, ed., *The Legacy of Mesopotamia*. Oxford: 85–106.

Danielewicz, J. 1990. "Deixis in Greek Choral Lyric." *QUCC* 63: 7–17.

Danielewicz, J. 2001. "Metatext and its Functions in Greek Lyric Poetry." In Harrison, ed., 2001: 46–61.

Daris, S. 1991. *Il lessico latino nel greco d'Egitto*, 2nd edn. Barcelona.

Darnell, J. C., F. W. Dobbs-Allsopp, M. J. Lundberg, P. K. McCarter, B. Zuckerman, and C. Manassa. 2005. *Two Early Alphabetic Inscriptions from the Wadi El-Hôl: New Evidence for the Origin of the Alphabet from the Western Desert of Egypt*. Boston. MA.

Dascal, M., et al., eds. 1992. *Sprachphilosophie. Ein internationales Handbuch zeitgenössischer Forschung*. Berlin and New York.

Daumas, F. 1972. "Les textes bilingues ou trilingues." *Textes et langages de l'Égypte pharaonique. Bibliothèque d'Étude*, 64.3: 41–5.

David, A. P. 2006. *The Dance of the Muses: Choral Theory and Ancient Greek Poetics*. Oxford.

De Boor, C., ed. 1978. *Georgius Monachus, Chronicon*. Corr. P. Wirth. Stuttgart.

De Borries, J., ed. 1911. *Phrynichi Sophistae Praeparatio Sophistica*. Leipzig.

De Bot, K. and B. Weltens. 1991. "Recapitulation, Regression and Language Loss." In H. Seliger and R. Vago, eds., *First Language Attrition: Structural and Theoretical Perspectives*. Cambridge: 31–51.

De Foucault, J.-A. 1972. *Recherches sur la langue et le style de Polybe*. Paris.

De Gregorio, G. 2000. "Materiali vecchi e nuovi per uno studio della minuscola greca fra VII e IX secolo." In Prato, ed., 2000: 83–151.

De Jong, I. J. F, and A. Rijksbaron, eds. 2006. *Sophocles and the Greek Language: Aspects of Diction, Syntax and Pragmatics*. Leiden.

De Jonge, C. C. 2008. *Between Grammar and Rhetoric: Dionysius of Halicarnassus on Language, Linguistics, and Literature*. Leiden and Boston, MA.

De Lange, N. 2007. "Jewish Greek." In Christidis, ed., 2007: 638–45.

De Lannoy, L. 2003. "L'atticisme de Philostrate II. Atticisme linguistique et admiration pour le passé grec." In H. Hokwerda, ed., *Constructions of Greek Past: Identity and Historical Consciousness from Antiquity to the Present*. Groningen: 69–77.

De Luna, M. E. 2003. *La comunicazione linguistica fra alloglotti nel mondo greco. Da Omero a Senofonte*. Florence.

De Rijk, L. M. 1986. *Plato's Sophist: A Philosophical Commentary*. Amsterdam, Oxford, and New York.

De Rosalia, A. 1991. "Il latino di Plutarco." In G. D'Ippolito and I. Gallo, eds., *Strutture formali dei "Moralia" di Plutarco. Atti del III Convegno plutarcheo Palermo, 3–5 maggio 1989*. Naples: 445–59.

Debrunner A. 1917. *Griechische Wortbildungslehre*. Heidelberg.

Debrunner, A., and A. Scherer 1969. *Geschichte der griechischen Sprache. 2: Grundfragen und Grundzüge des nachklassischen Griechisch*. Berlin.

Debut, J. 1984. "Les *Hermeneumata Pseudodositheana*. Une méthode d'apprentissage des langues pour grands débutants." *Koinonia* 8: 61–85.

Deferrari, R. 1916. *Lucian's Atticism: The Morphology of the Verb.* Princeton.

Deissmann, A. 1895. *Bibelstudien.* Marburg.

Demont, P. 1978 "Remarques sur le sens de *trepho.*" *REG* 91: 358–84.

Denniston, J. D. 1952. *Greek Prose Style.* Oxford.

Denniston, J. D. 1954. *The Greek Particles,* 2nd edn. Oxford.

Depauw, M. 2003. "Autograph Confirmation in Demotic Private Contracts." *CdÉ* 78: 66–111.

Derchain, P. 1955. "Une origine égyptienne de l'emploi du mot ϑαλλός = 'cadeau' dans les papyrus grecs d'Égypte." *CdÉ* 30: 324–6.

Derchain, P. 2001. "De la véracité d'Hérodote." *Enchoria* 27: 198–9.

Devine, A. M., and L. D. Stephens. 1984. *Language and Metre: Resolution, Porson's Bridge, and their Prosodic Basis* (American Philological Association, American Classical Studies No. 12). Oxford.

Devine, A. M., and L. D. Stephens. 1994. *The Prosody of Greek Speech.* New York and Oxford.

DeVries, K. 2000. "The Nearly Other: The Attic Vision of Phrygians and Lydians." In B. Cohen, ed., *Not the Classical Ideal: Athens and the Construction of the Other in Greek Art.* Leiden: 338–63.

Dewald, C., and J. Marincola, eds. 2006. *The Cambridge Companion to Herodotus.* Cambridge.

Di Benedetto, V. 2007. *Il richiamo del testo: Contributi di filologia e letteratura,* 4 vols. Pisa.

Di Cesare, D. 1996. "Die Geschmeidigkeit der Sprache. Zur Sprachauffassung und Sprachbetrachtung der Sophistik." In P. Schmitter, ed., *Sprachtheorien der abendländischen Antike* (Geschichte der Sprachtheorie 2). Tübingen: 87–118.

Dickey, E. 1995. "Forms of Address and Conversational Language in Aristophanes and Menander." *Mnemosyne* 48: 257–71.

Dickey, E. 1996. *Greek Forms of Address: From Herodotus to Lucian.* Oxford.

Dickey, E. 2001. "Κύριε, Δέσποτα, *Domine*: Greek Politeness in the Roman Empire." *JHS* 121: 1–11.

Dickey, E. 2002. *Latin Forms of Address: From Plautus to Apuleius.* Oxford.

Dickey, E. 2003a. "Ancient Bilingualism." *JRS* 93: 295–302.

Dickey, E. 2003b. "Latin Influence on the Greek of Documentary Papyri: An Analysis of its Chronological Distribution." *ZPE* 145: 249–57.

Dickey, E. 2004a. "The Greek Address System of the Roman Period and its Relationship to Latin." *CQ* 54: 494–527.

Dickey, E. 2004b. "Literal and Extended use of Kinship Terms in Documentary Papyri." *Mnemosyne* 57: 131–76.

Dickinson, O. 2006. *The Aegean from Bronze Age to Iron Age.* London.

Dieleman, J. 2005. *Priests, Tongues, and Rites: The London–Leiden Magical Manuscripts and Translation in Egyptian Ritual (100–300 CE).* Leiden.

Diels, H. 1899. *Elementum. Eine Vorarbeit zum griechischen und lateinischen Thesaurus.* Leipzig.

Dieterich, K. 1898. *Untersuchungen zur Geschichte der griechischen Sprache von der hellenistischen Zeit bis zum 10. Jahrh. n. Chr.* (Byzantinisches Archiv, Heft 1). Leipzig.

Dihle, A. 1977 "Der Beginn des Attizismus." *A&A* 23: 162–77.

Dihle, A. 1994. *Greek and Latin Literature of the Roman Empire: From Augustus to Justinian.* Trans. M. Malzahn. London and New York.

Dik, H. 1995. *Word Order in Ancient Greek: A Pragmatic Account of Word Order Variation in Herodotus.* Amsterdam.

Dik, H. 2007. *Word Order in Greek Tragic Dialogue.* Oxford.

Dinneen, L. 1929. *Titles of Address in Christian Greek Epistolography to 527 AD*. Chicago.

Donadoni, S. 1955. "Il greco di un sacerdote di Narmuthis." *Acme* 8: 73–83.

Donbaz, V. 1990. "Two Neo-Assyrian Stelae in the Antakya and Karamanmaraş Museums." *Annual Review of the Royal Inscriptions of Mesopotamia Project* 8: 5–24.

Dornseiff, F. 1921. *Pindars Stil*. Berlin.

Dover, K. J. 1968. *Lysias and the Corpus Lysiacum*. Berkeley and Los Angeles.

Dover, K. J. 1980. *Plato, Symposium. Edition and Commentary*. Cambridge.

Dover, K. J. 1993. *Aristophanes, Frogs*. Oxford.

Dover, K. J. 1997. *The Evolution of Greek Prose Style*. Oxford.

Dow, S. 1969. *Conventions in Editing: A Suggested Reformulation of the Leiden System* (*GRBS* Scholarly Aids 2). Durham.

Drettas, G. 1997. *Aspects pontiques*. Paris.

Drettas, G. 2007. "The Translation (Targum) of the Septuagint." Trans. W. J. Lillie. In Christidis, ed., 2007: 887–96.

Drews, R. 1988. *The Coming of the Greeks*. Princeton.

Drexler, H. 1972. *Herodot-Studien*. Hildesheim and New York.

Driessen, J. 2000. *The Scribes of the Room of the Chariot Tablets at Knossos. Interdisciplinary Approach to the Study of a Linear B Deposit*. Salamanca.

Drijvers, J. W. 1996. "Ammianus Marcellinus 15.13.1–2: Some Observations on the Career and Bilingualism of Strategius Musonianus." *CQ* 46: 532–7.

Dubois, L. 1995. *Inscriptions grecques dialectales de Grande Grèce* I : *Colonies eubéennes. Colonies ioniennes. Emporia*. Geneva.

Dubuisson, M. 1979. "Le latin des historiens grecs." *LEC* 47: 89–106.

Dubuisson, M. 1980. "Toi aussi, mon fils!" *Latomus* 39: 881–90.

Dubuisson, M. 1981a. "*Utraque lingua*." *Ant. Class.* 50: 274–86.

Dubuisson, M. 1981b. "Problèmes du bilinguisme romain." *LEC* 49: 27–45.

Dubuisson, M. 1982. "Y a-t-il une politique linguistique romaine?" *Ktèma* 7: 55–68.

Dubuisson, M. 1983. "Recherches sur la terminologie antique du bilinguisme." *Rev. Phil.* 57: 203–25.

Dubuisson, M. 1985. *Le latin de Polybe. Les implications historiques d'un cas de bilinguisme*. Paris.

Dubuisson, M. 1992a. "Le grec à Rome à l'époque de Cicéron. Extension et qualité du bilinguisme." *Annales ESC* 47: 187–206.

Dubuisson, M. 1992b. "Le contact linguistique gréco-romain: problèmes d'interférences et d'emprunts." *Lalies* 10: 91–109.

Dubuisson, M. 2002. "Le grec d'Auguste: notes pour un réexamen." In P. Defosse, ed., *Hommages à Carl Deroux. II. Prose et linguistique, Médecine*. Brussels: 152–63.

Dubuisson, M. 2005. "Le grec de la correspondance de Cicéron: questions préliminaires sur un cas de bilinguisme." *La linguistique* 41: 69–86.

Dué, C. 2009. ed. *Recapturing a Homeric Legacy: Images and Insights from the Venetus A Manuscript of the Iliad*. Cambridge, MA and Washington, DC.

Duffy, J., and J. Parker, eds. 1979. *The* Synodicon Vetus. Washington, DC.

Duhoux, Y. 1978. "Une analyse linguistique du linéaire A." In Y. Duhoux, ed., *Études minoennes* 1. Louvain: 65–129.

Duhoux, Y. 1989. "Le linéaire A. Problèmes de déchiffrement." In Y. Duhoux, T. G. Palaima, and J. Bennet, eds., *Problems in Decipherment*. Louvain-la-Neuve: 59–119.

Duhoux, Y. 1997. "Grec écrit et grec parlé: Une étude contrastive des particules aux Ve–IVe siècles." In Rijksbaron, ed., 1997: 15–48.

Duhoux, Y. 2000. *Le verbe grec ancien. Éléments de morphologie et de syntaxe historiques*, 2nd edn. Louvain.

Dunbar, N. 1995. *Aristophanes, Birds.* Oxford.

Dunkel, G. 1997. "Mono- and Disyllabic *ā* in the *Ṛgveda.*" In E. Pirart, ed., *Syntaxe des langues indo-iraniennes anciennes. Colloque international — Sitges (Barcelona) 4–5 mai 1993.* Sabadell (Barcelona): 9–27.

Dunkel, G. 2000. "Remarks on Code-Switching in Cicero's Letters to Atticus." *MH* 57: 122–9.

Dupont, F., and E. Valette-Cagnac, eds. 2005. *Façons de parler grec à Rome.* Paris.

Durante, M. 1976. *Sulla preistoria della tradizione poetica greca. Parte seconda: Risultanze della comparazione indoeuropea.* Rome.

Dyck, A. R., ed. 1995. *Epimerismi Homerici*, vol. 2. Berlin.

Dyovouniotis, K. 1924. "Μητροφάνους Κριτοπούλου, Ἀνέκδοτος γραμματικὴ τῆς ἁπλῆς Ἑλληνικῆς." *Ἐπιστημονικὴ Ἐπετηρὶς Θεολογικῆς Σχολῆς Πανεπιστημίου Ἀθηνῶν* 1: 97–123.

Earp, F. R. 1944. *The Style of Sophocles.* Cambridge.

Earp, F. R. 1948. *The Style of Aeschylus.* Cambridge.

Easterling, P. E. 1973. "Repetition in Sophocles." *Hermes* 101: 14–34.

Easterling, P. E. 1999. "Plain Words in Sophocles." In J. Griffin, ed., *Sophocles Revisited.* Oxford: 95–107.

Easterling, P. E. 2006. "Notes on Notes: The Ancient Scholia on Sophocles." In S. Eklund, ed., Συγχάρματα: *Studies in Honour of Jan Fredrik Kindstrand.* Uppsala: 21–36.

Eben, E. F. 2004. *The Phonology of Formulas: The Case of 'Resonant Lengthening' in Homer.* PhD dissertation, Cornell University.

Eck, W. 2000. "Latein als Sprache politischer Kommunikation in Städten der östlichen Provinzen." *Chiron* 30: 641–60.

Eck, W. 2004. "Lateinisch, Griechisch, Germanisch . . . ?: wie sprach Rom mit seinen Untertanen?" In L. De Ligt, E. A. Hemelrijk, and H. W. Singor, eds., *Roman Rule and Civic Life: Local and Regional Perspectives.* Amsterdam: 3–19.

Eckert, P., and S. McConnell-Ginet. 2003. *Language and Gender.* Cambridge.

Edwards, M. W. 1997. "Homeric Style and Oral Poetics." In Morris and Powell, eds., 1997: 261–83.

Egli, U. 1987. "Stoic Syntax and Semantics." In D. J. Taylor, ed., *The History of Linguistics in the Classical Period.* Amsterdam: 107–32.

Ehrlich, S. 1990. *Point of View: A Linguistic Analysis of Literary Style.* London and New York.

Eijk, Ph. J. van der. 1997. "Towards a Rhetoric of Ancient Scientific Discourse." In Bakker, ed., 1997: 77–129.

Einarson E. 1936. "On Certain Mathematical Terms in Aristotle's Logic." *AJPh* 57: 33–54, 151–72.

Eliot, T. S. 1920. *The Sacred Wood.* London.

Ellendt, F., and H. Genthe. 1872. *Lexicon Sophocleum*, 2nd edn. Berlin.

Erbse, H. 1950. *Untersuchungen zu den attizistischen Lexika.* Berlin.

Erman, A. 1893. "ὄνος ὑπὸ οἴνου." *Hermes* 28: 479–80.

Ervin-Tripp, S. 1972. "On Sociolinguistic Rules: Alternation and Co-Occurrence." In J. J. Gumperz and D. Hymes, eds., *Directions in Sociolinguistics: The Ethnography of Communication*, 2nd edn. Oxford: 213–50.

Evans, A. J. 1909. *Scripta Minoa: The Hieroglyphic and Primitive Linear Classes*, vol. 1. Oxford.

Evans, T. V. 2001. *Verbal Syntax in the Greek Pentateuch.* Oxford.

Evans, T. V. 2003. "The Last of the Optatives." *CP* 38: 70–80.

Evans, T. V. 2009. "Identifying the Language of the Individual in the Zenon Archive." In Evans and Obbink, eds., 2009.

Evans, T. V., and D. Obbink, eds. 2009. *The Language of the Papyri.* Oxford.

Exler, F. X. J. 1923. *The Form of the Ancient Greek Letter: A Study in Greek Epistolography.* Washington, DC.

Fabricius, C. 1962. *Zu den Jugendschriften des Johannes Chrysostomos.* Lund.

Fabricius, C. 1967. "Der sprachliche Klassizismus der griechischen Kirchenväter. Ein philologisches und geistesgeschichtliches Problem." *JbAChr* 10: 187–99.

Famerie, E. 1998. *Le latin et le grec d'Appien. Contribution à l'étude du lexique d'un historien grec de Rome.* Geneva.

Famerie, E. 1999. "La transposition de *quaestor* en grec." *Ant. Class.* 68: 211–25.

Fantham, E., H. P. Foley, N. Boymel Kampen, S. B. Pomeroy, and H. A. Shapiro. 1994. *Women in the Classical World: Image and Text.* New York and Oxford.

Fasold, R. 1984. *The Sociolinguistics of Society.* Oxford.

Fasold, R. 1990. "Language and Sex." In R. Fasold, *The Sociolinguistics of Language.* Oxford: 89–119.

Fauriel, C. 1824. *Chants populaires de la Grèce moderne,* vol. 1. Paris.

Federspiel, M. 1992. "Sur l'origine du mot ΣΗΜΕΙΟΝ en géométrie." *REG* 105: 385–407.

Federspiel, M. 1995. "Sur l'opposition *défini/indéfini* dans la langue des mathématiques grecques." *LEC* 63: 249–93.

Federspiel, M. 2003. "Sur quelques effets du 'principe d'abréviation' chez Euclide." *LEC* 71: 321–52.

Federspiel, M. 2005. "Sur l'expression linguistique du rayon dans les mathématiques grecques." *LEC* 73: 97–108.

Federspiel, M. 2006. "Sur le sens de ΜΕΤΑΛΑΜΒΑΝΕΙΝ et de ΜΕΤΑΛΗΨΙΣ dans les mathématiques grecques." *LEC* 74: 105–13.

Fehling, D. 1965. "Zwei Untersuchungen zur griechischen Sprachphilosophie." *Rh. Mus.* 108: 212–29.

Fehling, D. 1969. *Die Wiederholungsfiguren und ihr Gebrauch bei den Griechen vor Gorgias.* Berlin.

Felson, N. 2004. "Introduction." In N. Felson, ed., *The Poetics of Deixis in Alcman, Pindar, and Other Lyric* (*Arethusa* 37.3). Baltimore, MD: 253–66.

Ferguson, C. 1959. "Diglossia." *Word* 15: 325–40.

Ferguson, C. 1994. "Dialect, Register, and Genre: Working Assumptions About Conventionalization." In Biber and Finegan, eds., 1994: 15–30.

Fernández Marcos, N. 2001. *The Septuagint in Context,* trans. W. G. E. Watson. Leiden.

Ferrari, G. A. 1981. "La scrittura invisibile." *Aut-Aut* 184–5: 95–110.

Fewster, P. 2002. "Bilingualism in Roman Egypt." In Adams, Janse, and Swain, eds., 2002: 220–45.

Fillmore, C. J. 1982. "Towards a Descriptive Framework for Spatial Deixis." In R. J. Jarvella and W. Klein, eds., *Speech, Place, and Action.* New York: 31–59.

Fillmore, C. J. 1997. *Lectures on Deixis.* Stanford, CA.

Fillmore, C. J., and B. T. S. Atkins. 1992. "Towards a Frame-Based Lexicon: The Semantics of RISK and its Neighbors". In A. Lehrer and E. F. Kittay, eds., *Frames, Fields, and Contrasts: New Essays in Semantic and Lexical Organization.* Hillsdale, NJ: 75–120.

Fillmore, C. J., and B. T. S. Atkins. 2000. "Describing Polysemy: The Case of 'Crawl'." In Y. Ravin and C. Leacock, eds., *Polysemy: Theoretical and Computational Approaches*. Oxford: 91–110.

Finkelberg, M. 1990–1. "Minoan Inscriptions on Libation Vessels." *Minos* 25–6: 43–85.

Finkelberg, M. 2005. *Greek and Pre-Greeks: Aegean Prehistory and Greek Heroic Tradition*. Oxford.

Finkelberg, M. 2007. "More on κλέος ἄφθιτον." *CQ* 57: 341–50.

Finley, J. 1939. "The Origins of Thucydides' Style." *HSCPh* 50: 35–84.

Finley, M. I. 2004. *The World of Odysseus*, 2nd edn. London.

Firth, J. R. 1935. "The Technique of Semantics." *TPS*, 36–72.

Fischer, E., ed. 1974. *Die Ekloge des Phrynichos* (*SGLG* 1). Berlin and New York.

Fitzmyer, J. A. 1979. *A Wandering Aramean: Collected Aramaic Essays*. Missoula, MT.

Fleischman, S. 1990. *Tense and Narrativity: From Medieval Performance to Modern Fiction*. Austin, TX.

Fluck, H.-R. 1985. *Fachsprachen. Einführung und Bibliographie*, 3rd edn. Tübingen.

Fögen, T. 2000. *"Patrii sermonis egestas": Einstellungen lateinischer Autoren zu ihrer Muttersprache. Ein Beitrag zum Sprachbewußtsein in der römischen Antike*. Munich and Leipzig.

Fögen, T. 2001. "Ancient Theorizing on Nonverbal Communication." In R. M. Brend, A. K. Melby, and A. R. Lommel, eds., *LACUS Forum XXVII: Speaking and Comprehending*. Fullerton, CA: 203–16.

Fögen, T. 2003. "Metasprachliche Reflexionen antiker Autoren zu den Charakteristika von Fachtexten und Fachsprachen." In M. Horster and Ch. Reitz, eds., *Antike Fachschriftsteller. Literarischer Diskurs und sozialer Kontext*. Stuttgart: 31–60.

Fögen, T. 2004. "Gender-Specific Communication in Graeco-Roman Antiquity. With a Research Bibliography." *Historiographia Linguistica* 31: 199–276.

Foley, H. 2001. *Female Acts in Greek Tragedy*. Princeton.

Fonkič, B. L. 2000. "Aux origines de la minuscule stoudite." In Prato, ed., 2000: 169–86.

Fontenrose, J. 1978. *The Delphic Oracle: Its Responses and Operations with a Catalogue of Responses*. Berkeley, CA.

Forssman, B. 1966. *Untersuchungen zur Sprache Pindars*. Wiesbaden.

Forssman, B. 1974. "Zu homerisch ἀγγελίης 'Bote'." *MSS* 32: 41–64.

Forssman, B. 1991. "Schichten in der homerischen Sprache." In J. Latacz, ed., *Zweihundert Jahre Homer-Forschung, Rückblick und Ausblick*. Stuttgart: 259–88.

Forssman, B. 2004. "Greek Literary Languages." In *Brill's New Pauly*, vol. 5. Leiden: 1019–21.

Fortson, B. W. IV. 2004. *Indo-European Language and Culture: An Introduction*. Malden, MA.

Fournet, J. L. 1989. "Les emprunts du grec à l'égyptien." *BSLP* 84: 55–80.

Fournet, J. L. 1999. *Hellénisme dans l'Égypte du VIᵉ siècle. La bibliothèque et l'oeuvre de Dioscore d'Aphrodité*. Cairo.

Fowler, R. L. 1987. *The Nature of Early Greek Lyric: Three Preliminary Studies*. Toronto.

Foxhall, L., and J. K. Davies. 1984. *The Trojan War: Its Historicity and Context*. Bristol.

Fraenkel, E. 1952. "Griechisches und Italisches." *IF* 60: 131–55.

Fränkel, H. 1960. "Der kallimachische und der homerische Hexameter." In *Wege und Formen frühgriechischen Denkens*, 2nd edn. Munich: 100–156.

Frede, D., and B. Inwood, eds. 2005. *Language and Learning: Philosophy of Language in the Hellenistic Age*. Cambridge.

Frede, M. 1974. *Die stoische Logik*. Göttingen.

Frede, M. 1987. *Essays in Ancient Philosophy*. Oxford.

Frede, M. 1992. "Plato's Sophist on False Statements." In R. Kraut, ed., *The Cambridge Companion to Plato*. Cambridge: 397–424.

Frede, M. 1993. "The Stoic Doctrine of the Tenses of the Verb." In K. Döring and T. Ebert, eds., *Dialektiker und Stoiker. Zur Logik der Stoa und ihrer Vorläufer*. Stuttgart: 141–54.

Frede, M. 1994a. "The Stoic Notion of a Grammatical Case." *BICS* 39: 13–24.

Frede, M. 1994b. "The Stoic Notion of a Lekton." In S. Everson, ed., *Companions to Ancient Thought 3. Language*. Cambridge: 109–28.

Freyburger-Galland, M.-L. 1997. *Aspects du vocabulaire politique et institutionnel de Dion Cassius*. Paris.

Frisk, Hj. 1960–72. *Griechisches etymologisches Wörterbuch*. Heidelberg.

Frösén, J. 1974. *Prolegomena to a Study of the Greek Language in the First Centuries A.D.: The Problem of Koiné and Atticism*. Helsinki.

Führer, R., and M. Schmidt. 2001. "Homerus redivivus, Renzension: Homerus Ilias, recensuit/testimonia congessit Martin L. West." *Göttingische Gelehrte Anzeigen* 253 (1–2): 1–32.

Furfey, P. H. 1944. "Men's and Women's Languages." *American Catholic Sociological Review* 5: 218–23.

Furley, D., and J. M. Bremer. 2001. *Greek Hymns*, 2 vols. Tübingen.

Gabba, E. 1963. "Il latino come dialetto greco." In *Studi alessandrini in memoria di A. Rostagni*. Turin: 188–94.

Galjanić, A. 2008. "Greek Priamel and Enumerative Sets in Indo-European." In K. Jones-Bley et al., eds., *Proceedings of the 19th Annual UCLA Indo-European Conference, Los Angeles, November 2–3, 2007*. Washington, DC: 137–50.

Gallavotti, C. 1956. "Lettura di testi micenei." *PP* 11: 5–24.

Gallo, P. 1989. "Ostraka Demotici da Medinet Madi." *EVO* 12: 99–123.

Gallop, D. 1963. "Plato and the Alphabet." *The Philosophical Review* 72: 364–76.

García Ramón, J. L. 1975. *Les origines postmycéniennes du groupe dialectal éolien*. Suppl. *Minos* 6. Salamanca.

García Ramón, J. L. 1992. "Griechisch ἱερός und seine Varianten, vedisch iṣirá-." In R. Beekes, A. Lubotsky, and J. Weitenberg, eds., *Rekonstruktion und relative Chronologie. Akten der VIII. Fachtagung der indogermanischen Gesellschaft, Leiden, 31. August–4. September 1987*. Innsbruck: 183–205.

García Ramón, J. L. 2004. "Greek Dialects." In *Brill's New Pauly*, vol. 5. Leiden: 1011–17.

Gardiner, A. 1916. "The Egyptian Origin of the Semitic Alphabet." *JEg. Arch.* 3: 1–16.

Garman, M. 1990. *Psycholinguistics*. Cambridge.

Garofalo, I., ed. 1988. *Erasistrati Fragmenta. Collegit et digessit I. Garofalo*. Pisa.

Garrett, A. 1999. "A New Model of Indo-European Subgrouping and Dispersal." In S. Chang, L. Liaw, and J. Ruppenhofer, eds., *Proceedings of the Twenty-Fifth Annual Meeting of the Berkeley Linguistics Society*. Berkeley, CA: 146–56.

Garrett, A. 2006. "Convergence in the Formation of Indo-European Subgroups: Phylogeny and Chronology." In P. Forster and C. Renfrew, eds., *Phylogenetic Methods and the Prehistory of Languages*. Cambridge: 139–51.

Gaskin, R. 1997. "The Stoics on Cases, Predicates and the Unity of the Proposition." In R. Sorabji, ed., *Aristotle and After*. London: 91–108.

Gauly, B. M. 2004. *Senecas* Naturales Quaestiones. *Naturphilosophie für die römische Kaiserzeit*. Munich.

Geeraerts, D. 1998. *Diachronic Prototype Semantics*. Oxford.

Geiger, J. 1999. "Some Latin Authors from the Greek East." *CQ* 49: 606–17.

Geiger, J. 2002. "A Quotation from Latin in Plutarch?" *CQ* 52: 632–4.

Gelzer, T. 1979. "Klassizismus, Attizismus und Asianismus." In H. Flashar, ed., *Le classicisme à Rome aux 1ers siècles avant et après J.-C.* Geneva: 1–41.

Gentili, B. 1989. *Poesia e pubblico nella Grecia antica: da Omero al V secolo*, 2nd edn. Rome.

Gentner, D., and S. Goldin-Meadow, eds. 2003. *Language in Mind: Advances in the Study of Language and Thought*. Cambridge, MA.

George, C. H. 2005. *Expressions of Agency in Ancient Greek*. Cambridge.

Georgiev, V. 1963. *Les deux langues des inscriptions crétoises en linéaire A*. Sofia.

Gera, D. L. 2003. *Ancient Greek Ideas on Speech, Language and Civilization*. Oxford.

Getty Handbook 2002. *The J. Paul Getty Museum. Handbook of the Antiquities Collection*. Los Angeles.

Gibson, J. C. L. 1982. *Textbook of Syrian Semitic Inscriptions*, vol. 3. Oxford.

Gignac, F. T. 1970. "The Pronunciation of Greek Stops in the Papyri." *TAPA* 101: 185–202.

Gignac, F. T. 1976–81. *A Grammar of the Greek Papyri of the Roman and Byzantine Periods.* Vol. 1: *Phonology.* Vol. 2: *Morphology.* Milan.

Gignac, F. T. 1981. "Some Interesting Morphological Phenomena in the Language of the Papyri." *Proceedings of the XVI International Congress of Papyrology*. Chico, CA: 199–207.

Gildersleeve, B. L. 1890. *Pindar: The Olympian and Pythian Odes*, rev. edn. New York.

Gilleland, M. E. 1980. "Female Speech in Greek and Latin." *AJPh* 101: 180–3.

Glück, H. 1979. "Der Mythos von den Frauensprachen." *Osnabrücker Beiträge zur Sprachtheorie* 9: 60–95.

Godart, L., and J.-P. Olivier. 1976–85. *Recueil des inscriptions en linéaire A*, vols I–V. Paris.

Goheen, R. F. 1951. *The Imagery of Sophocles' Antigone*. Princeton.

Goldhill, S. 1997. "The Language of Tragedy: Rhetoric and Communication." In P. E. Easterling, ed., *The Cambridge Companion to Greek Tragedy*. Cambridge: 127–50.

Goldhill, S. 2002. *The Invention of Prose. Greece and Rome* (New Surveys in the Classics No. 32). Oxford.

Goltz, D. 1969. "Krankheit und Sprache." *Sudhoffs Archiv* 53: 225–69.

Goodwin, W. W. 1889. *Syntax of the Moods and Tenses of the Greek Verb*. London.

Goodwin, W. W. 1894. *A Greek Grammar*. London and New York.

Goody, J., and I. Watt. 1963. "The Consequences of Literacy." *Comparative Studies in Social History* 5: 304–45. Repr. in J. Goody, ed., *Literacy in Traditional Societies*. Cambridge 1968: 27–68.

Gordon, C. H. 1966. *Evidence for the Minoan Language*. Princeton.

Goudriaan, K. 1988. *Ethnicity in Ptolemaic Egypt*. Amsterdam.

Gould, J. 1989. *Herodotus*. London.

Graham, A. J. 1986. "The Historical Interpretation of Al Mina." *DHA* 12: 51–65.

Grayson, A. K. 1982. "Assyria: Ashur-Dan II to Ashur-Nirari V." In J. Boardman et al., eds., *CAH* 3.1, 2nd edn. Cambridge: 238–81.

Griffith, M. 1977. *The Authenticity of the Prometheus Bound*. Cambridge.

Griffith, M. 2001. "Antigone and her Sister(s): Embodying Women in Greek Tragedy." In Lardinois and McClure, eds., 2001: 117–36.

Gruen, E. S. 1992. *Culture and National Identity in Republican Rome*. Ithaca.

Guarducci, M. 1967. *Epigrafia Greca*. Rome.

Guarducci, M. 1987. *L'epigrafia greca dalle origini al tardo impero*. Rome.

Guillard, J. 1966. "Fragments inédits d'un antirrhétique de Jean le grammarien." *REB* 34: 171–81.

Gutas, D. 1998. *Greek Thought, Arabic Culture: The Graeco-Arabic Translation Movement in Baghdad and Early 'Abbāsid Society*. New York.

Hackett, J. 2004. "Phoenician and Punic." In Woodard, ed., 2004: 365–85.

Hackstein, O. 1997/8. "Sprachgeschichte und Kunstsprache: Der Perfekttyp βεβαρηότες im frühgriechischen Hexameter (und bei späteren Daktylikern)." *Glotta* 74: 21–53.

Hackstein, O. 2002. *Die Sprachform der homerischen Epen. Faktoren morphologischer Variabilität in literarischen Frühformen, Tradition, Sprachwandel, sprachliche Anachronismen.* Wiesbaden.

Hackstein, O. 2006. "La langue poétique indo-européenne: archaïsme et renouvellement dans les théonymes." In Pinault and Petit, eds., 2006: 95–108.

Hackstein, O. 2007. "La paréchèse et les jeux sur les mots chez Homère." In Blanc and Dupraz, eds., 2007: 103–13.

Hagedorn, D., and K. A. Worp. 1980. "Von κύριος zu δεσπότης. Eine Bemerkung zur Kaisertitulatur im 3./4. Jhdt." *ZPE* 39: 165–77.

Hajnal, I. 1995. *Studien zum mykenischen Kasussystem.* Berlin.

Hajnal, I. 1997. *Sprachschichten des mykenischen Griechisch. Zur Frage der Differenzierung zwischen "Mycénien spécial" und "Mycénien normal".* Salamanca.

Hajnal, I. 1998. *Mykenisches und homerisches Lexikon. Übereinstimmungen, Konvergenzen und der Versuch einer Typologie.* Innsbruck.

Hajnal, I. 2003a. "Methodische Vorbemerkungen zu einer Palaeolinguistik des Balkanraums." In A. Bammesberger and Th. Vennemann, eds., *Languages in Prehistoric Europe.* Heidelberg: 117–45.

Hajnal, I. 2003b. *Troia aus sprachwissenschaftlicher Sicht. Die Struktur einer Argumentation.* Innsbruck.

Hajnal, I. 2003c. "Der epische Hexameter im Rahmen der Homer-Troia-Debatte." In Ulf, ed., 2003: 217–31.

Hajnal, I. 2005. "Das Frühgriechische zwischen Balkan und Ägäis. Einheit oder Vielheit?" In G. Meiser and O. Hackstein, eds., *Sprachkontakt und Sprachwandel. Akten der XI. Fachtagung der indogermanischen Gesellschaft, 17.–23. September 2000.* Halle a. d. Saale: 185–214.

Hale, M. 2003. "Neogrammarian Sound Change." In B. D. Joseph and R. D. Janda, eds., *The Handbook of Historical Linguistics.* Malden, MA: 343–68.

Hale, M. 2007. *Historical Linguistics: Theory and Method.* Malden, MA.

Hall, E. 1989. *Inventing the Barbarian: Greek Self-Definition through Tragedy.* Oxford.

Hall, E. 1995. "Law Court Dramas: The Power of Performance in Greek Forensic Oratory." *BICS* 40: 39–58.

Hall, E. 1999. "Actor's Song in Tragedy." In S. Goldhill and R. Osborne, eds., *Performance Culture and Greek Democracy.* Cambridge: 96–122.

Hall, J. 1981. *Lucian's Satire.* New York.

Hallager, E. 1987. "The Inscribed Stirrup Jars: Implications for Late Minoan IIIB Crete." *AJA* 91: 171–90.

Hallager, E. 1996. *The Minoan Roundel and Other Sealed Documents in the Neopalatial Linear A Administration* (*Aegaeum* 14, vols. I–II). Liège.

Halliday, M. A. K. 1978. *Language as Social Semiotic: The Social Interpretation of Language and Meaning.* London.

Halliday, M. A. K., and R. Hasan. 1976. *Cohesion in English.* London.

Halliwell, S. 1986. *Aristotle's Poetics.* Repr. 1998. London.

Halliwell, S. 1988. *Plato, Republic 10: with translation and commentary.* Warminster.

Halliwell, S. 1997. "Between Public and Private: Tragedy and Athenian Experience of Rhetoric." In C. Pelling, ed., *Greek Tragedy and the Historian.* Oxford: 121–41.

Hamm, E.-M. 1957. *Grammatik zu Sappho und Alkaios.* Berlin.

Hansen, D. U., ed. 1998. *Das attizistische Lexikon des Moeris. Quellenkritische Untersuchung und Edition* (*SGLG* 9). Berlin and New York.

Hanson, A. E. 1991. "Ancient Illiteracy." In Beard et al., eds., 1991: 159–98.

Harris, W. V. 1989. *Ancient Literacy*. Cambridge.

Harrison, S. J., ed. 2001. *Texts, Ideas, and the Classics: Scholarship, Theory, and Classical Literature*. Oxford.

Harrison, T. 1998. "Herodotus' Conception of Foreign Languages." *Histos* 2. http://www. dur.ac.uk/Classics/histos/1998/harrison.html.

Harvey, A. E. 1957. "Homeric Epithets in Greek Lyric Poetry." *CQ* 7: 206–23.

Haslam, M. W. 1976. Review of Nagy 1974. *JHS* 96: 202–3.

Hatzidakis, G. N. 1892. *Einleitung in die neugriechische Grammatik*. Leipzig.

Hatzidakis, G. N. 1905–7. Μεσαιωνικὰ καὶ Νέα Ἑλληνικά. Athens.

Haug, D., and E. Welo. 2001. "The Proto-Hexameter Hypothesis: Perspectives for further Research." *SO* 76: 130–6.

Haugen, E. 1950. "The Analysis of Linguistic Borrowing." *Language* 26: 210–31.

Havers, W. 1906. "Das Pronomen der Jener-Deixis im Griechischen." *IF* 19: 1–98.

Hawkins, J. D. 1982. "The Neo-Hittite States in Syria and Anatolia." In J. Boardman et al., eds., *CAH* 3.1, 2nd edn. Cambridge: 372–441.

Hawkins, J. D. 1998. "Tarkasnawa King of Mira, Tarkondemos, Bofiazköy Sealings and Karabel." *Anat. St.* 48: 1–31.

Hawkins, S. 2004. *Studies in the Language of Hipponax*. PhD dissertation, Chapel Hill, NC.

Healey, J. F. 1990. "The Early Alphabet." In *Reading the Past: Ancient Writing from Cuneiform to the Alphabet*. Berkeley: 197–257.

Heath, M. 2004. *Menander: A Rhetor in Context*. Oxford.

Heinimann. F. 1945. *Nomos und Physis. Herkunft und Bedeutung einer Antithese im griechischen Denken des 5. Jahrhunderts*. Darmstadt.

Hellinger, M., and H. Bußmann, eds. 2001–3. *Gender Across Languages: The Linguistic Representation of Women and Men*, 3 vols. Amsterdam and Philadelphia.

Hellweg, R. 1985. *Stilistische Untersuchungen zu den Krankengeschichten der Epidemienbücher I und III des Corpus Hippocraticum*. Bonn.

Henderson, J. 1991. *The Maculate Muse: Obscene Language in Attic Comedy*, 2nd edn. New York and Oxford.

Henriksson, K.-E. 1956. *Griechische Büchertitel in der römischen Literatur*. Helsinki.

Herbermann, C.-P. 1996. "Antike Etymologie." In P. Schmitter, ed., *Sprachtheorien der abendländischen Antike*. Tübingen: 353–76.

Herbst, W. 1911. *Galeni Pergameni de Atticissantium studiis testimonia*. Leipzig.

Hesk, J. 2000. *Deception and Democracy in Classical Athens*. Cambridge.

Hesseling, D. 1903. *Les mots maritimes empruntés par le grec aux langues romanes*. Amsterdam.

Heubeck, A. 1972. "Syllabic *ṛ* in Mycenaean?" In M. S. Ruipérez, ed., *Acta Mycenaea: Proceedings of the Fifth International Colloquium on Mycenaean Studies*, 2. Salamanca: 55–79.

Heubeck, A. 1979. *Schrift*. Göttingen.

Heubeck, A. 1981. "Das Problem der homerischen Kunstsprache." *MH* 38: 65–80.

Heubeck, A. 1986. "Die Würzburger Alphabettafel." *WJA* n.s. 12: 7–20.

Hewlett, E. 1890. "On the Articular Infinitive in Polybius: I." *AJPh* 11: 267–90.

Hidber, T. 1996. *Das klassizistische Manifest des Dionys von Halikarnass. Die Praefatio zu De oratoribus veteribus. Einleitung, Übersetzung, Kommentar*. Stuttgart.

Hiersche, R. 1970. *Grundzüge der griechischen Sprachgeschichte bis zur klassischen Zeit*. Wiesbaden.

Hilgard, A. 1901. *Scholia in Dionysii Thracis artem grammaticam* (*Grammatici Graeci* 1.3). Leipzig.

Hinds, S. 1998. *Allusion and Intertext: Dynamics of Appropriation in Roman Poetry.* Cambridge.

Hinge, G. 2006. *Die Sprache Alkmans. Textgeschichte und Sprachgeschichte.* Wiesbaden.

Hinterberger, M. 2006. "How Should We Define Vernacular Literature?" In *Unlocking the Potential of Texts: Interdisciplinary Perspectives on Medieval Greek.* Cambridge, July 18–19: www.mml.cam.ac.uk/greek/grammarofmedieval greek/unlocking/Hinterberger.pdf.

Hinterberger, M. 2007a. "Die Sprache der byzantinischen Literatur. Der Gebrauch der synthetischen Plusquamperfektformen." In M. Hinterberger and E. Schiffer, eds., *Byzantinische Sprachkunst. Studien zur byzantinischen Literatur gewidmet Wolfram Hörandner zum 65. Geburtstag.* Berlin and New York: 107–142.

Hinterberger, M. 2007b. "»Ich wäre schon längst Mönch geworden, wenn nicht . . .« oder Die Macht des Kontrafaktischen." In K. Belke et al., eds., *Byzantina Mediterranea. Festschrift für Johannes Koder zum 65. Geburtstag.* Vienna: 245–56.

Hock, H. H. 1991. *Principles of Historical Linguistics,* 2nd edn. Berlin and New York.

Hock, H. H., and B. D. Joseph. 1996. *Language History, Language Change, and Language Relationship: An Introduction to Historical Comparative Linguistics.* Berlin and New York.

Hodot, R. 1990. *Le dialecte éolien d'Asie. La langue des inscriptions, VIIe s. a.C.–IVe s. p.C.* Paris.

Hoekstra, A. 1965. *Homeric Modifications of Formulaic Prototypes: Studies in the Development of Greek Epic Diction.* Amsterdam.

Hoenigswald, H. 2004. "Ἑλλήσποντος." In J. H. W. Penney, ed., *Indo-European Perspectives: Studies in Honour of Anna Morpurgo Davies.* Oxford: 179–81.

Hoffmann, C. 1991. *An Introduction to Bilingualism.* London.

Hoffmann, L. 1985. *Kommunikationsmittel Fachsprache. Eine Einführung,* 2nd edn. Tübingen.

Hoffmann, O. 1891–8. *Die griechischen Dialekte in ihrem historischen Zusammenhange mit den wichtigsten ihrer Quellen dargestellt.* 1. Band: *Der süd-achäische Dialekt* (1891); 2. Band: *Der nord-achäische Dialekt* (1893); 3. Band: *Der ionische Dialekt. Quellen und Lautlehre* (1898). Göttingen.

Hoffmann, O, A. Debrunner, and A. Scherer. 1969. *Geschichte der griechischen Sprache.* Berlin.

Høgel, C. 2002. *Symeon Metaphrastes: Rewriting and Canonization.* Copenhagen.

Holford-Strevens, L. A. 1993. "*Utraque lingua doctus*: Some Notes on Bilingualism in the Roman Empire." In H. D. Jocelyn, ed., *Tria Lustra. Essays and Notes Presented to John Pinsent.* Liverpool: 203–13.

Holmes, J. 1998. "Women Talk too Much." In L. Bauer and P. Trudgill, eds., *Language Myths.* Harmondsworth: 41–9.

Holmes, J., and M. Meyerhoff, eds. 2003. *The Handbook of Language and Gender.* Malden, MA.

Holst-Warhaft, G. 1992. *Dangerous Voices: Women's Laments and Greek Literature.* London and New York.

Holton, D. 2002. "Modern Greek: Towards a Standard Language or a New Diglossia?" In M. C. Jones and E. Esch, eds., *The Interplay of Internal, External and Extra-Linguistic Factors.* Berlin and New York: 169–79.

Holton, D. Forthcoming. "The Cambridge Grammar of Medieval Greek Project: Aims, Scope, Research Questions". In G. Mavromatis, ed., *Neograeca Medii Aevi VI,* Ioannina, October 2005.

Holton, D., ed. 1991. *Literature and Society in Renaissance Crete.* Cambridge.

Holton, D., P. Mackridge, and I. Philippaki-Warburton. 1997. *Greek: A Comprehensive Grammar of the Modern Language.* London.

Holton, D., P. Mackridge, and I. Philippaki-Warburton. 2004. *Greek: An Essential Grammar of the Modern Language*. London.

Hooker, J. T. 1968. "Non-Greek Elements in the Linear B Tablets." *IF* 73: 67–86.

Hooker, J. T. 1979. *The Origin of the Linear B Script*. Salamanca.

Hooker, J. T. 1980. *Linear B: An Introduction*. Bristol.

Hooker, J. T. 1988. "The Varieties of Minoan writing." *Cretan Studies* 1: 169–89.

Hopkins, K. 1991. "Conquest by Book." In Beard et al., eds., 1991: 133–58.

Hopkinson, N. 1982. "Juxtaposed Variants in Greek and Latin Poetry." *Glotta* 60: 162–77.

Hopper, P. J., and E. C. Traugott. 1993. *Grammaticalization*. Cambridge.

Hörandner, W., and E. Trapp. 1991. *Lexicographica Byzantina. Beiträge zum Symposion zur byzantinischen Lexikographie (Wien, 1.–4.3.1989)*. Vienna.

Hordern, J. H. 2002. *The Fragments of Timotheus of Miletus*. Oxford.

Horn, W. 1970. *Gebet und Gebetsparodie in den Komödien des Aristophanes*. Nuremberg.

Hornblower, S. 2002. "Herodotus and his Sources of Information." In Bakker, de Jong, and van Wees, eds., 2002: 373–86.

Horrocks, G. C. 1990. "Clitics in Greek: A Diachronic Review." In M. Roussou and S. Panteli, eds., *Greek outside Greece* II. Athens: 35–52.

Horrocks, G. C. 1995. "On Condition: Aspect and Modality." *PCPS* 41: 153–73.

Horrocks, G. C. 1997a. *Greek: A History of the Language and its Speakers*. London.

Horrocks, G. C. 1997b. "Homer's Dialect." In Morris and Powell, eds., 1997: 193–217.

Horsley, G. H. R. 1994. "Papyrology and the Greek Language: A Fragmentary Abecedarius of Desiderata for Future Study." In A. Bülow-Jacobsen, ed., *Proceedings of the 20th International Congress of Papyrologists*. Copenhagen.

Householder, F. W. 1959. "*pa-ro* and Mycenaean Cases." *Glotta* 38: 1–10.

Houwink ten Cate, Ph. H. J. 1961. *The Luwian Population Groups of Lycia and Cilicia Aspera during the Hellenistic Period*. Leiden.

Hubbard, M. E., trans. 1989. "Aristotle, *Poetics*." In D. A. Russell and M. Winterbottom, eds., *Ancient Literary Criticism: The Principal Texts in New Translations*, rev. edn. Oxford.

Hülser, K. 1987–8. *Die Fragmente zur Dialektik der Stoiker*, 4 vols. Stuttgart.

Hülser, K. 1992. "Stoische Sprachphilosophie." In Dascal et al., eds., 1992: 17–34.

Humbert, J. 1930. *La disparition du datif en grec (Du Ier au Xe siècle)*. Paris.

Hummel, P. 1993. *La syntaxe de Pindare*. Louvain and Paris.

Hunger, H. 1978. *Die hochsprachliche profane Literatur der Byzantiner*, 2 vols. Munich.

Hunger, H. 1981. *Anonyme Metaphrase zu Anna Komnene, Alexias XI–XIII. Ein Beitrag zur Erschliessung der byzantinischen Umgangssprache*. Vienna.

Hunger, H., and I. Ševčenko. 1986. *Des Nikephoros Blemmydes Βασιλικὸς Ἀνδριάς und dessen Metaphrase von Georgios Galesiotes und Georgios Oinaiotes. Ein weiterer Beitrag zum Verständnis der byzantinischen Schrift-Koine*. Vienna.

Hunter, R. 2006. "Homer and Greek Literature." In R. L. Fowler, ed., *The Cambridge Companion to Homer*. Cambridge: 235–53.

Hurwit, J. M. 1990. "The Words in the Image: Orality, Literacy, and Early Greek Art." *Word & Image* 6.2: 180–97.

Husson, G. 1982. "'Υπό dans le grec d'Égypte et la préposition égyptienne *ẖr*." *ZPE* 46: 227–30.

Husson, G. 1986. "A propos du mot λόχιον, 'lieu de naissance', attesté dans un papyrus d'Egypte." *Rev. Phil.* 60: 89–94.

Husson, G. 1999. "Κωμαστήριον et quelques termes d'architecture religieuse du grec d'Égypte." In A. Blanc and A. Christol, eds., *Langues en contact dans l'antiquité* (*Études anciennes* 19). Nancy and Paris: 125–30.

Hutchinson, G. O. 2001. *Greek Lyric Poetry: A Commentary on Selected Larger Pieces*. Oxford.

Hymes, D. 1974. *Foundations in Sociolinguistics: An Ethnographic Approach*. Philadelphia.

Ildefonse, F. 1997. *La naissance de la grammaire dans l'antiquité grecque*. Paris.

Immerwahr, H. R. 1971. "A Projected Corpus of Attic Vase Inscriptions." In *Acta of the Fifth International Congress of Greek and Latin Epigraphy, Cambridge, 1967*. Oxford: 53–60.

Immerwahr, H. R. 2006. "Nonsense Inscriptions and Literacy." *Kadmos* 45: 136–72.

Immisch, O., ed. 1927. *Gorgiae Helena*. Berlin and Leipzig.

Inwood, B., ed. 2003. *The Cambridge Companion to the Stoics*. Cambridge.

Isnardi Parente, M., ed. 1982. *Senocrate – Ermodoro: Frammenti*. Naples.

Italie, G. 1964. *Lexicon Aeschyleum*, rev. edn. Leiden.

Jacobsohn, H. 1908. "Der Aoristtyp ἄλτο und die Aspiration bei Homer." *Philol.* 67: 325–65.

Jacobsohn, H. 1909. "Πτολεμαῖος und der Wechsel von anlautendem πτ- und π- im Griechischen." *ZVS* 42: 264–86.

Jacquinod, B., et al., eds. 2000. *Études sur l'aspect verbal chez Platon*. Saint-Étienne.

Jakobson, R. 1960. "Closing Statement: Linguistics and Poetics." In Th. Sebeok, ed., *Style in Language*. Cambridge, MA: 350–77.

Jakobson, R., and L. Waugh. 1979. *The Sound Shape of Language*. Bloomington, IN.

Janko, R. 1992. "The Origins and Evolution of the Epic Diction." In *The Iliad. A Commentary*. Vol. IV: *Books 13–16*. Cambridge: 8–19.

Janko, R. 2000. *Philodemus*, On Poems, Book 1. *Introduction, Translation and Commentary*. Oxford.

Jannaris, A. N. 1897. *An Historical Greek Grammar chiefly of the Attic Dialect*. London. Repr. 1968. Hildesheim.

Janse, M. 1996–7. "Regard sur les études de linguistique byzantine (grec médiéval)." *Orbis* 39: 193–244.

Janse, M. 2000. "Convergence and Divergence in the Development of the Greek and Latin Clitic Pronouns." In R. Sornicola et al., eds., *Stability, Variation and Change of Word-Order Patterns over Time*. Amsterdam: 231–58.

Janse, M. 2002. "Aspects of Bilingualism in the History of the Greek Language." In Adams, Janse, and Swain, eds., 2002: 332–90.

Janse, M. 2007. "The Greek of the New Testament." In Christidis, ed., 2007: 646–53.

Jasanoff, J. H. 2003. *Hittite and the Indo-European Verb*. Oxford and New York.

Jeffery, L. 1990. *The Local Scripts of Archaic Greece: A Study of the Origin of the Greek Alphabet and its Development from the Eighth to the Fifth Centuries BC*, rev. edn., suppl. by A. Johnston. Oxford.

Jeffreys, M., and D. Doulavera. 1998. *Early Modern Greek Literature: General Bibliography (4.000 items) 1100–1700*. Sydney.

Jenkins, R. J. H. 1954. "The Classical Background of the *Scriptores post Theophanem*." *DOP* 8: 11–30.

Jenkins, R. J. H. 1963. "The Hellenistic Origins of Byzantine Literature." *DOP* 17: 37–52.

Jespersen, O. 1922. *Language: Its Nature, Development and Origin*. London.

Jiménez, L. Conti. 1999. "Zur Bedeutung von *tunchano* und *hamartano* bei Homer." *Glotta* 75: 50–62.

Jocelyn, H. D. 1999. "Code-Switching in the *Comoedia Palliata*." In G. Vogt-Spira and B. Rommel, eds., *Rezeption und Identität. Die kulturelle Auseinandersetzung Roms mit Griechenland als europäisches Paradeigma*. Stuttgart: 169–95.

Johnson, C. 1999. "Metaphor vs Conflation in the Acquisition of Polysemy: The Case of *See*." In M. K. Hiraga et al., eds., *Cultural, Psychological, and Typological Issues in Cognitive Linguistics*. Amsterdam: 155–70.

Johnson, J. 2000. *Thus Wrote 'Onchsheshonqy: An Introductory Grammar of Demotic*. Chicago.

Johnston, A. W. 1979. *Trademarks on Greek Vases*. Warminster.

Johnston, A. W. 1983. "The Extent and Use of Literacy; the Archaeological Evidence." In R. Hägg, ed., *The Greek Renaissance of the Eighth Century B.C.: Tradition and Innovation*. Stockholm: 63–8.

Johnston, A. W. 2006. *Trademarks on Greek Vases: Addenda*. Oxford.

Jones, H. S. 1925. "Preface 1925." LSJ: i–xiv.

Jones, R. E. 1986. *Greek and Cypriot Pottery: A Review of Scientific Studies*. Athens.

Joseph, B. 1990. *Morphology and Universals in Syntactic Change: Evidence from Medieval and Modern Greek*. New York.

Joseph, B. 2000. "Textual Authenticity: Evidence from Medieval Greek." In S. Herring et al., eds., *Textual Parameters in Older Languages*. Amsterdam: 309–29.

Joseph, B., and P. Pappas. 2002. "On Some Recent Views Concerning the Development of the Greek Future System." *BMGS* 26: 247–73.

Jouanna, J. 1984. "Rhétorique et médecine dans la Collection hippocratique." *REG* 97: 26–44.

Kahane, H., and R. Kahane. 1982. "The Western Impact on Byzantium: The Linguistic Evidence." *DOP* 36: 127–53.

Kahle, P. 1954. *Bala'izah, Coptic Texts from Deir el-Bala'iza in Upper Egypt*. London.

Kaimio, J. 1979. *The Romans and the Greek Language* (Commentationes Humanarum Litterarum 64). Helsinki.

Kajanto, I. 1963. *A Study of the Greek Epitaphs of Rome* (Acta Instituti Romani Finlandiae II/3). Helsinki.

Kapsomenos, S. G. 1953. "Das Griechische in Ägypten." *MH* 10.3/4: 248–63.

Kapsomenos, S. G. 1985. *Από την ιστορία της ελληνικής γλώσσας. Η ελληνική γλώσσα από τα ελληνιστικά ως τα νεώτερα χρόνια. Η ελληνική γλώσσα στην Αίγυπτο*. Thessaloniki.

Karageorghis, V. 2002. *Early Cyprus: Crossroads of the Mediterranean*. Los Angeles.

Karageorghis, V. 2003. "Heroic Burials in Cyprus and Other Mediterranean Regions." In N. C. Stampolidis and V. Karageorghis, eds., *ΠΛΟΕΣ. Sea Routes: Interconnections in the Mediterranean 16th–6th c. BC*. Athens: 339–51.

Karanastasis, A. 1997. *Γραμματική τῶν ἑλληνικῶν ἰδιωμάτων τῆς Κάτω Ἰταλίας*. Athens.

Kastovsky, D. 1992. "Semantics and Vocabulary." In R. M. Hogg, ed., *The Cambridge History of the English Language*. Vol. 1: *The Beginnings to 1066*. Cambridge: 290–408.

Katsouris, A. G. 1975. *Linguistic and Stylistic Characterization: Tragedy and Menander*. Ioannina.

Katz, J. T. 2003. "Oral Tradition in Linguistics." *Oral Tradition* 18: 261–2.

Katz, J. T. 2005a. "The Indo-European Context." In J. M. Foley, ed., *A Companion to Ancient Epic*. Malden, MA: 20–30.

Katz, J. T. 2005b. Review of Latacz 2004. *JAOS* 125: 422–5.

Katz, J. T. 2006a. "The Origin of the Greek Pluperfect." *Die Sprache* 46 (publ. 2008): 1–37.

Katz, J. T. 2006b. "The Riddle of the *sp(h)ij-*: The Greek Sphinx and her Indic and Indo-European Background." In Pinault and Petit, eds., 2006: 157–94.

Katz, J. T. 2007a. "The Epic Adventures of an Unknown Particle." In C. George et al., eds., *Greek and Latin from an Indo-European Perspective*. Cambridge: 65–79.

Katz, J. T. 2007b. "What Linguists are Good for." *CW* 100: 99–112.

Kavčič, J. 2005. *The Syntax of the Infinitive and the Participle in Early Byzantine Greek*. Ljubljana.

Kazazis, J. N. 2007. "Atticism." In Christidis, ed., 2007: 1200–20.

Kazhdan, A. P. 1984. *Studies on Byzantine Literature of the Eleventh and Twelfth Centuries*, in collaboration with Simon Franklin. Cambridge.

Kazhdan, A. P. 1999. *A History of Byzantine Literature (650–850)*; in collaboration with L. F. Sherry and C. Angelidi. Athens.

Kazhdan, A. P. 2006. *A History of Byzantine literature (850–1000)*, ed. C. Angelidi. Athens.

Kearsley, R. A. 1989. *The Pendent Semi-Circle Skyphos*. London.

Kearsley, R. A. 1999. "Greeks Overseas in the 8th Century B.C." In G. R. Tsetskhladze, ed., *Ancient Greeks, West and East*. Leiden: 109–34.

Kearsley, R. A., and T. V. Evans. 2001. *Greeks and Romans in Imperial Asia: Mixed Language Inscriptions and Linguistic Evidence for Cultural Interaction until the End of AD III (= IK 59)*. Bonn.

Key, M. R. 1975. *Male/Female Language. With a Comprehensive Bibliography*. Metuchen, NJ (2nd edn., Lanham, NJ 1996).

Kieckers, E. 1912. "Die Stellung der Verba des Sagens in Schaltesätzen im Griechischen und in verwandten Sprachen." *IF* 30: 145–85.

Kieckers, E. 1913. "Zu den Schaltesätzen im Lateinischen, Romanischen und Neuhochdeutschen." *IF* 32: 7–23.

Killen, J. T. 2006. "Thoughts on the Functions of the New Thebes Tablets." In S. Deger-Jalkotzy and O. Panagl, eds., *Die neuen Linear B-Texte aus Theben*. Vienna.

Kim, C.-H. 1985. *Form and Structure of the Familiar Greek Letter of Recommendation*. Ann Arbor, MI .

Kirchhoff, A. 1877. *Studien zur Geschichte des griechischen Alphabets*. Berlin.

Kissilier, M. 2004. "Κλιτικές προσωπικές αντωνυμίες στο Λειμωνάριον του Ιωάννου Μόσχου." *Proceedings of the 6th International Conference in Greek Linguistics, Rethymno 18–21 Sept. 2003*: www.philology.uoc.gr/conferences/6thICGL/ebook/h/kissilier.pdf.

Klaffenbach, G. 1966. *Griechische Epigraphik*, 2nd edn. Göttingen.

Kleinknecht, H. 1937. *Die Gebetsparodie in der Antike*. Stuttgart and Berlin.

Koller, H. 1955. "Stoicheion." *Glotta* 34: 161–74.

Konstantinidis, A., and X. Moschos, eds. and trans. 1907–95. Μέγα Λεξικόν τῆς ἑλληνικῆς γλώσσης. Athens.

Kontosopoulos, N. G. 1994. Διάλεκτοι και ιδιώματα της νέας Ελληνικής. Athens.

Koskenniemi, H. 1956. *Studien zur Idee und Phraseologie des griechischen Briefes bis 400 n. Chr.* Helsinki.

Kosman, L. A. 1975. "Perceiving that We Perceive: *On the Soul* III, 2." *Philosophical Review* 84.4: 499–519.

Kourou, N. 2003. "Rhodes: The Phoenician Issue Revisited." In N. C. Stampolidis and V. Karageorghis, eds., ΠΛΟΕΣ. *Sea Routes: Interconnections in the Mediterranean 16th–6th c. BC*. Athens: 249–62.

Kramarae, C. 1982. "Gender: How She Speaks." In E. Bouchard Ryan and H. Giles, eds., *Attitudes Towards Language Variation: Social and Applied Contexts*. London: 84–98.

Kramer, B. 1991. "Das Vertragregister von Theogenis." *Corpus Papyrorum Raineri*, vol. 18, *Griechische Texte* 13. Vienna: 69–70.

Kranz, W. 1933. *Stasimon. Untersuchungen zur Form und Gehalt der griechischen Tragödie*. Berlin.

Kraus, T. J. 1999. "'Slow Writers' – βραδέως γράφοντες: What, How Much, and How did they Write." *Eranos* 97: 86–97.

Kretschmer, P. 1909. "Zur Geschichte der griechischen Dialekte." *Glotta* 1: 1–59.

Kriaras, E., ed. 1967–. Λεξικό της Μεσαιωνικής Ελληνικής Δημώδους Γραμματείας (1100–1669), 18 vols. Thessaloniki.

Kroll, J. H. 2008. "Early Iron Age Balance Weights at Lefkandi, Euboea." *OJA* 27: 37–48.

Kroll, W. 1907. "Randbemerkungen." *Rh. Mus.* 62: 86–101.

Kuhn, A. 1853a. "Über das alte S und einige damit verbundene Lautentwicklungen. Vierter artikel. Die Verbindung des σ mit liquiden Buchstaben." *ZVS* 2: 260–75.

Kuhn, A. 1853b. "Über die durch Nasale erweiterten Verbalstämme." *ZVS* 2: 455–71.

Kurzová, H. 1968. *Zur syntaktischen Struktur des Griechischen: Infinitiv und Nebensatz.* Amsterdam.

La Roche, J. 1869. *Homerische Untersuchungen.* Leipzig.

La Roche, J. 1895. "Metrische Excurse zu Homer." *WS* 17: 165–79.

Laiou, A., and C. Morrisson. 2007. *The Byzantine Economy.* Cambridge.

Lakoff, G. 1987. *Women, Fire, and Dangerous Things: What Categories Reveal about the Mind.* Chicago.

Lakoff, R. 1973. "Language and Woman's Place." *Language in Society* 2: 45–80.

Lakoff, R. 1975. *Language and Woman's Place.* New York.

Lakoff, R. 2004. *Language and Woman's Place: Text and Commentaries,* ed. M. Bucholtz. New York.

Lallot, J. 1997. *Apollonius Dyscole. De la construction.* Paris.

Lallot, J. 1998. *La grammaire de Denys le Thrace,* 2nd edn. Paris.

Lambert, P. Y. 1994. *La langue gauloise.* Paris.

Lambert, R. D., and B. F. Freed, eds., 1982. *The Loss of Language Skills.* Rowley, MA.

Lampe, G. W. H. 1969. *A Patristic Greek Lexicon.* Oxford.

Lang, M. L. 1990. *Ostraka* (The Athenian Agora 25). Princeton.

Langholf, V. 1977. *Syntaktische Untersuchungen zu Hippokrates-Texten.* Wiesbaden.

Langslow, D. R. 2000. *Medical Latin in the Roman Empire.* Oxford.

Langslow, D. R. 2002. "Approaching Bilingualism in Corpus Languages." In Adams, Janse, and Swain, eds., 2002: 23–51.

Lanza, D. 1983. "Quelques remarques sur le travail linguistique du médecin." In F. Lasserre and P. Mudry, eds., *Formes de pensée dans la Collection hippocratique.* Geneva: 181–5.

Lardinois, A., and L. McClure, eds. 2001. *Making Silence Speak: Women's Voices in Greek Literature and Society.* Princeton.

Laroche, E. 1966. *Les noms des Hittites.* Paris.

Lasserre, F. 1979. "Prose grecque classicisante." In H. Flashar, ed., *Le classicisme à Rome aux Iers siècles avant et après J.-C.* Geneva: 135–63.

Latacz, J. 1998. "Zu Umfang und Art der Vergangenheitsbewahrung in der mündlichen Überlieferungsphase des griechischen Heldenepos." In J. von Ungern-Sternberg and H. Reinau, eds., *Vergangenheit in mündlicher Überlieferung.* Stuttgart: 153–83.

Latacz, J. 2000. "Formelhaftigkeit und Mündlichkeit." In Latacz et al. 2000: 39–59.

Latacz, J. 2001. *Troia und Homer. Der Weg zur Lösung eines alten Rätsels.* Munich and Berlin.

Latacz, J. 2003a. *Homer. Der erste Dichter des Abendlands,* 4th edn. Düsseldorf and Zürich.

Latacz, J. 2003b. *Homers Ilias. Gesamtkommentar. Band II: Zweiter Gesang* (B)*; Faszikel 2: Kommentar.* Munich.

Latacz, J. 2004. *Troy and Homer: Towards a Solution of an Old Mystery.* Oxford.

Latacz, J., et al. 2000. *Homer Ilias Gesamtkommentar. Prolegomena.* Leipzig.

Latte, K. 1915. "Zur Zeitbestimmung des Antiatticista." *Hermes* 50: 373–94.

Laum, B. 1928. *Das alexandrinische Akzentuationssystem unter Zugrundelegung der theoretischen Lehren der Grammatiker und mit Heranziehung der praktischen Verwendung in den Papyri.* Paderborn.

Law, V. 2003. *The History of Linguistics in Europe: From Plato to 1600.* Cambridge.

Layton, B. 2004. *Coptic Grammar. With Chrestomathy and Glossary: Sahidic Dialect,* Wiesbaden.

Lazzarini, M. L. 1977. "Le formule delle dediche votive nella Grecia arcaica." *Memorie della Accademia nazionale dei Lincei, classe di scienze morali, storiche e filologiche* ser. 8, 19: 47–354.

Lebeck, A. 1971. *The Oresteia: A Study in Language and Structure*. Washington, DC.

Legrand, E. 1874. Νικολάου Σοφιανοῦ τοῦ Κερκυραίου, Γραμματικὴ τῆς κοινῆς τῶν Ἑλλήνων γλώσσης. Paris.

Leiwo, M. 1995. "The Mixed Languages in Roman Inscriptions." In Solin et al., eds., 1995: 293–301.

Lejeune, M. 1971. *Mémoires de philologie mycénienne, deuxième série*. Rome.

Lejeune, M. 1972a. *Mémoires de philologie mycénienne, troisième série*. Rome.

Lejeune, M. 1972b. *Phonétique historique du mycénien et du grec ancien*. Paris.

Lemerle, P. 1971. *Le premier humanisme byzantin*. Paris.

Lemon, L. T., and M. J. Reis. 1965. *Russian Formalist Criticism: Four Essays*. Lincoln, NB.

Lendari, T., and I. Manolessou. 2003. "Η εκφορά του έμμεσου αντικειμένου στα μεσαιωνικά ελληνικά. Γλωσσολογικά και εκδοτικά προβλήματα." In *Studies in Greek Linguistics* 23. Thessaloniki: 394–405.

Lendle, O. 1967. "Cicero's ὑπόμνημα τῆς ὑπατείας." *Hermes* 95: 90–109.

Lennox, J. G. 2001. *Aristotle's Philosophy of Biology*. Cambridge.

Lepre, M. Z. 1979. *L'interiezione vocativale nei poemi omerici*. Rome.

Leumann, M. 1950. *Homerische Wörter*. Basel. Repr. 1993. Darmstadt.

Levick, B. 1967. *Roman Colonies in Southern Asia Minor*. Oxford.

Levick, B. 1995. "The Latin Inscriptions of Asia Minor." In Solin et al., eds., 1995: 393–402.

Levinson, S. C. 1983. *Pragmatics*. Cambridge.

Lewis, N. 1993. "The Demise of the Demotic Document: When and Why." *JEg. Arch.* 79: 276–81.

Lewis, N. 1999. *Life in Egypt under Roman Rule* (Classics in Papyrology 1). Oakville.

Lewis, N. 2001. *Greeks in Ptolemaic Egypt: Case Studies in the Social History of the Hellenistic World* (Classics in Papyrology 2). Oakville.

Lexiko. 1998. Λεξικό τῆς κοινῆς νεοελληνικῆς. Thessaloniki.

Liakos, A. 2007. "'From Greek into our Common Language': Language and History in the Making of Modern Greece." In Christidis, ed., 2007: 1287–95.

Liddell, H. G., and G. Scott. 1847. *A Greek–English Lexicon*. Oxford.

Liddell, H. G., and G. Scott. 1891. *A Greek–English Lexicon*, abridged edn. Oxford.

Lightfoot, J., ed. 1999. *Parthenius of Nicaea*. Oxford.

Lilja, S. 1968. *On the Style of the Earliest Greek Prose* (Commentationes Humanarum Litterarum 41.3). Helsinki.

Lissarrague, F. 1987. *Un flot d'images: une esthétique du banquet grec*. Paris.

Lloyd, G. E. R. 1979. *Magic, Reason, and Experience: Studies in the Origin and Development of Greek Science*. Cambridge.

Lloyd, G. E. R. 1983. *Science, Folklore, and Ideology: Studies in the Life Sciences in Ancient Greece*. Cambridge.

Lloyd, G. E. R. 2003. *In the Grip of Disease: Studies in the Greek Imagination*. Oxford.

Lloyd, M. 1992. *The Agon in Euripides*. Oxford.

Lloyd-Jones, H., and N. G. Wilson. 1990. *Sophoclea*. Oxford.

Long, A. A. 1968. *Language and Thought in Sophocles*. London.

Long, A. A., and D. N. Sedley. 1987. *The Hellenistic Philosophers*. Cambridge.

López Eire, A. 1991. *Atico, koiné y aticismo*. Murcia.

López Eire, A. 1996. *La lengua coloquial de la Comedia aristofánica*. Murcia.

López Férez, J. A. 2000. "Algunos datos sobre el léxico de los tratados hipocráticos." In J. A. López Férez, ed., *La lengua científica griega: orígenes, desarrollo e influencia en las lenguas modernas europeas*, 1. Madrid: 39–51.

Loprieno, A. 1995. *Ancient Egyptian: A Linguistic Introduction.* Cambridge.

Loprieno, A. 2004. "Ancient Egyptian and Coptic." In Woodard, ed., 2004: 160–217.

Lowry, M. 1979. *The World of Aldus Manutius.* Oxford.

Lucy, J. 1992. *Language Diversity and Thought: A Reformulation of the Linguistic Diversity Hypothesis.* Cambridge.

Lüddekens, E. 1980. "Ägypten." In G. Neumann and J. Untermann, eds., *Die Sprachen im Römischen Reich der Kaiserzeit.* Cologne and Bonn: 241–65.

Lüdtke, H. 1969. "Die Alphabetschrift und das Problem der Lautsegmentierung." *Phonetica* 20: 147–76.

Ludwich, A. 1885. *Aristarchs Homerische Textkritik nach den Fragmenten des Didymos dargestellt und beurteilt.* Zweiter Theil. Leipzig.

Lupaş, L. 1972. *Phonologie du grec attique.* The Hague and Paris.

Luria, S. 1957. "Über die Nominaldeklination in den mykenischen Inschriften." *PP* 12: 321–32.

Luzzatto, J. M. 2002–3. "Grammata e syrmata. Scrittura greca e produzione libraria tra VII e IX secolo." *Analecta Papyrologica* 14–15: 1–85.

Maas, P. 1912. "Metrische Akklamationen der Byzantiner". *BZ* 21: 28–51.

Mackridge, P. 1985. *The Modern Greek Language.* Oxford.

Mackridge, P. 1996. "The Medieval Greek Infinitive in the Light of Dialectal Evidence." In Konstantinides, K., et al., eds., *ΦΙΛΕΛΛΗΝ: Studies in Honour of R. Browning.* Venice: 191–204.

Mackridge, P. 2000. "The Position of the Weak Object Pronoun in Medieval and Modern Greek." *Yazyk i rechevaya deyatel'nost'* 3: 133–51.

Mackridge, P. 2009. *Language and National Identity in Greece, 1766–1976.* Oxford.

Macleod, C. W. 1983. *Collected Essays.* Oxford.

Madden, T. F. 1992. "The Fires of the Fourth Crusade in Constantinople, 1203–1204: A Damage Assessment." *BZ* 84–5: 72–93.

Maehler, H. 1983. "Die griechische Schule im ptolemäischen Ägypten." In Van 't Dack et al., eds., 1983: 191–203.

Maehler, H. 2004. *Bacchylides: A Selection.* Cambridge.

Magdalino, P. 1993. *The Empire of Manuel I Komnenos.* Cambridge.

Magdalino, P. 2006. *L'orthodoxie des astrologues.* Paris.

Magnelli, E. 1996. "Studi recenti sull'origine dell'esametro: Un profilo critico." In M. Fantuzzi and R. Pretagostini, eds., *Struttura e storia dell'esametro greco,* vol. 2. Rome: 111–37.

Magnien, V. 1922. "Emploi des démonstratifs chez Homère." *BSLP* 23: 156–83.

Malinowski, B. 1923. "The Problem of Meaning in Primitive Languages." In C. K. Ogden and I. A. Richards, *The Meaning of Meaning: A Study of the Influence of Language upon Thought and of the Science of Symbolism.* London and New York: 451–510 (10th edn: London, 1949: 296–336).

Mallory, J. P. 1989. *In Search of the Indo-Europeans: Language, Archaeology and Myth.* London.

Mallory, J. P. 1991. "Kurgan and Indo-European Fauna III: Birds." *JIES* 19: 223–34.

Mallory, J. P., and D. Q. Adams. 2006. *The Oxford Introduction to Proto-Indo-European and the Proto-Indo-European World.* Oxford.

Mallory, J. P., and D. Q. Adams, eds. 1997. *Encyclopedia of Indo-European Culture.* London.

Maloney, E. C. 1981. *Semitic Interference in Marcan Syntax.* Chico, CA.

Mandilaras, B. 1973. *The Verb in the Greek Non-Literary Papyri.* Athens.

Mango, C. 1971. "The Availability of Books in the Byzantine Empire, A.D. 750–850." In *Byzantine Books and Bookmen.* Washington, DC: 29–45.

Mango, C. 1977a. "The Liquidation of Iconoclasm and the Patriarch Photios." In Bryer and Herrin, eds., 1977: 133–40.

Mango, C. 1977b. "L'origine de la minuscule." In *La paléographie grecque et byzantine*. Paris: 175–80.

Mango, C. 1991. "Greek Culture in Palestine after the Arab Conquest." In Cavallo et al., eds., 1991: 149–60.

Mangoni, C. 1993. *Filodemo: Il quinto libro della Poetica (PHerc. 1425 e 1538)*. Naples.

Manolessou, I. 2005. "From Participles to Gerunds." In M. Stavrou and A. Terzi, eds., *Advances in Greek Generative Syntax*. Amsterdam: 241–83.

Manolessou, I. 2008. "On Historical Linguistics, Linguistic Variation and Medieval Greek". *BMGS* 32: 63–79.

Manolessou, I., and N. Toufexis. 2009. "Phonetic Change in Medieval Greek: Focus on Liquid Interchange." *Proceedings of the 8th International Conference on Greek Linguistics, Ioannina, August 30–September 2, 2007* www. linguist-uoi.gr/app/webroot/cd_web/.

Mansfeld, J. 1986. "Diogenes Laertius on Stoic Philosophy." *Elenchos* 7: 295–382.

Mansour, K. 2007. "Séquences dactyliques dans la prose d'Hérodote. Hexamètres, homérismes, formules." In Blanc and Dupraz, eds., 2007: 151–62.

Markopoulos, A. 2004. "New Evidence of the Date of Photios' *Bibliotheca*." In *History and Literature of Byzantium in the 9th–10th Centuries*. Aldershot.

Markopoulos, A. 2006. "De la structure de l'école byzantine. Le maître, les livres et le processus éducatif." In B. Mondrain, ed., *Lire et écrire à Byzance*. Paris: 85–96.

Markopoulos, A., ed. 2000. *Anonymi professoris epistulae*. Berlin and New York.

Markopoulos, Th. 2007. "Γραμματικοποίηση και γλωσσική ποικιλία: ο μέλλοντας στην εποχή της Κρητικής «Αναγέννησης» (16ος–17ος αι.)." *Studies in Greek Linguistics 27. Proceedings of the Annual Meeting of the Department of Linguistics, Aristotle University of Thessaloniki*, 251–63.

Markopoulos, Th. 2009. *The Future in Greek: From Ancient to Medieval*. Oxford.

Marrou, H.-I. 1965. *Histoire de l'éducation dans l'antiquité*, 6th edn. Paris.

Masson, É. 1967. *Recherches sur les plus anciens emprunts sémitiques en grec*. Paris.

Masson, O. 1983. *Les inscriptions chypriotes syllabiques*. Paris.

Mastronarde, D. J. 2002. *Euripides, Medea*. Cambridge.

Matasović, R. 1996. *A Theory of Textual Reconstruction in Indo-European Linguistics*. Frankfurt.

Mathiesen, T. J. 1999. *Apollo's Lyre: Greek Music and Music Theory in Antiquity and the Middle Ages*. Lincoln, NB.

Matthaios, S. 1999. *Untersuchungen zur Grammatik Aristarchs. Texte und Interpretation zur Wortartenlehre*. Göttingen.

Matthaios, S. 2002. "Neue Perspektiven für die Historiographie der antiken Grammatik: Das Wortartensystem der Alexandriner." In Swiggers and Wouters, eds., 2002: 161–220.

Mayser, E. 1906–. *Grammatik der griechischen Papyri der Ptolemäerzeit*. Leipzig.

McCabe, D. F. 1981. *The Prose-Rhythm of Demosthenes*. New York.

McCarter, P. K. 1975. *The Antiquity of the Greek Alphabet and the Early Phoenician Scripts*. Missoula, MT.

McCarter, P. K. 2004. "Hebrew." In Woodard, ed., 2004: 317–64.

McClure, L. 1999. *Spoken like a Woman: Speech and Gender in Athenian Drama*. Princeton.

McCormick, M. 1985. "The Birth of the Codex and Apostolic Lifestyle." *Scriptorium* 39: 150–8.

McCoskey, D. E. 2002. "Race before 'Whiteness': Studying Identity in Ptolemaic Egypt." *Critical Sociology* 28: 13–39.

McCoskey, D. E. 2004. "On Black Athena, Hippocratic Medicine and Roman Imperial Edicts: Egyptians and the Problem of Race in Classical Antiquity." In R. D. Coates, ed., *Race and Ethnicity: Across Time, Space, and Discipline*. Leiden: 297–330.

McLean, B. H. 2002. *An Introduction to Greek Epigraphy of the Hellenistic and Roman Periods from Alexander the Great down to the Reign of Constantine (323 BC–AD 337)*. Ann Arbor.

McLynn, N. 2009. "The Manna From Uncle: Basil of Caesarea's *Address to Young Men*." In R. Flower, C. Kelly, and M. Williams, eds., *Unclassical Traditions*. Cambridge: 54–72.

Meid, W. 1978. *Dichter und Dichtkunst in indogermanischer Zeit*. Innsbruck.

Meier-Brügger, M. 1986. "Homerisch μευ oder μοι?" In A. Etter, ed., *o-o-pe-ro-si. Festschrift für Ernst Risch zum 75. Geburtstag*. Berlin and New York: 346–54.

Meier-Brügger, M. 1992. *Griechische Sprachwissenschaft*. Berlin.

Meier-Brügger, M. 2003a. "Die homerische Kunstsprache." In Ulf, ed., 2003: 232–44.

Meier-Brügger, M. 2003b. *Indo-European Linguistics*. Berlin and New York.

Meillet, A. 1913. *Aperçu d'une histoire de la langue grecque*. Paris.

Meillet, A. 1923. *Les origines indo-européennes des mètres grecs*. Paris.

Meillet, A. 1975. *Aperçu d'une histoire de la langue grecque. Avec bibliographie mise à jour et complétée par O. Masson*, 8th edn. Paris.

Meillet, A. 1977. *Esquisse d'une histoire de la langue latine. Avec bibliographie mise à jour et complétée par J. Perrot*. Paris.

Meissner, T. 2007. "Notes on Mycenaean Spelling." *PCPS (CCJ)* 53: 96–111.

Meister, K. 1921. *Die homerische Kunstsprache*. Leipzig.

Meister, R. 1882–9. *Die griechischen Dialekte auf Grundlage von Ahrens' Werk: "De graecae linguae dialectis". 1. Band: Asiatisch-Äolisch, Boötisch, Thessalisch* (1882); *2. Band: Eleisch, Arkadisch, Kyprisch* (1889). Göttingen.

Melchert, H. C., ed. 2003. *The Luwians*. Leiden and Boston.

Melena, J. L. 1983. "Further Thoughts on Mycenaean *o-pa*." In A. Heubeck and G. Neumann, eds., *Res Mycenaeae*. Göttingen: 258–86.

Melena, J. L., and J.-P. Olivier. 1991. *TITHEMY. The Tablets and Nodules in Linear B from Tiryns, Thebes and Mycenae*. Suppl. *Minos* 12. Salamanca.

Mellink, M. J., ed. 1986. *Troy and the Trojan War: A Symposium Held at Bryn Mawr College, October 1984*. Bryn Mawr, PA.

Mette, H. J. 1952. *Parateresis. Untersuchungen zur Sprachtheorie des Krates von Pergamon*. Saale.

Meyer, G. 1923. *Die stilistische Verwendung der Nominalkomposition im Griechischen*. Leipzig.

Meyer, H. 1933. *Hymnische Stilelemente in der frühgriechischen Dichtung*. Würzburg.

Mickey, K. 1981. "Dialect Consciousness and Literary Language: An Example from Ancient Greek." *TPS*, 35–65.

Miklosich, F. 1870. "Die slavischen Elemente im Neugriechischen." *Sitzungsberichte der ph.-hist. Klasse der kaiserl. Akad. der Wissenschaften* 63: 529–66.

Millar, F. G. B. 1995. "Latin in the Epigraphy of the Roman Near East." In Solin et al., eds., 1995: 403–19.

Minon, S. 2007. *Les inscriptions éléennes dialectales (VIᵉ–IIᵉ siècle avant J.-C.)*, 3 vols. Geneva.

Mirambel, A. 1961. "Participe et gérondif en grec médiéval et moderne." *BSLP* 56: 46–79.

Mitteis, L., and U. Wilcken. 1912. *Grundzüge und Chrestomathie der Papyruskunde*, Bd. 1: *Historischer Teil*, 2. Hälfte: *Chrestomathie*. Leipzig and Berlin.

Moatti, C. 1997. *La raison de Rome. Naissance de l'esprit critique à la fin de la République*. Paris.

Moffatt, A. 1977. "Schooling in the Iconoclast Centuries." In Bryer and Herrin, eds., 1977: 85–92.

Monro, D. B., and T. W. Allen, eds. 1920. *Homeri Opera* I–II, 3rd edn. Oxford.

Montevecchi, O. 1957. "Dal paganesimo al Cristianesimo: aspetti dell'evoluzione della lingua greca nei papiri dell'Egitto." *Aegyptus* 37: 41–59. Also in Montevecchi 1999: 69–95.

Montevecchi, O. 1964. "Continuità ed evoluzione della lingua greca nella Settanta e nei papiri." *Actes du X* *Congrès international de papyrologues, Varsovie*: 39–49. Also in Montevecchi 1999: 121–33.

Montevecchi, O. 1996. "La lingua dei papiri e quella della versione dei LXX: Due realtà che se illuminano a vicenda." *Annali di Scienze Religiose* 1: 71–80.

Montevecchi, O. 1999. *Bibbia e papiri. Luce dai papiri sulla Bibbia greca*, a cura di A. Passoni Dell'Acqua. Barcelona.

Montevecchi, O. 2001. "Ioni nati in Egitto. La parabola della grecità nella valle del Nilo." *Atti del XXII Congresso Internazionale di Papirologia, Firenze 1998*. Florence: 983–94.

Moorhouse, A. C. 1959. *Studies in the Greek Negatives*. Cardiff.

Moorhouse, A. C. 1982. *The Syntax of Sophocles*. Leiden.

Moravcsik, Gy. 1943. *Byzantinoturcica 2. Sprachreste der Türkvölker in den Byzantinischen Quellen*. Budapest.

Moreau, Ph. 1995. "Paroles des hommes, paroles des femmes." In F. Dupont, ed., *Paroles romaines*. Nancy: 53–63.

Moretti, L. 1967–76. *Iscrizioni storiche ellenistiche* (Biblioteca di studi superiori 53 and 62). Florence.

Morgan, G. 1983. "Butz Triads: Towards a Grammar of Folk Poetry." *Folklore* 94: 44–56.

Morpurgo Davies, A. 1960. "Il genitivo miceneo e el sincretismo dei casi." *RANL* 15: 33–61.

Morpurgo Davies, A. 1966. "An Instrumental-Ablative in Mycenaean?" In Palmer and Chadwick, eds., 1966: 191–202.

Morpurgo Davies, A. 1985. "Mycenaean and Greek Language." In A. Morpurgo Davies and Y. Duhoux, eds., *Linear B. A 1984 Survey*. Louvain-la-Neuve: 75–125.

Morpurgo Davies, A. 1986. "The Linguistic Evidence: Is there Any?" In G. Cadogan, ed., *The End of the Early Bronze Age in the Aegean*. Leiden: 93–123.

Morpurgo Davies, A. 1987a. "Mycenaean and Greek Syllabification." In P. Ilievski and L. Crepajac, eds., *Tractata Mycenaea*. Skopje: 91–103.

Morpurgo Davies, A. 1987b. "The Greek Notion of Dialect." *Verbum* 10: 7–28. Repr. T. Harrison, ed., *Greeks and Barbarians*. London, 2002: 153–71.

Morpurgo Davies, A. 1987c. "Folk-Linguistics and the Greek Word." In G. Cardona and N.H. Zide, eds., *Festschrift for Henry Hoenigswald*. Tübingen: 263–80.

Morpurgo Davies, A. 2003. "Greek Language." *OCD*[3]: 653–6.

Morris, I., and B. Powell, eds. 1997. *A New Companion to Homer*. Leiden.

Morris, S. 1997. "Homer and the Near East." In Morris and Powell, eds., 1997: 599–623.

Morwood, J., and J. Taylor. 2002. *Pocket Oxford Classical Greek Dictionary*. Oxford.

Moser, A. 1988. *The History of the Perfect Periphrases in Greek*. PhD dissertation, University of Cambridge.

Mosley, D. J. 1971. "Greeks, Barbarians, Language and Contact." *Ancient Society* 2: 1–6.

Mountford, J. F., and R. P. Winnington-Ingram. 1970. "Music." In *OCD*[2]: 705–13.

Mourgues, J.-L. 1995. "Écrire en deux langues: bilinguisme et pratique de chancellerie sous le Haut-Empire." *DHA* 21: 105–29.

Moussy, C. 1969. *Recherches sur trepho*. Paris.

Moysiadis, Th. 2005. Ετυμολογία. Εισαγωγή στη μεσαιωνική και νεοελληνική ετυμολογία. Athens.

Mugler, Ch. 1958. *Dictionnaire historique de la terminologie géométrique des Grecs*. Paris.

Müller, C. W., K. Sier, and J. Werner, eds. 1992. *Zum Umgang mit fremden Sprachen in der griechisch-römischen Antike* (Palingenesia 36). Stuttgart.

Mullett, M. 1984. "Aristocracy and Patronage in the Literary Circles of Comnenian Constantinople." In M. Angold, ed., *The Byzantine Aristocracy: IX–XIII Centuries.* Oxford: 173–201.

Mumm, P.-A. 2004. "Zur Funktion des homerischen Augments." In *Analecta homini universali dicata. Festschrift für Oswald Panagl zum 65. Geburtstag,* 1.148–58. Stuttgart.

Munson, R. V. 2005. *Black Doves Speak: Herodotus and the Languages of Barbarians.* Washington, DC and Cambridge, MA.

Murray, A. T. 1999. *Homer, Iliad: Books 1–12,* rev. W. F. Wyatt. Cambridge, MA.

Murray, O. 1993. *Early Greece,* 2nd edn. Cambridge, MA.

Myres, J. L. 1933. "The Amathus Bowl: A Long-Lost Masterpiece of Oriental Engraving." *JHS* 53: 25–39.

Nabrings, K. 1981. *Sprachliche Varietäten.* Tübingen.

Nagy, G. 1963. "Greek-Like Elements in Linear A." *GRBS* 4: 181–211.

Nagy, G. 1968. "On Dialectal Anomalies in the Pylian Texts." *Atti e memorie del 1° Congresso internazionale di micenologia (Roma, 27 IX–3 X, 1967).* Rome: 663–79.

Nagy, G. 1970. *Greek Dialects and the Transformation of an Indo-European Process.* Cambridge, MA.

Nagy, G. 1972. Introduction, Parts I and II, and Conclusions. In F. W. Householder and G. Nagy, *Greek: A Survey of Recent Work* (Janua Linguarum Series Practica, 211). The Hague: 15–72.

Nagy, G. 1974. *Comparative Studies in Greek and Indic Meter* (Harvard Studies in Comparative Literature 33). Cambridge, MA.

Nagy, G. 1979. *The Best of the Achaeans: Concepts of the Hero in Archaic Greek Poetry.* Baltimore (rev. edn. 1999).

Nagy, G. 1990a. *Pindar's Homer: The Lyric Possession of an Epic Past.* Baltimore.

Nagy, G. 1990b. *Greek Mythology and Poetics.* Ithaca.

Nagy, G. 1996. *Poetry as Performance: Homer and Beyond.* Cambridge.

Nagy, G. 1998. "Is There an Etymology for the Dactylic Hexameter?" In J. Jasanoff, H. C. Melchert, and L. Oliver, eds., *Mír Curad: Studies in Honor of Calvert Watkins.* Innsbruck: 495–508. Rewritten as ch. 8 in Nagy 2004.

Nagy, G. 1999. "Epic as Genre." In M. Beissinger, J. Tylus, and S. Wofford, eds., *Epic Traditions in the Contemporary World: The Poetics of Community.* Berkeley and Los Angeles: 21–32.

Nagy, G. 2000. "Reading Greek Poetry Aloud: Evidence from the Bacchylides Papyri." *QUCC* 64: 7–28.

Nagy, G. 2002. *Plato's Rhapsody and Homer's Music: The Poetics of the Panathenaic Festival in Classical Athens.* Washington, DC.

Nagy, G. 2004. *Homer's Text and Language.* Urbana and Chicago.

Nagy, G. 2009. "Traces of an Ancient System of Reading Homeric Verse in the Venetus A." In Dué, ed., 2009: 133–57.

Naveh, J. 1973. "Some Semitic Epigraphical Considerations on the Antiquity of the Greek Alphabet." *AJA* 77: 1–8.

Naveh, J. 1987. *Early History of the Alphabet,* 2nd edn. Jerusalem.

Naveh, J. 1991. "Semitic Epigraphy and the Antiquity of the Greek Alphabet." *Kadmos* 30: 143–52.

Negbi, O. 1992. "Early Phoenician Presence in the Mediterranean Islands: A Reappraisal." *AJA* 96: 599–615.

Nehrbass, R. 1935. *Sprache und Stil der Iamata von Epidauros.* Leipzig.

Németh, A. Forthcoming. "Imperial Systematisation of the Roman Past: The Historical Excerpts Commissioned by Emperor Constantine VII (945–59)." In *Encyclopaedism before the Enlightenment: Proceedings of the Conference, St Andrews, June 13–15, 2007.* Cambridge.

Nesselrath, H.-G. 1997. *Einleitung in die griechische Philologie.* Stuttgart and Leipzig.

Nettl, B. 1965. *Folk and Traditional Music of the Western Continents.* Englewood Cliffs NJ.

Netz R. 1999. *The Shaping of Deduction in Greek Mathematics: A Study in Cognitive History.* Cambridge.

Netz R. 2007. *The Archimedes Codex.* London.

Neumann, G. 1961. *Untersuchungen zum Weiterleben hethitischen und luwischen Sprachgutes in hellenistischer und römischer Zeit.* Wiesbaden.

Neumann, G. 1988. *Phrygisch und Griechisch.* Vienna.

Newton, B. 1972. *The Generative Interpretation of Dialect: A Study of Modern Greek Phonology.* Cambridge.

Nicolas, C. 2005. Sic enim appello . . . *Essai sur l'autonymie terminologique gréco-latine chez Cicéron.* Louvain and Paris.

Niehoff-Panagiotidis, J. 1994. *Koine und Diglossie.* Wiesbaden.

Niemeier, W.-D. 2001. "Archaic Greeks in the Orient: Textual and Archaeological Evidence." *BASOR* 322: 11–32.

Nikiforidou, K. 1996. "Modern Greek ας: A Case Study in Grammaticalization and Grammatical Polysemy." *Studies in Language* 20.3: 599–632.

Norden, E. 1923. *Agnostos Theos. Untersuchungen zur Formengeschichte religiöser Rede*, rev. edn. Leipzig.

Norden, E. 1971. *Die antike Kunstprosa vom VI. Jahrhundert v. Chr. bis in die Zeit der Renaissance*, 2 vols. Darmstadt. Repr. of 2nd edn. 1909, and 3rd edn. 1915. Leipzig.

Nöthiger, M. 1971. *Die Sprache des Stesichorus und des Ibycus.* Zürich.

Nowottny, W. 1962. *The Language Poets Use.* London.

Nussbaum, A. J. 1998. *Two Studies in Greek and Homeric Linguistics.* Göttingen.

Nutton, V. 1992. "Healers in the Medical Market Place: Towards a Social History of Graeco-Roman Medicine." In A. Wear, ed., *Medicine in Society: Historical Essays.* Cambridge and New York: 15–58.

O'Neill, E. G. 1942. "The Localization of Metrical Word-Types in the Greek Hexameter." *YCS* 8: 105–78.

Oettinger, N. 1989–90. "Die 'dunkle Erde' im Hethitischen und Griechischen." *Die Welt des Orients* 20–1: 83–98.

Oliver, J. H. 1989. *Greek Constitutions of Early Roman Emperors from Inscriptions and Papyri.* London and New York.

Olivier, J.-M. 1989. *Répertoire des bibliothèques et des catalogues de manuscrits grecs de Marcel Richard.* Turnhout.

Olivier, J.-P. 1979. "L'origine de l'écriture linéaire B." *SMEA* 20: 43–52.

Olivier, J.-P. 1989. "The Possible Methods in Deciphering the Pictographic Cretan Script." In Y. Duhoux, T. G. Palaima, and J. Bennet, eds., *Problems in Decipherment.* Louvain-la-Neuve: 39–58.

Olivier, J.-P., and L. Godart. 1996. *Corpus hieroglyphicarum inscriptionum Cretae.* Paris.

Oréal, E. 1999. "Contact linguistique. Le cas du rapport entre le grec et le copte," *Lalies* 19: 289–306.

Pabón, J.-M. 1939. "El griego, lengua de la intimidad entre los Romanos." *Emerita* 7: 126–31.

Palaima, T. G. 1987. "Comments on Mycenaean Literacy." In J. T. Killen, J. L. Melena, and J.-P. Olivier, eds., *Studies in Mycenaean and Classical Greek Presented to J. Chadwick*. Salamanca: 499–510.

Palaima, T. G. 1988a. "The Development of the Mycenaean Writing System." In J.-P. Olivier and T. G. Palaima, eds., *Texts, Tablets and Scribes: Studies in Mycenaean Epigraphy and Economy offered to E. L. Bennett*. Suppl. *Minos* 10: 269–342.

Palaima, T. G. 1988b. *The Scribes of Pylos*. Rome.

Palaima, T. G. 2000–1. "Review of V. L. Aravantinos, L. Godart, and A. Sacconi, *Thèbes. Fouilles de la Cadmée I. Les tablettes en linéaire B de la Odos Pelopidou, Édition et commentaire*, Pisa/Rome, 2001." *Minos* 35–6: 474–86.

Palaima, T. G. 2004. "Sacrificial Feasting in the Linear B Documents." *Hesperia* 73: 217–46.

Palaima, T. G. 2006. " *65 = FAR?* or *ju?* and Other Interpretive Conundra in the New Thebes Tablets." In S. Deger-Jalkotzy and O. Panagl, eds., *Die neuen Linear B-Texte aus Theben*. Vienna.

Palau, A. Cataldi 2001. "Un nuovo codice della 'collezione filosofica'." *Scriptorium* 55: 249–74.

Palm, J. 1955. *Über Sprache und Stil des Diodoros von Sizilien. Ein Beitrag zur Beleuchtung der hellenistischen Prosa*. Lund.

Palmer, F. R. 2001. *Mood and Modality*, 2nd edn. Cambridge.

Palmer, L. R. 1945. *A Grammar of the Post-Ptolemaic Papyri*. London.

Palmer, L. R. 1963. *The Interpretation of Mycenaean Greek Texts*. Oxford.

Palmer, L. R. 1980. *The Greek Language*. London.

Palmer, L. R., and J. Chadwick, eds. 1966. *Proceedings of the Cambridge Colloquium on Mycenaean Studies*. Cambridge.

Panayotou, A. 1992a. Φωνητική και φωνολογία των ελληνικών επιγραφών της Μακεδονίας. Ελληνική Διαλεκτολογία 3: 5–32.

Panayotou, A. 1992b. "Εξέλιξη του ονόματος και του ρήματος της ελληνικής κατά την ελληνιστική, ρωμαϊκή και πρώιμη βυζαντινή περίοδο. Τα επιγραφικά δεδομένα της Μακεδονίας." In *Studies in Greek Linguistics* 13. Thessaloniki: 13–32.

Pandolfini, M., and A. Prosdocimi. 1990. *Alfabetari e insegnamento della scrittura in Etruria e nell'Italia antica*. Florence.

Pantelidis, N. 2001. "Πελοποννησιακός ιδιωματικός λόγος και κοινή νεοελληνική." In *Studies in Greek Linguistics* 21. Thessaloniki: 550–61.

Pantelidis, N. 2007. "Κοινή δημοτική: παρατηρήσεις στη διαδικασία διαμόρφωσής της." In *Studies in Greek Linguistics* 27. Thessaloniki: 337–47.

Papadopoulos, J. K. 1997. "Phantom Euboians." *JMA* 10: 191–219.

Pape, W., and G. E. Benseler. 1863–70. *Wörterbuch der griechischen Eigennamen*, 3rd edn. Braunschweig.

Pappas, P. 2004. *Variation and Morphosyntactic Change in Greek: From Clitics to Affixes*. Basingstoke.

Parker, L.P. E. 1997. *The Songs of Aristophanes*. Oxford.

Parry, M. 1971. *The Making of Homeric Verse: The Collected Papers of Milman Parry*, ed. A. Parry. Oxford.

Parsons, P. 2007. *City of the Sharp-Nosed Fish: Greek Lives in Roman Egypt*. London.

Passa, E. 2008. "La lingua dell'elegia e dell'epigramma su pietra." In Cassio, ed., 2008: 205–30.

Passoni dell'Acqua, A. 1981. "Ricerche sulla versione dei LXX e i papiri: I Pastophorion." *Aegyptus* 61: 171–211.

Pavese, C. O. 1972. *Tradizioni e generi poetici della Grecia arcaica.* Rome.

Pavese, C. O., and F. Boschetti. 2003. *A Complete Formular Analysis of the Homeric Poems.* Vol. 2: *Formular Edition, Text and Apparatus, Homeri* Ilias. Amsterdam.

Peek, W. 1955. *Griechische Vers-Inschriften.* Berlin.

Peek, W. 1957. *Verzeichnis der Gedicht-Anfänge und vergleichende Übersicht zu den Griechischen Versinschriften I.* Berlin.

Peek, W. 1969. *Inschriften aus dem Asklepieion von Epidauros.* Berlin.

Peek, W. 1972. *Neue Inschriften aus Epidauros.* Berlin.

Pelling, C. 2007. "Sophocles' Learning Curve." In C. Collard, P. Finglass, and N. J. Richardson, eds., *Hesperos: Essays in Honour of Martin West.* Oxford: 204–27.

Peremans, W. 1964. "Über die Zweisprachigkeit im ptolemäischen Ägypten." In H. Braunert, ed., *Studien zur Papyrologie und antiken Wirtschaftsgeschichte. F. Oertel zum achtigsten Geburtstag gewidmet.* Bonn: 49–60.

Peremans, W. 1981. "Les mariages mixtes dans l'Égypte des Lagides." In E. Bresciani, ed., *Scritti in onore di Orsolina Montevecchi.* Bologna: 273–81.

Peremans, W. 1983a. "Le bilinguisme dans les relations gréco-égyptiennes sous les Lagides." In Van 't Dack et al., eds., 1983: 253–80.

Peremans, W. 1983b. "Les hermeneis dans l'Égypte gréco-romaine." In G. Grimm, H. Heinen, and E. Winter, eds., *Das römisch-byzantinische Ägypten.* Mainz: 11–17.

Pérez Martín, I. 1996. *El patriarca Gregorio de Chipre (ca. 1240–1290) y la transmisión de los textos clásicos en Bizancio.* Madrid.

Pernigotti, S. 1998. "Qualque osservazioni sugli ostraka di Medinet Madi." In M. Capasso, ed., *Da Ercolano all'Egitto: ricerche varie di papirologia* (Papyrologica Lupiensia 7). Lecce: 117–30.

Pernot, L. 1981. *Les discours siciliens d'Aelius Aristide (Or. 5-6). Étude littéraire et paléographique, édition et traduction.* New York.

Pernot, L. 1993. *La rhétorique de l'éloge dans le monde gréco-romain,* 2 vols. Paris.

Perreault, J. Y. 1993. "Les emporia grecs du Levant: mythe ou réalité?" In A. Bresson and P. Rouillard, eds., *L'Emporion.* Paris: 59–83.

Perria, L. 1991. "Scrittura e ornamentazione nei codici della 'collezione filosofica'." *Rivista di studi bizantini e neoellenici* n.s. 28: 45–111.

Peruzzi, E. 1973. *Origini di Roma II.* Bologna.

Pestman, P. W. 1991. *1952–1992. Veertig jaar Griekse* Berichtigungslisten *in Leiden* (Uitgaven vanwege de stiching "Het Leids Papyrologisch Instituut" 12). Leiden.

Pestman, P. W. 1994. *The New Papyrological Primer,* 2nd edn. Leiden.

Peters, M. 1980. *Untersuchungen zur Vertretung der indogermanischen Laryngale im Griechischen.* Vienna.

Peters, M. 1995. "'Αμφιάραος und die attische Rückverwandlung." In M. Ofitsch and C. Zinko, eds., *Studia onomastica et indogermanica. Festschrift für Fritz Lochner von Hüttenbach zum 65. Geburtstag.* Graz: 185–202.

Peters, M. 1998. "Homerisches und Unhomerisches bei Homer und auf dem Nestorbecher." In J. Jasanoff, H. C. Melchert, and L. Olivier, eds., *Mír Curad: Studies in Honor of Calvert Watkins.* Innsbruck: 585–602.

Petersmann, H. 1983. "Die pragmatische Dimension in der Sprache des Chores bei den griechischen Tragikern." *A&A* 29: 95–106.

Petersmann, H. 1998. "Zur Sprach- und Kulturpolitik in der klassischen Antike." *SCI* 17: 87–101.

Petzl, G. 1994. *Die Beichtinschriften Westkleinasiens* (= *Ep. Anatolica* 22). Bonn.

Pfeiffer, R. 1968. *History of Classical Scholarship: From the Beginnings to the End of the Hellenistic Age.* Oxford.

Pfeijffer, I. L. 1999. *Three Aeginetan Odes of Pindar: A Commentary on Nemean V, Nemean III, and Pythian VIII*. Leiden.

Pinault, G.-J., and D. Petit, eds. 2006. *La langue poétique indo-européenne. Actes du colloque de travail de la Société des études indo-européennes (Indogermanische Gesellschaft/Society for Indo-European Studies), Paris, 22–24 octobre 2003*. Louvain.

Pinborg, J. 1975. "Classical Antiquity: Greece." *Current Trends in Linguistics* 13: 69–126.

Pintaudi R., and P. J. Sijpesteijn. 1989. "*Ostraka* di contenuto scolastico provenienti da Narmuthis." *ZPE* 76: 85–92.

Piteros, C., J.-P. Olivier, and J. L. Melena. 1990. "Les inscriptions en linéaire B des nodules de Thèbes (1982). La fouille, les documents, les possibilités d' interprétation." *BCH* 114: 103–84.

Plant, I. M., ed. 2004. *Women Writers of Ancient Greece and Rome: An Anthology*. Norman, OK.

Poccetti, P. 1986. "Lat. *bilinguis*." *AION (ling.)* 8: 193–205.

Poltera, O. 1997. *Le langage de Simonide*. Bern.

Popham, M. R. 2004. "Precolonization: Early Greek Contact with the East." In Tsetskhladze and De Angelis, eds., 2004: 11–34.

Popham, M. R., and I. S. Lemos. 1995. "A Euboean Warrior Trader." *OJA* 14: 151–7.

Porter, D. H. 1986. "The Imagery of Greek Tragedy: Three Characteristics." *SO* 61: 19–42.

Porter, J. I. 1989. "Philodemus on Material Difference." *Cron. Erc.* 19: 149–78.

Porter, J. I. 1993. "The Seductions of Gorgias." *CA* 12: 267–99.

Porter, J. I. 1995. "οἱ κριτικοί: A Reassessment." In J. G. J. Abbenes et al., eds., *Greek Literary Theory after Aristotle: A Collection of Papers in Honour of D. M. Schenkeveld*. Amsterdam: 83–109.

Porter, J. I. 2010. *The Origins of Aesthetic Inquiry*. Cambridge.

Pound, E. 1954. *Literary Essays*. London.

Powell, B. 1991. *Homer and the Origin of the Greek Alphabet*. Cambridge.

Prato, G., and G. de Gregorio, 2003. "Scrittura arcaizzante in codici profani e sacri della prima età paleologa." *RHM* 45: 59–102.

Prato, G., ed. 2000. *I manoscritti greci tra riflessione e debattito*. Florence.

Preminger, A., and T. V. F. Brogan, eds. 1993. *The New Princeton Encyclopedia of Poetry and Poetics*. Princeton.

Probert, P. 2003. *A New Short Guide to the Accentuation of Ancient Greek*. London.

Probert, P. 2006. *Ancient Greek Accentuation: Synchronic Patterns, Frequency Effects, and Prehistory*. Oxford.

Psaltes, S. 1913. *Grammatik der byzantinischen Chroniken*. Göttingen.

Puhvel, J. 1991. *Homer and Hittite*. Innsbruck.

Puhvel, J. 2002. *Epilecta Indoeuropaea: Opuscula selecta annis 1978–2001 excusa imprimis ad res Anatolicas attinentia*. Innsbruck.

Pulleyn, S. 1997. *Prayer in Greek Religion*. Oxford.

Pulvermüller, F. 2002. *The Neuroscience of Language*. Cambridge.

Pustejovsky, J., and B. Boguraev, eds., 1996. *Lexical Semantics: The Problem of Polysemy*. Oxford.

Quaegebeur, J. 1974. "The Study of Egyptian Proper Names in Greek Transcription: Problems and Perspectives." *Onoma* 18: 403–20.

Quaegebeur, J. 1978. "Mummy Labels: An Orientation." In Boswinkel and Pestman, eds., 1978: 232–59.

Quaegebeur, J. 1982. "De la préhistoire de l'écriture copte." *OLP* 13: 125–36.

Race, W. H. 1990. *Style and Rhetoric in Pindar's Odes*. Atlanta.

Raison, J., and M. Pope. 1977. *Index transnuméré du linéaire A*. Louvain.

Ravin, Y., and C. Leacock. 1998. "Polysemy: An Overview". In Y. Ravin and C. Leacock, eds., *Polysemy: Theoretical and Computational Approaches*. Oxford: 1–29.

Ray, J. 1995. "Soldiers to Pharaoh: The Carians of Southwest Anatolia." In Sasson, ed., 1995: 1185–94.

Ray, J. 2007. "Greek, Egyptian, and Coptic." In Christides, ed., 2007: 811–18.

Rayor, D. J., ed. 1991. *Sappho's Lyre: Archaic Lyric and Women Poets of Ancient Greece. Translated, with Introduction and Notes*. Berkeley.

Reardon, B. P. 1971. *Courants littéraires grecs des IIᵉ et IIIᵉ siècles après J.-C.* Paris.

Regenbogen O. 1961. "Eine Forschungsmethode antiker Naturwissenshaft." In F. Dirlmeier, ed., *Otto Regenbogen. Kleine Schriften*. Munich: 141–94.

Rémondon, R. 1964. "Problèmes du bilinguisme dans l'Égypte lagide" (*UPZ* I 148). *CdÉ* 39: 126–46.

Renehan, R. F. 1969. "Conscious Ambiguities in Pindar and Bacchylides." *GRBS* 19: 217–28.

Reynolds, L. D., ed. 1986. *Texts and Transmission: A Survey of the Latin Classics*. Oxford.

Rhodes, P. J., and D. Lewis. 1997. *The Decrees of the Greek States*. Oxford.

Richardson, N. 1993. *The Iliad: A Commentary*. Vol. VI: *Books 20–24*. Cambridge.

Richlin, A. 1997. "Gender and Rhetoric: Producing Manhood in the Schools." In W. J. Dominik, ed., *Roman Eloquence: Rhetoric in Society and Literature*. New York: 90–110.

Ridgway, D. 2004. "Phoenicians and Greeks in the West." In Tsetskhladze and De Angelis, eds., 2004: 35–46.

Rijksbaron, A. 1976. *Temporal and Causal Conjunctions in Ancient Greek*. Amsterdam.

Rijksbaron, A. 1988. "The Discourse Function of the Imperfect." In A. Rijksbaron et al., eds., *In the Footsteps of Raphael Kühner*. Amsterdam: 237–54.

Rijksbaron, A. 2002. *Syntax and Semantics of the Verb in Classical Greek: An Introduction*, 3rd edn. Amsterdam.

Rijksbaron, A. 2006. "On False Historic Presents in Sophocles (and Euripides)." In De Jong and Rijksbaron, eds., 2006: 127–50.

Rijksbaron, A., ed. 1997. *New Approaches to Greek Particles*. Amsterdam.

Risch, E. 1954. "Die Sprache Alkmans." *MH* 11: 20–37. Repr. Risch. 1981. *Kleine Schriften*, 314–31. Berlin.

Risch, E. 1955. "Die Gliederung der griechischen Dialekte in neuer Sicht." *MH* 12: 61–75.

Risch, E. 1959. "Frühgeschichte der griechischen Sprache." *MH* 16: 215–27.

Risch, E. 1966. "Les différences dialectales dans le mycénien." In Palmer and Chadwick, eds., 1966: 150–7.

Risch, E. 1974. *Wortbildung der homerischen Sprache*, 2nd edn. Berlin.

Risch, E. 1979. "Die griechischen Dialekte im 2. vorchristlichen Jahrtausend." *SMEA* 20: 91–111.

Risch, E. 1980. "Betrachtungen zur indogermanischen Nominalflexion." In *Festschrift Hansjakob Seiler*. Tübingen: 259–67.

Risch, E. 1987. "Zum Nestorbecher aus Ischia." *ZPE* 70: 1–9.

Risch, E. 1992. "À propos de la formation du vocabulaire poétique grec entre le 12e et le 8e siècle." In F. Létoublon, ed., *La langue et les textes en grec ancien. Actes du colloque Pierre Chantraine*. Amsterdam: 91.

Ritchie, W. 1964. *The Authenticity of the Rhesus of Euripides*. Cambridge.

Rix, H. 1992. *Historische Grammatik des Griechischen. Laut- und Formenlehre*, 2nd edn. Darmstadt.

Rix, H. 2005. Review of Hajnal 2003b. *Gnomon* 77: 385–8.

Rix, H., ed. 2001. *LIV: Lexikon der indogermanischen Verben*, 2nd edn. Wiesbaden.

Robb, K. 1994. *Literacy and Paideia in Ancient Greece*. New York.

Robert, L. (and J. Robert). 2007. *Choix d'écrits,* ed. D. Rousset et al. Paris.

Roberts, C. H., and T. C. Skeat. 1983. *The Birth of the Codex.* Oxford.

Roberts, E. S. 1887–1905. *An Introduction to Greek Epigraphy,* 2 vols. Cambridge.

Roberts, I. 1993. *Verbs and Diachronic Syntax: A Comparative History of English and French.* Dordrecht.

Robins, R. H. 1997. *A Short History of Linguistics,* 4th edn. London and New York.

Rochette, B. 1994. "Traducteurs et traductions dans l'Égypte gréco-romaine." *CdÉ* 69: 313–22.

Rochette, B. 1995. "Grecs et Latins face aux langues étrangères. Contribution à l'étude de la diversité linguistique dans l'antiquité classique." *RBPH* 73.1: 5–16.

Rochette, B. 1996a. "Sur le bilinguisme dans l'Égypte gréco-romaine." *CdÉ* 71: 153–68.

Rochette, B. 1996b. "Parce que je ne connais pas bien le grec . . . : P. Col. Zenon II 66." *CdÉ* 71: 311–16.

Rochette, B. 1996c. "Remarques sur le bilinguisme gréco-latin." *LEC* 64: 3–19.

Rochette, B. 1997. *Le latin dans le monde grec. Recherches sur la diffusion de la langue et des lettres latines dans les provinces hellénophones de l'Empire romain* (Collection Latomus 233). Brussels.

Rochette, B. 1998. "Le bilinguisme gréco-latin et la question des langues dans le monde gréco-romain. Chronique bibliographique." *RBPH* 76: 177–96.

Rochette, B. 2001. "À propos du grec δίγλωσσος." *Ant. Class.* 70: 177–84.

Rollinger, R. 1997. "Zur Bezeichnung von 'Griechen' in Keilschrifttexten." *RAAO* 91: 167–72.

Romaine, S. 1999. *Communicating Gender.* Mahwah, NJ and London.

Ronconi, F. 2007. *I manoscritti greci miscellanei.* Spoleto.

Ronconi, F. 2008. "Qualche riflessioni sulla provenienza dei modelli della 'collezione filosofica'." In D. Bianconi and L. Del Corso, eds., *Oltre la scrittura.* Paris: 125–42.

Ros, J. G. A. 1938. *Die ΜΕΤΑΒΟΛΗ (Variatio) als Stilprinzip des Thukydides.* Nijmegen.

Rosch, E. 1975. "Cognitive Representation of Semantic Categories". *Journal of Experimental Psychology: General* 104: 192–233.

Rose, V. 1886. *Aristotelis qui ferebantur librorum fragmenta collegit Valentinus Rose.* Leipzig.

Rosenqvist, J.-O. 1981. *Studien zur Syntax und Bemerkungen zum Text der Vita Theodori Syceotae.* Uppsala.

Rotolo, V. 1972. "La comunicazione linguistica fra alloglotti nell'antichità classica." In *Studi classici in onore di Q. Cataudella* I. Catania: 395–414.

Rotstein, A. 2004. "Aristotle, *Poetics* 1447a13–16 and Musical Contests." *ZPE* 149: 39–42.

Roux, G. 1992. *Ancient Iraq,* 3rd edn. London.

Ruge, H. 1969. *Zur Entstehung der neugriechischen Substantiv-Deklination.* Stockholm.

Ruijgh, C. J. 1961. "Le traitement des sonantes voyelles dans les dialectes grecs et la position du mycénien." *Mnemosyne* 14: 193–216.

Ruijgh, C. J. 1967. *Études sur la grammaire et le vocabulaire du grec mycénien.* Amsterdam.

Ruijgh, C. J. 1978. Review of García Ramón 1975. *Bibliotheca Orientalis* 30: 418–23. Repr. in C. J. Ruijgh, *Scripta Minora,* vol. 1. Amsterdam, 1991: 662–75.

Ruijgh, C. J. 1980. "De ontwikkeling van de lyrische kunsttaal, met name van het litteraire dialect van de koorlyriek." *Lampas* 13: 416–35.

Ruijgh, C. J. 2006. "The Use of the Demonstratives ὅδε, οὗτος and (ἐ)κεῖνος in Sophocles." In De Jong and Rijksbaron, eds., 2006: 151–61.

Ruipérez, M. S. 1952. "Desinencias medias primarias indo-europeas." *Emerita* 20: 8–31.

Ruiz-Montero, C. 1991. "Aspects of the Vocabulary of Chariton of Aphrodisias." *CQ* 41: 484–9.

Russell, D. A. 1991. *An Anthology of Greek Prose.* Oxford.

Rusten, J. S. 1989. *Thucydides Book II. Edition and Commentary.* Cambridge.

Rutherford, I. C. 1998. *Canons of Style in the Antonine Age: Idea-Theory in its Literary Context.* Oxford.

Rutherford, I. C. 2002. "Interference or Translationese? Some Patterns in Lycian–Greek Bilingualism." In Adams, Janse, and Swain, eds., 2002: 197–219.

Rutherford, R. B. 1995. *The Art of Plato.* Cambridge.

Rydbeck, L. 1967. *Fachprosa, vermeintliche Volkssprache und Neues Testament. Zur Beurteilung der sprachlichen Niveauunterschiede im nachklassischen Griechisch.* Uppsala.

Rydén, L. 1982. "Style and Historical Fiction in the Life of St. Andreas Salos." *JÖB* 32.3: 175–83.

Samel, I. 2000. *Einführung in die feministische Sprachwissenschaft*, 2nd edn. Berlin.

Sansone, D. 1993. "Towards a New Doctrine of the Article in Greek: Some Observations on the Definite Article in Plato." *CP* 88: 191–205.

Saporetti, C. 1990. "Testimonianze neo-assire relative alla Fenicia da Tiglat-pileser III ad Assurbanipal." In M. Botto, ed., *Studi storici sulla Fenicia. L'VIII e il VII secolo a.C.* Pisa: 109–243.

Sass, B. 1988. *The Genesis of the Alphabet and Its Development in the Second Millennium* BC. Wiesbaden.

Sass, B. 2005. *The Alphabet at the Turn of the Millennium.* Tel Aviv.

Sasson, J. M., ed. 1995. *Civilizations of the Ancient Near East*, 4 vols. New York.

Satzinger, H. 1984. "Die altkoptischen Texte." In P. Nagel, ed., *Graeco-Coptica.* Halle: 137–47.

Schaps, D. 1977. "The Woman Least Mentioned: Etiquette and Women's Names." *CQ.* 27: 323–30.

Schauer, M. 2002. *Tragisches Klagen. Form und Funktion der Klagedarstellung bei Aischylos, Sophokles und Euripides.* Tübingen.

Scheer, T. 2000. "Forschungen über die Frau in der Antike. Ziele, Methoden, Perspektiven." *Gymnasium* 107: 143–72.

Schiffrin, D. 1994. *Approaches to Discourse.* Oxford and Cambridge, MA.

Schironi, F. 2002. "Articles in Homer: A Puzzling Problem in Ancient Grammar." In Swiggers and Wouters, eds., 2002: 145–60.

Schloemann, J. 2002. "Entertainment and Democratic Distrust: The Audience's Attitude towards Oral and Written Oratory in Classical Athens." In I. Worthington and J. M. Foley, eds., *Epea and Grammata: Oral and Written Communication in Ancient Greece.* Leiden: 133–46.

Schmid, W. 1887–97. *Der Atticismus in seinen Hauptvertretern von Dionysius von Halikarnass bis auf den zweiten Philostratus*, 5 vols. Stuttgart.

Schmid, W. 1917. "Die sogenannte Aristidesrhetorik." *Rh. Mus.* 72: 113–69, 238–57.

Schmidhauser, A. U. 2000. *A Full Bibliography on Apollonius Dyscolus.* http://schmidhauser. us/apollonius.

Schmidhauser, A. U. Forthcoming. "Stoic Deixis." In A. Longo and M. Bonelli, eds., *Quid Est Veritas? Essays in Honour of Jonathan Barnes.* Naples.

Schmidt, M. 1860. Ἐπιτομὴ τῆς Καθολικῆς προσῳδίας Ἡρωδιανοῦ. Jena. Repr. 1983. Hildesheim.

Schmidt, V. 1968. *Sprachliche Untersuchungen zu Herondas. Mit einem kritisch-exegetischen Anhang.* Berlin.

Schmitt, R. 1967a. *Dichtung und Dichtersprache in indogermanischer Zeit.* Wiesbaden.

Schmitt, R. 1967b. "Medisches und persisches Sprachgut bei Herodot." *ZDMG* 117: 119–45.

Schmitt, R. 1977. *Einführung in die griechischen Dialekte.* Darmstadt.

Schmitt, R. 1978. *Die Iranier-Namen bei Aischylos.* Vienna.

Schmitt, R. 1992. "Assyria grammata und Ähnliches: Was wussten die Griechen von Keilschrift und Keilinschriften?" In Müller, Sier, and Werner, eds., 1992: 21–35.

Schmitt, R. 2004. "Old Persian." In Woodard, ed., 2004: 717–40.

Schmitt, R., ed. 1968. *Indogermanische Dichtersprache*. Darmstadt.

Schmitter, P. 2000. "Sprachbezogene Reflexionen im frühen Griechenland." In Auroux et al., eds., 2000: 345–66.

Schmitz, T. 1997. *Bildung und Macht. Zur sozialen und politischen Funktion der zweiten Sophistik in der griechischen Welt der Kaiserzeit*. Munich.

Schöpsdau, K. 1992. "Vergleiche zwischen Lateinisch und Griechisch in der antiken Sprachwissenschaft." In Müller, Sier, and Werner, eds., 1992: 115–36.

Schreiner, P. 1986. "Slavische Lexik bei byzantinischen Autoren." In R. Olesch and H. Rothe, eds., *Festschrift für Herbert Bräuner zum 65. Geburtstag*. Cologne: 479–90.

Schürr, D. 2007. "Formen der Akkulturation in Lykien: Griechisch-Lykische Sprachbeziehungen." In Chr. Schuler, ed., *Griechische Epigraphik in Lykien. Ein Zwischenbilanz* (= Österr. Akad. Wisschenschaften, Phil.-hist. Klasse. Denkschr., 354 = Ergänzungsbände zu den *Tituli Asiae Minoris*, 25). Vienna: 27–40.

Schwyzer, E. 1939. *Griechische Grammatik*, vol. 1. Munich.

Scott, D. A., R. D. Woodard, P. K. McCarter, B. Zuckerman, and M. Lundberg. 2005. "Greek Alphabet (MS 108)." In R. Pintaudi, ed., *Papyri Graecae Schøyen*. Florence: 149–60.

Seaford, R. 1996. *Euripides, Bacchae: Introduction, Translation and Commentary*. Warminster.

Sedley, D. 2003. *Plato's Cratylus*. Cambridge.

Segal, C. 1998. *Aglaia: The Poetry of Alcman, Sappho, Pindar, Bacchylides, and Corinna*. Lanham, MD.

Seiler, H-J. 1958. "Zur Systematik und Entwicklungsgeschichte der griechischen Nominaldeklination." *Glotta* 37: 41–67.

Setaioli, A. 2007. "Plutarch's Assessment of Latin as a Means of Expression." *Prometheus* 33: 156–66.

Ševčenko, I. 1981. "Levels of Style in Byzantine Prose." *JÖB* 31: 290–312.

Ševčenko, I. 1982. "Additional Remarks to the Report on Levels of Style." *JÖB* 32: 220–33.

Sherk, R. K. 1969. *Roman Documents from the Greek East: Senatus Consulta and Epistulae to the Age of Augustus*. Baltimore.

Sherratt, S. 2003. "Visible Writing: Questions of Script and Identity in Early Iron Age Greece and Cyprus." *OJA* 22: 225–42.

Shipp, G. P. 1953. "Greek in Plautus." *WS* 66: 105–12.

Shklovsky, V. 1965 [1917]. "Art as Technique." In Lemon and Reis, eds., 1965: 3–24.

Shoep, I. 1994. "Ritual, Politics, and Script on Minoan Crete." *Aegean Archaeology* 1: 7–25.

Sicking, C. M. J. 1991. "The Distribution of Aorist and Present Tense Stem Forms in Greek, Especially in the Imperative." *Glotta* 69: 14–43; 154–70.

Sicking, C. M. J. 1993. *Griechische Verslehre*. Munich.

Sicking, C. M. J. 1996. "Aspect Choice: Time Reference or Discourse Function?" In C. M. J. Sicking and P. Stork, *Two Studies in the Semantics of the Verb in Classical Greek*. Leiden: 1–118.

Sicking, C. M. J., and P. Stork. 1997. "The Grammar of the So-Called Historical Present in Ancient Greek." In Bakker, ed., 1997: 131–68.

Sihler, A. L. 1995. *New Comparative Grammar of Greek and Latin*. New York and Oxford.

Sijpesteijn, P. 1992. "The Meanings of ἤτοι in the Papyri." *ZPE* 90: 241–7.

Silk, M. S. 1974. *Interaction in Poetic Imagery: with Special Reference to Early Greek Poetry*. Cambridge.

Silk, M. S. 1980. "Aristophanes as a Lyric Poet." *YCS* 26: 99–151.

Silk, M. S. 1983. "LSJ and the Problem of Poetic Archaism: From Meanings to Iconyms." *CQ* 33: 303–30.

Silk, M. S. 1993. "Aristophanic Paratragedy." In A. H. Sommerstein et al., eds., *Tragedy, Comedy and the Polis*. Bari: 477–504.

Silk, M. S. 1996. "Tragic Language." In M. S. Silk, ed., *Tragedy and the Tragic*. Oxford: 458–96.

Silk, M. S. 1999. "Style, Voice and Authority in the Choruses of Greek Drama." *Drama* (Stuttgart/Weimar) 7: 1–26.

Silk, M. S. 2000. *Aristophanes and the Definition of Comedy*. Oxford.

Silk, M. S. 2001. "Pindar Meets Plato: Theory, Language, Value, and the Classics." In Harrison, ed., 2001: 26–45.

Silk, M. S. 2003. "Assonance, Greek." In *OCD*³: 193–4.

Silk, M. S. 2007. "Pindar's Poetry as Poetry: A Literary Commentary on *Olympian* 12." In S. Hornblower and C. A. Morgan, eds., *Pindar's Poetry, Patrons, and Festivals*. Oxford.

Silk, M. S. 2009. "The Invention of Greek: Poets, Macedonians and Others." In A. Georgakopoulou and M. S. Silk, eds., *Standard Languages and Language Standards: Greek, Past and Present*. Aldershot.

Silk, M. S. Forthcoming. *Poetic Language in Theory and Practice*. Oxford.

Silva, P. 2000. "Time and Meaning: Sense and Definition in the *OED*." In L. Mugglestone, ed., *Lexicography and the Oxford English Dictionary: Pioneers in the Untrodden Forest*. Oxford: 77–95.

Simelidis, C. 2009. *Selected Poems of Gregory of Nazianzus*. Göttingen.

Sirago, V.A. 1989. "La seconda sofistica come espressione culturale della classe dirigente del II sec." *ANRW* II.33.1: 36–78.

Skeat, T. C. 1994. "The Origin of the Christian Codex." *ZPE* 102: 236–68.

Skeat, T. C. 1999. "The Codex Sinaiticus, the Codex Vaticanus and Constantine." *JTS* 50: 583–625.

Skoda, F. 1988. *Médecine ancienne et métaphore. Le vocabulaire de l'anatomie et de la pathologie en grec ancien*. Paris.

Skopetea, E. 2007. "Ancient, Vernacular, and Purist Greek Language." In Christidis, ed., 2007: 1280–6.

Slater, W. J., ed. 1986. *Aristophanis Byzantii Fragmenta* (*SGLG* 6). Berlin and New York.

Slings, S. R. 1992. "Written and Spoken Language: An Exercise in the Pragmatics of the Greek Language." *CP* 87: 95–109.

Slings, S. R. 1997. "Figures of Speech and their Lookalikes: Two Further Exercises in the Pragmatics of the Greek Sentence." In Bakker, ed., 1997: 169–214.

Slings, S. R. 2002. "Oral Strategies in the Language of Herodotus." In Bakker, de Jong, and van Wees, eds., 2002: 53–77.

Sluiter, I. 1990. *Ancient Grammar in Context: Contributions to the Study of Ancient Linguistic Thought*. Amsterdam.

Sluiter, I. 1997. "The Greek Tradition." In W. van Bekkum, J. Houben, I. Sluiter, and K. Versteegh, eds., *The Emergence of Semantics in Four Linguistic Traditions: Hebrew, Sanskrit, Greek, Arabic*. Amsterdam and Philadelphia: 147–224.

Sluiter, I. 2000. "Language and Thought in Stoic Philosophy." In Auroux et al., eds., 2000: 375–84.

Smith, C. S. 2003. *Modes of Discourse: The Local Structure of Texts*. Cambridge.

Smith, J. A. 2003. "Clearing up Some Confusion in Callias' *Alphabet Tragedy*." *CP* 98: 313–29.

Smyth, H. W. 1887. "The Arcado-Cyprian Dialect." *TAPA* 18: 59–133.

Smyth, H. W. 1956. *Greek Grammar*. Rev. G. M. Messing. Cambridge, MA.

Snell, B. 1953. *The Discovery of the Mind*. Trans. T. G. Rosenmeyer. Cambridge, MA.

Snodgrass, A. 1971. *The Dark Age of Greece*. Edinburgh.

Snodgrass, A. 2000. "The Uses of Writing on Early Greek Painted Pottery." In N. K. Rutter and B. A. Sparkes, eds., *Word and Image in Ancient Greece*. Edinburgh: 22–34.

Snodgrass, A. 2004. "The Nature and Standing of the Early Western Colonies." In Tsetskhladze and De Angelis, eds., 2004: 1–10.

Snyder, J. M. 1990. *The Woman and the Lyre: Women Writers in Greece and Rome*. Carbondale, IL.

Solin, H. 2003. *Die griechischen Personennamen in Rom. Ein Namenbuch*, 2nd edn. Berlin.

Solin, H., O. Salomies, and U.-M. Liertz, eds. 1995. *Acta colloquii epigraphici Latini, Helsinki 3–6 September* (Commentationes Humanarum Litterarum 104). Helsinki.

Sommerstein, A. H. 1973. *The Sound Pattern of Ancient Greek*. Oxford.

Sommerstein, A. H. 1980. "The Naming of Women in Greek and Roman Comedy." *Quaderni di Storia* 11: 393–409.

Sommerstein, A. H. 1995. "The Language of Athenian Women." In F. de Martino and A. H. Sommerstein, eds., *Lo spettacolo delle voci*, 2. Bari: 61–85.

Sophocles, E. A. 1887. *Greek Lexicon of the Roman and Byzantine Periods, from* BC *146 to* AD *1100*. New York.

Sosin J., and J. G. Manning. 2003. "Palaeography and Bilingualism: P.Duk. inv. 320 and 675." *CdÉ* 78: 202–10.

Speck, P. 1974. *Die Kaiserliche Universität von Konstantinopel*. Munich.

Speck, P. 1984. "Ikonoklasmus und die Anfänge der makedonischen Renaissance." In *Varia* I: 175–210.

Stanford, W. B. 1939. *Ambiguity in Greek Literature*. Oxford.

Stanford, W. B. 1942. *Aeschylus in His Style*. Dublin.

Stanton, G. R. 1988. "τέχνον, παῖς, and Related Words in Koine Greek." In B. G. Mandilaras, ed., *Proceedings of the XVII International Congress of Papyrology*, I. Athens: 463–80.

Steiner, D. 1986. *The Crown of Song: Metaphor in Pindar*. London.

Steiner, D. 1994. *The Tyrant's Writ: Myths and Images of Writing in Ancient Greece*. Princeton.

Steiner, R. 1982. *Affricated Ṣade in the Semitic Languages*. New York.

Steriade, D. 1982. *Greek Prosodies and the Nature of Syllabification*. PhD dissertation, MIT.

Stevens, P. T. 1976. *Colloquial Expressions in Euripides*. Wiesbaden.

Stolper, M. W., and J. Tavernier. 2007. "An Old Persian Administrative Tablet from the Persepolis Fortification." *ARTA: Achaemenid Research on Texts and Archaeology*, 1–28.

Stray, C. 1998. *Classics Transformed: Schools, Universities and Societies in England, 1830–1960*. Oxford.

Strunk, K. 1982. "Vater Himmel–Tradition und Wandel einer sakralsprachlichen Formel." In J. Tischler, ed., *Serta Indogermanica. Festschrift für Günter Neumann*. Innsbruck: 427–38.

Strunk, K. 1994. "Der Ursprung des temporalen Augments—Ein Problem Franz Bopps aus heutiger Sicht." In R. Sternemann, ed., *Bopp-Symposium 1992 der Humboldt-Universität zu Berlin*. Heidelberg: 270–84.

Strunk, K. 1997. "Vom mykenischen bis zum klassischen Griechisch." In Nesselrath, ed., 1997: 135–55.

Sturtevant, E. H. 1940. *The Pronunciation of Greek and Latin*, 2nd edn. Philadelphia.

Swain, S. 1996. *Hellenism and Empire: Language, Classicism and Power in the Greek World*, AD *50–250*. Oxford.

Swain, S. 2002. "Bilingualism in Cicero? The Evidence of Code-Switching." In Adams, Janse, and Swain, eds., 2002: 128–67.

Swain, S. 2004. "Bilingualism and Biculturalism in Antonine Rome: Apuleius, Fronto, and Gellius." In L. Holford-Strevens and A. Vardi, eds., *The Worlds of Aulus Gellius*. Oxford: 3–40.

Sweetser, E. 1990. *From Etymology to Pragmatics: Metaphorical and Cultural Aspects of Semantic Structure*. Cambridge.

Swiderek, A. 1961. "Hellénion de Memphis. La rencontre de deux mondes." *Eos* 51: 55–63.

Swiderek, A. 1975. "Sarapis et les hellénomemphites." In J. Bingen et al., eds., *Le monde grec: pensée, littérature, histoire, documents. Hommages à Claire Préaux*. Brussels: 670–5.

Swiggers, P., and A. Wouters, eds. 2002. *Grammatical Theory and Philosophy of Language in Antiquity* (Orbis Supplementa 19). Louvain, Paris, and Sterling, VA.

Szemerényi, O. 1974. "The Origins of the Greek Lexicon: Ex Oriente Lux." *JHS* 94: 144–57.

Szemerényi, O. 1996. *Introduction to Indo-European Linguistics*. Oxford.

Tait, W. J. 1986. "Rush and Reed: The Pens of Egyptian and Greek Scribes." In *Proceedings of the 18th International Congress of Papyrology* 2. Athens: 477–81.

Talbot, M. M. 1998. *Language and Gender: An Introduction*. Cambridge.

Tambling, J. 1988. *What is Literary Language?* Milton Keynes.

Tannen, D. 1990. *You Just Don't Understand: Women and Men in Conversation*. New York.

Tanselle, G. T. 1989. *A Rationale of Textual Criticism*. Philadelphia.

Taylor, A. E. 1928. *A Commentary on Plato's Timaeus*. Oxford.

Taylor, J. 1995. *Linguistic Categorization: Prototypes in Linguistic Theory*, 2nd edn. Oxford.

Teffeteller, A. Forthcoming. *Mycenaeans and Anatolians in the Late Bronze Age: The Ahhijawa Question*.

Thesleff, H. 1966. "Scientific and Technical Style in Early Greek Prose." *Arctos* 4: 89–113.

Thesleff, H. 1967. *Studies in the Styles of Plato*. Helsinki.

Thissen, H. J. 1993. "Zum Umgang mit der ägyptischen Sprache in der griechisch-römischen Antike." *ZPE* 97: 239–52.

Thomas, R. 1989. *Oral Tradition and Written Record in Classical Athens*. Cambridge.

Thomas, R. 1992. *Literacy and Orality in Ancient Greece*. Cambridge.

Thomason, S. G. 2001. *Language Contact: An Introduction*. Edinburgh.

Thomason, S. G., and T. Kaufmann. 1988. *Language Contact, Creolization, and Genetic Linguistics*. Berkeley.

Thompson, D. J. 1988. *Memphis under the Ptolemies*. Princeton.

Thompson, R. J. E. 1996–7. "Dialects in Mycenaean and Mycenaean among the Dialects." *Minos* 31–2: 313–33.

Thompson, R. J. E. 2000. "Prepositional Usage in Arcado-Cypriot and Mycenaean: A Bronze Age Isogloss?" *Minos* 35: 395–430.

Thompson, R. J. E. 2002–3a. "*What the Butler Saw*: Some Thoughts on the Mycenaean *o- ~ jo-* Particle." *Minos* 37–8: 317–36.

Thompson, R. J. E. 2002–3b. "Special vs. Normal Mycenaean Revisited." *Minos* 37–8: 337–70.

Thompson, R. J. E. 2006. "Long Mid Vowels in Attic-Ionic and Cretan." *CCJ* 52: 81–101.

Thorne, B., and N. Henley, eds. 1975. *Language and Sex: Difference and Dominance*. Rowley, MA.

Threatte, L. 1980. *The Grammar of Attic Inscriptions*. Vol. 1: *Phonology*. Berlin and New York.

Threatte, L. 1996. *The Grammar of Attic Inscriptions*. Vol. 2: *Morphology*. Berlin and New York.

Thumb, A. 1901. *Die griechische Sprache im Zeitalter des Hellenismus*. Strasburg.

Thumb, A. 1909. *Handbuch der griechischen Dialekte*. Heidelberg.

Thumb, A., and E. Kieckers. 1932. *Handbuch der griechischen Dialekte*, i. Heidelberg.

Thumb, A., and A. Scherer. 1959. *Handbuch der griechischen Dialekte*, ii. Heidelberg.

Tichy, E. 1981. "Hom. ἀνδροτῆτα und die Vorgeschichte des daktylischen Hexameters." *Glotta* 59: 28–67.

Timpanaro, S. 2005. *The Genesis of Lachmann's Method*. Trans. G. W. Most. Chicago.

Tischler, Joh. 1977. *Kleinasiatische Hydronymie. Semantische und morphologische Analyse der griechischen Gewässernamen*. Wiesbaden.

Tonnet, H. 1988. *Recherches sur Arrien. Sa personnalité et ses écrits atticistes*, 2 vols. Amsterdam.

Tonnet, H. 2003. *Histoire du grec moderne*, 2nd ed. Paris.

Torallas Tovar, S. 2003. "La situación lingüística de las comunidades monásticas en el Egipto de los siglos IV y V." *CCO* 1: 233–45.

Torallas Tovar, S. 2004a. "Lexical Interference in Greek in Byzantine and Early Islamic Egypt." In P. Sijpesteijn and L. Sundelin, eds., *Papyrology and the History of Early Islamic Egypt*. Leiden: 143–78.

Torallas Tovar, S. 2004b. "The Context of Loanwords in Egyptian Greek." In P. Bádenas et al., eds., *Lenguas en contacto: el testimonio escrito*. Madrid: 57–67.

Torallas Tovar, S. 2005. *Identidad lingüística e identidad religiosa en el Egipto Grecorromano*. Barcelona.

Torallas Tovar, S. 2007. "Egyptian Loan Words in *Septuaginta* and the Papyri." In B. Palme, ed., *Akten des 23. Internationalen Papyrologenkongresses, Wien*. Vienna: 687–91.

Tosi, R. 1998. "Appunti sulla filologia di Eratostene di Cirene." *Eikasmos* 9: 327–46.

Toufexis, N. 2008. "Diglossia and Register Variation in Medieval Greek." *BMGS* 32: 203–19.

Tovar, A. 1964. "A Research Report on Vulgar Latin and its Local Variations." *Kratylos* 9: 113–34.

Trapp, E. 1988. *Studien zur byzantinischen Lexikographie*. Vienna.

Trapp, E. et al., eds. 1994–. *Lexikon zur byzantinischen Gräzität, besonders des 9.–12. Jahrhunderts* (Byzantina Vindobonensia 20). Vienna.

Traugott, E. C., and P. Dasher. 2000. *Regularity in Semantic Change*, Cambridge.

Treadgold, W. T. 1980. *The Nature of the* Bibliotheca *of Photius*. Washington, DC.

Treadgold, W. T., ed. 1984. *Renaissances before the Renaissance*. Stanford, CA.

Trenkner, S. 1960. *Le style καί dans le récit attique oral*. Assen.

Trevett, J. 1992. *Apollodorus, Son of Pasion*. Oxford.

Triantaphyllidis, M. 1909. *Lehnwörter der mittelgriechischen Literatur*. Marburg.

Triantaphyllidis, M. 1941. *Νεοελληνικὴ γραμματικὴ (τῆς δημοτικῆς)*. Athens.

Trosborg, A. 1997. "Text Typology: Register, Genre and Text Type." In A. Trosborg, ed., *Text Typology and Translation*. Amsterdam and Philadelphia: 3–23.

Trudgill, P. 2003. "Modern Greek Dialects: A Preliminary Classification." *JGL* 4: 45–63.

Trümpy, C. 1997. *Untersuchungen zu den altgriechischen Monatsnamen und Monatsfolgen*. Heidelberg.

Tsetskhladze, G. R., and F. De Angelis, eds. 2004. *The Archaeology of Greek Colonisation: Essays Dedicated to Sir John Boardman*, rev. edn. Oxford.

Turner, E. G. 1980. *Greek Papyri: An Introduction*. Oxford.

Tzamali, E. 1996. *Syntax und Stil bei Sappho*. Dettelbach.

Uhlig, G. 1883. *Dionysii Thracis ars grammatica* (*Grammatici Graeci* 1.1). Leipzig.

Ulf, Chr., ed. 2003. *Der neue Streit um Troia. Eine Bilanz*. Munich.

Usher, S. 1960. "Some Observations on Greek Historical Narrative from 400 to 1 BC: A Study in the Effect of Outlook and Environment on Style." *AJPh* 81: 358–72.

Usher, S. 1982. "The Style of Dionysius of Halicarnassus in the 'Antiquitates Romanae'." *ANRW* II.30.1: 817–38.

Vahlen, J. 1914. *Beiträge zu Aristoteles' Poetik*. Berlin.

Valakas, K. 2007. "The Use of Language in Greek Tragedy." In Christidis, ed., 2007: 1010–20.

Valette-Cagnac, E. 2003. "Plus grec que le grec des Athéniens. Quelques aspects du bilinguisme gréco-latin." *Mètis*, n.s. 1: 149–79.

van der Weiden, M. J. H. 1991. *The Dithyrambs of Pindar*. Amsterdam.

van Dieten, J.-L. 1979. "Bemerkungen zur Sprache der sog. vulgärgriechischen Niketasparaphrase." *Byzantinische Forschungen* 6: 37–77.

van Minnen, P. 1997. "The Performance and Readership of the *Persai* of Timotheus." *Arch. Pap.* 43: 246–60.

van 't Dack, E., P. van Dessel, and W. van Gucht, eds. 1983. *Egypt and the Hellenistic World*. Louvain.

Vandenabeele, F. 1985. "La chronologie des documents en linéaire A." *BCH* 109: 3–20.

Vandorpe, K. 2002a. *The Bilingual Family Archive of Dryton, His Wife Apollonia and their Daughter Senmouthis* (Collectanea Hellenistica IV). Brussels.

Vandorpe, K. 2002b. "Apollonia, a Businesswoman in a Multicultural Society (Pathyris, 2nd–1st centuries B.C.)." In H. Melaerts and L. Mooren, eds., *Le rôle et le statut de la femme en Égypte hellénistique, romaine et byzantine* (Studia Hellenistica 37). Louvain: 325–36.

Vassilaki, S. 2007. "Ἑλληνισμός." In Christidis, ed., 2007: 1118–29.

Vassis, I., ed. 2002. *Leon Magistros Choirosphaktes. Chiliostichos theologia*. Berlin.

Vegetti, M. 1983. "Metafora politica e imagine del corpo negli scritti ippocratici." In F. Lasserre and P. Mudry, eds., *Formes de pensée dans la Collection hippocratique*. Geneva: 459–69.

Venini, P. 1952. "La distribuzione chronologica delle parole greche nell'epistolario di Cicerone." *Rend. Ist. Lomb.* 85: 50–68.

Verdan, S., A. Kenzelmann Pfyffer, and Th. Theurillat. 2005. "Graffiti d'époque géométrique provenant du sanctuaire d'Apollon Daphnéphoros à Erétrie." *ZPE* 151: 51–83; 84–6.

Verdier, C. 1972. *Les éolismes non-épiques de la langue de Pindare*. Innsbruck.

Vergote, J. 1938. "Grec biblique." In L. Pirot, ed., *Supplément au Dictionnaire de la Bible*, vol. 3. Paris: 1319–69.

Vergote, J. 1984. "Bilinguisme et calques (translation loan words) en Égypte." In *Atti del XVII Congresso internazionale di papirologia*, vol. 3. Naples: 1385–89.

Versteegh, K. 1987. "Latinitas, Hellenismos, 'Arabiyya.'" In D. J. Taylor, ed., *The History of Linguistics in the Classical Period*. Amsterdam: 251–74.

Versteegh, K. 2002. "Dead or Alive? The Status of the Standard Language." In Adams, Janse, and Swain, eds., 2002: 52–74.

Vierros, M. 2003. "Everything is Relative: The Relative Clause Constructions of an Egyptian Scribe Writing Greek." In L. Pietilä-Castrén and M. Vesterinen, eds., *Grapta Poikila* I (Papers and Monographs of the Finnish Institute at Athens 8), 13–23.

Vierros, M. 2007. "The Language of Hermias, an Egyptian Notary from Pathyris (*c.* 100 BC)." In B. Palme, ed., *Akten des 23. internationalen Papyrologenkongresses, Wien*. Vienna: 719–23.

Villing, A. 2005. "Persia and Greece." In J. Curtis and N. Tallis, eds., *Forgotten Empire: The World of Ancient Persia*. Berkeley: 236–49.

Vine, B. 1998. *Aeolic ὄρπετον and Deverbative *-etó- in Greek and Indo-European*. Innsbruck.

Visser, E. 1997. "Die Formel als Resultat frühepischer Versifikationstechnik." In F. Létoublon, ed., *Hommage à Milman Parry*. Amsterdam: 159–72.

Vitrac, B. 2008. "Les formulas de la 'puissance' (δύναμις, δύνασθαι) dans les mathématiques grecs et dans les dialogues de Platon." In M. Crubellier et al., eds., *Dunamis. Autour de la puissance chez Aristote*. Louvain-la-Neuve: 73–148.

Voelz, J. W. 1984. "The Language of the New Testament." *ANRW* II.25.2: 893–977.

Vogt-Spira, G. 1991. "Vox und Littera. Der Buchstabe zwischen Mündlichkeit und Schriftlichkeit in der grammatischen Tradition." *Poetica* 23: 295–327.

Volk, K. 2002. "Κλέος ἄφθιτον Revisited." *CP* 97: 61–8.

Volkmann, R. 1885. *Die Rhetorik der Griechen und Römer in systematischer Übersicht*, 2nd edn. Leipzig.

Von Staden, H. 1989. *Herophilus: The Art of Medicine in Early Alexandria. Edition, Translation and Essays*. Cambridge.

Von Staden, H. 1996. "Body and Machine: Interactions between Medicine, Mechanics, and Philosophy in Early Alexandria." In *Alexandria and Alexandrianism*. Malibu: 85–106.

Von Staden, H. 1997. "Galen and the 'Second Sophistic'." In R. Sorabji, ed., *Aristotle and After*. London: 33–54.

Von Staden, H. 1998. "Andréas de Caryste et Philon de Byzance. Médecine et mécanique à Alexandrie." In G. Argoud and J.-Y. Guillaumin, eds., *Sciences exactes et sciences appliquées à Alexandrie (IIIe siècle av. J.-C –I^e siècle ap. J.-C.)*. Saint-Étienne: 147–72.

Vyzantios, S. D. 1835. *Λεξικὸν τῆς καθ' ἡμᾶς ἑλληνικῆς διαλέκτου*. Athens.

Wachter, R. 1999. "Evidence for Phrase Structure Analysis in Some Archaic Greek Inscriptions." In A. C. Cassio, ed., *Katà Diálekton. Atti del III Colloquio internazionale di dialettologia greca*. Napoli—Fiaiano d'Ischia, September 1996, 25–29 (AION, Dipartimento di studi del mondo classico e del Mediterraneo antico, sezione filologico-letteraria 19.). Naples: 365–82.

Wachter, R. 2000. "Grammatik der homerischen Sprache." In Latacz et al. 2000: 61–108.

Wachter, R. 2001. *Non-Attic Greek Vase Inscriptions*. Oxford.

Wachter, R. 2002. "Griechisch δόξα und ein frühes Solonzitat eines Töpfers in Metapont." In M. Fritz and S. Zeilfelder, eds., *Novalis Indogermanica. Festschrift für Günter Neumann zum 80. Geburtstag* (Grazer vergleichende Arbeiten 17). Graz: 497–511.

Wachter, R. 2004. "BA-BE-BH-BI-BO-BY-BΩ . . . Zur Geschichte des elementaren Schreibunterrichts bei den Griechen, Etruskern und Venetern." *ZPE* 146: 61–74.

Wachter, R. 2007. "Attische Vaseninschriften: Was ist von einer sinnvollen und realistischen Sammlung und Auswertung zu erwarten? (*AVI* 1)." In I. Hajnal and B. Stefan, eds., *Die altgriechischen Dialekte. Wesen und Werden. Akten des Kolloquiums Freie Universität Berlin, September, 19–22 2001*. Innsbruck: 479–98.

Wackernagel, J. 1912. *Über einige antike Anredeformen*. Göttingen.

Wackernagel, J. 1916. *Sprachliche Untersuchungen zu Homer*. Göttingen.

Wade-Gery, H. T. 1952. *The Poet of the Iliad*. Cambridge.

Wahlgren, S. 1995. *Sprachwandel im Griechisch der frühen römischen Kaiserzeit*. Göteborg.

Wahlgren, S. 2002. "Towards a Grammar of Byzantine Greek." *SO* 77: 201–4.

Wahlström, E. 1970. *Accentual Responsion in Greek Strophic Poetry* (Commentationes Humanarum Litterarum 47). Helsinki: 1–23.

Wakker, G. C. 1994. *Conditions and Conditionals: An Investigation of Ancient Greek*. Amsterdam.

Wallraff, M., ed. 2007. *Iulius Africanus, Chronographiae: The Extant Fragments*. Berlin and New York.

Walser, G. 2001. *The Greek of the Ancient Synagogue: An Investigation on the Greek of the Septuagint, Pseudepigrapha and the New Testament*. Lund.

Waltke, B. K., and M. O'Connor. 1990. *An Introduction to Biblical Hebrew Syntax*. Winona Lake, IN.

Ward, J. S. 2007. "Roman Greek: Latinisms in the Greek of Flavius Josephus." *CQ* 57: 632–47.

Ward, R. L. 1944. "Afterthoughts on *g* as ŋ in Latin and Greek." *Language* 20: 73–7.

Wasserstein, A., and D. J. Wasserstein. 2006. *The Legend of the Septuagint: From Classical Antiquity to Today*. Cambridge.

Wathelet, P. 1966. "La coupe syllabique et les liquides voyelles dans la tradition formulaire de l'épopée grecque." In Y. Lebrun, ed., *Linguistic Research in Belgium*. Wetteren: 101–73.

Watkins, C. 1963a. "Preliminaries to a Historical and Comparative Syntax of the Old Irish Verb." *Celtica* 6: 1–49.

Watkins, C. 1963b. "Indo-European Metrics and Archaic Irish Verse." *Celtica* 6: 194–249.

Watkins, C. 1976a. "Observations on the 'Nestor's Cup' Inscription." *HSCPh* 80: 25–40.

Watkins, C. 1976b. "Syntax and Metrics in the Dipylon Vase Inscription." In A. Morpurgo Davies and W. Meid, eds., *Studies in Greek, Italic, and Indo-European Linguistics Offered to Leonard R. Palmer*. Innsbruck: 431–41.

Watkins, C. 1979. "Old Irish *saithe*, Welsh *haid*: Etymology and Metaphor." *Études Celtiques* 16: 191–4.

Watkins, C. 1986. "The Language of the Trojans." In Mellink, ed., 1986: 45–62.

Watkins, C. 1987. "Linguistic and Archaeological Light on some Homeric Formulas." In N. Skomal and E. Polomé, eds., *Proto-Indo-European: The Archeology of a Linguistic Problem. Studies in Honor of Marija Gimbutas*. Washington, DC: 286–98.

Watkins, C. 1994. *Selected Writings*, 2 vols, ed. L. Oliver. Innsbruck.

Watkins, C. 1995. *How to Kill a Dragon: Aspects of Indo-European Poetics*. New York.

Watkins, C. 1998. "Homer and Hittite Revisited." In P. Knox and C. Foss, eds., *Style and Tradition: Studies in Honor of Wendell Clausen*. Stuttgart: 201–11.

Watkins, C. 2001. "An Indo-European Linguistic Area and its Characteristics: Ancient Anatolia. Areal Diffusion as a Challenge to the Comparative Method?" In A. Y. Aikhenvald and R. M. W. Dixon, eds., *Areal Diffusion and Genetic Inheritance*. Oxford: 44–63.

Watkins, C. 2002. "ΕΠΕΩΝ ΘΕΣΙΣ. Poetic Grammar: Word Order and Metrical Structure in the Odes of Pindar." In H. Hettrich, ed., *Indogermanische Syntax. Fragen und Perspektiven*. Wiesbaden: 319–37.

Watkins, C. 2007. "The Golden Bowl: Thoughts on the New Sappho and its Asianic Background." *CA* 26: 305–25.

Watzinger, C. 1905. *Griechische Holzsarkophage aus der Zeit Alexanders des Großen*. Leipzig.

Weidemann, H. 1996. "Grundzüge der aristotelischen Sprachtheorie." In P. Schmitter, ed., *Sprachtheorien der abendländischen Antike* (Geschichte der Sprachtheorie 2). Tübingen: 170–92.

Weinreich, U. 1953. *Languages in Contact: Findings and Problems*. New York. Repr. The Hague, 1974.

Weis, R. 1992. "Zur Kenntnis des Griechischen im Rom der republikanischen Zeit." In Müller, Sier, and Werner, eds., 1992: 137–42.

Weissenberger, B. 1895. *Die Sprache Plutarchs von Chaeronea und die pseudoplutarchischen Schriften*. Straubing.

Weissenberger, M. 1996. *Literaturtheorie bei Lukian. Untersuchung zum Dialog Lexiphanes*. Stuttgart and Leipzig.

Wendel, T. 1929. *Die Gesprächsanrede im griechischen Epos und Drama der Blütezeit*. Stuttgart.

Wenskus, O. 1982. *Ringkomposition, anaphorish-rekapitulierende Verbindung und anknüpfende Wiederholung im hippokratischen Corpus*, Frankfurt.

Wenskus, O. 1993. "Zitatzwang als Motiv für Codewechsel in der lateinischen Prosa." *Glotta* 71: 205–16.

Wenskus, O. 1998. *Emblematischer Codewechsel und Verwandtes in der lateinischen Prosa. Zwischen Nähesprache und Distanzsprache*. Innsbruck.

Wenskus, O. 2001. "Wie schreibt man einer Dame? Zum Problem der Sprachwahl in der römischen Epistolographie." *WS* 114: 215–32.

Werner, J. 1983. "Nichtgriechische Sprachen im Bewußtsein der antiken Griechen." In P. Händel et al., eds., *Festschrift für Robert Muth* (Innsbrucker Beiträge zur Kulturwissenschaft 22). Innsbruck: 583–95.

Werner, J. 1989. "Kenntnis und Bewertung fremder Sprachen bei den antiken Griechen I. Griechen und 'Barbaren': Zum Sprachbewußtsein und zum ethnischen Bewußtsein im frühgriechischen Epos." *Philol.* 133: 169–76.

Werner, J. 1992. "Zur Fremdsprachenproblematik in der griechisch-römischen Antike." In Müller, Sier, and Werner, eds., 1992: 1–20.

Werner, J. 1996. "Περὶ τῆς Ῥωμαϊκῆς διαλέκτου ὅτι ἐστὶν ἐκ τῆς Ἑλληνικῆς." In E. G. Schmidt, ed., *Griechenland und Rom. Vergleichende Untersuchungen*. Tbilisi, Erlangen, and Jena: 323–33.

West, M. L. 1973a. "Greek Poetry 2000–700 BC" *CQ* 23: 179–92.

West, M. L. 1973b. "Indo-European Metre." *Glotta* 51: 161–87.

West, M. L. 1974. Review of Nagy 1974. *Phoenix* 28: 457–9.

West, M. L. 1981. "Melos, Iambos, Elegie und Epigramm." In E. Vogt, ed., *Neues Handbuch der Literaturwissenschaft. Griechische Literatur*. Wiesbaden: 73–142.

West, M. L. 1982. *Greek Metre*. Oxford.

West, M. L. 1988. "The Rise of the Greek Epic." *JHS* 108: 151–72.

West, M. L. 1990. "Colloquialism and Naïve Style in Aeschylus." In E. Craik, ed., *Owls to Athens: Essays on Classical Subjects for Sir Kenneth Dover*. Oxford: 3–12.

West, M. L. 1992. *Ancient Greek Music*. Oxford.

West, M. L. 1997a. *The East Face of Helicon: West Asiatic Elements in Greek Poetry and Myth*. Oxford.

West, M. L. 1997b. "Homer's Meter." In Morris and Powell, eds., 1997: 218–37.

West, M. L. 1998. "Praefatio." In *Homerus Ilias, recensuit Martin L. West. Volumen prius rhapsodiae I–XII*. Stuttgart and Leipzig.

West, M. L. 2004. "An Indo-European Stylistic Feature in Homer." In A. Bierl, A. Schmitt, and A. Willi, eds., *Antike Literatur in neuer Deutung*. Munich: 33–49.

West, M. L. 2007. *Indo-European Poetry and Myth*. Oxford.

Westerink, L. 1986. "Leo the Philosopher: *Job* and other poems." *ICS* 11: 193–222.

Whitaker, C. W. A. 1996. *Aristotle's De Interpretatione: Contradiction and Dialectic*. Oxford.

Whitehead, D. 2000. *Hypereides: Translation, Edition, and Commentary*. Oxford.

Whitmarsh, T. 2005. *The Second Sophistic*. Oxford.

Wifstrand, A. 2005. *Epochs and Styles: Selected Writings on the New Testament, Greek Language and Greek Culture in the Post-Classical Era*. Tübingen.

Wilamowitz-Möllendorff, U. 1900. "Asianismus und Atticismus." *Hermes* 35: 1–52.

Wilcken, U. 1917. "Die griechischen Denkmäler vom Dromos des Serapeums von Memphis." *Jahrbuch* DAI 32: 149–203.

Wilcox, M. 1984. "Semitisms in the New Testament." *ANRW* II.25.2: 978–1029.

Willetts, R. F. 1967. *The Law Code of Gortyn*. Berlin.

Willi, A. 2003. *The Languages of Aristophanes: Aspects of Linguistic Variation in Classical Attic Greek*. Oxford.

Willi, A. 2008. *Sikelismos. Sprache, Kultur und Gesellschaft im griechischen Sizilien (8.–5. Jh. v. Chr.)*. Basel.

Willi, A., ed. 2002. *The Language of Greek Comedy*. Oxford.

Wilson, N. G. 1972–3. *Medieval Greek Bookhands: Examples Selected from Greek Manuscripts in Oxford Libraries*, 2 vols. Cambridge, MA.

Wilson, N. G. 1977. "Scholarly Hands of the Middle Byzantine Period." In *La paléographie grecque et byzantine*. Paris: 221–39.

Wilson, N. G. 1983a. "A Mysterious Byzantine Scriptorium: Ioannikios and his Colleagues." *Scrittura e Civiltà* 7: 161–76.

Wilson, N. G. 1983b. *Scholars of Byzantium*. London.

Wilson, N. G. 1992. *From Byzantium to Italy*. London.

Wilson, N. G. 1994. *Photius: The* Bibliotheca. London.

Wilson, N. G. 1996. *Scholars of Byzantium*, rev. edn. London.

Wipszycka, E. 1984. "Le Degré d'alphabétisation en Égypte byzantine." *REAug* 30: 279–96.

Wismann, H. 1979. "*Atomos Idea.*" *Neue Hefte für Philosophie* 15–16: 34–52.

Wisse, J. 1995. "Greeks, Romans, and the Rise of Atticism." In J. G. J. Abbenes, S. R. Slings, and I. Sluiter, eds., *Greek Literary Theory After Aristotle: A Collection of Papers in Honour of D. M. Schenkeveld*. Amsterdam: 125–34.

Witte, K. 1913. "Homeros, B) Sprache." In *Realenzyklopädie der classischen Altertumswissenschaft*, vol. 8. Stuttgart: 2213–47.

Witte, K. 1915. "Wortrhythmus bei Homer." *Rh. Mus.* 70: 481–523.

Witte, K. 1972. *Zur homerischen Sprache*. Darmstadt.

Wodtko, D. S., B. Irslinger, and C. Schneider. 2008. *Nomina im indogermanischen Lexikon*. Heidelberg.

Woodard, R. D. 1997a. *Greek Writing from Knossos to Homer: A Linguistic Interpretation of the Origin of the Greek Alphabet and the Continuity of Ancient Greek Literacy*. New York and Oxford.

Woodard, R. D. 1997b. "Linguistic Connections between Greeks and Non-Greeks." In J. E. Coleman and C. A. Walz, eds., *Greeks and Barbarians: Essays on the Interactions between Greeks and Non-Greeks in Antiquity and the Consequences for Eurocentrism*. Bethesda, MD: 29–60.

Woodard, R. D. 2004a. "Attic Greek." In Woodard, ed., 2004: 614–49.

Woodard, R. D. 2004b. "Greek Dialects." In Woodard, ed., 2004: 650–72.

Woodard, R. D., ed. 2004. *The Cambridge Encyclopedia of the World's Ancient Languages*. Cambridge.

Woodhead, A. G. 1981. *The Study of Greek Inscriptions*, 2nd edn. Cambridge.

Worp, K. A., and A. Rijksbaron. 1997. *The Kellis Isocrates Codex (P. Kell. III Gr. 95)* (Dakhleh Oasis Project: Monograph No. 5). Oxford.

Wyatt, W. F. 1992: "Homeric Hiatus," *Glotta* 70: 20–30.

Yaguello, M. 1978. *Les mots et les femmes. Essai d'approche socio-linguistique de la condition féminine*. Paris.

Youtie, H. C. 1950. "Greek Ostraka from Egypt." *TAPA* 81: 99–116 (= *Scriptiunculae*, vol. 1: 213–30).

Youtie, H. C. 1973a. "The Papyrologist: Artificer of Fact." In *Scriptiunculae*, vol. 1. Amsterdam: 9–23.

Youtie, H. C. 1973b. "'Bradeos graphon': Between Literacy and Illiteracy. In *Scriptiunculae*, vol. 2. Amsterdam: 629–51.

Youtie, H. C. 1974. *The Textual Criticism of Documentary Papyri. Prolegomena* (*BICS* Suppl. No. 33), 2nd edn. London.

Youtie, H. C. 1975. "ΥΠΟΓΡΑΦΕΥΣ: The Social Impact of Illiteracy in Graeco-Roman Egypt." *ZPE* 17: 201–21.

Yunis, H. 2001. *Demosthenes, On the Crown. Edition and Commentary*. Cambridge.

Yunis, H. ed. 2003. *Written Texts and the Rise of Literate Culture in Ancient Greece*. Cambridge.

Zgusta, L. 1964a. *Kleinasiatische Personennamen*. Prague.

Zgusta, L. 1964b. *Anatolische Personennamensippen*. Prague.

Zgusta, L. 1980. "Die Rolle des Griechischen im römischen Kaiserreich." In G. Neumann and J. Untermann, eds., *Die Sprachen im römischen Reich der Kaiserzeit*. Cologne: 121–45.

Zgusta, L. 1984. *Kleinasiatische Ortsnamen*. Heidelberg.

Zilliacus, H. 1935. *Zum Kampf der Weltsprachen im oströmischen Reich*. Helsinki. Repr. 1965. Amsterdam.

Zilliacus, H. 1949. *Untersuchungen zu den abstrakten Anredeformen und Höflichkeitstiteln im Griechischen*. Helsinki.

Zilliacus, H. 1953. *Selbstgefühl und Servilität. Studien zum unregelmässigen Numerusgebrauch im Griechischen*. Helsinki.

Zimmermann, B. 1987. *Untersuchungen zur Form und dramatischen Technik der aristophanischen Komödien*, vol. 3. Frankfurt.

Zirin, R. A. 1980. "Aristotle's Biology of Language." *TAPA* 110: 325–47.

Zurbach, J. 2006. "L'Ionie à l'époque mycénienne. Essai de bilan historique." *REA* 108: 271–97.

Index

Printed and bound by CPI Group (UK) Ltd, Croydon, CR0 4YY